# Business
# Plans
## Handbook

# Highlights

*Business Plans Handbook, Volume 8 (BPH-8)* is a collection of actual business plans compiled by entrepreneurs seeking funding for businesses throughout North America. For those looking for examples of how to approach, structure, and compose their own business plans, *BPH-8* presents 22 sample plans, including plans for the following businesses:

- Aftermarket Skate Store
- Charity Youth Hockey Tournament
- Chemical Manufacturer
- Convenience Store & Bait Shop
- Creative Agency
- Discount Internet Securities Broker
- Gourmet Foods Company

- Internet Marketplace
- Online Outdoor Company
- Racing Parts Store
- Rock Climber's Store & Cafe
- Ski Resort
- Structural Engineering Consulting Firm
- Teen Night Club

## FEATURES AND BENEFITS

*BPH-8* offers many features not provided by other business planning references including:

○ Twenty-two new business plans, each of which represent an owner's successful attempt at clarifying (for themselves and others) the reasons that the business should exist or expand and why a lender should fund the enterprise.

○ Two fictional plans that are used by business counselors at a prominent small business development organization as examples for their clients. (You will find these in the Business Plan Template Appendix.)

○ An expanded directory section that includes: listings for venture capital and finance companies, which specialize in funding start-up and second-stage small business ventures, and a comprehensive listing of Service Corps of Retired Executives (SCORE) offices. In addition, the Appendix also contains updated listings of all Small Business Development Centers (SBDCs); associations of interest to entrepreneurs; Small Business Administration (SBA) Regional Offices; and consultants specializing in small business planning and advice. It is strongly advised that you consult supporting organizations while planning your business, as they can provide a wealth of useful information.

○ A Small Business Term Glossary to help you decipher the sometimes confusing terminology used by lenders and others in the financial and small business communities.

○ A cumulative index, outlining each plan in the complete *Business Plans Handbook* series.

○ A Business Plan Template which serves as a model to help you construct your own business plan. This generic outline lists all the essential elements of a complete business plan and their components, including the Summary, Business History and Industry Outlook, Market Examination, Competition, Marketing, Administration and Management, Financial Information, and other key sections. Use this guide as a starting point for compiling your plan.

○ Extensive financial documentation required to solicit funding from small business lenders. *BPH-6* contains the most comprehensive financial data within the series to date. You will find examples of: Cash Flows, Balance Sheets, Income Projections, and other financial information included with the textual portions of the plan.

# Business
# Plans
# Handbook

A COMPILATION
OF ACTUAL
BUSINESS PLANS
DEVELOPED BY
BUSINESSES
THROUGHOUT
NORTH
AMERICA

VOLUME

# 8

Eric Hoss, Editor

GALE GROUP

Detroit
New York
San Francisco
London
Boston
Woodbridge, CT

Eric Hoss, *Editor and Project Coordinator*
Paul Lewon and Jeffrey Lee Matlock, *Technical Training Specialists*

Erin E. Braun, *Managing Editor*

Mary Beth Trimper, *Composition Manager*
Nekita McKee, *Buyer*

Mike Logusz, *Graphic Artist*
Kenn Zorn, *Product Design Manager*

Shelly Andrews, *Typesetter*

ISBN 0-7876-3421-2
ISSN 1084-4473

# Contents

## Business Plans

# Appendixes

# Introduction

Perhaps the most important aspect of business planning is simply *doing* it. More and more business owners are beginning to compile business plans even if they don't need a bank loan. Others discover the value of planning when they *must* provide a business plan for the bank. The sheer act of putting thoughts on paper seems to clarify priorities and provide focus. Sometimes business owners completely change strategies when compiling their plan, deciding on a different product mix or advertising scheme after finding that their assumptions were incorrect. This kind of healthy thinking and rethinking via business planning is becoming the norm. The editors of *Business Plans Handbook, Volume 8 (BPH-8)* sincerely hope that this latest addition to the series is a helpful tool in the successful completion of your business plan, no matter what the reason for creating it.

This eighth volume, like each volume in the series, offers genuine business plans used by real people. *BPH-8* provides 22 business plans used by actual entrepreneurs to gain funding support for their new businesses. The business and personal names and addresses and general locations have been changed to protect the privacy of the plan authors.

## NEW BUSINESS OPPORTUNITIES

As in other volumes in the series, *BPH-8* finds entrepreneurs engaged in a wide variety of creative endeavors. Examples in *BPH-8* include a proposal for a combination live bait and tackle/convenience retail store in a small but thriving lake resort; a company whose primary mission is to provide a welcome alternative the traditional ski resort experience; and a business that combines the sale of high-end rockclimbing gear with classic Northwest coffee for an intriguing consumer experience. In addition, several e-commerce-based plans are provided, including an Internet-based trading company, a business-to-business provider of aftermarket auto parts, and a company that provides a thorough tracking system for online purchases. Social entrepreneurship is also profiled in this volume, with plans for a charity hockey tournament and a non-alcohol teen nightclub for youths in the Midwest.

Comprehensive financial documentation has become increasingly important as today's entrepreneurs compete for the finite resources of business lenders. Our plans illustrate the financial data generally required of loan applicants, including Income Statements, Financial Projections, Cash Flows, and Balance Sheets.

## ENHANCED APPENDICES

In an effort to provide the most relevant and valuable information for our readers, we have updated the coverage of small business resources. For instance, you will find: a directory section, which includes listings of all of the Service Corps of Retired Executives (SCORE) offices; an informative glossary, which includes small business terms; and a cumulative index, outlining each plan profiled in the complete *Business Plans Handbook* series. In addition we have updated the list of Small Business Development Centers (SBDCs); Small Business Administration Regional Offices; venture capital and finance companies, which specialize in funding start-up and second-stage small business enterprises; associations of interest to entrepreneurs; and consultants, specializing in small business advice and planning. For your reference, we have also reprinted the business plan template, which provides a comprehensive overview of the essential components of a business plan and two fictional plans used by small business counselors.

## SERIES INFORMATION

If you already have the first seven volumes of *BPH*, with this eighth volume, you will now have a collection of over 200 real business plans (not including the one updated plan in the second volume, whose original appeared in the first, or the two fictional plans in the Business Plan Template Appendix section of the second, third, fourth, fifth, sixth, and seventh volumes); contact information for hundreds of organizations and agencies offering business expertise; a helpful business plan template; a foreword providing advice and instruction to entrepreneurs on how to begin their research; more than 1,500 citations to valuable small business development material; and a comprehensive glossary of terms to help the business planner navigate the sometimes confusing language of entrepreneurship.

## ACKNOWLEDGMENTS

The Editors wish to sincerely thank Palo Alto Software, makers of Business Plan Pro©, the premier business planning software tool, for providing the use of several business plans in this volume (Phone: 800-229-7526; Website: http://www.paloaltosoftware.com).

Special thanks are also in order for the many contributors to *BPH-8*, including Lisa A. Bastian, CBC, principal of Bastian Public Relations, www.bastianpr.com; Michelle LeCompte; Lisa D. Morrow J.D., Stephen Kinstler, Mark Kotcher, Lea Weber, and Professor. Jerome Katz of Saint Louis University's Entrepreneurship Program; Kent Bradshaw, Richard Burgess, Dr. Paul Kurko, Jason D. Levin, Jason Sears, Esther Schuller, Amy George, Alex Krishnan, Brink Melton, Ann Whitt, and Dr. Gary Cadenhead of the MOOT CORP® Competition, sponsored by the University of Texas at Austin; Jason P. Spellberg and Gaspar V. Makale of Colorado University's business planning courses; and Tobias Hemmerling and Jenn Bucci of Blue Sky West. Their diverse contributions and helpful suggestions were greatly appreciated.

The Editors would also like to express their gratitude to Shelly Andrews, Contributing Editor & Typesetter, for her talent, dedication, and hard work on behalf of this publication.

## COMMENTS WELCOME

Your comments on *BPH-8* are appreciated. Please direct all correspondence, suggestions for future volumes of *BPH*, and other recommendations to the following:

*Business Plans Handbook, Volume 8*
The Gale Group
27500 Drake Rd.
Farmington Hills, MI 48331-3535

Phone: (248)699-4253
Fax: 800-339-3374
Toll-Free: 800-347-GALE

# Advertising Agency

BUSINESS PLAN

BLUEISLAND.COM, INC.

1705 Washington Avenue
San Francisco, California 94105

*BlueIsland's featured product will be a user-friendly Internet website that provides free and fee-based services to meet the needs of its customers—advertising buyers and sellers. BlueIsland's first product line will be dedicated to reaching the highly fragmented buyers and sellers of advertising space in the radio advertising sector. BlueIsland.com's information-rich services reduce a buyer's time while enabling the development of a cost-effective advertising strategy.*

- EXECUTIVE SUMMARY
- PRODUCTS & SERVICES
- MARKET ANALYSIS
- TARGET MARKET
- MARKETING PLAN
- OPERATIONS PLAN
- MANAGEMENT
- FINANCIAL SUMMARY
- FINANCIAL STATEMENTS

## EXECUTIVE SUMMARY

Buying and creating advertising in any media is a time-intensive process reflecting hours of transactions between buyers, sellers, and creative agents. For example, if a buyer wants to advertise in the radio media, he targets a few radio stations with desired listener demographics, discusses contract options with a radio account executive, bids on an ad schedule, negotiates a price, creates ad copy, approves the final ad, and pays for the service. For a skilled buyer, this entire transaction can take up to 3 weeks to complete. For a local deli or sporting goods shop with little or no demographic information, small purchasing power, and less familiarity with radio advertising, this transaction process can take more than 3 weeks and cost the small business more money per ad than large ad agencies. For the seller, in this case the radio stations, the transactions' costs of dealing with such small customers can prove to be cost ineffective. BlueIsland.com is an Internet advertising infomediary ("adfomediary") that provides a one-stop shop for demographic information, ad rates, ad campaign schedule planning, ad buys, and creative development, reducing transaction time and costs for buyers and sellers of advertising spots.

## The Company

BlueIsland.com, Inc. ("the company") is a "C" corporation located in San Francisco, California. The company is located on the Internet at www.BlueIsland.com and is the first adfomediary dedicated to the needs of small businesses.

## Products & Services

BlueIsland's featured product will be a user-friendly Internet website that provides free and fee-based services to meet the needs of its customers—advertising buyers and sellers. BlueIsland's first product line will be dedicated to reaching the highly fragmented buyers and sellers of advertising space in the radio advertising sector. Qualified buyers and sellers are invited to join BlueIsland.com's community as members. Membership is free and provides users access to valuable customized services. Selling members receive opportunity to list ads and gain access to the buying community. Buyers receive access to up-to-the-minute aggregated, radio market information, ad campaign planning tools, creative services, ad space, buying discounts, monitoring services, and account management.

BlueIsland.com's information-rich services reduce a buyer's time while enabling the development of a cost-effective advertising strategy. In addition BlueIsland.com buyers receive unique buying discounts, usually reserved for major ad agencies and companies, and an opportunity to participate in discounted "over-capacity" ads.

BlueIsland.com serves as a third sales channel for radio stations, complementing their national and local sales efforts. Unlike traditional sales methods, the Internet offers radio stations access to a national market and 24-hour selling power. BlueIsland.com provides radio station members with a listing and brokerage service, access to customers, free marketing, and monthly value reports. These monthly BlueIsland.com value reports will include buyer profiles, competitive analysis, market analysis, and savings calculated.

## Market & Opportunity

BlueIsland.com represents the intersection of two growing U.S. markets: advertising and business-to-business electronic commerce. The advertising industry represents a $190 billion industry and is expected to grow at 5.7 percent compound annual growth. The radio advertising market is a $17.7 billion sector represented by more than 12,275 radio stations in 268 major markets. Approximately 75 percent of radio advertising is purchased at the local level.

Although there has been consolidation in the radio industry since the Telecommunication Act of 1996, the industry is still highly fragmented and growing at an 8.5 percent annual rate. In addition, radio stations have generally been slow to adopt Internet strategies.

Business-to-business e-commerce revenues for 1998 were $17 billion and are projected to grow to $1.7 trillion by 2003. It is projected that by the year 2002 almost one third of all business-to-business transactions will be performed via e-commerce (1998).

### Customers

As an intermediary agent BlueIsland.com has two primary customers: radio stations and small business advertisers. BlueIsland.com will target the top 4,000 radio stations, which represent 80 percent of the industry revenues. BlueIsland.com will target small, high-growth businesses as its primary market. In the U.S., there are currently 24 million small businesses with approximately 885,000 new firms each year. These businesses represent 47 percent of all sales in the U.S. According to research, approximately 41 percent of small businesses are online and one in three conducts business transactions on the Internet. Each of these firms represents an average of $3.79 million in annual revenues, significantly more than the $2.72 million average.

### Competitors

AllMedia.com and AdDeals.com are websites that have launched within the last 18 months that connect buyers and sellers of radio advertising space. However, BlueIsland.com is the only website with customized services and a pricing model to meet the needs of small businesses. In so doing, BlueIsland.com will expand the current advertising market.

## Marketing Strategy

BlueIsland.com's marketing efforts are centered on strategic partnerships, an educational advertising and public relations campaign, and a regional sales force. BlueIsland.com will forge a strategic partnership with the Radio Advertising Bureau, the national association that represents 4,300 radio stations and 80 percent of U.S. radio advertising revenues. BlueIsland.com will forge an alliance with the U.S. Chamber of Commerce, the world's largest business federation, representing nearly 3 million companies, 96 percent of which are small businesses. BlueIsland's marketing campaign will focus on driving volume to the website and converting visitors to buyers.

## The Start-up Plan

BlueIsland.com will follow a three-phase start-up plan. During the first phase, the BlueIsland.com team will create a demonstration site, refine product and services mix, and alpha test among focus groups of buyers and sellers. During the second phase, BlueIsland.com hopes to raise the required venture funding of $2 million to launch the site. The funds will be used to finalize the development of an integrated website, negotiate strategic alliances and radio station partnership agreements, launch a marketing and sales plan, and launch the website in San Francisco, California. To meet the objectives of the first two phases, BlueIsland.com will incrementally hire 16 additional staff and outsource the initial development of the website. The third phase will include a launch in 10 cities, including: San Francisco, Atlanta, Washington, Seattle, Minneapolis, Boston, New York, Chicago, and Miami.

## Management

BlueIsland's management team has extensive experience in the marketing, Internet, and high-tech sectors. LeeAnn Masters, Chief Executive Officer, has seven years of professional experience in the field of marketing for small businesses and national clients in the telecommunication, real estate, multimedia, and education industries. Ali Manon, Chief Operating Officer, has five years of experience in the high-tech industry in the areas of Internet strategy, program management, software design, and development. Wayne Stewart, Chief Technology

Officer, has three years' experience as a software developer and technology consultant. He has experience launching a successful technology consulting partnership dedicated to serving the needs of small businesses in San Francisco, California. He is currently pursuing his M.B.A. at the University of California at Berkeley, concentrating in information management and entrepreneurship. BlueIsland.com's team of consultants are experts in the small business, radio, advertising, high-tech, and Internet start-up fields.

**Financial Overview**

BlueIsland's five-year financials are displayed in the following table (see the Appendix for additional information). BlueIsland.com derives its primary revenue from the following sources:

- Transaction fees for brokering the sale of radio advertising spots. This is the primary revenue stream and the fee collected will be 5 percent of each transaction.
- Fees for value-added market research information provided to buyers.
- Advertisements and paid promotions.

Because of the high investment needs in year 1 and year 2, the company does not achieve profitability until year 3. By year 5 revenues will grow to $26.9 million with net income of $8.6 million. The company is seeking $2 million in first-round financing with a ROI for investors to be 70 percent.

**Financial Summary and Operating Statistics**

| Key Operating Statistics | Year 1 | Year 2 | Year 3 | Year 4 | Year 5 |
|---|---|---|---|---|---|
| Employees | 27 | 57 | 78 | 86 | 98 |
| **Financial Statistics** | | | | | |
| Revenue | $53,700 | $2,625,000 | $12,770,000 | $19,200,000 | $26,900,000 |
| Expenses | $4,130,597 | $8,029,597 | $9,584,866 | $11,685,887 | $13,213,244 |
| **Net Income** | **($4,076,897)** | **($5,404,597)** | **$2,070,337** | **$4,884,174** | **$8,896,391** |

# PRODUCTS & SERVICES

**Overview of Product**

BlueIsland's featured product will be an Internet website dedicated to being a "one-stop" advertising exchange for buyers and sellers of advertising spots. BlueIsland.com's provides a way for buyers and sellers to make more efficient decisions, thereby reducing transaction costs. BlueIsland's first stage rollout will be dedicated to reaching the highly fragmented buyers and sellers of advertising space in the $17.7 billion radio sector.

**Product Architecture**

BlueIsland.com will be an attractive, easy-to-use, and informative website designed to make each user's experience familiar and enjoyable. The site will be divided into two sections: buyers and sellers. The main page will showcase BlueIsland.com's value to customers, offer a news corner with articles and current events in the radio advertising industry, a demonstration site, a membership option, partner information, company information, and BlueIsland.com advertisers. The user will then have the opportunity to enter into their relevant area.

**Membership**

To access free basic services, BlueIsland.com visitors will be invited to join as members and complete a brief membership form. If interested in becoming a qualified buyer or seller of advertising space, members will be asked to complete a brief financial information form and authorize governing terms and conditions. This process will enable BlueIsland.com to establish a direct deposit account with the buyers' or sellers' financial institution. In addition to basic services, buyers can obtain access to value-added products and services, like competitive analysis or ad monitoring, on a cost per transaction basis.

## Services

The seller portion of the website will contain information particular to the needs and interests of radio stations. Those who have registered their station with BlueIsland.com will be presented with a customized home page with information particular to their individual station. They will have the ability to select from the following options:

**Radio Station Data**—The radio sales manager will edit and update the stations' descriptive information, including advertising space, times, radio promotions, advertising rates, and discount packages.

**Online Sales Calendar**—This service will allow radio sales agents to update the availability of spots for sale through BlueIsland.com. Once a spot is sold through BlueIsland.com, it will be immediately removed from the market. This will provide a real-time snapshot of available spots for sales agents. A station will also be able to view the schedule of sold spots by parameters like times, industry, and buyer demographics.

**Promote Special Offerings**—This option provides radio stations the ability to send special promotional offerings to target BlueIsland.com customers. These could include discounted sales of unsold spots or other promotional packages. The sales manager will be able to target these ads to particular individual clients that have purchased in the past or to customers who fit a certain profile or to all BlueIsland buyers. Those requesting mass broadcast will require the approval of BlueIsland staff before transmission.

**Reporting**—BlueIsland will provide the radio stations the opportunity to obtain a wealth of information about their customers and their purchasing habits. For example, a sales manager will be able to obtain demographic and purchasing data about the types of companies purchasing their ads. BlueIsland will also provide reports on numbers of "matches" their station's profile met, the frequency of purchases resulting through BlueIsland, and other information about their clients and competition.

## Benefits

Radio stations will enjoy significant advantages by accessing a third online sales channel, including: sales cost savings, access to new customers, free marketing, customer research, and real-time radio buying trends.

**Cost Savings:** BlueIsland.com will also enable radio sales managers to reduce their cost of sales and administrative costs, which currently represents 28 percent of sales. Typically, a radio station has a small sales staff to field calls from potential customers, answer questions about demographic profiles the station reaches, create various potential rate plans, and many other additional administrative duties. By listing this information with BlueIsland.com, they will not have to constantly field requests that can usually be answered on their information section of the website. Typically, the sales staff is engaged in a constant relay of faxing and phone calls in order to secure a single sale, causing the cost of customer acquisition to be unnecessarily high. A common problem is a sales manager's ability to screen out good leads from possible "information hunters."

**Valuable Customer Data & Analysis:** BlueIsland.com allows stations to gather better information about their specific and potential customers. Since all buyers utilizing the system will register with their business specific information, radio stations can better understand their customers' and non-customers' needs and buying habits. As a result, the radio station can respond quickly to opportunities and threats. This information, which is currently not systematically collected, will prove valuable market data for the radio station's competitive marketplace.

**New Market Opportunities:** Radio stations will be able to quickly react to market demands by changing their prices, offering promotional packages, and offering discounts for unsold ad space. Radio stations can trace purchase histories of their past clients and promote appropriate promotional packages to a much more targeted market. Due to the timeliness required of this disposable commodity, this savings in efficiency could ensure a station from losing revenues from unsold space. In addition, the 24-hour availability and borderless reach of the Internet will enable radio stations to access a much wider range of customers than ever before. Also, because BlueIsland.com's search function provides buyers with stations that meet the customer's needs, BlueIsland.com is helping to drive new buyers to the radio stations.

**Free Marketing:** Finally, BlueIsland.com will promote the radio advertising industry through a nationwide educational advertising campaign. Participating radio stations listed on the website will benefit from BlueIsland.com's promotion and capital investment.

## Buyer Services & Benefits

### Services

Buyers will be presented with a user interface that is customized to meet their needs. Buyers will also enjoy the following services and benefits:

**Research Stations**—Buyers can conduct research using the BlueIsland radio station database. Buyers can search by several criteria including station demographics, price (average cost per spot), specific region or city, listener reach, music format, and other criteria important in making purchasing decisions. The search will result in a listing of all station matching the criteria and the customer will be able to select stations they wish to continue using for further research. In addition, buyers will be able to select "value-added" research like competitive analysis (What is my competitor doing?) and niche customer segments (Help me reach the online customer).

**Plan Campaign**—Buyers will begin to plan their media campaign, selecting specific radio stations, availability, cost data, and discounts as parameters. A buyer can create a variety of different customized ad campaigns or select one of BlueIsland.com's pre-packaged options. Ultimately, a buyer can save this campaign to buy later or they can execute a "buy." If a buyer decides to buy, they enter into the buy phase of the service.

**Buy Media**—This option gives the media buyer a fully functioning transaction center to actually purchase ad spots. After selecting the options, a buyer can proceed to "check out" or close the deal. To complete a transaction, the media buyer must have verified financial information linked to their membership. Once a purchase is made, the buyer's account will be debited for the amount of purchase and will receive an invoice and confirmation number. The spots purchased will also be immediately removed from sale on the exchange. An e-mail notification will then be generated and transmitted to both the buyer and seller, confirming the transaction.

**Create My Spot®**—A buyer will be provided the option to build their ad online. Specific packages and prices will be offered as alternatives to using traditional production houses. A variety of example voices will be available for a user to choose from to build their ad. After submitting the copy of the ad text, BlueIsland will create a selection of three digital ads for the buyer and make it available for review online. A buyer can select from the ad online and submit it to BlueIsland.com for final delivery to the radio station.

**Client History**—The buyer will have the opportunity to track past schedules and purchases made with BlueIsland.com. A ROI calculator will provide the ability to observe actual benefits of advertising on the radio and include estimates of cost savings achieved by using BlueIsland.com's service.

**Monitor My Ads®**—This value-added service enables buyers to monitor whether a radio station actually executes the correct ad "on the air." This is a valuable service among the small business market and is currently not offered by a traditional advertising agency.

### Benefits

BlueIsland.com provides buyers tremendous advantages over the conventional methods of procuring ad space. The most substantial of these benefits has to be the efficiency and time saved in the process.

**Increase Advertising Cost-Effectiveness:** Through BlueIsland's search engine, a potential buyer will be able to better screen and target those stations that enable them to reach their market. This will increase the cost-effectiveness of advertising expenditures.

**Convenience:** A buyer will be able to search all radio station information including demographics, reach, and pricing at the click of a mouse. Typically, a business seeking to find information about particular radio stations would have to call every station they have an interest in purchasing space from. Through BlueIsland.com, they will not have to contact every station or purchase a costly database to evaluate the demographic profile, reach, and pricing structure of radio stations. All of this information will be provided in a convenient easy-to-use place. This will greatly reduce the amount of faxing and phone calls necessary to make a purchasing decision. In addition, BlueIsland.com serves as an account manager and repeat buyers can access their client history to simply repeat the past purchases for a future campaign.

**Discounts & Buying Power:** BlueIsland.com aggregates the buying power of small businesses and provides and automatic 10 percent discount below market rates, a benefit reserved primarily for major companies. Potential buyers will receive notification of ad sales and other promotions the radio stations are offering. This will enable customers with smaller advertising budgets to take advantage of opportunities to advertise at discounted rates.

**Independent Information:** BlueIsland.com also allows those new to this medium of advertising to learn more about the potential of radio. Many of the businesses that may want to advertise on the radio are simply not educated in the language or process of actually securing ad space. BlueIsland will allow a new potential customer the ability to educate themselves, screen potential markets, get costing estimates, and become more informed in general about the powerful nature of radio advertising.

BlueIsland.com will be able to expand its operations in the following ways:

- Targeting new customer markets
- Selling other advertising media, such as TV, print, Internet, and billboards
- Transmission of final ad spots to and from buyers and sellers
- Joint ventures with small business software packages such as QuickBooks to further integrate the back end process of the buyers and sellers

**Expansion Opportunities**

## MARKET ANALYSIS

### Market

BlueIsland.com's market intersects two industries: the $17 billion business-to-business electronic commerce industry and the $190 billion advertising industry. Although BlueIsland.com's vision is to become the small business hub for online advertising buying and selling, BlueIsland.com will initially just represent the transactions of the $17 billion radio industry. The competitive space we have defined for BlueIsland.com overlaps that of one direct competitor, AllMedia.com, and a number of indirect competitor groups. Our markets, customers, and competitors are further defined below.

### Business-to-Business E-commerce Market

Business-to-business e-commerce revenues for 1998 were $17 billion and are projected to grow to $1.7 trillion in 2003. It is projected that by the year 2002 almost one-third of all business-to-business transactions will be performed via e-commerce (1998). In 1998, 41 percent of small businesses used the Internet; this was double the use in 1996. According to a survey conducted by IBM and the U.S. Chamber of Commerce, 63 percent of small businesses (less than 100 employees) use the Internet for research, 37 percent use the Internet for online ordering, 30 percent use it for promotion/advertising, and 9 percent pay suppliers. Small businesses have been slow adopters in the e-commerce industry.

### Radio Industry Analysis

**Radio Stations**

The radio industry includes 12,275 radio stations in more than 238 major markets. Although there has been consolidation since the Telecommunications Act of 1996, the radio industry is still highly fragmented and managed by many small mom-and-pop operations. Radio stations derive 75-100 percent of their revenues from advertising. In 1999, the U.S. radio advertising market represents a $17.7 billion industry with expected 8.5 percent continued annual growth. This growth had been fueled by radio industry marketing campaigns, the growth of the Internet, and the use of radio as a primary communication medium to drive consumers to the web.

**Radio & Technology**

Radio stations have been slow to adopt the use of the Internet as a broadcast, advertising, or e-commerce medium. Realizing the lack of development of an Internet strategy among radio stations, CEO Gary Fries called on radio stations to be "E-Born" at the September 9, 1999 Annual Radio Advertising Bureau (RAB) conference. However, even Mr. Fries, like many radio station managers, is not seizing the power of the Internet as a channel to automate traditional sales and expand the market reach and size.

**Radio Advertising Process**

Approximately 75 percent of radio advertising is purchased at the local level. Buyers of radio advertising space include national advertising agencies, local advertising agencies, businesses, and media brokers (representative firms). Most radio stations have their own personnel to manage sales within their respective markets. However, national media representatives or "rep firms" are contracted to sell to national clients. There are currently two major radio "rep firms," Ray Communications and Anderson Radio Store.

Radio advertising can be purchased on a national network and individual local market spot basis either directly or through advertising agencies. Spot radio programming formats vary widely from market to market, from talk shows to music. Prices also vary depending on the size of the market, from $601 cost per thousand in New York City to $58 in San Francisco, California.

**Radio Listeners**

In 1996, 99 percent of all households owned a radio. Ninety-five percent of all adults not only listen to radio each week, they listen for more than 3 1/4 hours per day. One third of people surveyed indicate they listen to radio at work. Radio reaches over 80 percent of professionals and managers each day. Radio is also one of the only mediums that can reach the increasingly mobile American at home, from their commute to and from work, as well as throughout the day at the office.

**Consolidation**

**Radio Listeners: Research**

The 15 largest radio broadcasters, which own about 11 percent of all U.S. stations, accounted for about 42 percent of all industry advertising revenues in 1997, up from six percent of stations and 34 percent of revenues in 1996. With the relaxation of federal station ownership regulation, a radio station operator can own as many as eight stations in one market, but no more than five of one kind (AM or FM). The ensuing consolidation has allowed for the centralization of back-office functions such as sales, billing, and marketing, and investment in new product and sales efforts. The concentration of ownership across markets appeals to advertisers who can make one station "block" ad buy then negotiate on a station-by-station basis. This one-stop shopping concept boosts the attractiveness of radio as an advertising medium, no matter whether the advertiser is a local merchant or national advertiser.

**Advertising Agencies**

In 1998, there were approximately 30,000 advertising agencies in the United States, representing $21.9 billion in annual revenues. A majority of these firms are headquartered in major cities such as New York, Chicago, and Los Angeles. Although traditionally dominated by large, public corporations, most advertising agencies average only 11 employees. Advertising agencies vary greatly in size and scope. Smaller agency personnel are responsible for a variety of tasks, while those in larger agencies find their job duties to be more defined.

Advertising agencies are responsible for two main functions: the production of advertising materials (writing copy, graphics, audio, video, art) and strategic placements of the finished product in various media outlets (periodicals, newspapers, radio, television). The activities of ad agencies are divided into four broad groups: account management, the creative department, media buying, and research. Agencies generally receive compensation for production costs from the client, plus a standard 15 percent commission from the media source for the ad placement. However, this pricing structure is changing from a flat fee to a cost plus contract structure.

**TARGET MARKET**

BlueIsland.com is targeting radio stations and small businesses (below 500 employees) as the primary selling and buyer markets.

1. Radio Stations

   The 12,375 radio stations in the U.S. are BlueIsland.com's critical customers. BlueIsland.com will create a strategic alliance with Radio Advertising Bureau to reach their 4,800 members, which represent 80 percent of annual advertising revenues.

2. Small Businesses

   BlueIsland.com will target a cross section of small business segments that represent 1.) Industries that advertise on the radio, 2.) High-growth sectors, and 3.) Firms that are currently on the Internet. The top 10 industries that purchase radio include: retail, business and consumer service, automotive, entertainment, media, food, travel, hotel, real estate, computer, and snack sectors. Because the decision-making tools that support radio advertising purchases are currently costly, time consuming, and require familiarity with radio, BlueIsland.com's services will provide the most value to the buyers who are time, money, and data impoverished and are in a growth phase. High-growth small business sectors include high-tech and computer retail, new businesses, and the consumer service industry. Internet companies represent a niche within this sector and on average ".com" companies spend 60 percent of their advertising budget on radio. According to a study by Visa of 350 small businesses, 34 percent of small businesses are early technology adopters and represent those potential online customers. The profile of the owners of these businesses are typically 30-49 years old, and male. BlueIsland.com will seek owners meeting this profile.

**Competitor Analysis**

BlueIsland.com has defined a unique competitive space as the high-service, low-cost provider of advertising and advertising services for small businesses. However, the market is not devoid of competitors. Our key direct competitor includes radio advertising sales websites. BlueIsland.com also has identified indirect competitors: traditional radio sales people, media representative firms, advertising agencies, market research firms, and other advertising sales websites.

1. Direct Competitors

**Radio Advertising Sales Websites**—As of October 29, 1999, the major national online resellers included: AllMedia.com and AdDeals.com. AllMedia.com caters to the needs of 2,500 media buyers representing major clients and advertising agencies and sells premium television and radio advertising space. AllMedia uses an Internet and fax-based purchase system and operates on an auction-negotiation model. AllMedia does not offer discounts or comprehensive advertising tools.

AdDeals.com sells leftover advertising space in a number of mediums including: billboards, television, and radio. AdDeals does not offer discounts or comprehensive campaign planning tools and targets high-end media buyers.

2. Indirect Competitors

**Traditional Radio Sales**—Although the partnership of BlueIsland.com with radio stations is critical to the success, the continued traditional radio sales channels (local and representative firms) represent a competitive threat to BlueIsland.com. However, BlueIsland.com will position itself as the low-cost, convenient, high customer service center for small business.

**Advertising Agencies**—Advertising agencies, primarily small ad agencies, will compete with BlueIsland.com for customers. Although many small business ad agencies do not target a national market, they do offer highly customized services for their clients at the national level. BlueIsland.com will replace much of the outsourced services for a fraction of the price.

**Market Research Firms**—Market research firms that provide market research data to high-end media buyers will be threatened by our ability to aggregate data across the country and provide it to customers in the format that meets their campaign planning needs on an "as needed basis." There are a number of market research firms that service the radio industry including: ASDM, Telmar, Arbitron, and LNA Market Research.

**Advertising Websites Selling Other Media**—A number of websites offer services for the Internet, television, billboard, and outside advertising. Although not direct competitors, these sites are substitutes for radio advertising and do compete for ad dollars. However, most of these websites do not target small businesses, but rather fairly sophisticated or high-dollar customers.

Small business owners and small advertising agencies have needs that BlueIsland.com will meet better than our direct or indirect competitors:

**Meeting Customer Needs**

1. **Information**—Our customers need information on advertising buying decisions, ratings, customer/radio station demographics, reach, costs per rating, trends and ad space prices. BlueIsland.com will provide users with access to a depth of information not found elsewhere on the Internet or in other channels.

2. **Speed and Ease**—Our customers are using the Internet to increase the efficiency of their buying decisions and reduce transaction costs. BlueIsland.com will provide customers with a friendly, easy-to-use interface that delivers advertising package options to meet the needs of the client.

3. **Radio Ad Space Selection**—BlueIsland.com will forge partnerships to secure premium and discount advertising space from a majority of radio stations in the top 260 markets. In doing so, BlueIsland.com will provide the user with the best selection of spaces available for a discount.

4. **Pricing Options**—BlueIsland.com realizes that the technique of negotiation used in traditional advertising purchasing deals may provide the buyer with a discounted rate on advertising. Because BlueIsland.com's mission is to reduce transaction costs by eliminating negotiations, BlueIsland.com will price all ad space at 10 percent below market rate, discounts for bulk purchases, and deep discounts for "over capacity space." This will provide more flexibility to the customer at a discount in one-fourth the time of traditional pricing negotiations.

5. **Community**—BlueIsland.com will bring together a community of small business owners and marketing directors with experienced advertising agency account managers to provide one-on-one consulting. In addition, small businesses can participate on the company's chat board and exchange questions and ideas with each other.

**Customer Needs Fulfillment: BlueIsland.com vs. Competitors**

| Competitor Category | Types of Ad Space | | | Information Services | Pricing Options | Convenience | Speed | Level of Community |
|---|---|---|---|---|---|---|---|---|
| | Radio | TV | Internet | | | | | |
| AllMedia.com | X | X | | — | Negotiate | Medium | Medium | None |
| AdDeals.com | X | X | X | — | Auction - Discount | High | High | None |
| AdMaster.com | | | X | XXX | Fixed Price - Premium | High | High | Small |
| Advertising Agencies | X | X | X | XXX | Cost Plus - Premium | Medium | Medium | Small |
| Representative Firms | X | X | | XX | Cost Plus - Premium | Medium | Medium | Small |
| Radio Station Direct Sales | X | | | X | Negotiate | Low | Low | None |
| Market Research Providers | | | | XXX | Fixed Price - Bulk | Medium | Medium | Large |
| BlueIsland.com | X | | | XXX | Fixed Price - Discount | High | High | Large |

## MARKETING PLAN

### Marketing Objectives

BlueIsland.com will position itself as the premier, discount, online advertising, and advertising services hub for small businesses. Using leading-edge web technology, BlueIsland.com will initially offer customized products and services exclusively in the radio advertising industry. As a new competitor in an attractive market, BlueIsland.com's primary marketing objective is securing exclusive radio station partnerships. The second marketing objective is revenue growth. The key drivers of revenue are the number of ad spaces listed, the number of visitors, the value of information, transaction value, and the conversion rate. Accordingly, BlueIsland.com will focus on attracting visitors, providing high-quality service, and converting visitors to buyers. Our marketing objective is to attract 3 million visitors, 88,000 transactions with an average transaction size of $5,000, and capture 4 percent of the radio advertising market by year five.

### Value Proposition

The value propositions that BlueIsland.com will communicate to each of the customers within our target are outlined below. The goal is to attract first-time customers and provide them with enough value to convert them into repeat customers.

> Radio stations seek access to customers at a low cost. BlueIsland.com delivers: An online radio brokerage service which enables stations to customize marketing efforts for each buyer, reach new customers, and package buying options at a fraction of the cost of traditional methods.

> Small businesses seek easy, targeted, cost-effective advertising. BlueIsland.com delivers: A free and friendly website to manage market research, plan campaigns, buy ad space, obtain creative services, and monitor ads all in one place, in a fraction of the time and cost. It's the convenient way to buy radio advertising.

### Strategic Partnerships

Strategic partnerships are fundamental in the world of Internet commerce. BlueIsland.com's strategic alliances will help increase brand equity, create barriers to entry, reduce marketing expenses, and reduce the time-to-market.

**Radio Station Partnership Strategy**

A key to BlueIsland.com's success will be the strategic partnership forged with the Radio Advertising Bureau (RAB), the national association that represents 4,300 radio stations and 80 percent of U.S. radio advertising revenues. An BlueIsland.com partnership will provide RAB with a number of benefits, including revenue sharing, an Advisory Board role, website design control, free national educational marketing campaign about the value of radio advertising, zero-cost investment in the technological advancement of the entire industry, free technical training to members, and an opportunity to open a third sales channel for RAB's radio station members. The RAB partnership will provide BlueIsland.com with access to a majority of the radio advertising industry revenues, create instant credibility, reduce BlueIsland.com's time-to-market, and create a competitive advantage. BlueIsland.com will receive access to RAB's industry contacts, membership, cross-marketing opportunities, and editorial content.

**Radio Stations Direct**

BlueIsland.com will also target non-RAB member stations that represent mom-and-pop operations in the most wired cities in the top 250 radio markets nationwide. RAB will develop custom partnership and exclusivity agreements with each participating radio station. In addition, RAB will train salespeople and accounting personnel on the easy-to-use BlueIsland.com system.

### Market Research Firm

BlueIsland.com will forge a strategic partnership with ASDM, a provider of media and marketing information for the media industry. ASDM's new online database represents information on 9,400 radio stations, including demographic profiles, market information, formats, and price. This database is updated in real-time and costs $467 per year, and $210 per additional user in the same facility. BlueIsland.com will negotiate a partnership agreement including an up-front fee for use of the information with a cost per use beyond the fixed rate. ASDM's current customers are advertising agencies and major corporate marketing departments. This partnership will enable ASDM to access new small business customers efficiently and grow their market, at no additional investment or marketing cost.

### U.S. Chamber of Commerce

BlueIsland.com will forge an alliance with the U.S. Chamber of Commerce, the world's largest business federation, representing nearly three million companies, 96 percent of which are small businesses, and 3,000 local and state chambers. U.S. Chamber of Commerce aggregates the power of small businesses to fight for their interests and provide necessary products and services. Similarly, BlueIsland.com will enable the U.S. Chamber of Commerce to offer their members a discount for our services, while supporting a service which returns buying power to the small business. This partnership provides BlueIsland.com cooperative marketing opportunities (direct mail, website, and trade shows), access to the U.S. Chamber of Commerce membership list, and a competitive advantage.

### Promotion

BlueIsland.com's strategy to attract website visitors is supported by a strong promotions effort that combines advertising and public relations strategies. The promotional efforts will focus on building brand and "buzz" around the BlueIsland.com name.

1. Advertising: Creating Awareness & Use

   **Radio:** To secure discounted or free radio ad space, BlueIsland.com will leverage its partnerships with radio stations, allocating $100,000 for the initial launch in San Francisco. The radio advertising campaign will target major radio markets and wired cities and focus on educating the small business customer about the value of radio, radio listener demographics, and the value of BlueIsland.com.

   **Internet:** In addition, BlueIsland.com will trade radio spots with Internet advertising agencies, such as AdMaster, to secure discounted Internet ad space on major small business and ad agency websites. BlueIsland.com will allocate $50,000 for Internet ad purchases.

   **Print:** BlueIsland.com will also advertise in national periodicals, which target small businesses, such as *Inc.* magazine. BlueIsland.com will allocate $100,000 for the initial launch.

2. Grassroots: Creating the Buzz

   BlueIsland.com will use its e-mail access to its membership to send promotional e-mails about discount ads that meet the customer's needs. BlueIsland.com will also encourage radio stations to offer discounts to targeted customers who have logged on with specific radio stations. This brokering service will create demand for airtime and a partnership between BlueIsland.com and their buyers and sellers.

**Marketing & Sales Strategy**

BlueIsland.com will also establish alliance partnerships or "hot links" on other small business websites, providing a stream of revenue for the host for every customer generated by that link.

**Mascot Tour:** BlueIsland.com will create a brand mascot called "Tangerine" who will tour the country, talking about the "juice" on BlueIsland.com. Tangerine will visit partnering radio station's morning talk shows, attend trade shows, and participate in parades. Tangerine will write editorial content on the website for his location, and provide a diary of his travels around the country. BlueIsland.com's public relations strategy will focus on a "Tangerine Madness" national tour. Tangerine will visit high-growth start-up companies around the country to articulate the benefit of radio.

**Trade Shows:** BlueIsland.com will attend national and regional small business tradeshows around the country to demonstrate the website and promote the BlueIsland.com name and brand.

**Charity:** BlueIsland.com will donate pre-tax profits, time, and ad space to nonprofit charitable organizations addressing issues of electronic literacy, community development investment, and global climate change. BlueIsland.com will launch a GIFTAD campaign, which provides one free ad space to a charity of their choice for every 100 visitors. Visitors will be able to select from a list of potential recipients. BlueIsland.com will enable visitors to send an e-mail about this campaign to friends and family. Tangerine will also participate in charity events that reflect the recipient organization.

3. Sales: Creating Conversion

While also helping to attract visitors, the main thrust of BlueIsland.com's promotion effort will be on converting visitors. After reviewing other e-commerce models, BlueIsland.com will initially use a traditional sales staff to make sales calls directly on businesses and provide a free technical demonstration of BlueIsland.com. These sales forces will be deployed regionally. Since the highly fragmented small business buyers are not early Internet adopters of technology, we believe this is the easiest way to build visitors, customers, and loyalty.

BlueIsland.com will use a pull strategy, by issuing a weekly e-mail newsletter for its members showcasing the buying discounts, and "fire sales" available that week. In addition, BlueIsland.com will feature businesses that have saved money through BlueIsland.com, new advertising techniques, and radio wisdom.

In addition to discounts, BlueIsland.com will establish partnerships and links with other websites. In addition BlueIsland.com will list its web advertising for sale on AdMaster. This will be a source of revenues for BlueIsland.com and an opportunity to advertise to its target market.

To motivate visitor purchases, BlueIsland.com will use 25 percent of the promotion budget on discounts, special price packs, and other tactics that will reduce the cost to the consumer and increase conversion rates. BlueIsland.com has forecasted discounts to total 5 percent of sales.

**Pricing**

BlueIsland.com's pricing strategy will be consistent with the overall objective to attract visitors. Products are priced to meet the perceived value of what they represent to the target customer. The two products for purchase on BlueIsland.com are: 1.) Value-added market research data, and 2.) Radio advertising space. Pricing of these products is reflected in membership fees and transaction fees.

**Membership Fees:**
Buyers and sellers are required to join as Tangerine members to gain access to BlueIsland.com's basic market research information, planning tools, and buying tools. To drive traffic and encourage use, membership is free to both buyers and sellers. However, to execute a trade, buyers and sellers must "pre-qualify" by completing a brief financial membership and terms and conditions form.

**Advertising Space Prices:**
Using BlueIsland.com's status as an ad agency, BlueIsland.com will receive 15 percent discount on ad space. BlueIsland.com will then list the premium advertising space for a 10 percent discount. This price will only be available on BlueIsland.com's site (not traditional suppliers), and will be competitive with listings on any other websites. BlueIsland.com will also negotiate volume-buying discounts to automatically apply to a buyer's planning schedule.

BlueIsland.com will also offer discounted advertising space through electronic "fire sales" of leftover ad space. This advertising space will be priced by the radio station and will reflect an 11-75 percent discount on regular ad space. This space will be competitive with other online providers and will be sold on a first-come, first-serve basis.

**Information Transaction Fees:**
Within the research division, buyers will have access to extra market research data for an additional fee, which reflects a percentage of the price of the market research to BlueIsland.com. The information will be presented in a one-time transaction price of $29.99 per transaction and the information requested will be saved in the buyer's profile for future use.

**Commission Fees:**
BlueIsland.com will collect a 5 percent commission from radio stations for the use of BlueIsland.com as a sales channel. This fee is transparent to the buyer and seller.

BlueIsland.com will follow a three-phase start-up plan outlined below:                **OPERATIONS PLAN**

Phase One (Q1 2000)

- Create a demonstration website
- Refine product and services mix
- Secure seed funding
- Create proposal for strategic alliances
- Secure bids on website hosting and development work
- Alpha test prototype website on focus group buyer and sellers

Phase Two (Q2-Q3 2000)

- Secure venture funding
- Hire Director of Finance and Director of Marketing
- Secure strategic alliances with RAB, independent radio stations, and market research firms
- Secure strategic alliance with U.S. Chamber of Commerce
- Outsource website development
- Secure advertising and public relations agency
- Further refine website, add national market research data
- Launch marketing plan in San Francisco as "pilot launch site"
- Beta test website in San Francisco market with all participating radio stations
- Hire 16 personnel in the website development, customer service, marketing, and sales arena

Phase Three (Q4 2000)

- Go "live" with national website
- Launch national advertising and marketing campaign in top 10 major radio/wired city markets, including: San Francisco, Atlanta, Washington, Seattle, Minneapolis, Boston, New York, Chicago, and Miami
- Issue "value reports" for first month of operation to radio station partners

**MANAGEMENT**

BlueIsland's management team has extensive experience in the marketing, Internet, and high-tech sectors. LeeAnn Masters, Chief Executive Officer, has eight years of professional experience in the field of marketing for clients in the telecommunication, real estate, multimedia, and education industries. Masters has launched grassroots marketing campaigns, managed national tradeshows, and negotiated half a million in advertising sponsorships. Ali Manon, Chief Operating Officer, has five years of experience in the high-tech industry in the areas of strategic planning, program management, software design, and development. Manon launched and managed a small household chemical manufacturing company in India for three years. In addition, Manon served as program manager for CNET News and as Internet marketing strategist at Delphi. Manon holds a master's in operations research from International University, India. Wayne Stewart, Chief Technology Officer, has three years' experience as a software developer and technology consultant. He has experience launching a successful technology consulting partnership dedicated to serving the needs of small businesses in San Francisco, California. He is currently pursuing his M.B.A. at the University of California at Berkeley, concentrating in information management and entrepreneurship.

BlueIsland.com has also worked with a team of expert consultants, which include: Stacy Williams (Media Buyer, formerly with GSD&M); John Singleton (Vice President, TateOakland Public Relations and Advertising Agency); Michael Rossi (Sales Consultant, CitySearch.com); Robert Monroe (Owner, Restaurant Holding Company); Dr. Tasmanian (Marketing Professor specializing in Marketing and the Digital Age, the University of California Graduate School of Business, UC GSB); Ernest Bolmer (Small Business Finance Professor, UC GSB); and Professor Jeb Jenkins (Entrepreneurship Professor UC GSB). BlueIsland.com is currently assembling a highly skilled board of advisors representing expertise in the radio industry, advertising, media buying, small business and Internet start-up industries.

**FINANCIAL SUMMARY**

**Deal Structure**

BlueIsland.com is seeking $2 million in equity capital. In return for this investment, the investor will receive 11 percent of the outstanding common shares of BlueIsland.com.

The capital raised in this first round of equity financing will be used as follows:

| **First-round Financing** | **$2,000,000** |
|---|---|
| Development Cost | $1,000,000 |
| Marketing & Advertising | $500,000 |
| Salary Expense | $200,000 |
| Office space leasing and other expenses | $300,000 |
| **Total** | **$2,000,000** |

BlueIsland.com also intends to raise additional funds through second and third rounds of equity financing as follows:

**Oct 2000**

Second-round Financing                                    $4,000,000

**By end of 2nd quarter 2001**

Third-round Financing                                     $4,250,000

The capital raised through these two rounds will be used to provide the working capital requirements. The largest part of these will be the advertising and marketing expenses. The initial investors will be given the first option to take part in these subsequent rounds of financing.

BlueIsland.com will provide its investors a return on investment of 70 percent. The following table illustrates the calculation of the investor's returns:

**Investor Return**

**Investment Opportunity**

| | |
|---|---|
| Investment required | $2,000,000 |
| Equity Offered | 11% |
| Industry Revenue Multiple | 20 |
| Year 5 Revenue | $26,900,000 |
| Terminal Value in 5 years with the liquidity discount of 50% | $269,000,000 |
| Value of investment in Year 5 | $28,397,140 |
| Return on Investment | 70% |

Although BlueIsland.com represents a great investment opportunity, there are inherent risks in the development of this online product, including:

**Risk Analysis**

- Website traffic is lower than expected
- Small business online commerce is lower than anticipated
- Competition appears overnight
- Demand for advertising space outstrips available advertising space for sale
- Unmet product development schedule
- Unable to secure strategic partnerships for the terms articulated and must purchase ad space and marketing lists direct

There are two primary means of an exit strategy for BlueIsland.com's investors:

**Exit Strategy**

- **Initial Public Offering.** BlueIsland.com is forecasting an IPO approximately Q1 2003
- **Merger or acquisition.** BlueIsland.com views this as the most viable harvest strategy for both the founders and the investors if the right opportunity presents itself. BlueIsland.com is an attractive acquisition for an Internet advertising website like AdMaster.com, a competitor such as AllMedia.com, or a potential player who would like access to our dedicated customers. A comparable company recently sold for $198 million to an online advertising conglomerate

**FINANCIAL STATEMENTS**

**Assumptions**

**Funding dates**

BlueIsland.com's financial plans are based upon the assumption that seed funding will occur approximately by the end of the second quarter 2000. Business activities prior to funding will include site concept demonstrations, initial strategic partner negotiations, and a limited sales campaign targeted to San Francisco radio stations, small businesses, and small advertising agencies. The financial projections will slip commensurate with funding dates beyond second quarter 2000.

### Date for "live" site

The expected "go live" in a beta test format in the San Francisco market will be in the third quarter of 2000. After an initial beta and marketing test, the national "go live" date will be fourth quarter 2000. At that period, the site will be operational for buyers and sellers.

### BlueIsland.com employee growth plan

The growth plan for BlueIsland.com takes into consideration:

- Outsource public relations and advertising
- Initial website development and hosting to reduce the time-to-market

Outsourcing allows us the ability for rapid growth and keeps us agile to respond to market and competitive changes. We will focus our employees on those things key to customer satisfaction. The roles for which employees will be hired include marketing, sales, customer service, business development, human resources, finance, and general administration.

### Key hires in Q2 2000

- Chief Executive Officer
- Director of Finance or Chief Financial Officer

### BlueIsland.com Office locations

BlueIsland.com will be headquartered in San Francisco, California, and all of its employees will reside in the San Francisco area.

## Revenue Sources

| Revenue Sources | Fee Details | Description |
|---|---|---|
| Commission fees | 5% of the transaction fees | % of transaction fees for brokering the sale of radio advertising spots. Primary revenue stream. |
| Services fees | $29.99 per usage | % of transaction fees for brokering the sale of radio advertising spots. Primary revenue stream. |
| Advertising | $45 Cost per Thousand (CPM) | % of transaction fees for brokering the sale of radio advertising spots. Primary revenue stream. |

## Expenses

### Direct Website Costs

The direct costs of the site certainly grow larger as traffic on the BlueIsland.com site traffic increases, yet the costs do not grow in a linear fashion. The direct web-related expenses include the development of BlueIsland.com site, hosting, and technical support.

### External Development

Costs of external development include consultants, contractors, applications, and tools to develop and maintain the BlueIsland.com site. We plan to outsource a large percentage of the early development work and to bring a higher percentage in-house over time. The costs for external development are derived from quotes of website development firms and historic averages.

**Hosting (To be determined)**

**Internal Development and Technical Support**
The internal capabilities of BlueIsland.com will grow over time to develop, maintain, and support the site. Key hires will include site designers, database administrator, software engineers, and content editors. As the organization grows we will bring in graphic designers and internal IT support staff. Projected costs are $15,000 per person per quarter in the year 2000 with salary growth of $17,000 per person per quarter in 2001, and $18,000 per person per quarter in 2002. This group will have the dual role of developing the BlueIsland.com site and offering customer technical support as a second level of response to customer questions after the inside sales/customer support organization. We plan to be the benchmark in customer service, which means all employees have that as their charter starting at the time of first interview with BlueIsland.com. In addition to our monetary compensation, we are planning on offering liberal stock option plans for all of our employees.

**Non-Direct Costs**

**Sales and Marketing**
The biggest expenses for BlueIsland.com are the sales and marketing costs. These are the critical elements to grab and ultimately maintain the lead over our competition. For our sales force, we projected $20,000 per quarter per person to capture salary, benefits, and commissions. We also assumed $40,000 per year per salesperson for travel and living costs to account for the substantial travel associated with covering the geographical disperse areas. The major portion of our marketing expense includes advertising and paid promotions. For our marketing staff, we forecasted $12,000 per person per quarter including salary, bonuses, and benefits.

**Financial Services**
The financial services expense takes into consideration the staffing costs to support billing, invoicing, collection, and internal reporting. As BlueIsland.com functions as advertising exchange, most of the billing, invoicing, and fund transfer would be done online using state-of-the-art applications. Hence the employee growth plan forecast assumes a conservative growth for the financial services organization. We project $12,000 per quarter per person for the financial services group that would include salary and benefits.

**Human Resources & Other Expenses**
Human Resources will be outsourced to the extent possible to payroll and 401K service firms. BlueIsland.com will still need internal HR people for recruitment and interfacing with the service firms. The projected expenses $12,000 per quarter per person including salary, bonuses, and benefits. Administrative costs include receptionist and administrative assistants. We project expenses of $10,000 per quarter per person for salary, bonus, and benefits for these positions. Other expenses include general office costs such as supplies, copier leasing, drinks, etc. Cost is projected at $1,000 per quarter per employee.

Key hires for general management by end of second quarter 2000 will include:

- **CEO**—Cost assumed is $50,000 per quarter.
- **CFO**—Cost assumed is $40,000 per quarter.
- **Director of HR**—Cost assumed is $30,000 per person.

Office lease expenses were projected at $20 per square foot and assuming 150 square feet of space per employee. Depreciation expenses include personal computers, office furniture, and other equipment. Projected costs are based on $4,000 per employee depreciated over three years. Telecommunications and data communications expenses are projected at $1,000 per employee per quarter.

| | 2000 | 2001 | 2002 | 2003 | 2004 |
|---|---|---|---|---|---|
| Website development & technical support | $52,000 | $56,160 | $60,653 | $65,505 | $70,745 |
| Customer Service | $40,000 | $43,200 | $46,656 | $50,388 | $54,420 |
| Sales | $45,000 | $48,600 | $52,488 | $56,687 | $61,222 |
| Marketing | $45,000 | $48,600 | $52,488 | $56,687 | $61,222 |
| Finance | $40,000 | $43,200 | $46,656 | $50,388 | $54,420 |
| HR | $40,000 | $43,200 | $46,656 | $50,388 | $54,420 |
| Administrative | $32,000 | $34,560 | $37,325 | $40,311 | $43,536 |
| | | | | | |
| **Executives** | | | | | |
| CEO | $200,000 | $224,000 | $250,880 | $280,986 | $314,704 |
| CFO | $160,000 | $179,200 | $200,704 | $224,788 | $251,763 |
| Director | $120,000 | $134,400 | $150,528 | $168,591 | $188,822 |
| VP | $100,000 | $112,000 | $125,440 | $140,493 | $157,352 |

# Aftermarket Internet Applications

BUSINESS PLAN                    AUTOAFTERMARKET.COM

*133 West Parker Parkway*
*Indianapolis, Indiana 46206*

*AutoAftermarket.com offers business Internet solutions to the automotive aftermarket. Primary services will include full scale e-commerce websites and business-to-business systems to address the growing concern for doing business with automobile manufacturers. Our mission is to provide our clients with Internet business services that help them become more successful and a leader in their industry. This plan was provided by Mark Kotcher and was compiled in conjunction with the business planning courses of St. Louis University's Entrepreneurship Program.*

- EXECUTIVE SUMMARY

- COMPANY SUMMARY

- SERVICES

- MARKET ANALYSIS SUMMARY

- STRATEGY & IMPLEMENTATION SUMMARY

- MANAGEMENT SUMMARY

- FINANCIAL PLAN

- ASSUMPTIONS

## EXECUTIVE SUMMARY

Brian Kelley, Ford Motor Company's Vice President of Global Consumer Services, was recently quoted as saying, "Ford, General Motors, and DaimlerChrysler welcome the participation of automotive manufacturers and suppliers in this exchange...of strategic sourcing.... This combination will allow suppliers to channel their efforts through a single exchange and will reduce overall inventories, develop industry standards, and provide productivity to all participants." AutoAftermarket.com gladly accepts this invitation.

A web development company with a new twist on the industry will be formed at the beginning of fiscal year 2001 in Indianapolis, Indiana, located in one of the top 5 most networked counties and the second largest automobile producing cities in the United States. AutoAftermarket.com, an Internet consulting company specializing in e-commerce and business-to-business applications will be targeted towards automotive aftermarket manufacturers and large-scale distributors.

AutoAftermarket.com's goal is to become a pioneer applications service providers in automotive aftermarket Internet applications, a concept that has so far only been attempted by general web houses that don't necessarily understand the complexity of the industry.

At its inception, AutoAftermarket.com will be the only automotive aftermarket focused Internet company in its target market. We will have two databases on our own server that will allow consumers and other businesses to look up parts by the manufacturers' part number, or by application. This will enable the user to in effect look up parts in a virtual catalog. The possibilities for the customer will be limitless. This offering will give us a distinct competitive advantage because it will reduce startup costs for our customers dramatically.

The target market has been shown to spend heavily for one-time setup costs for Internet and Intranet applications based on AutoAftermarket.com's research. These figures are based on sales through web development companies without automotive experience. Our pricing structure is based on a conservative approach for worst-case scenarios. Prices and sales figures should be considered conservative and are subject to real market conditions.

John Teller, a May 2000 Indiana University M.B.A. graduate, with a focus in entrepreneurship and management, and a veteran in the automotive aftermarket, will manage AutoAftermarket.com, a sole proprietorship with one family investor. John has experience at the manufacturer, distributor, and jobber level throughout his career. The primary purpose of this plan is to obtain the funding necessary to get AutoAftermarket.com off the ground.

As will be discussed further, AutoAftermarket.com breaks even in the first year, despite using a conservative approach. Numbers in the first year are also based on lagging startup sales in the first 6 months. We are expecting some heavy development time to ensure that we are marketing the very best product. This relatively fast break-even occurs because our overhead costs are low and our primary costs are our salaries.

### Objectives

1. Sales of $317,000 in 2001 and over $800,000 by 2003.
2. Net income more than 30 percent of sales by the third year.

### Mission

AutoAftermarket.com offers business Internet solutions to the automotive aftermarket. Primary services will include full scale e-commerce websites and business-to-business systems to address the growing concern for doing business with automobile manufacturers.

Our mission is to provide our clients with Internet business services that help them become more successful and a leader in their industry. It is critical for us to be a pioneer and leader in automotive aftermarket Internet business solutions by providing our clients with services that help them and their customers become more successful.

**Keys to Success**

AutoAftermarket.com will specialize in automotive aftermarket Internet solutions. While other consulting firms in the region offer Internet solutions on a broad base, there are none that we know of who specialize in this area. With today's unpredictable economic environment within the automotive aftermarket, it is increasingly difficult for companies to successfully stay in business and remain profitable. This can be seen in the increasing trend of consolidation within the industry. Our services will differ from our competitors in that AutoAftermarket.com will offer creative, innovative, and effective solutions to these business problems. Too many consulting firms try to develop standard models to solve key business problems. We realize that business problems within a particular industry have a variety of solutions; what may be right for one business in a particular industry would not necessarily meet the needs of another business in another industry. This will be our distinct competitive advantage. We realize and understand the complex nature of the automotive aftermarket, and it is that fact that enables us to give the highest quality services to our clients.

**COMPANY SUMMARY**

AutoAftermarket.com is a new company that provides high-level, industry specific expertise in the automotive aftermarket. We will offer three services to our customers:

1. Business-to-business and business-to-consumer e-commerce solutions for the aftermarket, enabling companies to more effectively sell their parts worldwide.
2. Customized web-based design.
3. Web hosting on a state-of-the-art server with unparalleled speed.

**Company Ownership**

AutoAftermarket.com is a sole proprietorship owned by John Teller. John's father, Richard Teller, will own a stake in the business of which the details are not determined at this time. Richard will also make available a revolving line of credit up to $100,000 if the need arises. Richard has total assets in excess of $2 million and is willing to cosign up to $500,000 for the business. As of this writing, the company has not been chartered and is still considering alternatives of legal formation.

**Start-up Summary**

Total start-up expenses including hardware, software, furniture, miscellaneous supplies, and initial rent and salaries comes to $119,162. John and Richard will be contributing a total of $25,000 to the business.

| **Start-up Expenses** | |
|---|---|
| Legal | $1,000 |
| Stationery, etc. | $100 |
| Brochures | $10,000 |
| Salaries - 3 months | $43,749 |
| Furniture | $5,000 |
| Rent - 3 months | $4,932 |
| Software | $2,050 |
| Software License | $25,000 |
| Travel | $2,880 |
| Start-up Expenses | $570 |
| Expensed Equipment | $2,609 |
| **Total Start-up Expenses** | **$97,890** |

**Start-up Summary**

*continued*

| Start-up Assets Needed | |
|---|---|
| Cash Requirements | $0 |
| Other Short-term Assets | $0 |
| **Total Short-term Assets** | **$0** |
| | |
| **Long-term Assets** | **$21,272** |
| **Total Assets** | **$21,272** |
| | |
| **Total Start-up Requirements** | **$119,162** |
| **Left to finance:** | **$0** |
| | |
| **Start-up Funding Plan** | |
| **Investment** | |
| John Teller | $10,000 |
| Richard Teller | $15,000 |
| Other | $0 |
| **Total investment** | **$25,000** |
| | |
| **Short-term Liabilities** | |
| Unpaid Expenses | $0 |
| Short-term Loans | $0 |
| Interest-free Short-term Loa | $0 |
| Subtotal Short-term Liabiliti | $0 |
| Long-term Liabilities | $94,162 |
| **Total Liabilities** | **$94,162** |
| | |
| **Loss at Start-up** | **($97,890)** |
| **Total Capital** | **($72,890)** |
| **Total Capital and Liabilities** | **$21,272** |
| **Checkline** | **$0** |

**Company Locations and Facilities**

To keep our overhead costs low, AutoAftermarket.com will be located at the Technology Towers in Indianapolis. This technological incubator is located in downtown Indianapolis and has meeting rooms, telephone services, copier and fax services, secretarial services, fixed utilities (included in rent), and even low cost T-1 lines.

**SERVICES**

AutoAftermarket.com offers the expertise an automotive aftermarket corporation needs to have to develop their product distribution in new and innovative ways. This may be through a full-blown e-commerce website, or something as simple as a web page with an e-mail address.

**Service Description**

There is no doubt that the Internet has become an integral part of the U.S. culture over the past 10 years. Though it appears that the automotive aftermarket has been behind the times. With recent announcements in the automobile industry, it is evident that the automotive aftermarket will be receiving a full reality check on their competitiveness through the Internet.

On February 25, 2000, Ford, General Motors, and DaimlerChrysler announced that they are planning to combine their efforts to form a business-to-business integrated supplier exchange through a single global portal. This will create the world's largest virtual marketplace. Ford President and CEO Jacques Nasser stated: "Today's announcement is another example of how the Internet is transforming every piece of our company and our industry. It's exciting, it's dramatic, and it's only going to accelerate. By joining together, we can further increase the pace of implementation."

What this means for the automotive aftermarket is that if a company wants to be a strategic supplier for any of the car manufacturers, they must have a business-to-business strategy in place on the Internet. This is where AutoAftermarket.com comes in. Unlike our generic web-hosting competitors, AutoAftermarket.com will have all the tools required to interface with the largest automakers by utilizing a cataloging and part number database. This will dramatically reduce their startup costs and implementation time, putting them ahead of their competition.

The company will host a state-of-the-art website owned and maintained by AutoAftermarket.com where automotive aftermarket customers can host their site, have e-mail capabilities, and utilize a database that will enable corporations to sell their products and services online to any audience. We will have a staff that will design the web pages to their specifications and the backend technology that enables clean and effective online cataloging and e-commerce transactions.

Danny Chessin, Executive Vice President of Hahn Automotive (which happens to be in the Top 20 among automotive chains in the U.S.) states that "particularly in the auto parts business a real barrier of entry for 99 percent of the companies to get on the Internet is the cataloging issue." Hahn is currently the only company of 70,000 utilizing NPI/Triads' electronic catalog on the Internet for this very reason. We feel very confident that once AutoAftermarket.com develops this sophisticated database, potential customers will not be able to pass up this service.

Our vision is to make AutoAftermarket.com a clearinghouse for all automotive part transactions on the web. This will require our customers to have an inventory management and ordering system already in place. Fortunately, just about every manufacturer, distributor, and jobber in the United States have these systems in place.

AutoAftermarket.com will not only create the customer's web page, but will also have the cataloging and part number technology developed and on-hand, as well as having the capabilities to host the customer's website on our automotive aftermarket-dedicated server.

We plan to supplement these larger applications (i.e. projects that require more time) with web pages that don't at this time require an e-commerce application for small to medium-sized customers. Our product will be distinctive because we will have a graphic artist on staff with automotive aftermarket experience who can offer more creative artistic solutions than our competitors. Also, it will be to our customers' benefit to have their web page on AutoAftermarket.com because if they ever do want to conduct business online, the technology will already be in place.

These generally take less time and will be critical to the cash flow of AutoAftermarket.com. We believe that there is a significant market for manufacturers that want to put some of their "bright star" applications on their web page for DIYs or prospective distributor purchasing agents. A professional purchasing manager will be investigating all avenues of research to find out if their supplier is offering the best products and services possible. It is our belief that this market research will take place online.

An example of where this type of application has been successful in the automotive aftermarket can be found with Kelley Performance Products, maker of carburetors, fuel injectors, ignition systems, engine systems, and customized engine parts for racing and street applications. Kelley's embracement of the Internet has cut their costs and workload according to Mack Miller, communications manager. "It was basically born out of a major frustration I've had for many years to supply artwork to our customers quickly and effectively." Because of the

Internet, distributors and catalog companies can now acquire photos in minutes rather than waiting for Kelley to process film and duplication at a photo lab, and then package the artwork for shipment. Prior to their Internet implementation, Miller was spending approximately $50,000 to supply their customers with art.

A feasibility study of the Internet environment will be conducted for each customer with any service we offer. It is important to AutoAftermarket.com that we help enhance the selling process of our customers. Our knowledge of the automotive aftermarket, as well as the Internet, will be fully utilized to offer the best solution for our customer. It is our belief that we are not successful unless our customer is successful. The amount and type of customers that can benefit from an online system is limitless. We feel confident that once the customer spends the initial cost of getting on the Internet, both our companies will enjoy a profitable relationship by reaching more customers.

## Competitive Comparison

Internet consulting within the automotive aftermarket is virtually nonexistent. There is only one other company that we know of that claims to cater to the automotive industry. InternetSource, based in Charlotte, North Carolina, has a package known as "E.MBRACE" that gives manufacturers and distributors of automotive products an affordable way to conduct business profitably over the Internet. It is a package that can be "quickly incorporated into your existing business systems without extensive customization or IT staff." Although they claim to focus around the automotive aftermarket, there is not one person on their corporate staff that has any automotive experience.

Another industry participant worthy of mentioning is Network Partners Incorporated (NPI), based in Austin, Texas. They would be considered more of an alternative product than a direct competitor. NPI has been a supplier of computer systems to the automotive aftermarket for many years. Their market share of distributor-to-jobber automation services is estimated at around 60-70 percent. It is best designed for interactions between the distribution center and jobber stores, although some major service shops have it, too. It is basically an online perpetual inventory system that runs on their supplied machines. The hardware is quite expensive, as is the software, maintenance, and in-house consultant. There are many drawbacks besides the expense, including that the system is not in real time (overnight refresh) and it is not Windows-based. Regardless of its market share, it is known for being extremely user-unfriendly.

## Sales Literature

The business will begin with a detailed corporate brochure establishing the different services AutoAftermarket.com will offer. It will quote various industry experts detailing what advantages other corporations have recognized after automating their supply chain. This brochure will be developed as part of the startup expenses.

## Fulfillment

AutoAftermarket.com provides intellectual services and will employ three professionals with varying degrees of experience. One e-commerce professional with 5 plus years of experience will be hired for projects of medium to large magnitudes. A general web specialist will be hired with 3 years' industry experience for smaller applications as well as assisting the e-commerce professional. Also a graphic artist who has experience in the automotive aftermarket will be on staff so that AutoAftermarket.com can offer superior looking services. While all reports will be produced and edited by John Teller, the physical reports will be formatted, printed and bound by the secretarial services at Technology Towers. It is forecasted that another web specialist will be added in year two and another e-commerce professional will be added in year three.

The enterprise server where the physical data will reside is a PowerEdge 8450 supplied by Dell. It represents the highest performance in an industry-standard server with up to 8 Intel Pentium III Xeon processors. It is also armed with Intel's Profusion chipset which keeps the data moving with its advanced crossbar architecture. The machine we have selected comes with 4 Intel processors, 1 gigabyte RAM, twin 18-gigabyte SCSI hard drives, 10 hot-plug PCI slots, and the Linux operating system. We will also add 4 18-gigabyte hard drives every subsequent year. AutoAftermarket.com will be leasing this machine at $1,381 per month.

We will also be utilizing a NetForce 2200 manufactured by Procom Technology to provide instant storage for our internal network, as well as overflow for the web server. The model we have selected has 6 25-gigabyte hard drives. The NetForce 2200 acts as a data pump that offers file storage and sharing on the network, distributing 150 gigabytes of data more quickly than if it was stored on a general-purpose file server. It is designed for CAD/CAM or digital photo applications and will be a benefit to AutoAftermarket.com for a cost of $10,675.

AutoAftermarket.com will maintain the latest Windows and Macintosh capabilities including complete e-mail and corporate website on the Internet so that companies looking for our service will have a direct link to us. We will have state-of-the-art equipment, including 3 Compaq Presarios, 1 Macintosh, top-of-the-line peripherals, interoffice network, and all the latest software. Software packages will include Macromedia Dreamweaver UltraDev for e-commerce, ColdFusion for web development, the Adobe Publishing Collection for graphic art, and Acid Pro for online digital music.

Security issues will be a major technological issue, especially with regard to the e-commerce sites we will set up for manufacturers and distributors. We will plan on using all the latest data encryption techniques available throughout the industry. For locking up e-commerce security, we plan on using Entrust Technologies' patented certification revocation list distribution technology mainly because it is part of the Internet Engineering Task Force standards. We are also optimistic because they offer free licenses to parts of its patented technology.

If the customer plans on having high volumes of e-commerce transactions, we will also recommend that they get in touch with WebTrust Organization. Accountants who do on-site audits of e-commerce security systems, transaction integrity, and personal information administer this organization. The cost for a WebTrust seal will range from $5,000 to $100,000 per year depending on the site's amount of business. The accounting houses will then check in every 90 days to ensure that Net firms are up to compliance with all terms of the seal program.

We will also recommend that our customers look in to purchasing insurance to protect themselves against Internet hackers. There are many companies such as ACE USA, AIG, and Sedgwick that offer e-commerce insurance policies that cost between $25,000 and $125,000 in annual premiums for companies with less than $1 billion in revenues.

**Future Services**

We will continually expand our services based on industry trends and changing client needs. Some visionaries within the Internet industry believe that the Internet of the future will include utilities like cellular phones, microwaves, and even washing machines and refrigerators. The beauty is that for any of these items to interact over the Internet, a programmer's skills will be required. It will be critical for AutoAftermarket.com to stay abreast of all new technologies that will affect our customers.

**MARKET ANALYSIS SUMMARY**

AutoAftermarket.com will be focusing on manufacturers and distributors in the automotive aftermarket that want to increase their competitive edge, especially when supplying the automobile industry, and open up communication lines with their customers.

**Market
Segmentation**

The annual U.S. production of motor vehicle parts and accessories is valued at over $90 billion. The industry is made up of two principal sections: original equipment manufacturers (OEMs) and aftermarket suppliers. OEMs sell parts and components directly to automobile manufacturers for the production of new vehicles. Aftermarket suppliers manufacture and sell replacement parts for use in vehicles already on the road. The majority of automotive parts manufacturers sell to both OEMs and aftermarket companies.

**Target Market
Segment Strategy**

The target markets that we will focus on are the manufacturers and distributors of auto parts. During the first year we will pay particular attention to the manufacturers because of the urgency with the major automakers. The plan is to break down manufacturers into two categories: original equipment manufacturers and aftermarket manufacturers. Following is a list of 6 of the top 20 that we will be pursuing heavily as customers, due to their profile, selling patterns, and the existence of established contacts:

- Dana Corporation
- Delco Electronics Corporation
- TRW Incorporated
- Robert Bosch Corporation
- Nippondenso Company Limited
- ITT Automotive

We will also focus on some of the major aftermarket companies based on the same criteria such as the following:

- Tenneco Automotive
- Federal-Mogul Corporation
- Echlin, Incorporated
- Tenneco, Incorporated
- Monroe Auto Equipment Company

Segmenting the automotive distributors will be done by determining who is primarily oriented to the consumer (do-it-yourself) and who is oriented towards the professional installer. The do-it-yourself distributor will be more interested in reaching a large, nationwide audience for parts that can ship from any one of a hundred warehouses they own. We will recommend that they develop a program around free shipping just like Stan Roland does with Smartcars.com. Because of their increased volume and strategic sourcing, they are able to offer free shipping and significant discounts. Following are some of the chains we will target and the percentage of DIY business as reported by their CEO:

| | |
|---|---|
| Autozone | 90% |
| O'Reilly Auto Parts | 50% |
| R&L Warehouse (Federated) | 50% |
| Smyth Automotive (Pronto) | 40% |
| Hub City Warehouse | 40% |

The non-DIYer distributor will be more interested in improving their distribution chain than reaching the consumer, which we certainly can do through the Internet. However, AutoAftermarket.com sees this as an opportunity. Perhaps a distributor classified as "non-DIY" would benefit most by gaining DIY sales, a target market that they have never even identified. How could a company pass up the opportunity to increase their consumer sales without having to add additional sales people or a major advertising/marketing campaign? Following is a list of companies in our target market that we see as an excellent opportunity:

| | |
|---|---|
| Merrill Company | 15% |
| Barron Motor, Incorporated | 20% |
| Jarvis Supply Company (Federated) | 20% |
| Cape Warehouse (Pronto) | 20% |
| Pat Young Service Company | 25% |

During the first three years, AutoAftermarket.com will call on a 600-mile radius area around Indianapolis, including metropolitan areas such as Kansas City, Memphis, Detroit, Cleveland, Cincinnati, St. Louis, and Chicago. Many regional and national manufacturers, distributors, and specialty shops reside in this area. 61.6 percent of all manufacturers and 21.9 percent of all distributors listed in the "1999 Top 100 Auto Parts Chains" in the contiguous United States reside in this area primarily due to the strategic sourcing of car manufacturers. There is a limited offering of automotive aftermarket focused Internet consultants in the country, so there is a lot of potential opportunity.

**Market Needs**

By far, the greatest market need will come out of the major automakers' requirement of electronic strategic sourcing. As Harold R. Kutner, Group Vice President of General Motors Worldwide says, "It's the largest Internet business ever created. Nobody will be better. Nobody will be faster. Nobody will offer more to everyone involved." This no doubt will fuel the rest of the automotive aftermarket to become Internet-ready.

Another market need that AutoAftermarket.com will fulfill is the fact that the automotive aftermarket is in a major consolidation period. It is becoming more and more difficult to remain competitive. Many companies are looking for new and innovative ways to create additional sales. Another aspect of bringing automotive aftermarket companies online is that it will reduce the purchasing cycle, thereby directly reducing operating costs.

Another problem that AutoAftermarket.com tries to solve is to have more effective orders, i.e. fewer errors. Most companies experience a key-entry error rate of between 3-5 percent. Consequently, it is estimated that the handling of an error costs 5 to 10 times that of handling information transmitted correctly. A general rule of thumb for the cost of manually handling an incoming purchase order is somewhere between $50 and $75. Imagine eliminating just key-entry errors: this would save the customer 5 to 10 times that of $50 to $75. Also, by some estimates, the $75 handling charge when combined with an electronic ordering system can slash the cost of processing a purchase order to as little as $6.

**Market Trends**

The world's major auto manufacturers are currently restructuring their operations in North America, Europe, Asia, and Latin America. The parts manufacturers have responded to globalization by strategizing their operations to supply auto parts worldwide. This has resulted in a sharper focus by parts manufacturers on their core competencies in order to become more competitive. This in turn has changed the look of the automotive parts industry. Many automotive manufacturers have undergone strategic mergers and acquisitions in order to pool their resources and gain a competitive edge. Manufacturers who have been unable to do this have been forced to close their doors. The value of mergers and acquisitions soared annually, nearing a record $19 billion in 1997, up 27 percent from the previous year. Although this sounds like a weakness of the industry, AutoAftermarket.com will utilize this shortcoming as a selling point.

**Market Growth**

The automotive parts industry accounted for slightly over 4 percent ($157 billion) of total U.S. manufacturing shipments in 1997. It is projected that by 2003, industry shipments may approach $189 billion.

The compound annual growth rate for the past ten years was 9.5 percent. More recent years have seen increases of 5 and 6 percent, somewhat lower than previous. Traditionally, growth in the U.S. aftermarket has been directly related to the size and age of the vehicle fleet. As discussed previously, the primary reason for this relatively low level of growth has been the dramatic improvement of quality in U.S. auto manufacturers.

Domestically, firms have restructured themselves in an effort to maintain their competitive position with Japan. This consolidation of the market to become more competitive plays a key role in the future growth of the industry. To give an example, Dana Corporation between 1993 and 1996, completed 24 purchases or joint ventures. In 1998, they announced their acquisition of Echlin, creating a company worth $13 billion in annual sales.

Future growth for U.S. automotive firms will continue to be technology-driven with more and more government regulation. Fuel efficiency, safety, and environmental regulations will open up new windows in the parts market. Consolidation and competition will remain major issues for U.S. aftermarket suppliers over the long term. Many firms will become more competitive by automating their manufacturing and supply chain with Enterprise Resource Systems. Any ERP such as SAP and J. D. Edwards can and will link the entire industry to the Internet in some capacity, whether it's linking the supply chain together (B to B) or making products available to the end-user (B to C).

## Service Business Analysis

The consulting business consists of thousands of smaller consulting organizations and individual consultants for every one of the few dozen well-known companies.

Consulting participants range from major international name-brand consultants to tens of thousands of individuals. One of AutoAftermarket.com's challenges will be establishing itself as a "real" consulting company, positioned as a relatively risk-free corporate purchase.

## Distributing a Service

Consulting today is sold and purchased mainly on a word-of-mouth basis, with relationships and previous experience being by far the most important factor. Some of the smaller jobs tend to go out on bid with online sites such as E-Lance and Yahoo!

The larger, more well known Internet consulting firms like Razorfish and Web USA have locations in major cities and major markets, and executive-level managers or partners developing new business through industry associations, business associations, and chambers of commerce and industry.

## Competition and Buying Patterns

The traditional buying process for consulting services varies by type of client and by type of service. Businesses find and choose consulting firms using several methods. Referral businesses find consultants through their lending institutions, business or industry associations, friends or colleagues, and the Yellow Pages. Businesses contact these consulting firms to obtain proposals and price quotes for the required services. A consulting firm is chosen based on the needs of the client, such as price, quality of proposal, as well as the reputation, past experience, and level of expertise of the consulting firm.

This was verified by General Parts Incorporated, the largest member of the CARQUEST buying group and the largest privately owned corporation in North Carolina. When they realized the need for an online presence and an Intranet, they went by different referrals from people within the industry, as well as their internal IS people. After a number were referred, the process of interviewing began until a final decision was made.

Companies in the automotive aftermarket will not necessarily seek out Internet consultants who are focused towards the automotive aftermarket because, for all intents and purposes, they don't exist. This is the type of industry where AutoAftermarket.com must have an aggressive sales campaign with brochures, and advertisements in industry journals, and must be constantly making contacts. Fortunately, John Teller has many contacts throughout the industry. Also, John's father is well known, being an industry executive himself, so the Teller name has an excellent reputation.

**STRATEGY & IMPLEMENTATION SUMMARY**

Our main strategy is to emphasize the business-to-business automation as automotive aftermarket firms strive to become more competitive, especially with the automobile manufacturers. In a sense, we will be pioneering a relatively new market, so deviating from the strategy is not an option.

**Strategy Pyramids**

Underneath this strategy, our main tactics are utilizing industry experience, advanced technical knowledge based assets, and unparalleled communication and educational skills.

Our industry experience will aid us in understanding the customer and the customer's customer to bridge the communication gap between the jobber and professional installer. We will stay active in various trade organizations like the Automotive Warehouse Distributors Association and the Automotive Parts and Accessories Association to build and maintain relationships throughout the industry. We will constantly maintain our presence by targeting customers based on industry knowledge first, and technological skills second.

Our technological skills will help us get the job done after the program is sold. Part of a successful consulting business is to keep as close to the schedule as possible. It is much like law firms, all that matters are billable hours. It will be critical that our technical skills be excellent and to not go over 10 percent on projects. Otherwise, AutoAftermarket.com runs the risk of a tarnished reputation.

Our communication skills will be extremely important in educating the customer and the end user on how to utilize the system we have built. It is relatively easy to put together an Internet system that functions, but having the ability to educate the users is when the project is truly finished. Our focus on education will be another distinction of AutoAftermarket.com from the competition.

John has extensive training experience with PCs at the distributor level, as well as ERPs at the manufacturing level. In fact, John was part of the implementation training team in SAP/R3 for pricing database management, as well as sales analysis for Moog Automotive.

One of our major value propositions is that AutoAftermarket.com will have already spent the money, time, and resources to develop a sophisticated behind-the-scenes approach to cataloging and SKU database management. A single company to do this independently would be extremely expensive and time consuming. Our pooling of resources will benefit the customer in the end to get them faster to market.

**Value Proposition**

Another value proposition is that because of our excellent relationships with manufacturers, our database will be more up-to-date than anyone else in the industry. Most companies wait until the next issue of *Triad's Electronic Catalog* because it is a quarterly publication. But, AutoAftermarket.com's customers will be more up to date than anyone else in the industry because we will constantly update the database whenever new applications are released.

Our clients will benefit from a team of experts with experience in the aftermarket to come into their business for a specialized product that will help them become more effective selling entities. They will be happy to pay top dollar for industry-specific expertise, especially since it addresses critical competitive issues. Our e-commerce developments are a one-time variable cost, whereas the alternative is a management team including major additions to their MIS department that would be a fixed cost, and this person would not be as skilled at the specific job that we do.

## Competitive Edge

We start with a critical competitive edge: there is no competitor we know of that can claim anywhere near as much specific technological expertise, coupled by the fact that we have grown up in the industry with experience at all levels. Our positioning on this fact is very hard to match, but only if we maintain this focus in our strategy, sales and marketing, education, and industry relationships. It is important to note that hiring more generalized Internet consultants would tend to dilute the expertise that AutoAftermarket.com brings to the table.

Another competitive edge that will distinguish AutoAftermarket.com from the competition is that not only do we provide e-commerce publishing services, but we also have heavily invested in machine and database capital to ensure that our site runs at the greatest speed with the latest technologies. It will be updated every month for new applications and prices automatically because all e-commerce applications at AutoAftermarket.com run on the same database behind the scenes.

## Marketing Strategy

Part of our marketing strategy will be to offer our e-commerce service for free to a smaller company to prove to the industry what we can do. This customer must be chosen carefully, however, because we would not want to get into a 6-month implementation. It needs to be someone relatively local so that we may work with them more closely to iron out any bugs that may be in the system. One good candidate that we are considering is Superior Chassis located in Gary, Indiana. They have one main product line with a standard set of part numbers that would be relatively simple when compared to some of the larger, more complex companies. Because the automotive aftermarket works on a word-of-mouth basis, especially with IS consultants, we believe this would get our name out there.

Part of this marketing technique will require us to have a website at www.AutoAftermarket.com that shows our capabilities and what we are all about. We will also show links to the sites that reside on our system, such as Superior Chassis in our previous example. We feel confident that when word travels about our new service, prospects will jump on our website to at least check us out.

When we are going through this implementation process, we would like to have some press coverage as well. *Aftermarket Business* would more than likely want to carry the story, especially to address how the automotive aftermarket is responding to the automobile industry's massive changes. *Aftermarket Business* happens to be the largest publication of its kind and would be a great avenue to make our name heard, especially in light of a headline such as, "AutoAftermarket.com addresses Automakers e-commerce Issues: For free!!!" Imagine the number of hits our site would get in that day alone.

AutoAftermarket.com will have two brochures; one for manufacturers and one for distributors (consequently, the distributor version will be written generically enough to be used for other applications as well). The manufacturing brochure will include details of the automakers' requirements and why it is critical for them to have business-to-business capabilities. The distributor version will focus more towards doing business online, whether business-to-business or business-to-consumer and what they may be missing out on in the future.

We will also run a couple of ads throughout the year in trade magazines. One in particular that we would like to run is an ad focusing around online manufacturers. We may even look into working out an interview about how critical it is to be online in order to be a major automotive supplier.

Another marketing strategy that AutoAftermarket.com will utilize is to go directly to the automotive manufacturers and form a strategic alliance to gain some business through them. If we were able to establish an excellent rapport and reputation with one of them, it would make all the difference in pursuing new customers. Fortunately, John's grandfather, Walt Johnson, used to be the Vice President of Personnel at Ford Motor Company for many years. We feel confident that we could get a meeting together because of some old contact to try to be their "go-to" firm when a manufacturer is looking to get online. It will be very critical for us to get the first customer under our belt to show that we are capable.

We will also hold two free seminars per year to educate companies about what AutoAftermarket.com can do for them. One will be held in Indianapolis and the other will be held in Las Vegas at the Automotive Warehouse Distributors Association (AWDA) annual conference. We believe that showing people our capabilities face-to-face tends to be more effective.

For manufacturers and distributors of auto parts who intend to stay competitive by automating the selling transaction, AutoAftermarket.com offers very specialized, industry specific expertise. Unlike the general Internet consultants, AutoAftermarket.com can provide a superior Internet commerce solution along with a top-notch ASP designed to be immediately effective in the automotive aftermarket.

**Positioning Statement**

AutoAftermarket.com will be priced at the upper edge of what the market will bear, competing with general Internet consultants. The pricing fits with the general positioning of AutoAftermarket.com as high-level, industry specific expertise. We will require 50 percent up front with the balance at project completion.

**Pricing Strategy**

E-commerce consulting will be based on $130 per hour, and $90 per hour for general web design. Graphic design portions of projects will be priced around $40 per hour. These numbers were established through a pricing analysis based on general web-consulting, as well as price quotes throughout the industry.

We will be charging $150 per month for a company to host its e-commerce site on our server. For this service they receive e-mail capabilities, high-speed access for themselves as well as their customers, use of an unparalleled database and catalog, and unlimited service from our staff. For a general website, we will charge $50 per month, which seems to be the middle of the road for business site hosting.

For our service, we will also require that the company pay back to us 1 percent of all sales gained on our server. We believe that the market can bear 1 percent of its total earnings.

Our promotion strategy will be three-fold. Our primary strategy will be the high-quality brochure sent to strategic individuals as mentioned previously. We will also run a couple ads per year in various automotive trade magazines. Lastly, we will offer two free seminars once a year to be held in Indianapolis and Las Vegas for industry professionals to learn more about what the Internet can do for their aftermarket company. This demonstration should generate some major activity. Needless to say, there is no better sales tool than actual demonstrations.

**Promotion Strategy**

Business-to-business e-commerce services will be the key product offered to the OEM/ aftermarket manufacturers. Our main selling point will be that the system we will design will be tailored to their business strategy and will reduce operating costs considerably. According to Intersearch Corporation, most executives believe that an Internet-based electronic trading system would increase the accuracy of billing by 31 percent, increase the accuracy of orders by 29 percent, reduce the purchase cycle by 62 percent, and reduce operating costs associated with this cycle by 45 percent. Gartner Group takes this further by saying that the most successful Internet strategies are those where companies use the Web to strengthen the distribution chain. Once we have some projects completed, we will show potential customers what we have done previously.

Our other major product segment will be to build websites for aftermarket companies. These generally take less time to compile and are good for keeping the cash flow of the business in good standing. Our web pages will be better than the competition because of our vast experience with the automotive field. One of our selling points will be that our graphic artist has worked in the automotive parts manufacturing industry in a graphic arts capacity for over a year.

## Marketing Programs

Our most important method of gaining recognition throughout the industry will be networking with key executives through current relationships. We do not believe that a major advertising campaign will bring major inquiries on our services. However, we will run some ads in automotive trade magazines to at least get our name out in the industry. Our annual budget for magazine advertising will be no more than $7,500. We will plan to run a small ad every quarter in two automotive journals: one focused on manufacturing and one focused on distributors.

## Sales Strategy

Our key sales strategy will be to first send out the corporate brochure to highly qualified prospects within the industry. This will be followed closely by a phone call from John Teller to set up a meeting to discuss. In the first few months, John will be taking the e-commerce professional to these meetings so that he/she can demonstrate what they have done in the past and what they can do for the customer. Once a couple of customers have been established, John can make these calls independently (unless it is a major proposal) and use examples from what AutoAftermarket.com has done for other customers.

It will be vital to our business to sell quality based on technological background and business industry experience. We will also exploit the fact that most consultants are not an ASP, and virtually none of them have both an ASP and come from the automotive aftermarket. It is certainly not our intention to be the low cost provider. AutoAftermarket.com's services are much more valuable than the competition. Any Internet company can build a website, but only AutoAftermarket.com truly understands their customer and the industry. Business-to-business e-commerce only becomes truly effective when solutions are industry-specific.

## Sales Forecast

The following table and chart give a run-down on forecasted sales. We expect sales to be sluggish as AutoAftermarket.com tries to establish itself. We do expect sales to increase within a few months of startup. We are also forecasting higher increases at the beginning of each year due to budgets being established. The sales budget is based on $130 per hour for e-commerce work/business-to-business work, $90 per hour for general web programming, and $40 per hour for graphic design. The budget takes into account 70 percent efficiency.

Sales are considerably higher in years 2 and 3 due to adding one employee per year. We expect an increase in sales of 83.5 percent in year 2, and 61.5 percent in year 3. We are confident that once the word is out that there is an Internet consultant with automotive experience, our market niche will be booming.

| Sales | 2001 | 2002 | 2003 |
|---|---|---|---|
| Graphic Design | $46,072.00 | $59,156.00 | $59,565.00 |
| Web Development | $103,661.00 | $265,044.00 | $265,724.00 |
| E-Commerce | $149,737.00 | $192,258.00 | $387,172.00 |
| % Sales | $1,796.91 | $15,584.00 | $109,191.00 |
| Web Hosting - General | $8,974.40 | $28,673.00 | $28,697.00 |
| Web Hosting - E-Commerce | $7,137.17 | $12,525.00 | $25,272.00 |
| **Total Sales** | **$317,378.48** | **$573,240.00** | **$875,621.00** |

## Sales Programs

We do not want to run any promotions or discounts at this point. There is little point in offering discounts or free services to a virtually untapped market. As mentioned previously, our discounts will occur if there is added business or a long-term relationship is established.

## Strategic Alliances

The major strategic alliance that we want to form is with Ford Motor Company. If a manufacturer ever asks automakers where they can find a company to put them on the Internet, we want them referred to us.

## Milestones

The accompanying table lists important program milestones, with start and end dates, and budgets for each. The milestone schedule indicates our emphasis on planning for implementation.

What the table doesn't show is the commitment behind it. We will hold monthly follow-up meetings every month to discuss the variance and course corrections to ensure that everything is completed in a timely fashion.

| Milestone | Start Date | End Date | Budget |
|---|---|---|---|
| Purchase Hardware and Software | 12/1/00 | 1/1/01 | $25,931 |
| Set-up Office | 1/1/01 | 1/15/01 | $5,000 |
| Pursue Loan | 7/1/00 | 9/1/00 | $0 |
| Brochures | 10/1/00 | 11/1/00 | $10,000 |
| Hire Staff | 10/1/00 | 12/15/00 | $300 |
| New Hire - Web Design | 1/1/02 | 2/1/02 | $300 |
| New Hire - E-Commerce | 1/1/03 | 2/1/03 | $300 |
| New Computer Year 2 | 1/1/02 | 1/15/02 | $2,199 |
| New Computer Year 3 | 1/1/03 | 1/15/03 | $2,199 |
| **Totals** | | | **$46,229** |

## MANAGEMENT SUMMARY

The management team for at least the first few years will be John Teller, founder and owner of AutoAftermarket.com. As we grow, we may take on additional management expertise if the volume of business justifies it.

## Organizational Structure

Everyone in one respect or another will report to John Teller. However, the office will be structured so that everyone has enough room to grow and hone their individual skills to enhance their business success. To do this, the web designer (typically with less experience and expertise than the e-commerce professional) will report to the e-commerce manager. It is John's intent for this to be a mentor role so that the web developer could then step up and fulfill an e-commerce role some day. As mentioned previously, education is a critical success factor for AutoAftermarket.com.

The graphic designer will technically report to John, but it will be critical to foster a creative environment for this position. This artist should be making many graphic decisions on their own. This will be a fast-paced, facilitating role.

## Management Team

AutoAftermarket.com is a sole proprietorship owned by John Teller. John has the benefit of having grown up in the automotive aftermarket industry, holding positions at jobber stores, distribution centers, corporate offices, and manufacturers. He has gained a vast knowledge of information systems within an automotive aftermarket environment. He is certified for training in SAP-R/3 with Sales Information Systems and Pricing Database Management, which he accomplished while an integral part of an SAP implementation team for a leading automotive aftermarket manufacturer. John has a business management degree from Ohio State University and will have completed a specialized M.B.A. in management/entrepreneurship from Indiana University. He has held various positions of increasing responsibility in sales and marketing, as well as MIS consulting for a medium-sized distributor. AutoAftermarket.com will initially have four employees. Additional staff support will be obtained as further success of the company allows in subsequent years.

## Management Team Gaps

Certainly the biggest gap in the management team is the lack of a professional with a financial background. If enough volume were present, a chief financial officer would be considered to ensure that AutoAftermarket.com is on the right path. Unfortunately, cost just doesn't allow it in the short-term.

## Personnel Plan

The following table summarizes our personnel expenditures for the first three years, with compensation increasing from $175,000 the first year to about $345,000 in the third. We believe this plan is a fair compromise between fairness and expedience and meets the commitment of our mission statement. The detailed monthly personnel plan for the first year follows.

| Personnel | 2001 | 2002 | 2003 |
|---|---|---|---|
| Graphic Designer | $30,000 | $31,500 | $33,075 |
| Web Developer | $45,000 | $92,250 | $96,863 |
| E-Commerce Professional | $100,000 | $105,000 | $215,250 |
| Other | $0 | $0 | $0 |
| **Total Payroll** | **$175,000** | **$228,750** | **$345,188** |
| | | | |
| **Total Headcount** | **3** | **4** | **5** |
| **Total Payroll Expenditure** | **$175,000** | **$228,750** | **$345,188** |

## FINANCIAL PLAN

We are predicting that the business will grow at a relatively rapid rate. Fortunately, financing that growth will not be much of an issue due to a low number of fixed costs. Our major expense by far is salary at over 50 percent of the total expenditure per year. As long as collection goes well, these salaries will be covered with profits to spare. Part of our strategic plan is to offset the major e-commerce projects with smaller web design projects to keep our cash flow in good standing. Keep in mind that we are assuming start-up capital of $94,162. This will be the only long-term loan required for AutoAftermarket.com, at least for the first 3 years.

## Important Assumptions

AutoAftermarket.com recognizes that collection days are critical. We will make it a corporate goal to keep collections within 30 days. We are assuming that we will do a fairly good job at collecting. Interest rates, tax rates, and personnel compensation are based on conservative assumptions.

| General Assumptions | 2001 | 2002 | 2003 |
|---|---|---|---|
| Short-term Interest Rate % | 12.00% | 12.00% | 12.00% |
| Long-term Interest Rate % | 12.00% | 12.00% | 12.00% |
| Payment Days Estimator | 30 | 30 | 30 |
| Collection Days Estimator | 30 | 30 | 30 |
| Tax Rate % | 28.00% | 28.00% | 28.00% |
| Expenses in Cash % | 10.00% | 10.00% | 10.00% |
| Sales on Credit % | 50.00% | 50.00% | 50.00% |
| Personnel Burden % | 0.00% | 0.00% | 0.00% |

**Break-even Analysis**

| Break-even Analysis: | | | |
|---|---|---|---|
| Monthly Units Break-even | 19,519 | | |
| Monthly Sales Break-even | $19,519 | | |

| Assumptions: | | | |
|---|---|---|---|
| Average Per-Unit Revenue | $1.00 | | |
| Average Per-Unit Variable Cost | $0.02 | | |
| Estimated Monthly Fixed Cost | $19,129 | | |

**Projected Profit & Loss**

| | 2001 | 2002 | 2003 |
|---|---|---|---|
| Sales | $317,378.48 | $573,240.00 | $875,621.00 |
| Direct Cost of Sales | $0.00 | $0.00 | $0.00 |
| Production Payroll | $0.00 | $0.00 | $0.00 |
| Other | $0.00 | $0.00 | $0.00 |
| **Total Cost of Sales** | **$0.00** | **$0.00** | **$0.00** |
| | | | |
| Gross Margin | $317,378.48 | $573,240.00 | $875,621.00 |
| Gross Margin % | $1.00 | $1.00 | $1.00 |
| | | | |
| **Operating expenses:** | | | |
| Server Lease | $16,572.00 | $16,572.00 | $16,572.00 |
| Database Licenses | $1,500.00 | $26,500.00 | $26,500.00 |
| Advertising/Promotion | $7,500.00 | $8,250.00 | $9,075.00 |
| Travel | $11,520.00 | $15,322.00 | $20,378.00 |
| Payroll Expense | $174,999.96 | $228,750.00 | $345,187.50 |
| Depreciation | $4,254.00 | $4,694.40 | $5,134.40 |
| Payroll Tax Expense | $13,179.00 | $17,477.00 | $24,548.00 |
| Utilities | $0.00 | $0.00 | $0.00 |
| Insurance | $7,440.00 | $10,492.00 | $15,527.00 |
| Rent | $13,152.00 | $13,152.00 | $13,152.00 |
| Vehicle Expense | $4,500.00 | $4,500.00 | $4,500.00 |
| Office Expense | $696.00 | $870.00 | $1,044.00 |
| Phone Expense | $1,800.00 | $1,980.00 | $2,178.00 |
| Organization Dues | $150.00 | $150.00 | $150.00 |
| **Total Operating Expenses** | **$257,262.96** | **$348,709.40** | **$483,945.90** |
| | | | |
| Profit before Interest and Taxes | $60,115.52 | $224,530.60 | $391,675.10 |
| Interest Expense Long-term | $10,367.42 | $8,617.33 | $6,580.72 |
| Taxes Incurred | $13,929.47 | $60,455.71 | $107,826.43 |
| Net Profit | $35,818.63 | $155,457.55 | $277,267.95 |
| Net Profit/Sales | 11.29% | 27.12% | 31.67% |

**Projected Cash Flow**

|  | 2001 | 2002 | 2003 |
|---|---|---|---|
| Net Profit | $35,818.63 | $155,457.55 | $277,267.95 |
| Plus: |  |  |  |
| Depreciation | $4,254.00 | $4,694.40 | $5,134.40 |
| Change in Accounts Payable | $9,238.24 | $7,407.52 | $5,751.50 |
| Current Borrowing (repayment) | $0.00 | $0.00 | $0.00 |
| Increase (decrease) Other Liabilities | $0.00 | $0.00 | $0.00 |
| Long-term Borrowing (repayment) | ($14,612.42) | ($15,476.92) | ($18,466.60) |
| Capital Input | $0.00 | $0.00 | $0.00 |
| **Subtotal** | **$34,698.46** | **$152,082.55** | **$269,687.25** |
| Less: | $2,001.00 | $2,002.00 | $2,003.00 |
| Change in Accounts Receivable | $16,920.25 | $13,640.63 | $16,120.70 |
| Change in Inventory | $0.00 | $0.00 | $0.00 |
| Change in Other Short-term Assets | $0.00 | $0.00 | $0.00 |
| Capital Expenditure | $0.00 | $3,399.00 | $3,399.00 |
| Dividends | $0.00 | $0.00 | $0.00 |
| **Subtotal** | **$16,920.25** | **$17,039.63** | **$19,519.70** |
| **Net Cash Flow** | **$17,778.21** | **$135,042.93** | **$250,167.56** |
| **Cash Balance** | **$17,778.21** | **$152,821.14** | **$402,988.69** |

**Projected Balance Sheet**

**Assets**

| **Short-term Assets** | 2001 | 2002 | 2003 |
|---|---|---|---|
| Cash | $17,778.21 | $152,821.14 | $402,988.69 |
| Accounts Receivable | $16,920.25 | $30,560.88 | $46,681.57 |
| Inventory | $0.00 | $0.00 | $0.00 |
| Other Short-term Assets | $0.00 | $0.00 | $0.00 |
| **Total Short-term Assets** | **$34,698.46** | **$183,382.01** | **$449,670.26** |
|  |  |  |  |
| **Long-term Assets** |  |  |  |
| Capital Assets | $21,272.00 | $24,671.00 | $28,070.00 |
| Accumulated Depreciation | $4,254.00 | $8,948.40 | $14,082.80 |
| **Total Long-term Assets** | **$17,018.00** | **$15,722.60** | **$13,987.20** |
| **Total Assets** | **$51,716.46** | **$199,104.61** | **$463,657.46** |
|  |  |  |  |
| **Liabilities and Capital** |  |  |  |
| Accounts Payable | $9,238.24 | $16,645.77 | $22,397.27 |
| Short-term Notes | $0.00 | $0.00 | $0.00 |
| Other Short-term Liabilities | $0.00 | $0.00 | $0.00 |
| **Subtotal Short-term Liabilities** | **$9,238.24** | **$16,645.77** | **$22,397.27** |
|  |  |  |  |
| Long-term Liabilities | $79,549.58 | $64,072.66 | $45,606.06 |
| **Total Liabilities** | **$88,787.82** | **$80,718.43** | **$68,003.33** |
|  |  |  |  |
| Paid in Capital | $25,000.00 | $25,000.00 | $25,000.00 |
| Retained Earnings | ($97,890.00) | ($62,071.37) | $93,386.19 |
| Earnings | $35,818.63 | $155,457.55 | $277,267.95 |
| **Total Capital** | **($37,071.37)** | **$118,386.19** | **$395,654.14** |
| **Total Liabilities and Capital** | **$51,716.46** | **$199,104.61** | **$463,657.46** |
| **Net Worth** | **($37,071.37)** | **$118,386.19** | **$395,654.14** |

## Ratio Analysis

| Profitability Ratios: | 2001 | 2002 | 2003 | RMA |
|---|---|---|---|---|
| Gross Margin | 100.00% | 100.00% | 100.00% | 0 |
| Net Profit Margin | 11.29% | 27.12% | 31.67% | 0 |
| Return on Assets | 69.26% | 78.08% | 59.80% | 0 |
| Return on Equity | 0.00% | 131.31% | 70.08% | 0 |
| | | | | |
| **Activity Ratios** | | | | |
| AR Turnover | 9.38 | 9.38 | 9.38 | 0 |
| Collection Days | 19 | 30 | 32 | 0 |
| Inventory Turnover | 0 | 0 | 0 | 0 |
| Accts Payable Turnover | 9.97 | 9.97 | 9.97 | 0 |
| Total Asset Turnover | 6.14 | 2.88 | 1.89 | 0 |
| | | | | |
| **Debt Ratios** | | | | |
| Debt to Net Worth | 19.4 | 0.68 | 0.17 | 0 |
| Short-term Liability to Liability | 0.1 | 0.21 | 0.33 | 0 |
| | | | | |
| **Liquidity Ratios** | | | | |
| Current Ratio | 3.76 | 11.02 | 20.08 | 0 |
| Quick Ratio | 3.76 | 11.02 | 20.08 | 0 |
| Net Working Capital | $25,460 | $166,736 | $427,273 | 0 |
| Interest Coverage | 5.8 | 26.06 | 59.52 | 0 |
| | | | | |
| **Additional Ratios** | | | | |
| Assets to Sales | 0.16 | 0.35 | 0.53 | 0 |
| Debt/Assets | 172% | 41% | 15% | 0 |
| Current Debt/Total Assets | 18% | 8% | 5% | 0 |
| Acid Test | 1.92 | 9.18 | 17.99 | 0 |
| Asset Turnover | 6.14 | 2.88 | 1.89 | 0 |
| Sales/Net Worth | $0 | 4.84 | 2.21 | 0 |
| Dividend Payout | $0 | $0 | $0 | 0 |

## Analysis:

*"How profitable are we?"*

Return on Assets—The only reason that the return on assets ratio decreases over the three-year period is because the firm's cash position is so strong. Rest assured, 59.8 percent in year 3 is representative of an extremely profitable company.

*"How much are we really earning on the money we take in?"*

Net Profit Margin—Net profit shows a steady increase from 11.29 percent to 31.67 percent in year 3, exceeding AutoAftermarket's goal. By year 3, the firm is earning 32 cents on each dollar it takes in. This is representative of a high growth company.

*"Do we have enough money to pay our employees?"*

Current ratio—AutoAftermarket.com's high ratio is an indication of the firm's ability to service current obligations through its strong cash business.

*"Do we have enough equity or are we living mostly on borrowed money?"*

Debt to Net Worth—AutoAftermarket.com displays its long-term success by decreasing this ratio from a high of 19.4 to 0.17 in year 3. This proves that AutoAftermarket.com is not living on borrowed money; rather, its success is based on its equity.

*"How efficiently are we using our capital?"*

Total Asset Turnover—This ratio shows that AutoAftermarket.com did business with its capital 6.14 times in year 1 and 1.89 times by year 3.

**ASSUMPTIONS**

1. Sales forecast is based on the following rates per hour:
   i. E-Commerce                $130
   ii. Web Development           $90
   iii. Graphic Design           $40

   All forecasts assume a 70 percent efficiency, i.e., 30 percent of time spent will not be considered billable hours. Monthly sales figures are based in the number of available nonweekend workdays.

2. Salaries are based on market rates in the Indianapolis area. All hiring will be done in said area.

3. Salary increases are based in 5 percent per year.

4. Rent is based on $13.15 per square foot @ 1,000 square feet.

5. Phone expense is based on $150 per month ($35/month line, $7 x 4 rental units, $87 long distance charges). Subsequent years include a 10 percent increase for increased volume.

6. Insurance is based on the following:
   i.  Worker's Comp             $3.25 / $100 in salaries
   ii. Liability                 $5.25 / $1,000 in revenue

7. Utilities are included in the monthly rent.

8. Capital expenditures for computers in years 2 and 3 are based on the top of the line, most expensive retail machine available through Microwarehouse (http://www.warehouse.com).

9. Payroll tax expense based on the following:
   i.   FICA: Social Security      6.2% capped @ $72,600
   ii.  FICA: Medicare            1.45%
   iii. Unemployment: Federal     0.80%
   iv.  Unemployment: State       5.51% (average)

10. Office expense based on $50 supplies per month plus $8 T-1 Internet connection through the Technology Towers. Subsequent years are based on 25 percent and 20 percent increases respectfully.

11. Vehicle expense is based on $0.30 per mile at an average of 300 miles per week for 50 weeks (2 weeks vacation).

12. Travel expense is based on 2 major travels of 800 and 400 miles spending 8 nights a month out of town. Breakfasts, dinners, hotels, and incidentals such as the occasional entertainment of customers estimated at $120/day. Subsequent years increase by one third/year.

13. Organization dues based on membership to the following:
    i.   The HTML Writers' Guild                          $100/yr
    ii.  The International Webmasters Association     $50/yr

14. Advertising expense based on two ads @ $300 and $325 per month in industry publications to be determined. Subsequent year increases based on 10 percent increases annually.

15. Depreciation is calculated based on the direct method amortized over 5 years and is based on the following items:
    i.   Year 1: 3 Compaqs, 1 Mac, 1 Color Laserjet Printer, 1 Storage
    ii.  Year 2: 4 Compaqs, 1 Mac, 1 Color Laserjet Printer, 1 Storage
    iii. Year 3: 5 Compaqs, 1 Mac, 1 Color Laserjet Printer, 1 Storage

16. Taxes incurred are based on a 28 percent standard rate.

17. Interest expense based on 12 percent.

18. Accounts Receivable estimates based on 50 percent of sales on credit (50 percent is due up front).

**Start-up Costs:**

1. Legal costs are based on an estimate from J. Christian Goeke of Goeke and Hilliard for startup costs and various "boilerplate" agreement documents.

2. Brochure costs based on an estimate from Mulligan Printing.

3. Salaries based on 3 months payments.

4. Furniture estimated based on retail prices from Office Max.

5. Rent based on 3 months payments plus 1.5 months deposit.

6. Software based on the following:
    i.   Macromedia Dreamweaver UltraDev          $389.95
    ii.  ColdFusion 4.5                           $429.95
    iii. Adobe Publishing Collection              $949.95
    iv.  Acid Pro 2.0                             $279.95

7. Travel based on 3 months sales prospecting prior to startup.

8. Expensed equipment based on the following:
    i.   Epson 800 Scanner                        $699.95
    ii.  Toshiba 2.14 megapixel Digital Camera    $499.95
    iii. HP Photosmart P100                       $400.00
    iv.  HP Laserjet 2100                         $699.99
    v.   4 NIC Cards                              $260.00
    vi.  1 HUB                                     $49.00

9. Long-term assets based on the following:
    i.   1 Procom                               $10,675.00
    ii.  3 Compaq Presario 5888s                $6,597.00
    iii. 1 Macintosh                            $3,000.00
    iv.  QMS Magicolor 2 Laser Printer            $999.95

10. Start-up expense is comprised of $70 for filing with the state of Indiana, and $500 for recruitment on the web (Monster.com membership) and a weekly ad in the *Post Dispatch*.

# Aftermarket Skate Store

BUSINESS PLAN                                PEGASUS SPORTS INTERNATIONAL

*2200 Alta Vista Boulevard*
*Venice, California 90294-1366*

*Pegasus Sports International is planning on fulfilling the need for skating aftermarket products, a market we have identified, based on the large volume of skates that have been sold in the last five years. We will establish a service network for in-line skaters by providing products that help people incorporate more skating into their daily lifestyles. This business plan was compiled using Business Plan Pro, © 1999, Palo Alto Software, www.paloaltosoftware.com, 800-229-7526.*

- EXECUTIVE SUMMARY

- COMPANY SUMMARY

- PRODUCTS

- MARKET ANALYSIS SUMMARY

- STRATEGY & IMPLEMENTATION SUMMARY

- MANAGEMENT SUMMARY

- FINANCIAL PLAN

# AFTERMARKET SKATE STORE
## BUSINESS PLAN

**EXECUTIVE SUMMARY**

At Pegasus Sports International, our emphasis is to provide quality products at the fairest price. Our pricing is determined by the cost of production, customer demand, demographics, and sales. Our products will fulfill the needs of all levels of in-line skaters.

The uniqueness of our product line and the existing untapped market will pave the way for our success in the skating market.

We will schedule production based on our monthly sales which will keep production costs down.

It is of the utmost importance that we protect our inventions by applying for patents as soon as possible.

Our goal is to borrow $50,000 for ten years. The loan will be repaid in 120 equal payments, including interest and principal. Our present plan is to utilize the borrowed money for the first year's operating expenses, with cash inputs on a monthly basis. Such cash input will aid our advertising, operating costs, and salaries. We should reach our break-even point after our first year. Upon receiving our loan, we would like to incorporate the business, as this will protect our company, investors, lenders, products, and stockholders. We expect income to reach $473,000 the first year, $1,104,000 the second year, and $1,699,000 the third year.

**Objectives**

- To fulfill the aftermarket skate accessory demand with top quality products.
- To develop and manufacture SkaterAids by December 1999.
- To develop skate tours by spring 2000.
- To reach sales of $473,000 by the end of our first year in business, and reach sales of $39,000 monthly.
- To break even by the end of the first year in business.
- To encourage our customers to live healthy lives by making skating more fun and convenient for them.
- To offer skaters support through our website, such as interviews with Dr. Kaye, podiatrist, with answers to skater-specific foot problems.
- To develop a solid e-commerce market and to maximize our profit margin. We make full retail profit through e-commerce.

**Mission**

Pegasus Sports International is planning on fulfilling the need for skating aftermarket products, a market we have identified, based on the large volume of skates that have been sold in the last five years.

Pegasus Sports International will establish a service network for in-line skaters by providing products that help people incorporate more skating into their daily lifestyles. Our goal is to:

- Expand skating as an alternative to driving to do local errands.
- Form a network of skating enthusiasts with an emphasis on health and fitness.
- To encourage SkateSailing as a new international sport.
- To develop SkateAids and other new products.

**Keys to Success**

1. Developing quality in-line skating accessories through feedback from skaters.
2. Developing a niche market for our unique skating accessories.

3. Maximizing profits by selling through the Internet at full retail price.
4. Maintaining low overhead costs by monitoring and scheduling production.
5. Developing a network with other businesses and experts, such as podiatrist and skater Dr. Kaye, through interviews published on our website.

**COMPANY SUMMARY**

Pegasus Sports International was conceived by skaters who can devise practical ideas and designs for in-line skating accessories. Being avid health and fitness advocates, we promote in-line skating as a lifestyle.

Our products make the trip to the local store or coffee shop easier and an enjoyable way to get exercise. This will eliminate the stress of driving in traffic and having to search for parking.

The main problem skaters encounter is poor fit. Lateral ankle support is essential due to the narrow wheel footprint of in-line skates. Because of this, skate boots have to be worn tighter than shoes. We have invented a solution to this problem and are excited about its application to other footwear as well. There is a lack of inexpensive accessory products available. Other needs can be addressed with new products.

**Company Ownership**

Pegasus Sports International currently is a limited partnership.

Presently, **Sal M. Chavez** is chief executive officer and owns 80 percent of the company.

Presently, **Sandi M. Arnold** is vice president and owns 20 percent of the company.

Upon incorporating, **Sal M. Chavez** and **Sandi M. Arnold** will change their partnership agreement so Sandi and Sal will divide profits to 45 percent to Sandi and 55 percent to Sal.

Ten percent of Internet sales will go to **Beth Laird**, our webmaster and office administrator.

**Start-up Summary**

Our start-up cost has been $10,000. Primarily, the money has been for materials for prototypes, product development, trademark acquisition, rental equipment, operating and administrative costs, and establishing a website.

Upon receiving our loan for the first month, we plan on heavy advertising through the Internet, skating publications, and on-site events such as skating races.

The start-up costs are shown in the following table.

**Start-up Plan**
**Start-up Expenses**

| | |
|---|---|
| Legal | $671 |
| Office & Computer Supply | $1,453 |
| Advertising | $1,000 |
| Consultants | $20 |
| Insurance | $0 |
| Rent | $2,500 |
| Research and Development | $1,827 |
| Expensed Equipment | $233 |
| Other | $1,500 |
| **Total Start-up Expenses** | **$9,204** |

**Start-up Plan**

*continued*

| Start-up Assets Needed | |
|---|---|
| Cash Requirements | $10,000 |
| Start-up inventory | $1,500 |
| Other Short-term Assets | $0 |
| **Total Short-term Assets** | **$11,500** |
| Long-term Assets | $0 |
| **Total Assets** | **$11,500** |
| | |
| **Total Start-up Requirements:** | **$20,704** |
| **Left to finance:** | **$0** |

| Start-up Funding Plan | |
|---|---|
| **Investment** | |
| Paul Neugas | $3,000 |
| Garry Waldie | $3,000 |
| Sandi M. Arnold | $2,004 |
| Beth Laird | $3,000 |
| Lamiah G. Arnold/Trower | $3,000 |
| Sal M. Chavez | $2,000 |
| Other | $0 |
| **Total investment** | **$16,004** |

| Short-term Liabilities | |
|---|---|
| Unpaid Expenses | $200 |
| Short-term Loans | $4,500 |
| Interest-free Short-term Loans | $0 |
| Subtotal Short-term Liabilities | $4,700 |
| Long-term Liabilities | $0 |
| **Total Liabilities** | **$4,700** |
| | |
| Loss at Start-up | ($9,204) |
| Total Capital | $6,800 |
| **Total Capital and Liabilities** | **$11,500** |
| **Checkline** | **$0** |

**Company Locations and Facilities**

At present we are located in Venice, California. From our location, we will warehouse, package, and ship our products. We will find a larger site as the business expands.

We have manufacturers lined up to subcontract our large production jobs. We plan to produce products on a monthly basis to cut our need for a large inventory space.

**PRODUCTS**

Pegasus Sports International now offers several products:

- The first product we have developed is BladeBoots™, a cover for the wheels and frame of in-line skates, which allow skaters to enter places that normally would not allow them in. BladeBoots™ come with a small pouch and belt which converts to a well-designed skate carrier.
- The second product we have invented is our SkateSails. These sails are specifically designed for use while skating. Feedback that we have received from skaters indicate this could become a very popular sport. Trademarking this product is currently in progress.
- The third product will be referred to as SkateAid and will be in production by December.

Other ideas for products are under development, but we must hold back until we can protect ourselves through pending patent applications.

We have two products now being marketed on our website (http://www.pegasussportsint.com), with two more products to be introduced in the near future.

- BladeBoots™ are made from Cordura, a nylon composite cloth that is extremely durable. BladeBoots enable the skater to enter places that normally don't allow skates while wearing their skates. Our cost to manufacture is $10.00 per set, and they retail for $24.95 per set. The packaging is simple, inexpensive, elegant, and done in-house.
- SkateSails are made of Dacron. The window of the sail is made of carbon fiber-reinforced Mylar. This product is an original concept and design. Our sails come with an alpha design, known for being very stable and easy to use. We incorporated a swallow-tail design for better upwind performance, speed, and excellent maneuverability. We have a choice of three beautiful colors. The manufacturing cost is $100 and retails for $350 to $500, depending on size.
- We are developing SkateAids, a new product that we feel has a large potential in this market. The estimated cost to manufacture each unit is $10. They will retail for $45.00. This product is in its advanced development stage so a pending patent and trademark have been applied for.
- Our fourth product is a service: Skate Tours. We are currently working out details with Terry's Café, a skate outlet shop on Santa Monica Beach, and a major skate manufacturer. This tour will take skaters out to sail with SkateSails.

**Product Description**

Our products are unique in the existing skate accessory market. While there are other accessory companies, none produce products as versatile as ours. Our ideas come from listening to what other skaters have to say.

**Competitive Comparison**

For 1999, we are developing a company brochure which will include our products.

We are targeting our market by focusing on Internet sales. A large portion of our advertising budget will be used for Internet advertising such as banners and site-promoting services.

We also plan on a mass postcard mailing media blitz to skate shops and to advertise in most of the major in-line skate magazines by spring time.

**Sales Literature**

Our Venice, California, location is ideal, since Venice is considered the center and birthplace of roller skating. Major local skate shops in the area are now carrying our products.

Our supplier for Cordura is the major distributor on the West Coast. We have a supplier of Dacron (our sail cloth), and a source for aluminum.

All of our costs are at the manufacturer level, and the prices should drop as our production increases.

**Sourcing**

Pegasus Sports International is a progressive company that has been able to combine high-tech materials and innovative ideas to produce new products with no present competition. We now have a trademark on BladeBoots™, and we are in the process of acquiring trademarks on our other products along with corresponding patents. Some of our high-tech implementation will

**Technology**

be more noticeable when we introduce our SkateAid. This product should make skating more comfortable due to the new chemical products. Our SkateSails are made of aircraft-quality aluminum, the lightest and strongest of sail materials.

We have already designed the next two generations of sails, and this should keep us ahead of any spin-off products that will try to copy us.

**Future Products**

We are constantly talking with skaters in order to develop unique products. We feel that the new products we are developing will be very useful, functional, and practical. There are a few more concepts on the drawing board. SkateAids, the newest one, will be in production by December of 1999. This product is being developed with the aid of a foot doctor who is also an avid skater.

**MARKET ANALYSIS SUMMARY**

With 31 million skates sold and no support products available, we have an opportunity to reach a market of approximately 26 million recreational and fitness enthusiasts.

There is now a growing trend towards fitness skating. With this large potential market, our products will be there to address this need.

**Market Segmentation**

With a world skating market of over 31 million and steadily growing (statistics released by the Sporting Goods Manufacturers Association), our niche has been created. Our aim is to expand this market by promoting SkateSailing, a new sport which is popular at both Santa Monica and Venice Beach in California.

The Sporting Goods Manufacturers Association survey indicates that in-line skating now has more participation than football, softball, skiing, and snowboarding combined. The breakdown of participation in in-line skating is as follows: 1% percent speed (growing), 8% hockey (declining), 7% extreme/aggressive (declining), 22% fitness (nearly 7 million—the fastest growing), and 61% recreational (first-timers). Our products are targeting the fitness and recreational groups, as they are the fastest growing. These groups are gearing themselves towards health and fitness, and combined, they can easily grow to 85% (or 26 million) of the market in the next five years.

**Market Analysis**

| Potential Customers | Growth | 1999 | 2000 | 2001 | 2002 | 2003 | CAGR |
|---|---|---|---|---|---|---|---|
| Recreational | | 61% | 58% | 54% | 47% | 40% | -10.01% |
| Fitness | | 22% | 27% | 30% | 35% | 40% | 16.12% |
| Speed | | 2% | 5% | 8% | 15% | 17% | 83.48% |
| Hockey | | 8% | 5% | 4% | 2% | 2% | -29.29% |
| Extreme | | 7% | 5% | 4% | 1% | 1% | -38.52% |
| **Total** | **0.13%** | **1** | **1** | **1** | **1** | **1** | **0.13%** |

**Target Market Segment Strategy**

Our target market is the recreational skater and the health and fitness enthusiast. This segment can be reached over the Internet and through skate magazine advertising.

We plan on developing the skate shop market through an inexpensive postcard method.

BladeBoots™ and SkateSails are now sold at the two major skate shops in Santa Monica and Venice, California. Surveys indicate that in the fitness and speed market, the average age is 34 years old, breaking down to 48 percent women, 52 percent men, an average of 1.8 years of college education, an average household income of $52,600, and 71 percent skate on four-wheel in-line skates.

We recognize the need for accessories for the growing market of skaters.                    **Market Needs**

- We promote SkateSailing as a new sport by providing excursions to wide open areas. A major skate company is willing to lend us the new large-wheel skates for our SkateSailing excursions. However, conventional in-line skates will work just as well.
- Soon we will offer SkateAids. The sheer number of existing skates purchased has created a whole new market for products to help increase the life of skates.

We have learned what skaters need for accessories by interviewing experienced skaters.

A person does not have to make time to exercise if skating becomes a lifestyle and is worked into daily activities. Skating is fun and a great cardiovascular workout at the same time.

We will distinguish ourselves by marketing products not previously available to skaters. The    **Market Trends**
emphasis in the past has been to sell skates and very few replacement parts.

The number of skaters is not restricted to any one single country, continent, or age group, so there is a world market. We have products for virtually every group of skaters.

The fastest growing segment of this sport is the fitness skater. Therefore, our marketing is being directed to service this group. BladeBoots™ will enable them to enter establishments without having to remove their skates. BladeBoots will be aimed at the recreational skater, the largest segment; however, SkateAids are great for everyone.

There is one more way the sport of skating will grow, and that is through SkateSailing. This sport is primarily for the medium to advanced skater. The growth potential for this sport is tremendous. The sails we've manufactured so far have ended up in Europe. The same thing happened with windsurfing. It started out here in Santa Monica but did not take off until it had already grown big in Europe. More and more groups are getting together on skate excursions in cities all over the world. For example, San Francisco has night group skating that numbers in the hundreds of people. The market trends are showing continued growth in all directions of skating.

With the price of skates going down due to competition by so many skate companies, the    **Market Growth**
market has had steady growth throughout the world, with 22.5 million in 1995 to over 31 million in 1997.

By January 2000 we will get the growth statistics for this year; it is estimated to be over 35 million. More and more people are discovering, and in many cases rediscovering, the health benefits and fun of skating

Skate sales have undergone tremendous growth and distribution throughout the country.    **Industry Analysis**

Presently, we will concentrate on Internet marketing. This will maximize our profit.

The Internet is probably the best communication medium for skaters all over the world, and we believe this is the best way to retail our products. The sales on the World Wide Web are now over $28 billion, as quoted by Forrester Research, in e-commerce.

**Industry Participants**

The number of skate companies is very large as many shoe companies have joined in; however, the major and biggest companies are Rollerblade®, Roces®, Solomon®, and K2®.

Some companies make skate bags whose price is in the $20 range. None of them address the problem of entrance to areas that will not allow you to enter while wearing skates, and those products are for the most part bulky and impractical to skate with.

**Distribution Patterns**

We plan on shipping our products using express mail at the U.S. Post Office as our way of distribution, because it is the least expensive way; however, some credit companies demand a shipping receipt and those will be handled by established shippers.

We are also in touch with a few foreign distribution companies that have contacted us and are interested in our products.

**Competition and Buying Patterns**

Each segment of skating has its own buying patterns depending on its own needs.

**Main Competitors**

Pegasus Sports International is forming its own market. While there are a few companies that do make sails and foils that a few skaters are using, ours is the only one that is truly designed for and by skaters. Our few competitors' sails are not designed for skating, but for windsurfing or for skateboards. In the case of foils, storage and carrying are not practical.

We need the capital to protect our inventions through patent application and trademark registration. Our other products do not have competition at this time.

**STRATEGY & IMPLEMENTATION SUMMARY**

Our involvement in roller skating goes back more than 25 years in Venice, California. We have the reputation and experience that has gained respect from some of the most skilled skaters. We remain close to the skating community through contact with the local skate shops and by giving lessons. Close contact with the public has put us in a unique position to be able to get feedback from skaters of all types on our products and ideas, designed for them.

**Value Proposition**

At Pegasus Sports International our emphasis is on quality at a fair price. Our pricing is determined by the cost of production and customer demand, so we pace production by need.

Speed skating's demographics show affluent and prime candidates for our higher ticket items. We develop our products for all skaters, but some of our products are more segment-specific, such as our SkateSails which are more for the experienced to expert skater. For example, the speed skating segment is only 1.5 percent of the entire market, but this is roughly 7 million skaters.

**Competitive Edge**

Our company's competitive edge exists because we are the only company addressing the needs that have resulted from the extensive sales of in-line skates. We wish to fill the need for items which could double the life of a pair of skates.

Accessories such as BladeBoots™ encourage people and make it more convenient to include skating into their lifestyles.

There are several other projects we are currently working on that will broaden our product line and open up our market even more. We will be more than glad to discuss in length some of our future confidential plans, upon request.

**Marketing Strategy**

The key to our marketing strategy is focusing on the speed, health and fitness, and recreational skaters. We can cover about 80 percent of the skating market since we produce products geared towards each segment.

The speed and fitness skaters are an average age of 34 years old with a salary of about $54,000 a year and an average of two years of college. This is our SkateSail market. We are in the process of designing more advanced safety equipment that is well-suited for skate sailing, in the future.

Our BladeBoots™ and SkateAids are items that can be useful to all segments of the market.

**Positioning Statements**

We design our products for the skaters who depend on their skating products to be well-designed and practical. We want to help lengthen and improve the life of our customers' investment—their skates.

The present skate companies concentrate on new skate sales with no support for products already sold, and that is our forte.

**Pricing Strategy**

Pegasus Sports' products are priced to encourage the customer to impulse buy, experiment, and repeat buy.

SkateSails are priced from $350 to $500. Lower-priced items are BladeBoots™ at $24.95 and SkateAids for $45.00.

**Promotion Strategy**

Our long-range goal is to gain enough visibility to expand the product line into other industries and other regions, and to generate inquiries from potential inventors. To do that we need $50,000, or a line of credit.

We also plan on promoting our goods at various skating races held throughout the country.

**Distribution Strategy**

We plan to enter the now extensive specialty skate shop market with SkateAid. We feel this is the competitive edge skate shops need to compete with the large chain discount distributors. The additional products, such as BladeBoots™ and SkateSails, should also help stimulate skate shop sales.

**Sales Strategy**

For now, our products are sold through our web site (http://www.pegasussportsint.com). This earns us full retail price.

In nine months, we will gear sales towards the skate shops with SkateAids. Through retail skate shops, we will increase our sales.

Visibility will be very important, and we will gain exposure at skate racing events. We will target our advertising through the major in-line skate magazines and on the Internet.

**Sales Forecast**

We feel that our sales forecasting is conservative. We will steadily increase sales as our advertising budget allows. Please refer to the Sales Forecast chart in the Appendix portion of this plan.

**Sales Forecast**

*continued*

| Sales Forecast Unit Sales | FY2000 | FY2001 | FY2002 |
|---|---|---|---|
| BladeBoots | 1,140 | 2,200 | 3,400 |
| SkateSails | 1,072 | 2,100 | 3,200 |
| SkateAid | 1,560 | 7,000 | 11,000 |
| **Total Unit Sales** | **3,772** | **11,300** | **17,600** |
| | | | |
| **Unit Prices** | | | |
| BladeBoots | $24.95 | $24.95 | $24.95 |
| SkateSails | $350.00 | $350.00 | $350.00 |
| SkateAid | $45.00 | $45.00 | $45.00 |
| | | | |
| **Sales** | | | |
| BladeBoots | $28,443 | $54,890 | $84,830 |
| SkateSails | $375,200 | $735,000 | $1,120,000 |
| SkateAid | $70,200 | $315,000 | $495,000 |
| **Total Sales** | **$473,843** | **$1,104,890** | **$1,699,830** |
| | | | |
| **Direct Unit Costs** | | | |
| BladeBoots | $10.00 | $10.00 | $10.00 |
| SkateSails | $100.00 | $100.00 | $100.00 |
| SkateAid | $7.00 | $7.00 | $7.00 |
| | | | |
| **Direct Cost of Sales** | | | |
| BladeBoots | $11,400 | $22,000 | $34,000 |
| SkateSails | $107,200 | $210,000 | $320,000 |
| SkateAid | $10,920 | $49,000 | $77,000 |
| **Subtotal Direct Cost of Sales** | **$129,520** | **$281,000** | **$431,000** |

**Sales Programs**

Our sales program consists of Internet advertising and skating magazine ads in order to target our market. On the Internet, banner advertising utilizing link exchange services and high search engine placement will be our primary method of selling.

We presently accept credit card orders through our website. We plan to capture the impulse buyer market, which makes up 80 percent of all Internet sales.

**Strategic Alliances**

Cooperation between Pegasus Sports International and the local skate shops in both Venice and Santa Monica, California, is very good. We hope that our growth will be mutual, since some of our products are designed for the skate shops.

Since Terry's Café in Santa Monica is situated in a parking lot, where skate sailing can be taught and SkateSails can be sold, this can be our home site where we also can arrange the skate sailing excursions.

**Milestones**

Sal M. Chavez will concentrate on sales and promotion, teaching skate sailing lessons in addition to overseeing product development.

Sandi M. Arnold will be in charge of production by making sure we have ordered the products needed to maintain a smooth production. Sandi will see to it that our orders will be filled and shipped to their destination.

Beth A. Laird will be in charge of the administrative functions. Her duties will be to run the office. Beth is also our webmaster and will maintain and update our website.

We will work as a team and help each other with all the work required for a smooth running company. Together, we will do whatever it takes to succeed.

**Milestones**

| Milestone | Start Date | End Date | Budget | Manager | Department |
|---|---|---|---|---|---|
| Sal Chavez | 10/10/1998 | 10/10/1998 | $20,000 | CEO | Sales/Research |
| Sandi Arnold | 1/1/1998 | 1/1/1998 | $15,600 | Vice Pres. | Production |
| Beth Laird | 1/1/1998 | 1/1/1998 | 0 | Admin. | Administrative |
| Other | | | | | |
| **Totals** | | | **$35,600** | | |

**MANAGEMENT SUMMARY**

Our group has very diverse talents that seem to complement each other well. Our common bond is our love for skating and fitness. We will create small businesses by teaching independent producers how to make our products. We have developed partnerships so we can control production quality and maintain exclusivity of all products produced.

**Organizational Structure**

Pegasus Sports International is organized in three main functional areas: production, sales, and administrative. We all have our assigned jobs but can and will help each other in other areas whenever necessary.

Sal and Sandi will continue to cooperate on product development. Sal Chavez and Sandi Arnold, as owners, are willing to accept the wages of $20,000-Sandi and $15,000-Sal, for the first year in order to help Pegasus Sports International to grow past the break-even point, with the expectations of a steady growth in salary as Pegasus Sports International becomes more successful.

**Management Team**

**Sal M. Chavez, CEO,** has over 23 years of skating experience and is the main force behind our company having earned the respect and good standing of the skating community. He has not driven an automobile in five years, instead skating for all his transportation needs. Because of skating instead of driving, he has not only regained his health, but is now in the best health condition ever thanks to skating. He has worked as a designer of skate products in the past for companies such as ZFlex, Dog Town, and Cheap Skates. This has given him some insight into product development. For the last three years, he worked selling skates at local skate shops and has developed a feel for skaters' needs and market trends. In college, he majored in chemistry and physics, which has helped tremendously in identifying and developing products that are applicable to our needs.

**Sandi M. Arnold, vice president,** loves skating for fitness and speed, which is a real asset for the company. Her ability in the inventing process is invaluable. Sandi's ability to input ideas when developing products and production procedures makes her a perfect partner in our endeavors.

**Beth Laird,** our administrator and webmaster, has been skating for many years. Beth has been doing our administration work and has been helping to make Pegasus Sports International a reality. Her computer and organizational skills are an imperative part of our development.

**Management Team Gaps**

To maintain a lower start-up budget, Sal and Sandi will be the only salaried employees until at least nine months into our operation. We wish to bring Beth into a salaried position as soon as possible. Beth will receive a 10 percent commission on website orders until the company can afford to hire her full-time. Beth will receive 10 percent of Pegasus Sports International ownership.

## Personnel Plan

The personnel plan calls for increasing headcount by one more employee by April 2000 since an increase in forecasted sales necessitate more administrative help.

Our aim is to increase salary and compensation in line with a projected increase in sales and profits. Our overall personnel costs will be $35,000 for the first 12 months, which includes principals only. The present personnel cost figure is subject to change as business demands it.

**Personnel Plan**

| Personnel | FY2000 | FY2001 | FY2002 |
|---|---|---|---|
| Payroll | $26,244 | $75,600 | $100,000 |

## FINANCIAL PLAN

Our goal is to borrow $50,000 for 10 years. Our present plan is to utilize the borrowed money for the first year's operating capital, with cash input on a monthly basis. Such cash input will aid our operating costs and salaries. We should reach our break-even point after our first year. Upon receiving our loan, we would like to incorporate, as this will protect our company, investors, lenders, products, and stockholders. We expect sales to reach $473,843 after the first year, $1,104,890 after our second year, and $1,699,830 after the third year.

If sales don't measure up to our expectations, this could add an additional six months and an influx of another $20,000, which could be carried by credit card, but we don't expect this to happen.

These are our strong points:

- We want to finance growth mainly through cash flow. We recognize that this means we will will have to grow at a slower pace than we would like, but this will enable us to build sales through investing in more advertising.
- Our most important asset is inventory turnover. Our ability to schedule production from month to month will help to control inventory costs.
- Collection is not a problem, since we will be credited payment to our bank account in two days by American Merchant Center for all our credit card sales over the Internet.

## Important Assumptions

The financial plan depends on important assumptions, most of which are shown in the following General Assumptions table. The key underlying assumptions are:

- A slow-growth economy, without major recession.
- No unforeseen changes in technology to make our products immediately obsolete.
- Access to equity capital and financing sufficient to maintain our financial plan as presented in this table.

| General Assumptions | FY2001 | FY2002 | FY2003 |
|---|---|---|---|
| Short-term Interest Rate % | 12.00% | 12.00% | 0.00% |
| Long-term Interest Rate % | 10.50% | 10.50% | 10.00% |
| Payment Days Estimator | 30 | 30 | 30 |
| Collection Days Estimator | 2 | 2 | 2 |
| Inventory Turnover Estimator | 12 | 12 | 12 |
| Tax Rate % | 25.00% | 25.00% | 25.00% |
| Expenses in Cash % | 10.00% | 10.00% | 10.00% |
| Sales on Credit % | 2.50% | 10.00% | 10.00% |
| Personnel Burden % | 10.00% | 10.00% | 10.00% |

- The most important indicator is inventory turnover. We have to make sure that turnover stays above 10, or we are clogged with inventory.
- Collection is not a problem, since payment to our bank is two days after receiving our orders via credit card. However, by October 1999, we will initiate skate shop sales and experience an approximately 30-45 day average payment delay. This could cause a change in cash flow, but can be easily managed.

Key Financial Indicators

The following is a simplified breakdown of our first year's break-even analysis:

Break-even Analysis

| | |
|---|---|
| First Year's Projected Sales: | $473,843 |
| Less 25% Tax: | - 11,846 |
| | **$461,997** |
| Less Production Costs: | -129,520 |
| | **$332,477** |
| Less Operating Costs: | - 71,450 |
| **Profit:** | **$261,027** |
| Plus Loan: | $50,000 |
| **Cash at end of the first year:** | **$311,027** |
| Production Costs for Year 2001: | -281,065 |
| **Projected Profit First Year:** | **$29,962** |

For more detail, see the Projected Profit and Loss table in the Appendix.

| **Break-even Analysis:** | |
|---|---|
| Monthly Units Break-even | 11 |
| Monthly Sales Break-even | $3,889 |

| **Assumptions:** | |
|---|---|
| Average Per-Unit Revenue | $350 |
| Average Per-Unit Variable Cost | $80 |
| Estimated Monthly Fixed Cost | $3,000 |

Our goal is to borrow $50,000 for the total of ten years. Our present plan is to utilize the borrowed money for the first year's operating expenses, with cash input on a monthly basis. Such cash input will aid in our advertising, operating costs, and salaries. This loan should help us maintain production and operating costs while developing our customer base and sales. Should sales lag, we plan to maintain solvency with credit card financing. We should reach our break-even point after our first year. We expect sales to hit $473,843 the first year, $1,104,870 our second year, and $1,699,830 the third year. Our sales projection is very conservative, considering the sales potential.

Projected Profit and Loss

**Profit and Loss (Income Statement)**

| | FY2000 | FY2001 | FY2002 |
|---|---|---|---|
| Sales | $473,843 | $1,104,890 | $1,699,830 |
| Direct Cost of Sales | $129,520 | $281,000 | $431,000 |
| Production Payroll | $0 | $0 | $0 |
| | $0 | | |
| **Total Cost of Sales** | **$129,520** | **$281,000** | **$431,000** |
| | | | |
| Gross Margin | $344,323 | $823,890 | $1,268,830 |
| Gross Margin % | 72.67% | 74.57% | 74.64% |

**Projected Profit and Loss**

*continued*

| | FY2000 | FY2001 | FY2002 |
|---|---|---|---|
| Advertising/Promotion (including website) | $12,000 | $25,000 | $35,000 |
| Travel | $1,800 | $7,000 | $10,000 |
| Miscellaneous | $1,250 | $1,300 | $1,500 |
| Payroll Expenses | $0 | $0 | $0 |
| Payroll Burden | $0 | $0 | $0 |
| Depreciation | $0 | $0 | $0 |
| Leased Equipment | $1,800 | $5,000 | $10,000 |
| Utilities | $600 | $1,500 | $2,000 |
| Insurance | $6,000 | $12,000 | $12,000 |
| Rent | $10,800 | $12,000 | $15,000 |
| Contract/Consultants | $3,600 | $3,000 | $3,000 |
| **Total Operating Expenses** | **$37,850** | **$66,800** | **$88,500** |
| | | | |
| Profit Before Interest and Taxes | $280,229 | $757,090 | $1,180,330 |
| Interest Expense Short-term | $1,059 | $2,713 | $0 |
| Interest Expense Long-term | $0 | $1,811 | $5,175 |
| Taxes Incurred | $76,353 | $188,141 | $293,789 |
| Extraordinary Items | $0 | $0 | $0 |
| Net Profit | $209,377 | $564,424 | $881,366 |
| Net Profit/Sales | 48.34% | 51.08% | 51.85% |

**Projected Cash Flow**

- We want to finance our first year's growth through a loan.
- The most important indicator is inventory turnover. Our ability to schedule production from month to month will help control inventory costs.
- Collection is not a problem since we will be credited payment to our bank account in two days by American Merchants Center, our credit card company for Internet sales.
- Selling our products over the Internet will allow us full retail price and maximize our profit.

| Projected Cash Flow | FY2000 | FY2001 | FY2002 |
|---|---|---|---|
| Net Profit | $229,060 | $564,424 | $881,366 |
| Plus: | | | |
| Depreciation | $0 | $0 | $0 |
| Change in Accounts Payable | $44,311 | $54,587 | $48,644 |
| Current Borrowing (repayment) | $7,992 | $20,235 | $20,235 |
| Increase (decrease) Other Liabilities | $0 | $0 | $0 |
| Long-term Borrowing (repayment) | $0 | $34,500 | $34,500 |
| Capital Input | $50,000 | $39,000 | $45,000 |
| **Subtotal** | **$331,363** | **$712,746** | **$1,029,745** |
| Less: | | | |
| Change in Accounts Receivable | $0 | $0 | $0 |
| Change in Inventory | $24,450 | $52,050 | $41,637 |
| Change in Other Short-term Assets | $2,000 | $0 | $0 |
| Capital Expenditure | $0 | $0 | $0 |
| Dividends | $0 | $0 | $0 |
| **Subtotal** | **$26,450** | **$52,050** | **$41,637** |
| **Net Cash Flow** | **$304,913** | **$660,696** | **$988,108** |
| **Cash Balance** | **$314,913** | **$975,609** | **$1,963,717** |

As shown on the balance sheet in the following table, we expect a healthy growth in net worth to more than $1,664,260 by the end of the third year.

**Projected Balance Sheet**

**Projected Balance Sheet**

**Assets**

| Short-term Assets | FY2000 | FY2001 | FY2002 |
|---|---|---|---|
| Cash | $314,913 | $975,609 | $1,963,717 |
| Accounts Receivable | $0 | $0 | $0 |
| Inventory | $25,950 | $78,000 | $119,637 |
| Other Short-term Assets | $2,000 | $2,000 | $2,000 |
| **Total Short-term Assets** | **$342,863** | **$1,055,609** | **$2,085,354** |
| | | | |
| **Long-term Assets** | | | |
| Capital Assets | $0 | $0 | $0 |
| Accumulated Depreciation | $0 | $0 | $0 |
| **Total Long-term Assets** | **$0** | **$0** | **$0** |
| **Total Assets** | **$342,863** | **$1,055,609** | **$2,085,354** |
| | | | |
| **Liabilities and Capital** | | | |
| Accounts Payable | $44,511 | $99,098 | $147,742 |
| Short-term Notes | $12,492 | $32,727 | $52,962 |
| Other Short-term Liabilities | $0 | $0 | $0 |
| **Subtotal Short-term Liabilities** | **$57,003** | **$131,825** | **$200,704** |
| **Long-term Liabilities** | **$0** | **$34,500** | **$69,000** |
| **Total Liabilities** | **$57,003** | **$166,325** | **$269,704** |
| | | | |
| Paid in Capital | $66,004 | $105,004 | $150,004 |
| Retained Earnings | ($9,204) | $219,856 | $784,280 |
| Earnings | $229,060 | $564,424 | $881,366 |
| **Total Capital** | **$285,860** | **$889,284** | **$1,815,651** |
| **Total Liabilities and Capital** | **$342,863** | **$1,055,609** | **$2,085,354** |
| **Net Worth** | **$285,860** | **$889,284** | **$1,815,651** |

**Business Ratios**

Standard business ratios are included in the table. The ratio shows a plan for balanced and healthy growth.

**Ratio Analysis**

| Profitability Ratios: | FY2000 | FY2001 | FY2002 | RMA |
|---|---|---|---|---|
| Gross Margin | 72.67% | 74.57% | 74.64% | 0 |
| Net Profit Margin | 48.34% | 51.08% | 51.85% | 0 |
| Return on Assets | 66.81% | 53.47% | 42.26% | 0 |
| Return on Equity | 80.13% | 63.47% | 48.54% | 0 |
| | | | | |
| **Activity Ratios** | | | | |
| AR Turnover | 0.00 | 0.00 | 0.00 | 0 |
| Collection Days | 0 | 0 | 0 | 0 |
| Inventory Turnover | 9.44 | 5.41 | 4.36 | 0 |
| Accts Payable Turnover | 5.48 | 5.48 | 5.48 | 0 |
| **Total Asset Turnover** | **1.38** | **1.05** | **0.82** | **0** |
| | | | | |
| **Debt Ratios** | | | | |
| Debt to Net Worth | 0.20 | 0.19 | 0.15 | 0 |
| Short-term Liability to Liability | 1.00 | 0.79 | 0.74 | 0 |
| | | | | |
| **Liquidity Ratios** | | | | |
| Current Ratio | 6.01 | 8.01 | 10.39 | 0 |
| Quick Ratio | 5.56 | 7.42 | 9.79 | 0 |
| Net Working Capital | $285,860 | $923,784 | $1,884,651 | 0 |
| Interest Coverage | 289.27 | 167.34 | 228.08 | 0 |
| | | | | |
| **Additional Ratios** | | | | |
| Assets to Sales | 0.72 | 0.96 | 1.23 | 0 |
| Debt/Assets | 17% | 16% | 13% | 0 |
| Current Debt/Total Assets | 17% | 12% | 10% | 0 |
| Acid Test | 5.56 | 7.42 | 9.79 | 0 |
| Asset Turnover | 1.38 | 1.05 | 0.82 | 0 |
| Sales/Net Worth | 1.66 | 1.24 | 0.94 | 0 |
| Dividend Payout | $0 | $0 | $0 | $0 |

*This page left intentionally blank to accommodate tabular matter following.*

## APPENDIX

## Projected Balance Sheet

**Assets**

| **Short-term Assets** | **Starting Balances** | **Oct** | **Nov** | **Dec** | **Jan** | **Feb** |
|---|---|---|---|---|---|---|
| Cash | $10,000 | $23,038 | $32,897 | $49,104 | $64,904 | $85,210 |
| Accounts Receivable | $0 | $0 | $0 | $0 | $0 | $0 |
| Inventory | $1,500 | $600 | $1,160 | $3,095 | $3,400 | $8,225 |
| Other Short-term Assets | $0 | $0 | $0 | $0 | $0 | $0 |
| **Total Short-term Assets** | **$11,500** | **$23,638** | **$34,057** | **$52,199** | **$68,304** | **$93,435** |
| | | | | | | |
| **Long-term Assets** | | | | | | |
| Capital Assets | $0 | $0 | $0 | $0 | $0 | $0 |
| Accumulated Depreciation | $0 | $0 | $0 | $0 | $0 | $0 |
| **Total Long-term Assets** | **$0** | **$0** | **$0** | **$0** | **$0** | **$0** |
| **Total Assets** | **$11,500** | **$23,638** | **$34,057** | **$52,199** | **$68,304** | **$93,435** |
| | | | | | | |
| **Liabilities and Capital** | | | | | | |
| Accounts Payable | $200 | $2,484 | $5,621 | $10,850 | $11,399 | $18,238 |
| Short-term Notes | $4,500 | $5,166 | $5,832 | $6,498 | $7,164 | $7,830 |
| Other Short-term Liabilities | $0 | $0 | $0 | $0 | $0 | $0 |
| **Subtotal Short-term Liabilities** | **$4,700** | **$7,650** | **$11,453** | **$17,348** | **$18,563** | **$26,068** |
| **Long-term Liabilities** | **$0** | **$0** | **$0** | **$0** | **$0** | **$0** |
| **Total Liabilities** | **$4,700** | **$7,650** | **$11,453** | **$17,348** | **$18,563** | **$26,068** |
| | | | | | | |
| Paid in Capital | $16,004 | $26,004 | $31,004 | $36,004 | $41,004 | $45,004 |
| Retained Earnings | ($9,204) | ($9,204) | ($9,204) | ($9,204) | ($9,204) | ($9,204) |
| Earnings | $0 | ($812) | $804 | $8,051 | $17,941 | $31,567 |
| **Total Capital** | **$6,800** | **$15,988** | **$22,604** | **$34,851** | **$49,741** | **$67,367** |
| **Total Liabilities and Capital** | **$11,500** | **$23,638** | **$34,057** | **$52,199** | **$68,304** | **$93,435** |
| **Net Worth** | **$6,800** | **$15,988** | **$22,604** | **$34,851** | **$49,741** | **$67,367** |

| Mar | Apr | May | Jun | Jul | Aug | Sep |
|---|---|---|---|---|---|---|
| $88,726 | $106,800 | $129,756 | $153,864 | $187,831 | $226,340 | $276,210 |
| $0 | $0 | $0 | $0 | $0 | $0 | $0 |
| $8,810 | $9,555 | $11,920 | $12,475 | $18,000 | $20,710 | $25,950 |
| $0 | $0 | $0 | $0 | $0 | $2,000 | $2,000 |
| **$97,536** | **$116,355** | **$141,676** | **$166,339** | **$205,831** | **$249,050** | **$304,160** |
| | | | | | | |
| $0 | $0 | $0 | $0 | $0 | $0 | $0 |
| $0 | $0 | $0 | $0 | $0 | $0 | $0 |
| **$0** | **$0** | **$0** | **$0** | **$0** | **$0** | **$0** |
| **$97,536** | **$116,355** | **$141,676** | **$166,339** | **$205,831** | **$249,050** | **$304,160** |
| | | | | | | |
| $15,373 | $16,735 | $21,716 | $20,893 | $33,151 | $36,625 | $44,511 |
| $8,496 | $9,162 | $9,828 | $10,494 | $11,160 | $11,826 | $12,492 |
| $0 | $0 | $0 | $0 | $0 | $0 | $0 |
| **$23,869** | **$25,897** | **$31,544** | **$31,387** | **$44,311** | **$48,451** | **$57,003** |
| **$0** | **$0** | **$0** | **$0** | **$0** | **$0** | **$0** |
| **$23,869** | **$25,897** | **$31,544** | **$31,387** | **$44,311** | **$48,451** | **$57,003** |
| | | | | | | |
| $48,004 | $51,004 | $54,004 | $57,004 | $60,004 | $63,004 | $66,004 |
| ($9,204) | ($9,204) | ($9,204) | ($9,204) | ($9,204) | ($9,204) | ($9,204) |
| $46,324 | $63,011 | $84,782 | $107,480 | $104,653 | $180,019 | $229,060 |
| **$85,124** | **$104,811** | **$129,582** | **$155,280** | **$191,453** | **$233,819** | **$285,860** |
| **$108,993** | **$130,708** | **$161,126** | **$186,667** | **$235,764** | **$282,270** | **$342,863** |
| **$85,124** | **$104,811** | **$129,582** | **$155,280** | **$191,453** | **$233,819** | **$285,860** |

**Projected Cash Flow**

| | Oct | Nov | Dec | Jan | Feb | Mar |
|---|---|---|---|---|---|---|
| Net Profit | ($812) | $1,616 | $7,247 | $9,889 | $13,626 | $14,757 |
| Plus: | | | | | | |
| Depreciation | $0 | $0 | $0 | $0 | $0 | $0 |
| Change in Accounts Payable | $2,284 | $3,137 | $5,229 | $550 | $6,839 | ($2,866) |
| Current Borrowing (repayment) | $666 | $666 | $666 | $666 | $666 | $666 |
| Increase (decrease) Other Liabilities | $0 | $0 | $0 | $0 | $0 | $0 |
| Long-term Borrowing (repayment) | $0 | $0 | $0 | $0 | $0 | $0 |
| Capital Input | $10,000 | $5,000 | $5,000 | $5,000 | $4,000 | $3,000 |
| **Subtotal** | **$12,138** | **$10,419** | **$18,142** | **$16,105** | **$25,131** | **$15,558** |
| Less: | | | | | | |
| Change in Accounts Receivable | $0 | $0 | $0 | $0 | $0 | $0 |
| Change in Inventory | ($900) | $560 | $1,935 | $305 | $4,825 | $585 |
| Change in Other Short-term Assets | $0 | $0 | $0 | $0 | $0 | $0 |
| Capital Expenditures | $0 | $0 | $0 | $0 | $0 | $0 |
| Dividends | $0 | $0 | $0 | $0 | $0 | $0 |
| **Subtotal** | **($900)** | **$560** | **$1,935** | **$305** | **$4,825** | **$585** |
| **Net Cash Flow** | **$13,038** | **$9,859** | **$16,207** | **$15,800** | **$20,306** | **$14,973** |
| **Cash Balance** | **$23,038** | **$32,897** | **$49,104** | **$64,904** | **$85,210** | **$100,183** |

| Apr | May | Jun | Jul | Aug | Sep |
|---|---|---|---|---|---|
| $16,687 | $21,771 | $22,698 | $33,173 | $39,366 | $49,041 |
| | | | | | |
| $0 | $0 | $0 | $0 | $0 | $0 |
| $1,362 | $4,981 | ($823) | $12,258 | $3,474 | $7,885 |
| $666 | $666 | $666 | $666 | $666 | $666 |
| $0 | $0 | $0 | $0 | $0 | $0 |
| $0 | $0 | $0 | $0 | $0 | $0 |
| $3,000 | $3,000 | $3,000 | $3,000 | $3,000 | $3,000 |
| **$21,715** | **$30,418** | **$25,541** | **$49,097** | **$46,506** | **$60,593** |
| | | | | | |
| $0 | $0 | $0 | $0 | $0 | $0 |
| $745 | $2,365 | $555 | $5,525 | $2,710 | $5,240 |
| $0 | $0 | $0 | $0 | $2,000 | $0 |
| $0 | $0 | $0 | $0 | $0 | $0 |
| $0 | $0 | $0 | $0 | $0 | $0 |
| **$745** | **$2,365** | **$555** | **$5,525** | **$4,710** | **$5,240** |
| **$20,970** | **$28,053** | **$24,986** | **$43,572** | **$41,796** | **$55,353** |
| **$121,153** | **$149,206** | **$174,192** | **$217,764** | **$259,560** | **$314,913** |

**General Assumptions**

|                              | Oct    | Nov    | Dec    | Jan    | Feb    | Mar    |
|------------------------------|--------|--------|--------|--------|--------|--------|
| Short-term Interest Rate %   | 12.00% | 12.00% | 12.00% | 12.00% | 12.00% | 12.00% |
| Long-term Interest Rate %    | 10.50% | 10.50% | 10.50% | 10.50% | 10.50% | 10.50% |
| Payment Days Estimator       | 30     | 30     | 30     | 30     | 30     | 30     |
| Collection Days Estimator    | 2      | 2      | 2      | 2      | 2      | 2      |
| Inventory Turnover Estimator | 12.00  | 12.00  | 12.00  | 12.00  | 12.00  | 12.00  |
| Tax Rate %                   | 25.00% | 25.00% | 25.00% | 25.00% | 25.00% | 25.00% |
| Expenses in Cash %           | 10.00% | 10.00% | 10.00% | 10.00% | 10.00% | 10.00% |
| Sales on Credit %            | 0.00%  | 0.00%  | 0.00%  | 0.00%  | 0.00%  | 0.00%  |
| Personnel Burden %           | 10.00% | 10.00% | 10.00% | 10.00% | 10.00% | 10.00% |

**Personnel Plan**

| Personnel | Oct | Nov | Dec | Jan     | Feb     | Mar     |
|-----------|-----|-----|-----|---------|---------|---------|
| Payroll   | $0  | $0  | $0  | $2,916  | $2,916  | $2,916  |

| Apr | May | Jun | Jul | Aug | Sep |
|---|---|---|---|---|---|
| 12.00% | 12.00% | 12.00% | 12.00% | 12.00% | 12.00% |
| 10.50% | 10.50% | 10.50% | 10.50% | 10.50% | 10.50% |
| 30 | 30 | 30 | 30 | 30 | 30 |
| 2 | 2 | 2 | 2 | 2 | 2 |
| 12.00 | 12.00 | 12.00 | 12.00 | 12.00 | 12.00 |
| 25.00% | 25.00% | 25.00% | 25.00% | 25.00% | 25.00% |
| 10.00% | 10.00% | 10.00% | 10.00% | 10.00% | 10.00% |
| 0.00% | 0.00% | 0.00% | 10.00% | 10.00% | 10.00% |
| 10.00% | 10.00% | 10.00% | 10.00% | 10.00% | 10.00% |

| Apr | May | Jun | Jul | Aug | Sep |
|---|---|---|---|---|---|
| $2,916 | $2,916 | $2,916 | $2,916 | $2,916 | $2,916 |

**Profit and Loss (Income Statement)**

| | Oct | Nov | Dec | Jan | Feb | Mar |
|---|---|---|---|---|---|---|
| Sales | $2,924 | $7,473 | $17,698 | $22,598 | $29,622 | $31,721 |
| Direct Cost of Sales | $805 | $2,060 | $4,820 | $6,190 | $8,225 | $8,810 |
| Production Payroll | $0 | $0 | $0 | $0 | $0 | $0 |
| | $0 | $0 | $0 | $0 | $0 | $0 |
| **Total Cost of Sales** | **$805** | **$2,060** | **$4,820** | **$6,190** | **$8,225** | **$8,810** |
| Gross Margin | $2,119 | $5,413 | $12,878 | $16,408 | $21,397 | $22,911 |
| Gross Margin % | 72.47% | 72.44% | 72.77% | 72.61% | 72.23% | 72.23% |
| | | | | | | |
| Advertising/Promotion (including website) | $1,000 | $1,000 | $1,000 | $1,000 | $1,000 | $1,000 |
| Travel | $150 | $150 | $150 | $150 | $150 | $150 |
| Miscellaneous | $100 | $150 | $100 | $100 | $100 | $100 |
| Payroll Expense | $0 | $0 | $0 | $0 | $0 | $0 |
| Payroll Burden | $0 | $0 | $0 | $0 | $0 | $0 |
| Depreciation | $0 | $0 | $0 | $0 | $0 | $0 |
| Leased Equipment | $150 | $150 | $150 | $150 | $150 | $150 |
| Utilities | $50 | $50 | $50 | $50 | $50 | $50 |
| Insurance | $500 | $500 | $500 | $500 | $500 | $500 |
| Rent | $900 | $900 | $900 | $900 | $900 | $900 |
| Other Payroll | $0 | $0 | $0 | $0 | $0 | $0 |
| Contract/Consultants CPA | $300 | $300 | $300 | $300 | $300 | $300 |
| **Total Operating Expenses** | **$3,150** | **$3,200** | **$3,150** | **$3,150** | **$3,150** | **$3,150** |
| | | | | | | |
| Profit Before Interest and Taxes | ($1,031) | $2,213 | $9,728 | $13,258 | $18,247 | $19,761 |
| Interest Expense Short-term | $52 | $58 | $65 | $72 | $78 | $85 |
| Interest Expense Long-term | $0 | $0 | $0 | $0 | $0 | $0 |
| Taxes Incurred | ($271) | $539 | $2,416 | $3,296 | $4,542 | $4,919 |
| Extraordinary Items | $0 | $0 | $0 | $0 | $0 | $0 |
| **Net Profit** | **($812)** | **$1,616** | **$7,247** | **$9,889** | **$13,626** | **$14,757** |
| **Net Profit/Sales** | **-27.77%** | **21.63%** | **40.95%** | **43.76%** | **46.00%** | **46.52%** |

| Apr | May | Jun | Jul | Aug | Sep |
|---|---|---|---|---|---|
| $35,046 | $44,196 | $45,994 | $65,492 | $76,466 | $94,613 |
| $9,555 | $11,920 | $12,475 | $18,000 | $20,710 | $25,950 |
| $0 | $0 | $0 | $0 | $0 | $0 |
| $0 | $0 | $0 | $0 | $0 | $0 |
| **$9,555** | **$11,920** | **$12,475** | **$18,000** | **$20,710** | **$25,950** |
| $25,491 | $32,276 | $33,519 | $47,492 | $55,756 | $68,663 |
| 72.74% | 73.03% | 72.88% | 72.52% | 72.92% | 72.57% |
| | | | | | |
| $1,000 | $1,000 | $1,000 | $1,000 | $1,000 | $1,000 |
| $150 | $150 | $150 | $150 | $150 | $150 |
| $100 | $100 | $100 | $100 | $100 | $100 |
| $0 | $0 | $0 | $0 | $0 | $0 |
| $0 | $0 | $0 | $0 | $0 | $0 |
| $0 | $0 | $0 | $0 | $0 | $0 |
| $150 | $150 | $150 | $150 | $150 | $150 |
| $50 | $50 | $50 | $50 | $50 | $50 |
| $500 | $500 | $500 | $500 | $500 | $500 |
| $900 | $900 | $900 | $900 | $900 | $900 |
| $0 | $0 | $0 | $0 | $0 | $0 |
| $300 | $300 | $300 | $300 | $300 | $300 |
| **$3,150** | **$3,150** | **$3,150** | **$3,150** | **$3,150** | **$3,150** |
| | | | | | |
| $22,341 | $29,126 | $30,369 | $44,342 | $52,606 | $65,513 |
| $92 | $98 | $105 | $112 | $118 | $125 |
| $0 | $0 | $0 | $0 | $0 | $0 |
| $5,562 | $7,257 | $7,566 | $11,058 | $13,122 | $16,347 |
| $0 | $0 | $0 | $0 | $0 | $0 |
| **$16,687** | **$21,771** | **$22,698** | **$33,173** | **$39,366** | **$49,041** |
| **47.61%** | **49.26%** | **49.35%** | **50.65%** | **51.48%** | **51.83%** |

**Sales Forecast**

| Unit Sales | Oct | Nov | Dec | Jan | Feb | Mar |
|---|---|---|---|---|---|---|
| BladeBoots | 20 | 35 | 40 | 50 | 70 | 75 |
| SkateSails | 5 | 15 | 40 | 52 | 70 | 75 |
| SkateAid | 15 | 30 | 60 | 70 | 75 | 80 |
| **Total Unit Sales** | **40** | **80** | **140** | **172** | **215** | **230** |

| Unit Prices | | | | | | |
|---|---|---|---|---|---|---|
| BladeBoots | $24.95 | $24.95 | $24.95 | $24.95 | $24.95 | $24.95 |
| SkateSails | $350.00 | $350.00 | $350.00 | $350.00 | $350.00 | $350.00 |
| SkateAid | $45.00 | $45.00 | $45.00 | $45.00 | $45.00 | $45.00 |

| Sales | | | | | | |
|---|---|---|---|---|---|---|
| BladeBoots | $499 | $873 | $998 | $1,248 | $1,747 | $1,871 |
| SkateSails | $1,750 | $5,250 | $14,000 | $18,200 | $24,500 | $26,250 |
| SkateAid | $675 | $1,350 | $2,700 | $3,150 | $3,375 | $3,600 |
| **Total Sales** | **$2,924** | **$7,473** | **$17,698** | **$22,598** | **$29,622** | **$31,721** |

| Direct Unit Costs | | | | | | |
|---|---|---|---|---|---|---|
| BladeBoots | $10.00 | $10.00 | $10.00 | $10.00 | $10.00 | $10.00 |
| SkateSails | $100.00 | $100.00 | $100.00 | $100.00 | $100.00 | $100.00 |
| SkateAid | $7.00 | $7.00 | $7.00 | $7.00 | $7.00 | $7.00 |

| Direct Cost of Sales | | | | | | |
|---|---|---|---|---|---|---|
| BladeBoots | $200 | $350 | $400 | $500 | $700 | $750 |
| SkateSails | $500 | $1,500 | $4,000 | $5,200 | $7,000 | $7,500 |
| SkateAid | $105 | $210 | $420 | $490 | $525 | $560 |
| **Subtotal Direct Cost of Sales** | **$805** | **$2,060** | **$4,820** | **$6,190** | **$8,225** | **$8,810** |

| Apr | May | Jun | Jul | Aug | Sep |
|---|---|---|---|---|---|
| 75 | 80 | 125 | 160 | 175 | 235 |
| 80 | 100 | 100 | 150 | 170 | 215 |
| 115 | 160 | 175 | 200 | 280 | 300 |
| **270** | **340** | **400** | **510** | **625** | **750** |

| | | | | | |
|---|---|---|---|---|---|
| $24.95 | $24.95 | $24.95 | $24.95 | $24.95 | $24.95 |
| $350.00 | $350.00 | $350.00 | $350.00 | $350.00 | $350.00 |
| $45.00 | $45.00 | $45.00 | $45.00 | $45.00 | $45.00 |

| | | | | | |
|---|---|---|---|---|---|
| $1,871 | $1,996 | $3,119 | $3,992 | $4,366 | $5,863 |
| $28,000 | $35,000 | $35,000 | $52,500 | $59,500 | $75,250 |
| $5,175 | $7,200 | $7,875 | $9,000 | $12,600 | $13,500 |
| **$35,046** | **$44,196** | **$45,994** | **$65,492** | **$76,466** | **$94,613** |

| | | | | | |
|---|---|---|---|---|---|
| $10.00 | $10.00 | $10.00 | $10.00 | $10.00 | $10.00 |
| $100.00 | $100.00 | $100.00 | $100.00 | $100.00 | $100.00 |
| $7.00 | $7.00 | $7.00 | $7.00 | $7.00 | $7.00 |

| | | | | | |
|---|---|---|---|---|---|
| $750 | $800 | $1,250 | $1,600 | $1,750 | $2,350 |
| $8,000 | $10,000 | $10,000 | $15,000 | $17,000 | $21,500 |
| $805 | $1,120 | $1,225 | $1,400 | $1,960 | $2,100 |
| **$9,555** | **$11,920** | **$12,475** | **$18,000** | **$20,710** | **$25,950** |

# Charity Youth Hockey Tournament

BUSINESS PLAN                                    LUCKY PUCKS

*223 Grand Trunk Street*
*Cleveland, Ohio 44113*

*Lucky Pucks is a nonprofit corporation, chartered in Ohio, whose charitable concern is to supply research funds to aid in the search for a cure for spinal cord injuries. Lucky Pucks also is a high school hockey tournament. Its two goals: To fund research using revenues from charitable activities and to standardize and formalize tournament procedures in order that they may be easily reproduced in other cities. This plan was provided by Stephen Kinstler and was compiled in conjunction with the business planning courses of St. Louis University's Entrepreneurship Program.*

- EXECUTIVE SUMMARY

- BUSINESS DESCRIPTION

- TARGET MARKET

- THE CHARITY INDUSTRY

- MANAGEMENT

- CORPORATE GOALS & FINANCIALS

## EXECUTIVE SUMMARY

Every 35 minutes someone is told that they will never walk again. That works out to be over 10,000 people a year. Lucky Pucks does not believe in the word "never." Unless, it is "never give up."

Lucky Pucks is a charity youth hockey tournament. It was founded in order to fund research to help find a cure for spinal cord injuries (SCI). Despite the alarmingly low amounts of money spent on spinal cord injury research, recent medical advances have projected the timeline to finding a cure at 5-10 years.

If you were to compare government research money spent on SCI research to AIDS research, something amazing occurs. Government spending on SCI research was $17 million dollars in 1994. With 250,000 SCI patients in the U.S., this works out to be $68 per person. Government grants to the National Institute of Health in 1994 to study AIDS research was $1.4 billion. There are now 501,310 reported cases of AIDS in the U.S. This works out to be $2,792.68 per person. President Clinton authorized a grant March 6, 1996 to assist 50,000 AIDS patients so they could afford medicine of $55 million. This works out to $945.45 per person. There exists some disparity in these numbers. The lack of funding for spinal cord injury research may be due to the fact that spinal cord injuries are considered permanent. Likewise, at this time, there is no cure for AIDS.

Lucky Pucks held its inaugural tournament in Cleveland on October 8, 1995. The event attracted an attendance of 6,700 for the entire daylong event. The event raised $25,000 after expenses. The money was given to the Spinal Cord Society to fund research projects, and to St. John's Mercy Hospital to provide advanced patient care. Lucky Pucks appeals to the Cleveland hockey fan, specifically those that attend high school hockey games. Fans tend to fall into three categories: high school students, parents of the players, and youth hockey players. They account for nearly all of the 300 fans that a Mid-States Club Hockey Association game averages for each high school game. The household income for members of this market is above $35,000 a year. In order to raise more research funds, Lucky Pucks must expand. Next year we will include 32 local high school teams. In 1998, we will add seven other cities and hold an eight-city tournament in February of 1998 in Cleveland. In addition, each city will have its own local operation benefiting an area rehabilitation hospital and the Spinal Cord Society. Lucky Pucks will help set up those operations in the other seven cities. Eventually, we will have a tournament in each of the 26 cities that has a National Hockey League franchise. We are setting lofty goals for ourselves, but compared to making the disabled walk again, our goals pale in comparison.

Lucky Pucks has proven that it can be successful. Last year we were able to raise a significant amount of money when only 8 teams were competing. This year we will have 32 teams. The increase in participation of high school teams will provide nearly three times the funds for research over last year's total. In addition to raising research funds, Lucky Pucks is dedicated to raising the level of disability awareness in Cleveland. Just by getting out in the public, the disabled person is able to provide a noticeable presence in the community. We can make a difference. Never? Never heard of the word.

Lucky Pucks: Incorporated January 12, 1995 as a 501(3) "C" corporation. This designation is possible because Lucky Pucks is a nonprofit corporation that is centered on a single event.

Founder and current president: J. B. Buckholtz.

Relevant Statistics:

- There are between 10,000 to 14,000 spinal cord injuries every year.
- 82 percent are men between the ages of 17-24.
- Major causes of injury are automobile accidents, falls, diving accidents, and gunshots.
- Around 52 percent of all spinal cord injuries are quadriplegics, having no leg or hand control.
- Medical costs per year can range from $10,000 a year for a low-level paraplegic, like Mike Utley, to $400,000 a year for a very high-level quadriplegic, like Christopher Reeve.
- There are approximately 250,000 Americans disabled by a spinal cord injury.

Promising research has shown that paralysis is reversible. Reasonable estimates predict a time frame for finding a cure at 5-10 years, with funding of $200 million. Current funding by the government totaled $17 million in 1994. Private funding in that same year was approximately $10 million.

**BUSINESS DESCRIPTION**

Lucky Pucks is a nonprofit corporation, chartered in Ohio, whose charitable concern is to supply research funds to aid in the search for a cure for spinal cord injuries. Joe Buckholtz founded the organization in 1995 after his son sustained a spinal cord injury. Mr. Buckholtz was alarmed when he learned of the present state of government funding. Currently, the government is spending approximately $17 million a year to aid spinal cord injury research projects. Private funds for research projects for spinal cord injuries were estimated at $10 million in 1994 and should rise slightly in 1995. Many estimates establish a timetable of five years needed to find a cure. Presently, research projects are unable to be run concurrently due to lack of adequate funding.

Lucky Pucks receives a majority of funding from a high school hockey tournament that is held once a year. The event is held at the Sparling Center in Cleveland, Ohio. Volunteers that have various ties to the local hockey community run the tournament. Members of the organizing committee hold various positions in local hockey and athletic organizations, including Fans, Inc., Mid-States Hockey, the referee's association, Monroe Athletic Association, and the Reds Alumni Association. Lucky Pucks has two organizations that are the recipients of their charitable funds. They are St. John's Mercy Hospital in Cleveland and the Spinal Cord Society in Muskegon, Michigan. The former provides care for spinal cord patients and the latter is concerned primarily with finding a cure for spinal cord injury.

The tournament in 1996 will be expanded to include a two-week tournament format at local rinks with the finals at the Sparling Center. Last year's tournament involved only eight teams playing at the Sparling Center. Facility rental was a major expense. In 1996, the facility rental will be lower this year due to the involvement of Cleveland Reds personnel. They have provided Lucky Pucks with increased access to ice time in the Cleveland area at a lower cost. In addition, the tournament will be expanded from the original eight teams, to all varsity high school hockey teams in the Cleveland metropolitan area. Each team is invited to participate in three games at no direct cost to the team. They will, however, be asked to sell $2,500 in tickets. A private donation of $4,500 will be divided among the two top ticket selling teams, $3,000 to the top seller and $1,500 to the second best seller. These organizations can use the money in any way they see fit. As of March 1996, 32 out of 42 teams have committed to play in the tournament to take place in late September, early October of 1996.

Lucky Pucks has a list of corporate sponsors that are vital to its success. KHSR, All-Sports radio, has expressed its interest in becoming the exclusive radio provider for the tournament. In return, they will provide publicity for the tournament with a value at approximately $20,000. The *Cleveland Suburban Journals* is also a sponsor that provided a series of articles publicizing the event last year. They will once again provide their support. An aspect of the tournament that proved to be lucrative was the auction of sports memorabilia from sports stars, including Brett Hull and Wayne Gretzky. In addition, T-shirts sold at a rather brisk pace, adding to total revenue.

Lucky Pucks has two goals: To fund research using revenues from charitable activities and to standardize and formalize tournament procedures in order that they may be easily reproduced in other cities. By 1997, Lucky Pucks will be expanded to include seven other cities in North America that have a strong amateur hockey program, a progressive rehabilitation center for spinal cord injuries, and, preferably, an NHL franchise hockey team. Currently, there are 26 cities that have franchises in the National Hockey League in the United States and Canada.

## TARGET MARKET

Lucky Pucks is a high school hockey tournament. Fans of high school hockey consist primarily of high school students, families of players, and youth hockey players. There are fans that do not fit easily into these categories. They include alumni of the various high schools and fans of the professional hockey team, the Pittsburgh Sharks. This group would also make up part of the audience for the tournament. However, they cannot easily be segmented. In addition, they do not make up a sizable portion of those most likely to see a typical high school hockey team. Fans who attend a high school hockey game can be generally classified into these categories:

Target Market:

   High school students: 75 percent Male and 25 percent Female
   Age: 14-18
   Family income: $35,000 and up
   This includes players, siblings and peers.

   Parents of players: 50 percent Male and 50 percent Female
   Age: 35-49
   Family income: $35,000 and up
   This group can include extended family members also.

   Youth hockey players: 90 percent Male and 10 percent Female
   Age: 7-13
   Family income: $35,000 and up

   Other: 80 percent Male and 20 percent Female
   Age: 25-35
   Income: $25,000 and up

   *Other includes high school alumni and hockey fans.

The figures that comprise the target market are approximately 50 percent parents, 30 percent high school students, 10 percent youth hockey players, and 10 percent other. Target market size: 375,000.

Most hockey players, parents of players, and fans of hockey fall into the common societal designation of middle-class.

## Total Market

The average Cleveland high school hockey game is viewed by approximately 300 people, according to Mid-States Club Hockey Association, the governing body of high school hockey in the Cleveland area. According to my personal experience, the typical Mid-States player comes from a middle-class background, attends high school at a private school or in a somewhat affluent public school district and has parents with income in excess of $35,000. The high cost of equipment and available ice time is a deterrent to more involvement by children.

Last year when the tournament was held involving the eight invited schools, Lucky Pucks was able to attract 6,700 people for the daylong event. A cursory look around confirmed that the majority of attendees fit within our target market categories. Hockey is indeed strong within the Cleveland metropolitan area. There are currently 42 high school varsity teams, 25 junior varsity teams, 13 youth hockey clubs serving children from the age of 5-17, 2 senior men's leagues, and 15 ice skating rinks. The explosion in the popularity of hockey is most evident in the number of skating rinks opened within the past four years. Community skating rinks were erected in Willow Groves, St. Martins, and South Park, and two private operations were begun in Fairlane and Southhampton. The cost of ice time is between $110 an hour at the Cleveland county rinks of Cuyahoga, Lorain, and Summit to $135 an hour. Operations generally begin at 7:00 A.M. and continue throughout the day until 1:30 A.M. This is year round. Ice is available for rent, but the only times available are usually after 11:00 P.M.

Total contributions to charities in 1994 totaled $129.9 billion. This was up 3.6 percent from 1993. Contributions had been consistently headed downward until that time. Corporate donations, adjusted for inflation, declined by $1 billion from 1989 to 1994, or roughly 0.13 percent annually, says the American Association of Fund Raising Counsel, a New York trade group. The recent increase is due in large part to the stabilization of the economy that has occurred. Coupled with this increase in charitable giving has come an increased competition for charity dollars. Internal Revenue Service figures show that from 1975 to 1990, the nonprofit sector grew from 6 percent of the gross domestic product to 10 percent, while revenues climbed 227 percent—more than four times as fast as the rest of the economy. In addition, corporate donations programs are no longer viewed as just giving cash, but are now considered a vital aspect of a firm's marketing plan. The industry has been characterized by these two major changes.

**THE CHARITY INDUSTRY**

Corporate downsizing has caused companies to rethink their donation programs and concentrate on those activities that will give them the greatest return. Adjusted for inflation, total corporate giving dipped 2 percent in 1994, to $6.1 billion, says the American Association of Fund Raising Counsel Trust for Philanthropy. That's part of a slide under way since 1987 that has resulted from factors ranging from the 1986 tax reform to greater cost-consciousness. Social responsibility was done previously to make a company's directors feel good. Today, it must make that company look good as well. A new Conference Board report calls this new approach "strategic philanthropy" or "financially sound goodwill." The study surveyed 463 U.S. companies and found that companies taking a more businesslike approach to charity reported a better image, increased employee loyalty, and improved customer ties. Cause-marketing advocates say such campaigns can meet traditional marketing goals, such as boosting market share, pumping up the sales force, or improving a weak public image, while helping causes the customer cares about. A 1993 survey by Roper Starch Worldwide, sponsored by cause-marketing specialist Cone Communications in Boston, found that 66 percent of 1,981 consumers polled claimed they were likely to switch brands if the purchase supported a cause of concern to them. The effects of strategic gift-giving cannot be ignored. A charity must provide a comprehensive benefits package to attract corporate funds. Corporate social responsibility attracts the most media attention, but corporate donations make up a very small percentage (4.7 percent in 1993) of total giving. This compares to 81.8 percent for private donations and 13.4 percent for government and foundations.

**Charity Competition**

An increase in the number of charities has led to an increase in the competition for charitable donations. Nearly 60 percent of all nonprofits nationwide have been founded since 1970, and their proliferation has intensified competition for both private donations and dwindling government funds. The private philanthropist is by far the largest giver of charitable funds. In 1993, the corporate world gave a total of $5.92 billion. This pales in comparison to private donations that totaled $102.55 billion that same year. Yet, the fallout in the corporate sector has carried over into personal giving. Today, charities have begun to offer benefits in addition to a feeling of goodwill. A charity has to distinguish itself in order to attract funds.

Lucky Pucks must compete for funds with many charities. They include the Salvation Army, United Way, the March of Dimes, and the Variety Club, to name a few. These competitors are better capitalized, better known, and better supported by the community. Yet, these charities do not address spinal cord injuries or its research. A challenge to Lucky Pucks is the idea that individual oriented spinal cord injury fundraisers present. The challenge is to convince donors that the money does not go to an individual, but to the research cause. The reason the misinterpretation occurs is simple: many people have been asked for money to help defray the medical costs of an individual. Lucky Pucks is the first organization in Cleveland to concentrate on the welfare and recovery of all spinal cord patients through progressive research projects.

Spinal cord injuries require surgery, critical care, and long rehabilitation. Even with insurance, the costs to a family are staggering. In an effort to help defray these costs, many families rely on one-time fundraisers in order to make ends meet. In the area of spinal cord research, there is little fundraising. Most people do not get involved until someone they know is affected. In addition, a spinal cord patient is not likely to become an active member of the community until they have gone through a mourning period. Through personal experience it is normally one year, with additional advances made in the third and fourth years. Some never recover emotionally.

The major challenge to fundraising for research is a lack of understanding and a lack of a strong presence among the injured themselves. In the past, a spinal-cord-injured person had no hope for a recovery. Medical science considered the condition irreversible. This pessimistic outlook is finally changing. People are now realizing that we can eliminate this affliction. But fundraising efforts can be hampered by the injured themselves. An injured person does not return to being the same person they were before the accident. Everything is more difficult. They prefer instead to remain in their homes where things are more accessible. A person will not venture out because of two reasons. First, it is hard to come to terms that the individual needs much more help than they used to. Second, the physical structure of a community is not accessible. Although the Americans with Disabilities Act is meant to eliminate these obstacles, many barriers still exist. To effect change, the disabled must take it upon themselves to establish an identifiable presence in the community.

The lessons of the Americans with Disabilities Act will not last if the changes they have made are not utilized. The cause of AIDS research was helped immensely by the associations that it had. Many high-profile people were victims of AIDS. Even though many of us do not know anyone with AIDS, we are familiar with famous people that have been afflicted. Spinal cord injuries have not affected a large number of well-known people. Recent injuries to the actor Christopher Reeve, football stars Mike Utley and Dennis Byrd, and hockey player Travis Roy have brought spinal cord injuries to the forefront. These four men bring home the devastating effects a spinal cord injury can have. Each one was considered to be in tremendous physical shape. Each one was considered to be in the prime of his life. Each one was injured competing in a sport they loved.

Lucky Pucks is in direct competition with many larger more established charities. We do not have the resources to compete with these organizations on a large scale. Instead, we have established a niche in which to operate. We have the opportunity to establish ourselves as the premier organization to raise funds for spinal cord injuries. Many fundraising activities are done locally with little impact beyond the community. A strong national drive can link each community effort and make a difference in the lives of many. Lucky Pucks faces competition from other smaller charities, such as golf tournaments, church bazaars, etc. Each charity tries to attract funds by associating a reward with the donation, i.e. a round of golf or crafts. Lucky Pucks offers a donor the opportunity to view quality hockey in Cleveland's premier facility, the Sparling Center. The price for tickets to a professional hockey game at the Kiel ranges from $35 to $55.

As a charity, Lucky Pucks brings together high school hockey teams in a forum that did not exist before. For $10 at the Sparling Center or $3 at local venues, people are able to see their favorite team play and evaluate the competition that they will face in the upcoming season. Before the tournament, a fan would have to travel to rinks throughout the city in order to evaluate his team's chances, each time at a cost of three dollars per game and at facilities with vastly different levels of comfort and cleanliness. The event at the Sparling Center will allow a hockey fan to enjoy seven games throughout the day at a cost of $10 for adults and $5 for students. The games prior to the finals will be held at the Johnson Recreation Complex and at the North County Recreation Complex. Each game at these facilities will be at a cost of $3 for admission.

Lucky Pucks controls expenses in order to provide the maximum funding possible for research. Eighty percent of revenue exceeding expenses are distributed to St. John's Mercy Hospital and the Spinal Cord Society. In the first three years of operation, high levels of expenses will limit Lucky Pucks. This is due to the initial costs of start-up. Each of the first three years involves substantial expansion. This results in high travel and promotion and travel expense, high phone expense, and high postage cost. In the third year, Lucky Pucks will hold an additional tournament in late February in Cleveland. This will involve eight cities. Lucky Pucks will assist each city in implementing a local "franchise." Each city will be independently operated. To maintain the integrity of the tournament and its goals, representatives of the local Spinal Cord Society chapter will closely monitor each new host city. Each chapter is well established in their area. Lucky Pucks will utilize this strong infrastructure to reach the local spinal cord community and local businesses. The quality of the tournament will be maintained by a strict set of guidelines established by Lucky Pucks and the Cleveland chapter of the Spinal Cord Society. The revenue over expenses that they earn will be divided among a local rehabilitation facility and the Spinal Cord Society home office in Michigan. The additional revenue for the Cleveland chapter of Lucky Pucks will come from hosting the eight-city tournament.

Because the hockey season is not year-round, there is a lull period when there is little exposure for the tournament. Most of our revenue comes in only a few months of each year. Lucky Pucks is implementing an education program to teach the public about disabilities. The effect is twofold. There is a greater understanding of how disabilities affect our lives and Lucky Pucks remains a visible presence year round. This program is provided at no cost to interested groups. There are a variety of speakers available to organizations. The organization can choose the speaker that would be most suitable for its needs.

In order to reduce costs, Lucky Pucks does not maintain central offices. All general meetings are held at Monroe Ice Rink. The director of sales for Lucky Pucks is the facility manager at the rink. All meeting rooms are provided at no cost. Lucky Pucks does maintain a separate mailing address. This is a post office box. Meetings of the board are normally held at a member's household. Lucky Pucks does not intend to have any paid staff positions at this time.

**Charitable Operations**

**MANAGEMENT**

Volunteers control Lucky Pucks. Each position is filled by a qualified volunteer based on prior experience, ties to the hockey community and awareness of the devastating effects of a spinal cord injury. They are president, sales coordinator, volunteer coordinator, tournament coordinator, and executive director.

**President: Joseph Buckholtz.** Joe is the founder of Lucky Pucks and is the director of manufacturing for Cleveland Shoe Company. Joe is also president of the Hockey Referee's Association in Cleveland and holds a position with the Cleveland chapter of the Spinal Cord Society. He has had vast experience with the Red Cross and is currently involved with setting up a new blood bank is Cleveland. The position of president includes the responsibilities of meeting with prospective sponsors, speaking at local hockey functions about the tournament, and acting as spokesperson at media events.

**Sales Coordinator: Dan Simpson.** Dan is a journeyman plumber with Ajax Plumbing Company. In addition, he is the facility manager for Monroe Ice Rink. He is responsible for all functions at the rink and coordinating ice times for Monroe Americans Hockey Club, Mid-States High School Hockey Association, and other local clubs. He is responsible for overseeing the sales of tickets for the tournament and is invaluable when it comes to contacts with all the local clubs in the Cleveland area.

**Volunteer Coordinator: Betty Singer.** Betty was formerly with Fan's Club Inc., a local no-for-profit organization instrumental in bringing the Browns football team to Cleveland. She has extensive experience with the facility operations at the Sparling Center. As volunteer coordinator, she is responsible for organizing the volunteer corps throughout the tournament and for events surrounding the days before and after the tournament.

**Tournament Coordinator: George Hill.** George is the president of Hill Shoe Company. In addition, he has just recently retired from the Board of Directors for the Mid-States Club Hockey Association. Among his many duties with MSCHA, George was responsible for organizing the championship tournament, the Cleveland Reds Challenge Cup, at the Cleveland Arena and at the Sparling Center. His extensive knowledge of tournament operations is invaluable to the Lucky Pucks charity hockey tournament.

**Executive Director: Michael Whistler.** Mike is an M.B.A. student at Ohio State University. In addition to working for Whistler Plumbing as a communications coordinator, Mike speaks about disabilities at public functions in elementary schools and for parents' organizations. Mike is responsible for communications that are sent by Lucky Pucks and also maintains Lucky Pucks's databases.

**Volunteers**

Lucky Pucks is a large operation that would not be successful without the assistance of its volunteers. Volunteers are drawn primarily from in and around the Cleveland hockey community. Some of the notable volunteers:

**Bruce Affleck** is the director of sales for the Cleveland Reds. He is a former professional hockey player and a current member of the Reds broadcast team on KTRV-TV Channel 20 and with regional sports provider, Top Sports. He acts as a liaison between Lucky Pucks and the Cleveland Reds and their alumni.

**Nicholas Bastion** is the owner of a local sports merchandise company. He is responsible for Lucky Pucks merchandise, including hats, T-shirts, and sweatshirts.

**Kyle Buckholtz** is the son of the founder of Lucky Pucks. Kyle acts as a spokesperson for Lucky Pucks.

Additional volunteers:

> Announcing and play-by-play: KHSR radio
> Referee services: Ohio Ice Hockey Officials Association
> Security: At the Sparling Center, Sparling Security Services
> At the local rinks, off-duty police or county park rangers
> First aid: St. John's Mercy Medical Staff
> Support services: volunteers

A nonpaid volunteer fills each position at Lucky Pucks. Each member of the board was selected for their extensive knowledge of the local hockey community and their dedication to eliminating spinal cord injuries. Each volunteer has witnessed the devastating effect that spinal cord injuries can have on the injured and their families. Each volunteer is well aware of the progress that has been made in research in the last few years, and each volunteer is dedicated to finding a cure and making a difference in the lives of many.

1. To at least double the amount of research funds given each year to support spinal cord injury research.
2. To expand from one city to eight cities, and possibly each NHL city with the assistance of the NHL.
3. To educate the public about disabilities and the effect that they have on the community.

**CORPORATE GOALS & FINANCIALS**

**Statement of Revenue, Expenses and Changes in Fund Balance**
**For the fiscal year ending March 15, 1996**

| | Mar | Apr | May | Jun | Jul | Aug |
|---|---|---|---|---|---|---|
| **Revenue** | $1,000.00 | $0.00 | $0.00 | $0.00 | $0.00 | $0.00 |
| | | | | | | |
| **Expenses** | | | | | | |
| Ice Rental-Sparling Center | $0.00 | $0.00 | $0.00 | $0.00 | $0.00 | $0.00 |
| Insurance | $0.00 | $0.00 | $0.00 | $0.00 | $0.00 | $0.00 |
| Rings | $0.00 | $0.00 | $0.00 | $0.00 | $0.00 | $0.00 |
| Printing | $0.00 | $0.00 | $678.00 | $0.00 | $0.00 | $0.00 |
| Office Products | $0.00 | $0.00 | $0.00 | $0.00 | $0.00 | $0.00 |
| Phone | $0.00 | $0.00 | $0.00 | $24.38 | $13.00 | $13.00 |
| Signs | $0.00 | $0.00 | $0.00 | $0.00 | $0.00 | $195.00 |
| Shirts | $0.00 | $0.00 | $0.00 | $0.00 | $0.00 | $0.00 |
| Program-Printing | $0.00 | $0.00 | $0.00 | $0.00 | $0.00 | $0.00 |
| Program-Artwork | $0.00 | $0.00 | $0.00 | $0.00 | $0.00 | $0.00 |
| P.O. Box | $0.00 | $0.00 | $31.00 | $0.00 | $0.00 | $0.00 |
| Trophies | $0.00 | $0.00 | $0.00 | $0.00 | $0.00 | $0.00 |
| Postage Meter | $0.00 | $0.00 | $0.00 | $0.00 | $0.00 | $0.00 |
| Postage | $0.00 | $0.00 | $0.00 | $0.00 | $0.00 | $0.00 |
| Volunteer Snacks | $0.00 | $0.00 | $0.00 | $0.00 | $0.00 | $0.00 |
| Travel & Promotion | $0.00 | $0.00 | $0.00 | $0.00 | $0.00 | $0.00 |
| Pictures | $0.00 | $0.00 | $0.00 | $0.00 | $0.00 | $0.00 |
| Funds repayment | $0.00 | $0.00 | $0.00 | $0.00 | $0.00 | $0.00 |
| | | | | | | |
| **Excess of Revenue over expenses before donations** | $1,000.00 | $0.00 | ($709.00) | ($733.38) | ($746.38) | ($954.38) |
| | | | | | | |
| **Donations** | | | | | | |
| Spinal Cord Society | $0.00 | $0.00 | $0.00 | $0.00 | $0.00 | $0.00 |
| St. John's Mercy | $0.00 | $0.00 | $0.00 | $0.00 | $0.00 | $0.00 |
| Variety Club | $0.00 | $0.00 | $0.00 | $0.00 | $0.00 | $0.00 |
| | | | | | | |
| **Fund Balance** | $1,000.00 | $0.00 | ($709.00) | ($733.38) | ($746.38) | ($954.38) |

| Sep | Oct | Nov | Dec | Jan | Feb |
|---|---|---|---|---|---|
| **$13,434.96** | **$53,739.83** | **$0.00** | **$0.00** | **$0.00** | **$0.00** |
| | | | | | |
| $0.00 | $31,020.93 | $0.00 | $0.00 | $0.00 | $0.00 |
| $0.00 | $1,575.00 | $0.00 | $0.00 | $0.00 | $0.00 |
| $0.00 | $0.00 | $0.00 | $1,725.00 | $0.00 | $0.00 |
| $200.86 | $0.00 | $0.00 | $0.00 | $0.00 | $260.00 |
| $1,383.24 | $0.00 | $0.00 | $0.00 | $0.00 | $0.00 |
| $13.00 | $13.00 | $13.00 | $13.00 | $13.00 | $13.00 |
| $0.00 | $0.00 | $0.00 | $0.00 | $0.00 | $0.00 |
| $0.00 | $890.28 | $0.00 | $0.00 | $0.00 | $0.00 |
| $0.00 | $1,000.00 | $0.00 | $0.00 | $0.00 | $0.00 |
| $0.00 | $800.00 | $0.00 | $0.00 | $0.00 | $0.00 |
| $0.00 | $0.00 | $58.00 | $0.00 | $0.00 | $0.00 |
| $0.00 | $298.00 | $0.00 | $0.00 | $0.00 | $0.00 |
| $0.00 | $0.00 | $0.00 | $128.00 | $0.00 | $127.47 |
| $0.00 | $0.00 | $267.74 | $0.00 | $0.00 | $0.00 |
| $0.00 | $128.57 | $0.00 | $0.00 | $0.00 | $0.00 |
| $0.00 | $0.00 | $0.00 | $0.00 | $300.00 | $326.31 |
| $0.00 | $0.00 | $230.64 | $0.00 | $0.00 | $0.00 |
| $1,000.00 | $0.00 | $0.00 | $0.00 | $0.00 | $0.00 |
| | | | | | |
| **$10,883.48** | **$28,897.53** | **$25,422.37** | **$6,212.15** | **$5,899.15** | **$5,172.37** |
| | | | | | |
| $0.00 | $0.00 | $10,000.00 | $0.00 | $0.00 | $0.00 |
| $0.00 | $0.00 | $10,000.00 | $0.00 | $0.00 | $0.00 |
| $0.00 | $0.00 | $250.00 | $0.00 | $0.00 | $0.00 |
| | | | | | |
| **$10,883.48** | **$28,897.53** | **$8,078.15** | **$6,212.15** | **$5,899.15** | **$5,172.37** |

**Statement of Revenue, Expenses and Changes in Fund Balance
For the fiscal year ending March 15, 1996**

| | | |
|---|---|---|
| **Revenue** | | **$68,174.79** |
| | | |
| **Expenses** | | |
| Ice Rental-Sparling Center | $31,020.93 | |
| Insurance | $1,575.00 | |
| Rings | $1,725.00 | |
| Printing | $1,138.86 | |
| Office Products | $1,383.24 | |
| Phone | $128.38 | |
| Signs | $195.00 | |
| Shirts | $890.28 | |
| Program-Printing | $1,000.00 | |
| Program-Artwork | $800.00 | |
| P.O. Box | $89.00 | |
| Trophies | $298.00 | |
| Postage Meter | $255.47 | |
| Postage | $267.74 | |
| Volunteer Snacks | $128.57 | |
| Travel & Promotion | $626.31 | |
| Pictures | $230.64 | |
| Funds repayment | $1,000.00 | **$42,752.42** |
| | | |
| **Excess of Revenue over expenses before donations** | | **$25,422.37** |
| | | |
| **Donations** | | |
| Spinal Cord Society | $10,000.00 | |
| St. John's Mercy | $10,000.00 | |
| Variety Club | $250.00 | **$20,250.00** |
| | | |
| **Fund Balance** | | **$5,172.37** |

## Balance Sheet
## March 15, 1996

**Assets**
**Current Assets**

| | | |
|---|---|---|
| Cash | $5,140.37 | |
| Office Supplies | $75.00 | |
| **Total Current Assets** | | **$5,215.37** |

**Fixed Assets**

| | | |
|---|---|---|
| Office Equipment | $100.00 | |
| **Total Fixed Assets** | | **$100.00** |

| | | |
|---|---|---|
| **Total Assets** | | **$5,315.37** |

**Liabilities and Fund Balance**
Current Liabilities

| | | |
|---|---|---|
| Accounts Payable | $143.00 | |
| **Total Liabilities** | | **$143.00** |

**Fund Balance**

| | | |
|---|---|---|
| General Fund | $5,172.37 | $5,172.37 |
| **Total Liabilities and Fund Balance** | | **$5,315.37** |

**Notes to Financial Statements Year 1**

**Notes for Statement of Revenue, Expenses and Change in Fund Balance, Year 1.**

**Revenue**

- Initial revenue in March of 1995 was a $1,000 advance by Joseph Buckholtz
- Revenue only occurred in September and October
- Components of revenue:

| | |
|---|---|
| Ticket sales | $53,770.00 |
| Sales of Reds Tickets | $8,000.00 |
| Donations | $1,400.00 |
| Raffle tickets | $1,649.00 |
| Program-Sales and Ads | $2,188.00 |
| Merchandise sales | $975.00 |
| Interest income | $192.79 |
| **Total Revenue** | **$68,174.79** |

- Raffle ticket sales are for three Brett Hull autographed hockey sticks
- Merchandise sales include T-shirts and sweatshirts
- Program sales includes purchase price and ad revenue
- Reds ticket sales were the result of a Reds' donation of tickets for three exhibition games at the beginning of the season for sale by Lucky Pucks
- Interest is calculated on monthly balance at approximately 3.75 percent annual interest

**Expenses**

- Postage was paid only in November. The owner of Cleveland Shoe Company deferred the expense until after the tournament.
- Travel and Promotion include a Redliners Banquet (Cleveland Reds Booster Club) and the Mid-States Club Hockey Association Championship Tournament and Dinner.
- Rings expense is for the purchase of championship rings for the winning team.
- Insurance costs are for the one day event and do not carry over into the next year.

**Notes to the Statement of Cash Flows**

**Disbursements**

- Donations to charity include $10,000 to St. John's Mercy Hospital, $10,000 to the Spinal Cord Society, and $250 to the Variety Club.

**Notes to the Balance Sheet**

**Fixed Assets**

- Office equipment is a fax machine. Depreciation is allocated for one year. This is due to the rapid obsolescence of electronic equipment and low salvage costs.

**Description of Cash Flows**

In year 1, Lucky Pucks was a one-day tournament involving eight high school hockey teams. The event was moderately successful and showed much promise for the next year.

## Statement of Revenue, Expenses and Change in Fund Balance
## For the year ending March 15, 1997

| | | |
|---|---|---|
| **Revenue** | | **$140,000.00** |
| | | |
| **Expenses** | | |
| Ice rental | $46,160.00 | |
| Insurance | $5,000.00 | |
| Local Rink Expense | $5,040.00 | |
| Rings | $1,800.00 | |
| Printing & Signs | $4,800.00 | |
| Office Products | $2,000.00 | |
| Phone | $500.00 | |
| Merchandise | $1,000.00 | |
| Program-Printing & Art | $2,500.00 | |
| P.O. Box | $100.00 | |
| Trophies | $100.00 | |
| Postage Meter & Postage | $1,100.00 | |
| Volunteer Snacks | $250.00 | |
| Travel & Promotion | $2,000.00 | |
| Pictures | $850.00 | |
| Vehicle Purchase | $20,000.00 | |
| Trademark expense | $500.00 | **$93,700.00** |
| | | |
| **Excess of revenue over expenses before donations** | | **$46,300.00** |
| | | |
| **Donations** | | |
| Spinal Cord Society (75%) | | $30,000.00 |
| St. John's Mercy (25%) | | $10,000.00 |
| | | |
| **Excess of revenue over expenses** | | **$6,300.00** |
| | | |
| General Fund-Beginning | | $5,172.37 |
| General Fund-Ending | | $11,472.37 |

**Balance Sheet**
**Year 2**

**Assets**
**Current Assets**

| | | |
|---|---|---|
| Cash | $11,872.37 | |
| Office Supplies | $100.00 | |
| Merchandise | $150.00 | |
| **Total Current Assets** | | **$12,122.37** |

**Fixed Assets**

| | | |
|---|---|---|
| Office Equipment | $300.00 | |
| **Total Fixed Assets** | | **$300.00** |

| | | |
|---|---|---|
| **Total Assets** | | **$12,422.37** |

**Liabilities and Fund Balances**

**Current Liabilities**

| | | |
|---|---|---|
| Accounts Payable | $950.00 | |
| **Total Liabilities** | | **$950.00** |

**Fund Balances**

| | | |
|---|---|---|
| General Fund | $11,472.37 | $11,472.37 |
| **Total Liabilities and Fund Balance** | | **$12,422.37** |

**Notes for Statement of Revenue, Expenses and Change in Fund Balance.**

**Revenue**

- Revenue consists of the one-day finals at the Sparling Center and the two-week tournament beforehand.
- Components of revenue:

| | |
|---|---|
| Ticket sales-Sparling Center | $70,000.00 |
| Ticket sales-Quarter & semi-finals | $50,400.00 |
| Raffles | $35,000.00 |
| Merchandise sales | $2,500.00 |
| Memorabilia auction | $2,500.00 |
| Programs | $5,000.00 |
| Interest | $700.00 |
| **Total** | **$166,100.00** |

- Revenue from the Sparling Center event is based on the target sales level for each high school. This is $2,500.
    32 teams @ $2,500 each = $80,000 - $10,000 for sales allowances = $70,000
- Revenue from quarterfinals and semi-finals is based on the average attendance at a high school hockey game multiplied by the number of games, 56.
    56 games @ 300 people per game @ $3 per game attendance = $50,400
- Raffles are for vehicles to be given away. Sales for one raffle will take place before the tournament. Sales will be limited to 250 tickets at a cost of $100 each. The second raffle will have sales starting before the tournament lasting the duration of the tournament. Each ticket will cost $1.00. Expected number of sales is 10,000.
- Merchandise includes T-shirts, sweatshirts, and hats.
- Program revenue includes the cost of the program and ad revenue.
- Interest income is calculated on the monthly fund balance at approximately 4 percent annual interest.

**Expenses**

- Insurance needs are increased due to the expanded tournament size.
- Local rink expense includes scorekeepers, ticket takers, additional security, and incidentals.
- Increase in phone expense is the result of long distance calls to eight prospective Lucky Pucks expansion cities and long distance calls resulting from travel.
- Trophy expense is lower because only a nameplate will be attached instead of purchasing new trophies.
- Travel and promotion are higher due to a regional hockey event in Colorado Springs.
- Vehicle purchase is for the prizes for the raffle. The vehicle will have to be purchased, but at a substantially lower price from the dealer.
- Donations are no longer equally divided by the two charities. At the request of St. John's Mercy, percentages are shifted in order to provide more money for research. The Spinal Cord Society is to receive around 75 percent and St. John's Mercy Hospital is to receive around 25 percent.

**Notes to the Statement of Cash Flows**

**Disbursements**

- Donations reflect the change in allotment at the request of St. John's Mercy.
- Travel and promotion increased due to trip to USA Hockey (national amateur hockey association) meeting in Colorado.

**Notes to the Balance Sheet**

**Fixed Assets**

- Office equipment is a fax machine and copier. Depreciation is allocated for one year. This is due to the rapid obsolescence of electronic equipment and low salvage cost.

**Description of Cash Flows**

In year two, Lucky Pucks will be expanded to 32 teams. Thirty-two is the number of teams that elected to participate out of a total of 42 possible teams. Additional cash flows will be experienced because the expanded format will include elimination games at local rinks prior to the one-day event at the Sparling Center.

## Break-even Analysis-Facility Rental Year 2

### Quarter & semi-final games:

Ice Rental

- 32 teams requiring 56 sessions @ $110 each session = $6,160 cost for ice rental at local ice rinks

Cost per game of scorekeepers, ticket-takers, and security = $90 a game

- $90 per game (56 games) = $5,040

Attendance needed each game to break even

- $11,200 total cost / 56 games / $3 per person = 67 persons needed per game

**Break-even point for local rink attendance = 67 people per game**

Average attendance per high school game according to the MSCHA= 300

Sparling Center

Ice Rental at the Sparling Center
- Cost for rental of Sparling Center = $40,000
- Average ticket price = $7.50
- Break-even attendance $40,000 / $7.50 = 5,333 people per game

**Break-even attendance for the Sparling Center = 5,333 people per game**

Attendance last year for the entire day was 6,700.

## Statement of Revenue, Expenses and Change in Fund Balance
## For the year 3 ending March 15, 1998

| | | |
|---|---|---|
| **Revenue** | | $200,000.00 |
| | | |
| **Expenses** | | |
| Ice rental | $76,720.00 | |
| Insurance | $6,000.00 | |
| Local Rink Expense | $5,600.00 | |
| Rings | $3,500.00 | |
| Printing & Signs | $6,000.00 | |
| Office Products | $2,000.00 | |
| Phone | $800.00 | |
| Merchandise | $1,800.00 | |
| Program-Printing & Art | $4,500.00 | |
| P.O. Box | $120.00 | |
| Trophies | $400.00 | |
| Postage Meter & Postage | $1,500.00 | |
| Volunteer Snacks | $400.00 | |
| Travel & Promotion | $2,500.00 | |
| Pictures | $1,000.00 | |
| Vehicle Purchase | $22,000.00 | **$134,840.00** |
| | | |
| **Excess of revenue over** | | |
| **expenses before donations** | | **$65,160.00** |
| | | |
| **Donations** | | |
| Spinal Cord Society (75%) | | $45,000.00 |
| St. John's Mercy (25%) | | $15,000.00 |
| | | |
| **Excess of revenue** | | |
| **over expenses** | | **$5,160.00** |
| | | |
| General Fund-Beginning | | $11,472.37 |
| General Fund-Ending | | $16,632.37 |

**Balance Sheet
Year 3**

**Assets**
**Current Assets**

| | | |
|---|---|---|
| Cash | $16,582.37 | |
| Office Supplies | $200.00 | |
| Merchandise | $350.00 | |
| **Total Current Assets** | | **$17,132.37** |

**Fixed Assets**

| | | |
|---|---|---|
| Office Equipment | $500.00 | |
| **Total Fixed Assets** | | **$500.00** |
| **Total Assets** | | **$17,632.37** |

**Liabilities and Fund Balances**

**Current Liabilities**

| | | |
|---|---|---|
| Accounts Payable | $1,000.00 | |
| **Total Liabilities** | | **$1,000.00** |

**Fund Balances**

| | | |
|---|---|---|
| General Fund | $16,632.37 | **$16,632.37** |
| **Total Liabilities and Fund Balance** | | **$17,632.37** |

### Notes for Statement of Revenue, Expenses and Change in Fund Balance.

#### Revenue

- Revenue consists of the two-week tournament beforehand, the one-day finals at the Sparling Center and the eight-city tournament in February of 1998.
- Components of revenue:

| | |
|---|---|
| Ticket sales-Sparling Center | $125,000.00 |
| Ticket sales-Quarter and semi-finals | $58,800.00 |
| Raffles | $37,500.00 |
| Merchandise sales | $4,000.00 |
| Memorabilia auction | $3,500.00 |
| Programs | $8,000.00 |
| Interest | $862.00 |
| **Total** | **$237,662.00** |

- Ticket sales at the Sparling Center events are split between the two events. The Cleveland tournament will raise $75,000, a $5,000 increase from last year.

The regional tournament in February will raise $50,000. This is based on original tournament figures.

- Quarter and semi-final ticket sales are based on the participation of 32 teams with an average attendance of 350 people per game.
- Merchandise sales will see an increase due to the session in February.
- Memorabilia will increase due to the February tournament.
- Program sales will be expanded to cover two separate programs.
- Interest is based on a 4 percent annual interest rate.

#### Expenses

- Ice rental includes an additional day at the Sparling Center.
- Increase in phone expense is the result of long distance calls to eight Lucky Pucks expansion cities and long distance calls resulting from travel.
- Trophy expense is higher because of purchasing new trophies for the eight-city tournament.
- Travel and promotion are higher due to trips to two regional hockey events, one in Chicago and one in Colorado Springs and to the eight cities to assist in starting their own tournament.
- Vehicle purchase is for the prizes for the raffle. The vehicle will have to be purchased, but at a substantially lower price from the dealer, the increased cost is due to inflation.
- Donations are no longer equally divided by the two charities. At the request of St. John's Mercy, percentages are shifted in order to provide more money for research.

#### Notes to the Statement of Cash Flows

#### Disbursements

- Travel and promotion in April increased for Chicago Showcase Hockey Tournament, a national event involving high school hockey.
- Travel and promotion increased due to trip to USA Hockey (national amateur hockey association) meeting in Colorado in July.
- Travel and promotion is substantially higher due to travel between the participating cities.

Notes to the Balance Sheet

**Fixed Assets**

- Office equipment is for a copier and replacing a fax machine. Depreciation is allocated for one year. This is due to the rapid obsolescence of electronic equipment and low salvage cost.

**Description of Cash Flows**

In year 3, Lucky Pucks plans to expand to seven other cities. Each city will run a Lucky Pucks independent of the others. Our organization will help each city organize their event, but each city will be able to format the tournament to best suit the needs of their city. The extra cash flow in February is the result of a regional tournament being played in Cleveland involving the victors in each city vying for the national crown.

## Break-even Analysis-Facility Rental Year 3

Quarter & semi-final games:

Ice Rental

- 32 teams requiring 56 sessions @ $120 each session = $6,720 cost for ice rental at local ice rinks

Cost per game of scorekeepers, ticket takers, security $100 a game

- $100 a game (56 games) = $5,600

Attendance needed each game to break-even

- $12,320 total cost / 56 games / $3 per person = 74 persons needed per game

**Break-even point for local rink attendance = 74 people per game**

Average attendance per high school game according to the MSCHA= 300

Sparling Center

Ice Rental at the Sparling Center—Cleveland Tournament

- Cost for rental of Sparling Center = $40,000
- Average ticket price = $7.50
- Break-even attendance = $40,000 / $7.50 = 5,333 people per game

**Break-even attendance for the Sparling Center = 5,333 people per game**

Attendance for the first year for the entire day was 6,700

Ice Rental at the Sparling Center—Regional Tournament

- Cost for rental of Sparling Center = $30,000
- Average ticket price = $7.50
- Break-even attendance $30,000 / $7.50 = 4,000 people per game

In year 3, Lucky Pucks will expand to eight cities, including Cleveland. Each city will, with the guidance of Lucky Pucks, establish their own charitable tournament. Each city will be independent of each other. This will allow the city to tailor the tournament to best meet the needs of the city. The overall impact on Lucky Pucks—Cleveland will be twofold. One, travel and correspondence expense will be abnormally high as each city begins establishing the tournament. Second, revenue for Lucky Pucks—Cleveland will be augmented as a result of an additional tournament being held in Cleveland involving the winners of the tournament in each city. This event will have a national flavor. Currently, no high school hockey association is involved in a national tournament. For instance, the Mid-States High School Hockey Association in Cleveland has a championship tournament each year. Yet, it cannot be considered a state tournament because they do not include high school teams from other cities, if they even exist. In addition, there are teams from Illinois in Mid-States. ESPN television has expressed an interest in televising a tournament that will involve teams from different cities. The expansion will involve these seven cities:

| | |
|---|---|
| Boston | Detroit |
| Chicago | Philadelphia |
| Cleveland | Pittsburgh |
| Denver | |

Each city was selected after meeting the following criteria:

1. Strength of amateur hockey program in the area
2. Strength and support of the professional hockey team in the area
3. Regional location in order to keep travel costs low
4. Prominence of a progressive rehabilitation hospital in the area
5. Strength of a Spinal Cord Society chapter in the city

The ultimate goal is to have a tournament in each National Hockey League city. There are currently 26 teams. As of this date, the National Hockey League does not have a league-wide charity to sponsor. The NHL has stated that Lucky Pucks must prove themselves as a viable charity before they will consider us as a league-wide charity. Hence, there is a need to expand to eight total cities. The commissioner of the NHL was formerly with the National Basketball Association. During his tenure, the NBA established a direct link to the youth involved in basketball. They did this by sponsoring local tournaments and starting a nationwide stay-in-school program. Mr. Soule, the NHL commissioner, is considering Lucky Pucks as a possible avenue to reach the youth and the hockey community. It is with this goal in mind that Lucky Pucks will operate. According to the American Paralysis Association, spinal cord injuries can be eliminated if the level of funding reaches $200 million dollars. With this amount of funding, they predict a cure in five years. It is paramount that Lucky Pucks be instrumental in this drive. We can make a difference. A cure for spinal cord injuries is a definite possibility. No goal is too high for our organization, we have come so far, and we just need to reach a little higher.

**How will Lucky Pucks control the integrity of the tournament after expansion?**

The key to maintaining sufficient control over the operations in other cities is to use the existing infrastructure of the city's chapter of the Spinal Cord Society. Lucky Pucks will work with the local chapter in helping to set up the tournament. In addition, a representative from Lucky Pucks will be present to oversee the operations of the tournament and aid in the collecting of proceeds from the tournament. The regional structure of the tournament will reduce travel expenses. Lucky Pucks is looking for people that have a personal involvement in the disabled community. This is where the Spinal Cord Society affiliation will prove most helpful. Individuals must be trustworthy, compassionate, and visionary. These individuals will work with Lucky Pucks in establishing and operating their own tournament. In addition to these individuals, the Cleveland Reds will help Lucky Pucks in creating a relationship with the local hockey franchise and the hockey community in the expansion city.

### Where does my money go?

In the first year, thirty percent of the funds raised by the tournament were given to spinal cord injury research. The high expenses are due to the fact that this was the inaugural tournament. Lucky Pucks does not plan to maintain that ratio. The percentage in Year 2 is 39 percent and Year 3 is 40 percent. The goal of Lucky Pucks is to return 75 percent of its revenue to research projects and hospitals after expansion is complete. Years 1 to 3 are substantially lower than the target goal. Many expenses are abnormally high in these years because of the expense associated with expansion. Yet, the ratios for years two and three can be significantly improved if the event draws more than the conservative estimates and if the major expenses are subsidized by corporate underwriting.

### Who will get the money that is raised by Lucky Pucks?

The bulk of the money raised by Lucky Pucks will be given to the Spinal Cord Society to fund research projects. They have a valuable link to the research community and will be able to best maximize the research dollar. The remaining funds will go to a hospital in the expansion city. These funds will be used for progressive patient care and for purchase of rehabilitation equipment. Some of the proceeds will be used to attract the more successful programs of rehabilitation to the hospital.

### Why not give all the money to the Spinal Cord Society?

Lucky Pucks's goal in each city is to establish a tie between the tournament and the community. By assisting in local programs, each new city's tournament will have an impact within the community. In addition, Lucky Pucks needs to be recognized as making a difference, within the area of spinal cord injury research and within the community itself. The money for local programs will be used to fund research projects within the community. Currently, there are commercially available products to aid in SCI care. Three programs that are receiving national attention are the Ergis Bike and the ParaStep program. Of the two, only the Ergis Bike is available in Cleveland. The Ergis Bike aids in the maintaining of muscle mass and range of motion below the injury level. The drawback is that the bike is expensive to operate and very few insurance companies will pay for the service. Local funds can be used to subsidize an SCI patient's medical bills. Second, the ParaStep system uses electrical stimulation of muscle tissue to facilitate lower level movement. An SCI patient is hooked up to the device and the muscles are electrically stimulated to expand and contract. The project is very expensive and costly to operate. The program is not readily available in the Cleveland area and use of the system would require travel to the nearest site in Columbus, Ohio. Although this seems to be a short drive away, coordinating a trip for a SCI patient can be very daunting. The third possible program is called biofeedback. Sensors are attached to muscles below the injury level and the patient is told to try and move these muscles. The sensors register any muscle signal that is sent by the brain. By repetition, a patient is able to learn how to access these muscles and strengthen them. Improvements can be made in the functional levels of SCI patients and help increase their level of independence. This system is also beneficial to stroke patients in learning how to regain their lost functions. By helping fund these types of programs, Lucky Pucks will create a vital link to the disabled community, and to the community as a whole, and show donors the change that their contribution is helping to make.

**How much money does Lucky Pucks need?**

Lucky Pucks would like to become a large contributor in the area of spinal cord injury research. To do so, Lucky Pucks must limit major expenditures. Currently, the largest expense—ice time—is in need of corporate underwriting. Reducing this expenditure would result in a larger margin between revenue and expenses. The difference would be reflected in a larger contribution to spinal cord research. Current expenses that are subsidized by corporate support are primarily in the area of media and publicity. Other subsidized expenses can be found in the area of accounting services, legal work, and tournament operations.

**How much does spinal cord injury research need?**

According to various estimates, mainly from the American Paralysis Association, SCI can be cured within five years if the funding is in place. Consensus opinion places the need for funding at around $200 million. Current funding is well below that figure. In fact, many research projects are unable to run concurrent projects due to the lack of sufficient funding.

# Chemical Manufacturer

BUSINESS PLAN

CHEMALYZE INC.

*7201 Rocky Mountain Way*
*Denver, Colorado 80202*

*Chemalyze is developing a chemical analyzer and Sensor Cartridge, based upon the Micro-Tongue™ technology, which can instantly analyze complex chemical solutions. Chemalyze's analyzer and Sensor Cartridge will enable economical, real-time analysis of many complex chemical solutions, instantly identifying the presence and quantity of multiple chemicals within a mixture. This plan was provided by Kent Bradshaw, Richard Burgess, Dr. Paul Kunko, and Jason D. Levin; and was compiled in conjunction with the MOOT CORP® competition sponsored by the University of Texas at Austin.*

- EXECUTIVE SUMMARY

- CHEMALYZE PROVIDES THE SOLUTION

- MARKETING STRATEGY

- MANUFACTURING STRATEGY

- MANAGEMENT

- FINANCIAL OVERVIEW

- APPENDICES

## EXECUTIVE SUMMARY

### The Vision

Chemalyze is developing a chemical analyzer and Sensor Cartridge, based upon the Micro-Tongue™ technology, which can instantly analyze complex chemical solutions. This major breakthrough in analyzer technology enables fine chemical manufacturers to:

- Significantly improve product quality
- Increase manufacturing efficiency
- Rapidly respond to processing problems

These benefits will save millions of dollars annually by reducing downtime and improving plant utilization.

In addition, numerous medical applications need real-time, on-the-spot, easy-to-use chemical analysis, which can save lives and reduce expensive hospital laboratory costs.

### The Gap in the Market

Many liquid processing industries do not have the technology available for real-time measurement of product quality. The current approach is to remove a sample from the manufacturing process and perform a laboratory test. The time delay in this approach could result in high volumes of product currently in production being rejected, thrown away, or re-processed. These inefficiencies can have a significant impact on a company's bottom line. Product costs can account for 40 percent of sales revenues. The online analyzers currently available are very expensive, have limited applications and accuracy, require skilled operators, and generate delays in providing results.

### Meeting the Market's Needs

Chemalyze's analyzer and Sensor Cartridge will enable economical, real-time analysis of many complex chemical solutions, instantly identifying the presence and quantity of multiple chemicals within a mixture. The results can be fed directly into a process control computer, allowing customers to consistently produce high-quality products on time, every time.

### Implementation

**Marketing and Distribution Strategy**

The initial market niche for Chemalyze's analyzer within the U.S. is estimated to be worth greater than $500 million with annual sales of its Sensor Cartridge worth close to $130 million (see Primary Market). Chemalyze intends to enter this market by partnering with large process control original equipment manufacturers (OEMs) that supply instrumentation to fine chemical manufacturers, pharmaceutical companies, and biotechnological companies. Chemalyze's goal is to design, develop, and beta-test analyzers through industrial collaborations and then sublicense the analyzer design to its OEM partner who will manufacture, market, and distribute the analyzers. Chemalyze will ramp up its Sensor Cartridge manufacturing and act as a sole supplier of Sensor Cartridges to the customers of its OEM partners. Other potential markets include but are not limited to food and beverage processing, medical diagnostics, and environmental testing.

**Manufacturing Strategy**

The analyzer consists of a customized housing into which the Sensor Cartridge can be placed and exposed to liquid chemicals within a process plant. The Sensor Cartridge contains a small silicon chip that holds chemically adapted beads housed in a disposable plastic cartridge. These beads react by producing a color pattern when exposed to different chemicals. Chemalyze will design and produce the chemical receptors to be placed on the beads and purchase the remaining components for the Sensor Cartridge from subcontractors. Chemalyze will NOT assemble the final analyzer instrument but will sublicense to a larger OEM partner. Chemalyze will neither incur the capital costs of developing a manufacturing facility for the instrumentation nor the expense of marketing or distributing the analyzer. However, the design, development, and manufacture of the bead chemistry that makes up the added value provided by the Sensor Cartridge will remain proprietary to Chemalyze.

**Financial Strategy**

Chemalyze is seeking seed capital of $1,500,000 for initial company operations to:

- Secure the license for the Micro-Tongue™ from the University of Colorado
- Hire a seasoned CEO and management team
- Develop a pre-manufacturing prototype from its proven analyzer technology
- Continue negotiations with potential industrial partners and customers
- Begin alpha-testing with select corporate collaborators
- Fund continuous development of the Micro-Tongue™ within the inventors' labs

Formal operations will begin in the second half of 1999. About one year later, Chemalyze will raise an additional $8 million in private equity, corporate partnerships, and federal grants to:

- Begin full-scale product development (designing novel chemical receptors)
- Commence receptor bead production
- Identify outside vendors and contract the design and manufacture of the Sensor Cartridge
- Develop corporate partnership efforts

Chemalyze intends to raise another $12 million in follow-on investment in the third year of operations to scale-up its chemistry development and new product development efforts. Chemalyze projects $57 million in revenue with $11 million in net income by year six. The initial investor will receive an equity stake in the company and preferential rights to invest in subsequent equity rounds.

**Management**

Chemalyze was founded by four graduate students from the University of Colorado Graduate School of Business. Its current president and chief executive officer, Roger Dalton, has over 6 years' experience in both academic research and industrial drug development. Roger spent 4 years as a scientist in a start-up gene therapy company. More recently, he worked in business development at a functional genomics company alongside the DNA microchip product development team. He is currently completing his M.B.A. at the University of Colorado.

Chemalyze's vice president and chief financial officer, Joshua Small, is a registered CPA with 5 years of public accounting experience. Joshua spent 3 years as a senior consultant at Citibank, then joined KPMG Peat Marwick as a supervising senior before returning to Colorado to pursue his M.B.A. at the University of Colorado. While completing his degree, he has been working for Trinity Bank, a venture banking firm.

Two of Chemalyze's founders are fulfilling advisory roles. Sidney Pittman, a chemical engineer with a decade of experience in operations and marketing high-tech products, is consulting with Chemalyze as a strategy consultant. Dr. John Barnes has spent the last 8 years performing pharmacology research and is consulting with Chemalyze as a market analyst.

Chemalyze is further strengthened by its collaboration with the four researchers that invented the Micro-Tongue™ at the University of Colorado. These partners are Drs. Brian Boleyn, an associate professor of chemistry and biochemistry, Ernest MacDonald, an associate professor of chemistry, Ian Kirkland, a professor of electrical engineering, and Lee Shu, an assistant professor of chemistry and biochemistry. Each inventor is an active member of Chemalyze's Scientific Advisory Board.

Chemalyze's advisers consist of an impressive group of seasoned businesspeople, including Ronald Mullen, former president of Presario Computers and chairman of the board of LakeTel, Dr. Andrew Rolla, former CEO of Avington Technologies Corporation and Smith Opthalmics; and Jennifer Zweig, president of the Chem.com Group.

## The Problem

Many of the products we use every day—from sodas to the fertilizer we put on our lawns to prescription drugs—are made from complex mixtures of many chemicals.

These products are manufactured in sophisticated processing plants. Despite the sophistication of these plants, companies often do not know if the composition of their product is correct until a final laboratory test is performed at the end of the process. If a mistake has been made, the result could be millions of dollars worth of poor quality product that either needs expensive reprocessing or must simply be thrown away (see Primary Market).

Processing companies cannot completely measure product streams during production because the technology currently available for online process analysis consists of basic analyzers that usually measure only one aspect of the product. This information alone is insufficient for highly efficient process control. To truly know the composition of an intermediate or final product, a sample must be removed from the process stream and taken to a laboratory for analysis. These tests take a lot of time, during which high volumes of expensive product could be lost. Hence, there is a tremendous need for chemical manufacturing companies to be able to measure the complex mixtures within their processing plants in a real-time manner. Such technology would enable them to produce high quality products on time, every time.

## The Solution

The solution to this gap in the market is at hand. Chemalyze Inc. is partnered with world-class researchers at the University of Colorado who are developing the first Micro-Tongue™. The Micro-Tongue™ is an analyzer that mimics the human tongue using novel chemical microsensor technology. This recent scientific breakthrough in real-time measurement of complex chemical solutions is a vast improvement over current analyzer technology.

The Micro-Tongue™ consists of a light source that shines onto chemically adapted polymer beads arranged on a small silicon wafer, which is known as a Sensor Chip. These beads change color based on the presence and quantity of specific chemicals. Currently the receptors are sensitive to 1 part per million, however, 1 part per billion sensitivity is expected. The color pattern is captured by a digital camera and the resulting video signal is converted into data using a video capture board and a personal computer.

This data output is in a format compatible for input into a process control computer. The polymer beads can be chemically adapted to detect specific chemical compounds within virtually any chemical solution. The capabilities of the technology range from the measurement of simple chemical compounds like calcium carbonate in water (which effects water hardness), to complex organic compounds, such as hemoglobin in blood and proteins in food.

**CHEMALYZE PROVIDES THE SOLUTION**
**The Company**

Chemalyze Inc. is a privately-held Delaware "C" corporation operating in the state of Colorado since October 1998, founded by Joshua Small, Sidney Pittman, John Barnes, and Roger Dalton to commercialize the Micro-Tongue™. Chemalyze aims to be the leading niche developer of real-time chemical analyzers to industrial and medical markets within seven years. Chemalyze will provide added value to these markets with real-time, sensitive, and accurate analytical hardware that is on the leading edge of chemical analyzer technology.

**The Product Benefits**

Chemalyze's initial product is a real-time liquid analyzer focused on the needs of fine chemical, pharmaceutical, and biotechnological manufacturing companies. These companies produce many complex chemical mixtures of high added value in their manufacturing processes. Chemalyze's analyzer can assess the presence and quantity of multiple chemicals in a process mixture, enabling such companies to:

- Measure multiple chemicals simultaneously
- Generate real-time results with laboratory level accuracy
- Use a compact instrument installed onsite
- Convert these results into a digital output suitable for direct input into a process control computer

The key end-user benefits are:

- Consistent quality with less waste
- Improved efficiency and utilization by reducing the quality control bottlenecks
- Increased customer satisfaction from better products without delivery delays

**Industry Need for Chemalyze's Technology**

Recently, the National Institute of Standards and Technology (NIST) reviewed the field of chemical measurement and identified a multitude of needs and challenges for future development (see this report on NIST's website at http://www.nist.gov/cstl/hndocs/ChemMeasmain.html). The NIST report recognized the "enabling" capability of chemical analysis for several applications. NIST developed a list of seven key application areas in need of chemical measurement improvements, which included process control and product development, but found the current state of technology to be less than optimal, stating that "real-time analytical measurements are not generally available, either on-line or off-line."

According to the report, the reason most real-world chemical measurements are conducted off-line is that many sophisticated methods of chemical analysis are not finding their way from the laboratory to research and development (R&D) and manufacturing facilities. This system needs to change, based on chemical manufacturers' desires for reduced costs, increased efficiency, increased speed to market and improved product quality. NIST expects the changes to be realized as "robust techniques for real-time, highly reliable analyses in practical environments." These new solutions will be sensors that respond quickly to change in complex manufacturing environments. Current methods, such as Gas Chromatography and Mass Spectrometry, are too slow to adapt to the above dynamic manufacturing trends (see Competition).

The NIST report further defined industry needs against a likely time frame. Short-term needs (less than 3 years) include a systems approach (integrated sampling, online detection, signal transmission, data handling, and maintenance), real-time compositional information for liquid phase streams, increased speed of analysis, sensitivity, and selectivity. Medium and long-term needs include high reliability, a PC-based generic user interface, real-time trace analysis, and miniaturization. All of these needs are addressed by Chemalyze's Micro-Tongue™ technology.

## Market Analysis

Sales of process control systems are experiencing strong growth. Sales in 1997 were $3.86 billion and are expected to reach $4.6 billion by the year 2000 and $5.75 billion by 2004. The chemical analyzer industry is slated for rapid expansion, growing at an annual rate of 7.8 percent from $1.45 billion in 1991 to $3.10 billion in 2001. This market is split almost evenly between liquid and gas analysis. Nearly half this total market is for process control. Within this market, revenues for online analyzers will grow at a similar rate and should reach $1.3 billion in 2000, up from $880 million in 1993 (*Chemical & Engineering News*, March 1995, Vol. 73, 11, p. 25). Typical industries that use process control analyzers are:

Process Industries

- Fine chemicals
- Chemical intermediaries
- Pharmaceuticals
- Biologicals
- Medicinals
- Detergents
- Fertilizers
- Soft drinks, Spirits, Malt beverages
- Explosives testing
- Paints and dyestuffs
- Food flavorings
- Personal care products (e.g. fragrances and cosmetics)

Clinical Diagnostic Systems

- Diagnostic testing
- Point-of-care testing

Environmental Management Systems

- Monitoring water quality
- Waste stream management

Chemalyze's primary market is process control analyzers for the fine chemicals industry. After Chemalyze has developed a strong presence in this market it will broaden its R&D efforts and marketing efforts to include medical diagnostics. Chemalyze will assess other market opportunities on a case-by-case basis and focus on those industries that are the most price-insensitive and where Chemalyze can quickly deliver the most value and capture the most profit.

## Primary Market

Worldwide prescription pharmaceutical sales reached $265 billion in 1997, and the market is continuing to grow. However, profit margins are threatened by strict industry requirements on processes, ever changing government regulations, and increasing competitive pressures. In response, pharmaceutical companies are spending increasing amounts on R&D to combat rising manufacturing costs, which are currently estimated at 24 percent of sales ("The Drug Industry and PBM companies in 1995," Cool, K.). Of the $21.1 billion spent on R&D in 1998, 9 percent was spent on process improvements totaling $1.91 billion (*Pharmaceutical Researchers & Manufacturers of America*, 1998 Industry Report). The process improvement investments are classically price-insensitive. Pharmaceutical manufacturers have indicated that Chemalyze's technology could provide an opportunity to improve their processes by significantly reducing manufacturing costs. This can be achieved by improving upon current quality control methods and relieving chemical analysis bottlenecks within the process.

The market opportunity for Chemalyze's technology among pharmaceutical manufacturers has been determined by assessing the process control requirements of the small, medium, and large manufacturers in the U.S. today. Of the 700 pharmaceutical firms in the U.S., we have estimated that 35 percent of those companies have small process plant manufacturing facilities, 35 percent have medium facilities, and 30 percent have large manufacturing plants. To identify the pharmaceutical manufacturer's return on investment from the introduction of Chemalyze's technology we estimated its impact of these different size plant.

### Small Process Facility

Based upon discussions with senior managers at biopharmaceutical manufacturers, Chemalyze estimates that 15-20 percent of a small facility's capacity is lost yearly from product quality problems at a cost of $250,000. With Analyzer 1 in place on one plant line, a firm of this size would save approximately $180,000/year by reducing total number of lost batches by 66 percent. With Analyzer 2 in place, such a firm would save approximately $60,000/year by eliminating one lab technician needed to perform Quality Control (QC) experimentation for Food and Drug Administration (FDA) compliance. Thus, the total savings estimated per small plant line are approximately $240,000 per year.

If a small process manufacturing facility has 2 plant lines that need 2 analyzers each, as well as having one pilot plant facility which may use 1 analyzer, then the total number of analyzers for a small process facility is equal to 5 analyzers, with a total savings of $480,000.

### Medium Process Facility

Chemalyze has estimated that a medium facility will have a similar production scheme as a small facility only it would include 6 plant lines rather than 2. Assuming each of 6 lines requires 2 analyzers—adding 3 extra analyzers for a larger pilot plant—the total number of analyzers for a medium process facility is equal to 15 analyzers, with a total savings of $1,440,000.

### Large Process Facility

A large process facility would have a more complex system for production and would work on a much larger scale than both a small and medium facility. Chemalyze has estimated that a large process facility with 1 plant line utilizing 4 feed lines to produce one final product could utilize 5 Chemalyze QC analyzers. This total does not include additional analyzers necessary for pilot scale experimentation. If we assume that a large facility has a throughput volume 10 times that of a small facility and Chemalyze's analyzers can similarly prevent 66 percent of the 15-20 percent lost batches, then the savings, if linearly scaled, would be approximately $2 million per annum.

### Market Size

The estimated size of the pharmaceutical manufacturing market niche for Chemalyze's Micro-Tongue™ technology (see also Marketing Strategy for details on industry structure) is shown in the following table.

**Analyzer Market Size**

| Plant Type | Plant Lines[1] | No. of Analyzers | Analyzers/ Pilot Plant[2] | Total Analyzers/ Plant | No. of Companies | Total Analyzers |
|---|---|---|---|---|---|---|
| Small | 2 | 2 | 1 | 5 | 250 | 1,250 |
| Medium | 6 | 2 | 3 | 15 | 250 | 3,750 |
| Large | 1 | 5 | 5 | 10 | 200 | 2,000 |
| **Total Analyzers** | | | | | | **7,000** |
| **Total Value[5]** | | | | | | **$420,000,000** |

**Sensor Chip Market Size**

**No. of Manufacturing Runs**

| Per Line/ Year | Per Plant/ Year[3] | Sensor Chips/ Year[4] |
|---|---|---|
| 10 | 20 | 25,000 |
| 20 | 120 | 450,000 |
| 20 | 20 | 40,000 |
| **Total Sensor Chips** | | **515,000** |
| **Total Value[6]** | | **$128,750,000** |

[1.] Number of manufacturing lines within a process plant.

[2.] Each manufacturing plant typically has pilot plants for product development.

[3.] = (Plant Lines) x (No. of Manufacturing Runs per Line/Year)

[4.] = (Total Analyzers/Plant) x (No. of Companies) x (No. of Manufacturing Runs per Plant/Year)

[5.] = (7,000 analyzers) x ($60,000; mean price of analyzers in market)

[6.] = (515,000 sensor chips annually) x ($250; estimated sales price of sensor chip)

Based upon the previous set of assumptions for the number of QC analyzers that a given pharmaceutical manufacturing firm would use our calculations indicate a national market for approximately 7,000 analyzers. However, analyzer system sales represent only one source of revenue. Chemalyze's technology incorporates a disposable element (a Sensor Cartridge), that needs to be replaced after each manufacturing run. As a result, the maximum Sensor Cartridge sales for this market would total over .5 million units per year. These calculations assume a relatively low number of analyzers per plant and ignore the many contract pharmaceutical manufacturers, who will also have multiple applications for Chemalyze's technology.

It is also important to note that this market estimation only considers the number of available plant lines in the pharmaceutical industry within the U.S. and does not take into account the number of plant lines in biotechnology and other types of fine chemical processing facilities (e.g. producers of chemical intermediaries to supply other manufacturers and users). In fact, large pharmaceutical companies spend 16 percent of their R&D budget (approximately $3 billion) on outsourcing pharmaceutical development and manufacturing to contract pharmaceutical manufacturers ("The Pharma Giants: Ready for the 21st Century?", Eagan, R., Hayes, R., 1998). Chemalyze expects that when the other potential buyers in the fine chemicals market are evaluated that the total market within the U.S. for Chemalyze's analyzers and Sensor Cartridges will increase substantially.

**Secondary Market**

The most attractive future market for Chemalyze's technology, once the technology has been fully developed, is the Point-of-Care (POC) medical diagnostics market. Medical diagnostics consists of the detection of substances in body fluids (e.g. real-time HIV testing). Fast and accurate analyses are essential for emergency medicine and high quality patient care. The estimated worldwide market for medical diagnostics in 1997 was $19.5 billion. These revenues are generated primarily from testing in hospitals and commercial labs, which account for $15.5

billion of the medical diagnostics market (POC Testing/IVD - Industry Report, Sutro & Co. Inc., 1/29/98).

Current federal regulations specify extensive and expensive training for commercial laboratory personnel. These labs are a significant source of hospital overhead. A handheld version of Chemalyze's technology will provide nurses and physicians with on-the-spot analyses, saving lives and eliminating much of the expense of laboratory testing.

Analyzer technologies that compete with Chemalyze's Micro-Tongue™ are:

**Competition**

- Physical property meters and single chemical sensors
- Gas chromatography (GC)
- Mass spectrometry (MS) and Raman spectrometry
- High performance liquid chromatography (HPLC)

These technologies either have severe limitations in the complexity of the chemical solutions they can analyze or they do not provide real-time analysis. Given the Micro-Tongue's™ capabilities these technologies are considered less of a direct threat and more complementary to Chemalyze. This is because its analyzer can be associated with these existing systems to provide another dimension on their current analytical capabilities.

**1. Physical property meters and single chemical sensors**

**Competing Technologies**

A sensor system designed to measure pH, conductivity, or to identify a single chemical in a solution can only measure one aspect of the process. A pH meter only tells you if your solution is acidic or alkaline. An ion conductivity probe only tells you of the electrical conductivity of your solution. Gas sensors only tell you how much of a particular gas, e.g. dissolved oxygen, is in your solution. Even the systems that companies claim can sense multiple chemicals have severe limitations, both in the number of chemicals detected and type of chemical that can be detected. This contrasts with Chemalyze's technology, which enables the user to sense multiple chemicals in a complex solution simultaneously, and in real time.

**2. Gas Chromatography (GC)**

GC vaporizes a liquid sample and identifies different compounds through their molecular weight. It is mainly used to test for purity. This technology can be used online but requires an additional $20,000 to $50,000 expenditure (on top of a $20,000 initial capital equipment cost) and does not enable real-time data acquisition and analysis, as it takes 5 to 10 minutes to analyze a sample. However, with the assistance of a highly trained operator, GC can analyze virtually any chemical mixture.

**3. Mass Spectrometry (MS)**

MS uses ionization technology to analyze the liquid sample. It is a laboratory based, expensive (ranging from $50,000 to $150,000) and complicated method for identifying compounds in a mixed solution. However, MS technology has also been in use for a number of years and has established itself as the benchmark in some industries for a limited range of chemicals. It has been used online but requires a few minutes to analyze the samples and eliminates the opportunity to evaluate data in real time. The key disadvantage with MS technology is that it cannot be used with water-based solutions, which are very common in pharmaceutical production.

**4. Raman Spectrometry**

The latest spectrometry technology is known as Raman spectrometry. It is not fully established as an online process analysis technology. Raman measures the scatter of light by different compounds and can effectively monitor compounds in water based solutions. The main disadvantage is its limited sensitivity, although this may improve over time.

### 5. High Performance Liquid Chromatography (HPLC)

HPLC uses separation techniques based upon molecular weight to identify chemical compounds. HPLC systems occupy the price range in between GC and MS technology at $100,000 each. HPLC methods are often slow and expensive to scale up and cannot distinguish between similar chemical compounds.

The closest comparable product to Chemalyze's analyzer is an HPLC unit, which is online in pharmaceutical manufacturing environments but cannot provide real-time results. In addition, the results from an HPLC unit need to be interpreted by a highly trained operator. Chemalyze's system provides easily understandable output that can feed directly into a process control computer or a standard PC. However, a new class of companies is developing electronic "nose" technology for analyzers to detect multiple chemical compounds in gaseous form; these companies present a more serious threat. Chemalyze has identified three companies in this space—Aromascan, Inc., Cyrano Sciences, Inc., and Illumina, Inc.

The scientific principles of the electronic nose are similar to the Micro-Tongue™, but are applied to vapors rather than liquids. This particular difference is where Chemalyze's Micro-Tongue™ has an advantage in liquid process control environments or any liquid-based chemical analysis. The polymers that are used for the electronic nose are not effective when immersed in a liquid solution, as they absorb liquid at a significantly slower rate than the polymers used in the Micro-Tongue™. Also, the fragile construction of most electronic nose analyzers makes them impractical for use in liquid process streams.

**Competing Multi-Chemical Sensor Companies**

- **Illumina Inc.** is a start-up located in San Diego, California, developing "electronic nose" technology where latex beads are arrayed on the end of a fiber optic bundle. These beads fluoresce in response to the chemical composition of the vapor they are exposed to. A light source sends light down the length of the bundle and the bead's fluorescence is registered by a digital camera. Illumina is targeting the genomics industry's drug discovery and development efforts. Its technology cannot be used in a liquid stream due to the fragile construction of the fiber optic head, and can only be used with vapors under very mild process conditions. They recently raised $750,000 in seed capital and potentially $8 million in follow-on investment from CW Group and ARCH Ventures.

- **Cyrano Sciences Inc.** is a start-up located in Pasadena, California, developing a handheld electronic nose. When the nose comes in contact with a vapor the polymer receptors react by swelling and electrodes translate this activity into a digital impulse, which is analyzed by computer. The prototype is slightly larger than a handheld calculator. Cyrano expects to sell each instrument for $5,000 and each chip for a few dollars. Currently, Cyrano's technology deals only with vapors. They are focusing on process control systems with intent on applying its technology to medical diagnostics in the future. Cyrano recently raised $3 million in seed capital and obtained $9 million more from J&J Development Corporation, Marquette Venture Partners, and Oak Investment Partners.

- **Aromascan, Inc.** represents the oldest commercial effort in developing electronic nose technology. It sells a benchtop analyzer that requires individual preparation of each sample to be placed into test tubes in a rack that is then systematically rotated through the sensor system. Aromascan is a publicly held company operating in the United Kingdom. They currently sell four instruments ranging from $30,000 for a benchtop system to $70,000 for an autosampler. The company has been in operation for 4 years and is focusing primarily on the polyurethane process industry and the personal care products industry.

**Comparison of Competing Technologies**

| Technology | On-Line Analysis | Real-Time Analysis | CHEMICAL SENSING | | SENSING MEDIUM | | Price |
|---|---|---|---|---|---|---|---|
| | | | Single | Multiple | Liquid | Gas | |
| Micro-Tongue | yes | yes | | X | X | | $6,000 |
| Electronic Nose | yes | yes | | X | | X | $15,000 |
| Physical Property Meters and Single Chemical Sensors | yes | yes | X | | X | X | $1,000-$5,000 |
| Gas Chromatography | yes | no | | X | X | X | $20,000-$50,000 |
| Mass Spectrometry | yes | no | | X | X | | $50,000-$100,000 |
| Raman Spectrometry | yes | no | | X | X | | $100,000 + |
| High Performance Liquid Chromatography | yes | no | | X | X | | $100,000 + |

## MARKETING STRATEGY

### Overview

Chemalyze intends to focus its initial efforts on applying the Micro-Tongue™ technology to the pharmaceutical process control industry and build market share within that specific niche.

Chemalyze will then broaden the scope of its market strategy to include the medical diagnostics market. This expansion will be achieved through the initial design, development, manufacture and sale of handheld, point-of-care blood and urine analyzers.

### Primary Customer Analysis & Entry Strategy

Pharmaceutical manufacturers develop new drugs and other pharmaceutical products through laboratory research and development programs. Such product development flows from a laboratory process to mass production via the construction of a small scale manufacturing plant (known as a pilot plant). This pilot plant is used for further experimentation and process optimization, before the company completes the conceptual design of the full-scale plant.

By adopting Chemalyze's analyzer technology at the pilot plant stage, pharmaceutical companies will realize immediate savings through developing a more efficient design. These savings will be multiplied in new and existing full-scale plants from both improved efficiencies and reduced reprocessing costs (see Primary Market). Chemalyze's technology will also improve project economics for conceptual projects. This will make larger plants significantly more cost effective and profitable, thus making some projects viable that were previously uneconomical.

There is an immediate need where Chemalyze's analyzer technology can be applied: every pharmaceutical facility must clean its tanks and pipes. Furthermore, the FDA requires that each facility monitor and document the amount of detergent leftover in the process equipment after each cleanin— referred to as residuals. These residuals have to be tested to assure that they are not contaminating the final product that is packaged and sold on the market. The current cleaning process requires that the system be shut down and the inside of the tanks swabbed. These swabs are then sent to a laboratory that performs an analysis to determine the amount of residual left in the tank or pipe after cleaning. This process takes time and requires that the facility be shut down 1-3 days. Chemalyze can provide a real-time analytical system to monitor the amount of residual left in each plant line, which decreases manufacturing down time and improves plant utilization. Such improvements can be worth far more than the savings detailed in Primary Market when one takes into account the market value of the final product and the lost opportunity cost associated with failed batches. Furthermore, Chemalyze's technology can be utilized at the end of the process as a final QC for lot release testing to test for any trace elements that may be carried over in the product processing. In some of our discussions with process plant operators it became clear that there are not only bottlenecks within the process but that there are also bottlenecks at the final QC release test.

**Strategic Alliances**

To achieve its vision, Chemalyze will partner with corporations that have distinctive competencies in the development and manufacture of chemical analyzer systems. These companies include:

- Leading liquid process automation and control specialists. These companies can provide 1) technical collaboration to enable Chemalyze to develop an analyzer that complements their control systems, 2) capital resources to fund development costs, and 3) well-established distribution channel to pharmaceutical manufacturers. In return, Chemalyze will become an exclusive supplier of Sensor Cartridges to the selected partner, giving the control specialist a significant competitive advantage in process quality control of complex chemical processes.

- Major manufacturers of chemical analyzer (e.g. HPLC) equipment. Chemalyze's analyzer will be a complementary product that expands the capabilities of their existing chemical analyzer systems.

**Core Competency**

Chemalyze's core competency is in developing real-time analytical platforms for complex chemical solutions. It is not a high volume instrumentation manufacturer, but rather a company that develops customized analytical sensing technology for different industrial applications. Hence, when Chemalyze has developed a pre-production prototype analyzer it will license this product to a major instrument manufacturer and will outsource the design and manufacture of the Sensor Cartridges. However, Chemalyze will continue to develop the Sensor Beads (for residuals testing) and customized beads (for a customer's proprietary chemistries) for its clients. Thus, the core of the proprietary Sensor Cartridge technology (the Sensor Beads) will continue to be developed and manufactured i- house. See Manufacturing Strategy for further detail.

**Expansion Strategy into Secondary Markets**

Chemalyze will exploit its experience in the fine chemicals industry to leverage its technological competence in other markets that can benefit from multi-chemical sensing. Sensor Cartridges and the Sensor Beads will then be customized for these new markets, again with licensing granted to a large-scale manufacturer when a pre-production prototype analyzer has been developed.

Medical diagnostics is a major secondary market for the company due to its need for real-time chemical analysis of complex chemical solutions. Chemalyze will work toward developing the Micro-Tongue™ into a handheld device that is capable of performing blood and urine analyses in the emergency room. In discussing this opportunity with emergency room physicians and clinical laboratory nurses it has become clear that there is a need for fast response chemical analysis in the emergent care environment to help save lives. Hospital management will also have a keen interest in Chemalyze's technology, as it will result in significant savings in laboratory overhead costs and the resulting reduction in personnel.

**Sales Strategy**

**Pricing:** Our initial estimates of the price sensitivity of the primary market for the Micro-Tongue™ show that our potential customer base spends anywhere between $25,000 and

$150,000 for sophisticated analyzers. Chemalyze will not only compete on price but will differentiate itself from the current state-of-the-art by offering customized products designed to suit the particular needs of the customer. Chemalyze has estimated a product price of $60,000 per analyzer unit for financial projection purposes. Sensor Cartridges, which will need to be replaced after each manufacturing run, will be priced at $250 per unit.

**Positioning:** Chemalyze will position the Micro-Tongue™ technology as a leading edge technology for fine chemical process and quality control. It complements existing chemical analysis technology. In the case of HPLC, Chemalyze's analyzer can be adapted to work with existing instrumentation and add to the current analytical methods. Thus, providing a fourth dimension chemical analysis [specific to the chemical(s) of interest and highly selective]. It will also be developed into a cost-effective, highly accurate handheld instrument for performing medical diagnostics in emergency care environments.

**Promotion:** Chemalyze will sublicense the analyzer to OEM partners and co-development customers. The partners will be responsible for mass marketing the analyzers and pushing the technology through their channels. Chemalyze will identify and focus on a key player in each respective market niche that would benefit from Chemalyze's technology and prosper from the unfair competitive advantage that this selective technology offers.

Chemalyze will work closely with its inventors, supporting the research needed to develop chemical receptors for later markets. As well, it will support the publishing of these efforts in prestigious research journals to position the product as a breakthrough in chemical analyzer technology.

An informational website (http://www.chemalyze.net) is in place and a product hotline will be set up to promote awareness and support new and prospective customers. Supporting promotional material such as video demonstrations of the technology and an exhibition demonstration model will also be developed. Acceptance of the technology by fine chemical manufacturing companies will result in the analyzer being adopted for use in pilot plants, quality control laboratories, specified in new process plants and for retrofitting on existing plants. In part, this approach implements a pull strategy, whereby the Process R&D groups for manufacturers (the early adopters) will adopt the technology in the early stages of development and specify the analyzer in their scale-up designs for use in the large scale process facility.

**Place:** Instrument distribution will be through an OEM that has successfully penetrated the markets that Chemalyze sees as its early adopters. This approach gives Chemalyze's technology access to established and accepted buying channels. The Sensor Cartridges will be shipped direct from Chemalyze to the OEM partner's customers using standard shipping subcontractor services such as UPS, DHL, and Federal Express.

## Service and Warranties

Chemalyze will deal with faulty Sensor Cartridges by replacing them directly. The system designed by the OEM partner will be modular, making removal and replacement of hardware parts simple and fast. Thus, whenever a system fails or breaks, the OEM partner can ship a replacement part directly to the customer. This feature allows the unit to be serviced by the client's personnel, thus reducing the need for a large customer service staff. However, Chemalyze's partner may choose to support the analyzer using their own service systems and warranty programs.

## MANUFACTURING STRATEGY

### Overview

The manufacturing process will primarily consist of in-house chemical receptor R&D and Sensor Bead production. An early stage pre-production prototype analyzer will be developed at Chemalyze but no assembly lines or systems will be created to support instrumentation manufacturing.

When the pre-production prototype is completed, volume manufacturing, marketing, and distribution of the analyzer will be licensed to an expert from whom Chemalyze would expect an 8-10 percent royalty from gross revenues. Chemalyze will design a receptor bead manufacturing facility to produce the beads for the Sensor Cartridges. The polymer beads that are chemically impregnated to make the Sensor Beads can be readily purchased from a number of polymer resin manufacturers for pennies per 1,000 (e.g. Novabiochem sells 450,000 beads for $170). The etched silicon chip can be purchased from a number of micro-electromagnetic systems (MEMS) suppliers (e.g. one such vendor, AMMi, quoted a price of $6 per 1cm2 silicon chip for a 10,000 unit order and a $3 cost per chip for a 250,000 unit order). The Sensor Cartridge can be designed by an outside design firm and the manufacturing can be subcontracted to plants overseas to reduce parts costs.

Initially, Chemalyze intends to develop Sensor Cartridges for many applications across the fine chemicals process industry, such as residuals testing for detergents and other trace elements. Eventually, Chemalyze will provide the R&D effort and customization of the Micro-Tongue™ to fit its clients' particular process needs—conceivably creating partnerships that protect each firm's proprietary chemistry.

Although the polymer beads in their current state are reversible and can be reused, Chemalyze intends to first market the Sensor Cartridge as disposable elements to avoid issues of re-calibration. As the technology develops and Chemalyze improves upon its product R&D, the Sensor Cartridges will be designed to be reusable, to provide the client added value, and increase the barrier to entry from competition. This development may also provide an opportunity to increase Sensor Cartridge prices.

## Manufacturing Process

The key stages of the manufacturing process are as follows:

- **Develop beads for insertion into Sensor Cartridge.** Chemalyze's development team will construct the necessary chemical receptors needed for the Sensor Beads to react to the specific chemical compounds identified through initial product marketing to pharmaceutical companies. A batch of beads will then be chemically impregnated. Chemalyze's development team will also work directly with specific corporate partners to identify proprietary chemistries that are specific to the partner and build receptors for their specific use.

- **Produce Sensor Chips.** The beads will then be inserted into pre-formed wafers (purchased from a MEMS vendor) using a "pick and place" machine in a "clean" environment by a subcontractor.

- **Assemble Sensor Cartridge components.** The newly produced chips will be encased in a disposable removable cartridge (designed and manufactured by a subcontractor) that can be inserted into the analyzer body (designed by the OEM), which consists of a light source and a CCD chip (to capture the image) enclosed in an insulated casing. A video capture board (to convert the analog visual signal into data) and the relevant software will also be included in the final packaging of the analyzer provided by the OEM partner.

Chemalyze will develop a list of preferred vendors for each outsourced component to assure security of supply. In addition, Chemalyze will carry sufficient safety stock of critical components. Chemalyze believes that the polymer beads, silicon wafers, and plastic cartridge housing will be relatively inexpensive on a large scale and will not add significantly to inventory levels.

Chemalyze's suppliers will not represent a competitive threat to Chemalyze, as each vendor will only be involved in providing a specific aspect of the product, and will be chosen so that they do not have the capability or market exposure to develop a competitive product.

Chemalyze's offices, laboratories, manufacturing, and storage will need to be located in at least a 15,000-square-foot facility. If such a facility doesn't readily exist in Denver, Chemalyze is prepared to work with design engineers, architects, and a builder to build-to-suit as a last resort. Chemalyze is pursuing the option of co-opting with another local start-up that will need lab space and HVAC systems, in order to share overhead costs.

Chemalyze's management team is highly motivated and talented, with complementary skills and experience. However, Chemalyze recognizes that the team needs additional expertise and skills to grow the company rapidly into a market leader. Thus, Chemalyze intends to actively recruit a seasoned CEO, chief scientific officer, and vice president of product marketing to help fill in the gaps of the current management team.

**Management**

Chemalyze's president and chief executive officer, Roger Dalton, has worked for two start-up biotechnology companies. Most recently, Roger worked for ABC Genes, Inc. in business development, focusing on the market analysis and product development strategy for an emerging DNA microchip technology. Roger will be responsible for licensing the technology from the UT system, as well as coordinating the business development and developing a long-term strategy for corporate growth at Chemalyze.

Chemalyze's vice president and chief financial officer, Joshua Small, will play a key role in securing financing for the company. He brings significant financial and accounting experience to Chemalyze, Inc. having worked as a senior consultant with Citibank. Currently, Joshua is working for Trinity Bank, where he has gained relevant experience working with venture capital firms and venture-backed companies. Joshua is a CPA licensed in Colorado.

In addition, Chemalyze is partnered with the inventors of the Micro-Tongue™ technology at the University of Colorado. Ernest MacDonald, Ph.D. is an associate professor of chemistry and is responsible for combining the organic synthetic chemistry developed by Brian Boleyn, Ph.D., associate professor of chemistry, micro-machining techniques developed by Ian Kirkland, Ph.D., associate professor of electrical engineering, and the detection methodology developed by Lee Shu, Ph.D., assistant professor of chemistry to create the Micro-Tongue™. Chemalyze has been working closely with this multi-disciplinary team of world-class scientists to commercialize the Micro-Tongue™. The inventors will remain actively involved in the creative development of Chemalyze and are eager to support Chemalyze's product development into the future.

Chemalyze's advisers consist of seasoned businesspeople that are bringing their complementary skills to bear on the hurdles that Chemalyze faces. These advisers include Mr. Ronald Mullen, former President of Presario Computers and chairman of LakeTel, Dr. Andrew Rolla, former CEO of Avington Technologies Corporation and Smith Opthalmics, and Ms. Jennifer Zweig, president of the Chem.com Group.

Chemalyze has also been working with a team of consultants to develop its marketing strategy and build upon its understanding of the potential for the Micro-Tongue™ within different commercial markets. Sidney Pittman is a chartered chemical engineer and has 10 years of industry experience, primarily in small technology companies selling to large blue chip corporations such as Mobil Oil and Phillips Petroleum. His experience also includes four years in plant design and operations. Sidney will aid in developing manufacturing and marketing strategies for Chemalyze, Inc. John Barnes, Ph.D., will help identify specific product market opportunities that utilize his scientific strengths developed during his research work in pharmacology, as well as his product development experience with St. Luke's Medical, Inc. Both Sidney and John are co-founders of Chemalyze, Inc. Roger, Joshua, Sidney, and John currently hold 100 percent ownership of the company.

## Regulatory Environment

In order to develop and market process control technology to the pharmaceutical industry, Chemalyze will have to provide experimental evidence that shows its technology is robust, reliable, sensitive, and reproducible enough to be used in closely monitored manufacturing environments. However, there are no regulatory compliance issues that Chemalyze would have to address prior to marketing its technology in pharmaceutical process control applications. The customer would be required to validate the use of the instrument and provide the Food and Drug Administration (FDA) with relevant documentation to this effect. Chemalyze will develop protocols with the customer to support the FDA approval process. The FDA's main concern is reproducibility and efficacy. Chemalyze already has data demonstrating the consistency and accuracy (e.g. reproducibility) of its technology.

With regard to marketing Chemalyze's technology for use within hospitals in the U.S., Chemalyze would have to gain regulatory approval through the FDA. The Code of Federal Regulations (CFR) provides guidelines for both the classification of medical devices, as well as the regulatory guidelines necessary to gain approval for the marketing of such devices. Since there is very little way of determining to what extent Chemalyze's instruments will require FDA approval until the instrument is actually designed and built, we will assume that the instrument will require the maximum testing and regulatory approval for a Class II medical device.

Chemalyze will make every effort to remain in contact with the FDA during the period of early development and testing to identify what guidelines Chemalyze needs to follow to obtain regulatory approval. This is a straightforward process and Chemalyze does not consider the regulatory process to be a critical issue.

## Intellectual Property

The University of Colorado has filed 2 provisional patent applications with the United States Patent and Trademark Office (USPTO). The first office action for the first provisional application was recently submitted to the USPTO by the university's lawyers. The university, its lawyers, and Chemalyze believe that a patent for this technology could be issued as early as June of 2000. We are working with the Office of Technology Licensing and Intellectual Property for the University of Colorado system to obtain a favorable license to this technology for our specified fields of use. We have the full support of the University of Colorado researchers who invented this technology.

## FINANCIAL OVERVIEW

**Seed Stage: Present - Jan. 2000**

Chemalyze is currently in the concept stage and has several milestones to reach before it begins full operations. We plan on achieving the following goals by the end of 1999:

- Obtain the license for the technology from the University of Colorado
- Perform research on detailed product specifications
- Build a pre-manufacture prototype for one application
- Establish a joint venture or co-development arrangement with at least one corporate partner
- Begin making Sponsored Research Agreement (SRA) payments to University of Colorado to maintain R&D efforts

- Hire a seasoned CEO
- Hire veteran product development scientists
- Hire a vice president of product marketing

In order to achieve these milestones, the company is seeking $1,500,000 investment from an investor or group of investors in exchange for an equity share of the company. The seed investors will have preferential rights in subsequent equity rounds.

**Start-up Stage: Feb. 2000 - Feb. 2001**

Once the above milestones are met, Chemalyze will require $8,000,000 in start-up capital. The company plans on obtaining these funds from venture investors and/or a joint venture with a corporate partner. It is also pursuing SBIR (Small Business Innovation and Research grants) funding and NIST ATP (National Institute of Standards and Technology Advanced Technology Program grant) awards to supplement the equity capital raised in the prior round.

The funds will be used to purchase the capital equipment needed to start operations and to hire relevant personnel to develop the beta versions of the product. (See Financial Statements for a list of staffing and capital expenditures, respectively).

The milestones for completing the start-up stage are:

- Hire the senior management, relevant executives, and other staff. This will include more industrial scientists to continue Sensor Cartridge development, and the requisite support staff.
- Build out the first phase of a facility.
- Purchase equipment to complete the R&D laboratory and set-up receptor chemistry manufacturing.
- Identify vendors to design and manufacture the Sensor Cartridge (includes arraying beads).
- Identify and begin beta testing with companies in the pharmaceutical industry. This step will be achieved with the support of our corporate partner and is the beginning of our revenue stream.
- Identify and create a corporate partnership agreement with an OEM to manufacture, market, and distribute Chemalyze's analyzers.

**Development Stage and Product Launch: Feb. 2002 and onward**

At this point we will have completed successful beta testing of our product. We will ramp up our manufacturing operations of the Sensor Cartridge. Our OEM partners will start a full-scale marketing campaign. This stage will require another round of financing for additional personnel, laboratory and manufacturing equipment, and for working capital purposes. A final $12,000,000 round of financing is needed before Chemalyze generates positive cash flows in 2004.

**Exit Strategy**

Chemalyze will have healthy levels of revenue and net income in FY 2004 and FY 2005. At this point, investors should be able to achieve liquidity through an initial public offering or through acquisition by a company in the process control industry.

**Licensing and cross-licensing**                                    **Critical Risks**

Chemalyze must license the Micro-Tongue™ technology from the University of Colorado. Chemalyze has the backing of the inventors of the technology and has a high probability of gaining a license for the technology within specified fields of use. Chemalyze will organize itself and implement strategies to protect itself and proactively avoid operating within the scope of issued patents thus, preventing infringement lawsuits from the current competition.

**A patent for the Micro-Tongue™ must be issued for Chemalyze to operate.**

Chemalyze will retain the services of an intellectual property (IP) law firm to perform an infringement study on patent USPTO #4,312,700 (technology developed at Tufts University and licensed exclusively to Illumina, Inc.) and USPTO #4,350,405 (technology developed at Caltech and licensed exclusively to Cyrano Sciences, Inc.). Both patents are issued for electronic nose technology. However, Chemalyze feels that honest diligence is necessary to confirm its freedom to operate.

If, after a patent is issued for the Micro-Tongue™ and Chemalyze obtains a license from the University of Colorado, its attorneys feel that there are issues around possible infringement (either against Chemalyze's property or by Chemalyze), Chemalyze will develop cross-licensing relationships with Illumina and Cyrano. This action serves the interest of all parties by enabling each the freedom to operate and eliminating the likelihood of costly legal entanglements in the future.

To further differentiate its IP portfolio and improve its ability to protect its technology, Chemalyze will continue to expand its IP portfolio by patenting its novel chemical receptors and Sensor Cartridge design.

*This page left intentionally blank to accommodate tabular matter following.*

**APPENDICES**

## Income Statement

|  | FYE 6/30/00 | | | | | |
|---|---|---|---|---|---|---|
|  | 1Q | 2Q | 3Q | 4Q | Total | % |
| **Units Sold** | | | | | | |
| Systems | 0 | 0 | 0 | 0 | 0 | 0 |
| Aggregate Systems | 0 | 0 | 0 | 0 | 0 | 0 |
| Chips | 0 | 0 | 0 | 0 | 0 | 0 |
| | | | | | | |
| **Revenue** | | | | | | |
| System Royalties (from OEM) | 0 | 0 | 0 | 0 | 0 | 0% |
| Sensor Chips | 0 | 0 | 0 | 0 | 0 | 0% |
| Contract and Grants | 0 | 0 | 300,000 | 0 | 300,000 | 100% |
| **Total Revenue** | **0** | **0** | **300,000** | **0** | **300,000** | **100%** |
| | | | | | | |
| **Cost of Sales** | | | | | | |
| Sensor Chips | 0 | 0 | 0 | 0 | 0 | 0% |
| Contract and Grants | 0 | 0 | 0 | 0 | 0 | 0% |
| **Gross Margin** | **0** | **0** | **300,000** | **0** | **300,000** | **100%** |
| | | | | | | |
| **Operating Expenses** | | | | | | |
| Royalty to University | 0 | 0 | 0 | 0 | 0 | 0% |
| Research & Development | 30,000 | 30,000 | 52,357 | 169,880 | 282,238 | 94% |
| Sales & Marketing | 0 | 0 | 94,804 | 94,804 | 189,608 | 63% |
| General and Administration | 107,017 | 189,658 | 199,497 | 204,417 | 700,589 | 234% |
| Sponsored Research | 450,000 | 0 | 300,000 | 0 | 750,000 | 250% |
| **Total Operating Expenses** | **587,017** | **219,658** | **646,659** | **469,101** | **1,922,435** | **641%** |
| | | | | | | |
| EBIT | (587,017) | (219,658) | (346,659) | (469,101) | (1,622,435) | -541% |
| | | | | | | |
| Interest Expense | (67) | (128) | (5,713) | (8,161) | (14,069) | -5% |
| **EBT** | **(587,084)** | **(219,786)** | **(352,372)** | **(477,262)** | **(1,636,504)** | **-546%** |
| Income taxes | 0 | 0 | 0 | 0 | 0 | 0% |
| **Net Income (Loss)** | **(587,084)** | **(219,786)** | **(352,372)** | **(477,262)** | **(1,636,504)** | **-546%** |

|  |  | **FYE 6/30/01** |  |  |  |
| --- | --- | --- | --- | --- | --- |
| **1Q** | **2Q** | **3Q** | **4Q** | **Total** | **%** |
|  |  |  |  |  |  |
| 0 | 20 | 30 |  |  |  |
| 0 | 20 | 50 | 50 |  |  |
| 0 | 232 | 820 | 1,052 |  |  |
|  |  |  |  |  |  |
| 0 | 0 | 96,000 | 144,000 | 240,000 | 5% |
| 0 | 0 | 58,083 | 205,000 | 263,083 | 5% |
| 1,875,000 | 0 | 2,875,000 | 0 | 4,750,000 | 90% |
| **1,875,000** | **0** | **3,029,083** | **349,000** | **5,253,083** | **100%** |
|  |  |  |  |  |  |
| 0 | 0 | 278,419 | 315,289 | 593,708 | 11% |
| 1,687,500 | 0 | 1,687,500 | 0 | 3,375,000 | 64% |
| **187,500** | **0** | **1,063,164** | **33,711** | **1,284,375** | **24%** |
|  |  |  |  |  |  |
| 0 | 0 | 12,327 | 87,673 | 100,000 | 2% |
| 417,923 | 618,476 | 550,176 | 683,067 | 2,269,642 | 43% |
| 140,155 | 160,155 | 280,802 | 326,767 | 907,879 | 17% |
| 277,129 | 302,044 | 391,361 | 395,259 | 1,365,793 | 26% |
| 450,000 | 0 | 300,000 | 0 | 750,000 | 14% |
| **1,285,208** | **1,080,675** | **1,534,665** | **1,492,767** | **5,393,314** | **103%** |
|  |  |  |  |  |  |
| (1,097,708) | (1,080,675) | (471,501) | (1,459,056) | (4,108,939) | -78% |
|  |  |  |  |  |  |
| (7,988) | (7,642) | (8,409) | (9,879) | (33,919) | -1% |
| **(1,105,695)** | **(1,088,317)** | **(479,910)** | **(1,468,935)** | **(4,142,858)** | **-79%** |
| 0 | 0 | 0 | 0 | 0 | 0% |
| **(1,105,695)** | **(1,088,317)** | **(479,910)** | **(1,468,935)** | **(4,142,858)** | **-79%** |

## Income Statement

*continued*

| | 1Q | 2Q | 3Q | 4Q | Total | |
|---|---|---|---|---|---|---|
| | | | FYE 6/30/02 | | | |
| **Units Sold** | | | | | | |
| Systems | 30 | 34 | 41 | 45 | 300 | |
| Aggregate Systems | 80 | 114 | 155 | 200 | 200 | |
| Chips | 1,435 | 2,091 | 2,877 | 3,793 | 10,195 | |
| | | | | | | |
| **Revenue** | | | | | | |
| System Royalties (from OEM) | 144,000 | 163,200 | 196,800 | 216,000 | 720,000 | 4% |
| Sensor Chips | 358,750 | 522,750 | 719,208 | 948,125 | 2,548,833 | 16% |
| Contract and Grants | 6,375,000 | 0 | 6,375,000 | 0 | 12,750,000 | 80% |
| **Total Revenue** | **6,877,750** | **685,950** | **7,291,008** | **1,164,125** | **16,018,833** | **100%** |
| | | | | | | |
| **Cost of Sales** | | | | | | |
| Sensor Chips | 500,887 | 513,655 | 582,758 | 631,239 | 2,228,540 | 14% |
| Contract and Grants | 5,737,500 | 0 | 5,737,500 | 0 | 11,475,000 | 72% |
| **Gross Margin** | **639,363** | **172,295** | **970,750** | **532,886** | **2,315,294** | **14%** |
| | | | | | | |
| **Operating Expenses** | | | | | | |
| Royalty to University | 40,220 | 54,876 | 73,281 | 93,130 | 261,507 | 2% |
| Research & Development | 639,866 | 639,866 | 691,755 | 691,755 | 2,663,241 | 17% |
| Sales & Marketing | 443,273 | 483,523 | 495,802 | 510,109 | 1,932,706 | 12% |
| General & Admin. | 444,926 | 448,590 | 453,191 | 458,153 | 1,804,860 | 11% |
| Sponsored Research | 0 | 0 | 0 | 0 | 0 | 0% |
| **Total Operating Expenses** | **1,568,284** | **1,626,854** | **1,714,028** | **1,753,147** | **6,662,313** | **42%** |
| | | | | | | |
| EBIT | (928,922) | (1,454,560) | (743,277) | (1,220,261) | (4,347,020) | -27% |
| | | | | | | |
| Interest Expense | (18,113) | (19,849) | (20,974) | (22,362) | (81,298) | -1% |
| **EBT** | **(947,035)** | **(1,474,409)** | **(764,251)** | **(1,242,623)** | **(4,428,318)** | **-28%** |
| Income taxes | 0 | 0 | 0 | 0 | 0 | 0% |
| **Net Income (Loss)** | **(947,035)** | **(1,474,409)** | **(764,251)** | **(1,242,623)** | **(4,428,318)** | **-28%** |

| FYE 6/30/03 | | FYE 6/30/04 | | FYE 6/30/05 | |
|---|---|---|---|---|---|
| 600 | | 1,000 | | | |
| 500 | | 1,100 | | 2,100 | |
| 41,000 | | 90,200 | | 172,200 | |
| | | | | | |
| 1,440,000 | 6% | 2,880,000 | 8% | 4,800,000 | 8% |
| 10,250,000 | 42% | 22,550,000 | 59% | 43,050,000 | 76% |
| 12,750,000 | 52% | 12,750,000 | 33% | 9,000,000 | 16% |
| **24,440,000** | **100%** | **38,180,000** | **100%** | **56,850,000** | **100%** |
| | | | | | |
| 3,970,336 | 16% | 6,594,013 | 17% | 12,077,381 | 21% |
| 11,475,000 | 47% | 11,475,000 | 30% | 8,100,000 | 14% |
| **8,994,664** | **37%** | **20,110,987** | **53%** | **36,672,619** | **65%** |
| | | | | | |
| 935,200 | 4% | 2,034,400 | 5% | 3,828,000 | 7% |
| 3,962,692 | 16% | 4,577,657 | 12% | 5,785,086 | 10% |
| 3,553,993 | 15% | 5,997,858 | 16% | 10,514,054 | 18% |
| 2,021,454 | 8% | 2,357,924 | 6% | 2,873,176 | 5% |
| 0 | 0% | 0 | 0% | 0 | 0% |
| **10,473,339** | **43%** | **14,967,839** | **39%** | **23,000,316** | **40%** |
| | | | | | |
| (1,478,675) | -6% | 5,143,149 | 13% | 13,672,303 | 24% |
| | | | | | |
| (145,205) | -1% | (201,687) | -1% | (194,722) | -0% |
| **(1,623,880)** | **-7%** | **4,941,461** | **13%** | **13,477,581** | **24%** |
| 0 | 0% | 0 | 0% | 2,634,993 | 5% |
| **(1,623,880)** | **-7%** | **4,941,461** | **13%** | **10,842,588** | **19%** |

## Balance Sheet

|                              | **FY 6/30/00** | | | |
|------------------------------|-----------|-----------|-------------|-------------|
|                              | **1Q**    | **2Q**    | **3Q**      | **4Q**      |
| **ASSETS**                   |           |           |             |             |
| **Current Assets**           |           |           |             |             |
| Cash                         | 784,800   | 473,297   | 8,198,949   | 6,730,576   |
| Net A/R                      | 0         | 0         | 0           | 0           |
| Inventory                    | 0         | 0         | 0           | 0           |
| **Total Current Assets**     | **784,800** | **473,297** | **8,198,949** | **6,730,576** |
|                              |           |           |             |             |
| Gross Fixed Assets           | 10,000    | 20,000    | 70,500      | 1,021,500   |
| Less Acc. Depr.              | 567       | 1,700     | 5,356       | 16,833      |
| **Net Fixed Assets**         | **9,433** | **18,300** | **65,144**  | **1,004,667** |
|                              |           |           |             |             |
| Other Assets                 | 140,000   | 240,000   | 340,000     | 400,000     |
|                              |           |           |             |             |
| **TOTAL ASSETS**             | **934,233** | **731,597** | **8,604,094** | **8,135,242** |
|                              |           |           |             |             |
| **LIABILITIES**              |           |           |             |             |
| **Short Term Liabilities**   |           |           |             |             |
| A/P                          | 10,900    | 14,300    | 38,400      | 57,450      |
| Salaries Payable             | 5,833     | 15,417    | 25,630      | 38,130      |
| Taxes Payable                | 0         | 0         | 0           | 0           |
| Line of Credit               | 0         | 0         | 0           | 0           |
| CP- LT Debt                  | 1,528     | 2,917     | 101,991     | 97,611      |
| **Total Short Term Liabilities** | **18,261** | **32,633** | **166,021** | **193,191** |
|                              |           |           |             |             |
| Long Term Debt               | 3,056     | 5,833     | 397,315     | 378,556     |
|                              |           |           |             |             |
| **TOTAL LIABILITIES**        | **21,317** | **38,467** | **563,335** | **571,746** |
|                              |           |           |             |             |
| **Equity**                   |           |           |             |             |
| Preferred Stock              | 1,500,000 | 1,500,000 | 9,200,000   | 9,200,000   |
| Retained Earnings            | (587,084) | (806,870) | (1,159,242) | (1,636,504) |
| Total Equity                 | 912,916   | 693,130   | 8,040,758   | 7,563,496   |
|                              |           |           |             |             |
| **LIABILITIES & EQUITY**     | **934,233** | **731,597** | **8,604,094** | **8,135,242** |

**FY 6/30/01**

| 1Q | 2Q | 3Q | 4Q |
|---|---|---|---|
| 5,139,481 | 3,684,016 | 2,734,534 | 1,113,968 |
| 0 | 0 | 126,770 | 247,253 |
| 0 | 0 | 58,425 | 106,600 |
| **5,139,481** | **3,684,016** | **2,919,729** | **1,467,820** |
| | | | |
| 1,535,000 | 1,966,500 | 2,479,000 | 2,618,000 |
| 45,400 | 87,878 | 147,167 | 218,947 |
| **1,489,600** | **1,878,622** | **2,331,833** | **2,399,053** |
| | | | |
| 470,000 | 470,000 | 470,000 | 470,000 |
| | | | |
| **7,099,081** | **6,032,638** | **5,721,562** | **4,336,873** |
| | | | |
| | | | |
| 101,550 | 128,500 | 194,917 | 217,617 |
| 68,911 | 85,974 | 119,005 | 130,599 |
| 0 | 0 | 0 | 0 |
| 0 | 0 | 82,400 | 160,714 |
| 99,162 | 95,116 | 94,111 | 87,991 |
| **269,623** | **309,590** | **490,433** | **596,920** |
| | | | |
| 371,657 | 353,565 | 341,556 | 319,315 |
| | | | |
| **641,281** | **663,154** | **831,989** | **916,235** |
| | | | |
| | | | |
| 9,200,000 | 9,200,000 | 9,200,000 | 9,200,000 |
| (2,742,199) | (3,830,517) | (4,310,427) | (5,779,362) |
| 6,457,801 | 5,369,483 | 4,889,573 | 3,420,638 |
| | | | |
| **7,099,081** | **6,032,638** | **5,721,562** | **4,336,873** |

## Balance Sheet

*continued*

| | FY 6/30/02 | | | |
| --- | --- | --- | --- | --- |
| | 1Q | 2Q | 3Q | 4Q |
| **ASSETS** | | | | |
| **Current Assets** | | | | |
| Cash | 8,010,124 | 6,555,802 | 5,731,019 | 4,179,287 |
| Net A/R | 348,728 | 479,358 | 636,727 | 793,691 |
| Inventory | 27,323 | 36,681 | 74,159 | 106,600 |
| **Total Current Assets** | **8,386,174** | **7,071,841** | **6,441,905** | **5,079,579** |
| | | | | |
| Gross Fixed Assets | 2,940,000 | 2,940,000 | 3,035,000 | 3,342,000 |
| Less Acc. Depr. | 353,506 | 488,064 | 629,078 | 771,064 |
| **Net Fixed Assets** | **2,586,494** | **2,451,936** | **2,405,922** | **2,570,936** |
| | | | | |
| Other Assets | 470,000 | 470,000 | 470,000 | 470,000 |
| | | | | |
| **TOTAL ASSETS** | **11,442,669** | **9,993,778** | **9,317,827** | **8,120,515** |
| | | | | |
| **LIABILITIES** | | | | |
| **Short Term Liabilities** | | | | |
| A/P | 234,425 | 236,117 | 258,867 | 259,717 |
| Salaries Payable | 142,412 | 142,412 | 153,437 | 154,815 |
| Taxes Payable | 0 | 0 | 0 | 0 |
| Line of Credit | 226,673 | 311,583 | 413,872 | 515,899 |
| CP- LT Debt | 179,630 | 165,935 | 156,681 | 143,699 |
| **Total Short Term Liabilities** | **783,139** | **856,046** | **982,856** | **1,074,130** |
| | | | | |
| Long Term Debt | 685,926 | 638,537 | 600,028 | 554,065 |
| | | | | |
| **TOTAL LIABILITIES** | **1,469,065** | **1,494,583** | **1,582,884** | **1,628,195** |
| | | | | |
| **Equity** | | | | |
| Preferred Stock | 16,700,000 | 16,700,000 | 16,700,000 | 16,700,000 |
| Retained Earnings | (6,726,397) | (8,200,806) | (8,965,057) | (10,207,680) |
| Total Equity | 9,973,603 | 8,499,194 | 7,734,943 | 6,492,320 |
| | | | | |
| **LIABILITIES & EQUITY** | **11,442,669** | **9,993,778** | **9,317,827** | **8,120,515** |

| FYE 6/30/03 | FYE 6/30/04 | FYE 6/30/05 |
|---|---|---|
| 2,377,470 | 6,036,252 | 14,348,660 |
| 1,928,850 | 4,195,950 | 7,895,250 |
| 225,500 | 218,777 | 408,975 |
| **4,531,820** | **10,450,980** | **22,652,885** |
| | | |
| 3,478,000 | 3,552,000 | 3,552,000 |
| 1,076,097 | 1,186,564 | 1,297,031 |
| **2,401,903** | **2,365,436** | **2,254,969** |
| | | |
| 470,000 | 470,000 | 470,000 |
| | | |
| **7,403,722** | **13,286,416** | **25,377,854** |
| | | |
| | | |
| 523,308 | 833,706 | 1,549,515 |
| 169,791 | 185,877 | 195,171 |
| 0 | 0 | 658,748 |
| 1,253,753 | 2,000,000 | 2,000,000 |
| 120,588 | 90,088 | 58,421 |
| **2,067,439** | **3,109,671** | **4,461,855** |
| | | |
| 467,843 | 366,843 | 263,509 |
| | | |
| **2,535,282** | **3,476,514** | **4,725,364** |
| | | |
| 16,700,000 | 16,700,000 | 16,700,000 |
| (11,831,560) | (6,890,098) | 3,952,490 |
| 4,868,440 | 9,809,902 | 20,652,490 |
| | | |
| **7,403,722** | **13,286,416** | **25,377,854** |

## Statement of Cashflow

| | 1Q | 2Q | 3Q | 4Q | Total |
|---|---|---|---|---|---|
| | | | **FYE 6/30/00** | | |
| **BEGINNING CASH** | **0** | **784,800** | **473,297** | **8,198,949** | **0** |
| | | | | | |
| **Sources of Cash** | | | | | |
| Net Income | (587,084) | (219,786) | (352,372) | (477,262) | (1,636,504) |
| Add Depreciation/Amortization | 567 | 1,133 | 3,656 | 11,478 | 16,833 |
| Issuance of Stock | 1,500,000 | 0 | 7,700,000 | 0 | 9,200,000 |
| | | | | | |
| **Plus Changes In:** | | | | | |
| Accounts Payable | 10,900 | 3,400 | 24,100 | 19,050 | 57,450 |
| Salaries Payable | 5,833 | 9,583 | 10,213 | 12,500 | 38,130 |
| Taxes Payable | 0 | 0 | 0 | 0 | 0 |
| Additions to Line of Credit | 0 | 0 | 0 | 0 | 0 |
| Additions to Long-Term Debt | 4,861 | 4,722 | 498,889 | 2,889 | 511,361 |
| **Total Sources of Cash** | **935,078** | **(200,947)** | **7,884,486** | **(431,346)** | **8,187,270** |
| | | | | | |
| **Uses of Cash** | | | | | |
| **Less Changes In:** | | | | | |
| A/R | 0 | 0 | 0 | 0 | 0 |
| Inventory | 0 | 0 | 0 | 0 | 0 |
| Gross Fixed Assets | 150,000 | 110,000 | 150,500 | 1,011,000 | 1,421,500 |
| Reductions Line of Credit | 0 | 0 | 0 | 0 | 0 |
| Reductions to Long-Term Debt | 278 | 556 | 8,333 | 26,028 | 35,194 |
| **Total Uses** | **150,278** | **110,556** | **158,833** | **1,037,028** | **1,456,694** |
| | | | | | |
| **CHANGES IN CASH** | **784,800** | **(311,503)** | **7,725,652** | **(1,468,373)** | **6,730,576** |
| | | | | | |
| **ENDING CASH** | **784,800** | **473,297** | **8,198,949** | **6,730,576** | **6,730,576** |

|  | **FYE 6/30/01** |  |  |  |
|---|---|---|---|---|
| **1Q** | **2Q** | **3Q** | **4Q** | **Total** |
| **6,730,576** | **5,139,481** | **3,684,016** | **2,734,534** | **6,730,576** |
|  |  |  |  |  |
| (1,105,695) | (1,088,317) | (479,910) | (1,468,935) | (4,142,858) |
| 28,567 | 42,478 | 59,289 | 71,781 | 202,114 |
| 0 | 0 | 0 | 0 | 0 |
|  |  |  |  |  |
| 44,100 | 26,950 | 66,417 | 22,700 | 160,167 |
| 30,781 | 17,063 | 33,031 | 11,594 | 92,469 |
| 0 | 0 | 0 | 0 | 0 |
| 0 | 0 | 82,400 | 78,314 | 160,714 |
| 19,653 | 5,556 | 13,778 | 500 | 39,486 |
| **(982,594)** | **(996,271)** | **(224,995)** | **(1,284,047)** | **(3,487,908)** |
|  |  |  |  |  |
| 0 | 0 | 126,770 | 120,483 | 247,253 |
| 0 | 0 | 58,425 | 48,175 | 106,600 |
| 583,500 | 431,500 | 512,500 | 139,000 | 1,666,500 |
| 0 | 0 | 0 | 0 | 0 |
| 25,000 | 27,694 | 26,792 | 28,861 | 108,347 |
| **608,500** | **459,194** | **724,486** | **336,519** | **2,128,700** |
|  |  |  |  |  |
| **(1,591,094)** | **(1,455,466)** | **(949,481)** | **(1,620,566)** | **(5,616,608)** |
|  |  |  |  |  |
| **5,139,481** | **3,684,016** | **2,734,534** | **1,113,968** | **1,113,968** |

## Statement of Cashflow

*continued*

| | 1Q | 2Q | FYE 6/30/02 3Q | 4Q | Total |
|---|---|---|---|---|---|
| **BEGINNING CASH** | 1,113,967 | 8,010,123 | 6,555,802 | 5,731,019 | 1,113,967 |
| **Sources of Cash** | | | | | |
| Net Income | (94,7035) | (1,474,409) | (764,251) | (1,242,623) | (4,428,317) |
| Add Depreciation/Amortization | 134,558 | 134,558 | 141,014 | 141,986 | 552,117 |
| Issuance of Stock | 7,500,000 | 0 | 0 | 0 | 7,500,000 |
| **Plus Changes In:** | | | | | |
| Accounts Payable | 16,809 | 1,691 | 22,750 | 850 | 42,100 |
| Salaries Payable | 11,813 | 0 | 11,025 | 1,378 | 24,216 |
| Taxes Payable | 0 | 0 | 0 | 0 | 0 |
| Additions to Line of Credit | 281,853 | 84,910 | 102,290 | 102,027 | 571,079 |
| Additions to Long-Term Debt | 490,639 | 0 | 2,917 | 0 | 493,556 |
| **Total Sources of Cash** | **7,488,637** | **(1,253,249)** | **(484,256)** | **(996,382)** | **4,754,749** |
| **Uses of Cash** | | | | | |
| **Less Changes In:** | | | | | |
| A/R | 101,475 | 130,631 | 157,369 | 156,965 | 546,439 |
| Inventory | (79,277) | 9,358 | 37,477 | 32,441 | 0 |
| Gross Fixed Assets | 322,000 | 0 | 95,000 | 307,000 | 724,000 |
| Reductions Line of Credit | 215,894 | 0 | 0 | 0 | 215,894 |
| Reductions to Long-Term Debt | 32,389 | 61,083 | 50,681 | 58,944 | 203,097 |
| **Total Uses** | **592,481** | **201,072** | **340,527** | **555,350** | **1,689,430** |
| **CHANGES IN CASH** | **6,896,155** | **(1,454,321)** | **(824,782)** | **(1,551,732)** | **3,065,319** |
| **ENDING CASH** | **8,010,123** | **6,555,802** | **5,731,019** | **4,179,287** | **4,179,287** |

| FYE 6/30/03 | FYE 6/30/04 | FYE 6/30/05 |
|---|---|---|
| **4,179,287** | **2,377,469** | **6,036,252** |
| | | |
| (1,623,879) | 4,941,461 | 10,842,588 |
| 305,033 | 110,467 | 110,467 |
| 0 | 0 | 0 |
| | | |
| 263,592 | 310,398 | 715,808 |
| 14,976 | 16,086 | 9,294 |
| 0 | 0 | 658,748 |
| 737,853 | 746,248 | 0 |
| 0 | 0 | 0 |
| **(302,426)** | **6,124,660** | **12,336,905** |
| | | |
| 1,135,158 | 2,267,100 | 3,699,300 |
| 118,900 | (6,723) | 190,198 |
| 136,000 | 74,000 | 0 |
| 0 | 0 | 0 |
| 109,333 | 131,500 | 135,000 |
| **1,499,392** | **2,465,877** | **4,024,497** |
| | | |
| **(1,801,817)** | **3,658,782** | **8,312,407** |
| | | |
| **2,377,469** | **6,036,252** | **14,348,660** |

# Convenience Store & Bait Shop

BUSINESS PLAN                    THE DOCK STORE

*South 6018 Rebecca Road*
*Lake Zurich, Ohio 45325*

*The Dock Store, LLC details how it will be success-
ful as the only combination live bait and tackle/
convenience retail store in a small but thriving lake
resort. This business/marketing plan was prepared
to help the company obtain a $248,090 small bus-
iness loan for development-related costs.*

- EXECUTIVE SUMMARY

- COMPANY SUMMARY

- CONVENIENCE & BAIT SHOP OVERVIEW

- MARKET ANALYSIS SUMMARY

- STRATEGY & IMPLEMENTATION SUMMARY

- PROMOTION PLAN SUMMARY

- FINANCIAL PLAN SUMMARY

# CONVENIENCE STORE & BAIT SHOP
# BUSINESS PLAN

**EXECUTIVE SUMMARY**

The Dock Store is a start-up convenience food and bait shop operation, located in Lake Zurich, Ohio. Our location is on the main road leading to one of two public boat launches, approximately a half mile from the lakeshore. Our store will be the only live bait and tackle retail store for five miles, and the only convenience and beverage retail operation for five miles. This ideal retail outlet location will carry "made-on-site" sandwich/soup food items amongst staple type grocery products. These activities are the basis of the Dock Store and the makings of a highly profitable venture.

Management of the Dock Store is presently seeking funds to develop and grow the business in a phased approach, as highlighted within this planning tool. Future growth opportunities include the area's only boat rental operations, expansion of food product offerings and development of a sit-down area for dining. This plan only details the funds needed to develop Phase I activities at this time.

The president, Mr. Jim Black, has an extensive knowledge of Lake Zurich and has identified a niche market retail opportunity to make this venture highly successful, combining his 20 years of work experience in a variety of businesses.

The foundation for this plan is a combination of primary and secondary research, upon which the marketing strategies are built. Discussions and interviews were held with a variety of individuals and other area retail small businesses to develop financial and proforma detail. We consulted census data, county business patterns, and other directories to develop the market potential and competitive situation.

The Dock Store shall provide the southern portion of Lake Zurich with the only bait, tackle, and food and grocery items for miles. Seasonal new job opportunities for area residents shall be created. Store hours of operation are from 5:00 A.M. to 9:00 P.M., seven days a week, year round. Hours may be extended as needed during peak summer season. As growth warrants, store floor space, bait, and seating area expansion can be realized (Phase II).

**Business Plan Purpose**

### Introduction

In today's highly competitive environment, formal business planning is an essential element in achieving business success. A well-written business plan is primarily a communication tool to be used in obtaining financing. In certain instances, particularly with our early stage company, this business plan also serves as a strategic plan.

Considering that lenders are inundated by numerous investment opportunities from which they choose only a few, this business plan describes our story and how we intend to grow with your assistance. The Dock Store management has made an in-depth analysis of its opportunities and weaknesses and has concluded that the company has an excellent chance to succeed. Please do not hesitate to address any questions, comments or concerns to Mr. Jim Black.

### Methodology for business planning

Sophisticated business planning helps management answer questions such as: What will be our record of achievement? How have we fared compared to our competitors? Are we setting realistic and attainable goals and objectives?

Constructive and useful business planning requires a broad-based understanding of changes taking place in the marketplace in which the company competes, or plans to compete, and the ever-changing financial markets. In-depth technical skills in a variety of disciplines such as tax, financial analysis, sales, marketing, and managing growth are critical components in assessing a company's opportunities and risks.

**Developing the business plan**

The management of the Dock Store has developed this disciplined planning methodology to help the company anticipate its start-up economic requirements and other critical information, and it has arrived at this realistic plan.

**Guidance from outside professionals**

Jim Black has sought out assistance and advisors to the Dock Store in developing this business plan. However, Jim will maintain an active management involvement in every aspect of the formation of this business. This planning tool reflects his concept of the future for the Dock Store.

The experienced professionals Mr. Black has retained have assisted the company in:

- Helping develop a realistic business plan
- Reviewing financial projections incorporating all of the assumptions and quantitative data presented in the business plan
- Assisting in structuring funding options and lending offerings
- Conducting market research
- Researching growth potential for convenience stores
- Identifying competitive forces and products
- Offering creative marketing approaches

1. Attract $248,090 of SBA backed commercial funding
2. Focus ideas and establish goals
3. Identify and quantify objectives
4. Track and direct growth
5. Create benchmarks for measuring success

**Five Objectives of The Dock Store**

The Dock Store was recently formed as a start-up retail operation in Lake Zurich, Ohio. We shall serve our neighbors and the fishing/boating communities in providing convenience groceries, made-on-site sandwiches, and bait and tackle shopping experience. The location had been previously a convenience store operation for nearly 47 years. Our food items, groceries, and bait will fill a niche vacated by closure of this operation three years ago. The integration of market niche analysis and other disciplines will result in an innovative and needed retail operation for the entire south portion of Lake Zurich.

The Dock Store will provide residents and guests to the southern portion of Lake Zurich with a quality and dependable retail operation from which they may purchase food items, groceries, bait, and tackle on a year-round basis. The Dock Store shall try to provide its quality food and fishing products in a comprehensive and cost competitive manner, while providing our customers the finest service available.

**Mission Statement**

This business plan serves to detail the direction, vision, and planning necessary to achieve our goal for providing a superior grocery and carryout food item selection. The extensive live bait and fishing tackle supplies are selected to the fishing patterns and variety of the Lake Zurich fish population.

**COMPANY SUMMARY**

**Company
Ownership**

Jim Black and the late Mr. Frank Black (uncle to Jim) founded the Dock Store in 2000 as an Ohio Limited Liability Corporation (LLC). The Dock Store is being reopened, after an extensive renovation, to address the needs of southern Lake Zurich. Jim is also completing the FastTrac entrepreneurial training program to fine-tune his skills.

The Dock Store has relied upon several key professionals to assist it: Mr. Darryl Keegan, attorney; Ms. Lisa Walker, accounting; and Mr. Frank O'Brien, business development specialist. Each person has assisted the Dock Store in the development, strategic planning, and marketing phases.

**Management &
Organizational
Summary**

Jim Black will manage all aspects of the business and service development to ensure effective customer responsiveness while monitoring day-to-day operations; inventory and retail merchandise mix/cost control, etc. Qualified and trained clerks personally trained by Jim in customer service skills will provide additional support services. Support staff will be added as seasonal or extended hours mandate.

**Corporate
Development Plan**

For purposes of this business plan document, the Dock Store's Phase I and Phase II growth are defined below:

> **Phase I**—This phase involves renovation, preparation, and development of the Dock Store's Lake Zurich, Ohio, operation. The Dock Store is housed at South 6018 Rebecca Road in Lake Zurich, Ohio, 45325. Its 1,200-square-foot retail selling space will reopen in a restored 50-year-old building that housed a general store operation for nearly 47 years. Previously ownership lost interest in the operation and voluntarily closed it.

> Jim Black's new operation will establish its own identity by servicing the local community and area fishing/boating enthusiasts. Our locations cannot be missed since traffic passes in front of our store on the way to and from one of two public boat launches. The Dock Store will develop key "base staples," groceries (bread, milk, etc.) and convenience health and beauty necessities, beverages, packaged goods, cigarettes, and fishing tackle and bait. Through proper product placement, space allocation, and in-store promotion, sales space will be geared towards high profit margin products.

> The preparation and sale of carryout soup/sandwich food items will fill a niche need for the area's year-round residents. With snowmobile and ice fishing in the winter, beach, fishing, and boating in the spring, summer, and fall, the Lake area remains a tourist and sportsmen's paradise year round.

> Phase I capital (start-up) funds are documented later on in this business plan.

> **Phase II**—Continue implementation of sales, advertising, and marketing strategies developed in Phase I. Expand the physical plant with a garage and bait store attachment. Several types of boats could be rented, the bait area removed for the convenience store portion of the building, allowing for an expansion of each line. Identify and pursue other business service opportunities, like expanded food service/seating and/or video rental, fax services, etc.

> The Dock Store anticipates additional support staff and efforts to meet additional demands brought about by Phase II expansion growth. This plan does not contain funding needs for this Phase.

> Initially, the Dock Store management will focus its efforts in Phase I activities. Phase II efforts depend upon the timely development of Phase I and the analysis of its customer

service base. The Dock Store's growth will directly impact the rate at which Phase II activities are considered.

We are located just blocks from Lake Zurich, which has several golf courses, two ski hills, water recreation activities, numerous dining establishments, various retail and specialty shops, art galleries, theater entertainment venues, and the beauty and serenity of Lake Zurich, a famous Midwest tourist destination for nearly 135 years. The city of Lake Zurich began to prosper in the 1870s after becoming famous as a resort area. Many homes and estates date back to this era. Enormous "summer cottages" were built on the lakeshore and some are still in evidence today. The essence of Lake Zurich is its down-home charm. Through the economic boom era of the 1990s, the area surrounding the Dock Store has seen several subdivisions spring up, filled with year-round residents enjoying the beauty of this area.

Potawatomi Indians inhabited the area in the early 1800s and named it "Kish-Way-Kee-Tow" meaning "clear water." The lake originated from an Ohio glacier, and most of its water comes from rainfall, springs, and streams, most of which originate at the western end of the lake. The lake has a surface of 4,458 acres and is 9 miles long and 3.7 miles wide. It is Ohio's second-deepest lake, making it a fishing destination for generations. A path along the lakeshore is about 26 miles in length and is enjoyed by hikers year round.

**Geographical Considerations**

U.S. convenience 1997 in-store sales (excluding gasoline and tackle related) were $52.8 billion and the store count reached 90,192 location store operations. Data summary by Midwest and U.S. listing product category is provided below.

**CONVENIENCE & BAIT SHOP OVERVIEW**

| Product | Midwest | U.S. |
|---|---|---|
| Tobacco | 3,172,806 | 13,298,130 |
| Beverage | 1,404,609 | 5,887,111 |
| Beer | 1,598,556 | 6,700,000 |
| Foodservice | 1,501,709 | 6,294,084 |
| Candy | 775,664 | 3,251,029 |
| Grocery | 774,405 | 3,245,749 |
| Dairy | 823,396 | 3,451,084 |
| GM | 629,574 | 2,638,722 |
| Snacks | 532,726 | 2,232,806 |
| Newspaper | 290,544 | 1,217,750 |
| HBC | 242,686 | 1,017,167 |
| Pckg. baked | 218,128 | 914,236 |
| Other food | 387,517 | 1,624,195 |
| Services | 241,679 | 1,012,944 |

*Figures are U.S. 1997 Dollar Sales (000)
Source: Convenience.net
Source: http://www.c-store.com/report97.htm

Beverages include packaged juices, sodas, drinks (sold in bottles, cans, etc.). Does not include fountain sodas or drinks. Food service includes fast food, other freshly prepared foods, fresh coffee, fountain sodas, drinks, and slush. Grocery includes packaged foods such as cereal, pasta, baby foods, frozen foods, canned foods, sugar, flour, condiments, cooking oils, etc. Dairy includes milk, ice cream, butter/margarine, yogurt, etc. Other foods include packaged meats, packaged deli salads/foods. Midwest region is defined as: Illinois, Indiana, Michigan, Ohio, Iowa, Kansas, Minnesota, Montana, Nebraska, North Dakota, South Dakota.

In Ohio, the average convenience store gross annual sales volume exceeds that of the U.S. and region totals, as shown below.

| State & Region | Sales $MM | C-Stores # | C-Stores Density | Sales/ C-Stores |
|---|---|---|---|---|
| OH | 1,061 | 1,665 | 3,104 | $637 |
| Midwest | 7,369 | 13,059 | 3,360 | $564 |
| U.S. | 52,785 | 90,192 | 2,967 | $585 |

*Sources: Convenience.net c-store database; U.S. Commerce Dept.; Bureau of the Census.*

Convenience store data in the above chart is for in-store sales only as of 12/31/97—gasoline and tackle related sales are excluded in this analysis. Retail density is the relationship between total population (1997) and the number of convenience stores. It is expressed as the number of potential customers in a state for each convenience store.

Our Dock Store's first year annualized proforma sales including tackle and bait sales is $517,558 falling conservatively below the U.S., Midwest, and Ohio State 1997 industry summary totals. The previous pattern of growth is a 7.1 percent increase from 1998 figures. Grocery store December 1999 sales (which include convenience stores) increased 2.0 percent from November 1999 but grew 7.1 percent from December 1998. The association predicts future growth patterns to remain similar at a 7 to 9 percent annual rate of expansion.

The Dock Store has identified a niche market growth opportunity. As research revealed product placement, word-of-mouth recommendations, food product tasting promotions and other referrals will be the primary way in which our store will gain steady growth. The Yellow Pages and other newspaper advertising will establish name recognition and prompt customers to call for information or pricing. Between 1990 and 1996, an estimated 6,400 people moved into Generals County (Southeast Ohio Regional Planning Commission Annual Report 1996).

Local growth in the residential areas surrounding the Dock Store is evidence to this growth pattern. Sustained growth throughout the Greater Generals County area, and the development of a new shopping center in Lake Zurich, will continue to bring additional people to the area, resulting in continued growth for the Dock Store.

**Competitive Advantage**

Strengths of the Dock Store include:

1. Jim Black's broad base of experience in different types of work environments. For example, Jim's fishing knowledge of Lake Zurich will bring in customers trying to understand the Lake's "hot spots."
2. Jim's emphasis on quality and timely response to meet consumer demands, while controlling operational costs will ensure the pier's success.
3. Location, Location, Location. The only convenience and bait/tackle operation on the southern end of the Lake and for five miles in either direction.
4. The carryout food niche is nonexistent in this area of Lake Zurich.
5. The ability to stock items requested by local residents.
6. Future growth potential (Phase II).

**Keys to Success**

1. A service designed specifically for the area
2. Total quality food and customer service
3. Controlled overhead and operational costs
4. Regular and ongoing customer feedback
5. Inventory and DNR technology/software capacity
6. Dedicated management and trained support staff

Forces and trends in the market environment affect the Dock Store and Bait Shop, like all businesses. These include economic, competitive, legal/political, technology, and record-keeping issues.

- **Economic Environment**—Positive forces include the generally prosperous economy that is currently in place, full employment, rising wages and low inflation, leading more people and businesses to be willing to purchase prepared foods rather than preparing meal from scratch at home. The strong stock market means people are making more money, primarily in the form of capital gains, and disposable income is up. For example, in 1996 alone there were 95 new business start-ups in Generals County (County Business Patterns, U.S. Department of Commerce, Bureau of the Census 1995). The Dock Store is proud to grow with the strong national, state, and local economy.
- **Legal/Political Environment**—Town of Lake Zurich supports the reopening of this needed business venture and has issued and approved building permits and licenses to support use of the property.
- **Technology and Recordkeeping Environment**—Use of computerized scales and cash registers will capture and generate accounting/inventory detail. Computer programs greatly simplify the financial recordkeeping and tax preparation with which all businesses must comply. The Dock Store will outsource the accounting tax functions, however, Jim will maintain the daily financial records in-house and generate the reports from his office.

In southeastern Ohio (source through Midwest Directories) the competition is as follows:

**Other General Store-like Businesses**
- Country Store - 6 miles
- Kipp's Store - 70 miles
- Citgo Fontana Convenience Station - 10 miles

**Large Full-service Stores**
- Sentry - 4 miles
- Wal-Mart (limited bait supply) - 3.5 miles

**Bait and Tackle Stores**
- Lake Zurich Bait and Tackle - 8 miles

The Dock Store has identified a niche in the area market—that of a small, customer-oriented convenience food and staples, bait and tackle, carryout-prepared general food store operation. A review of other area competitors' retail mix shows none with the extensive selection of bait and tackle offered by the Dock Store.

A threat to be aware of is the emergence of new competitors. The barriers to entry are a comparable location, a subsequent investment, and the time and dedication of ownership.

Overall, the environment appears very positive for the Dock Store and Bait Shop. The forces driving market demand, mainly economic, are strong, with industry growth healthy and new residents moving into the area resulting in a greater demand for carryout food service.

All business is helped by advertising and referrals, so for the first few years the Dock Store will need to be aggressive in getting new customers, who will then pass the word on, and the business can begin to experience sustained growth.

---

**MARKET ANALYSIS SUMMARY**

**Competitive Environment Summary**

**STRATEGY & IMPLEMENTATION SUMMARY**

**Target Markets:**
- Residents to the southern Lake Zurich area
- Lake enthusiasts (boating, fishing, beachgoers)

**Positioning and Product Strategy:** The Dock Store will aim to attract area resident and lake enthusiasts who need convenience food items or personal health staples, carryout food items, and tackle/bait needs.

**Distribution Strategy:** Customers can contact the Dock Store by telephone, fax, and by dropping in. The Dock Store's nearest competitors' are five miles around the lake in either direction. The store can stock request items for regular area residents.

## Mix & Pricing Strategy

The Dock Store will offer the top 31 best-selling industry items as determined by Convenience Net Association, plus bait and Lake Zurich area specific products.

List of 32 Line Categories

| | |
|---|---|
| Alternative Snacks | Ice |
| Automotive Products | Liquor |
| Bait and Tackle | Lottery/Gaming |
| Beer | Nonedible Grocery |
| Candy | Other Dairy |
| Cigarettes | Other Tobacco |
| Cold Dispensed Beverages | Packaged Beverages (Non-Alcohol) |
| Edible Grocery | Packaged Bread |
| Fishing Licenses | Packaged Ice Cream/Novelties |
| Fluid Milk Products | Packaged Sandwich/Deli Products |
| Food Service | Packaged Sweet Snacks |
| Frozen Foods | Perishable Grocery |
| General Merchandise | Publications |
| Health and Beauty Care | Salty Snacks |
| Homemade Food Items | Store Services |
| Hot Dispensed Beverages | Wine |

The product listing takes into account regularly requested items and the ability to offer standing order items for area residents as space requirements allow.

## Services & Support Philosophy

Giving careful consideration to customer responsiveness, the Dock Store's goal will be to meet and exceed every service expectation of its food products and retail merchandise. Quality service and quick responsiveness will be the philosophy guiding a customer approach to the Dock Store.

## PROMOTION PLAN SUMMARY

Promotion strategies will be focused to the target market segment. Given the importance of word-of-mouth/referrals among the areas resident. We shall strive to service all our customers to gain their business regularly, which is the recipe for our long-term success. We shall focus on direct resident marketing, publicity, trial food demonstrations, and advertising as proposed.

## Marketing Plan

**Grocery and Restaurant Segment**—To build name recognition and to announce the entry of the Dock Store, we will offer a mail package consisting of a tri-fold brochure containing a coupon for a free cup of coffee to welcome our new customers. From those identified local residential customers we shall ask them to complete a survey and ask them of their perception of the store, any specific product or food items that they would like to see, etc. Those customers returning completed surveys would receive a gift or discount.

The local residential lists can be obtained from the Yellow Pages, the city clerk, or through International Business Lists, Inc. (Chicago, Ilinois) and is compiled from Secretary of State registrations, business license applications, announcements from newspaper clippings, and tax records.

**Local Carryout Food Products**—Local newspapers for advertising to build name recognition and to announce any weekly or monthly food specials will be introduced.

The Dock Store will develop a one-page menu/newsletter to be handed out to customers to take home with them as they visit the store. The menu/newsletter can be used to update clients on pricing and food special promotional developments, but also serves as a reminder of what sets the Dock Store apart—homemade quality and freshness. The newsletter would contain fishing area "hot spot' information and other tips. The menu/newsletter can be produced in-house and for the cost of paper and computer time.

**Publicity and Public Relations**—A news release will be sent to area newspapers and magazines announcing the launch of the Dock Store and Bait Shop. Jim Black may join the area Chamber of Commerce as a means of networking in the community. Becoming a sponsor in a community event (various parades, blood drives, etc.) is a low-cost way (average $100) of increasing awareness and building goodwill in the community.

**Customer Reward Program**—For the carryout customer and as a means of building business by word-of-mouth, present customers should be encouraged and rewarded as repeat customers. This can be accomplished by offering a free lunch meal, by raffle of a weekly customer business card or name slip as a means to generate excitement.

**Advertising**—Advertising is utilized primarily to attract new customers. It also serves to build awareness and name recognition of the company in general—important for word-of-mouth referrals ("Oh yes, I've seen their ads before").

- *Local Lake Zurich & Generals County Shopper/Sunday Shopper*—advertising in this Wednesday and Sunday primarily classified newspaper reaches over 33,000 homes and businesses in the county twice each week. A 12-week schedule (24 insertions) commencing upon store opening would be the initial placement. A six-week, every-other-week schedule (12 insertions) is also proposed for the peak season to promote specials.

- *Yellow Pages—Ameritech PagesPlus, Greater Generals County Telephone Directory.* Research indicated that new residents or people who don't have many personal acquaintances will look to the Yellow Pages to establish a list of potential businesses to call upon. Even a small 2" x 2" boxed ad can create awareness and attract the desired target client, above and beyond the ability of a simple listing. Ameritech Yellow Pages covers the relevant markct area, delivering over 30,000 copies to residents and businesses. Midwest Directories covers greater Generals County, with 90,000 circulation, but is considered a second-tier directory to Ameritech.

- Additional places to post advertising include playbills for local theater groups.

**Example Promotion Budget**
**2000 (Amount Included in Start-Up Funds)**

| | |
|---|---|
| Company brochure and newsletter | $150 |
| *(B&W, 1,000 quantity, stock paper, in-house produced)* | |
| Postage (mailing 150 residents, twice) | $100 |
| Newspaper advertising | $750 |
| Yellow Pages advertising | $200 |
| **Total for 2000** | **$1,200** |

**Evaluation &
Control Strategies**

Objectives have been established for the Dock Store so that actual performance can be measured against them. Thus, at the end of its first year, the Dock Store should have:

- $517,558 in total revenue
- Gross profit margin of 17.1 percent, or $88,592 before taxes.

Each subsequent year, new objectives will be set for these benchmarks and actual performance will be measured against them. If actual performance falls short of objectives, investigation will be made into the cause and plans adjusted accordingly.

Each subsequent year's budget should adjust spending toward the types of promotion that are accounting for the most new customers. Continuing customer satisfaction polling (questioning) shall be conducted throughout the life of the business. The feedback shall be evaluated and changes made accordingly.

**Identify
Opportunities
(SWOT Analysis)**

A SWOT (Strengths, Weaknesses, Opportunities, Threats) analysis can help answer questions that can determine the success or failure of a business entity. Retailers and pier store partners can develop the SWOT analysis together, and formal data is not typically needed. SWOT provides overall insights and observations to populate each of the four analytical areas. Key areas for examination include such factors as operations, facilities, location, employees, price/promotions, assortment, etc.:

- **Strengths:** What are the retailer's key category strengths? What factors are responsible for the retailer's current category success?
- **Weaknesses:** What are the retailer's key category weaknesses? What factors hinder category performance?
- **Opportunities:** What key internal opportunities could improve category performance?
- **Threats:** What are the key external threats to the retailer's category performance?

Dock Store management has identified the following as its SWOT analysis.

**Strengths:**

- The location of the Dock Store is in the heart of an upscale neighborhood and is in close proximity to a popular boat launch and public beach with ample parking facilities.
- The facility has been established as a retail grocery store for 47 years. The nearest competition is 5 miles from the Dock Store and does not carry live bait and tackle and has a minimal inventory of convenience goods.
- The Dock Store will be extensively renovated, with many upgrades already completed. After completion of this project the premises should not require any extensive upkeep until future expansion of the business (Phase II).
- The Dock Store has the ability to change inventory with the seasonal requirements.
- The owner has been a contractor for 10 years.

**Weaknesses:**

- The store has been closed for three years; therefore, I would have to reestablish a client base. I also would need to access what the client needs are in the area.
- Off-season effect.
- Lack of developmental capital to complete Phase I start-up.

**Opportunities:**

- Phase II expansion.
- Owner lives on the site of the business.
- Seasonal changes in inventory.
- Guide business will attract sales in both fishing and convenience goods.

**Threats:**

- New competition if any land was rezoned nearby.
- Economic downturn may cause decline in the number of people traveling to the area.

The following proforma contains the Dock Store's projections for a Ten-Year Basis.

**FINANCIAL PLAN SUMMARY**

**Phase I Funding Amounts Sought**

We are seeking $248,090 in developmental costs for the start-up of this convenience store, bait/tackle, and carryout food business. This schedule defines the financial needs to develop a successful business and is the basis for the financial start-up capital amounts listed in the Ten-Year Proforma.

The following schedules highlight the anticipated remaining developmental costs and the first-year Dock Store capital expenditures and assumptions.

| Capital Summary Overview | |
|---|---|
| Land, Building, and Improvements | $162,700 |
| Equipment & Installation Expenses | $30,740 |
| Development Expense (detail below) | $44,650* |
| First Quarter Working Capital | |
| (Mortgage, labor, and operating expense) | $10,000 |
| **Total** | **$248,090** |

| *Developmental Start-Up Expenses Detail | |
|---|---|
| Marketing, Advertising, and Promotion | $1,000 |
| Accounting | $400 |
| Permitting Legal and Consulting | $1,000 |
| Association Dues & Office Expense Start-Up | $250 |
| Engineering and Architect Fees | $500 |
| Bags and Supplies | $1,500 |
| Beginning Inventory | $39,000 |
| Unforeseen Contingency | $1,000 |
| **Total** | **$44,650** |
| **Owners' Equity Contribution to Date** | **$54,675** |

Phase II growth amounts will be developed and sought at a later date, based upon needs to be determined at that time.

**Financial Plan
Assumptions**

1. The following assumptions have been incorporated into the Dock Store Proforma statements.
2. All operating costs are based on the Dock Store's management research of similar operating companies.
3. Automated informational systems will reduce the Dock Store staff requirements.
4. Food and grocery inventory expense is 65 percent of revenue sales; tackle/bait inventory expense is 55 percent of revenue sales.
5. Developmental start-up costs are amortized over a five-year period.
6. Home office or other apartment expenses are not included.
7. Overhead and operations costs are calculated on an annual basis.
8. The Dock Store founders' salary is based on a fixed monthly salary expense basis.
9. All fixed and variable labor costs are scheduled to rise annually at 7.5 percent.
10. All revenues are figured to rise annually at 10 percent.
11. Administrative and office expenses rise at an annual rate of 2.5 percent.
12. Operating costs increase at 5 percent annually.
13. Loan amount interest rate at 9 percent.

# Creative Agency

BUSINESS PLAN

OCEANIA CREATIVE PRINT & INTERACTIVE

*1200 Forester Drive*
*Indianapolis, Indiana 46204*

*Oceania Creative is in the business of providing premium consulting, brand communications, and visual design services. The Oceania mission is to provide consulting and graphic production services to selected prospect clients primarily in the manufacturing industry. Through the application of knowledge, business relationships, and effective service delivery and continued success of Oceania clients, we will become recognized as a premier industry provider of communications services.*

- EXECUTIVE SUMMARY

- TARGET MARKET

- COMPANY TEAM

- COMPETITIVE LANDSCAPE

- PROJECTED 5-YEAR FINANCIALS

# CREATIVE AGENCY
# BUSINESS PLAN

## EXECUTIVE SUMMARY

Purpose of the document is to provide a high-level, executive overview of Oceania Creative Print and Interactive business plan for the year 2001-2005. This document is to be used as information and business planning purposes in attaining a second round of credit-based capital.

## Description of the Business

Oceania Creative is in the business of providing premium consulting, brand communications, and visual design services.

## Mission

The Oceania mission is simple. Oceania will provide consulting and graphic production services to selected prospect clients primarily in the manufacturing industry.

## Vision

Through the application of knowledge, business relationships, and effective service delivery and continued success of Oceania clients, we will become recognized as a premier industry provider of communications services.

## Business Problem

The manufacturing industry, particularly, old-line heavy equipment, agricultural, and transportation have difficult business issues related to high-end communications services.

In the manufacturing environment, companies are striving to be competitive in all aspects of manufacturing. This means processes and technology must work together harmoniously and must be integrated. Even world-class companies have found many improvement opportunities in communications processes and market perceptions.

Communications services supported by proven concepts, tools, and methodologies by our experienced designers and consultants, our process accommodates the client's needs. Our communications and marketing experts help the client manage operational change and focus on integrated resource management.

We are committed to creative concepts and tangible results, evaluation, and continuous improvement. With the client's leadership, OC's business approach helps them achieve their vision of world-class market communications.

Examples of our service offerings:

- Communications consulting
- Brand management
- Customized executive sales event specialties
- Traditional graphic design services
- Internet/web-based design and production services

Benefits of using Oceania Services:

- Increased market responsiveness
- Increased customer retention
- Improved brand management and leveragability
- Improved communications processes and decision making
- Improved market awareness

Target prospect market companies include the following list of companies with primary locations and/or headquarters based in the Midwest. The Midwest is defined as a six-state area including, Michigan, Ohio, Indiana, Illinois, Wisconsin, and northern Kentucky. The states of Minnesota and Missouri will be considered a secondary market due to time, travel, and budgetary requirements in pursuing business in these areas. However, for the right prospect with the right project, with the right level of revenue commitment, we will consider investing in pursuing the business in that geographic area.

Target companies listed below are primary targets:

- Tier one automotive suppliers
- Tier two automotive suppliers
- Diversified chemical and industrial suppliers
- Diversified financial and insurance services providers
- Food and food services companies (over $500 million revenue)

**Market Size**

The current market size analysis, based on identified prospects and selected categories of current and projected spending, has estimated this market at more than $750 million in current communications spending.

*Note: Detailed industry and analysis methodology information available on request.*

**Revenue Model**

Oceania revenue will be based on client needs and market competitive service rates.

Examples of client billing models include:

- Project-based fixed price agreements
- Consulting (one-time and ongoing brand leadership services)
- Design and production services (project and ongoing design maintenance)

**COMPANY TEAM**

Expected margins are estimated at 30-35 percent for graphic production services and 50-65 percent for consulting services. Production services are required to align our companies with client to provide ongoing management and design services to carry projects from concept to delivery.

The Oceania team is comprised of seasoned design, consulting, and management professionals. Experience is our hallmark. The Oceania team has an average of 10 years of experience in communications, marketing, and related disciplines, and 12 years in professional brand and executive communications strategy consulting experience.

Each team member brings industry relationships. Oceania has an expectation of its sales and consulting personnel to leverage these relationships in a meaningful manner and to demonstrate a direct relationship to revenue contributions.

We intend to continue to compensate our entire team with an outstanding package of ongoing salary with individually based bonus and fringe packages. These packages will be based on performance and return to the Oceania enterprise, primarily revenue-based packages for sales professionals and relationship-expansion-based incentives for our consulting professionals.

*Note: Professional profiles available on request.*

**Market Awareness**

We plan to achieve industry and client recognition and establish a market reputation by providing superior service delivery and enabling business performance for our clients. Achieving our strategic vision will play a major role in our long-term success and ongoing profitability.

**Community Involvement**

Oceania Creative will play an active role in community-based organizations to support important arts-based programs as well as continued involvement in business-based professional organizations. Participation in community and business organizations is critical to business success and employee satisfaction. We are actively researching and engaging leading organizations to determine which organizations will best serve the goals of the community at large, our organization, and associated business community partners.

The following is a short list of professional organizations we have sponsored or have participated in.

- American Institute of Graphic Arts
- American Marketing Association
- Direct Marketing Association
- Executive Men's Clubs
- Executive Women's Clubs
- Executive Golf Organizations

**COMPETITIVE LANDSCAPE**

Each year competition in this market space gets stronger and stronger. Our competitive advantage will be our superior service delivery and client satisfaction; however, in this environment it may not be enough. Thus our focus on leveraging industry and client relationships will become tantamount to continued revenue growth.

This market has a unique competitive model. Companies we will compete against in our day-to-day operations and sales pursuit will range from 3-person high-level consultant partnerships to established, multimillion-dollar advertising agencies such as Ogilvy and business management consultancies such as Accenture and Deloitte & Touche. However, members of our team will exercise high-level relationships particularly with the business management consultancies. Our leadership team has participated with these organizations within high-level engagements—a true win/win environment for revenue generation.

**Success to Date**

Oceania has had many successful engagements and client experiences to date. Two of which address attainment of strategic intent.

**Tangible Results**

**Client Acquisition**
Over the first 16 months of our business operations, Oceania has engaged 35 companies at the Senior Manager through Vice President level with business engagements resulting from 15 percent of those pursued relationships. This has resulted in a 50 percent win rate for sales pursuits.

**Market Awareness**
Recently, our company has been asked to participate as speakers at several communications/marketing/design industry conferences. Attaining speaker-level positioning at these conferences is a preliminary indicator or our success in achieving market-leading (top-of-mind) executive perceptions.

**Organizational results**

Over the past 18 months we believe we have assembled a team of 18 highly focused, nimble professionals. Our continued success will be predicated on the basis of our ability to work comprehensively as a team with a high degree of individual performance successes.

All financial projections are estimates and further detailed information and individual services-level reporting are outlined in additional documentation. All financial expectations are based on current level of success, sales performance, and a robust economic environment. A five-year expansion in the U.S. economy has contributed to a robust environment for communications services. This economic environment cannot be predicted or expected for years upcoming. All dollars are listed in millions.

**PROJECTED 5-YEAR FINANCIALS**

| *Pre-2000 not reflected* | 2000 | 2001 | 2002 | 2003 | 2004 | 2005 | Total |
|---|---|---|---|---|---|---|---|
| **Revenue** | | | | | | | |
| Consulting | 1.0 | 2.0 | 3.2 | 5.5 | 7.5 | 10.2 | 29.4 |
| Production services | 1.2 | 1.7 | 2.3 | 3.1 | 4.0 | 5.5 | 17.8 |
| Other creative services | 0.5 | 1.2 | 2.5 | 3.0 | 3.5 | 4.0 | 14.7 |
| **Total Revenue** | **2.7** | **4.9** | **8.0** | **11.6** | **15.0** | **19.7** | **61.9** |
| | | | | | | | |
| **Expenses** | | | | | | | |
| Professional and business operations salary/compensation | 1.5 | 2.2 | 3.2 | 4.5 | 5.7 | 6.7 | 23.8 |
| Facilities/comm/equip. | 1.0 | 1.5 | 2.0 | 2.5 | 3.0 | 3.5 | 13.5 |
| **Total Expenses** | **2.5** | **3.7** | **5.2** | **7.0** | **8.7** | **10.2** | **37.3** |
| | | | | | | | |
| **Total profit:** | **0.2** | **1.2** | **2.7** | **4.6** | **7.7** | **9.7** | **24.6** |

*Note #1: This table does not represent distribution of partner and investor profit distribution. Nor does it represent financial impact of financial institution operating capital interest.*

*All issues related to Note #1 shall be conducted in detail with written approval of officers on the company.*

# Dentist

BUSINESS PLAN

STANLEY M. KRAMER, DDS, LLC

*43110 Gillette Street*
*Omaha, Nebraska 68110*

*The goal of this business is to provide high quality general dentistry with a moderate to high price using the highest technology possible. Prices will be justified by the advanced technology used and the lifestyle conveniences that the dental practice will offer. The dental practice will be positioned as a place one can get high quality dental work in an environment of convenience and technology.*

- EXECUTIVE SUMMARY

- MARKETING PLAN

- OPERATIONAL & ORGANIZATIONAL PLAN

- FINANCIAL POLICY

- FINANCIAL PLAN

- FINANCIAL STATEMENTS

- POSSIBLE PITFALLS

- POSITIVE POINTS

- APPENDIX

## EXECUTIVE SUMMARY

I am preparing this business plan to discuss the dental practice that I am planning to purchase upon my graduation from dental school. Upon graduating, I will do an associateship with the potential for buyout, in a practice in Nebraska. This will allow me to spend one year determining if Nebraska is where I want to live long-term and will familiarize me with the practice that I could possibly buy. After the year is over, if I am pleased with what the practice has to offer, I will buy it. If I am not satisfied with its performance, I will have spent time researching other practices that are or will be going up for sale. After approximately a year of my building up the current client base, my father, who is also a dentist, is planning to move to Nebraska to work with me as an associate. He will sell his current home and practice and work for me until he decides to retire. This arrangement works in both my father's and my favor. This allows me to work with a dentist who has over 25 years of experience in the practice and business of dentistry. This gives my father an opportunity to make a comparable living to what he is currently making without the responsibilities of an entrepreneur. As he nears retirement (he is currently 52 years old), he will reduce his hours and patients.

In evaluating a location for a dental practice we are looking for an area of growth and culture, namely an affluent, western suburb of Omaha, Nebraska. We have chosen this general area for various reasons. The main reason being that we love all that this area has to offer in raising a family. Further we feel strongly about living in a location that you would also desire to spend your retirement in. The suburbs of Omaha are growing rapidly and do not have enough dentists to meet the needs of the people. I plan to buy a practice in a highly traveled, suburban area of Omaha that has the patient and facility capacity for two active dentists. In 1995, almost 20 percent of all private dental practices were two-dentist practices, so this should not be too difficult to find ("Key Dental Facts," p. 17). Working with the retiring dentist will allow me to learn his practice management style and to foster a relationship with the client base. This is very important, as with many businesses, the client list and work force is the most valuable asset of a dental practice. Also this affords me the opportunity to understand the management philosophy of the past dentist, so I will be able to make gradual changes that do not cause too much dissension from the staff. If a dental practice with capacity for two dentists cannot be found, I will buy a single practice office and expand it to suit two dentists. I will use savings accumulated during my year as an associate to pay for the down payment of the business loan and finance the business through a bank, the Small Business Administration, or through a broker.

My father should not have great difficulty selling his practice, as his is the largest practice in the area. Also, there are dental brokers that buy practices to sell them at a higher price. In the worst-case scenario, my father could sell his practice to one of these brokers.

## Company Description

## Purpose of the Service

My goal is to provide high quality general dentistry with a moderate to high price using the highest technology possible. My prices will be justified by the advanced technology used and the lifestyle conveniences that the dental practice will offer. The dental practice will be positioned as a place one can get high quality dental work in an environment of convenience and technology. Due to the increase in two-income families, many service-oriented professions are leaning toward differentiating themselves on the basis of convenience. This is what I intend to do when I have completely taken over this business from its previous owner and have hired an associate, namely my father. For instance, we plan to have two shifts, an early morning shift and an evening shift in which the practice will be fully functional from 7 A.M. to 7 P.M. or later on various days of the week. We also plan to work rotating weekends to offer Saturday service twice a month. We feel that the main beneficiaries to these services are professional, high-income individuals that do not feel that they can take time out from work to go to the dentist. We are also considering hiring part-time help to do filing and various other work during the day and to act as a sitter so that parents can leave their kids while they are receiving dental care.

Possible related services include:

- Tooth Whitening
- Smoking Abstainment Treatments
- Practice Management Seminars
- Dental School Instruction
- Tempromanibular Joint Disorder Treatment
- Implant services
- Free screenings for children in severely/profoundly retarded care centers and schools
- Having a yearly "Sealant Day" and "Dental Awareness Day" at local grade schools
- Nursing home screenings

**Related Services and Spin-offs**

Stanley M. Kramer, DDS, LLC is still in the idea stage as I will not have my dental license until August 2001 and my father has not actively looked for a purchaser for his practice. Between now and when I graduate, I plan to accept a position with a retiring dentist with a contract giving me first option to buy the practice.

**Stage of Development**

A restrictive covenant will be included in my contract with the former dentist. This non-competitive clause will ensure that the dentist does not sell me the practice and then set up a practice next door. It also ensures that I do not work with the dentist and then set up a practice down the street using the patient base I have seen while working with him. Further, we will not participate in any HMOs or Managed Care Insurance, as it is my belief that these cost dentists more than it makes them and reduces their treatment alternatives (see Appendix).

**Service Limitations**

In June 2001, after passing the Central Regional Dental Test required by the American Dental Association, I will receive a license to practice dentistry in the central region of the United States, which includes Nebraska. My father has already applied for and received his Nebraska license. The practice will apply for any applicable city, county, or township licenses that apply, a Drug Enforcement Agency permit to prescribe controlled substances, and any applicable licenses for such items as administration of general anesthesia or conscious sedation. Compliance with the Occupational Safety and Health Association (OSHA) standards set by the previous owner must be maintained.

**Government Approvals**

I will purchase malpractice insurance to protect myself against any malpractice suits raised. Even the best, most conscientious dentist can be sued; therefore, malpractice insurance is an essential part of dentistry. The type of malpractice or professional liability insurance I will buy is an occurrence policy. If the policy would expire before a claim arises, the insurance company will still defend the dentist and pay any settlement or court-awarded judgement that occurred while the policy was in force that does not exceed the limits of the policy. Disability insurance provides continuing income in the event that an injury or illness prevents me from practicing. Adequate amounts of disability income and medical expense insurance will be maintained to cover the costs of treatment and ongoing family expenses until re-entry into active practice is

**Service Liability**

possible. The insurer will require proof that you are in good health, as no company will cover potentially disabling conditions present prior to the date coverage is issued. It is essential that I purchase as much non-term type disability insurance as possible while I am young and healthy—waiting until I am older could cause me to be uninsurable or cause my premiums to be astronomical. I will also carry business liability and property insurance and any other insurance we deem necessary after receiving counsel from my lawyer and insurance agent. Health insurance and workers' compensation will be provided for our employees and myself as part of their benefit package. We feel that this is mandatory to ensure that they do not leave the practice for one that does offer these benefits.

## MARKETING PLAN

### Current Market Size & Growth Potential

The dental profession is one with a very low failure rate and a high propensity for profit. These were two areas I examined before selecting a profession. According to the American Dental Association (ADA), dental offices are the third highest-ranking category of start-up business most likely to survive. The average income of a dentist is in the highest 8 percent of U.S. family income. As the growing population becomes better educated and more wealthy, people demand better dental care ("Starting Your Dental Practice," p. 4). Annual spending for dental services has risen from $13.3 to $45.8 billion, an increase of 244.4 percent, from 1980 to 1995 ("Key Dental Facts," p. 8). The advancements in cosmetic dentistry provide new venues of service for the general dentist to offer. Also, with the increase in non-capitation dental insurance, many people who could not previously afford dental work are now part of the patient pool. Of the total population over the age of 2, 40.5 percent are covered by private dental insurance. Sixty percent of those with dental insurance have an annual income of $35,000 or more and 51.4 percent have an education level of 13 or more years. Also, 45.4 percent of all American children ages 5-17 are covered by dental insurance ("Key Dental Facts," p. 9).

The average dentist to patient ratio is 1 to 1,600-1,700 ("Starting Your Dental Practice," 9). Nebraska as a state has a ratio of 1 to 2050 and an expected population growth of 11 percent by the year 2001. Further, 21 percent of the general dentists in Nebraska are over 55 years old and many are looking to sell their practices and retire. Nebraska is a very educated state with 24.9 percent of its residents having a college degree and over 75 percent of its residents working in white-collar positions. The average household income in Nebraska was $34,938 in 1996 and is projected to increase by 10.8 percent by the year 2001 to $41,328 (ADA County Reports).

**Various demographic profiles in Nebraska:**

| | Nebraska | Douglas County | Washington County | Cass County | Saunders County | Sarpy County |
|---|---|---|---|---|---|---|
| Population in 1996 | 3,833,144 | 459,920 | 499,680 | 18,021 | 493,656 | 310,568 |
| 1990 to 1996 Population Growth Rate | 16.4 | 17.5 | 6.9 | 39.9 | 12.6 | 17.2 |
| Projected Population by 2001 | 4,251,171 | 513,189 | 522,617 | 22,141 | 535,764 | 345,977 |
| 1996 to 2001 Projected Population Growth Rate | 10.9 | 11.6 | 4.6 | 22.8 | 8.5 | 11.4 |
| Median Household Income 1996 | 28,087 | 42,033 | 28,409 | 39,450 | 43,330 | 33,045 |
| Average Household Income 1996 | 34,938 | 53,177 | 38,343 | 45,372 | 50,797 | 38,409 |
| % Change in Number of Active Dentists in area | 3.9 | 1.6 | -2.1 | 37.5 | -2.8 | 37 |
| Total Number of General Dentists | 1,869 | 251 | 322 | 10 | 256 | 105 |
| General Dentists Under 35 | 224 | 33 | 36 | 2 | 29 | 17 |
| General Dentists 35 to 44 | 644 | 115 | 108 | 2 | 85 | 41 |
| General Dentists 45 to 54 | 611 | 69 | 85 | 4 | 83 | 29 |
| General Dentists 55 to 64 | 267 | 21 | 60 | 2 | 36 | 13 |
| General Dentists over 65 | 123 | 13 | 33 | 0 | 23 | 5 |
| Patients per Dentist ratio 1996 | 2051 | 1832 | 1552 | 1802 | 1928 | 2958 |
| Number of dentists that will be in retiring age within next 10 years | 1001 | 103 | 178 | 6 | 142 | 47 |
| % of dentists that will be in retiring age within next 10 years | 54 | 41 | 55 | 60 | 55 | 45 |

**Customer Profile**

- Middle to high income
- College educated
- White collar
- Married with children
- All ages
- Two-income families

**Target Market**

- Current patients of the practice we purchase (2,500 to 3,000 patients)
- Professionals that need the convenience factors we will offer
- Stay-at-home mothers that need a place to keep their children while they receive dental work
- All other dental patients who will pay a premium for convenience

**Customer Benefits**

Various customer benefits include:

- Two highly skilled dentists to be treated by, one with over 25 years of experience and the other with the boundless energy and enthusiasm of a recent graduate
- Extended hours on various nights of the week
- Saturday hours two times a month
- Childcare while receiving dental work
- Use of advanced technology in treatment and patient education
- Discounts for referrals

**Market Penetration**

Current patients of the practice purchased will receive letters of notification of the change in practice ownership and management. I will give my background and experience information and tell the patient that I hope to maintain their business. I will set up a "Meet the Doctor" picnic, where all patients will be invited. We will also offer free family consultations to discuss any concerns the patient might have. We will also advertise our benefits in the local papers and telephone books and send out direct-mail information advertising our practice. Current patients will be given referral cards that give both the current patient and patient referred a discount for services after the new patient has received a cleaning and consultation. Advertisements will be taken out in the local paper promoting discounts on whitening procedures. Once the patient comes in for whitening, I will sit down with the patient and discuss other ways to improve the aesthetics of their teeth. If they like the service that they are given, they may become patients or at least give good word-of-mouth advertisement. Other incentives will be given to attract new patients and maintain current ones.

**Internal Marketing**

The goal of Internal Marketing is to make current patients continue their patronage and to encourage them to refer our services. This can be done by first and foremost treating them with respect. This office will also give each patient the highest quality dental treatment possible, while offering competitive prices. Treatment is to be presented to patients by the doctor only. Treatment will be presented by encouraging the patient to ask questions and asking open-ended questions to prompt discussion. Visual aids will be used when necessary and intraoral pictures will also be utilized. A benefit for the patient will be given to help them see the need for treatment (i.e. "So that tooth doesn't fracture further and cause you more expense and pain, I recommend we start a crown on that tooth as soon as possible.").

To stimulate referrals from existing patients at the end of the dental appointment we stress to them their importance in our dental office and request that they refer family and friends to our office. In order to maintain a strong patient base and retain active patients, a patient should have either a restorative appointment and recall appointment or be in the recall system to call on a specific month for a specific procedure. Various other ways to promote our office to already active clients and induce them to refer our practice to others include:

- Be on time and if you cannot, personally apologize to the patient for any inconveniences this has caused him or her
- Greet patients by name (both dentist and staff)
- Install a music system
- Have multiple telephone lines
- Call patients at home after significant treatment to ensure patient is doing well
- Install a "good-bye" mirror so patients can check their appearance before leaving the office
- Offer coffee or other beverages
- Keep reading material current
- Provide referral cards which offers both the referring current patient and the new patient a discount of certain services
- Have personal information written on a notecard attached to chart to give dentist conversational topics
- Send a special note for occasions such as weddings, graduations, birthdays, etc.
- Decorate office internally and externally for holidays
- Have toys for children to play with
- Give patients magnets, toothbrushes, etc. with dental practice name and logo
- Give a picnic, barbecue, or other outdoor event during the summer for your patients

External Marketing deals with promoting the dental practice to potential patients. This can take the form of referrals, free publicity, or advertising. Examples of each of these are:

- Yellow page listing
- Send a welcome letter to new residents in community
- Run newspaper advertisements
- Become involved with local Chamber of Commerce
- Hold an open house event to show off new office, meet new staff, or celebrate the practice's anniversary
- Participate in career days for area students
- Get acquainted with community leaders
- Join civic, religious, and community organizations
- Patronize your patients' businesses
- Offer to write a monthly column on dental health issues or a Question/Answer column

For a detailed summary of industry trends, refer to the industry analysis included in the Appendix.

- Decrease in dentists participating in managed care organizations
- Increase in consolidation or networking of practices
- Retirement of baby boomer dentists causing a future shortage in dentists
- Increase in gross profits for dental practices
- Globalization of the dental industry
- Advancements in technology and invention of products that aid in treatment

The philosophy of my dental practice will be to provide high quality general dentistry in a comfortable setting, with a moderate to high price using the highest technology possible. Prices will be justified by the advanced technology used and the lifestyle conveniences that the dental practice will offer. With use of an interactive, multi-media educational system, I will present my patients with multiple treatment alternatives and let them choose the alternative that best suits their lifestyle and budget. I will emphasize preventative dentistry and continually suggest cosmetic procedures. Any dental work that is too complex to be treated at my practice will be referred out to a specialist. I will foster a relationship with various specialists in the area, so they will refer patients in need of general dentistry to me as well. Further, I will not participate in any capitation insurance, as it is my feeling that these plans cost dentists more than it makes them.

The dental practice will be positioned as a place to get high quality dental work in an environment of convenience and technology. Due to the increase in two-income families, many service-oriented professions are leaning toward differentiating themselves on the basis of convenience. This is what I intend to do. For instance, I plan to have flexible, "people" hours on various days of the week so that not all patients have to leave work to have their dental work done. I also plan to work rotating weekends to offer Saturday service twice a month. I feel that the main beneficiaries to these services are professional, high-income individuals that do not feel that they can take time out from work to go to the dentist. We are also considering hiring part-time help to do filing and various other work during the day and to act as a sitter so that parents can leave their kids while they are receiving dental care.

The office will be run as a team, with each employee playing an integral part in the success or failure of the business. Employees will be given whatever tools and training is deemed necessary to carry out their assignments. An emphasis on process improvement will be instilled in each of the "teammates" by offering bonuses or special privileges. Teammates will be rewarded both monetarily and non-monetarily for jobs well done. Effective communication will be stressed in the office. This will cut down on misunderstandings and miscommunications among patients, employees, and doctor. Weekly meetings will be held to discuss the weekly agenda, and to give a report of last week's happenings. Teammates will be given the opportunity to add input at these meetings in the form of suggestions, comments, and complaints. Teammates will have defined tasks, but are to be open to doing whatever requests outside of their set guidelines need to be done to bring success to the practice. Finally, I plan to offer many perks to my employees to keep them satisfied and willing to give the practice 100 percent.

## Job Description— Dentist

1. The Dentist is responsible for all procedures that are covered by his license and not those of the hygienist and assistant.
2. The Dentist is responsible for all human resource aspects of the practice.
3. The Dentist is responsible for the management aspects of the practice.
4. The Dentist will form a relationship with both the clients and staff.
5. All major purchases or decisions must receive final authorization from the doctor.
6. The Dentist will sign all checks.
7. The Dentist will be punctual to all appointments. Should the case arise where he cannot see the patient on time, he will personally apologize to the patient for any inconvenience.
8. The Dentist will call all patients receiving significant treatment the night of the appointment to ensure that the patient is doing well.
9. The Dentist will join civic and religious organizations to be of benefit to the community.
10. The Dentist will actively, yet with taste, market the practice.
11. The Dentist will treat employees and patients in a fair and unbiased manner.
12. The Dentist will provide high quality dental work with an emphasis on technology and education for himself, his staff, and his customers.
13. The Dentist will work to make the practice an enjoyable environment in which to work

## Job Description— Assistant

1. Study and become familiar with Office Philosophy and agreements in the office.
2. Be observant, and considerate, friendly and generally in good humor. Make patients feel at ease and welcome as a guest in your facility.
3. Upon arriving in the morning, get prepared for the day prior to the morning meeting.
   a. Set up trays
   b. Check treatment room drawers, stock as needed.
5. Go through charts and review the treatment patients are scheduled for today and treatment pending. At this time always check what type of anesthesia each patient will need. Be prepared to discuss charts at morning meeting.
6. Greet patient in reception room and escort to proper treatment room.
7. Seat patients, desensitize areas of treatment, take necessary study models, prepare Rx blanks, select shades for composites and PFMs, take impressions for temps, mark and adjust temps, remove cement from temps, orthodontic bands and crown and bridges; place matrix bands, and perform other procedures to prepare patient for doctor as instructed by the doctor.
8. Be with the doctor to assist with all treatment.
9. Give patients POST treatment instructions as needed (orally and/or written).
10. Complement the dentistry procedures performed by the doctor. Show the patients their case before and after the insertion in the mouth.
11. Dismiss patient and escort them to the front desk with chart. If the business office is busy ask the patient to have a seat in the reception room. The business coordinator will be with them ASAP.

12. Compliment the behavior of a child to the child and the parent. This helps to child be more confident.
13. Spray and clean room after each patient; change headrest cover, light handles, etc. Follow all sterilization procedures as mandated by OSHA.
14. Prepare all instruments and handpieces for sterilization by autoclave or cold sterilization.
15. Close all treatment rooms at the end of the day. Make sure all equipment is shut off.
16. Have a general knowledge of the business office and be familiar with business office verbal skills.
17. Know how to schedule appointments.
18. Do a bi-weekly inventory and order necessary items.
19. Prepare and participate in weekly staff meeting.
20. Study and become familiar with all OSHA requirements. Take all precautions as trained and have a completed HBV vaccination series. Wear protective equipment as required.

## Duties to Perform As Needed

- Take, develop, and mount x-rays
- Record any x-rays taken in chart, type name and date on label
- Prepare Rx blanks of Meds
- Take diagnostic cast and pour in proper stone
- Trim models and label
- Keep lab cases labeled and organized
- Clean cement from newly cemented PFM, FGC, temps, etc.
- Place matrix bands and wedges
- Make vacuforms
- Make customtrays
- Make temp crown
- Remove and place orthodontic elastics
- Calm apprehensive patients
- Keep current with up-to-date dentistry
- Check supplies and keep inventory current
- Help business office when time permits
- Empty the trash
- Stock drawers
- Run cleaner through the vacuum system each night.
- Lubricate drills
- All other reasonable requests by the doctor

## Daily Duties

1. Check level of water in autoclave and add, if needed
2. Run autoclave during day as needed
3. Oil and autoclave handpieces after each patient
4. Oil prophy handpieces daily
5. Check trash at the end of the day and empty if needed
6. General operatory cleaning
7. Take intraoral pictures as needed
8. Prepare charts for morning meeting
9. Check developer reservoir tanks and refill
10. Prepare trays for procedures and assist doctor

**Weekly Duties**

1. Change solutions in ultrasonic cleaner
2. Autoclave lab burs
3. Clean autoclave per manufacturer's instructions for weekly maintenance
4. Restock all drawers and check inventory

**Job Description—
Dental Hygienist**

1. Study and become familiar with Office Philosophy and Agreements in the office.
2. Organize yourself physically, mentally, and emotionally, always dress in a professional manner, leave your private and family concerns at home, and make a mental check of your day.
3. Be observant, considerate, friendly, and generally in good humor. Make patients feel at ease and welcome as a guest in your facility.
4. Upon arriving in the morning, get prepared for the day prior to the morning meeting.
5. Go through charts, review the treatment patients are scheduled for today and treatment pending. At this time always check what type of anesthesia each patient will need. Be prepared to discuss charts at morning meeting.
6. Greet patient in reception room and escort to proper treatment room.
7. Use correct verbal skills.
8. Dismiss patient; escort to front desk with chart. If business coordinator is busy ask patient to have a seat in reception room. Business coordinator will be with ASAP.
9. Spray and clean room after each patient, change headrest cover, light handles, etc. Follow all sterilization procedures as mandated by OSHA.
10. Prepare all your instruments and handpieces for sterilization by autoclave or cold sterilization.
11. Close your treatment room at the end of the day, making sure all equipment is shut off.
12. Have a general knowledge of the business office and be familiar with business office procedures.
13. Know how to schedule an appointment on the computer.
14. Prepare and participate in weekly staff meetings.
15. Take all OSHA precautions as trained, have a completed HBV vaccination series. Wear protective equipment as required.
16. The dental hygienist may not perform any of the clinical duties without the dentist in the facility.
17. Help to maintain and keep the recall system current.

**Clinical Duties**

1. Polish restoration.
2. Perform root planing and soft tipsier curettage.
3. Apply topical anesthetics and topical medicaments.
4. Record existing conditions through the use of radiographs.
5. Perform intraoral dental laboratory tests, including but not limited to, oral cytology smears, pulp vitality test, and caries tests.
6. Apply pit and fissure sealant to teeth, as prescribed by the dentist.
7. Do intraoral irrigation and sulcular irrigation.
8. Remove overhanging margins without the use of rotary instruments.
9. Oral prophylaxis with slow speed handpiece.
10. Give topical fluoride application.
11. Complete all other reasonable requests from doctor.

1. Organize yourself physically, mentally, and emotionally; always dress in a professional manner; leave your private and family concerns at home, and make a mental check of your day.
2. Study and become familiar with office philosophy and agreements in the office.
3. Be observant, considerate, friendly, and generally in good humor. Make patients feel at ease and welcome as guest in our facility.

## Appointment Scheduling

1. Set appointment hours in accordance with appointment scheduling guidelines and daily goals.
2. See that the dental hygiene schedule is completely filled.
3. Follow up on all broken appointments.
4. Keep a short call list.
5. Fill broken and canceled appointments.
6. Confirm patient's appointments at least 2 days prior to appointment date.
7. Copy the daily schedule and post it in each treatment room.
8. Greet all patients courteously when arriving and make sure the charts are in the proper place.
9. Promptly indicate to the staff when the next patient has arrived.
10. See that the phone is answered before the third ring at all times.
11. See that the desk is covered at all times.
12. Complete all other reasonable requests from doctor.

## Financial Control

1. Check records each day to approach any patients who owe a balance.
2. Take responsibility for requesting and collecting money "over the counter" daily.
3. See that each record is posted and filed as it comes through. Be responsible for the accuracy of the day sheet and records.
4. Print and submit insurance for patients when appropriate.
5. Make financial arrangements with patients in accordance with the financial policy
6. Follow up on all insurance not paid within 6 weeks. Maintain the insurance system.
7. Send monthly statements.
8. Follow up on past due accounts; set arrangements for past due balances. Make collection calls and send accounts to collections with doctor's approval.
9. See that each payment received in the mail is posted to the accounts receivable system. Be responsible for the accuracy of the accounts receivable system.
10. See that the bank deposit slip matches the daysheet total.
11. Make definite financial arrangements with all new patients and patients requiring extensive treatment in accordance with the financial policy of the office.
12. Work the delinquent payment record.
13. Be in charge of all correspondence regarding collections, insurance, etc.
14. Determine approximate patient portion of insurance procedures.
15. Notify patients of overpayments and send refunds.

## Marketing

1. Keep the new patient book current
2. Prepare new patient letters for Dr. Kramer
3. Tank referral sources, letters, etc.

**Office Procedures**

1. Be responsible for the preventive maintenance system (recall system).
2. Be responsible for preventive maintenance follow-up.
3. Organize and maintain file systems for quick retrieval of information.
4. See that all backlog paperwork is completed before closing the office on Friday.
5. Maintain the supply system and inventory for business office items.
6. Keep Dr. Kramer informed and current on all aspects of the office, patient status, recommendations, etc.
7. Be responsible for own desk appearance.
8. Put together new patients' records and charts. Coordinate patient flow.
9. As changes occur in schedule, change schedules in the treatment rooms.
10. Check and straighten the reception area.

## Job Description— Janitorial Staff

The janitorial staff is an outside agency that comes in one day per week and cleans the office. They are responsible for:

- Vacuuming the entire office
- Mopping floors
- Cleaning the bathroom (sink and toilet)
- Washing exterior and interior windows, mirrors, etc.
- Emptying trash
- Dusting shelves and countertops
- Cleaning out operatory sinks and lab sinks

All other maintenance of the dental equipment is the responsibility of the office staff.

## Infrastructure Members

**Accountant:** to prepare tax returns and advise on various practice financial decisions. $50 to $100/hour.

**Lawyer:** to help with start up legalities and incorporation, to act as representation in case of litigation and to advise on various business decisions. $75 to $150/hour depending on experience with dental practices.

**Insurance Agent:** for malpractice and liability insurance. Commissions only.

## FINANCIAL POLICY

### Third-Party Insurance Policies

This office does not and never will participate in capitation and/or reduced fee-for-service programs. Any phone calls, mail, or solicitors for such plans are to be turned away. Patients who have non-capitation insurance will be required to have an insurance card and the insurance company must be called and verified before they are considered for assignment of benefits. Once a patient has been verified, the following information needs to be retrieved from the insurance company: address to mail claims to; deductibles, if any, and what they apply to; excluded treatments (i.e. crowns are not covered); if the payments are usual and customary or fee schedule; and if prophys are limited per year. All this information can be provided to the patients as needed.

Assignment of benefits will be taken again, only if verification has been approved. Otherwise, the patient is considered "cash paying" until verification can be established.

Patients who receive treatment with insurance will be told up front (before treatment begins) as to their estimated portion of the bill. That portion is due on the date of service; no exceptions are to be given. Patients need to be aware that the amount they are paying is an estimated portion based on what their insurance has told us, and if insurance does not pay or pays less, they are responsible for the balance. We gladly process insurance forms for patients. Insurance claims are to be submitted each day as the charges are posted. Narratives and X-rays need to be mailed with larger claims and all crown and bridge cases. Periodontal charting should be sent with all periodontal cases.

Claims are to be filed in duplicate. One copy goes to the insurance company and one is filed by month and in ABC order. As claims are paid, the EOB (explanation of benefits) is to be attached to our copy and filed in a separate file under "paid claims" for that month. Claims not paid within 5 weeks must be called on and proper steps taken to expedite payment. Also, Visa and Mastercard will be accepted. For treatment plans of considerable amounts, we will help the patient file for financing through a bank.

**Financial Arrangements**

1. A 5 percent discount is given to patients whose treatment plan is over $250 and pay cash up front.
2. If a patient needs to come back 5 times to complete a $1,000 treatment plan, then payments would be $200 each visit.
3. Treatment plans under $250 are expected on the day of service.
4. Any other arrangements must be made directly through Dr. Kramer.

**Appointment Philosophy and Procedures**

The appointment book is the map of our day and is to be used in a specific manner. All procedures have been timed and a schedule of times is attached to the schedule book. Only in instances that Dr. Kramer or the hygienist request additional time are these guidelines to be changed.

1. Always try and fill the schedule to capacity and keep a short call list.
2. The schedule is also to be filled to our daily production goals.
3. Patients that cancel less than 24 hours in advance or no-show are to be warned the first time and charged a $25 fee the second time.

**FINANCIAL PLAN**

The practice will be set up as a Limited Liability Company (LLC). This will be done to receive the limited liability of a corporation with the option of selecting taxation as either a partnership or as a corporation. Upon counsel with my lawyer and accountant, I will decide which setup offers me the best result in regards to taxes.

I am looking at a practice worth approximately $250,000. One shortcut method to determine the selling price of a practice is to take the average of the last three years gross sales and divide it by two. To purchase the practice I will take out a $300,000 ten-year loan at a negotiable rate (I used 15 percent in my financials) that gives me the opportunity of renewal every three years and has no penalty for early repayment. I am estimating that $250,000 will go for the practice, $30,000 will be used for any start-up costs (such as updates to building or equipment), and the remaining $20,000 will be used to maintain positive cash flows at start-up and to be used in case of any unforeseen problems. I don't foresee any problems attaining a loan, as there are many brokerage companies that will fully finance your dental practice with no down payment if you can prove that there will be no significant decline in gross sales resulting from the purchase of the practice. Another financing possibility is that the current owner of the practice could seller-finance some or the entire sales price. This would allow 100 percent financing without titled collateral, but would preclude a higher than market rate. Similarly, a dental broker could finance the project with the same general benefits and drawbacks of the seller-finance option.

Also, we could approach a bank for the loan, which will generally ask for a 20 percent down payment, titled collateral, and an aggressive amortization rate, but a lower interest rate than the other options.

In doing my financial statements, I have had to make many assumptions and use many numbers, averages, and percentages given by the American Dental Association (ADA). Some of the numbers seem either too high or too low, but I used them to maintain consistency. For instance, in the first five years of business, marketing and legal/professional costs will probably be higher than the national average. I think that insurance will be much higher than the amount attained by using the percentage given by the ADA. Also, the average patient charge per patient includes dentists who do all of their own hygiene work, dentists who accept capitation insurance, and dentists who do public health dentistry only. Therefore, the $183.56 national average as stated by the ADA seems very low.

The number of total employees the practice will have upon my purchase is dependent on the structure prior to my buyout. My first year in practice, I will need one full-time assistant and one full-time bookkeeper/receptionist. Until I feel I have a sufficient client base, I will do much of my hygiene work. One hygienist will work one or two days a week dependent upon need and on a percent of work completed basis. This will give the hygienist greater incentive to see more patients and to insure the recall system works efficiently. Building the patient base to have enough patients to allow for two dentists will take about a year and a half. Optimal full-time employment upon my father joining the practice is two full-time assistants, one full-time bookkeeper/receptionist, and one hygienist with the same conditions. After the larger client base has been established, which will probably take about a year of working with my father, another hygienist will be added so that there will be a hygienist in the office four days a week and my father and I will not need to see any hygiene patients which will make our per patient charge increase. If need arises, one part-time office helper will be employed.

As we will be living in the central region of the United States, I have used the wage rates quoted in the *Journal of the American Dental Association* for dental employees in that region. Median hourly salary for a receptionist/bookkeeper is $11.65/hour. The average hourly wage for an experienced chairside assistant is $11.00. Finally, a hygienist in the central area will make around $200 a day. This sounds like a lot, but hygienists often rotate between practices as to support a broader client base.

My father and I will discuss a contract whereby he receives a certain percentage of his gross production, probably 40 percent the first year. With working the same hours per week that he currently does and seeing fewer patients, he will make a comparable salary to what he pays himself in Lincoln. Lincoln is a farming and industrial community that does not see the benefits of the highly profitable aesthetic dentistry. Although my father has the largest practice in the area, he does not make as much money as comparable practices in more educated areas due to the demand for restorative dentistry only. Working for Stanley allows his father, Jeremiah, to make as much money as he wants, while only working the amount of hours that suits his lifestyle. Also, he will not have the risk or responsibility associated with running a business, but will have significant input, as he has so many years of practice experience. The money he will make by selling his practice can be invested to use in his retirement.

We will establish written bylaws that address issues such as how the relationship between my father and I will be handled. As my parents will probably help with a small portion of the down payment on the loan, both my mother and father will receive a percentage of profits based on their contribution. The other portion of ownership will be divided between my wife and myself. We will have guidelines on buying back and selling ownership shares. This is to ensure the business does not suffer from problems within the family.

My family is a very close one that is intent on building our futures together. We have held many discussions concerning the control and management of the practice and are in agreement to this point. Before my father actually decides to move and sell his practice, we will sit down and write up an agreement about practice management. We will have a lawyer that is familiar with dental practices and family businesses look it over and add suggestions. Me and my wife will have the final say in matters pertaining to the practice, as we will have a greater share of ownership. As I have not had as much experience managing a practice, my parents' input will be greatly appreciated and sought. A policy of mutual respect between the four of us and documented policies will make our working relationship as positive as our personal one.

My first year after buying the practice, I will be able to see about seven patients per day and will work five days a week. The average cost per patient visit is $183.56 for a normal solo practice. Using these numbers, I should have an average monthly gross income of $25,000 and first-year gross income of approximately $275,000 based on having four weeks' vacation. My client base should be somewhere around 2,000 to 2,500 (a small drop from initial patient base) active patients, and I expect to exceed the average growth rate of 32 new patients per month for new dentists. I should have patient capacity for my father within two years. My financial statements assume that Dr. Jeremiah Kramer will join the practice after two years. I have also included income statements that show the practice's standings if my father and my dream of working together does not become a reality. Note: the practice still garners a reasonable profit, but not nearly as significant as the one earned with both dentists practicing. An exit strategy has not yet been planned, as this business will be the main source of income for my father for many years. When my father decides to retire, I will either hire another associate or rent out his facility to another doctor or specialist.

Customers will be charged the going industry price for the geographic area of practice plus a premium for the convenience-based value-added services. An example of a price list for services from the May 1996 issue of *Dental Economics* for the central region is as follows. We will use prices similar to these plus a premium for some treatments.

**Price List**

| | | | |
|---|---|---|---|
| Initial oral exam, adult—excluding radiographs | $27 | Inlay, porcelain, 1 surface | $344 |
| Comprehensive oral exam, adult | 38 | Full-cast, high-noble metal crown | 511 |
| Emergency oral exam | 31 | Porcelain fused to high-noble metal crown | 514 |
| Panoramic film | 48 | Porcelain fused to noble metal crown | 491 |
| Intraoral X-rays, complete series— including BWX | 59 | Prefabricated stainless-steel crown, permanent | 129 |
| BWX—four films | 28 | Cast post and core, in addition to crown | 159 |
| Intraoral, periapical, first film | 11 | Crown buildup, including any pins | 110 |
| Intraoral, periapical, each additional film | 9 | Replacement crown | 45 |
| Prophylaxis, adult | 44 | Labial veneer-laminate | 232 |
| Limited oral exam, problem-focused | 25 | Labial veneer (porcelain laminate)—lab | 415 |
| Initial oral exam, child | 24 | Complete upper denture | 694 |
| Prophylaxis, child | 30 | Complete lower denture | 696 |
| Fluoride, child-excluding prophylaxis | 17 | Upper denture reline, chairside | 146 |
| Periodic oral exam, child | 19 | Lower denture reline, chairside | 148 |
| Pit and fissure sealant, per tooth | 23 | Extraction, single tooth | 61 |

## Price List

*continued*

| | | | |
|---|---|---|---|
| Periodic oral exam, adult | 20 | One root canal, exclusive of restoration | 283 |
| BWX—two films | 19 | Two root canals, exclusive of restoration | 345 |
| Amalgam restoration, 1 surface, permanent | 55 | Three root canals, exclusive of restoration | 438 |
| Amalgam restoration, 2 surfaces, permanent | 72 | Periodontal scaling with gingival inflammation | 80 |
| Amalgam restoration, 3 surfaces, permanent | 89 | Gingival curettage, per quadrant | 119 |
| Composite resin restoration, 1 surface, anterior | 65 | Periodontal root planing, per quadrant | 111 |
| Composite resin restoration, 1 surface, posterior | 75 | Teeth-whitening, per arch | 161 |
| Inlay, metallic, 1 surface | 323 | Infection-control fee | 18 |

## FINANCIAL STATEMENTS

- Percentages given by "Building a Financial Foundation for your Practice," an article from ADA Dental Practice Library.
- Sales estimate based on a 48-week year with benefits paid for 52 weeks.
- Years 3-5 are shown both including and excluding Dr. Jeremiah Kramer, DDS.

*This page left intentionally blank to accommodate tabular matter following.*

## Income Statement—Year 1, June 2002-May 2003

| INCOME: | Jun | Jul | Aug | Sep | Oct | Nov |
|---|---|---|---|---|---|---|
| Dr. Stanley Kramer | 22,917 | 22,917 | 22,917 | 22,917 | 22,917 | 22,917 |
| Hygienist | 6,720 | 6,720 | 6,720 | 6,720 | 6,720 | 6,720 |
| Gross Sales | 29,637 | 29,637 | 29,637 | 29,637 | 29,637 | 29,637 |
| Cash Receipts (90%) | 26,673 | 26,673 | 26,673 | 26,673 | 26,673 | 26,673 |
| Accounts Receivable (10%) | 2,964 | 2,964 | 2,964 | 2,964 | 2,964 | 2,964 |
| Cost of Goods Sold | | | | | | |
| Lab Fees (9%) | -2,667 | -2,667 | -2,667 | -2,667 | -2,667 | -2,667 |
| Dental Supplies (6%) | -1,778 | -1,778 | -1,778 | -1,778 | -1,778 | -1,778 |
| **GROSS INCOME:** | **25,191** | **25,191** | **25,191** | **25,191** | **25,191** | **25,191** |
| | | | | | | |
| **EXPENSES:** | | | | | | |
| Advertising (3%) | 889 | 889 | 889 | 889 | 889 | 889 |
| Insurance (3%) | 889 | 889 | 889 | 889 | 889 | 889 |
| Interest Expense (F) | 3,750 | 3,750 | 3,750 | 3,750 | 3,750 | 3,750 |
| Legal & Professional Services (F) | 833 | 833 | 833 | 833 | 833 | 833 |
| Office Supplies (6%) | 1,778 | 1,778 | 1,778 | 1,778 | 1,778 | 1,778 |
| Mortgage (F) | 2,500 | 2,500 | 2,500 | 2,500 | 2,500 | 2,500 |
| Taxes & Licenses (10% of salary) | 417 | 417 | 417 | 417 | 417 | 417 |
| Utilities (2%) | 593 | 593 | 593 | 593 | 593 | 593 |
| | | | | | | |
| **Wages** | | | | | | |
| Professional (F) | 4,167 | 4,167 | 4,167 | 4,167 | 4,167 | 4,167 |
| Hygienist (.25 of production) | 1,680 | 1,680 | 1,680 | 1,680 | 1,680 | 1,680 |
| Salaried & Benefits (21%) | 4,813 | 4,813 | 4,813 | 4,813 | 4,813 | 4,813 |
| | | | | | | |
| Other Expenses (F) | 417 | 417 | 417 | 417 | 417 | 417 |
| **TOTAL EXPENSES:** | **22, 725** | **22,725** | **22,725** | **22,725** | **22,725** | **22,725** |
| **NET PROFIT (LOSS):** | **2,466** | **2,466** | **2,466** | **2,466** | **2,466** | **2,466** |

**Stanley at 7 patients a day at an average of $183.56/patient**

| | |
|---|---|
| 1 Hygienist at 7 patients a day for 2 days a week averaging $120/patient | $80,640 |
| 1 Assistant 40 hours/week at $11.00/hour for 52 weeks | 22,880 |
| 1 Receptionist/bookkeeper 40 hours/week at $11.65/hour at 52 weeks | 24,232 |
| **Weekly wage of Assistant and Receptionist before benefits** | **47,112** |

| Dec | Jan | Feb | Mar | Apr | May | Total |
|---|---|---|---|---|---|---|
| 22,917 | 22,917 | 22,917 | 22,917 | 22,917 | 22,917 | 275,000 |
| 6,720 | 6,720 | 6,720 | 6,720 | 6,720 | 6,720 | 80,640 |
| 29,637 | 29,637 | 29,637 | 29,637 | 29,637 | 29,637 | 355,640 |
| 26,673 | 26,673 | 26,673 | 26,673 | 26,673 | 26,673 | 320,076 |
| 2,964 | 2,964 | 2,964 | 2,964 | 2,964 | 2,964 | 35,564 |
| | | | | | | |
| -2,667 | -2,667 | -2,667 | -2,667 | -2,667 | -2,667 | -32,008 |
| -1,778 | -1,778 | -1,778 | -1,778 | -1,778 | -1,778 | -21,338 |
| **25,191** | **25,191** | **25,191** | **25,191** | **25,191** | **25,191** | **302,294** |
| | | | | | | |
| 889 | 889 | 889 | 889 | 889 | 889 | 10,669 |
| 889 | 889 | 889 | 889 | 889 | 889 | 10,669 |
| 3,750 | 3,750 | 3,750 | 3,750 | 3,750 | 3,750 | 45,000 |
| 833 | 833 | 833 | 833 | 833 | 833 | 10,000 |
| 1,778 | 1,778 | 1,778 | 1,778 | 1,778 | 1,778 | 21,338 |
| 2,500 | 2,500 | 2,500 | 2,500 | 2,500 | 2,500 | 30,000 |
| 417 | 417 | 417 | 417 | 417 | 417 | 5,000 |
| 593 | 593 | 593 | 593 | 593 | 593 | 7,113 |
| | | | | | | |
| 4,167 | 4,167 | 4,167 | 4,167 | 4,167 | 4,167 | 50,000 |
| 1,680 | 1,680 | 1,680 | 1,680 | 1,680 | 1,680 | 20,160 |
| 4,813 | 4,813 | 4,813 | 4,813 | 4,813 | 4,813 | 57,750 |
| | | | | | | |
| 417 | 417 | 417 | 417 | 417 | 417 | 5,000 |
| **22,725** | **22,725** | **22,725** | **22,725** | **22,725** | **22,725** | **272,700** |
| **2,466** | **2,466** | **2,466** | **2,466** | **2,466** | **2,466** | **29,594** |

## Statement of Cash Flows—Year 1, June 2002-May 2003

|  | Jun | Jul | Aug | Sep | Oct | Nov |
|---|---|---|---|---|---|---|
| **Cash Inflows** | | | | | | |
| Beginning Cash Balance | 20,000 | 19,503 | 19,005 | 18,508 | 18,010 | 17,513 |
| Loan for Start-up costs | 30,000 | | | | | |
| Cash Receipts | 26,673 | 26,673 | 26,673 | 26,673 | 26,673 | 26,673 |
| **Total Cash Inflows** | **76,673** | **46,176** | **45,678** | **45,181** | **44,683** | **44,186** |
| | | | | | | |
| **Cash Disbursements** | | | | | | |
| Start-up costs | 30,000 | | | | | |
| Lab Fees (9%) | 2,667 | 2,667 | 2,667 | 2,667 | 2,667 | 2,667 |
| Dental Supplies (6%) | 1,778 | 1,778 | 1,778 | 1,778 | 1,778 | 1,778 |
| Advertising (3%) | 889 | 889 | 889 | 889 | 889 | 889 |
| Insurance (3%) | 889 | 889 | 889 | 889 | 889 | 889 |
| Interest Expense (F) | 3,750 | 3,750 | 3,750 | 3,750 | 3,750 | 3,750 |
| Legal & Professional Services (F) | 833 | 833 | 833 | 833 | 833 | 833 |
| Office Supplies (6%) | 1,778 | 1,778 | 1,778 | 1,778 | 1,778 | 1,778 |
| Mortgage (F) | 2,500 | 2,500 | 2,500 | 2,500 | 2,500 | 2,500 |
| Taxes & Licenses (10% of salary) | 417 | 417 | 417 | 417 | 417 | 417 |
| Utilities (2%) | 593 | 593 | 593 | 593 | 593 | 593 |
| Wages | | | | | | |
| Professional (F) | 4,167 | 4,167 | 4,167 | 4,167 | 4,167 | 4,167 |
| Hygienist | 1,680 | 1,680 | 1,680 | 1,680 | 1,680 | 1,680 |
| Salaried & Benefits | 4,813 | 4,813 | 4,813 | 4,813 | 4,813 | 4,813 |
| Other Expenses (F) | 417 | 417 | 417 | 417 | 417 | 417 |
| **Total Disbursements** | **57,170** | **27,170** | **27,170** | **27,170** | **27,170** | **27,170** |
| | | | | | | |
| **Remaining Cash at Month End** | **19,503** | **19,005** | **18,508** | **18,010** | **17,513** | **17,015** |

| Dec | Jan | Feb | Mar | Apr | May |
|---|---|---|---|---|---|
| 17,015 | 16,518 | 16,020 | 15,523 | 15,025 | 14,528 |
| 26,673 | 26,673 | 26,673 | 26,673 | 26,673 | 26,673 |
| **43,688** | **43,191** | **42,693** | **42,196** | **41,698** | **41,201** |
| | | | | | |
| 2,667 | 2,667 | 2,667 | 2,667 | 2,667 | 2,667 |
| 1,778 | 1,778 | 1,778 | 1,778 | 1,778 | 1,778 |
| 889 | 889 | 889 | 889 | 889 | 889 |
| 889 | 889 | 889 | 889 | 889 | 889 |
| 3,750 | 3,750 | 3,750 | 3,750 | 3,750 | 3,750 |
| 833 | 833 | 833 | 833 | 833 | 833 |
| 1,778 | 1,778 | 1,778 | 1,778 | 1,778 | 1,778 |
| 2,500 | 2,500 | 2,500 | 2,500 | 2,500 | 2,500 |
| 417 | 417 | 417 | 417 | 417 | 417 |
| 593 | 593 | 593 | 593 | 593 | 593 |
| | | | | | |
| 4,167 | 4,167 | 4,167 | 4,167 | 4,167 | 4,167 |
| 1,680 | 1,680 | 1,680 | 1,680 | 1,680 | 1,680 |
| 4,813 | 4,813 | 4,813 | 4,813 | 4,813 | 4,813 |
| 417 | 417 | 417 | 417 | 417 | 417 |
| **27,170** | **27,170** | **27,170** | **27,170** | **27,170** | **27,170** |
| | | | | | |
| **16,518** | **16,020** | **15,523** | **15,025** | **14,528** | **14,030** |

**Balance Sheet—
Year 1-5**

| | Year 1 | Year 2 | Year 3 | Year 4 | Year 5 |
|---|---|---|---|---|---|
| **Assets:** | | | | | |
| Cash | 14,030 | 27,228 | 53,494 | 39,471 | 55,598 |
| Accounts Receivable | 35,564 | 48,872 | 75,908 | 79,432 | 91,902 |
| Building and Equipment | 250,000 | 250,000 | 250,000 | 250,000 | 250,000 |
| **Total Assets** | **299,594** | **326,100** | **379,402** | **368,903** | **397,500** |
| | | | | | |
| **Liabilities and Owners Equity:** | | | | | |
| Note Payable | 270,000 | 240,000 | 210,000 | 180,000 | 150,000 |
| Owners Equity | 29,594 | 56,505 | 102,174 | 65,409 | 108,029 |
| Retained Earnings | 0 | 29,594 | 56,505 | 102,174 | 65,409 |
| | 0 | 0 | 10,723 | 21,321 | 74,062 |
| **Total Liabilities** | **299,594** | **326,100** | **379,402** | **368,903** | **397,500** |
| | | | | | |
| Difference | 0 | 0 | 0 | 0 | 0 |

*This page left intentionally blank to accommodate tabular matter following.*

## Income Statement—Year 2, June 2003-May 2004

| INCOME: | Jun | Jul | Aug | Sep | Oct | Nov |
|---|---|---|---|---|---|---|
| Dr. Stanley Kramer | 29,370 | 29,370 | 29,370 | 29,370 | 29,370 | 29,370 |
| Hygienist | 6,720 | 6,720 | 6,720 | 6,720 | 6,720 | 6,720 |
| Gross Sales | 36,090 | 36,090 | 36,090 | 36,090 | 36,090 | 36,090 |
| Cash Receipts (90%) | 32,481 | 32,481 | 32,481 | 32,481 | 32,481 | 32,481 |
| Accounts Receivable (10%) | 3,609 | 3,609 | 3,609 | 3,609 | 3,609 | 3,609 |
| | | | | | | |
| **Cost of Goods Sold** | | | | | | |
| Lab Fees (9%) | (3,248) | (3,248) | (3,248) | (3,248) | (3,248) | (3,248) |
| Dental Supplies (6%) | (2,165) | (2,165) | (2,165) | (2,165) | (2,165) | (2,165) |
| **GROSS INCOME:** | **30,676** | **30,676** | **30,676** | **30,676** | **30,676** | **30,676** |
| | | | | | | |
| **EXPENSES:** | | | | | | |
| Advertising (3%) | 1,083 | 1,083 | 1,083 | 1,083 | 1,083 | 1,083 |
| Insurance (3%) | 1,083 | 1,083 | 1,083 | 1,083 | 1,083 | 1,083 |
| Interest Expense (F) | 3,750 | 3,750 | 3,750 | 3,750 | 3,750 | 3,750 |
| Legal & Professional Services (F) | 833 | 833 | 833 | 833 | 833 | 833 |
| Office Supplies (6%) | 2,165 | 2,165 | 2,165 | 2,165 | 2,165 | 2,165 |
| Mortgage (F) | 2,500 | 2,500 | 2,500 | 2,500 | 2,500 | 2,500 |
| Taxes & Licenses (10% of salary) | 500 | 500 | 500 | 500 | 500 | 500 |
| Utilities (2%) | 722 | 722 | 722 | 722 | 722 | 722 |
| | | | | | | |
| **Wages** | | | | | | |
| Professional (F) | 5,000 | 5,000 | 5,000 | 5,000 | 5,000 | 5,000 |
| Hygienist (.26 of production) | 1,747 | 1,747 | 1,747 | 1,747 | 1,747 | 1,747 |
| Salaried & Benefits (21%) | 6,168 | 6,168 | 6,168 | 6,168 | 6,168 | 6,168 |
| Other Expenses (F) | 417 | 417 | 417 | 417 | 417 | 417 |
| **TOTAL EXPENSES:** | **25,967** | **25,967** | **25,967** | **25,967** | **25,967** | **25,967** |
| | | | | | | |
| **NET PROFIT (LOSS):** | **4,709** | **4,709** | **4,709** | **4,709** | **4,709** | **4,709** |

| Dec | Jan | Feb | Mar | Apr | May | Total |
|---|---|---|---|---|---|---|
| 29,370 | 29,370 | 29,370 | 29,370 | 29,370 | 29,370 | 352,435 |
| 6,720 | 6,720 | 6,720 | 6,720 | 6,720 | 6,720 | 80,640 |
| 36,090 | 36,090 | 36,090 | 36,090 | 36,090 | 36,090 | 433,075 |
| 32,481 | 32,481 | 32,481 | 32,481 | 32,481 | 32,481 | 389,768 |
| 3,609 | 3,609 | 3,609 | 3,609 | 3,609 | 3,609 | 43,308 |
| | | | | | | |
| (3,248) | (3,248) | (3,248) | (3,248) | (3,248) | (3,248) | (38,977) |
| (2,165) | (2,165) | (2,165) | (2,165) | (2,165) | (2,165) | (25,985) |
| **30,676** | **30,676** | **30,676** | **30,676** | **30,676** | **30,676** | **368,114** |
| | | | | | | |
| 1,083 | 1,083 | 1,083 | 1,083 | 1,083 | 1,083 | 12,992 |
| 1,083 | 1,083 | 1,083 | 1,083 | 1,083 | 1,083 | 12,992 |
| 3,750 | 3,750 | 3,750 | 3,750 | 3,750 | 3,750 | 45,000 |
| 833 | 833 | 833 | 833 | 833 | 833 | 10,000 |
| 2,165 | 2,165 | 2,165 | 2,165 | 2,165 | 2,165 | 25,985 |
| 2,500 | 2,500 | 2,500 | 2,500 | 2,500 | 2,500 | 30,000 |
| 500 | 500 | 500 | 500 | 500 | 500 | 6,000 |
| 722 | 722 | 722 | 722 | 722 | 722 | 8,662 |
| | | | | | | |
| 5,000 | 5,000 | 5,000 | 5,000 | 5,000 | 5,000 | 60,000 |
| 1,747 | 1,747 | 1,747 | 1,747 | 1,747 | 1,747 | 20,966 |
| 6,168 | 6,168 | 6,168 | 6,168 | 6,168 | 6,168 | 74,011 |
| 417 | 417 | 417 | 417 | 417 | 417 | 5,000 |
| **25,967** | **25,967** | **25,967** | **25,967** | **25,967** | **25,967** | **311,608** |
| | | | | | | |
| **4,709** | **4,709** | **4,709** | **4,709** | **4,709** | **4,709** | **56,505** |

## Statement of Cash Flows—Year 2, June 2003-May 2004

|  | Jun | Jul | Aug | Sep | Oct | Nov |
|---|---|---|---|---|---|---|
| **Cash Inflows** | | | | | | |
| Beginning Cash Balance | 14,030 | 15,130 | 16,230 | 17,330 | 18,430 | 19,530 |
| Cash Receipts | 32,481 | 32,481 | 32,481 | 32,481 | 32,481 | 32,481 |
| **Total Cash Inflows** | **46,511** | **47,611** | **48,711** | **49,811** | **50,910** | **52,010** |
| | | | | | | |
| **Cash Disbursements** | | | | | | |
| Lab Fees (9%) | 3,248 | 3,248 | 3,248 | 3,248 | 3,248 | 3,248 |
| Dental Supplies (6%) | 2,165 | 2,165 | 2,165 | 2,165 | 2,165 | 2,165 |
| Advertising (3%) | 1,083 | 1,083 | 1,083 | 1,083 | 1,083 | 1,083 |
| Insurance (3%) | 1,083 | 1,083 | 1,083 | 1,083 | 1,083 | 1,083 |
| Interest Expense (F) | 3,750 | 3,750 | 3,750 | 3,750 | 3,750 | 3,750 |
| Legal & Professional Services (F) | 833 | 833 | 833 | 833 | 833 | 833 |
| Office Supplies (6%) | 2,165 | 2,165 | 2,165 | 2,165 | 2,165 | 2,165 |
| Mortgage (F) | 2,500 | 2,500 | 2,500 | 2,500 | 2,500 | 2,500 |
| Taxes & Licenses (10% of salary) | 500 | 500 | 500 | 500 | 500 | 500 |
| Utilities (2%) | 722 | 722 | 722 | 722 | 722 | 722 |
| | | | | | | |
| **Wages** | | | | | | |
| Professional (F) | 5,000 | 5,000 | 5,000 | 5,000 | 5,000 | 5,000 |
| Hygienist | 1,747 | 1,747 | 1,747 | 1,747 | 1,747 | 1,747 |
| Salaried & Benefits | 6,168 | 6,168 | 6,168 | 6,168 | 6,168 | 6,168 |
| Other Expenses (F) | 417 | 417 | 417 | 417 | 417 | 417 |
| | | | | | | |
| **Total Disbursements** | **31,381** | **31,381** | **31,381** | **31,381** | **31,381** | **31,381** |
| | | | | | | |
| **Remaining Cash at Month End** | **15,130** | **16,230** | **17,330** | **18,430** | **19,530** | **20,629** |

|          | Dec    | Jan    | Feb    | Mar    | Apr    | May    |
|----------|--------|--------|--------|--------|--------|--------|
|          | 20,629 | 21,729 | 22,829 | 23,929 | 25,029 | 26,129 |
|          | 32,481 | 32,481 | 32,481 | 32,481 | 32,481 | 32,481 |
|          | **53,110** | **54,210** | **55,310** | **56,410** | **57,509** | **58,609** |
|          |        |        |        |        |        |        |
|          | 3,248  | 3,248  | 3,248  | 3,248  | 3,248  | 3,248  |
|          | 2,165  | 2,165  | 2,165  | 2,165  | 2,165  | 2,165  |
|          | 1,083  | 1,083  | 1,083  | 1,083  | 1,083  | 1,083  |
|          | 1,083  | 1,083  | 1,083  | 1,083  | 1,083  | 1,083  |
|          | 3,750  | 3,750  | 3,750  | 3,750  | 3,750  | 3,750  |
|          | 833    | 833    | 833    | 833    | 833    | 833    |
|          | 2,165  | 2,165  | 2,165  | 2,165  | 2,165  | 2,165  |
|          | 2,500  | 2,500  | 2,500  | 2,500  | 2,500  | 2,500  |
|          | 500    | 500    | 500    | 500    | 500    | 500    |
|          | 722    | 722    | 722    | 722    | 722    | 722    |
|          |        |        |        |        |        |        |
|          | 5,000  | 5,000  | 5,000  | 5,000  | 5,000  | 5,000  |
|          | 1,747  | 1,747  | 1,747  | 1,747  | 1,747  | 1,747  |
|          | 6,168  | 6,168  | 6,168  | 6,168  | 6,168  | 6,168  |
|          | 417    | 417    | 417    | 417    | 417    | 417    |
|          | **31,381** | **31,381** | **31,381** | **31,381** | **31,381** | **31,381** |
|          | **21,729** | **22,829** | **23,929** | **25,029** | **26,129** | **27,228** |

## Income Statement—Year 3 with Dr. Jeremiah Kramer, DDS
## June 2004-May 2005

| INCOME: | Jun | Jul | Aug | Sep | Oct | Nov |
|---|---|---|---|---|---|---|
| Dr. Stanley Kramer | 33,041 | 33,041 | 33,041 | 33,041 | 33,041 | 33,041 |
| Dr. Jeremiah Kramer | 23,496 | 23,496 | 23,496 | 23,496 | 23,496 | 23,496 |
| Hygienist | 6,720 | 6,720 | 6,720 | 6,720 | 6,720 | 6,720 |
| Gross Sales | 63,257 | 63,257 | 63,257 | 63,257 | 63,257 | 63,257 |
| Cash Receipts (90%) | 56,931 | 56,931 | 56,931 | 56,931 | 56,931 | 56,931 |
| Accounts Receivable (10%) | 6,326 | 6,326 | 6,326 | 6,326 | 6,326 | 6,326 |
| | | | | | | |
| **Cost of Goods Sold** | | | | | | |
| Lab Fees (9%) | (5,693) | (5,693) | (5,693) | (5,693) | (5,693) | (5,693) |
| Dental Supplies (6%) | (3,795) | (3,795) | (3,795) | (3,795) | (3,795) | (3,795) |
| **GROSS INCOME:** | **53,768** | **53,768** | **53,768** | **53,768** | **53,768** | **53,768** |
| | | | | | | |
| **EXPENSES:** | | | | | | |
| Advertising (3%) | 1,898 | 1,898 | 1,898 | 1,898 | 1,898 | 1,898 |
| Insurance (3%) | 1,898 | 1,898 | 1,898 | 1,898 | 1,898 | 1,898 |
| Interest Expense (F) | 3,750 | 3,750 | 3,750 | 3,750 | 3,750 | 3,750 |
| Legal & Professional Services (F) | 833 | 833 | 833 | 833 | 833 | 833 |
| Office Supplies (6%) | 3,795 | 3,795 | 3,795 | 3,795 | 3,795 | 3,795 |
| Mortgage (F) | 2,500 | 2,500 | 2,500 | 2,500 | 2,500 | 2,500 |
| Taxes & Licenses (10% of salary) | 750 | 750 | 750 | 750 | 750 | 750 |
| Utilities (2%) | 1,265 | 1,265 | 1,265 | 1,265 | 1,265 | 1,265 |
| | | | | | | |
| **Wages** | | | | | | |
| Dr. Stanley Kramer (F) | 7,500 | 7,500 | 7,500 | 7,500 | 7,500 | 7,500 |
| Dr. Jeremiah Kramer (.45 of production) | 11,895 | 11,895 | 11,895 | 11,895 | 11,895 | 11,895 |
| Hygienist (.27 of production) | 1,814 | 1,814 | 1,814 | 1,814 | 1,814 | 1,814 |
| Salaried & Benefits (21%) | 6,939 | 6,939 | 6,939 | 6,939 | 6,939 | 6,939 |
| Other Expenses (F) | 417 | 417 | 417 | 417 | 417 | 417 |
| **TOTAL EXPENSES:** | **45,254** | **45,254** | **45,254** | **45,254** | **45,254** | **45,254** |
| **NET PROFIT (LOSS):** | **8,514** | **8,514** | **8,514** | **8,514** | **8,514** | **8,514** |

| | |
|---|---|
| **Stanley at 9 patients a day at an average of $183.56/per patient** | **396,490** |
| Jeremiah at 8 patients a day, 4 days a week for 48 weeks at $183.56/patient | 281,948 |
| 1 Hygienist at 7 patients a day for 2 days a week averaging $120/patient | 80,640 |
| 2 assistants 40 hours a week at $11.00/hour for 52 weeks | 45,760 |
| 1 receptionist/ bookkeeper 40 hours a week at $11.65/hour at 52 weeks | 24,232 |
| **Weekly wage of assistant and receptionist before benefits** | **69,992** |

| Dec | Jan | Feb | Mar | Apr | May | Total |
|---|---|---|---|---|---|---|
| 33,041 | 33,041 | 33,041 | 33,041 | 33,041 | 33,041 | 396,490 |
| 23,496 | 23,496 | 23,496 | 23,496 | 23,496 | 23,496 | 281,948 |
| 6,720 | 6,720 | 6,720 | 6,720 | 6,720 | 6,720 | 80,640 |
| 63,257 | 63,257 | 63,257 | 63,257 | 63,257 | 63,257 | 759,078 |
| 56,931 | 56,931 | 56,931 | 56,931 | 56,931 | 56,931 | 683,170 |
| 6,326 | 6,326 | 6,326 | 6,326 | 6,326 | 6,326 | 75,908 |
| | | | | | | |
| (5,693) | (5,693) | (5,693) | (5,693) | (5,693) | (5,693) | (68,317) |
| (3,795) | (3,795) | (3,795) | (3,795) | (3,795) | (3,795) | (45,545) |
| **53,768** | **53,768** | **53,768** | **53,768** | **53,768** | **53,768** | **645,216** |
| | | | | | | |
| 1,898 | 1,898 | 1,898 | 1,898 | 1,898 | 1,898 | 22,772 |
| 1,898 | 1,898 | 1,898 | 1,898 | 1,898 | 1,898 | 22,772 |
| 3,750 | 3,750 | 3,750 | 3,750 | 3,750 | 3,750 | 45,000 |
| 833 | 833 | 833 | 833 | 833 | 833 | 10,000 |
| 3,795 | 3,795 | 3,795 | 3,795 | 3,795 | 3,795 | 45,545 |
| 2,500 | 2,500 | 2,500 | 2,500 | 2,500 | 2,500 | 30,000 |
| 750 | 750 | 750 | 750 | 750 | 750 | 9,000 |
| 1,265 | 1,265 | 1,265 | 1,265 | 1,265 | 1,265 | 15,182 |
| | | | | | | |
| 7,500 | 7,500 | 7,500 | 7,500 | 7,500 | 7,500 | 90,000 |
| 11,895 | 11,895 | 11,895 | 11,895 | 11,895 | 11,895 | 142,736 |
| 1,814 | 1,814 | 1,814 | 1,814 | 1,814 | 1,814 | 21,773 |
| 6,939 | 6,939 | 6,939 | 6,939 | 6,939 | 6,939 | 83,263 |
| 417 | 417 | 417 | 417 | 417 | 417 | 5,000 |
| **45,254** | **45,254** | **45,254** | **45,254** | **45,254** | **45,254** | **543,043** |
| **8,514** | **8,514** | **8,514** | **8,514** | **8,514** | **8,514** | **102,174** |

## Income Statement—Year 3 without Dr. Jeremiah Kramer, DDS
## June 2004-May 2005

| INCOME: | Jun | Jul | Aug | Sep | Oct | Nov |
|---|---|---|---|---|---|---|
| Dr. Stanley Kramer | 33,041 | 33,041 | 33,041 | 33,041 | 33,041 | 33,041 |
| Hygienist | 6,720 | 6,720 | 6,720 | 6,720 | 6,720 | 6,720 |
| Gross Sales | 39,761 | 39,761 | 39,761 | 39,761 | 39,761 | 39,761 |
| Cash Receipts (90%) | 35,785 | 35,785 | 35,785 | 35,785 | 35,785 | 35,785 |
| Accounts Receivable (10%) | 3,976 | 3,976 | 3,976 | 3,976 | 3,976 | 3,976 |
| | | | | | | |
| **Cost of Goods Sold** | | | | | | |
| Lab Fees (9%) | (3,578) | (3,578) | (3,578) | (3,578) | (3,578) | (3,578) |
| Dental Supplies (6%) | (2,386) | (2,386) | (2,386) | (2,386) | (2,386) | (2,386) |
| **GROSS INCOME:** | **33,797** | **33,797** | **33,797** | **33,797** | **33,797** | **33,797** |
| | | | | | | |
| **EXPENSES:** | | | | | | |
| Advertising (3%) | 1,193 | 1,193 | 1,193 | 1,193 | 1,193 | 1,193 |
| Insurance (3%) | 1,193 | 1,193 | 1,193 | 1,193 | 1,193 | 1,193 |
| Interest Expense (F) | 3,750 | 3,750 | 3,750 | 3,750 | 3,750 | 3,750 |
| Legal & Professional Services (F) | 833 | 833 | 833 | 833 | 833 | 833 |
| Office Supplies (6%) | 2,386 | 2,386 | 2,386 | 2,386 | 2,386 | 2,386 |
| Mortgage (F) | 2,500 | 2,500 | 2,500 | 2,500 | 2,500 | 2,500 |
| Taxes & Licenses (10% of salary) | 500 | 500 | 500 | 500 | 500 | 500 |
| Utilities (2%) | 795 | 795 | 795 | 795 | 795 | 795 |
| | | | | | | |
| **Wages** | | | | | | |
| Dr. Stanley Kramer (F) | 5,000 | 5,000 | 5,000 | 5,000 | 5,000 | 5,000 |
| Hygienist (.27 of production) | 1,814 | 1,814 | 1,814 | 1,814 | 1,814 | 1,814 |
| Salaried & Benefits (21%) | 6,939 | 6,939 | 6,939 | 6,939 | 6,939 | 6,939 |
| Other Expenses (F) | 417 | 417 | 417 | 417 | 417 | 417 |
| **TOTAL EXPENSES:** | **27,319** | **27,319** | **27,319** | **27,319** | **27,319** | **27,319** |
| **NET PROFIT (LOSS):** | **6,477** | **6,477** | **6,477** | **6,477** | **6,477** | **6,477** |

| | |
|---|---|
| **Stanley at 9 patients a day at an average of $183.56/patient** | **396,490** |
| 1 Hygienist at 7 patients a day for 2 days a week averaging $120/patient | 80,640 |
| 1 assistant 40 hours a week at $11.00/hour for 52 weeks | 22,880 |
| 1 receptionist/ bookkeeper 40 hours a week at $11.65/hour at 52 weeks | 24,232 |
| **Weekly wage of assistant and receptionist before benefits** | **47,112** |

| Dec | Jan | Feb | Mar | Apr | May | Total |
|---|---|---|---|---|---|---|
| 33,041 | 33,041 | 33,041 | 33,041 | 33,041 | 33,041 | 396,490 |
| 6,720 | 6,720 | 6,720 | 6,720 | 6,720 | 6,720 | 80,640 |
| 39,761 | 39,761 | 39,761 | 39,761 | 39,761 | 39,761 | 477,130 |
| 35,785 | 35,785 | 35,785 | 35,785 | 35,785 | 35,785 | 429,417 |
| 3,976 | 3,976 | 3,976 | 3,976 | 3,976 | 3,976 | 47,713 |
| | | | | | | |
| (3,578) | (3,578) | (3,578) | (3,578) | (3,578) | (3,578) | (42,942) |
| (2,386) | (2,386) | (2,386) | (2,386) | (2,386) | (2,386) | (28,628) |
| **33,797** | **33,797** | **33,797** | **33,797** | **33,797** | **33,797** | **405,561** |
| | | | | | | |
| 1,193 | 1,193 | 1,193 | 1,193 | 1,193 | 1,193 | 14,314 |
| 1,193 | 1,193 | 1,193 | 1,193 | 1,193 | 1,193 | 14,314 |
| 3,750 | 3,750 | 3,750 | 3,750 | 3,750 | 3,750 | 45,000 |
| 833 | 833 | 833 | 833 | 833 | 833 | 10,000 |
| 2,386 | 2,386 | 2,386 | 2,386 | 2,386 | 2,386 | 28,628 |
| 2,500 | 2,500 | 2,500 | 2,500 | 2,500 | 2,500 | 30,000 |
| 500 | 500 | 500 | 500 | 500 | 500 | 6,000 |
| 795 | 795 | 795 | 795 | 795 | 795 | 9,543 |
| | | | | | | |
| 5,000 | 5,000 | 5,000 | 5,000 | 5,000 | 5,000 | 60,000 |
| 1,814 | 1,814 | 1,814 | 1,814 | 1,814 | 1,814 | 21,773 |
| 6,939 | 6,939 | 6,939 | 6,939 | 6,939 | 6,939 | 83,263 |
| 417 | 417 | 417 | 417 | 417 | 417 | 5,000 |
| **27,319** | **27,319** | **27,319** | **27,319** | **27,319** | **27,319** | **327,834** |
| **6,477** | **6,477** | **6,477** | **6,477** | **6,477** | **6,477** | **77,727** |

## Statement of Cash Flows—Year 3, June 2004-May 2005

|  | Jun | Jul | Aug | Sep | Oct | Nov |
|---|---|---|---|---|---|---|
| **Cash Inflows** | | | | | | |
| Beginning Cash Balance | 27,228 | 29,417 | 31,606 | 33,795 | 35,984 | 38,173 |
| Cash Receipts | 56,931 | 56,931 | 56,931 | 56,931 | 56,931 | 56,931 |
| **Total Cash Inflows** | **84,159** | **86,348** | **88,537** | **90,726** | **92,915** | **95,103** |
| | | | | | | |
| **Cash Disbursements** | | | | | | |
| Lab Fees (9%) | 5,693 | 5,693 | 5,693 | 5,693 | 5,693 | 5,693 |
| Dental Supplies (6%) | 3,795 | 3,795 | 3,795 | 3,795 | 3,795 | 3,795 |
| Advertising (3%) | 1,898 | 1,898 | 1,898 | 1,898 | 1,898 | 1,898 |
| Insurance (3%) | 1,898 | 1,898 | 1,898 | 1,898 | 1,898 | 1,898 |
| Interest Expense (F) | 3,750 | 3,750 | 3,750 | 3,750 | 3,750 | 3,750 |
| Legal & Professional Services (F) | 833 | 833 | 833 | 833 | 833 | 833 |
| Office Supplies (6%) | 3,795 | 3,795 | 3,795 | 3,795 | 3,795 | 3,795 |
| Mortgage (F) | 2,500 | 2,500 | 2,500 | 2,500 | 2,500 | 2,500 |
| Taxes & Licenses (10% of salary) | 750 | 750 | 750 | 750 | 750 | 750 |
| Utilities (2%) | 1,265 | 1,265 | 1,265 | 1,265 | 1,265 | 1,265 |
| | | | | | | |
| **Wages** | | | | | | |
| Dr. Stanley Kramer (F) | 7,500 | 7,500 | 7,500 | 7,500 | 7,500 | 7,500 |
| Dr. Jeremiah Kramer | 11,895 | 11,895 | 11,895 | 11,895 | 11,895 | 11,895 |
| Hygienist | 1,814 | 1,814 | 1,814 | 1,814 | 1,814 | 1,814 |
| Salaried & Benefits | 6,939 | 6,939 | 6,939 | 6,939 | 6,939 | 6,939 |
| Other Expenses (F) | 417 | 417 | 417 | 417 | 417 | 417 |
| | | | | | | |
| **Total Disbursements** | **54,742** | **54,742** | **54,742** | **54,742** | **54,742** | **54,742** |
| | | | | | | |
| **Remaining Cash at Month End** | **29,417** | **31,606** | **33,795** | **35,984** | **38,173** | **40,361** |

| | Dec | Jan | Feb | Mar | Apr | May |
|---|---|---|---|---|---|---|
| | 40,361 | 42,550 | 44,739 | 46,928 | 49,117 | 51,306 |
| | 56,931 | 56,931 | 56,931 | 56,931 | 56,931 | 56,931 |
| | **97,292** | **99,481** | **101,670** | **103,859** | **106,048** | **108,236** |
| | | | | | | |
| | 5,693 | 5,693 | 5,693 | 5,693 | 5,693 | 5,693 |
| | 3,795 | 3,795 | 3,795 | 3,795 | 3,795 | 3,795 |
| | 1,898 | 1,898 | 1,898 | 1,898 | 1,898 | 1,898 |
| | 1,898 | 1,898 | 1,898 | 1,898 | 1,898 | 1,898 |
| | 3,750 | 3,750 | 3,750 | 3,750 | 3,750 | 3,750 |
| | 833 | 833 | 833 | 833 | 833 | 833 |
| | 3,795 | 3,795 | 3,795 | 3,795 | 3,795 | 3,795 |
| | 2,500 | 2,500 | 2,500 | 2,500 | 2,500 | 2,500 |
| | 750 | 750 | 750 | 750 | 750 | 750 |
| | 1,265 | 1,265 | 1,265 | 1,265 | 1,265 | 1,265 |
| | | | | | | |
| | 7,500 | 7,500 | 7,500 | 7,500 | 7,500 | 7,500 |
| | 11,895 | 11,895 | 11,895 | 11,895 | 11,895 | 11,895 |
| | 1,814 | 1,814 | 1,814 | 1,814 | 1,814 | 1,814 |
| | 6,939 | 6,939 | 6,939 | 6,939 | 6,939 | 6,939 |
| | 417 | 417 | 417 | 417 | 417 | 417 |
| | | | | | | |
| | **54,742** | **54,742** | **54,742** | **54,742** | **54,742** | **54,742** |
| | | | | | | |
| | **42,550** | **44,739** | **46,928** | **49,117** | **51,306** | **53,494** |

## Income Statement—Year 4 with Dr. Jeremiah Kramer, DDS
## June 2005-May 2006

| INCOME: | Jun | Jul | Aug | Sep | Oct | Nov |
|---|---|---|---|---|---|---|
| Dr. Stanley Kramer | 33,041 | 33,041 | 33,041 | 33,041 | 33,041 | 33,041 |
| Dr. Jeremiah Kramer | 26,433 | 26,433 | 26,433 | 26,433 | 26,433 | 26,433 |
| Hygienist | 6,720 | 6,720 | 6,720 | 6,720 | 6,720 | 6,720 |
| Gross Sales | 66,194 | 66,194 | 66,194 | 66,194 | 66,194 | 66,194 |
| Cash Receipts (90%) | 59,574 | 59,574 | 59,574 | 59,574 | 59,574 | 59,574 |
| Accounts Receivable (10%) | 6,619 | 6,619 | 6,619 | 6,619 | 6,619 | 6,619 |
| | | | | | | |
| **Cost of Goods Sold** | | | | | | |
| Lab Fees (9%) | (5,957) | (5,957) | (5,957) | (5,957) | (5,957) | (5,957) |
| Dental Supplies (6%) | (3,972) | (3,972) | (3,972) | (3,972) | (3,972) | (3,972) |
| **GROSS INCOME:** | **56,264** | **56,264** | **56,264** | **56,264** | **56,264** | **56,264** |
| | | | | | | |
| **EXPENSES:** | | | | | | |
| Advertising (3%) | 1,986 | 1,986 | 1,986 | 1,986 | 1,986 | 1,986 |
| Insurance (3%) | 1,986 | 1,986 | 1,986 | 1,986 | 1,986 | 1,986 |
| Interest Expense (F) | 3,750 | 3,750 | 3,750 | 3,750 | 3,750 | 3,750 |
| Legal & Professional Services (F) | 833 | 833 | 833 | 833 | 833 | 833 |
| Office Supplies (6%) | 3,972 | 3,972 | 3,972 | 3,972 | 3,972 | 3,972 |
| Mortgage (F) | 2,500 | 2,500 | 2,500 | 2,500 | 2,500 | 2,500 |
| Taxes & Licenses (10% of salary) | 958 | 958 | 958 | 958 | 958 | 958 |
| Utilities (2%) | 1,324 | 1,324 | 1,324 | 1,324 | 1,324 | 1,324 |
| | | | | | | |
| **Wages** | | | | | | |
| Dr. Stanley Kramer (F) | 9,583 | 9,583 | 9,583 | 9,583 | 9,583 | 9,583 |
| Dr. Jeremiah Kramer (.5 of production) | 14,685 | 14,685 | 14,685 | 14,685 | 14,685 | 14,685 |
| Hygienist (.28 of production) | 1,882 | 1,882 | 1,882 | 1,882 | 1,882 | 1,882 |
| Salaried & Benefits (21%) | 6,939 | 6,939 | 6,939 | 6,939 | 6,939 | 6,939 |
| Other Expenses (F) | 417 | 417 | 417 | 417 | 417 | 417 |
| **TOTAL EXPENSES:** | **50,814** | **50,814** | **50,814** | **50,814** | **50,814** | **50,814** |
| **NET PROFIT (LOSS):** | **5,451** | **5,451** | **5,451** | **5,451** | **5,451** | **5,451** |

| | |
|---|---|
| **Stanley at 9 patients a day at an average of $183.56/patient** | **396,490** |
| **Jeremiah at 9 patients a day, 4 days a week for 48 weeks at $183.56/patient** | **317,192** |
| 1 Hygienist at 7 patients a day for 2 days a week averaging $120/patient | 80,640 |
| 2 assistants 40 hours a week at $11.00/hour for 52 weeks | 45,760 |
| 1 receptionist/ bookkeeper 40 hours a week at $11.65/hour at 52 weeks | 24,232 |
| 1 receptionist/ bookkeeper 20 hours a week at $11.65/hour at 52 weeks | 12,116 |
| **Weekly wage of assistant and receptionist before benefits** | **82,108** |

| | Dec | Jan | Feb | Mar | Apr | May | Total |
|---|---|---|---|---|---|---|---|
| | 33,041 | 33,041 | 33,041 | 33,041 | 33,041 | 33,041 | 396,490 |
| | 26,433 | 26,433 | 26,433 | 26,433 | 26,433 | 26,433 | 317,192 |
| | 6,720 | 6,720 | 6,720 | 6,720 | 6,720 | 6,720 | 80,640 |
| | 66,194 | 66,194 | 66,194 | 66,194 | 66,194 | 66,194 | 794,322 |
| | 59,574 | 59,574 | 59,574 | 59,574 | 59,574 | 59,574 | 714,890 |
| | 6,619 | 6,619 | 6,619 | 6,619 | 6,619 | 6,619 | 79,432 |
| | | | | | | | |
| | (5,957) | (5,957) | (5,957) | (5,957) | (5,957) | (5,957) | (71,489) |
| | (3,972) | (3,972) | (3,972) | (3,972) | (3,972) | (3,972) | (47,659) |
| | **56,264** | **56,264** | **56,264** | **56,264** | **56,264** | **56,264** | **675,174** |
| | | | | | | | |
| | 1,986 | 1,986 | 1,986 | 1,986 | 1,986 | 1,986 | 23,830 |
| | 1,986 | 1,986 | 1,986 | 1,986 | 1,986 | 1,986 | 23,830 |
| | 3,750 | 3,750 | 3,750 | 3,750 | 3,750 | 3,750 | 45,000 |
| | 833 | 833 | 833 | 833 | 833 | 833 | 10,000 |
| | 3,972 | 3,972 | 3,972 | 3,972 | 3,972 | 3,972 | 47,659 |
| | 2,500 | 2,500 | 2,500 | 2,500 | 2,500 | 2,500 | 30,000 |
| | 958 | 958 | 958 | 958 | 958 | 958 | 11,500 |
| | 1,324 | 1,324 | 1,324 | 1,324 | 1,324 | 1,324 | 15,886 |
| | | | | | | | |
| | 9,583 | 9,583 | 9,583 | 9,583 | 9,583 | 9,583 | 115,000 |
| | 14,685 | 14,685 | 14,685 | 14,685 | 14,685 | 14,685 | 176,218 |
| | 1,882 | 1,882 | 1,882 | 1,882 | 1,882 | 1,882 | 22,579 |
| | 6,939 | 6,939 | 6,939 | 6,939 | 6,939 | 6,939 | 83,263 |
| | 417 | 417 | 417 | 417 | 417 | 417 | 5,000 |
| | **50,814** | **50,814** | **50,814** | **50,814** | **50,814** | **50,814** | **609,765** |
| | **5,451** | **5,451** | **5,451** | **5,451** | **5,451** | **5,451** | **65,409** |

## Income Statement—Year 4 without Dr. Jeremiah Kramer, DDS
## June 2005-May 2006

| INCOME: | Jun | Jul | Aug | Sep | Oct | Nov |
|---|---|---|---|---|---|---|
| Dr. Stanley Kramer | 36,712 | 36,712 | 36,712 | 36,712 | 36,712 | 36,712 |
| Hygienist | 6,720 | 6,720 | 6,720 | 6,720 | 6,720 | 6,720 |
| Gross Sales | 43,432 | 43,432 | 43,432 | 43,432 | 43,432 | 43,432 |
| Cash Receipts (90%) | 39,089 | 39,089 | 39,089 | 39,089 | 39,089 | 39,089 |
| Accounts Receivable (10%) | 4,343 | 4,343 | 4,343 | 4,343 | 4,343 | 4,343 |
| Cost of Goods Sold | | | | | | |
| Lab Fees (9%) | (3,909) | (3,909) | (3,909) | (3,909) | (3,909) | (3,909) |
| Dental Supplies (6%) | (2,606) | (2,606) | (2,606) | (2,606) | (2,606) | (2,606) |
| **GROSS INCOME:** | **36,917** | **36,917** | **36,917** | **36,917** | **36,917** | **36,917** |
| | | | | | | |
| **EXPENSES:** | | | | | | |
| Advertising (3%) | 1,303 | 1,303 | 1,303 | 1,303 | 1,303 | 1,303 |
| Insurance (3%) | 1,303 | 1,303 | 1,303 | 1,303 | 1,303 | 1,303 |
| Interest Expense (F) | 3,750 | 3,750 | 3,750 | 3,750 | 3,750 | 3,750 |
| Legal & Professional Services (F) | 833 | 833 | 833 | 833 | 833 | 833 |
| Office Supplies (6%) | 2,606 | 2,606 | 2,606 | 2,606 | 2,606 | 2,606 |
| Mortgage (F) | 2,500 | 2,500 | 2,500 | 2,500 | 2,500 | 2,500 |
| Taxes & Licenses (10% of salary) | 500 | 500 | 500 | 500 | 500 | 500 |
| Utilities (2%) | 869 | 869 | 869 | 869 | 869 | 869 |
| | | | | | | |
| **Wages** | | | | | | |
| Dr. Stanley Kramer (F) | 5,000 | 5,000 | 5,000 | 5,000 | 5,000 | 5,000 |
| Hygienist (.28 of production) | 1,882 | 1,882 | 1,882 | 1,882 | 1,882 | 1,882 |
| Salaried & Benefits (21%) | 7,710 | 7,710 | 7,710 | 7,710 | 7,710 | 7,710 |
| Other Expenses (F) | 417 | 417 | 417 | 417 | 417 | 417 |
| **TOTAL EXPENSES:** | **28,672** | **28,672** | **28,672** | **28,672** | **28,672** | **28,672** |
| | | | | | | |
| **NET PROFIT (LOSS):** | **8,246** | **8,246** | **8,246** | **8,246** | **8,246** | **8,246** |

| | |
|---|---|
| **Stanley at 10 patients a day at an average of $183.56/patient** | **440,544** |
| 1 Hygienist at 7 patients a day for 2 days a week averaging $120/patient | 80,640 |
| 1 assistant 40 hours a week at $11.00/hour for 52 weeks | 22,880 |
| 1 receptionist/ bookkeeper 40 hours a week at $11.65/hour at 52 weeks | 24,232 |
| **Weekly wage of assistant and receptionist before benefits** | **47,112** |

| Dec | Jan | Feb | Mar | Apr | May | Total |
|---|---|---|---|---|---|---|
| 36,712 | 36,712 | 36,712 | 36,712 | 36,712 | 36,712 | 440,544 |
| 6,720 | 6,720 | 6,720 | 6,720 | 6,720 | 6,720 | 80,640 |
| 43,432 | 43,432 | 43,432 | 43,432 | 43,432 | 43,432 | 521,184 |
| 39,089 | 39,089 | 39,089 | 39,089 | 39,089 | 39,089 | 469,066 |
| 4,343 | 4,343 | 4,343 | 4,343 | 4,343 | 4,343 | 52,118 |
| | | | | | | |
| (3,909) | (3,909) | (3,909) | (3,909) | (3,909) | (3,909) | (46,907) |
| (2,606) | (2,606) | (2,606) | (2,606) | (2,606) | (2,606) | (31,271) |
| **36,917** | **36,917** | **36,917** | **36,917** | **36,917** | **36,917** | **443,006** |
| | | | | | | |
| | | | | | | |
| 1,303 | 1,303 | 1,303 | 1,303 | 1,303 | 1,303 | 15,636 |
| 1,303 | 1,303 | 1,303 | 1,303 | 1,303 | 1,303 | 15,636 |
| 3,750 | 3,750 | 3,750 | 3,750 | 3,750 | 3,750 | 45,000 |
| 833 | 833 | 833 | 833 | 833 | 833 | 10,000 |
| 2,606 | 2,606 | 2,606 | 2,606 | 2,606 | 2,606 | 31,271 |
| 2,500 | 2,500 | 2,500 | 2,500 | 2,500 | 2,500 | 30,000 |
| 500 | 500 | 500 | 500 | 500 | 500 | 6,000 |
| 869 | 869 | 869 | 869 | 869 | 869 | 10,424 |
| | | | | | | |
| | | | | | | |
| 5,000 | 5,000 | 5,000 | 5,000 | 5,000 | 5,000 | 60,000 |
| 1,882 | 1,882 | 1,882 | 1,882 | 1,882 | 1,882 | 22,579 |
| 7,710 | 7,710 | 7,710 | 7,710 | 7,710 | 7,710 | 92,514 |
| 417 | 417 | 417 | 417 | 417 | 417 | 5,000 |
| **28,672** | **28,672** | **28,672** | **28,672** | **28,672** | **28,672** | **344,059** |
| | | | | | | |
| **8,246** | **8,246** | **8,246** | **8,246** | **8,246** | **8,246** | **98,947** |

## Statement of Cash Flows—Year 4, June 2005-May 2006

|  | Jun | Jul | Aug | Sep | Oct | Nov |
|---|---|---|---|---|---|---|
| **Cash Inflows** | | | | | | |
| Beginning Cash Balance | 53,494 | 52,326 | 51,157 | 49,988 | 48,820 | 47,651 |
| Cash Receipts | 59,574 | 59,574 | 59,574 | 59,574 | 59,574 | 59,574 |
| **Total Cash Inflows** | **113,069** | **111,900** | **110,731** | **109,563** | **108,394** | **107,225** |
| | | | | | | |
| **Cash Disbursements** | | | | | | |
| Lab Fees (9%) | 5,957 | 5,957 | 5,957 | 5,957 | 5,957 | 5,957 |
| Dental Supplies (6%) | 3,972 | 3,972 | 3,972 | 3,972 | 3,972 | 3,972 |
| Advertising (3%) | 1,986 | 1,986 | 1,986 | 1,986 | 1,986 | 1,986 |
| Insurance (3%) | 1,986 | 1,986 | 1,986 | 1,986 | 1,986 | 1,986 |
| Interest Expense (F) | 3,750 | 3,750 | 3,750 | 3,750 | 3,750 | 3,750 |
| Legal & Professional Services (F) | 833 | 833 | 833 | 833 | 833 | 833 |
| Office Supplies (6%) | 3,972 | 3,972 | 3,972 | 3,972 | 3,972 | 3,972 |
| Mortgage (F) | 2,500 | 2,500 | 2,500 | 2,500 | 2,500 | 2,500 |
| Taxes & Licenses (10% of salary) | 958 | 958 | 958 | 958 | 958 | 958 |
| Utilities (2%) | 1,324 | 1,324 | 1,324 | 1,324 | 1,324 | 1,324 |
| | | | | | | |
| **Wages** | | | | | | |
| Dr. Stanley Kramer (F) | 9,583 | 9,583 | 9,583 | 9,583 | 9,583 | 9,583 |
| Dr. Jeremiah Kramer | 14,685 | 14,685 | 14,685 | 14,685 | 14,685 | 14,685 |
| Hygienist | 1,882 | 1,882 | 1,882 | 1,882 | 1,882 | 1,882 |
| Salaried & Benefits | 6,939 | 6,939 | 6,939 | 6,939 | 6,939 | 6,939 |
| Other Expenses (F) | 417 | 417 | 417 | 417 | 417 | 417 |
| | | | | | | |
| **Total Disbursements** | **60,743** | **60,743** | **60,743** | **60,743** | **60,743** | **60,743** |
| | | | | | | |
| **Remaining Cash at Month End** | **52,326** | **51,157** | **49,988** | **48,820** | **47,651** | **46,483** |

| | Dec | Jan | Feb | Mar | Apr | May |
|---|---|---|---|---|---|---|
| | 46,483 | 45,314 | 44,145 | 42,977 | 41,808 | 40,639 |
| | 59,574 | 59,574 | 59,574 | 59,574 | 59,574 | 59,574 |
| | **106,057** | **104,888** | **103,719** | **102,551** | **101,382** | **100,213** |
| | | | | | | |
| | 5,957 | 5,957 | 5,957 | 5,957 | 5,957 | 5,957 |
| | 3,972 | 3,972 | 3,972 | 3,972 | 3,972 | 3,972 |
| | 1,986 | 1,986 | 1,986 | 1,986 | 1,986 | 1,986 |
| | 1,986 | 1,986 | 1,986 | 1,986 | 1,986 | 1,986 |
| | 3,750 | 3,750 | 3,750 | 3,750 | 3,750 | 3,750 |
| | 833 | 833 | 833 | 833 | 833 | 833 |
| | 3,972 | 3,972 | 3,972 | 3,972 | 3,972 | 3,972 |
| | 2,500 | 2,500 | 2,500 | 2,500 | 2,500 | 2,500 |
| | 958 | 958 | 958 | 958 | 958 | 958 |
| | 1,324 | 1,324 | 1,324 | 1,324 | 1,324 | 1,324 |
| | | | | | | |
| | 9,583 | 9,583 | 9,583 | 9,583 | 9,583 | 9,583 |
| | 14,685 | 14,685 | 14,685 | 14,685 | 14,685 | 14,685 |
| | 1,882 | 1,882 | 1,882 | 1,882 | 1,882 | 1,882 |
| | 6,939 | 6,939 | 6,939 | 6,939 | 6,939 | 6,939 |
| | 417 | 417 | 417 | 417 | 417 | 417 |
| | **60,743** | **60,743** | **60,743** | **60,743** | **60,743** | **60,743** |
| | **45,314** | **44,145** | **42,977** | **41,808** | **40,639** | **39,471** |

## Income Statement—Year 5, June 2006-May 2007

| INCOME: | Jun | Jul | Aug | Sep | Oct | Nov |
|---|---|---|---|---|---|---|
| Dr. Stanley Kramer | 36,712 | 36,712 | 36,712 | 36,712 | 36,712 | 36,712 |
| Dr. Jeremiah Kramer | 26,433 | 26,433 | 26,433 | 26,433 | 26,433 | 26,433 |
| Hygienist #1 | 6,720 | 6,720 | 6,720 | 6,720 | 6,720 | 6,720 |
| Hygienist #2 | 6,720 | 6,720 | 6,720 | 6,720 | 6,720 | 6,720 |
| Gross Sales | 76,585 | 76,585 | 76,585 | 76,585 | 76,585 | 76,585 |
| Cash Receipts (90%) | 68,926 | 68,926 | 68,926 | 68,926 | 68,926 | 68,926 |
| Accounts Receivable (10%) | 7,658 | 7,658 | 7,658 | 7,658 | 7,658 | 7,658 |
| | | | | | | |
| **Cost of Goods Sold** | | | | | | |
| Lab Fees (9%) | (6,893) | (6,893) | (6,893) | (6,893) | (6,893) | (6,893) |
| Dental Supplies (6%) | (4,595) | (4,595) | (4,595) | (4,595) | (4,595) | (4,595) |
| **GROSS INCOME:** | **65,097** | **65,097** | **65,097** | **65,097** | **65,097** | **65,097** |
| | | | | | | |
| **EXPENSES:** | | | | | | |
| Advertising (3%) | 2,298 | 2,298 | 2,298 | 2,298 | 2,298 | 2,298 |
| Insurance (3%) | 2,298 | 2,298 | 2,298 | 2,298 | 2,298 | 2,298 |
| Interest Expense (F) | 3,750 | 3,750 | 3,750 | 3,750 | 3,750 | 3,750 |
| Legal & Professional Services (F) | 833 | 833 | 833 | 833 | 833 | 833 |
| Office Supplies (6%) | 4,595 | 4,595 | 4,595 | 4,595 | 4,595 | 4,595 |
| Mortgage (F) | 2,500 | 2,500 | 2,500 | 2,500 | 2,500 | 2,500 |
| Taxes & Licenses (10% of salary) | 1,083 | 1,083 | 1,083 | 1,083 | 1,083 | 1,083 |
| Utilities (2%) | 1,532 | 1,532 | 1,532 | 1,532 | 1,532 | 1,532 |
| | | | | | | |
| **Wages** | | | | | | |
| Dr. Stanley Kramer (F) | 10,833 | 10,833 | 10,833 | 10,833 | 10,833 | 10,833 |
| Dr. Jeremiah Kramer (.5 of production) | 14,685 | 14,685 | 14,685 | 14,685 | 14,685 | 14,685 |
| Hygienist #1 (.28 of production) | 1,882 | 1,882 | 1,882 | 1,882 | 1,882 | 1,882 |
| Hygienist #2 (.25 of production) | 1,680 | 1,680 | 1,680 | 1,680 | 1,680 | 1,680 |
| Salaried & Benefits (21%) | 7,710 | 7,710 | 7,710 | 7,710 | 7,710 | 7,710 |
| Other Expenses (F) | 417 | 417 | 417 | 417 | 417 | 417 |
| **TOTAL EXPENSES:** | **56,094** | **56,094** | **56,094** | **56,094** | **56,094** | **56,094** |
| **NET PROFIT (LOSS):** | **9,002** | **9,002** | **9,002** | **9,002** | **9,002** | **9,002** |

| | |
|---|---|
| **Stanley at 10 patients a day at an average of $183.56/patient** | **440,544** |
| **Jeremiah at 9 patients a day, 4 days a week for 48 weeks at $183.56/patient** | **317,192** |
| 2 Hygienist at 7 patients a day for 2 days a week averaging $120/patient | 161,280 |
| 2 assistants 40 hours a week at $11.00/hour for 52 weeks | 45,760 |
| 1 receptionist/ bookkeeper 40 hours a week at $11.65/hour at 52 weeks | 24,232 |
| 1 receptionist/ bookkeeper 20 hours a week at $11.65/hour at 52 weeks | 12,116 |
| **Weekly wage of assistant and receptionist before benefits** | **82,108** |

| Dec | Jan | Feb | Mar | Apr | May |
|---|---|---|---|---|---|
| 36,712 | 36,712 | 36,712 | 36,712 | 36,712 | 36,712 |
| 26,433 | 26,433 | 26,433 | 26,433 | 26,433 | 26,433 |
| 6,720 | 6,720 | 6,720 | 6,720 | 6,720 | 6,720 |
| 6,720 | 6,720 | 6,720 | 6,720 | 6,720 | 6,720 |
| 76,585 | 76,585 | 76,585 | 76,585 | 76,585 | 76,585 |
| 68,926 | 68,926 | 68,926 | 68,926 | 68,926 | 68,926 |
| 7,658 | 7,658 | 7,658 | 7,658 | 7,658 | 7,658 |
| (6,893) | (6,893) | (6,893) | (6,893) | (6,893) | (6,893) |
| (4,595) | (4,595) | (4,595) | (4,595) | (4,595) | (4,595) |
| **65,097** | **65,097** | **65,097** | **65,097** | **65,097** | **65,097** |
| 2,298 | 2,298 | 2,298 | 2,298 | 2,298 | 2,298 |
| 2,298 | 2,298 | 2,298 | 2,298 | 2,298 | 2,298 |
| 3,750 | 3,750 | 3,750 | 3,750 | 3,750 | 3,750 |
| 833 | 833 | 833 | 833 | 833 | 833 |
| 4,595 | 4,595 | 4,595 | 4,595 | 4,595 | 4,595 |
| 2,500 | 2,500 | 2,500 | 2,500 | 2,500 | 2,500 |
| 1,083 | 1,083 | 1,083 | 1,083 | 1,083 | 1,083 |
| 1,532 | 1,532 | 1,532 | 1,532 | 1,532 | 1,532 |
| 10,833 | 10,833 | 10,833 | 10,833 | 10,833 | 10,833 |
| 14,685 | 14,685 | 14,685 | 14,685 | 14,685 | 14,685 |
| 1,882 | 1,882 | 1,882 | 1,882 | 1,882 | 1,882 |
| 1,680 | 1,680 | 1,680 | 1,680 | 1,680 | 1,680 |
| 7,710 | 7,710 | 7,710 | 7,710 | 7,710 | 7,710 |
| 417 | 417 | 417 | 417 | 417 | 417 |
| **56,094** | **56,094** | **56,094** | **56,094** | **56,094** | **56,094** |
| **9,002** | **9,002** | **9,002** | **9,002** | **9,002** | **9,002** |

## Income Statement—Year 5 without Dr. Jeremiah Kramer, DDS
## June 2006-May 2007

| INCOME: | Jun | Jul | Aug | Sep | Oct | Nov |
|---|---|---|---|---|---|---|
| Dr. Stanley Kramer | 36,712 | 36,712 | 36,712 | 36,712 | 36,712 | 36,712 |
| Hygienist #1 | 6,720 | 6,720 | 6,720 | 6,720 | 6,720 | 6,720 |
| Hygienist #2 | 6,720 | 6,720 | 6,720 | 6,720 | 6,720 | 6,720 |
| Gross Sales | 50,152 | 50,152 | 50,152 | 50,152 | 50,152 | 50,152 |
| Cash Receipts (90%) | 45,137 | 45,137 | 45,137 | 45,137 | 45,137 | 45,137 |
| Accounts Receivable (10%) | 5,015 | 5,015 | 5,015 | 5,015 | 5,015 | 5,015 |
| | | | | | | |
| **Cost of Goods Sold** | | | | | | |
| Lab Fees (9%) | (4,514) | (4,514) | (4,514) | (4,514) | (4,514) | (4,514) |
| Dental Supplies (6%) | (3,009) | (3,009) | (3,009) | (3,009) | (3,009) | (3,009) |
| **GROSS INCOME:** | **42,629** | **42,629** | **42,629** | **42,629** | **42,629** | **42,629** |
| | | | | | | |
| **EXPENSES:** | | | | | | |
| Advertising (3%) | 1,505 | 1,505 | 1,505 | 1,505 | 1,505 | 1,505 |
| Insurance (3%) | 1,505 | 1,505 | 1,505 | 1,505 | 1,505 | 1,505 |
| Interest Expense (F) | 3,750 | 3,750 | 3,750 | 3,750 | 3,750 | 3,750 |
| Legal & Professional Services (F) | 833 | 833 | 833 | 833 | 833 | 833 |
| Office Supplies (6%) | 3,009 | 3,009 | 3,009 | 3,009 | 3,009 | 3,009 |
| Mortgage (F) | 2,500 | 2,500 | 2,500 | 2,500 | 2,500 | 2,500 |
| Taxes & Licenses (10% of salary) | 500 | 500 | 500 | 500 | 500 | 500 |
| Utilities (2%) | 1,003 | 1,003 | 1,003 | 1,003 | 1,003 | 1,003 |
| | | | | | | |
| **Wages** | | | | | | |
| Dr. Stanley Kramer (F) | 5,000 | 5,000 | 5,000 | 5,000 | 5,000 | 5,000 |
| Hygienist #1 (.28 of production) | 1,882 | 1,882 | 1,882 | 1,882 | 1,882 | 1,882 |
| Hygienist #2 (.25 of production) | 1,680 | 1,680 | 1,680 | 1,680 | 1,680 | 1,680 |
| Salaried & Benefits (21%) | 7,710 | 7,710 | 7,710 | 7,710 | 7,710 | 7,710 |
| Other Expenses (F) | 417 | 417 | 417 | 417 | 417 | 417 |
| **TOTAL EXPENSES:** | **31,292** | **31,292** | **31,292** | **31,292** | **31,292** | **31,292** |
| **NET PROFIT (LOSS):** | **11,337** | **11,337** | **11,337** | **11,337** | **11,337** | **11,337** |

| | |
|---|---|
| **Stanley at 10 patients a day at an average of $183.56/patient** | **440,544** |
| 1 Hygienist at 7 patients a day for 2 days a week averaging $120/patient | 80,640 |
| 1 Hygienist at 7 patients a day for 2 days a week averaging $120/patient | 80,640 |
| 1 assistant 40 hours a week at $11.00/hour for 52 weeks | 22,880 |
| 1 receptionist/ bookkeeper 40 hours a week at $11.65/hour at 52 weeks | 24,232 |
| 1 receptionist/ bookkeeper 20 hours a week at $11.65/hour at 52 weeks | 12,116 |
| **Weekly wage of assistant and receptionist before benefits** | **59,228** |

| Dec | Jan | Feb | Mar | Apr | May | Total |
|---|---|---|---|---|---|---|
| 36,712 | 36,712 | 36,712 | 36,712 | 36,712 | 36,712 | 440,544 |
| 6,720 | 6,720 | 6,720 | 6,720 | 6,720 | 6,720 | 80,640 |
| 6,720 | 6,720 | 6,720 | 6,720 | 6,720 | 6,720 | 80,640 |
| 50,152 | 50,152 | 50,152 | 50,152 | 50,152 | 50,152 | 601,824 |
| 45,137 | 45,137 | 45,137 | 45,137 | 45,137 | 45,137 | 541,642 |
| 5,015 | 5,015 | 5,015 | 5,015 | 5,015 | 5,015 | 60,182 |
| | | | | | | |
| (4,514) | (4,514) | (4,514) | (4,514) | (4,514) | (4,514) | (54,164) |
| (3,009) | (3,009) | (3,009) | (3,009) | (3,009) | (3,009) | (36,109) |
| **42,629** | **42,629** | **42,629** | **42,629** | **42,629** | **42,629** | **511,550** |
| | | | | | | |
| 1,505 | 1,505 | 1,505 | 1,505 | 1,505 | 1,505 | 18,055 |
| 1,505 | 1,505 | 1,505 | 1,505 | 1,505 | 1,505 | 18,055 |
| 3,750 | 3,750 | 3,750 | 3,750 | 3,750 | 3,750 | 45,000 |
| 833 | 833 | 833 | 833 | 833 | 833 | 10,000 |
| 3,009 | 3,009 | 3,009 | 3,009 | 3,009 | 3,009 | 36,109 |
| 2,500 | 2,500 | 2,500 | 2,500 | 2,500 | 2,500 | 30,000 |
| 500 | 500 | 500 | 500 | 500 | 500 | 6,000 |
| 1,003 | 1,003 | 1,003 | 1,003 | 1,003 | 1,003 | 12,036 |
| | | | | | | |
| 5,000 | 5,000 | 5,000 | 5,000 | 5,000 | 5,000 | 60,000 |
| 1,882 | 1,882 | 1,882 | 1,882 | 1,882 | 1,882 | 22,579 |
| 1,680 | 1,680 | 1,680 | 1,680 | 1,680 | 1,680 | 20,160 |
| 7,710 | 7,710 | 7,710 | 7,710 | 7,710 | 7,710 | 92,514 |
| 417 | 417 | 417 | 417 | 417 | 417 | 5,000 |
| **31,292** | **31,292** | **31,292** | **31,292** | **31,292** | **31,292** | **375,509** |
| **11,337** | **11,337** | **11,337** | **11,337** | **11,337** | **11,337** | **136,042** |

## Statement of Cash Flows—Year 5, June 2006-May 2007

|  | Jun | Jul | Aug | Sep | Oct | Nov |
|---|---|---|---|---|---|---|
| **Cash Inflows** | | | | | | |
| Beginning Cash Balance | 39,471 | 40,815 | 42,159 | 43,503 | 44,847 | 46,191 |
| Cash Receipts | 68,926 | 68,926 | 68,926 | 68,926 | 68,926 | 68,926 |
| **Total Cash Inflows** | **108,397** | **109,741** | **111,085** | **112,429** | **113,773** | **115,117** |
| | | | | | | |
| **Cash Disbursements** | | | | | | |
| Lab Fees (9%) | 6,893 | 6,893 | 6,893 | 6,893 | 6,893 | 6,893 |
| Dental Supplies (6%) | 4,595 | 4,595 | 4,595 | 4,595 | 4,595 | 4,595 |
| Advertising (3%) | 2,298 | 2,298 | 2,298 | 2,298 | 2,298 | 2,298 |
| Insurance (3%) | 2,298 | 2,298 | 2,298 | 2,298 | 2,298 | 2,298 |
| Interest Expense (F) | 3,750 | 3,750 | 3,750 | 3,750 | 3,750 | 3,750 |
| Legal & Professional Services (F) | 833 | 833 | 833 | 833 | 833 | 833 |
| Office Supplies (6%) | 4,595 | 4,595 | 4,595 | 4,595 | 4,595 | 4,595 |
| Mortgage (F) | 2,500 | 2,500 | 2,500 | 2,500 | 2,500 | 2,500 |
| Taxes & Licenses (10% of salary) | 1,083 | 1,083 | 1,083 | 1,083 | 1,083 | 1,083 |
| Utilities (2%) | 1,532 | 1,532 | 1,532 | 1,532 | 1,532 | 1,532 |
| | | | | | | |
| **Wages** | | | | | | |
| Dr. Stanley Kramer (F) | 10,833 | 10,833 | 10,833 | 10,833 | 10,833 | 10,833 |
| Dr. Jeremiah Kramer | 14,685 | 14,685 | 14,685 | 14,685 | 14,685 | 14,685 |
| Hygienist #1 | 1,882 | 1,882 | 1,882 | 1,882 | 1,882 | 1,882 |
| Hygienist #2 | 1,680 | 1,680 | 1,680 | 1,680 | 1,680 | 1,680 |
| Salaried & Benefits | 7,710 | 7,710 | 7,710 | 7,710 | 7,710 | 7,710 |
| Other Expenses (F) | 417 | 417 | 417 | 417 | 417 | 417 |
| | | | | | | |
| **Total Disbursements** | **67,582** | **67,582** | **67,582** | **67,582** | **67,582** | **67,582** |
| | | | | | | |
| **Remaining Cash at Month End** | **40,815** | **42,159** | **43,503** | **44,847** | **46,191** | **47,535** |

| Dec | Jan | Feb | Mar | Apr | May |
|---|---|---|---|---|---|
| 47,535 | 48,879 | 50,223 | 51,566 | 52,910 | 54,254 |
| 68,926 | 68,926 | 68,926 | 68,926 | 68,926 | 68,926 |
| **116,461** | **117,805** | **119,149** | **120,493** | **121,837** | **123,181** |
| | | | | | |
| 6,893 | 6,893 | 6,893 | 6,893 | 6,893 | 6,893 |
| 4,595 | 4,595 | 4,595 | 4,595 | 4,595 | 4,595 |
| 2,298 | 2,298 | 2,298 | 2,298 | 2,298 | 2,298 |
| 2,298 | 2,298 | 2,298 | 2,298 | 2,298 | 2,298 |
| 3,750 | 3,750 | 3,750 | 3,750 | 3,750 | 3,750 |
| 833 | 833 | 833 | 833 | 833 | 833 |
| 4,595 | 4,595 | 4,595 | 4,595 | 4,595 | 4,595 |
| 2,500 | 2,500 | 2,500 | 2,500 | 2,500 | 2,500 |
| 1,083 | 1,083 | 1,083 | 1,083 | 1,083 | 1,083 |
| 1,532 | 1,532 | 1,532 | 1,532 | 1,532 | 1,532 |
| | | | | | |
| 10,833 | 10,833 | 10,833 | 10,833 | 10,833 | 10,833 |
| 14,685 | 14,685 | 14,685 | 14,685 | 14,685 | 14,685 |
| 1,882 | 1,882 | 1,882 | 1,882 | 1,882 | 1,882 |
| 1,680 | 1,680 | 1,680 | 1,680 | 1,680 | 1,680 |
| 7,710 | 7,710 | 7,710 | 7,710 | 7,710 | 7,710 |
| 417 | 417 | 417 | 417 | 417 | 417 |
| **67,582** | **67,582** | **67,582** | **67,582** | **67,582** | **67,582** |
| **48,879** | **50,223** | **51,566** | **52,910** | **54,254** | **55,598** |

**Possible Pitfalls**

**Locating a suitable practice**—There is the possibility that the perfect practice does not exist in our desired location. Further, the practice that I do the associateship with may not be optimal for purchase. In that case I will survey the area for a practice to buy or a location to build. Living in the area will give me latitude to do this.

**Not being asked to buy the practice from the present owner**—If the owner does not like my work or decides not to retire, I will weigh my options. I could buy another practice, build a practice or possibly do a partial buyout of the current practice. Fortunately, this decision will be made after I have had a year's experience with the owner to assess his practice, the area, and my goals for the future without any capital outlay.

**Not having a "quality" client base**—I feel that it is optimal to buy a practice with a good client base. Sometimes the goodwill of the client base is overstated. By working in a practice, I will have the opportunity to assess the quality of the clients. If I decide not to buy the practice that I am doing an associateship in, I will have built up a client pool of my own that will hopefully follow me to my new practice.

**Not having large enough initial client base**—We will select a practice only after intense study of its active patient base, collection percentage, etc.

**Possibility of clashing management styles between previous owners and new owners**—We feel that patients will adapt to our style provided we make it a policy to show sincere concern for our patients' well being. Also, we realize that it is likely that the practice will lose a percentage of its original patients in the beginning.

**Possibility of clashing management styles of new owners**—An office manual will be constructed prior to purchase of the practice to determine whether management philosophies are compatible. Any discrepancies will be discussed and documented with employees having say in outcome.

**Positive Aspects**

- Market conditions are right for location selected
- Pre-existing client base
- A business agreement that meets both my father's and my personal and professional goals
- Industry trends are favorable (see Appendix)

**APPENDIX**

**Managed Care**

As in the medical profession, over the past couple of years, the dental industry has been bombarded with Preferred Provider Organizations (PPO) and Dental Health Maintenance Organizations (DHMO). Not surprising, after a couple years' trial of these services, many dentists are going back to traditional, independent practices. In 1995, 44 percent of dentists surveyed participated in at least one PPO and 19 percent participated in a DHMO as compared to 37.1 percent and 15.5 percent respectively in 1996 (Kehoe, pp. 28-29). Dr. Gordon Christensen, a leading researcher, clinician, and lecturer in dentistry, feels that the move to managed care has "degenerated the quality of dentistry, particularly the dentistry delivered by less-mature dentists" and that it has only proven beneficial for those patients that might not have had access to dentistry previously (Bonner, p.74). He predicts a movement away from managed care in the next 15 years as the American public becomes disgruntled with the poor quality and reduced alternatives offered by managed care much like it has in the medical profession. "We will see free-enterprise dentistry finally win, and therefore, the American public wins because quality will remain. This will happen because of the elective nature of many dental services, and the lack of most managed care programs to provide care in the elective area" (Bonner, p. 78).

One current trend in the dental industry is the linking together or networking of separate dental practices. This is called consolidation and is normally instigated by nondentist entrepreneurs who have recognized a potential income source in uniting dentists with managed care organizations (MCO). The dentists either act as salaried employees to the MCO or get paid a percentage of the collections or production. Obviously this is not the scenario that the dentist hoped for when attending eight years of school. This is only an alternative that the dentist will consider when faced with the choice of staying in private practice and losing a large percentage of the patient base to managed care or joining managed care and losing money. Consolidators act as brokers that see to it that the MCO gets the much needed managed care dental providers and that the dentists get a fair contract. This is done by networking dental practices. The consolidator is called a network administrator and he/she "evaluates the proposed contract, negotiates the terms and sets up the agreement." These consolidations are very similar to the activity taking place in the physician managed-care networks.

There are various benefits derived from the use of consolidation networks. Dentists in the managed care network receive an increase in patients. Although most consolidations that have been made include already practicing dentists, many recent graduates see it as an appealing alternative. The main benefit that they see is the elimination of the expenses associated with setting up a practice. Also it greatly reduces the necessity of making business decisions. As many dental students have had little or no business experience or instruction, and have had an education based almost entirely in science, the prospect of running a business is frightening. Speculators expect a trend toward recent graduates joining MCO networks right out of school. One other benefit of the networks is that consolidators focus on using "economies of scale" to save money. Network dental offices within a given location will see reduced lab expenses, supplies and equipment costs by volume purchasing.

Consolidation also has many obstacles. Neither dentists nor patients of managed care have as much freedom of choice in the dental care given or received. As dentistry is becoming more elective and is offering more alternatives for each diagnosis, both the patient and dentist want more freedom of choice. There is also the question of legal liability for treatment. If the dentist is merely acting as an employee of a MCO, who is liable in a case of malpractice? "Managed care companies usually cannot be directly sued for malpractice because they do not practice dentistry, but rather 'arrange' for treatment or pay for services. Consolidation companies may work with network dentists as independent contractors or employees. If a dentist is an employee or 'agent' of a company, that company may be held liable." Finally, some states have laws stating that only a dentist can own a dental practice. "Challenges to the law are expected to be made by consolidators in 'dentist-ownership only' states."

As the baby boomers are starting to turn 50, there is much interest in the effect that this will have on dentistry. Many dentists retire between the ages of 55 and 65 and as the baby boomers near these ages, there are many questions that need to be answered about the competitive factors involved. For instance, will there be a surplus of dental practices for sale in the next 10 years, making a shift to a buyer's market? Imtiaz Manji, president of ExperDent Consultants, Inc. says that eventually the dental practice market will be a buyer's market. He speculates that the only practices that will sell at close to what their value is today are those that have "exceptionally well-managed patient bases and goodwill assets" (Manji, p. 12).

Another question concerning the retirement of baby boomer dentists is whether there will be a shortage of dentists in 10 years. This question can be looked at by discussing the number of active dentists that will be over 50 in 10 years and the number of dental students graduating in the next few years. In 1996, there were 152,575 professionally active dentists in the United States. Of the active dentists, only 45,580 or 30 percent were under age 40. That means that

## Consolidation

## Baby Boomer Dentists Retiring

within 10 years, 70 percent of the current active dentists will either be retired or preparing for retirement. Will this number be offset by an abnormally high market influx of recent graduates? Currently there are 55 dental schools in the United States and the current trend is that it is more likely for a school to close down that for a new school to be instituted. In 1996, there were 16,570 undergraduate dental students of which 3,810 graduated. Applications to dental schools have increased from 5,123 to 8,872 between 1990 and 1996; however, class sizes have remained relatively the same size ("Key Dental Facts, pp. 14-16).

## Bigger Bottom Line

The current trend in dentistry is increased wealth. Between 1995 and 1996, 73.2 percent of dentists noted increased take home pay, 76.8 percent reported their gross personal income increased by a median of 10 percent, and more than 50 percent of respondents claimed unchanged or decreased overhead costs. When the dentists surveyed were asked the reason for this increase in wealth, they typically diagnosed it as a "combination of working harder, working smarter, and increasing fees" (Kehoe, p. 28).

## Globalization

As we enter a new millennium, we are forced to expand our viewpoint to include the international perspective. "Globalization can be defined as a process of change stemming from a combination of increasing cross-border activity and information technology enabling virtually instantaneous communication worldwide." There is a greater global immigration among dentists, and countries are becoming more lenient with their accreditation of immigrant dentists. Furthermore, many students are receiving their education internationally. The Internet has become an integral part of international communication among dentists. The more developed nations claim to be becoming more "Americanized" in dentistry. This is important since American dentistry has led the way in most dental advancements in the last several decades. There is also a push for the developed nations to make dental practices and education available to underdeveloped countries due to a great feeling of international social responsibility among the dental profession. This push toward globalization is opening vistas worldwide in such avenues as business opportunities, education and training, and social conscious.

## Technology

More and more dentists are embracing the new innovations that have reached the industry. Nearly 93 percent of respondents to a survey done by Dental Practice and Finance magazine use computers in the daily operations of their practice. As the doctor's income level increased, so did the spending on new technologies. A listing of percentages of high-tech instrumentation used by respondents is as follows ("Examining Incomes," p. 32):

| | |
|---|---|
| Intraoral video camera | 37.1% |
| Air abrasion cavity preparation systems | 5.0% |
| Digital radiography | 2.8% |
| Cosmetic imaging software | 5.5% |

## New Products

In an interview conducted with Dr. Gordon Christensen, he addressed the most important changes in dentistry in the last 15 years and how they will affect the next 15 years. In his discussion, he talks of an abundance of new product innovation and dental procedure improvements that are shaping dentistry of the future. For instance, the vast use of fluoride in community water and by direct application to teeth by means of toothpaste and rinses has greatly controlled the cases of gross caries that have been seen in past generations. This has promoted dentistry to a point of being largely preventative rather than restorative. With the new preventative stance taken, doctors can spend more time doing some form of aesthetic or cosmetic dentistry, which is where the true profit comes into play. For example, due to preventative measures, the average person retains his or her teeth longer. Since people age 50 and older have more discretionary money, they are more prone to take advantage of new products and processes, such as tooth whitening and implants. As the baby boomers hit this age, dentists will see an even bigger trend toward aesthetic and cosmetic services. Dr. Christensen gives a listing of the areas that have seen the most change in dentistry over the last 15 years. This list includes (Bonner, p. 74):

**20 Areas That Have Changed Dentistry Over the Last 15 Years**

1. Infection control
2. Orthognathic surgery
3. Adult orthodontics
4. Lighted handpieces
5. Magnifying Loupes
6. Aesthetic Dentistry
7. Bleaching teeth
8. Composite resin restoration
9. Controlling caries among children
10. The maturation of dental implants
11. Intraoral cameras
12. Digital radiography
13. Ceramic restorations in fixed prosthodontics
14. Polymer-based fixed prosthodontic restorations
15. The maturation of class II resins
16. Microscopic endodontics
17. Air abrasion
18. Resin-reinforced glass ionomers
19. The refinement of impression materials
20. Managed Care

**Bibliography**

Bonner, Phillip. "A Look at the Past and Future: Interview with Gordon Christensen, DDS, Ph.D." *Dentistry Today*, December 1997.

Dental County Reports. American Dental Association.

"Examining the Incomes of High-tech Dentists." *Dental Practice and Finance,* Nov./Dec. 1997, pp. 32-33.

Kehoe, Bob. "Building a Bigger Bottom Line." *Dental Practice and Finance,* Nov./Dec. 1997, pp. 28-36.

"Key Dental Facts." *American Dental Association,* Survey Center, September 1997.

Manji, Imtiaz. "Practically Speaking: Solving Management Challenges." *Dental Practice and Finance*, Nov./Dec. 1997, p. 12.

"Starting Your Dental Practice: A Complete Guide." *American Dental Association*, Practice Management, Series, 1996.

# Discount Internet Securities Broker

BUSINESS PLAN                                 E-BEST-TRADE.COM

*580 Washington Boulevard*
*Chicago, Illinois 60661*

*This company raised $1 million (at $.20 per share) and an additional $400,000 in loans using this plan written in May 1999. A revised version will likely raise between $2 million and $3 million by the first quarter of 2001. Technology Consultants, Inc., a business planning and strategy firm for early-stage technology companies, supplied the plan.*

- EXECUTIVE SUMMARY

- COMPANY DESCRIPTION

- COMPANY PRODUCTS & SERVICES

- MANAGEMENT

- MARKETING & SALES STRATEGY

- MARKET ANALYSIS

- FINANCIAL PLAN

## EXECUTIVE SUMMARY

The financial services industry has two unique market windows converging in the next six months that e-best-trade.com Incorporated ("e-best-trade.com") is positioned to assume a leadership role:

1. Discount Internet Securities Brokers are grabbing customers and trading volume from traditional full-service brokers at an increasing pace.
2. Extended trading hours on NASDAQ and the NYSE by early fall 1999 will require brokerages to double their staff to meet client requirements to trade and access portfolio and company information—or build their own online trading system.

## The e-best-trade.com Solution

For $500 a month and $1.00 per trade, e-best-trade.com Incorporated can offer broker-dealers a "Schwab(c)-like" turnkey discounted online trading service. There are currently no directly competing services to the e-best-trade.com offering and the alternative—to build in-house—is technologically complex with costs ranging from $250,000 to over $1,000,000.

This service can be quickly implemented and is fully customizable so that the client thinks the trading is occurring at the broker-dealer site and server. All client portfolios and client information appears on the site. The e-best-trade.com system is one of the most secure on the market, using technology from GlobalEye Security Systems as a foundation for solid transaction and server security.

In the U.S., there are more than 5,500 securities firms with more than 62,000 branch offices. With over 130 stock exchanges globally, it's expected that the number of broker-dealers comprising the target market exceeds 50,000 firms.

The company requires U.S. $4 million over the next year to do a market trial and launch the service nationally. A fully functioning pilot of the system is installed at AMXStock.com, a broker-dealer and e-best-trade.com customer. Within four weeks of funding, the system will be ready to market trial with AMXStock's 100 brokers. Within a month, parallel trials will occur in Chicago and New York. Following this, e-best-trade.com will direct market to 2,000 of the largest mid-sized broker-dealers not already online, and commence international expansion and publicity to establish it as a leader in providing this service.

The company's founder is Dr. Theodore Singer, who has a Ph.D. in engineering, mathematics and computer science from M.I.T. and more than 30 years of experience. Dr. Singer has assembled a strong management team with broad experience in the securities and high-tech industries.

## COMPANY DESCRIPTION

e-best-trade.com Incorporated was chartered in the state of Oregon for the purpose of developing, marketing and acting as a service bureau for Internet-based securities trading systems. The company has exclusive rights to a suite of secure server and transaction software developed specifically for the brokerage industry. This suite of software combines with proprietary trading and clearing systems to produce a turnkey, secure, Web-based discount brokerage trading system targeted to small- and medium-sized broker-dealers who do not have the resources to develop their own online systems.

## Location and Facilities

e-best-trade.com will contract out all R&D to GlobalEye Security Systems (GES). GES operates out of premises in Montreal, Quebec. The facility has state-of-the-art computer testing and assembly space and an Internet Service Provider (ISP) location with 10MB fiber optics "pipe." The facility is alarmed and visited nightly at least 6 times on a random basis by a local security company.

e-best-trade.com has an established management office in Portland and will initially operate "identity" sales offices in Chicago and New York. Within 24 months, the company expects to have full offices in those cities, as well as representatives in Chicago alliances with firms in Toronto, Hong Kong, and Sydney.

*Goal: to be the de-facto standard for Web-based brokerage systems solutions within 24 months of market launch, through savvy marketing, alliance, and business operations strategies.*

**Company Objectives and Mission**

To achieve the above goal, the company's objectives are set out in phases.

**In Phase I,** the objective was to design an online brokerage trading system that would incorporate all the functionality of current Web-based systems and also be extremely secure and portable to many clients, either through selling the software or on an out-sourced service bureau basis. This objective was achieved in March 1998.

**In Phase II,** the objective was to find a broker-dealer client who would be willing to work through and refine the system and also act as a demo site for e-best-trade.com capabilities. In addition, patent processes for the software would be started. The demo/client site was achieved by signing AMXStock.com as a customer in June 1998; the patent process is underway and still pending.

**Current Status, June 1, 1999**

**In Phase III,** the objective is to raise capital ($500K) to add third-party quote systems, refine the AMXStock.com site to make it a world-class Internet destination. The management team that has already agreed to join the company will be brought on board on a full- and part-time basis as funds permit. The product will undergo a full market trial in Chicago, New York, and, pending regulatory issues, Toronto. In this phase, the emphasis will be on building the operations and administrative infrastructure and technical support systems so that clients, once signed, can be swiftly implemented and brought online. This phase is already underway and with funding will be completed by August 15, 1999.

**In Phase IV,** the objective is to raise additional capital ($1.5 million) to launch the product in the U.S. and Canada through an intensive telemarketing, hosted events, and advertising campaign to capitalize on the "extended hours" trading in September. In this Phase, the company wants to ensure that sales growth does not outstrip the ability of development, operations, and technical teams to properly support existing and new clients. The company expects that there will be a number of "evolutions" of the available product, and will build automated upgrade systems for existing clients. An aggressive, but steady growth pattern will continue until March 2000.

**In Phase V,** additional capital will be required for additional staff, facilities, and international expansion ($2 million). This will occur with the assistance of a public relations and advertising campaign, and hiring experienced high level staff to manage this process. The company will increase sales and support staff and develop full offices in Chicago, New York, Toronto, and Sydney. The company expects to grow by alliance or merger with well established firms in London, Hong Kong, and other international investment hubs that have support staff and financial systems experience and customers. The company expects to expand into other financial verticals such as insurance and financial planning advisors with products specific to industry needs. This phase is expected to last until June 2001.

**Phase VI,** the future. The company will continue to expand internationally, developing specific products to handle the more than 130 stock exchanges globally and the increasing need of investors to have access to truly global investment opportunities.

## Responsibility & Mission

e-best-trade.com has a responsibility to return a profit to the company's stockholders, then establish a process whereby future investors may reap substantial profits. To fulfill this responsibility, the company's management team must produce a quality, leading-edge software and service offering that is cost effective and competitive. Company profits should follow closely.

Due to the nature of this business, the end user is generally not the paying customer. So, this technology and service must be managed in a dignified and responsible manner so that the company's customers are able to retain and grow their client base.

The Mission of e-best-trade.com will be to perform these functions with uncompromising integrity, excellence, and service with utmost respect towards the firms and individuals we serve.

## The Company's Developmental Stage

The company has progressed from the idea stage to the product development and pilot stage, Phases I and II, with founders seed money. The company is in Phase III of its plan and seeks funding to complete the last phases of making the service market-ready, conducting a market trial and establishing the management team and infrastructure. As soon as Phase III is completed, the company plans to enter Phase IV, market launch, and will be seeking additional funds according to the Financial Plan section later in this document.

## COMPANY PRODUCTS & SERVICES

e-best-trade.com gives small to medium-sized broker-dealers an online stock trading system with functionality similar to E-Trade© or Schwab© for $500 a month and $1.00 per trade.

Transaction security is the most important and highly sought-after element in the growth of online financial applications. Available security software utilizing public key and SSL (secure sockets layer) encryption protocols can be cumbersome, may inhibit speed of transactions, and if penetrated have inherent adverse side effects. e-best-trade.com's software combines patent-pending transaction and server security with proprietary security trading and clearing functions. It allows full service broker-dealers or financial advisers the ability to offer feature-rich and very secure online discounted trading and remain profitable.

e-best-trade.com customers will be able to offer clients access to their portfolios over the Internet, allow interaction with their brokers to buy and sell, and will also allow them to take advantage of discount trading.

## System Features

The online trading system has been designed with customization tools that make installation straightforward and fast. Features of the system include:

- Fully customizable to broker-dealer's image and client servicing requirements
- Speedy installation—can be operational in less than a week
- Quotes, charts, news, and client portfolio
- Online trading with real-time quotes
- Online registration and client information

**Board of Directors**

There are currently three members of the Board of Directors who have agreed to act until changed by the company stockholders at the first annual stockholders meeting. It's expected that three additional directors will be appointed as soon as the company begins formal operation.

| Name | Experience and Qualifications |
|---|---|
| Dr. Theodore Singer | President, GlobalEye Security Systems Inc. |
| Henry Muster | President, AMXStock.com |
| Jennifer Heartly | Managing Partner, Beechknoll Consulting Inc. |

**Dr. Theodore Singer**, Founder and Chief Technology Officer

Dr. Singer holds a Ph.D. in engineering and applied mathematics and computer sciences from M.I.T. (1974), where he worked at the internationally famous Morningstar Research Institute conducting many projects. From 1976 to 1983, he was a college professor of Computer and Engineering Sciences. His industry experience includes MIS, software design, and consulting for major companies in the U.S. and Canada. He did extensive research in large project management and consulted on famous IT projects such as Project Atlantis-M.

Dr. Singer founded GlobalEye Security Systems Inc., a computer firm specializing in network integration and innovative software solutions. He was responsible for the company's rise from a small home operation to a successful company with sales in excess of $10 million.

**Henry Muster**, Director

Mr. Muster holds a M.S. in mathematics (San Diego University, 1965) and an Executive M.B.A. (University of Notre Dame, 1987). He has over 30 years' professional experience in finance, management, and engineering. As President and CEO of AMXStock.com he directs and manages a broker-dealer with a wide range of products, services, and contacts.

**Jennifer Heartly**, President and CEO

Ms. Heartly holds an M.B.A. and is a Certified Management Consultant. Since 1994, she has consulted on technology management issues in the U.S. and Canada and has managed over $200 million in technology acquisitions and contracts.

Ms. Heartly is on the board of Capital Ventures Inc., and has most recently specialized in taking technology startups from concept to financing stages. She has extensive experience opening international high-tech markets through direct, agency, and reseller channels.

Ms. Heartly has been involved with technology since 1981, as a systems analyst supporting the brokerage offerings for Data Keys in New York City. Subsequently, with Morris Ltd. she managed telecommunications for the New York Stock Exchange and Zoe Securities. With Mission Data Systems, she worked closely with Michael Roberts to develop an early ISDN brokerage system in conjunction with TRG Telephone Systems. As acting Director of the Eastern seaboard Branch of the Timber S Group, she was responsible for all the financial modeling and analysis for its comprehensive New York Stock Exchange project.

**Nicholas Moster**, Vice President, Sales and Marketing

Mr. Moster has more than 15 years' high-tech sales and international equity trading experience in more than seven countries around the world. In 1984, with a degree from the European Securities Institute, he became a Director and Partner in four private companies headquartered in Paris, France.

In 1989, he moved to Singapore as a Company Director and Institutional Business Manager for the Keystone Group. He provided consulting to nearly all of the respective members of the Singapore Stock Exchange and then further afield to include Malaysia, Hong Kong, the Philippines, and surrounding South East Asian countries working with brokerage firms and government-managed equity funds.

In 1993 he moved to New York City working as a Senior Account Manager for the Timbe S Group. Interfacing with each of the listed companies on the New York Stock Exchange, he later incorporated his expertise to assist Canadian Companies with the foreign listings in the U.S. on the NASDAQ and the NYSE. Mr. Moster now resides in Toronto working in the technology sector specializing in Strategic Account Management at a senior level for Internet "startup" companies. He plans to join the company within a month of initial funding.

**Jeremy Birch**, President, Development and Operations

Mr. Birch has been involved in the business and deployment sides of technology since 1981. He holds an M.B.A. focusing on Finance and Entrepreneurial studies and an undergraduate majoring in economics and computer science. He spent three years developing business plans, financial plans, and business analysis reports for high-tech companies in their early stages of development and three years' head office accounting and IT management in a multinational corporation.

Since 1988 he has provided outsourced IT management services to a number of small clients and a large corporate client ($1 million annual IT budget). He is the primary designer and developer of over 50 custom financial, accounting, and investment analysis software applications. His investment activities include short-term trading of technology and resource stocks, a general partner in one commercial software company, and a limited partner in a software development fund.

Mr. Birch's current projects include an all-inclusive corporate intranet site development, Y2K readiness preparation, and computerizing a custom stock trading system and a graphical data based economic/market data trends website. He plans to join the company within two months of initial funding, working part-time in the interim until he completes his current work.

**Gene Benson**, Vice President, Administration

Following 20 years with Delta Airlines, during which time he was responsible for developing North America's first self-service airline ticketing kiosks, Mr. Benson continued to combine his expertise and knowledge providing new services to the travel and tourism sectors. As joint founder and Vice President, Sales and Marketing of an online "e-Commerce" company, Mr. Benson provided new capabilities to major vacation resorts in North America, including online sales ranging from accommodation reservations to lift-ticket sales.

From 1993 to 1995 he was Vice President, Business Development for a Toronto tourism information system which was part of a larger Ontario provincial tourism initiative. From

1989 to 1993 he concentrated on interactive multimedia technologies and developed an electronic "duty free" shopping center located within hotels. It served an international clientele on behalf of international airlines.

**Mark Waddle**, Acting Director of Technology

Mr. Waddle holds a B.S. in Physics (University of Chicago, 1995) and is currently head of MIS systems for GlobalEye Security Systems Inc. He is experienced in UNIX, Novell, and NT and is a C programming specialist. Mr. Waddle plans to work with the company until Mr. Birch comes on board in order to transition development work smoothly. He will remain as a full-time employee of GlobalEye Security Systems, e-best-trade.com's outsourced development and data center in Montreal, Quebec.

The company's marketing and sales strategy is to promote and support its quickly installable online trading system as a solution to NASDAQ and NYSE extended trading hours and the loss of clients by broker-dealers to discount Web-based trading firms.

## MARKETING & SALES STRATEGY

The company's initial target market is the small- to medium-sized broker-dealers and brokers that do not have online systems in the U.S. and Canada. There are 5,500 broker-dealers in the U.S. with over 60,000 branch offices.

### Target Markets

Within a month of initial funding, e-best-trade.com will be ready to market to broker-dealers and brokers in both the U.S. and Canada. Due to regulatory constraints, the Canadian product will have to be modified. However, there is an immediate opportunity for mutual fund sales through both small brokerages and financial advisors.

NYSE and NASDAQ have announced extended trading hours to be implemented by early fall, extending trading to twelve hours a day from the current six. For full service brokerage firms without an online trading option, this means huge costs in staffing and support personnel to maintain trading for clients while the markets are open. Similar announcements are expected at other major exchanges around the world.

### Strategic Market Opportunity

The company feels that there is a window of opportunity to take advantage of this timing, and has set its market launch to occur prior to extended trading. With funding in place, it is critical that the company pursue its marketing objectives as soon as possible.

These accounts will be managed by the President and Sales Vice President, as they generally require executive level contacts.

### Partnerships and Alliances

**GlobalEye Security Systems**

e-best-trade.com has a partnership with GlobalEye Security Systems and exclusive rights to its products for the financial industry. GlobalEye Security Systems was conceived to meet the need of secure commerce on the Internet. GlobalEye has low cost top layer products designed to remove the threat of intruders being able to break in and compromise an Internet server and its data as it travels over the Internet. When used in combination these products provide the most secure and effective electronic commerce applications available. GlobalEye Systems will provide data center, development, and technical support until the company is sufficiently funded to build its own infrastructure and systems.

**AMXStock.com**

The company has formed a strategic alliance with AMXStock.com of Chicago which has been a pilot site for the development of the online trading system. AMXStock.com has over 100 brokers who will comprise the first market trial of the company's Internet trading solution. Based on this trial, expected to start a month after funding occurs, the company will revise and refine its product and continue trials in Chicago and Toronto until market launch late August.

**WI International**

The company has also formed an alliance with Dr. Mark Woo of Woo International (WI). WI will be assisting in e-best-trade.com's international market expansion and future investment. With its affiliates in many different countries, WI has a global network for marketing, joint venture, partnership, and investment for high-tech products. In foreign countries, WI has a particularly strong market base in Germany, Japan, Korea, Taiwan, and China.

**Future considerations**

The company intends to pursue alliances with international firms actively developing business in the brokerage services sector in Austral-Asia, Europe, and South America. The company Sales Vice President has extensive international experience with firms in Asia and Australia, and it's expected that much of his effort in the early part of Year Two will be to develop these alliances and manage the relationship with WI.

## Marketing Vehicles

**Direct Contact**

Prior to market launch, a complete list of prospects will be gathered and an intensive telemarketing campaign will commence, so that sales activities can begin as soon as there is a completed online system. e-best-trade.com has an up-to-date, accurate listing of 4,000 of these broker-dealers, and will be narrowing and enhancing the list with contact names, phone numbers, and e-mail addresses over the next three months to the top 2,000 prospects.

Use of demo websites and e-mail as marketing tools will greatly shorten the sales cycle. Hosted group information sessions will allow a larger number of brokers to be handled than through individual meetings.

The company's strategy is to first sell the largest broker-dealers not on the Internet, then through the broker-dealer set up a series of group information sessions for its brokers, with appropriate follow-up and marketing materials. The company plans to hire a telemarketing person by July to research and begin this process to contact each of the first 2,000 prospective broker-dealers. The company expects that as many as 25 percent of the prospective clients for the service will not require an in-person visit, and that a strong telemarketing program will yield excellent results.

**Advertisement and Promotion Objectives**

The company is using a moderate advertising and public relations strategy from August to October 1999 until a core of solid broker-dealers and dealers have been signed and the sales process is well underway. Two approaches will be used. Full-page advertisements in national financial papers (WSJ) will announce the availability of the service to brokers and broker-dealers. Full-page advertisements in national newspapers (*USA Today*) will announce the availability to clients of those brokers. An aggressive but low-key approach will yield excellent market penetration in conjunction with an excellent website that showcases the features of the system.

Other direct mail, fax, and regional advertising and PR efforts will emphasize the following:

- Security of the service using the GlobalEye Security Systems software versus security measures used by most of the other online brokerage and finance offerings
- Raise the awareness of the general low level of security that is currently available in e-commerce and financial transactions
- Promote e-best-trade.com as the "first to market" with this innovative solution to the small to medium-sized brokerage problems caused by extended trading and migration of clients to discount houses
- Encourage investment interest
- Implement a "pull" strategy to encourage brokerage clients to ask their brokers and broker-dealers why they don't have an "affordable" online solution

## Marketing Materials and Online Presence

The bulk of the marketing budget will be spent on increasing the functionality and design appeal of e-best-trade.com's online demo site and alliance sites of software suppliers such as GlobalEye Security Systems Inc. A standard e-mail message will be developed that links to reports showing the increased migration of customers away from traditional broker-dealers, security issues reports, and e-best-trade.com online's demo site.

Initially, the demo site will be AMXStock.com, since this will serve to act as a reference of a real customer. The company intends to develop its own demo site within three months of initial funding, once it has a customer list and track record sufficiently impressive to promote.

## Conferences and Trade Shows

Within six months, the company intends to seek out speaking engagements at financial trade shows and conferences, emphasizing the same points as in the advertising section. It intends to position itself as a market leader and innovator in the area of secure brokerage systems and intends to raise industry awareness of the possible threats to personal and business privacy and transactions. Through this approach, the company expects to be able to assist its customers in their ability to retain clients and start to reverse the migration to the larger online brokerage offerings currently on the market.

## Sales Force and Structure

All company personnel will be considered members of the sales team. The administrative assistant and support personnel who implement the systems will all have an active role in customer relations and customer satisfaction. The company intends to conduct training for all personnel who may have customer contact to ensure that top-level communication occurs at all times.

The in-field sales force will be made up five regionally located sales professionals. The regions are the East Coast, West Coast, Central Plains, Canada (including the Pacific Northwest), and International (based in San Diego). Each salesperson will live in the geographical area in which they are responsible to reduce travel expense and build a local presence. Additional sales people will be added as the company develops demand.

The company has budgeted for web-based contact and customer management software to handle the widely dispersed organization.

## Pricing and Profitability

Pricing for e-best-trade.com services are set to be affordable to individual brokers, yet return excellent profitability once a core group of customers has been signed up. Current competitive pricing is for the broker-dealer to build their own system, estimated to cost at least $250,000 and as much as $1,000,000.

e-best-trade.com's profit will be based on a monthly fee of $500 per broker. This will allow the broker to quickly have an online offering and a look customized based on color, logo, and fonts. Additional customization will be billed at an hourly rate of $80 an hour and average customization charges are expected to be $2,000, although the range will be from $500 to $50,000.

Per transaction price will be $1.00 per trade, payable by the broker-dealer. The broker-dealer will add this cost to its billing of the per-trade cost to each broker.

Variable costs average 26 percent as a percentage of sales over the first four years. The company believes that this percentage will be reduced once there is a core group of customers to achieve economies of scale.

For large broker-dealers with a large complement of in-house sales staff, the company expects to offer volume pricing on the monthly service charge. It also anticipates restructuring the pricing to accommodate business practices in different countries.

## MARKET ANALYSIS

### Size and Growth Trends

There are more than 500 brokerage companies on the Internet. By the end of 1999, an estimated 10 million brokerage accounts will be able to trade online. Despite the tremendous growth in this market, only 6 percent of investors are currently trading online, but 58 percent are either currently using the Internet, or plan to go online within one year.

There are currently 5,500 full service broker-dealers serving the U.S.'s eight stock exchanges. These firms have over 62,000 branch offices (source NASD). Virtually all of the broker-dealers will require Internet trading services in the immediate future to retain their client base.

**Maturity of Industry**

The era of the full-service brokerage charging high premiums for trading is in its "sunset" phase. A number of recent studies support the need for full-service broker-dealers to have an online presence. The vast community of small to medium-sized brokerage firms are likely to suffer if they are not able to sustain an attractive cost structure, high levels of service, quality offerings, and advice for full-service investors in the future.

"The implication is that unless full-service firms begin to realign their services to include high-quality online offerings, investors who believe they are not getting personalized service from their brokers will quickly become candidates for these hybrid, direct competitors" (ABN AMRO study).

Globally there are over 130 stock exchanges (see Appendix B). At this stage, the company has not been able to obtain figures on the exact number of broker-dealers worldwide, but by conservative estimates it is over 50,000 firms, all of whom will require an online presence as the global Internet services market expands.

### Competition

e-best-trade.com has researched exhaustively and has not found a direct competitor to this service. There is one firm based in Atlanta, Georgia, that offers a similar service who could potentially migrate to the e-best-trade.com offering.

FireBird Securities of Atlanta is offering entrepreneurs the chance to operate their own Internet brokerage operation via a franchise system. FireBird provides entrepreneurs with the Internet dealing software customized with their company logo, color scheme, and specific requirements. FireBird also provides franchisees with a network of executing brokers throughout the world, to which orders to buy/sell stocks are automatically routed via its franchise system.

FireBird's system also allows traditional broker-dealers to have a "private-label" online system. The company is in the process of determining pricing and more information on FireBird to understand how large a threat they may be in the future.

**Future Competition**

There are a number of firms that offer solutions for broker-dealers to build their own systems, and numerous consulting and web development firms who offer similar services, but no one has a service offering with an outsourced solution. It is possible that a number of firms may enter the market once e-best-trade.com establishes that there is a viable, lucrative opportunity. Below are the various groups that may in future provide competitive offerings.

**Broker-dealers**

A few clearing firms have set up systems to market to their correspondents and a number of broker-dealers already have online solutions. It would be relatively straightforward to offer their current service to broker-dealers and brokers in a similar manner to e-best-trade.com.

Some of the better broker-dealer sites include Hickory & Kendall, a national firm with an impressive online site, and Fidelity. These sites are well designed, are quick loading, and have a wealth of investment information and portfolio management tools.

The company believes that most broker-dealers will not compromise their broker relationships by offering online trading to other broker-dealers or brokers. Issues of confidentiality, client lists and competition issues will more than likely prevent this group from becoming a strong competitor. The company will position itself as providing a much more secure trading environment, and publicizing the current e-commerce security threats will be critical to keeping a market leadership role.

**Brokerage Development Firms**

There are many firms that offer development tools and packages to allow traditional brokers to offer online services. Among these, the ones the company found that were most viable were:

- **Queenlink** is a division of Quarks, Litter & Post (QLP) Securities Corporation, a leading investment banking and securities firm with total capital of over $8 billion and total assets of over $80.3 billion. QLP is a publicly traded company on the New York Stock Exchange. It has a product sold as a reliable solution for offering access to account information, trading capability, news, quotes, and other content on the World Wide Web. A customized version of this product enables financial organizations to offer online services to their clients, and offers Internet-based tools that investment professionals need to effectively service clients.

- **Michaels Ltd.** based in Nevada with a sales office in New York, has a product called LMP/NetWebbing. It provides financial firms with a vehicle in which to utilize the Internet as a low-cost, highly effective communication methodology, providing headquarters system access to all professionals via the Internet/Intranet. Michaels has a joint venture with a major computer corporation to provide build online brokerage solutions for broker-dealers.

- **K&K Investments, Inc.,** a Florida corporation, provides a comprehensive solution to transact online securities trading including site hosting, website design, and development, client/server interfaces, and database interaction. K&K was incorporated in 1994 and placed its first online trading site on the Internet in 1996.

The company believes that these firms and firms similar to them have the in-house expertise and sales forces to effectively compete with e-best-trade.com in the future. It is questionable whether these companies would want to jeopardize their current client relationships by offering a directly competing service. Queenlink in particular may be a possible partner or acquirer of e-best-trade.com in the future and the company will pursue this once marketing is well established and underway.

## FINANCIAL PLAN

### Introduction, General Discussion

As the accompanying spreadsheets show, e-best-trade.com projects profitability within 36 months of its first raise. The financials show revenues of U.S. $13 million after 24 months of operations. These revenues should increase to U.S. $37 million by the end of the fourth year, resulting in a pre-tax profit of over U.S. $7 million.

e-best-trade.com's financial benchmarks conservatively assume a twenty-four-month startup phase to complete all products, initiate corporate infrastructure and offices, and commence initial market entry, with indications of related costs.

Online broker revenues are expected to steadily increase, providing e-best-trade.com with U.S. $442K in net profit by the end of the second year. As the Implementation discussion below explains, the financials, which are based on very conservative assumptions, contemplate four lifts, with a public offering thereafter.

e-best-trade.com is also in discussions with interested financiers in proposed deals which would take the company public in its initial phase and provide substantially all of the financing necessary to achieve full operations through the positive cash flow projections. e-best-trade.com, as of the development of this business plan, is not committed to a particular financing vehicle.

## Implementation of the Financial Plan

### Overview

In the next four years, e-best-trade.com has milestone objectives as follows:

| | |
|---|---|
| April 1999 | Infrastructure in place |
| June 1999 | First financing in place ($500K) |
| July 1999 | e-best-trade.com in market trial in Chicago |
| August 1999 | Second financing in place ($1.5 million) |
| | e-best-trade.com market launch |
| | |
| October 1999 | Over 100 brokers online |
| December 1999 | Over 200 brokers online; third financing in place ($2 million) |
| May 2001 | Over 1,800 brokers online; gross revenues over $13 million |
| May 2003 | Gross revenues of $37 million; pre-tax profits of $7.1 million |

### Investment Required

e-best-trade.com requires a total investment of U.S. $4 million. Capital will be raised in three different "lifts." U.S. $500K will be used to finalize the infrastructure and market test and fully develop the marketing plan. U.S. $1.5 million will be utilized to develop the company infrastructure and continue the marketing effort until a core group of customers are on board.

U.S. $2 million will be used to begin advertising and marketing, establish the company as a market leader, and also expand the sales and technical teams. The company also expects to move the product line into new vertical markets. e-best-trade.com expects to be in a position to pursue an IPO within 12 to 24 months, assuming it doesn't raise its full financing through an early merger with a public company—an option it's exploring.

There are significant start-up costs that must be incurred to make e-best-trade.com into a long-term viable company. It is critical to get to the marketplace now and to create brand identification so that as the market matures, e-best-trade.com will be synonymous with secure affordable online brokerage solutions on the Internet.

**Corporate Value**

Using very conservative revenue numbers and very aggressive costs, by the end of the second year the value of the company should be in the order of U.S. $52 million, based on a conservative market valuation of four times revenue. The target for the end of the four-year period is nearly three times that value. With a projected pre-tax profit of U.S. $7.1 million by the end of year four, at an average 10 times EBIT, the standard valuation currently used for pricing technology Initial Public Offerings, e-best-trade.com will be valued at U.S. $71 million. It is important to note that Internet companies, particularly those with positive cash flow and products that have applicability in non-Internet markets, are valued by the markets far more generously than by a conservative multiple of cash flow or earnings.

**Worst-Case Scenario**

e-best-trade.com, of course, does not believe its business will fail, but it has nonetheless contemplated a worst-case scenario. As we already have working software and are on the way to establishing the first market trial, it is our contention that the company will become marginally viable at the worst. If this case is evident early in the first year, then the company will fall back into an operational mode to capitalize on the strengths and build a smaller company and concentrate on the most profitable of the four product lines.

## Revenues and Cost of Sales to Year-End 1999

| | Jun | Jul | Aug | Sep | Oct | Nov |
|---|---|---|---|---|---|---|
| **Revenues** | | | | | | |
| New Accounts (signed previous month) | | 2 | 30 | 50 | 50 | 50 |
| Total Accounts | | 2 | 32 | 82 | 132 | 182 |
| Monthly ($500) | | $1,000 | $15,000 | $25,000 | $25,000 | $25,000 |
| Trans/broker/month ($200) | | $400 | $6,400 | $16,400 | $26,400 | $36,400 |
| Average Customization ($1,000) | | $2,000 | $30,000 | $50,000 | $50,000 | $50,000 |
| **Totals** | | **$3,400** | **$51,400** | **$91,400** | **$101,400** | **$111,400** |
| | | | | | | |
| **Cost of Revenues** | | | | | | |
| Sales Commission ($200) | | $400 | $6,000 | $10,000 | $10,000 | $10,000 |
| Quote System Costs | $4,000 | $2,500 | $2,500 | $2,500 | $2,500 | $2,500 |
| Incremental Quote costs/Broker ($50) | | $100 | $1,600 | $4,100 | $6,600 | $9,100 |
| | | | | | | |
| Number of Analysts required | 1 | 1 | 1 | 3 | 4 | 6 |
| Analyst Cost ($5,000) | $5,000 | $5,000 | $5,000 | $15,000 | $20,000 | $30,000 |
| **Totals** | **$9,000** | **$7,900** | **$13,500** | **$27,500** | **$32,500** | **$42,500** |
| | | | | | | |
| **Revenues less Cost of Sales** | **($9,000)** | **($4,500)** | **$37,900** | **$63,900** | **$68,900** | **$68,900** |

## Pre-Tax Income to Year-End 1999

| | Jun | Jul | Aug | Sep | Oct | Nov |
|---|---|---|---|---|---|---|
| **Total Revenue** | | **$3,400** | **$51,400** | **$91,400** | **$101,400** | **$111,400** |
| Less: Cost of Sales | $9,000 | $7,900 | $13,500 | $27,500 | $32,500 | $42,500 |
| | | | | | | |
| **Gross Profit** | **($9,000)** | **($4,500)** | **$37,900** | **$63,900** | **$68,900** | **$68,900** |
| | | | | | | |
| **Expenses** | | | | | | |
| Advertising & Marketing | $10,000 | $50,000 | $500,000 | $500,000 | $250,000 | $50,000 |
| Data Line | $200 | $200 | $200 | $500 | $500 | $500 |
| Insurance | $100 | $2,000 | $2,000 | $3,000 | $3,000 | $3,000 |
| Amortization | $167 | $313 | $2,521 | $2,708 | $2,771 | $3,604 |
| Legal & Accounting | $1,000 | $5,000 | $5,000 | $5,000 | $2,500 | $2,500 |
| Conferences, Memberships | $1,000 | $1,500 | $1,500 | $1,500 | $1,500 | $1,500 |
| Office Expenses | | $500 | $500 | $3,000 | $3,000 | $5,000 |
| 15% Payroll taxes & benefits | | $6,405 | $8,015 | $10,614 | $11,258 | $11,914 |
| 20% Bonuses | | | | | | |
| SkyHook Data/Technical Services | $20,000 | $20,000 | $20,000 | $20,000 | $20,000 | $20,000 |
| Telecommunications | $1,000 | $1,000 | $1,000 | $1,000 | $1,000 | $1,000 |
| Training & Professional Development | $2,500 | $2,500 | $2,500 | $2,500 | $500 | $500 |
| Travel & Moving | $5,000 | $5,000 | $10,000 | $15,000 | $20,000 | $30,000 |
| Wages | $36,450 | $42,700 | $53,433 | $70,758 | $75,054 | $79,429 |
| | | | | | | |
| **Total Expenses** | **$77,417** | **$137,118** | **$606,669** | **$635,580** | **$391,083** | **$208,948** |
| | | | | | | |
| **Pretax Income (Loss)** | **($86,417)** | **($141,618)** | **($568,769)** | **($571,680)** | **($322,183)** | **($140,048)** |

**Dec**

50
232
$25,000
$46,400
$50,000
**$121,400**

$10,000
$2,500
$11,600

7
$35,000
**$47,500**

**$73,900**

**Dec**
**$121,400**
$47,500

**$73,900**

$50,000
$500
$3,000
$3,667
$2,500
$1,500
$5,000
$14,031
$18,708
$20,000
$1,000
$500
$20,000
$93,538

**$233,942**

**($160,042)**

**Pre-Tax Income to Year-End 1999**

|  | Year 1 | Year 2 | Year 3 | Year 4 |
|---|---|---|---|---|
| **Gross Profits** | **$817,000** | **$10,585,300** | **$18,085,300** | **$28,485,300** |
| Disbursements | $3,786,455 | $10,142,955 | $14,574,161 | $21,337,546 |
| Hardware/Software |  |  |  |  |
|   Purchases | $323,000 | $455,400 | $667,020 | $947,126 |
| Add: Amortization | $40,454 | $76,200 | $152,400 | $304,800 |
| **Subtotal** | **$4,149,909** | **$10,674,555** | **$15,393,581** | **$22,589,472** |
| Tax Payable |  |  |  | $1,429,551 |
| **Net Cash After Tax** | **($3,332,909)** | **$442,345** | **$3,511,139** | **$5,718,203** |
| **Financing Cash Flow** |  |  |  |  |
|   Sale of Stock | $4,000,000 |  |  |  |
| Beginning Cash Balance |  | $667,091 | $1,109,436 | $4,620,575 |
| **Ending Cash Balance** | **$667,091** | **$1,109,436** | **$4,620,575** | **$10,338,778** |

**Assumptions Used in Brokerage Revenues:**

- Potential to attract at least 10 percent of the broker-dealers by Year Two, yielding a minimum of 500 broker-dealers in the U.S.
- Pilot, market trial, and the first 50 commercial users within one year.
- 200 direct trades per month per broker.
- Monthly fees of $500 per month per broker.
- $1.00 per transaction will be billed to each broker-dealer and added to trading charges from the broker-dealer to the brokers.

# Energy Solutions Company

BUSINESS PLAN

ABAKA ENERGY SOLUTIONS

*1200 Manistee Way*
*Portland, Oregon 97209*

*Abaka Energy Solutions will empower the world's underdeveloped communities through the application of solar and wind energy technologies. The company will become the world's leading provider of renewable energy (RE) products and services, with projects potentially spanning all seven continents by 2014. This business plan was provided by Jason P. Spellberg and Gaspar V. Makale, and was compiled in conjunction with the business plan preparation courses at the University of Colorado.*

- EXECUTIVE SUMMARY

- COMPANY OVERVIEW

- PRODUCTS & SERVICES

- INDUSTRY & MARKETPLACE ANALYSIS

- MARKETING STRATEGY

- OPERATIONS STRATEGY

- DEVELOPMENT STRATEGY

- MANAGEMENT TEAM

- FINANCIAL SUMMARY

- OFFERING

- APPENDICES & FINANCIAL STATEMENTS

## EXECUTIVE SUMMARY

### Company Overview

Abaka Energy Solutions will empower the world's underdeveloped communities through the application of solar and wind energy technologies. The company will become the world's leading provider of renewable energy (RE) products and services, with projects potentially spanning all seven continents by 2014.

### Industry & Marketplace Analysis

One third of the world's population has no electricity. The majority of these people live in rural, remote areas of the world's poorest nations. Global development is a multi-billion dollar industry, with the World Bank providing huge sums of money to fund large-scale projects. In the past ten years, global electricity demand has grown by 40 percent. During this time, the use of RE has expanded at ten times the rate of fossil fuels. Experts predict that the world's electricity demand could triple by 2020, a colossal increase that will be fuelled by the industrialization of developing countries. As a specialty provider and integrator of RE systems designed for developing communities, Abaka will position itself to capitalize on this explosive trend. Abaka will establish its first project in Karagwe, Tanzania, which lies near the western shore of Lake Victoria, deep in sub-Saharan Africa.

### Products & Services

Abaka will introduce affordable electricity to Karagwe by offering attractive financing options for solar electric systems. This will enable families to make purchases in small monthly installments, in the same way that a consumer would buy an automobile in the United States. In addition, Abaka will construct a 15,000-watt solar/ wind power station and community center, where services such as electric coffee processing, water pumping, refrigeration, computing, telecommunications access, and Internet browsing will be sold. This community center will also serve as a nucleus of education, where Karagwe residents will be exposed to a contagious spirit of entrepreneurship. The services provided here will enable, motivate, and educate people to start new businesses. In this way, Abaka's presence in Karagwe will substantially boost the region's economic prosperity.

### Marketing Strategy

Karagwe is a dispersed farming community of 350,000 people. The area is so remote that power lines may never be extended there, and only 2 percent of the population has electricity. Abaka's target customer is a Karagwe family that earns about $700 per year. A basic solar electric system will be priced at $288, or $24 per month. Market research conducted in Karagwe strongly suggests that this price is feasible, despite the fact that it represents 45 percent of a typical family's annual income. Currently, Karagwe families use crude and dangerous kerosene lamps to light their homes, and expensive dry-cell batteries to power their radios. A solar electric system is safer, more reliable, provides better lighting, and promises better value than the alternatives mentioned above. Construction of the power station and community center will advertise Abaka's dedication to a sustainable, long-term presence within the community. Abaka has partnered with a local company called the Seattle Solar Electronics Workshop (SSEW). Working with SSEW, Abaka will sponsor informational forums to educate customers about the economic benefits of financing, the technology behind solar electricity, and the use of electricity in cultivating a prosperous economy.

| | |
|---|---|
| In October 2000, Abaka will begin building the power station and community center. | **Operations and Development** |
| An expert in the RE field has been recruited to design this station, and to oversee its construction. SSEW will run all operations of the business in Karagwe, including inventory handling, payment collection, product distribution, and maintenance repair. All power systems will be sold to customers as pre-packaged kits, assembled by SSEW employees. | |
| Liam Stiller, Abaka's founder, is completing his M.B.A. in Entrepreneurship at the University of Oregon. He has traveled extensively in East Africa, and has forged a business partnership with Ghin Patel, owner of SSEW. As permanent employees, the founders will seek, identify, and finance lucrative new project opportunities all over the world. Mr. Patel will also oversee Abaka's operations in Karagwe. | **Management Team** |
| In Karagwe, solar kit financing will generate almost $800,000 of net income, and $2.7 million in accumulated cash, by 2006. Abaka will seek $1 million in a single round of seed financing to fund the construction of the power station and community center. Abaka will seek this capital from private accredited investors, nonprofit relief agencies, or possibly as a partnership with a global technology company interested in penetrating emerging markets. Abaka's presence in Karagwe will drastically improve the community's prosperity, thereby building real demand for electronics and telecommunications products and services. In exchange for capital and strategic support, Abaka will offer an investor equity, and will additionally offer a partner company direct, unlimited access to these markets at the grass-roots level. Abaka is dedicated to improving the lives of the world's underprivileged people by promoting the use of clean renewable energy. Therefore, Abaka also offers investors association with this noble initiative. | **Summary of Financials and Offering to Investors** |
| The commitment of Abaka Energy Solutions will be to spread technologies for harnessing renewable energy (RE). The term "renewable" refers to sources of energy that can never be diminished or exhausted, such as wind and sun. The most common commercial RE technologies are photovoltaic (PV) modules, wind turbines, and, increasingly, fuel cells, which produce electricity from solar radiation, wind, and hydrogen, respectively. | **COMPANY OVERVIEW** |
| To become the world leader in the creation, development, and deployment of technologies that converge the advancement of human civilization with that of the environmental condition. | **Vision Statement** |
| To profitably and sustainably introduce renewable energy into the world's underdeveloped communities. | **Three-Year Mission Statement** |
| Abaka Energy Solutions will be organized as a Delaware C-corporation, with an executive office in Portland, Oregon, USA, during the first quarter of 2000. The company will serve as a for-profit holding, investing, and consulting agency, and will work in partnership with developing communities to establish sustainable RE projects all over the world. | **Current Status** |
| Abaka will immediately specialize in providing electricity and electric services for rural communities, and will utilize two different business strategies to distribute power. First, Abaka will sell solar electric systems for home and commercial applications by allowing customers to finance the cost of these systems over time. Second, the company will offer end-user services | **Market & Services** |

direct to customers by establishing electrified community centers in the heart of their villages. At these centers, people will be able to purchase services ranging from crop processing to refrigeration to telecommunications access to internet browsing.

**Objectives**

Abaka's first RE project will be in Karagwe, Tanzania, a remote agricultural community in East Africa. The company will aggressively expand into a global provider of RE products and services by seeking new opportunities in other parts of Africa, as well as in Asia and Latin America. By 2014, Abaka will be the world's undisputed leading provider of RE products and services, and will operate Research & Development divisions for creating innovative novel technologies that address the environmental crises of the twenty-first century. This business plan will present Abaka's strategy for getting started, by establishing a profitable and sustainable RE business in Karagwe, Tanzania.

**PRODUCTS & SERVICES**

**Description of Services**

Abaka will offer financing packages for home and commercial-scale solar electric systems. The retail price of a small solar electric system in rural Africa is around $800. Abaka will enable Karagwe customers to purchase systems in affordable monthly installments, similar to the way most people in the United States purchase automobiles. These financing options will be especially popular in poor communities such as Karagwe, where affordability drives a preventative wedge in a customer's ability to buy. This business plan will mainly describe the financing aspect of Abaka's operation in Karagwe.

To solidify people's confidence in these financing options, and to demonstrate the company's dedication to the community, a 15,000-watt solar/ wind power station and community center will be constructed in Karagwe. A number of end-user services will eventually be provided at this community center, such as coffee bean processing, food storage and refrigeration, battery charging, water distilling, computing, telecommunications access, and Internet browsing. In addition, an educational center will be instituted, where customers will learn how to use electricity and technology to start new businesses, or to expand existing ones. Most of these services will be provided within a year after Abaka's initial establishment in Karagwe, but eventually they will generate as much as 75 percent of the company's revenue. All of these services will be designed to help Karagwe residents augment their incomes. In this way, Abaka hopes to foster economic activity, and thus prosperity, within the community. This business plan will not describe the community center aspect of Abaka's operation in detail, but the offering of these services is part of the company's long-range plan for development in Karagwe.

**Proprietary Rights**

In Karagwe, and in all other project sites, Abaka will seek partnership with a local organization to help with operations, marketing, legal negotiations, and other important aspects of conducting business. Abaka's partner in Karagwe is a natively owned company called the Seattle Solar Electronics Workshop (SSEW). SSEW was founded in April 1999 by Mr. Ghin Patel, a Tanzanian electrical engineer and entrepreneur. Mr. Patel and Mr. Stiller, Abaka's founder, are close friends, and have been in business together for close to two years. It is virtually impossible for any foreign company to conduct effective or sustainable business in a poor, developing community without trustworthy local contacts. Besides SSEW, there is no company in Karagwe that has the technical capability, or the entrepreneurial innovation, to establish a joint venture of this kind. As such, Abaka is confident that no other foreign company will be able to enter this market.

Although fifty years of market exposure have proven RE technologies to be unequivocally reliable and durable, the commercial RE industry is still in its infancy, and the electricity markets in developing parts of the world remain almost completely untapped. A business solution is needed to meet the challenge of profitably selling this expensive, high technology equipment to people with meager incomes. In the past five years, a number of strategies have been implemented in rural, developing markets with astounding success. Almost all of these models have extended a micro-credit or financing option to their customers. These successful companies, which will be further discussed in the Industry Analysis section, have proven the efficacy of the business model that Abaka will apply in Karagwe.

**Stage of Development**

As an RE service provider targeting emerging markets, Abaka will compete in the industry known as Renewables for Sustainable Village Power (RSVP). RSVP is a small, but fast-growing subset of the gigantic global energy industry, which is currently experiencing an economic revolution. One significant characteristic of this revolution has been astonishing growth. Over the past ten years, for instance, the world's demand for electricity has increased by 40 percent. Experts predict that, as industrialization sweeps developing countries, current demand could triple by 2020. Because so many new electricity users live in remote areas, most of this increased demand has been, and will continue to be, serviced by RE. As a result, renewables are by far the fastest growing segment of world energy use.

**INDUSTRY & MARKETPLACE ANALYSIS**

**Industry Analysis**

The second trend of importance is privatization and deregulation. Over the past five years, this has been a global contagion, especially in developing countries, where governments continue to implement aggressive policies designed to attract foreign investment. Tanzania, for instance, adopted the National Investment Promotion and Protection Act in 1990, which guaranteed the privatization of several key industries, including energy. The opening of these economies has sparked the proliferation of scores of small, entrepreneurial energy companies striving to profitably satisfy the need for rural energy development. Some, such as the Grameen Bank of Bangladesh, the Solar Electric Light Fund of Thailand, and Soluz of the Dominican Republic, have developed profitable business models based on selling solar electric systems through micro-credit arrangements. Meanwhile, large companies such as Enron, Shell Oil, and British Petroleum/ Amoco have established dedicated RE divisions, and are aggressively executing multi-million-dollar RE projects in places such as Indonesia and South Africa.

But despite this recent surge of activity, the RSVP industry still faces some imposing challenges. For example, the vast majority of people who most need RE technologies still cannot afford them. Substantial increases in end-user purchasing power have remained elusive, and, as a result, sales are not close to what they could be. Consequently, RE manufacturers have been unable to drive economies of scale enough to cost-compete with fossil fuels. Another problem is the lack of skilled RE technicians in developing countries. There are only a handful of training centers in the world teaching RE system installation. Finally, international turmoil remains an imposing obstacle. In many countries, political and economic instability has prevented the long-term investment and presence needed to sustain RE projects.

These challenges are typical of any global industry that is only just beginning to mature, and real progress is being made to address them. Over the past decade, for instance, PV production costs have been reduced by 80 percent (an additional 50 to 75 percent is required to cost-compete with coal-fired electricity). Furthermore, experts predict that economic and industrial development in emerging countries will lead to a 100 percent increase in world income by 2020. As prosperity builds demand for electricity, RE training centers are being established in the developing world, such as the highly respected Institute for Solar Training in Karagwe. Furthermore, despite civil wars and social unrest, there are scores of developing countries, like

Tanzania, where political stability harbors fantastic economic opportunity. Many experts predict that this global "Energy Revolution" contains the seed that will become the world's premier growth industry of the twenty-first century.

**Marketplace Analysis**

**Tanzania.** Tanzania is the largest and most peaceful nation in East Africa. The country has demonstrated over 38 years of political stability, and is governed by a multiparty democracy based on English common law. Tanzania has posted an average annual economic growth rate of 3.5 percent over the past ten years, however inflation currently lingers at 13 percent. Tanzania's GDP is expected to grow at 5 percent annually through 2002. Agriculture is the nation's primary industry, accounting for 56 percent of its GDP, and employing over 90 percent of its workforce. Only 24 percent of Tanzania's population live in urban areas, meaning that the country's 32 million people are widely dispersed over an area more than twice the size of California. Between 1986 and 1991, demand for electricity in Tanzania grew at an average annual rate of 10.2 percent, a trend that is expected to continue. Over 75 percent of Tanzania's electricity consumers are served by hydroelectric power, and the country experiences generation shortfalls during drought conditions. Almost all of Tanzania's electricity usage is confined to its urban areas.

**Karagwe.** Karagwe is a remote farming community in the northwestern corner of Tanzania, about 100 kilometers from the western shore of Lake Victoria, at a geographic position of two degrees south latitude. The region experiences two dependable rainy seasons per year, and receives an annual average of about five peak sun hours per day, roughly 10 percent more than Denver, Colorado. About 350,000 people, or 60,000 households, live in this region, which is situated on a wide, sloping ridge at an elevation of 1,650 meters (5,400 feet) above sea level. The prominence of this ridge above the surrounding plain leaves it exposed to the tropical trade winds, which consistently blow from the west. There are few regions in the world that boast such abundant RE natural resources. Almost every household in Karagwe is surrounded by a plantation of several hectares, and coffee is the community's chief cash crop. The average yearly income is about $700 per family, and, though this is strikingly poor by Western standards, Karagwe is one of Tanzania's most prosperous rural communities.

**Customer Analysis**

Karagwe is an extremely dispersed village, with 350,000 people living in an area of 3,200 square kilometers. As a result, only 1.4 percent of Karagwe's most centralized homes and businesses are electrified by the regional utility grid, while 0.6 percent are electrified with solar power. The remaining 98 percent have no hope of seeing the grid extended to their homes during the next ten years. Residents of Karagwe realize that modernization cannot take place without electricity, and that access to electricity will significantly enhance their economic prosperity and quality of life. As a result, it is no surprise that 100 percent of the fifty or so Karagwe residents surveyed during the summer of 1999 indicated a strong desire to participate in a financing program that would allow them to afford a solar electric system.

Karagwe families live in large houses, typically constructed of brick and concrete. Each house has three to five bedrooms, a kitchen, a living room, a washroom, and an animal pen. Families submit no property taxes or mortgage payments. Furthermore, because Karagwe is a farming community, residents spend very little on food, except for the few items, such as rice and fish that must be imported from surrounding districts. Very few people in this village possess an automobile, and those who do earn three to ten times more than the average yearly income. Aside from a handful of bars, restaurants, grocery stores, and weekly farmers' markets, Karagwe offers very little for the consumer. Because there is not much in this community to spend money on, Karagwe families tend to retain a purchasing power that is greater than half of their annual income. Nevertheless, due in large part to the inflationary pressures and banking crises that have plagued Tanzania ever since the 1960s, people are generally unfamiliar with the concept of saving money. Only in the past few years have stabilized banks begun to earn the trust of Tanzanian consumers, and in the rural parts of the country, this trend is proceeding quite slowly.

Despite these simplistic financial tendencies, the typical Karagwe resident is quite sophisticated, and understands the benefits of solar electricity. Karagwe is home to Africa's most distinguished solar training facility, where Abaka's Africa Operations Officer, Mr. Ghin Patel, is chief of faculty. Because of the international recognition of this school, Karagwe residents know that solar electricity represents a clean, safe, and reliable way to power their homes. Unfortunately, however, even a small solar electric system costs about $800 retail in Africa, and only the richest families can afford this price. As a result, most families continue to light their homes with crude kerosene lamps, and to power their radios with inefficient dry cell batteries. Nevertheless, the demand for solar electric systems latently exists in Karagwe, and it is up to Abaka to tap this market potential by making these systems affordable for the average Karagwe family.

**Competing Technologies.** Because solar electric systems are so expensive in Karagwe, they are viewed as luxury items. Almost every family would love to have one, but affordability is a preventative issue. As such, people must use more conventional methods of lighting their homes. Kerosene and dry cell batteries are readily available in Karagwe, but neither item is particularly cheap. Kerosene sells for about fifty cents per liter, and a typical family uses four to six liters per month; many organizations, such as schools and health clinics, use twenty to fifty liters per month. Dry cell batteries retail for about $3.00, and may last two or three weeks at the rate most families use their radios. Some families also own gasoline gensets, while still others own automobile batteries, which they charge with gensets, or at a grid station in the central part of the village. Abaka's chief competition in Karagwe is certainly kerosene and disposable batteries, and solar has several advantages over them. First, kerosene lamps are crude and dangerous; it is easy to find an adult in Karagwe who has been burned, at some point in his or her life, by a kerosene lamp leaking, spilling, or completely exploding. Furthermore, kerosene lamps provide lighting that is only somewhat better than a large candle, and they tend to be noisy and smelly during operation. Dry cell batteries are expensive because they must be replaced so frequently, and their disposal poses a serious environmental threat. Also, many appliances cannot be powered with batteries. A solar electric system, on the other hand, is clean and safe, and provides the familiar fluorescent, white light that can illuminate an entire room. Furthermore, a solar electric system can be used to power any electric appliance. It offers modularity, flexibility, and expandability, so that one single power source can be used for the house's every electrical need. Additionally, these systems are extremely reliable, and require only minimal maintenance on, and periodic replacement of, the battery. If well maintained, a solar electric system will last for thirty years. Solar electric systems are more expensive than conventional alternatives in the short-term, but in the long run provide a far superior value for the money.

Aside from Abaka's partner, SSEW, there are no businesses or organizations providing solar electricity in Karagwe. Furthermore, there is not a single organization in all of northwestern Tanzania that offers financing for solar electric systems. The national utility, the Tanzania Electric Supply Company (TANESCO), has no intention of expanding the utility grid into the periphery of Karagwe for at least ten years. Furthermore, this company has no understanding of solar electricity, and maintains only a minimal presence in Karagwe. TANESCO is not equipped to effectively compete in this marketplace.

**Competitor Analysis**

**Competing Service Providers**

## MARKETING STRATEGY

### Target Market Strategy

In order to make solar electricity affordable, Abaka will offer families and businesses the option of paying for their system in twelve monthly installments. The smallest kit offered will be priced at $24.00 per month. This translates into a year-end price of $288, which is a tremendous saving over retail. Because people in this region maintain a purchasing power equivalent to about 50 percent of their annual income, Abaka's principal target market is families that earn at least $600 per year. It is estimated that roughly one-third of Karagwe's households earn this amount or more, meaning that Abaka's primary target market in Karagwe consists of about 19,000 families.

### Service Strategy

**Financing Terms.** Many micro-credit programs have failed in developing communities because customers have been allowed to default on their loans. It can be extremely difficult both logistically and financially to repossess equipment in remote villages of foreign countries. To circumvent this problem, Abaka will offer "pre-financing" plans to its customers. Under the terms of these pre-financing options, customers will have to pay their entire balance before Abaka will give them a system. There are two reasons why this is necessary in Karagwe. First, people in developing countries often do not understand the concept of credit, and, especially when an American company is the lender, regularly assume that "credit" means "free." Second, industrialized nations have repeatedly allowed governments and businesses in the developing world to default on their debt. People in these communities, Karagwe included, are accustomed to receiving free handouts from the World Bank and industrialized governments. It is unlikely that Abaka can establish a high-growth, sustainable business in Karagwe if expensive electrical systems are provided, but money is not collected. As such, customers will pay for their systems first, in entirety, before they receive them; no exceptions will be allowed.

Because the financing plans will have one-year terms, Abaka must offer customers something while they pay for their electric systems. This is where the community center will be useful. During the terms of their financing contracts, Abaka's customers will be allowed to utilize all services at this community center free of charge. These privileges will end upon fulfillment of the financing agreement, or if a customer defaults on several payments. This strategy will allow Abaka to collect money before distributing systems, and will encourage customers to fulfill their financing agreements. Abaka will gladly accept down payments for customers desiring shorter financing terms.

**Solar Electric Kits.** Abaka's solar electric systems will be sized to meet the needs of a typical Karagwe household.

Very few Karagwe homes have the need to power anything more extravagant than a few fluorescent lights and a radio, and therefore these systems will be small by Western standards. Each system will come with a solar panel, a deep-cycle battery, a charge controller, lights, a radio, wiring, connectors, and mounting materials. In order to serve the expected high demand for affordable solar electric systems in Karagwe, all systems will be sold as pre-assembled kits. These kits will be designed to be so simple that end-users will be able to perform the installations themselves. In this way, Abaka will minimize the size of its technical staff. Initially, there will be three kit sizes offered. The following table presents a spec and price comparison of Abaka's introductory product line. For homes or businesses requiring more power, customized systems will also be available. Furthermore, as the community becomes more prosperous, people will develop more extravagant tastes for electric appliances and equipment, such as television sets, satellite dish receivers, refrigerators, and computers. Abaka will continuously readjust this product line according to customers' power needs. In addition, attractive trade-in and scale-up plans will be offered to customers in subsequent years, so that smaller systems can be traded in and upgraded to larger ones.

**Abaka's Initial Product Line**

| Kit | Size | Components | Price/Month | Price/Year | Gross Margin |
|-----|------|-----------|-------------|------------|--------------|
| 1 | 13 watts | 1 light, 1 radio | $24.00 | $288.00 | 72.46% |
| 2 | 30 watts | 2 lights, 1 radio | $48.00 | $576.00 | 80.00% |
| 3 | 48 watts | 3 lights, 1 radio | $72.00 | $864.00 | 94.59% |

Abaka will price these kits as low as possible while still yielding an attractive profit. Based on Prouffer's experience in Indonesia between 1994 and 1998, it is expected that a family living in an impoverished, rural agricultural community will surrender about half of its yearly income for a necessary item such as reliable electricity. With the pricing strategy that Abaka has adopted, Karagwe consumers will pay less than half of what a comparable solar electric system would cost from a typical African retailer.

**Pricing Strategy**

The community center will be used as Abaka's administrative office and distribution hub. Most of the components of the solar electric kits will be shipped by sea from suppliers in the U.S. or Europe to the Indian Ocean port of Dar es Salaam, then trucked overland to Karagwe. Abaka will also attempt to identify reliable suppliers in South Africa to reduce its dependence on overseas shipping. Upon arrival in Karagwe, SSEW will be responsible for assembling all components into complete solar electric kits, ready for installation. When customers have satisfied their payment schedules, they will be cordially thanked for their business, and invited to pick up their kits from the community center. At this time, customers will be given written instructions on how to install and maintain their new systems. During their payment period, and throughout their duration of ownership, all Abaka customers will be invited to attend free educational workshops on using, maintaining, optimizing, and expanding their solar electric systems.

**Distribution Strategy**

Abaka will rely greatly on publicity and word-of-mouth advertising to promote these financing plans. The construction of a 15,000-watt solar/wind power station and community center will be tremendous news in Karagwe, and will therefore serve as a very useful promotional tool. Residents will be unable to avoid noticing the sheer scale of this project. Over 100 people will be employed in this undertaking, and every newspaper and radio station in the region will publicly monitor its progress. Like many rural agricultural villages, Karagwe is a tight-knit community, and people tend to be extremely social. Abaka will have to do little to instigate excitement and conversation about this project. Once built, the generating facility, featuring a 10,000-watt wind turbine perched on an eighty-foot tower, and a 5,000-watt array of sleek solar panels mounted on a 10,000-square-foot scaffold, will serve as a constant advertisement of the electricity that Abaka offers.

**Advertising & Promotion Strategy**

Due to the visibility of this project, Abaka will ensure that high standards of professionalism are maintained at all times. Embroidered uniforms will be distributed to the SSEW technicians that maintain and operate the community center. New, high-quality equipment will be purchased, and the community center itself will have a clean, modern design. Service will be prompt and courteous, and technicians will be well trained and well paid. To complement the publicity aspect, Abaka will also post billboards in the heavily trafficked "downtown" area of the Karagwe district. The main purpose of these billboard advertisements will be to inform and remind customers of scheduled educational training sessions and technical demonstrations being held at the community center. In addition, posters will be used to announce new service offerings or price adjustments, as needed. Finally, professionally printed brochures, featuring concise descriptions of the financing plans offered, as well as general information about solar energy, will be widely distributed.

**Sales Strategy**

Ghin Patel, the founder and executive officer of SSEW, is a native of Karagwe, and has been installing solar energy systems there for eight years. Mr. Patel's expert reputation is common knowledge in the community. All sales and operational responsibilities will be contracted to SSEW, taking advantage of Mr. Patel's contacts and stature in Karagwe as a solar energy professional. Because SSEW's name is already well known to the community, customers will be dealing directly with a local company that they trust. A customer service office and reception desk will be established at the community center, and SSEW will collect payments at this location. In exchange for these services, and for using the SSEW name to generate trust and loyalty, Abaka will pay SSEW a contracting fee based on sales volume. Therefore, SSEW will have an incentive to aggressively generate sales by subscribing new customers, in whatever fashion they deem appropriate or effective.

**Marketing & Sales Forecasts**

Abaka's projected target market in Karagwe is about 19,000 families. There are 58,000 families in the region without electricity. However, these pre-financing plans will be expensive. Furthermore, customers will have to pay all of their monthly installments before receiving any equipment. Abaka recognizes that this will initially dissuade many potential customers. However, the construction of the power station and community center, as well as the partnership with SSEW, will help to reinforce Abaka's trustworthiness, and should neutralize some of these concerns. In addition, Abaka will allow subscribed customers to use the community center for free during their contract term. This means that customers will be able to enjoy free access to computers, refrigeration, water distilling, coffee bean processing, telecommunications access, and other services, for up to a year. Abaka anticipates subscribing about 250 families in 2001, the first year of operation. After one year, Karagwe residents will witness the delivery of solar electric systems purchased the previous year by their friends, neighbors, and relatives. The demand for these financing contracts will therefore increase exquisitely over the next five years, as Abaka's trustworthiness becomes confirmed, and its presence accepted, by the community. Furthermore, similar projects in other parts of the world have demonstrated that the availability of energy systems motivates people to increase their income by working harder, and then to save more of that income, in anticipation of having something valuable to buy. As a result, more Karagwe families will be able and willing to afford Abaka's financing plans over time, and the growth rates built into Abaka's revenue forecasts reflect this expectation. The following table shows sales and revenue forecasts for the years 2001-2006.

|  | 2001 | 2002 | 2003 | 2004 | 2005 | 2006 |
|---|---|---|---|---|---|---|
| Units Sold | 250 | 750 | 1,875 | 3,750 | 5,625 | 8,438 |
| Revenues | $84,240 | $252,720 | $631,800 | $1,263,600 | $1,895,400 | $2,843,100 |

**OPERATIONS STRATEGY**

Bim Stiletto, a primary schoolteacher in Karagwe, arrives home after a long day of work. It is nighttime in Africa, and pitch black envelops the quiet community. There are no street lights, no glows in the neighbors' windows; only the brilliant stars of the Southern Cross provide illumination. But on this night, Mr. Stiletto arrives to find his house teeming with activity. The solar electric system he spent a year buying has finally arrived, and his family is already putting it to good use. His wife is busily cooking in the kitchen, his eldest son studiously doing homework, and his two youngest children playing Monopoly, all possible due to the streaming radiance provided by the fluorescent lamp in the living room. Had this been a typical night in a typical Karagwe house, Mr. Stiletto would have to wait his turn to use one of the household's two kerosene lamps, for he has about thirty exams to grade. In other words, he would be up late, long after his family had retired for the night. But as he greets his family working and playing under this new artificial sun, Mr. Stiletto realizes that the "typical" Karagwe evening has now changed forever.

Customers will start their lifetime relationship with Abaka upon receipt of their first solar electric kit. In time, they will learn to effectively apply the full potential of solar energy, and they will completely replace archaic kerosene lamps and dry cell batteries with the solar electricity that will become the routine hallmark of the future for communities like Karagwe.

All of Abaka's operations in Karagwe will be contracted out to SSEW. Mr. Ghin Patel, founder and CEO of SSEW, will serve as Abaka's Chief Operating Officer for this project. Mr. Patel will facilitate dealings with the Tanzanian government, as well as with Karadea, an influential UN-funded nongovernment organization that will be heavily utilized, both in the construction of the power station and in ongoing operations.

SSEW will be responsible for conducting the following activities in Karagwe:

**Scope of Operations**

- Operating and maintaining the power station and community center
- Placing supply orders and maintaining inventory
- Overseeing and orchestrating solar kit assembly and distribution
- Collecting customer payments
- Servicing customer repair calls and manufacturer's warranties
- Printing and distributing advertisements, such as billboards, posterboards, and brochures
- Subscribing new customers and up-grading current and past customers
- Organizing informational forums and instructional demonstrations

Abaka will negotiate the most attractive supply agreements possible, and all purchases will be made directly from manufacturers at wholesale prices. Additionally, all shipping will occur via ocean, to the Tanzanian port of Dar es Salaam. Supplies will be trucked overland to Karagwe from the Indian Ocean coast. To avoid import duties, all batteries will be purchased in bulk directly from the Acme Exide Company, a Tanzania manufacturer. Lights, charge controllers, wiring, connectors, and radios will be purchased in bulk from wholesale suppliers in the United States, Europe, or South Africa. Solar modules will be purchased directly from WorldSolar, Inc, a Eugene, Oregon- based company with production facilities in India. Wind turbines and towers will be purchased from and installed by Rossimond Light & Power, of Forrestville, Wisconsin. Building and security materials will be purchased in the United States, South Africa, or Kenya. Abaka will be able to legally avoid all import duties through Mr. Patel's association with Karadea, which enjoys complete exemption from most Tanzanian tariff laws. A temporary workforce of about 100 will be hired in Karagwe to build the power station and community center. Rossimond Light & Power will design, oversee, and orchestrate the construction project, with all Abaka officers present to oversee progress and to direct funding.

After the power station and community center are completed, a full-time workforce of three to five maintenance technicians and two to four security agents will be hired and paid directly by SSEW for salaries in excess of $1,000 per year. Rossimond Light & Power will thoroughly train SSEW technicians on proper maintenance and operation of the power station. Insurance on hard assets will be purchased from a trustworthy agency in Tanzania.

**Ongoing Operations**

SSEW will be charged with the responsibility of maintaining customer relations and satisfaction. This will include subscribing new customers and taking care of existing ones. SSEW will provide free maintenance or repair visits to customers' homes for one year after the equipment's initial installation. Additionally, SSEW will help and encourage customers to upgrade to larger power systems. Used components in good working condition will be accepted as trade-in for credit on a larger system. Furthermore, customers will be encouraged to return their used batteries to SSEW, which will send them out for proper recycling. Price credits towards the purchase of new batteries will be given to all customers who dispose of their old batteries in this manner.

SSEW will be in charge of hiring and maintaining a trained local workforce. Because Mr. Patel has taught at the Institute for Solar Training for six years, he knows who the most competent technicians are, and how to find them in East Africa. Abaka will provide the financial resources to help Mr. Patel attract these technicians to Karagwe.

**Operating Expenses**

The following table shows Abaka's anticipated operating expenses from 2001-2006.

| Operating Expenses | 2001 | 2002 | 2003 | 2004 | 2005 | 2006 |
|---|---|---|---|---|---|---|
| SSEW Contracting Fees | 5,000 | 10,000 | 20,000 | 40,000 | 80,000 | 160,000 |
| Maintenance Expenses | 3,000 | 3,150 | 3,308 | 3,473 | 3,647 | 3,829 |
| Marketing Expenses | 3,000 | 3,600 | 4,320 | 5,184 | 6,221 | 7,465 |
| Insurance and Security | 8,000 | 8,000 | 8,000 | 8,000 | 8,000 | 8,000 |
| **Total** | **$19,000** | **$24,750** | **$35,628** | **$56,657** | **$97,867** | **$179,294** |

**DEVELOPMENT STRATEGY**

Abaka will assemble a legal team and incorporate during the first quarter of 2000. After completing and revising the business plan, the company will begin to seek grants and investments from accredited private investors, multi-national relief agencies, and, possibly, from large corporations.

There will be some need for product development and prototyping in Karagwe. Solar electric systems consist of four main components. The solar panel harnesses photon energy from the sun, converting radiation into electricity. This electricity is then conditioned by a charge controller before it is sent to a battery for storage. The charge controller regulates the battery's state of charge, preventing it from being damaged. The appliance, then, receives its power directly from the battery. This system has been used and perfected for well over fifty years, and Abaka's kits will not deviate from this simple design. Nevertheless, Abaka's solar electric systems will be sold as pre-assembled kits. Because customers will be expected to perform their own installations, Abaka will need to test customer reaction to these kits. Specifically, Abaka will assemble several versions in order to develop a packaging method that optimizes simplicity for the customer. Prototype testing will be conducted simultaneously with the construction of the power station and will take less than one month to complete.

Once in Karagwe, Abaka and SSEW will focus on developing market demand for the financing services. Because these financing plans will be expensive, and because no equipment will be distributed until all payments have been received, it will take time for Abaka to earn the trust of Karagwe's consumers. However, Abaka is convinced that this can be done within one year. First, utilization of SSEW, a Karagwe company that people already know and trust, will help to lend credibility to Abaka's promises. Second, the power station and community center will represent a symbol of Abaka's long-term commitment to the community. Finally, Abaka will lead by example; when working solar kits are delivered to the first wave of customers, Abaka's trustworthiness will be ultimately confirmed. By this time, Karagwe's demand for these systems will be growing fantastically.

Project Karagwe will be launched in five major phases, during the following estimated dates:

Phase 1  Incorporation: Finalize business plan, incorporate, file with the U.S. SEC, build project website: January-March 2000

Phase 2  Venture Financing: $1 million for construction of power station and community center, and to jump-start operations: February-September 2000

Phase 3  Construction of power station and community center: October-December 2000

Phase 4  Optimize solar kit packaging and assembly: November 2000

Phase 5  Subscribe customers to solar kit financing plans: December 2000

Abaka estimates that the company will need $2,000 to $5,000 for incorporation and legal fees, which will be paid by Mr. Stiller during the first quarter of 2000.

Abaka's principal founders, Liam Stiller and Ghin Patel, will control the majority of the company's equity. Abaka will employ both Mr. Stiller and Mr. Patel on a full-time basis. A Board of Directors will be assembled if and when investors demand one. A Board of Advisers has been compiled in the meanwhile. This Board is composed of experts with extensive experience relevant to the area of international rural development. All of these advisers have agreed to lend their assistance free of charge. Please see the Appendix for a detailed description of Abaka's Board of Advisers, and Appendix F for the resume of one of Abaka's founders.

**Liam Stiller, Executive Officer.** Mr. Stiller is Abaka's primary visionary. He will earn his M.B.A. degree in entrepreneurship from the University of Oregon in May 2000. He has taken formal coursework in both PV and wind system design and installation at International Natural Energy (INE), arguably the most respected and well-known RE training facilities in the world. Mr. Stiller has many contacts in the industry, and knows key people at the Renewable Energy Sources Laboratory (RESL), the Public Service Company of Oregon, WorldSolar, Inc., Energy Choices Africa, and the Tanzania Investment Center. He has traveled extensively in East Africa, and conducted market research on solar financing in Karagwe while doing an internship for SSEW during the summer of 1999.

**Ghin Patel, Africa Operations Officer.** Mr. Patel, Abaka's principal co-founder, will serve as the company's Officer for Africa Operations. Mr. Patel is a native of Karagwe, Tanzania, and is a master electrician. In 1999, he founded the Seattle Solar Electronics Workshop (SSEW) with financial backing from Mr. Stiller. SSEW offers a wide range of electrical services in the Karagwe area and beyond. Mr. Patel has installed over 500 solar electric systems in his career, and he has taught the PV systems design and installation course at the Institute for Solar Training for six years. For the last three of those years, Mr. Patel has served as the school's resident chief of staff. The school itself is located in Karagwe, and is operated and funded by one of Tanzania's most important non-government organizations, the Karagwe Development Association (KARADEA), with which Mr. Patel has very close ties. In a period of only eight years, the Institute for Solar Training has arguably become the most respected solar energy technical school in the southern Hemisphere. Mr. Patel has earned the distinction "Fundi," which, in Kiswahili means "Master Technician." He is unquestionably Tanzania's premier installer of PV systems, and one of the most admired men in Karagwe.

**Administrative Expenses**

The following table shows Abaka's expected administrative expenses for 2001-2006.

| Administrative Expenses | 2001 | 2002 | 2003 | 2004 | 2005 | 2006 |
|---|---|---|---|---|---|---|
| Salary, Mr. Stiller | 30,000 | 36,000 | 43,200 | 51,840 | 62,208 | 74,650 |
| Benefits, Mr. Stiller | 3,000 | 3,600 | 4,320 | 5,184 | 6,221 | 7,465 |
| Salary, Mr. Patel | 2,500 | 3,000 | 3,600 | 4,320 | 5,184 | 6,221 |
| Travel Expenses | 4,000 | 4,800 | 5,760 | 6,912 | 8,294 | 9,953 |
| Legal & Accounting Services | 4,000 | 4,800 | 5,760 | 6,912 | 8,294 | 9,953 |
| Office Expenses | 500 | 600 | 720 | 864 | 1,037 | 1,244 |
| **Total** | **$44,000** | **$52,800** | **$63,360** | **$76,032** | **$91,238** | **$109,486** |

## FINANCIAL SUMMARY

### Assumptions

The financial statements presented in the Appendix reflect only Abaka's forecasted sales of pre-financing contracts in Karagwe. Revenues generated from community center services are not included in these forecasts, nor are potential revenues generated from projects in locations other than Karagwe. In addition, the financial statements assume that Abaka makes no capital expenditures during the explicit period of 2001-2006. Due to the nature of the pre-financing plans, the bulk of customer payments will be collected before kit components will be ordered. This will have a positive effect on net income and cash flow. The following table presents Abaka's expected operational calendar and shows why reported net income and cash flow will be increased by the nature of the pre-financing plans.

**Operational Calendar**

| | |
|---|---|
| Sign-Up New Customers | Year 0 - Nov. to Dec. |
| Collect Monthly Payments | Year 1 - Jan. to Dec. |
| Order Kit Components | Year 1 - Sep. to Oct. |
| Assemble Kits | Year 1 - Oct. to Dec. |
| Distribute Kits | Year 2 - Jan. to Feb. |
| Charge off Cost of Kits Sold | Year 2 - Jan. to Feb. |

### Capital Requirements

Abaka requires $800,000 in start-up capital for the construction of the power station and community center. An additional infusion of $200,000 in cash at the end of 2000 will be needed to jump-start operations; this includes a significant safety cushion in case of financial emergency.

### Ratio Analysis

The following table shows Abaka's comparative financial ratios for operational years 2001-2006. The increasing return on equity figures demonstrate that Abaka does not plan to seek further external capital to expand the operation in Karagwe. The return on assets figures do not increase as substantially, because this analysis assumes that Abaka does not expend any cash during the first six years of operation.

| Financial Ratios | 2001 | 2002 | 2003 | 2004 | 2005 | 2006 |
|---|---|---|---|---|---|---|
| **Profitability** | | | | | | |
| Cost of Kits Sold | 0.00% | 19.04% | 22.84% | 28.55% | 38.07% | 38.07% |
| Operating Expenses | 74.79% | 30.69% | 15.67% | 10.50% | 9.98% | 10.16% |
| Gross Margin | -74.75% | 14.57% | 44.97% | 51.04% | 44.63% | 45.86% |
| Profit Margin | -74.75% | 8.74% | 26.98% | 30.63% | 26.78% | 27.52% |
| Return on Equity | -6.30% | 2.21% | 17.05% | 38.70% | 50.76% | 78.23% |
| Return on Assets | -6.36% | 1.99% | 11.18% | 16.77% | 15.87% | 17.11% |

| Activity | 2001 | 2002 | 2003 | 2004 | 2005 | 2006 |
|---|---|---|---|---|---|---|
| Total Asset Turnover | 0.09 | 0.23 | 0.41 | 0.55 | 0.59 | 0.62 |
| Fixed Asset Turnover | 0.12 | 0.39 | 1.13 | 2.63 | 4.74 | 8.88 |
| **Liquidity** | | | | | | |
| Quick Ratio | 4.19 | 2.14 | 1.53 | 1.4 | 1.46 | 1.49 |

**Ratio Comparisons.** There are no comparable businesses that release their financial ratios to the public. Most of the activity in the rural development industry is driven and subsidized by industrialized governments and World Bank contracts. There are several private enterprises that have been largely successful in this realm, but their financial statements are not available for comparison.

**Financial Risks**

**Currency Translation.** All of Abaka's revenues will be collected in Tanzanian shillings, and almost every shilling collected will have to be converted into U.S. dollars in order to meet the company's major expense accounts. Although the Tanzanian shilling has deflated considerably against the dollar over the past eighteen months, this trend may not continue. As far as the founders know, there are no market-based instruments available for hedging this currency risk. As such, all financial forecasts assume that Abaka will lose 5 percent of its revenue to currency exchange fluctuations and expenses. In order to minimize exposure, almost all collected Tanzanian money will be immediately converted into U.S. dollars by establishing a corporate forex account at the Tanzania National Bank. This account will allow for currency exchange at a competitive market rate, and will also enable Abaka to automatically wire transfer all funds directly into a corporate account at either Citibank or the Chase Manhattan Bank in Eugene. This will be Abaka's short-term answer to contending with currency risk. For the long-term, Abaka will neutralize currency risk by diversifying its operations and holdings into other areas of the world.

**Political and Economic Stability.** The countries surrounding Tanzania's western border have experienced a great deal of strife over the past ten years, characterized by anarchy, exodus, bloody violence, and massive inflation. In Tanzania, these regional pressures have contributed to high unemployment and double-digit inflation. Nevertheless, Tanzania has demonstrated 38 years of political stability, during which time the government has transferred power peacefully on three different occasions, most recently in 1994. There is a substantial World Bank presence in Tanzania, as well as in Kenya and Uganda. The Tanzanian government has set up an Investment Center to aid foreigners in identifying lucrative opportunities in Tanzania. Consistent with this measure, the government has also adopted extremely liberal tax and import laws in an effort to attract foreign investment. Abaka is confident that the political and economic climate in Tanzania is becoming more and more favorable for business every day, and that real progress is being made to protect Tanzania's economy and infrastructure from the instability occurring in neighboring regions.

**Coffee.** Karagwe residents depend heavily on coffee for their revenue. Economically, coffee harvests can be affected by climate or market prices, and this cannot be ignored as a potential threat to Abaka's success in Karagwe. However, Abaka's presence in Karagwe will drastically improve the region's prosperity, and the community center will help to spark an entrepreneurial spirit by providing new opportunities for small businesses in Karagwe. In short, Abaka's commitment for a long-term, value-enhancing presence in Karagwe will itself significantly neutralize this risk by helping the community to diversify and expand its economy. Furthermore, Abaka will explore the possibility of accepting coffee as payment for solar kits, which might prove to be another effective strategy for neutralizing currency translation risk.

**Cross-Cultural.** There is an operational risk inherent whenever a company in one country attempts to do business in another. This "distance" risk will be mitigated in Karagwe through the partnership with SSEW, which will handle all day-to-day operations of the business. Additionally, Abaka will maintain a full-time Oregon-based staff, as well as an expanding travel budget, so that Karagwe, and future sites in other countries, will be visited on a regular basis.

**Exit Strategy**

This proposed project in Karagwe will require a long-term commitment. In Karagwe, Abaka will generate cash flows that will be used to finance project expansions into other areas of the world, such as West Africa, Asia, and Latin America. Once Abaka's concept has been proven, and the potential for further growth demonstrated, Abaka will most likely exit via a management buyout. Another real possibility will be to take the company public. Demonstration of substantial and sustainable growth, combined with the establishment of a global brand name recognition, should make this a viable exit option. In the past decade, several mutual funds have been established that explicitly invest with environmental companies, and this demonstrates that there is a public capital market willing to purchase equity in a company like Abaka. In any case, Abaka does not foresee an exit occurring until at least 2006.

For a comprehensive background on the challenges of conducting business in Tanzania, please see the author's paper entitled "Tanzania: Developing Strategies for Effective Business Practices," available in Adobe Acrobat format from the Abaka website, www.Abaka.com.

**OFFERING**

**Investment Requirements**

Mr. Stiller has already invested $8,000 in administrative, travel, and research expenses to write this business plan. In the near future, Abaka will require an additional $2,000 to $5,000 for incorporation and legal expenses, plus $1 million in seed venture financing to launch the project in Karagwe. The following table presents an itemized breakdown of the venture financing needed.

**Itemization of Investment Needed**

**Power Station**

| | |
|---|---|
| 5,000-Watt Solar Array | $50,000 |
| 10,000-Watt Wind Generator | $50,000 |
| Power Conditioning Equipment | $50,000 |
| Power Storage Equipment | $50,000 |
| Security Equipment | $10,000 |
| Wiring and Connectors | $10,000 |
| Labor | $30,000 |
| **Total Cost of Power Station** | **$250,000** |

**Community Center**

| | |
|---|---|
| Coffee and Fruit Processors | $175,000 |
| Refrigeration & Freezing Equipment | $80,000 |
| Computing and Telecommunications Center | $100,000 |
| Water Pumping Facility | $60,000 |
| Convention Center and Theatre | $25,000 |
| Battery Charging Station | $20,000 |
| 2 Work Vans | $20,000 |
| Workshops | $15,000 |
| Office Space | $5,000 |
| Furniture | $5,000 |
| Security Equipment | $5,000 |

| | |
|---|---|
| Labor | $40,000 |
| **Total Cost of Community Center** | **$550,000** |

**Totals**

| | |
|---|---|
| Power Station | $250,000 |
| Community Center | $550,000 |
| Cash for Operations | $200,000 |
| **Total Venture Round B Investment** | **$1,000,000** |

In addition, the company will seek assistance in further developing legal, distribution, marketing, and financial strategies for conducting business internationally. Therefore, Abaka will require significant strategic support, as well as capital, in launching this venture.

The following table shows the valuation analysis for Abaka's project in Karagwe. This estimation is based on expected net income in 2006 multiplied by a factor of three. This multiple reflects Abaka's expectation that the services offered at the community center will be 75 percent of total net income. This valuation analysis unequivocally confirms Abaka's intention to provide a positive return to its investors. This is consistent with the company's mission statement, which mandates that Abaka will profitably empower underprivileged communities through the application of RE.

**Project Valuation**

**Net Income-Based Valuation 2006**

| | |
|---|---|
| Expected Revenue from Pre-Financing Program | $2,843,100 |
| Expected Revenue from Community Center | $8,529,300 |
| **Total Expected Revenue** | **$11,372,400** |
| Expected Profit Margin | 27.52% |
| Expected Net Income | $3,129,282 |
| P/ E Multiple 10 Expected Valuation | $31,292,815 |
| Discount Rate | 50% |
| **Present Value, Year 2000** | **$2,243,115** |

**Offering**

Abaka's required $1 million capital investment will be obtained through a venture round financing period conducted during the first half of 2000. Abaka will attempt to obtain the majority of this capital either from an environmental project investment agency or in the form of a partnership with a large, multinational corporation interested in penetrating emerging market. Ideally, this will be an electronics or telecommunications company that has substantial financial, marketing, and legal resources. Potential corporate partners include companies such as General Electric, Philips, Sharp, Magnavox, Toshiba, Thompson's of France, and a host of streamlined, globally-aggressive telecommunications companies. Abaka will also seek and accept financing from private, accredited investors, in accordance with all U.S. and Tanzanian securities laws.

Abaka will prefer to structure this investment agreement as an exchange of services partnership agreement, but, if necessary, equity can and will be granted in return for capital. Because the founders want to maintain cash flows for use in future project expansions, and not to buy back common stock, Abaka will attempt to retain 67 percent of its equity in the control of management throughout both rounds of financing. Additionally, the company will explore the possibility of leveraging a partnership or equity investment with a loan from a government or nonprofit relief agency such as USAID or the Africa Project Development Fund.

The markets in which Abaka will operate have a tremendous long-term potential for economic development. Abaka has the knowledge and the local contacts to bring electricity and prosperity to these regions. Eventually, these markets will develop a substantial demand for electronics, telecommunication, and information technologies. Abaka's ideal investor and/or corporate partner will have the vision and the desire to penetrate these markets early and aggressively. They will have the resources to provide significant financial, logistical, operational, marketing, and legal support. In exchange, a partner company will be granted exclusive supply and branding rights for all products and services that Abaka offers. In addition, Abaka will actively help a partner company to market its product(s) at the grassroots level by employing locals to build a loyal, long-term customer base within their communities. By providing underdeveloped communities with affordable and dependable electricity, Abaka will help pave the way for prosperity and economic development to permeate emerging markets all over the world.

## APPENDICES

**Global Entrepreneurial RE Enterprises**

| Organization | Type | Location |
|---|---|---|
| CAT Consultancy | Profit | Wales |
| Cinergy Global Power | Profit | United Kingdom |
| E & Company | Profit | New Jersey, USA |
| Econergy International Corporation | Profit | Oregon, USA |
| Energy & Environmental Ventures, LLC | Profit | New England, USA |
| Energy Alternatives Africa | Profit | Kenya |
| Energy Power Resources, Ltd. | Profit | England |
| Enersol | Nonprofit | New England, USA |
| Global Impressions, Ltd. | Profit | United Kingdom |
| Hyder | Profit | Wales |
| Intermediate Technology Consultants | Profit | United Kingdom |
| Nykomb Synergetics AB | Profit | Sweden |
| Plenum Energy | Profit | Germany |
| PowerGen | Profit | United States |
| Ramboll | Profit | Denmark |
| Solar Bank International | Profit | United States |
| Soluz | Profit | New England, USA |
| SunTree | Profit | Israel |
| The Grameen Bank/Grameen Shakti | Nonprofit/Profit | Bangladesh |
| TradeWind Insurance | Profit | United States |

## Survey

During the Summer of 1999, Mr. Stiller conducted an informal survey of Karagwe citizens. As an American, it is very difficult to obtain reliable information from people there, because they will always try to make themselves sound poorer than they really are, in the hope of receiving a handout or "sponsorship." Therefore, questions concentrated on qualitative measures rather than quantitative. In other words, discussion of actual dollar figures was avoided. Nevertheless, a good measure of Karagwe's demand for solar electricity, and why it is not being met, was obtained from these conversations. In some cases, a translator was used. The following questions were posed, generally in this order:

1. What other electrical appliances do you own?
2. How do you feel about the currently available energy sources in Karagwe?
3. What do you know about solar energy?
4. Do you know Ghin Patel?

5. Why is solar energy not used more readily in Karagwe?

6. In which village do you live?

7. How big is your house?

8. How do you light your house and power your radios?

9. What would you use solar energy for, if you could get it?

It is important to note that these questions were not posed in a formal interview environment, but during casual conversation with almost every local that Mr. Stiller met. Most of these conversations took place on the streets, in bars and restaurants, or on shuttle rides between villages. Overwhelmingly, the results of these conversations demonstrated that, in Karagwe, solar power is viewed as an expensive luxury item that only the richest families possess.

Furthermore, it was clear that almost every individual had a basic understanding of what solar energy is, and what it can do. The most important message of these conversations is that a tremendous latent demand for solar energy exists in Karagwe, and that the major obstacle impeding its widespread use is affordability.

**Mary Flinger.** Ms. Flinger has developed RE policy in Bangladesh, in Egypt, and in many parts of Latin America. She worked at RESL's International Programs Division for three years, and graduated from International Natural Energy's RE education program. Most significantly, Ms. Flinger was instrumental in aiding the Grameen Bank of Bangladesh to develop a working micro-finance plan for solar electric systems. The Grameen model is now regarded to be the most successful solar leasing program in the history of the industry, and the bank has become one of the most fortuitous lending institutions in the world with a 95 percent pay-back rate. Ms. Flinger is currently earning her M.B.A. degree at New York University in New York. Her experience developing a successful business plan to bring affordable solar energy systems to families in Bangladesh will be extremely valuable to this project.

**Jane Winger.** Ms. Winger has over six years of experience in the energy industry, as well as several years' experience in the global development field. Currently, she is employed by Energy Resources International (ERI), where she develops training curriculum for electric utility managers in developing countries. This curriculum, which has been implemented in Ghana, Brazil, and Mexico, teaches utility managers strategies for maximizing energy efficiency. Ms. Winger is currently earning her M.B.A. degree in entrepreneurship and marketing from the University of Oregon. She played an instrumental roe in the preparation of this business plan, and, as one of Abaka's most accessible advisers, will maintain close involvement with Abaka in years to come. At some point in the future, Ms. Winger may join the company's full-time staff.

**Rudolph Heisemann.** Mr. Bartholf is a director at Energy Resourcs International (ERI), and has over twenty years of experience in the RE industry. During his impressive career, Mr. Bartholf has provided strategic planning, project development, and technical assistance as a consultant to numerous organizations all over the world. Prior to joining ERI, Mr. Bartholf served as a Senior Program Officer at Prouffer International, a nonprofit development assistance organization. While at Prouffer, Mr. Bartholf spearheaded the development of RE projects in several Asian countries. His advice on technical and economic matters, as well as his contacts within the industry, will prove highly valuable to Abaka.

**Miller Fried.** Mr. Byrne is a British ex-patriot who has been installing solar electric systems off and on in eastern and southern Africa for twelve years. Currently, he is working with the Maasai people in Arusha, Tanzania, on a large-scale solar project to electrify several remote community centers and schools on tribal lands. Mr. Byrne is literally in the trenches, both as a system installer and integrator, and as a fundraiser. He has important contacts with non-

**Board of Advisors**

government organizations throughout Europe and Africa, and knows key RE producers and distributors. His assistance with the Tanzanian government, with suppliers and distributors, and with private fundraisers, will prove vital to Abaka's success in Karagwe. He will also serve as an ideal sounding board for idea testing.

**Justin Sangria, Ph.D.** Dr. Sangria is a Professor of Finance at the University of Oregon. He specializes in the area of risk management, particularly as it relates to international finance and currency exchange. A native of Peru, Professor Sangria has consulted for numerous banks in Latin America on currency hedging, and has developed financial strategies to help these banks effectively conduct business across international borders. Professor Sangria's expertise in this realm will help Abaka to manage the serious financial risks associated with doing business in Tanzania.

**Felicia Strong, M.B.A.** Ms. Strong has worked in the U.S. RE industry for over seven years in both the public and private sectors. Most recently, she worked for Kyocera Solar International, one of the world's largest producers of PV technology, as well as for the U.S. Export Council for RE. She is now working for Prouffer International. Ms. Strong has lived and worked in Brazil, and knows the global RE industry as well as anybody. She will aid in developing strategies for executing this business plan, and in locating potential investors.

**Joseph Rosenthal, Ph.D.** Dr. Rosenthal is a Senior Economist at the National Energy Sources Laboratory (NESL) in Eugene, Oregon. He has been the Senior Analyst of NESL's International and Village Power Program for nine years, and has worked in the RE field since 1978. He specializes in conducting feasibility and optimization analyses for RE projects in developing nations. Dr. Rosenthal will continue to assist Abaka by reviewing and editing the business plan, by providing fresh ideas and approaches, and by connecting Abaka's management team with other key people in the industry.

**Samuel Obago.** Mr. Obago is a native of Kenya, and is the Chief Operations Officer at Energy Choices Africa (ECA), probably Kenya's pre-eminent large-scale RE consulting firm. He has seven years of hands-on experience installing solar electric systems. For ECA, Mr. Obago evaluates project financing and feasibility, and negotiates contracts with the World Bank and other international lenders. He is fluent in Kiswahili, and knows key people in East African government, financial, and nonprofit organizations.

**Jake Rossimond,** owner of Rossimond Power and Light, has been designing, installing, repairing, and building wind generators for twenty years. He is perhaps the nation's best-known specialist in the commercial wind energy industry, and has worked on RE development projects in 23 foreign countries. He has consulted for NESL, as well as numerous other energy organizations all over the world, and has taught the wind energy class at INE for the past six years. In addition to serving as a consultant for the business plan, he has agreed to oversee the design and construction of Abaka's power station and community center in Karagwe.

**Mitchell Bumholtz.** Mr. Bumholtz served two years in Paraguay with the Peace Corps, and has since graduated from INE's RE education program. He has consulted for the World Conservation Project, and for the past two years has been instrumental in the establishment of a large-scale commercial wind power project in New England. Mr. Bumholtz has been a dedicated proponent of this project since its inception, and may join the Abaka management team as a full-time employee within a year.

**Jimmy Wise.** Mr. Wise has been an Executive Director of International Natural Energy (INE), arguably the world's most respected RE training center, since 1991. He has been training people in RE installation since 1981, and has nearly thirty years of experience as a licensed general contractor in solar home building and design. During his career, Mr. Wise has taught solar installation in developing countries all over the world. He has agreed to assist with the on-site design and construction of Abaka's power station and community center.

**Jacob Black, Ph.D.** Dr. Black is a Senior Analyst at NESL's International Programs Division. He has over twenty years of experience advising and consulting on RE projects in sub-Saharan Africa, and has traveled extensively in the region. As one of Abaka's most accessible and supporting advisers, Dr. Black will continue to provide constructive criticism, new ideas, and liaison with potential consultants and investors.

**OBJECTIVE:** To build Abaka Energy Solutions into a global provider of renewable energy products and services

**Resume of Liam Stiller**

### EDUCATION & EXPERIENCE
**University of Oregon**
Master's Degree in Business Administration
Expected Graduation, May 2000
- Major in Entrepreneurship; 3.7 cumulative GPA
- Awarded $3,500 in merit-based fellowships for study in Entrepreneurship
- Helped WorldSolar, Inc. of Eugene, OR develop a marketing strategy for introducing their solar module into East Africa as an independent project for M.B.A. credit
- Teaching Assistant, M.B.A. Business Statistics course

**Seattle Solar Electronics Workshop,** Karagwe, Kagera, Tanzania
Summer Internship, June-August 1999
- Conducted the feasibility analysis for the Abaka business concept
- Forged a business partnership with Ghin Patel, Tanzania's leading installer of solar electric systems
- Made contacts with key industry people including Samuel Obago and Miller Fried, as well as officials at the Karagwe Development Association (KARADEA), the Tanzania Foreign Investment Center, the Tanzania Revenue Authority, the Tanzania Electric Supply Company, and the Africa Projects Development Fund

**International Natural Energy,** Eugene, OR
Renewable Energy Education Program, June-August 1998
- Completed coursework in PV system design and installation
- Helped to install a 1.5 kW grid-tied PV system on a home in Edwards, CO
- Completed coursework in the fundamentals of wind generator operation and installation
- Helped to install a 1.5 kW wind generator on a remote home near Fairplay, CO

**Amgen, Inc.,** Portland OR
Department of Inflammation November 1993-May 1998
Research Associate in Cell Biology & Immunology
- Worked on over 20 project teams to develop novel therapeutics for treating inflammatory diseases
- Responsible for researching the effects of drugs on cells and organ systems, reporting data at team meetings, contributing to strategies for drug development, and coordinating cell biology research efforts with those of other departments
- Supervised 3 student interns to help with research and project implementation
- Wrote 2 and co-authored 7 scientific papers
- Promoted twice for ability to work in teams, handle multiple responsibilities, conduct sound science, function without supervision, and take primary initiative
- Presented data in front of 200 cell biologists at the international Keystone Symposium

University of Chicago, Chicago, IL
Bachelor's Degree in History & Immunology, Graduated June 1993
- Chairman of fraternity committee; led the most successful recruitment program on campus
- Chairman of Philanthropy committee; led an effort which raised $79,000 for cancer research, and honored by the Saturn Corporation for dedication to community service

### ADDITIONAL INFORMATION
- Skilled in Microsoft Office, including Access databases, as well as using Excel spreadsheets for financial analyses and optimization modeling (maximizing profits or minimizing costs using the Solver function)
- Written and conversational literacy in Spanish
- Able to travel extensively, and to remote locations (have been to 17 countries on 4 continents); self-sufficient and culturally adaptive

## FINANCIAL STATEMENTS

### Pricing Strategy and Sales & Revenue Forecasts

| Pricing of Financing Contracts | Plan 1 | | Plan 2 | | Plan 3 | |
|---|---|---|---|---|---|---|
| | per month | per contract | per month | per contract | per month | per contract |
| Price | $24.00 | $288 | $48.00 | $576 | $72.00 | $864 |
| Gross Profit Margin | | 72.46% | | 80.00% | | 94.59% |

| Anticipated Sales Breakdown | Plan 1 | Plan 2 | Plan 3 |
|---|---|---|---|
| Percent of Total Sales | 85% | 13% | 2% |

| Sales Forecasts | 2001 | 2002 | 2003 | 2004 | 2005 | 2006 |
|---|---|---|---|---|---|---|
| Sales Growth Rate | 200% | 150% | 100% | 50% | 50% | |
| Kit Sales, Plan 1 | 213 | 638 | 1,594 | 3,188 | 4,781 | 7,172 |
| Kit Sales, Plan 2 | 33 | 98 | 244 | 488 | 731 | 1,097 |
| Kit Sales, Plan 3 | 5 | 15 | 38 | 75 | 113 | 169 |
| **Total Kits Sold** | **250** | **750** | **1,875** | **3,750** | **5,625** | **8,438** |

| Total Customers Served, 2001-2006 | | 20,688 |
|---|---|---|

| Revenue Forecasts | 2001 | 2002 | 2003 | 2004 | 2005 | 2006 |
|---|---|---|---|---|---|---|
| Plan 1 | $61,200 | $183,600 | $459,000 | $918,000 | $1,377,000 | $2,065,500 |
| Plan 2 | $18,720 | $56,160 | $140,400 | $280,800 | $421,200 | $631,800 |
| Plan 3 | $4,320 | $12,960 | $32,400 | $64,800 | $97,200 | $145,800 |
| **Total Revenue** | **$84,240** | **$252,720** | **$631,800** | **$1,263,600** | **$1,895,400** | **$2,843,100** |

### Pro-Forma Cost of Kits Sold and Inventory Holding Schedule

| Cost of Kits Sold | Plan 1 | | Plan 2 | | Plan 3 | |
|---|---|---|---|---|---|---|
| | Description | Cost | Description | Cost | Description | Cost |
| Photovoltaic Module | 13 Watt | $69.00 | 30 Watt | $125.00 | 48 Watt | $171.00 |
| Battery | 12 V, 20 Amp-Hr | $20.00 | 12 V, 60 Amp-Hr | $60.00 | 12 V, 100 Amp-Hr | $100.00 |
| Charge Controller | 2.5 Amp | $30.00 | 5 Amp | $50.00 | 5 Amp | $50.00 |
| Loads | 1 light, 1 radio | $10.00 | 2 lights, 1 radio | $15.00 | 3 lights, 1 radio | $20.00 |
| Connectors & Wiring | | $15.00 | | $25.00 | | $35.00 |
| Mounting | | $10.00 | | $15.00 | | $20.00 |
| Shipping (Whole Kit) | | $13.00 | | $30.00 | | $48.00 |
| **Total Unit Cost** | | **$167.00** | | **$320.00** | | **$444.00** |

| Inventory Holding Schedule | 2001 | 2002 | 2003 | 2004 | 2005 | 2006 |
|---|---|---|---|---|---|---|
| Inventory at Beginning of Year | 0 | 250 | 750 | 1,875 | 3,750 | 5,625 |
| Kits Installed During Year | 0 | 250 | 750 | 1,875 | 3,750 | 5,625 |
| New Kits Ordered at End of Year | 250 | 750 | 1,875 | 3,750 | 5,625 | 8,438 |
| Inventory at End of Year (Units) | 250 | 750 | 1,875 | 3,750 | 5,625 | 8,438 |
| **Inventory at End of Year (Value)** | **$48,108** | **$144,323** | **$360,806** | **$721,613** | **$1,082,419** | **$1,623,628** |

## Consolidated Pro-Forma Financial Statements, 2001-2006

| Income Statement | 2001 | 2002 | 2003 | 2004 | 2005 | 2006 |
|---|---|---|---|---|---|---|
| Revenue | $84,240 | $252,720 | $631,800 | $1,263,600 | $1,895,400 | $2,843,100 |
| Cost of Kits Sold | $0 | $48,108 | $144,323 | $360,806 | $721,613 | $1,082,419 |
| **Gross Profit** | **$84,240** | **$204,613** | **$487,478** | **$902,794** | **$1,173,788** | **$1,760,681** |
| | | | | | | |
| CSEW Contracting Fee | $5,000 | $10,000 | $20,000 | $40,000 | $80,000 | $160,000 |
| Administrative Expense | $44,000 | $52,800 | $63,360 | $76,032 | $91,238 | $109,486 |
| Maintenance Expense | $3,000 | $3,150 | $3,308 | $3,473 | $3,647 | $3,829 |
| Marketing Expense | $3,000 | $3,600 | $4,320 | $5,184 | $6,221 | $7,465 |
| Insurance & Security Expense | $8,000 | $8,000 | $8,000 | $8,000 | $8,000 | $8,000 |
| **Total Operating Expenses** | **$63,000** | **$77,550** | **$98,988** | **$132,689** | **$189,106** | **$288,780** |
| | | | | | | |
| Operating Profit | $21,240 | $127,063 | $388,490 | $770,105 | $984,682 | $1,471,901 |
| Currency Exchange Loss | $4,212 | $10,231 | $24,374 | $45,140 | $58,689 | $88,034 |
| Depreciation Expense | $80,000 | $80,000 | $80,000 | $80,000 | $80,000 | $80,000 |
| Earnings Before Income Taxes | ($62,972) | $36,832 | $284,116 | $644,965 | $845,992 | $1,303,867 |
| Income Tax Expense | $0 | $14,733 | $113,646 | $257,986 | $338,397 | $521,547 |
| **Net Income** | **($62,972)** | **$22,099** | **$170,470** | **$386,979** | **$507,595** | **$782,320** |

**Balance Sheet**

**Assets**

| | 2001 | 2002 | 2003 | 2004 | 2005 | 2006 |
|---|---|---|---|---|---|---|
| Cash | $206,874 | $313,492 | $588,437 | $1,091,318 | $1,701,810 | $2,614,063 |
| Inventory | $48,108 | $144,323 | $360,806 | $721,613 | $1,082,419 | $1,623,628 |
| Equity in CSEW | $4,000 | $4,000 | $4,000 | $4,000 | $4,000 | $4,000 |
| Total Current Assets | $258,982 | $461,815 | $953,244 | $1,816,930 | $2,788,228 | $4,241,691 |
| Property, Plant, & Equipment | $800,000 | $800,000 | $800,000 | $800,000 | $800,000 | $800,000 |
| Accumulated Depreciation | $80,000 | $160,000 | $240,000 | $320,000 | $400,000 | $480,000 |
| Net Fixed Assets | $720,000 | $640,000 | $560,000 | $480,000 | $400,000 | $320,000 |
| **Total Assets** | **$978,982** | **$1,101,815** | **$1,513,244** | **$2,296,930** | **$3,188,228** | **$4,561,691** |

**Liabilities**

| | 2001 | 2002 | 2003 | 2004 | 2005 | 2006 |
|---|---|---|---|---|---|---|
| Accounts Payable | $48,108 | $144,323 | $360,806 | $721,613 | $1,082,419 | $1,623,628 |
| Accrued Expenses | $4,846 | $5,965 | $7,614 | $10,207 | $14,547 | $22,214 |
| Accrued Taxes Payable | $0 | $3,400 | $26,226 | $59,535 | $78,092 | $120,357 |
| Total Liabilities | $52,954 | $153,688 | $394,647 | $791,355 | $1,175,057 | $1,766,199 |
| Stockholders' Equity | $1,009,000 | $1,009,000 | $1,009,000 | $1,009,000 | $1,009,000 | $1,009,000 |
| Retained Earnings | ($82,972) | ($60,873) | $109,597 | $496,576 | $1,004,171 | $1,786,492 |
| **Total Liabilities & Stockholders' Equity** | **$978,982** | **$1,101,815** | **$1,513,244** | **$2,296,930** | **$3,188,228** | **$4,561,691** |

**Statement of Cash Flows**

| | 2001 | 2002 | 2003 | 2004 | 2005 | 2006 |
|---|---|---|---|---|---|---|
| Beginning Cash | $185,000 | $206,874 | $313,492 | $588,437 | $1,091,318 | $1,701,810 |
| Net Income | ($62,972) | $22,099 | $170,470 | $386,979 | $507,595 | $782,320 |
| Change in Inventory | ($48,108) | ($96,215) | ($216,484) | ($360,806) | ($360,806) | ($541,209) |
| Depreciation Add-Back | $80,000 | $80,000 | $80,000 | $80,000 | $80,000 | $80,000 |
| Change in Accounts Payable | $48,108 | $96,215 | $216,484 | $360,806 | $360,806 | $541,209 |
| Change in Accrued Expenses | $4,846 | $1,119 | $1,649 | $2,592 | $4,340 | $7,667 |
| Change in Accrued Taxes Payable | $0 | $3,400 | $22,826 | $33,309 | $18,556 | $42,265 |
| Total Adjustments to Cash Balance | $21,874 | $106,618 | $274,945 | $502,881 | $610,492 | $912,253 |
| **Ending Cash** | **$206,874** | **$313,492** | **$588,437** | **$1,091,318** | **$1,701,810** | **$2,614,063** |

*This page left intentionally blank to accommodate tabular matter following.*

## Consolidated Monthly Pro-Forma Financial Statements, Year 2001

| Income Statement | Jan | Feb | Mar | Apr | May | Jun | Jul |
|---|---|---|---|---|---|---|---|
| Revenue | $7,020 | $7,020 | $7,020 | $7,020 | $7,020 | $7,020 | $7,020 |
| Cost of Kits Sold | $0 | $0 | $0 | $0 | $0 | $0 | $0 |
| Gross Profit | $7,020 | $7,020 | $7,020 | $7,020 | $7,020 | $7,020 | $7,020 |
| | | | | | | | |
| CSEW Contracting Fee | $417 | $417 | $417 | $417 | $417 | $417 | $417 |
| Administrative Expense | $3,667 | $3,667 | $3,667 | $3,667 | $3,667 | $3,667 | $3,667 |
| Maintenance Expense | $250 | $250 | $250 | $250 | $250 | $250 | $250 |
| Marketing Expense | $750 | $0 | $0 | $750 | $0 | $0 | $750 |
| Insurance & Security Expense | $667 | $667 | $667 | $667 | $667 | $667 | $667 |
| **Total Operating Expenses** | **$5,750** | **$5,000** | **$5,000** | **$5,750** | **$5,000** | **$5,000** | **$5,750** |
| | | | | | | | |
| Currency Exchange Loss | $351 | $351 | $351 | $351 | $351 | $351 | $351 |
| Depreciation Expense | $6,667 | $6,667 | $6,667 | $6,667 | $6,667 | $6,667 | $6,667 |
| Earnings Before Income Taxes | ($5,748) | ($4,998) | ($4,998) | ($5,748) | ($4,998) | ($4,998) | ($5,748) |
| Income Tax Expense | $0 | $0 | $0 | $0 | $0 | $0 | $0 |
| Income Tax Credit | $0 | $0 | $0 | $0 | $0 | $0 | $0 |
| **Net Income** | **($5,748)** | **($4,998)** | **($4,998)** | **($5,748)** | **($4,998)** | **($4,998)** | **($5,748)** |

**Balance Sheet**

**Assets**

| | Jan | Feb | Mar | Apr | May | Jun | Jul |
|---|---|---|---|---|---|---|---|
| Cash | $191,669 | $192,588 | $194,257 | $195,926 | $196,845 | $198,514 | $200,183 |
| Inventory | $0 | $0 | $0 | $0 | $0 | $0 | $0 |
| Equity in CSEW | $4,000 | $4,000 | $4,000 | $4,000 | $4,000 | $4,000 | $4,000 |
| Total Current Assets | $195,669 | $196,588 | $198,257 | $199,926 | $200,845 | $202,514 | $204,183 |
| Property, Plant, & Equipment | $800,000 | $800,000 | $800,000 | $800,000 | $800,000 | $800,000 | $800,000 |
| Accumulated Depreciation | $6,667 | $13,333 | $20,000 | $26,667 | $33,333 | $40,000 | $46,667 |
| Net Fixed Assets | $793,333 | $786,667 | $780,000 | $773,333 | $766,667 | $760,000 | $753,333 |
| **Total Assets** | **$989,002** | **$983,255** | **$978,257** | **$973,259** | **$967,512** | **$962,514** | **$957,516** |

**Liabilities**

| | Jan | Feb | Mar | Apr | May | Jun | Jul |
|---|---|---|---|---|---|---|---|
| Accounts Payable | $0 | $0 | $0 | $0 | $0 | $0 | $0 |
| Accrued Expenses | $5,750 | $5,000 | $5,000 | $5,750 | $5,000 | $5,000 | $5,750 |
| Accrued Taxes Payable | $0 | $0 | $0 | $0 | $0 | $0 | $0 |
| Total Liabilities | $5,750 | $5,000 | $5,000 | $5,750 | $5,000 | $5,000 | $5,750 |
| Stockholders' Equity | $1,009,000 | $1,009,000 | $1,009,000 | $1,009,000 | $1,009,000 | $1,009,000 | $1,009,000 |
| Retained Earnings | ($25,748) | ($30,745) | ($35,743) | ($41,491) | ($46,488) | ($51,486) | ($57,234) |
| **Total Liabilities & Stockholders' Equity** | **$989,002** | **$983,255** | **$978,257** | **$973,259** | **$967,512** | **$962,514** | **$957,516** |

**Statement of Cash Flows**

| | Jan | Feb | Mar | Apr | May | Jun | Jul |
|---|---|---|---|---|---|---|---|
| Beginning Cash | $185,000 | $191,669 | $192,588 | $194,257 | $195,926 | $196,845 | $198,514 |
| Net Income | ($5,748) | ($4,998) | ($4,998) | ($5,748) | ($4,998) | ($4,998) | ($5,748) |
| Change in Inventory | $0 | $0 | $0 | $0 | $0 | $0 | $0 |
| Depreciation Add-Back | $6,667 | $6,667 | $6,667 | $6,667 | $6,667 | $6,667 | $6,667 |
| Change in Accounts Payable | $0 | $0 | $0 | $0 | $0 | $0 | $0 |
| Change in Accrued Expenses | $5,750 | ($750) | $0 | $750 | ($750) | $0 | $750 |
| Change in Accrued Taxes Payable | $0 | $0 | $0 | $0 | $0 | $0 | $0 |
| **Total Adjustments to Cash Balance** | **$6,669** | **$919** | **$1,669** | **$1,669** | **$919** | **$1,669** | **$1,669** |
| **Ending Cash** | **$191,669** | **$192,588** | **$194,257** | **$195,926** | **$196,845** | **$198,514** | **$200,183** |

| Aug | Sep | Oct | Nov | Dec | Year |
|---|---|---|---|---|---|
| $7,020 | $7,020 | $7,020 | $7,020 | $7,020 | $84,240 |
| $0 | $0 | $0 | $0 | $0 | $0 |
| $7,020 | $7,020 | $7,020 | $7,020 | $7,020 | $84,240 |
|  |  |  |  |  |  |
| $417 | $417 | $417 | $417 | $417 | $5,000 |
| $3,667 | $3,667 | $3,667 | $3,667 | $3,667 | $44,000 |
| $250 | $250 | $250 | $250 | $250 | $3,000 |
| $0 | $0 | $750 | $0 | $0 | $3,000 |
|  |  |  |  |  |  |
| $667 | $667 | $667 | $667 | $667 | $8,000 |
| **$5,000** | **$5,000** | **$5,750** | **$5,000** | **$5,000** | **$63,000** |
|  |  |  |  |  |  |
| $351 | $351 | $351 | $351 | $351 | $4,212 |
| $6,667 | $6,667 | $6,667 | $6,667 | $6,667 | $80,000 |
| ($4,998) | ($4,998) | ($5,748) | ($4,998) | ($4,998) | ($62,972) |
| $0 | $0 | $0 | $0 | $0 | $0 |
| $0 | $0 | $0 | $0 | $0 | $0 |
| **($4,998)** | **($4,998)** | **($5,748)** | **($4,998)** | **($4,998)** | **($62,972)** |
|  |  |  |  |  |  |
|  |  |  |  |  |  |
| $201,102 | $202,771 | $204,440 | $205,359 | $207,028 |  |
| $0 | $0 | $0 | $0 | $48,108 |  |
| $4,000 | $4,000 | $4,000 | $4,000 | $4,000 |  |
| $205,102 | $206,771 | $208,440 | $209,359 | $259,136 |  |
| $800,000 | $800,000 | $800,000 | $800,000 | $800,000 |  |
| $53,333 | $60,000 | $66,667 | $73,333 | $80,000 |  |
| $746,667 | $740,000 | $733,333 | $726,667 | $720,000 |  |
| **$951,769** | **$946,771** | **$941,773** | **$936,026** | **$979,136** |  |
|  |  |  |  |  |  |
|  |  |  |  |  |  |
| $0 | $0 | $0 | $0 | $48,108 |  |
| $5,000 | $5,000 | $5,750 | $5,000 | $5,000 |  |
| $0 | $0 | $0 | $0 | $0 |  |
| $5,000 | $5,000 | $5,750 | $5,000 | $53,108 |  |
| $1,009,000 | $1,009,000 | $1,009,000 | $1,009,000 | $1,009,000 |  |
| ($62,231) | ($67,229) | ($72,977) | ($77,974) | ($82,972) |  |
|  |  |  |  |  |  |
| **$951,769** | **$946,771** | **$941,773** | **$936,026** | **$979,136** |  |
|  |  |  |  |  |  |
|  |  |  |  |  |  |
| $200,183 | $201,102 | $202,771 | $204,440 | $205,359 |  |
| ($4,998) | ($4,998) | ($5,748) | ($4,998) | ($4,998) |  |
| $0 | $0 | $0 | $0 | ($48,108) |  |
| $6,667 | $6,667 | $6,667 | $6,667 | $6,667 |  |
| $0 | $0 | $0 | $0 | $48,108 |  |
| ($750) | $0 | $750 | ($750) | $0 |  |
|  |  |  |  |  |  |
| $0 | $0 | $0 | $0 | $0 |  |
|  |  |  |  |  |  |
| **$919** | **$1,669** | **$1,669** | **$919** | **$1,669** |  |
| **$201,102** | **$202,771** | **$204,440** | **$205,359** | **$207,028** |  |

## Consolidated Monthly Pro-Forma Financial Statements, Year 2002

| Income Statement | Jan | Feb | Mar | Apr | May | Jun | Jul |
|---|---|---|---|---|---|---|---|
| Revenue | $21,060 | $21,060 | $21,060 | $21,060 | $21,060 | $21,060 | $21,060 |
| Cost of Kits Sold | $48,108 | $0 | $0 | $0 | $0 | $0 | $0 |
| Gross Profit | ($27,048) | $21,060 | $21,060 | $21,060 | $21,060 | $21,060 | $21,060 |
| | | | | | | | |
| CSEW Contracting Fee | $833 | $833 | $833 | $833 | $833 | $833 | $833 |
| Administrative Expense | $4,400 | $4,400 | $4,400 | $4,400 | $4,400 | $4,400 | $4,400 |
| Maintenance Expense | $263 | $263 | $263 | $263 | $263 | $263 | $263 |
| Marketing Expense | $900 | $0 | $0 | $900 | $0 | $0 | $900 |
| Insurance & Security Expense | $667 | $667 | $667 | $667 | $667 | $667 | $667 |
| Total Operating Expenses | $7,063 | $6,163 | $6,163 | $7,063 | $6,163 | $6,163 | $7,063 |
| | | | | | | | |
| Currency Exchange Loss | $1,053 | $1,053 | $1,053 | $1,053 | $1,053 | $1,053 | $1,053 |
| Depreciation Expense | $6,667 | $6,667 | $6,667 | $6,667 | $6,667 | $6,667 | $6,667 |
| Earnings Before Income Taxes | ($41,830) | $7,178 | $7,178 | $6,278 | $7,178 | $7,178 | $6,278 |
| Income Tax Expense | $0 | $2,871 | $2,871 | $2,511 | $2,871 | $2,871 | $2,511 |
| Income Tax Credit | $16,732 | $0 | $0 | $0 | $0 | $0 | $0 |
| Net Income | ($25,098) | $4,307 | $4,307 | $3,767 | $4,307 | $4,307 | $3,767 |

**Balance Sheet**

| | Jan | Feb | Mar | Apr | May | Jun | Jul |
|---|---|---|---|---|---|---|---|
| Cash | $190,659 | $203,604 | $217,448 | $225,551 | $238,495 | $252,340 | $257,931 |
| Inventory | $0 | $0 | $0 | $0 | $0 | $0 | $0 |
| Equity in CSEW | $4,000 | $4,000 | $4,000 | $4,000 | $4,000 | $4,000 | $4,000 |
| Total Current Assets | $194,659 | $207,604 | $221,448 | $229,551 | $242,495 | $256,340 | $261,931 |
| Property, Plant, & Equipment | $800,000 | $800,000 | $800,000 | $800,000 | $800,000 | $800,000 | $800,000 |
| Accumulated Depreciation | $86,667 | $93,333 | $100,000 | $106,667 | $113,333 | $120,000 | $126,667 |
| Net Fixed Assets | $713,333 | $706,667 | $700,000 | $693,333 | $686,667 | $680,000 | $673,333 |
| Total Assets | $907,993 | $914,271 | $921,448 | $922,884 | $929,162 | $936,340 | $935,264 |

**Liabilities**

| | Jan | Feb | Mar | Apr | May | Jun | Jul |
|---|---|---|---|---|---|---|---|
| Accounts Payable | $0 | $0 | $0 | $0 | $0 | $0 | $0 |
| Accrued Expenses | $7,063 | $6,163 | $6,163 | $7,063 | $6,163 | $6,163 | $7,063 |
| Accrued Taxes Payable | $0 | $2,871 | $5,742 | $2,511 | $5,382 | $8,253 | $2,511 |
| Total Liabilities | $7,063 | $9,034 | $11,905 | $9,574 | $11,545 | $14,416 | $9,574 |
| Stockholders' Equity | $1,009,000 | $1,009,000 | $1,009,000 | $1,009,000 | $1,009,000 | $1,009,000 | $1,009,000 |
| Retained Earnings | ($108,070) | ($103,763) | ($99,456) | ($95,690) | ($91,383) | ($87,076) | ($83,310) |
| Total Liabilities & Stockholders' Equity | $907,993 | $914,271 | $921,448 | $922,884 | $929,162 | $936,340 | $935,264 |

**Statement of Cash Flows**

| | Jan | Feb | Mar | Apr | May | Jun | Jul |
|---|---|---|---|---|---|---|---|
| Beginning Cash | $207,028 | $190,659 | $203,604 | $217,448 | $225,551 | $238,495 | $252,340 |
| Net Income | ($25,098) | $4,307 | $4,307 | $3,767 | $4,307 | $4,307 | $3,767 |
| Change in Inventory | $48,108 | $0 | $0 | $0 | $0 | $0 | $0 |
| Depreciation Add-Back | $6,667 | $6,667 | $6,667 | $6,667 | $6,667 | $6,667 | $6,667 |
| Change in Accounts Payable | ($48,108) | $0 | $0 | $0 | $0 | $0 | $0 |
| Change in Accrued Expenses | $2,063 | ($900) | $0 | $900 | ($900) | $0 | $900 |
| Change in Accrued Taxes Payable | $0 | $2,871 | $2,871 | ($3,231) | $2,871 | $2,871 | ($5,742) |
| Total Adjustments to Cash Balance | ($16,369) | $12,945 | $13,845 | $8,102 | $12,945 | $13,845 | $5,591 |
| Ending Cash | $190,659 | $203,604 | $217,448 | $225,551 | $238,495 | $252,340 | $257,931 |

| Aug | Sep | Oct | Nov | Dec | Year |
|---|---|---|---|---|---|
| $21,060 | $21,060 | $21,060 | $21,060 | $21,060 | $252,720 |
| $0 | $0 | $0 | $0 | $0 | $48,108 |
| $21,060 | $21,060 | $21,060 | $21,060 | $21,060 | $204,613 |
| | | | | | |
| $833 | $833 | $833 | $833 | $833 | $10,000 |
| $4,400 | $4,400 | $4,400 | $4,400 | $4,400 | $52,800 |
| $263 | $263 | $263 | $263 | $263 | $3,150 |
| $0 | $0 | $900 | $0 | $0 | $3,600 |
| $667 | $667 | $667 | $667 | $667 | $8,000 |
| **$6,163** | **$6,163** | **$7,063** | **$6,163** | **$6,163** | **$77,550** |
| | | | | | |
| $1,053 | $1,053 | $1,053 | $1,053 | $1,053 | $12,636 |
| $6,667 | $6,667 | $6,667 | $6,667 | $6,667 | $80,000 |
| | | | | | |
| $7,178 | $7,178 | $6,278 | $7,178 | $7,178 | $34,427 |
| $2,871 | $2,871 | $2,511 | $2,871 | $2,871 | $30,502 |
| $0 | $0 | $0 | $0 | $0 | $16,732 |
| **$4,307** | **$4,307** | **$3,767** | **$4,307** | **$4,307** | **$20,656** |
| | | | | | |
| | | | | | |
| $270,875 | $284,720 | $290,311 | $303,255 | $317,100 | |
| $0 | $0 | $0 | $0 | $144,323 | |
| $4,000 | $4,000 | $4,000 | $4,000 | $4,000 | |
| $274,875 | $288,720 | $294,311 | $307,255 | $465,422 | |
| $800,000 | $800,000 | $800,000 | $800,000 | $800,000 | |
| $133,333 | $140,000 | $146,667 | $153,333 | $160,000 | |
| $666,667 | $660,000 | $653,333 | $646,667 | $640,000 | |
| **$941,542** | **$948,720** | **$947,644** | **$953,922** | **$1,105,422** | |
| | | | | | |
| | | | | | |
| $0 | $0 | $0 | $0 | $144,323 | |
| $6,163 | $6,163 | $7,063 | $6,163 | $6,163 | |
| $5,382 | $8,253 | $2,511 | $5,382 | $8,253 | |
| $11,545 | $14,416 | $9,574 | $11,545 | $158,738 | |
| $1,009,000 | $1,009,000 | $1,009,000 | $1,009,000 | $1,009,000 | |
| ($79,003) | ($74,696) | ($70,930) | ($66,623) | ($62,316) | |
| | | | | | |
| **$941,542** | **$948,720** | **$947,644** | **$953,922** | **$1,105,422** | |
| | | | | | |
| | | | | | |
| $257,931 | $270,875 | $284,720 | $290,311 | $303,255 | |
| $4,307 | $4,307 | $3,767 | $4,307 | $4,307 | |
| $0 | $0 | $0 | $0 | ($144,323) | |
| $6,667 | $6,667 | $6,667 | $6,667 | $6,667 | |
| $0 | $0 | $0 | $0 | $144,323 | |
| ($900) | $0 | $900 | ($900) | $0 | |
| | | | | | |
| $2,871 | $2,871 | ($5,742) | $2,871 | $2,871 | |
| | | | | | |
| **$12,945** | **$13,845** | **$5,591** | **$12,945** | **$13,845** | |
| **$270,875** | **$284,720** | **$290,311** | **$303,255** | **$317,100** | |

# Gourmet Foods Company

BUSINESS PLAN

GOOD EARTH FOODS COMPANY

*1705 Stubbleton Road*
*Bismarck, North Dakota 58502*

*People are smarter about the foods they eat these days, and more consumers have turned to organic food products for personal health and reasons of quality. The Good Earth Foods Company will provide high-quality organic foods and ready-made convenience items for people who are too busy for complex food preparation but who care about what they eat.*

- EXECUTIVE SUMMARY

- STATE OF THE INDUSTRY

- MISSION

- MARKETING STRATEGY

- COMPANY FOUNDER PROFILE

- FINANCIALS

# GOURMET FOODS COMPANY
## BUSINESS PLAN

## EXECUTIVE SUMMARY

### Introduction

Good Earth Foods Company has formed to meet the growing demand for unique, organic, partially prepared, specialty convenience foods.

Good Earth Foods is initially focusing on the development, production, and marketing of dry spice products, which is detailed in this document. Other food product development opportunities will be addressed in future amendments to this business plan that will provide additional profit with expanded market share.

Good Earth Foods has retained legal counsel and has developed a business relationship agreement with a volume food manufacturer to partner with in ongoing business operations. In addition to establishing a relationship with a food production producer, Good Earth Foods has sought out and secured professional services firms to evaluate, validate quality, and longevity of products and product life cycle. These additional professional services will allow Good Earth Foods Company to ensure food quality compliance with state, federal, local, and industry group certifications.

Our line of products will conform to the guidelines established by the California Organic Foods Act of 1994.

## STATE OF THE INDUSTRY

The organic and gourmet convenience foods market in the U.S. and Canada is emerging at an accelerating rate.

Organic foods, gourmet convenience products, and partially prepared specialty items, once a novelty, have grown to become an integral part of the overall consumer shopping environment. This serves to indicate a consumer's commitment to personal health, quality food consumption, and intelligent shopping.

Consumer expectations for food convenience and high quality food products is rapidly "pushing" old-line food manufacturers into new exciting food trends and convenience areas.

The consumer food industry is quickly becoming ready for mass market, customized, organic food products.

## MISSION

GEFC is characterized as a developer of unique organic products catering to the discriminating consumer who demands a high degree of creativity, quality, and convenience.

Before the end of the year 2002, GEFC will be recognized as a highly visible company in the customized, gourmet food, dry spice product marketplace. We will have introduced products aimed directly at industry-standard product brands and will become known for high quality, consistent taste, and easy-to-prepare products. Our anticipated revenues will exceed $7,000,000. GEFC will actively seek to develop new products and promote expansion into other additional market opportunities.

## MARKETING STRATEGY

Create an essence of high quality premium products through the delivery of high quality merchandise consumer food shoppers can count on time and time again. We will approach the market as a premium manufacturer of premium products with the highest quality organic ingredients. Our reputation will be unmatched in our product segments. We will position ourselves head-to-head with other industry brand leaders while maintaining a degree of perceived "smallness." Our customers demand the very best and we will provide it.

Our sales, merchandising, and distribution strategies will play a linchpin role in the success of our company. Our ability to foster relationships within the retail and distribution value chain will challenge traditional business models.

In order for Good Earth Foods Company to attain its vision as described in our mission statement, the following primary goals need to be achieved in year one of operations.

- Develop two products and release to retail marketplace
- Establish marketing and consumer image processes
- Establish distribution process for promotions and product release
- Establish two additional products into development pipeline
- Participate with industry-leading trade associations for relationship and brand development opportunities
- Leverage market recognition of the quality of our product and develop demand for our products featuring similar uniqueness

**Expected Accomplishments— Year One**

Our strategy is to focus first on those prospective consumers who understand food, appreciate high quality food products, and earn a high degree of income. These customers will be the basis for working out price points, product development, and expected consumer volumes.

**Customer Profile**

We believe a ready-made market exists for our products and those in the premium, convenience food category.

The demographics of the typical Good Earth Food Company consumer are:

- Over $42,000 annual income
- Business person with little time for complex food preparation
- Equally split between male and female, age 32-40 years old
- Highly educated regarding food ingredients
- Creative spirit with love for outdoors
- Shop primarily in high-end grocery stores and specialty shops

**Smith Specialty Foods:** Unveiled a new product line with similar characteristics in February 2000. These products included organic certifications. The demonstration of these products was being featured in high-end retail grocery chains. It is not known whether the features of these products include similar ingredient formulas.

**Competition**

Since this company is also a start-up we consider them a direct competitor not only in product, but brand image as well. There has been no information in the marketplace suggesting this company has gained greater market share than us.

**Target Gourmet:** Unveiled a new line of products with similar characteristics in March 2000. Their product line release included a demonstration of organic products mixed with traditionally processed ingredients. Like the Smith Specialty Foods demonstration, it was not shown that their product line has any significant market share beyond our own.

**The Organic Food Market:** A 500-person organic product-oriented grocery chain. This company, which has developed its own line of "store brand" products in the past, should be viewed as a partner as well as a tier II competitor. They have stated that they wish to continually develop competitively branded products but will market them as a moderately processed brand. This company will play a major role in our "retail shelf" strategy. This company has expressed interest in our products and is currently evaluating volume commitments from our manufacturing partners.

## Industry Participation & Relationships

The importance of industry relationships and participation in consortiums in this marketspace cannot be underestimated. Industry relationships are an absolute requirement for competing. The organic industry and marketplace should be seen as a multi-faceted, multi-layered marketspace. Relationships and industry presence at each of these levels plays a critical role in attaining success in this market.

GEFC currently participates and will continue to participate in food industry consortiums and standards setting/development organizations. This participation will allow GEFC to play a role in establishing industry standards and brand precedence. Participation in industry organizations will also allow GEFC to leverage research and development conducted by other participants and maintain a "pulse" on market trends and the competitive environment. GEFC will be able to use association with these organizations to establish market presence and develop an industry leadership position.

## Sales Promotions

Good Earth Foods Company will take advantage of and leverage all media outlets available. While we feel that, based on market research, our target audience and consumer base is highly fragmented and distributed across regional markets, a highly focused sales and media promotions strategy will, in part, drive short- and long-term brand and sales success. The following list of opportunities will shape our sales promotions plans into a highly targeted marketing communications, sales promotion, and media plan.

- Traditional media: Television and newspaper advertising will target specific local buyers
- Targeted consumer event sponsorship will provide awareness and firsthand experience with products
- In-store specialty displays will promote seasonal and regional programs to drive retail sales
- Direct contact product demonstration in participating grocery locations will address a highly focused segment of the consumer population
- Online retail networking with other new media consumer food product properties will provide a source of prescreened, targeted prospective consumers
- Promote multi-cultural, social, and economic diversity to extend product reach and marketshare

## Product Pricing

Our products will be priced at competitive market rates for premium products. Our products will be presented alongside competitive products and priced at a slightly higher "sticker" price resulting in a higher profit margin.

This also will promote a higher degree of cost basis/profit benefit to our retailers and increase brand perceptions among targeted consumers. Our products are expected to drive a 5-7 percent margin rate among our specialty retailers and high-end grocery chains that normally operate on a 3-5 percent profit margin basis. This pricing strategy dovetails with stated marketing strategies to result in greater retail attractiveness, thus resulting in enhanced market share for GEFC.

According to the opportunities and requirements for Good Earth Foods Company described in this business plan, and based on what we feel are sound business assumptions, our initial total capital requirements total $13,000,000. This sum of initial "seed" capital will enable Good Earth Foods Company to develop a high-energy, high-quality start-up company specializing in desirable food products. Investment monies will be used primarily for brand development, food packaging, manufacturing and distribution, and ongoing operations. Based on percentage of investment contributions, Good Earth Foods Company is willing to entertain option share ownership arrangements with the investor community.

## Business Operations

- Engaged real estate specialties to locate and complete contract for product development and test space
- Relocated offices from leveraged office space to current site location
- Attracted local culinary talent to provide consultation for product manufacturability and desirability
- Formed LLC business organization within Burleigh County, North Dakota
- Engaged local financial and legal institutions to provide services at discount rates (negotiated potential for account growth)
- Established business relationships with industry-leading trade organizations
- Engaged and finalized manufacturing agreement with certified organic food processor
- Began discussions with retail food consumer grocery chains, gourmet food distributors, and specialty food catalog distributors (traditional and new media outlets)

## Product Development, Sales and Marketing

- Initial product development                                      05/2000
- Initial packaging design completed                              06/2000
- Initial product and packaging testing with target market consumers    06/2001

## Mr. John Langolf

As founder of the Good Earth Foods Company, Mr. Langolf is responsible for all marketing, sales, and business development activities, as well as customer delivery and service and product concept/development.

### Professional Experience (Private)

Mr. Langolf has helped many clients achieve communications success in a wide range of capacities ranging from providing day-to-day sales tools and graphics systems consulting, to establishing and maintaining direct-mail promotional plans and corporate identity.

### Professional Experience (Corporate)

After beginning his career with Kraft Foods as a food packaging engineer in May 1990, Mr. Langolf progressed through a series of management and executive positions, playing an active role for many high-level product line development efforts and product rollouts.

In October 1998, John moved to Sacramento, California, to establish and head the global product development team for Sunshine Organic Foods. While in that position, John was recognized as an outstanding achiever by an outside consulting firm performing a food industry best practices audit. Sunshine Organic included customers like Safeway Stores, Albertson's Inc, and Organic Brands.

### Education

Mr. Langolf is a graduate of the University of California, in Berkeley, California, with a B.S. degree in agricultural engineering. While completing his master's work at the University of Oregon, in Eugene, Oregon, Mr. Langolf was distinguished with numerous agricultural industry awards for leadership in research and organic food processing methods.

### Personal

John and his wife, Susan, and their two children reside in Bismarck, North Dakota.

Mr. Langolf enjoys, golf, kayaking, and wildlife photography in his leisure time.

## FINANCIALS

| Expense/Investment Line Items | 2000 | 2001 | 2002 | 2003 |
|---|---|---|---|---|
| **Business Management/Leadership** | | | | |
| Executive Business Operations | $150,000 | $175,000 | $200,000 | $250,000 |
| Financial Operations | $175,000 | $200,000 | $250,000 | $300,000 |
| Day-to-Day Operational Leadership | $120,000 | $120,000 | $130,000 | $140,000 |
| | | | | |
| **Functional Operations Leadership** | | | | |
| Legal & Industry Counselors | $250,000 | $200,000 | $200,000 | $150,000 |
| Sales & Marketing | $200,000 | $250,000 | $300,000 | $350,000 |
| Marketing/PR (budget includes salary) | $200,000 | $225,000 | $250,000 | $275,000 |
| Advertising/Marketing Specialties | $125,000 | $150,000 | $175,000 | $200,000 |
| Administration and Human Resources Support | $75,000 | $77,000 | $79,000 | $81,000 |
| Food Prep, Test, Kitchen Staff | $200,000 | $200,000 | $250,000 | $300,000 |
| | | | | |
| **Technology and Systems Requirements** | | | | |
| Desktop and office automation (software and hardware) | $100,000 | $125,000 | $133,750 | $143,113 |
| External Package Design and manufacturing consultation | $125,000 | $150,000 | $100,000 | $100,000 |
| Website (Concept, design, and production) | $75,000 | $100,000 | $75,000 | $75,000 |
| Communications (Voice and Data) | $25,000 | $30,000 | $36,000 | $36,000 |
| Space/Facilities | $100,000 | $100,000 | $100,000 | $100,000 |
| Specialized Kitchen and Test Equipment | $100,000 | $120,000 | $80,000 | $60,000 |
| Product Development Operations | $75,000 | $100,000 | $125,000 | $150,000 |
| | | | | |
| **Total** | **$2,095,000** | **$2,322,000** | **$2,483,750** | **$2,710,113** |

| | 2004 | 5-Year Total |
|---|---|---|
| | $260,000 | $1,035,000 |
| | $350,000 | $1,275,000 |
| | $160,000 | $670,000 |
| | | |
| | $150,000 | $950,000 |
| | $400,000 | $1,500,000 |
| | $300,000 | $1,250,000 |
| | $300,000 | $950,000 |
| | $83,000 | $395,000 |
| | $350,000 | $1,200,000 |
| | | |
| | $153,130 | $654,993 |
| | $100,000 | $575,000 |
| | $75,000 | $400,000 |
| | $43,200 | $170,200 |
| | $100,000 | $500,000 |
| | $50,000 | $410,000 |
| | $200,000 | $650,000 |
| | **$3,074,330** | **$12,685,193** |

# Internet Marketplace

BUSINESS PLAN

ABC INTERNET MARKETPLACE, INC.

*16001 Institution Avenue*
*Burlington, Vermont 05401*

*ABC Internet Marketplace, Inc. will provide a sophisticated web-based tool that will help manufacturers save money by managing the market risk in their purchases. Using focused business strategies led by respected industry professionals, ABC sets a course for success.*

- EXECUTIVE SUMMARY

- COMPANY OVERVIEW

- PRODUCTS & SERVICES

- THE MARKET

- OPERATIONS

- THE MANAGEMENT TEAM

- FINANCIALS

- APPENDICES

## EXECUTIVE SUMMARY

ABC Internet Marketplace, Inc. of Burlington, Vermont, is proud to announce a successful breakthrough in the application of financial tools for the manufacturing sector.

ABC Marketplace provides a unique vehicle to insulate manufacturers from business uncertainties and losses through a mechanism that disseminates true prices and materials availability now and in the future.

This business plan describes our sophisticated Web-based financial market and trading platform, which allows manufacturers to manage risk caused by changes in product prices, trade tariffs, interest rates, and currency exchange rates.

ABC Marketplace will apply its pilot phase of the project to the electronic industry, which in 1998 reached $500 billion in revenues within the United States. Forecasts through 2005 anticipate uninterrupted growth in the electronics industry. This situation has evolved because of the increased demand for electronic products in industrialized nations. Worldwide revenues for 2005 are forecast at $1.5 trillion, which represents an average growth rate of 15 percent.

## Management Team

The ABC Marketplace management team has a proven record of several successful startup companies and has expeditiously guided numerous multimillion-dollar programs. Our management staff has served as executive officers at several Fortune 1000 companies as well as at smaller corporations.

The ABC Marketplace team consists of professionals well versed in an array of required disciplines. Each member of the team is a significant contributor to a particular element of this venture and was hired for that expertise as well as for his or her fit with the other staff members.

The principals of ABC Marketplace have a long-established relationship with a number of reliable and reputable distributors and manufacturers, many of which will assist in the final testing process of the ABC system. These valuable resources will serve as our preliminary subjects during the final development stage of the system.

## Market Environment

Our first trading market will be the electronics industry, specifically, semiconductor manufacturers. The market for new applications of semiconductor products shows no direct dependency on sustained general economic status. Though the market for semiconductor products is complex, we find that this market grows regardless of national economic conditions.

The cornerstone of this business plan is the application of financial tools in the manufacturing sector. Using proven commodity trading techniques to minimize financial losses, we will be able to manage risk as never before in the manufacturing environment. The advent of the Internet has made it possible for the development of a unique system that will combine all the necessary building blocks for a financial market and trading platform over the Internet.

## Financial Forecasts

ABC Marketplace is expected to grow rapidly after the first year of its operations and to achieve revenues of $921 million by the fifth year of its operation.

Estimated sales during the first year of operations are $5.2 million (starting in 2000), rising to $99.6 million and $305.2 million in the second and third year, respectively.

Gross margin in the fourth and fifth year is calculated to be 75 percent, and post-tax income about 40 percent. Positive cash flow is expected in the latter half of the second year.

The business opportunity presented here is to capitalize on a long-recognized market need that could not be suitably addressed through traditional tools.

Although there have been rapid gains in productivity in almost all aspects of manufacturing due to advances in technology and management techniques, the buying-selling process has generally lagged behind because of a lack of modern tools. One of the essential reasons for this is the high cost of owning and maintaining the infrastructure required to create a common global platform, an essential component for such a risk management system.

The Internet and the ever-increasing acceptance of it as a serious tool for commerce have removed most of the barriers to the creation of a common global platform. The combination of the Internet and our implementation of advanced risk management concepts in manufacturing has created a wholly new opportunity for manufacturing firms. Informal marketing surveys and the enthusiasm of significant members of the manufacturing sector attest to the interest in and need for our proprietary service.

The total required capital to bring the service to beta testing (Phase II) and on to full implementation (Phase III) is estimated at $16 million, with a positive cash flow expected in the latter half of the second year of operation.

The investors are expected to realize a return on investment on the order of five to ten times that investment in approximately three to four years, at which time the company will go public or sell out to a strategic buyer.

In summary, using innovative technology and an experienced and seasoned management team, this business plan identifies an opportunity to enter a marketplace that has enormous potential for revenue and profit growth.

**COMPANY OVERVIEW**

**History**

ABC Internet Marketplace, Inc., headquartered in Burlington, Vermont, is seeking financing of $16 million over the next two years to expand its existing operations.

Founded by Fred McKenzie, Patrick Ogilvey, and Kishore Manji in March 1996 as a Vermont "C" corporation, ABC Marketplace is primarily in the business of operating a financial market and trading platform for the manufacturing sector. The company's founders recognized that technology was key to bringing their idea to fruition and that a technology partner was needed to develop the product. In August 1998, ABC selected Mindware Pertech, Inc. as its technology partner. Mindware Pertech, Inc. in turn purchased 28 percent of ABC Marketplace stock and joined the board of directors.

In January 1999, the board of ABC Marketplace felt the need to add additional business talent in order to move the project from developmental stage to full implementation. To achieve this, ABC invited Kishore Manji to join the company's board of directors.

The ownership of ABC Marketplace, Inc. is structured as follows.

**STOCK OWNERSHIP**

| Owner | % of stock |
|---|---|
| Fred McKenzie | 41.00% |
| Mindware Pertech, Inc | 21.00% |
| Kishore Manji | 20.00% |
| Robert Kline | 13.00% |
| Others | 5.00% |

**Business Problems**

Almost all manufacturers are exposed to losses in three areas:

1. Increased cost of in-process materials (IPMs), that is, raw materials
2. Inventory write-downs due to obsolescence or price changes
3. Production losses due to the short supply, or lack of supply, of IPMs

ABC Marketplace provides a unique vehicle to insulate manufacturers from these uncertainties by providing a mechanism by which true prices and materials availability are disseminated now and in the future.

Our sophisticated Web-based platform with proprietary tools allows manufacturers to manage risks caused by changes in underlying product prices, trade tariffs, interest rates, and currency exchange rates.

ABC Marketplace derives its earnings from trade commission, currency translation, sale of data, and subscription to the technology index created by the exchange.

**Risk Management Defined**

Risk, an element of uncertainty, is a relatively broad term in manufacturing. Its significance has recently become known mainly because of uncertainties resulting from international trading activities. Manufacturers are aware of the risk involved in building up inventory; they know that should the market go soft, an untimely liquidation can be very costly. Those who build "on order" assume a similar risk; a sudden increase in the price of raw materials reduces profits.

Risk management has become a fundamental tool to minimize these financial losses. Although the need for such a tool has long been known, the technology for implementation has never before existed. Now that the Internet has made it possible for the creation of such a platform, ABC Marketplace has developed a unique system that will combine all the necessary building blocks for such a financial market and trading platform.

**Key Goals and Objectives**

Rapid advance in technology and the break up of trade barriers have created a true global economy, which in turn has created uncertainties in the pricing structure of manufactured products. Such uncertainties result from underlying changes in product prices, trade tariffs, interest rates, and currency fluctuation—all of them leading to volatile markets around the globe.

These uncertainties are most visible in the global electronics market. ABC Marketplace will initially target the semiconductor sector in the global electronics market, starting with integrated chip (IC) makers and their users. The semiconductor sector alone generates $150 billion among some 10,000 manufacturers worldwide.

In addition to the electronics market, ABC Marketplace will soon target other manufacturing sectors such as chemicals and pharmaceuticals. Eventually, we will expand to still other sectors—for example, telecommunication and construction.

**PRODUCTS & SERVICES**

Earnings at manufacturing firms are frequently affected by inventory write-downs due to softening of the market or increased cost of in-process materials (IPMs), technology changes (obsolescence), or production losses stemming from a short supply of IPMs. The loss in production not only affects earnings, it also causes serious erosion of market share.

This in turn affects cash flow, which can then seriously threaten the viability of any manufacturing firm. Long-term viability of a manufacturing firm is also affected by restricted or closed markets, which result in artificial—that is, inflated or depressed—prices.

Even though there have been rapid gains in productivity in most aspects of manufacturing due to advances in technology and management techniques, the buying-selling process has generally lagged behind because of a lack of modern tools. One of the essential reasons for this deficiency is the high cost of owning and maintaining the infrastructure required to create a common global platform necessary to eliminate the risk of doing business globally.

The acceptance of the Internet as a serious tool for commerce has removed most of the barriers to the creation of a common global platform. E-commerce, along with our implementation of advanced risk management concepts in manufacturing, has opened a new opportunity for manufacturing firms.

ABC Marketplace addresses these business uncertainties by providing an open market for manufacturers and distributors that will mitigate much of this uncertainty through risk management.

ABC Marketplace has developed a state-of-the-art, Web-based, double auction system that uses highly sophisticated and efficient algorithms to automate continuous bid and offer matching with real-time clearing. Our platform includes an integrated automated physical delivery system and automated currency translation system with currency exchange and banking.

ABC Marketplace provides the following services:

1. A spot and forward buying-selling platform for a new class of commodities
2. A risk management vehicle for the manufacturing and distribution business
3. The convenience and efficiency of a trading platform with integrated clearing service
4. The incorporation of currency translation into commodity prices
5. The convenience of working over the Internet
6. A unique platform that brings together buyers, sellers, investors, and speculators across many continents and time zones
7. Business hours from Sunday 9:00 P.M. through Friday 7:00 P.M. EST
8. Product index and global market data

An illustrative scenario:

The standard method of buying or selling generally fixes the price for delivery sometime in the future. In mid-January 1998, the spot market price for 16 MB EDO DRAM in the U.S. market was $3.10 (OEM quantity). If the order for 20,000 devices with delivery date of 30 days was placed (or received) in mid-January, it is expected that a payment of $3.10 x 20,000 = $62,000 be made by mid-February 1998. The open market price at that time was $2.65.

In mid-February when the delivery is made, the spot price is $2.65 and the contract is worth $53,000. The difference of $9,000 resulting from the price drop is due to the risk that the manufacturer or consumer took by assuming the price stability.

ABC Internet Marketplace allows the manufacturer and the consumer (OEM) to pass on this unwanted risk to an intermediary who is willing to take such risks. Forward pricing is a mechanism by which the risk element is passed on to an intermediary. In this example, on January 16, 1998, the spot price was $3.10 and the 30-day forward price was $2.88 (per device with minimum quantity of 1000). The 30-day forward price is the adjusted price for 30-day delivery. The order (buy or sell) for 20,000 devices is executed based on 30-day forward price. The new contract price is then $57,600 ($2.88 x 20,000). The difference between the order date price $62,000 and delivery date price $57,600 is narrowed from the original $9,000 to $4,400, and the savings is more than 50 percent.

**Product Points**

ABC has a comprehensive system platform for trading:

1. **Product development and trade:** The products for trade are developed on the basis of market share, multiple sources of production, universality of consumption, and uniformity of product specification.
2. **Financial clearinghouse:** This facility ensures funds are available between the parties, clears the trade, and maintains the performance bond.
3. **Commerce:** Spot transaction of products is a link to global warehouses. The clearinghouse guarantees the delivery of items being traded. For this purpose, modest-size warehouse spaces will operate as bonded warehouses. The warehouses will be outsourced to major carriers.
4. **Safeguards:** ABC Marketplace ensures customer satisfaction by incorporating several essential safety measures, including:
   a. **Guaranteed trade:** All trades are sent to an automated clearinghouse to check the matched orders between the buyer and the seller. The clearinghouse verifies the amount of the contract and credit, and debits the buyer's and the seller's accounts. The clearinghouse routinely computes the required performance bond that needs to be maintained by the buyer and the seller for enforcing the contracts. (Adjustment on the amount of performance bond will be made daily.)
   b. **Guaranteed delivery:** All spot or cash transactions are based on items available in our designated bonded warehouse. Forward and futures contracts that result in deliveries will be available five days before the contract expiration date. The point of delivery is the nearest designated warehouse to the buyer.
   c. **Quality assurance:** All original suppliers are ISO 9000 compliant, and their goods are routinely inspected, certified, and graded by internationally recognized quality inspectors.
   d. **Warranty:** The original manufacturer's warranty will be sent to the buyers.

**Patents and Intellectual Properties**

ABC Internet Marketplace does not use or depend on any external intellectual properties. However, since ABC is the first to market these products, many of our proprietary technologies will be patented. These patents and technologies will keep us ahead of any future "me-to" or mimicked implementations.

**How ABC Marketplace Operates**

ABC Marketplace provides an open market for manufacturers and distributors to address their business uncertainties through risk management. It provides up-to-the-minute prices and availability of manufactured products.

ABC Marketplace performs three basic functions:

1. Discovers a true market price for products
2. Provides a vehicle for risk management
3. Provides real-time global market data and a technology index

A continuous double-sided auction allows that a "true" price of a product be established. A hedging mechanism helps the manufacturer to plan a stable production schedule and to competitively price the product.

ABC Marketplace has developed a state-of-the-art, Web-based, continuous double auction system that uses highly sophisticated and efficient algorithms to automate bid and offer matching with real-time clearing. Our platform also includes an integrated automated physical delivery system and an automated currency translation system with currency exchange and banking.

Two internationally respected market leaders in package delivery services and global banking manage our delivery system and banking services.

ABC Marketplace provides all this functionality through an automated communication network system for online transactional and analytical processing, and uses the Internet as its backbone.

ABC Internet Marketplace will build a reputation for superior customer service and attention to customer satisfaction. Its essential benefits include the following:

### Wide Range of Services

ABC Internet Marketplace has the ability to provide a variety of services within its overall service of commodity trading. ABC Marketplace will allow customers to buy and sell products. ABC Marketplace will also be positioned to provide instant global market data to manufacturers, thereby enabling them to extract the most commonly used historical data on process and trade volume. Buyers and sellers can use the market data instantly, and as soon as a transaction clears it will be instantly available on the ABC Web site.

### Integrated Services

ABC Marketplace provides an interface with the existing Web-based account management of a financial institution for an online clearing that is an integral part of the trading platform. By so doing, the clearing functions will include the creation of virtual fiduciary accounts for traders, cash management, and international treasury management and audit trail.

### Personalized Services

Each ABC customer will have access to a service representative who is solely responsible for the customer's account. In addition, following any trade and clearing, there will be value-added services such as currency conversion and integrated delivery management that can be applied to e-commerce applications.

### Customer Solutions

ABC Marketplace provides customers with solutions to managing business risk. We are the first future trading platform to include:

1. A two-sided continuous auction forum (bid and asks)
2. Real-time spots and forwards pricing for in-process materials (IPMs)
3. Integrated trade execution, clearing, and settlement
4. Integrated currency exchange at the interbank rate
5. An integrated physical delivery system for spot market transactions

### One-Stop Trading

The system provides seamless integration between order matching, order execution, and clearing (leading to order confirmation) in an online environment. The concept of real-time clearing is central to the process of global trading. A centralized clearinghouse enables the marketplace to operate worldwide with maximum efficiency and at a low maintenance cost.

**Customer Benefits and Value**

**ABC Market's Unique Selling Points**

## THE MARKET

### Customer Description

ABC serves a wide range of customers, primarily those engaged in manufacturing, distribution, investors, and derivatives. A profile of a typical customer would be:

- Fair understanding of the product being traded
- Familiarity with the market that uses the product
- Understanding of the manufacturing process
- Familiarity with the concept of currency forward, product
- Familiarity with performance bond and margin requirements

### CUSTOMER PROFILE

| Customer Profile | Items | 1999 projected | 2000 projected | 2001 projected | 2002 projected | 2003 projected |
|---|---|---|---|---|---|---|
| **Fortune 1000** | ICs | $620,000 | $16,433,700 | $90,523,600 | $111,463,625 | $191,625,000 |
| | Interconnect | $0 | $1,350,000 | $9,418,000 | $13,473,625 | $43,800,000 |
| | Passives | $0 | $405,000 | $7,756,000 | $9,186,563 | $19,710,000 |
| | Chemicals | $0 | $0 | $7,977,600 | $4,899,500 | $13,140,000 |
| | Others | $0 | $0 | $1,108,000 | $1,469,850 | $4,927,500 |
| **$5 million companies** | ICs | $3,853,500 | $60,475,500 | $125,758,000 | $281,721,250 | $410,625,000 |
| | Interconnect | $0 | $12,094,500 | $16,620,000 | $39,196,000 | $131,400,000 |
| | Passives | $0 | $4,563,220 | $14,958,000 | $20,210,438 | $29,565,000 |
| | Chemicals | $0 | $0 | $15,512,000 | $22,047,750 | $26,280,000 |
| | Others | $0 | $0 | $1,662,000 | $3,674,625 | $4,927,500 |
| **Distributors** | ICs | $470,100 | $1,827,100 | $4,210,400 | $10,043,975 | $13,140,000 |
| | Interconnect | $0 | $226,500 | $554,000 | $1,469,850 | $2,190,000 |
| | Passives | $0 | $181,200 | $443,200 | $918,656 | $1,095,000 |
| | Chemicals | $0 | $0 | $221,600 | $293,970 | $1,095,000 |
| | Others | $0 | $0 | $0 | $0 | $5,475,000 |
| **Brokers/Investors** | ICs | $308,200 | $1,283,500 | $7,534,400 | $9,799,000 | $13,687,500 |
| | Interconnect | $0 | $226,500 | $121,880 | $3,062,187 | $3,285,000 |
| | Passives | $0 | $120,800 | $886,400 | $1,837,312 | $3,285,000 |
| | Chemicals | $0 | $17,677 | $554,000 | $975,800 | $1,095,000 |
| | Others | $0 | $0 | $0 | $244,975 | $1,095,000 |
| **Total** | | **$5,251,800** | **$99,205,197** | **$305,819,080** | **$535,988,951** | **$921,442,500** |

### Target Market

In Phase I, ABC Internet Marketplace will focus on semiconductor makers and consumers. The global aspect of this market, coupled with rapid technological changes, has created a particularly volatile market. This is an ideal market for ABC Marketplace. According to the International Semiconductor Association, the semiconductor market generated $150 billion in revenues in 1994.

The three major marketplaces for ABC Marketplace are NAFTA, the Pacific Rim, and the European Union (EU). Within these markets, there are about 10,000 manufacturers. We expect 3,800 of these manufacturers to become members of ABC Marketplace. Many small to medium-size manufacturers are expected to be attracted by the low-cost opportunity that ABC Marketplace provides to showcase and sell their products in an open market.

**Electronics Market Segments (in $billion)**

| Segment by Industry Sector | | | | | | | Projected | | |
|---|---|---|---|---|---|---|---|---|---|
| | **1998** | | **1999** | | **2000** | | **2001** | |
| Semiconductors | $130 | 68% | $137 | 68% | $180 | 70% | $210 | 73% |
| Interconnects | $22 | 16% | $25 | 16% | $38 | 15% | $42 | 15% |
| Passives | $22 | 11% | $23 | 11% | $27 | 10% | $21 | 7% |
| Chemicals | $10 | 5% | $10 | 5% | $12 | 5% | $14 | 5% |
| **Total Market** | **$184** | 100% | **$165** | 100% | **$257** | 100% | **$287** | 100% |

Accurate data from trade publications and official trade associations were used in all pro forma projections, charts, and graphs. All information was obtained from the U.S. Department of Commerce, Semiconductor Industry Association, Institute for Interconnect and Packaging Circuits, and *Ward's Business Reference Book.*

**Market Size** (margin: **Market Size**)

| | $ billions |
|---|---|
| U.S. market for in-process-materials (IPM) (1993) | $1,046 |
| Electronics (NAFTA) (1998) | $490 |
| Semiconductors, worldwide | $130 |

The expected number of participants, worldwide, is estimated as follows.

| Type of Organization | Number | Total Users |
|---|---|---|
| Large manufacturers (15 users per manufacturer)* | 500 | 7,500 |
| Medium/small manufacturers (3 users per manufacturer)* | 3,000 | 9,000 |
| Small independent distributors | 1,200 | 1,200 |
| Major electronics distributors (30 users per distributor)* | 40 | 1,200 |
| Brokers/resellers | 1,500 | 1,500 |
| **Total number of participants** | | **20,400** |

*\*The number of users is based on product groups and location. The above numbers may be considered conservative.*

During the first three years, ABC Internet Marketplace plans to target the electronics industry. According to the U.S. Department of Commerce, in 1998, this industry generated just under $500 billion in revenues. Judging from the market share of Japan, Pacific Rim, and Europe, the global market for this industry can easily top $1 trillion. For the first year of its operations, ABC Marketplace will restrict itself to the semiconductor sector. According to the Semiconductor Industry Association, U.S. manufacturers accounted for nearly $137 billion in revenues during 1997. In the second year of its operation, ABC Marketplace will expand its offerings to include interconnects, passive components, chemicals, and wafer production. IPC (Institute for Interconnect and Packaging Circuits) data for interconnects sales among U.S.-based manufacturers for 1998 was $22 billion, and the global market for interconnects is estimated to be much higher.

In the third year of operation, ABC Marketplace will expand into chemicals and plastics. This sector, according to *Ward's Business Reference Book,* 1993 (Volumes 3 and 4), generated $115 billion in sales. This will be followed by expansion into pharmaceuticals and nonferrous and ferrous metals.

ABC Marketplace will attract customers and electronic traders (ETs) from Fortune 1000 companies, businesses with at least 20 percent of electronic content and over $5 million in revenues, component brokers, distributors, individuals, and businesses with an interest in speculative markets. According to *Ward's Business Reference Book*, 1993 (Volumes 3 and 4), there are 252 publicly traded electronics companies and 208 computer manufacturers (SIC 36 and 35). Similarly, the 1994 U.S. Department of Commerce SICS classification lists some 369,145 manufacturing-related companies.

SIC code 36 lists 3606 companies in California, 981 in Illinois, and 727 in Vermont, whereas SIC code 38 lists 2124 companies in California, 54 in Illinois, and 643 in Vermont. ABC Marketplace has based its business plans on 10,000 manufacturing companies worldwide that are primarily or partially (minimum 20 percent electronics content) involved with electronics.

One of the principal goals for ABC Marketplace is to attract major OEM industries (notably the auto and aerospace industries) for which electronics constitutes a significant component. However, to be attractive to such players, ABC Marketplace must trade 20 percent of all products that collectively contribute to 80 percent of OEM purchases. (We plan to address this issue beyond the third year of operation.)

**Target Market**

| Segment by Industry Sector | Year 1 1999 | Year 2 2000 | Year 3 2001 | Year 4 2002 | Year 5 2003 |
|---|---|---|---|---|---|
| Semiconductors | 100% | 76% | 69% | 77% | 70% |
| Interconnects | 0% | 21% | 17% | 12% | 19% |
| Passives | 0% | 3% | 8% | 5% | 6% |
| Chemicals | 0% | 0% | 6% | 6% | 5% |
| **Total** | **100%** | **100%** | **100%** | **100%** | **100%** |

## MARKET SEGMENT

**End of**

| SEGMENTS | Year 1 | Year 2 | Year 3 | Year 4 | Year 5 |
|---|---|---|---|---|---|
| Fortune 1000 companies | $619,920 | $1,895,818 | $101,167,500 | $161,540,000 | $342,736,000 |
| $5 million sales companies | $4,322,220 | $81,376,900 | $172,200,000 | $290,500,000 | $466,396,000 |
| Distributors | $77,490 | $4,090,400 | $6,457,000 | $18,904,500 | $21,984,000 |
| Brokers | $154,980 | $9,236,200 | $18,942,000 | $35,750,000 | $50,000,000 |
| Investors | $77,490 | $3,067,900 | $8,500,000 | $28,650,000 | $40,000,000 |
| **Total** | **$5,252,100** | **$99,667,218** | **$307,266,500** | **$535,344,500** | **$921,116,000** |

## Competition

### Industry Information

As stated in the opening section of this plan, ABC Marketplace is creating a new market for the trading of contracts, especially as pertains to small and medium-size businesses. Consequently, verifiable industry statistics are difficult to come by. However, some generalizations are as follows:

- The futures marketplace is growing dramatically
- Manufacturers are looking for ways to reduce operating risk
- Businesses are becoming more globally oriented

## Competitive Information

ABC Marketplace intends to become the most significant player in the marketplace. Consequently, ABC chose its strategic locations and marketing strategy carefully.

Management has pooled their creative resources and industry knowledge to create ABC's much sought-after service. The reputation of these individuals assures our customers that they will receive only the best professional expertise.

## Current Competition

No other company performs all the critical functions that ABC Internet Marketplace performs. ABC Marketplace differentiates itself from the cash market—the only market available at this time—by introducing forward pricing and risk management practices. The introduction of the forward market will undoubtedly change the way manufacturers conduct business.

The largest regional broker that can become a potential competitor to ABC Marketplace is NECX, which has been in business for the past 12 years and has revenues of more than $300 million. However, ABC Marketplace intends to close the gap within five years. The 3 percent market share that NECX has maintained is due to the minimal competition it faces in the electronic brokerage market. Once ABC Marketplace commences its aggressive marketing campaign, we expect to capture a dramatic increase in the size of the market.

The following table provides a synopsis of the competitive environment.

**Competition**

| Business Type | Electronic Trading & Futures | Electronic Trading & Futures | Independent Distributor | Electronic Trading/ Auctioning | Electronic Trading |
|---|---|---|---|---|---|
| **Size of Business** | Startup | Large | Medium | Startup | Startup |
| **Geographical Presence** | Global | U.S./select locations | U.S./select countries | North American | N/A |
| **Number of Employees (payroll)** | 140 (within 5 yrs.) | N/A | 133 | 25 | N/A |
| **Years in Business** | 2 | 6 | 12 | 3 | N/A |
| **Market Share** | 15% (within 5 yrs.) | 5% | 3% | 0% | N/A |
| **1998 Sales** | Startup | N/A | $340 million | Startup | Startup |
| **Growth Rate** | 150% (year to year) | 20% | 10% | 30% | 10% |
| **Advertising & PR Budget** | 35% of projected sales | Negligible | 5% of sales | N/A | N/A |
| **Greatest Strength** | Risk management | Established customer | Established market | Auction/clearing | N/A |

*continued on next page*

| Key Weakness | Untested market | Open cry dependency | Brokering only | No liquidity established | Regulatory measures applied |
|---|---|---|---|---|---|
| Cost | $1.00 per trade | $1.00 per trade | Commission as % of sales | Commission as % of sales | N/A |
| Range of Service | Complete | Complete | Limited | Limited | N/A |
| Profitability | 60% | Poor | 10-20% | 20-30% | Below average |
| Strength of Sales Force | Startup | Minimal | High | Low | Low |
| Standing in Industry | First of its kind | First of its kind | Top broker | Startup | N/A |
| Future Potential | Will include all markets that trade in nonproprietary, commoditylike products | Trades all commodities already in the market | Limited to electronics market | Limited to electronics market | N/A |

### Competitive Advantage

ABC Marketplace has, and can maintain, a competitive advantage for several reasons.

One reason is ABC Marketplace's ability to offer a one-stop trading service. This applies to customers seeking online clearing and currency translation, which is not available in today's marketplace.

Another ABC Marketplace competitive advantage is its extensive in-house software development programs. ABC has developed its own proprietary software, which allows us to offer more services to our customers—services that are not currently available in the marketplace.

Finally, ABC Marketplace has a cost advantage over its competitors. As the lowest-cost trading platform, ABC Marketplace offers the most cost-effective way to initiate trades.

## Marketing Strategy

### Philosophy

ABC Marketplace's marketing strategy has been shaped by the personal experiences of Kishore Manji and Fred McKenzie. Both Mr. Veeravagu and Mr. McKenzie have extensive experience in the manufacturing industry. They have firsthand knowledge of the negative impact on earnings due to price changes that result in inventory write-downs or increased cost of in-process materials, technology changes (obsolescence), and production losses due to the short supply of IPMs.

They have conducted a number of informal oral surveys to determine what their customers look for while trying to minimize the risk in buy or sell contracts. The results of this survey—along with several brainstorming sessions with industry leaders in the manufacturing, financial, and banking sectors—indicated that price stability, currency exchange, and efficient delivery service are the key elements that customers desire.

Therefore, based on their research, the founders of ABC Marketplace hypothesized that trading and risk management services for the manufacturing industry will be a promising and lucrative business venture.

**Goals & Objectives**

**Marketing Tactics**

In our preliminary phase, ABC will conduct a live test period at no charge to the users. This will allow ABC to compile certain market research data. These primary data will address the degree of liquidity of the market in general as well as verify some specific issues:

1. The concentration ratio for buyers and sellers
2. The range of price movement
3. The current degree of forward market pricing
4. The size of existing brokers and dealers
5. The extent of cash market

ABC Internet Marketplace has set its marketing objectives on capturing 14 percent of the electronic market in the next five years. This will be achieved in three phases. In Phase I, we have planned an aggressive marketing campaign through direct selling to reach the middle-tier manufacturing firms, distributors, and brokers. In Phase II, we will concentrate sales efforts on Fortune 1000 corporations and investors. And in Phase III, we will focus on adding new products and segments to the target market, which in turn will dramatically increase the number of transactions per visit, rather than on trying to continuously increase the number of users or electronic traders.

The direct sales effort will obtain support from a focused public relations and awareness campaign. The focus of this effort will be manufacturers, industry experts, financial consultants, and traders. We will reach these groups through sponsorship, seminars, and the Web.

Because of the global implications of trade and in order to maximize the trade volume in different time zones, ABC Marketplace will develop independently operated regional "trading centers." These centers will serve the additional purpose of maintaining local contacts with customers and users. This will also ensure that no single trading center has an advantage over another trading center.

ABC Marketplace expects to increase its market share from 1.25 percent in the third year to 5.5 percent in the fourth year and 14 percent in the fifth year.

**Advertising**

The advertising efforts of ABC Internet Marketplace will concentrate on PR activity, trade shows, seminars, the Internet, TV/CNBC, various financial magazines, and direct mail. The advertising budget will be 3 percent of gross sales in the first 12 months of operation. The following table represents the projected advertising efforts, month by month, for the first year. Over five years, the advertising budget will amount to $130 million.

**Advertising (Figures in '000)**

| Type of Media | Jul 1999 | Aug 1999 | Sep 1999 | Oct 1999 | Nov 1999 | Dec 1999 |
|---|---|---|---|---|---|---|
| Internet | $75 | $100 | $150 | $150 | $150 | $150 |
| Trade publications | $0 | $150 | $200 | $150 | $150 | $150 |
| Direct sales/seminar | $75 | $200 | $100 | $150 | $150 | $0 |
| **Total Spending** | **$150** | **$450** | **$450** | **$450** | **$450** | **$300** |

**Advertising (Figures in '000)**

| Type of Media | Jan 2000 | Feb 2000 | Mar 2000 | Apr 2000 | May 2000 | June 2000 | Jan-Jun Total |
|---|---|---|---|---|---|---|---|
| Internet | $100 | $100 | $100 | $100 | $150 | $150 | $700 |
| Trade publications | $100 | $100 | $150 | $150 | $150 | $150 | $800 |
| Direct sales/seminar | $50 | $150 | $150 | $150 | $100 | $150 | $750 |
| **Total Spending** | **$250** | **$350** | **$400** | **$400** | **$400** | **$450** | **$2,250** |

## Sales Promotions

The sales promotion aspect of ABC Marketplace will consist of collateral material for the account executives. This includes brochures, videos, and multimedia CBTs. An incentive program has been established that awards each account executive points for recruiting users and bonus points for transaction volumes generated from these users during the first 12 months from signup. These points are redeemed for cash at the end of each month.

In addition to the sales incentives, ABC Marketplace will participate in trade shows that cater to electronic manufacturers, component distributors, and brokers. The budget for sales promotions is set at 9 percent of gross sales.

## Pricing

ABC Marketplace will price its services around transactions. This will permit users to pay as they go. The pricing schedule is as follows.

**PRICE SCHEDULE**

| | Transaction | Fee |
|---|---|---|
| 1.00 | Inquiry per product | |
| 1.01 | Less than 1 million daily inquiry | $0.050 |
| 1.02 | More than 1 million daily inquiry | $0.025 |
| 2.00 | Placing orders per item per contract | $0.100 |
| 3.00 | Order execution and clearing per item | $0.900 |
| 4.00 | Updating order | No Charge |
| 5.00 | Order execution acknowledged per item | $0.050 |
| 6.00 | Currency translation/trade | $1.000 |
| 7.00 | Historical data | $25/page |

As a part of our marketing strategy, the price schedule has been set significantly lower than that of competitors in the industry. The low transaction fee will encourage greater participation.

In addition to the transaction fee, ABC Marketplace will receive revenues from the sale of market data. ABC Marketplace will market this data at $25.00 per page.

## Sales Approach

Both Kishore Manji and Fred McKenzie have extensive industry experience, which they will certainly use to generate leads for the sales team. Kishore Manji, in particular, plans to follow up with many of his industry associates and recruit them as members of ABC Internet Marketplace.

As part of their expansion plans, the founders intend to bring onboard a senior industry executive with electronics industry expertise and knowledge to strengthen the sales team. We intend to buy "mailing lists" for organizations such as Semiconductor Industry Association and trade publications. These lists will provide the sales team with detailed information on manufacturing companies, distributors, brokers, and (OEMs). The sales representatives will contact the owners, CFOs, and CEOs of these companies and follow up with a "vision in process" package and closing call. Additionally, the founders and the sales representatives will attend every possible event that would have industry contacts in attendance. This form of networking has proven to be very effective.

ABC Marketplace plans to adopt "solutions selling" as its selling system. The sales process will use the following four channels:

**Executive sales:** Kishore Manji will head this program with strong support by Fred McKenzie.

**Direct sales:** ABC Marketplace plans to hire experienced sales staff to call directly on prospects. The bulk of ABC Marketplace members will come through direct sales. Kishore Manji will manage the team.

**Web-based selling:** ABC Marketplace plans extensive use of Web resources to focus sales through direct-response advertising.

**Telemarketing:** ABC Marketplace plans to hire experienced sales staff who can handle inbound and outbound sales calls. Inbound calls will come from Web advertisements and seminars. The sales staff will also place outbound calls.

We also plan to conduct a highly publicized orientation and training program to certify electronic traders, who will be the core users or hedgers. Such certification will have the advantage of controlling the number of traders as well as reorienting corporate buying and selling practices toward an open market concept. An added advantage will be a built-in premium that will be associated with the service.

 a. **Bronze (10,000 seats):** Holders of these seats can trade only the limited items classified under any specific subgroup—for example, all items under ICs.
 b. **Silver (1600 seats):** Owners can trade a particular group of products—for example, all subgroups of semiconductors, but not another subgroup such as plastics.
 c. **Gold (150 seats):** Owners can trade any products. Each manufacturer, distributor, or broker is entitled to buy a seat at a price determined by ABC Marketplace. All members must be certified before buying a seat.

The next tables provide an overview of the business that is expected.

## Sales Targets

| Description | Q3 2000 | Q4 2000 | Q1 2001 | Q2 2001 | Year Total |
|---|---|---|---|---|---|
| Commission | $11,550 | $269,755 | $1,054,742 | $1,966,140 | $3,302,187 |
| Market Data | $3,465 | $80,927 | $316,422 | $589,842 | $990,656 |
| Other Sales | $0 | $0 | $0 | $0 | $0 |
| Others | $0 | $0 | $421,897 | $786,456 | $1,208,353 |
| **Gross Sales** | **$15,015** | **$350,682** | **$1,793,061** | **$2,158,757** | **$5,501,195** |

## Sales Targets

| Description | Q3 2001 | Q4 2001 | Q1 2002 | Q2 2002 | Year Total |
|---|---|---|---|---|---|
| Commission | $5,301,186 | $9,971,907 | $16,997,475 | $26,345,319 | $58,615,887 |
| Market Data | $1,590,356 | $2,991,572 | $5,099,243 | $7,903,596 | $17,584,766 |
| Other Sales | $80,000 | $295,000 | $480,000 | $700,000 | $1,555,000 |
| Others | $2,120,474 | $3,988,763 | $6,798,990 | $10,538,128 | $23,446,355 |
| **Gross Sales** | **$9,092,016** | **$17,247,242** | **$29,375,708** | **$45,487,042** | **$101,202,008** |

## Sales Targets

| Description | Q3 2002 | Q4 2002 | Q1 2003 | Q2 2003 | Year Total |
|---|---|---|---|---|---|
| Commission | $33,722,502 | $41,534,295 | $48,302,265 | $57,117,555 | $180,676,617 |
| Market Data | $10,116,751 | $12,460,289 | $14,490,680 | $17,135,267 | $54,202,985 |
| Other Sales | $950,000 | $1,160,000 | $1,255,000 | $1,350,000 | $4,715,000 |
| Others | $13,489,001 | $16,613,718 | $19,320,906 | $22,847,022 | $72,270,647 |
| **Gross Sales** | **$58,278,253** | **$71,768,302** | **$83,368,851** | **$213,415,405** | **$311,865,249** |

## Sales Targets

| Description | Q3 2003 | Q4 2003 | Q1 2004 | Q2 2004 | Year Total |
|---|---|---|---|---|---|
| Commission | $62,993,568 | $72,889,608 | $82,570,620 | $96,952,185 | $315,405,981 |
| Market Data | $18,898,070 | $21,866,882 | $24,771,186 | $29,085,656 | $94,621,794 |
| Other Sales | $1,475,000 | $1,710,000 | $1,940,000 | $2,175,000 | $7,300,000 |
| Others | $25,197,427 | $29,155,843 | $33,028,248 | $38,780,874 | $126,162,392 |
| **Gross Sales** | **$108,564,066** | **$125,622,334** | **$142,310,054** | **$376,496,453** | **$543,490,168** |

## Sales Targets

| Description | Q3 2004 | Q4 2004 | Q1 2005 | Q2 2005 | Year Total |
|---|---|---|---|---|---|
| Commission | $111,471,360 | $133,774,740 | $148,802,940 | $150,866,760 | $544,915,800 |
| Market Data | $33,441,408 | $40,132,422 | $44,640,882 | $45,260,028 | $163,474,740 |
| Research Data | $2,250,000 | $2,250,000 | $2,250,000 | $2,250,000 | $9,000,000 |
| Others | $44,588,544 | $53,509,896 | $59,521,176 | $60,346,704 | $217,966,320 |
| **Gross Sales** | **$191,751,312** | **$229,667,058** | **$255,214,998** | **$258,723,492** | **$935,356,860** |

The founders of ABC Internet Marketplace believe that a professionally managed launch will generate great excitement for the company and its services. ABC Marketplace plans to hire a professional PR consulting firm to market the launch effectively through press conferences and press releases, TV/CNBC interviews of the founders, presentations to professional groups, and focused prelaunch informational mailings.

The following table represents the cost allocation for public relations activities for the first 12-month period. The budget for these promotions is set at 6 percent of gross sales.

**Public Relation (Figures in '000)**

| Type of Media | Jul 1999 | Aug 1999 | Sept 1999 | Oct 1999 | Nov 1999 | Dec 1999 |
|---|---|---|---|---|---|---|
| PR Firm | $0 | $20 | $20 | $20 | $20 | $20 |
| TV/CNBC | $0 | $0 | $0 | $0 | $0 | $0 |
| **Total Spending** | $0 | $20 | $20 | $20 | $20 | $20 |

**Public Relation (Figures in '000)**

| Type of Media | Jan 2000 | Feb 2000 | Mar 2000 | Apr 2000 | May 2000 | Jun 2000 | Year Total |
|---|---|---|---|---|---|---|---|
| PR Firm | $10 | $10 | $10 | $10 | $5 | $10 | $155 |
| TV/CNBC | $10 | $10 | $10 | $10 | $15 | $20 | $75 |
| **Total Spending** | $20 | $20 | $20 | $20 | $20 | $30 | $220 |

Every business faces risks in today's economy, and ABC Internet Marketplace is no exception. Although risk management through futures trading is now common in traditional commodities, extending the concept of risk management to other disciplines is a new idea. We will be competing against established distributors and large brokers. Many large manufacturing companies maintain long-term contracts with their suppliers and thus may not feel the need for our services.

The risk elements are largely attributed to the newness of the concept to a manufacturing environment. The selling arm of more traditional manufacturing sectors equates open market with low price. The well-known method of static pricing passed on to the customer through the established distribution channel will be challenged by the open market. Additionally:

1. Brand-name producers will resist being associated with generic products. The benefits of the marketplace will eventually remove the major producers' resistance to change. They will then have to decide to participate in the open market or risk the loss of market share. We believe that once our marketplace has reached its critical mass, this concern will cease to exist.

2. The less critical element in this concept is the assumption that corporate purchasers will have difficulty in foregoing their close and convenient relationship with their suppliers in favor of an open market. The marketplace has safeguards that will guarantee the suppliers' quality, reliability, and promised delivery. The marketplace provides services beyond those currently offered by distribution channels. The purchasers will be reminded that such services will be given at no extra charge, whereas the present suppliers will certainly add that to the cost of the goods.

3. Most manufacturers are familiar with "contract" purchase, but the idea of "forward" pricing and "hedging" will have to be considered a new business practice.

**Publicity and Public Relations**

**Description of Risks**

4. ABC Marketplace is a global trading environment. Its operation may affect some country currency and/or export-import laws and regulations. It may also have as yet unknown regulatory implications.

5. The viability of an open market will depend on the volume of trade. This implies that the market must have a sufficient number of traders to affect the market price. This critical mass of traders is essential to make the market alive. Our marketing strategy is based on recruiting and training electronic traders (as well as enlisting the present traders within the industry). A significant cost is earmarked for this task.

6. ABC Marketplace assumes the position of an intermediary when immediate matches are not found and a trader defaults. Offsetting those positions may lead to certain monetary losses.

## Contingency Plans

Since the pilot phase concentrates on an initial free-of-charge test phase, we believe any contingency plan will be better devised during and after such tests.

ABC Internet Marketplace has considered the business risks in detail and has developed an effective multilayered strategy systematically addressing each of these risks.

During the startup phase, ABC Marketplace intends to focus its marketing and selling energies on the $5 million-plus manufacturing and distribution businesses. This market generates more than 50 percent of the overall market and remains largely ignored by both manufacturers and consumers. The clear ability of ABC Marketplace to allow electronic traders to maximize profits through risk management in a global market and at a very low cost will ensure the participation of significant users. The efficiency, ease of logistics, and low cost of this concept ensures the success of ABC Marketplace.

As a part of its marketing strategy, ABC Marketplace will invest in public relations, trade shows, and seminars to reach out to all possible players in the ABC Marketplace. Many of these activities will be directed at brokers and investors. Investors have been very active in the futures market and will be happy to expand their investment into a new market formerly unavailable to them.

Not only will ABC Marketplace be successful in attracting traditional players, potentially, all financial and brokerage firms are likely to find this new market attractive.

The very low cost of operation and the nature of the business virtually ensure a high level of trading in any economic climate. Further, ABC Internet Marketplace plans to secure a $5 million line of credit at a favorable rate of interest. In the unlikely event that sufficient revenue is not generated, or should there be a downturn, this line of credit will allow ABC to withdraw cash when needed. In addition to the credit line, the business will set aside 5 percent of the net earnings in a nonpenalty interest-bearing account. This account will be accessed only if there is an emergency cash flow problem.

## OPERATIONS

ABC Internet Marketplace is a collection of database servers, as well as Web servers, housed in a physical location known as a center (or node). The customers inquire or order via the World Wide Web. The data is collected, processed, and stored in our databases. The processed data is then sent back to customers via the Web in the form of market data or executed trade. If an order is executed, the database "clears" the trade within an escrow account. This is accomplished by transferring money from a customer's fiduciary account to an escrow account via its link to a financial institution. The customer is required to deposit money in the fiduciary account before a trade can be executed.

If the physical delivery is to be made, the database collects the supplier's input and upon order confirmation generates a pro forma bill of lading. The bill of lading will be transmitted to an international carrier for release of goods and immediate dispatch.

**Center locations:** ABC Marketplace consists of 28 interconnected centers in different geographical locations. The location of a center is based on the marketplace of the product and the product's proximity to producers and consumers. For example, for electronics components, we have chosen Taiwan, Japan, Singapore, Germany, and the United States. Each center operates during its local time and has on-site personnel. Sensitive data are interchanged among the centers via VPN (includes clearing); otherwise, all centers are available to users for all transactions on the Web. Although the clearing is performed in a single location, the settlement takes place in the center where the match has been made.

**Center resources:** Each center is equipped with its local database server, Web server, data bank, and other auxiliaries. A database administrator will head the locally operated databases.

Each center will be operated by a number of product specialists whose main function is to monitor the products' sources of supply and update the specification of the products. The number of product specialists will roughly equal one individual for one sub-subgroup of product (for example, for passive components, there will be one individual responsible for ceramic capacitors). The product specialist will also act as a liaison between the manufacturer (producer) and ABC Marketplace. The product specialists will routinely dispatch an inspection team to designated warehouses so as to ensure product quality.

**Center management:** A regional marketing manager directs all operations, including customer service, sales, and employee affairs. Any professional service such as equipment leasing or advertising will be performed on the regional level. Except for the accountant, all staff members are compensated on salary and commission.

**Fiduciary account for the first center:** ABC Marketplace intends to open a general fiduciary account with BankBoston and to install the Microlink. ACH transactions will be set up for the users of ABC Marketplace in the United States. A user intending to deposit money into the ABC fiduciary account will initiate the process through the ABC trading platform. The process of initiating the ACH transaction will occur at regular intervals. Each deposit will be associated with a unique identifier allocated to the particular user. ABC Marketplace will also use a similar setup, the Bostonnet, for collecting information on the wire transfers. This will be especially valuable for international users for whom an ACH transaction cannot be set up.

**Delivery of physicals:** ABC Marketplace will require suppliers that wish to list their offers to deliver their goods to our designated bonded warehouse. These warehouses are subleased areas from the select locations within the existing international carrier-bonded warehouses.

## ABC Marketplace's Future Plans

From the start of operations, ABC will benefit from a consistent high-growth pattern. The company has been fortunate to have identified and hired extremely qualified and motivated senior management. Senior management has concentrated its attention on the development of the ABC platform software system and believes this will be the primary reason for the company's success. ABC is currently pursuing the completion of the beta version of the software program.

Upon achieving the funding referred to in this plan, ABC intends to fully test its trading platform system and then proceed with its companywide expansion. ABC will proceed with additional expansion in products and geographical locations as revenue increases with trading activity.

### System History

ABC Marketplace has been in development since early 1998. In August 1998, ABC Marketplace contracted with Mindware Pertech, Inc., an international consulting firm specializing in client server and Internet development, to code the system.

The product development team at ABC Internet Marketplace is headed by Martha Pranik, Ph.D. in computer science (JU). Mr. Delip Gupta, Ph.D. in economics (Princeton) and a team of project managers, project leaders, and programmers all assist Mrs. Pranik.

### System Status

The alpha version was delivered in early June 1999 and is now being tested. The beta version, which is in development, will require four months to develop and will include all bug fixes, interfaces to the bank, and a package delivery service.

### System Plans

ABC Marketplace will allocate $6 million over the next five years toward system development. ABC Marketplace is acutely aware of the need to continually provide additional functionality and incorporate technologies that will improve performance. Furthermore, in the near future, ABC Marketplace plans to include multilanguage support.

## THE MANAGEMENT TEAM
### Officers and Directors

**Fred McKenzie—Chairman of the Board.** Fred McKenzie is the creator of ABC Market, a risk management application tool for manufacturers and distributors. He founded ABC Internet Marketplace in 1996. As chairman of the board, Mr. McKenzie oversees all strategic and operational functions of the company, including the product development conducted by an eight-member team.

In 1980, Mr. McKenzie established Futura Trading, Inc. in Vermont. The company traded industrial commodities in energy, electrical, electronics, and computer sectors. Among its major customers were the U.S. Agency for International Development (USAID), the International Reconstruction and Development Bank (part of World Bank), the Defense Information Service Agency (DISA), the General Service Administration (GSA), and numerous private companies. The company was heavily involved in global buying and the logistics of moving the commodities from the source of supply (copper from Chile) to processing plants (United States) to consumer markets (Switzerland).

As part of improving customer service, and to take advantage of available technology, Futura Trading developed a computerized procurement system in 1982 for rural electrification. The system reduced the procurement cycle from months to days, allowing projects to be completed in a timely manner.

As president of Futura Trading, Mr. McKenzie arranged for a joint development of the first electronic catalog for chips with General Electric Information Service (GEIS) in Boston. The program became operational on GE's private network in 1986.

Prior to Futura Trading, Mr. McKenzie was managing director of Nordon Manufacturing Company in Iran. The factory produced electrical equipment and control systems for industrial applications. The 10,000-square-meter facility employed 75 people and, by 1978, had generated about $10 million in revenue.

Mr. McKenzie, a graduate of Syracuse University, obtained his Series-3 NASD Certificate and is registered as a commodity trading advisor (CTA) with Commodity Futures Trading Commission.

**Kishore Manji—Chief Executive Officer, Director.** Mr. Veeravagu is a 16-year veteran in the manufacturing and information technology arena. Mr. Veeravagu was the senior vice president of sales and marketing for Mindware Pertech, Inc. As the vice president and then as the senior vice president at Mindware, Mr. Veeravagu successfully sold to and signed multiyear contracts with large to medium-size firms (GE Capital, Occidental Petroleum, HSA, Cumberland Farms, and Safeway Stores, among others). He was responsible for changing the indirect business model at Mindware to a direct one, thereby achieving not only a rapid revenue growth but also a significantly higher profit margin.

Before Mindware Pertech, Inc., Mr. Veeravagu was responsible for setting up Altos India's contract manufacturing business from the ground up. Mr. Veeravagu was based in Austin, Texas, where he signed his first contract manufacturing agreement with Mr. Michael Dell of Dell Computer Corporation; this contract was signed even before the manufacturing plant had been set up. Over the next three years, Mr. Veeravagu grew the business for Altos India to $200 million to become the 25th largest contract manufacturing firm in the world.

During his tenure at Altos, Mr. Veeravagu felt the urgent need for tools and processes to manage risk resulting out of in-process material (IPM) supply management. Too often, he would face cost increases that could not be passed on to his customers, IPM shortages, and IPM obsolescence. In 1998, Mr. Veeravagu and Mr. McKenzie met, and Mr. Veeravagu instantly knew that he had his solution in Mr. McKenzie's idea and agreed to invest in ABC.

Prior to Altos India, Mr. Veeravagu in his various capacities with Pertech Computers was responsible for market analysis, product development, product marketing, sales, and sales management of such brands as Brother Electronic Typewriters, PCL Computers (IBM PC compatibles, the largest brand in India), WordPerfect, Ingress, and so on. Before he moved to Altos, he headed the sales management group of a 600-person sales operation with 48 offices in India. Mr. Veeravagu brings with him extensive experience in managing global operations, logistics, market development, and sales. Mr. Veeravagu has a long and successful record of accomplishments in translating ideas to successful businesses both in the international and domestic arena. Mr. Veeravagu received his B.A. in commerce with honors from University of Delhi.

**Robert R. Kline—Chief Technology Officer, Director.** One of the founders of the company, Mr. Kline has the most up-to-date knowledge and expertise in using transactional business in an Internet environment. As a network consultant, he has provided management assistance to numerous companies in improving the efficiency of their enterprise networking. Mr. Kline completed four years of college preparatory courses at the prestigious Ecole Des Roches Bluche, Switzerland. He received his B.A. in business administration from American College of Switzerland. Mr. Kline is fluent in French, German, and Spanish.

**Patrick Ogilvey—Chief Financial Officer.** Mr. Ogilvey has been the purchaser or principal stockholder of more than 15 corporations engaged in manufacturing, wholesaling, publishing, transportation, and banking. Mr. Ogilvey has more than 20 years of experience in finance, merchant banking, and investment banking. Before joining ABC Internet Marketplace, he was executive vice president of finance at General Electrical Construction Group. Mr. Ogilvey graduated from Boston College with a B.S. in finance, and the University of Chicago Graduate School of Business with an M.B.A. in corporate finance. He also holds a M.A. in organizational psychology.

**Sue Hu—Director.** Dr. Hu holds tenure at TuABC University, Department of Electrical Engineering and Computer Science. She has supervised an impressive number of research projects, both for masters and Ph.D. candidates, as well as conducting her own independent work with industry and the government. Dr. Hu obtained her Ph.D. in computer engineering from Drexel University and is a member of the Institute of Electrical and Electronics Engineers.

**Outside Professionals**

Foley, Hoag & Eliot—attorney
Ernst & Young—accountants
BankBoston—banker
Mindware Pertech—technical advisors

## FINANCIALS

### Overview

ABC has not generated any revenue since inception. The founders and friends have furnished all equity funding to date. Mindware Pertech has supplemented this with the purchase of 28 percent of the stock.

The company is now seeking equity financing for $5 million in the form of common stock and $6 million in preferred stock. This equity will be used to support the company's expansion plans as well as furnish financing to support the marketing of its trading system. Additionally, ABC is proposing to open a line of credit for $5 million with its bank or, alternatively, to identify private sources of subordinated debt.

### Pro Forma Financials

The appendixes show five years of pro forma financials for the company (Income Statements and Balance Sheets). A detailed explanation of revenue generation is provided in the sales section of this document. Detailed and full assumptions are appended.

### Use of Proceeds

The company is proposing to sell 1 million common stock shares for $5.00 per share for a total of $5 million. In addition, the company is offering 600,000 preferred stock shares for $10.00 per share for a total of $6 million. The sources of funds and use of proceeds from this offer will be used as follows:

**SOURCES OF FUNDS**

| | |
|---|---|
| Common Stock | $5,000,000 |
| Preferred Stock | $6,000,000 |
| Debt/Line of Credit | $5,000,000 |
| **TOTAL** | **$16,000,000** |

**USE OF PROCEEDS**

| | |
|---|---|
| Marketing | $8,000,000 |
| Operations | $3,000,000 |
| Line of Credit | $5,000,000 |
| **TOTAL** | **$16,000,000** |

### Future Financing Plans and Financial Exits

As discussed in the business plan, ABC intends to expand its existing operations by the addition of 28 system centers. Concurrent with this expansion, ABC intends to expand the number of products being traded to 400. Within three years, ABC will be able to support any additional financing needs through retained earnings.

Management believes that within three years from the inception of this financing, it will be prepared to undertake an IPO. This will depend upon market conditions at that time and the profitability of the company.

Management is pleased to entertain further discussions with serious investors concerning its expansion and operating plans.

The company's founders, officers, and directors own all the current stock of ABC Internet Marketplace. The company's articles of incorporation provide for the issuance of preferred stock in a form as determined by its board of directors. No such preferred stock is currently outstanding. The company currently operates as a "C" corporation in the Commonwealth of Vermont. With the exception of the sale of 28 percent of the company to Mindware Pertech, Inc., ABC has not been involved in any material transactions with its shareholders.

**Capitalization**

**APPENDICES**

**Five-Year Projections— Income Statement ('000)**

| | FY 2000 | FY 2001 | FY 2002 | FY 2003 | FY 2004 |
|---|---|---|---|---|---|
| Revenue | $5,253 | $99,677 | $305,228 | $542,687 | $921,189 |
| Expenses | | | | | |
| G&A | $4,942 | $9,930 | $19,035 | $42,454 | $83,044 |
| Sales, Marketing & Services | $7,412 | $14,897 | $28,553 | $63,682 | $124,566 |
| **Total** | **$12,354** | **$24,827** | **$47,588** | **$106,136** | **$207,610** |
| Operating Income | -$7,101 | $74,850 | $257,640 | $436,551 | $713,579 |
| Interest/Other Expenses | $0 | $510 | $510 | $510 | $510 |
| Income Before Taxes | $0 | $74,340 | $257,130 | $436,041 | $713,069 |
| Income Taxes | $0 | $26,019 | $89,996 | $152,614 | $249,574 |
| **Net Income** | **-$7,101** | **$48,321** | **$167,135** | **$283,427** | **$463,495** |

**Five-Year Projections— Balance Sheet ('000)**

| | FY 2000 | FY 2001 | FY 2002 | FY 2003 | FY 2004 |
|---|---|---|---|---|---|
| **Assets** | | | | | |
| Cash | $6,370 | $72,073 | $226,657 | $510,415 | $974,241 |
| Accounts Receivable | 140 | 3,000 | 9,150 | 12,352 | 16,675 |
| Other Assets | 5,000 | 5,000 | 5,000 | 5,000 | 5,000 |
| **Total** | **$11,510** | **$80,073** | **$240,807** | **$527,767** | **$995,916** |
| PP&E | $400 | $1,100 | $1,900 | $2,650 | $3,150 |
| Prepaid Costs | 100 | 100 | 100 | 100 | 100 |
| | $500 | $1,200 | $2,000 | $2,750 | $3,250 |
| **Total Assets** | **$12,010** | **$81,273** | **$242,807** | **$530,517** | **$999,166** |

**Five-Year
Projections—
Balance Sheet ('000)**

*continued*

| Liabilities | | | | | |
|---|---|---|---|---|---|
| Accounts Payable | $9,883 | $4,965 | $9,518 | $21,227 | $41,522 |
| Senior Revolver | 5000 | 5000 | 5000 | 5000 | 5000 |
| Accrued Expenses | 100 | 800 | 1200 | 1600 | 2200 |
| **Total** | **$14,983** | **$10,765** | **$15,718** | **$27,827** | **$48,722** |
| | | | | | |
| Other Liabilities | $0 | $510 | $765 | $510 | $510 |
| | | | | | |
| **Total Liabilities** | **$14,983** | **$11,275** | **$16,483** | **$28,337** | **$49,232** |
| | | | | | |
| **Shareholders' Equity** | | | | | |
| Common Stock | $5,000 | $5,000 | $5,000 | $5,000 | $5,000 |
| Preferred Stock | 6000 | 6000 | 6000 | 6000 | 6000 |
| Paid in Capital | 1500 | 1500 | 1500 | 1500 | 1500 |
| Retained Earnings | ($15,473) | $57,498 | $213,824 | $489,680 | $937,434 |
| **Total** | **-2,973** | **69,998** | **226,324** | **502,180** | **949,934** |
| | | | | | |
| **Total Liabilities and Equity** | **$12,010** | **$81,273** | **$242,807** | **$530,517** | **$999,166** |

**Notes and
Assumptions to
Forecast**

The forecast included in this business plan represents the projected results of operation and financial conditions for the five-year period. Accordingly, the forecast reflects management's judgment of the expected conditions and its expected course of action as of October 1, 1999. The company's financial reporting periods commence on January 1 and end on December 31.

**Forecast**

*Accounting Policies*

The forecast has been prepared on the accrual basis of accounting, in conformance with generally accepted accounting principles.

*Tax Assumptions*

The forecast assumptions are based upon the current federal tax regulations and the regulations in effect in the state of Vermont.

*Operating Expenses*

Operating expenses as a percentage of sales are reduced to reflect economies of scale in later years.

**Balance Sheet**

*Accounts Receivable*

Accounts receivable assumes a 60-day aging.

*Fixed Assets*

Depreciation on existing fixed assets is calculated over a five-year life.

*Accounts Payable*

Substantially all expenditures are assumed to be paid as incurred. Certain other expenses are assumed to be paid in 45 days.

**Supplemental Information**

THIS BUSINESS PLAN HAS BEEN PREPARED BY THE MANAGEMENT TEAM OF ABC INTERNET MARKETPLACE, INC., AND IS BEING FURNISHED TO SELECT INDIVIDUALS FOR THE SOLE PURPOSE OF PROVIDING POTENTIAL FINANCING TO THE COMPANY. THIS BUSINESS PLAN IS A CONFIDENTIAL DOCUMENT THAT CONTAINS IDEAS, CONCEPTS, METHODS, AND OTHER PROPRIETARY INFORMATION. READERS ARE TO TREAT THE INFORMATION CONTAINED HEREIN AS CONFIDENTIAL AND MAY NOT COPY OR DIVULGE ANY OF THESE MATERIALS WITHOUT THE WRITTEN PERMISSION OF ABC INTERNET MARKETPLACE, INC.

ABC INTERNET MARKETPLACE, INC.

# Leasing Company

BUSINESS PLAN

LEASING GROUP

120 Johnston Boulevard
Minneapolis, Minnesota 55401

*A significant competitive opportunity exists in small ticket leasing, primarily due to companies like Sprint and Intel who have tried to dominate the small ticket market with their size. In the process, they have become too big and slow to effectively respond to the needs of vendors. Small ticket leasing continues to be a viable and profitable business for those national leasing companies that are focused, highly automated, competitively funded, and effectively managed.*

- EXECUTIVE SUMMARY

- MARKET COMPETITION

- PROJECTIONS & ESTIMATES

- RESUMES

- FINANCIALS

## EXECUTIVE SUMMARY
### Leasing Industry Overview

Based on Equipment Leasing Association (ELA) statistics, there was $466 billion of capital equipment purchased in 1994, of which $140 billion (30 percent) was leased. New lease volume in the small ticket market, defined as transactions less than $100,000, was in excess of $7.2 billion in direct finance leases and $772 million in operating leases. These totals represented increases over 1993 of 16.6 percent for direct finance leases and 6.6 percent for operating leases. ELA estimates that 34 percent of the new lease volume generated by finance leases in 1994, was in office machines (20 percent), computers (9 percent), and telecommunications (5 percent).

National small ticket leasing companies have had their greatest success generating business in the office machine, computer, and telecommunication equipment markets. These lessors have had limited success in other markets, such as medical/dental, machine tool, printing, automotive aftermarket, etc.

The limitations in these markets are primarily due to the differences that exist in originating business with office automation product vendors versus vendors selling other types of equipment. Office automation product vendors are very familiar with leasing, and in the majority of cases, they handle all of the selling aspects of the lease with the lessee. Vendors selling other types of equipment generally expect the leasing company to handle the entire leasing sales process with the lessee. In effect, the vendor is only providing the leasing company with a referral.

Most national small ticket leasing companies, due to their assembly line approach of generating and processing business, find it cumbersome to originate business from vendor relationships of this nature. Markets where the vendor requires the leasing company to originate the lease directly with the vendor's customers are usually best served by small, niche-oriented leasing companies generating lease volumes in the $10 to $50 million range.

Small ticket leasing continues to be a viable and profitable business for those national leasing companies that are focused, highly automated, competitively funded, and effectively managed. ELA's 1994 Survey of Industry Activity and Business Operations supports the profitable opportunities that exist in small ticket leasing.

The successful small ticket leasing company today and in the future will be the one which effectively addresses the following five business issues:

- Technology capabilities
- Processing efficiency
- Asset management in niche markets
- Training
- Sales structure and support

## MARKET COMPETITION

A significant competitive opportunity exists in small ticket leasing, primarily due to companies like Sprint and Intel who have tried to dominate the small ticket market with their size. In the process, they have become too big and slow to effectively respond to the needs of vendors. By trying to penetrate so many different equipment markets to achieve their growth goals, they have only compounded this problem. They have also developed cost structures which make it difficult to achieve acceptable profit targets as a small ticket lessor in today's competitive environment.

In addition, many competitors, in an effort to gain market share, have made extremely aggressive residual assumptions to offer very low fair market value lease rates to vendors. This practice in the long run will prove to have a negative impact on earnings by their not being able to realize their booked residuals.

Listed below are the primary small ticket leasing competitors broken down in three ties based on their estimated annual lease sales volume:

**ANNUAL SALES OVER $300 MILLION**

- Copelco
- Sprint
- Intel
- Tokai
- TechLease

**ANNUAL SALES BETWEEN $150 AND $299 MILLION**

- Finova
- Sanwa
- Lear
- Doran Credit

**ANNUAL SALES BELOW $149 MILLION**

- Verta Leasing
- Lyon Financial/Business Credit Leasing
- Advanta
- Great American Leasing
- Rockford Industries
- Orix Credit Alliance
- Vanguard Financial Services
- Trans Leasing

I propose to create an industry-leading small ticket leasing company by developing a successful partnership alliance between:

**Strategic Leasing Partnership Plan**

- American Finance Inc.—Equity
- ABX Capital—Warehouse lines and securitization
- Jim O'Hara—Experienced management capabilities

There would be a three-point plan to build the company's business. In order of priority, they are:

1. Direct origination in the office automation product markets based on a highly automated sales and processing database management strategy. Sales structure would center around a proactive inside sales team generating business from vendors and any existing lessees, with a small group of highly skilled outside salespeople originating new business from large vendors who have annual lease volumes in excess of $1.8 million. The product focus would be on commercial finance leases, consumer finance leases, and inventory finance. The majority of leases would be under $100,000, with an average size lease between $5,000 and $25,000 and average lease terms ranging 12 to 60 months.
2. Acquisitions of or joint ventures with niche-oriented leasing companies specializing in the medical/dental, printing, machine tool, and automotive aftermarket equipment markets.

3. Processing and portfolio management services on a fee income basis for leasing companies and vendors.

This plan accomplishes several critical success factors in building a profitable leasing company:

- Provides an effective cost structure that, through technology, achieves a highly efficient service level to originate and process large volumes of business within the office automation product markets.
- Allows for diversification into new markets without expensive start-up sales, processing, and learning curve costs. Centralization of fixed processing costs, combined with competitive funding capability, enables acquisitions and joint venture to improve market share and increase profitability.
- Fee income business spreads fixed processing costs over a wide base, resulting in increased profit margins while providing an additional income source.
- Achieves a blended gross portfolio yield between 13 percent and 15 percent, in addition to significant fee and residual income.

**PROJECTIONS & ESTIMATES**

Lease income projections are included for the years 1996 though 2001. These projections assume conservative revenue, expense, and reserve estimates to make the pre-tax profit calculations as accurate as possible. They also reflect realistic sales growth projections for a start-up leasing company year to year. For comparison purposes, a five year financial forecast has been included. This is an actual forecast from an existing small ticket leasing company which has had a solid history of profitability.

Inventory finance projections have been prepared for $10 million, $25 million, and $50 million; all assume an average note size of $10,000. They also make realistic assumptions to reflect an accurate projection of potential profitability.

Finally, the lease processing system cost estimates provide the amount of investment required in technology to develop a leading edge lease processing system.

**RESUMES**

**JAMES O'HARA**

**EXPERIENCE**

**BUDGET LEASING CORPORATION,** Boston, Massachusetts, 1995

**THE BUDGET FUNDING GROUP, INC.,** Boston, Massachusetts, 1993 to 1994

Budget Leasing Corporation (BLC) is an independent third-party equipment leasing company, operating under the trade name Verta Leasing, with sales over $200 million. BLC specializes in small ticket to low-middle market leasing and inventory financing, focusing on manufacturers and vendors in the copier/fax, telecommunication, and personal computer markets. The Budget Funding Group (BFG), a privately held corporation, was divided in 1995 into three separate operating companies, one of which was BLC.

**President/Chief Executive Officer, 1995**

Complete profit and loss responsibility with the objective of preparing BLC for a future public offering. Reported to the Chairman of the Board and served as a member of the Board of Directors. Appointed to the Executive Committee, the senior operating committee of the Board.

- Returned the company to profitability in 1995 from a position of loss in 1994.
- Reduced fixed costs by over $1.8 million by restructuring across all functional areas. Simultaneously improved efficiency and productivity through implementation of cross-functional teams and enhanced system automation.
- Restructured lending relationships, resulting in a cost of funds savings to the company of over 200 basis points.

**Executive Vice President, Sales, 1994 to 1995**

**Vice President, Sales, 1993 to 1994**

Directed the sales and marketing functions for Verta Leasing and Resort Funding with sales in excess of $250 million. Led a 32-person staff in the accomplishment of aggressive sales goals. Diversified the company into new markets and strengthened national account programs with Konica, Mita, Sharp, Copystar, Danka, Toshiba, Monroe, Riso, and Telrad.

- Achieved 115 percent growth in leasing sales volume in two-year period, from $71 million to $153 million.
- Increased inventory finance sales volume by 63 percent, from $35 million to $57 million.
- Successfully repositioned the sales organization to expand into the telecommunication and personal computer leasing markets.
- Developed a new market by implementing BFG's first consumer leasing program.

**DORAN CREDIT,** Auburn Hills, Michigan, 1990 to 1993

Small ticket to low-middle market third-party lessor, with emphasis on the personal computer products marketplace. Subsidiary of Doran Corporation, a Fortune 100 company.

**Vice President, Sales, Dealer Products Group**

Responsible as a member of the management committee to provide a 20 percent return on equity to parent company. Managed a productive team of 30 sales and management professionals. Strategically extended the sales division into new markets. Led the profitable growth of a $100 million sales organization with national account responsibility for CompaqComputer, MicroTech, Intelligent Electronics, and Graybar.

- Increased profitability by 133 percent, from $1.5 million in 1990 to $3.5 million in 1992.
- Built an inside salesforce of 11, generating $40 million in sales.

Restructured the sales staff to increase efficiency while reducing sales costs by over $1 million.

**GENESEE LEASING,** Minneapolis, Minnesota, 1988 to 1990

Genesee Leasing was a captive leasing company to Citizens' Business (CBS), one of the nation's leading Hewlett Packard office equipment dealers.

**Vice President, Sales**

Generated additional leasing business by marketing directly to our existing lessee base. Increased leasing business in all CBS branches by creating new marketing and leasing sales training programs.

- Increased leasing revenue 47 percent in one-year period.

**WILMINGTON LEASING,** Charlotte, North Carolina, 1987 to 1988

A third-party, small ticket leasing company providing a funding source for brokers and other leasing companies.

**Regional Manager, Broker Development**

Generated leasing transactions under $100,000 by providing a debt source to independent third-party lessors and leasing brokers.

Reached 450 percent of Quota and ranked third of ten regional managers company-wide.

**CORPORATE CREDIT LEASING,** Cincinnati, Ohio, 1983 to 1986

A small ticket, third-party leasing company which originated business with manufacturers, vendors, and lessees. Subsidiary of Budson Sales Enterprises, a billion-dollar food distribution company.

**National Sales Manager**

Developed business nationally by establishing a productive network of vendors. Created and implemented all company leasing programs and advertising. Recruited and managed the national sales force.

- Increased lease bookings from $600,000 per month to $3.8 million per month.
- Increased total lease receivables outstanding from $3.6 million to $89.5 million.

**DIAMOND LEASING CORPORATION,** Indianapolis, Indiana, 1979 to 1983

A subsidiary of the Diamond Finance Company, a publicly traded consumer finance company.

**Regional Sales Representative, 1981 to 1983**

**Operations Manager, 1979 to 1980**

Developed and maintained a productive network of vendors in a defined territory through the sale of Diamond Leasing's programs and services.

- #1 produce in applications and bookings out of ten sales representatives nationally in 1982 and 1983.
- Set up and managed the first branch office for Diamond Leasing in the Midwest.

**EDUCATION**

**Michigan State University, East Lansing, Michigan,** Bachelor's Degree in Business Administration

**Amembal and Isom,** The Creative Financing Alternative, Leasing for Profit

**Doran University,** Management Training

**KENNETH INGRAM**

Management Executive, General Counsel with more than 10 years experience in contract negotiations, legal department management, cost reduction, and strategic planning, who boosted revenues $480K by increasing collections 40 percent within 16 months.

Decision-maker with track record of promoting corporate growth through solid management skills.

- 40 percent reduction in overhead costs achieved ($200K annually) by restructuring departments.
- $9 million saved by skillfully negotiating $90 million in equipment leases.

Key player in successfully reorganizing company in bankruptcy; $20 million in sales achieved.

Proven ability to enhance company's competitive advantage by implementing effective business strategies.

- More than $30K in potential savings by streamlining procedures, improving response time in highly competitive market.
- 15 percent reduction in timeline for collection turnaround and enhanced productivity.

Accomplished at implementing innovative procedures and systems to achieve superior results.

- Improved efficiencies and increased productivity by reorganizing legal department operating procedures.
- Tracked more than 1,000 cases after selecting/designing case management software system with MIS Department.

Willing to relocate. Age 35. Computer literate.


**EDUCATION**

M.B.A., 3.2 GPA, Yale University, 1990

J.D., Dean's List, Columbia University College of Law, 1984

B.A., Dean's List, New York University, 1980


**PROFESSIONAL EXPERIENCE**

General Counsel, 1995-present, **THE BUDGET FUNDING GROUP, INC.,** Boston, Massachusetts, 1994 to present

- Report to CEO of newly formed leasing corporation. Serve as Corporate Secretary.
- Increase revenues by streamlining collection processes. Review federal/state laws for proposed financing.
- Manage commercial collections and litigation processes. Member of corporate credit committee.

Associate General Counsel (Funding Group), 1994-1995

- Determined average litigation cost and identified revenue trends and productivity of department personnel over 3 years.
- Managed 4 paralegals, associate counsel, and support staff. Recruited/supervised outside counsel in 20+ states.

Corporate Counsel, MIC CORPORATION, Boston, Massachusetts, 1991 to 1994

- Negotiated $16 million in settlements for bankruptcy estates. Reviewed SEC filings.
- Performed due diligence review of potential liabilities of parent and subsidiaries for reorganization plan.
- Research included intercompany guarantees, indemnity agreements and expected value of remarketing agreements.
- Assisted in company-wide implementation of Corporate Ethics Policy. Supervised 4 paralegals and 7 analysts.
- Advised Human Resources on WARN Act compliance, ADA, FMLA and Massachusetts Labor Law.
- Determined whether to assume or reject 20-year real estate during bankruptcy proceedings.

Corporate Counsel, CYBERNOSTICS, INC., Richmond, Virginia, 1987 to 1988

- Interim manager after Chapter 11 filing. Appeared at hearings and reported to outside counsel/creditor's committee.
- Negotiated $50 million in leveraged leases as well as workouts and settlements with creditors.
- Supported bankruptcy counsel in analysis of $90 million in filed claims.

Vice President/Senior Counsel, Secretary, MAKON CORPORATION, Richmond, Virginia, 1984 to 1987

- Negotiated more than 200 leases. As securities principal, managed NASD-registered broker-dealer subsidiary.
- Supervised Regulation D offerings registration in 25 states. Reduced costs by performing attorney functions in-house.

---

## FINANCIALS

**Financial Data for All Small-Ticket Respondents, 1994**

*Average balance sheet data per respondent at the end of fiscal year 1994*
*(35 respondents)*

| | |
|---|---|
| Net earning assets (e.g. loan and net lease receivables) | $603,124,290 |
| Other assets (e.g. investments; property plants & equipment; other nonearning assets) | $49,939,740 |
| **Total assets** | **$653,064,030** |
| | |
| Short-term debt (including current portion of long-term debt) | $114,514,700 |
| Long-term debt, less current portion | $385,373,900 |
| Other current liabilities (e.g. accounts and taxes payable; accrued payroll/employee benefits) | $32,683,140 |
| Other long-term liabilities (e.g. retirement benefits, deferred income taxes) | $39,424,170 |
| **Total liabilities** | **$571,995,900** |
| | |
| **Owner equity** | **$81,068,130** |

*Average borrowings data per respondent for fiscal year 1994*
*(35 respondents)*

| | |
|---|---|
| External borrowings | $436,916,629 |
| Borrowing from affiliates | $62,971,971 |
| **Total borrowing** | **$499,888,600** |

*Average income statement data per respondent for fiscal year 1994*
*(39 respondents)*

| | |
|---|---|
| Lease revenue | $45,240,130 |
| Loan revenue | $23,031,410 |
| Fee income and other revenue | $5,502,615 |
| **Total revenue** | **$73,774,155** |
| | |
| Interest expense | $24,550,870 |
| Operating expense (general and administrative, selling, etc.) | $21,332,360 |
| Depreciation expense-operating leases | $8,459,846 |
| Provision for bad debt | $4,324,769 |
| **Total expenses** | **$58,667,845** |
| | |
| Income before taxes on income | $15,106,310 |
| | |
| Provision for taxes on income: | |
| Current portion (credit) | $3,064,333 |
| Deferred portion | $1,580,974 |
| **Total provision for taxes on income** | **$4,645,307** |
| **Net income** | **$10,461,003** |

## Portfolio Analysis Model

| Input | Input Items | |
|---|---|---|
| **Lease Parameters** | | |
| Target Period | Jan-01 to Dec-01 | |
| Credit Applications Processed | 24,107 | |
| Contracts Booked | 13,500 | |
| Target Rate Factor | 0.02922 | |
| Term | 42 | months |
| Equipment Cost | $135,000,000.00 | dollars |
| Residual (Based on Matrix) | 5.62% | of equipment cost. |
| Security Deposits | 0 | payment(s) |
| | | |
| **Debt Parameters** | | |
| Leverage Percentage | 100.00% | |
| Note Amount | $135,000,000.00 | |
| Commissions Paid (if appl) | 0.00% | = $0.00 |
| Net Note Proceeds | $135,000,000.00 | |
| Cost of Capital | 6.75% | for xx months. |
| | | |
| **Up-front Expenses** | | |
| Sales Expenses | 1.00% | of equipment cost. |
| Commissions to Manf/Vendor | 0.00% | of equipment cost. |
| Allowance for Bad Debt | 3.00% | of equipment cost. |

| **Ongoing Expenses** | **$ Per Contract** | **Period % Breakout** |
|---|---|---|
| Credit Apps >$25,000 | $24.00 | => 96.0% |
| Credit Apps <$25,000 | $36.00 | => 4.0% |
| Processing Expenses (Cap) | $50.00 | => 99.0% |
| | $100.00 | => 1.0% |
| Invoicing Costs | $4.80 | per contract per month. |

| **Income** | | |
|---|---|---|
| Doc Fee | $29.40 | = $49.00 x 60% |
| Risk Fee | 0.00076 | = .19% x 40% |

## Calculations

| | |
|---|---|
| **Monthly Note Payment** | **3,617,899.47** |
| **Monthly Lease Stream** | **3,944,700.00** |
| **Effective Lease Interest Rate** | **14.02%** |
| Pre-Tax Income (Loss) | 16,621,857.73 |
| (percentage of orig cost) | 12.3% |
| **Average Annual R.O.E.** | **2.11%** |
| **Booked Residual Value** | **7,583,625.00** |

**Up-front Expenses**

| | |
|---|---|
| Bad Debt Expense | 4,050,000.00 |
| Commissions to Manf/Vendor | 0.00 |
| Selling Expenses | 1,350,000.00 |
| **Total Up-Front Expenses** | **5,400,000.00** |

**Ongoing Expenses**

| | |
|---|---|
| Monthly Invoicing Exp | 64,800.00 |
| Monthly Credit Amort | 14,050.94 |
| Monthly Processing Amort | 16,232.14 |
| **Monthly Processing Total** | **95,083.08** |

**Up-front Income**

| | |
|---|---|
| Documentation Fees | 396,900.00 |

**Ongoing Fee Income**

| | |
|---|---|
| Monthly Risk Fees | 102,600.00 |

## Actual 5-Year Forecast of an Existing Small Ticket Leasing Company

|  | **FORECASTS FOR:** | | | | |
|---|---|---|---|---|---|
| **INCOME (Rounded to thousands)** | **1993** | **1994** | **1995** | **1996** | **1997** |
| LEASE INCOME | 32,564 | 31,956 | 34,264 | 36,849 | 39,405 |
| INTEREST EXPENSE | (14,579) | (13,500) | (14,478) | (15,570) | (16,650) |
| NET LEASE INCOME | 17,985 | 18,456 | 19,786 | 21,279 | 22,755 |
| FEE INCOME | 5,848 | 6,025 | 6,532 | 6,888 | 7,338 |
| RESIDUAL GAIN | 6,272 | 5,895 | 5,300 | 5,000 | 5,000 |
| TOTAL OTHER INCOME | 12,120 | 11,920 | 11,832 | 11,888 | 12,338 |
| **TOTAL OPERATING INCOME** | **$30,105** | **$30,376** | **$31,618** | **$33,167** | **$35,093** |
| | | | | | |
| **SALES EXPENSES** | | | | | |
| SALARIES | 1,224 | 1,224 | 1,110 | 1,110 | 1,200 |
| COMMISSIONS | 576 | 624 | 680 | 680 | 680 |
| FRINGES | 392 | 392 | 355 | 355 | 384 |
| OTHER EXPENSES | 1,440 | 1,400 | 1,300 | 1,300 | 1,450 |
| **TOTAL SALES EXPENSES** | **$3,632** | **$3,640** | **$3,445** | **$3,445** | **$3,714** |
| | | | | | |
| **ADMIN. EXPENSES** | | | | | |
| COMPENSATION | 3,600 | 3,708 | 3,700 | 3,710 | 3,810 |
| FRINGES | 1,152 | 1,187 | 1,184 | 1,187 | 1,219 |
| RENT/UTILITIES | 1,236 | 1,040 | 1,060 | 1,080 | 1,100 |
| TELEPHONE/POSTAGE | 840 | 850 | 830 | 850 | 850 |
| DEPRECIATION | 528 | 500 | 490 | 485 | 470 |
| DATA PROCESSING | 2,760 | 1,500 | 1,400 | 1,550 | 1,600 |
| OTHER EXPENSES | 1,920 | 1,900 | 1,900 | 1,920 | 1,920 |
| **TOTAL ADMIN. EXPENSES** | **$12,036** | **$10,685** | **$10,564** | **$10,782** | **$10,969** |
| | | | | | |
| **TOTAL SALES & ADMIN. EXP.** | **$15,668** | **$14,325** | **$14,009** | **$14,227** | **$14,683** |
| | | | | | |
| PROVISION FOR BAD DEBT | 8,660 | 8,100 | 8,687 | 9,342 | 9,990 |
| OUTSIDE COMMISSIONS | 2,700 | 3,000 | 3,500 | 3,500 | 3,500 |
| DEFERRED IDC NEW BUSINESS | (4,860) | (5,400) | (6,300) | (6,300) | (6,300) |
| **NET EXPENSES** | **$22,168** | **$20,025** | **$19,896** | **$20,769** | **$21,873** |
| | | | | | |
| **PRE-TAX PROFIT/(LOSS)** | **$7,937** | **$10,351** | **$11,722** | **$12,398** | **$13,220** |
| | | | | | |
| INCOME TAX EXPENSE | 3,016 | 3,933 | 4,454 | 4,710 | 5,024 |
| | | | | | |
| **AFTER-TAX PROFIT/(LOSS)** | ***$4,921** | ***$6,418** | ***$7,268** | **$7,688** | **$8,196** |
| | | | | | |
| VOLUME | 108,000 | 120,000 | 140,000 | 140,000 | 140,000 |
| ASSETS | 243,405 | 259,589 | 278,000 | 299,000 | 319,000 |
| ROA | 2.02% | 2.47% | 2.61% | 2.57% | 2.57% |
| O.LIAB & D.T. | 26,000 | 27,000 | 28,000 | 30,000 | 33,000 |
| DEBT | 186,347 | 199,362 | 214,286 | 230,571 | 245,143 |
| EQUITY | 31,058 | 33,227 | 35,714 | 38,429 | 40,857 |
| ROE | 15.84% | 19.32% | 20.35% | 20.00% | 20.06% |
| NIL | 217,405 | 232,589 | 250,000 | 269,000 | 286,000 |

*Profit goals achieved were over 100% of plan for 1993-1995.*

## Lease Processing System Cost Estimates

| | |
|---|---:|
| Complete Automated Credit Scoring System | $175,000 |
| Back End Leasing Software | $100,000 |
| System Setup and Development Costs | $150,000 |
| Structured Query Language Server Software | $65,000 |
| Structured Query Language Database Server | $50,000 |
| Document Imaging System | $50,000 |
| Miscellaneous System Hardware and Software | $25,000 |
| Remote Access System | $10,000 |
| Backup System | $10,000 |
| Printers (per unit installed) | $5,000 |
| Optical Storage System | $5,000 |
| Workstations (per user) | $3,000 |
| Fax Servers (per unit installed) | $2,500 |
| Local Area Network (per user) | $300 |
| (Includes wiring, concentrators, network cards, and software) | |
| **TOTAL COST:** | **$650,800** |

- Total includes only one printer, work station, fax server, and local area network user. These costs would vary depending on number of employees.
- One printer is needed for approximately every 20 people.

## IFS Pricing Model

| Input | Input Items: | |
|---|---|---|
| **Lease Parameters** | | |
| Credit Applications Processed | 0 | |
| Contracts Booked | 5,000 | |
| Interest Rate | 25.01% | |
| Term | 4 | months |
| Equipment Cost | $50,000,000.00 | dollars |
| Terms | 30 | days net to Manufacturer |
| Manufacturer's Discount | 5.00% | |
| Add-on Percentage | 0.00% | |
| Amount Funded | $47,500,000.00 | payment(s) |
| | | |
| **Debt Parameters** | | |
| Leverage Percentage | 100.00% | |
| Total Amount Borrowed | $35,000,000.00 | |
| Commissions Paid | 0.00% | = $0.00 |
| Net Proceeds | $35,000,000.00 | (Equal to Manf. Funding) |
| Cost of Capital | 6.75% | for xx months. |
| | | |
| **Up-front Expenses** | | |
| Sales Expenses | 0.25% | of equipment cost. |
| Commissions Paid to Ven/Manf | 0.00% | of equipment cost. |
| Allowance for Bad Debt | 0.50% | of equipment cost. |
| | | |
| **Ongoing Expenses** | | |
| Credit Applications (Cap) | $50.00 | per application processed |
| Processing Expenses (Cap) | $46.00 | per contract booked |
| Invoicing Costs | $5.00 | per contract per month. |

## Calculations

| | |
|---|---|
| **Monthly Debt Payment** | **8,873,391.97** |
| **Monthly Note Stream** | **12,500,000.00** |
| **Rate Factor** | **0.25000** |
| **Pre-Tax Income (Loss)** | **1,051,432.11** |
| **Average Annual R.O.A.** | **0.84%** |

**Up-front Expenses**

| | |
|---|---|
| Bad Debt Expense | (250,000.00) |
| Manf. Commissions Paid | 0.00 |
| Selling Expenses | (125,000.00) |
| Credit Expenses | (250,000.00) |
| Processing Expenses | (230,000.00) |
| **Total Up-Front Expenses** | **(855,000.00)** |

**Ongoing Expenses**

| | |
|---|---|
| Monthly Invoicing Exp | (25,000.00) |
| **Monthly Processing Total** | **(25,000.00)** |

## Rebate Analysis:

Set Maximum Percentage of Income you wish to rebate back to Dealer: 75%.

| Period | Profit Available | Maximum Rebate % | Profit remaining after Rebate based on percentage used. |
|---|---|---|---|
| 1 | $1,423,125.00 | 2.13% | $355,781.25 |
| 2 | $1,250,055.41 | 1.88% | $312,513.85 |
| 3 | $1,126,065.75 | 1.69% | $281,516.44 |
| 4 | $1,051,432.11 | 1.58% | $262,858.03 |
| 5 | $0.00 | 0.00% | $0.00 |
| 6 | $0.00 | 0.00% | $0.00 |

# Online Job Service

BUSINESS PLAN

CAREERCONNECTIONS.COM

*3614 Western Highway*
*Cleveland, Ohio 44113*

*Our passion for developing recruiting innovations creates a world of ideas without boundaries. By aspiring to the highest standards of quality in everything we do, we will become a business without competition. At CareerConnections we don't view ourselves as being in the Internet recruiting business. We are in the business of helping employers find a diverse group of qualified candidates to make successful hiring decisions.*

- WHO WE ARE & WHAT WE STAND FOR

- EXECUTIVE SUMMARY

- BIOGRAPHIES

- INTERNET RECRUITING MARKET OVERVIEW

- COMPETITIVE OVERVIEW

- OUR CLIENTS

- MARKETING STRATEGY

- FINANCIAL OVERVIEW

- CRITICAL SUCCESS FACTORS

- TOP FORTY MARKETS

**WHO WE ARE &
WHAT WE STAND
FOR**

CareerConnections is in the business of helping employment professionals find qualified candidates and successfully fill openings. We are experts in pioneering high-tech and nontraditional recruiting solutions. Our Virtual Job Fairs provide a low cost, high-impact means of reaching individuals in targeted geographic markets across the Midwest.

CareerConnections Virtual Job Fairs merge the immediacy of the Internet with the power of focused radio advertising to connect with qualified candidates. Through the strategic link between the Internet and radio, we are able to mobilize the attention of employed, experienced candidates and ignite the interest of passive job seekers.

As partners to the human resources team, we are committed to helping employers raise their corporate profiles and communicate their unique identities. We also dedicate ourselves to the serious task of attracting and maintaining a diverse workforce.

Human resources professionals applaud us for the muscle we add to their recruiting efforts. Candidates appreciate us for our quick and convenient access to a wide range of companies and their openings.

CareerConnections hosts Virtual Job Fairs in specific cities in the Midwest, where we commit ourselves to markets often neglected by other online employment services. Upcoming Virtual Job Fair markets include Chicago, Cincinnati, Cleveland, Toledo, Detroit, Grand Rapids, Indianapolis, and Milwaukee.

**Our Vision**

Our passion for developing recruiting innovations creates a world of ideas without boundaries. By aspiring to the highest standards of quality in everything we do, we will become a business without competition.

**Our Mission**

At CareerConnections we don't view ourselves as being in the Internet recruiting business. We are in the business of helping employers find a diverse group of qualified candidates to make successful hiring decisions. Our search strategies are creative, cost-effective, and dynamic.

**Our Principles**

1. We build trusting relationships with clients through hard work and integrity.
2. We value innovation and continually strive to develop better ways to support our clients.
3. We keep our promises, respect one another, share rewards, and make time to have fun.
4. We view our clients and shareholder as partners. When our partners succeed, so do we.
5. We are tenacious.

CareerConnections's vision, mission, and principles are the cornerstone of our culture.

**EXECUTIVE
SUMMARY**

**Emerging Market for Employee Recruiting**

- Companies seeking to find more dynamic recruiting methods...convenience of "Internet recruiting" in demand
- Candidates identified effectively and cost efficiently...without expensive recruiters or print advertising
- Significant growth potential exists in market...over 91,000 U.S. businesses with over 100 employees

**CareerConnections Virtual Job Fairs Represent Attractive New Channel for Reaching Passive Job Seekers...**

- Recruiting employed, experienced candidates is a key objective for every employer
- Opportunity to leverage power of Internet with targeted radio advertising focused on local markets
- Clearly the largest untapped recruiting channel for employers...market potential $2 billion plus

**We've Gotten Started...but Must Increase Resources to Capture Market Share Quickly...**

- Market penetration dependent on investment in telemarketing, advertising, and technology capability
- Reduce expenses and increase control by bringing website/systems development and sales functions in-house
- Explore strategic acquisition of a business to business telemarketing company to shorten growth cycle
- Enhance our image as a technology company...establish Boston corporate office by September 30, 2000

**CareerConnections's Pro Forma Looks Solid...Phased Approach to Growth...**

- Forecasting $315,000 revenues in 2000...growing to $11,250,000 by 2003
- Targeting $6,775,000 pre-tax income over next 4 years...30 percent pre-tax profits
- Assumptions realistic...significant upside if Internet recruiting estimates hold true

CareerConnections strategically links the strength of the Internet with the power of targeted radio advertising to capture the attention of employed, experienced candidates conveniently and affordably.

**BIOGRAPHIES**

**Management**

**Gerald Simons—President & Chief Executive Officer**

Gerry Simons has over twenty years experienced in the financial services industry. Mr. Simons has held various senior leadership positions with GM Credit, Nissan Financial Services, Citibank Capital Corporation, and Lear Credit. He has had P/L management responsibility for businesses in excess of $200 million and responsibility for sales budgets in excess of $400 million. His expertise includes development of Internet strategies within the equipment leasing industry. Mr. Simons holds his Bachelor of Arts degree in business administration from Ohio State University.

**Jill Monroe—Vice President Product Development**

Jill Monroe is the author of *Job Hunters' Sourcebook: Where to Find Employment Leads and Other Job Search Resources* (Gale Research Inc.). Under her authorship, *Job Hunters' Sourcebook* was the recipient of two prominent publishing awards. Ms. Monroe has over twenty years of broad human resources management experience, with specialized knowledge in staffing, compensation, benefits, and employee relations. She has held senior human resources positions with Bonior Consulting Group and Ogilvy & Mather. Ms. Monroe holds her Bachelor of Communications degree from Ohio State University. Ms. Monroe is also a former board member of the Human Resources Association of Greater Cleveland.

**Frederick Paul—Vice President Operations**

Fred Paul has thirteen years of sales, managerial, and entrepreneurial experience. Mr. Paul was National Sales Manager for Mercury Interactions, a subsidiary of ABC Broadcasting. He was responsible for managing all national sales programs associated with ABC's national recruitment website. Mr. Paul began his career with Standard & Poors, where he was named Broker of the Year for three consecutive years. He started his own company, Creative Auto Detailing, and successfully built it into three locations before selling the company in 1996. Mr. Paul has his Bachelor of Arts degree in business administration from Northwestern University.

### Suzanne Rintimacki—Vice President Business Development

Suzanne Rintimacki has three years of successful sales and business development experience with ABC Broadcasting. Ms. Schumacher was National Director of Sales and Business Development, and was responsible for creating and implementing nationally ABC's Wonder Job Fair product. She successfully executed nine events, generating over $500 thousand in revenue. In 1997 she implemented the ABC JobConnect for ABC Radio Cleveland, generating $1.1 million in revenue, and was honored as the number one market nationally for ABC Radio.

## Advisory Board

### Troy Bennett—Dunston & Ray P.L.C.

Troy Bennett has been a practicing attorney with Dunston & Ray for twelve years and is a partner specializing in Commercial and Product Liability, Commercial Landlord-Tenant, and Securities Litigation. Mr. Bennett is a member of the Litigation Section of the American Bar, State Bar of Ohio, and Cleveland Bar Association. He holds his Juris Doctorate Law degree from Columbia College Law School and his Bachelor of Arts degree from College of the Holy Cross. CareerConnections has engaged Dunston & Ray as its law firm.

### Jonathon Williams—Morgan & Reilly, LLP

Jonathon Williams has been a practicing Certified Public Accountant with Morgan & Reilly for seventeen years and is a partner specializing in tax and consulting services to corporations. Mr. Williams is a member of the American Institute of Certified Public Accountants and the Ohio Association of Certified Public Accountants. He holds his Master of Science degree from Ohio State University and his Bachelor of Business Administration, Accounting degree from Ohio University. CareerConnections has engaged Morgan & Reilly as its accounting firm.

### Phillip Owens—Citibank

Phillip Owens is Vice President and Deposit Relationship Manager for Citibank. Mr. Owens has over eleven years of banking relationship management experience. He holds his Juris Doctorate Law degree from Ohio College of Law and his Bachelor of Science degree from Ohio University. CareerConnections has engaged Citibank as its primary deposit bank.

### Yoko Una—The Smith Group

Yoko Una has over twenty-five years of broad human resources management experience. Ms. Una has held senior human resources leadership positions with Macmillan, General Motors, and the University of Ohio. She is an active member and former officer and board member of the Society for Human Resources Management, Human Resources Association of Greater Cleveland, and Academy for Academic Personnel Administration. She is also a former board member of the College and University Personnel Association and Metro Cleveland Equal Opportunity Forum. Ms. Dolan-Greene holds her Master in Public Administration degree from the University of Virginia and her Bachelor of Arts degree from University of Arkansas.

### Sydney Atwater—Atwater Communications, Inc.

Syd Atwater has over eighteen years' experience as a broadcast executive. Mr. Atwater is president of his own company, specializing in radio broadcasting and consulting services. He is an active member and former officer and board member of the Ohio Association of Broadcasters and the Pittsburg Area Radio Broadcasters Association. Mr. Atwater holds his Juris Doctorate Law degree from Ohio State Law School and his Bachelor of Arts degree from the University of Michigan.

**Kevin Freeman—Vision Information Technologies**

Kevin Freeman is the President & CEO of Vision Information Technologies, which he founded in 1997, specializing in website development and maintenance. Mr. Segura developed and patented VisionPro, a dynamic website development software which allows companies to self-manage their websites without technical expertise. His company has over 60 clients including such companies as GM Sales, Highland Brands, Michigan State University, and Monroe County. Mr. Freeman is a board member of the Hispanic Business Alliance, Hispanic Engineers Business Corporation, University of Ohio Computer & Information Science Professional Advisory Board, Economic Club of Cleveland, and Society of Hispanic Professional Engineers. He holds his Bachelor of Science degree in Computer Science from the University of Ohio.

Companies are aggressively looking for new ways to lower costs and generate better results.

| **INTERNET RECRUITING MARKET OVERVIEW** |

**Online Recruiting Spending (millions)**

| 1999 | $265 |
| 2000 | $525 |
| 2001 | $895 |
| 2002 | $1,340 |
| 2003 | $1,740 |

**Number of Recruiters Using Online Ads (thousands)**

| 1999 | 24 |
| 2000 | 38 |
| 2001 | 56 |
| 2002 | 90 |
| 2003 | 125 |

Today, the Internet recruiting market is in its infancy, but the future opportunity is substantial as more companies seek to increase their Internet capabilities.

**Online Ad Spending Per Recruiter (thousands)**

| 1999 | $11 |
| 2000 | $14 |
| 2001 | $16 |
| 2002 | $15 |
| 2003 | $14 |

**Online Spending as a Percentage of Print Ads**

| 1999 | 2.9% |
| 2000 | 5.6% |
| 2001 | 9.2% |
| 2002 | 14.3% |
| 2003 | 19.8% |

Overall Internet recruiting market is growing an average of 62 percent per year.

## COMPETITIVE OVERVIEW

Resume posting boards currently dominate Internet recruiting and have made a large investment to grow.

**Employment Website Market**
**Most Popular Employment Websites**

| | |
|---|---|
| Monster | 3.9% |
| CareerPath | 1.7% |
| CareerMosaic | 1.5% |
| HotJobs | 1.4% |
| CareerBuilder | 0.5% |

**Largest Resume Posting Websites**
**(Percentage of Job Postings in thousands)**

| | |
|---|---|
| Monster | 371 |
| CareerPath | 340 |
| CareerBuilder | 180 |
| Headhunter.net | 169 |
| HotJobs | 150 |

### Competitive Analysis

The top forty employment website companies offer similar products and compete for the same market share. Resume posting companies charge $150-$250 per job posting (packages generally range from $5,000-$50,000). There are over three million jobs posted on the Internet today. Approximately 71 percent of job board website resumes are from unemployed job seekers. Print employment ads are expensive and reach only 12 percent of adults with household incomes over $50,000.

## Scorecard

CareerConnection's strategy of targeting passive job seekers in local markets with focused virtual job fairs gives us a significant competitive advantage.

**Virtual Job Fair Competitors**

| | Client Customized Radio Ads | Promoted through Local Radio | Targeted Demographics | Investment Required |
|---|---|---|---|---|
| CareerConnections.com | Yes | Yes | Yes | $995-$4,995 |
| Jobs.com | No | CBS Stations only | No | $2,000-$8,500 |
| CareerMosaic | No | No | No | $4,500 |

**Resume Posting Board Competitors**

| | Promoted through Local Radio | Targets Passive Job Seekers | Provides Current Resumes from Local Market | Requires Labor Intensive Process | Creates Sense of Urgency |
|---|---|---|---|---|---|
| CareerConnections.com | Yes | Yes | Yes | No | Yes |
| Monster | No | No | No | Yes | No |
| CareerPath | No | No | No | Yes | No |
| CareerBuilder | No | No | No | Yes | No |
| Headhunter.net | No | No | No | Yes | No |
| HotJobs | No | No | No | Yes | No |

Some "experts" say that the larger a resume database gets the more difficult and time consuming it becomes to search.

Monster.com's founder and CEO, Jeff Taylor, admits that big resume services like his can be a black hole for job listings and resumes. "I think the matching process is begging for innovation."

**Aloha Cottage Health Services**

"This was our first Virtual Job Fair. It was so informative and we got a great response. We're already planning for the next event!"

*Joanne Clarkston*
*Aloha Cottage Health Services*
*Human Resources Manager*

**SelectCare**

"Of all the Internet recruiting we are currently doing, the Virtual Job Fair made it possible for us to target specific demographics and get results!"

*Lori Collins*
*SelectCare Individual Financial Services*
*Human Resources Specialist*

**Greyhound Transportation International**

"The CareerConnections Virtual Job Fair got us results! We will be participating in all of the Virtual Job Fairs in 2000."

*Julie Jones*
*Greyhound Transportation International*
*Human Resources*

**Macmillan**

"I just wanted to let you know that it was a pleasure working with you on the Virtual Job Fair. We were extremely pleased with the results, ease of use, and the excellent customer service."

*John Reynolds*
*Macmillan*
*Human Resources Manager*

**Parklane Chevrolet**

"We received numerous resumes for several different positions. From sales to automotive technicians, we had a large number of qualified candidates to choose from."

*Reginald Stanley*
*Parklane Chevrolet*
*Human Resources Manager*

**IBM**

"We received 45 qualified resumes for several different positions at IBM. So far we have hired 25 people from just one CareerConnections Virtual Job Fair!"

*Henry Lincoln*
*IBM*
*Staffing*

**Our Clients—Cleveland, January 2000**

1. Compuware
2. Art Van
3. Macmillan
4. 7Eleven
5. IBM
6. Frito Lay
7. SelectCare
8. Creative Solutions
9. Proto-Tech
10. Eisenhower Center
11. Qualex
12. Army
13. CCX
14. Kinko's
15. Ameritech
16. CTS
17. CPI
18. Aloha Cottage Health Services
19. CDI Information Technology Services
20. ACSIA
21. E&E Manufacturing
22. Central Transportation International
23. Village Life Care Retirement Community
24. Parklane Chevrolet
25. Domino's Pizza
26. Enterprise Rent-a-Car
27. Sagemark Consulting

**Our Clients—Boston, April 2000**

1. Children's Hospital, Toledo, Ohio
2. Macmillan
3. Firestone Tire & Service Centers
4. AirTouch Cellular
5. Anthem Life
6. Dominion
7. Safelite Auto Glass
8. Idea Integration
9. IBM
10. Huckleberry House Inc.
11. Cardinal Health Inc.
12. Uniprise
13. United Healthcare
14. Kmart
15. Executive Jet

1. Little Caesars' Pizza
2. Ameritech
3. Macmillan
4. Valvoline
5. Firestone Tire & Service Centers
6. Citibank
7. IBM
8. Overland Park
9. SelectCare
10. CCX
11. Comerica
12. Olympia Entertainment
13. Kelly Services
14. CTS
15. Alcoa
16. Steak 'n Shake
17. Parklane Chevrolet
18. Sports & Entertainment Dome
19. Compuware
20. Ohio Bank
21. ICA
22. Vision Information Technologies
23. IKON
24. Morgan & Reilly L.L.P.
25. BT Boulevard Retirement Community
26. Enterprise Rent-a-Car
27. ACSIA
28. Parkedale Pharmaceuticals
29. TEK systems
30. Carhartt
31. Army
32. Aloha Cottags Health Services
33. Verizon Wireless

**Our Clients— Cleveland, June 2000**

1. WFDA Sports Radio AM 1010
2. FM 103
3. ABC
4. The Light 1420
5. LIV
6. V96.3 FM Jazz
7. WDEQ Newsradio 830
8. WONK 93.9 FM Cleveland's Soft Rock
9. 106.9 Smooth Rock WSTE
10. 95.5 FM Cleveland's Talkradio
11. WADR 91.9
12. WXYZ 1260 AM
13. FM 102.7 WCKL
14. 970 WBOR The Voice of Ohio
15. 104 WNOC
16. 93.3 Solid Rock
17. WRN

**Radio Station Alliances**

18. 87 XYS
19. 109.9 Country Life

**MARKETING STRATEGY**

**To take Internet recruiting beyond job boards to integrated solutions.**

How it works.

1. Build relationships with human resources professional on a personal level
   - Become actively involved in the Society for Human Resource Management (SHRM)
   - Target 430 local chapters nationally with over 200,000 members
   - Utilize SHRM member directories and other strategic human resources lists to reach decision makers

2. Implement a pro-active database management sales plan to maximize our sales results
   - Use Treasure Chest 5.0 database software to segment the market and achieve a competitive sales advantage
   - Develop qualified leads through a focused lead generation telemarketing program
   - Augment our database sales effort by high impact marketing techniques through email, SHRM banner ads, etc.

3. Use the power of radio to create awareness with human resources professionals and passive job seekers
   - Reach human resources decision makers prior to a Virtual Job Fair with a pre-emptive radio campaign
   - Promote each ten-day Virtual Job Fair with intensive radio advertising (300-350 spots) to link with passive job seekers
   - Promote our clients and their opportunities through development of customized radio ads

4. Assure that our website is fast and convenient to use
   - Provide sophisticated company profiling
   - Maintain an effective direct link between candidates and companies
   - Provide automated job postings

CareerConnections's marketing strategy is aggressive, disciplined, and efficient.

**FINANCIAL OVERVIEW**

**Number of Virtual Job Fairs**

| | |
|---|---|
| 2000 | 7 |
| 2001 | 48 |
| 2002 | 96 |
| 2003 | 150 |

**Projected Revenue (thousands)**

| | |
|---|---|
| 2000 | $315 |
| 2001 | $3,025 |
| 2002 | $6,624 |
| 2003 | $11,250 |

**Projected Pre-tax Income (thousands)**

| | |
|---|---|
| 2000 | $130 |
| 2001 | $1,262 |
| 2002 | $1,987 |
| 2003 | $3,375 |

| Projected Net Income | The Math | | | | | The Math |
|---|---|---|---|---|---|---|
| **(000's)** | **2000** | **%** | | **2001** | **%** | |
| **Revenues** | | | | | | |
| VJFs | $315 | 100 | | $3,025 | 100 | |
| **Expenses** | | | | | | |
| Equipment | $10 | 3 | | $90 | 3 | |
| VJFs | $160 | 51 | | $1,566 | 52 | |
| • Radio Advertising | | | | | | |
| • Event Promotion | | | | | | |
| • Compensation | | | | | | |
| Operating | $15 | 5 | | $107 | 4 | |
| **Total** | **$185** | **59** | | **$1,763** | **59** | |
| **Pre-Tax Income** | **$130** | **41** | | **$1,262** | **41** | |
| **Taxes** | **$46** | **15** | | **$442** | **15** | |
| **Net Income** | **$84** | **27** | | **$820** | **27** | |

Equity injection required to achieve future growth.

**CRITICAL SUCCESS FACTORS**

To compete and succeed in the top forty markets, a minimum of $1,000,000 in additional capitalization is essential.

**How the money will be invested**

| | |
|---|---|
| Enhancement to the website | $35,000 |
| Computers, software, network server | $30,000 |
| Phone system | $25,000 |

**Key Staff Additions**

| | | |
|---|---|---|
| 1. National Account Relationship Manager | $80,000 | |
| 2. Inside Sales Manager | $60,000 | |
| 3. Seven Inside Salespeople | $280,000 | |
| 4. Two Administrative/Customer Service People | $85,000 | |
| | $120,000 | |
| | | $625,000 |

**Working Capital**

| | | |
|---|---|---|
| 1. Boston Corporate Office | | |
| 2. Advertisement and Promotion for Growth | | |
| 3. Establish Benefit Plan | | |
| 4. Miscellaneous Operating Expenses | | |
| | | $285,000 |

## TOP FORTY MARKETS

1. New York
2. Los Angeles
3. Chicago
4. San Francisco
5. Philadelphia
6. Dallas
7. Cleveland
8. Boston
9. Washington, DC
10. Houston
11. Atlanta
12. Miami
13. Seattle
14. San Diego
15. Phoenix
16. Minneapolis
17. New Jersey
18. St. Louis
19. Baltimore
20. Tampa
21. Pittsburgh
22. Denver
23. Detroit
24. Portland
25. Cincinnati
26. San Jose
27. Riverside
28. Sacramento
29. Kansas City
30. Milwaukee
31. San Antonio
32. Providence
33. Toledo
34. Salt Lake City
35. Norfolk
36. Charlotte
37. Indianapolis
38. Orlando
39. Las Vegas
40. New Orleans

# Online Merchant

BUSINESS PLAN

## E-RETURN SOLUTIONS

*43600 Wonderland Boulevard*
*Kansas City, Missouri 64105*

*E-Return Solutions offers a unique and proprietary solution to managing the receipt, handling, and resale of returned merchandise for electronic commerce and multi-channel retailers. E-Return provides these retailers with the opportunity to entirely outsource the burdensome, complex, and costly chore of managing product returns. This plan was provided by Jason Sears and Esther Schuller and was compiled in conjunction with the MOOT CORP® competition sponsored by the University of Texas at Austin.*

- EXECUTIVE SUMMARY

- THE OPPORTUNITY

- SOLUTION & VALUE

- TECHNICAL INFRASTRUCTURE OVERVIEW

- MARKETING & SALES STRATEGY

- COMPETITION & RISKS

- GROWTH & HARVEST

- MANAGEMENT TEAM & BOARD OF ADVISORS

- FINANCIALS

- APPENDICES

## EXECUTIVE SUMMARY

*"There's going to be a fallout this holiday season. Most online merchants don't preserve customer relationships."*

It is common knowledge that the next evolution of online commerce involves developing sustainable customer relationships, but what exactly does that mean for retailers? Many sophisticated online retailers have initiated customized delivery solutions using consumer profiles developed from an online shoppers' clicks and purchases, but that is only the beginning. It is imperative that retailers ensure that the online experience provides comparable customer service as that provided in the traditional brick-and-mortar channel. In fact, 87 percent of shoppers who spent at least $2,000 online during the past six months will abandon a website if they encounter bad customer service. E-Return Solutions addresses a traditionally neglected aspect of this customer service—managing the return process.

E-commerce companies, hoping to grow market share, are feverishly pursuing customer acquisition and brand recognition strategies. These companies are in a relentless race to become the recognized online leader; however, lost amid their frantic efforts to drive sales, many of these companies have failed to address a critical aspect of their business—logistics, and in particular reverse logistics. Reverse logistics is the process of managing the receipt, handling, and disposition of returned merchandise.

With return rates for the online apparel industry ranging from 18-50 percent, an estimated $3.6 to $10.1 billion in returns will be generated by 2003. With online apparel sales expected to increase 13 times in the next five years, the handling of returned merchandise—typically handled by most companies as an exception process—will become extremely cost-intensive and disruptive. E-Return manages the receipt, handling, and resale of returned merchandise for e-commerce and multi-channel apparel manufacturers and retailers, and allows companies to remain focused on driving sales.

While the handling of returned merchandise has contributed to retailer frustration for many years, the explosion in e-commerce has presented a new set of challenges to the retail industry. Multi-channel retailing (the practice of selling merchandise through numerous channels such as brick-and-mortar, online, and/or mail-order catalogs) involves managing multiple forward distribution and fulfillment strategies—each of which involves specific shipping economies, packaging practices, and inventory management requirements. Complicating the process even further, returns involve processing and valuing damaged merchandise, aggregating and preparing merchandise for resale, and mitigating damaged relationships with frustrated customers.

The industry is enormous, the problem is substantial, and E-Return has created the solution. E-Return will become the industry standard for e-commerce returns, beginning with the apparel industry and ultimately penetrating diverse markets including the toys and games and home furnishings industries. No other reverse logistics provider offers a comprehensive solution that addresses all return concerns from improved customer care to increased bottom line profitability. In a nutshell, E-Return lowers our clients' cost, increases their revenues, and helps ensure customer loyalty. E-Return is the answer.

## The Solution

E-Return offers a unique and proprietary solution to managing the receipt, handling, and resale of returned merchandise for electronic commerce and multi-channel retailers. E-Return provides these retailers with the opportunity to entirely outsource the burdensome, complex, and costly chore of managing product returns. E-Return is designed to meet the requirements of their industry and utilizes specialized processing techniques and the latest technology to deliver:

- Top-notch customer support
- The most efficient handling of returned merchandise
- The optimization of merchandise resale and alternative methods of disposition through the use of a sophisticated and dynamic business-to-business exchange

Our solution is divided into four components: (1) customer care, (2) operations, (3) product disposition, and (4) post-transaction supply chain management. As the first company to offer all of these critical components, E-Return provides the following value to its clients:

- Improved customer satisfaction and sustainability
- Improved financial returns on returned merchandise
- Reduced processing costs
- Increased sales and profitability
- Improved asset utilization

Based on estimated revenues and costs over a five-year horizon, E-Return will require $3.5 million to launch and fund the company's growth until the second round of financing, which is scheduled to raise an additional $8 million by late 2001. The initial $3.5 million of funding will be used to expand the management team and sales force, lease fixed assets, develop and purchase necessary technology, and secure two charter customers.

## Funding Requirements

E-Return's founding team and current management includes:

## The Management Team

- **Anthony Ray, President**—Mr. Ray's background is in management consulting at KPMG and Center for Applied Strategy (CAST). He has advised emerging-growth and established companies in the services and technology industries on information technology, operations, and marketing strategies. Mr. Ray is pursuing his M.B.A. and his Juris Doctor joint-degree from the University of Missouri at Kansas City. He received a B.A. in Economics from Columbia University at New York.

- **Barton Fitz, Director of Marketing and Sales**—Mr. Fitz has marketing and sales experience in both the financial services and consumer goods industries. At IBM, he developed national marketing and sales programs for corporate and consumer clients. Mr. Fitz received a B.S. degree in finance from New York University, and is pursuing his M.B.A. at the University of Missouri at Kansas City.

- **Robert Romano, CPA, Director of Finance**—Mr. Romano's experience includes audit and financial analysis with Ernst & Young and later with Shell Oil's global internal audit division. His experience includes initial and secondary public stock offerings. Mr. Romano completed his B.S. degree in accountancy at the University of Michigan and is pursuing his M.B.A. at the University of Missouri at Kansas City.

- **Rachel Summers, Director of Strategic Operations**—Ms. Summers's experience includes designing, implementing, and managing operations and financial processes and controls for Credit Suisse Financial Products as well as emerging-growth companies. Ms. Summers has a B.B.A. degree in finance from the University of Missouri at Kansas City and is pursuing her M.B.A. from the same university.

- **Justin Roberts, Director of Technology**—Mr. Roberts's technical and managerial experience includes software development, database modeling, and systems management projects working for multiple companies located throughout the U.S. Mr. Roberts received a B.S. degree in mathematics from the University of Illinois at Urbana and is pursuing his M.B.A. at the University of Missouri at Kansas City.

## Board of Advisors

- **William Fanchon**—Mr. Fanchon is founder and president of CFO Services, Inc. which provides business consulting services including merger and acquisition advisory services, financial and credit analysis, business valuations, loan procurement, business planning and strategic planning to small to mid-size businesses. Mr. Fanchon serves on the advisory board of multiple start-up ventures in the Kansas City area.

- **Jason Williams**—Mr. Williams has over 18 years of retail management experience in merchandising and operations. Mr. Williams is Director of Retail Operations for MGM Grand Hotel and Casino. Additional retail experience includes Bullocks department store, a division of R. H. Macy Corporation, where he served as divisional merchandise manager and general manager.

- **Abdul Ruiz**—Dr. Ruiz received his Ph.D. in MIS from Indiana State University and is currently a professor in the MIS department at the University of Missouri at Kansas City. Dr. Ruiz's research involves various aspects and components of online markets and exchanges.

## Professional Advisors

- **Thompson, Wall, & Heidenreich**—currently filing a provisional patent on the E-Return Interface Exchange (ERIE), Merchant Interface Application (MIA), and the Secondary Market Exchange (SME).

## THE OPPORTUNITY

## An Introduction to Reverse Logistics

According to Forrester Research, the apparel industry will be inundated with over 550 million returned garments in the year 2000 that will cost an estimated $3 billion to process. Of these, 19 million returns will be generated by the online channel alone, based on Gartner Group estimates of 20 percent return rates and sales of $5.6 billion for apparel purchased online. Given their immediate focus on customer acquisition and order fulfillment, apparel manufacturers will be unable to manage the returned merchandise in a timely or cost-effective manner. Consequently, manufacturers will suffer from symptoms of poor reverse logistics management including:

- Substantial customer dissatisfaction with the returns process and subsequent loss of customer loyalty
- Excessive handling and processing costs due to the lack of accurate reporting capabilities, merchandise handling technologies, and standard procedures
- Significant loss of revenue due to the inability to recapture the costs of the returned merchandise

Reverse logistics is the process of managing the receipt, handling, and disposition of returned merchandise. Distinguished from forward distribution and order fulfillment, the reverse logistics function is comprised of a set of unique, complex, and time-sensitive tasks. Optimal performance of these tasks—which includes reviewing product quality, crediting customer accounts, and immediate resale of the merchandise—requires specialized operations and information systems.

Although returns represent a significant cost component of a manufacturer's total logistics costs, it was only recently that reverse logistics began to receive the attention of executive management. Reasons for this include:

- Reverse logistics do not directly generate revenue
- Manufacturers focus resources on staying ahead of the fashion curve
- Capital expenditures on reverse logistics do not offer a return on assets
- E-commerce manufacturers focus on acquiring customers and establishing a web presence

With the explosion of online and mail-order retailing, and the excessive high rates of product returns associated with these channels, manufacturers are beginning to realize the importance of an effective reverse logistics function. As competition continues to increase, apparel manufacturers will be forced to embrace innovative strategies that go beyond offering the lowest prices and user-friendly websites to include enhancing customer care and minimizing logistics costs beyond the initial purchase.

Traditional reverse logistics practices are especially impractical and ineffective for e-commerce retailers ("e-tailers") and mail-order catalog apparel manufacturers primarily because they contribute to poor customer care, operational inefficiency, and minimal financial return on returned apparel.

**Current Reverse Logistics in Electronic Commerce and Mail-Order Environment**

### Poor Customer Care

Contrary to customer demands, online and mail-order apparel manufacturers do not offer the same level of service and convenience for merchandise returns as provided by brick-and-mortar retailers. Customers are often confronted with a difficult and time-consuming ordeal when returning items purchased on the web or by catalog.

Typically, the consumer must retrieve the retailer's return address from the website or customer service representative, re-package and label the return item, bring the package to the USPS or UPS office during business hours, and wait in line for proper postage. The consumer must then track the product until the retailer acknowledges receipt to ensure subsequent credit on the return.

Unsurprisingly, a recent E-Return survey found that 95 percent of online consumers are dissatisfied with current e-tailers' return policies. Moreover, 66 percent of online consumers factor the e-tailer's return policy into their purchasing decisions, suggesting that companies unable to improve customer service risk significant loss of sales.

Current e-tailer and mail-order return policies also result in excessive obsolescence costs. Apparel, due to constantly changing seasonal requirements and fashion trends, is subject to high obsolescence costs. The Reverse Logistics Executive Council reports that obsolescence diminishes the value of clothing by approximately 10-20 percent every 30 days. Consumers confronted with the inconvenience of returning merchandise purchased online or via a mail-order catalog will often hold an item the maximum time allowed by the manufacturers before returning an item. The estimated duration of this holding period ranges from 3-8 weeks, potentially costing manufacturers up to 40 percent of the returned garment's original value.

### Inefficient and Costly Handling Procedures

Most warehouses are designed for forward distribution. Thus, handling returned items is an exception process with a low priority. Returned items may remain in the warehouse for weeks before it is processed, further increasing obsolescence costs and diminishing the clothing's resale value. Many warehouses are not equipped with the technology or personnel to efficiently handle individually returned garments. Receiving, sorting, and repackaging returns is a time-intensive process that detracts from the manufacturer's ability to fulfill orders, and costs an estimated 2-3 times as much per item as forward distribution.

**Minimal Financial Returns**

Once the returned items have been processed, manufacturers typically hold the garments in their warehouses until there is a substantial inventory build-up, at which time the merchandise is liquidated at local clearance sales. These clearance sales are intended to simply move the merchandise out of the warehouse and, therefore, fail to maximize recovery on these assets.

## SOLUTION AND VALUE

### The Solution

E-Return offers the first total reverse logistics and product disposition service specifically designed to manage returned merchandise for e-tailers and multi-channel apparel manufacturers. While E-Return never assumes title of the manufacturer's merchandise, it does offer the most sophisticated and advanced service available to ensure minimal operations costs and maximum financial return on the merchandise.

Our service is composed of four components:

1. Customer care
2. Operations
3. Product disposition
4. Post-transaction supply chain management

Combined, the components represent a total solution that relieves the manufacturer of the costly and time-consuming reverse logistics process, while providing premier customer service and optimal performance.

**Customer Care**

The customer care component of E-Return's solution will enable the retailer's online customer to link to the E-Return website, designed as a seamless interface to the retailer's site, and automatically receive a return merchandise authorization (RMA) number for the merchandise to be returned. Customers only need to write the RMA number on the pre-paid and pre-addressed E-Return return label, which is included with the original package, and can then conveniently place the package in the mail from their home or office. Also, online customers will automatically receive an e-mail confirmation once E-Return has received and reviewed the returned merchandise.

The returns process for mail-order catalog customers is essentially the same. These customers will also receive a pre-paid and pre-addressed mailing label with their purchase. If, however, the RMA cannot be assigned online because the manufacturer is not accessible online or the customer does not have access to the Internet, the customer need only call the manufacturer's customer service department to obtain the RMA number. The package can then conveniently be mailed to E-Return.

**Operations**

E-Return's operations component will incorporate both a web-based interface that seamlessly communicates with our client's website and a centralized return center (CRC) equipped with leading-edge technology and resources dedicated to the most-efficient processing of returned merchandise. Once the returned merchandise has been received, E-Return will immediately identify, inspect, and sort the clothing for resale or other disposition. E-Return's CRC staff will utilize a combination of bar-coding, warehousing technology, and inventory management systems to ensure rapid processing and precise control of the merchandise. Since E-Return's focus is the management of merchandise returns, the processing of returns is the highest priority. This enables a substantial reduction in obsolescence costs due to inefficiency or oversight.

### Product Disposition

After the merchandise has been sorted, E-Return will prepare it for resale or other disposition. E-Return's custom-built product management and disposition management applications will allow the apparel manufacturer to establish and modify merchandise resale and disposition policies in real-time to reflect each manufacturer's branding and re-distribution strategy, product life cycles, and goals for maximizing financial returns on the returned garments.

E-Return will also design a dynamic business-to-business exchange to facilitate the resale and charitable contribution of returned merchandise to secondary markets, thereby avoiding inventory build-up at the manufacturer's warehouse and the potential for loss due to shrinkage. The exchange is continually updated to reflect available merchandise both in the warehouse and currently in shipment from the customer. The manufacturer will determine the parameters of each sale to the secondary market. The exchange will also govern the donation and destruction of items according to the disposition parameters established by the manufacturer.

### Post-Transaction Supply Chain Management

E-Return's solution creates the only information system available that provides the manufacturer with complete post-transaction supply chain management and control capabilities. From the moment the customer generates an RMA until the resale or alternative disposition of the merchandise, the manufacturer has access to real-time knowledge of the volume and value of merchandise in the reverse logistics channel. Consequently, the manufacturer will be empowered to better control manufacturing quality, inventory, product life cycles and customer satisfaction.

As the first and only provider of reverse logistics services designed for e-commerce and multi-channel apparel manufacturers, E-Return is uniquely positioned to improve every aspect of managing returned merchandise.

**The Value Proposition**

### Reduced Processing Costs

E-Return incorporates the benefits of a centralized operation, a highly-efficient merchandise handling process, and innovative technology to reduce the manufacturer's reverse logistics costs by an average of 22 percent per item, based on estimated labor costs and overhead. These cost-savings directly impact our client's bottom line.

### Increased Sales

E-Return's services will result in increased and more profitable sales by facilitating the returns process and improving the manufacturer's ability to cross-sell merchandise. E-Return minimizes the unpleasantness and inconvenience of returning products, thereby restoring customer confidence in the manufacturer and increasing the likelihood of future sales.

### Improved Financial Return on Merchandise

E-Return's system will improve our client's average recovery on returned merchandise by an estimated 5-10 percent by minimizing customer and warehouse holding times. Our convenient and easy-to-use process encourages online customers to promptly ship return items. In fact, E-Return will automatically generate reminders to customers who have registered a return but have forgotten or neglected to mail the merchandise. Once received at E-Return's centralized return center, the merchandise will be immediately processed and prepared for resale or an alternative disposition.

Moreover, E-Return's web-based, business-to-business exchange will provide secondary marketers the opportunity to bid-up the purchase price on the returned merchandise—further increasing the manufacturer's cost recovery.

### Enhanced Customer Care

E-Return's system will greatly enhance the manufacturer's ability to provide customer care by improving the convenience and ease of returning merchandise by providing the consumer with an easy-to-use, web-based interface that automatically registers the return and generates an RMA number. Also, customers will be provided with return labels that include a return address and pre-paid postage and will be notified upon E-Return's receipt of the merchandise.

E-Return's system enables manufacturers to customize return policies for online and direct mail customers by dictating the shipping and restocking charges for each customer. This allows the manufacturer to reward loyal customers and discourage the abuse of favorable return policies.

### Improved Supply Chain Management

E-Return's unique system allows the manufacturer to manage the post-transaction portion of the supply chain, tracking returned merchandise from the moment it is registered into the system until its ultimate disposition. Post-transaction supply chain management provides numerous benefits to the manufacturer including improved manufacturing quality control, inventory and product life cycle management, and customer satisfaction.

### Improved Asset Utilization

The main challenge in today's rapidly changing e-commerce and multi-channel environment is not to commit to assets that do not support a company's core competency or limit its flexibility, according to Andersen Consulting's supply chain management practice. E-Return will provide e-commerce and multi-channel apparel manufacturers with the first opportunity to capitalize on a reverse logistics solution specifically designed to satisfy their requirements without requiring significant capital expenditure.

## Customer Care, Operations, & Product Disposition

E-Return's approach to reverse logistics eliminates the hassle of managing returns and improves our client's bottom line. The company's unique "one touch" handling process reduces our client's returns processing costs by an average of 22 percent, based on conservative wage estimates for employees to receive, credit, handle, and redirect returned items and for on- and off-site warehouse space. E-Return also reduces obsolescence costs by reducing customer return and merchandise handling time. Finally, E-Return increases the resale value of the returned merchandise by first aggregating the apparel and then making it instantly available to secondary markets through E-Return's dynamic secondary market business-to-business exchange.

## TECHNICAL INFRASTRUCTURE OVERVIEW

E-Return's technical infrastructure, explained in the following section, will combine off-the-shelf software with internally developed proprietary components to provide a comprehensive and unique solution.

## Customer Care

### Point of Origin

E-tailers and mail-order catalog manufacturers using E-Return's solution will be given return slips to include with all online and mail-order catalog purchases. Each slip will contain a pre-addressed mailing label, convenient pre-paid postage, and instructions to the online customer on how to return merchandise.

To initiate the return process, online customers will visit E-Return's web interface, reached via the e-tailer's website, to initiate the return process and to specify the item(s) to be returned. The website, branded with our client's colors and logo, first requests the customer to specify what item is being returned and why it is being returned, and then automatically generates a Return Merchandise Authorization (RMA) number. This allows E-Return to immediately capture critical merchandise data at the moment the consumer makes the decision to send the items back to the e-tailer.

Mail-order returns will be similarly handled, except that the call center representative will log on to the website rather than the customer.

**E-Return's Return Notification Application (ERRNA)**
E-Return's Return Notification Application (ERRNA) is the web-based application referred to above designed to capture critical information on the returned merchandise at its point of origin. The ERRNA will use the customer's invoice number to generate an XML-based request to our client's site requesting the contents of the invoice(s). Please see Appendix E for additional information on the use of this technology.

The ERRNA application will:

- allow customers to specify what merchandise they intend to return
- issue invoice-content requests to our client
- generate a Return Merchandise Authorization (RMA) number
- enable the e-tailer and mail-order catalog manufacturer to provide preferential treatment to individual consumers on a transaction-by-transaction basis. Our clients can then identify preferential customers to waive shipping and handling costs or, conversely, penalize "return abusers" with additional restocking charges.
- save all customer return information for later use at the Customer Return Center Management System (CRCMS)

**E-Return Interface Engine (ERIE)**
The E-Return Interface Engine (ERIE) is a Java-based server-side application that will be installed on our clients' (the e-tailers') web server. The ERIE will act as the interface between the ERRNA and the database of customer and invoice information, translating requests for customer information into a suitable query format and then transmitting the results.

**Shipping and Transportation**                                                    **Operations**
E-Return will outsource shipping and transportation to third-party carriers.

**Receiving and Processing**
Upon receipt of the merchandise, E-Return will record the RMA number and the associated shipping costs for the merchandise. E-Return clients are notified electronically of shipping charges incurred on behalf of each customer for charge-back purposes. At this time, each item will be tagged with a E-Return bar code tag. The bar code tag will be scanned into the Warehouse Management System and will track both the original RMA number and the individual customer SKU number of each item throughout the entire system.

Products will be individually inspected and identified as one of three categories: good, flawed, or destroyed. This information will be entered into the warehouse information systems via a touch-screen and will dictate how the merchandise should be handled within E-Return's warehouse.

### Warehousing (CRC)

Initially, E-Return intends to locate its Centralized Return Center (CRC) in Jefferson City, Missouri. Jefferson City provides affordable warehouse space and labor, as well as access to the technical expertise required for systems development. The CRC will be an estimated 20,000 square feet to provide sufficient capacity for E-Return's initial clients.

### Central Return Center Management System (CRCMS)

E-Return will use an off-the-shelf Warehouse Management System (WMS) since a number of these systems are currently available and offer the combined functionality of bar code recognition and customizable inventory locations. Internal development staff will identify, document, and develop the additional E-Return requirements not sufficiently addressed by the chosen WMS.

Among the technology utilized to ensure complete and accurate inventory tracking will be stationary and portable bar code scanners, bar code printers, and rolling workstations equipped with touch-screen functionality. These technologies will allow scalability associated with increased processing volumes.

## Product Disposition

Once the merchandise has been identified and sorted, it will be ready for resale or alternative disposition. E-Return's disposition services as designed are unique and innovative and will give the client the ability to dictate disposition policies in real-time that incorporate marketing strategies and the particular garment's stage in its product cycle.

E-Return will establish relationships with numerous retailers in the secondary market, at which point each secondary marketer will be "graded" according to their individual resale practices. For example, franchised outlets may receive a high grade since merchandise is resold in a controlled environment while exporters unable to guarantee retailing practices will receive a lower grade. E-Return's clients will then identify which grades of secondary marketers are allowed to purchase returned merchandise.

E-Return's clients can also direct certain merchandise to be donated to the charities of their choice. In these instances, E-Return will track the value of the merchandise contributed so that our clients can realize the tax benefits and goodwill of these donations.

Finally, any merchandise not resold or donated will be destroyed or recycled. In each case, the disposition process will be administered according to environmental regulations. Destruction expenses will be passed through to the client.

### Merchant Interface Application (MIA)

Using the MIA, the E-Return's client will communicate the disposition policies by label, product line, or SKU. The variables captured by the system include holding duration, resale restrictions prohibiting sales to specific secondary marketers, and donation/destruction thresholds. These parameters are then transmitted to the CRC Management System (CRCMS) and the Secondary Market Exchange (SME).

### Secondary Market Exchange (SME)

E-Return's dynamic business-to-business exchange, the SME, will manage the posting of merchandise to the secondary markets as it becomes available. The auction-style exchange will identify the merchandise, the duration of the exchange for that merchandise, and the minimum bid price. This minimum bid price will be calculated based on the merchandise pricing logic specified by our client. Once a particular exchange period closes, the SME will identify the highest bidder, debit the appropriate vendor's account, and post a work order to the CRCMS to have the merchandise shipped.

The SME will also allow our client to pre-select charities for the contribution of returned merchandise. Charities requesting particular merchandise may submit a merchandise request through the SME system. In addition to immediately designating merchandise for contribution, e-tailers and manufacturers can specify rules through the SME that specify that once returned merchandise reaches the end of its pre-determined resale holding duration, or its value drops below a designated level, the merchandise should be shipped to a specified charity.

E-Return will engage the apparel market through a three-phase marketing approach, illustrated and explained below.

**MARKETING &
SALES STRATEGY
Marketing Approach**

### Phase 1—Refine the approach

During Phase 1, E-Return will conduct extensive market research to further define our target customers and better understand their specific needs. Phase 1 will be executed without promotion to avoid unnecessary attention from potential competition.

Concurrent with the secondary research, we will utilize contacts provided by our advisory board members, investors, and our own previous research to identify and obtain two charter customers by September 2000. E-Return will work closely with our charter customers to further develop our promotions and sales strategies. E-Return will hire a vice president of marketing and sales with substantial apparel industry experience and contacts to oversee the development of our client base and marketing campaign.

### Phase 2—Inform the marketplace

Phase 2 will commence in November 2000, just before the holiday season, and last until March of 2001. E-Return will use information gathered from our charter customers to refine product and service offerings. To augment post-holiday sales efforts, E-Return will actively begin personal contact with our prospects prior to the holiday season. Concurrently, E-Return will conduct several awareness and brand-building activities including mass mailings, advertisements in key industry publications, and participation in industry trade shows. We will also actively promote the success of our charter customers. We anticipate hiring a sales manager during January 2001 in preparation for Phase 3.

### Phase 3—Sell the solution

After successfully managing the holiday season for our two charter customers, E-Return will initiate full-scale sales efforts, as part of Phase 3, in March of 2001. Initially, all efforts will target the manufacturer's e-commerce and mail-order catalog sales. Because it is the e-commerce channel that presents the most difficult challenges for our clients, selling our e-commerce solution will be a logical entry point to establishing a relationship with our clients.

### Phase 4—Up-sell existing clients

Once E-Return has established strong relationships with its clients and has proven the value of its services, we will, starting in 2003, up-sell our clients and begin to handle returned merchandise from all of their channels including those by mail-order customers and brick-and-mortar retailers. According to the American Apparel Manufacturers Association, these two channels will generate over 500 million returned garments in 2003.

The apparel industry represents an attractive opportunity for E-Return for several reasons. First, online apparel sales are rapidly growing. According to Forrester Research, online retail apparel sales next year will approach $5.6 billion, resulting in approximately 19 million returned garments. This number will swell to 67 million returned garments by 2003. E-Return expects to process about 8-12 percent of this online apparel return market. The mail-order

**Market Size**

channel is growing more than 6 percent annually, and will generate an estimated 50 million returned garments by 2003.

Second, the apparel industry experiences relatively high return rates due to seasonal factors and the subjective nature of the merchandise. Third, returned garments are relatively easy to manage from a reverse logistics perspective, mainly due to their less complex nature and consequent ease with which irregular and defective garments are identified. Finally, apparel suffers from high obsolescence costs as styles change from one season to the next—a costly problem minimized by E-Return's solution.

## Customer Profile

E-Return will initially target mid-tier apparel manufacturers that either plan to sell—or have already begun to sell—merchandise online or through mail-order catalogs. These manufacturers will be the most unprepared to administer the complexities of e-commerce and multi-channel reverse logistics management.

## Product Positioning and Pitch

E-Return has spoken with apparel manufacturers, industry analysts, and online consumers. Based on this research and continued feedback, E-Return will position itself as the only provider of comprehensive reverse logistics services catering to e-commerce and multi-channel apparel manufacturers. Our marketing and sales pitch will emphasize our ability to enhance customer care and improve financial recovery on returned merchandise. E-Return will work with its charter customers to further refine the marketing efforts and sales pitch to better reflect potential clients' needs.

Once E-Return enlists a client, the manufacturer will be unlikely to defect to a would-be competitor because of the relationship-oriented nature of the business, our apparel focus, switching costs relating the technical systems' interfaces, and a reluctance to sacrifice their customers' return experience.

## Pricing

E-Return will utilize a multi-schemed pricing model that reflects the company's various services. Our pricing is designed to align E-Return's incentives with those of the apparel manufacturer. In addition to per-item processing fees, commissions are charged as a percentage of sales to secondary marketers. Clients are billed on a monthly basis.

## Customer Acquisition

**Costing Model**

> *"I have spent some time in the last few months listening to apparel purveyors—brick-and-mortar, pure-play, catalog, retail, some or all of those—talk about returns, and they seem not to have anywhere to go for statistics either."*

Retailers are generally unaware of their actual reverse logistics costs. Consequently, E-Return must educate prospective clients about the costs and complexities associated with this function. E-Return's sales representatives will act as consultants to our clients' technical, accounting, and operations management. Utilizing E-Return's costing model, sales representatives will be able to quantify the true costs of processing, aggregating, and re-selling returned merchandise for each individual client. The model will include the indirect costs associated with a returned good, including warehouse space, labor costs, obsolescence costs, and shrinkage.

**Obtaining "Charter" Customers**
E-Return will target several small to mid-size apparel manufacturers as "charter" customers with whom we can work to finalize the system requirements. In exchange for their willingness

to partner with E-Return during the developmental stage and subsequent publicity campaigns, E-Return will customize and implement our charter customers' systems at no charge and substantially discount initial processing fees.

### Costs of Obtaining a New Client

E-Return will begin awareness and brand advertising in November 2000. Periodical advertising and direct mail will be utilized to establish initial contact. Awareness will also be generated through direct phone calls to potential clients before the holiday season. Advertising will increase after the holidays as we will marry the E-Return brand to the anticipated pain associated with post-holiday returns.

Direct sales calls will begin in March of 2001. From the first meeting to the close of the sale (about 3 months), we expect the sales process to include about four meetings between the client and E-Return's management team. E-Return estimates the cost of acquiring a customer to be approximately $40,000. This figure includes all sales-related expenses, including travel, client education, and on-site tours of E-Return's facilities.

E-Return intends to form strategic partnerships with freight providers and complementary technology firms, including vendors specializing in CRM, point-of-sale, and business-to-business exchange software. These relationships will provide increased cost savings and customer acquisition rates for our clients.

## Partnerships and Strategic Alliances

## Promotion

### Capitalizing on the "Charter" Client

Once E-Return proves its ability to effectively manage its "charter" clients' return processes through the peak merchandise returns period following Christmas 2000, the company will aggressively advertise its success through public relations campaigns and sales literature designed to give potential clients a "reason to believe."

### Direct Mailings and Web Presence

E-Return will conduct a focused direct-mailing initiative for a select group of small to mid-size multi-channel and purely e-commerce retailers. We will concentrate more marketing dollars to fewer prospects using simple, image-oriented direct mail composed of rich mailings and customized sales literature.

E-Return will also maintain a website that publicizes the company's services and demonstrates how the customer interface portion of our system facilitates the return process for the end-consumer. E-Return's website will feature a costing model that enables our prospective clients to estimate their current reverse logistics costs.

### Advertising and Public Relations

E-Return will build industry awareness and brand recognition by advertising in trade publications that cater to operations/logistics executives as well as appropriate mainstream periodicals. In addition, E-Return will aggressively publicize its success with the company's charter clients and participate in industry trade shows and conferences. Finally, E-Return will explore the feasibility of producing a "Best of Breed in the Industry" newsletter to promote the company's services and the benefits of administering effective reverse logistics.

## COMPETITION & RISKS
### Current and Potential Competition

The following table lists E-Return's current and potential competition by category. Although several companies offer partial reverse logistics solutions to retailers, E-Return offers the only solution combining the benefits of customer care, real-time merchandise disposition control, and total post-transaction supply chain management. For those companies currently handling this function in-house, the process is burdensome, ineffective and especially costly. When made aware of the E-Return solution, these companies will recognize the value of outsourcing their reverse logistics.

**Current and Potential Competition**

| Category of Logistics Provider | Multi-Channel, Reverse Logistics Provider | General Logistics Providers | Reverse Logistics Specialists | E-commerce Logistics Specialists | Shippers and Transportation Companies |
|---|---|---|---|---|---|
| Examples | E-Return | Consolidated Freight, USF Logistics | GENCO, Consolidated Freightways | NetShip, iShip | United States Postal Service, FedEx, UPS |
| Reverse Logistics Emphasis | X | X | X | | X |
| Apparel Industry Emphasis | X | | | | |
| Merchandise Processing Capability | X | | X | | |
| Multi-channel Capability | X | X | X | X | |
| Customer Care Capability | X | | | X | |
| Real-time Disposition Control Capability | X | | | | |
| Secondary Market Exchange | X | | | | |
| Total Post-Transaction SCM | X | | | | |

### Competitive Advantage and Sustainability

E-Return's competitive advantage stems from our ability to differentiate ourselves as the only reverse logistics specialist providing multi-channel support exclusive to the apparel industry. As such, the company will capitalize on its "first mover advantage" to establish a proven record of performance before the competition will be able to provide comparable services.

Several factors will help E-Return to sustain its competitive advantage. High barriers to entry include first mover advantages as well as proprietary technology and processes that are difficult, expensive, and time-consuming for competitors to emulate, thus creating a significant timing advantage. High switching costs associated with switching service providers include systems integration and data transfer will protect our customer base. Customized services, extended service contracts, and relationship management will extend the duration of our customers and will protect margins.

### Risks

Despite E-Return's expectation to become a leading reverse logistics provider, the company understands the risks associated with the venture. These risks are:

- **Sensitive Launch Time:** E-Return must aggressively pursue and develop a "charter" customer and consequent customer base while it has the first mover advantage.
- **Significant Launch and Ramp-up Costs:** E-Return will incur significant costs

associated with leasing fixed assets and developing technology before the company can generate profits.

- **Seasonal Nature of the Business:** E-Return plans to accommodate the seasonal spikes in merchandise volume with temporary staffing and additional shifts.
- **Potential Competition:** E-Return must aggressively market itself as the only company providing a comprehensive solution for multi-channel retailers. E-Return will develop strong customer relationships and extended service contracts as well as create strong brand equity that will make it difficult for competitors to establish a market presence.

### Phase 0: Pre-Launch (January 2000 - June 2000)

Pre-launch will be funded by internal sources. These efforts will focus on four areas: (1) coordinating legal preparation for launch, (2) completing of prototype and commencement of development of technical Phase 1, (3) conducting market research to develop client prospect list and refine approach, and (4) developing key relationships with potential charter customers and disposition channel partners.

### Time Frame Event

| | |
|---|---|
| Jan '00 | Commence prototype development |
| Feb '00 | Develop initial web page content and marketing strategy for charter purposes |
| May '00 | Develop relationships with disposition channel partners |
| May '00 | Identify and develop relationships with target charter customers |
| May '00 | Prototype complete |
| May '00 | 50 percent of technical Phase 1 development complete—E-Return Return Notification Application (ERRNA) and E-Return Interface Engine (ERIE) |

### USE OF FUNDS: $3.5 million in Series A funding

E-Return will use $3.5 million in Series A funding to complete technical Phase 1 and begin Phase 2—over a 15-18 month period—for eight primary purposes: (1) completing technical Phase 1 development, (2) establishing warehouse and office set-up and staffing, (3) developing an interactive website, (4) acquiring and testing of two charter customers, (5) commencing technical Phase 2 development, (6) ramping-up sales force, (7) building market and brand recognition, and (8) acquiring additional customers.

### Phase 1: Launch (June 2000 - February 2001)

### Time Frame Event

| | |
|---|---|
| **Jun '00** | **Raise $3.5 million in Series A funding** |
| Jun '00 | Technology Development team ramp-up |
| Jun '00 | Outsource interactive website |
| Aug '00 | First charter customer acquired |
| Aug '00 | Initiate warehouse lease and begin preliminary set-up |
| Sep '00 | Second charter customer acquired |
| Oct '00 | Warehouse set-up complete |
| Nov '00 | Complete Merchant Interface Application version 1 (MIA1) |
| Nov '00 | Technical Phase 1 implementation |
| Nov '00 | Finalize technology set-up and training of charter customers |
| Nov '00 | Final testing operation and information flow |
| Nov '00 | Begin pre-holiday mass advertising campaign |
| Jan '01 | Commence Phase 2 technology development efforts |

| Jan '01 | Sales force ramp-up |
| Jan '01 | Post-holiday target marketing and brand awareness campaign |
| Feb '01 | Initiate preliminary design sessions with existing customers and management |
| Feb '01 | Commence development of Merchant Interface Application version 2 (MIA2) |
| Feb '01 | Complete customer training literature |

**Phase 2: Early Growth (March 2001 - March 2003)**

**Time Frame Event**

| Mar '01 | Charter customers are converted to full paying customers |
| Mar '01 | Develop network of secondary markets for B2B exchange |
| Mar '01 | Begin direct selling efforts to build customer base |
| Sep '01 | Commence development of Secondary Market Exchange (SME) |

**USE OF FUNDS: $8 million in funding**

E-Return will use $8 million in funding—over a 30-36 month rapid-growth period—for four primary purposes: (1) expand warehouse and office set-up, (2) implement second shift of employee and management staffing, (3) complete technical Phase 2 development, and (4) continue to acquire customers. E-Return expects to be cash-positive in March 2004.

**Time Frame Event**

| **Oct '01** | **Raise $8 million in Series B funding** |
| Oct '01 | Warehouse equipment investment |
| Nov '01 | Warehouse employee ramp-up |
| Jan '02 | Sales force ramp-up |
| Feb '02 | Post-Christmas target marketing and brand awareness campaign |
| Aug '02 | Complete customized reporting and analysis tools training information |
| Aug '02 | Expansion to larger warehouse and employee hiring increase |
| Oct '02 | Technical Phase 2 implementation |
| Dec '02 | Implement second shift for holiday and busy seasons |
| Jan '03 | Up-sell existing client base to include brick-and-mortar channel returns |

**Phase 3: Emerging Growth (March 2003 - June 2005)**

Phase 3 will focus on effectively managing E-Return's continued growth. By March 2004, E-Return will establish itself as the reverse logistics provider for the apparel industry. Year 5 will show enormous revenue growth with E-Return handling returns for all of our clients' distribution channels (online, catalog, and brick-and-mortar).

E-Return will develop plans to apply its proprietary software and handling processes to other industries including toys and games and home furnishings. In addition, Back Track will begin to license its proprietary technology to large multi-channel retailers or non-targeted industries for in-house merchandise handling and access to E-Return's Secondary Market Exchange (SME).

**Phase 4: Harvest**

In 2005, E-Return will earn revenues of $50.8 million and will process over 11 million articles of clothing for 47 clients. By this time, expansion efforts into several industries will have begun.

E-Return will be a prime candidate for strategic acquisition by general logistics providers or transportation providers seeking to expand their service offerings. E-Return will also be an attractive acquisition target for supply chain management software vendors. In addition, E-Return's expertise in managing the growing e-commerce and multi-channel returns market will make the company a strong IPO candidate.

### The Founders and Management Team

E-Return's founding team represents a solid mix of professional experience and qualifications necessary to develop, launch, and grow an innovative technology and services company in a new logistics environment. Detailed bios on the management team members may be found in Appendix B.

### Board of Advisors

E-Return's Board of Advisors currently consists of three individuals. Detailed bios for these individuals may be found in Appendix B. In addition, E-Return is currently pursuing additions to the Board of Advisors to provide experience in the areas of retail logistics and apparel sales.

E-Return has also been introduced to a former chief executive of a leading catalog retailer and is actively pursuing an advisory relationship with this individual.

E-Return has modeled revenue for our launch market: the apparel industry. Later stage-expansion opportunities into other markets, including toys and games and home furnishings have not been included. In addition, E-Return has not included revenues from the licensing of its proprietary technology for in-house merchandise handling and access to E-Return's Secondary Market Exchange (SME). The table below shows market size, market growth, and market share estimates as well as pricing assumptions:

|  | Year 1 | Year 2 | Year 3 | Year 4 | Year 5 |
|---|---|---|---|---|---|
| Online Apparel Market Size | $9.7B | $13.7B | $20.1B | $28.3B | $39.5B |
| Online Apparel Market Growth | 71.40% | 41.60% | 40.00% | 40.00% | 40.00% |
| Penetration of Online Market | 0.10% | 1.00% | 5.00% | 11.00% | 17.00% |
| E-commerce Units Handled | De minimus | 160,000 | 1,200,000 | 5,004,000 | 11,448,000 |
| Revenue | $0.0MM | $0.8MM | $5.7MM | $22.7MM | $50.9MM |

*Note: Market information obtained from Forrester Research, Gomez Advisors, and Harris Interactive.*

Our gross margin forecasts are the key drivers of value. Gross margins have been calculated utilizing cost analyses for technology development, infrastructure establishment, and initial customer acquisition costs. Costs of operation include the following expense items:

- Warehouse leasing costs (approximately 30 percent)
- Warehouse equipment depreciation (approximately 15 percent)
- All manual labor associated with handling the goods (approximately 55 percent)

In addition, as allowed by FASB principles, software development costs are capitalized and amortized over a period of 36 months. At the point in which the software is "substantially complete" (approximately mid 2002), E-Return will begin to amortize these costs accordingly

**MANAGEMENT TEAM & BOARD OF ADVISORS**

**FINANCIALS**

**Revenue**

**Expenses**

as costs of operation. The IT Development Costs identified as operating costs will be costs associated with system maintenance and software upgrades based upon our clients' needs.

In addition, analyses of comparable fulfillment and distribution companies' costs were utilized in identifying our costs. These industry comparisons have been adjusted to reflect the cost reduction effects of E-Return's industry specialization, high utilization of assets and information technology, and a unique one-touch handling and disposition process.

**Assumptions**

Other major assumptions are in the notes of the financial statements in Appendix A. Assumptions include:

- Financial model assumes a five-year horizon with a terminal value calculation.
- Our most likely financial scenario. E-Return performed sensitivity analyses surrounding our key success factors. As such, our funding requests are based upon our worst case scenario, which include information technology overruns, higher warehouse leasing and operating costs, and lastly higher costs of customer acquisition.
- Initial IT development costs are capitalized and amortized in accordance with FASB requirements. In addition to the cost of operations, future IT Development Costs will be expensed as incurred.

**Summary of Financial Results (Most Likely Scenario)**

|  | Year 1 | Year 2 | Year 3 | Year 4 | Year 5 |
|---|---|---|---|---|---|
| Sales | $0.0MM | $0.8MM | $5.7MM | $22.7MM | $50.9MM |
| Gross Margin | ($0.4MM) | $0.2MM | $1.5MM | $7.2MM | $17.7MM |
| % | — | 22.80% | 26.30% | 31.90% | 34.80% |
| EBITDA | ($1.2MM) | ($0.9MM) | ($0.5MM) | $3.5MM | $11.4MM |
| % | — | -116.40% | -8.60% | 15.20% | 22.30% |
| EBIT | ($1.2MM) | ($1.2MM) | ($1.0MM) | $2.5MM | $10.0MM |
| % | — | -151.20% | -17.50% | 11.10% | 19.70% |
| Cash balance | $1.0MM | $6.5MM | $3.1MM | $3.8MM | $8.3MM |

**The value of E-Return (including a summary of investor returns)**

|  | Year 0 | Year 1 | Year 2 | Year 3 | Year 4 | Year 5 |
|---|---|---|---|---|---|---|
| Operating cash flows | ($41) | ($2,502) | ($2,144) | ($3,369) | $1,472 | $4,469 |
| Financing/ Investing Cash flow |  |  |  |  |  |  |
| Equity cash flow | $3,500 |  | $8,000 |  |  | $90,854 |
| Cash flows to investor |  |  |  |  |  | ($33,363) |
| IRR % | 57% |  |  |  |  |  |

*(in thousands of dollars)*

The value of the business has been based on cash flows available to equity holders, discounted at a 40 percent post-tax cost of equity. Included in these cash flows is the assumption that the business is sold at the end of year 5. The terminal value for the business (net of debt) has been estimated as $90.9 million, and is based on a terminal earnings multiple of 8 times EBITDA.

This valuation is conservative given that E-Return will be expanding into several different industries subsequent to year 5.

Detailed financial forecasts (which include profit and loss), balance sheets, and cash flow statements are included in the Financial Forecast at the conclusion of this plan.

E-Return is seeking $3.5 million in initial funding from investors who are familiar with the retail and apparel industry, to finance technology development, warehouse infrastructure development, working capital, and customer acquisition. In return for this investment, E-Return's investors will receive:

- 35 percent equity position in E-Return
- Two seats on the Board of Directors
- An internal rate of return of 57 percent

**Assumptions and Financial Decisions:**

1. Software development costs are capitalized and amortized over a period of 36 months. At the point in which the operations software is "substantially complete" (approximately mid 2002), E-Return will begin to amortize these costs accordingly as costs of operation. Additional IT development costs, which are identified as operating costs, will be associated with system maintenance and software upgrades.

2. E-Return's financing request is based upon our worst-case financial position. Sensitivity analyses were performed surrounding the following factors:

- Price reductions for services rendered—upwards to 20 percent
- Gross margin decreases upwards to 10 percent
- Online apparel market penetration rate reductions of 10 percent
- Increased operating expenses in relation to labor and warehouse expenses of approximately 15 percent
- Additional time required to obtain customers
- Other minor shifts in cost and in revenue growths

Due to the time and effort required to raise additional levels of capital, the E-Return team has consciously requested funding based upon the worst-case scenarios identified above. As such, should the most-likely financial situation occur, E-Return intends to utilize the additional cash flow to expand operations quicker.

3. E-Return utilized the following conservative revenue assumptions:

Online apparel purchases will not all be returned via shipping as many e-tailers have established return policies to their brick-and-mortar locations. As such, our estimates utilize that approximately 35 percent of all online apparel returns will be returned via shipping (E-Return). The other 65 percent will be returned via other means.

- Online retailers will experience a 15 percent rate of return for online purchases.
- Minimal revenues will be recognized by E-Return for those items processed by our charter customers.
- Revenues from other channels (brick-and-mortar and mail order) will occur over a period of 2 years after our customers' satisfaction with our high level of service.

| Projected Apparel Sales by Channel | 2001 | 2002 | 2003 | 2004 | 2005 |
|---|---|---|---|---|---|
| E-commerce | $9,692 | $13,729 | $20,181 | $28,253 | $39,555 |
| Mail Order | $13,251 | $14,112 | $15,029 | $16,006 | $17,046 |
| Brick-and-Mortar | $165,017 | $165,758 | $164,197 | $161,129 | $154,950 |

*Note: Market information obtained from Forrester Research, Gomez Advisors, and Harris Interactive.*

### The Founders and Management Team

#### Anthony Ray, President

Mr. Ray is responsible for coordination of company growth and strategy, communications, and intellectual property.

Mr. Ray's experience includes consulting to established and emerging growth companies in the technology, services, and financial sectors with the Center for Applied Strategy (CAST), a West Coast-based management consulting firm specializing in marketing, information technology, and operations strategy and as a senior consultant for KPMG Consulting. Mr. Ray developed information technology strategies to improve operations and enhance customer service, designed marketing strategies and competition assessments in support of product development, market penetration, and acquisition strategies, and enhanced business operations with reengineering and organizational effectiveness strategies. Mr. Ray is pursuing a M.B.A. and a Juris Doctor joint-degree from the University of Missouri at Kansas City. He received a B.A. in economics from Columbia University.

#### Barton Fitz, Director of Marketing and Sales

Mr. Fitz is responsible for marketing and sales, customer acquisition, and relationship development.

Mr. Fitz's experience includes marketing and sales for the commercial banking and consumer goods industries. While working with the Middle Valley National Bank in Missouri, Mr. Fitz was responsible for the creation of multiple product launch campaigns and institution-wide sales programs. In addition, he designed and developed the bank's Internet site, which included online account access and applications. For IBM, Mr. Fitz developed a strategy and an integrated national marketing plan to penetrate target channels and developed a co-marketing strategy to enhance brand equity positions of the firm and its independent distributors. Mr. Fitz has a B.S. degree in finance from New York University and is pursuing an M.B.A. degree at the University of Missouri at Kansas City.

#### Robert Romano, CPA, Director of Finance

Mr. Romano is responsible for finance, accounting, and client profitability measurements.

Mr. Romano has over six years of accounting and finance experience with Ernst & Young and Shell Oil. His work included the preparation of an S-1 initial public offering filing as well as a second public stock offering. His experience also included comfort letter, 10K, 10Q, and 8K audit services for well-recognized clients in the insurance, financial services, and manufacturing industries. Lastly, Mr. Romano performed numerous employee benefit plan audits and in doing so gained familiarity with ERISA regulations. Mr. Romano's operational and financial control experience included import/export, manufacturing, and information systems operations. He was extensively involved with the SAP Human Resource and Payroll system implementation. Mr. Romano completed with highest honors his B.S. degree in accountancy at the University ofMichigan and is pursuing his M.B.A. at the University of Missouri at Kansas City.

### Rachel Summers, Director of Strategic Operations

Ms. Summers is responsible for operations and logistics.

Ms. Summers's experience includes designing, implementing, and managing operations and financial processes and controls for a top-tier financial institution as well as emerging-growth companies. In this capacity, Ms. Summers developed operations and financial processes for global inter-company reconciliation at Credit Suisse Financial Products including transaction level tracking and reconciling and the standardization, timely, and efficient operation of complex procedures. She established and automated financial and operations procedures to manage 100 percent growth at the European headquarters for Weiden & Kennedy, Inc. Ms. Summers developed short- and long-term strategic plans for product and market expansion of Internet start-up, GoPDA.com, through complete solutions for vertical markets and business-to-business opportunities. Ms. Summers received a B.B.A. in finance from the University of Missouri at Kansas City, where she is currently pursuing an M.B.A.

### Justin Roberts, Director of Technology

Mr. Roberts is responsible for building E-Return's technical infrastructure, including the development of all new applications, and customer technical implementation and support.

Mr. Roberts brings over 6 years of technical and management experience. He has directed software development teams of up to 10 people in the custom design and development of applications to track, relocate, and redistribute fixed assets for the transportation industry. Mr. Roberts's experience includes the application of Java-based XML integrator technologies in developing web-based applications including the various components and communication protocols that these solutions require and the use of Microsoft's ASP technology to access SQL Server databases. Mr. Roberts has experience managing both full-time and part-time developers to ensure completion of all deliverables under tight time constraints. Mr. Roberts received a B.S. degree in mathematics and operations research from the University of Illinois at Urbana and is pursuing an M.B.A. at the University of Missouri at Kansas City.

### Board of Advisors

### Profile of William Fanchon

Mr. Fanchon is a full-time faculty member employed as a Senior Lecturer in the Department of Finance at the University of Missouri at Kansas City. Mr. Fanchon has been a voting faculty member since 1980 and instructed over 8,000 students. He has taught multiple sections of the undergraduate small business finance class, multiple sections of the graduate corporate finance classes for small business as well as sections of the graduate Entrepreneurial Process class and graduate Entrepreneurial Harvest class. Mr. Fanchon is associate director of the Center for Small and Middle-Sized Companies which coordinates the Community Minority Business Advancement Program, a 45-hour, 15-session business fundamental courses to minority businessmen and businesswomen in St. Louis, Independence, Springfield, and Kansas City each year. Mr. Fanchon is a regular lecturer in UT's Management Development Programs and Executive Education Programs and has lectured in custom programs at Shell Oil, IBM, Halliburton, M.D. Anderson, Fisher Rosemount, Banco do Brazil, Wayne Dresser, and Dell

Computer. He teaches in Executive Education public programs such as Management Institute and Management Challenge programs as well as topical programs such as finance and accounting for nonfinancial managers. He has participated in seminars with the University of Missouri's Executive Program for Agricultural Producers, Small Business Administration, Cen-Tex Certified Development Companies, and Businesses Invest in Growth. He has also traveled to Mexico to lecture in the ITESM Monterey Tech executive education programs as well as the ITESM Ph.D. program. Mr. Fanchon has also served as faculty advisor to the University of Missouri Finance Association and has received numerous teaching awards.

William Fanchon is founder and president of CFO Services, Inc., a Kansas City-based small business financial consulting firm. CFO Services provides an array of business consulting services to owner/managers of private, closely held, and family small and middle-sized businesses. Services include merger and acquisition advisory services, financial and credit analysis, business valuations, loan procurement, SBA loan packaging, loan restructuring, feasibility studies, business planning and strategic planning. Mr. Fanchon has served as an expert witness in divorce cases, dissenting shareholder suits, bankruptcy cases, and business litigation cases. CFO Services has a client list of over 650 small and middle-sized businesses ranging from annual revenues of $100,000 to over $100 million that cross all industry lines including retail, wholesale, manufacturing, construction, high tech, low tech, and service.

William Fanchon has been assisting small business owners in Kansas City since 1977. He incorporated his sole proprietorship, FMC Associates, to form CFO Services, Inc. in 1989. In addition to his consulting practice, Mr. Fanchon is co-owner and vice-president of Hill Country Printing, Inc. Mr. Fanchon serves as an advisory director of a Kansas City independent bank, a recycling company, and a manufacturing company. He also holds a Kansas City real estate salespersons' license.

William Fanchon received his B.B.A. and M.B.A. from the University of Missouri at Kansas City and majored in finance.

### Profile of Jason Williams

Mr. Williams brings over 18 years of retail management experience, both merchandising and operations, to E-Return. Currently, Mr. Williams oversees MGM's $30MM annual retail sales operations for all MGM locations. In addition, Mr. Williams's previous experience includes responsibilities as the divisional merchandise manager and general manager for Bullocks department store (a division of R. H. Macy Corporation). Prior to that role, Mr. Williams was the general manager for the Nevada Merchandise Division of the Marriott Corporation. This position entailed management responsibility for 27 stores in the greater Las Vegas area.

Mr. Williams completed his bachelor's degree in business administration at the University of California at Berkeley.

### Profile of Abdul Ruiz

Dr. Ruiz is currently an assistant professor in the Management Science and Information Systems Department at the University of Missouri at Kansas City. He is currently teaching Digital Economy and Commerce at the graduate level. His previous teaching experience includes Management Information Systems at the undergraduate level at Indiana State University and Telecommunications for Managers at the graduate level at Columbia College at Chicago.

Dr. Ruiz's research and areas of interest include the economics of information systems and electronic commerce. In particular, his work focuses on the economic characteristics of information goods and how firms producing these goods decide to compete and/or exist efficiently in the market place. Dr. Ruiz provides E-Return with valuable insight into the complexities of business to business exchanges.

Dr. Ruiz received his Ph.D. in MIS from Indiana State University with a specialization in telecommunications, economics of information systems, electronic commerce, and database management.

**APPENDIX C: Consumer Survey Results**

1. What would it take for you to begin purchasing clothing from an online store?
   - Free return shipping—very important
   - Easy return policy—very important
   - Having brick-and-mortar store for return—somewhat important
2. At what point would an online return policy discourage you from purchasing?
   - = existence of a mandatory 7-day return policy
   - = had to pay shipping costs
   - = need to acquire an RMA
3. 2/3 of consumers say that a return policy affects their decisions of from which store to purchase.
4. What is most frustrating about a company's return policy?
   - Had to pay shipping costs for returns
   - Getting to the post office to mail return
   - Not knowing the status of a return
5. 100 percent of respondents indicated they want a pre-printed return label to be included with the merchandise.
6. Only 9 percent of respondents like the idea of calling customer service to request an RMA.
7. 95 percent indicated they expect to individually receive better customer service because they have made multiple purchases from the online store.
8. When asked to score the importance of the return policy in choosing an apparel store, the average consumer score was 4.4 (on a scale from 1-5 with 5 = extremely important).
9. 78 percent feel that customer service is worse in the e-commerce market space compared to the traditional brick-and-mortar channel.
10. 70 percent need more assurances that their returns will be handled properly because they are purchasing the item online rather than in the traditional brick-and-mortar channel.
11. Rather than returning an item because it is defective or because the wrong item was sent, 80 percent of the returns are the result of the item not being what the consumer expected it to be.

Straight from the consumer's mouth...

"Because I am worried about the return policy, I will probably not buy clothing online."

"If the [return] policy is bad, I will shop elsewhere."

*Note: 66 of 80 survey participants responding.*

**APPENDIX D: A Note on E-Return's Technical Infrastructure**

As part of its technology solution, E-Return will rely on the use of XML for the transfer of data between organizations. Critical to the adoption of XML are the Document Definition Types (DTDs). DTDs are essentially the mapping of data so that both parties in a data transfer transaction are "speaking the same language." The concept of sharing document definitions is aimed at ensuring that each end of the document exchange is using the same standard.

There are standards being developed in all industries, and the apparel industry in which E-Return operates is no different. The DTDs that exist define invoice content, inventory details, and other similar information.

Recognizing that no one standard is recognized as the dominant standard for the industry, E-Return's solution is designed to handle multiple DTD types. As part of the initial implementation phase, E-Return works with a merchant to determine the appropriate or desired DTD to be used for their customized solution. This step of the implementation phase is required for the organizations and merchants who are sophisticated enough to be using XML interfaces in their business operations. These organizations may be using similar technology in the interaction with their suppliers. E-Return would simply leverage the existing technology already in place. The Merchant Interface Engine is simply an XML integrator that is used to translate XML requests into merchant specific queries to their databases.

Recognizing the importance of being familiar with the standards that govern the exchange of invoice and RMA information between businesses, E-Return intends to participate in the development of the DTD standards when possible.

## APPENDIX E: The Status of E-Return's Intellectual Property

As part of E-Return Solutions' technical infrastructure, the company intends to build several novel and non-obvious software applications. Accordingly, E-Return has engaged Thompson, Wall, & Heidenrich to manage the protection of its intellectual property. E-Return is currently filing a provisional patent on its E-Return Interface Exchange (ERIE), Merchant Interface Application (MIA), and the Secondary Market Exchange (SME).

## APPENDIX F: E-Return's Fee and Commission Schedule

| Name of Fee/Commission | Description | Fee Type | Fee Amount |
|---|---|---|---|
| System Implementation Fee | • Covers system customization and implementation, client education, and all systems consulting | • Flat <br> • One-time | $50,000 |
| System Service and Maintenance Fee | • Covers system maintenance <br> • Covers supply chain reporting capabilities | • Incremental <br> • Periodic | • $2,500 - $4,000 per month |
| Merchandise Processing Fee | • Covers processing of all items received by the CRC | • Transaction-based | • $1.00-$4.00 per item* |
| Secondary Market Resale Commission | • Covers costs of secondary market interface and holding costs | • Percentage of resale price | • 7.5 - 12.5%** |

*\* The higher charge reflects the additional costs of receiving and processing individual garments.*
*\*\* The commission rate fluctuates to accommodate clients' varying holding requirements.*

*This page left intentionally blank to accommodate tabular matter following.*

## Profit and Loss Analysis (000's): Year 1—2001

| Revenues | Jul | Aug | Sep | Q1 | Oct | Nov | Dec | Q2 |
|---|---|---|---|---|---|---|---|---|
| Set-Up Revenues | $0.0 | $0.0 | $0.0 | $0.0 | $0.0 | $0.0 | $0.0 | $0.0 |
| Service Fee Revenues | $0.0 | $0.0 | $0.0 | $0.0 | $0.0 | $0.0 | $0.0 | $0.0 |
| Online Revenue | $0.0 | $0.0 | $0.0 | $0.0 | $0.0 | $0.0 | $0.0 | $0.0 |
| Brick-and-Mortar Revenues | $0.0 | $0.0 | $0.0 | $0.0 | $0.0 | $0.0 | $0.0 | $0.0 |
| Mail-Order Revenues | $0.0 | $0.0 | $0.0 | $0.0 | $0.0 | $0.0 | $0.0 | $0.0 |
| Disposition Revenue from Retailers | $0.0 | $0.0 | $0.0 | $0.0 | $0.0 | $0.0 | $0.0 | $0.0 |
| **Total Revenues** | **$0.0** | **$0.0** | **$0.0** | **$0.0** | **$0.0** | **$0.0** | **$0.0** | **$0.0** |
| | | | | | | | | |
| Cost of Operations (See Assumptions for Details) | $4.3 | $30.1 | $20.0 | $54.3 | $20.0 | $26.8 | $24.8 | $71.5 |
| | | | | | | | | |
| Gross Margin | ($4.3) | ($30.1) | ($20.0) | ($54.3) | ($20.0) | ($26.8) | ($24.8) | ($71.5) |
| | | | | | | | | |
| **Operating Expenses** | | | | | | | | |
| IT Development Costs | $0.0 | $0.0 | $0.0 | $0.0 | $0.0 | $0.0 | $0.0 | $0.0 |
| Marketing | ($24.0) | ($4.5) | ($26.5) | ($55.0) | ($17.0) | ($6.5) | ($4.5) | ($28.0) |
| Selling Costs | ($0.3) | ($0.3) | ($20.3) | ($20.8) | ($10.3) | ($10.3) | ($0.3) | ($20.8) |
| General & Administrative Costs | ($19.5) | ($19.5) | ($19.5) | ($58.5) | ($19.5) | ($21.8) | ($21.8) | ($63.1) |
| **Total Operating Expenses** | **($43.8)** | **($24.3)** | **($66.3)** | **($134.3)** | **($46.8)** | **($38.5)** | **($26.5)** | **($111.8)** |
| | | | | | | | | |
| EBITDA | ($48.0) | ($54.3) | ($86.2) | ($188.6) | ($66.7) | ($65.3) | ($51.3) | ($183.3) |
| | | | | | | | | |
| Depreciation | ($1.1) | ($1.1) | ($1.1) | ($3.4) | ($1.1) | ($1.1) | ($1.1) | ($3.4) |
| | | | | | | | | |
| EBIT | ($49.1) | ($55.5) | ($87.4) | ($192.0) | ($67.9) | ($66.4) | ($52.4) | ($186.7) |
| | | | | | | | | |
| Interest Expense | $0.0 | $0.0 | $0.0 | $0.0 | $0.0 | $0.0 | $0.0 | $0.0 |
| | | | | | | | | |
| EBT | ($49.1) | ($55.5) | ($87.4) | ($192.0) | ($67.9) | ($66.4) | ($52.4) | ($186.7) |
| | | | | | | | | |
| Taxes | $0.0 | $0.0 | $0.0 | $0.0 | $0.0 | $0.0 | $0.0 | $0.0 |
| | | | | | | | | |
| NPAT | ($49.1) | ($55.5) | ($87.4) | ($192.0) | ($67.9) | ($66.4) | ($52.4) | ($186.7) |
| | | | | | | | | |
| **Financial Summary Ratios** | | | | | | | | |
| Gross Margin % | n/a | n/a | n/a | n/a | n/a | n/a | n/a | n/a |
| EBITDA % | n/a | n/a | n/a | n/a | n/a | n/a | n/a | n/a |
| EBT % | n/a | n/a | n/a | n/a | n/a | n/a | n/a | n/a |
| NPAT % | n/a | n/a | n/a | n/a | n/a | n/a | n/a | n/a |

| | Jan | Feb | Mar | Q3 | Apr | May | Jun | Q4 | Total |
|---|---|---|---|---|---|---|---|---|---|
| | $0.0 | $0.0 | $0.0 | $0.0 | $0.0 | $0.0 | $0.0 | $0.0 | $0.0 |
| | $0.0 | $0.0 | $0.0 | $0.0 | $0.0 | $0.0 | $0.0 | $0.0 | $0.0 |
| | $0.0 | $0.0 | $0.0 | $0.0 | $0.0 | $0.0 | $0.0 | $0.0 | $0.0 |
| | | | | | | | | | |
| | $0.0 | $0.0 | $0.0 | $0.0 | $0.0 | $0.0 | $0.0 | $0.0 | $0.0 |
| | $0.0 | $0.0 | $0.0 | $0.0 | $0.0 | $0.0 | $0.0 | $0.0 | $0.0 |
| | | | | | | | | | |
| | $0.0 | $0.0 | $0.0 | $0.0 | $0.0 | $0.0 | $0.0 | $0.0 | $0.0 |
| | **$0.0** | **$0.0** | **$0.0** | **$0.0** | **$0.0** | **$0.0** | **$0.0** | **$0.0** | **$0.0** |
| | | | | | | | | | |
| | $27.8 | $23.8 | $23.8 | $75.3 | $27.6 | $27.6 | $27.6 | $82.8 | $283.9 |
| | ($27.8) | ($23.8) | ($23.8) | ($75.3) | ($27.6) | ($27.6) | ($27.6) | ($82.8) | ($283.9) |
| | | | | | | | | | |
| | $0.0 | $0.0 | $0.0 | $0.0 | $0.0 | $0.0 | $0.0 | $0.0 | $0.0 |
| | ($29.5) | ($6.5) | ($4.5) | ($40.5) | ($9.0) | ($4.5) | ($6.5) | ($20.0) | ($143.5) |
| | ($10.3) | ($20.3) | ($20.3) | ($50.8) | ($10.3) | ($10.3) | ($10.3) | ($30.8) | ($123.0) |
| | ($21.8) | ($21.8) | ($21.8) | ($65.3) | ($21.8) | ($21.8) | ($21.8) | ($65.3) | ($252.2) |
| | **($61.5)** | **($48.5)** | **($46.5)** | **($156.6)** | **($41.0)** | **($36.5)** | **($38.5)** | **($116.1)** | **($518.7)** |
| | | | | | | | | | |
| | ($89.3) | ($72.3) | ($70.3) | ($231.9) | ($68.6) | ($64.1) | ($66.1) | ($198.8) | ($802.6) |
| | | | | | | | | | |
| | ($1.1) | ($1.1) | ($1.1) | ($3.4) | ($1.1) | ($1.1) | ($1.1) | ($3.4) | ($13.6) |
| | | | | | | | | | |
| | ($90.4) | ($73.4) | ($71.4) | ($235.3) | ($69.7) | ($65.2) | ($67.2) | ($202.2) | ($816.3) |
| | | | | | | | | | |
| | $0.0 | $0.0 | $0.0 | $0.0 | $0.0 | $0.0 | $0.0 | $0.0 | $0.0 |
| | | | | | | | | | |
| | ($90.4) | ($73.4) | ($71.4) | ($235.3) | ($69.7) | ($65.2) | ($67.2) | ($202.2) | ($816.3) |
| | | | | | | | | | |
| | $0.0 | $0.0 | $0.0 | $0.0 | $0.0 | $0.0 | $0.0 | $0.0 | $0.0 |
| | | | | | | | | | |
| | ($90.4) | ($73.4) | ($71.4) | ($235.3) | ($69.7) | ($65.2) | ($67.2) | ($202.2) | ($816.3) |
| | | | | | | | | | |
| | n/a | n/a | n/a | n/a | n/a | n/a | n/a | n/a | n/a |
| | n/a | n/a | n/a | n/a | n/a | n/a | n/a | n/a | n/a |
| | n/a | n/a | n/a | n/a | n/a | n/a | n/a | n/a | n/a |
| | n/a | n/a | n/a | n/a | n/a | n/a | n/a | n/a | n/a |

## Profit and Loss Analysis (000's): Years 2-5—2002-2005

|  | 2002/Q1 | 2002/Q2 | 2002/Q3 | 2002/Q4 | Total 2002 |
|---|---|---|---|---|---|
| **Revenues** | | | | | |
| Set-Up Revenues | $0.0 | $0.0 | $0.0 | $0.0 | $0.0 |
| Service Fee Revenues | $30.0 | $30.0 | $30.0 | $30.0 | $120.0 |
| Online Revenue | $26.5 | $44.2 | $79.6 | $26.5 | $177.0 |
| Brick-and-Mortar Revenues | $348.6 | $581.1 | $1,045.9 | $348.6 | $2,324.3 |
| Mail-Order Revenues | $79.2 | $131.9 | $237.5 | $79.2 | $527.7 |
| Disposition Revenue from | | | | | |
|   Retailers | $0.0 | $0.0 | $0.0 | $0.0 | $0.0 |
| **Total Revenues** | **$484.3** | **$787.2** | **$1,393.0** | **$484.3** | **$3,149.0** |
| | | | | | |
| Cost of Operations | | | | | |
|   (See Assumptions for Details) | $351.9 | $586.5 | $1,055.7 | $351.9 | $2,346.0 |
| | | | | | |
| Gross Margin | $132.4 | $200.7 | $337.3 | $132.4 | $803.0 |
| | | | | | |
| **Operating Expenses** | | | | | |
| IT Development Costs | ($47.2) | ($47.2) | ($23.6) | ($39.4) | ($157.4) |
| Marketing | ($28.3) | ($47.2) | ($94.5) | ($18.9) | ($188.9) |
| Selling Costs | ($15.7) | ($15.7) | ($15.7) | ($15.7) | ($63.0) |
| General & Administrative Costs | ($55.1) | ($55.1) | ($55.1) | ($55.1) | ($220.4) |
| **Total Operating Expenses** | **($146.4)** | **($165.3)** | **($188.9)** | **($129.1)** | **($629.8)** |
| | | | | | |
| EBITDA | ($14.0) | $35.4 | $148.4 | $3.3 | $173.2 |
| | | | | | |
| Depreciation | ($48.0) | ($48.0) | ($48.0) | ($48.0) | ($192.1) |
| | | | | | |
| EBIT | ($62.0) | ($12.6) | $100.4 | ($44.7) | ($18.9) |
| | | | | | |
| Interest Expense | $0.0 | $0.0 | $0.0 | $0.0 | $0.0 |
| | | | | | |
| EBT | ($62.0) | ($12.6) | $100.4 | ($44.7) | ($18.9) |
| | | | | | |
| Taxes | $0.0 | $0.0 | $0.0 | $0.0 | $0.0 |
| | | | | | |
| NPAT | ($62.0) | ($12.6) | $100.4 | ($44.7) | ($18.9) |
| | | | | | |
| **Financial Summary Ratios** | | | | | |
| Gross Margin % | 27.3% | 25.5% | 24.2% | 27.3% | 25.5% |
| EBITDA % | -2.9% | 4.5% | 10.7% | 0.7% | 5.5% |
| EBT % | -12.8% | -1.6% | 7.2% | -9.2% | -0.6% |
| NPAT % | -12.8% | -1.6% | 7.2% | -9.2% | -0.6% |

| 2003/Q1 | 2003/Q2 | 2003/Q3 | 2003/Q4 | Total 2003 | 2004 | 2005 |
|---|---|---|---|---|---|---|
| $37.5 | $37.5 | $37.5 | $37.5 | $150.0 | $250.0 | $350.0 |
| $52.5 | $52.5 | $52.5 | $52.5 | $210.0 | $360.0 | $570.0 |
| $195.1 | $325.2 | $585.4 | $195.1 | $1,300.8 | $4,370.8 | $8,741.6 |
| $968.7 | $1,614.5 | $2,906.0 | $968.7 | $6,457.9 | $11,847.9 | $24,029.8 |
| $217.3 | $362.1 | $651.8 | $217.3 | $1,448.3 | $3,338.2 | $5,516.7 |
| | | | | | | |
| $0.0 | $0.0 | $0.0 | $0.0 | $0.0 | $0.0 | $0.0 |
| **$1,471.1** | **$2,391.8** | **$4,233.2** | **$1,471.1** | **$9,567.0** | **$20,166.8** | **$39,208.0** |
| | | | | | | |
| | | | | | | |
| $247.8 | $366.8 | $407.4 | $368.4 | $7,003.1 | $14,419.3 | $28,033.8 |
| | | | | | | |
| $384.6 | $641.0 | $1,153.8 | $384.6 | $2,564.0 | $5,747.6 | $11,174.3 |
| | | | | | | |
| | | | | | | |
| ($86.1) | ($86.1) | ($43.1) | ($71.8) | ($287.0) | ($403.3) | ($784.2) |
| ($229.6) | ($229.6) | ($57.4) | ($57.4) | ($574.0) | ($806.7) | ($1,176.2) |
| ($23.9) | ($23.9) | ($23.9) | ($23.9) | ($95.7) | ($100.8) | ($196.0) |
| ($215.3) | ($215.3) | ($215.3) | ($215.3) | ($861.0) | ($1,815.0) | ($3,528.7) |
| **($554.9)** | **($554.9)** | **($339.6)** | **($368.3)** | **($1,817.7)** | **($3,125.9)** | **($5,685.2)** |
| | | | | | | |
| ($170.3) | $86.1 | $814.2 | $16.3 | $746.2 | $2,621.7 | $5,489.1 |
| | | | | | | |
| ($69.5) | ($69.5) | ($69.5) | ($69.5) | ($278.1) | ($587.2) | ($491.9) |
| | | | | | | |
| ($239.8) | $16.6 | $744.6 | ($53.3) | $468.1 | $2,034.5 | $4,997.2 |
| | | | | | | |
| $0.0 | $0.0 | $0.0 | $0.0 | $0.0 | $0.0 | $0.0 |
| | | | | | | |
| ($239.8) | $16.6 | $744.6 | ($53.3) | $468.1 | $2,034.5 | $4,997.2 |
| | | | | | | |
| $0.0 | ($6.0) | ($268.1) | $0.0 | $0.0 | ($570.4) | ($1,799.0) |
| | | | | | | |
| ($239.8) | $10.6 | $476.6 | ($53.3) | $468.1 | $1,464.1 | $3,198.2 |
| | | | | | | |
| | | | | | | |
| 26.1% | 26.8% | 27.3% | 26.1% | 26.8% | 28.5% | 28.5% |
| -11.6% | 3.6% | 19.2% | 1.1% | 7.8% | 13.0% | 14.0% |
| -16.3% | 0.7% | 17.6% | -3.6% | 4.9% | 10.1% | 12.7% |
| -16.3% | 0.4% | 11.3% | -3.6% | 4.9% | 7.3% | 8.2% |

## Balance Sheet Analysis (000's): Year 1—2001

| | Current Position | Investment Adjustments | Post Investment | Jul | Aug | Sep | Q1 | Oct | Nov |
|---|---|---|---|---|---|---|---|---|---|
| **Current Assets** | | | | | | | | | |
| Cash | $0 | $1,500 | $1,500 | $1,432 | $1,237 | $1,112 | $1,112 | $959 | $856 |
| Receivables | $0 | $0 | $0 | $0 | $0 | $0 | $0 | $0 | $0 |
| Other | $0 | $0 | $0 | $10 | $10 | $10 | $10 | $10 | $10 |
| **Total Current Assets** | **$0** | **$1,500** | **$1,500** | **$1,442** | **$1,247** | **$1,122** | **$1,122** | **$969** | **$866** |
| | | | | | | | | | |
| **Non-Current Assets** | | | | | | | | | |
| Property, plant, and equipment (including software & hardware) | $41 | $0 | $41 | $61 | $202 | $241 | $241 | $327 | $364 |
| Accumulated depreciation | $0 | $(1) | $(2) | $(3) | $(3) | $(5) | $(6) | $(7) | $(7) |
| Net Assets | $41 | $0 | $41 | $60 | $199 | $237 | $237 | $322 | $358 |
| **Total Assets** | **$41** | **$1,500** | **$1,541** | **$1,502** | **$1,446** | **$1,359** | **$1,359** | **$1,291** | **$1,225** |
| | | | | | | | | | |
| **Current Liabilities** | | | | | | | | | |
| Payables | $0 | $0 | $0 | $10 | $10 | $10 | $10 | $10 | $10 |
| Revolving Line of Credit | $0 | $0 | $0 | $0 | $0 | $0 | $0 | $0 | $0 |
| Other Current Liabilities | $0 | $0 | $0 | $0 | $0 | $0 | $0 | $0 | $0 |
| **Total Current Liabilities** | **$0** | **$0** | **$0** | **$10** | **$10** | **$10** | **$10** | **$10** | **$10** |
| | | | | | | | | | |
| **Non-Current Liabilities** | | | | | | | | | |
| Long-Term Borrowings | $0 | $0 | $0 | $0 | $0 | $0 | $0 | $0 | $0 |
| Other Liabilities | $0 | $0 | $0 | $0 | $0 | $0 | $0 | $0 | $0 |
| **Total Liabilities** | **$0** | **$0** | **$0** | **$10** | **$10** | **$10** | **$10** | **$10** | **$10** |
| **Net Assets** | **$41** | **$1,500** | **$1,541** | **$1,492** | **$1,436** | **$1,349** | **$1,349** | **$1,281** | **$1,215** |
| | | | | | | | | | |
| Issued Capital | $250 | $1,500 | $1,750 | $1,750 | $1,750 | $1,750 | $1,750 | $1,750 | $1,750 |
| Retained Earnings | $(209) | $0 | $(209) | $(258) | $(314) | $(401) | $(401) | $(469) | $(535) |
| **Total Shareholders Equity** | **$41** | **$0** | **$1,541** | **$1,492** | **$1,436** | **$1,349** | **$1,349** | **$1,281** | **$1,215** |

| | Dec | Q2 | Jan | Feb | Mar | Q3 | Apr | May | Jun | Q4 | Total |
|---|---|---|---|---|---|---|---|---|---|---|---|
| | $775 | $775 | $656 | $555 | $455 | $455 | $351 | $258 | $162 | $162 | $162 |
| | $0 | $0 | $0 | $0 | $0 | $0 | $0 | $0 | $0 | $0 | $0 |
| | $10 | $10 | $10 | $10 | $10 | $10 | $10 | $10 | $10 | $10 | $10 |
| | **$785** | **$785** | **$666** | **$565** | **$465** | **$465** | **$361** | **$268** | **$172** | **$172** | **$172** |
| | | | | | | | | | | | |
| | $394 | $394 | $423 | $453 | $483 | $483 | $517 | $547 | $576 | $576 | $576 |
| | $(8) | $(9) | $(10) | $(10) | $(11) | $(12) | $(14) | $(14) | $(14) | $(14) | $(14) |
| | $387 | $387 | $415 | $444 | $472 | $472 | $506 | $534 | $563 | $563 | $563 |
| | **$1,172** | **$1,172** | **$1,082** | **$1,008** | **$937** | **$937** | **$867** | **$802** | **$735** | **$735** | **$735** |
| | | | | | | | | | | | |
| | $10 | $10 | $10 | $10 | $10 | $10 | $10 | $10 | $10 | $10 | $10 |
| | $0 | $0 | $0 | $0 | $0 | $0 | $0 | $0 | $0 | $0 | $0 |
| | $0 | $0 | $0 | $0 | $0 | $0 | $0 | $0 | $0 | $0 | $0 |
| | $10 | $10 | $10 | $10 | $10 | $10 | $10 | $10 | $10 | $10 | $10 |
| | | | | | | | | | | | |
| | $0 | $0 | $0 | $0 | $0 | $0 | $0 | $0 | $0 | $0 | $0 |
| | $0 | $0 | $0 | $0 | $0 | $0 | $0 | $0 | $0 | $0 | $0 |
| | $10 | $10 | $10 | $10 | $10 | $10 | $10 | $10 | $10 | **$10** | **$10** |
| | **$1,172** | **$1,162** | **$1,072** | **$998** | **$927** | **$927** | **$857** | **$792** | **$725** | **$725** | **$725** |
| | | | | | | | | | | | |
| | $1,750 | $1,750 | $1,750 | $1,750 | $1,750 | $1,750 | $1,750 | $1,750 | $1,750 | $1,750 | $1,750 |
| | $(588) | $(588) | $(678) | $(752) | $(823) | $(823) | $(893) | $(958) | $(1,025) | $(1,025) | $(1,025) |
| | **$1,162** | **$1,162** | **$1,072** | **$998** | **$927** | **$927** | **$857** | **$792** | **$725** | **$725** | **$725** |

## Balance Sheet Analysis (000's): Years 2-5—2002-2005

|  | 2002/Q1 | 2002/Q2 | 2002/Q3 | 2002/Q4 | Total 2002 | 2003/Q1 | 2003/Q2 | 2003/Q3 |
|---|---|---|---|---|---|---|---|---|
| **Current Assets** | | | | | | | | |
| Cash | $511 | $416 | $365 | $1,987 | $1,987 | $1,513 | $1,517 | $1,803 |
| Receivables | $319 | $519 | $918 | $319 | $319 | $970 | $1,577 | $2,791 |
| Other | $10 | $10 | $10 | $10 | $10 | $0 | $0 | $0 |
| **Total Current Assets** | **$840** | **$945** | **$1,293** | **$2,317** | **$2,317** | **$2,483** | **$3,094** | **$4,594** |
| | | | | | | | | |
| **Non-Current Assets** | | | | | | | | |
| Property, plant, and equipment | | | | | | | | |
|   (including software & hardware) | $624 | $704 | $804 | $834 | $834 | $1,486 | $1,673 | $1,746 |
| Accumulated depreciation | $(62) | $(110) | $(158) | $(206) | $(206) | $(275) | $(345) | $(414) |
| Net Assets | $562 | $594 | $646 | $629 | $629 | $1,211 | $1,328 | $1,332 |
| **Total Assets** | **$1,402** | **$1,539** | **$1,939** | **$2,945** | **$2,945** | **$3,693** | **$4,423** | **$5,926** |
| | | | | | | | | |
| **Current Liabilities** | | | | | | | | |
| Payables | $240 | $389 | $689 | $240 | $240 | $727 | $1,183 | $2,093 |
| Revolving Line of Credit | $500 | $500 | $500 | $0 | $0 | $500 | $500 | $500 |
| Other Current Liabilities | $0 | $0 | $0 | $0 | $0 | $0 | $0 | $0 |
| **Total Current Liabilities** | **$740** | **$889** | **$1,189** | **$240** | **$240** | **$1,227** | **$1,683** | **$2,593** |
| | | | | | | | | |
| **Non-Current Liabilities** | | | | | | | | |
| Long-Term Borrowings | $0 | $0 | $0 | $0 | $0 | $0 | $0 | $0 |
| Other Liabilities | $0 | $0 | $0 | $0 | $0 | $0 | $265 | $381 |
| Total Liabilities | $740 | $889 | $1,189 | $240 | $240 | $1,227 | $1,948 | $2,974 |
| **Net Assets** | **$663** | **$650** | **$750** | **$2,706** | **$2,706** | **$2,466** | **$2,475** | **$2,952** |
| | | | | | | | | |
| Issued Capital | $1,750 | $1,750 | $1,750 | $3,750 | $3,750 | $3,750 | $3,750 | $3,750 |
| Retained Earnings | $(1,087) | $(1,100) | $(1,000) | $(1,044) | $(1,044) | $(1,284) | $(1,274) | $(797) |
| **Total Shareholders Equity** | **$663** | **$650** | **$750** | **$2,706** | **$2,706** | **$2,466** | **$2,476** | **$2,953** |

| 2003/Q4 | Total 2003 | 2004 | 2005 |
|---|---|---|---|
| $1,415 | $1,415 | $2,630 | $5,138 |
| $970 | $970 | $3,315 | $6,445 |
| $0 | $0 | $0 | $0 |
| **$2,385** | **$2,385** | **$5,946** | **$11,583** |
| | | | |
| | | | |
| $1,803 | $1,803 | $2,052 | $2,452 |
| $(484) | $(484) | $(1,071) | $(1,563) |
| $1,319 | $1,319 | $981 | $889 |
| **$3,704** | **$3,704** | **$6,927** | **$12,472** |
| | | | |
| $727 | $727 | $2,486 | $4,834 |
| $0 | $0 | $0 | $0 |
| $0 | $0 | $0 | $0 |
| **$727** | **$727** | **$2,486** | **$4,834** |
| | | | |
| $0 | $0 | $0 | $0 |
| $77 | $77 | $77 | $77 |
| $804 | $804 | $2,563 | $4,911 |
| **$2,899** | **$2,899** | **$4,363** | **$7,561** |
| | | | |
| $3,750 | $3,750 | $3,750 | $3,750 |
| $(850) | $(850) | $614 | $3,812 |
| **$2,900** | **$2,900** | **$4,364** | **$7,562** |

## Cash Flow Statement: Year 1—2001

**BackTrack Solutions (Most Likely Scenario)**

| Cashflow Analysis | 1/1 thru 6/30 2000 $ | Jul 01 $ Jul 00 | Aug 01 $ Aug 00 | Sep 01 $ Sep 00 | Oct 01 $ Oct 00 | Nov 01 $ Nov 00 | Dec 01 $ Dec 00 | Jan 01 $ Jan 01 | Feb 01 $ Feb 01 |
|---|---|---|---|---|---|---|---|---|---|
| | | | | | | Forecast | | | |
| Opening Balance Cash (7/1/xx) | $41 | $1,500 | $1,432 | $1,237 | $1,112 | $959 | $856 | $775 | $656 |
| EBITDA | | ($48) | ($54) | ($86) | ($67) | ($65) | ($51) | ($89) | ($72) |
| Less Interest | | $0 | $0 | $0 | $0 | $0 | $0 | $0 | $0 |
| Less Tax | | $0 | $0 | $0 | $0 | $0 | $0 | $0 | $0 |
| Less Change in Working Capital | | $0 | $0 | $0 | $0 | $0 | $0 | $0 | $0 |
| Less CAPEX | ($41) | ($20) | ($140) | ($39) | ($86) | ($37) | ($30) | ($30) | ($30) |
| Long-term Debt | | $0 | $0 | $0 | $0 | $0 | $0 | $0 | $0 |
| Financing Activity | $1,500 | $0 | $0 | $0 | $0 | $0 | $0 | $0 | $0 |
| Dividends Paid | | $0 | $0 | $0 | $0 | $0 | $0 | $0 | $0 |
| **Closing Balance Cash (6/30/xx)** | **$1,500** | **$1,432** | **$1,237** | **$1,112** | **$959** | **$856** | **$775** | **$656** | **$555** |

## Cash Flow Statement: Years 2-5—2002-2005

| Cashflow Analysis | 2002/Q1 $ Jul-Sep | 2002/Q2 $ Oct-Dec | 2002/Q3 $ Jan-Mar | 2002/Q4 $ Apr-Jun | 2003/Q1 $ Jul-Sep | 2003/Q2 $ Oct-Dec |
|---|---|---|---|---|---|---|
| Opening Balance Cash (7/1/xx) | $162 | $511 | $416 | $365 | $1,987 | $1,513 |
| EBITDA | ($14) | $35 | $148 | $3 | ($170) | $86 |
| Less Interest | $0 | $0 | $0 | $0 | $0 | $0 |
| Less Tax | $0 | $0 | $0 | $0 | $0 | $0 |
| Less Change in Working Capital | $410 | ($50) | ($100) | ($350) | $347 | $106 |
| Less CAPEX | ($47) | ($80) | ($100) | ($30) | ($652) | ($187) |
| Long-term Debt | $0 | $0 | $0 | $0 | $0 | $0 |
| Financing Activity | $0 | $0 | $0 | $2,000 | $0 | $0 |
| Dividends Paid | $0 | $0 | $0 | $0 | $0 | $0 |
| **Closing Balance Cash (6/30/xx)** | **$511** | **$416** | **$365** | **$1,987** | **$1,513** | **$1,517** |

| Mar 01 | Apr 01 | May 01 | Jun 01 |
| $ | $ | $ | $ |
| Mar 01 | Apr 01 | May 01 | Jun 01 |
|---|---|---|---|
| $555 | $455 | $351 | $258 |
| ($70) | ($69) | ($64) | ($66) |
| $0 | $0 | $0 | $0 |
| $0 | $0 | $0 | $0 |
| $0 | $0 | $0 | $0 |
| ($30) | ($35) | ($30) | ($30) |
| $0 | $0 | $0 | $0 |
| $0 | $0 | $0 | $0 |
| $0 | $0 | $0 | $0 |
| **$455** | **$351** | **$258** | **$162** |

| 2003/Q3 | 2003/Q4 | 2004 | 2005 |
| $ | $ | $ | $ |
| Jan-Mar | Apr-Jun | | |
|---|---|---|---|
| $1,517 | $1,803 | $1,415 | $2,630 |
| $814 | $16 | $2,622 | $5,489 |
| $0 | $0 | $0 | $0 |
| $0 | $0 | ($570) | ($1,799) |
| ($455) | ($348) | ($586) | ($783) |
| ($73) | ($56) | ($250) | ($400) |
| $0 | $0 | $0 | $0 |
| $0 | $0 | $0 | $0 |
| $0 | $0 | $0 | $0 |
| **$1,803** | **$1,415** | **$2,630** | **$5,138** |

# Online Outdoor Company

BUSINESS PLAN                    OUTDOORSMAN.COM

*1400 Main St., Suite 3*
*Alpena, Michigan 49707*

*The success of this company will depend largely on the ability to attract its target audiences to shop online. E-mailed subscriptions and other marketing efforts will promote the Outdoorsman.com website and its targeted brand offerings.*

- BUSINESS PLAN

- MARKET APPROACH

- FINANCIAL STRATEGY

- PLAN FOR COMMUNITY LAUNCH

- ORGANIZATIONAL STRUCTURE

- BUSINESS CHALLENGES

**BUSINESS PLAN**

**Vision & Mission**

Outdoorsman.com will create an online community focused on serving and supporting the well established, easily identifiable market of the outdoor sporting lifestyle of anglers and hunters. The Outdoorsman.com web portal will serve the highly brand conscious and affiliation of loyal individuals and organizations whose members live the sporting lifestyle by providing a comprehensive clearinghouse of value-added, special interest content, valuable information resources, e-commerce capabilities, and user information sharing opportunities through the use of advanced technologies.

**The Hook**

Outdoorsman.com will build an online consumer database of 7.5 million subscribers within the first 18 months of launch. The portal site will have four main areas of unique offerings:

- Maps, way-point marking through GPS and integrated wireless devices, including emerging PDAs used in the hunting and fishing lifestyle. Outdoorsman.com will concentrate on becoming the place to come for all location finding/recording devices and associated product information.

- The use of a subscription-based e-mail newsletter/news alert system will bring the subscriber's love of the outdoors to him/her on a daily basis or as the news breaks. This service would attain the status of the "CNN" of the sportsman's lifestyle to be known as Outdoorsman News Network (WONN) through cable, and traditional media/news reporting affiliations.

- The Outdoorsman.com consumer brand will also be built surrounding the pervasive availability of content and brand e-commerce/e-retailing aspects of the site. Unique negotiated equipment and service arrangements will be made with highly recognized brand sporting goods suppliers, where Outdoorsman will act as the members' advocate and generate commissions and fees. Affiliates will also be sought in the travel, lodging, and guide and related industries. In addition to the affiliate program, special purchases and auction type sales will be offered to the members.

- All the above items will be done with the concentration of effort focused at advanced and emerging technologies that can be used in the hunting and angling markets.

**Market Sizing & Demographic Background**

One in six Americans are anglers. Of these 34 million anglers, 75 percent are male and 80 percent are between 16-54 years of age. In 1996, $38 billion was spent on fishing equipment and trips. Half of the anglers in the U.S. have attended college.

Of the 14 million hunters in the U.S. 90 percent are male, 80 percent are between 16-54, and 85 percent have a grade 12 education or more. Hunters spend $10 billion annually on equipment and trips.

From a technology adoption perspective, of the 80 percent of anglers and hunters aged 16-54 (or 38 million individuals), approximately 60 percent (or 19 million) have Internet access today. This would suggest that anglers and hunters aged 16-54 who have Internet access today spend approximately $28 billion on equipment and trips. This is Outdoorsman.com's targeted and growing membership audience.

Additional demographics available regarding cross-section of multi-interest individuals and cross-community related interests demonstrate enormous market potential beyond the initially targeted user interest base. Essentially, the user base expands into lifestyle requirements that follow hand-in-hand with the fishing and hunting lifestyle.

Outdoorsman.com has engaged significant content and data research services to establish a profile for pursuit of potential/prospect user base.

**MARKET APPROACH**

**1995 - 1998 Federal Bureau of Outdoor Recreation study on outdoor Activities and Interest.** This report has enabled the leadership to establish a potential user group size and user demographic profile by general interests and cross-sport interests and specifically by region, income, sex, and financial/spending orientation.

Market data has also been acquired through the purchase of private mailing list services providing the subscription and user profile content of leading outdoor and sporting magazine readership.

The Outdoorsman.com primary user communities include the following U.S. states based on population density of potential prospects fitting the target market profile. These states are New Jersey, Pennsylvania, Michigan, New York, Texas, Florida, California, Missouri, Michigan, and Ohio.

**Regional Market Considerations**

These findings have been validated firsthand through focus group and interviews conducted with targeted users in the sporting and outdoor life communities.

Initially, Outdoorsman.com marketing and awareness will rely on the power of targeted online messaging tools, strategies, and word-of-mouth references, followed up with directed traditional media promotional strategies, such as outdoor advertising, periodicals, and network and cable sponsorships.

**Targeted Marketing Promotional Strategy**

**Critical Success Factors to Successful Marketing Approach**
- Ability to attract and leverage current outdoor industry leaders for content and co-brand association
- Leverage branding efforts in marketplace across multiple media and technologies

The following marketing model outlines examples of immediately available marketing and promotional opportunities consistent with targeted Outdoorsman.com user base. Promotional strategies must be executed at a high level for continuous top-of-mind coverage, but should be nimble and leverageable for seasonal and regional differences and user brand preferences.

| Opportunity | Classification | Examples |
| --- | --- | --- |
| Periodicals | Traditional media | Print ads - in *Fisherman/Bowhunter* |
| Co-branding with demographics | Traditional media | Anheuser-Busch/ bar coasters, etc. |
| NASCAR events | Traditional media | Give-aways including bumper stickers, T-shirts etc. |
| Big Buck/Big Fish Contests | Online Media | Submit bragging photos |
| Win a free truck | Online Media | Subscribe and win truck with logo |
| Fishing Tournaments | Unique branding opportunity | National potential |
| Outdoorsman.com Boat | Unique branding opportunity | Logo covered boat visiting anglers giving stuff away at local lakes, etc. |
| Boat launch/wetland sponsorships | Unique branding opportunity | Goodwill to sportsmen and environment |
| Charitable Events | Unique branding opportunity | Lake Huron River Crab Salmon Stakes |
| Professional Speaker Sponsorships | National/Local | Jimmy Houston seminar series |
| Game Dinners | Local | Local restaurant promotions |
| Co-sponsorships | National | Ducks Unlimited, etc. |

*continued on next page*

| Giveaways | National | Matchboxes, bumper stickers, coasters, bottle coolers, key chains, coffee cups |
| Poster Campaign | Local | Tackle and bait shops, sporting goods stores, boat dealers, etc. |

**Revenue**

These are the primary revenue streams that will sustain Outdoorsman.com.

Direct revenues:

- Auctions
- Specials Deals
- Commissions from travel, e-sales
- Advertising banners
- Advertising focused on special needs of recipients of outbound materials
- Private-brand Outdoorsman.com products

Indirect revenues:

- Commissions from state and local governments
- Online commerce affiliations

**FINANCIAL STRATEGY**

**Funding Requirements**

Outdoorsman.com is requesting between $12-15 million for the development, launch, and 5-year ongoing expense outlook of the company expenses.

Additional funding requirements will potentially be required for consumer brand and related, currently unseen partnership development opportunity investments.

**Community Framework**

The Outdoorsman.com community strategy is centered around a targeted user demographic.

These targeted users have very specific interests and the site will have a high degree of credibility with the user base. Although users have specific interests, more often than not these interests change seasonally. The Outdoorsman.com site is designed to accommodate the interest shift.

As demonstrated in focus user group testing, a hard-core Bass fisherman using the Freshwater Fishing community found himself filling out an insurance quote form on the Boats and Marine section then purchasing a rod through an affiliate partner and then looking for a map to purchase through TopoZone.

**Growth/Exit Strategy**

The following growth/exit strategies indicate potential market opportunities for the Outdoorsman.com enterprise.

**Option #1**

Concept: Develop operational concept site, build business plan, put concept and plan up for sale.

This type of relationship would allow investment and competitor community to leverage concept and work performed and would result in a one-time windfall for Outdoorsman.com partners and advisors. Potential for follow-up consultation and director-level follow-on employment possible.

**Option #2**

Concept: Launch site, build independent consumer brand, put up for sale.

This type of relationship would primarily require launch and rapid deployment of brand awareness and gaining user base to make "attractive" to investment and/or competitor community to result in a sale of business and brand operations.

**Option #3**

Concept: Launch site and build independent consumer brand (national/global).

This type of relationship would require significant effort with business incubation and relationship development for national marketing and rollout management. Effective development of consumer brand could result in enormous revenue opportunities through e-commerce from partners and advertising revenues.

Demonstrated success could result in follow-on execution of Options #3 and #4.

**Option #3-A**

Concept: Launch site and build small-scale, independent consumer brand (national/global).

Entirely dependent on private funding and development resource availability, this type of web enterprise would be dependent on resource commitment and grassroots marketing efforts. Although small in scale and development, this enterprise could have significant impact on the sporting community but would be much slower to grasp significant revenues based on slower user growth rate resulting from significantly lower market penetration.

**Option #4**

Concept: Launch site and partner with name brand Internet portal/lifestyle community to extend content reach, community focus, and brand recognition, i.e., become a prime or sub-community within the established consumer brand. For example,

- Yahoo! Outdoorsman
- AOL Outdoorsman
- Excite Outdoorsman
- etc.

The portal would reap benefits from having a preconstructed lifestyle portal ready-to-go and have intellectual capital in place, while enabling Outdoorsman.com to build an enormous user base and create opportunity for revenue potential in the form of stock equity, flat-out cash purchase, or privately funded operating capital.

**Option #5**

Concept: Develop relationship with "privately" branded product manufacturer. Essentially create a private label portal focused around the sportsman lifestyle, i.e.,

- Jeep Outdoorsman.com
- Ford Outdoorsman.com
- etc.

This type of relationship would result in loss of individual brand but would provide private funding and allow the private brand to leverage work done to date. Privately branded product company reaps financial reward by leveraging online product already in place and Outdoorsman reaps windfall for flat-out cash purchase, or privately funded operating capital and continued employment with product manufacturer while retaining direction and leadership for community integrity.

## PLAN FOR COMMUNITY LAUNCH

Tactical execution activities will continue as follows in support of public Internet "soft" launch in March 2000 timeframe. Site will be launched no later than mid March. Site will have an estimated 75 percent portion of initial "look and feel" issues resolved, 75-90 percent portion of content/links available, 70 percent of interactive functional issues resolved, and 80 percent of revenue-generating affiliate partner programs in activation.

### Accomplishments

Outdoorsman.com was recently conceived and is in the development phase. Based on the current calendar year the following has been accomplished:

- A prototype site has been developed and is up and running in a privately hosted environment
- Prospective customer and partner lists have been developed and several have been contacted for establishing an emerging business relationship
- Agreements have been drafted with several vendor partners to offer ecommerce opportunities within the online community
- A business plan has been established and is being communicated to the investment community at large to acquire funding to proceed
- A core business management team has been created, consisting of business and technical professionals
- Focus groups have been established and are currently providing ongoing insight and consumer end-user feedback into the online community development cycle. Initial market acceptance tests have indicated a warm welcome of the concept for potential

## ORGANIZATIONAL STRUCTURE

The Outdoorsman.com organizational structure is intended to be a flexible version of a traditional organization structure. It is our belief that a learning and cross-functional organization is key to our success. Any one member of the Outdoorsman leadership or staff team community must be able to perform related tasks when business needs or technical crises arise. Following the list below you will find profiles of the founding partners and additional leadership team.

- President/Founder
- Internet Commerce Management
- Sales
- Marketing/Brand Management
- Legal (outsourced)
- Chief Technology Officer
- Application Development
- Technical Infrastructure
- Ongoing Technical Operations

The Outdoorsman team is made up of outdoor enthusiasts, and business and technical professionals. Our team is committed to the outdoor lifestyle. The following profiles of our founders, leadership, and advisory teams illustrate the outdoor experiences and professional expertise of the Outdoorsman team.

### Dave Miller, Founder and President

Dave Miller is the founder and thought leader behind the Outdoorsman community portal. Dave has guided the Outdoorsman team to its launch and is the lead concept champion. Dave has 14 years of high-tech industry experience, specializing in sales and marketing concept development, consumer behavior, and user interface development. Dave has held many leadership positions within the high-tech community and concurrently holds a marketing management position with a leading high-tech services company. He brings his unique brand of creative talent and multiple years of professional business influences to the Outdoorsman creative and business strategy.

Dave has been a member of the sporting community for over 20 years and has extensive experience in fishing, boating, wildlife photography, and other outdoor activities. A Midwest native, he has also lived in northern California, western Montana, and his particular interests include pursuit of Pacific Coastal Steelhead, fishing western Montana's Blue Ribbon trout streams, exploring Michigan's Great Lakes, and preparing fish and game dishes for his family.

### Robert Olsen, Founding Partner and Chief Technology Officer

Robert brings technology leadership to Outdoorsman. The Outdoorsman community portal is developed with Bob's Internet and implementation expertise. Bob's extensive, eleven-year career in application development, technical implementation, and database management has enabled our website and launch schedule. Throughout his high-tech career, Bob has held technical leadership and senior project implementation positions in bringing many web-based conceptual ideas into reality. His knowledge of digital technologies and development languages enables Outdoorsman to leverage his unique, "blue sky" perspective.

Bob has spent many years enjoying the outdoors lifestyle. Bob is a native of Michigan and brings knowledge and experiences of Michigan's "northern coasts" and communities.

### Wendy Pepper, Design and Creative Development Director

Wendy brings creative vision and visual management skills to the Outdoorsman community. She has developed and manages the overall visual integrity and brand imagery of the Outdoorsman.com community. Wendy's eleven-year career in design development, brand image implementation, and technical management has enabled Outdoorsman to leverage its brand across multiple computing and media platforms. Her leadership, creative excellence, and professional expertise brings the visual energy of the Outdoorsman community to life.

A Midwest native, Wendy spends many hours in the outdoors of the northern Midwest, particularly Michigan's upper peninsula and outlying island destinations.

| **Advisory Panel** | A highly qualified advisory panel has been established, and they have signed commitments for a period of one year to provide insight to users, sporting trends, and online ecommerce purchasing behavior of outdoor-type goods and services. Panel member detail and profile information is available upon request to a limited audience. |
|---|---|

**BUSINESS CHALLENGES**

- Acquiring strategic investment and consistent funding stream
- Tactical and strategic site development and content planning
- Research and development of content/link generation
- User functionality and programming development and execution
- Development of identity and consumer brand acceptance
- Identification, development, and execution of effective marketing communications
- Identifying and executing ongoing affiliate revenue generation, advertising, and ecommerce revenue stream

## Launch and Operating Investment Assumptions

| Direct Expenses | 2001 | 2002 | 2003 | 2004 |
|---|---|---|---|---|
| **Business Operating Structure** | | | | |
| **Executive Leadership** | | | | |
| Chief Executive Officer (CEO) | $175,000 | $190,000 | $200,000 | $250,000 |
| Chief Financial Officer (and support) | $225,000 | $300,000 | $350,000 | $375,000 |
| Chief Technology Officer (CTO) | $120,000 | $120,000 | $130,000 | $140,000 |
| **Business Operations Leadership** | | | | |
| Legal (outside counsel) | $500,000 | $350,000 | $250,000 | $200,000 |
| Sales staff | $200,000 | $300,000 | $400,000 | $50,000 |
| Marketing/PR (including salary) | $250,000 | $300,000 | $350,000 | $400,000 |
| Advertising | $500,000 | $60,000 | $700,000 | $750,000 |
| Administrative support | $75,000 | $77,000 | $79,000 | $81,000 |
| HR Services | $100,000 | $107,000 | $114,490 | $122,504 |
| **Technical Operations and Facilities** | | | | |
| Application Development Team | $200,000 | $214,000 | $228,980 | $245,009 |
| Infrastructure/Systems Administration | $400,000 | $325,000 | $325,000 | $325,000 |
| Communications/Web Hosting | $25,000 | $30,000 | $36,000 | $36,000 |
| Space/Facilities (partner provided) | | | | |
| **Total** | **$2,770,000** | **$2,373,000** | **$3,163,470** | **$2,974,513** |

*Revenue expectations available on request.*
*Assumes company formed on 1/1/2001.*

| | 2005 | TOTAL |
|---|---|---|
| | $260,000 | $1,075,000 |
| | $400,000 | $1,650,000 |
| | $160,000 | $670,000 |
| | | |
| | $200,000 | $1,500,000 |
| | $600,000 | $1,550,000 |
| | $450,000 | $1,750,000 |
| | $800,000 | $2,810,000 |
| | $83,000 | $395,000 |
| | $131,080 | $575,074 |
| | | |
| | $262,159 | $1,150,148 |
| | $325,000 | $1,700,000 |
| | $43,200 | $170,200 |
| | | |
| | **$3,714,439** | **$14,995,422** |

# Racing Parts Store

BUSINESS PLAN

SOUTHEAST RACING PARTS

*4315 Dale Jarrett Avenue*
*Raleigh, North Carolina 27612*

*Southeast Racing Parts is dedicated to providing racing products that combine quality performance with value pricing. We wish to establish a successful partnership with our customers, our employees, and our suppliers that respects the interests and goals of each party. Our target market will be the entry-level/novice racer. This business plan was compiled using Business Plan Pro, © 1999, Palo Alto Software, www.paloaltosoftware.com, 800-229-7526.*

- EXECUTIVE SUMMARY

- COMPANY SUMMARY

- PRODUCTS & SERVICES

- MARKET ANALYSIS SUMMARY

- STRATEGY & IMPLEMENTATION SUMMARY

- MANAGEMENT SUMMARY

- FINANCIAL PLAN

## EXECUTIVE SUMMARY

We believe there is room for smaller companies in the retail racing parts market. A smaller firm is more personalized and more responsive, which allows the decisionmaking process to be streamlined, reducing delays. The person you deal with is the decisionmaker, the person that calls the shots. People enjoy working with folks on a personal level; that's part of what smaller firms have to offer. And with all the technology available, we can get a bigger piece of the market by going out and attaining our own business.

We need to be aware of the service aspect of our sales, along with new racer rules and regulations, and not allow ourselves to become self-satisfied in an industry that is constantly changing.

The continued boom of the hardcore racing market, along with the sport of racing itself, is most reassuring. However, it will take hard work, dedication, proper inventory control, and a well-positioned advertising and promotion program to be successful.

### Objectives

1. To make Southeast Racing Parts the number one destination for the purchase of entry-level/novice racing supplies in the Carolinas.
2. To achieve an initial gross profit margin of at least 30 percent, increasing that by at least 1 percent per year until reaching our final target of 33 percent.
3. To sell $350,000 in product the first year.
4. To maintain a solid growth rate of 30 percent per year for the first five years.

### Mission

Southeast Racing Parts is dedicated to providing racing products that combine quality performance with value pricing. We wish to establish a successful partnership with our customers, our employees, and our suppliers that respects the interests and goals of each party.

Constantly striving to supply what the consumer is asking for, we will continually review what is available in the marketplace, and what isn't. Improving on what is available and providing new products and services to the areas of need will help ensure our success in a market driven by consumer demand.

Success will ultimately be measured by our customers choosing us because of their belief in our ability to meet or exceed their expectations of price, service, and selection.

### Keys to Success

To succeed in this business, we must:

- Be an active member of the racing community; i.e., attend functions at local race tracks, attend regional and national trade shows.
- Deliver our products promptly.
- Work with our customers on a personal level, as opposed to the "What's your customer number?" mentality of large mail order firms.

## COMPANY SUMMARY

Southeast Racing Parts is a new company, which upon commencement of operations will provide entry-level oval track racers with affordable products and quality service.

### Company Ownership

Southeast Racing Parts is a North Carolina corporation, subchapter "S", owned entirely by Tim and Molly Jones.

Our start-up costs are listed on the following page. Major costs include $12,500 for computer hardware, software, and setup support; $1,600 for rent, $2,500 for a telephone system, approximately $1,300 for office equipment and furniture, approximately $2,700 for parts shelving and other warehouse equipment, $2,800 for leasehold improvements, and $7,000 for a company pickup truck.

The company will start out with about three months' inventory on hand. This means the majority of company assets will consist of inventory and the starting cash balance will not be significant.

You will find that we have approximately $60,625 additional funding needed. The purpose of this plan is to secure financing for that amount.

Later in this plan, when you view the Projected Balance Sheet, Projected Cash Flow, and the Projected Profit and Loss, you will notice that we do not show any debt or interest expense. However, by examining these same charts, you will see that we project a sufficient amount of earnings to service a debt load.

Upon negotiations of debt amount and terms, modified charts will be provided upon request.

**Start-up Summary**

**Start-up Plan**
**Start-up Expenses**

| | |
|---|---|
| Legal | $0 |
| Decals | $725 |
| Rent | $1,600 |
| Stationery, forms, etc. | $300 |
| Expensed equipment | $0 |
| Other | $0 |
| **Total Start-up Expenses** | **$2,625** |

**Start-up Assets Needed**

| | |
|---|---|
| Cash Requirements | $1,000 |
| Start-up inventory | $50,000 |
| Other Short-term Assets | $0 |
| **Total Short-term Assets** | **$51,000** |
| **Long-term Assets** | **$29,000** |
| **Total Assets** | **$80,000** |

| | |
|---|---|
| Total Start-up Requirements: | $82,625 |
| Left to finance: | $60,625 |

**Start-up Funding Plan**
**Investment**

| | |
|---|---|
| Personal Investment | $20,000 |
| Other | $0 |
| **Total Investment** | **$20,000** |

**Short-term Liabilities**

| | |
|---|---|
| Unpaid Expenses | $2,000 |
| Short-term Loans | $0 |
| Interest-free Short-term Loans | $0 |
| Subtotal Short-term Liabilities | $2,000 |
| Long-term Liabilities | $0 |
| **Total Liabilities** | **$2,000** |

**Start-up Summary**

*Continued*

| Loss at Start-up | $58,000 |
|---|---|
| Total Capital | $78,000 |
| Total Capital and Liabilities | $80,000 |
| Checkline | $0 |

**Company Location**

Southeast Racing Parts will be located at 4315 Dale Jarrett Avenue, Raleigh, North Carolina. This location will afford us good visibility along with convenient access for traveling race teams wishing to stop at our location.

Another advantage of this location is the recent announcement of a go-cart/entertainment complex, which will be located directly across the street. This complex will attract many potential customers to our immediate vicinity.

By locating in close proximity to Charlotte, Southeast Racing Parts will enjoy a large built-in customer base. The skyrocketing popularity of NASCAR Winston Cup racing in the last 15 years has only strengthened its role as the hub for most race teams and all the related businesses they've spawned.

The sport's explosion has been so boundless that University of North Carolina at Charlotte researchers conducted a study of the industry to try to determine its impact. The study, completed in December 1996, found that in its surrounding counties, NASCAR racing is responsible for about 2,000 jobs producing more than $200 million in expenditures annually—figures that many in the industry consider conservative in 1998. Many of the people employed within the industry, along with their children, other relatives, and friends, take up racing as a hobby.

Another benefit of the area is that it is centrally located near the East Coast. The Carolinas and parts of Virginia and Georgia will have the benefit of overnight UPS ground service. A large portion of the East Coast and southeastern United States would be serviced in two days by UPS ground service.

**Company Facility**

We will initially be leasing 3,000 square feet of a new 10,000-square-foot building. As needs dictate, our office and/or warehouse facilities could be expanded into an additional 2,500 square feet.

We will be sharing this facility with another business that is also involved in racing, and their business attracts many of the local racers. In light of this, we will meet many potential customers simply because of our association with them.

This location will consist of a showroom, office space, and warehousing. All deliveries and shipments will be serviced at this location. We will also have ample parking available.

**PRODUCTS & SERVICES**

Southeast Racing Parts will sell racing products to the entry-level/novice racer. These products will include engine and chassis parts along with safety and set-up equipment. Services that we will provide include coil spring rating, along with a scaling service for race cars.

**Product and Service Description**

Southeast Racing Parts will assist its customers in selecting the best parts for their application at a price that meets or exceeds their expectations. In the event of a problem, we will be there to assist and counsel the customer to a speedy solution.

We will carry or have quick access to most major lines of racing equipment. We will also carry generic "plain label" merchandise that we will market under our own performance name. Private labeling will allow us, in most cases, to greatly increase our profit margins since the procurement costs are much lower for these types of items.

Even though our target market is the entry-level racer, our product mix will be sufficient to fill most of the needs of even the most hard-core racer. With leisure time at a premium, our reputation for having needed items in stock will save our customers both time and money. We will be open Monday through Saturday with hours yet to be determined.

Our experience has shown that most entry-level racers' preference is for low prices. We believe we can offer products that indeed are lower in price without sacrificing the performance and safety concerns that our customers will demand. Southeast Racing Parts will provide precisely the level of service that today's entry-level racer requires.

**Competitive Comparison**

Within our niche, we only have one significant competitor. They, however, do not carry engine parts, which should give us an edge in that respect.

In general, however, our competition is not in our targeted portion of the market. This competition consists mainly of these three groups:

1. NASCAR Winston Cup suppliers
2. Asphalt late model chassis builders
3. National mail order suppliers

More discussion is included later in this plan on competitive businesses.

**Sales Literature**

To drive sales initially, Southeast Racing Parts will utilize an existing supply catalog. This four-color catalog will have a different cover with the Southeast Racing Parts logo, phone number, etc., printed on it.

After much research, we found that the product mix in this catalog most closely resembles the needs of the consumer niche that we are focusing upon. An agreement was reached to supply these catalogs to us at no charge. This precludes the need to invest in catalog production at the outset. In turn, we will be using the catalog company as a supplier for some of the inventory lines that we carry. We have developed a price sheet to be enclosed with each catalog.

We will produce flyers in-house on an as-needed basis. These will primarily be to showcase new products and/or to advertise special sales promotions. The flyers will be distributed in the same fashion as the catalogs.

**Catalog Distribution**

Following are planned means of catalog distribution:

1. Give away in-store
2. Enclose in mail order shipments
3. Personally hand out at area race tracks
4. Distribute at local trade shows and auctions
5. Sell for $3 through local racing newspaper business card advertisements
6. Upon the release of a new catalog, we would need to check into the financial feasibility of utilizing direct mail as a means of bulk distribution

**Sourcing**

This is an area that we feel we will enjoy a distinct advantage over much of our competition. Because of our past work experience in purchasing, we have a vast number of supplier contacts within the racing industry. We have good, long-term, solid relationships with many of these vendors which, in many cases, will allow us to achieve decreased cost-of-goods and/or additional terms. Many of these suppliers have already committed to special deals for us, such as waiving their buy-in requirements, additional payment terms, sales referrals, etc.

We will purchase our inventory from both regional wholesalers and direct from the manufacturers. We will use the regional wholesalers more initially because of their ability to service us faster. This will lower our margins slightly; however, we feel that the upside will be that it will allow us to turn our inventory faster. As our sales volume increases, we will shift our buying patterns away from the wholesalers and purchase more of our inventory direct, which will result in increased profits.

## Technology

All computer hardware and software systems that will be utilized by Southeast Racing Parts have been carefully and diligently evaluated. We will use off-the-shelf, PC-based software for accounting purposes including AR/AP, inventory, purchasing, sales, and returns. We will start out with three workstations and expand upon that as necessary.

Many of the computer systems used in the racing industry today are outmoded and obsolete. The major suppliers are reluctant to change because of the huge capital expense to change over their systems at one time. Hence, they keep going with the old and outdated.

By choosing this software, our training costs will be reduced tremendously. Much of the software used by competitors takes weeks to learn and master. Southeast Racing Parts's use of this software will enable a basic, computer-literate employee to learn the system in one day.

This system will speed our order entry process, assist us in sales forecasting, and allow us to give a higher level of customer service.

## Future Products and Services

We must remain on top of new products and trends. The most important factor in developing future products is market need. Our understanding of the needs in our market niche is one of our competitive advantages.

As stated earlier, we will have our own private label brand. Not only are profit margins better than name brands, but these accessories will help build name identity and awareness for Southeast Racing Parts when they are used on the race track. As our sales volume increases, this will be an area that we can expand.

Another natural area for expansion in the future would be the implementation of a website. On-line commerce is becoming an increasingly attractive option, due to relatively low cost of operation, the global reach of the medium, and the increasing security. Our business model could quite easily expand to include a form of Internet commerce in a variety of racing equipment.

## MARKET ANALYSIS SUMMARY

Currently, the market for racing parts and accessories is rapidly expanding. Performance Racing Industry completed an estimate for total number of racers. The resulting number was 385,000 people who competed in an organized auto race at least once in the past year. The estimate includes all forms of auto racing: drag, stock car, open wheel, modified, sports car, autocross, formula car, tractor pull, and off-road.

Overall, it is estimated that the total retail market for hardcore racing products is $1.5 billion annually and it still continues to grow.

The only real threat to our venture would be a similar new entry to the marketplace. This opportunity may best be described as one ready and waiting for the first entrant who arrives with a well-conceived plan, sufficient industry experience, and the required capitalization.

The racing industry is in a boom period. While there are many items from various vendors available, Southeast Racing Parts has approached the market as a specialty retailer—a provider of parts and services to the entry-level racer.

Our target customer in this segment will have a wide range of racing and automotive skills, but our most important target customers are relatively unsophisticated at racing. We will be able to serve this customer well not only by offering them parts at an affordable price, but also by giving them advice that ensures they get the task done correctly, therefore improving their on-track performance.

**Market Segmentation**

Our segment definition is in and of itself strategic. We are not intending to satisfy all users of racing equipment, but rather those who are just starting out and those who are struggling to keep up. We can save our customers time and money, not so much within our pricing structure, but by assessing their needs and directing them toward the proper product. Racers, by nature, tend to desire a high-end product, when often a low to mid-end product will do as well, or sometimes even a better job. By always dealing in an honest and ethical manner, we will build customer loyalty and word-of-mouth sales that many of our competitors are lacking.

**Target Market Segment Strategy**

Since our target market is the entry-level racer, the most important needs are service, price, and availability, in that order. One of the key points of our strategy is to focus on target segments that know and understand these needs and are willing for us to fulfill those needs.

**Market Needs**

Trends are in our favor. We have identified four major trends that help us:

**Market Trends**

1. Motorsports in general, and circle track racing in particular, have experienced explosive growth in the 1990s. Most experts attribute this growth to greatly expanded television coverage of motorsports events. This coverage exposes many more potential participants to the sport. By focusing on affordable entry-level racing, we feel that Southeast Racing Parts will be filling a niche in the market.
2. This area has experienced tremendous population growth in the past decade, approximately 25 percent. As racing and the local population grow hand-in-hand, it should make many more potential customers available to us.
3. There are a lot of fathers dreaming their son will be the next Jeff Gordon. In fact, there are tens of thousands of serious young kart racers who have chosen this sport over baseball, football, or basketball. They'll be the ones that fill the fields in the next decade.
4. Finally, there is the aging Baby Boomer generation. Many have discharged their duties to their children, who have grown and moved on, and now there is money and time again. They turn to something they always wanted to do, or return to the sport they loved, and they go racing.

With expanded television coverage and an enormous base of grassroots motorsports activity, auto racing is a thriving industry, as well as the fastest growing sport in America.

**Industry Analysis**

As with baseball, it could be argued that auto racing has grown to such popularity because of its vital grassroots foundation. Our customers will be the Little Leagues and softball leagues of auto racing. Outsiders to the racing industry must understand that racers may be the most obsessive consumers of any industry. Because of the pressure to win, they avidly purchase new technology. In most race cars, several parts will become obsolete in the course of a season, even though they function perfectly well.

Racers are hard on their investment, too. New tires might be a weekly purchase, and several engine freshening expenditures might be called for in a season. A good whack at the outside wall, and a racing retailer has a customer or two for shocks, a-arms, fasteners, hubs, and more.

Racers spend what it takes to win; they are not out merely to enjoy the ride. Any person who has spent any time at all in the racing pit has heard the guy in front of him in the snack bar line describe how he postponed a key household expense—the telephone bill or a new household appliance—to purchase a new right rear tire, or other critical racing part.

To service this sport, there are thousands of small businesses across the country skilled in the ways of horsepower and hooking it to the ground. Whether they make their money from parts or services, retailing or building engines, these businesses make it an easy and convenient matter to go racing. Without these local ambassadors of speed, it is hard to imagine the existence of auto racing in a large scale.

**Industry Participants**

We are part of the Performance Racing Industry, which includes several kinds of businesses.

**Speed Shops:** Most of these are small, sometimes part-time, ventures run from the individual's home. Sometimes they will service a local race track; however, they usually carry a very minimal amount of inventory and are usually operated by a racer or an ex-racer depending solely upon a small circle of friends or acquaintances as customers. They normally are short on business and marketing skills.

**Engine and Chassis Builders:** Typically these are well-respected firms supplying engines and chassis to the racing industry. Their customer profile lies in the mid to upper end of the market. They offer superb technical support; however, it is only available to customers utilizing their engine or chassis. They stock parts to service their engine or chassis, but are usually limited in areas beyond that. Normally their pricing structure is slightly above average.

**Mail Order:** The racing industry is served increasingly by large mail order firms that offer aggressive pricing on racing components. They are usually impersonal, and have little or no technical support available. For the purely price-driven buyer who purchases parts and expects no support, these firms offer a good option.

**Others:** There are many other channels through which people buy their racing parts, usually variations of the main three types above.

**Distribution Patterns**

Generally, traditional distribution channels are followed. The products are bought from distributors and/or direct from the manufacturers who have little say in how products are marketed. As in most industries, price levels decrease as volume increases.

**Competition and Buying Patterns**

We feel that racers understand the concept of service and availability, and they are much more likely to pay for it when the offering is clearly stated.

There is no doubt that we will compete much more against the large mail order outfits than against any small local suppliers. We have good indications that racers/customers would pay

5-15 percent more for a long-term relationship with a vendor providing quality service and support. To this point, the racer thinks about price because that's what he sees emphasized by the mail order companies.

Availability is of utmost importance. Buyers tend to want immediate, local solutions to their problems and/or needs.

By positioning ourselves at the lower end of the market, we will present ourselves to consumers just getting into racing, and we will sell to a base of customers that we can grow with together.

**Main Competitors**

- Professional Racing Store

The above is targeted towards the professional (NASCAR Winston Cup, etc.) market. They carry a totally different product mix to service that market. Their prices are high, and their interest in selling to the entry-level market is basically nonexistent.

- Performance Motorsports

This is a late-model chassis builder not targeting the entry-level market. Basically, they stock inventory that's used just on their own cars. They are located in the Motorsports Center business park which is in an out-of-the-way, hard-to-find location.

- The Pit Stop Shop

They are a large drag racing mail order firm that is skimming the circle track gravy. Since Southeast Racing Parts will cater to the circle track market, we believe that whatever local circle track customers they have will switch suppliers. We will have more knowledge and experience to suit their needs.

- Motorsports and More

These are the mega mail order firms. Customers seem to use them only for price, and because of a lack of local suppliers. We can offer faster delivery times, along with knowledge and experience in their type of racing. We believe a small share of their circle track market would be obtainable. These companies do not enjoy a loyal circle track customer base.

- Buddy's Used Racing Parts

As implied in their name, they sell used parts, so in most cases they're not usable for our target market. They also sell a limited amount of new parts; however, because of their name, most people are not aware of this. Also, they are located in an area which was described as a poor location.

- Target Racing

They are the only local competitor that we could identify that was targeting our niche. Following are what we feel are some of our competitive advantages: We feel that we are in a much better location. They utilize a black and white flyer as their main sales tool, and we will have a professional four-color catalog. Also, they concentrate mainly on chassis and safety equipment, where we will also offer a full array of engine parts.

The S.I.C. code for Southeast Racing Parts is 5531, Speed Shop—retail.         **Standard Industrial Classification**

**STRATEGY &
IMPLEMENTATION
SUMMARY**

Our strategy is based on serving the niche of entry-level racers well. This area is full of small race teams that can't get products or services from the major vendors who focus only on professional race teams.

Also:

- What begins as a customized version of a standard product, tailored to the needs of local racers, can eventually become a niche product that will fill the needs of similar racers across the country.
- We are planning our marketing strategy so that we can eventually reach specific kinds of racers across broad geographic lines.
- We focus on satisfying the needs of entry-level race teams.
- We focus on follow-on technology that we can take to the masses, as opposed to leading edge technology that aims at the professional race teams.

**Marketing Strategy**

The retail marketing strategy of Southeast Racing Parts centers on creating a corporate identity that clearly defines our market niche in terms that benefit our customer. Other specific strategies that will be used follow:

1. Print Ads—Keeping the Southeast Racing Parts name in front of the customer while getting established will be necessary. We plan on running limited space ads in the local racing newspapers to keep our name and phone number in front of the consumer. We may attempt to showcase a single product in an effort to return revenue from the ad. Our past experience has been that showing measurable revenue from these types of ads is difficult. In the future we plan on utilizing *Stock Car Racing* and *Circle Track* (both national magazines) as a method of increasing our sales revenue.

2. Press Releases—The local racing papers: the *Racing News*, *Late Model Digest*, *Dirt Late Model Digest*, and the *Pit List* have offered to run releases and/or stories concerning the opening of Southeast Racing Parts. *Stock Car Racing* magazine has also extended us the same offer. We will also use the above media to run new product releases.

3. Race Car Sponsorship—Entry-level racers can be persuaded into running the Southeast Racing Parts logo on their race car in exchange for a token discount on purchases and/ or for receiving technical support.

4. Decals—We will have decals manufactured with the Southeast Racing Parts logo. We will include the decals with all of the orders that we ship. Entry-level racers in particular enjoy displaying decals on their race cars, haulers, tool boxes, etc.

5. Apparel—We know several people in the area who produce NASCAR apparel. A line of premium Southeast Racing Parts apparel could be designed and produced in very short runs to reduce inventory costs. These can be sold or given away with qualifying purchases to further expose the Southeast Racing Parts name.

6. Grand Opening—A Grand Opening is the most successful of any in-store promotions. With manufacturer support, a large number of door prizes can be given away while instantly building a mailing list. Loss leader pricing on a few high volume consumable products will attract in-store traffic. Vendors will subsidize loss leader pricing with a rebate or kickback. Appearances by local racing celebrities would also expose potential customers to Southeast Racing Parts.

7. Trade Shows—We will exhibit at approximately four local trade shows annually. Revenue that we produce at the shows will outweigh our expenses for attending.

8. Word of Mouth—By giving first-time customers great service and a fair price, the word is sure to spread. Also, the many industry and racer contacts that we already have in the area will prove to be most beneficial in spreading the word.

All marketing decisions with regard to specific media choices, frequency, size, and expenditures will be conducted on an on-going basis with careful considerations of returns generated.

## Pricing Strategy

Our customers are especially sensitive to value. We must ensure that our price and service are perceived to be a good value to the racers. However, in the nearly thirty years of experience that we have accumulated in the racing industry, one message rings true: someone can always beat you on price.

Therefore, our pricing strategy is to be competitive within the various product categories, but not to rely on the selling price to overshadow the other advantages of doing business with our company. We will sell ourselves on the basis of a diverse line of quality products, that are readily available, reasonably priced, and backed up by our extraordinary customer service. The products will be checked prior to shipment and all promised shipping dates will be met.

We will strive for a gross profit margin of 30 percent, increasing that to 33 percent by year four.

## Promotion Strategy

Our most important vehicle for sales promotion will be our catalog, which is discussed later in this plan.

## Distribution Strategy

Our customers will buy our products at our location. However, we anticipate a significant amount of mail order sales in order to meet or exceed our Sales Forecast. We will receive orders by mail, phone, or fax, process them immediately, and ship the goods via United Parcel Service.

In the event we are out of an item or we don't stock it, many of our vendors have offered drop shipping as a service to us. This will allow us to keep our service at a high level, yet let us keep our inventory levels in check.

In the future, electronic commerce with a secure website will be thoroughly investigated for feasibility.

## Sales Strategy

Because Southeast Racing Parts is a new entity, we understand that we will have to prove our company's worth to racers in order to earn their respect and business.

Most importantly, we need to sell our company, not necessarily the products. We will need to push our service and support capabilities.

## Sales Forecast

The following table and related charts show our present sales forecast. We are projecting sales to grow at the rate of 30 percent for the next three years.

Our seasonality, as shown in the chart, is a factor in the racing industry. We will tend to sell much better in the period January through June, while sales trail off in late summer and fall.

Management feels these forecasts are highly attainable.

| Sales Forecast | | | |
|---|---|---|---|
| **Sales** | **FY2000** | **FY2001** | **FY2002** |
| Inventory Sales | $350,219 | $455,285 | $591,870 |
| Internet marketing | $16,800 | $16,800 | $16,800 |
| Other | $0 | $0 | $0 |
| **Total Sales** | **$367,019** | **$472,085** | **$608,670** |
| | | | |
| **Direct Cost of Sales** | | | |
| Inventory Sales | $245,154 | $314,147 | $402,472 |
| Internet marketing | $0 | $0 | $0 |
| Other | $0 | $0 | $0 |
| **Subtotal Cost of Sales** | **$245,154** | **$314,147** | **$402,472** |

**Sales Forecast Details**

When Performance Racing Industry completed its annual survey, the resulting figure for total number of racers was 385,000. Within the survey they also found that 150,000 of those were oval track racers. The survey also showed $1.5 billion in annual retail sales for all segments, with 48 percent of that total ($720 million) derived from the oval track segment. By dividing that number ($720 million) by the number of oval track racers (150,000), the average annual retail purchases of oval track racers equals $4,800. From our past experience, we believe that each customer we have would spend on average 25 percent of that figure ($1,200) with our company. Finally, by dividing our first year sales forecast ($350,000) by $1,200 (average annual customer purchases), it shows that we will need 292 customers to support the sales forecast numbers. We believe, by and large, that these are realistic and attainable numbers.

**Strategic Alliances**

We have the ability to build strong strategic alliances with many of our suppliers, some of which are listed below.

- Smith Racing. They will do "whatever they can" to help us succeed. Possibly supply us with a show car to display in our showroom.
- Motorsport Industries. They will set us up as a W.D. without the buy-in requirement.
- Raleigh Products, Inc. They will set us up as a W.D. and could also be persuaded into extending us special terms.
- Racing Accessories, Etc. They will set us up as a W.D and help out as needed with additional terms.
- Jalopy Shop. They have set us up as a dealer and will drop ship when needed.
- A&I Industries. They will work with us by drop shipping direct to our customers and also by acting as a "paper" warehouse so that we may order direct from the manufacturer for a nominal billing fee.
- Racemore, Inc. They will supply us with used testing equipment at no charge. They have indicated that they would also extend special terms and/or dating on initial stocking order.
- Winner's Circle. They will supply us with their 94-page 4-color catalog at no charge.

The following two local warehouses will help us immensely in keeping our own inventory levels in check, while still giving our customers fast service:

- Andy's Storage
- Wherehouse

Approached properly, these vendors and many others will assist Southeast Racing Parts in becoming a force in the marketplace.

We are a small company owned and operated by Tim and Molly Jones, husband and wife, as a subchapter "S" corporation.

　　Tim Jones—President

Tim will be the main salesperson. He will also be responsible for shipping and receiving, inventory management, and the marketing and promotion of products. Tim will assist with recordkeeping and cost containment.

　　Molly Jones—Corporate Secretary

Molly will maintain the company records and be in direct communication with the accountant and other advisors. She will also be in charge of the computer system and perform all of the desktop publishing for the company. She will assist as needed with sales, shipping and receiving, and customer service related issues.

In addition to her regular duties, Molly will be doing Internet marketing from her office at Southeast Racing Parts. We anticipate that 20 hours every week will be dedicated to this marketing. The revenue that will be generated by this is reflected in the Sales Forecast.

The initial management team depends on the founders themselves, with little back-up. We plan on hiring additional personnel as the need for them arises, and as we have the ability to pay them.

Tim and Molly not only have the desire to succeed, but will bring a wealth of knowledge and experience to the Southeast Racing Parts team. They have nearly thirty years of combined experience in the racing industry and have both performed nearly all facets of daily operations for a racing business.

**Management Team**

We depend on professionals, particularly our CPA, for some key management help. We have retained a local CPA to help us with financial and business management questions since we don't have a strong background in those areas. Also, we are short on experience concerning human resource issues; however, we plan on utilizing our network of business associates to advise us when the need arises.

**Management Team Gaps**

The cornerstone of the personnel plan is to maximize productivity and minimize the labor burden on the company's operating expenses. As we grow, we expect to see steady increases in our personnel to match the increases in sales.

**Personnel Plan**

**Personnel Plan**

| Personnel | FY2000 | FY2001 | FY2002 |
|---|---|---|---|
| Tim Jones | $16,800 | $20,160 | $24,192 |
| Molly Jones | $9,600 | $11,520 | $13,824 |
| Salesperson (PT) | $0 | $8,000 | $8,000 |
| Salesperson (FT) | $0 | $0 | $20,000 |
| Other | $0 | $0 | $0 |
| **Total Payroll** | **$26,400** | **$39,680** | **$66,016** |
| | | | |
| Total Headcount | 2 | 3 | 4 |
| Payroll Burden | $3,960 | $5,952 | $9,902 |
| **Total Payroll Expenditures** | **$30,360** | **$45,632** | **$75,918** |

## FINANCIAL PLAN

- Salaries and rent are the two major expenses, while depreciation is another significant cost that will increase as the company develops.
- We want to finance growth mainly through cash flow. We recognize that this means we will have to grow slowly.
- It should be noted that the owners of Southeast Racing Parts do not intend to take any profits out of the business until the long-term debt has been satisfied. Whatever profits remain after the debt payments will be used to finance growth, mainly through the acquisition of additional inventory.

## Important Assumptions

Key assumptions for Southeast Racing Parts:

- We do not sell anything on credit.
- We assume the continued popularity of auto racing in America.
- Monthly sales are the largest indicator for this business. There are some seasonal variations, with the months January through June being the highest sales months.
- We assume access to capital and financing sufficient to maintain our financial plan as shown in the tables.

| General Assumptions | FY2000 | FY2001 | FY2002 |
|---|---|---|---|
| Short-term Interest Rate % | 10.00% | 10.00% | 10.00% |
| Long-term Interest Rate % | 10.00% | 10.00% | 10.00% |
| Payment Days Estimator | 30 | 30 | 30 |
| Collection Days Estimator | 45 | 45 | 45 |
| Inventory Turnover Estimator | 7 | 7 | 7 |
| Tax Rate % | 25.00% | 25.00% | 25.00% |
| Expenses in Cash % | 10.00% | 10.00% | 10.00% |
| Sales on Credit % | 0.00% | 0.00% | 0.00% |
| Personnel Burden % | 15.00% | 15.00% | 15.00% |

## Key Financial Indicators

The key indicators in our plan illustrate increasing sales, control of costs, and increasing profit margins.

## Break-even Analysis

For our break-even analysis, we assume running costs of approximately $6,000 per month, which includes payroll, rent, utilities, and an estimation of other running costs.

Based on a 30 percent margin, we need to sell about $20,000 per month to break even, according to our assumptions.

Our sales forecast indicates that monthly sales are expected to be much greater than the break-even point mentioned in the table.

| Break-even Analysis: | |
|---|---|
| Monthly Units Break-even | 20,000 |
| Monthly Sales Break-even | $20,000 |

| Assumptions: | |
|---|---|
| Average Per-Unit Revenue | $1.00 |
| Average Per-Unit Variable Cost | $0.70 |
| Estimated Monthly Fixed Cost | $6,000 |

The detailed monthly Profit and Loss (Income Statement) is included in the appendix for this plan. The annual estimates are included on the following page.

We expect income to hit $36,000 at the end of the first year of business. It should increase to around $60,000 by the third year as the reputation of our business, its employees, and services become apparent to the local racers. Second year revenues anticipate the addition of one part-time employee, along with one full-time employee in the third year.

The credit card surcharge expense was based upon 50 percent of sales being paid for with plastic, and assuming a 2 percent service fee.

The inbound freight charges were based upon 2 percent of cost of goods for year one, 1.75 percent for year two, and 1.5 percent for year three.

Depreciation was figured upon $29,000 in expensed equipment at the rate of seven years.

**Projected Profit and Loss**

### Profit and Loss (Income Statement)

|                               | FY2000    | FY2001    | FY2002    |
|-------------------------------|-----------|-----------|-----------|
| Sales                         | $367,019  | $472,085  | $608,670  |
| Direct Cost of Sales          | $245,154  | $314,147  | $402,472  |
| **Total Cost of Sales**       | **$245,154** | **$314,147** | **$402,472** |
|                               |           |           |           |
| Gross Margin                  | $121,865  | $157,938  | $206,198  |
| Gross Margin %                | 33.20%    | 33.46%    | 33.88%    |
|                               |           |           |           |
| **Operating Expenses:**       |           |           |           |
| Advertising/Promotion         | $1,800    | $2,340    | $3,042    |
| Vehicle Expense               | $1,700    | $1,850    | $2,000    |
| Credit Card Surcharge         | $3,498    | $4,547    | $5,911    |
| Inbound freight charges       | $4,906    | $5,497    | $6,036    |
| Payroll Expense               | $26,400   | $39,680   | $66,016   |
| Payroll Burden                | $3,960    | $5,952    | $9,902    |
| Depreciation                  | $4,140    | $4,140    | $4,140    |
| Leased Equipment              | $0        | $0        | $0        |
| Telephone                     | $2,650    | $3,445    | $4,478    |
| Office Supplies               | $600      | $780      | $1,014    |
| Utilities                     | $2,400    | $2,400    | $2,400    |
| Security/alarm                | $360      | $360      | $360      |
| Insurance                     | $840      | $840      | $840      |
| Rent                          | $19,200   | $19,200   | $19,200   |
| Accounting Costs              | $1,500    | $1,500    | $1,500    |
| **Total Operating Expenses**  | **$73,954** | **$92,531** | **$126,839** |
|                               |           |           |           |
| Profit Before Interest and Taxes | $47,911 | $65,407   | $79,359   |
| Interest Expense Short-term   | $0        | $0        | $0        |
| Interest Expense Long-term    | $0        | $0        | $0        |
| Taxes Incurred                | $11,978   | $16,352   | $19,840   |
| Extraordinary Items           | $0        | $0        | $0        |
| **Net Profit**                | **$35,933** | **$49,055** | **$59,519** |
| **Net Profit/Sales**          | **9.79%** | **10.39%** | **9.78%** |

## Projected Cash Flow

Cash flow projections are critical to our success. The following table shows cash flow for the first three years, and the chart illustrates monthly cash flow in the first year. Monthly cash flow projections are included in the appendix.

| Projected Cash Flow | FY2000 | FY2001 | FY2002 |
|---|---|---|---|
| Net Profit | $59,519 | $0 | $0 |
| Plus: | | | |
| Depreciation | $4,140 | $4,140 | $4,140 |
| Change in Accounts Payable | $24,362 | ($37,434) | $0 |
| Current Borrowing (repayment) | $0 | $0 | $0 |
| Increase (decrease) Other Liabilities | $0 | $0 | $0 |
| Long-term Borrowing (repayment) | $0 | $0 | $0 |
| Capital Input | $0 | $0 | $0 |
| **Subtotal** | **$64,435** | **($37,434)** | **$0** |
| | | | |
| Less: | | | |
| Change in Accounts Receivable | $0 | $0 | $0 |
| Change in Inventory | ($5,093) | ($12,638) | $16,179 |
| Change in Other Short-term Assets | $0 | $0 | $0 |
| Capital Expenditure | $0 | $0 | $0 |
| Dividends | $0 | $0 | $0 |
| **Subtotal** | **($5,093)** | **$12,638** | **$16,179** |
| **Net Cash Flow** | **$69,528** | **$47,158** | **$55,911** |
| **Cash Balance** | **$70,528** | **$117,686** | **$173,594** |

## Projected Balance Sheet

The table shows the annual balance sheet results, with a healthy projected increase in net worth. Detailed monthly projections are in the appendix.

| Assets | | | |
|---|---|---|---|
| **Short-term Assets** | **FY2000** | **FY2001** | **FY2002** |
| Cash | $67,121 | $117,686 | $173,596 |
| Accounts Receivable | $0 | $0 | $0 |
| Inventory | $44,907 | $57,546 | $73,725 |
| Other Short-term Assets | $0 | $0 | $0 |
| **Total Short-term Assets** | **$115,435** | **$175,231** | **$247,321** |
| | | | |
| **Long-term Assets** | | | |
| Capital Assets | $29,000 | $29,000 | $29,000 |
| Accumulated Depreciation | $4,140 | $8,280 | $12,420 |
| Total Long-term Assets | $24,860 | $20,720 | $16,580 |
| **Total Assets** | **$140,295** | **$195,951** | **$263,901** |
| | | | |
| **Liabilities and Capital** | | | |
| Accounts Payable | $26,362 | $32,963 | $41,394 |
| Short-term Notes | $0 | $0 | $0 |
| Other Short-term Liabilities | $0 | $0 | $0 |
| Subtotal Short-term Liabilities | $0 | $0 | $0 |
| Long-term Liabilities | $0 | $0 | $0 |
| **Total Liabilities** | **$0** | **$0** | **$0** |

| Paid in Capital | $20,000 | $80,625 | $80,625 |
|---|---|---|---|
| Retained Earnings | $58,000 | $93,933 | $142,989 |
| Earnings | $35,933 | $49,055 | $59,519 |
| **Total Capital** | **$113,933** | **$162,989** | **$222,507** |
| **Total Liabilities and Capital** | **$140,295** | **$195,951** | **$263,901** |
| **Net Worth** | **$113,933** | **$162,989** | **$222,507** |

**Business Ratios**

**Ratio Analysis**

| **Profitability Ratios:** | **FY2000** | **FY2001** | **FY2002** |
|---|---|---|---|
| Gross Margin | 33.20% | 33.46% | 33.88% |
| Net Profit Margin | 9.79% | 10.39% | 9.78% |
| Return on Assets | 26.25% | 25.44% | 22.90% |
| Return on Equity | 31.54% | 30.10% | 26.75% |

| **Activity Ratios** | | | |
|---|---|---|---|
| AR Turnover | 0.00 | 0.00 | 0.00 |
| Collection Days | 0 | 0 | 0 |
| Inventory Turnover | 5.17 | 6.13 | 6.13 |
| Accts Payable Turnover | 9.86 | 9.86 | 9.86 |
| **Total Asset Turnover** | **2.62** | **2.41** | **2.31** |

| **Debt Ratios** | | | |
|---|---|---|---|
| Debt to Net Worth | 0.23 | 0.20 | 0.19 |
| Short-term Liability to Liability | 1.00 | 1.00 | 1.00 |

| **Liquidity Ratios** | | | |
|---|---|---|---|
| Current Ratio | 4.38 | 5.32 | 5.97 |
| Quick Ratio | 2.68 | 3.57 | 4.19 |
| Net Working Capital | $89,073 | $142,269 | $205,927 |
| Interest Coverage | 0.00 | 0.00 | 0.00 |

| **Additional Ratios** | | | |
|---|---|---|---|
| Assets to Sales | 0.38 | 0.42 | 0.43 |
| Debt/Assets | 19% | 17% | 16% |
| Current Debt/Total Assets | 19% | 17% | 16% |
| Acid Test | 2.68 | 3.57 | 4.19 |
| Asset Turnover | 2.62 | 2.41 | 2.31 |
| **Sales/Net Worth** | **3.22** | **2.90** | **2.74** |

## Projected Balance Sheet

**Assets**

| Short-term Assets | Starting Balances | Aug | Sep | Oct | Nov | Dec |
|---|---|---|---|---|---|---|
| Cash | $1,000 | $13,545 | $30,050 | $46,815 | $43,111 | $46,055 |
| Accounts Receivable | $0 | $0 | $0 | $0 | $0 | $0 |
| Inventory | $50,000 | $38,800 | $24,960 | $29,952 | $26,957 | $24,261 |
| Other Short-term Assets | $0 | $0 | $0 | $0 | $0 | $0 |
| Total Short-term Assets | $51,000 | $52,345 | $55,010 | $76,767 | $70,068 | $70,315 |
| | | | | | | |
| **Long-term Assets** | | | | | | |
| Capital Assets | $29,000 | $29,000 | $29,000 | $29,000 | $29,000 | $29,000 |
| Accumulated Depreciation | $0 | $345 | $690 | $1,035 | $1,380 | $1,725 |
| Total Long-term Assets | $29,000 | $28,655 | $28,310 | $27,965 | $27,620 | $27,275 |
| **Total Assets** | **$80,000** | **$81,000** | **$83,320** | **$100,128** | **$97,688** | **$97,590** |
| | | | | | | |
| **Liabilities and Capital** | | | | | | |
| Accounts Payable | $2,000 | $2,688 | $3,707 | $22,981 | $14,281 | $12,980 |
| Short-term Notes | $0 | $0 | $0 | $0 | $0 | $0 |
| Other Short-term Liabilities | $0 | $0 | $0 | $0 | $0 | $0 |
| Subtotal Short-term Liabilities | $2,000 | $2,688 | $3,707 | $22,981 | $14,281 | $12,980 |
| Long-term Liabilities | $0 | $0 | $0 | $0 | $0 | $0 |
| **Total Liabilities** | **$2,000** | **$2,688** | **$3,707** | **$22,981** | **$14,281** | **$12,980** |
| | | | | | | |
| Paid in Capital | $20,000 | $20,000 | $20,000 | $20,000 | $20,000 | $20,000 |
| Retained Earnings | $58,000 | $58,000 | $58,000 | $58,000 | $58,000 | $58,000 |
| Earnings | $0 | $312 | $1,613 | $3,752 | $5,408 | $6,611 |
| **Total Capital** | **$78,000** | **$78,312** | **$79,613** | **$81,752** | **$83,408** | **$84,611** |
| **Total Liabilities and Capital** | **$80,000** | **$81,000** | **$83,320** | **$100,128** | **$97,688** | **$97,590** |
| **Net Worth** | **$78,000** | **$78,312** | **$79,613** | **$81,752** | **$83,408** | **$84,611** |

| Jan | Feb | Mar | Apr | May | Jun | Jul |
|---|---|---|---|---|---|---|
| $52,193 | $53,767 | $56,943 | $60,029 | $64,240 | $59,543 | $67,121 |
| $0 | $0 | $0 | $0 | $0 | $0 | $0 |
| $27,900 | $32,085 | $38,501 | $46,202 | $55,442 | $49,898 | $44,907 |
| $0 | $0 | $0 | $0 | $0 | $0 | $0 |
| $80,093 | $85,851 | $95,444 | $98,538 | $110,234 | $113,105 | $115,435 |
| | | | | | | |
| $29,000 | $29,000 | $29,000 | $29,000 | $29,000 | $29,000 | $29,000 |
| $2,070 | $2,415 | $2,760 | $3,105 | $3,450 | $3,795 | $4,140 |
| $26,930 | $26,585 | $26,240 | $25,895 | $25,550 | $25,205 | $24,860 |
| **$103,638** | **$108,433** | **$115,455** | **$124,433** | **$135,784** | **$138,310** | **$140,295** |
| | | | | | | |
| $20,599 | $23,496 | $29,170 | $34,746 | $41,435 | $25,362 | $22,955 |
| $0 | $0 | $0 | $0 | $0 | $0 | $0 |
| $0 | $0 | $0 | $0 | $0 | $0 | $0 |
| $20,599 | $23,496 | $29,170 | $34,746 | $41,435 | $25,362 | $22,955 |
| $0 | $0 | $0 | $0 | $0 | $0 | $0 |
| **$20,599** | **$23,496** | **$29,170** | **$34,746** | **$41,435** | **$25,362** | **$22,955** |
| | | | | | | |
| $20,000 | $20,000 | $20,000 | $20,000 | $20,000 | $20,000 | $20,000 |
| $58,000 | $58,000 | $58,000 | $58,000 | $58,000 | $58,000 | $58,000 |
| $8,424 | $10,940 | $14,514 | $19,379 | $25,797 | $31,284 | $35,933 |
| **$86,424** | **$88,940** | **$92,514** | **$97,379** | **$103,797** | **$109,284** | **$113,933** |
| **$103,683** | **$108,433** | **$115,455** | **$124,433** | **$135,784** | **$138,310** | **$140,295** |
| **$86,424** | **$88,940** | **$92,514** | **$97,379** | **$103,797** | **$109,284** | **$113,933** |

## Projected Cash Flow

| | Aug | Sep | Oct | Nov | Dec | Jan |
|---|---|---|---|---|---|---|
| Net Profit | $312 | $1,301 | $2,139 | $1,656 | $1,203 | $1,814 |
| Plus: | | | | | | |
| Depreciation | $345 | $345 | $345 | $345 | $345 | $345 |
| Change in Accounts Payable | $688 | $1,019 | $19,274 | ($8,700) | ($1,301) | $7,620 |
| Current Borrowing (repayment) | $0 | $0 | $0 | $0 | $0 | $0 |
| Increase (decrease) Other Liabilities | $0 | $0 | $0 | $0 | $0 | $0 |
| Long-term Borrowing (repayment) | $0 | $0 | $0 | $0 | $0 | $0 |
| Capital Input | $0 | $0 | $0 | $0 | $0 | $0 |
| **Subtotal** | **$1,345** | **$2,665** | **$21,758** | **($6,699)** | **$247** | **$9,778** |
| Less: | | | | | | |
| Change in Accounts Receivable | $0 | $0 | $0 | $0 | $0 | $0 |
| Change in Inventory | ($11,200) | ($13,840) | $4,992 | ($2,995) | ($2,697) | $3,639 |
| Change in Other Short-term Assets | $0 | $0 | $0 | $0 | $0 | $0 |
| Capital Expenditure | $0 | $0 | $0 | $0 | $0 | $0 |
| Dividends | $0 | $0 | $0 | $0 | $0 | $0 |
| **Subtotal** | **($11,200)** | **($13,840)** | **$4,992** | **($2,995)** | **($2,697)** | **$3,639** |
| **Net Cash Flow** | **$12,545** | **$16,505** | **$16,766** | **($3,704)** | **$2,943** | **$6,139** |
| **Cash Balance** | **$13,545** | **$30,050** | **$46,815** | **$43,111** | **$46,055** | **$52,193** |

| Feb | Mar | Apr | May | Jun | Jul |
|---|---|---|---|---|---|
| $2,516 | $3,574 | $4,865 | $6,418 | $5,487 | $4,649 |
| | | | | | |
| $345 | $345 | $345 | $345 | $345 | $345 |
| $2,897 | $5,674 | $5,576 | $6,688 | ($16,073) | ($2,407) |
| $0 | $0 | $0 | $0 | $0 | $0 |
| $0 | $0 | $0 | $0 | $0 | $0 |
| $0 | $0 | $0 | $0 | $0 | $0 |
| $0 | $0 | $0 | $0 | $0 | $0 |
| **$5,758** | **$9,592** | **$10,787** | **$13,451** | **($10,241)** | **$2,587** |
| | | | | | |
| $0 | $0 | $0 | $0 | $0 | $0 |
| $4,185 | $6,417 | $7,701 | $9,240 | ($5,544) | ($4,990) |
| $0 | $0 | $0 | $0 | $0 | $0 |
| $0 | $0 | $0 | $0 | $0 | $0 |
| $0 | $0 | $0 | $0 | $0 | $0 |
| **$4,185** | **$6,417** | **$7,701** | **$9,240** | **($5,544)** | **($4,990)** |
| **$1,573** | **$3,176** | **$3,086** | **$4,211** | **($4,697)** | **$7,578** |
| **$53,767** | **$56,943** | **$60,029** | **$64,240** | **$59,543** | **$67,121** |

## General Assumptions

|                               | Aug     | Sep     | Oct     | Nov     | Dec     | Jan     |
|-------------------------------|---------|---------|---------|---------|---------|---------|
| Short-term Interest Rate %    | 10.00%  | 10.00%  | 10.00%  | 10.00%  | 10.00%  | 10.00%  |
| Long-term Interest Rate %     | 10.00%  | 10.00%  | 10.00%  | 10.00%  | 10.00%  | 10.00%  |
| Payment Days Estimator        | 30      | 30      | 30      | 30      | 30      | 30      |
| Collection Days Estimator     | 45      | 45      | 45      | 45      | 45      | 45      |
| Inventory Turnover Estimator  | 7.00    | 7.00    | 7.00    | 7.00    | 7.00    | 7.00    |
| Tax Rate %                    | 25.00%  | 25.00%  | 25.00%  | 25.00%  | 25.00%  | 25.00%  |
| Expenses in Cash %            | 10.00%  | 10.00%  | 10.00%  | 10.00%  | 10.00%  | 10.00%  |
| Sales on Credit %             | 0.00%   | 0.00%   | 0.00%   | 0.00%   | 0.00%   | 0.00%   |
| Personnel Burden %            | 15.00%  | 15.00%  | 15.00%  | 15.00%  | 15.00%  | 15.00%  |

## Personnel Plan

| Personnel                   | Aug     | Sep     | Oct     | Nov     | Dec     | Jan     |
|-----------------------------|---------|---------|---------|---------|---------|---------|
| Tim Jones                   | $1,400  | $1,400  | $1,400  | $1,400  | $1,400  | $1,400  |
| Molly Jones                 | $800    | $800    | $800    | $800    | $800    | $800    |
| Salesperson (PT)            | $0      | $0      | $0      | $0      | $0      | $0      |
| Salesperson (FT)            | $0      | $0      | $0      | $0      | $0      | $0      |
| Other                       | $0      | $0      | $0      | $0      | $0      | $0      |
| **Total Payroll**           | **$2,200** | **$2,200** | **$2,200** | **$2,200** | **$2,200** | **$2,200** |
|                             |         |         |         |         |         |         |
| **Total Headcount**         | **2**   | **2**   | **2**   | **2**   | **2**   | **2**   |
| **Payroll Burden**          | **$330** | **$330** | **$330** | **$330** | **$330** | **$330** |
| **Total Payroll Expenditures** | **$2,530** | **$2,530** | **$2,530** | **$2,530** | **$2,530** | **$2,530** |

| Feb | Mar | Apr | May | Jun | Jul |
|---|---|---|---|---|---|
| 10.00% | 10.00% | 10.00% | 10.00% | 10.00% | 10.00% |
| 10.00% | 10.00% | 10.00% | 10.00% | 10.00% | 10.00% |
| 30 | 30 | 30 | 30 | 30 | 30 |
| 45 | 45 | 45 | 45 | 45 | 45 |
| 7.00 | 7.00 | 7.00 | 7.00 | 7.00 | 7.00 |
| 25.00% | 25.00% | 25.00% | 25.00% | 25.00% | 25.00% |
| 10.00% | 10.00% | 10.00% | 10.00% | 10.00% | 10.00% |
| 0.00% | 0.00% | 0.00% | 0.00% | 0.00% | 0.00% |
| 15.00% | 15.00% | 15.00% | 15.00% | 15.00% | 15.00% |

| Feb | Mar | Apr | May | Jun | Jul |
|---|---|---|---|---|---|
| $1,400 | $1,400 | $1,400 | $1,400 | $1,400 | $1,400 |
| $800 | $800 | $800 | $800 | $800 | $800 |
| $0 | $0 | $0 | $0 | $0 | $0 |
| $0 | $0 | $0 | $0 | $0 | $0 |
| $0 | $0 | $0 | $0 | $0 | $0 |
| **$2,200** | **$2,200** | **$2,200** | **$2,200** | **$2,200** | **$2,200** |
| 2 | 2 | 2 | 2 | 2 | 2 |
| **$330** | **$330** | **$330** | **$330** | **$330** | **$330** |
| **$2,530** | **$2,530** | **$2,530** | **$2,530** | **$2,530** | **$2,530** |

## Profit and Loss (Income Statement)

| | Aug | Sep | Oct | Nov | Dec | Jan |
|---|---|---|---|---|---|---|
| Sales | $17,400 | $22,200 | $26,360 | $23,864 | $21,617 | $24,650 |
| Direct Cost of Sales | $11,200 | $14,560 | $17,472 | $15,725 | $14,152 | $16,275 |
| **Total Cost of Sales** | **$11,200** | **$14,560** | **$17,472** | **$15,725** | **$14,152** | **$16,275** |
| | | | | | | |
| Gross Margin | $6,200 | $7,640 | $8,888 | $8,139 | $7,465 | $8,375 |
| Gross Margin % | 35.63% | 34.41% | 33.72% | 34.11% | 34.53% | 33.98% |
| | | | | | | |
| **Operating expenses:** | | | | | | |
| Advertising/Promotion | $150 | $150 | $150 | $150 | $150 | $150 |
| Vehicle Expense | $150 | $150 | $150 | $125 | $125 | $125 |
| Credit Card Surcharge | $160 | $208 | $249 | $224 | $202 | $232 |
| Inbound freight charges | $224 | $292 | $350 | $314 | $284 | $326 |
| Payroll Expense | $2,200 | $2,200 | $2,200 | $2,200 | $2,200 | $2,200 |
| Payroll Burden | $330 | $330 | $330 | $330 | $330 | $330 |
| Depreciation | $345 | $345 | $345 | $345 | $345 | $345 |
| Leased Equipment | $0 | $0 | $0 | $0 | $0 | $0 |
| Telephone | $150 | $156 | $187 | $168 | $150 | $174 |
| Office Supplies | $50 | $50 | $50 | $50 | $50 | $50 |
| Utilities | $200 | $200 | $200 | $200 | $200 | $200 |
| Security/alarm | $30 | $30 | $30 | $30 | $30 | $30 |
| Insurance | $70 | $70 | $70 | $70 | $70 | $70 |
| Rent | $1,600 | $1,600 | $1,600 | $1,600 | $1,600 | $1,600 |
| Accounting Costs | $125 | $125 | $125 | $125 | $125 | $125 |
| **Total Operating Expenses** | **$5,784** | **$5,906** | **$6,036** | **$5,931** | **$5,861** | **$5,957** |
| | | | | | | |
| Profit before Interest and Taxes | $416 | $1,734 | $2,852 | $2,208 | $1,604 | $2,418 |
| Interest Expense Short-term | $0 | $0 | $0 | $0 | $0 | $0 |
| Interest Expense Long-term | $0 | $0 | $0 | $0 | $0 | $0 |
| Taxes Incurred | $104 | $434 | $713 | $552 | $401 | $605 |
| Extraordinary Items | $0 | $0 | $0 | $0 | $0 | $0 |
| Net Profit | $312 | $1,301 | $2,139 | $1,656 | $1,203 | $1,814 |
| Net Profit/Sales | 1.79% | 5.86% | 8.11% | 6.94% | 5.57% | 7.36% |

| | Feb | Mar | Apr | May | Jun | Jul |
|---|---|---|---|---|---|---|
| | $28,137 | $33,484 | $39,901 | $47,602 | $42,981 | $38,823 |
| | $18,716 | $22,459 | $26,951 | $32,341 | $29,107 | $26,196 |
| | **$18,716** | **$22,459** | **$26,951** | **$32,341** | **$29,107** | **$26,196** |
| | | | | | | |
| | $9,421 | $11,025 | $12,950 | $15,261 | $13,874 | $12,627 |
| | 33.48% | 32.93% | 32.46% | 32.06% | 32.28% | 32.52% |
| | | | | | | |
| | $150 | $150 | $150 | $150 | $150 | $150 |
| | $125 | $150 | $150 | $150 | $150 | $150 |
| | $267 | $320 | $385 | $462 | $415 | $374 |
| | $374 | $450 | $540 | $646 | $582 | $524 |
| | $2,200 | $2,200 | $2,200 | $2,200 | $2,200 | $2,200 |
| | $330 | $330 | $330 | $330 | $330 | $330 |
| | $345 | $345 | $345 | $345 | $345 | $345 |
| | $0 | $0 | $0 | $0 | $0 | $0 |
| | $200 | $240 | $288 | $346 | $311 | $280 |
| | $50 | $50 | $50 | $50 | $50 | $50 |
| | $200 | $200 | $200 | $200 | $200 | $200 |
| | $30 | $30 | $30 | $30 | $30 | $30 |
| | $70 | $70 | $70 | $70 | $70 | $70 |
| | $1,600 | $1,600 | $1,600 | $1,600 | $1,600 | $1,600 |
| | $125 | $125 | $125 | $125 | $125 | $125 |
| | **$6,066** | **$6,260** | **$6,463** | **$6,704** | **$6,558** | **$6,428** |
| | | | | | | |
| | $3,355 | $4,765 | $6,487 | $8,557 | $7,316 | $6,199 |
| | $0 | $0 | $0 | $0 | $0 | $0 |
| | $0 | $0 | $0 | $0 | $0 | $0 |
| | $839 | $1,191 | $1,622 | $2,139 | $1,829 | $1,550 |
| | $0 | $0 | $0 | $0 | $0 | $0 |
| | $2,516 | $3,574 | $4,865 | $6,418 | $5,487 | $4,649 |
| | 8.94% | 10.67% | 12.19% | 13.48% | 12.77% | 11.98% |

## Sales Forecast

| Sales | Aug | Sep | Oct | Nov | Dec | Jan |
|---|---|---|---|---|---|---|
| Inventory Sales | $16,000 | $20,800 | $24,960 | $22,464 | $20,217 | $23,250 |
| Internet marketing | $1,400 | $1,400 | $1,400 | $1,400 | $1,400 | $1,400 |
| Other | $0 | $0 | $0 | $0 | $0 | $0 |
| **Total Sales** | **$17,400** | **$22,200** | **$26,360** | **$23,864** | **$21,617** | **$24,650** |
| | | | | | | |
| **Direct Cost of Sales** | | | | | | |
| Inventory Sales | $11,200 | $14,560 | $17,472 | $15,725 | $14,152 | $16,275 |
| Internet marketing | $0 | $0 | $0 | $0 | $0 | $0 |
| Other | $0 | $0 | $0 | $0 | $0 | $0 |
| **Subtotal Cost of Sales** | **$11,200** | **$14,560** | **$17,472** | **$15,725** | **$14,152** | **$16,275** |

| | Feb | Mar | Apr | May | Jun | Jul |
|---|---|---|---|---|---|---|
| | $26,737 | $32,084 | $38,501 | $46,202 | $41,581 | $37,423 |
| | $1,400 | $1,400 | $1,400 | $1,400 | $1,400 | $1,400 |
| | $0 | $0 | $0 | $0 | $0 | $0 |
| | **$28,137** | **$33,484** | **$39,901** | **$47,602** | **$42,981** | **$38,823** |
| | | | | | | |
| | $18,716 | $22,459 | $26,951 | $32,341 | $29,107 | $26,196 |
| | $0 | $0 | $0 | $0 | $0 | $0 |
| | $0 | $0 | $0 | $0 | $0 | $0 |
| | **$18,716** | **$22,459** | **$26,951** | **$32,341** | **$29,107** | **$26,196** |

# Rock Climber's Store & Café

BUSINESS PLAN

THE BOULDER STOP

*1455 Portland Street*
*Bend, Oregon 97701*

*This store will offer rock climbing gear to people heading to Smith Rock State Park. It is hoped this will become a regular stop for their three main target markets: weekend warriors, hard-core climbers, and the curious. The Boulder Stop will offer mrechandise that complements that of our competition, and their café, which will offer specialty Northwest coffees, will further distinguish them. This business plan was compiled using Business Plan Pro, © 1998, Palo Alto Software, www.paloaltosoftware.com, 800-229-7526.*

- EXECUTIVE SUMMARY

- COMPANY SUMMARY

- PRODUCTS

- MARKET ANALYSIS SUMMARY

- STRATEGY & IMPLEMENTATION SUMMARY

- MANAGEMENT SUMMARY

- FINANCIAL PLAN

# ROCK CLIMBER'S STORE & CAFÉ
# BUSINESS PLAN

## EXECUTIVE SUMMARY

- The Boulder Stop will offer high-end rock climbing gear and classic Northwest coffee. We will purchase the gear wholesale and have it shipped via FedEx and UPS, both of which serve the Bend/Redmond business community. We will buy our freshly roasted coffee beans from Espresso Harvest, a Bend area distributor and reseller of gourmet coffee beans.
- The store is located one mile from Smith Rock State Park in the central Oregon desert. It is conveniently located in an area frequented by national and international tourists.
- 50 percent of profits will go to the owner, 25 percent to employees, and 25 percent to Smith Rock State Park restoration projects.
- This plan outlines the rewards—community and financial—of investment in the Boulder Stop.

## Objectives

1. To make the Boulder Stop a local favorite for tourists, hikers, and climbers on their way to/from Smith Rock.
2. To achieve the largest market share in the region for rock climbing gear. We will use State of Oregon economic data to compile an estimate of market share goals for 1998.
3. To be an active and vocal member of the community, and to provide continual re-investment through sponsorship of community activities and celebrations. We will sponsor five or more events during the year, including fun climbs, family bouldering, and celebrity hosted competitions.
4. To achieve a 65 percent gross margin within the first year. Our conservative projected gross margin is 45 percent .
5. To achieve a net profit of $30,000 by year two. We will re-invest these profits in our business and our community's future.

## Mission

The Boulder Stop is an equipment store and café specializing in premium rock climbing gear and coffee/espresso drinks. We believe rock climbing should be safe and fun. We understand that rock climbers need a healthy dose of the newest gear, fresh snacks, and raw caffeine.

Our goal is to be the centrifuge for rock climbers living in and visiting central Oregon. Smith Rock State Park is one of the finest rock climbing parks in the world. Our staff is fluent in several languages, including Spanish, German, and French. Locals and tourists alike will long for our hip, lively shop because of our staff, our setting, our gear, and our coffee.

We believe it is important to remain an active member of the community—to impact people's lives in more ways than deriving a profit from them. We host community events that bring out the best in people.

We will be the region's destination for those who want to know all there is to know about rock climbing gear, safety, rules, and events. The future of rock climbing in central Oregon will be determined by our level of commitment.

## Keys to Success

To succeed in this business we must:

- Sell products that are of the highest reliability and quality. We must offer as many or more premium products than REI offers online and through their Eugene and Portland stores. This means we must carry all premium brands of harnesses, active protection, passive protection, helmets, ice-climbing gear, camping gear, and mountaineering gear.

- Offer loss leaders and other promotions that bring customers into the store to buy goods, explore our line of services, and sign up for future events.
- Provide for the satisfaction of 100 percent of our customers and vendors. Both are very valuable to us and we will design a customer care plan to manage complaints, implement employee and customer feedback, manage supplier accounts, and predict potential conflicts.
- Be an active member of the community: i.e., host sportclimbing and rock climbing events.
- Negotiate valuable contracts with great distributors such as Trago, Petzl, Black Diamond, Beal, Ushba Mountain Works, and others. To maintain a high margin business plan, we must negotiate a good cost structure.

The Boulder Stop is a purveyor of premium coffee and gear. The café is located one mile from Smith Rock State Park in central Oregon.

The Boulder Stop was incorporated in the state of Oregon on January 1, 1997. It is privately held and managed by Luke Walsh. The company has established a central office at 1455 Portland St., Bend, OR 97701. This location is designed for purchasing, storage, and contract negotiations. Service purchases will be forwarded to this office for review and approval. All PO authorizations will also be approved at this office.

**COMPANY SUMMARY**

The Boulder Stop is a privately held corporation. Luke Walsh owns 60 percent of the Boulder Stop and his wife, Lisa, owns 40 percent . This company operates under the jurisdiction of the state of Oregon and the United States of America as an "S" Corporation. If the company shows steady exponential growth, the owners will prepare the company for re-establishment as a "C" corporation. As a "C" corporation, the owners will not be taxed at the higher maximum personal rate of 39.6 percent , but rather the company will be taxed at the maximum corporate rate of 34 percent . If the owners elect to administer the Boulder Stop as a "C" corporation, it will not be taken lightly. A company that moves from "S" to "C" status must remain in "C" status for a minimum of five years.

At the moment, the owners wish to benefit from the single taxation of an "S" corporation.

**Company Ownership**

Our incorporation costs are listed below, as well as the cost of retaining a marketing consultant to manage local impact-management teams and to issue a community impact report to major public and private agencies within the region. Their job will be to inform the Boulder Stop owners about how to effectively communicate with the community leaders. Our lawyer will be responsible for preempting any local government conflicts having to do with zoning and/or permit allowance.

**Start-up Summary**

There will be other normal business costs such as a $1,000,000 liability umbrella, rent, interior design costs, and opening day promotions.

The largest equipment purchase will be that of a Conti brand commercial espresso machine. This machine, named "The TwinStar," comes with an 18-month warranty on parts and 12 months warranty on labor. Their espresso machines are world renowned for their high quality and performance features. The machine will push steam through the espresso grounds at temperatures set by the user.

The company will start with two months' inventory on hand. The majority of company assets will reside in inventory. The starting cash balance will be $3,000.

The purpose of this business plan is to secure a $11,700 SBA loan. This loan appears in the long-term liability row of the following Start-up costs table.

**Start-up Costs**

**Start-up Expenses**

| | |
|---|---|
| Legal | $300 |
| Marketing consultant | $4,500 |
| Business and liability insurance | $600 |
| First month's payment + deposit | $2,500 |
| Design costs | $3,500 |
| First week promotion | $1,100 |
| Expensed equipment | $3,500 |
| Other | $0 |
| **Total Start-up Expenses** | **$16,000** |

**Start-up Assets Needed**

| | |
|---|---|
| Cash Requirements | $3,000 |
| Start-up inventory | $7,000 |
| Other Short-term Assets | $1,000 |
| **Total Short-term Assets** | **$11,000** |

| | |
|---|---|
| **Long-term Assets** | $0 |
| **Total Assets** | **$11,000** |

| | |
|---|---|
| **Total Start-up Requirements:** | **$27,000** |
| **Left to finance:** | **$0** |

**Start-up Funding Plan**

**Investment**

| | |
|---|---|
| Luke Walsh | $10,900 |
| Lisa Walsh | $2,900 |
| Other | $0 |
| Other | $0 |
| **Total investment** | **$13,800** |

**Short-term Liabilities**

| | |
|---|---|
| Unpaid Expenses | $500 |
| Short-term Loans | $0 |
| Interest-free Short-term Loans | $1,000 |
| **Subtotal Short-term Liabilities** | **$1,500** |
| Long-term Liabilities | $11,700 |
| **Total Liabilities** | **$13,200** |

| | |
|---|---|
| Loss at Start-up | ($16,000) |
| Total Capital | ($2,200) |
| Total Capital and Liabilities | $11,000 |
| Checkline | $0 |

**Company Locations and Facilities**

The company office is located in the owner's residence, 1455 Portland St., Bend, Oregon 97701. The office is about 1,000 square feet and has ample space for the first three years of growth. Deliveries and shipments are serviced through the store located at 432 Smith Rock Drive, Redmond, OR 97756. The 5,000-square-foot retail building is owned by the Boulder Stop and there is no excess storage capacity.

Espresso is the big money maker for the Boulder Stop, with coffee peripherals coming in at a close second. The rock climbing gear is a long-term sales project that will rely on future catalog and "word-of-mouth" sales to achieve a positive return on investment.

The Boulder Stop sells high-quality rock climbing gear to serious climbers. The gear is checked by knowledgeable employees who use and recommend equipment to customers and management. The gear is purchased from well-known manufacturers like Black Diamond, Boreal, and Petzl. Management will rely on employees and customers to shorten the feedback loop in product and service offerings. Climbing gear is delivered every Thursday via UPS.

Straight espresso bean rebuys arrive on Mondays and Thursdays, ensuring the freshest beans possible. Modified rebuys begin on the first of each month. The owner will oversee all purchases, shipments, and deliveries.

**PRODUCTS & SERVICES**

The Boulder Stop sells the entire raft of coffee drinks: lattes, mochas, cappuccino, espresso, and a delicious house blend. The coffee and espresso beans are freshly roasted by Espresso Harvest. Our team of two part-time high school students will create the beverages for customers. They will be trained in "The Art of Making the Proper Espresso Beverage" at Espresso Harvest, which hosts such classes once a month.

**Product Description**

The Boulder Stop also sells carabiners, friends, nuts, ropes, webbing, shoes, and harnesses; our product mix is sufficient to satisfy even the most hard-core enthusiast. Below is a listing of some high-end products that we market:

- Black Diamond Camalot Camming Device - $50 to $100
- Wild Country Forged Friends with Sling - $35 to $65
- Hugh Banner HMS Locking Carabiner - $12 to $17
- The North Face Bouldering Sweatshirt, Men's - $85 to $105
- Mammut Flash Duodess 10.5mm Dry Rope - $185 to $200
- Boreal Ace Rock Shoes - $150 to $170

All products are quality checked when they arrive and quality checked before the customer takes them home.

The Boulder Stop has several advantages over its leading competitor.

**Competitive Comparison**

1. Newer inventory and more modern interior fixtures.

2. Espresso drinks are made available to consumers while they shop, increasing marketing message impact. Our competitor offers the shopping experience that lacks the thrill of being able to sit down with friends, munch on a cookie, drink espresso, and "talk shop."

3. The Boulder Stop is a fun, spacious store catering to both the climbing pros and the inexperienced. Our competitor, Rockage, is an exclusive Pro shop that discourages some newcomers to the sport. Our positioning encourages those just getting started, a one-stop destination for equipment advice and purchasing opportunities, technique and safety instruction, and conversation with other enthusiasts.

4. We expect a high degree of expertise and enthusiasm from our employees and we compensate them accordingly. All employees are hired for their expertise and enthusiasm and will be paid at a rate well above the minimum wage to facilitate low-turnover and long-term loyalty.

**Sales Literature**

The Boulder Stop will use advertising and sales programs to get the word out to customers.

- 2,000 four-color brochures to be distributed throughout Bend and area facilities: outdoor clothing shops, hotels, ranger stations, chambers of commerce, tourism council offices, area eateries, and other tourist-frequented spots one month before the grand opening in May.
- Half-page newspaper advertisements in Oregon regional newspapers, advertising the following sales promotion: introductory rock-climbing classes, two days for $100 per person. Copy: magazine and newspaper advertisements.
- Web promotions: we will administer a website at www.boulder-stop.com. This website will present promotional material such as new marketing programs, product white papers, and contests. The site will allow for immediate purchase of gear online and will use a secure server to process transactions through Cybercash.

**Sourcing**

Sourcing is critical for any enterprise, especially a retail operation. The Espresso Harvest will be our coffee vendors, and will handle many in-store merchandising issues for their line of coffee products. Operational supplies for the coffee bar will be purchased from the regional supply wholesaler, who will handle special merchandising issues, such as point-of-sale materials. The sport and recreation inventory will be sourced directly from manufacturers like Black Diamond, Boreal, and Petzl.

We will solidify relationships with vendors so that we may achieve decreased cost-of-goods. Our competitor buys from some of the same vendors we do, yet we believe that through marketing programs and strategic alliances we will gain more loyalty from these vendors. This is our long-term strategy for gaining a sourcing competitive advantage.

Advertising costs are outsourced. Most sales promotion and public relations work is handled in-house by Luke. Luke will write all product white-papers and combine those with literature supplied by the manufacturer.

Future seminars and climbing clinics will be handled either by the owner or by several certified and experienced tour and adventure professionals. We will use local contacts to research the availability of celebrity climbers to sponsor some of these clinics and events. We believe this tactic will build a grassroots network of climbers that will help us to differentiate the Boulder Stop as a "hang-out" for serious and curious climbers.

**Technology**

We use off-the-shelf, PC-based software for accounting purposes, including AR/AP, inventory, purchasing, sales, and returns.

Our business plan is generated on an annual basis using Business Plan Pro from Palo Alto Software, and reviewed quarterly for evaluation. Further functionality is provided by Palo Alto Software's companion package, Marketing Plan Pro, which allows us to make the most use of our marketing dollars by focusing our communications on target markets and enhancing our marketing knowledge.

We are in the process of implementing a website for the Boulder Stop. Online commerce is becoming an increasingly attractive option due to the relatively low cost-of-goods, the global reach of the medium, and the increasing security. Our business model could quite conceivably expand to include a form of Internet commerce in a variety of adventure equipment.

Future expansion may allow for a horizontal increase of our product line by offering additional product categories: water sport gear, camping gear, and mountain biking accessories. We won't rule out the possibility of vertically integrating through our own line of climbing gear and/or espresso. We will also explore new services such as gear storage lockers, cellular phone rentals, and same-day guide services.

**Future Products**

One dream the owner has is to develop an Internet environment within the store, not to remove people from those surrounding them, but to help them stay in touch with friends, family, and the latest information about rock climbing.

Consumer expenditures for rock climbing equipment rose to $4,000,000 in central Oregon in 1997. We expect sales to increase steadily as Oregon's population grows and the rock climbing industry becomes increasingly popular.

**MARKET ANALYSIS SUMMARY**

The western Oregon presence of several large universities helps fuel our business, as does the status of Smith Rock as an international destination spot for rock climbing enthusiasts. Individuals from as far away as Japan, Europe, South America, and Australia seek out Smith Rock as a beautiful and challenging sport and rock climbing destination. We count worldwide readers of such publications as *Rock & Ice* magazine and *Outdoor Adventure* among our target audience.

Our three main target markets are weekend warriors, hard-core climbers, and the curious. We predict that the number of hard-core climbers will grow faster than the number of weekend warriors. Climbing is becoming more and more technical, an "Insider's sport," and we believe this will fuel the growth of dedicated, highly sophisticated climbers.

This market analysis is somewhat conservative when compared with Oregon's predicted population growth of 2 percent per year and Bend's 5 percent average gains over the last five years.

- The weekend warriors purchase during weekends. When these climbers are on a rock wall, they want to look cool. They want to hang out with their friends at Smith Rock and enjoy a nice pre-climb or post-climb espresso drink or ice cream cone. Weekend warriors plan special events with family members and friends. This market is our target for special events and climbing services such as tours and fun climbs.

**Market Segmentation**

- Hard-core climbers are very fickle about the gear they use. This segment is very brand loyal and provides the company with powerful word-of-mouth marketing. They are highly sophisticated climbers who know the jargon and want to let everyone know they are serious about the sport and its image.

- The curious want to stop in for a gander on their way to their campsites or hotel rooms. They may be into hiking Smith Rock State Park, or just taking a driving tour, it doesn't matter. They may be travelers or locals, depending upon the season and the event.

**Market Analysis**

| Potential Customers | Growth | 1997 | 1998 | 1999 | 2000 | 2001 | CAGR |
|---|---|---|---|---|---|---|---|
| Weekend warriors | 2% | 40,000 | 40,600 | 41,209 | 41,827 | 42,454 | 1.50% |
| Hard-core climbers | 2% | 2,300 | 2,337 | 2,374 | 2,412 | 2,451 | 1.60% |
| The curious | 2% | 30,000 | 30,570 | 31,151 | 31,743 | 32,346 | 1.90% |
| Other | 0% | 0 | 0 | 0 | 0 | 0 | 0.00% |
| **Total** | **1.67%** | **72,300** | **73,507** | **74,734** | **75,982** | **77,251** | **1.67%** |

**Target Market Segment Strategy**

We will focus on the highly discriminating hard-core climber segment first, because these are the opinion leaders. Both the weekend warrior and the curious will follow the hard-core climbers. If we can attract and keep the hard-core climbers, then they will attract others. To attract hard-core climbers, we will carry all the best high-tech gear, know the jargon, use the latest technology, and become a "futurist" product and services company.

We want to clearly differentiate the weekend warriors from the hard-core climbers. Less competitive, or at least at a different competitive level, these climbers are usually at Smith Rock to hike or explore. They respect the hard-core climbers, but don't want to be classified as having "rock on the brain." Twenty to 30 percent of these climbers will respond to family events by bringing their families, the other 70-80 percent climb with friends and occasionally try to outdo each other. This market is highly susceptible to getting stuck in a coffee shop with friends, they will talk about their latest romance, conflicts with other friends, the future, or the fine espresso at the Boulder Stop. We will market the weekend warriors with a combination of amateur climbing events and family fun climbs.

**Market Needs**

There are two important underlying needs, and the combination of gear and coffee serves both. In many ways the Boulder Stop mimics the positioning of a ski lodge; selling crucial gear while providing a place for coffee, snacks, and talk.

1. There is a real need for a highly professional provider of climbing gear near the Smith Rock location. People forget to pack exactly what they need, and things break.
2. There is also a practical need for coffee, a meeting place, and conversation. This is the activity focus of the location.

**Market Trends**

Trends are in our favor. There are three major trends at work in our market:

- Outdoor sports in general and rock climbing in particular are gaining exposure. The rock climbing gyms in the Silicon Valley, Seattle, Eugene, and other locations are clear evidence of this trend.
- Central Oregon is becoming a major vacation destination and recreation spot.
- The gourmet coffee trend started in the Northwest, and is spreading throughout the nation. A growing number of people look to their high-end coffee drinks as a way to enjoy a moment, and as an integral part of any outing or activity.

**Market Growth**

- Vacation spending in Oregon is growing more than 25 percent per year.
- Over the last five years, spending on climbing has grown faster than spending on skiing or mountain biking, although from a much smaller base. The industry will experience 130 percent growth over the next three years.
- Coffee spending is up 15 percent this year.

The rock-climbing industry is expanding faster than ever. Although climbing gear is priced at a premium, people buy it because it provides them with adventurous and, naturally, safer climbs.

High profit margins on coffee sales and low overhead costs lead to high profit margins in the espresso industry. Expansion of coffee and espresso retail outlets has increased exponentially in the last five years as large companies such as Starbucks have increased their reach to the East Coast in cities such as Boston, New York, and Washington D.C.

**Industry Analysis**

The rock climbing gear industry is still fairly young. Climbing stores are generally small in size and community oriented. These stores seek to attract the most knowledgeable $6-8/hour employees. There are some bigger players that serve a larger, less targeted community with rock gear and gear for dozens of other outdoor sports. These national participants are consistent about their message and carry an impressive array of gear, but only the largest stores combine an espresso shop with the "Yuppie" shopping experience.

Participants in the espresso market are big name retailers. These retailers focus on the standardized model. Under this model, a buyer will get the same service and same beverage in New York as the one they will get in downtown Bend. This leads to a backlash of sorts, as local consumers move to industry participants that differentiate their companies from the national standardized model. The product becomes localized and the buyer recognizes the value of supporting a business that keeps its profits in the community that created the profit.

**Industry Participants**

Traditional distribution channels are followed. The products are bought from wholesalers who have little say in how products are marketed, beyond the occasional sales promotion display provided via the manufacturer. This is beneficial in keeping the marketing and product costs low, while maintaining profit margins of 60 percent or more.

Customers are very brand oriented and affect the distribution patterns (rebuys) on the retail end. As consumers become increasingly aware of the Internet's potential, they will begin to buy product directly from the manufacturer. This will not hurt our business because a.) we have a website, direct distribution model of our own and b.) our location and convenience create an advantage for us. We will create in-store kiosks linked to our website. For now we will build on the strengths of location. If distribution patterns shift to a direct model, we build our business under the direct model.

**Distribution Patterns**

Climbers demand knowledgeable employees in a convenient location.

- Comparison: Rock Stop has placed its stores in urban industrial areas. Mountain Gear, a wholesaler, implements a similar strategy that draws the suburban dweller out of the house. This strategy keeps these customers isolated from the competition.
- Products and services are the most important factors when selling rock climbing gear. Brand name products sell well in stores that maintain a good selection, good location, and knowledgeable, friendly employees.
- Espresso shops need to be fast, efficient, and friendly. Fortunately, there are no espresso shops in close proximity to the Boulder Stop.

**Competition and Buying Patterns**

Our nearest competitor is Sportswhere. Our next closest competitor is Blue Mountain Climbing Gear, located in Redmond, 7 miles from our store. Neither of these retailers offers espresso to their customers.

**Main Competitors**

- Sportswhere sells limited gear (clothes), they do not promote, or otherwise market their products extensively. They sell ice cream and carry more GenX apparel than the Boulder Stop. In fact, their biggest strength may be that they may potentially become our ally. We see their products as complementary to ours: Ice Cream vs. Espresso. Their biggest weakness is limited store space.
- Blue Mountain Climbing Gear will be our toughest competitor, for they have already established themselves in the rock climbing community. They have a very experienced and knowledgeable staff of expert climbers, and are located on highway 97, 2 miles from Smith Rock. They carry 75-80 percent of the same gear that we do.

## STRATEGY & IMPLEMENTATION SUMMARY

The Boulder Stop uses a strategy of total market service.

Assumptions:

1. Every person is a potential customer and all our potential markets will experience growth.
2. Marketing to one segment of the population will lead to an expansion in overall market growth.

## Strategy Pyramids

Our main strategy is to develop the Boulder Stop experience as part of the rock climbing activity. We don't intend to be just a store, but rather a rock climbing cultural center for regulars and visitors to Smith Rock.

Underneath this strategy, our first tactic emphasizes the needs of the hard-core climber. We assume that participation of the hard-core set will generate interest for others.

## Value Proposition

The Boulder Stop gives Smith Rock visitors the highest quality climbing gear, good coffee, and a place to meet, in a convenient locale.

## Competitive Edge

Our location is a very important competitive edge. It will be difficult for our competitors to match our location.

The other competitive edge in development is our reputation and involvement with the community. The Boulder Stop is part of the Smith Rock experience, like the photography store used to be, in Yosemite Valley. That is why we are developing a community of employees who are rock climbers, and promoting rock climbing events, bulletin boards, etc. This advantage is important to us because our prices are slightly higher than other cafés and other gear stores in Oregon.

## Marketing Strategy

Our marketing strategy will focus on three segments. Those three segments are described in the following subtopics.

- The plan will benchmark our objectives for sales promotion, mass selling, and personal selling.
- We are focusing our marketing effort on the weekend warriors and the hard-core climbing community. We will implement a strategy that treats these customers as a community. This means our marketing resources will be centered around both sales promotions (events, displays) and personal sales (customer service, friendly atmosphere).
- The marketing budget will not exceed $5,000 per year.
- Marketing promotions will be consistent with the mission statement.

For climbers who need a place to stop for gear and coffee near Smith Rock, the Boulder Stop offers high quality climbing gear, gourmet espresso drinks, and a comfortable place to meet and talk. Unlike our competitors, our store is near the park and offers exactly what most climbers and tourists need.

**Positioning Statements**

We will encourage impulse buying, therefore it is important that we maintain a flexible pricing strategy.

**Pricing Strategy**

- Our pricing strategy will be based on competitive parity guidelines. We will not exceed competitors' prices by more than 10 percent , and if a customer sees a price elsewhere for less, we will give it to them for that price.
- Price says a lot about a product. The products that are innovative and not available elsewhere in the region will be marked up to meet the demand curve. We are not afraid of premium pricing a premium product.
- Espresso beverages will be priced slightly above the industry average. Although we will still make money off our house coffee (not espresso), we consider this a "loss leader" product. Word-of-mouth advertising brings customers in for the house coffee, simply to make them aware of our additional products and services.

The Boulder Stop will implement a strong sales promotion strategy. Advertising will be secondary.

**Promotion Strategy**

- We will pay to $4,000 to determine the needs of the surrounding population and how the company may best meet those needs with promotions, literature, and other marketing programs.
- Promotional campaigns will be partially outsourced.
- Advertising will be consistent.
- Sales promotions and public relation strategies will work together to inform customers of new products, to encourage an image of community involvement for the Boulder Stop, and to limit environmental impact.

The customers will buy our products directly from the store, in the store. We will also generate sales through our website and its secure server and we will ship all ordered products from the store. All telephone orders will be taken at the store through either our singletoll free line or the local number. Mail orders will be processed at the main office in Bend and shipped from the store. All debits and credits, order transactions, charge backs, and price discounts will be accounted for on the SBT Accounting system at the Bend office.

**Distribution Strategy**

We will appeal to the weekend warriors by hosting fun events like the "Fun Summer Climb." Our part-time sales clerks, also trained in the ways of promotional tactics, will call businesses within the Bend area and establish additional sponsors for these events. They will close the sale immediately, if possible, enter the closure into the software accounting system, and provide post sales follow-up.

**Sales Strategy**

For in-store sales, our strategy will be to maintain as much on-site point-of-purchase literature as is physically possible. Our part-timers will be responsible for informing customers of the products and creating the best fit between customer and product. Our salespeople will understand that selling is about filling a need, not pressuring the customer to buy. Seventy to 80 percent of returns will be sent back to the distributor or vendor.

**Sales Forecast**

The following table and chart give a rundown on forecasted sales. We expect sales to increase at a rate of 1-2 percent per month for each product in the first few months.

November through January will be slow months for the Boulder Stop. For February through March, we expect 1 percent monthly sales growth becoming 2 percent growth as we reach the second summer. In 1999 and 2000, we expect solid 20-25 percent sales growth as the Boulder Stop becomes well-known in central Oregon. 1999 and 2000 costs will decrease 4-7 percent due to lower agency and efficiency costs.

Note: For company purchases, the per-unit price of inventory purchases includes cost of shipping.

**Sales Forecast**

| Sales | FY1998 | FY1999 | FY2000 |
|---|---|---|---|
| Carabiners | $16,784 | $20,141 | $25,176 |
| Ropes | $9,791 | $11,749 | $14,686 |
| Books and Magazines | $1,798 | $2,158 | $2,697 |
| Cookies | $1,573 | $1,888 | $2,360 |
| Espresso regulars | $57,695 | $69,233 | $86,542 |
| Espresso shakes | $7,418 | $8,901 | $11,127 |
| Gear rentals | $1,961 | $2,353 | $2,941 |
| Other | $0 | $0 | $0 |
| **Total Sales** | **$97,019** | **$116,423** | **$145,529** |
| | | | |
| **Direct Cost of Sales** | | | |
| Carabiners | $9,754 | $8,779 | $7,462 |
| Ropes | $6,069 | $5,462 | $4,643 |
| Books and Magazines | $1,300 | $1,170 | $995 |
| Cookies | $748 | $673 | $572 |
| Espresso regulars | $30,148 | $27,134 | $23,064 |
| Espresso shakes | $4,547 | $4,092 | $3,479 |
| Gear rentals | $1,286 | $1,158 | $984 |
| Other | $0 | $0 | $0 |
| **Subtotal Cost of Sales** | **$53,854** | **$48,468** | **$41,198** |

**Sales Programs**

Sales programs will include sales awards for highest sales and customer service awards for those employees who best exemplify the Boulder Stop's commitment to customers. The owner will award these valuable employees yearly with a $200-300 vacation to the Sunriver Resort in Bend.

- We will request rebate info from manufacturers and use those rebates to drive traffic to the store. We will also offer coupons in local area newspapers. These coupons will offer buyers from 100 to 50 percent off any espresso drink and/or buy-one-get-one-free espresso programs.
- We will offer gear rentals all week. This will let climbers who don't have 100 percent of the gear climb with their friends, creating goodwill and repeat customers. We will not rent carabiners, ropes, or cams; only shoes, bags, and helmets.

**Milestones**

The milestone table shows purchasing, sales, and marketing goals. The owner will conduct straight rebuys while touching base with Espresso Harvest. We have paid a deposit of $700 (06/28/97) to establish a 30-day grace period on all purchases from Espresso Harvest. There is no franchise fee and Espresso Harvest will donate advertising, consulting, and literature, provided that 40 percent of sales from Espresso Harvest mugs, cups, and T-shirts go directly to Espresso Harvest, Inc.

**Milestones**

| Milestone | Start Date | End Date | Budget | Manager | Department |
|---|---|---|---|---|---|
| COGS | 6/30/98 | 7/30/98 | $4,000 | Luke Walsh | Purchasing |
| Meet with rep | 6/25/98 | 6/30/98 | $700 | Luke Walsh | Sales |
| Complete advertising | 6/26/98 | 6/26/98 | $500 | Luke Walsh | Marketing |
| COGS | 7/30/98 | 8/30/98 | $4,000 | Luke Walsh | Purchasing |
| Perry Claw Rock Festival | 8/23/98 | 9/23/98 | $650 | Luke Walsh | Marketing |
| COGS | 8/30/98 | 9/30/98 | $4,000 | Luke Walsh | Purchasing |
| Straight rebuy | 9/30/98 | 9/30/98 | $4,000 | Luke Walsh | Purchasing |
| Straight rebuy | 10/30/98 | 10/30/98 | $2,500 | Luke Walsh | Purchasing |
| Straight rebuy | 11/30/98 | 11/30/98 | $500 | Luke Walsh | Purchasing |
| Other | 1/1/98 | 1/1/98 | $0 | ABC | Department |
| Totals | | | $20,850 | | |

## MANAGEMENT SUMMARY

The owner of the Boulder Stop believes very strongly that relationships should be forthright, work should be structured with enough room for creativity, and pay should be commensurate with the amount and quality of work completed. The company is young enough that the only manager this philosophy applies to is the president.

The president will assess the productivity of the two part-time employees every six months.

## Organizational Structure

The Boulder Stop is not departmentalized. The owner, Luke Walsh, is also the president, CFO, and lead manager. The company makes all decisions in accordance with the company mission. Employees are given specific tasks based upon their creativity, knowledge, and social ability.

## Management Team

**Luke Walsh: Manager and founder.**

Luke spent four years selling shoes and apparel for Nordstrom, Inc. He graduated from the University of Oregon in 1997 with a degree in Business Management. Luke's success at Nordstrom, the university, and in building a network of close friends has hinged upon his "common sense" approach to solving ambiguous problems, his ability to identify strengths and weaknesses in the marketplace and exploit them, as well as his commitment to building strong relationships through trust, not politics. These skills, combined with formal business training make him an ideal community leader and business owner.

## Personnel Plan

The personnel plan is included in the following table. It shows the owner's salary (Other) followed by two part-time salaries for espresso servers/gear experts. Part-time employees will not be included in the profit-sharing program until they have worked with the company for twelve months. All part-time employees will start at $8/hr and receive full health benefits.

**Personnel Plan**

*continued*

**Personnel Plan**

| Personnel | FY1998 | FY1999 | FY2000 |
|---|---|---|---|
| Part-time employee #1 | $4,700 | $4,935 | $5,182 |
| Part-time employee #2 | $4,700 | $4,935 | $5,182 |
| Other | $0 | $0 | $0 |
| **Total Payroll** | **$9,400** | **$9,870** | **$10,364** |
| | | | |
| Total Headcount | 0 | 0 | 0 |
| Payroll Burden | $376 | $395 | $415 |
| **Total Payroll Expenditure** | **$9,776** | **$10,265** | **$10,778** |

**Financial Plan**

- Growth will be moderate, cash balance always positive.
- Marketing will remain at or below 15 percent of sales.
- The company will invest residual profits into company expansion and personnel.

**Important Assumptions**

We do not sell anything on credit. The personnel burden is very low because benefits are not paid to part-timers. And the short-term interest rate is extra ordinarily low because of the owner's long-standing relationship with the USAA Credit Union.

**General Assumptions**

| | FY1998 | FY1999 | FY2000 |
|---|---|---|---|
| Short-term Interest Rate % | 7.00% | 7.00% | 7.00% |
| Long-term Interest Rate % | 7.50% | 7.50% | 7.50% |
| Payment Days Estimator | 35 | 35 | 35 |
| Collection Days Estimator | 30 | 30 | 30 |
| Inventory Turnover Estimator | 12.00 | 12.00 | 12.00 |
| Tax Rate % | 30.00% | 30.00% | 30.00% |
| Expenses in Cash % | 25.00% | 25.00% | 25.00% |
| Sales on Credit % | 0.00% | 0.00% | 0.00% |
| Personnel Burden % | 4.00% | 4.00% | 4.00% |

**Break-even Analysis**

For our Break-even Analysis, we have chosen $3.00 to represent our average revenue per unit. Although revenue from ropes and other gear amount to significantly more revenue per unit, such items skew the revenue curve toward less units sold. We want to engage in a practical analysis of precisely what it will take to turn the company profitable by using the P&L statement. The Break-even Analysis is a gauge by which we can measure our monthly revenue streams to predict long-term profitability.

According to the analysis, we will break-even at approximately $6,000 in monthly sales.

**Break-even Analysis:**

| | |
|---|---|
| Monthly Units Break-even | 2,000 |
| Monthly Sales Break-even | $6,000 |

**Assumptions:**

| | |
|---|---|
| Average Per-Unit Revenue | $3.00 |
| Average Per-Unit Variable Cost | $0.75 |
| Estimated Monthly Fixed Cost | $4,500 |

We predict advertising costs and consulting costs will go up in the next three years. This will give the Boulder Stop a profit-to-sales ratio of nearly 31 percent by the year 2000. Normally, a start-up concern will operate with negative profits through the first two years. We will avoid that kind of operating loss by knowing our competitors, our target markets, industry direction, and the products we sell.

Note that we predict we will exceed our objective of 65 percent gross margin by the year 2000.

| Profit and Loss (Income Statement) | FY1998 | FY1999 | FY2000 |
|---|---|---|---|
| Sales | $97,019 | $116,423 | $145,529 |
| Direct Cost of Sales | $53,854 | $48,468 | $41,198 |
| Production Payroll | $0 | $0 | $0 |
| Other | $0 | $0 | $0 |
| | | | |
| **Total Cost of Sales** | **$53,854** | **$48,468** | **$41,198** |
| Gross Margin | $43,165 | $67,955 | $104,331 |
| Gross Margin % | 44.49% | 58.37% | 71.69% |
| | | | |
| **Operating expenses:** | | | |
| Advertising/Promotion | $3,740 | $3,100 | $3,500 |
| Travel | $300 | $0 | $0 |
| Miscellaneous | $0 | $0 | $0 |
| Payroll Expense | $9,400 | $9,870 | $10,364 |
| Payroll Burden | $376 | $395 | $415 |
| Depreciation | $1,200 | $1,236 | $1,273 |
| Leased Equipment | $0 | $0 | $0 |
| Utilities | $1,569 | $1,616 | $1,665 |
| Insurance | $780 | $803 | $828 |
| Lease | $20,400 | $21,012 | $21,642 |
| Other | $0 | $0 | $0 |
| | | | |
| **Total Operating Expenses** | **$37,765** | **$38,032** | **$39,686** |
| Profit Before Interest and Taxes | $5,400 | $29,922 | $64,645 |
| Interest Expense Short-term | $0 | $0 | $0 |
| Interest Expense Long-term | $770 | $572 | $356 |
| Taxes Incurred | $1,389 | $8,805 | $19,287 |
| Extraordinary Items | $0 | $0 | $0 |
| Net Profit | $3,241 | $20,546 | $45,003 |
| Net Profit/Sales | 3.34% | 17.65% | 30.92% |

**Projected Profit and Loss**

**Projected Cash Flow**

We are positioning ourselves in the market as a medium risk concern with steady cash flows. Accounts payable is paid at the end of each month while sales are in cash, and this gives the Boulder Stop an excellent cash flow structure. Solid Net Working Capital and intelligent marketing will secure a cash balance of $31,000 by January 1, 2000. Any amounts above $10,000 will be invested into semi-liquid stock portfolios to decrease the opportunity cost of cash held. The interest will show up as Dividends in the Projected Cash Flow table and will be updated quarterly.

**Projected Cash Flow**

|  | FY1998 | FY1999 | FY2000 |
|---|---|---|---|
| Net Profit | $3,241 | $20,546 | $45,003 |
| Plus: |  |  |  |
| Depreciation | $1,200 | $1,236 | $1,273 |
| Change in Accounts Payable | $9,997 | ($719) | $786 |
| Current Borrowing (repayment) | $0 | $0 | $0 |
| Increase (decrease) Other Liabilities | $0 | $0 | $0 |
| Long-term Borrowing (repayment) | ($2,640) | ($2,880) | ($2,880) |
| Capital Input | $0 | $0 | $0 |
| **Subtotal** | **$11,798** | **$18,182** | **$42,610** |
| Less: |  |  |  |
| Change in Accounts Receivable | $0 | $0 | $0 |
| Change in Inventory | $2,821 | ($982) | ($1,326) |
| Change in Other ST Assets | $0 | $0 | $0 |
| Capital Expenditure | $0 | $0 | $0 |
| Dividends | $0 | $0 | $0 |
| Subtotal | $2,821 | ($982) | ($1,326) |
| Net Cash Flow | $8,978 | $19,164 | $43,935 |
| **Cash Balance** | **$11,978** | **$31,142** | **$75,078** |

**Projected Balance Sheet**

All of our tables will be updated monthly to reflect past performance and future assumptions. Future assumptions will not be based on past performance but rather economic cycle activity, regional industry strength, and future cash flow possibilities. We expect solid growth in Net Worth beyond the year 2000.

**Projected Balance Sheet**
**Assets**

| **Short-term Assets** | FY1998 | FY1999 | FY2000 |
|---|---|---|---|
| Cash | $11,032 | $28,390 | $73,735 |
| Accounts Receivable | $0 | $0 | $0 |
| Inventory | $9,821 | $8,838 | $7,513 |
| Other Short-term Assets | $1,000 | $1,000 | $1,000 |
| Total Short-term Assets | $21,853 | $38,229 | $82,247 |
| Long-term Assets |  |  |  |
| Capital Assets | $0 | $0 | $0 |
| Accumulated Depreciation | $1,200 | $2,436 | $3,709 |
| Total Long-term Assets | ($1,200) | ($2,436) | ($3,709) |
| **Total Assets** | **$20,653** | **$35,793** | **$78,538** |

| Liabilities and Capital | FY1998 | FY1999 | FY2000 |
|---|---|---|---|
| Accounts Payable | $9,552 | $7,026 | $7,649 |
| Short-term Notes | $0 | $0 | $0 |
| Other Short-term Liabilities | $1,000 | $1,000 | $1,000 |
| **Subtotal Short-term Liabilities** | **$10,552** | **$8,026** | **$8,649** |
| | | | |
| Long-term Liabilities | $9,060 | $6,180 | $3,300 |
| **Total Liabilities** | **$19,612** | **$14,206** | **$11,949** |
| | | | |
| Paid in Capital | $13,800 | $13,800 | $13,800 |
| Retained Earnings | ($16,000) | ($12,759) | $7,787 |
| Earnings | $3,241 | $20,546 | $45,003 |
| **Total Capital** | **$1,041** | **$21,587** | **$66,589** |
| **Total Liabilities and Capital** | **$20,653** | **$35,793** | **$78,538** |
| **Net Worth** | **$1,041** | **$21,587** | **$66,589** |

**Projected Balance Sheet**

*continued*

We expect our net profit margin, gross margin, and ROA to increase steadily over the three-year period. ROE will decrease due to lower equity needs and higher cash inflow. Our net working capital will increase to almost $74,000 by year three, proving that we have the cash flows to remain a going concern. The following table shows these important financial ratios.

**Business Ratios**

**Ratio Analysis**

| Profitability Ratios: | FY1998 | FY1999 | FY2000 | RMA |
|---|---|---|---|---|
| Gross Margin | 44.49% | 58.37% | 71.69% | 0 |
| Net Profit Margin | 3.34% | 17.65% | 30.92% | 0 |
| Return on Assets | 15.69% | 57.40% | 57.30% | 0 |
| Return on Equity | 311.31% | 95.18% | 67.58% | 0 |
| | | | | |
| **Activity Ratios** | | | | |
| AR Turnover | 0.00 | 0.00 | 0.00 | 0 |
| Collection Days | 0 | 0 | 0 | 0 |
| Inventory Turnover | 6.40 | 5.20 | 5.04 | 0 |
| Accounts Payable Turnover | 6.72 | 10.43 | 10.43 | 0 |
| Total Asset Turnover | 4.70 | 3.25 | 1.85 | 0 |
| | | | | |
| **Debt Ratios** | | | | |
| Debt to Net Worth | 18.84 | 0.66 | 0.18 | 0 |
| Short-term Liability to Liability | 0.54 | 0.56 | 0.72 | 0 |
| | | | | |
| **Liquidity Ratios** | | | | |
| Current Ratio | 2.07 | 4.76 | 9.51 | 0 |
| Quick Ratio | 1.14 | 3.66 | 8.64 | 0 |
| Net Working Capital | $11,301 | $30,203 | $73,598 | 0 |
| Interest Coverage | 7.01 | 52.36 | 181.84 | 0 |
| | | | | |
| **Additional Ratios** | | | | |
| Assets to Sales | 0.21 | 0.31 | 0.54 | 0 |
| Debt/Assets | 95% | 40% | 15% | 0 |
| Current Debt/Total Assets | 51% | 22% | 11% | 0 |
| Acid Test | 1.14 | 3.66 | 8.64 | 0 |
| Asset Turnover | 4.70 | 3.25 | 1.85 | 0 |
| Sales/Net Worth | 93.19 | 5.39 | 2.19 | 0 |
| Dividend Payout | $0 | $0 | $0 | $0 |

## APPENDIX

## Projected Balance Sheet

**Assets**

| Short-term Assets | Starting Balances | May | Jun | Jul | Aug | Sep |
|---|---|---|---|---|---|---|
| Cash | $3,000 | $10,046 | $14,369 | $16,708 | $18,790 | $20,484 |
| Accounts Receivable | $0 | $0 | $0 | $0 | $0 | $0 |
| Inventory | $7,000 | $3,805 | $3,729 | $3,654 | $3,581 | $3,402 |
| Other Short-term Assets | $1,000 | $1,000 | $1,000 | $1,000 | $1,000 | $1,000 |
| **Total Short-term Assets** | **$11,000** | **$14,851** | **$19,097** | **$21,362** | **$23,372** | **$24,887** |
| | | | | | | |
| **Long-term Assets** | | | | | | |
| Capital Assets | $0 | $0 | $0 | $0 | $0 | $0 |
| Accumulated Depreciation | $0 | $100 | $200 | $300 | $400 | $500 |
| Total Long-term Assets | $0 | ($100) | ($200) | ($300) | ($400) | ($500) |
| **Total Assets** | **$11,000** | **$14,751** | **$18,897** | **$21,062** | **$22,972** | **$24,387** |
| | | | | | | |
| **Liabilities and Capital** | | | | | | |
| Accounts Payable | $500 | $2,995 | $5,556 | $5,909 | $5,954 | $5,459 |
| Short-term Notes | $0 | $0 | $0 | $0 | $0 | $0 |
| Other Short-term Liabilities | $1,000 | $1,000 | $1,000 | $1,000 | $1,000 | $1,000 |
| **Subtotal Short-term Liabilities** | **$1,500** | **$3,995** | **$6,556** | **$6,909** | **$6,954** | **$6,459** |
| Long-term Liabilities | $11,700 | $11,480 | $11,260 | $11,040 | $10,820 | $10,600 |
| **Total Liabilities** | **$13,200** | **$15,475** | **$17,816** | **$17,949** | **$17,774** | **$17,059** |
| | | | | | | |
| Paid in Capital | $13,800 | $13,800 | $13,800 | $13,800 | $13,800 | $13,800 |
| Retained Earnings | ($16,000) | ($16,000) | ($16,000) | ($16,000) | ($16,000) | ($16,000) |
| Earnings | $0 | $1,476 | $3,281 | $5,313 | $7,397 | $9,527 |
| **Total Capital** | **($2,200)** | **($724)** | **$1,081** | **$3,113** | **$5,197** | **$7,327** |
| **Total Liabilities and Capital** | **$11,000** | **$14,751** | **$18,897** | **$21,062** | **$22,972** | **$24,387** |
| **Net Worth** | **($2,200)** | **($724)** | **$1,081** | **$3,113** | **$5,197** | **$7,327** |

| Oct | Nov | Dec | Jan | Feb | Mar | Apr |
|---|---|---|---|---|---|---|
| $20,563 | $21,488 | $19,401 | $18,599 | $20,938 | $13,302 | $11,032 |
| $0 | $0 | $0 | $0 | $0 | $0 | $0 |
| $2,552 | $1,914 | $1,435 | $1,005 | $10,667 | $9,821 | $9,821 |
| $1,000 | $1,000 | $1,000 | $1,000 | $1,000 | $1,000 | $1,000 |
| **$24,114** | **$24,402** | **$21,836** | **$20,603** | **$32,605** | **$24,122** | **$21,853** |
|  |  |  |  |  |  |  |
| $0 | $0 | $0 | $0 | $0 | $0 | $0 |
| $600 | $700 | $800 | $900 | $1,000 | $1,100 | $1,200 |
| ($600) | ($700) | ($800) | ($900) | ($1,000) | ($1,100) | ($1,200) |
| **$23,514** | **$23,702** | **$21,036** | **$19,703** | **$31,605** | **$23,022** | **$20,653** |
|  |  |  |  |  |  |  |
| $3,867 | $3,210 | $1,586 | $1,356 | $16,347 | $9,918 | $9,552 |
| $0 | $0 | $0 | $0 | $0 | $0 | $0 |
| $1,000 | $1,000 | $1,000 | $1,000 | $1,000 | $1,000 | $1,000 |
| **$4,867** | **$4,210** | **$2,586** | **$2,356** | **$17,347** | **$10,918** | **$10,552** |
| $10,380 | $10,160 | $9,940 | $9,720 | $9,500 | $9,280 | $9,060 |
| **$15,247** | **$14,370** | **$12,526** | **$12,076** | **$26,847** | **$20,198** | **$19,612** |
|  |  |  |  |  |  |  |
| $13,800 | $13,800 | $13,800 | $13,800 | $13,800 | $13,800 | $13,800 |
| ($16,000) | ($16,000) | ($16,000) | ($16,000) | ($16,000) | ($16,000) | ($16,000) |
| $10,467 | $11,532 | $10,710 | $9,827 | $6,958 | $5,024 | $3,241 |
| **$8,267** | **$9,332** | **$8,510** | **$7,627** | **$4,758** | **$2,824** | **$1,041** |
| **$23,514** | **$23,702** | **$21,036** | **$19,703** | **$31,605** | **$23,022** | **$20,653** |
| **$8,267** | **$9,332** | **$8,510** | **$7,627** | **$4,758** | **$2,824** | **$1,041** |

## Projected Cash Flow

| | May | Jun | Jul | Aug | Sep | Oct |
|---|---|---|---|---|---|---|
| Net Profit | $1,476 | $1,806 | $2,031 | $2,085 | $2,130 | $940 |
| Plus: | | | | | | |
| Depreciation | $100 | $100 | $100 | $100 | $100 | $100 |
| Change in Accounts Payable | $2,495 | $2,561 | $353 | $45 | ($495) | ($1,592) |
| Current Borrowing (repayment) | $0 | $0 | $0 | $0 | $0 | $0 |
| Increase (decrease) Other Liabilities | $0 | $0 | $0 | $0 | $0 | $0 |
| Long-term Borrowing (repayment) | ($220) | ($220) | ($220) | ($220) | ($220) | ($220) |
| Capital Input | $0 | $0 | $0 | $0 | $0 | $0 |
| **Subtotal** | **$3,851** | **$4,247** | **$2,264** | **$2,010** | **$1,515** | **($772)** |
| Less: | | | | | | |
| Change in Accounts Receivable | $0 | $0 | $0 | $0 | $0 | $0 |
| Change in Inventory | ($3,195) | ($76) | ($75) | ($73) | ($179) | ($851) |
| Change in Other Short-term Assets | $0 | $0 | $0 | $0 | $0 | $0 |
| Capital Expenditure | $0 | $0 | $0 | $0 | $0 | $0 |
| Dividends | $0 | $0 | $0 | $0 | $0 | $0 |
| **Subtotal** | **($3,195)** | **($76)** | **($75)** | **($73)** | **($179)** | **($851)** |
| Net Cash Flow | $7,046 | $4,323 | $2,339 | $2,083 | $1,694 | $78 |
| **Cash Balance** | **$10,046** | **$14,369** | **$16,708** | **$18,790** | **$20,484** | **$20,563** |

| Nov | Dec | Jan | Feb | Mar | Apr |
|---|---|---|---|---|---|
| $1,065 | ($821) | ($883) | ($2,869) | ($1,934) | ($1,783) |
| | | | | | |
| $100 | $100 | $100 | $100 | $100 | $100 |
| ($657) | ($1,625) | ($230) | $14,991 | ($6,428) | ($366) |
| $0 | $0 | $0 | $0 | $0 | $0 |
| $0 | $0 | $0 | $0 | $0 | $0 |
| ($220) | ($220) | ($220) | ($220) | ($220) | ($220) |
| $0 | $0 | $0 | $0 | $0 | $0 |
| **$288** | **($2,566)** | **($1,233)** | **$12,002** | **($8,483)** | **($2,269)** |
| | | | | | |
| $0 | $0 | $0 | $0 | $0 | $0 |
| ($638) | ($478) | ($431) | $9,662 | ($846) | $0 |
| $0 | $0 | $0 | $0 | $0 | $0 |
| $0 | $0 | $0 | $0 | $0 | $0 |
| $0 | $0 | $0 | $0 | $0 | $0 |
| **($638)** | **($478)** | **($431)** | **$9,662** | **($846)** | **$0** |
| $926 | ($2,088) | ($802) | $2,340 | ($7,637) | ($2,269) |
| **$21,488** | **$19,401** | **$18,599** | **$20,938** | **$13,302** | **$11,032** |

## General Assumptions

|  | May | Jun | Jul | Aug | Sep | Oct |
|---|---|---|---|---|---|---|
| Short-term Interest Rate % | 7.00% | 7.00% | 7.00% | 7.00% | 7.00% | 7.00% |
| Long-term Interest Rate % | 7.50% | 7.50% | 7.50% | 7.50% | 7.50% | 7.50% |
| Payment Days Estimator | 35 | 35 | 35 | 35 | 35 | 35 |
| Collection Days Estimator | 30 | 30 | 30 | 30 | 30 | 30 |
| Inventory Turnover Estimator | 12.00 | 12.00 | 12.00 | 12.00 | 12.00 | 12.00 |
| Tax Rate % | 30.00% | 30.00% | 30.00% | 30.00% | 30.00% | 30.00% |
| Expenses in Cash % | 25.00% | 25.00% | 25.00% | 25.00% | 25.00% | 25.00% |
| Sales on Credit % | 0.00% | 0.00% | 0.00% | 0.00% | 0.00% | 0.00% |
| Personnel Burden % | 4.00% | 4.00% | 4.00% | 4.00% | 4.00% | 4.00% |

## Personnel Plan

| Personnel | May | Jun | Jul | Aug | Sep | Oct |
|---|---|---|---|---|---|---|
| Part-time employee #1 | $500 | $500 | $500 | $500 | $500 | $500 |
| Part-time employee #2 | $500 | $500 | $500 | $500 | $500 | $500 |
| Other | $0 | $0 | $0 | $0 | $0 | $0 |
| **Total Payroll** | $1,000 | $1,000 | $1,000 | $1,000 | $1,000 | $1,100 |
|  |  |  |  |  |  |  |
| Total Headcount | 0 | 0 | 0 | 0 | 0 | 0 |
| Payroll Burden | $40 | $40 | $40 | $40 | $40 | $44 |
| **Total Payroll Expenditures** | $1,040 | $1,040 | $1,040 | $1,040 | $1,040 | $1,144 |

| Nov | Dec | Jan | Feb | Mar | Apr |
|---|---|---|---|---|---|
| 7.00% | 7.00% | 7.00% | 7.00% | 7.00% | 7.00% |
| 7.50% | 7.50% | 7.50% | 7.50% | 7.50% | 7.50% |
| 35 | 35 | 35 | 35 | 35 | 35 |
| 30 | 30 | 30 | 30 | 30 | 30 |
| 12.00 | 12.00 | 12.00 | 12.00 | 12.00 | 12.00 |
| 30.00% | 30.00% | 30.00% | 30.00% | 30.00% | 30.00% |
| 25.00% | 25.00% | 25.00% | 25.00% | 25.00% | 25.00% |
| 0.00% | 0.00% | 0.00% | 0.00% | 0.00% | 0.00% |
| 4.00% | 4.00% | 4.00% | 4.00% | 4.00% | 4.00% |

| Nov | Dec | Jan | Feb | Mar | Apr |
|---|---|---|---|---|---|
| $550 | $0 | $0 | $0 | $550 | $550 |
| $550 | $0 | $0 | $0 | $550 | $550 |
| $0 | $0 | $0 | $0 | $0 | $0 |
| $0 | $0 | $0 | $1,100 | $1,100 | $1,100 |
| 0 | 0 | 0 | 0 | 0 | 0 |
| $0 | $0 | $0 | $44 | $44 | $44 |
| $0 | $0 | $0 | $1,144 | $1,144 | $1,144 |

## Projected Profit and Loss (Income Statement)

| | May | Jun | Jul | Aug | Sep | Oct |
|---|---|---|---|---|---|---|
| Sales | $9,715 | $9,909 | $10,207 | $10,309 | $9,793 | $7,345 |
| Direct Cost of Sales | $3,805 | $3,729 | $3,654 | $3,581 | $3,402 | $2,552 |
| Production Payroll | $0 | $0 | $0 | $0 | $0 | $0 |
| Other | $0 | $0 | $0 | $0 | $0 | $0 |
| | | | | | | |
| **Total Cost of Sales** | **$3,805** | **$3,729** | **$3,654** | **$3,581** | **$3,402** | **$2,552** |
| Gross Margin | $5,910 | $6,180 | $6,552 | $6,727 | $6,391 | $4,793 |
| Gross Margin % | 60.83% | 62.37% | 64.20% | 65.26% | 65.26% | 65.26% |
| | | | | | | |
| **Operating expenses:** | | | | | | |
| Advertising | $700 | $500 | $250 | $650 | $250 | $250 |
| Travel | $0 | $0 | $300 | $0 | $0 | $0 |
| Miscellaneous | $0 | $0 | $0 | $0 | $0 | $0 |
| Payroll Expenses | $1,000 | $1,000 | $1,000 | $1,000 | $1,000 | $1,100 |
| Payroll Burden | $40 | $40 | $40 | $40 | $40 | $44 |
| Depreciation | $100 | $100 | $100 | $100 | $100 | $100 |
| Leased Equipment | $0 | $0 | $0 | $0 | $0 | $0 |
| Utilities | $120 | $121 | $121 | $122 | $122 | $122 |
| Insurance | $70 | $70 | $70 | $70 | $70 | $70 |
| Lease | $1,700 | $1,700 | $1,700 | $1,700 | $1,700 | $1,700 |
| Other | $0 | $0 | $0 | $0 | $0 | $0 |
| Contract/Consultants | $0 | $0 | $0 | $0 | $0 | $0 |
| | | | | | | |
| **Total Operating Expenses** | **$3,730** | **$3,531** | **$3,581** | **$3,682** | **$3,282** | **$3,386** |
| | | | | | | |
| Profit Before Interest and Taxes | $2,180 | $2,650 | $2,971 | $3,046 | $3,109 | $1,407 |
| Interest Expense Short-term | $0 | $0 | $0 | $0 | $0 | $0 |
| Interest Expense Long-term | $72 | $70 | $69 | $68 | $66 | $65 |
| Taxes Incurred | $632 | $774 | $871 | $893 | $913 | $403 |
| Extraordinary Items | $0 | $0 | $0 | $0 | $0 | $0 |
| **Net Profit** | **$1,476** | **$1,806** | **$2,031** | **$2,085** | **$2,130** | **$940** |
| **Net Profit/Sales** | **15.19%** | **18.22%** | **19.90%** | **20.22%** | **21.75%** | **12.79%** |

| Nov | Dec | Jan | Feb | Mar | Apr |
|---|---|---|---|---|---|
| $5,509 | $1,377 | $1,239 | $10,296 | $10,502 | $10,817 |
| $1,914 | $478 | $431 | $10,667 | $9,821 | $9,821 |
| $0 | $0 | $0 | $0 | $0 | $0 |
| $0 | $0 | $0 | $0 | $0 | $0 |
| **$1,914** | **$478** | **$431** | **$10,667** | **$9,821** | **$9,821** |
| $3,595 | $899 | $809 | ($370) | $682 | $997 |
| 65.26% | 65.26% | 65.26% | -3.60% | 6.49% | 9.22% |
| $0 | $0 | $0 | $540 | $250 | $350 |
| $0 | $0 | $0 | $0 | $0 | $0 |
| $0 | $0 | $0 | $0 | $0 | $0 |
| $0 | $0 | $0 | $1,100 | $1,100 | $1,100 |
| $0 | $0 | $0 | $44 | $44 | $44 |
| $100 | $100 | $100 | $100 | $100 | $100 |
| $0 | $0 | $0 | $0 | $0 | $0 |
| $160 | $160 | $160 | $115 | $123 | $123 |
| $50 | $50 | $50 | $70 | $70 | $70 |
| $1,700 | $1,700 | $1,700 | $1,700 | $1,700 | $1,700 |
| $0 | $0 | $0 | $0 | $0 | $0 |
| $0 | $0 | $0 | $0 | $0 | $0 |
| **$2,010** | **$2,010** | **$2,010** | **$3,669** | **$3,387** | **$3,487** |
| $1,585 | ($1,111) | ($1,201) | ($4,039) | ($2,705) | ($2,490) |
| $0 | $0 | $0 | $0 | $0 | $0 |
| $64 | $62 | $61 | $59 | $58 | $57 |
| $456 | ($352) | ($379) | ($1,230) | ($829) | ($764) |
| $0 | $0 | $0 | $0 | $0 | $0 |
| **$1,065** | **($821)** | **($883)** | **($2,869)** | **($1,934)** | **($1,783)** |
| **19.33%** | **-59.64%** | **-71.27%** | **-27.86%** | **-18.42%** | **-16.48%** |

## Sales Forecast

| Sales | May | Jun | Jul | Aug | Sep | Oct |
|---|---|---|---|---|---|---|
| Carabiners | $1,680 | $1,714 | $1,765 | $1,783 | $1,694 | $1,270 |
| Ropes | $980 | $1,000 | $1,030 | $1,040 | $988 | $741 |
| Books and Magazines | $180 | $184 | $189 | $191 | $181 | $136 |
| Cookies | $158 | $161 | $165 | $167 | $159 | $119 |
| Espresso regulars | $5,775 | $5,891 | $6,067 | $6,128 | $5,821 | $4,366 |
| Espresso shakes | $743 | $757 | $780 | $788 | $748 | $561 |
| Gear rentals | $200 | $204 | $210 | $212 | $202 | $151 |
| Other | $0 | $0 | $0 | $0 | $0 | $0 |
| **Total Sales** | **$9,715** | **$9,909** | **$10,207** | **$10,309** | **$9,793** | **$7,345** |
| | | | | | | |
| **Direct Cost of Sales** | | | | | | |
| Carabiners | $735 | $720 | $706 | $692 | $657 | $493 |
| Ropes | $490 | $480 | $471 | $461 | $438 | $329 |
| Books and Magazines | $120 | $118 | $115 | $113 | $107 | $80 |
| Cookies | $42 | $41 | $40 | $40 | $38 | $28 |
| Espresso regulars | $1,980 | $1,940 | $1,902 | $1,864 | $1,770 | $1,328 |
| Espresso shakes | $363 | $356 | $349 | $342 | $325 | $243 |
| Gear rentals | $75 | $74 | $72 | $71 | $67 | $50 |
| Other | $0 | $0 | $0 | $0 | $0 | $0 |
| **Subtotal Cost of Sales** | **$3,805** | **$3,729** | **$3,654** | **$3,581** | **$3,402** | **$2,552** |

| Nov | Dec | Jan | Feb | Mar | Apr |
|---|---|---|---|---|---|
| $953 | $238 | $214 | $1,783 | $1,818 | $1,873 |
| $556 | $139 | $125 | $1,040 | $1,061 | $1,093 |
| $102 | $26 | $23 | $191 | $195 | $201 |
| $89 | $22 | $20 | $167 | $170 | $176 |
| $3,275 | $819 | $737 | $6,128 | $6,250 | $6,438 |
| $421 | $105 | $95 | $788 | $804 | $828 |
| $113 | $28 | $26 | $200 | $204 | $210 |
| $0 | $0 | $0 | $0 | $0 | $0 |
| **$5,509** | **$1,377** | **$1,239** | **$10,296** | **$10,502** | **$10,817** |
| | | | | | |
| $370 | $92 | $83 | $1,747 | $1,730 | $1,730 |
| $246 | $62 | $55 | $1,019 | $1,009 | $1,009 |
| $60 | $15 | $14 | $187 | $185 | $185 |
| $21 | $5 | $5 | $164 | $162 | $162 |
| $996 | $249 | $224 | $6,005 | $5,945 | $5,945 |
| $183 | $46 | $41 | $772 | $764 | $764 |
| $38 | $9 | $8 | $772 | $25 | $25 |
| $0 | $0 | $0 | $0 | $0 | $0 |
| **$1,914** | **$478** | **$431** | **$10,667** | **$9,821** | **$9,821** |

# Ski Resort

BUSINESS PLAN

MOUNTJOY, LLC

*84 Junction Way*
*Ogden, Utah 84111*

*Mountjoy will provide a welcome alternative to the traditional ski resort experience. By supplying extra-wide powder skis to its clients, the company will enable them to glide through the area's pristine powder with confidence. Mountjoy's experienced and well-trained guides will provide expert instruction. The company's private on-mountain cabin will serve as an elegant setting for a catered lunch. With superior customer service and attention to detail, Mountjoy will deliver an experience that is unequaled in the marketplace.*

- EXECUTIVE SUMMARY

- MANAGEMENT

- MARKETING

- INDUSTRY & MARKETPLACE ANALYSIS

- MARKETING STRATEGY

- MARKETING COMMUNICATIONS

- DEVELOPMENT

- OPERATIONS

- FINANCIAL SUMMARY

- APPENDIX

# SKI RESORT
# BUSINESS PLAN

## EXECUTIVE SUMMARY

### Mission

Mountjoy will provide its clients with the best powder skiing experience in America.

### Company Overview

Founded by Emmett Metterley in January of 1999, Mountjoy is positioned to bring the highest level of service to the ski industry. The company has negotiated to purchase the assets of Ogden Powder Cats (OPC), an established snowcat ski company in Ogden, Utah, with a sixteen-year operating history. Acquiring OPC's assets will give Mountjoy exclusive commercial access to the best powder skiing and snowboarding terrain in the state. Located immediately north of the Powder Mountain Ski Area, OPC's 10,000-acre Forest Service permit area receives over 600 inches of the lightest snow in Utah every year. With Mountjoy's professional management, the company will transform OPC into a world-class operation.

Mountjoy will provide a welcome alternative to the traditional ski resort experience. By supplying extra-wide powder skis to its clients, the company will enable them to glide through the area's pristine powder with confidence. For those clients who require assistance with their powder skiing or snowboarding technique, Mountjoy's experienced and well-trained guides will provide expert instruction. The company's private on-mountain cabin will serve as an elegant setting for a catered lunch. With superior customer service and attention to detail, Mountjoy will deliver an experience that is unequaled in the marketplace.

### Industry

The market for adventure skiing has grown substantially over the last decade as more consumers actively seek experiences that involve physical challenges in outdoor environments. Mountjoy will capitalize on this trend by providing untracked snow conditions within a full-service environment that allows its clients to indulge in their powder skiing or snowboarding fantasies.

### Market

Mountjoy's target market consists of skiers and snowboarders who enjoy deep powder conditions and consider themselves to be of intermediate, advanced, or expert ability. Visitors are already attracted to Ogden by its reputation for champagne powder, and Mountjoy will offer the ultimate powder experience without the ski area's crowds or lift lines. The size of the local target market is estimated at 600,000 skier visits per year, and Mountjoy plans to capture one half of one percent of this market by its fifth year of operation.

### Competition

Mountjoy will not be the only snowcat ski company in Utah, but it will be the only one located within ninety miles of Ogden. The company's exclusive Forest Service permit will prevent any direct competitors from entering the local market.

### Development

Mountjoy has organized as a Utah Limited Liability Company and closed on a first round of financing in the amount of $700,000.

### Operations

Mountjoy will earn its first revenues during the 1999/2000 season. With two new snowcats, a renovated cabin, and terrain that is three times larger than OPC's current usage area,

Mountjoy will be positioned to deliver on its promise of providing the best powder skiing and snowboarding experience in America. A comprehensive marketing campaign will be designed to increase market demand and justify the addition of a third snowcat during the company's third year of operation.

| Fiscal Year | 2000 | 2001 | 2002 | 2003 | 2004 |
|---|---|---|---|---|---|
| Revenue | 446,075 | 541,666 | 710,932 | 895,780 | 1,081,655 |
| Cost of Services | 162,590 | 246,997 | 315,453 | 381,096 | 394,745 |
| Operating Expenses | 208,617 | 189,986 | 211,381 | 234,211 | 256,303 |
| Interest Expenses | 61,669 | 59,367 | 55,537 | 44,131 | 33,291 |
| **Net Income** | **13,199** | **45,316** | **128,566** | **252,100** | **397,315** |

**Financial Projections**

### Emmett Metterley, Chief Executive Officer, Manager, Member

**MANAGEMENT**

Mr. Metterley has worked in the outdoor recreation industry in Europe, Canada, and the United States for 15 years and holds a master's degree in Wilderness Risk Management and an M.B.A. in Entrepreneurship from the University of Utah. He is a Level II mountain guide and has led ascents throughout Switzerland, France, Canada, and the United States. Mr. Metterley has taught skiing in St. Moritz, Switzerland, and Mont Tremblant, Canada, home of the prestigious Northern Rocks Ski School. As an instructor in Provo, Utah, he refined a new method of teaching telemark skiing originally developed by Mr. Morgan Smithson of the Provo Ski Company. Mr. Metterley is a certified Level III avalanche forecaster with the American Avalanche Institute, the highest certification available. He is also certified as a Wilderness First Responder and has been an active rescuer since 1986. He served as the Operating Officer for Club Hagenstrasse in Provo, a multi-million dollar German ski-tour company catering to an affluent clientele. In this capacity, he personally guided clients on snowcat skiing tours. Mr. Metterley successfully founded and grew a nonprofit organization in Heber City, Utah, dedicated to outdoor education and skill building.

A profile of the company's advisory board may be found in the Appendix.

**MARKETING**

**Service Description**

Mountjoy's Forest Service permit area near Pioneer Trail in the Wasatch National Forest will offer 10,000 acres of Ogden's legendary champagne powder. With more than 600 inches of snowfall per year, this area features Utah's deepest snowpack. Mountjoy's open glades and world-class tree skiing will offer challenging terrain for intermediate through expert skiers and snowboarders.

Mountjoy will provide its clients with specialized Volant powder skis and B-Line snowboards in order to maximize their enjoyment of the deep, untracked snow. By assuming OPC's Professional Ski Instructors of America (PSIA) ski school certification, Mountjoy will enable its guides to offer clients high quality instruction. With powder skis and expert coaching, every client will be equipped with the resources necessary to ensure an enjoyable day on the mountain.

Prior to skiing, clients will be asked to visit Mountjoy's office in order to fit their boots to the company's powder skis, complete a short questionnaire regarding their skiing ability and sign a liability waiver. On the morning of their trip, clients may elect to depart from Mountjoy's office or arrange for one of the company's vans to pick them up directly from their lodging. In either case, their powder skis will have already been adjusted and loaded onto the vans. After a short drive to the company's staging area within the Wasatch National Forest, clients and their guides will board heated snowcats and begin a twenty-five minute journey into the heart of Mountjoy's ski terrain.

During the initial ride up the mountain, the lead guide in each snowcat will distribute digital avalanche transceivers and small backpacks to each client that contain snow shovels, water, and room for personal items such as cameras, camcorders, or additional layers of clothing. By the time the guide has finished explaining Mountjoy's safety procedures, the snowcat will have reached the top of the first run.

Depending on the experience level of the clients, the lead guide will either demonstrate appropriate powder skiing technique on a forgiving slope or escort clients directly to Mountjoy's more advanced terrain. Each lead guide will be accompanied by a second guide who follows clients down the hill, providing additional assistance and coaching when necessary.

After a morning of approximately five runs, clients will ski to Mountjoy's on-mountain cabin, where they will be greeted with a catered lunch including hot soup and beverages. The cabin will feature a dining area, comfortable reading chairs, and a restroom. Those who feel too tired to continue skiing in the afternoon may choose to sit by the warm stove and enjoy a book from Mountjoy's library or ride with their snowcat operator in the front of the vehicle.

The afternoon will typically consist of five additional runs, allowing most clients to ski 10,000 vertical feet per day. In most cases, clients will have finished skiing by 4:00 P.M. and will arrive at Mountjoy's office or their lodging by 4:30 P.M.

Within two weeks of their trip, clients will receive letters of thanks from Mr. Metterley that contain return postcards inviting them to provide feedback on the quality of Mountjoy's services.

A table of Mountjoy's proposed services is provided below:

**Mountjoy's Services**

**Terrain**

> 600 inches of snowfall per year
> Deepest and lightest snow in Utah
> 10,000 acres of open glades and tree skiing
> - 10% expert
> - 60% advanced
> - 30% intermediate

**Amenities**

> Door-to-door transportation available
> Custom fitted ski equipment
> - Extra-wide powder skis in two configurations
>   -Alpine
>   -Telemark
> Client safety equipment
> - Digital avalanche transceivers
> - Snow shovels
> - Avalanche probes
> Private on-mountain cabin
> - Dining area
> - Library and reading chairs
> - Restroom

**Food**

Lunch
- Hot beverages
- Catered gourmet food

After-ski
- Hot cider
- Fresh Cookies

**Learning**

Snow safety presentations
Local history and geography
Ski and snowboard instruction
- Demonstration and coaching
- Videotaping and review

**INDUSTRY & MARKETPLACE ANALYSIS**

**Industry Analysis**

Mountjoy will compete in the recreational services industry. Between 1995 and 1996, consumer spending in the industry rose by 78 percent. In a 1995 Gallup Poll survey on the use of recreation and leisure time, 79 percent of respondents in the high income bracket listed "seeking adventure" and "being with nature" as primary motivations. The adventure travel segment alone accounts for over $10 billion in annual revenue and is the fastest growing segment of the travel industry. W. Norman, President of the Travel Industry Association believes that "American[s]... are looking for new ways to challenge themselves, to push their physical energies to the edge and face nature at its boldest moments."

The ski industry is responding to this trend with significant investments in services that appeal to adventure skiers and snowboarders. Peterson Resorts has purchased a snowcat ski company that offers backcountry skiing on Peterson Pass. In addition, Category III, Peterson's newest expansion area, is intended to attract adventure skiers with ungroomed slopes designed to simulate backcountry conditions. Ogden's Pioneer Ridge expansion is targeted toward a similar market, as are Winter Park's Circle Cross, The Ridge at Provo, and Provo's Highlands Peak and Highlands Bowl areas. Like Peterson Resorts, the Provo Ski Company has also acquired a neighboring snowcat ski operation.

Snowcat and helicopter ski companies are becoming increasingly popular with consumers. Canadian Mountain Holidays (CMH), the largest helicopter ski operation in the world, consistently sells out its fleet of thirty helicopters every year. During the 1996/1997 season, the helicopter skiing business in British Columbia alone amounted to more than 55,000 skier visits, or approximately $55 million in revenue. Intrawest Resorts, the largest ski company in North America, acquired CMH in January of 1999, signaling its confidence in the growth potential of the adventure skiing market.

Not only are consumers demanding better ski conditions, but they are spending more money on their ski vacations as well. The National Ski Areas Association reports that total industry profits per skier increased more than 50 percent from 1995 to 1996. On average, destination skiers spend three times more money than day skiers and typically ski six days per trip, making them the most profitable consumer group on the mountain. Because they tend to return to the same resort year after year, destination skiers are a more profitable long-term revenue source than day skiers. The 1997/1998 Profile of Utah Skiing reports that the median income of Utah skiers increased by 16 percent from prior season levels to $87,200 per household. Moreover, the number of skiers who report incomes over $100,000 increased by 6 percent during the same twelve month period to 43 percent of all Utah skiers. These consumers are capable of paying what is necessary to ensure an enjoyable ski vacation.

## Marketplace Analysis

Approximately 80 percent of Ogden's winter visitors are destination skiers. Recognizing the revenue potential of this market, the American Skiing Company recently purchased the Ogden Ski Area and its surrounding properties. During 1998 alone, the company spent $9 million expanding the mountain's terrain and investing in local real estate. By December of 1999, it will have completed construction of the Grand Summit, Ogden's largest luxury hotel and condominium project to date.

According to the local Chamber of Commerce, Ogden draws more than 350,000 visitors to the area each winter. The resort boasts 1.05 million skier visits per season, ranking it as the fourth most popular ski area in Utah. Its world renowned reputation for powder skiing draws winter visitors who care more about the quality of ski conditions then they do about shopping, nightlife, or any other activities that are unrelated to skiing.

## Customer Analysis

Mr. Metterley has spent years working in the outdoor recreation industry. Throughout his experience, the increasing market demand for a high level of service has become apparent. Mountjoy will address this demand with the best service offering in the industry at a price that is competitive with other snowcat ski companies and is significantly less expensive than helicopter skiing.

Mountjoy's target market is the intermediate to expert Ogden skier or snowboarder who seeks adventure and deep powder conditions. The size of this market is considerable, as demonstrated in the figure below using data obtained from the 1997 National Skier/Boarder Opinion Survey:

| Powder Mountain Ski Area 1997/1998 skier visits (1.05 million) | × | Skiers who seek adventure or new challenges (79%) | × | Skiers rated intermediate or above in ability (73%) | = | Size of local market **605,535** |
|---|---|---|---|---|---|---|

With only 1,450 skier visits per season, OPC currently has a local market penetration of only two tenths of one percent. Mountjoy's management projects a market penetration of one half of one percent by its fifth year of operations.

As skiers and snowboarders become less tolerant of the long lift lines and poor snow conditions available at ski resorts, they are seeking alternative service providers who can guarantee excellent snow conditions and truly memorable experiences. Mountjoy is uniquely positioned to deliver on this promise.

## Competitor Analysis

Mountjoy will face competition from helicopter ski companies, other snowcat ski operators and traditional ski resorts. For clients to receive the same level of service from a helicopter ski company, they would spend three to four times as much money and would assume the higher risk associated with transportation via helicopter. Existing snowcat operators charge comparable prices to Mountjoy, but offer significantly less terrain, inferior snow conditions and lower levels of service. Ski resorts deliver a completely different experience and simply cannot provide comparable powder skiing conditions. Detailed descriptions of Mountjoy's primary competitors may be found in the Appendix.

With a Special Use Permit from the Forest Service, Mountjoy will secure an effective monopoly within the Ogden area. Because Forest Service policy allows only one such permit per forest zone, it will be impossible for direct competitors to enter the local market. As the only snowcat ski company within ninety miles of Ogden, Mountjoy will enjoy an enviable position.

Barriers to Entry

MARKETING<br>STRATEGY<br>Positioning

Mountjoy's primary points of differentiation will be its superior service and snow conditions. With the deepest and lightest snow in Utah, Mountjoy's future permit area is recognized throughout the industry as the best powder skiing terrain in America. The benefits of an on-mountain cabin, custom-fitted powder skis and well-trained guides will further enhance the experience.

The figure below illustrates Mountjoy's positioning with respect to its primary competitors.

| Company | Service | Price Per Day | Location | Size of Permit Area |
|---|---|---|---|---|
| Mountjoy | Snowcat | $245 | Ogden | 10,000 acres |
| Johnson Ridge Snowcat Tours | Snowcat | $125 | Ski Cooper | 1,200 acres |
| Peterson Snowtours | Snowcat | $255 | Ptarmigan Pass | 1,200 acres |
| Provo Mountain Powder Tours | Snowcat | $245 | Provo Mountain | 800 acres |
| Heli-Ski | Helicopter | $630 | Telluride | N/A |

No other snowcat or helicopter ski companies in Utah currently offer services that are as comprehensive as those proposed by Mountjoy. The company will always enjoy the advantage of its superior terrain, and will continually strive to improve its excellent service.

Pricing

Mountjoy's basic daily rate will be $245 per person. A detailed pricing structure is given in the table below.

| Single-day tickets | | Multi-day tickets | |
|---|---|---|---|
| Full day | $245 | 5 full days | $1,000 |
| Full day with instruction | $255 | 10 full days | $1,700 |
| Half day | $180 | 5 half days | $750 |
| Half day with instruction | $200 | 10 half days | $1,200 |

Partnerships

Mountjoy will cultivate the established relationship between OPC and the Powder Mountain Ski Area. A strong relationship with Mountjoy will complement the on-mountain offerings of the Powder Mountain Ski Area, whose customers often wish for more diverse activities and better powder skiing conditions than are available at the resort. In fact, Bobby Krug, Ogden's director of skiing, a former Olympic Gold Medalist and World Champion, has been referring clients to OPC for a number of years. Mountjoy expects to continue this friendly relationship and will recommend that its clients visit the resort prior to their snowcat skiing experience in order to acclimate to the high altitude environment.

Mountjoy will provide its clients with specialized powder skis made by Volant. This company manufactures some of the world's most respected powder skis and has entered into an exclusive supplier relationship with Mountjoy. In return for very competitive pricing, the company's clients and guides will ski exclusively on Volant skis, and Mountjoy will feature Volant's name and trademark on all of its marketing materials. The company has entered into similar agreements with B-Line snowboards, Marker, and Smith.

Mountjoy is also currently negotiating a partnership with the German ski association (Deutscher Ski Verband [DSV]). This relationship will allow Mountjoy to capitalize on the significant marketing capabilities of this powerful and well-organized association. The president of the DSV has expressed great interest in a formal relationship that would bring large groups of German skiing enthusiasts to Mountjoy on an annual basis.

## MARKETING COMMUNICATIONS

Mountjoy has budgeted $87,000 for marketing expenses during its first year of operation and an increasing amount thereafter. The company's initial marketing resources will be devoted to capturing the established local and national markets. Beginning in the second year of operation, the company intends to broaden its efforts to include international markets as well.

## Trade Name

The company's option agreement with OPC includes the right for Mountjoy to use the Ogden Powder Cats trade name and client list. During its sixteen-year history, OPC has developed a loyal client base and a mailing list of more than two thousand names.

## Direct Mail

Mountjoy will develop a high quality color brochure designed to convey the personalization and exceptional quality of the company's services. All of Mountjoy's marketing materials, including its brochures, will be designed with a common look and will feature the OPC Internet address and redesigned logo. The cost of brochure design, layout, printing, and postage is estimated to be $28,500 during the first year. Brochures will be sent to prospective and repeat clients accompanied by personalized letters from the CEO. These names will be identified from OPC's client list and from mailing lists purchased from the Powder Mountain Ski Area at an approximate cost of ten cents per name.

## Internet Web Site

In order to serve those members of the target market who actively search for information using the Internet, Mountjoy will redesign OPC's existing we site (www.ogdenpowdercats.com). The new site will include more detailed information than is given in the company's brochure and will allow potential clients to contact Mountjoy via e-mail. The cost of website development is not expected to exceed $5,000.

## Public Relations

In addition to the company's direct-mail campaign, Mountjoy will initiate a press relations campaign that targets local, national, and international newspaper and magazine writers. The company will send brochures and letters to publications such as the *Ogden Post*, the *Rocky Mountain News*, the *Wall Street Journal*, the *New York Times*, *Men's Journal*, *Outside*, *Ski*, *Skiing*, and *Powder*. One to two weeks after brochures and letters have been sent, Mountjoy will contact the appropriate representatives, offering complimentary ski days for those correspondents who would like to experience Mountjoy's service.

## Advertising

Mountjoy will advertise on the local Ogden television channel at a cost of approximately $5,600 per season, place company brochures in local hotels, advertise in local newspapers, and pay for listings in *Ogden Visitor's Guide* and *Ogden Magazine*.

## Personal Selling

The CEO will conduct regional sales presentations for prospective corporate clients during the off-season. These exclusive presentations will be held by invitation only and will give the founders an opportunity to demonstrate Mountjoy's high degree of service. Beginning in the second year of operation, presentations will also be held abroad in order to capitalize on the CEO's extensive network of international contacts.

The company will produce videotapes that include an introduction to Mountjoy's services and footage of spectacular powder skiing in the company's permit area. These tapes will run continuously in Mountjoy's office for the benefit of walk-in clients and will be available to prospective clients upon request.

**Videotape Production**

Mountjoy will cultivate relationships with Ogden lodging concierges and accredited travel agents, rewarding them for client referrals with free ski days and commissions where appropriate.

**Commissions**

Mountjoy will schedule complimentary moonlight descents once per month for influential members of the Ogden community and for those who have referred a substantial number of clients to Mountjoy. Occurring on Friday evenings and synchronized as closely as possible with the rising of the full moon, these events will take place after regular business hours. Guests will be transported via snowcat to the top of a gently sloping hill. The CEO will lead the group with a blazing torch down to the company's cabin where a roaring fire, hot drinks and a catered dinner will be available. For those who wish to make repeated descents, a snowcat will be on call to transport them back to the top of the hill. The entire event will be designed to showcase Mountjoy's high standards of service and to generate goodwill and future sales.

**Moonlight Descents**

Within two weeks of each client's visit, Mountjoy will send a personalized letter of thanks that includes a return postcard requesting feedback and suggestions for improving the service. During late summer of every year, the company will send brochures to its former clients informing them of changes and improvements for the upcoming season and inviting them to return.

**Post-Service Follow-Up**

Mountjoy will actively support local clubs and charitable organizations by donating free ski days and hosting special events.

**Sponsorship**

## DEVELOPMENT

Mountjoy's development activities can be divided into two phases as outlined below. The development period began January 1, 1999 and ends December 14, 1999. Phase I activities were funded with seed money contributed by the founder. Phase II began with the exercise of Mountjoy's option to purchase OPC's assets. It has been funded by the proceeds of the companies first round of financing.

**Timeline**

| 1999 | | | |
|---|---|---|---|
| **Jan 1** | | **Jun 1** | **Dec 15** |
| | *Phase I* | *Phase II* | |
| Organization | | Office Space | |
| Seed Funding | | Insurance | |
| Legal Counsel | | Marketing and Sales | |
| Option Agreement | | Vehicles | |
| Due Diligence | | Snowcats | |
| Exercise of Option | | Equipment | |
| Closing | | | |

**Phase I (January 1, 1999 to May 31, 1999)**

### Organization

Mountjoy organized as a Utah Limited Liability Company (LLC) on January 11, 1999.

### Seed Funding

Mountjoy's Phase I expenses are funded by a $100,000 capital contribution from its founder, Mr. Metterley. These funds have covered all expenses incurred during Phase I of the development period.

### Legal Counsel

Mountjoy has retained Jackson, Smith, and Barney as its legal counsel. Based in Provo, Utah, the firm specializes in corporate law.

### Option Agreement

Mountjoy signed an option agreement with OPC on January 26, 1999 that entitles the company to purchase OPC's assets, trade name, and client list at the end of the 1998/1999 winter season. The option was exercised by Mountjoy on May 31, 1999.

### Due Diligence

In January of 1999, Mr. Metterley began an ongoing due diligence process facilitated by the current proprietors of OPC. Mr. Metterley has been briefed with regard to management and sales tasks, and has joined current OPC employees in guiding ski trips. This process will continue throughout the development period.

### Closing

Mountjoy will close on its purchase of OPC's assets on Friday, August 20, 1999.

**Phase II (June 1, 1999 to December 14, 1999)**

### Office Space

Mountjoy will lease permanent office space in Ogden, Utah. Office renovations are expected to last as long as two months and cost $30,000. The approximately 1,000-square-foot facility will be used for administrative duties and storage of ski equipment.

### Insurance

Mountjoy will acquire a comprehensive array of insurance policies prior to commencing operations, including general business insurance, key man insurance, snowcat and vehicle insurance, health insurance, workers' compensation insurance, general liability insurance and property damage insurance for the company's on-mountain cabin.

### Marketing and Sales

Mountjoy will begin its marketing and sales campaign during the summer of 1999. Details may be found in the Marketing section.

### Vehicles

The company will sell OPC's existing vans and will lease two vans on a seasonal basis.

### Snowcats

Because OPC's aging snowcats are incapable of climbing steep slopes and are unsuitable for Mountjoy's improved service level, the company will replace them with two newer leased models built by Bombardier. An experienced fabricator will be retained to build custom twelve-passenger cabins at an estimated cost of $30,000 each.

### Equipment

The company will purchase all outdoor equipment necessary to conduct its business prior to commencing operations. This includes technical, communications, and safety equipment as well as specialized Volant powder skis.

**OPERATIONS**

**Personnel**

### Management

Emmett Metterley serves as Mountjoy's Chief Executive Officer. He will begin drawing a $60,000 annual salary beginning June 1, 1999.

### Guides

During its first two operating seasons, Mountjoy will employ six guides on a full-time basis. In addition, the company will maintain relationships with qualified part-time guides who are able to work when needed. All guides will be trained in ski and snowboard instruction, mountain safety procedures, snow stability evaluation techniques, and customer service skills. Mountjoy's lead guides will possess at least five years of industry experience, Emergency Medical Technician certification, and training in snowcat operation and maintenance. Guides will be compensated at a rate of $90 to $110 per day.

### Administrative Assistant

Mountjoy will employ a seasonal administrative assistant beginning November 1, 1999 at the equivalent of an annual salary of $25,000. The assistant's duties will include answering the company phone, accepting reservations from clients and performing general administrative tasks.

**Service Delivery**

### Transportation

Mountjoy will transport its clients from their lodging or the company's office directly to its staging area in the Wasatch National Forest. Morning half-day trips will depart at 7:15 A.M., full-day trips at 7:45 A.M., and afternoon half-day trips at noon.

### Equipment

In order to ensure their comfort, Mountjoy will request that clients use their own ski boots and poles. Prior to skiing, clients will visit Mountjoy's office in order to allow for custom fitting of their boots to the company's powder skis. In addition to powder skis, Mountjoy will provide each client with a small backpack, digital avalanche transceiver, shovel, avalanche probe, and personal water bottle. The company will also keep a limited number of telemark skis on hand for those clients who are skilled in their use. Snowboarding clients will be asked to provide their own boots and boards.

### Cabin

After a thorough remodeling during the summer of 1999, Mountjoy's on-mountain cabin will be ideally suited to provide a welcome respite after a morning of powder skiing. Its features will include a dining table, cast iron stove, comfortable reading chairs, and a modern propane-fired incinerating toilet.

**Safety Procedures**

All guides will use two-way radios to remain in constant communication with each other and the company's office. Guides will carry comprehensive first-aid kits in their backpacks and will keep large items such as rescue sleds and oxygen canisters in the snowcats. In an emergency, injured parties may be transported down the mountain in a snowcat or flown directly to the hospital via helicopter.

The company's guides will conduct regular snowpack and snow stability evaluations supervised by Mr. Metterley, a certified Level III avalanche forecaster. Using meteorological data, snow pits, and advanced stability measures, they will carefully monitor the snow conditions on all of the area's major slopes. The thoroughness of these procedures will allow Mountjoy to expand its operations into more challenging terrain than is currently utilized by OPC.

**Growth**

Mountjoy's fifteen-square-mile permit area will encompass approximately 10,000 acres and will be five to ten times larger than the permit areas of competing Utah snowcat ski operators. The company's exceptional service quality and aggressive marketing strategy are projected to generate enough demand by the third year of operation to require the addition of a third snowcat.

## FINANCIAL SUMMARY

### Income Statement

The following chart summarizes the projected financial performance of Mountjoy over the five-year period ending in April of 2004.

| For the year ending April 30 (Amounts in Dollars) | 2000 | 2001 | 2002 | 2003 | 2004 |
|---|---|---|---|---|---|
| Revenue | 446,075 | 541,666 | 710,937 | 895,780 | 1,081,655 |
| Cost of Services | 162,590 | 246,997 | 315,453 | 365,339 | 394,745 |
| **Gross Margin** | **283,485** | **294,669** | **395,483** | **530,442** | **686,910** |
| | | | | | |
| % of Revenue | 64% | 54% | 56% | 59% | 64% |
| Operating Expenses | 208,617 | 189,986 | 211,381 | 234,211 | 256,303 |
| % of Revenue | 47% | 35% | 30% | 26% | 24% |
| Interest Expense | 61,669 | 59,367 | 55,537 | 44,131 | 33,291 |
| Net Income/(Loss) | 13,199 | 45,316 | 128,566 | 252,100 | 397,315 |
| % of Revenue | 3% | 8% | 18% | 28% | 37% |

The Balance Sheet provides an overview of the company's use of the proceeds of its first round of financing.

**Balance Sheet**

| April 30 (Amounts in Dollars) | 2000 | 2001 | 2002 | 2003 | 2004 |
|---|---|---|---|---|---|
| **Current Assets** | | | | | |
| Cash | 192,655 | 185,702 | 163,176 | 222,401 | 371,924 |
| Accounts receivable | 16,828 | 20,280 | 26,618 | 33,539 | 40,498 |
| **Total Current Assets** | **209,482** | **205,983** | **189,794** | **255,940** | **412,422** |
| | | | | | |
| **Intangible Assets** | | | | | |
| Goodwill/Non-compete | 195,000 | 195,000 | 195,000 | 195,000 | 195,000 |
| Organization costs | 13,000 | 13,000 | 13,000 | 13,000 | 13,000 |
| Accumulated amortization | 13,961 | 29,561 | 45,161 | 60,761 | 75,494 |
| **Net Intangible Assets** | **194,039** | **178,439** | **162,839** | **147,239** | **132,506** |
| | | | | | |
| Fixed assets | 395,457 | 428,165 | 582,550 | 647,558 | 710,066 |
| Accumulated depreciation | 29,137 | 101,722 | 190,816 | 274,971 | 331,553 |
| **Net fixed assets** | **366,320** | **326,443** | **391,734** | **372,587** | **378,513** |
| | | | | | |
| **Total Assets** | **769,841** | **710,865** | **744,367** | **775,766** | **923,441** |
| | | | | | |
| **Liabilities** | | | | | |
| Total Current Liabilities | 18,642 | 20,921 | 23,484 | 26,231 | 28,750 |
| Bank Loan Liability | 551,484 | 493,669 | 430,272 | 360,757 | 284,532 |
| Capital Lease Liability | 102,422 | 71,793 | 88,988 | 35,897 | 18,889 |
| **Total Liabilities** | **672,548** | **586,383** | **542,745** | **422,884** | **332,170** |
| | | | | | |
| **Members' Capital** | | | | | |
| Beginning of period capital balance | 106,228 | 151,066 | 258,192 | 446,664 | 736,616 |
| Contributions | - | - | - | - | - |
| Net income/ (loss) | -8,935 | -8,458 | -5,144 | 7,057 | 13,581 |
| Distributions | - | -18,126 | -51,426 | -100,840 | -158,926 |
| **Total Members' Capital** | **97,293** | **124,482** | **201,622** | **352,882** | **591,271** |
| | | | | | |
| **Total Liabilities and Members' Capital** | **769,841** | **710,865** | **744,367** | **775,766** | **923,441** |

## Statement of Cash Flows

| For the year ending April 30 (Amounts in Dollars) | 2000 | 2001 | 2002 | 2003 | 2004 |
|---|---|---|---|---|---|
| **Cash flows from operating activities:** | | | | | |
| Net income/(Loss) | 13,199 | 45,316 | 128,566 | 252,100 | 397,315 |
| | | | | | |
| **Adj. to reconcile net income/(loss) to cash** | | | | | |
| Depreciation and amortization | 87,682 | 88,185 | 104,694 | 99,755 | 71,315 |
| | | | | | |
| **Changes in operating assets and liabilities:** | | | | | |
| (Increase)/decrease in | | | | | |
| accounts receivable | (16,828) | (3,453) | (6,338) | (6,921) | (6,959) |
| Increase/(decrease) in | | | | | |
| accounts payable | 16,356 | 2,279 | 2,563 | 2,747 | 2,519 |
| **Net cash provided/(used) by operating activities** | **100,409** | **132,326** | **229,486** | **347,681** | **464,191** |
| | | | | | |
| **Cash flows from investing activities:** | | | | | |
| Purchase of fixed assets | (310,457) | (32,708) | (89,385) | (65,008) | (62,508) |
| Other investing activities | (175,000) | - | - | - | - |
| **Net cash provided/(used) by investing activities** | **(485,457)** | **(32,708)** | **(89,385)** | **(65,008)** | **(62,508)** |
| | | | | | |
| **Cash flows from financing activities:** | | | | | |
| Principal payments | (76,094) | (88,444) | (111,201) | (122,607) | (93,233) |
| Contributions | 640,000 | - | - | - | - |
| Distributions | - | (18,126) | (51,426) | (100,840) | (158,926) |
| **Net cash provided/(used) by financing activities** | **563,906** | **(106,570)** | **(162,627)** | **(223,447)** | **(252,159)** |
| | | | | | |
| Net increase/(decrease) in cash | 178,858 | (6,952) | (22,527) | 59,226 | 149,523 |
| Cash - beginning of period | 13,796 | 192,655 | 185,702 | 163,176 | 222,401 |
| | | | | | |
| **Cash-end of period** | **192,655** | **185,702** | **163,176** | **222,401** | **371,924** |

## Use of Proceeds

The company will use the proceeds of the first round of financing (i.e., $700,000) in the following manner:

1. $305,000 (approximately one half of the proceeds) will be used by the company to purchase the assets of Ogden Powder Cats, a Utah corporation ("OPC"), pursuant to the terms and conditions of an option agreement dated January 26, 1999. As more fully described in "The Business Plan," this transaction will provide the company with its initial working assets and will allow it to assume OPC's former Special Use Permit in the Wasatch National Forest.

2. $200,000 will be used by the company for other capital expenditures, including, but not limited to:

   a. The replacement of snowcats.
   b. Powder skis and safety equipment for clients.
   c. Lease of an additional van.
   d. The renovation of the on-mountain cabin.

3. $145,000 (approximately one-quarter of the proceeds) will be used by the company for working capital. These funds will be roughly allocated as follows:

   a. Marketing expenditures (budgeted at approximately $90,000).
   b. Office lease (approximately $20,000).
   c. Reserve ($35,000).

### John Wise

Mr. Wise is Chairman of the Board of Managers of SPAS and a founding Member of the Stone Pine Companies. Mr. Wise is also Chairman and Chief Executive Officer of FCM Fiduciary Capital Management Company, a registered investment advisor, and Consolidated Capital of North America, Inc., a company involved in steel fabrication and steel service center operations. Mr. Wise was Chief Executive Officer of Laidlaw Holdings, Inc., an investment services company, from January 1995 until November 1996. For more than 15 years prior to July 1990, Mr. Wise was engaged in investment banking activities with Shearson Lehman Hutton Inc. and its predecessor, E. F. Hutton & Company, Inc. Mr. Wise served in various capacities with Shearson and E. F. Hutton, including Executive Vice President and Director, Managing Director, Head of Direct Investment Origination and Manager of Corporate Finance. Mr. Wise also serves as Chairman of the Board of Directors of Silver Screen Management, Inc. and International Film Investors, Inc., which manage film portfolios. Mr. Wise is also a director of MacDonald Pharmaceuticals, Inc., a publicly held company, LMC Corporation, a privately held manufacturer of low ground pressure vehicles, Hamilton Lane Advisors, HSLP Investment Management LLC, and Rockland Lane Private Equity Fund PLC, an Irish Stock Exchange listed investment partnership. Mr. Wise graduated from the University of Michigan in 1965 with a B.S. degree in Business and Economics and from Harvard Business School in 1968 with an M.B.A. in Finance.

### Christopher Walker

Mr. Walker is a Partner of Utah Venture Management (UVM), a venture capital firm located in Logan, Utah. He is Vice President of UVM Equity Fund V, a new $6 million venture fund investing in start-up companies throughout Utah and New Mexico. Mr. Walker was formerly Executive Vice President of the Logan Technology Incubator, a not-for-profit business whose mission is to council and fund promising technology-based start-up companies during the early stages of their development. Mr. Walker holds an M.B.A. from the University of Utah.

### Maxwell Stokes

Mr. Stokes holds an M.B.A. in Entrepreneurship from the University of Utah. He is the Marketing Director for TeleConnect, Inc., a high-tech telecommunications start-up company in Ogden, Utah. His responsibilities include establishing a market penetration strategy, evaluating new markets, analyzing the competitive nature of the industry, and spearheading a marketing communications campaign. Prior to his work at TeleConnect, he was a consultant with RRC Associates, a market research firm specializing in the ski industry. Clients of Mr. Stokes at RRC included Peterson Resorts, Intrawest Resorts, and Booth Creek Holdings.

### Casey and Rita Madison

Mr. and Mrs. Madison founded Ogden Powder Cats in 1983. During the past sixteen years, their business has grown substantially. They have signed a noncompete agreement that prohibits them from competing with Mountjoy within the state of Utah and have also pledged their support as consultants to Mountjoy while the company establishes its presence in the marketplace. Mr. and Mrs. Madison are currently training Mr. Metterley in the operation of Ogden Powder Cats.

**James Calloway**

Mr. Calloway is President and Founder of the Adventure Travel Society. His company offers marketing consulting services to adventure travel and outdoor recreation firms worldwide. He has 25 years of experience in the outdoor recreation and tourism industry. Mr. Calloway has acted as a liaison for the outdoor industry, government agencies, and the private sector in the United States and around the world. He has also served as a recreation planning consultant to corporations and governments. Mr. Calloway founded the annual Congress on Adventure Travel and Ecotourism, the premier international industry event. He served as Executive Director of the Western River Guides Association for eight years, co-founded American Rivers, and was Chairman of American Wildlands.

**Jack Bolten**

Mr. Bolten is an Associate Professor in the University of Utah's College of Business. He has held a variety of senior management positions during his career in business, including Director of the acquisition and new ventures department for Owens-Illinois, President of a manufacturing subsidiary of General Electric, and Founder of National Computer Graphics, a software development company in the graphic arts and CAD/CAM markets. Mr. Bolten continues to provide management advice to Utah start-up companies. He holds an M.B.A. from the Wharton School of the University of Pennsylvania.

**Jeffrey Wismer**

Mr. Wismer is a certified public accountant and former associate of Deloitte & Touche LLP, a national public accounting firm. While at Deloitte & Touche, Mr. Wismer planned and supervised audit engagements for a wide variety of public and private companies. His financial accounting experience is complemented by several years of tax return preparation during which he was responsible for completing individual and partnership tax returns. Since leaving Deloitte & Touche, Mr. Wismer has served as a strategic marketing consultant for several nonprofit organizations and entrepreneurial start-ups.

## Competitor Profiles

**Provo Mountain Powder Tours**

Like Mountjoy, the snowcat operation on Provo mountain utilizes a 12-passenger snowcat with two guides. Passengers are treated to an early morning ride on the gondola to the top of Provo mountain to reach the company's staging area. Because their permit area only encompasses 1,400 acres of mostly southward facing terrain, true powder conditions are short lived. Rates for the 1998/99 season are $245 per person per day and include the use of Volant powder skis.

The quality of service is as close as any competitors come to Mountjoy but the overall experience still does not compare. With less than fifteen percent of Mountjoy terrain, only half as much snow of greatly inferior quality, and without the luxury of an on-mountain cabin, Provo Mountain Powder Tours finds it difficult to live up to the high standards expected by its well-heeled clients.

**Johnson Ridge Snowcat Tours**

Johnson Ridge operates a single, 12-person snowcat near Ski Cooper, approximately 90 miles from Ogden. The service is priced at $125 per seat.

Johnson Ridge is positioned at the lowest price point for snowcat skiing in the area. Its service appeals to those who require transportation into the backcountry but do not want to pay for additional services. Johnson Ridge offers only 1,800 acres of inferior terrain and often marginal snow conditions, yet typically sells out every season. The popularity of this service demonstrates that a substantial market exists for snowcat skiing in Utah and much of it is currently unserviced.

### Heli-Ski

Heli-Ski is the only helicopter supported ski service in Utah. Based in Grand Junction, approximately 300 miles from Ogden, it flies its customers to a permit area in the Sawatch mountains. Passenger space is sold at $625 per seat, and up to five groups of three customers each may be shuttled by a single helicopter. Heli-Ski also charters its helicopter and guide to single customer groups for $6,500 per day.

Heli-Ski provides a service similar to a flying bus, but is significantly more expensive than all other providers in Utah. While helicopters are undoubtedly quicker than snowcats, helicopter skiing involves lengthy waits at the bottom of a run, while additional groups who share the same helicopter are being shuttled to the top of their run. Due to the logistical problems associated with using one four-passenger helicopter among twenty skiers, Heli-Ski guarantees no more than 10,000 vertical feet per day. In addition, the operation of a helicopter may prove to be a serious liability, as evidenced by the pending lawsuit against Heli-Ski due to its recent crash with clients on board.

### Peterson Snowtours

Peterson Resorts, Inc. owns Peterson Snowtours, a snowcat skiing operation that allows customers to backcountry ski on Peterson Pass, approximately 90 miles from Ogden. The service includes round-trip transportation by van, lunch, the use of powder skis, and one guide for up to ten customers. Rates for the 1998/99 season are $240 per person per day.

Mountjoy offers a superior service at a similar price point. Not only do Mountjoy's clients benefit from the company's addition of a second guide for every group, but Mountjoy's terrain is far superior to that offered by Peterson Snowtours. Peterson Pass is well known as a snowmobile Mecca and is subjected to considerable traffic noise from the interstate. Moreover, the snow in this terrain is often compacted by wind and prone to very high avalanche danger.

# Structural Engineering Consulting Firm

BUSINESS PLAN                    STRUCTUREALL LTD.

*306 Pine Trail Way*
*Yellowknife, Northwest Territories, Canada*

*StructureAll's mission is to provide clients across Canada's Northwest Territories with structural engineering services for all types of buildings, from concept planning through completion, with a highly skilled professional team working together, using common sense and practical experience. This business plan was compiled using Business Plan Pro, © 1999, Palo Alto Software, www.paloaltosoftware.com, 800-229-7526.*

- EXECUTIVE SUMMARY

- COMPANY SUMMARY

- SERVICES

- MARKET ANALYSIS SUMMARY

- STRATEGY & IMPLEMENTATION SUMMARY

- MANAGEMENT SUMMARY

- FINANCIAL PLAN

# STRUCTURAL ENGINEERING CONSULTING FIRM
## BUSINESS PLAN

**EXECUTIVE SUMMARY**

StructureAll Ltd. will be formed as a consulting firm specializing in structural engineering services. A home office in Yellowknife, Northwest Territories, will be established the first year of operations to reduce start-up costs. The founder of the firm is a professional engineer with eighteen years of progressive and responsible experience.

Initial start-up costs amount to $20,000. Of this total, $13,000 is required for start-up expenses while the balance is to to be placed in the company accounts as working capital. We have secured an investor (Russ Renneberg, P. Eng.) who will contribute $10,000 toward start-up costs. This investment has been indicated in Long-Term Loans in the Projected Cash Flow chart. The loan will be repaid over a three-year period.

Projected sales and profits for the first three years of operation are summarized below:

| Year | Sales ($) | Profits ($) | Sales/Profit (%) |
|------|-----------|-------------|------------------|
| 1 | $118,000 | $9,150 | 7.80% |
| 2 | $130,000 | $12,650 | 9.80% |
| 3 | $138,000 | $15,100 | 11.00% |

The firm will specialize in providing three-dimensional modeling and visualization to our clients. State-of-the-art analysis and design tools will be an integral part of the business plan. Implementation of a quality control and assurance program will provide a focus for production work.

**Objectives**

1. Revenues of $118,000 the first year, approaching $138,000 at the end of three years.
2. Achieve 20 percent of market value at the end of the third year of operation.
3. Increase gross margin to 80 percent by the third year of operations.

**Mission**

Our mission is to provide clients across Canada's North with structural engineering services for all types of buildings, from concept planning through completion, with a highly skilled professional team working together, using common sense and practical experience.

**Keys to Success**

1. Provide professional quality services on time and on budget.
2. Develop a follow-up strategy to gauge performance with all clients.
3. Implement and maintain a quality control and assurance policy.

**COMPANY SUMMARY**

StructureAll Ltd. is a new company which provides professional engineering design services for clients which manage, maintain, and plan for residential, commercial, and industrial type buildings. Our focus will be the public sector market in remote communities across Canada's North.

**Company Ownership**

StructureAll Ltd. will be created as a limited liability company. The company will be privately owned by Philip D. Nolan. Leslie C. Goit will also be listed as a Director.

**Start-up Summary**

Our start-up expenses amount to $13,000, which allows for initial legal expenses, licenses, permits, stationery, specialty software, office equipment, and furniture. In addition to these start-up costs, an initial balance of $7,000 will be placed in the company accounts. The software purchases include an allowance of $5,000 for AutoCADD® 2000, $1,800 for National Master Specifications, and $200 for Quickbooks® (accounting package).

Philip Nolan will contribute $10,000 toward the overall start-up costs. The balance of the start-up costs ($10,000) will be provided through a colleague and friend who operates W&R Foundations Ltd. This investment has been indicated as a three-year loan in the Projected Cash Flow table.

**Start-up Plan**
**Start-up Expenses**

| | |
|---|---|
| Professional Liability Insurance | $1,200 |
| Website Development | $600 |
| Legal Services | $500 |
| Business Licenses | $1,000 |
| Permit Holder (NAPEGG) | $500 |
| Software Purchases | $7,000 |
| Stationery | $600 |
| Office Furniture | $600 |
| Office Equipment | $500 |
| Other | $500 |
| **Total Start-up Expenses** | **$13,000** |

**Start-up Assets Needed**

| | |
|---|---|
| Cash Requirements | $7,000 |
| Start-up inventory | $0 |
| Other Short-term Assets | $0 |
| **Total Short-term Assets** | **$7,000** |

| | |
|---|---|
| Long-term Assets | $0 |
| **Total Assets** | **$7,000** |

| | |
|---|---|
| Total Start-up Requirements: | $20,000 |
| Left to finance: | $0 |

**Start-up Funding Plan**
**Investment**

| | |
|---|---|
| Philip D. Nolan | $10,000 |
| Russ Renneberg, P. Eng. | $10,000 |
| Other | $0 |
| **Total investment** | **$20,000** |

**Short-term Liabilities**

| | |
|---|---|
| Unpaid Expenses | $0 |
| Short-term Loans | $0 |
| Interest-free Short-term Loans | $0 |
| Subtotal Short-term Liabilities | $0 |
| Long-term Liabilities | $0 |
| **Total Liabilities** | **$0** |

| | |
|---|---|
| **Loss at Start-up** | **($13,000)** |
| **Total Capital** | **$7,000** |
| **Total Capital and Liabilities** | **$7,000** |
| **Checkline** | **$0** |

**Company Locations and Facilities**

We will establish a home office in Yellowknife, Northwest Territories, in order to reduce start-up costs. The office space is estimated to be 150 square feet. We will be installing a dedicated fax line as well as a high-speed Internet connection. An interactive website will also be developed which will serve as a marketing tool. The domain name of "structureall.com" has already been reserved.

**SERVICES**

StructureAll Ltd. offers complete structural engineering services. We will focus on buildings with the following "Use and Occupancies":

- residential
- commercial
- industrial

The company is "project" oriented where each project involves:

- renovations
- rehabilitation
- additions
- new construction

We offer innovative and economical design services, maintaining state-of-the-art design technology. We meet client needs on projects of all sizes and smaller, special design projects.

**Service Description**

**Project Consulting:** Proposed and billed on a per-project and per-milestone basis, project consulting offers a client company a way to harness our specific qualities and use our expertise to develop and/or implement plans, from conceptual planning to turnover. Proposal costs will be associated with each project.

**Forensic Investigations:** Proposed and billed on a per-project and per-milestone basis, our investigations will serve the public and private sector markets. We will focus on troubleshooting buildings where damage and or failure has occurred. Our reports will outline the description of the problem, the nature of the mechanism which has caused damage or failure, and a list of options for remedial action including estimated budget costs for implementation.

**Project Management:** Our project management services include defining client needs, preparing bid documents, tendering, bid analysis, construction review, payment certification, contract administration, and warranty inspections. Projects include new facilities, renovations, repairs, and remodeling.

**Dispute Resolution:** We draw upon our broad range of construction and contract administration experience to provide dispute resolution services, including arbitration, mediation and expert reports for litigation. This work is supported by forensic engineering services to identify the cause of failures.

**Restoration Engineering:** We provide condition survey, design, and construction review services for the repair of building structures.

**Home Inspections:** We will provide prospective homeowners with an assessment of the various systems in a residential home, including foundations, framing, building envelope and efficiency, mechanical systems, electrical systems, and general safety issues. We provide a photographic record along with a thorough written report.

StructureAll Ltd. offers their clients superior service accompanied with state-of-the-art analysis and design capabilities. We will offer three-dimensional visualization services to reduce the possibility of spatial conflicts with architectural elements and other engineering disciplines. In comparison, our competitors rely mostly on two-dimensional models.

We will implement a quality assurance and control program for all projects undertaken. This document will serve to focus on the standards which will be achieved and a means of measuring performance.

A systematic manner of sorting and retrieving a library of structural elements and assemblies will be implemented. Slide libraries will be available from a tool bar within AutoCADD for quick access. We will adopt the layering standards of the American Institute of Architects (AIA). In comparison, our competitors do not have an integrated database.

StructureAll Ltd. will adopt the filing systems developed by the AIA. All project information will be tracked using an integrated database management system.

A brochure system, which covers a broad spectrum of the target market segment, will be developed during the initial year of operations. This system will be modular in nature and include many "boiler plate" sections which may be edited to suit specific needs. Brochure inserts will be maintained as individual sheets to facilitate their assembly in any custom situation.

Our website will be developed the first year of operations and will include a description of our services, the areas which we plan to serve, contact information, a list of representative projects, and a brief biography of Philip D. Nolan. An Internet domain name has already been reserved for this purpose http://www.structureall.com.

A series of templates will be developed for project proposals. The format for all proposals will include:

- Cover letter
- Scope of services for each project
- Fee (if requested)
- Firm's qualifications to provide services (overview)
- Project Team (describes each person's tasks and qualifications)
- Philosophy of design approach
- Relevant experience
- Schedule to provide services

We will turn to qualified professionals to supplement computer-aided design and drafting (CADD) services, specialty connection designs, and analysis support services which are areas that we can afford to contract out without risking the core values provided to the clients.

We have fostered several alliances with suppliers of structural elements, including glued laminated lumber, pre-engineered dimension lumber trusses, engineered lumber, and steel to facilitate this strategy.

In the second year of operations, we intend to secure a storefront presence in Yellowknife. At this stage, we will seek qualified northern engineering students to provide them with work experience in a structural engineering office environment.

**Technology**

StructureAll Ltd. will maintain complete and comprehensive Windows®-based analysis tools for structural design. An integrated computer-aided design and drafting tool permits several evaluations to be made on a structure at minimal cost.

StructureAll Ltd. will maintain an Internet website complete with file transfer protocol (ftp) capabilities.

**Future Services**

**Quality Control and Assurance:** Serving the needs of the welding industry, we will ensure that certified firms and their employee welders are qualified to perform specific welds in accordance with the requirements of the Canadian Welding Bureau (CWB) as a certified welding inspector. We are currently in the process of completing a comprehensive home study program offered through the CWB for this purpose.

There are four firms presently in the Northwest Territories which require these services in order to maintain their certification with the CWB. On-site inspections are required four times per year.

**Fabrication and Detailing Drawings:** Serving the special needs of steel and concrete construction, StructureAll Ltd. will be working toward offering these services to contractors in the future.

**Accident Reconstruction Services:** We will act as a storefront for a well respected engineering firm in Edmonton (Renneberg and Wallace Ltd.) who have the knowledge and expertise to conduct this type of work. We will learn how to gather basic information from an accident site and act as a local representative to facilitate and expedite these services.

**Toll-Free Communications:** We will provide our clients a toll-free number to access 24 hours a day in the second year of operations.

**MARKET ANALYSIS SUMMARY**

StructureAll Ltd. will focus on traditional architect/engineering (A/E) contracts. The owner will usually contract the A/E to perform planning and design services. These design services include preparation of plans, specifications, and estimates.

Construction services may be limited to occasional field visits and certain contract administration requirements. Typically, these types of projects distribute total design fees among the professionals involved in accordance with the following guideline:

- Architecture Design (65%)
- Structural Design (10%)
- Mechanical Design (15%)
- Electrical Design (10%)

Our most important clients will be established architectural/engineering firms who require structural engineering services.

**Market Segmentation**

The market for engineering services may be summarized with the following groups:

1. **Established Architectural and Engineering firms:** Typically, the structural portions of any building project involve a prime consultant who pre-selects their team members and promotes their strengths in a proposal call to prospective clients. Our strategy is to offer these established firms a viable resource from which to draw upon. We can undertake the entire structural engineering process or provide assistance to their own in-house staff.

2. **Territorial and Federal Governmental Departments:** The Government of the Northwest Territories (GNWT) and the newly created Nunavut Territory retain consultants for a variety of purposes. We intend to position ourselves as a local firm offering expertise in consulting, project management, forensic, and restoration engineering. The Federal Government also retains consultants for similar purposes.

3. **Law Firms:** We will market our services to the legal community to provide dispute resolution services, including arbitration, mediation and expert reports for litigation. This work is supported by forensic engineering services to identify the cause of failures.

4. **Contractors:** We will offer design/build services to contractors for the multitude of potential projects which the Territorial Government and Nunavut Territory have recently undertaken. Contractors occasionally require structural engineers to submit sealed alternatives for equivalents to construction details.

5. **Municipal Governments:** Remote Municipal Governments in the Territories can expect to have more autonomy with respect to infrastructure growth and development in the years to come. This initiative is part of the GNWT mandate. We will promote our services to the local municipal governments for this purpose. To attract this market potential, we will offer to train those students in each community who are interested in engineering as a career choice. On the local front, the city of Yellowknife often provides recommendations to builders and homeowners for structural engineering services related to renovations, additions, and new construction.

6. **Private Individuals:** We will focus attention on homeowners in Yellowknife who are renovating or contemplating an addition to their residence. We will also promote home inspections to those parties contemplating the purchase of a home.

7. **Realtors:** In conjunction with home inspections, we will make all the Realtors aware of this service.

The Potential Market Chart and the Market Analysis Table are based on percentages which each of these groups could contribute to the services offered. This manner of describing the potential market is more appropriate for this type of business. As can be seen, the established architectural/engineering firms account for 65 percent of the potential market with the other participants claiming the balance in smaller proportions.

**Market Analysis**

| Potential Customers | Growth | 1999 | 2000 | 2001 | 2002 | 2003 | CAGR |
|---|---|---|---|---|---|---|---|
| Architectural/Engineering firms | 0% | 65 | 65 | 65 | 65 | 65 | 0.00% |
| Territorial/Federal Governments | 0% | 10 | 10 | 10 | 10 | 10 | 0.00% |
| Law firms | 0% | 5 | 5 | 5 | 5 | 5 | 0.00% |
| Contractors | 0% | 5 | 5 | 5 | 5 | 5 | 0.00% |
| Municipal Governments | 0% | 5 | 5 | 5 | 5 | 5 | 0.00% |
| Private Individuals | 0% | 5 | 5 | 5 | 5 | 5 | 0.00% |
| Realtors | 0% | 5 | 5 | 5 | 5 | 5 | 0.00% |
| Other | 0% | 0 | 0 | 0 | 0 | 0 | 0.00% |
| **Total** | **0.00%** | **100** | **100** | **100** | **100** | **100** | **0.00%** |

**Service Business Analysis**

The following sections describe in more detail these aspects of the service business environment:

- Business Participants
- Competition and Buying Patterns
- Main Competitors

**Business
Participants**

The majority of consulting services cater to the needs of the Territorial Governments. The Territorial Governments operate on a budget of approximately $1,170 million per year, based on the 1998/1999 Main Estimates. Of this total, approximately $1,028 million is spent on Operating and Maintenance Expenditures while $142 million is allocated to Capital Expenditures.

Within the Capital Expenditures, Buildings and Works is a sub-category. This is the area of the annual operating budget from which all building design consultants must draw upon. Our analysis of the 1998/1999 Main Estimates indicates a total expenditure of $59,339,000. A typical A/E contract derives fee estimates from total budgets. For this analysis, we will apply 9 percent as a guideline for design fees. This yields a figure of about $5,340,000 in design fees available for distribution to the consulting industry.

The major clients within the Territorial Governments include:

- Department of Education
- Department of Transportation
- Department of Municipal and Community Affairs

Our competition matrix indicates a total of 102 persons within the consulting field in the Territories. This total has been subdivided into the types of positions these people hold. Based on reasonable estimates of salary expectations including 30 percent burdens for administration yields a value of about $7,800,000. This figure represents an estimate of the revenues required to sustain engineering consultants in the Territories.

From this evaluation, the Territorial Governments account for close to 70 percent of design fees while other participants in the building marketplace account for the balance. The Territorial Governments retain consultants for the following types of buildings:

- Schools
- Health Centers
- Community Halls
- Arenas
- Warehouses
- Firehalls

These types of buildings are constructed on a rotating basis across several communities in the Northwest Territories. In addition to new construction, rehabilitation, renovations, and additions are also in demand.

Typically, the Territorial Governments issue a proposal call to consultants to service these needs. StructureAll will position itself as a Structural Sub-Consultant or resource to the Prime Consultant.

StructureAll Ltd. will also promote its services as structural specialists and project managers to the Territorial Governments.

**Competition and
Buying Patterns**

Pricing of projects and billing rates are surprisingly variable. In consulting at this level, it is easier to be priced too low than too high. Clients and potential clients expect to pay substantial fees for the best quality professional advice. The nature of the billing, however, is sensitive. Clients are much more likely to be offended when a job starts at $20K and ends up at $30K because of overruns, than if the same job started at $30K or even $35K.

Clients rarely compare consultants directly, looking for two, or more, possible providers of a proposed project or job. Usually they follow word-of-mouth recommendations and either go for the job or not, rather than selecting from a menu of possible providers.

The most important element of general competition, by far, is what it takes to keep clients for repeat business. It is worth making huge concessions in any single project to maintain a client relationship that brings the client back for future projects.

**Main Competitors**

1. **Ferguson Simek Clark (FSC Group):** This well-established architectural and multi-discipline engineering firm would be our main competitor. This firm has branch offices in Iqaluit, Northwest Territories, and Whitehorse, Yukon, besides a head office located in Yellowknife. Their principal strength is undertaking a project from inception through to completion under one roof. Their weakness stems from an understaffed structural engineering group. At present, there is only one structural engineer who services the needs of all their in-house architects and outside clients. The drafting aspects of any project rely upon recollection and modification of past projects typically. There is no systematic manner in which standard block libraries are maintained or updated. They underutilize the programs at their disposal for structural analysis and design.
2. **A. D. Williams Engineering Ltd. (ADWEL):** This multi-discipline engineering firm is well established in Yellowknife. Their head office is located in Edmonton, Alberta. They can draw on additional resources from the core group as required to meet the demands of project schedules. At present, there is no resident structural engineer on staff in Yellowknife.
3. **Girvan and Associates:** This is a small one-person architectural and engineering firm which specializes in providing services for residential construction projects. Ian Girvan services the private sector mostly. It is our hope that we can form a strategic alliance to carry out consulting work jointly as needs and occasions arise.
4. **B. Nelson Engineer:** Mr. Nelson is a former partner with FSC Group who has resurfaced in the Territories to provide structural engineering services. His strength is his working relationship with existing architectural firms. His weakness stems from not having an established presence in the Territories. At present, he is working out of the offices of a mechanical engineering firm (Thorn Engineering Ltd.).

**STRATEGY & IMPLEMENTATION SUMMARY**

StructureAll Ltd. will focus on the Western Arctic area initially. We believe the creation of Nunavut will still provide opportunities for structural engineering services; however, a separate Association of Professional Engineers for Nunavut is anticipated.

We are also licensed to practice in the Yukon Territories, although we have not planned for any aggressive marketing in this area.

The target client is usually an architect manager.

**Competitive Edge**

StructureAll Ltd. offers the following competitive edge:

- State-of-the-art modeling, design, analysis, and drafting capabilities
- Quality control and assurance program
- An Internet website (http:\\www.structureall.com and e-mail, info@structureall.com)

**Marketing Strategy**

The sections which follow describe in more detail our positioning statement, pricing, and promotion strategy.

**Positioning Statement**

For established engineering and architectural firms in Yellowknife who require structural engineering sub-consultant services, StructureAll Ltd. offers a competitive and economical option. Projects may be delegated to StructureAll Ltd. directly or arrangements can be made to supplement and assist their own in-house staff.

**Pricing Strategy**

Most consulting work is billed on an hourly basis to pre-determined levels dictated by project schedule milestones. We have assigned a rate of $80/hour for basic consulting services and $40/hour for drafting services. These are conservative values for the consulting market. We have used conservative unit rates to remain more competitive.

**Promotion Strategy**

We will be using the Internet extensively in our sales promotion. Together with a well targeted direct mail and e-mail campaign, we will make all the major players in the marketplace aware of our presence.

We will focus our limited advertising budgets to promote community sponsored events. We will also offer technical services at discount rates to nonprofit organizations.

When traveling to remote communities, we will contact the local principals in elementary, middle, and high schools offering them a speaker on structural engineering as a career choice.

StructureAll Ltd. will apply for the Northwest Territories Business Incentive Policy. This policy is directed at those firms resident in the Northwest Territories and provides incentives with respect to evaluation of services.

**Sales Strategy**

Success in a consulting market is focused on client service and typically translates into repeat business. We will avoid the pitfall of buying a project, only to find that the scope of work far exceeds renumeration.

When a potential client questions the cost of a project, we explain the benefits and refer to our proposal which clearly outlines the tasks to be performed. If the budget is for less money, then we must offer less service.

Billing rates are not negotiated. One exception to this rule would be for not-for-profit organizations where marketing can be traded for services in kind.

**Sales Forecast**

The following table and chart summarizes forecasted sales. We expect sales to remain at a constant level after three months of operation. We predict the first two months of operations will be slow. Revenues will be limited while a generic quality management plan is formulated and basic office administration tasks are completed.

Direct unit costs for the first year have been set at 30 percent of unit revenues, which yields a 70 percent gross margin. In the third year of operations, we plan to increase gross margin to 80 percent as a result of providing a more efficient service to our clients.

Our unit rate for basic consulting services has been set at $80/hour. This is a conservative assumption based on published salary guideline levels for engineering professionals. Our unit rate for CADD services is $40/hour.

**Sales Forecast**

| Unit Sales | FY2000 | FY2001 | FY2002 |
|---|---|---|---|
| Project Consulting | 690 | 750 | 800 |
| Project Management | 240 | 260 | 280 |
| Home Inspections | 96 | 110 | 120 |
| Computer-aided Drafting Services | 890 | 1,000 | 1,050 |
| Other | 0 | 0 | 0 |
| **Total Unit Sales** | **1,916** | **2,120** | **2,250** |

| Unit Prices | FY2000 | FY2001 | FY2002 |
|---|---|---|---|
| Project Consulting | $80.00 | $80.00 | $80.00 |
| Project Management | $80.00 | $80.00 | $80.00 |
| Home Inspections | $80.00 | $80.00 | $80.00 |
| Computer-aided Drafting Services | $40.00 | $40.00 | $40.00 |
| Other | $0.00 | $0.00 | $0.00 |

| Sales | FY2000 | FY2001 | FY2002 |
|---|---|---|---|
| Project Consulting | $55,200 | $60,000 | $64,000 |
| Project Management | $19,200 | $20,800 | $22,400 |
| Home Inspections | $7,680 | $8,800 | $9,600 |
| Computer-aided Drafting Services | $35,600 | $40,000 | $42,000 |
| Other | $0 | $0 | $0 |
| **Total Sales** | **$117,680** | **$129,600** | **$138,000** |

| Direct Unit Costs | FY2000 | FY2001 | FY2002 |
|---|---|---|---|
| Project Consulting | $24.00 | $20.00 | $16.00 |
| Project Management | $24.00 | $20.00 | $16.00 |
| Home Inspections | $24.00 | $20.00 | $16.00 |
| Computer-aided Drafting Services | $12.00 | $10.00 | $8.00 |
| Other | $0.00 | $0.00 | $0.00 |

| Direct Cost of Sales | FY2000 | FY2001 | FY2002 |
|---|---|---|---|
| Project Consulting | $16,560 | $15,000 | $12,800 |
| Project Management | $5,760 | $5,200 | $4,480 |
| Home Inspections | $2,304 | $2,200 | $1,920 |
| Computer-aided Drafting Services | $10,680 | $10,000 | $8,400 |
| Other | $0 | $0 | $0 |
| **Subtotal Direct Cost of Sales** | **$35,304** | **$32,400** | **$27,600** |

**Milestones**

The accompanying table lists important program milestones, with dates and managers in charge, and budgets for each. The milestone schedule indicates our emphasis on planning for implementation.

What the table doesn't show is the commitment behind it. Our business plan includes complete provisions for plan vs. actual analysis, which will be updated monthly to compare the variance and plan for course corrections.

**Milestones**

| | Start Date | End Date | Budget | Manager | Department |
|---|---|---|---|---|---|
| Complete incorporation | 04/01/99 | 04/15/99 | $500 | PN | Administrative |
| Acquire Tradename for Internet site | 03/06/99 | 03/06/99 | $400 | PN | Administrative |
| Submit Business License Application to City | 04/01/98 | 04/16/98 | $250 | PN | Administrative |
| Aquire WCB Coverage | 04/01/98 | 04/16/98 | $50 | PN | Administrative |
| Apply for Staad-Pro Core financing | 04/01/99 | 04/16/99 | n/a | PN | Administrative |
| Aquire E&O Insurance | 04/01/98 | 04/16/98 | $1,200 | PN | Administrative |
| Other | n/a | n/a | n/a | PN | n/a |
| **Totals** | | | **$2,400** | | |

## MANAGEMENT SUMMARY

StructureAll Ltd. will initially have one employee who is also acting as general manager. Phil Nolan will be responsible for all daily operations in the firm.

## Management Team

Philip Nolan, P. Eng. has eighteen years of progressive and responsible engineering experience. Phil will be responsible for soliciting clients, marketing, promotion, and all daily aspects of running the business. He graduated from McGill University in Montreal, Quebec, in 1981 with a Bachelor of Engineering degree.

Following graduation in 1981, Phil worked for consulting engineers in Toronto, Ontario, on a variety of transportation planning projects.

In 1982, Phil moved to Yellowknife where he worked for the GNWT as a project engineer. Phil gained experience working on a host of community development and transportation related projects, including Little Buffalo River Bridge, Bridge Inspections, and Bridge Rehabilitations. Phil was with the GNWT for six years.

From 1988 to 1991, Phil worked for Foundation Company of Canada Ltd., a large multinational contracting firm as a project engineer where he gained experience in the use of explosives at the Magpie River Hydro Development and continued gaining experience on several bridge projects.

In 1992, Phil worked for Reid Crowther & Partners Ltd. out of Edmonton, Alberta, on a host of bridge design and rehabilitation projects, including the Whitemud Ravine Pedestrian Bridges.

From 1993 to 1995, Phil was self-employed as a private consultant offering services in quality control and assurance for building construction where he gained considerable experience in Preserved Wood Foundations and their use in residential and commercial applications.

In May of 1995, Phil joined the Ferguson Simek Clark (FSC) team of professionals and was responsible for all structural design, including quality control and assurance services for schools, arenas, health centers, and other buildings.

Phil will be the principal designer of all projects at StructureAll Ltd. Phil is currently working on a contract basis for Ferguson Simek Clark.

## Management Team Gaps

StructureAll Ltd. will require administrative support to ensure clients are billed on a timely basis. We will be looking to an outside source for ensuring the books are kept in order and up to date.

Self sufficiency in computer-aided drafting capabilities will require Phil to become more familiar with AutoCADD 2000 as a drafting tool. We will invest in continuing education to fulfill this need. We have accounted for this in the business plan.

The following table summarizes our personnel expenditures for the first three years, with compensation increasing from $50K the first year to $70K in the third. The detailed monthly personnel plan for the first year is included in the appendices.

| Personnel Plan | FY2000 | FY2001 | FY2002 |
|---|---|---|---|
| Payroll | $50,000 | $60,000 | $70,000 |

The financial plan depends on important assumptions, most of which are shown in the following table as annual assumptions. The monthly assumptions are included in the appendices.

Some of the more important underlying assumptions are:

- We assume a strong economy, without major recession.
- We assume the creation of Nunavut will not dramatically change the delivery of engineering services.
- Interest rates, tax rates, and personnel burdens are based on conservative assumptions.

| General Assumptions | FY2000 | FY2001 | FY2002 |
|---|---|---|---|
| Short-term Interest Rate % | 10.00% | 10.00% | 10.00% |
| Long-term Interest Rate % | 10.00% | 10.00% | 10.00% |
| Payment Days Estimator | 30 | 30 | 30 |
| Collection Days Estimator | 45 | 45 | 45 |
| Inventory Turnover Estimator | 6 | 6 | 6 |
| Tax Rate % | 15.00% | 15.00% | 15.00% |
| Expenses in Cash % | 10.00% | 10.00% | 10.00% |
| Sales on Credit % | 100.00% | 100.00% | 100.00% |
| Personnel Burden % | 15.00% | 15.00% | 15.00% |

We foresee modest growth in sales and a marginal reduction in operating expenses for the first three years.

The following table and chart summarize our break-even analysis. With estimated monthly fixed costs of $6,500, billing targets of $10,000 per month will cover our costs. We don't really expect to reach break-even until a few months into the business operation.

The break-even assumes unit variable costs at 30 percent of unit revenue. The unit revenue value of $60/hour is an aggregate measure for all the types of services which will be offered.

**Break-even Analysis:**

| | |
|---|---|
| Monthly Units Break-even | 238 |
| Monthly Sales Break-even | $14,286 |

**Assumptions:**

| | |
|---|---|
| Average Per-Unit Revenue | $60 |
| Average Per-Unit Variable Cost | $18 |
| Estimated Monthly Fixed Cost | $10,000 |

**Personnel Plan**

**FINANCIAL PLAN**

**Important Assumptions**

**Key Financial Indicators**

**Break-even Analysis**

**Projected Profit and Loss**

The gross margin for a service-based business is a reflection of the efficiency at which those services are offered. In the initial year of operations, we have targeted a gross margin of 70 percent. This is not an unreasonable figure for a consulting business. For the second and third year of operations, we have targeted gross margins of 75 percent and 80 percent to indicate overall improved efficiency at service delivery.

In order to fulfill the requirements of the mission statement and simultaneously reduce start-up costs, we have made arrangements to purchase software on quarterly repayment options:

- Staad-Pro Core is a structural engineering design and drafting suite offered through Research Engineers Ltd. This program fulfills the need to carry out three-dimensional analysis and design requirements and is a key feature of the business plan. This program supports Canadian codes and standards. We have contacted the authorized Canadian reseller (Detech Corporation Ltd.) and will made arrangements to purchase this tool on four payments of $1,550 over the first year of operations.

- Errors and Omissions Insurance is required for all consultants working on behalf of the Territorial Governments. Through Falconair Insurance, we have received a quotation of $1,200/year for this coverage. The first year's premium payments are included in the start-up costs, with subsequent years indicated at the same annual premium.

- Website hosting fees are included as quarterly payments to Internic.com, the web host. This service provides the company with a valuable marketing tool. As part of this service, we will have at our disposal file transfer protocol capabilities. This feature permits us to place electronic media on the Internet for our clients and strategic allies.

- Rent for storefront office space has been included in the profit and loss table for the second and third years of operations. An allowance of $500 per month has been indicated for Contracts and Sub-Consultants.

Net Profit/Sales is determined to be 7.8 percent the first year, increasing to 9.8 percent the second year and 11 percent the third year.

**Profit and Loss (Income Statement)**

|  | **FY2000** | **FY2001** | **FY2002** |
|---|---|---|---|
| Sales | $117,680 | $129,600 | $138,000 |
| Direct Cost of Sales | $35,304 | $32,400 | $27,600 |
| Production Payroll | $0 | $0 | $0 |
| Other | $0 | $0 | $0 |
| **Total Cost of Sales** | **$35,304** | **$32,400** | **$27,600** |
|  |  |  |  |
| Gross Margin | $82,376 | $97,200 | $110,400 |
| Gross Margin % | 70.00% | 75.00% | 80.00% |
|  |  |  |  |
| Advertising/Promotion | $850 | $1,000 | $1,000 |
| Engineering Association Annual Fees | $600 | $750 | $750 |
| Continuing Education | $900 | $900 | $900 |
| Yellow Pages/White Pages | $500 | $500 | $500 |
| Miscellaneous | $600 | $600 | $600 |
|  |  |  |  |
| Payroll Expense | $50,000 | $60,000 | $70,000 |
| Payroll Burden | $0 | $0 | $0 |
| Depreciation | $1,800 | $1,800 | $1,800 |
| Website Hosting Fees | $380 | $380 | $380 |
| Telephone/Fax | $2,400 | $2,400 | $2,400 |
| Software Purchases (Staad-Pro Core) | $6,200 | $300 | $300 |
| Utilities | $1,200 | $1,200 | $1,200 |
| Errors and Omissions Insurance | $0 | $1,200 | $1,200 |
| Rent | $0 | $4,800 | $4,800 |
| Contract/Consultants | $6,000 | $6,000 | $6,000 |
|  |  |  |  |
| **Total Operating Expenses** | **$71,430** | **$81,830** | **$91,830** |
|  |  |  |  |
| Profit Before Interest and Taxes | $10,946 | $15,370 | $18,570 |
| Interest Expense Short-term | $0 | $0 | $0 |
| Interest Expense Long-term | $179 | $495 | $830 |
| Taxes Incurred | $1,615 | $2,231 | $2,661 |
| Extraordinary Items | $0 | $0 | $0 |
| Net Profit | $9,152 | $12,644 | $15,079 |
| Net Profit/Sales | 7.78% | 9.76% | 10.93% |

**Projected Cash Flow**

Cash flow projections are critical to our success. The monthly cash flow is shown in the illustration, with one bar representing the cash flow per month, and the other the monthly balance. The first few months are critical. It may be necessary to inject additional capital in this time-frame if the need arises. The annual cash flow figures are included here and the more important detailed monthly numbers are included in the appendices.

**Projected Cash Flow**

|  | FY2000 | FY2001 | FY2002 |
|---|---|---|---|
| Net Profit | $9,152 | $12,644 | $15,079 |
| Plus: |  |  |  |
| Depreciation | $1,800 | $1,800 | $1,800 |
| Change in Accounts Payable | $3,677 | $513 | ($401) |
| Current Borrowing (repayment) | $0 | $0 | $0 |
| Increase (decrease) Other Liabilities | $0 | $0 | $0 |
| Long-term Borrowing (repayment) | $3,300 | $3,300 | $3,400 |
| Capital Input | $0 | $0 | $0 |
| **Subtotal** | **$17,930** | **$18,257** | **$19,878** |
| Less: |  |  |  |
| Change in Accounts Receivable | $15,360 | $1,556 | $1,096 |
| Change in Inventory | $0 | $0 | $0 |
| Change in Other Short-term Assets | $0 | $0 | $0 |
| Capital Expenditure | $0 | $0 | $0 |
| Dividends | $0 | $0 | $0 |
| **Subtotal** | **$15,360** | **$1,556** | **$1,096** |
| Net Cash Flow | $2,570 | $16,701 | $18,781 |
| **Cash Balance** | **$9,570** | **$26,271** | **$45,052** |

**Projected Balance Sheet**

The balance sheet in the following table shows managed but sufficient growth of net worth and a sufficiently healthy financial position. The monthly estimates are included in the appendices.

**Projected Balance Sheet**
**Assets**

| **Short-term Assets** | FY2000 | FY2001 | FY2002 |
|---|---|---|---|
| Cash | $9,570 | $26,271 | $45,052 |
| Accounts Receivable | $15,360 | $16,916 | $18,012 |
| Inventory | $0 | $0 | $0 |
| Other Short-term Assets | $0 | $0 | $0 |
| Total Short-term Assets | $24,930 | $43,186 | $63,064 |
|  |  |  |  |
| **Long-term Assets** |  |  |  |
| Capital Assets | $0 | $0 | $0 |
| Accumulated Depreciation | $1,800 | $3,600 | $5,400 |
| Total Long-term Assets | ($1,800) | ($3,600) | ($5,400) |
| **Total Assets** | **$23,130** | **$39,586** | **$57,664** |
|  |  |  |  |
| **Liabilities and Capital** |  |  |  |
| Accounts Payable | $3,677 | $4,190 | $3,789 |
| Short-term Notes | $0 | $0 | $0 |
| Other Short-term Liabilities | $0 | $0 | $0 |
| **Subtotal Short-term Liabilities** | **$3,677** | **$4,190** | **$3,789** |
| Long-term Liabilities | $3,300 | $6,600 | $10,000 |
| **Total Liabilities** | **$6,977** | **$10,790** | **$13,789** |

|  | FY2000 | FY2001 | FY2002 |
|---|---|---|---|
| Paid in Capital | $20,000 | $20,000 | $20,000 |
| Retained Earnings | ($13,000) | ($3,848) | $8,796 |
| Earnings | $9,152 | $12,644 | $15,079 |
| **Total Capital** | **$16,152** | **$28,796** | **$43,875** |
| **Total Liabilities and Capital** | **$23,130** | **$39,586** | **$57,664** |
| **Net Worth** | **$16,152** | **$28,796** | **$43,875** |

**Projected Balance Sheet**

*continued*

The following table shows the projected business ratios. We expect to maintain healthy ratios for profitability, risk, and return.

**Business Ratios**

**Ratio Analysis**

| Profitability Ratios: | FY2000 | FY2001 | FY2002 | RMA |
|---|---|---|---|---|
| Gross Margin | 70.00% | 75.00% | 80.00% | 0 |
| Net Profit Margin | 7.78% | 9.76% | 10.93% | 0 |
| Return on Assets | 39.57% | 31.94% | 26.15% | 0 |
| Return on Equity | 56.66% | 43.91% | 34.37% | 0 |

| Activity Ratios | | | | |
|---|---|---|---|---|
| AR Turnover | 7.66 | 7.66 | 7.66 | 0 |
| Collection Days | 24 | 45 | 46 | 0 |
| Inventory Turnover | 0.00 | 0.00 | 0.00 | 0 |
| Accounts Payable Turnover | 13.88 | 12.17 | 12.17 | 0 |
| **Total Asset Turnover** | **5.09** | **3.27** | **2.39** | **0** |

| Debt Ratios | | | | |
|---|---|---|---|---|
| Debt to Net Worth | 0.43 | 0.37 | 0.31 | 0 |
| Short-term Liability to Liability | 0.53 | 0.39 | 0.27 | 0 |

| Liquidity Ratios | | | | |
|---|---|---|---|---|
| Current Ratio | 6.78 | 10.31 | 16.64 | 0 |
| Quick Ratio | 6.78 | 10.31 | 16.64 | 0 |
| Net Working Capital | $21,252 | $38,996 | $59,275 | 0 |
| Interest Coverage | 61.24 | 31.05 | 22.37 | 0 |

| Additional Ratios | | | | |
|---|---|---|---|---|
| Assets to Sales | 0.20 | 0.31 | 0.42 | 0 |
| Debt/Assets | 30% | 27% | 24% | 0 |
| Current Debt/Total Assets | 16% | 11% | 7% | 0 |
| Acid Test | 2.60 | 6.27 | 11.89 | 0 |
| Asset Turnover | 5.09 | 3.27 | 2.39 | 0 |
| Sales/Net Worth | 7.29 | 4.50 | 3.15 | 0 |
| Dividend Payout | $0 | $0 | $0 | 0 |

## Projected Balance Sheet

**Assets**

| Short-term Assets | Starting Balances | Apr | May | Jun | Jul | Aug |
|---|---|---|---|---|---|---|
| Cash | $7,000 | $4,108 | $596 | $2,337 | $3,217 | $3,554 |
| Accounts Receivable | $0 | $7,840 | $12,782 | $13,374 | $14,760 | $15,360 |
| Inventory | $0 | $0 | $0 | $0 | $0 | $0 |
| Other Short-term Assets | $0 | $0 | $0 | $0 | $0 | $0 |
| **Total Short-term Assets** | **$7,000** | **$11,948** | **$13,379** | **$15,711** | **$17,977** | **$18,914** |
| | | | | | | |
| **Long-term Assets** | | | | | | |
| Capital Assets | $0 | $0 | $0 | $0 | $0 | $0 |
| Accumulated Depreciation | $0 | $150 | $300 | $450 | $600 | $750 |
| Total Long-term Assets | $0 | ($150) | ($300) | ($450) | ($600) | ($750) |
| **Total Assets** | **$7,000** | **$11,798** | **$13,079** | **$15,261** | **$17,377** | **$18,164** |
| | | | | | | |
| **Liabilities and Capital** | | | | | | |
| Accounts Payable | $0 | $4,467 | $3,460 | $3,500 | $5,011 | $3,796 |
| Short-term Notes | $0 | $0 | $0 | $0 | $0 | $0 |
| Other Short-term Liabilities | $0 | $0 | $0 | $0 | $0 | $0 |
| **Subtotal Short-term Liabilities** | **$0** | **$4,467** | **$3,460** | **$3,500** | **$5,011** | **$3,796** |
| Long-term Liabilities | $0 | $275 | $550 | $825 | $1,100 | $1,375 |
| **Total Liabilities** | **$0** | **$4,742** | **$4,010** | **$4,325** | **$6,111** | **$5,171** |
| | | | | | | |
| Paid in Capital | $20,000 | $20,000 | $20,000 | $20,000 | $20,000 | $20,000 |
| Retained Earnings | ($13,000) | ($13,000) | ($13,000) | ($13,000) | ($13,000) | ($13,000) |
| Earnings | $0 | $56 | $2,069 | $3,936 | $4,266 | $5,993 |
| **Total Capital** | **$7,000** | **$7,056** | **$9,069** | **$10,936** | **$11,266** | **$12,993** |
| **Total Liabilities and Capital** | **$7,000** | **$11,798** | **$13,079** | **$15,261** | **$17,377** | **$18,164** |
| **Net Worth** | **$7,000** | **$7,056** | **$9,069** | **$10,936** | **$11,266** | **$12,993** |

| Sep | Oct | Nov | Dec | Jan | Feb | Mar |
|---|---|---|---|---|---|---|
| $5,706 | $6,687 | $6,665 | $7,517 | $8,629 | $8,649 | $9,570 |
| $15,360 | $15,360 | $15,360 | $15,360 | $15,360 | $15,360 | $15,360 |
| $0 | $0 | $0 | $0 | $0 | $0 | $0 |
| $0 | $0 | $0 | $0 | $0 | $0 | $0 |
| **$21,066** | **$22,047** | **$22,025** | **$22,877** | **$23,989** | **$24,009** | **$24,930** |
| | | | | | | |
| $0 | $0 | $0 | $0 | $0 | $0 | $0 |
| $900 | $1,050 | $1,200 | $1,350 | $1,500 | $1,650 | $1,800 |
| ($900) | ($1,050) | ($1,200) | ($1,350) | ($1,500) | ($1,650) | ($1,800) |
| **$20,166** | **$20,997** | **$20,825** | **$21,527** | **$22,489** | **$22,359** | **$23,130** |
| | | | | | | |
| $3,798 | $4,922 | $4,114 | $3,672 | $4,890 | $4,045 | $3,677 |
| $0 | $0 | $0 | $0 | $0 | $0 | $0 |
| $0 | $0 | $0 | $0 | $0 | $0 | $0 |
| **$3,798** | **$4,922** | **$4,114** | **$3,672** | **$4,890** | **$4,045** | **$3,677** |
| $1,650 | $1,925 | $2,200 | $2,475 | $2,750 | $3,025 | $3,300 |
| **$5,448** | **$6,847** | **$6,314** | **$6,147** | **$7,640** | **$7,070** | **$6,977** |
| | | | | | | |
| $20,000 | $20,000 | $20,000 | $20,000 | $20,000 | $20,000 | $20,000 |
| ($13,000) | ($13,000) | ($13,000) | ($13,000) | ($13,000) | ($13,000) | ($13,000) |
| $7,718 | $7,150 | $7,511 | $8,380 | $7,849 | $8,289 | $9,152 |
| **$14,718** | **$14,150** | **$14,511** | **$15,380** | **$14,849** | **$15,289** | **$16,152** |
| **$20,166** | **$20,997** | **$20,825** | **$21,527** | **$22,489** | **$22,359** | **$23,130** |
| **$14,718** | **$14,150** | **$14,511** | **$15,380** | **$14,849** | **$15,289** | **$16,152** |

## Projected Cash Flow

| | Apr | May | Jun | Jul | Aug | Sep |
|---|---|---|---|---|---|---|
| Net Profit | $56 | $2,013 | $1,867 | $331 | $1,727 | $1,725 |
| Plus: | | | | | | |
| Depreciation | $150 | $150 | $150 | $150 | $150 | $150 |
| Change in Accounts Payable | $4,467 | ($1,007) | $40 | $1,510 | ($1,215) | $2 |
| Current Borrowing (repayment) | $0 | $0 | $0 | $0 | $0 | $0 |
| Increase (decrease) Other Liabilities | $0 | $0 | $0 | $0 | $0 | $0 |
| Long-term Borrowing (repayment) | $275 | $275 | $275 | $275 | $275 | $275 |
| Capital Input | $0 | $0 | $0 | $0 | $0 | $0 |
| **Subtotal** | **$4,948** | **$1,431** | **$2,332** | **$2,266** | **$937** | **$2,152** |
| Less: | | | | | | |
| Change in Accounts Receivable | $7,840 | $4,942 | $592 | $1,386 | $600 | $0 |
| Change in Inventory | $0 | $0 | $0 | $0 | $0 | $0 |
| Change in Other Short-term Assets | $0 | $0 | $0 | $0 | $0 | $0 |
| Capital Expenditure | $0 | $0 | $0 | $0 | $0 | $0 |
| Dividends | $0 | $0 | $0 | $0 | $0 | $0 |
| **Subtotal** | **$7,840** | **$4,942** | **$592** | **$1,386** | **$600** | **$0** |
| Net Cash Flow | ($2,892) | ($3,511) | $1,740 | $880 | $337 | $2,152 |
| Cash Balance | $4,108 | $596 | $2,337 | $3,217 | $3,554 | $5,706 |

## General Assumptions

| | Apr | May | Jun | Jul | Aug | Sep |
|---|---|---|---|---|---|---|
| Short-term Interest Rate % | 10.00% | 10.00% | 10.00% | 10.00% | 10.00% | 10.00% |
| Long-term Interest Rate % | 10.00% | 10.00% | 10.00% | 10.00% | 10.00% | 10.00% |
| Payment Days Estimator | 30 | 30 | 30 | 30 | 30 | 30 |
| Collection Days Estimator | 45 | 45 | 45 | 45 | 45 | 45 |
| Inventory Turnover Estimator | 6.00 | 6.00 | 6.00 | 6.00 | 6.00 | 6.00 |
| Tax Rate % | 15.00% | 15.00% | 15.00% | 15.00% | 15.00% | 15.00% |
| Expenses in Cash % | 10.00% | 10.00% | 10.00% | 10.00% | 10.00% | 10.00% |
| Sales on Credit % | 100.00% | 100.00% | 100.00% | 100.00% | 100.00% | 100.00% |
| Personnel Burden % | 15.00% | 15.00% | 15.00% | 15.00% | 15.00% | 15.00% |

## Personnel Plan

| | Apr | May | Jun | Jul | Aug | Sep |
|---|---|---|---|---|---|---|
| Payroll | $2,500 | $2,500 | $3,000 | $4,000 | $4,000 | $4,000 |

| Oct | Nov | Dec | Jan | Feb | Mar |
|---|---|---|---|---|---|
| ($568) | $361 | $869 | ($531) | $440 | $863 |
| | | | | | |
| $150 | $150 | $150 | $150 | $150 | $150 |
| $1,125 | ($808) | ($442) | $1,218 | ($845) | ($368) |
| $0 | $0 | $0 | $0 | $0 | $0 |
| $0 | $0 | $0 | $0 | $0 | $0 |
| $275 | $275 | $275 | $275 | $275 | $275 |
| $0 | $0 | $0 | $0 | $0 | $0 |
| **$982** | **($22)** | **$852** | **$1,112** | **$20** | **$920** |
| | | | | | |
| $0 | $0 | $0 | $0 | $0 | $0 |
| $0 | $0 | $0 | $0 | $0 | $0 |
| $0 | $0 | $0 | $0 | $0 | $0 |
| $0 | $0 | $0 | $0 | $0 | $0 |
| $0 | $0 | $0 | $0 | $0 | $0 |
| **$0** | **$0** | **$0** | **$0** | **$0** | **$0** |
| $982 | ($22) | $852 | $1,112 | $20 | $920 |
| $6,687 | $6,665 | $7,517 | $8,629 | $8,649 | $9,570 |

| Oct | Nov | Dec | Jan | Feb | Mar |
|---|---|---|---|---|---|
| 10.00% | 10.00% | 10.00% | 10.00% | 10.00% | 10.00% |
| 10.00% | 10.00% | 10.00% | 10.00% | 10.00% | 10.00% |
| 30 | 30 | 30 | 30 | 30 | 30 |
| 45 | 45 | 45 | 45 | 45 | 45 |
| 6.00 | 6.00 | 6.00 | 6.00 | 6.00 | 6.00 |
| 15.00% | 15.00% | 15.00% | 15.00% | 15.00% | 15.00% |
| 10.00% | 10.00% | 10.00% | 10.00% | 10.00% | 10.00% |
| 100.00% | 100.00% | 100.00% | 100.00% | 100.00% | 100.00% |
| 15.00% | 15.00% | 15.00% | 15.00% | 15.00% | 15.00% |

| Oct | Nov | Dec | Jan | Feb | Mar |
|---|---|---|---|---|---|
| $5,000 | $5,000 | $5,000 | $5,000 | $5,000 | $5,000 |

## Profit and Loss (Income Statement)

| | Apr | May | Jun | Jul | Aug | Sep |
|---|---|---|---|---|---|---|
| Sales | $7,840 | $8,640 | $9,040 | $10,240 | $10,240 | $10,240 |
| Direct Cost of Sales | $2,352 | $2,592 | $2,712 | $3,072 | $3,072 | $3,072 |
| Production Payroll | $0 | $0 | $0 | $0 | $0 | $0 |
| Other | $0 | $0 | $0 | $0 | $0 | $0 |
| **Total Cost of Sales** | **$2,352** | **$2,592** | **$2,712** | **$3,072** | **$3,072** | **$3,072** |
| | | | | | | |
| Gross Margin | $5,488 | $6,048 | $6,328 | $7,168 | $7,168 | $7,168 |
| Gross Margin % | 70.00% | 70.00% | 70.00% | 70.00% | 70.00% | 70.00% |
| | | | | | | |
| Advertising/Promotion | $200 | $100 | $50 | $50 | $50 | $50 |
| Engineering Association Annual Fees | $0 | $0 | $0 | $0 | $0 | $0 |
| Continuing Education | $75 | $75 | $75 | $75 | $75 | $75 |
| Yellow Pages/White Pages | $0 | $0 | $0 | $0 | $0 | $0 |
| Miscellaneous | $50 | $50 | $50 | $50 | $50 | $50 |
| Payroll Expenses | $2,500 | $2,500 | $3,000 | $4,000 | $4,000 | $4,000 |
| Payroll Burden | $0 | $0 | $0 | $0 | $0 | $0 |
| Depreciation | $150 | $150 | $150 | $150 | $150 | $150 |
| Website Hosting Fees | $95 | $0 | $0 | $95 | $0 | $0 |
| Telephone/Fax | $200 | $200 | $200 | $200 | $200 | $200 |
| Software Purchases (Staad-Pro Core) | $1,550 | $0 | $0 | $1,550 | $0 | $0 |
| Utilities | $100 | $100 | $100 | $100 | $100 | $100 |
| Errors and Omissions Insurance | $0 | $0 | $0 | $0 | $0 | $0 |
| Rent | $0 | $0 | $0 | $0 | $0 | $0 |
| Contract/Consultants | $500 | $500 | $500 | $500 | $500 | $500 |
| **Total Operating Expenses** | **$5,420** | **$3,675** | **$4,125** | **$6,770** | **$5,125** | **$5,125** |
| | | | | | | |
| Profit Before Interest and Taxes | $68 | $2,373 | $2,203 | $398 | $2,043 | $2,043 |
| Interest Expense Short-term | $0 | $0 | $0 | $0 | $0 | $0 |
| Interest Expense Long-term | $2 | $5 | $7 | $9 | $11 | $14 |
| Taxes Incurred | $10 | $355 | $329 | $58 | $305 | $304 |
| Extraordinary Items | $0 | $0 | $0 | $0 | $0 | $0 |
| Net Profit | $56 | $2,013 | $1,867 | $331 | $1,727 | $1,725 |
| Net Profit/Sales | 0.71% | 23.30% | 20.65% | 3.23% | 16.86% | 16.84% |

| Oct | Nov | Dec | Jan | Feb | Mar |
|---|---|---|---|---|---|
| $10,240 | $10,240 | $10,240 | $10,240 | $10,240 | $10,240 |
| $3,072 | $3,072 | $3,072 | $3,072 | $3,072 | $3,072 |
| $0 | $0 | $0 | $0 | $0 | $0 |
| $0 | $0 | $0 | $0 | $0 | $0 |
| **$3,072** | **$3,072** | **$3,072** | **$3,072** | **$3,072** | **$3,072** |
| | | | | | |
| $7,168 | $7,168 | $7,168 | $7,168 | $7,168 | $7,168 |
| 70.00% | 70.00% | 70.00% | 70.00% | 70.00% | 70.00% |
| | | | | | |
| $100 | $50 | $50 | $50 | $50 | $50 |
| $0 | $600 | $0 | $0 | $0 | $0 |
| $75 | $75 | $75 | $75 | $75 | $75 |
| $0 | $0 | $0 | $0 | $500 | $0 |
| $50 | $50 | $50 | $50 | $50 | $50 |
| $5,000 | $5,000 | $5,000 | $5,000 | $5,000 | $5,000 |
| $0 | $0 | $0 | $0 | $0 | $0 |
| $150 | $150 | $150 | $150 | $150 | $150 |
| $95 | $0 | $0 | $95 | $0 | $0 |
| $200 | $200 | $200 | $200 | $200 | $200 |
| $1,550 | $0 | $0 | $1,550 | $0 | $0 |
| $100 | $100 | $100 | $100 | $100 | $100 |
| $0 | $0 | $0 | $0 | $0 | $0 |
| $0 | $0 | $0 | $0 | $0 | $0 |
| $500 | $500 | $500 | $500 | $500 | $500 |
| **$7,820** | **$6,725** | **$6,125** | **$7,770** | **$6,625** | **$6,125** |
| | | | | | |
| ($652) | $443 | $1,043 | ($602) | $543 | $1,043 |
| $0 | $0 | $0 | $0 | $0 | $0 |
| $16 | $18 | $21 | $23 | $25 | $28 |
| ($100) | $64 | $153 | ($94) | $78 | $152 |
| $0 | $0 | $0 | $0 | $0 | $0 |
| ($568) | $361 | $869 | ($531) | $440 | $863 |
| -5.55% | 3.53% | 8.49% | -5.19% | 4.30% | 8.43% |

## Sales Forecast

| Unit Sales | Apr | May | Jun | Jul | Aug | Sep |
|---|---|---|---|---|---|---|
| Project Consulting | 50 | 50 | 50 | 60 | 60 | 60 |
| Project Management | 20 | 20 | 20 | 20 | 20 | 20 |
| Home Inspections | 8 | 8 | 8 | 8 | 8 | 8 |
| Computer-aided Drafting Services | 40 | 60 | 70 | 80 | 80 | 80 |
| Other | 0 | 0 | 0 | 0 | 0 | 0 |
| **Total Unit Sales** | **118** | **138** | **148** | **168** | **168** | **168** |
| | | | | | | |
| **Unit Prices** | | | | | | |
| Project Consulting | $80.00 | $80.00 | $80.00 | $80.00 | $80.00 | $80.00 |
| Project Management | $80.00 | $80.00 | $80.00 | $80.00 | $80.00 | $80.00 |
| Home Inspections | $80.00 | $80.00 | $80.00 | $80.00 | $80.00 | $80.00 |
| Computer-aided Drafting Services | $40.00 | $40.00 | $40.00 | $40.00 | $40.00 | $40.00 |
| Other | $0.00 | $0.00 | $0.00 | $0.00 | $0.00 | $0.00 |
| | | | | | | |
| **Sales** | | | | | | |
| Project Consulting | $4,000 | $4,000 | $4,000 | $4,800 | $4,800 | $4,800 |
| Project Management | $1,600 | $1,600 | $1,600 | $1,600 | $1,600 | $1,600 |
| Home Inspections | $640 | $640 | $640 | $640 | $640 | $640 |
| Computer-aided Drafting Services | $1,600 | $2,400 | $2,800 | $3,200 | $3,200 | $3,200 |
| Other | $0 | $0 | $0 | $0 | $0 | $0 |
| **Total Sales** | **$7,840** | **$8,640** | **$9,040** | **$10,240** | **$10,240** | **$10,240** |
| | | | | | | |
| **Direct Unit Costs** | | | | | | |
| Project Consulting | $24.00 | $24.00 | $24.00 | $24.00 | $24.00 | $24.00 |
| Project Management | $24.00 | $24.00 | $24.00 | $24.00 | $24.00 | $24.00 |
| Home Inspections | $24.00 | $24.00 | $24.00 | $24.00 | $24.00 | $24.00 |
| Computer-aided Drafting Services | $12.00 | $12.00 | $12.00 | $12.00 | $12.00 | $12.00 |
| Other | $0.00 | $0.00 | $0.00 | $0.00 | $0.00 | $0.00 |
| | | | | | | |
| **Direct Cost of Sales** | | | | | | |
| Project Consulting | $1,200 | $1,200 | $1,200 | $1,440 | $1,440 | $1,440 |
| Project Management | $480 | $480 | $480 | $480 | $480 | $480 |
| Home Inspections | $192 | $192 | $192 | $192 | $192 | $192 |
| Computer-aided Drafting Services | $480 | $720 | $840 | $960 | $960 | $960 |
| Other | $0 | $0 | $0 | $0 | $0 | $0 |
| **Subtotal Direct Cost of Sales** | **$2,352** | **$2,592** | **$2,712** | **$3,072** | **$3,072** | **$3,072** |

| Oct | Nov | Dec | Jan | Feb | Mar |
|---|---|---|---|---|---|
| 60 | 60 | 60 | 60 | 60 | 60 |
| 20 | 20 | 20 | 20 | 20 | 20 |
| 8 | 8 | 8 | 8 | 8 | 8 |
| 80 | 80 | 80 | 80 | 80 | 80 |
| 0 | 0 | 0 | 0 | 0 | 0 |
| **168** | **168** | **168** | **168** | **168** | **168** |
| | | | | | |
| $80.00 | $80.00 | $80.00 | $80.00 | $80.00 | $80.00 |
| $80.00 | $80.00 | $80.00 | $80.00 | $80.00 | $80.00 |
| $80.00 | $80.00 | $80.00 | $80.00 | $80.00 | $80.00 |
| $40.00 | $40.00 | $40.00 | $40.00 | $40.00 | $40.00 |
| $0.00 | $0.00 | $0.00 | $0.00 | $0.00 | $0.00 |
| | | | | | |
| $4,800 | $4,800 | $4,800 | $4,800 | $4,800 | $4,800 |
| $1,600 | $1,600 | $1,600 | $1,600 | $1,600 | $1,600 |
| $640 | $640 | $640 | $640 | $640 | $640 |
| $3,200 | $3,200 | $3,200 | $3,200 | $3,200 | $3,200 |
| $0 | $0 | $0 | $0 | $0 | $0 |
| **$10,240** | **$10,240** | **$10,240** | **$10,240** | **$10,240** | **$10,240** |
| | | | | | |
| $24.00 | $24.00 | $24.00 | $24.00 | $24.00 | $24.00 |
| $24.00 | $24.00 | $24.00 | $24.00 | $24.00 | $24.00 |
| $24.00 | $24.00 | $24.00 | $24.00 | $24.00 | $24.00 |
| $12.00 | $12.00 | $12.00 | $12.00 | $12.00 | $12.00 |
| $0.00 | $0.00 | $0.00 | $0.00 | $0.00 | $0.00 |
| | | | | | |
| $1,440 | $1,440 | $1,440 | $1,440 | $1,440 | $1,440 |
| $480 | $480 | $480 | $480 | $480 | $480 |
| $192 | $192 | $192 | $192 | $192 | $192 |
| $960 | $960 | $960 | $960 | $960 | $960 |
| $0 | $0 | $0 | $0 | $0 | $0 |
| **$3,072** | **$3,072** | **$3,072** | **$3,072** | **$3,072** | **$3,072** |

# Student Services Consulting Firm

BUSINESS PLAN

GRAD STUDENT EXCHANGE
CONSULTANTS INTERNATIONAL

*46705 Northwest Boulevard*
*Seattle, Washington 98121*

*Grad Student Exchange Consultants International is a professional consulting firm specializing in providing placement information for prospective graduate students interested in attending colleges and universities in the United States. Our goal is to assist overseas students in their search for graduate programs designed to meet their individual needs. We are committed to providing honest and accurate information in accordance with the admission standards of each institution.*

- EXECUTIVE SUMMARY

- BUSINESS OBJECTIVES

- PROMOTIONAL STRATEGIES

- FINANCIALS

## EXECUTIVE SUMMARY

### Mission and Vision Statement

Grad Student Exchange Consultants International (GSECI) is a professional consulting firm specializing in providing placement information for prospective graduate students interested in attending colleges and universities in the United States. Our goal is to adequately and successfully perform our services to overseas students, assisting them in their search for graduate programs designed to meet their individual needs. We are committed to providing honest and accurate information in accordance with the admission standards of each institution.

### The Nature of the Business and Services Provided

Each year thousands of students from Japan, Taiwan, China, and other Pacific Rim countries seek information regarding admissions to graduate programs in the United States. Because there are a multitude of programs available across the world, the task of finding a suitable institution can be overwhelming and time-consuming for the student. The institution's academic reputation is not the only factor in deciding which program would meet the needs of the student, but also the environment of the institution, such as the population, the cost of living, and the very process for applying to become a member of that community. GSECI would be able to provide adequate information the student would need to ensure an effortless arrival of a decision binding and successful application acceptance for the future.

GSECI's major focus is in providing higher education in the United States with limited reach into the adjacent Canadian market. These services include, but are not limited to, the following:

**1. Research Facilities and Database Services**

Our research capabilities include a complete database of the thousands of graduate programs and their admissions standards currently available in the United States. Depending upon the type of services the client desires, we will provide up-to-the-minute, accurate background information on the institution(s) of their choice. Included in the research process are enrollment information, criteria for admissions, and a thorough explanation of the program(s) offered through each institution. This information can be transmitted to the student either via telefax, traditional hardcopy, or electronic personal mail, or a 1-800-customer support number. The extent of our research is left up to the decision of the client. GSECI is committed to serving the client by assisting them in this arduous process.

**2. Application Process**

GSECI will assist students with the application process, including how to obtain the necessary documents, such as entrance Visas and financial statements, which are required by each institution. Upon completion of the application, GSECI can provide additional assistance by reviewing the application and, if necessary, make appropriate suggestions and recommendations to ensure a polished, professional application is received by the institution. In addition, also included in the application process, GSECI will assure that all applications and the accompanying documents are promptly forwarded to the appropriate institution.

**3. Customer Support**

There will be a continuous follow-up to facilitate communication between our staff, agent, and the client base. Overseas agents/representatives will be available to answer questions and to provide clients with on-site support. An 800-customer support number with a VRU voice response unit with integrated database connectivity will be provided so the client can be kept up-to-date with the progress of their application.

Our dedication to our clients does not stop when clients are accepted by their desired institutions; we offer the client a three-month period of support in which they can call our 800 number in the event they have questions about their initial months in the United States.

Once the GSECI North American business office has been established, and China, Japan, and Taiwan resources are scouted and staffed, we will be expanding both the countries served and the services available. Future business objectives include:

**BUSINESS OBJECTIVES**

1.  GSECI will look to expand to other countries of the Pacific Rim, such as Korea and the Southeast Asia countries.
2.  GSECI will afford students in the United States the same opportunity to access institutions within the United States.
3.  GSECI will also expand services to include assistance in locating suitable housing.
4.  GSECI also seeks to introduce students in United States graduate exchange programs to programs in Pacific Rim countries.

GSECI offers a wide array of service packages (all fees in U.S. currency and exclude international trade tariffs, etc.) GSECI will not selectively source which colleges and/or universities are represented. The intent of GSECI business plan will include all accredited colleges, universities, and technical institutions.

**Services Offered**

**#1 Basic Package:**
*   3 school searches
*   Application forms requested and sent to the client by GSECI

Fee: $75.00 - $100.00
$25.00 per additional school

**#2 Basic Plus Package:**
*   3-5 school searches
*   Application forms requested and sent to the client by GSECI
*   1/2 hour consultative session with agent/consultant

Fee: $150.00
$20.00 per additional school

**#3 Deluxe Package:**
*   3-5 school searches
*   Application forms requested and sent to the client by GSECI. Consultations on applications and appropriate suggestions and guidance.
*   Complete consultant follow-up with the institution, including status of application, such as deadlines.

Fee: $200.00
$40.00 per additional school

*Note: Included with all packages is an additional three months of limited customer support. GSECI will also offer special incentives for referrals.*

**1. Advertising and Brand Communications**

**PROMOTIONAL STRATEGIES**

GSECI believes that college and localized educational newspapers will provide our firm with the best source of advertising because it is inexpensive and accessible to most of our target audience, which are prospective and current college students. We will also make use of bulletin boards, department offices, career centers, educational online communities, and Internet relationship marketing programs.

**2. Other Strategies**

GSECI will offer one free search with each contact made for the first three months of operation, saving each of our prospective clients anywhere between $20.00 and $40.00.

**Place**

GSECI is a Limited Liability Partnership with its central office located in Seattle, Washington. An existing office is ready for immediate occupancy, which is owned by one of the partners. The cost to start GSECI is moderate for an international start-up. A partner-owner office facility will contribute the main office facilities for a one-year time period. These facilities currently have existing phone lines and other office equipment, such as computers, fax machines, and various office furniture. The cost of these facilities will be contributed for a one-year start-up period by a limited partner holding an 1/8 share in GSECI future profits. Ongoing costs for facilities management and basic business tools, including but not limited to the above mentioned items, will be negotiated one year from the date of GSECI incorporation. Leveraging these facilities will allow us to begin start-up operations very quickly and enable our initial run at client acquisition and revenue generation process.

GSECI's overseas representatives will work from their own home office facilities and be paid a commission according to each account acquired. This arrangement is seen as "agent" framework and each "agent" will negotiate commission rates independently with an Officer of GSECI.

**Potential Liabilities/ Barriers to Success**

While the market for our services is burgeoning, GSECI cannot ignore potential pitfalls of operating an international business. The following short list of issues may have impact on our ability to compete:

- Economic environment in United States and Pacific Rim countries
- Political environment in United States in relationship to trade with Asia
- United States Immigration and Naturalization policies
- United States federal investment in student transfer and endowment policies

**Conclusion**

GSECI is devoted to promoting cultural diversity and breaking down the barriers of international education. Because the demand for higher education is apparent worldwide, the services offered by GSECI will benefit many students from many countries. Through the introduction of the United States to other countries, and vice versa, cultural differences can one day be accepted worldwide. Through education, GSECI will pave the way toward heightened communication between students of an international and national exchange.

| OPERATING MANAGEMENT | 2001 | 2002 | 2003 | 2004 | 2005 | TOTAL |
|---|---|---|---|---|---|---|
| Founder and President [Salary] | $35,000 | $75,000 | $82,000 | $85,000 | $90,000 | $397,000 |
| **OPERATIONS** | | | | | | |
| Legal counsel | $5,000 | $2,500 | $2,500 | $2,500 | $2,500 | $15,000 |
| 5 sales agents (training, travel, etc.) | $50,000 | $35,000 | $35,000 | $35,000 | $35,000 | $190,000 |
| Marketing/PR/Adv/ 1-800# (w/salary) | $75,000 | $60,000 | $50,000 | $50,000 | $50,000 | $285,000 |
| Clerical support (shared resource) | $20,000 | $22,000 | $24,000 | $32,000 | $35,000 | $133,000 |
| Computers, phones, desks, etc. | $0 | $15,000 | $16,050 | $17,174 | $18,376 | $66,599 |
| Office space rental/insurance | $0 | $10,000 | $12,000 | $14,000 | $16,000 | $52,000 |
| **OTHER** | | | | | | |
| Business insurance | $1,000 | $1,000 | $1,250 | $1,250 | $1,500 | $5,000 |
| Health insurance (2 persons) | $10,000 | $12,000 | $14,000 | $15,000 | $15,000 | $96,000 |
| **TOTAL** | **$196,000** | **$232,500** | **$236,800** | **$251,924** | **$263,376** | **$1,180,599** |

# Teen Night Club

BUSINESS PLAN

VENTURES

40 Pebblestone Court
Rockville, Missouri 65804

*This nonalcohol teen nightclub is aiming to give bored Midwestern teens another choice of where to go when they're tired of seeing movies and walking around the mall. Ventures will play Top 40s hits, screen the latest music videos, and serve a variety of sodas and tasty fruit drinks. Having no direct competition, Ventures anticipates popularity with the local teen population. This plan was provided by Lisa D. Morrow, J.D., and was compiled in conjunction with the business planning courses of St. Louis University's Entrepreneurship Program.*

- BUSINESS DESCRIPTION

- INTRODUCTION

- ORGANIZATIONAL FORM

- MARKETING

- MANAGEMENT

- ACCOUNTING

- RISKS

- FINANCIALS

## BUSINESS DESCRIPTION

Ventures, a nonalcohol nightclub, will cater to the 15- to 20-year-old age group. Ventures will be 7,000-8,000 square feet, accommodating around 650-700 people.

## INTRODUCTION

During the past ten years, a new concept has been blazing the trails. Nonalcohol nightclubs have been popping up throughout the United States, as well as in other parts of the world. The majority of these nightclubs cater to teenagers by giving them a high-energy place where they can socialize and dance to the hottest Top 40 hits. In some locations, these clubs constitute the only entertainment for this age group.

Ventures, a nonalcohol nightclub, will cater to the 15- to 20-year-old age group in Bates County and these surrounding counties: Cass, Johnson, Henry, Hickory, St. Clair, and Vernon. Ventures will be the only nightclub catering to this age group in the Bates area. Ventures' goal is to furnish new answers to this age group's complaints of "nothing to do and nowhere to go." Instead of serving alcohol, Ventures will boast a menu of sodas, shakes, and several speciality drinks consisting of a variety of fruit juices and syrups.

## ORGANIZATIONAL FORM

Ventures will be a family-owned business organized as a limited liability company. The principal owners will be David and Mary Jensen. Mary Jensen will be the decisionmaking partner while David Jensen will be a silent partner. The ownership split will be 60 percent for Mary Jensen and 40 percent for David Jensen. This organization will provide the owners the liability protections of a corporation and the flexibility and tax advantages of a partnership entity.

## MARKETING

### Target Market

Ventures' target market consists of individuals between the ages of 15-20 who listen to Top 40 radio stations and live within an hour's drive from Rockville, Missouri. According to recent research, this age group has the "time, money, and a steady desire to be entertained."

Ventures' market consists of over 120,000 individuals in seven counties:

| | |
|---|---|
| Bates County | 23,000 |
| Cass County | 3,232 |
| Henry County | 1,076 |
| Hickory County | 84,347 |
| Johnson County | 2,110 |
| St. Clair County | 8,128 |
| Vernon County | 416 |
| **Total** | **122,309** |

### Market Profile

Ventures' target market consists largely of high school teens and recent grads who listen to radio stations that play Top 40s tunes. Most of Ventures' target market will possess a driver's license. These kids tend to spend the majority of their money on clothing, food, and entertainment. Their primary entertainment options include going to the movies, buying CDs, and going on dates. Mediamark Research Inc. (MRI) surveyed a sample of teens and found that 28 percent of the teens go out either with friends or on a date at least once a week. Since this age group has a need for entertainment, Ventures will provide a place where they can bring their dates, dance to the hottest music, watch the latest videos, and hang out with their friends.

The majority of these teens tend to listen to Top 40s music. According to the Aribtron Company, most of the people in the 12-24 age group in the St. Louis metropolitan area listen to either straight rhythm and blues or a mixture of Top 40s hits. To draw the most customers, Ventures will cater to Z107.7 listeners because the radio station plays a variety of Top 40s music, including rhythm and blues, pop, alternative, and rap. By playing these types of music, Ventures will appeal to a wider audience by allowing its customers to dance to various types of music without isolating any one particular type.

Teenage spending has steadily increased since 1953 and it will continue every year. Gale Research, Inc. has determined that teens average about $40.00 of disposable income a week. Out of this amount, teens spend about 15 percent, or $6.00, for entertainment and about 8 percent, or $3.20, on fast food. Based on this data, Ventures will charge an entrance fee of $5.00. Ventures will provide more entertainment options for a longer period of time than any other entertainment venue. Thus, Ventures needs to keep the entrance fee in accordance with the amount teens usually pay for this type of entertainment. Ventures will be able to make additional revenue on the drinks, snacks, and video games that they will provide.

While the $5.00 entrance fee is less than what the local movie theaters charge ($6.50), it is more than the cost of just hanging out at the local malls. By charging less than the movies, Ventures will become a less costly alternative that will provide heart-thumping entertainment for a longer period of time than a movie. And, although Ventures will cost more than the price of just hanging out at the malls, it will nonetheless be an attractive alternative: it will allow teens the opportunity to dance to base-thumping music, listen to the hottest musical artists, watch the most popular videos, play the most exciting videos games, and visit their favorite DJ during live radio remotes.

Teenage Research Unlimited did a study in 1996 in which they surveyed teens, asking what makes places/brands cool to them and where do they learn trends. In answering the question, the teens reported the following (in part):

- 47 percent stated if it's for people of my age
- 39 percent stated advertising
- 24 percent stated if cool friends or peers use it
- 18 percent stated if it's a new place/brand.

In answering the question, "Where do teens learn trends?," the teens reported the following (in part):

- 47 percent stated friends
- 21 percent stated myself
- 14 percent stated advertising
- 13 percent stated "coolest" people in school
- 9 percent stated DJ (radio)
- 6 percent stated celebrities

In keeping with the above data, Ventures plans to advertise in the following ways. First, as any new nightclub would do, Ventures plans to have a huge grand opening celebration. Ventures will reach its target market by placing radio ads on Z107.7. In addition to ads, this station will also do lives remotes for the grand opening and on weekends. The radio station will also give away free passes for each of their radio spots, including the grand opening. This will be the most

**Pricing and Advertising**

expensive form of advertising that Ventures will employ. Ventures advertising budget will be 15 percent of its monthly revenue. The radio ads will cost an average of $140 each, depending on the time slot. The live remotes will cost about $2,500. This cost includes two live "call-ins" per hour, 8-10 exclusive promotional announcement slots to begin airing three days prior to appearance, giveaways, the services of the on-air DJ, promotional banners, and the radio station's van. These live remotes will generally occur about 3-4 times a month. This may seem like a lot; however, several alcohol clubs hold these types of live remotes every weekend. Also, once the radio station establishes that you will advertise with them, the cost of these live remotes drops substantially. Plus, these live remotes draw large crowds because customers can hang out with their favorite DJ, while receiving free giveaways or concert tickets.

Secondly, in order to increase revenue during the week, Ventures plans to pre-sell these nights to the local radio stations, soft drink bottlers, and clothing manufacturers. These companies will sponsor a night in order to reach its target market and thus build Ventures' audience base. This will guarantee cash flow. For example, Pepsi might sponsor a night where people are invited to participate in an indoor triathlon. The first 100 get in free; contest entrants get Pepsi t-shirts; other club-goers win free Pepsi drinks, trophies, and other such prizes. Pepsi supplies everything and Ventures only supplies the use of the building.

Finally, Ventures will set up a panel of "experts." This panel will consist of teens within Ventures' target market. Ventures will announce a contest on Z107.7 in which they will have a chance to be one of the teen experts for the new club Ventures. Ventures will use this panel to pass out flyers and to advise on choosing decorations, special events, and contests. These experts will receive a Ventures employee shirt, free passes, and discount on special event prices. The flyers' cost will be included in the advertising budget for Ventures.

## Competitors

Ventures considers any goods or services that teens would rather spend their money on for entertainment purposes as our competition. At the same time, Ventures also feels that we have no direct competition because no type of nightclub that caters to teens is currently in operation in our target area. Our indirect competitors consist of the following: several movie theaters, a monthly D.A.R.E. dance, several alcohol bars, and any "free" hangout spots such parking lots and parks within our target radius.

Mediamark Research Inc. conducted a survey on teen spending on entertainment and leisure. The teens reported that, in the past 90 days, 85 percent of them attended a movie in the following time frame:

- 8 percent attended once a week
- 25 percent attended 2-3 times a month
- 23 percent attended once a month
- 28 percent attended less than once a month

If this sample holds true, then Ventures would suffer little competition from the movie theater because only a small percentage of kids attend the movies on a regular basis because of the general lack of entertainment options that movie theaters supply. Teens usually receive an allowance from their parents and, in general, look for ways to make the allowance go further. Ventures will provide more entertainment options for a longer period of time. Ventures customers can dance to base-thumping dance music, watch the hottest videos on several monitors throughout the building, play the latest video games, or just sit and socialize with their friends.

D.A.R.E. holds a monthly dance for the local teens. These dances only occur once a month during the school year. D.A.R.E. holds no summer activities. However, Ventures will contact

D.A.R.E. to see if they would like to hold their monthly dance at Ventures. This way they will have no overhead and Ventures will be able to maintain revenue.

Ventures anticipates that the alcohol bars will try to copy its concept by having all age nights or teen nights. Some of Ventures target market will undoubtedly attend these nights at first just to experience the new atmosphere. Also, Ventures does not anticipate the bars converting since they make most their money by serving alcohol, especially on the weekends. During this period of change, Ventures plans to institute the following new concepts and ideas in which to retain the customers that it has:

- Talent shows
- Battle of the local high school bands competitions
- Cheerleading competitions
- Performances by local teen bands
- Promotions and contests for gift certificates and makeovers

As for the "free" hangout spots, Ventures will have a hard time competing with them since Ventures will charge an entrance fee. However, Ventures can strive to make its establishment "the" place to be and thus making it the place to be seen. By implementing the above advertising campaigns, Ventures will let its customers know that it's a great place to socialize with friends and also they will have great music playing in the background.

## MANAGEMENT

Mary Jensen, along with an experienced manager, will initially manage the club. Ms. Jensen is currently learning the field of bar management from an established bar manager with seven years of experience, as well as building a library of books on bar management. She has nine years of experience with teens in her work as a teacher and a tutor. She has also volunteered in the past with youth organizations such as Matthew Dicky. Once Ventures is up and running, a full-time manager and a part-time assistant manager will take over the day-to-day operations. This manager will be experienced in running a nightclub and supervising employees.

## ACCOUNTING

Ventures will have a primarily cash business. Ventures will have basic cash registers and will collect the drawers at random times. This will keep theft by employees low and will hold each employee accountable. After collecting the drawers, either the owner or manager will fill out an accountability sheet. This sheet will list the employee's name, total receipts turned in, server's cash, amount in credit cards (if applicable), manager's adjustments, and whether the drawer is over or short. This will be checked against the register's tape to determine the above amounts.

## RISKS

Teen clubs tend to suffer some risks. First, situations could occur involving patrons fighting. Ventures' goal is to prevent this type of occurrence by employing security and having these individuals pat down customers and lock up bags and coats. If such occurrences should happen, though, then it will be the bouncers' job to break up the fight, escort the fighting customer from the premises, and, if needed, call the police for assistance. Fighting inevitably occurs in clubs, and thus the public will not generally be alarmed. Ventures will just follow the above procedure to make it known that it will not tolerate such behavior.

Finally, Ventures could be closed down by the police for some drug or alcohol violation. If this occurs, Ventures will shut down and reopen under a new name. Ventures will simply change its name and form a new limited liability company. Under a new name, Ventures can continue to make revenue, profits, and continue to pay back loan monies.

**FINANCIALS**

### Start-up and Loan Information

| | |
|---|---|
| Construction/Bar renovations | $20,000 |
| Furniture | $16,000 |
| Video, lighting, stereo equipment | $35,000 |
| Advertising | $4,000 |
| First Month Rent | $5,334 |
| Phone | $150 |
| Insurance | $1,223 |
| Building Permit | $50 |
| Pretzel Machine | $200 |
| Nacho Machine | $175 |
| Popcorn Machine | $300 |
| Snacks | $1,000 |
| Ice Cream/Milk | $1,000 |
| Sodas Dispenser | $0 |
| Soda Products | $330 |
| Ice Machine | $200 |
| Freezer | $1,165 |
| Paper and Disposable Products | $700 |
| Shake Mixer | $2,000 |
| Business License | $15 |
| Video Games | $0 |
| Working Capital | $30,000 |
| **Total** | **$118,842** |
| Owners' Contribution | $0 |

### Operating Budget

| | Year 1 | Year 2 |
|---|---|---|
| Rent | $6,400 | $6,400 |
| Salaries | $36,360 - $167,400 | $41,400 - $192,600 |
| Social Security Tax | $5,406 - $17,708 | $5,437 - $192,600 |
| Phone | $1,800 | $1,800 |
| Paper and Disposables | $6,000 | $6,000 |
| Insurance | | |
|     Worker's Comp | $1,182 - $5,441 | $1,346 - $6,260 |
|     Liability | $1,273 - $5,859 | $1,449 - $6,741 |
| Electric | $48,000 | $48,000 |
| Water | $9,600 | $9,600 |
| Office Supplies | $3,000 | $3,000 |
| Advertising/Promotions | $29,088 - $133,920 | $33,120 - $154,080 |
| Radio Personality | $7,200 | $7,200 |
| Theft Replacement | $1,212 - $5,580 | $1,380 - $6,420 |
| Ice Machine | $2,400 | $2,400 |
| Exterminating Expense | $528 | $528 |
| Recorded Music Fees | $4,500 | $4,500 |

## Construction Costs

This is an estimate for renovations and bar constructions. This price is based on bulk buying and sweat equity.

## Bar Furniture

This includes point of sale equipment, shelves, and furniture. This price is based on bulk buying and sweat equity.

## Video, Lighting, and Stereo Equipment

This is an estimate for lighting, video, and stereo equipment, electrical modifications, and signs.

## Advertising

This includes promotional advertising (grand opening expenses including radio spots, passes given away on the radio and by the staff, and flyers).

## First Month Rent

Based on $8.00 x 8,000 square feet per 12 months.

## Phone

Estimate from GTE.

## Insurance

This is just the content insurance. The worker's compensation and liability will be on the income statement since they are based on salaries and revenue.

## Building Permit

Estimate from Rockville City Hall

## Pretzel, Nacho, and Popcorn Machines

This is from Bates Restaurant and Bar Supply.

## Snacks

This is an estimate for the Nacho chips, popcorn, and pretzel retail. Wholesale will be much lower once I find a vendor.

## Ice Cream and Milk

This is an estimate for ice cream and milk for the shakes. I haven't determined the exact menu yet so it will be difficult to determine how much I will need. So I just based this amount on a large quantity.

## Soda Dispenser and Products

This is an estimate from Coke and Pepsi. Sodas will range from $35-55 for five gallons and water and juice will range about $55.00 for five gallons. The company will run the lines for free if you buy their products.

## Ice Machine

This is an estimate for leasing an ice machine from Fowlers Leasing Company.

## Freezer

This is from Bates Restaurant and Bar Supply.

## Paper and Disposable Products

This is an estimate for napkins, toilet tissues, hand towels, and for two different sizes of plastic cups (one for sodas/drinks and one for shakes).

**Shake Mixer**

This is from Bates Restaurant and Bar Supply.

**Business License**

Rockville City Hall

**Video Games**

BFC, in Brentwood, stated that they deliver and maintain the games while the company provided the security/space and they split the cash boxes 50/50. No deposit is required.

**Owner's contribution**

The owners are planning on applying for a veteran's small business loan through the Small Business Administration once they have acquired 25 percent of the start of capital.

## Notes for Year One Operating Budget

The expenses listed below are based on the gross revenue of (low) $242,400, (med) $492,000, and (high) $1,116,000.

**Rent**

Based on $8.00 x 8,000 square feet per 12 months.

**Salaries**

Salaries were calculated at 15 percent of gross revenue.

**Social Security Tax**

Based on 7.6 percent of the above salaries.

**Phone**

Based on GTE phone service and it included making long distance calls with the county and target market since they are in 314, 636, and 573 area codes.

**Paper and Disposable Supplies**

Based on the cost of napkins, toilet tissues, hand towels, and disposable cups. This is an average from several Internet sites specializing in these goods.

**Insurance**

1. Worker's Comp insurance is based on $3.25 per hundred dollars of salaries.
2. Liability insurance is based on $5.25 per thousand of gross revenue.
3. Content insurance is $1,223 per year. This year's content insurance was paid out of the start-up costs. These figures were supplied by Martin Labors Insurance Company located in Rockville, Missouri.

**Electric and Water**

Based on an average of usage.

**Office Supplies**

An average based on the use of register tape, paper, ink, and order slips.

**Advertising/Promotions**

Calculated at 12 percent of gross revenue. This will pay for flyers, radio ads, and live radio remotes.

**Radio Personality**

Based on 2 monthly appearances at $300.00 each.

### Theft Replacement

Calculated at .5 percent of total gross revenue. This will pay to replace items such as menus, decorations, and other damaged or missing items.

### Ice Machine

This is an estimate for leasing an ice machine from Fowlers Leasing Company.

### Exterminating Expense

This is based on exterminating for pests every other month at the cost of $88.

### Recorded Music Fees

These fees are for the playing of recorded music. This will average about $4,500 a year.

The expenses listed below are based on the gross revenue of (low) $276,400, (med) $564,000, and (high) $1,284,000.

**Notes for Year Two Operating Budget**

### Rent

Based on $8.00 x 8,000 square feet per 12 months.

### Salaries

Salaries were calculated at 15 percent of gross revenue.

### Social Security Tax

Based on 7.6 percent of the above salaries.

### Phone

Based on GTE phone service and it included making long distance calls with the county and target market since they are in 314, 636, and 573 area codes.

### Paper and Disposable Supplies

Based on the cost of napkins, toilet tissues, hand towels, and disposable cups. This is an average from several Internet sites specializing in these goods.

### Insurance

1. Worker's Comp insurance is based on $3.25 per hundred dollars of salaries.
2. Liability insurance is based on $5.25 per thousand of gross revenue.
3. Content insurance is $1,223 per year. This year's content insurance was paid out of the start-up costs. These figures were supplied by Martin Labors Insurance Company located in Rockville, Missouri.

### Electric and Water

Based on an average of usage.

### Office Supplies

An average based on the use of register tape, paper, ink, and order slips.

### Advertising/Promotions

Calculated at 12 percent of gross revenue. This will pay for flyers, radio ads, and live radio remotes.

### Radio Personality

Based on 2 monthly appearances at $300.00 each.

### Theft Replacement

Calculated at .5 percent of total gross revenue. This will pay to replace items such as menus, decorations, and other damaged or missing items.

### Ice Machine

This is an estimate for leasing an ice machine from Fowlers Leasing Company.

**Exterminating Expense**

This is based on exterminating for pests every other month at the cost of $88.

**Recorded Music Fees**

These fees are for the playing of recorded music. This will average about $4,500 a year.

# Appendix A - Business Plan Template

# Business Plan Template

## USING THIS TEMPLATE

A business plan carefully spells out a company's projected course of action over a period of time, usually the first two to three years after the start-up. In addition, banks, lenders, and other investors examine the information and financial documentation before deciding whether or not to finance a new business venture. Therefore, a business plan is an essential tool in obtaining financing and should describe the business itself in detail as well as all important factors influencing the company, including the market, industry, competition, operations and management policies, problem solving strategies, financial resources and needs, and other vital information. The plan enables the business owner to anticipate costs, plan for difficulties, and take advantage of opportunities, as well as design and implement strategies that keep the company running as smoothly as possible.

This template has been provided as a model to help you construct your own business plan. Please keep in mind that there is no single acceptable format for a business plan, and that this template is in no way comprehensive, but serves as an example.

The business plans provided in this section are fictional and have been used by small business agencies as models for clients to use in compiling their own business plans.

## GENERIC BUSINESS PLAN

Main headings included below are topics that should be covered in a comprehensive business plan. They include:

### Business Summary

**Purpose**
Provides a brief overview of your business, succinctly highlighting the main ideas of your plan.

**Includes**

- ○ Name and Type of Business
- ○ Description of Product/Service
- ○ Business History and Development
- ○ Location
- ○ Market
- ○ Competition
- ○ Management
- ○ Financial Information
- ○ Business Strengths and Weaknesses
- ○ Business Growth

## Table of Contents

**Purpose**

Organized in an Outline Format, the Table of Contents illustrates the selection and arrangement of information contained in your plan.

**Includes**

- ◯ Topic Headings and Subheadings
- ◯ Page Number References

## Business History and Industry Outlook

**Purpose**

Examines the conception and subsequent development of your business within an industry specific context.

**Includes**

- ◯ Start-up Information
- ◯ Owner/Key Personnel Experience
- ◯ Location
- ◯ Development Problems and Solutions
- ◯ Investment/Funding Information
- ◯ Future Plans and Goals
- ◯ Market Trends and Statistics
- ◯ Major Competitors
- ◯ Product/Service Advantages
- ◯ National, Regional, and Local Economic Impact

## Product/Service

**Purpose**

Introduces, defines, and details the product and/or service that inspired the information of your business.

**Includes**

- ◯ Unique Features
- ◯ Niche Served
- ◯ Market Comparison
- ◯ Stage of Product/Service Development
- ◯ Production
- ◯ Facilities, Equipment, and Labor
- ◯ Financial Requirements
- ◯ Product/Service Life Cycle
- ◯ Future Growth

## Market Examination

**Purpose**

Assessment of product/service applications in relation to consumer buying cycles.

**Includes**

- Target Market
- Consumer Buying Habits
- Product/Service Applications
- Consumer Reactions
- Market Factors and Trends
- Penetration of the Market
- Market Share
- Research and Studies
- Cost
- Sales Volume and Goals

## Competition

**Purpose**

Analysis of Competitors in the Marketplace.

**Includes**

- Competitor Information
- Product/Service Comparison
- Market Niche
- Product/Service Strengths and Weaknesses
- Future Product/Service Development

## Marketing

**Purpose**

Identifies promotion and sales strategies for your product/service.

**Includes**

- Product/Service Sales Appeal
- Special and Unique Features
- Identification of Customers
- Sales and Marketing Staff
- Sales Cycles
- Type of Advertising/Promotion
- Pricing
- Competition
- Customer Services

## Operations

**Purpose**

Traces product/service development from production/inception to the market environment.

**Includes**

- Cost Effective Production Methods
- Facility
- Location
- Equipment
- Labor
- Future Expansion

## Administration and Management

**Purpose**

Offers a statement of your management philosophy with an in-depth focus on processes and procedures.

**Includes**

- Management Philosophy
- Structure of Organization
- Reporting System
- Methods of Communication
- Employee Skills and Training
- Employee Needs and Compensation
- Work Environment
- Management Policies and Procedures
- Roles and Responsibilities

## Key Personnel

**Purpose**

Describes the unique backgrounds of principle employees involved in business.

**Includes**

- Owner(s)/Employee Education and Experience
- Positions and Roles
- Benefits and Salary
- Duties and Responsibilities
- Objectives and Goals

## Potential Problems and Solutions

### Purpose
Discussion of problem solving strategies that change issues into opportunities.

### Includes
○Risks
○Litigation
○Future Competition
○Economic Impact
○Problem Solving Skills

## Financial Information

### Purpose
Secures needed funding and assistance through worksheets and projections detailing financial plans, methods of re-payment, and future growth opportunities.

### Includes
○Financial Statements
○Bank Loans
○Methods of Repayment
○Tax Returns
○Start-up Costs
○Projected Income (3 years)
○Projected Cash Flow (3 Years)
○Projected Balance Statements (3 years)

## Appendices

### Purpose
Supporting documents used to enhance your business proposal.

### Includes
○Photographs of product, equipment, facilities, etc.
○Copyright/Trademark Documents
○Legal Agreements
○Marketing Materials
○Research and or Studies
○Operation Schedules
○Organizational Charts
○Job Descriptions
○Resumes
○Additional Financial Documentation

# Food Distributor

FICTIONAL BUSINESS PLAN

## COMMERCIAL FOODS, INC.

*3003 Avondale Ave.*
*Knoxville, TN 37920*

*October 31, 1992*

*This plan demonstrates how a partnership can have a positive impact on a new business. It demonstrates how two individuals can carve a niche in the specialty foods market by offering gourmet foods to upscale restaurants and fine hotels. This plan is fictional and has not been used to gain funding from a bank or other lending institution.*

- STATEMENT OF PURPOSE

- DESCRIPTION OF THE BUSINESS

- MANAGEMENT

- PERSONNEL

- LOCATION

- PRODUCTS AND SERVICES

- THE MARKET

- COMPETITION

- SUMMARY

- INCOME STATEMENT

- FINANCIAL STATEMENTS

# FOOD DISTRIBUTOR
# BUSINESS PLAN

**STATEMENT OF
PURPOSE**

Commercial Foods, Inc. seeks a loan of $75,000 to establish a new business. This sum, together with $5,000 equity investment by the principals, will be used as follows:

| | |
|---|---|
| Merchandise inventory | $25,000 |
| Office fixture/equipment | 12,000 |
| Warehouse equipment | 14,000 |
| One delivery truck | 10,000 |
| Working capital | 39,000 |
| **Total** | **$100,000** |

**DESCRIPTION OF
THE BUSINESS**

Commercial Foods, Inc. will be a distributor of specialty food service products to hotels and upscale restaurants in the geographical area of a 50 mile radius of Knoxville. Richard Roberts will direct the sales effort and John Williams will manage the warehouse operation and the office. One delivery truck will be used initially with a second truck added in the third year.

We expect to begin operation of the business within 30 days after securing the requested financing.

**MANAGEMENT**

A. Richard Roberts is a native of Memphis, Tennessee. He is a graduate of Memphis State University with a Bachelor's degree from the School of Business. After graduation, he worked for a major manufacturer of specialty food service products as a detail sales person for five years, and, for the past three years, he has served as a product sales manager for this firm.

B. John Williams is a native of Nashville, Tennessee. He holds a B.S. Degree in Food Technology from the University of Tennessee. His career includes five years as a product development chemist in gourmet food products and five years as operations manager for a food service distributor.

Both men are healthy and energetic. Their backgrounds complement each other, which will ensure the success of Commercial Foods, Inc. They will set policies together and personnel decisions will be made jointly. Initial salaries for the owners will be $1,000 per month for the first few years. The spouses of both principals are successful in the business world and earn enough to support the families.

They have engaged the services of Foster Jones, CPA, and William Hale, Attorney, to assist them in an advisory capacity.

**PERSONNEL**

The firm will employ one delivery truck driver at a wage of $8.00 per hour. One office worker will be employed at $7.50 per hour. One part-time employee will be used in the office at $5.00 per hour. The driver will load and unload his own trucks. Mr. Williams will assist in the warehouse operation as needed to assist one stock person at $7.00 per hour. An additional delivery truck and driver will be added the third year.

**LOCATION**

The firm will lease a 20,000 square foot building at 3003 Avondale Ave., in Knoxville, which contains warehouse and office areas equipped with two-door truck docks. The annual rental is $9,000. The building was previously used as a food service warehouse and very little modification to the building will be required.

The firm will offer specialty food service products such as soup bases, dessert mixes, sauce bases, pastry mixes, spices, and flavors, normally used by upscale restaurants and nice hotels. We are going after a niche in the market with high quality gourmet products. There is much less competition in this market than in standard run of the mill food service products. Through their work experiences, the principals have contacts with supply sources and with local chefs.

**PRODUCTS AND SERVICES**

We know from our market survey that there are over 200 hotels and upscale restaurants in the area we plan to serve. Customers will be attracted by a direct sales approach. We will offer samples of our products and product application data on use of our products in the finished prepared foods. We will cultivate the chefs in these establishments. The technical background of John Williams will be especially useful here.

**THE MARKET**

We find that we will be only distributor in the area offering a full line of gourmet food service products. Other foodservice distributors offer only a few such items in conjunction with their standard product line. Our survey shows that many of the chefs are ordering products from Atlanta and Memphis because of a lack of adequate local supply.

**COMPETITION**

Commercial Foods, Inc. will be established as a foodservice distributor of specialty food in Knoxville. The principals, with excellent experience in the industry, are seeking a $75,000 loan to establish the business. The principals are investing $25,000 as equity capital.

**SUMMARY**

The business will be set up as an "S" Corporation with each principal owning 50% of the common stock in the corporation.

Attached is a three year pro forma income statement we believe to be conservative. Also attached are personal financial statements of the principals and a projected cash flow statement for the first year.

|                          | 1st Year | 2nd Year | 3rd Year |
|--------------------------|----------|----------|----------|
| Gross Sales              | 300,000  | 400,000  | 500,000  |
| Less Allowances          | 1,000    | 1,000    | 2,000    |
| Net Sales                | 299,000  | 399,000  | 498,000  |
| Cost of Goods Sold       | 179,400  | 239,400  | 298,800  |
| Gross Margin             | 119,600  | 159,600  | 199,200  |
| **Operating Expenses**   |          |          |          |
| Utilities                | 1,200    | 1,500    | 1,700    |
| Salaries                 | 76,000   | 79,000   | 102,000  |
| Payroll Taxes/Benefits   | 9,100    | 9,500    | 13,200   |
| Advertising              | 3,000    | 4,500    | 5,000    |
| Office Supplies          | 1,500    | 2,000    | 2,500    |
| Insurance                | 1,200    | 1,500    | 1,800    |
| Maintenance              | 1,000    | 1,500    | 2,000    |
| Outside Services         | 3,000    | 3,000    | 3,000    |
| Whse Supplies/Trucks     | 6,000    | 7,000    | 10,000   |
| Telephone                | 900      | 1,000    | 1,200    |
| Rent                     | 9,000    | 9,500    | 9,900    |
| Depreciation             | 2,500    | 2,000    | 3,000    |
| **Total Expenses**       | 114,400  | 122,000  | 155,300  |
| **Other Expenses**       |          |          |          |
| Bank Loan Payment        | 15,000   | 15,000   | 15,000   |
| Bank Loan Interest       | 6,000    | 5,000    | 4,000    |
| **Total Expenses**       | **120,400** | **142,000** | **174,300** |
| **Net Profit (Loss)**    | **(800)** | **17,600** | **24,900** |

**PRO FORMA INCOME STATEMENT**

**FINANCIAL STATEMENT I**

| Assets | | Liabilities | |
|---|---|---|---|
| Cash | 15,000 | | |
| 1991 Olds | 11,000 | Unpaid Balance | 8,000 |
| Residence | 140,000 | Mortgage | 105,000 |
| Mutual Funds | 12,000 | Credit Cards | 500 |
| Furniture | 5,000 | Note Payable | 4,000 |
| Merck Stock | 10,000 | | |
| | 182,200 | | 117,500 |
| **Net Worth** | | | **64,700** |
| | **182,200** | | **182,200** |

**FINANCIAL STATEMENT II**

| Assets | | Liabilities | |
|---|---|---|---|
| Cash | 5,000 | | |
| 1992 Buick Auto | 15,000 | Unpaid Balance | 12,000 |
| Residence | 120,000 | Mortgage | 100,000 |
| U.S. Treasury Bonds | 5,000 | Credit Cards | 500 |
| Home Furniture | 4,000 | Note Payable | 2,500 |
| AT&T Stock | 3,000 | | |
| | 147,000 | | 115,000 |
| **Net Worth** | | | **32,000** |
| | **147,000** | | **147,000** |

# Hardware Store

FICTIONAL BUSINESS PLAN

## OSHKOSH HARDWARE, INC.

*123 Main St.*
*Oshkosh, WI 54901*

*June 1994*

*The following plan outlines how a small hardware store can survive competition from large discount chains by offering products and providing expert advice in the use of any product it sells. This plan is fictional and has not been used to gain funding from a bank or other lending institution.*

- EXECUTIVE SUMMARY

- THE BUSINESS

- THE MARKET

- SALES

- MANAGEMENT

- GOALS IMPLEMENTATION

- FINANCE

- JOB DESCRIPTION-GENERAL MANAGER

- QUARTERLY FORECASTED BALANCE SHEETS

- QUARTERLY FORECASTED STATEMENTS OF EARNINGS AND RETAINED EARNINGS

- QUARTERLY FORECASTED STATEMENTS OF CHANGES IN FINANCIAL POSITION

- FINANCIAL RATIO ANALYSIS

- DETAILS FOR QUARTERLY STATEMENTS OF EARNINGS

## EXECUTIVE SUMMARY

Oshkosh Hardware, Inc. is a new corporation that is going to establish a retail hardware store in a strip mall in Oshkosh, Wisconsin. The store will sell hardware of all kinds, quality tools, paint, and housewares. The business will make revenue and a profit by servicing its customers not only with needed hardware but also with expert advice in the use of any product it sells.

Oshkosh Hardware, Inc. will be operated by its sole shareholder, James Smith. The company will have a total of four employees. It will sell its products in the local market. Customers will buy our products because we will provide free advice on the use of all of our products and will also furnish a full refund warranty.

Oshkosh Hardware, Inc. will sell its products in the Oshkosh store staffed by three sales representatives. No additional employees will be needed to achieve its short and long range goals. The primary short range goal is to open the store by October 1, 1994. In order to achieve this goal a lease must be signed by July 1, 1994 and the complete inventory ordered by August 1, 1994.

Mr. James Smith will invest $30,000 in the business. In addition, the company will have to borrow $150,000 during the first year to cover the investment in inventory, accounts receivable, and furniture and equipment. The company will be profitable after six months of operation and should be able to start repayment of the loan in the second year.

## THE BUSINESS

The business will sell hardware of all kinds, quality tools, paint, and housewares. We will purchase our products from three large wholesale buying groups.

In general our customers are homeowners who do their own repair and maintenance, hobbyists, and housewives. Our business is unique in that we will have a complete line of all hardware items and will be able to get special orders by overnight delivery. The business makes revenue and profits by servicing our customers not only with needed hardware but also with expert advice in the use of any product we sell. Our major costs for bringing our products to market are cost of merchandise of 36%, salaries of $45,000, and occupancy costs of $60,000.

Oshkosh Hardware, Inc.'s retail outlet will be located at 1524 Frontage Road, which is in a newly developed retail center of Oshkosh. Our location helps facilitate accessibility from all parts of town and reduces our delivery costs. The store will occupy 7500 square feet of space. The major equipment involved in our business is counters and shelving, a computer, a paint mixing machine, and a truck.

## THE MARKET

Oshkosh Hardware, Inc. will operate in the local market. There are 15,000 potential customers in this market area. We have three competitors who control approximately 98% of the market at present. We feel we can capture 25% of the market within the next four years. Our major reason for believing this is that our staff is technically competent to advise our customers in the correct use of all products we sell.

After a careful market analysis, we have determined that approximately 60% of our customers are men and 40% are women. The percentage of customers that fall into the following age categories are:

|          |     |
|----------|-----|
| Under 16: | 0%  |
| 17-21:   | 5%  |
| 22-30:   | 30% |
| 31-40:   | 30% |

| 41-50: | 20% |
| 51-60: | 10% |
| 61-70: | 5% |
| Over 70: | 0% |

The reasons our customers prefer our products is our complete knowledge of their use and our full refund warranty.

We get our information about what products our customers want by talking to existing customers. There seems to be an increasing demand for our product. The demand for our product is increasing in size based on the change in population characteristics.

**SALES**

At Oshkosh Hardware, Inc. we will employ three sales people and will not need any additional personnel to achieve our sales goals. These salespeople will need several years experience in home repair and power tool usage. We expect to attract 30% of our customers from newspaper ads, 5% of our customers from local directories, 5% of our customers from the yellow pages, 10% of our customers from family and friends, and 50% of our customers from current customers. The most cost effect source will be current customers. In general our industry is growing.

**MANAGEMENT**

We would evaluate the quality of our management staff as being excellent. Our manager is experienced and very motivated to achieve the various sales and quality assurance objectives we have set. We will use a management information system that produces key inventory, quality assurance, and sales data on a weekly basis. All data is compared to previously established goals for that week, and deviations are the primary focus of the management staff.

**GOALS**
**IMPLEMENTATION**

The short term goals of our business are:

1. Open the store by October 1, 1994
2. Reach our breakeven point in two months
3. Have sales of $100,000 in the first six months

In order to achieve our first short term goal we must:

1. Sign the lease by July 1, 1994
2. Order a complete inventory by August 1, 1994

In order to achieve our second short term goal we must:

1. Advertise extensively in Sept. and Oct.
2. Keep expenses to a minimum

In order to achieve our third short term goal we must:

1. Promote power tool sales for the Christmas season
2. Keep good customer traffic in Jan. and Feb.

The long term goals for our business are:

1. Obtain sales volume of $600,000 in three years
2. Become the largest hardware dealer in the city
3. Open a second store in Fond du Lac

The most important thing we must do in order to achieve the long term goals for our business is to develop a highly profitable business with excellent cash flow.

**FINANCE**

Oshkosh Hardware, Inc. Faces some potential threats or risks to our business. They are discount house competition. We believe we can avoid or compensate for this by providing quality products complimented by quality advice on the use of every product we sell. The financial projections we have prepared are located at the end of this document.

**JOB DESCRIPTION: GENERAL MANAGER**

The General Manager of the business of the corporation will be the president of the corporation. He will be responsible for the complete operation of the retail hardware store which is owned by the corporation. A detailed description of his duties and responsibilities is as follows:

Train and supervise the three sales people. Develop programs to motivate and compensate these employees. Coordinate advertising and sales promotion effects to achieve sales totals as outlined in budget. Oversee purchasing function and inventory control procedures to insure adequate merchandise at all times at a reasonable cost.

**Sales Finance**

Prepare monthly and annual budgets. Secure adequate line of credit from local banks. Supervise office personnel to insure timely preparation of records, statements, all government reports, control of receivables and payables, and monthly financial statements.

**Administration**

Perform duties as required in the areas of personnel, building leasing and maintenance, licenses and permits, and public relations.

**QUARTERLY FORECASTED BALANCE SHEETS**

| | Beg. Bal. | 1st Qtr | 2nd Qtr | 3rd Qtr | 4th Qtr |
|---|---|---|---|---|---|
| **Assets** | | | | | |
| Cash | 30,000 | 418 | (463) | (3,574) | 4,781 |
| Accounts Receivable | 0 | 20,000 | 13,333 | 33,333 | 33,333 |
| Inventory | 0 | 48,000 | 32,000 | 80,000 | 80,000 |
| Other Current Assets | 0 | 0 | 0 | 0 | 0 |
| Total Current Assets | 30,000 | 68,418 | 44,870 | 109,759 | 118,114 |
| Land | 0 | 0 | 0 | 0 | 0 |
| Building & Improvements | 0 | 0 | 0 | 0 | 0 |
| Furniture & Equipment | 0 | 75,000 | 75,000 | 75,000 | 75,000 |
| Total Fixed Assets | 0 | 75,000 | 75,000 | 75,000 | 75,000 |
| Less Accum. Depreciation | 0 | 1,875 | 3,750 | 5,625 | 7,500 |
| Net Fixed Assets | 0 | 73,125 | 71,250 | 69,375 | 67,500 |
| Intangible Assets | 0 | 0 | 0 | 0 | 0 |
| Less Amortization | 0 | 0 | 0 | 0 | 0 |
| Net Intangible Assets | 0 | 0 | 0 | 0 | 0 |
| Other Assets | 0 | 0 | 0 | 0 | 0 |
| **Total Assets** | **30,000** | **141,543** | **116,120** | **179,134** | **185,614** |

| | Beg. Bal. | 1st Qtr | 2nd Qtr | 3rd Qtr | 4th Qtr |
|---|---|---|---|---|---|
| **Liabilities and Shareholders' Equity** | | | | | |
| Short-Term Debt | 0 | 0 | 0 | 0 | 0 |
| Accounts Payable | 0 | 12,721 | 10,543 | 17,077 | 17,077 |
| Dividends Payable | 0 | 0 | 0 | 0 | 0 |
| Income Taxes Payable | 0 | (1,031) | (2,867) | (2,355) | (1,843) |
| Accrued Compensation | 0 | 1,867 | 1,867 | 1,867 | 1,867 |
| Other Current Liabilities | 0 | 0 | 0 | 0 | 0 |
| Total Current Liabilities | 0 | 13,557 | 9,543 | 16,589 | 17,101 |
| Long-Term Debt | 0 | 110,000 | 110,000 | 160,000 | 160,000 |
| Other Non-Current Liabilities | 0 | 0 | 0 | 0 | 0 |
| Total Liabilities | 0 | 123,557 | 119,543 | 176,589 | 177,101 |
| Common Stock | 30,000 | 30,000 | 30,000 | 30,000 | 30,000 |
| Retained Earnings | 0 | (12,014) | (33,423) | (27,455) | (21,487) |
| Shareholders' Equity | 30,000 | 17,986 | (3,423) | 2,545 | 8,513 |
| Total Liabilities & Shareholders' Equity | 30,000 | 141,543 | 116,120 | 179,134 | 185,614 |

| | Beg. Actual | 1st Qtr | 2nd Qtr | 3rd Qtr | 4th Qtr | Total |
|---|---|---|---|---|---|---|
| Total Sales | 0 | 60,000 | 40,000 | 100,000 | 100,000 | 300,000 |
| Goods/Services | 0 | 21,600 | 14,400 | 36,000 | 36,000 | 108,000 |
| Gross Profit | 0 | 38,400 | 25,600 | 64,000 | 64,000 | 192,000 |
| Operating Expenses | 0 | 47,645 | 45,045 | 52,845 | 52,845 | 198,380 |
| Fixed Expenses | | | | | | |
| Interest | 0 | 1,925 | 1,925 | 2,800 | 2,800 | 9,450 |
| Depreciation | 0 | 1,875 | 1,875 | 1,875 | 1,875 | 7,500 |
| Amortization | 0 | 0 | 0 | 0 | 0 | 0 |
| Total Fixed Expenses | 0 | 3,800 | 3,800 | 4,675 | 4,675 | 16,950 |
| Operating Profit (Loss) | 0 | (13,045) | (23,245) | 6,480 | 6,480 | (23,330) |

**BUSINESS PLAN TEMPLATE**

**QUARTERLY FORECASTED STATEMENTS OF EARNINGS AND RETAINED EARNINGS**

| | Beg. Actual | 1st Qtr | 2nd Qtr | 3rd Qtr | 4th Qtr | Total |
|---|---|---|---|---|---|---|
| Other Income (Expense) | 0 | 0 | 0 | 0 | 0 | 0 |
| Interest Income | 0 | 0 | 0 | 0 | 0 | 0 |
| Earnings (Loss) Before Taxes | 0 | (13,045) | (23,245) | 6,480 | 6,480 | (23,330) |
| Income Taxes | 0 | (1,031) | (1,836) | 512 | 512 | (1,843) |
| Net Earnings | 0 | (12,014) | (21,409) | 5,968 | 5,968 | (21,487) |
| Retained Earnings, Beginning | 0 | 0 | (12,014) | (33,423) | (27,455) | 0 |
| Less Dividends | 0 | 0 | 0 | 0 | 0 | 0 |
| Retained Earnings, Ending | 0 | (12,014) | (33,423) | (27,455) | (21,487) | (21,487) |

**QUARTERLY FORECASTED STATEMENTS OF CHANGES IN FINANCIAL POSITION**

| | Beg. Bal. | 1st Qtr | 2nd Qtr | 3rd Qtr | 4th Qtr | Total |
|---|---|---|---|---|---|---|
| *Sources (Uses) of Cash* | | | | | | |
| Net Earnings (Loss) | 0 | (12,014) | (21,409) | 5,968 | 5,968 | (21,487) |
| Depreciation & Amortization | 0 | 1,875 | 1,875 | 1,875 | 1,875 | 7,500 |
| Cash Provided by Operations | 0 | (10,139) | (19,534) | 7,834 | 7,834 | (13,987) |
| Dividends | 0 | 0 | 0 | 0 | 0 | 0 |
| *Cash Provided by (Used For) Changes in* | | | | | | |
| Accounts Receivable | 0 | (20,000) | 6,667 | (20,000) | 0 | (33,333) |
| Inventory | 0 | (48,000) | 16,000 | (48,000) | 0 | (80,000) |
| Other Current Assets | 0 | 0 | 0 | 0 | 0 | 0 |
| Accounts Payable | 0 | 12, | 721 | (2,178) | 6,534 0 | 17,077 |
| Income Taxes | 0 | (1,031) | (1,836) | 512 | 512 | (1,843) |
| Accrued Compensation | 0 | 1,867 | 0 | 0 | 0 | 1,867 |
| Dividends Payable | 0 | 0 | 0 | 0 | 0 | 0 |
| Other Current Liabilities | 0 | 0 | 0 | 0 | 0 | 0 |

| | Beg. Bal. | 1st Qtr | 2nd Qtr | 3rd Qtr | 4th Qtr | Total |
|---|---|---|---|---|---|---|
| Other Assets | 0 | 0 | 0 | 0 | 0 | 0 |
| **Net Cash Provided by (Used For)** | | | | | | |
| Operating Activities | 0 | (54,443) | 18,653 | (60,954) | 512 | (96,233) |
| *Investment Transactions* | | | | | | |
| Furniture & Equipment | 0 | (75,000) | 0 | 0 | 0 | (75,000) |
| Land | 0 | 0 | 0 | 0 | 0 | 0 |
| Building & Improvements | 0 | 0 | 0 | 0 | 0 | 0 |
| Intangible Assets | 0 | 0 | 0 | 0 | 0 | 0 |
| Net Cash from Investment Transactions | 0 | (75,000) | 0 | 0 | 0 | (75,000) |
| *Financing Transactions* | | | | | | |
| Short-Term Debt | 0 | 0 | 0 | 0 | 0 | 0 |
| Long-Term Debt | 0 | 110,000 | 0 | 50,000 | 0 | 160,000 |
| Other Non-Current Liabilities | 0 | 0 | 0 | 0 | 0 | 0 |
| Sale of Common Stock | 30,000 | 0 | 0 | 0 | 0 | 0 |
| Net Cash from Financing Transactions | 30,000 | 110,000 | 0 | 50,000 | 0 | 160,000 |
| Net Increase (Decrease) in Cash | 30,000 | (29,582) | (881) | (3,111) | 8,355 | (25,219) |
| Cash, Beginning of Period | 0 | 30,000 | 418 | (463) | (3,574) | 30,000 |
| Cash, End of Period | 30,000 | 418 | (463) | (3,574) | 4,781 | 4,781 |

## FINANCIAL RATIO ANALYSIS

| | Beg. Actual | 1st Qtr | 2nd Qtr | 3rd Qtr | 4th Qtr |
|---|---|---|---|---|---|
| **Overall Performance** | | | | | |
| Return on Equity | 0.00 | (66.80) | 625.45 | 234.50 | 70.10 |
| Return on Total Assets | 0.00 | (8.49) | (18.44) | 3.33 | 3.22 |
| Operating Return | 0.00 | (9.22) | (20.02) | 3.62 | 3.49 |
| | | | | | |
| **Profitability Measures** | | | | | |
| Gross Profit Percent | 0.00 | 64.00 | 64.00 | 64.00 | 64.00 |
| Profit Margin (AIT) | 0.00 | (20.02) | (53.52) | 5.97 | 5.97 |
| Operating Income per Share | 0.00 | 0.00 | 0.00 | 0.00 | 0.00 |
| Earnings per Share | 0.00 | 0.00 | 0.00 | 0.00 | 0.00 |
| | | | | | |
| **Test of Investment Utilization** | | | | | |
| Asset Turnover | 0.00 | 0.42 | 0.34 | 0.56 | 0.54 |
| Equity Turnover | 0.00 | 3.34 | (11.69) | 39.29 | 11.75 |
| Fixed Asset Turnover | 0.00 | 0.82 | 0.56 | 1.44 | 1.48 |
| Average Collection Period | 0.00 | 30.00 | 30.00 | 30.00 | 30.00 |
| Days Inventory | 0.00 | 200.00 | 200.00 | 200.00 | 200.00 |
| Inventory Turnover | 0.00 | 0.45 | 0.45 | 0.45 | 0.45 |
| Working Capital Turns | 0.00 | 1.09 | 1.13 | 1.07 | 0.99 |
| | | | | | |
| **Test of Financial Condition** | | | | | |
| Current Ratio | 0.00 | 5.05 | 4.70 | 6.62 | 6.91 |
| Quick Ratio | 0.00 | 1.51 | 1.35 | 1.79 | 2.23 |
| Working Capital Ratio | 1.00 | 0.43 | 0.33 | 0.57 | 0.60 |
| Dividend Payout | 0.00 | 0.00 | 0.00 | 0.00 | 0.00 |
| | | | | | |
| **Financial Leverage** | | | | | |
| Total Assets | 1.00 | 7.87 | (33.92) | 70.39 | 21.80 |

| | Beg. Actual | 1st Qtr | 2nd Qtr | 3rd Qtr | 4th Qtr |
|---|---|---|---|---|---|
| Debt/Equity | 0.00 | 6.87 | (34.92) | 69.39 | 20.80 |
| Debt to Total Assets | 0.00 | 0.87 | 1.03 | 0.99 | 0.95 |

**Year-End Equity History**

| | Beg. Actual | 1st Qtr | 2nd Qtr | 3rd Qtr | 4th Qtr |
|---|---|---|---|---|---|
| Shares Outstanding | 0 | 0 | 0 | 0 | 0 |
| Market Price per Share (@20x's earnings) | 0.00 | 0.00 | 0.00 | 0.00 | 0.00 |
| Book Value per Share | 0.00 | 0.00 | 0.00 | 0.00 | 0.00 |

**Altman Analysis Ratio**

| | Beg. Actual | 1st Qtr | 2nd Qtr | 3rd Qtr | 4th Qtr |
|---|---|---|---|---|---|
| 1.2x (1) | 1.20 | 0.47 | 0.37 | 0.62 | 0.65 |
| 1.4x (2) | 0.00 | (0.12) | (0.40) | (0.21) | (0.16) |
| 3.3x (3) | 0.00 | (0.35) | (0.72) | 0.07 | 0.07 |
| 0.6x (4) | 0.00 | 0.00 | 0.00 | 0.00 | 0.00 |
| 1.0x (5) | 0.00 | 0.42 | 0.34 | 0.56 | 0.54 |
| Z Value | 1.20 | .042 | (.041) | 1.04 | 1.10 |

**Sales**

**Dollars Sales Forecasted**

| | Beg. Act. | 1st Qtr | 2nd Qtr | 3rd Qtr | 4th Qtr | Total | %Sales | Fixed |
|---|---|---|---|---|---|---|---|---|
| Product 1 | 0 | 60,000 | 40,000 | 100,000 | 100,000 | 300,000 | | |
| Product 2 | 0 | 0 | 0 | 0 | 0 | 0 | | |
| Product 3 | 0 | 0 | 0 | 0 | 0 | 0 | | |
| Product 4 | 0 | 0 | 0 | 0 | 0 | 0 | | |
| Product 5 | 0 | 0 | 0 | 0 | 0 | 0 | | |
| Product 6 | 0 | 0 | 0 | 0 | 0 | 0 | | |
| Total Sales | 0 | 60,000 | 40,000 | 100,000 | 100,000 | 300,000 | | |

**DETAILS FOR QUARTERLY STATEMENTS OF EARNINGS**

**BUSINESS PLAN TEMPLATE**

**DETAILS FOR QUARTERLY STATEMENTS OF EARNINGS**

*...continued*

| | Beg. Act. | 1st Qtr | 2nd Qtr | 3rd Qtr | 4th Qtr | Total | %Sales | Fixed |
|---|---|---|---|---|---|---|---|---|
| Cost of Sales | | | | | | | | |
| Dollar Cost Forecasted | | | | | | | | |
| Product 1 | 0 | 21,600 | 14,400 | 36,000 | 36,000 | 108,000 | 36.00% | 0 |
| Product 2 | 0 | 0 | 0 | 0 | 0 | 0 | 0.00% | 0 |
| Product 3 | 0 | 0 | 0 | 0 | 0 | 0 | 0.00% | 0 |
| Product 4 | 0 | 0 | 0 | 0 | 0 | 0 | 0.00% | 0 |
| Product 5 | 0 | 0 | 0 | 0 | 0 | 0 | 0.00% | 0 |
| Product 6 | 0 | 0 | 0 | 0 | 0 | 0 | 0.00% | 0 |
| Total Cost of Sales | 0 | 21,600 | 14,400 | 36,000 | 36,000 | 108,000 | | |
| Operating Expenses | | | | | | | | |
| Payroll | 0 | 12,000 | 12,000 | 12,000 | 12,000 | 48,000 | 0.00% | 12,000 |
| Paroll Taxes | 0 | 950 | 950 | 950 | 950 | 3,800 | 0.00% | 950 |
| Advertising | 0 | 4,800 | 3,200 | 8,000 | 8,000 | 24,000 | 8.00% | 0 |
| Automobile Expenses | 0 | 0 | 0 | 0 | 0 | | 0.00% | 0 |
| Bad Debts | 0 | 0 | 0 | 0 | 0 | 0 | 0.00% | 0 |
| Commissions | 0 | 3,000 | 2,000 | 5,000 | 5,000 | 15,000 | 5.00% | 0 |
| Computer Rental | 0 | 1,200 | 1,200 | 1,200 | 1,200 | 4,800 | 0.00% | 1,200 |
| Computer Supplies | 0 | 220 | 220 | 220 | 220 | 880 | 0.00% | 220 |
| Computer Maintenance | 0 | 100 | 100 | 100 | 100 | 400 | 0.00% | 100 |
| Dealer Training | 0 | 1,000 | 1,000 | 1,000 | 1,000 | 4,000 | 0.00% | 1,000 |
| Electricity | 0 | 3,000 | 3,000 | 3,000 | 3,000 | 12,000 | 0.00% | 3,000 |
| Employment Ads and Fees | 0 | 0 | 0 | 0 | 0 | 0 | 0.00% | 0 |
| Entertainment: Business | 0 | 1,500 | 1,500 | 1,500 | 1,500 | 6,000 | 0.00% | 1,500 |
| General Insurance | 0 | 800 | 800 | 800 | 800 | 32,000 | 0.00% | 800 |
| Health & W/C Insurance | 0 | 0 | 0 | 0 | 0 | 0 | 0.00% | 0 |
| Interest: LT Debt | 0 | 2,500 | 2,500 | 2,500 | 2,500 | 10,000 | 0.00% | 2,500 |
| Legal & Accounting | 0 | 1,500 | 1,500 | 1,500 | 1,500 | 6,000 | 0.00% | 1,500 |
| Maintenance & Repairs | 0 | 460 | 460 | 460 | 460 | 1,840 | 0.00% | 460 |

| | Beg. Act. | 1st Qtr | 2nd Qtr | 3rd Qtr | 4th Qtr | Total | %Sales | Fixed |
|---|---|---|---|---|---|---|---|---|
| Office Supplies | 0 | 270 | 270 | 270 | 270 | 1,080 | 0.00% | 270 |
| Postage | 0 | 85 | 85 | 85 | 85 | 340 | 0.00% | 85 |
| Prof. Development | 0 | 0 | 0 | 0 | 0 | 0 | 0.00% | 0 |
| Professional Fees | 0 | 1,000 | 1,000 | 1,000 | 1,000 | 4,000 | 0.00% | 1,000 |
| Rent | 0 | 8,000 | 8,000 | 8,000 | 8,000 | 2,000 | 0.00% | 8,000 |
| Shows & Conferences | 0 | 0 | 0 | 0 | 0 | 0 | 0.00% | 0 |
| Subscriptions & Dues | 0 | 285 | 285 | 285 | 285 | 1,140 | 0.00% | 285 |
| Telephone | 0 | 1,225 | 1,225 | 1,225 | 1,225 | 4,900 | 0.00% | 1,225 |
| Temporary Employees | 0 | 0 | 0 | 0 | 0 | 0 | 0.00% | 0 |
| Travel Expenses | 0 | 750 | 750 | 750 | 750 | 3,000 | 0.00% | 750 |
| Utilities | 0 | 3,000 | 3,000 | 3,000 | 3,000 | 12,000 | 0.00% | 3,000 |
| Research & Development | 0 | 0 | 0 | 0 | 0 | 0 | 0.00% | 0 |
| Royalties | 0 | 0 | 0 | 0 | 0 | 0 | 0.00% | 0 |
| Other 1 | 0 | 0 | 0 | 0 | 0 | 0 | 0.00% | 0 |
| Other 2 | 0 | 0 | 0 | 0 | 0 | 0 | 0.00% | 0 |
| Other 3 | 0 | 0 | 0 | 0 | 0 | 0 | 0.00% | 0 |
| | | | | | | | | |
| Total Operating Expenses | 0 | 47,645 | 45,045 | 52,845 | 52,845 | 198,380 | | |
| | | | | | | | | |
| Percent of Sales | 0.00% | 79.41 | 112.61 | 52.85 | 52.85 | 66.13 | | |

**DETAILS FOR QUARTERLY STATEMENT OF EARNINGS**

*...continued*

**BUSINESS PLAN TEMPLATE**

# Appendix B - Organizations, Agencies and Consultants

# Organizations, Agencies, & Consultants

*A listing of Associations and Consultants of interest to entrepreneurs, followed by the 10 Small Business Administration Regional Offices, Small Business Development Centers, Service Corps of Retired Executives offices, and Venture Capital & Finance companies.*

## ASSOCIATIONS

*This section contains a listing of associations and other agencies of interest to the small business owner. Entries are listed alphabetically by organization name.*

American Association for Consumer
Benefits
PO Box 100279
Ft. Worth, TX 76185
Free: (800)872-8896
Fax: (817)377-5633
Jerry Clark, Contact

American Association of Family
Businesses
PO Box 547217
Surfside, FL 33154
Phone: (305)864-1184
Fax: (305)864-1187
Craig Gordon, Pres.

American Women's Economic
Development Corporation
216 East 45th St.
New York, NY 10169
Phone: (212)692-9100
Fax: (212)692-9296
Suzanne Tufts, Pres. & CEO

Association for Enterprise
Opportunity
70 E Lake St., Ste. 1120
Chicago, IL 60601
Phone: (312)357-0177
Fax: (312)357-0180
E-mail: aeochicago@ad.com
Christine M. Benuzzi, Exec. Dir.

Association of Small Business
Development Centers
3108 Columbia Pike No. 300
Arlington, VA 22204-4304
Phone: (703)271-8700
Fax: (703)271-8701
E-mail: info@asbdc-us.org

Website: http://www.asbdc-us.org
James King, Pres.

BEST Employers Association
2515 McCabe Way
Irvine, CA 92614
Phone: (714)756-1000
Free: (800)854-7417
Fax: (714)553-0883
Donald R. Lawrenz, Exec. Sec.

Business Market Association
4131 N. Central Expy., Ste. 720
Dallas, TX 75204
R. Mark King, Pres.

Employers of America
520 S. Pierce, Ste. 224
Mason City, IA 50401
Phone: (641)424-3187
Free: (800)728-3187
Fax: (641)424-1673
E-mail: employer@employerhelp.org
Website: http://
www.employerhelp.org
Jim Collison, Pres.

Family Firm Institute
221 N. Beacon St.
Boston, MA 02135-1943
Phone: (617)789-4200
Fax: (617)789-4220
E-mail: ffi@ffi.org
Website: http://www.ffi.org

Group Purchasing Association
Plaza Tower, 35th Fl.
1001 Howard Ave.
New Orleans, LA 70113-2002
Phone: (504)529-2030
Fax: (504)558-0929
E-mail: lenn@firstgpa.com

International Association of Business
701 Highlander Blvd., Ste. 110
Arlington, TX 76015-4325
Phone: (817)465-2922
Fax: (817)467-5940
Paula Rainey, Pres.

International Association for Business
Organizations
PO Box 30149
Baltimore, MD 21270
Phone: (410)581-1373
Rudolph Lewis, Exec. Officer

International Council for Small
Business
c/o Jefferson Smurfit Center for
Entrepreneurial Studies
St. Louis University
3674 Lindell Blvd.
St. Louis, MO 63108
Phone: (314)977-3628
Fax: (314)977-3627
E-mail: icsb@slu.edu
Website: http://www.icsb.org
Sharon Bower, Sec.

National Alliance for Fair
Competition
3 Bethesda Metro Center, Ste. 1100
Bethesda, MD 20814
Phone: (410)235-7116
Fax: (410)235-7116
E-mail: ampesq@aol.com
Website: http://www.nafcc.org
Tony Ponticelli, Exec. Dir.

National Association of Business
Leaders
PO Box 766
Bridgeton, MO 63044
Phone: (314)344-1111
Fax: (314)298-9110
E-mail: nabl@nabl.com
Website: http://www.nabl.com/
John Wcigcl, Contact

National Association for Business
Organizations
PO Box 30149
Baltimore, MD 21270
Phone: (410)581-1373
Website: http://www.ameribiz.com/
quicklink.htm
Rudolph Lewis, Pres.

National Association of Private
Enterprise
7819 Shelburne Cir.
Spring, TX 77379-4687
Phone: (281)655-5412
Free: (800)223-6273
Fax: (281)257-3244
E-mail: info@nape.org
Website: http://www.nape.org
Laura Squiers, Exec. Dir.

National Association for the Self-
Employed
PO Box 612067
DFW Airport
Dallas, TX 75261-2067
Free: (800)232-NASE
Fax: (800)551-4446
Website: http://www.nase.org
Bennie Thayer, Pres. & CEO

National Association of Small
Business Investment Companies
666 11th St. NW, No. 750
Washington, DC 20001
Phone: (202)628-5055
Fax: (202)628-5080
E-mail: nasbic@nasbic.org
Website: http://www.nasbic.org
Lee W. Mercer, Pres.

National Business Association
PO Box 700728
Dallas, TX 75370
Phone: (972)458-0900
Free: (800)456-0440
Fax: (972)960-9149
E-mail:
p.archibald@nationalbusiness.org
Website: http://
www.nationalbusiness.org
Pat Archibald, Pres.

National Business Owners
Association
820 Gibbon St. Ste. 204
Alexandria, VA 22314
Phone: (202)737-6501
Free: (888)755-NBOA
Fax: (877)626-2329
E-mail: govaffairs@nboa.org
Website: http://www.nboa.com
Thomas Rumfelt, Chm.

National Center for Fair Competition
8421 Frost Way
Annandale, VA 22003
Phone: (703)280-4622
Fax: (703)280-0942

E-mail: kentonp1@aol.com
Kenton Pattie, Pres.

National Federation of Independent
Business
53 Century Blvd., Ste. 300
Nashville, TN 37214
Phone: (615)872-5800
Free: (800)NFIBNOW
Fax: (615)872-5353
Website: http://www.nfib.com
Fred Holladay, VP & CFO

National Small Business United
1156 15th St. NW, Ste. 1100
Washington, DC 20005
Phone: (202)293-8830
Free: (800)345-6728
Fax: (202)872-8543
E-mail: nsbu@nsbu.org
Website: http://www.nsbu.org
Todd McCraken, Pres.

Research Institute for Small and
Emerging Business
722 12th St. NW
Washington, DC 20005
Phone: (202)628-8382
Fax: (202)628-8392
E-mail: info@riseb.org
Website: http://www.riseb.org
Mark Schultz, CEO/Pres.

Score Association
Service Corps of Retired Executives
Association
409 3rd St. SW, 6th Fl.
Washington, DC 20024
Phone: (202)205-6762
Free: (800)-634-0245
Fax: (202)205-7636
Website: http://www.score.org
W. Kenneth

Small Business Legislative Council
1010 Massachusetts Ave. NW
Washington, DC 20001
Phone: (202)639-8500
Fax: (202)296-5333
John Satagaj, Pres.

Small Business Network
PO Box 30149
Baltimore, MD 21270
Phone: (410)581-1373
E-mail: natibb@ix.netcom.com
Rudolph Lewis, CEO

Small Business Service Bureau
554 Main St.

PO Box 15014
Worcester, MA 01608
Phone: (508)756-3513
Fax: (508)770-0528
Website: http://www.sbsb.com
Francis R. Carroll, Pres.

Small Business Survival Committee
1920 L St., NW, Ste. 200
Washington, DC 20036
Phone: (202)785-0238
Fax: (202)822-8118
Website: http://www.sbsc.org
Christopher Wysocki, Pres.

Support Services Alliance
PO Box 130
Schoharie, NY 12157-0130
Phone: (518)295-7966
Free: (800)322-3920
Fax: (518)295-8556
E-mail: comments@ssainfo.com
Website: http://www.ssainfo.com
Gary Swan, Pres.

# CONSULTANTS

*This section contains a listing of consultants specializing in small business development. It is arranged alphabetically by country, then by state or province, then by firm name.*

## CANADA

### Alberta

Common Sense Solutions
3405 16A Ave.
Edmonton, AB, Canada
Phone: (403)465-7330
Fax: (403)465-7380
E-mail:
gcoulson@comsensesolutions.com
Website: http://
www.comsensesolutions.com

Varsity Consulting Group
School of Business
University of Alberta
Edmonton, AB, Canada T6G 2R6
Phone: (780)492-2994
Fax: (780)492-5400
Website: http://www.bus.ualberta.ca/
vcg

Viro Hospital Consulting
42 Commonwealth Bldg., 9912 - 106
St. NW
Edmonton, AB, Canada T5K 1C5
Phone: (403)425-3871
Fax: (403)425-3871
E-mail: rpb@freenet.edmonton.ab.ca

### British Columbia

Andrew R. De Boda Consulting
1523 Milford Ave.
Coquitlam, BC, Canada V3J 2V9
Phone: (604)936-4527
Fax: (604)936-4527
E-mail: deboda@intergate.bc.ca
Website: http://
www.ourworld.compuserve.com/
homepages/deboda

The Sage Group Ltd.
980 - 355 Burrard St.
744 W Haistings, Ste. 410
Vancouver, BC, Canada V6C 1A5
Phone: (604)669-9269
Fax: (604)669-6622

SRI Strategic Resources Inc.
4330 Kingsway, Ste. 1600
Burnaby, BC, Canada V5H 4G7
Phone: (604)435-0627
Fax: (604)435-2782
E-mail: inquiry@sri.bc.ca
Website: http://www.sri.com

Tikkanen-Bradley
1345 Nelson St., Ste. 202
Vancouver, BC, Canada V6E 1J8
Phone: (604)669-0583
E-mail:
webmaster@tikkanenbradley.com
Website: http://
www.tikkanenbradley.com

### Ontario

Begley & Associates
RR 6
Cambridge, ON, Canada N1R 5S7
Phone: (519)740-3629
Fax: (519)740-3629
E-mail: begley@in.on.ca
Website: http://www.in.on.ca/
~begley/index.htm

CRO Engineering Ltd.
1895 William Hodgins Ln.
Carp, ON, Canada K0A 1L0
Phone: (613)839-1108

Fax: (613)839-1406
E-mail: J.Grefford@ieee.ca
Website: http://www.geocities.com/
WallStreet/District/7401/

The Cynton Company
17 Massey St.
Brampton, ON, Canada L6S 2V6
Phone: (905)792-7769
Fax: (905)792-8116
E-mail: cynton@home.com
Website: http://
www.memberts.home.com/cynton

Harrison Associates
BCE Pl.
181 Bay St., Ste. 3740
PO Box 798
Toronto, ON, Canada M5J 2T3
Phone: (416)364-5441
Fax: (416)364-2875

HST Group Ltd.
430 Gilmour St.
Ottawa, ON, Canada K2P 0R8
Phone: (613)236-7303
Fax: (613)236-9893

JPL Business Consultants
82705 Metter Rd.
Wellandport, ON, Canada L0R 2J0
Phone: (905)386-7450
Fax: (905)386-7450
E-mail:
plamarch@freenet.npiec.on.ca

Task Enterprises
Box 69, RR 2 Hamilton
Flamborough, ON, Canada L8N 2Z7
Phone: (905)659-0153
Fax: (905)659-0861

TCI Convergence Ltd. Management
Consultants
99 Crown's Ln.
Toronto, ON, Canada M5R 3P4
Phone: (416)515-4146
Fax: (416)515-2097
E-mail: tci@inforamp.net
Website: http://tciconverge.com/
index.1.html

Ken Wyman & Associates Inc.
64B Shuter St., Ste. 200
Toronto, ON, Canada M5B 1B1
Phone: (416)362-2926
Fax: (416)362-3039
E-mail: kenwyman@compuserve.com

### Quebec

The Zimmar Consulting Partnership
Inc.
Westmount
PO Box 98
Montreal, QC, Canada H3Z 2T1
Phone: (514)484-1459
Fax: (514)484-3063

### Saskatchewan

Trimension Group
No. 104-110 Research Dr.
Innovation Place, SK, Canada S7N
3R3
Phone: (306)668-2560
Fax: (306)975-1156
E-mail: trimension@trimension.ca
Website: http://www.trimension.ca

## UNITED STATES

### Alabama

Business Planning Inc.
300 Office Park Dr.
Birmingham, AL 35223-2474
Phone: (205)870-7090
Fax: (205)870-7103

Tradebank of Eastern Alabama
546 Broad St., Ste. 3
Gadsden, AL 35901
Phone: (205)547-8700
Fax: (205)547-8718
E-mail: mansion@webex.com
Website: http://www.webex.com/~tea

### Alaska

AK Business Development Center
3335 Arctic Blvd., Ste. 203
Anchorage, AK 99503
Phone: (907)562-0335
Free: 800-478-3474
Fax: (907)562-6988
E-mail: twilson@customcpu.com
Website: http://www.customcpu.com/
commercial/abdc

Business Matters
PO Box 287
Fairbanks, AK 99707
Phone: (907)452-5650

## Arizona

Carefree Direct Marketing Corp.
8001 E Serene St.
Carefree, AZ 85377-3737
Phone: (480)488-4227
Fax: (480)488-2841

CMAS
5125 N 16th St.
Phoenix, AZ 85016
Phone: (602)395-1001
Fax: (602)604-8180

Comgate Telemanagement Ltd.
706 E Bell Rd., Ste. 105
Phoenix, AZ 85022
Phone: (602)485-5708
Fax: (602)485-5709
E-mail: comgate@netzone.com
Website: http://www.comgate.com

LMC Services
8711 E Pinnacle Peak Rd., No. 340
Scottsdale, AZ 85255-3555
Phone: (602)585-7177
Fax: (602)585-5880
E-mail: louws@earthlink.com

Gary L. McLeod
PO Box 230
Sonoita, AZ 85637
Fax: (602)455-5661

Moneysoft Inc.
1 E Camelback Rd. #550
Phoenix, AZ 85012
Free: 800-966-7797
E-mail: mbray@moneysoft.com

Sauerbrun Technology Group Ltd.
7979 E Princess Dr., Ste. 5
Scottsdale, AZ 85255-5878
Phone: (602)502-4950
Fax: (602)502-4292
E-mail: info@sauerbrun.com
Website: http://www.sauerbrun.com

Harvey C. Skoog
PO Box 26439
Prescott Valley, AZ 86312
Phone: (520)772-1714
Fax: (520)772-2814

Trans Energy Corp.
1739 W 7th Ave.
Mesa, AZ 85202
Phone: (602)921-0433
Fax: (602)967-6601
E-mail: aha@getnet.com

Van Cleve Associates
6932 E 2nd St.
Tucson, AZ 85710
Phone: (602)296-2587
Fax: (602)296-2587

## California

3C Systems Co.
16161 Ventura Blvd., Ste. 815
Encino, CA 91436
Phone: (818)907-1302
Fax: (818)907-1357
E-mail: mark@3CSysCo.com
Website: http://www.3CSysCo.com

Acumen Group Inc.
Phone: (650)949-9349
Fax: (650)949-4845
E-mail: acumen-g@ix.netcom.com
Website: http://pw2.netcom.com/
~janed/acumen.html

Aerospcace.Org
PO Box 28831
Oakland, CA 94604-8831
Phone: (510)530-9169
Fax: (510)530-3411
Website: http://www.aerospace.org

Bay Area Tax Consultants and
Bayhill Financial Consultants
1150 Bayhill Dr., Ste. 1150
San Bruno, CA 94066-3004
Phone: (415)952-8786
Fax: (415)588-4524
E-mail: baytax@compuserve.com
Website: http://www.baytax.com/

Beblie, Brandt & Jacobs Inc.
16 Technology, Ste. 164
Irvine, CA 92618
Phone: (714)450-8790
Fax: (714)450-8799
E-mail: darcy@bbjinc.com
Website: http://198.147.90.26

Bell Springs Publishing
PO Box 1240
Willits, CA 95490
Phone: (707)459-6372
E-mail: bellsprings@sabernet

Norris Bernstein, CMC
9309 Marina Pacifica Dr. N
Long Beach, CA 90803
Phone: (562)493-5458
Fax: (562)493-5459
E-mail: norris@ctecomputer.com

Brincko Associates Inc.
1801 Avenue of the Stars, Ste. 1054
Los Angeles, CA 90067
Phone: (310)553-4523
Fax: (310)553-6782

Burnes Consulting
20537 Wolf Creek Rd.
Grass Valley, CA 95949
Phone: (530)346-8188
Free: 800-949-9021
Fax: (530)346-7704
E-mail: kent@burnesconsulting.com
Website: http://
www.burnesconsulting.com

California Business Incubation
Network
101 W Broadway, No. 480
San Diego, CA 92101
Phone: (619)237-0559
Fax: (619)237-0521

Carrera Consulting Group, a division
of Maximus
2110 21st St., Ste. 400
Sacramento, CA 95818
Phone: (916)456-3300
Fax: (916)456-3306
E-mail:
central@carreraconsulting.com
Website: http://
www.carreraconsulting.com

Cast Management Consultants
1620 26th St., Ste. 2040N
Santa Monica, CA 90404
Phone: (310)828-7511
Fax: (310)453-6831

Career Paths-Thomas E. Church &
Associates Inc.
PO Box 2439
Aptos, CA 95001
Phone: (408)662-7950
Fax: (408)662-7955
E-mail: church@ix.netcom.com
Website: http://www.careerpaths-
tom.com

Comprehensive Business Services
3201 Lucas Cir.
Lafayette, CA 94549
Phone: (925)283-8272
Fax: (925)283-8272

Cuma Consulting Management
Box 724
Santa Rosa, CA 95402

Phone: (707)785-2477
Fax: (707)785-2478

The E-Myth Academy
131B Stony Cir., Ste. 2000
Santa Rosa, CA 95401
Phone: (707)569-5600
Free: 800-221-0266
Fax: (707)569-5700
E-mail: info@e-myth.com
Website: http://www.e-myth.com

Fluor Daniel Inc.
3353 Michelson Dr.
Irvine, CA 92612-0650
Phone: (949)975-2000
Fax: (949)975-5271
E-mail:
sales.consulting@fluordaniel.com
Website: http://
www.fluordanielconsulting.com

Freeman, Sullivan & Co.
131 Steuart St., Ste. 500
San Francisco, CA 94105
Phone: (415)777-0707
Free: 800-777-0737
Fax: (415)777-2420
Website: http://www.fsc-research.com

Global Tradelinks
451 Pebble Beach Pl.
Fullerton, CA 92835
Phone: (714)441-2280
Fax: (714)441-2281
E-mail: info@globaltradelinks.com
Website: http://
www.globaltradelinks.com

G.R. Gordetsky Consultants Inc.
11414 Windy Summit Pl.
San Diego, CA 92127
Phone: (619)487-4939
Fax: (619)487-5587
E-mail: gordet@pacbell.net

Grid Technology Associates
20404 Tufts Cir.
Walnut, CA 91789
Phone: (909)444-0922
Fax: (909)444-0922
E-mail: grid_technology@msn.com

Helfert Associates
1777 Borel Pl., Ste. 508
San Mateo, CA 94402-3514
Phone: (415)377-0540
Fax: (415)377-0472

Highland Associates
16174 Highland Dr.

San Jose, CA 95127
Phone: (408)272-7008
Fax: (408)272-4040

Horizon Consulting Services
1315 Garthwick Dr.
Los Altos, CA 94024
Phone: (415)967-0906
Fax: (415)967-0906

House Agricultural Consultants
PO Box 1615
Davis, CA 95617-1615
Phone: (916)753-3361
Fax: (916)753-0464
E-mail: infoag@houseag.com
Website: http://www.houseag.com/

Hutchinson Consulting and
Appraisals
23245 Sylvan St., Ste. 103
Woodland Hills, CA 91367
Phone: (818)888-8175
Free: 800-977-7548
Fax: (818)888-8220
E-mail: hcac.@sprintmall.com

Ideas Unlimited
2151 California St., Ste. 7
San Francisco, CA 94115
Phone: (415)931-0641
Fax: (415)931-0880

Independent Research Services
PO Box 2426
Van Nuys, CA 91404-2426
Phone: (818)993-3622

The Information Group Inc.
4675 Stevens Creek Blvd., Ste. 100
Santa Clara, CA 95051
Phone: (408)985-7877
Fax: (408)985-2945
E-mail: dvincent@tig-usa.com
Website: http://www.tig-usa.com

Ingman Co. Inc.
7949 Woodley Ave., Ste. 120
Van Nuys, CA 91406-1232
Phone: (818)375-5027
Fax: (818)894-5001

Innovative Technology Associates
3639 E Harbor Blvd., Ste. 203E
Ventura, CA 93001
Phone: (805)650-9353

Inspired Arts Inc.
4225 Executive Sq., Ste. 1160
La Jolla, CA 92037
Phone: (619)623-3525

Free: 800-851-4394
Fax: (619)623-3534
E-mail: info@inspiredarts.com
Website: http://www.inspiredarts.com

Intelequest Corp.
722 Gailen Ave.
Palo Alto, CA 94303
Phone: (415)968-3443
Fax: (415)493-6954
E-mail: frits@iqix.com

International Health Resources
PO Box 329
North San Juan, CA 95960-0329
Phone: (530)292-1266
Fax: (530)292-1243
Website: http://
www.futureofhealthcare.com

JB Associates
21118 Gardena Dr.
Cupertino, CA 95014
Phone: (408)257-0214
Fax: (408)257-0216
E-mail: semarang@sirius.com

Keck & Co. Business Consultants
410 Walsh Rd.
Atherton, CA 94027
Phone: (650)854-9588
Fax: (650)854-7240
E-mail: info@keckco.com
Website: http://www.keckco.com

Kremer Management Consulting
PO Box 500
Carmel, CA 93921
Phone: (408)626-8311
Fax: (408)624-2663
E-mail: ddkremer@aol.com

The Laresis Companies
PO Box 3284
La Jolla, CA 92038
Phone: (619)452-2720
Fax: (619)452-8744

Larson Associates
PO Box 9005
Brea, CA 92822
Phone: (714)529-4121
Fax: (714)572-3606
E-mail: ray@consultlarson.com
Website: http://
www.consultlarson.com

Ben W. Laverty III, PhD, REA, CEI
4909 Stockdale Hwy., Ste. 132
Bakersfield, CA 93309
Phone: (661)283-8300

Free: 800-833-0373
Fax: (661)283-8313
E-mail: cstc@cstcsafety.com
Website: http://www.cstcsafety.com/
cstc

Lindquist Consultants-Venture
Planning
225 Arlington Ave.
Berkeley, CA 94707
Phone: (510)524-6685
Fax: (510)527-6604

Management Consultants
Sunnyvale, CA 94087-4700
Phone: (408)773-0321

The Market Connection
4020 Birch St., Ste. 203
Newport Beach, CA 92660
Phone: (714)731-6273
Fax: (714)833-0253

Marketing Services Management
PO Box 1377
Martinez, CA 94553
Phone: (510)370-8527
Fax: (510)370-8527
E-mail: markserve@biotechnet.com

McLaughlin & Associates
66 San Marino Cir.
Rancho Mirage, CA 92270
Phone: (760)321-2932
Fax: (760)328-2474
E-mail: jackmcla@aol.com

MCS Associates
18300 Von Karman, Ste. 1000
Irvine, CA 92612
Phone: (949)263-8700
Fax: (949)553-0168
E-mail: info@mcsassociates.com

Russell Miller Inc.
300 Montgomery St., Ste. 900
San Francisco, CA 94104
Phone: (415)956-7474
Fax: (415)398-0620
E-mail: rmi@pacbell.net
Website: http://www.rmisf.com

Muller Associates
PO Box 7264
Newport Beach, CA 92658
Phone: (714)646-1169
Fax: (714)646-1169

Mykytyn Consulting Group Inc.
185 N Redwood Dr., Ste. 200
San Rafael, CA 94903

Phone: (415)491-1770
Fax: (415)491-1251
E-mail: info@mcgi.com
Website: http://www.mcgi.com

NEXUS - Consultants to Management
PO Box 1531
Novato, CA 94948
Phone: (415)897-4400
Fax: (415)898-2252
E-mail: jimnexus@aol.com

Omega Management Systems Inc.
3 Mount Darwin Ct.
San Rafael, CA 94903-1109
Phone: (415)499-1300
Fax: (415)492-9490
E-mail: omegamgt@ix.netcom.com

On-line Career and Management
Consulting
420 Central Ave., No. 314
Alameda, CA 94501
Phone: (510)864-0336
Fax: (510)864-0336
E-mail: career@dnai.com
Website: http://www.dnai.com/
~career

ORDIS Inc.
6815 Trinidad Dr.
San Jose, CA 95120-2056
Phone: (408)268-3321
Free: 800-446-7347
Fax: (408)268-3582
E-mail: ordis@ordis.com
Website: http://www.ordis.com

Out of Your Mind...and Into the
Marketplace
13381 White Sands Dr.
Tustin, CA 92780-4565
Phone: (714)544-0248
Free: 800-419-1513
Fax: (714)730-1414
E-mail: lpinson@aol.com
Website: http://www.business-
plan.com

Palo Alto Management Group Inc.
2672 Bayshore Pky., Ste. 701
Mountain View, CA 94043
Phone: (415)968-4374
Fax: (415)968-4245
E-mail: mburwen@pamg.com

Pioneer Business Consultants
9042 Garfield Ave., Ste. 312
Huntington Beach, CA 92646
Phone: (714)964-7600

PKF Consulting
425 California St., Ste. 1650
San Francisco, CA 94104
Phone: (415)421-5378
Fax: (415)956-7708
E-mail: callahan@pkfc.com
Website: http://www.pkfonline.com

RAINWATER-GISH & Associates,
Business Finance & Development
317 3rd St., Ste. 3
Eureka, CA 95501
Phone: (707)443-0030
Fax: (707)443-5683

RCL & Co.
PO Box 1143
737 Pearl St., Ste. 201
La Jolla, CA 92038
Phone: (619)454-8883
Fax: (619)454-8880

Reilly, Connors & Ray
1743 Canyon Rd.
Spring Valley, CA 91977
Phone: (619)698-4808
Fax: (619)460-3892
E-mail: davidray@adnc.com

The Ribble Group
27601 Forbes Rd., Ste. 52
Laguna Niguel, CA 92677
Phone: (714)582-1085
Fax: (714)582-6420
E-mail: ribble@deltanet.com

Ridge Consultants Inc.
100 Pringle Ave., Ste. 580
Walnut Creek, CA 94596
Phone: (925)274-1990
Fax: (510)274-1956
E-mail: info@ridgecon.com
Website: http://www.ridgecon.com

RJR Associates
1639 Lewiston Dr.
Sunnyvale, CA 94087
Phone: (408)737-7720
Fax: (408)737-7720
E-mail: bobroy@netcom
Website: http://www.rjroy.mcni.com

J.H. Robinson & Associates
20695 Deodar Dr., Ste. 100
Yorba Linda, CA 92886-3169
Phone: (714)970-1279

Rubenstein/Justman Management
Consultants
2049 Century Park E, 24th Fl.

Los Angeles, CA 90067
Phone: (310)282-0800
Fax: (310)282-0400
E-mail: info@rjmc.net
Website: http://www.rjmc.net

F.J. Schroeder & Associates
1926 Westholme Ave.
Los Angeles, CA 90025
Phone: (310)470-2655
Fax: (310)470-6378
E-mail: fjsacons@aol.com
Website: http://www.mcninet.com/
GlobalLook/Fjschroe.html

Schwafel Associates
333 Cobalt Way, Ste. 21
Sunnyvale, CA 94086
Phone: (408)720-0649
Fax: (408)720-1796
E-mail: schwafel@ricochet.net
Website: http://www.patca.org

Darrell Sell and Associates
Los Gatos, CA 95030
Phone: (408)354-7794
E-mail: darrell@netcom.com

William M. Shine Consulting Service
PO Box 127
Moraga, CA 94556-0127
Phone: (510)376-6516

Stanford Resources Inc.
20 Great Oaks Blvd., Ste. 200
San Jose, CA 95119
Phone: (408)360-8400
Fax: (408)360-8410
E-mail: stanres@ix.netcom.com
Website: http://
www.stanfordresources.com

Staubs Business Services
23320 S Vermont Ave.
Torrance, CA 90502-2940
Phone: (310)830-9128
Fax: (310)830-9128
E-mail: Harry_L_Staubs@Lamg.com

Strategic Business Group
800 Cienaga Dr.
Fullerton, CA 92835-1248
Phone: (714)449-1040
Fax: (714)525-1631

Technical Management Consultants
3624 Westfall Dr.
Encino, CA 91436-4154
Phone: (818)784-0626
Fax: (818)501-5575
E-mail: tmcrs@aol.com

Technology Properties Ltd. Inc.
4010 Moore Park, St. 215
San Jose, CA 95117
Phone: (408)243-9898
Fax: (408)296-6637

W and J Partnership
PO Box 2499
18876 Edwin Markham Dr.
Castro Valley, CA 94546
Phone: (510)583-7751
Fax: (510)583-7645
E-mail:
wamorgan@wjpartnership.com
Website: http://
www.wjpartnership.com

Welling & Woodard Inc.
1067 Broadway
San Francisco, CA 94133
Phone: (415)776-4500
Fax: (415)776-5067

Western Management Associates
8351 Vicksburg Ave.
Los Angeles, CA 90045-3924
Phone: (310)645-1091
Free: (888)788-6534
Fax: (310)645-1092
E-mail: CFOForRent@att.net
Website: http://www.expert-
market.com/cfoforrent

Leslie J. Zambo
3355 Michael Dr.
Marina, CA 93933
Phone: (408)384-7086
Fax: (408)647-4199
E-mail:
104776.1552@compuserve.com

## Colorado

Ameriwest Business Consultants Inc.
PO Box 26266
Colorado Springs, CO 80936
Phone: (719)380-7096
Fax: (719)380-7096
E-mail: email@abchelp.com
Website: http://www.abchelp.com

Associated Enterprises Ltd.
13050 W Ceder Dr., Unit 11
Lakewood, CO 80228
Phone: (303)988-6695
Fax: (303)988-6739
E-mail: ael1@classic.msn.com

Sam Boyer & Associates
4255 S Buckley Rd., No. 136

Aurora, CO 80013
Free: 800-785-0485
Fax: (303)766-8740
E-mail: samboyer@samboyer.com
Website: http://www.samboyer.com/

GVNW Consulting Inc.
2270 La Montana Way
Colorado Springs, CO 80936
Phone: (719)594-5800
Fax: (719)599-0968
Website: http://www.gvnw.com

Johnson & West Management
Consultants Inc.
7612 S Logan Dr.
Littleton, CO 80122
Phone: (303)730-2810
Fax: (303)730-3219

M-Squared Inc.
755 San Gabriel Pl.
Colorado Springs, CO 80906
Phone: (719)576-2554
Fax: (719)576-2554

TenEyck Associates
1760 Cherryville Rd.
Greenwood Village, CO 80121-1503
Phone: (303)758-6129
Fax: (303)761-8286

Thornton Financial FNIC
1024 Centre Ave., Bldg. E
Fort Collins, CO 80526-1849
Phone: (970)221-2089
Fax: (970)484-5206

The Vincent Co. Inc.
200 Union Blvd., Ste. 210
Lakewood, CO 80228
Phone: (303)989-7271
Free: 800-274-0733
Fax: (303)989-7570
E-mail: vincent@vincentco.com
Website: http://www.vincentco.com

Western Capital Holdings Inc.
7500 E Arapahoe Rd., Ste. 395
Englewood, CO 80112
Phone: (303)290-8482
Fax: (303)770-1945

## Connecticut

Cowherd Consulting Group Inc.
106 Stephen Mather Rd.
Darien, CT 06820
Phone: (203)655-2150
Fax: (203)655-6427

Follow-up News
185 Pine St., Ste. 818
Manchester, CT 06040
Phone: (860)647-7542
Free: 800-708-0696
Fax: (860)646-6544
E-mail: Followupnews@aol.com

Greenwich Associates
8 Greenwich Office Park
Greenwich, CT 06831-5149
Phone: (203)629-1200
Fax: (203)629-1229
E-mail: lisa@greenwich.com
Website: http://www.greenwich.com

Charles L. Hornung Associates
52 Ned's Mountain Rd.
Ridgefield, CT 06877
Phone: (203)431-0297

JC Ventures Inc.
4 Arnold St.
Old Greenwich, CT 06870-1203
Phone: (203)698-1990
Free: 800-698-1997
Fax: (203)698-2638

Lovins & Associates Consulting
309 Edwards St.
New Haven, CT 06511
Phone: (203)787-3367
Fax: (203)624-7599
E-mail: Alovinsphd@aol.com
Website: http://www.lovinsgroup.com

Manus
100 Prospect St., S Tower
Stamford, CT 06901
Phone: (203)326-3880
Free: 800-445-0942
Fax: (203)326-3890
E-mail: manus1@aol.com
Website: http://
www.RightManus.com

Stratman Group Inc.
40 Tower Ln.
Avon, CT 06001-4222
Phone: (860)677-2898
Free: 800-551-0499
Fax: (860)677-8210

### Delaware

Daedalus Ventures Ltd.
PO Box 1474
Hockessin, DE 19707
Phone: (302)239-6758

Fax: (302)239-9991
E-mail: daedalus@mail.del.net

Focus Marketing
61-7 Habor Dr.
Claymont, DE 19703
Phone: (302)793-3064

The Formula Group
PO Box 866
Hockessin, DE 19707
Phone: (302)456-0952
Fax: (302)456-1354
E-mail: formula@netaxs.com

Selden Enterprises Inc.
2502 Silverside Rd., Ste. 1
Wilmington, DE 19810-3740
Phone: (302)529-7113
Fax: (302)529-7442
E-mail: selden2@bellatlantic.net
Website: http://
www.seldenenterprises.com

### District of Columbia

Bruce W. McGee and Associates
7826 Eastern Ave. NW, Ste. 30
Washington, DC 20012
Phone: (202)726-7272
Fax: (202)726-2946

McManis Associates Inc.
1900 K St. NW, Ste. 700
Washington, DC 20006
Phone: (202)466-7680
Fax: (202)872-1898
Website: http://www.mcmanis-
mmi.com

Smith, Dawson & Andrews Inc.
1000 Connecticut Ave., Ste. 302
Washington, DC 20036
Phone: (202)835-0740
Fax: (202)775-8526
E-mail: webmaster@sda-inc.com
Website: http://www.sda-inc.com

### Florida

Agrippa Enterprises Inc.
PO Box 175
Venice, FL 34284-0175
Phone: (941)355-7876
E-mail: webservices@agrippa.com
Website: http://www.agrippa.com

Avery Business Development
Services
2506 St. Michel Ct.
Ponte Vedra Beach, FL 32082

Phone: (904)285-6033
Fax: (904)285-6033

T.C. Brown & Associates
8415 Excalibur Cir., Apt. B1
Naples, FL 34108
Phone: (941)594-1949
Fax: (941)594-0611
E-mail: tcater@naples.net.com

Center for Simplified Strategic
Planning Inc.
PO Box 3324
Vero Beach, FL 32964-3324
Phone: (561)231-3636
Fax: (561)231-1099
Website: http://www.cssp.com

Comprehensive Franchising Inc.
2465 Ridgecrest Ave.
Orange Park, FL 32065
Phone: (904)272-6567
Free: 800-321-6567
Fax: (904)272-6750
E-mail: theimp@cris.com
Website: http://
www.franchise411.com

Dufresne Consulting Group Inc.
10014 N Dale Mabry, Ste. 101
Tampa, FL 33618-4426
Phone: (813)264-4775
Fax: (813)264-9300
Website: http://www.dcgconsult.com

William V. Hall
1925 Brickell, Ste. D-701
Miami, FL 33129
Phone: (305)856-9622
Fax: (305)856-4113
E-mail:
williamvhall@compuserve.com

Host Media Corp.
3948 S 3rd St., Ste. 191
Jacksonville Beach, FL 32250
Phone: (904)285-3239
Fax: (904)285-5618
E-mail:
msconsulting@compuserve.com
Website: http://
www.mediaservicesgroup.com

Hunter G. Jackson Jr. - Consulting
Environmental Physicist
PO Box 618272
Orlando, FL 32861-8272
Phone: (407)295-4188
E-mail: hunterjackson@juno.com

F.A. McGee Inc.
800 Claughton Island Dr., Ste. 401
Miami, FL 33131
Phone: (305)377-9123

F. Newton Parks
210 El Brillo Way
Palm Beach, FL 33480
Phone: (561)833-1727
Fax: (561)833-4541

RLA International Consulting
713 Lagoon Dr.
North Palm Beach, FL 33408
Phone: (407)626-4258
Fax: (407)626-5772

E.N. Rysso & Associates
202 Caroline St., Ste. 103
Cape Canaveral, FL 32920-2706
Phone: (407)783-7588
Fax: (407)783-7580
E-mail: erysso@aol.com

Eric Sands Consulting Services
6193 Rock Island Rd., Ste. 412
Fort Lauderdale, FL 33319
Phone: (954)721-4767
Fax: (954)720-2815

Strategic Business Planning Co.
PO Box 821006
South Florida, FL 33082-1006
Phone: (954)704-9100
Fax: (954)438-7333
E-mail: info@bizplan.com
Website: http://www.bizplan.com

Taxplan Inc.
Mirasol International Ctr.
2699 Collins Ave.
Miami Beach, FL 33140
Phone: (305)538-3303

Whalen & Associates Inc.
4255 Northwest 26 Ct.
Boca Raton, FL 33434
Phone: (561)241-5950
Fax: (561)241-7414
E-mail: drwhalen@ix.netcom.com

## Georgia

Business Ventures Corp.
1650 Oakbrook Dr., Ste. 405
Norcross, GA 30093
Phone: (770)729-8000
Fax: (770)729-8028

Tom C. Davis & Associates, P.C.
3189 Perimeter Rd.

Valdosta, GA 31602
Phone: (912)247-9801
Fax: (912)244-7704
E-mail: mail@tcdcpa.com
Website: http://www.tcdcpa.com/

Informed Decisions Inc.
100 Falling Cheek
Sautee Nacoochee, GA 30571
Phone: (706)878-1905
Fax: (706)878-1802
E-mail: skylake@compuserve.com

Marketing Spectrum Inc.
115 Perimeter Pl., Ste. 440
Atlanta, GA 30346
Phone: (770)395-7244
Fax: (770)393-4071

## Illinois

ACE Accounting Service Inc.
3128 N Bernard St.
Chicago, IL 60618
Phone: (773)463-7854
Fax: (773)463-7854

AON Corp.
123 N Wacker Dr.
Chicago, IL 60606
Phone: (312)701-3924
Free: 800-438-6487
Fax: (312)701-3900
Website: http://www.aon.com

BioLabs Inc.
15 Sheffield Ct.
Lincolnshire, IL 60069
Phone: (847)945-2767

Camber Business Strategy
Consultants
PO Box 986
Palatine, IL 60078-0986
Phone: (847)705-0101
Fax: (847)705-0101

Center for Workforce Effectiveness
500 Skokie Blvd., Ste. 222
Northbrook, IL 60062
Phone: (847)559-8777
Fax: (847)559-8778
E-mail: office@cwelink.com
Website: http://www.cwelink.com

China Business Consultants Group
931 Dakota Cir.
Naperville, IL 60563
Phone: (630)778-7992
Fax: (630)778-7915
E-mail: cbcq@aol.com

Phil Faris Associates
86 Old Mill Ct.
Barrington, IL 60010
Phone: (847)382-4888
Fax: (847)382-4890
E-mail: pfaris@meginsnet.net

FMS Consultants
5801 N Sheridan Rd., Ste. 3D
Chicago, IL 60660
Phone: (773)561-7362
Fax: (773)561-6274

Francorp Inc.
20200 Governors Dr.
Olympia Fields, IL 60461
Phone: (708)481-2900
Free: 800-372-6244
Fax: (708)481-5885
E-mail: francorp@aol.com
Website: http://www.francorpinc.com

Clyde R. Goodheart
15 Sheffield Ct.
Lincolnshire, IL 60069
Phone: (847)945-2767

Grant Thornton
800 1 Prudential Plz.
130 E Randolph St.
Chicago, IL 60601
Phone: (312)856-0001
Fax: (312)861-1340
E-mail: gtinfo@gt.com
Website: http://
www.grantthornton.com

Grubb & Blue Inc.
2404 Windsor Pl.
Champaign, IL 61820
Phone: (217)366-0052
Fax: (217)356-0117

Human Energy Design Systems
620 Roosevelt Dr.
Edwardsville, IL 62025
Phone: (618)692-0258
Fax: (618)692-0819

William J. Igoe
3949 Earlston Rd.
Downers Grove, IL 60515
Phone: (630)960-1418

Kingsbury International Ltd.
5341 N Glenwood Ave.
Chicago, IL 60640
Phone: (773)271-3030
Fax: (773)728-7080
E-mail: jetlag@mcs.com
Website: http://www.kingbiz.com

MacDougall & Blake Inc.
1414 N Wells St., Ste. 311
Chicago, IL 60610-1306
Phone: (312)587-3330
Fax: (312)587-3699
E-mail: jblake@compuserve.com

Management Planning Associates Inc.
2275 Half Day Rd., Ste. 350
Bannockburn, IL 60015-1277
Phone: (847)945-2421
Fax: (847)945-2425

James C. Osburn Ltd.
2701 W Howard St.
Chicago, IL 60645
Phone: (773)262-4428
Fax: (773)262-6755

Partec Enterprise Group
5202 Keith Dr.
Richton Park, IL 60471
Phone: (708)503-4047
Fax: (708)503-9468

Rockford Consulting Group Ltd.
Century Plz., Ste. 206
7210 E State St.
Rockford, IL 61108
Phone: (815)229-2900
Free: 800-667-7495
Fax: (815)229-2612
E-mail:
rligus@RockfordConsulting.com
Website: http://
www.RockfordConsulting.com

RSM McGladrey Inc.
1699 E Woodfield Rd., Ste. 300
Schaumburg, IL 60173-4969
Phone: (847)518-7070
Fax: (847)517-7067
Website: http://
www.rsmmcgladrey.com

Seven Continents Technology
787 Stonebridge
Buffalo Grove, IL 60089
Phone: (708)577-9653
Fax: (708)870-1220

Smith Associates
1320 White Mountain Dr.
Northbrook, IL 60062
Phone: (847)480-7200
Fax: (847)480-9828

A.D. Star Consulting
320 Euclid
Winnetka, IL 60093

Phone: (847)446-7827
Fax: (847)446-7827
E-mail: startwo@worldnet.att.net

Tarifero & Tazewell Inc.
211 S Clark
Chicago, IL 60690
Phone: (312)665-9714
Fax: (312)665-9716

TWD and Associates
431 S Patton
Arlington Heights, IL 60005
Phone: (847)398-6410
Fax: (847)255-5095
E-mail: tdoo@aol.com

## Indiana

Ketchum Consulting Group
8021 Knue Rd., Ste. 112
Indianapolis, IN 46250
Phone: (317)845-5411
Fax: (317)842-9941

MDI Management Consulting
1519 Park Dr.
Munster, IN 46321
Phone: (219)838-7909
Fax: (219)838-7909

Midwest Marketing Research
PO Box 1077
Goshen, IN 46527
Phone: (219)533-0548
Fax: (219)533-0540
E-mail: 103365.654@compuserve

Modular Consultants Inc.
3109 Crabtree Ln.
Elkhart, IN 46514
Phone: (219)264-5761
Fax: (219)264-5761
E-mail: sasabo5313@aol.com

## Iowa

Grandview Marketing
15 Red Bridge Dr.
Sioux City, IA 51104
Phone: (712)239-3122
Fax: (712)258-7578
E-mail: eandrews@pionet.net

Management Solutions, L.C.
3815 Lincoln Pl. Dr.
Des Moines, IA 50312
Phone: (515)277-6408
Fax: (515)277-3506
E-mail: wasunimers@uswest.net

McCord Consulting Group Inc.
4533 Pine View Dr. NE
PO Box 11024
Cedar Rapids, IA 52410
Phone: (319)378-0077
Fax: (319)378-1577
E-mail: mccord@quixnet.net
Website: http://
www.mccordgroup.com

## Kansas

Assessments in Action
513A N Mur-Len
Olathe, KS 66062
Phone: (913)764-6270
Free: (888)548-1504
Fax: (913)764-6495
E-mail: lowdene@qni.com
Website: http://www.assessments-in-action.com

## Maine

Edgemont Enterprises
PO Box 8354
Portland, ME 04104
Phone: (207)871-8964
Fax: (207)871-8964

Pan Atlantic Consultants
5 Milk St.
Portland, ME 04101
Phone: (207)871-8622
Fax: (207)772-4842
E-mail: pmurphy@maine.rr.com
Website: http://www.panatlantic.net

## Maryland

Burdeshaw Associates Ltd.
4701 Sangamore Rd.
Bethesda, MD 20816-2508
Phone: (301)229-5800
Fax: (301)229-5045
E-mail: jstacy@burdeshaw.com
Website: http://www.burdeshaw.com

Clemons & Associates Inc.
5024-R Campbell Blvd.
Baltimore, MD 21236
Phone: (410)931-8100
Fax: (410)931-8111
E-mail: info@clemonsmgmt.com
Website: http://
www.clemonsmgmt.com

Michael E. Cohen
5225 Pooks Hill Rd., Ste. 1119 S
Bethesda, MD 20814
Phone: (301)530-5738
Fax: (301)530-2988
E-mail: mecohen@crosslin.net

Hammer Marketing Resources
179 Inverness Rd.
Severna Park, MD 21146
Phone: (410)544-9191
Fax: (410)544-9189
E-mail: bhammer@gohammer.com
Website: http://www.gohammer.com

Imperial Group Ltd.
305 Washington Ave., Ste. 204
Baltimore, MD 21204-6009
Phone: (410)337-8500
Fax: (410)337-7641

Leadership Institute
3831 Yolando Rd.
Baltimore, MD 21218
Phone: (410)366-9111
Fax: (410)243-8478
E-mail: behconsult@aol.com

Software Solutions International Inc.
9633 Duffer Way
Gaithersburg, MD 20886
Phone: (301)977-3743
Fax: (301)330-4136

Strategies Inc.
8 Park Center Ct., Ste. 200
Owings Mills, MD 21117
Phone: (410)363-6669
Fax: (410)363-1231
E-mail: strategies@strat1.com
Website: http://www.strat1.com

Andrew Sussman & Associates
13731 Kretsinger
Smithsburg, MD 21783
Phone: (301)824-2943
Fax: (301)824-2943

Swartz Consulting
PO Box 4301
Crofton, MD 21114-4301
Phone: (301)262-6728

World Development Group Inc.
5272 River Rd., Ste. 650
Bethesda, MD 20816-1405
Phone: (301)652-1818
Fax: (301)652-1250
E-mail: wdg@has.com
Website: http://www.worlddg.com

**Massachusetts**

Bain & Co.
2 Copley Pl.
Boston, MA 02116
Phone: (617)572-2000
Fax: (617)572-2427
E-mail: corporate.inquiries@bain.com
Website: http://www.bain.com

Business Planning and Consulting
Services
20 Beechwood Ter.
Wellesley, MA 02482
Phone: (617)237-9151
Fax: (617)237-9151

The Company Doctor
14 Pudding Stone Ln.
Mendon, MA 01756
Phone: (508)478-1747
Fax: (508)478-0520

Consulting Resources Corp.
6 Northbrook Park
Lexington, MA 02420
Phone: (781)863-1222
Fax: (781)863-1441
E-mail: res@consultingresources.net
Website: http://
consultingresources.net

Data and Strategies Group Inc.
190 N Main St.
Natick, MA 01760
Phone: (508)653-9990
Fax: (508)653-7799
E-mail: dsginc@dsggroup.com
Website: http://www.dsggroup.com

The Enterprise Group
73 Parker Rd.
Needham, MA 02494
Phone: (617)444-6631
Fax: (617)433-9991
E-mail: lsacco@world.std.com
Website: http://www.enterprise-
group.com

Geibel Marketing and Public
Relations
PO Box 611
Belmont, MA 02478-0005
Phone: (617)484-8285
Fax: (617)489-3567
E-mail: jgeibel@geibelpr.com
Website: http://www.geibelpr.com

IEEE Consultants' Network
255 Bear Hill Rd.

Waltham, MA 02451
Phone: (617)890-5294
Fax: (617)890-5290

Information & Research Associates
PO Box 3121
Framingham, MA 01701
Phone: (508)788-0784

Interim Management Associates
21 Avon Rd.
Wellesley, MA 02482
Phone: (781)237-0024

Kalba International Inc.
1601 Trapelo Rd.
Waltham, MA 02451-7333
Phone: (781)466-8450
Fax: (781)466-8440
E-mail: info@kalbainternational.com
Website: http://
www.kalbainternational.com

Jeffrey D. Marshall
102 Mitchell Rd.
Ipswich, MA 01938-1219
Phone: (508)356-1113
Fax: (508)356-2989

Mehr & Co.
62 Kinnaird St.
Cambridge, MA 02139
Phone: (617)876-3311
Fax: (617)876-3023
E-mail: mehrco@aol.com

Monitor Company Inc.
2 Canal Park
Cambridge, MA 02141
Phone: (617)252-2000
Fax: (617)252-2100
Website: http://www.monitor.com

Planning Technologies Group LLC
92 Hayden Ave.
Lexington, MA 02421
Phone: (781)778-4678
Fax: (781)861-1099
E-mail: ptg@plantech.com
Website: http://www.plantech.com

PSMJ Resources Inc.
10 Midland Ave.
Newton, MA 02458
Phone: (617)965-0055
Free: 800-537-7765
Fax: (617)965-5152
E-mail: psmj@tiac.net
Website: http://www.psmj.com

Scheur Management Group
255 Washington St., Ste. 100
Newton, MA 02458-1611
Phone: (617)969-7500
E-mail: smgnow@scheur.com
Website: http://www.scheur.com

VMB Associates Inc.
115 Ashland St.
Melrose, MA 02176
Phone: (781)665-0623
Fax: (425)732-7142
E-mail: vmbinc@aol.com

Walden Consultants Ltd.
252 Pond St.
Hopkinton, MA 01748
Phone: (508)435-4882
Fax: (508)435-3971
Website: http://
www.waldenconsultants.com

## Michigan

Altamar Group Ltd.
6810 S Cedar, Ste. 2-B
Lansing, MI 48911
Phone: (517)694-0910
Free: 800-443-2627
Fax: (517)694-1377

Fox Enterprises
6220 W Freeland Rd.
Freeland, MI 48623
Phone: (517)695-9170
Fax: (517)695-9174
E-mail: foxjw@concentric.net
Website: http://www.cris.com/~foxjw

Francis & Co.
17200 W 10 Mile Rd., Ste. 207
Southfield, MI 48075
Phone: (248)559-7600
Fax: (248)559-5249

Walter Frederick Consulting
1719 South Blvd.
Ann Arbor, MI 48104
Phone: (313)662-4336
Fax: (313)769-7505

G.G.W. and Associates
1213 Hampton
Jackson, MI 49203
Phone: (517)782-2255
Fax: (517)782-2255

JGK Associates
14464 Kerner Dr.

Sterling Heights, MI 48313
Phone: (810)247-9055

Private Ventures Inc.
16000 W 9 Mile Rd., Ste. 504
Southfield, MI 48075
Phone: (248)569-1977
Free: 800-448-7614
Fax: (248)569-1838
E-mail: pventuresi@aol.com

Rehmann, Robson PC
5800 Gratiot
Saginaw, MI 48605
Phone: (517)799-9580
Fax: (517)799-0227
Website: http://www.rrpc.com

Sheffieck Consultants Inc.
23610 Greening Dr.
Novi, MI 48375-3130
Phone: (248)347-3545
Fax: (248)347-3530
E-mail: cfsheff@concentric.net

## Minnesota

Amdahl International
724 1st Ave. SW
Rochester, MN 55902
Phone: (507)252-0402
Fax: (507)252-0402
E-mail: amdahl@best-service.com
Website: http://www.wp.com/
amdahl_int

Consatech Inc.
PO Box 1047
Burnsville, MN 55337
Phone: (612)953-1088
Fax: (612)435-2966

DRI Consulting
7715 Stonewood Ct.
Edina, MN 55439
Phone: (612)941-9656
Fax: (612)941-2693
E-mail: dric@dric.com
Website: http://www.dric.com

Enterprise Consulting Inc.
PO Box 1111
Minnetonka, MN 55345
Phone: (612)949-5909
Fax: (612)906-3965

Health Fitness Corp.
3500 W 80th St., Ste. 130
Bloomington, MN 55431

Phone: (612)831-6830
Fax: (612)831-7264

Kinnon Lilligren Associates Inc.
6211 Oakgreen Ave. S
Hastings, MN 55033-9153
Phone: (612)436-6530
Fax: (612)436-6530

Robert F. Knotek
14960 Ironwood Ct.
Eden Prairie, MN 55346
Phone: (612)949-2875

Markin Consulting
12072 87th Pl. N
Maple Grove, MN 55369
Phone: (612)493-3568
Fax: (612)493-5744
E-mail:
markin@markinconsulting.com
Website: http://
www.markinconsulting.com

Minnesota Cooperation Office for
Small Business & Job Creation Inc.
5001 W 80th St., Ste. 825
Minneapolis, MN 55437
Phone: (612)830-1230
Fax: (612)830-1232
E-mail: mncoop@msn.com
Website: http://www.mnco.org

Power Systems Research
1365 Corporate Center Curve, 2nd Fl.
St. Paul, MN 55121
Phone: (612)905-8400
Free: (888)625-8612
Fax: (612)454-0760
E-mail: Barb@Powersys.com
Website: http://www.powersys.com

Small Business Success
PO Box 21097
St. Paul, MN 55121-0097
Phone: (612)454-2500
Fax: (612)456-9138

## Missouri

Business Planning and Development
Corp.
4030 Charlotte St.
Kansas City, MO 64110
Phone: (816)753-0495
E-mail: humph@bpdev.demon.co.uk
Website: http://
www.bpdev.demon.co.uk

CFO Service
10336 Donoho
St. Louis, MO 63131
Phone: (314)750-2940
E-mail: jskae@cfoservice.com
Website: http://www.cfoservice.com

### Nebraska

Heartland Management Consulting
Group
1904 Barrington Pky.
Papillion, NE 68046
Phone: (402)339-2387
Fax: (402)339-1319

International Management Consulting
Group Inc.
1309 Harlan Dr., Ste. 205
Bellevue, NE 68005
Phone: (402)291-4545
Free: 800-665-IMCG
Fax: (402)291-4343
E-mail: imcg@neonramp.com
Website: http://
www.mgtconsulting.com

### Nevada

The DuBois Group
865 Tahoe Blvd., Ste. 108
Incline Village, NV 89451
Phone: (775)832-0550
Free: 800-375-2935
Fax: (775)832-0556
E-mail: DuBoisGrp@aol.com

Technology Consultants, Inc.
5300 W. Sahara Ave.
Ste. 106
Las Vegas, NV 89146
Free: (888)737-4727
Fax: (877)511-3833
E-mail: spraggs@sfu.ca
Cynthia Spraggs

### New Hampshire

BPT Consulting Associates Ltd.
12 Parmenter Rd., Ste. B-6
Londonderry, NH 03053
Phone: (603)437-8484
Free: (888)278-0030
Fax: (603)434-5388
E-mail: bptcons@tiac.net
Website: http://
www.bptconsulting.com

Wolff Consultants
10 Buck Rd.
Hanover, NH 03755
Phone: (603)643-6015

### New Jersey

Aurora Marketing Management Inc.
66 Witherspoon St., Ste. 600
Princeton, NJ 08542
Phone: (908)904-1125
Fax: (908)359-1108
E-mail: aurora2@voicenet.com
Website: http://
www.auroramarketing.net

R.W. Bankart & Associates
20 Valley Ave., Ste. D-2
Westwood, NJ 07675-3607
Phone: (201)664-7672

Henry Branch Associates
2502 Harmon Cove Tower
Secaucus, NJ 07094
Phone: (201)866-2008
Fax: (201)601-0101
E-mail: hbranch161@aol.com

ConMar International Ltd.
283 Dayton-Jamesburg Rd.
Dayton, NJ 08810
Phone: (908)274-1100
Fax: (908)274-1199

Robert Gibbons & Company Inc.
46 Knoll Rd.
Tenafly, NJ 07670-1050
Phone: (201)871-3933
Fax: (201)871-2173
E-mail: crisisbob@aol.com

John Hall & Company Inc.
PO Box 187
Glen Ridge, NJ 07028
Phone: (201)680-4449
Fax: (201)680-4581
E-mail: jhcompany@aol.com

KLW New Products
156 Cedar Dr.
Old Tappan, NJ 07675
Phone: (201)358-1300
Fax: (201)664-2594
E-mail: lrlarsen@usa.net
Website: http://
www.klwnewproducts.com

Kumar Associates Inc.
1004 Cumbermeade Rd.
Fort Lee, NJ 07024

Phone: (201)224-9480
Fax: (201)585-2343
E-mail: kassoc@idt.net

Market Focus
PO Box 402
Maplewood, NJ 07040
Phone: (973)378-2470
Fax: (973)378-2470
E-mail: mcss66@marketfocus.com

PA Consulting Group
315A Enterprise Dr.
Plainsboro, NJ 08536
Phone: (609)936-8300
Fax: (609)936-8811
E-mail: info@paconsulting.com
Website: http://www.pa-
consulting.com

PMC Management Consultants Inc.
11 Thistle Ln.
Three Bridges, NJ 08887-0332
Phone: (908)788-1014
Fax: (908)806-7287
E-mail: int@pmc-management.com
Website: http://www.wwpmc-
management.com

Schkeeper Inc.
130-6 Bodman Pl.
Red Bank, NJ 07701
Phone: (732)219-1965
Fax: (732)530-3703

Smart Business Supersite
88 Orchard Rd., CN-5219
Princeton, NJ 08543
Phone: (908)321-1924
Fax: (908)321-5156
E-mail: irv@smartbiz.com
Website: http://www.smartbiz.com

Tracelin Associates
1171 Main St., Ste. 6K
Rahway, NJ 07065
Phone: (732)381-3288

Vanguard Communications Corp.
100 American Rd.
Morris Plains, NJ 07950
Phone: (201)605-8000
Fax: (201)605-8329
Website: http://www.vanguard.net/

### New Mexico

InfoNewMexico
2207 Black Hills Rd., NE

Rio Rancho, NM 87124
Phone: (505)891-2462
Fax: (505)896-8971

Vondle & Associates Inc.
4926 Calle de Tierra, NE
Albuquerque, NM 87111
Phone: (505)292-8961
Fax: (505)296-2790
E-mail: vondle@aol.com

## New York

M. Clifford Agress
891 Fulton St.
Valley Stream, NY 11580
Phone: (516)825-8955
Fax: (516)825-8955

Boice Dunham Group
30 W 13th St.
New York, NY 10011
Phone: (212)752-5550
Fax: (212)752-7055

Elizabeth Capen
27 E 95th St.
New York, NY 10128
Phone: (212)427-7654
Fax: (212)876-3190

ComputerEase Co.
9 Hachaliah Brown Dr.
Somers, NY 10589
Phone: (914)277-5317
Fax: (914)277-5317
E-mail: crawfordc@juno.com

Consortium House
139 Wittenberg Rd.
Bearsville, NY 12409
Phone: (914)679-8867
Fax: (914)679-9248
E-mail: eugenegs@aol.com
Website: http://www.chpub.com

Delta Planning Inc.
PO Box 425
Denville, NY 07834
Phone: (913)625-1742
Free: 800-672-0762
Fax: (973)625-3531
E-mail: DeltaP@worldnet.att.net
Website: http://deltaplanning.com

Haver Analytics
60 E 42nd St., Ste. 2424
New York, NY 10017
Phone: (212)986-9300
Fax: (212)986-5857

E-mail: data@haver.com
Website: http://www.haver.com

Innovation Management Consulting
Inc.
209 Dewitt Rd.
Syracuse, NY 13214-2006
Phone: (315)425-5144
Fax: (315)445-8989
E-mail: missonneb@axess.net

The Jordan, Edmiston Group Inc.
150 E 52nd Ave., 18th Fl.
New York, NY 10022
Phone: (212)754-0710
Fax: (212)754-0337

Destiny Kinal Marketing Consultancy
105 Chemung St.
Waverly, NY 14892
Phone: (607)565-8317
Fax: (607)565-4083

KPMG International
345 Park Ave.
New York, NY 10154-0102
Phone: (212)758-9700
Fax: (212)758-9819
Website: http://www.kpmg.com

Mahoney Cohen Consulting Corp.
111 W 40th St., 12th Fl.
New York, NY 10018
Phone: (212)490-8000
Fax: (212)790-5913

Management Insight
96 Arlington Rd.
Buffalo, NY 14221
Phone: (716)631-3319
Free: 800-643-3319
Fax: (716)631-0203
E-mail:
michalski@foodserviceinsight.com
Website: http://
www.foodserviceinsight.com

Management Practice Inc.
342 Madison Ave.
New York, NY 10173-1230
Phone: (212)867-7948
Fax: (212)972-5188
Website: http://www.mpiweb.com

Marketing Resources Group
71-58 Austin St.
Forest Hills, NY 11375
Phone: (718)261-8882

Moseley Associates Inc.
342 Madison Ave., Ste. 1414

New York, NY 10016
Phone: (212)213-6673
Fax: (212)687-1520

North Star Enterprises
670 N Terrace Ave.
Mount Vernon, NY 10552
Phone: (914)668-9433

Overton Financial
7 Allen Rd.
Peekskill, NY 10566
Phone: (914)737-4649
Fax: (914)737-4696

Powers Research and Training
Institute
PO Box 78
Bayville, NY 11709
Phone: (516)628-2250
Fax: (516)628-2252
E-mail:
powercocch@compuserve.com
Website: http://
www.nancypowers.com

Practice Development Counsel
60 Sutton Pl. S
New York, NY 10022
Phone: (212)593-1549
Fax: (212)980-7940
E-mail: pwhaserot@pdcounsel.com
Website: http://www.pdcounsel.com

Progressive Finance Corp.
3549 Tiemann Ave.
Bronx, NY 10469
Phone: (718)405-9029
Free: 800-225-8381
Fax: (718)405-1170

Samani International Enterprises,
Marions Panyaught Consultancy
2028 Parsons
Flushing, NY 11357-3436
Phone: (917)287-8087
Fax: 800-873-8939
E-mail: vjp2@compuserve.com
Website: http://www.dorsai.org/~vjp2

Stromberg Consulting
2500 Westchester Ave.
Purchase, NY 10577
Phone: (914)251-1515
Fax: (914)251-1562
E-mail:
strategy@stromberg_consulting.com
Website: http://
www.stromberg_consulting.com

Unique Value International Inc.
575 Madison Ave., 10th Fl.
New York, NY 10022-1304
Phone: (212)605-0590
Fax: (212)605-0589

Valutis Consulting Inc.
5350 Main St., Ste. 7
Williamsville, NY 14221-5338
Phone: (716)634-2553
Fax: (716)634-2554
E-mail: valutis@localnet.com
Website: http://
www.valutisconsulting.com

The Van Tulleken Co.
126 E 56th St.
New York, NY 10022
Phone: (212)355-1390
Fax: (212)755-3061
E-mail: newyork@vantqlleken.com

Vencon Management Inc.
301 W 53rd St.
New York, NY 10019
Phone: (212)581-8787
Fax: (212)397-4126
Website: http://www.venconinc.com

Wave Hill Associates
2621 Palisade Ave., Ste. 15-C
Bronx, NY 10463
Phone: (718)549-7368
Fax: (718)601-9670

Werner International Inc.
55 E 52nd, 29th Fl.
New York, NY 10055
Phone: (212)909-1260
Fax: (212)909-1273
E-mail: richard.downing@rgh.com
Website: http://www.wernertex.com

Zimmerman Business Consulting Inc.
44 E 92nd St., Ste. 5-B
New York, NY 10128
Phone: (212)860-3107
Fax: (212)860-7730
E-mail: ljzzbci@aol.com

## North Carolina

Best Practices, LLC
6320 Quadrangle Dr., Ste. 200
Chapel Hill, NC 27514
Phone: (919)403-0251
Fax: (919)403-0144
E-mail: best@best:in/class

Website: http://www.best-in-
class.com

Norelli & Co.
Bank of America Corporate Ctr.
100 N Tyron St., Ste. 5160
Charlotte, NC 28202-4000
Phone: (704)376-5484
Fax: (704)376-5485
E-mail: consult@norelli.com
Website: http://www.norelli.com

## North Dakota

Center for Innovation
4300 Dartmouth Dr.
PO Box 8372
Grand Forks, ND 58202
Phone: (701)777-3132
Fax: (701)777-2339
E-mail: bruce@innovators.net
Website: http://www.innovators.net

## Ohio

Alliance Management International
Ltd.
1440 Windrow Ln.
Cleveland, OH 44147-3200
Phone: (440)838-1922
Fax: (440)838-0979
E-mail: bgruss@amiltd.com
Website: http://www.amiltd.com

Bastian Public Relations
499 Clemray Dr.
Cincinnati, OH 45231
Phone: (513)772-4533
Fax: (513)772-3180
E-mail: lisa@bastianpr.com
Website: www.bastianpr.com
Lisa Bastian

Bozell Kamstra Public Relations
1301 E 9th St., Ste. 3400
Cleveland, OH 44114
Phone: (216)623-1511
Fax: (216)623-1501
E-mail:
jfeniger@cleveland.bozellkamstra.com
Website: http://
www.bozellkamstra.com

Cory Dillon Associates
111 Schreyer Pl. E
Columbus, OH 43214
Phone: (614)262-8211
Fax: (614)262-3806

Empro Systems Inc.
4777 Red Bank Expy., Ste. 1
Cincinnati, OH 45227-1542
Phone: (513)271-2042
Fax: (513)271-2042

Holcomb Gallagher Adams
300 Marconi, Ste. 303
Columbus, OH 43215
Phone: (614)221-3343
Fax: (614)221-3367
E-mail: riadams@acme.freenet.oh.us

Transportation Technology Services
208 Harmon Rd.
Aurora, OH 44202
Phone: (330)562-3596

Robert A. Westman & Associates
8981 Inversary Dr. SE
Warren, OH 44484-2551
Phone: (330)856-4149
Fax: (330)856-2564

Young & Associates
PO Box 711
Kent, OH 44240
Phone: (330)678-0524
Free: 800-525-9775
Fax: (330)678-6219
Website: http://www.younginc.com

## Oklahoma

Innovative Partners LLC
4900 Richmond Sq., Ste. 100
Oklahoma City, OK 73118
Phone: (405)840-0033
Fax: (405)843-8359
E-mail: ipartners@juno.com

## Oregon

INTERCON - The International
Converting Institute
5200 Badger Rd.
Crooked River Ranch, OR 97760
Phone: (541)548-1447
Fax: (541)548-1618
E-mail:
johnbowler@crookedriverranch.com

Management Technology Associates
Ltd.
1750 NW Naito Pky., Ste. 113
Portland, OR 97209
Phone: (503)224-5220
Fax: (503)224-6704
E-mail: lcuster@mta-ltd.com
Website: http://www.mgmt-tech.com

Talbott ARM
HC 60, Box 5620
Lakeview, OR 97630
Phone: (541)635-8587
Fax: (503)947-3482

## Pennsylvania

Advantage Associates
434 Avon Dr.
Pittsburgh, PA 15228
Phone: (412)343-1558
Fax: (412)362-1684
E-mail: ecocba1@aol.com

Autech Products
1289 Revere Rd.
Morrisville, PA 19067
Phone: (215)493-3759
Fax: (215)493-9791
E-mail: autech4@yahoo.com

James W. Davidson Company Inc.
23 Forest View Rd.
Wallingford, PA 19086
Phone: (610)566-1462

GRA Inc.
115 West Ave., Ste. 201
Jenkintown, PA 19046
Phone: (215)884-7500
Fax: (215)884-1385
E-mail: gramail@gra-inc.com
Website: http://www.gra-inc.com

Healthscope Inc.
400 Lancaster Ave.
Devon, PA 19333
Phone: (610)687-6199
Fax: (610)687-6376
E-mail: health@voicenet.com
Website: http://www.healthscope.net/

Elayne Howard & Associates Inc.
3501 Masons Mill Rd., Ste. 501
Huntingdon Valley, PA 19006-3509
Phone: (215)657-9550

Mifflin County Industrial
Development Corp.
Mifflin County Industrial Plz.
6395 SR 103 N
Bldg. 50
Lewistown, PA 17044
Phone: (717)242-0393
Fax: (717)242-1842
E-mail: mcide@acsworld.net

Regis J. Sheehan & Associates
291 Foxcroft Rd.

Pittsburgh, PA 15220
Phone: (412)279-1207

## Puerto Rico

Diego Chevere & Co.
Ste. 301, Metro Parque 7
Caparra Heights, PR 00920
Phone: (787)782-9595
Fax: (787)782-9532

Manuel L. Porrata and Associates
898 Munoz Rivera Ave., Ste. 201
Rio Piedras, PR 00927
Phone: (809)765-2140
Fax: (809)754-3285

## South Carolina

Aquafood Business Associates
PO Box 16190
Charleston, SC 29412
Phone: (803)795-9506
Fax: (803)795-9477

Minus Stage
Box 4436
Rock Hill, SC 29731
Phone: (803)328-0705
Fax: (803)329-9948

Profit Associates Inc.
PO Box 38026
Charleston, SC 29414
Phone: (803)763-5718
Fax: (803)763-5719
E-mail: bobrog@awod.com
Website: http://www.awod.com/
gallery/business/proasc

Strategic Innovations International
12 Executive Ct.
Lake Wylie, SC 29710
Phone: (803)831-1225
Fax: (803)831-1177
E-mail: stratinnov@aol.com
Website: http://
www.strategicinnovations.com

## Tennessee

Business Choices
1114 Forest Harbor, Ste. 300
Hendersonville, TN 37075-9646
Phone: (615)822-8692
Free: 800-737-8382
Fax: (615)822-8692
E-mail: bz-ch@juno.com

Growth Consultants of America
3917 Trimble Rd.
Nashville, TN 37215
Phone: (615)383-0550
Fax: (615)269-8940
E-mail: 70244.451@compuserve.com

Daniel Petchers & Associates
8820 Fernwood CV
Germantown, TN 38138
Phone: (901)755-9896

RCFA Healthcare Management
Services, LLC
9648 Kingston Pke., Ste. 8
Knoxville, TN 37922
Phone: (865)531-0176
Free: 800-635-4040
Fax: (865)531-0722
E-mail: info@rcfa.com
Website: http://www.rcfa.com

## Texas

Business Resource Software Inc.
2013 Wells Branch Pky., Ste. 305
Austin, TX 78728
Free: 800-423-1228
E-mail: info@brs-inc.com
Website: http://www.brs-inc.com

Business Strategy Development
Consultants
PO Box 690365
San Antonio, TX 78269
Phone: (210)696-8000
Free: 800-927-BSDC
Fax: (210)696-8000

Erisa Adminstrative Services Inc.
12325 Haymeadow Dr., Bldg. 4
Austin, TX 78750-1847
Phone: (512)250-9020
Fax: (512)250-9487
Website: http://www.cserisa.com

R. Miller Hicks & Co.
1011 W 11th St.
Austin, TX 78703
Phone: (512)477-7000
Fax: (512)477-9697
E-mail: millerhicks@rmhicks.com
Website: http://www.rmhicks.com

High Technology Associates -
Division of Global Technologies Inc.
1775 St. James Pl., Ste. 105
Houston, TX 77056

Phone: (713)963-9300
Fax: (713)963-8341
E-mail: hta@infohwy.com

Integrated Cost Management Systems
Inc.
2261 Brookhollow Plz. Dr., Ste. 104
Arlington, TX 76006
Phone: (817)633-2873
Fax: (817)633-3781
E-mail: abm@icms.net
Website: http://www.icms.net

MasterCOM
103 Thunder Rd.
Kerrville, TX 78028
Phone: (830)895-7990
Fax: (830)443-3428
E-mail:
jmstubblefield@mastertraining.com
Website: http://
www.mastertraining.com

Perot Systems
12404 Park Central Dr.
Dallas, TX 75251
Phone: (972)340-5000
Free: 800-688-4333
Fax: (972)455-4100
E-mail: corp.comm@ps.net
Website: http://
www.perotsystems.com

Pragmatic Tactics Inc.
3303 Westchester Ave.
College Station, TX 77845
Phone: (409)696-5294
Free: 800-570-5294
Fax: (409)696-4994
E-mail: ptactics@aol.com
Website: http://www.ptatics.com

PROTEC
4607 Linden Pl.
Pearland, TX 77584
Phone: (281)997-9872
Fax: (281)997-9895
E-mail: p.oman@ix.netcom.com

ReGENERATION Partners
3838 Oak Lawn Ave.
Dallas, TX 75219
Phone: (214)559-3999
Free: 800-406-1112
Website: http://www.regeneration-
partners.com

Tom Welch, CPC
6900 San Pedro Ave., Ste. 147
San Antonio, TX 78216-6207

Phone: (210)737-7022
Fax: (210)737-7022
E-mail: bplan@iamerica.net
Website: http://
www.moneywords.com

Lori Williams
1000 Leslie Ct.
Arlington, TX 76012
Phone: (817)459-3934
Fax: (817)459-3934

## Utah

Business Management Resource
PO Box 521125
Salt Lake City, UT 84152-1125
Phone: (801)272-4668
Fax: (801)277-3290
E-mail: pingfong@worldnet.att.net

## Virginia

AMX International Inc.
1420 Spring Hill Rd. , Ste. 600
McLean, VA 22102-3006
Phone: (703)690-4100
Fax: (703)643-1279
E-mail: amxmail@amxi.com
Website: http://www.amxi.com

Federal Market Development
5650 Chapel Run Ct.
Centreville, VA 20120-3601
Phone: (703)502-8930
Free: 800-821-5003
Fax: (703)502-8929

Huff & Stuart
2107 Graves Mills Rd., Ste. C
Forest, VA 24551
Phone: (804)316-9356
Free: (888)316-9356
Fax: (804)316-9357
Website: http://www.wealthnet.net

Elliott B. Jaffa
2530-B S Walter Reed Dr.
Arlington, VA 22206
Phone: (703)931-0040
E-mail: trainingdoctor@excite.com

Koach Enterprises - USA
5529 N 18th St.
Arlington, VA 22205
Phone: (703)241-8361
Fax: (703)241-8623

McLeod & Co.
410 1st St.

Roanoke, VA 24011
Phone: (540)342-6911
Fax: (540)344-6367
Website: http://www.mcleodco.com/

Charles Scott Pugh (Investor)
4101 Pittaway Dr.
Richmond, VA 23235-1022
Phone: (804)560-0979
Fax: (804)560-4670

John C. Randall and Associates Inc.
PO Box 15127
Richmond, VA 23227
Phone: (804)746-4450
Fax: (804)747-7426

Salzinger & Company Inc.
8000 Towers Crescent Dr., Ste. 1350
Vienna, VA 22182
Phone: (703)442-5200
Fax: (703)442-5205
E-mail: info@salzinger.com
Website: http://www.salzinger.com

The Small Business Counselor
12423 Hedges Run Dr., Ste. 153
Woodbridge, VA 22192
Phone: (703)490-6755
Fax: (703)490-1356

## Washington

Burlington Consultants
10900 NE 8th St., Ste. 900
Bellevue, WA 98004
Phone: (425)688-3060
Fax: (425)454-4383
E-mail:
partners@burlingtonconsultants.com
Website: http://
www.burlingtonconsultants.com

Business Planning Consultants
S 3510 Ridgeview Dr.
Spokane, WA 99206
Phone: (509)928-0332
Fax: (509)921-0842
E-mail: bpci@nextdim.com

Dan Collin
3419 Wallingord Ave N. #2
Seattle, WA 98103
Phone: (206)634-9469
E-mail: dc@dancollin.com
Website: http://members.home.net/
dcollin/

ECG Management Consultants Inc.
1111 3rd Ave., Ste. 2700

Seattle, WA 98101-3201
Phone: (206)689-2200
Fax: (206)689-2209
E-mail: ecg@ecgmc.com
Website: http://www.ecgmc.com

Independent Automotive Training
Services
PO Box 334
Kirkland, WA 98071-0344
Phone: (425)822-5715
E-mail: ltunney@autosvccon.com
Website: http://www.autosvccon.com

Kahle Associate Inc.
6203 204th Dr. NE
Redmond, WA 98053
Phone: (425)836-8763
Fax: (425)868-3770
E-mail:
randykahle@kahleassociates.com
Website: http://
www.kahleassociates.com

Northwest Trade Adjustment
Assistance Center
900 4th Ave., Ste. 2430
Seattle, WA 98164-1003
Phone: (206)622-2730
Free: 800-667-8087
Fax: (206)622-1105
E-mail: matchingfunds@nwtaac.org

St. Charles Consulting Group
1420 NW Gilman Blvd.
Issaquah, WA 98027
Phone: (425)557-8708
Fax: (425)557-8731
E-mail:
info@stcharlesconsulting.com
Website: http://
www.stcharlesconsulting.com

Perry L. Smith Consulting
800 Bellevue Way NE, Ste. 400
Bellevue, WA 98004-4208
Phone: (425)462-2072
Fax: (425)462-5638

## Wisconsin

White & Associates Inc.
5349 Somerset Ln. S
Greenfield, WI 53221
Phone: (414)281-7373
Fax: (414)281-7006
E-mail: wnaconsult@aol.com

# SMALL BUSINESS ADMINISTRATION REGIONAL OFFICES

*This section contains a listing of Small Business Administration offices arranged numerically by region. Service areas are provided. Contact the appropriate office for a referral to the nearest field office, or visit the Small Business Administration online at www.sba.gov.*

## Region 1

U.S. Small Business Administration
10 Causeway St.
Boston, MA 02222-1093
Phone: (617)565-8415
Fax: (617)565-8420
Serves Connecticut, Maine,
Massachusetts, New Hampshire,
Rhode Island, and Vermont.

## Region 2

U.S. Small Business Administration
26 Federal Plaza, Ste. 3108
New York, NY 10278
Phone: (212)264-1450
Fax: (212)264-0038
Serves New Jersey, New York, Puerto
Rico, and the Virgin Islands.

## Region 3

Serves Delaware, the District of
Columbia, Maryland, Pennsylvania,
Virginia, and West Virginia. For the
nearest field office, visit the Small
Business Administration online at
www.sba.gov.

## Region 4

U.S. Small Business Administration
233 Peachtree St. NE
Harris Tower 1800
Atlanta, GA 30303
Phone: (404)331-4999
Fax: (404)331-2354
Serves Alabama, Florida, Georgia,
Kentucky, Mississippi, North
Carolina, South Carolina, and
Tennessee.

## Region 5

U.S. Small Business Administration
500 W. Madison St., Ste. 1240
Chicago, IL 60661-2511
Phone: (312)353-5000
Fax: (312)353-3426
Serves Illinois, Indiana, Michigan,
Minnesota, Ohio, and Wisconsin.

## Region 6

U.S. Small Business Administration
4300 Amon Carter Blvd.
Dallas/Fort Worth, TX 76155
Phone: (817)885-6581
Fax: (817)885-6588
Serves Arkansas, Louisiana, New
Mexico, Oklahoma, and Texas.

## Region 7

U.S. Small Business Administration
323 W. 8th St., Ste. 307
Kansas City, MO 64105-1500
Phone: (816)374-6380
Fax: (816)374-6339
Serves Iowa, Kansas, Missouri, and
Nebraska.

## Region 8

U.S. Small Business Administration
721 19th St., Ste. 400
Denver, CO 80202
Phone: (303)844-0500
Fax: (303)844-0506
Serves Colorado, Montana, North
Dakota, South Dakota, Utah, and
Wyoming.

## Region 9

U.S. Small Business Administration
455 Market St., Ste. 2200
San Francisco, CA 94105
Phone: (415)744-2118
Fax: (415)744-2119
Serves American Samoa, Arizona,
California, Guam, Hawaii, Nevada,
and the Trust Territory of the Pacific
Islands.

## Region 10

U.S. Small Business Administration
1200 6th Ave., Ste. 1805
Seattle, WA 98101-1128
Phone: (206)553-5676

Fax: (206)553-2872
Serves Alaska, Idaho, Oregon, and
Washington.

# SMALL BUSINESS DEVELOPMENT CENTERS

*This section contains a listing of all Small Business Development Centers organized alphabetically by state/U.S. territory name, then by agency name.*

## Alabama

Alabama A & M University
University of Alabama at Huntsville
NE Alabama Regional Small
Business Development Center
PO Box 168
225 Church St., NW
Huntsville, AL 35804-0168
Phone: (205)535-2061
Fax: (205)535-2050
Jeff Thompson

Alabama International Trade Center
University of Alabama
SBDC Bidgood Hall, Rm. 201
PO Box 870396
Tuscaloosa, AL 35487-0396
Phone: (205)348-7621
Fax: (205)348-6974
E-mail: aitc@aitc.cba.ua.edu
Brian Davis

Alabama Small Business
Development Consortium
Office of the State Director
University of Alabama at
Birmingham
2800 Milan Court, Ste. 124
Medical Towers Bldg.
Birmingham, AL 35211
Phone: (205)943-6750
Fax: (205)943-6752
E-mail: sandefur@uab.edu
Website: http://www.asbdc.org
John Sandefur, Director

Alabama Small Business Procurement
System
University o f Alabama at
Birmingham
SBDC
1717 11th Ave. S., Ste. 419
Birmingham, AL 35294-4410

Phone: (205)934-7260
Fax: (205)934-7645
Charles Hobson

Alabama State University
SBDC
915 S. Jackson St.
Montgomery, AL 36104-5714
Phone: (334)229-4138
Fax: (334)269-1102
Lorenza G. Patrick

Auburn University
SBDC
108 College of Business
Auburn, AL 36849-5243
Phone: (334)844-4220
Fax: (334)844-4268
Garry Hannem

Jacksonville State University
Small Business Development Center
114 Merrill Hall
700 Pelham Rd. N.
Jacksonville, AL 36265
Phone: (205)782-5271
Fax: (205)782-5179
Pat Shaddix

Troy State University
Small Business Development Center
Bibb Graves, Rm. 102
Troy, AL 36082-0001
Phone: (205)670-3771
Fax: (205)670-3636
Janet W. Kervin

University of Alabama
Alabama International Trade Center
Small Business Development Center
Bidgood Hall, Rm. 250
Box 870397
Tuscaloosa, AL 35487-0396
Phone: (205)348-7011
Fax: (205)348-9644
Paavo Hanninen

University of Alabama at
Birmingham
Alabama Small Business
Development Consortium
SBDC
1717 11th Ave. S., Ste. 419
Birmingham, AL 35294-4410
Phone: (205)934-7260
Fax: (205)934-7645
John Sandefur

University of Alabama at
Birmingham
SBDC
1601 11th Ave. S.
Birmingham, AL 35294-2180
Phone: (205)934-6760
Fax: (205)934-0538
Brenda Walker

University of North Alabama
Small Business Development Center
Box 5248, Keller Hall
Florence, AL 35632-0001
Phone: (205)760-4629
Fax: (205)760-4813

University of South Alabama
Small Business Development Center
College of Business, Rm. 8
Mobile, AL 36688
Phone: (334)460-6004
Fax: (334)460-6246

University of West Alabama
SBDC
Station 35
Livingston, AL 35470
Phone: (205)652-3665
Fax: (205)652-3516
Paul Garner

## Alaska

Kenai Peninsula Small Business
Development Center
PO Box 3029
Kenai, AK 99611-3029
Phone: (907)283-3335
Fax: (907)283-3913
Mark Gregory

University of Alaska (Anchorage)
Small Business Development Center
430 W. 7th Ave., Ste. 110
Anchorage, AK 99501
Phone: (907)274-7232
Free: 800-478-7232
Fax: (907)274-9524
E-mail: anjaf@uaa.alaska.edu
Jan Fredricks, Director

University of Alaska (Fairbanks)
Small Business Development Center
510 Second Ave., Ste. 101
Fairbanks, AK 99701
Phone: (907)474-6700
Fax: (907)474-1139
Billie Ray Allen

University of Alaska (Juneau)
Small Business Development Center
612 W. Willoughby Ave., Ste. A
Juneau, AK 99801
Phone: (907)463-1732
Fax: (907)463-3929
Norma Strickland

University of Alaska (Matanuska-
Susitna)
Small Business Development Center
201 N. Lucile St., Ste. 2-A
Wasilla, AK 99654
Phone: (907)373-7232
Fax: (907)373-7234
Timothy Sullivan

## Arizona

Arizona Small Business Development
Center Network
Maricopa County Community College
SBDC
2411 W 14th St., Ste. 132
Tempe, AZ 85281
Phone: (480)731-8722
Fax: (480)731-8729
E-mail: york@maricopa.bitnet
Website: http://
www.dist.maricopa.edu/sbdc
Michael York

Arizona Western College
Small Business Development Center
Century Plz., No. 152
281 W. 24th St.
Yuma, AZ 85364
Phone: (520)341-1650
Fax: (520)726-2636
John Lundin

Central Arizona College
Pinal County Small Business
Development Center
8470 N. Overfield Rd.
Coolidge, AZ 85228
Phone: (520)426-4341
Fax: (520)426-4363
Carol Giordano

Cochise College
Small Business Development Center
901 N. Colombo, Rm. 308
Sierra Vista, AZ 85635
Phone: (520)515-5478
Fax: (520)515-5437
E-mail: sbdc@trom.cochise.cc.az.us
Shelia Devoe Heidman

Coconino County Community
College
Small Business Development Center
3000 N. 4th St., Ste. 25
Flagstaff, AZ 86004
Phone: (520)526-5072
Fax: (520)526-8693
Mike Lainoff

Eastern Arizona College
SBDC
622 College Ave.
Thatcher, AZ 85552-0769
Phone: (520)428-8590
Fax: (520)428-8591
Frank Granberg

Eastern Arizona College
Small Business Development Center
622 College Ave.
Thatcher, AZ 85552-0769
Phone: (520)428-8590
Fax: (520)428-8462
Greg Roers

Maricopa Community Colleges
Arizona Small Business Development
Center Network
2411 W. 14th St., Ste. 132
Tempe, AZ 85281
Phone: (602)731-8720
Fax: (602)731-8729
Michael York

Mohave Community College
Small Business Development Center
1971 Jagerson Ave.
Kingman, AZ 86401
Phone: (520)757-0894
Fax: (520)757-0836
Kathy McGehee

Northland Pioneer College
Small Business Development Center
PO Box 610
Holbrook, AZ 86025
Phone: (520)537-2976
Fax: (520)524-2227
Mark Engle

Pima Community College
Small Business Development and
Training Center
4905-A E. Broadway Blvd., Ste. 101
Tucson, AZ 85709-1260
Phone: (520)206-4906
Fax: (520)206-4585
Linda Andrews

Yavapai College
Small Business Development Center
Elks Building
117 E. Gurley St., Ste. 206
Prescott, AZ 86301
Phone: (520)778-3088
Fax: (520)778-3109
Richard Senopole

## Arkansas

Arkansas State University
Small Business Development Center
College of Business
Drawer 2650
Jonesboro, AR 72467
Phone: (870)972-3517
Fax: (501)972-3868
Herb Lawrence

Genesis Technology Incubator
SBDC Satellite Office
University of Arkansas - Engineering
Research Center
Fayetteville, AR 72701-1201
Phone: (501)575-7473
Fax: (501)575-7446
Bob Penquite

Henderson State University
Small Business Development Center
1100 Henderson St.
PO Box 7624
Arkadelphia, AR 71923
Phone: (870)230-5224
Fax: (870)230-5236
Jeff Doose

Mid-South Community College
SBDC
2000 W. Broadway
PO Box 2067
West Memphis, AR 72303-2067
Phone: (870)733-6767

Small Business Development Center
1109 S. 16th St.
PO Box 2067
Ft. Smith, AR 72901
Phone: (501)785-1376
Fax: (501)785-1964
Vonelle Vanzant

University of Arkansas at Fayetteville
Small Business Development Center
Business Administration Bldg., Ste.
106
Fayetteville, AR 72701
Phone: (501)575 5148

Fax: (501)575-4013
Ms. Jimmie Wilkins

University of Arkansas at Little Rock
SBDC
Little Rock Technology Center Bldg.
100 S. Main St., Ste. 401
Little Rock, AR 72201
Phone: (501)324-9043
Fax: (501)324-9049
Website: http://www.ualr.edu/
~sbdcdept/
Janet Nye

University of Arkansas at Little Rock,
Regional Office (Fort Smith)
Small Business Development Center
1109 S. 16th St.
PO Box 2067
Ft. Smith, AR 72901
Phone: (501)785-1376
Fax: (501)785-1964
Byron Branch

University of Arkansas at Little Rock,
Regional Office (Harrison)
Small Business Development Center
818 Hwy. 62-65-412 N
PO Box 190
Harrison, AR 72601
Phone: (870)741-8009
Fax: (870)741-1905
Bob Penquite

University of Arkansas at Little Rock,
Regional Office (Hot Springs)
Small Business Development Center
835 Central Ave., Box 402-D
Hot Springs, AR 71901
Phone: (501)624-5448
Fax: (501)624-6632
Richard Evans

University of Arkansas at Little Rock,
Regional Office (Magnolia)
Small Business Development Center
600 Bessie
PO Box 767
Magnolia, AR 71753
Phone: (870)234-4030
Fax: (870)234-0135
Mr. Lairie Kincaid

University of Arkansas at Little Rock,
Regional Office (Pine Bluff)
Small Business Development Center
The Enterprise Center III
400 Main, Ste. 117
Pine Bluff, AR 71601

Phone: (870)536-0654
Fax: (870)536-7713
Russell Barker

University of Arkansas at Little Rock,
Regional Office (Stuttgart)
Small Business Development Center
301 S. Grand, Ste. 101
PO Box 289
Stuttgart, AR 72160
Phone: (870)673-8707
Fax: (870)673-8707
Larry Lefler

## California

Accelerate Technology Assistance
Small Business Development Center
4199 Campus Dr.
University Towers, Ste. 240
Irvine, CA 92612-4688
Phone: (714)509-2990
Fax: (714)509-2997
Tiffany Haugen

Alpine SBDC
PO Box 265
3 Webster St.
Markleeville, CA 96120
Phone: (916)694-2475
Fax: (916)694-2478

Amador SBDC
222 N. Hwy. 49
PO Box 1077
Jackson, CA 95642
Phone: (209)223-0351
Fax: (209)223-5237
Ron Mittelbrunn

Butte College
Small Business Development Center
260 Cohasset Rd., Ste. A
Chico, CA 95926
Phone: (916)895-9017
Fax: (916)895-9099
Kay Zimmerlee

Calaveras SBDC
PO Box 431
3 N. Main St.
San Andreas, CA 95249
Phone: (209)754-1834
Fax: (209)754-4107

California Small Business
Development Center
California Trade and Commerce
Agency

801 K St., Ste 1700
Sacremento, CA 95814
Phone: (916)324-5068
Free: 800-303-6600
Fax: (916)322-5084
Website: http://commerce.ca.gov/
business/small/starting/sb_sbdcl.html
Kim Neri

California Trade and Commerce
Agency
California SBDC
801 K St., Ste. 1700
Sacramento, CA 95814
Phone: (916)324-5068
Fax: (916)322-5084
Kim Neri

Cascade Small Business Development
Center
737 Auditorium Dr., Ste. A
Redding, CA 96001
Phone: (916)247-8100
Fax: (916)241-1712
Carole Enmark

Central California
Small Business Development Center
3419 W. Shaw Ave., Ste. 102
Fresno, CA 93711
Phone: (209)275-1223
Fax: (209)275-1499
Dennis Winans

Central California/Visalia Satellite
SBDC
430 W. Caldwell Ave., Ste. D
Visalia, CA 93277
Phone: (209)625-3051
Fax: (209)625-3053
Randy Mason

Central Coast Small Business
Development Center
6500 Soquel Dr.
Aptos, CA 95003
Phone: (408)479-6136
Fax: (408)479-6166
Teresa Thomae

Coachella Valley SBDC
Palm Springs Satellite Center
501 S. Palm Canyon Dr., Ste. 222
Palm Springs, CA 92264
Phone: (619)864-1311
Fax: (619)864-1319
Brad Mix

Contra Costa SBDC
2425 Bisso Ln., Ste. 200
Concord, CA 94520
Phone: (510)646-5377
Fax: (510)646-5299
Debra Longwood

East Bay Small Business
Development Center
519 17th. St., Ste. 210
Oakland, CA 94612
Phone: (510)893-4114
Fax: (510)893-5532
Napoleon Britt

East Los Angeles SBDC
5161 East Pomona Blvd., Ste. 212
Los Angeles, CA 90022
Phone: (213)262-9797
Fax: (213)262-2704

Eastern Los Angeles County Small
Business Development Center
375 S. Main St., Ste. 101
Pomona, CA 91766
Phone: (909)629-2247
Fax: (909)629-8310
Toni Valdez

Export SBDC/El Monte Outreach
Center
10501 Valley Blvd., Ste. 106
El Monte, CA 91731
Phone: (818)459-4111
Fax: (818)443-0463
Charles Blythe

Export SBDC Satellite Center
5700 Ralston St., Ste. 310
Ventura, CA 93003
Phone: (805)658-2688
Fax: (805)658-2252
Heather Wicka

Export Small Business Development
Center of Southern California
110 E. 9th, Ste. A669
Los Angeles, CA 90079
Phone: (213)892-1111
Fax: (213)892-8232
Gladys Moreau

Gavilan College Small Business
Development Center
7436 Monterey St.
Gilroy, CA 95020
Phone: (408)847-0373
Fax: (408)847-0393
Peter Graff

Gold Coast SBDC
5700 Ralston St., Ste. 310
Ventura, CA 93003
Phone: (805)658-2688
Fax: (805)658-2252
Joe Higgins

Greater Sacramento SBDC
1410 Ethan Way
Sacramento, CA 95825
Phone: (916)563-3210
Fax: (916)563-3266
Cynthia Steimle

Greater San Diego Chamber of
Commerce
Small Business Development Center
4275 Executive Sq., Ste. 920
La Jolla, CA 92037
Phone: (619)453-9388
Fax: (619)450-1997
Hal Lefkowitz

High Desert SBDC
Victorville Satellite Center
15490 Civic Dr., Ste. 102
Victorville, CA 92392
Phone: (619)951-1592
Fax: (619)951-8929
Janice Harbaugh

Imperial Valley Satellite SBDC
Town & Country Shopping Center
301 N. Imperial Ave., Ste. B
El Centro, CA 92243
Phone: (619)312-9800
Fax: (619)312-9838
Debbie Trujillo

Inland Empire Business Incubator
SBDC
155 S. Memorial Dr.
Norton Air Force Base, CA 92509
Phone: (909)382-0065
Fax: (909)382-8543
Chuck Eason

Inland Empire Small Business
Development Center
1157 Spruce St.
Riverside, CA 92507
Phone: (909)781-2345
Free: 800-750-2353
Fax: (909)781-2353
Teri Ooms

International Trade Office
SBDC
3282 E. Guasti Rd., Ste. 100

Ontario, CA 91761
Phone: (909)390-8071
Fax: (909)390-8077
John Hernandez

Napa Valley College Small Business
Development Center
1556 First St., Ste. 103
Napa, CA 94559
Phone: (707)253-3210
Fax: (707)253-3068
Chuck Eason

North Coast
Small Business Development Center
520 E St.
Eureka, CA 95501
Phone: (707)445-9720
Fax: (707)445-9652
Duff Heuttner

North Coast Small Business
Development Center
207 Price Mall, Ste. 500
Crescent City, CA 95531
Phone: (707)464-2168
Fax: (707)465-6008
Fran Clark

North Los Angeles Small Business
Development Center
4717 Van Nuys Blvd., Ste. 201
Van Nuys, CA 91403-2100
Phone: (818)907-9922
Fax: (818)907-9890
Wilma Berglund

Orange County Small Business
Development Center
901 E. Santa Ana Blvd., Ste. 101
Santa Ana, CA 92701
Phone: (714)647-1172
Fax: (714)835-9008
Gregory Kishel

Pasadena Satellite
SBDC
2061 N. Los Robles, Ste. 106
Pasadena, CA 91104
Phone: (818)398-9031
Fax: (818)398-3059
David Ryal

Pico Rivera SBDC
9058 E. Washington Blvd.
Pico Rivera, CA 90660
Phone: (310)942-9965
Fax: (310)942-9745
Beverly Taylor

Pomona SBDC
375 S. Main St., Ste. 101
Pomona, CA 91766
Phone: (909)629-2247
Fax: (909)629-8310
Paul Hischar

Redwood Empire Small Business
Development Center
520 Mendocino Ave., Ste. 210
Santa Rosa, CA 95401
Phone: (707)524-1770
Fax: (707)524-1772
Charles Robbins

San Francisco SBDC
711 Van Ness, Ste. 305
San Francisco, CA 94102
Phone: (415)561-1890
Fax: (415)561-1894
Tim Sprinkles

San Joaquin Delta College Small
Business Development Center
445 N. San Joaquin, 2nd Fl.
Stockton, CA 95202
Phone: (209)474-5089
Fax: (209)474-5605
Gillian Murphy

Sierra College Small Business
Development Center
560 Wall St., Ste. J
Auburn, CA 95603
Phone: (916)885-5488
Fax: (916)823-2831
Mary Wollesen

Silicon Valley SBDC
298 S. Sunnyvale Ave., Ste. 204
Sunnyvale, CA 94086
Phone: (408)736-0680
Fax: (408)736-0679
Eliza Minor

South Central LA/Satellite
SBDC
3650 Martin Luther King Blvd., Ste.
246
Los Angeles, CA 90008
Phone: (213)290-2832
Fax: (213)290-7191
Cope Norcross

Southwest Los Angeles County
Westside Satellite
SBDC
3233 Donald Douglas Loop S., Ste. C
Santa Monica, CA 90405

Phone: (310)398-8883
Fax: (310)398-3024
Sue Hunter

Southwest Los Angeles County Small
Business Development Center
21221 Western Ave., Ste. 110
Torrance, CA 90501
Phone: (310)787-6466
Fax: (310)782-8607
Susan Hunter

Southwestern College
Small Business Development and
International Trade Center
900 Otay Lakes Rd., Bldg. 1600
Chula Vista, CA 91910
Phone: (619)482-6393
Fax: (619)482-6402
Mary Wylie

Valley Sierra SBDC
Merced Satellite
1632 N St.
Merced, CA 95340
Phone: (209)725-3800
Fax: (209)383-4959
Nick Starianoudakis

Valley Sierra Small Business
Development Center
1012 11th St., Ste. 300
Modesto, CA 95354
Phone: (209)521-6177
Fax: (209)521-9373
Kelly Bearden

Weill Institute Small Business
Development Center
1706 Chester Ave., Ste. 200
Bakersfield, CA 93301
Phone: (805)322-5881
Fax: (805)322-5663
Jeffrey Johnson

West Company SBDC
367 N. State St., Ste. 208
Ukiah, CA 95482
Phone: (707)468-3553
Fax: (707)468-3555
Sheilah Rogers

Yuba College SBDC
PO Box 1566
15145 Lakeshore Dr.
PO Box 4550
Lakeport, CA 95453
Phone: (707)263-0330
Fax: (707)263-8516
George McQueen

Yuba/Sutter Satellite
SBDC
10th and E St.
PO Box 262
Marysville, CA 95901
Phone: (916)749-0153
Fax: (916)749-0155
Sandra Brown-Abernathy

## Colorado

Adams State College
Small Business Development Center
School of Business, Rm. 105
Alamosa, CO 81102
Phone: (719)587-7372
Fax: (719)587-7603
Mary Hoffman

Aims Community College
Greeley/Weld Chamber of Commerce
Small Business Development Center
902 7th Ave.
Greeley, CO 80631
Phone: (970)352-3661
Fax: (970)352-3572
Ron Anderson

Boulder Chamber of Commerce
Small Business Development Center
2440 Pearl St.
Boulder, CO 80302
Phone: (303)442-1475
Fax: (303)938-8837
Marilynn Force

Colorado Mountain College
(Glenwood Springs)
Small Business Development Center
831 Grand Ave.
Glenwood Springs, CO 81601
Phone: (970)928-0120
Free: 800-621-1647
Fax: (970)947-9324
Alisa Zimmerman

Colorado Northwestern Community
College
Small Business Development Center
50 College Dr.
Craig, CO 81625
Phone: (970)824-7078
Fax: (970)824-1134
Ken Farmer

Colorado Office of Economic
Development
Small Business Development Center
1625 Broadway, Ste. 1710

Denver, CO 80202
Phone: (303)892-3809
Fax: (303)892-3848
Website: http://www.state.co.us/
gov_dir/oed/sbdc/sbdc-list.html
Ms. Mary Madison, Director

Community College of Aurora
Small Business Development Center
9905 E. Colfax
Aurora, CO 80010-2119
Phone: (303)341-4849
Fax: (303)361-2953
E-mail: asbdc@henge.com
Randy Johnson

Community College of Denver
Greater Denver Chamber of
Commerce
Small Business Development Center
1445 Market St.
Denver, CO 80202
Phone: (303)620-8076
Fax: (303)534-3200
Tamela Lee

Delta Montrose Vocational School
Small Business Development Center
1765 US Hwy. 50
Delta, CO 81416
Phone: (970)874-8772
Free: (888)234-7232
Fax: (970)874-8796
Bob Marshall

Fort Lewis College
Small Business Development Center
136-G Hesperus Hall
Durango, CO 81301-3999
Phone: (970)247-7009
Fax: (970)247-7623
Jim Reser

Front Range Community College (Ft.
Collins)
Small Business Development Center
125 S. Howes, Ste. 105
Ft. Collins, CO 80521
Phone: (970)498-9295
Fax: (970)204-0385
Frank Pryor

Front Range Community College
(Westminster)
Small Business Development Center
3645 W. 112th Ave.
Westminster, CO 80030
Phone: (303)460-1032
Fax: (303)469-7143
Leo Giles

Lamar Community College
Small Business Development Center
2400 S. Main
Lamar, CO 81052
Phone: (719)336-8141
Fax: (719)336-2448
Dan Minor

Mesa State College
Small Business Development Center
304 W. Main St.
Grand Junction, CO 81505-1606
Phone: (970)243-5242
Fax: (970)241-0771
Julie Morey

Morgan Community College (Ft.
Morgan)
Small Business Development Center
300 Main St.
Ft. Morgan, CO 80701
Phone: (970)867-3351
Fax: (970)867-3352
Dan Simon

Morgan Community College
(Stratton)
Small Business Development Center
PO Box 28
Stratton, CO 80836
Phone: (719)348-5596
Fax: (719)348-5887
Roni Carr

Office of Business Development
Colorado SBDC
1625 Broadway, Ste. 1710
Denver, CO 80202
Phone: (303)892-3809
Free: 800-333-7798
Fax: (303)892-3848
Lee Ortiz

Pikes Peak Community College
Small Business Development Center
Colorado Springs Chamber of
Commerce
CITTI Bldg.
1420 Austin Bluff Pkwy.
Colorado Springs, CO 80933
Phone: (719)592-1894
Fax: (719)533-0545
E-mail: sbdc@mail.uccs.edu
Iris Clark

Pueblo Community College (Canon
City)
Small Business Development Center
3080 Main St.

Canon City, CO 81212
Phone: (719)275-5335
Fax: (719)275-4400
Elwin Boody

Pueblo Community College Small
Business Development Center
900 W. Orman Ave.
Pueblo, CO 81004
Phone: (719)549-3224
Fax: (719)549-3338
Rita Friberg

Red Rocks Community College Small
Business Development Center
777 S. Wadsworth Blvd., Ste. 254
Bldg. 4
Lakewood, CO 80226
Phone: (303)987-0710
Fax: (303)987-1331
Jayne Reiter

Small Business Development Center
1726 Cole Blvd., Bldg. 22, Ste. 310
Golden, CO 80401
Phone: (303)277-1840
Fax: (303)277-1899
Jayne Reiter

Small Business Development Center
Arapahoe Community College
South Metro Chamber of Commerce
7901 S. Park Plz., Ste. 110
Littleton, CO 80120
Phone: (303)795-5855
Fax: (303)795-7520
Selma Kristel

Trinidad State Junior College
Small Business Development Center
136 W. Main St.
Davis Bldg.
Trinidad, CO 81082
Phone: (719)846-5645
Fax: (719)846-4550
Dennis O'Connor

## Connecticut

Bridgeport Regional Business Council
Small Business Development Center
10 Middle St., 14th Fl.
Bridgeport, CT 06604-4229
Phone: (203)330-4813
Fax: (203)366-0105
Juan Scott

Eastern Connecticut State University
Small Business Development Center
83 Windham St.

Williamantic, CT 06226-2295
Phone: (860)465-5349
Fax: (860)465-5143
Richard Cheney

Greater New Haven Chamber of
Commerce
Small Business Development Center
195 Church St.
New Haven, CT 06510-2009
Phone: (203)782-4390
Fax: (203)787-6730
Pete Rivera

Middlesex County Chamber of
Commerce
SBDC
393 Main St.
Middletown, CT 06457
Phone: (860)344-2158
Fax: (860)346-1043
John Serignese

Naugatuck Valley Development
Center
Small Business Development Center
100 Grand St., 3rd Fl.
Waterbury, CT 06702
Phone: (203)757-8937
Fax: (203)757-8937
Ilene Oppenheim

Quinebaug Valley Community
Technical College
Small Business Development Center
742 Upper Maple St.
Danielson, CT 06239-1440
Phone: (860)774-1133
Fax: (860)774-7768
Roger Doty

Southwestern Area Commerce and
Industry Association (SACIA)
Small Business Development Center
1 Landmark Sq., Ste. 230
Stamford, CT 06901
Phone: (203)359-3220
Fax: (203)967-8294
Harvey Blomberg

University of Connecticut
Small Business Development Center
2 Bourn Place, U - 94
Storrs, CT 06269-5094
Phone: (860)486-4135
Fax: (860)486-1576
E-mail: CSBDCinformationsmall
businessadministration.uconn.edu

Website: http://www.sbdc.uconn.edu
Dennis Gruell, Director

University of Connecticut (Greater
Hartford Campus)
Small Business Development Center
1800 Asylum Ave.
West Hartford, CT 06117
Phone: (860)570-9107
Fax: (860)570-9107
Dennis Gruel

University of Connecticut (Groton)
Small Business Development Center
Administration Bldg., Rm. 300
1084 Shennecossett Rd.
Groton, CT 06340-6097
Phone: (860)405-9009
Fax: (860)405-9041
Louise Kahler

## Delaware

Delaware State University
School of Business Economics
SBDC
1200 N. Dupont Hwy.
Dover, DE 19901
Phone: (302)678-1555
Fax: (302)739-2333
Jim Crisfield

Delaware Technical and Community
College
SBDC
Industrial Training Bldg.
PO Box 610
Georgetown, DE 19947
Phone: (302)856-1555
Fax: (302)856-5779
William F. Pfaff

Small Business Resource &
Information Center
SBDC
1318 N. Market St.
Wilmington, DE 19801
Phone: (302)571-1555
Fax: (302)571-5222
Barbara Necarsulmer

University of Delaware
Delaware Small Business
Development Center Network
One Innovation Way, Ste. 301
Newark, DE 19711
Phone: (302)831-1555
Free: 800-222-2279
Fax: (302)831-1423

E-mail: newark@delawaresbdc.org
Website: http://
www.delawaresbdc.org/
Clinton Tymes

## District of Columbia

Friendship House/Southeastern
University
SBDC
921 Pennsylvania Ave., SE
Washington, DC 20003
Phone: (202)547-7933
Fax: (202)806-1777
Elise Ashby

George Washington University
East of the River Community
Development Corp.
SBDC
3101 MLK Jr. Ave., SE, 3rd Fl.
Washington, DC 20032
Phone: (202)561-4975
Howard Johnson

Howard University
George Washington Small Business
Legal Clinic
SBDC
2000 G St., NW, Ste. 200
Washington, DC 20052
Phone: (202)994-7463
Jose Hernandez

Howard University
Office of Latino Affairs
SBDC
2000 14th St., NW, 2nd Fl.
Washington, DC 20009
Phone: (202)939-3018
Fax: (202)994-4946
Jose Hernandez

Howard University
SBDC
Satellite Location
2600 6th St., NW, Rm. 125
Washington, DC 20059
Phone: (202)806-1550
Fax: (202)806-1777
Terry Strong

Howard University
Small Business Development Center
2600 6th St., NW
Rm. 128
Washington, DC 20059
Phone: (202)806-1550

Fax: (202)806-1777
Vicki Johnson

Marshall Heights Community
Development Organization
SBDC
3917 Minnesota Ave., NE
Washington, DC 20019
Phone: (202)396-1200
Terry Strong

Washington District Office
Business Information Center
SBDC
1110 Vermont Ave., NW, 9th Fl.
Washington, DC 20005
Phone: (202)737-0120
Fax: (202)737-0476
Johnetta Hardy

## Florida

Brevard Community College
(Melbourne)
Small Business Development Center
3865 N. Wickham Rd.
Melbourne, FL 32935
Phone: (407)632-1111
Fax: (407)634-3721
Victoria Peak

Central Florida Development Council
Small Business Development Center
600 N. Broadway, Ste. 300
Bartow, FL 33830
Phone: (941)534-4370
Fax: (941)533-1247
Marcela Stanislaus

Dania Small Business Development
Center
46 SW 1st Ave.
Dania, FL 33304-3607
Phone: (954)987-0100
Fax: (954)987-0106
William Healy

Daytona Beach Community College
Florida Regional SBDC
1200 W. International Speedway
Blvd.
Daytona Beach, FL 32114
Phone: (904)947-5463
Fax: (904)258-3846
Brenda Thomas-Ramos

Edison Community College
Small Business Development Center
8099 College Pkwy. SW

Ft. Myers, FL 33919
Phone: (941)489-9200
Fax: (941)489-9051
Dan Regelski

Florida Agricultural and Mechanical
University
Small Business Development Center
1157 E. Tennessee St.
Tallahassee, FL 32308
Phone: (904)599-3407
Fax: (904)561-2049
Patricia McGowan

Florida Atlantic University (Boca
Raton)
Small Business Development Center
777 Glades Rd.
Bldg. T9
Boca Raton, FL 33431
Phone: (561)362-5620
Fax: (561)362-5623
Nancy Young

Florida Atlantic University
Commercial Campus
Small Business Development Center
1515 W. Commercial Blvd., Rm. 11
Ft. Lauderdale, FL 33309
Phone: (954)771-6520
Fax: (954)351-4120
Marty Zients

Florida Gulf Coast University
Small Business Development Center
17595 S. Tamiami Trail, Ste. 200
Midway Ctr.
Ft. Myers, FL 33908-4500
Phone: (941)948-1820
Fax: (941)948-1814
Dan Regleski

Florida International University
Small Business Development Center
University Park
CEAS-2620
Miami, FL 33199
Phone: (305)348-2272
Fax: (305)348-2965
Marvin Nesbit

Florida International University
(North Miami Campus)
Small Business Development Center
Academic Bldg. No. 1, Rm. 350
NE 151 and Biscayne Blvd.
Miami, FL 33181
Phone: (305)919-5790

Fax: (305)919-5792
Roy Jarrett

Florida Small Business Development
Center
University of West Florida
UWF Downtown Center
19 W. Garden St., Ste. 300
Pensacola, FL 32501
Phone: (850)595-5480
Free: 800-644-SBDC
Fax: (850)595-5487
E-mail: fsbdc@uwf.edu
Website: http://www.sbdc.uwf.edu
Larry Strain, Director

Gulf Coast Community College
SBDC
2500 Minnesota Ave.
Lynn Haven, FL 32444
Phone: (850)271-1108
Fax: (850)271-1109
Doug Davis

Indian River Community College
Small Business Development Center
3209 Virginia Ave., Rm. 114
Ft. Pierce, FL 34981-5599
Phone: (561)462-4756
Fax: (561)462-4796
Marsha Thompson

Miami Dade Community College
Small Business Development Center
6300 NW 7th Ave.
Miami, FL 33150
Phone: (305)237-1906
Fax: (305)237-1908
Frederic Bonneau

Minority Business Development
Center
SBDC
5950 West Oakland Park Blvd., Ste.
307
Ft. Lauderdale, FL 33313
Phone: (954)485-5333
Fax: (954)485-2514

Ocala Small Business Development
Center
110 E. Silver Springs Blvd.
PO Box 1210
Ocala, FL 34470-6613
Phone: (352)622-8763
Fax: (352)651-1031
E-mail: sbdcoca@mercury.net
Philip Geist

Okaloosa-Walton Community
College
SBDC
1170 Martin Luther King, Jr. Blvd.
Ft. Walton Beach, FL 32547
Phone: (850)863-6543
Fax: (850)863-6564
Jane Briere, Mgr.

Palm Beach Gardens
Florida Atlantic University
SBDC
Northrop Center
3970 RCA Blvd., Ste. 7323
Palm Beach Gardens, FL 33410
Phone: (407)691-8550
Fax: (407)692-8502
Steve Windhaus

Procurement Technical Assistance
Program
University of West Florida
Small Business Development Center
19 W. Garden St., Ste. 302
Pensacola, FL 32501
Phone: (850)595-5480
Fax: (850)595-5487
Martha Cobb

Seminole Community College
SBDC
100 Weldon Blvd.
Sanford, FL 32773
Phone: (407)328-4722
Fax: (407)330-4489
Wayne Hardy

UCF Brevard Campus
Small Business Development Center
1519 Clearlake Rd.
Cocoa, FL 32922
Phone: (407)951-1060

University of Central Florida
Small Business Development Center
College of Business Administration,
Ste. 309
PO Box 161530
Orlando, FL 32816-1530
Phone: (407)823-5554
Fax: (407)823-3073
Al Polfer

University of North Florida
(Gainesville)
Small Business Development Center
505 NW 2nd Ave., Ste. D
PO Box 2518
Gainesville, FL 32602-2518

Phone: (352)377-5621
Fax: (352)372-0288
Lalla Sheehy

University of North Florida
(Jacksonville)
Small Business Development Center
College of Business
Honors Hall, Rm. 2451
4567 St. John's Bluff Rd. S
Jacksonville, FL 32224
Phone: (904)620-2476
Fax: (904)620-2567
E-mail: smallbiz@unf.edu
Lowell Salter

University of South Florida—CBA
SBDC Special Services
4202 E. Fowler Ave., BSN 3403
1111 N. Westshore Dr., Annex B
Tampa, FL 33620
Phone: (813)974-4371
Fax: (813)974-5020
Dick Hardesty

University of South Florida (Tampa)
Small Business Development Center
1111 N. Westshore Dr., Annex B, Ste.
101-B
4202 E. Fowler Ave., BSN 3403
Tampa, FL 33607
Phone: (813)554-2341
Free: 800-733-7232
Fax: (813)554-2356
Irene Hurst

University of West Florida
Florida SBDC Network
19 West Garden St., Ste. 300
Pensacola, FL 32501
Phone: (850)595-6060
Fax: (850)595-6070
E-mail: fsbdc@uwf.edu
Jerry Cartwright

## Georgia

Clayton State College
Small Business Development Center
PO Box 285
Morrow, GA 30260
Phone: (770)961-3440
Fax: (770)961-3428
E-mail: sbdcmorr@uga.cc.uga.edu
Bernie Meincke

DeKalb Chamber of Commerce
DeKalb Small Business Development
Center

750 Commerce Dr., Ste. 201
Decatur, GA 30030-2622
Phone: (404)373-6930
Fax: (404)687-9684
E-mail: sbdcdec@uga.cc.uga.edu
Eric Bonaparte

Floyd College
Small Business Development Center
PO Box 1864
Rome, GA 30162-1864
Phone: (706)295-6326
Fax: (706)295-6732
E-mail: sbdcrome@uga.cc.uga.edu
Drew Tonsmeire

Gainesville Small Business
Development Center
500 Jesse Jewel Pkwy., Ste. 304
Gainesville, GA 30501-3773
Phone: (770)531-5681
Fax: (770)531-5684
E-mail: sbdcgain@uga.cc.uga.edu
Ron Simmons

Georgia Southern University
Small Business Development Center
325 S. Main St.
PO Box 8156
Statesboro, GA 30460-8156
Phone: (912)681-5194
Fax: (912)681-0648
E-mail: sbdcstat@uga.cc.uga.edu
Mark Davis

Georgia State University
Small Business Development Center
University Plz.
Box 874
Atlanta, GA 30303-3083
Phone: (404)651-3550
Fax: (404)651-1035
E-mail: sbdcatl@uga.cc.uga.edu
Lee Quarterman

Kennesaw State University
Small Business Development Center
1000 Chastain Rd.
Kennesaw, GA 30144-5591
Phone: (770)423-6450
Fax: (770)423-6564
E-mail: sbdcmar@uga.cc.uga.edu
Carlotta Roberts

Morris Brown College
Small Business Development Center
643 Martin Luther King, Jr., Dr. NW
Atlanta, GA 30314
Phone: (404)220-0205

Fax: (404)688-5985
Ray Johnson

NE Georgia District
SBDC
1180 E. Broad St.
Athens, GA 30602-5412
Phone: (706)542-7436
Fax: (706)542-6823
Gayle Rosenthal

NW Georgia District
University of Georgia
SBDC
1180 E. Broad St.
Athens, GA 30602-5412
Phone: (706)542-6756
Fax: (706)542-6776

Southeast Georgia District (Macon)
Small Business Development Center
401 Cherry St., Ste. 701
PO Box 13212
Macon, GA 31208-3212
Phone: (912)751-6592
Fax: (912)751-6607
E-mail: sbdcmac@uga.cc.uga.edu
Denise Ricketson

University of Georgia
Chicopee Complex
Georgia SBDC
1180 E. Broad St.
Athens, GA 30602-5412
Phone: (706)542-6762
Fax: (706)542-6776
E-mail: sbdcath@uga.cc.uga.edu
Hank Logan

University of Georgia
SBDC
1770 Indian Trail Rd., Ste. 410
Norcross, GA 30093
Phone: (770)806-2124
Fax: (770)806-2129
E-mail: sbdclaw@uga.cc.edu
Robert Andoh

University of Georgia
Small Business Development Center
230 S. Jackson St., Ste. 333
Albany, GA 31701-2885
Phone: (912)430-4303
Fax: (912)430-3933
E-mail: sbdcalb@uga.cc.uga.edu
Sue Ford

University of Georgia
Small Business Development Center
Chicopee Complex

1180 E. Broad St.
Athens, GA 30602-5412
Phone: (706)542-6762
Fax: (706)542-6776
Website: http://www.sbdc.uga.edu
Hank Logan

University of Georgia
Small Business Development Center
1054 Claussen Rd., Ste. 301
Augusta, GA 30907-3215
Phone: (706)737-1790
Fax: (706)731-7937
E-mail: sbdcaug@uga.cc.uga.edu
Jeff Sanford

University of Georgia (Brunswick)
Small Business Development Center
1107 Fountain Lake Dr.
Brunswick, GA 31525-3039
Phone: (912)264-7343
Fax: (912)262-3095
E-mail: sbdcbrun@uga.cc.uga.edu
David Lewis

University of Georgia (Columbus)
Small Business Development Center
North Bldg., Rm. 202
928 45th St.
Columbus, GA 31904-6572
Phone: (706)649-7433
Fax: (706)649-1928
E-mail: sbdccolu@uga.cc.uga.edu
Jerry Copeland

University of Georgia (Savannah)
Small Business Development Center
450 Mall Blvd., Ste. H
Savannah, GA 31406-4824
Phone: (912)356-2755
Fax: (912)353-3033
E-mail: sbdcsav@uga.cc.uga.edu
Lynn Vos

University of Georgia (Valdosta)
Small Business Development Center
Baytree W. Professional Offices
1205 Baytree Rd., Ste. 9
Valdosta, GA 31602-2782
Phone: (912)245-3738
Fax: (912)245-3741
E-mail: sbdcval@uga.cc.uga.edu
Suzanne Barnett

University of Georgia (Warner
Robins)
Small Business Development Center
151 Osigian Blvd.
Warner Robins, GA 31088

Phone: (912)953-9356
Fax: (912)953-9376
E-mail: sbdccwr@uga.cc.uga.edu
Ronald Reaves

## Guam

Pacific Islands SBDC Network
UOG Station
303 University Dr.
Mangilao, GU 96923
Phone: (671)735-2590
Fax: (671)734-2002
Dr. Sephen L. Marder

Pacific Islands Small Business
Development Center
University of Guam
UOG Station
Mangilao, GU 96923
Phone: (671)735-2590
Fax: (671)734-2002
Mr. Jack Peters

## Hawaii

Kauai Community College
Small Business Development Center
3-1901 Kaumualii Hwy.
Lihue, HI 96766-9591
Phone: (808)246-1748
Fax: (808)246-5102
Randy Gringas

Kona Circuit Rider
SBDC
200 West Kawili St.
Hilo, HI 96720-4091
Phone: (808)933-3515
Fax: (808)933-3683
Rebecca Winters

Maui Community College
Small Business Development Center
Maui Research and Technology
Center
590 Lipoa Pkwy., No. 130
Kihei, HI 96779
Phone: (808)875-2402
Fax: (808)875-2452
David B. Fisher

University of Hawaii at Hilo
Business Research Library
SBDC
590 Lipoa Pkwy., No. 128
Kihei, HI 96753
Phone: (808)875-2400
Fax: (808)875-2452

University of Hawaii at Hilo
Hawaii SBDC
200 W. Kawili St.
Hilo, HI 96720-4091
Phone: (808)974-7515
Fax: (808)974-7683
Darryl Mleynek

University of Hawaii at Hilo
Small Business Development Center
200 W. Kawili St.
Hilo, HI 96720-4091
Phone: (808)974-7515
Fax: (808)974-7683
Website: http://www.maui.com/
~sbdc/hilo.html
Dr. Darryl Mleynek

University of Hawaii at West Oahu
SBDC
130 Merchant St., Ste. 1030
Honolulu, HI 96813
Phone: (808)522-8131
Fax: (808)522-8135
Laura Noda

## Idaho

Boise State University
College of Business
Idaho SBDC
1910 University Dr.
Boise, ID 83725
Phone: (208)385-1640
Free: 800-225-3815
Fax: (208)385-3877
James Hogge

Boise State University
Small Business Development Center
1910 University Dr.
Boise, ID 83725
Phone: (208)385-3875
Free: 800-225-3815
Fax: (208)385-3877
Robert Shepard

Boise State University
Small Business Development Center
1910 University Dr.
Boise, ID 83725
Phone: (208)426-1640
Free: 800-225-3815
Fax: (208)426-3877
Website: http://www.idbsu.edu/isbdc/
James Hogge

College of Southern Idaho
Small Business Development Center

315 Falls Ave.
PO Box 1238
Twin Falls, ID 83303
Phone: (208)733-9554
Fax: (208)733-9316
Cindy Bond

Idaho Small Business Development
Center
305 E. Park St., Ste. 405
PO Box 1901
McCall, ID 83638
Phone: (208)634-2883
Larry Smith

Idaho State University (Idaho Falls)
Small Business Development Center
2300 N. Yellowstone
Idaho Falls, ID 83401
Phone: (208)523-1087
Free: 800-658-3829
Fax: (208)523-1049
Betty Capps

Idaho State University (Pocatello)
Small Business Development Center
1651 Alvin Ricken Dr.
Pocatello, ID 83201
Phone: (208)232-4921
Free: 800-232-4921
Fax: (208)233-0268
Paul Cox

Lewis-Clark State College
Small Business Development Center
500 8th Ave.
Lewiston, ID 83501
Phone: (208)799-2465
Fax: (208)799-2878
Helen Le Boeuf-Binninger

North Idaho College
SBDC
525 W. Clearwater Loop
Post Falls, ID 83854
Phone: (208)769-3296
Fax: (208)769-3223
John Lynn

## Illinois

Asian American Alliance
SBDC
222 W. Cermak, No. 302
Chicago, IL 60616
Phone: (312)326-2200
Fax: (312)326-0399
Emil Bernardo

Back of the Yards Neighborhood
Council
Small Business Development Center
1751 W. 47th St.
Chicago, IL 60609-3889
Phone: (773)523-4419
Fax: (773)254-3525
Bill Przybylski

Black Hawk College
Small Business Development Center
301 42nd Ave.
East Moline, IL 61244-4038
Phone: (309)755-2200
Fax: (309)755-9847
Donna Scalf

Bradley University
Small Business Development Center
141 N. Jobst Hall, 1st Fl.
Peoria, IL 61625-0001
Phone: (309)677-2992
Fax: (309)677-3386
Roger Luman

Chicago Small Business Development
Center
DCCA / James R. Thompson Center
100 W. Randolph, Ste. 3-400
Chicago, IL 60601-3219
Phone: (312)814-6111
Fax: (312)814-5247
Carson A. Gallagher

College of DuPage
Small Business Development Center
425 22nd St.
Glen Ellyn, IL 60137-6599
Phone: (630)942-2771
Fax: (630)942-3789
David Gay

College of Lake County
Small Business Development Center
19351 W. Washington St.
Grayslake, IL 60030-1198
Phone: (847)223-3633
Fax: (847)223-9371
Linda Jorn

Cooperative Extension Service
SBDC
Building 11, Ste. 1105
2525 E. Federal Dr.
Decatur, IL 62526-1573
Phone: (217)875-8284
Fax: (217)875-8288
Bill Wilkinson

Danville Area Community College
Small Business Development Center
28 W. North St.
Danville, IL 61832-5729
Phone: (217)442-7232
Fax: (217)442-6228
Ed Adrain

Department of Commerce &
Community Affairs
Illinois SBDC
620 East Adams St., Third Fl.
Springfield, IL 62701
Phone: (217)524-5856
Fax: (217)524-0171
Jeff Mitchell

East St. Louis Small Business
Development Center
Federal Building
650 Missouri Ave., Ste. G32
East St. Louis, IL 62201-2955
Phone: (618)482-3833
Fax: (618)482-3859
Robert Ahart

Eighteenth Street Development Corp.
Small Business Development Center
1839 S. Carpenter
Chicago, IL 60608-3347
Phone: (312)733-2287
Fax: (312)733-8242
Maria Munoz

Elgin Community College
Small Business Development Center
1700 Spartan Dr.
Elgin, IL 60123-7193
Phone: (847)888-7488
Fax: (847)931-3911
Craig Fowler

Evanston Business and Technology
Center
Small Business Development Center
1840 Oak Ave.
Evanston, IL 60201-3670
Phone: (847)866-1817
Fax: (847)866-1808
Rick Holbrook

Governors State University
Small Business Development Center
College of Business, Rm. C-3370
University Park, IL 60466-0975
Phone: (708)534-4929
Fax: (708)534-1646
Christine Cochrane

Greater North Pulaski Development
Corp.
Small Business Development Center
4054 W. North Ave.
Chicago, IL 60639-5223
Phone: (773)384-2262
Fax: (773)384-3850
Kaushik Shah

Illinois Central College
Procurement Technical Assistance
Center
Small Business Development Center
124 SW Adams St., Ste. 300
Peoria, IL 61602-1388
Phone: (309)676-7500
Fax: (309)676-7534
Susan Gorman

Illinois Department of Commerce and
Community Affairs
Small Business Development Center
620 E. Adams St., 3rd Fl.
Springfield, IL 62701
Phone: (217)524-5700
Fax: (217)524-0171
E-mail:
mpetrill@commerce.state.il.us
Website: http://
www.comerce.state.il.us
Jeff Mitchell, Director

Illinois Eastern Community College
Small Business Development Center
401 E. Main St.
Olney, IL 62450-2119
Phone: (618)395-3011
Fax: (618)395-1922
Debbie Chilson

Illinois Valley Community College
Small Business Development Center
815 N. Orlando Smith Ave., Bldg. 11
Oglesby, IL 61348-9692
Phone: (815)223-1740
Fax: (815)224-3033
Boyd Palmer

Industrial Council of Northwest
Chicago
Small Business Development Center
2023 W. Carroll
Chicago, IL 60612-1601
Phone: (312)421-3941
Fax: (312)421-1871
Melvin Eiland

John A. Logan College
Small Business Development Center

700 Logan College Rd.
Carterville, IL 62918-9802
Phone: (618)985-3741
Fax: (618)985-2248
Richard Fyke

John Wood Community College
Procurement Technical Assistance
Center
Small Business Development Center
301 Oak St.
Quincy, IL 62301-2500
Phone: (217)228-5511
Fax: (217)228-5501
Edward Van Leer

Joliet Junior College
Small Business Development Center
Renaissance Center, Rm. 312
214 N. Ottawa St.
Joliet, IL 60431-4097
Phone: (815)727-6544
Fax: (815)722-1895
Denise Mikulski

Kankakee Community College
Small Business Development Center
River Rd., Box 888
Kankakee, IL 60901-7878
Phone: (815)933-0376
Fax: (815)933-0217
Kelly Berry

Kaskaskia College
Small Business Development Center
27210 College Rd.
Centralia, IL 62801-7878
Phone: (618)532-2049
Fax: (618)532-4983
Richard McCullum

Latin American Chamber of
Commerce
Small Business Development Center
3512 W. Fullerton St.
Chicago, IL 60647-2655
Phone: (773)252-5211
Fax: (773)252-7065
Ed Diaz

Lewis and Clark Community College
SBDC
5800 Godfrey Rd.
Godfrey, IL 62035
Phone: (618)466-3411
Fax: (618)466-0810
Bob Duane

Lincoln Land Community College
Small Business Development Center

100 N. 11th St.
Springfield, IL 62703-1002
Phone: (217)789-1017
Fax: (217)789-9838
Freida Schreck

Maple City Business and Technology
Center
Small Business Development Center
620 S. Main St.
Monmouth, IL 61462-2688
Phone: (309)734-4664
Fax: (309)734-8579
Carol Cook

McHenry County College
Small Business Development Center
8900 U.S. Hwy. 14
Crystal Lake, IL 60012-2761
Phone: (815)455-6098
Fax: (815)455-9319
Susan Whitfield

Moraine Valley Community College
Small Business Development Center
10900 S. 88th Ave.
Palos Hills, IL 60465-0937
Phone: (708)974-5468
Fax: (708)974-0078
Hilary Gereg

North Business and Industrial Council
(NORBIC)
SBDC
2500 W. Bradley Pl.
Chicago, IL 60618-4798
Phone: (773)588-5855
Fax: (773)588-0734
Tom Kamykowski

Rend Lake College
Small Business Development Center
Rte. 1
Ina, IL 62846-9801
Phone: (618)437-5321
Fax: (618)437-5677
Lisa Payne

Richard J. Daley College
Small Business Development Center
7500 S. Pulaski Rd., Bldg. 200
Chicago, IL 60652-1299
Phone: (773)838-0319
Fax: (773)838-0303
Jim Charney

Rock Valley College
Small Business Development Center
1220 Rock St.

Rockford, IL 61101-1437
Phone: (815)968-4087
Fax: (815)968-4157
Shirley DeBenedetto

Sauk Valley Community College
Small Business Development Center
173 Illinois, Rte. 2
Dixon, IL 61021-9188
Phone: (815)288-5511
Fax: (815)288-5958
John Nelson

Shawnee Community College
Small Business Development Center
Shawnee College Rd.
Ullin, IL 62992
Phone: (618)634-9618
Fax: (618)634-2347
Donald Denny

Southeastern Illinois College
Small Business Development Center
303 S. Commercial
Harrisburg, IL 62946-2125
Phone: (618)252-5001
Fax: (618)252-0210
Becky Williams

Southern Illinois University at
Carbondale
Small Business Development Center
150 E. Pleasant Hill Rd.
Carbondale, IL 62901-4300
Phone: (618)536-2424
Fax: (618)453-5040
Dennis Cody

Southern Illinois University at
Edwardsville
Small Business Development Center
Campus Box 1107
Edwardsville, IL 62026-0001
Phone: (618)692-2929
Fax: (618)692-2647
Alan Hauff

University of Illinois at Urbana-
Champaign
International Trade Center
Small Business Development Center
428 Commerce W.
1206 S. 6th St.
Champaign, IL 61820-6980
Phone: (217)244-1585
Fax: (217)333-7410
Tess Morrison

Waubonsee Community College
(Aurora Campus)
Small Business Development Center
5 E. Galena Blvd.
Aurora, IL 60506-4178
Phone: (630)801-7900
Fax: (630)892-4668
Linda Garrison-Carlton

Western Illinois University
Small Business Development Center
214 Seal Hall
Macomb, IL 61455-1390
Phone: (309)298-2211
Fax: (309)298-2520
Dan Voorhis

Women's Business Development
Center
Small Business Development Center
8 S. Michigan, Ste. 400
Chicago, IL 60603-3302
Phone: (312)853-3477
Fax: (312)853-0145
Joyce Wade

## Indiana

Batesville Office of Economic
Development
SBDC
132 S. Main
Batesville, IN 47006
Phone: (812)933-6110

Bedford Chamber of Commerce
SBDC
1116 W. 16th St.
Bedford, IN 47421
Phone: (812)275-4493

Blackford County Economic
Development
SBDC
PO Box 43
Hartford, IN 47001-0043
Phone: (317)348-4944

Bloomfield Chamber of Commerce
SBDC
c/o Harrah Realty Co.
23 S. Washington St.
Bloomfield, IN 47424
Phone: (812)275-4493

Bloomington Area Regional Small
Business Development Center
216 Allen St.
Bloomington, IN 47403

Phone: (812)339-8937
Fax: (812)335-7352
David Miller

Brookville Chamber of Commerce
SBDC
PO Box 211
Brookville, IN 47012
Phone: (317)647-3177

Brown County Chamber of
Commerce
SBDC
PO Box 164
Nashville, IN 47448
Phone: (812)988-6647

Clark County Hoosier Falls
Private Industry Council Workforce
1613 E. 8th St.
Jeffersonville, IN 47130
Phone: (812)282-0456

Clay Count Chamber of Commerce
SBDC
12 N. Walnut St.
Brazil, IN 47834
Phone: (812)448-8457

Clinton Chamber of Commerce
SBDC
292 N. 9th St.
Clinton, IN 47842
Phone: (812)832-3844

Clinton County Chamber of
Commerce
SBDC
207 S. Main St.
Frankfort, IN 46041
Phone: (317)654-5507

Columbia City Chamber of
Commerce
SBDC
112 N. Main St.
Columbia City, IN 46725
Phone: (219)248-8131

Columbus Regional Small Business
Development Center
4920 N. Warren Dr.
Columbus, IN 47203
Phone: (812)372-6480
Free: 800-282-7232
Fax: (812)372-0228
Jack Hess

Connerville SBDC
504 Central

Connersville, IN 47331
Phone: (317)825-8328

Crawford County
Private Industry Council Workforce
SBDC
Box 224 D, R.R. 1
Marengo, IN 47140
Phone: (812)365-2174

Decatur Chamber of Commerce
SBDC
125 E. Monroe St.
Decatur, IN 46733
Phone: (219)724-2604

City of Delphi Community
Development
SBDC
201 S. Union
Delphi, IN 46923
Phone: (317)564-6692

East Central Indiana Regional Small
Business Development Center
401 S. High St.
PO Box 842
Muncie, IN 47305
Phone: (765)284-8144
Fax: (765)751-9151
Barbara Armstrong

Economic Development Office
SBDC
46 E. Market St.
Spencer, IN 47460
Phone: (812)829-3245

First Citizens Bank
SBDC
515 N. Franklin Sq.
Michigan City, IN 46360
Phone: (219)874-9245

Greater Lafayette Regional Area
Small Business Development Center
122 N. 3rd
Lafayette, IN 47901
Phone: (765)742-2394
Fax: (765)742-6276
Susan Davis

Greater Martinsville Chamber of
Commerce
SBDC
210 N. Marion St.
Martinsville, IN 46151
Phone: (317)342-8110

Greencastle Partnership Center
SBDC
2 S. Jackson St.
Greencastle, IN 46135
Phone: (317)653-4517

Greensburg Area Chamber of
Commerce
SBDC
125 W. Main St.
Greensburg, IN 47240
Phone: (812)663-2832

Hammond Development Corp.
SBDC
649 Conkey St.
Hammond, IN 46324
Phone: (219)853-6399

Harrison County
Development Center
SBDC
405 N. Capitol, Ste. 308
Corydon, IN 47112
Phone: (812)738-8811

Henry County Economic
Development Corp.
SBDC
1325 Broad St., Ste. B
New Castle, IN 47362
Phone: (317)529-4635

Indiana SBDC Network
One North Capitol, Ste. 420
Indianapolis, IN 46204
Phone: (317)264-6871
Fax: (317)264-3102
E-mail: sthrash@in.net
Stephen Thrash

Indianapolis Regional Small Business
Development Center
342 N. Senate Ave.
Indianapolis, IN 46204-1708
Phone: (317)261-3030
Fax: (317)261-3053
Glenn Dunlap

Jay County Development Corp.
SBDC
121 W. Main St., Ste. A
Portland, IN 47371
Phone: (219)726-9311

Jennings County Chamber of
Commerce
SBDC
PO Box 340
North Vernon, IN 47265
Phone: (812)346-2339

Kendallville Chamber of Commerce
SBDC
228 S. Main St.
Kendallville, IN 46755
Phone: (219)347-1554

Kokomo-Howard County Regional
Small Business Development Center
106 N. Washington
Kokomo, IN 46901
Phone: (317)454-7922
Fax: (317)452-4564
E-mail: sbdc5@holli.com
Kim Moyers

Lake County Public Library
Small Business Development Center
1919 W. 81st. Ave.
Merrillville, IN 46410-5382
Phone: (219)756-7232

LaPorte Small Business Development
Center
414 Lincolnway
La Porte, IN 46350
Phone: (219)326-7232

Linton/Stockton Chamber of
Commerce
SBDC
PO Box 208
Linton, IN 47441
Phone: (812)847-4846

Minority Business Development
Project Future
SBDC
South Bend, IN 46634
Phone: (219)234-0051

Mitchell Chamber of Commerce
SBDC
1st National Bank
Main Street
Mitchell, IN 47446
Phone: (812)849-4441

Montgomery County Chamber of
Commerce
SBDC
211 S. Washington St.
Crawfordsville, IN 47933
Phone: (317)654-5507

Mt. Vernon Chamber of Commerce
SBDC
405 E. 4th St.
Mt. Vernon, IN 47620
Phone: (812)838-3639

Northeast Indiana Regional Small
Business Development Center
1830 Wayne Trace
Fort Wayne, IN 46803
Phone: (219)426-0040
Fax: (219)424-0024
E-mail: sbdc@mailfwi.com
Nick Adams

Northlake Small Business
Development Center
487 Broadway, Ste. 201
Gary, IN 46402
Phone: (219)882-2000

Northwest Indiana Regional Small
Business Development Center
Small Business Development Center
6100 Southport Rd.
Portage, IN 46368
Phone: (219)762-1696
Fax: (219)763-2653
Mark McLaughlin

Orange County
Private Industry Council Workforce
SBDC
326 B. N. Gospel
Paoli, IN 47454-1412
Phone: (812)723-4206

Porter County
SBDC
911 Wall St.
Valparaiso, IN 46383
Phone: (219)477-5256

Purdue University
SBDC
Business & Industrial Development
Center
1220 Potter Dr.
West Lafayette, IN 47906
Phone: (317)494-5858

Randolph County Economic
Development Foundation
SBDC
111 S. Main St.
Winchester, IN 47394
Phone: (317)584-3266

Richmond-Wayne County Small
Business Development Center
33 S. 7th St.
Richmond, IN 47374
Phone: (765)962-2887
Fax: (765)966-0882
Cliff Fry

Rochester and Lake Manitou
Chamber of Commerce
Fulton Economic Development
Center
SBDC
617 Main St.
Rochester, IN 46975
Phone: (219)223-6773

Rushville Chamber of Commerce
SBDC
PO Box 156
Rushville, IN 46173
Phone: (317)932-2222

St. Mary of the Woods College
SBDC
St. Mary-of-the-Woods, IN 47876
Phone: (812)535-5151

Scott County
Private Industry Council Workforce
SBDC
752 Lakeshore Dr.
Scottsburg, IN 47170
Phone: (812)752-3886

Seymour Chamber of Commerce
SBDC
PO Box 43
Seymour, IN 47274
Phone: (812)522-3681

South Bend Regional Small Business
Development Center
300 N. Michigan
South Bend, IN 46601
Phone: (219)282-4350
Fax: (219)236-1056
Jim Gregar

Southeastern Indiana Regional Small
Business Development Center
975 Industrial Dr.
Madison, IN 47250
Phone: (812)265-3127
Fax: (812)265-5544
E-mail: seinsbdc@seidata.com
Rose Marie Roberts

Southern Indiana Regional Small
Business Development Center
1613 E. 8th St.
Jeffersonville, IN 47130
Phone: (812)288-6451
Fax: (812)284-8314
Patricia Stroud

Southern Indiana Small Business
Development Center

Private Industry Council Workforce
4100 Charleston Rd.
New Albany, IN 47150
Phone: (812)945-0266
Fax: (812)948-4664
Gretchen Mahaffey

Southwestern Indiana Regional Small
Business Development Center
100 NW 2nd St., Ste. 200
Evansville, IN 47708
Phone: (812)425-7232
Fax: (812)421-5883
Kate Northrup

Sullivan Chamber of Commerce
SBDC
10 S. Crt. St.
Sullivan, IN 47882
Phone: (812)268-4836

Tell City Chamber of Commerce
SBDC
645 Main St.
Tell City, IN 47586
Phone: (812)547-2385
Fax: (812)547-8378

Terre Haute Area Small Business
Development Center
School of Business, Rm. 510
Terre Haute, IN 47809
Phone: (812)237-7676
Fax: (812)237-7675
William Minnis

Tipton County Economic
Development Corp.
SBDC
136 E. Jefferson
Tipton, IN 46072
Phone: (317)675-7300

Union County Chamber of Commerce
SBDC
102 N. Main St., No. 6
Liberty, IN 47353-1039
Phone: (317)458-5976

Vevay/Switzerland Country
Foundation
SBDC
PO Box 193
Vevay, IN 47043
Phone: (812)427-2533

Vincennes University
SBDC
PO Box 887

Vincennes, IN 47591
Phone: (812)885-5749

Wabash Area Chamber of Commerce
Wabash Economic Development
Corp.
SBDC
67 S. Wabash
Wabash, IN 46992
Phone: (219)563-1168

Washington County
Private Industry Council Workforce
SBDC
Hilltop Plaza
Salem, IN 47167
Phone: (812)883-2283

Washington Davies County
SBDC
1 Train Depot St.
Washington, IN 47501
Phone: (812)254-5262
Fax: (812)254-2550
Mark Brochin

## Iowa

DMACC Small Business
Development Center
Circle West Incubator
PO Box 204
Audubon, IA 50025
Phone: (712)563-2623
Fax: (712)563-2301
Lori Harmening

Drake University
Small Business Development Center
2507 University Ave.
Des Moines, IA 50311-4505
Phone: (515)271-2655
Fax: (515)271-1899
Benjamin Swartz

Eastern Iowa Small Business
Development Center
304 W. 2nd St.
Davenport, IA 52801
Phone: (319)322-4499
Fax: (319)322-8241
Jon Ryan

Indian Hills Community College
Small Business Development Center
525 Grandview Ave.
Ottumwa, IA 52501
Phone: (515)683-5127

Fax: (515)683-5263
Bryan Ziegler

Iowa Central Community College
SBDC
900 Central Ave., Ste. 4
Ft. Dodge, IA 50501
Phone: (515)576-5090
Fax: (515)576-0826
Todd Madson

Iowa Lakes Community College
(Spencer)
Small Business Development Center
1900 N. Grand Ave., Ste. 8
Hwy. 71 N
Spencer, IA 51301
Phone: (712)262-4213
Fax: (712)262-4047
John Beneke

Iowa SBDC
137 Lynn Ave.
Ames, IA 50014
Phone: (515)292-6351
Free: 800-373-7232
Fax: (515)292-0020
Ronald Manning

Iowa State University
Small Business Development Center
137 Lynn Ave., Ste. 5
Ames, IA 50014-7198
Phone: (515)292-6351
Free: 800-373-7232
Fax: (515)292-0020
Website: http://www.iowasbdc.org/
staff.html
Ronald Manning

Iowa State University
Small Business Development Center
ISU Branch Office
Bldg. 1, Ste. 615
2501 N. Loop Dr.
Ames, IA 50010-8283
Phone: (515)296-7828
Free: 800-373-7232
Fax: (515)296-6714
Steve Carter

Iowa Western Community College
Small Business Development Center
2700 College Rd., Box 4C
Council Bluffs, IA 51502
Phone: (712)325-3260
Fax: (712)325-3408
Ronald Helms

Kirkwood Community College
Small Business Development Center
2901 10th Ave.
Marion, IA 52302
Phone: (319)377-8256
Fax: (319)377-5667
Steve Sprague

North Iowa Area Community College
Small Business Development Center
500 College Dr.
Mason City, IA 50401
Phone: (515)422-4342
Fax: (515)422-4129
Richard Petersen

Northeast Iowa Small Business
Development Center
770 Town Clock Plz.
Dubuque, IA 52001
Phone: (319)588-3350
Fax: (319)557-1591
Charles Tonn

Southeastern Community College
Small Business Development Center
Drawer F
West Burlington, IA 52655
Phone: (319)752-2731
Free: 800-828-7322
Fax: (319)752-3407
Deb Dalziel

Southwestern Community College
Small Business Development Center
1501 W. Townline Rd.
Creston, IA 50801
Phone: (515)782-4161
Fax: (515)782-3312
Robin Beech Travis

University of Iowa
Small Business Development Center
108 Papajohn Business
Administration Bldg., Ste. S-160
Iowa City, IA 52242-1000
Phone: (319)335-3742
Free: 800-253-7232
Fax: (319)353-2445
Paul Heath

University of Northern Iowa
Small Business Development Center
8628 University Ave.
Cedar Falls, IA 50614-0032
Phone: (319)273-2696
Fax: (319)273-7730
Lyle Bowlin

Western Iowa Tech Community
College
Small Business Development Center
4647 Stone Ave.
PO Box 5199
Sioux City, IA 51102-5199
Phone: (712)274-6418
Free: 800-352-4649
Fax: (712)274-6429
Dennis Bogenrief

## Kansas

Allen County Community College
SBDC
1801 N. Cottonwood
Iola, KS 66749
Phone: (316)365-5116
Fax: (316)365-3284
Susan Thompson

Benedictine College
SBDC
1020 N. 2nd St.
Atchison, KS 66002
Phone: (913)367-5340
Fax: (913)367-6102
Don Laney

Butler County Community College
Small Business Development Center
600 Walnut
Augusta, KS 67010
Phone: (316)775-1124
Fax: (316)775-1370
Dorinda Rolle

Cloud County Community College
SBDC
2221 Campus Dr.
PO Box 1002
Concordia, KS 66901
Phone: (913)243-1435
Fax: (913)243-1459
Tony Foster

Coffeyville Community College
SBDC
11th and Willow Sts.
Coffeyville, KS 67337-5064
Phone: (316)251-7700
Fax: (316)252-7098
Charles Shaver

Colby Community College
Small Business Development Center
1255 S. Range
Colby, KS 67701
Phone: (913)462-3984

Fax: (913)462-8315
Robert Selby

Dodge City Community College
Small Business Development Center
2501 N. 14th Ave.
Dodge City, KS 67801
Phone: (316)227-9247
Fax: (316)227-9200
Wayne E. Shiplet

Emporia State University
Small Business Development Center
130 Cremer Hall
Emporia, KS 66801
Phone: (316)342-7162
Fax: (316)341-5418
Lisa Brumbaugh

Fort Hayes State University
Kansas Small Business Development
Center State Office
214 SW 6th St., Ste. 205
Topeka, KS 66603
Phone: (785)296-6514
Fax: (785)291-3261
E-mail: ksbdc@cjnetworks.com
Debbie Bishop

Ft. Hays State University
Small Business Development Center
109 W. 10th St.
Hays, KS 67601
Phone: (785)628-6786
Fax: (785)628-0533
Clare Gustin

Ft. Scott Community College
SBDC
2108 S. Horton
Ft. Scott, KS 66701
Phone: (316)223-2700
Fax: (316)223-6530
Steve Pammenter

Garden City Community College
SBDC
801 Campus Dr.
Garden City, KS 67846
Phone: (316)276-9632
Fax: (316)276-9630
Bill Sander

Hutchinson Community College
Small Business Development Center
815 N. Walnut, Ste. 225
Hutchinson, KS 67501
Phone: (316)665-4950
Free: 800-289-3501

Fax: (316)665-8354
Clark Jacobs

Independence Community College
SBDC
Arco Bldg.
11th and Main St.
Independence, KS 67301
Phone: (316)332-1420
Fax: (316)331-5344
Preston Haddan

Johnson County Community College
Small Business Development Center
CEC Bldg., Rm. 223
Overland Park, KS 66210-1299
Phone: (913)469-3878
Fax: (913)469-4415
Kathy Nadiman

Kansas SBDC
214 SW 6th St., Ste. 205
Topeka, KS 66603-3261
Phone: (785)296-6514
Fax: (785)291-3261
E-mail: ksbdc@cjnetworks.com
Debbie Bishop

Kansas State University (Manhattan)
Small Business Development Center
College of Business Administration
2323 Anderson Ave., Ste. 100
Manhattan, KS 66502-2947
Phone: (785)532-5529
Fax: (785)532-5827
Fred Rice

Labette Community College
SBDC
200 S. 14th
Parsons, KS 67357
Phone: (316)421-6700
Fax: (316)421-0921
Mark Turnbull

Neosho County Community College
SBDC
1000 S. Allen
Chanute, KS 66720
Phone: (316)431-2820
Fax: (316)431-0082
Duane Clum

Ottawa University
SBDC
College Ave., Box 70
Ottawa, KS 66067
Phone: (913)242-5200
Fax: (913)242-7429
Lori Kravets

Pittsburg State University
Small Business Development Center
Shirk Hall
1501 S. Joplin
Pittsburg, KS 66762
Phone: (316)235-4920
Fax: (316)232-6440
Kathryn Richard

Pratt Community College
Small Business Development Center
Hwy. 61
Pratt, KS 67124
Phone: (316)672-5641
Fax: (316)672-5288
Pat Gordon

Salina Area Chamber of Commerce
Small Business Development Center
PO Box 586
Salina, KS 67402
Phone: (785)827-9301
Fax: (785)827-9758
James Gaines

Seward County Community College
Small Business Development Center
1801 N. Kansas
PO Box 1137
Liberal, KS 67901
Phone: (316)629-2650
Fax: (316)629-2689
Dale Reed

University of Kansas
Small Business Development Center
734 Vermont St., Ste. 104
Lawrence, KS 66044
Phone: (785)843-8844
Fax: (785)865-8878
Randy Brady

Washburn University of Topeka
SBDC
School of Business
101 Henderson Learning Center
Topeka, KS 66621
Phone: (785)231-1010
Fax: (785)231-1063
Don Kingman

Wichita State University
SBDC
1845 Fairmont
Wichita, KS 67260
Phone: (316)689-3193
Fax: (316)689-3647
Joann Ard

Wichita State University
Small Business Development Center
1845 N. Fairmont
Wichita, KS 67260-0148
Phone: (316)978-3193
Fax: (316)978-3647
E-mail: sbdc@wsunub.uc.twsu.edu.
Clair Gustin, Director

## Kentucky

Bellarmine College
Small Business Development Center
School of Business
600 W. Main St., Ste. 219
Louisville, KY 40202
Phone: (502)574-4770
Fax: (502)574-4771
Thomas G. Daley

Eastern Kentucky University
South Central Small Business
Development Center
The Center for Rural Development,
Ste. 260
2292 S. Hwy. 27
Somerset, KY 42501
Phone: (606)677-6120
Fax: (606)677-6083
Kathleen Moats

Moorehead State University
Pikeville Small Business
Development Center
3455 N. Mayo Trail, No. 4
110 Village St.
Pikeville, KY 41501
Phone: (606)432-5848
Fax: (606)432-8924
Michael Morley

Morehead State University
Small Business Development Center
309 Combs Bldg.
UPO 575
Morehead, KY 40351
Phone: (606)783-2895
Fax: (606)783-5020
Keith Moore

Morehead State University College of
Business
Boyd-Greenup County Chamber of
Commerce
SBDC
1401 Winchester Ave., Ste. 305
207 15th St.
Ashland, KY 41101
Phone: (606)329-8011

Fax: (606)324-4570
Kimberly A. Jenkins

Murray State University
Owensboro Small Business
Development Center
3860 U.S. Hwy. 60 W
Owensboro, KY 42301
Phone: (502)926-8085
Fax: (502)684-0714
Mickey Johnson

Murray State University
West Kentucky Small Business
Development Center
College of Business and Public
Affairs
PO Box 9
Murray, KY 42071
Phone: (502)762-2856
Fax: (502)762-3049
Rosemary Miller

Murray State University
(Hopkinsville)
Small Business Development Center
300 Hammond Dr.
Hopkinsville, KY 42240
Phone: (502)886-8666
Fax: (502)886-3211
Michael Cartner

Northern Kentucky University
SBDC
BEP Center 463
Highland Heights, KY 41099-0506
Phone: (606)572-6524
Fax: (606)572-6177
Sutton Landry

Small Business Development Center
Lexington Central Library, 4th Fl.
140 E. Main St.
Lexington, KY 40507-1376
Phone: (606)257-7666
Fax: (606)257-1751
Debbie McKnight

Southeast Community College
SBDC
1300 Chichester Ave.
Middlesboro, KY 40965-2265
Phone: (606)242-2145
Fax: (606)242-4514
Kathleen Moats

University of Kentucky
Center for Business Development
225 C.M. Gatton Business and
Economics Bldg.

Lexington, KY 40506-0034
Phone: (606)257-7668
Fax: (606)323-1907
Website: http://gatton.gws.uky.edu/
KentuckyBusiness/ksbdc/ksbdc.htm
Janet S. Holloway, Director

University of Kentucky
Center for Entrepreneurship
Kentucky SBDC
225 Gatton Business and Economics
Bldg.
Lexington, KY 40506-0034
Phone: (606)257-7668
Fax: (606)323-1907
Janet S. Holloway

University of Kentucky
(Elizabethtown)
Small Business Development Center
133 W. Dixie Ave.
Elizabethtown, KY 42701
Phone: (502)765-6737
Fax: (502)769-5095
Lou Ann Allen

University of Louisville
Center for Entrepreneurship and
Technology
Small Business Development Center
Burhans Hall, Shelby Campus, Rm.
122
Louisville, KY 40292
Phone: (502)588-7854
Fax: (502)588-8573
Lou Dickie

Western Kentucky University
Bowling Green Small Business
Development Center
2355 Nashville Rd.
Bowling Green, KY 42101
Phone: (502)745-1905
Fax: (502)745-1931
Richard S. Horn

## Louisiana

Alexandria SBDC
Hibernia National Bank Bldg., Ste.
510
934 3rd St.
Alexandria, LA 71301
Phone: (318)484-2123
Fax: (318)484-2126
Kathey Hunter

Louisiana Electronic Assistance
Program
SBDC
NE Louisiana, College of Business
Administration
Monroe, LA 71209
Phone: (318)342-1215
Fax: (318)342-1209
Dr. Jerry Wall

Louisiana International Trade Center
SBDC
World Trade Center, Ste. 2926
2 Canal St.
New Orleans, LA 70130
Phone: (504)568-8222
Fax: (504)568-8228
Ruperto Chavarri

Louisiana State University at
Shreveport
Small Business Development Center
College of Business Administration
1 University Dr.
Shreveport, LA 71115
Phone: (318)797-5144
Fax: (318)797-5208
Peggy Cannon

Louisiana Tech University
Small Business Development Center
College of Business Administration
Box 10318, Tech Sta.
Ruston, LA 71272
Phone: (318)257-3537
Fax: (318)257-4253
Tracey Jeffers

Loyola University
Small Business Development Center
College of Business Administration
Box 134
New Orleans, LA 70118
Phone: (504)865-3474
Fax: (504)865-3496
Ronald Schroeder

McNeese State University
Small Business Development Center
College of Business Administration
Lake Charles, LA 70609
Phone: (318)475-5529
Fax: (318)475-5012
Paul Arnold

Nicholls State University
Small Business Development Center
College of Business Administration
PO Box 2015

Thibodaux, LA 70310
Phone: (504)448-4242
Fax: (504)448-4922
Weston Hull

Northeast Louisiana University
Small Business Development Center
College of Business Administration,
Rm. 2-57
Monroe, LA 71209
Phone: (318)342-5506
Fax: (318)342-5510
E-mail: brbaker@alpha.nlu.edu
Website: http://isbdc.net1.nlu.edu
Dr. John Baker

Northwestern State University
Small Business Development Center
College of Business Administration
Natchitoches, LA 71497
Phone: (318)357-5611
Fax: (318)357-6810
Mary Lynn Wilkerson

Southeastern Louisiana University
Small Business Development Center
College of Business Administration
Box 522, SLU Sta.
Hammond, LA 70402
Phone: (504)549-3831
Fax: (504)549-2127
William Joubert

Southern University
Capital Small Business Development
Center
1933 Wooddale Blvd., Ste. E
Baton Rouge, LA 70806
Phone: (504)922-0998
Fax: (504)922-0024
Gregory Spann

Southern University at New Orleans
Small Business Development Center
College of Business Administration
New Orleans, LA 70126
Phone: (504)286-5308
Fax: (504)286-5131
Jon Johnson

University of New Orleans
Small Business Development Center
1600 Canal St., Ste. 620
New Orleans, LA 70112
Phone: (504)539-9292
Fax: (504)539-9205
Norma Grace

University of Southwestern Louisiana
Acadiana Small Business
Development Center
College of Business Administration
Box 43732
Lafayette, LA 70504
Phone: (318)262-5344
Fax: (318)262-5296
Kim Spence

## Maine

Androscoggin Valley Council of
Governments
Small Business Development Center
125 Manley Rd.
Auburn, ME 04210
Phone: (207)783-9186
Fax: (207)783-5211
Jane Mickeriz

Belfast Satellite
Waldo County Development Corp.
SBDC
67 Church St.
Belfast, ME 04915
Phone: (207)942-6389
Free: 800-339-6389
Fax: (207)942-3548

Biddeford Satellite
Biddeford-Saco Chamber of
Commerce and Industry
SBDC
110 Main St.
Saco, ME 04072
Phone: (207)282-1567
Fax: (207)282-3149

Brunswick Satellite
Midcoast Council for Business
Development
SBDC
8 Lincoln St.
Brunswick, ME 04011
Phone: (207)882-4340

Coastal Enterprises Inc.
SBDC
Weston Bldg.
7 N. Chestnut St.
Augusta, ME 04330
Phone: (207)621-0245
Fax: (207)622-9739
Robert Chiozzi

Coastal Enterprises, Inc. (Wiscasset)
Small Business Development Center
Water St.

PO Box 268
Wiscasset, ME 04578
Phone: (207)882-4340
Fax: (207)882-4456
James Burbank

East Millinocket Satellite
Katahdin Regional Development
Corp.
SBDC
58 Main St.
East Millinocket, ME 04430
Phone: (207)746-5338
Fax: (207)746-9535

East Wilton Satellite
Robinhood Plaza
Rte. 2 & 4
East Wilton, ME 04234
Phone: (207)783-9186
Fax: (207)783-9186

Eastern Maine Development Corp.
Small Business Development Center
1 Cumberland Pl., Ste. 300
PO Box 2579
Bangor, ME 04402-2579
Phone: (207)942-6389
Free: 800-339-6389
Fax: (207)942-3548
Ron Loyd

Fort Kent Satellite
SBDC
Aroostook County Registry of Deeds
Elm and Hall Sts.
Fort Kent, ME 04743
Phone: (207)498-8736
Free: 800-427-8736
Fax: (207)498-3108

Houlton Satellite
SBDC
Superior Court House
Court St.
Houlton, ME 04730
Phone: (207)498-8736
Free: 800-427-8736
Fax: (207)498-3108

Lewiston Satellite
Business Information Center (BIC)
SBDC
Bates Mill Complex
35 Canal St.
Lewiston, ME 04240
Phone: (207)783-9186
Fax: (207)783-5211

Machias Satellite
Sunrise County Economic Council
(Calais Area)
SBDC
63 Main St.
PO Box 679
Machias, ME 04654
Phone: (207)454-2430
Fax: (207)255-0983

Northern Maine Development
Commission
Small Business Development Center
2 S. Main St.
PO Box 779
Caribou, ME 04736
Phone: (207)498-8736
Free: 800-427-8736
Fax: (207)498-3108
Rodney Thompson

Rockland Satellite
SBDC
331 Main St.
Rockland, ME 04841
Phone: (207)882-4340
Fax: (207)882-4456

Rumford Satellite
River Valley Growth Council
Hotel Harris Bldg.
23 Hartford St.
Rumford, ME 04276
Phone: (207)783-9186
Fax: (207)783-5211

Skowhegan Satellite
SBDC
Norridgewock Ave.
Skowhegan, ME 04976
Phone: (207)621-0245
Fax: (207)622-9739

South Paris Satellite
SBDC
166 Main St.
South Paris, ME 04281
Phone: (207)783-9186
Fax: (207)783-5211

Southern Maine Regional Planning
Commission
Small Business Development Center
255 Main St.
PO Box Q
Sanford, ME 04073
Phone: (207)324-0316
Fax: (207)324-2958
Joseph Vitko

University of Southern Maine
Maine SBDC
96 Falmouth St.
PO Box 9300
Portland, ME 04104-9300
Phone: (207)780-4420
Fax: (207)780-4810
E-mail: msbdc@portland.maine.edu
Charles Davis

University of Southern Maine
Small Business Development Center
15 Surrenden St.
PO Box 9300
Portland, ME 04103
Phone: (207)780-4420
Fax: (207)780-4810
E-mail: msbdc@portland.maine.edu
Website: http://www.usm.maine.edu/
~sbdc
Charles Davis, Director

Waterville Satellite
Thomas College
SBDC
Administrative Bldg. - Library
180 W. River Rd.
Waterville, ME 04901
Phone: (207)621-0245
Fax: (207)622-9739

York Satellite
York Chamber of Commerce
SBDC
449 Rte. 1
York, ME 03909
Phone: (207)363-4422
Fax: (207)324-2958

## Maryland

Anne Arundel, Office of Economic
Development
SBDC
2666 Riva Rd., Ste. 200
Annapolis, MD 21401
Phone: (410)224-4205
Fax: (410)222-7415
Mike Fish

Arundel Center N.
SBDC
101 Crain Hwy., NW, Rm. 110B
Glen Burnie, MD 21061
Phone: (410)766-1910
Fax: (410)766-1911
Mike Fish

Baltimore County Chamber of
Commerce
SBDC
102 W. Pennsylvania Ave., Ste. 402
Towson, MD 21204
Phone: (410)832-5866
Fax: (410)821-9901
John Casper

Carrol County Economic
Development Office
SBDC
125 N. Court St., Rm. 101
Westminster, MD 21157
Phone: (410)857-8166
Fax: (410)848-0003
Michael Fish

Cecil County Chamber of Commerce
SBDC
135 E. Main St.
Elkton, MD 21921
Phone: (410)392-0597
Fax: (410)392-6225
Maurice Brown

Central Maryland
SBDC
1420 N. Charles St., Rm 142
Baltimore, MD 21201-5779
Phone: (410)837-4141
Fax: (410)837-4151
Barney Wilson

Charles County Community College
Southern Maryland SBDC
SBDC
Mitchell Rd.
PO Box 910
LaPlata, MD 20646-0910
Phone: (301)934-7580
Free: 800-762-7232
Fax: (301)934-7681
Betsy Cooksey

Community College at Saint Mary's
County
SBDC
PO Box 98, Great Mills Rd.
Great Mills, MD 20634
Phone: (301)868-6679
Fax: (301)868-7392
James Shepherd

Eastern Region - Upper Shore SBDC
PO Box 8
Wye Mills, MD 21679
Phone: (410)822-5400
Free: 800-762SBDC

Fax: (410)827-5286
Patricia Ann Marie Schaller

Frederick Community College
SBDC
7932 Opossumtown Pike
Frederick, MD 21702
Phone: (301)846-2683
Fax: (301)846-2689
Mary Ann Garst

Garrett Community College
SBDC
Mosser Rd.
McHenry, MD 21541
Phone: (301)387-6666
Fax: (301)387-3096
Sandy Major

Hagerstown Junior College
SBDC
Technology Innovation Center
11404 Robinwood Dr.
Hagerstown, MD 21740
Phone: (301)797-0327
Fax: (301)777-7504
Tonya Fleming Brockett

Hartford County Economic
Development Office
SBDC
220 S. Main St.
Bel Air, MD 21014
Phone: (410)893-3837
Fax: (410)879-8043
Maurice Brown

Howard County Economic
Development Office
SBDC
6751 Gateway Dr., Ste. 500
Columbia, MD 21044
Phone: (410)313-6552
Fax: (410)313-6556
Ellin Dize

Landover SBDC
7950 New Hampshire Ave., 2nd Fl.
Langley Park, MD 20783
Phone: (301)445-7324
Fax: (301)883-6479
Avon Evans

Maryland Department of Economic
and Employment Development
Small Business Development Center
Program Control Center
217 E. Redwood St., Ste. 936
Baltimore, MD 21202

Phone: (410)767-2000
Fax: (410)333-4460
A. Thomas McLamore, Director

Maryland Small Business
Development Center
7100 Baltimore Ave., Ste. 401
College Park, MD 20740
Phone: (301)403-8300
Fax: (301)403-8303
James N. Graham

Maryland Small Business
Development Center
SBDC
7100 Baltimore Ave., Ste. 401
College Park, MD 20740
Phone: (301)403-8300
Fax: (301)403-8303
Website: http://www.mbs.umd.edu/
sbdc
James M. Graham

Prince George's County Minority
Business Opportunities Commission
Suburban Washington Region Small
Business Development Center
1400 McCormick Dr., Ste. 282
Upper Marlboro, MD 20774
Phone: (301)883-6491
Fax: (301)883-6479
Avon Evans

Salisbury State University
Eastern Shore Region Small Business
Development Center
Power Professional Bldg., Ste. 170
Salisbury, MD 21801
Phone: (410)546-4325
Free: 800-999-7232
Fax: (410)548-5389
Marty Green

University of Maryland
SBDC
College of Business and Management
College Park, MD 20742-1815
Phone: (301)405-2144
Fax: (301)314-9152

Western Maryland Small Business
Development Center
Western Region, Inc.
3 Commerce Dr.
Cumberland, MD 21502
Phone: (301)724-6716
Free: 800-457-7232
Fax: (301)777-7504
Sam LaManna

**Massachusetts**

Boston College
Capital Formation Service
SBDC
Rahner House
96 College Rd.
Chestnut Hill, MA 02167
Phone: (617)552-4091
Fax: (617)552-2730
Don Reilley

Clark University
Central Massachusetts Small Business
Development Center Regional Office
Dana Commons
950 Main St.
Worcester, MA 01610
Phone: (508)793-7615
Fax: (508)793-8890
Laurence March

International Trade Center
University of Massachusetts Amherst
SBDC
205 School of Management
Amherst, MA 01003-4935
Phone: (413)545-6301
Fax: (413)545-1273

Massachusetts Export Center
World Trade Center, Ste. 315
Boston, MA 02210
Phone: (617)478-4133
Free: 800-478-4133
Fax: (617)478-4135
Paula Murphy

Metropolitan Boston Small Business
Development Center Regional Office
Rahner House
96 College Rd.
Chestnut Hill, MA 02167
Phone: (617)552-4091
Fax: (617)552-2730
Dr. Jack McKiernan

Minority Business Assistance Center
SBDC
University of Massachusetts (Boston)
College of Management, 5th Fl.
Boston, MA 02125-3393
Phone: (617)287-7750
Fax: (617)287-7767
Hank Turner

North Shore Massachusetts Small
Business Development Center
Regional Office

197 Essex St.
Salem, MA 01970
Phone: (508)741-6343
Fax: (508)741-6345
Frederick Young

Southeastern Massachusetts Small
Business Development Center
Regional Office
200 Pocasset St.
PO Box 2785
Fall River, MA 02722
Phone: (508)673-9783
Fax: (508)674-1929
Clyde Mitchell

University of Massachusetts
Massachusetts SBDC
205 School of Management
Amherst, MA 01003-4935
Phone: (413)545-6301
Fax: (413)545-1273
John Ciccarelli

University of Massachusetts
Small Business Development Center
School of Management, Rm. 205
Amherst, MA 01003-4935
Phone: (413)545-6301
Fax: (413)545-1273
Ms. Georgeanna Parhen, Director

Western Massachusetts Small
Business Development Center
Regional Office
101 State St., Ste. 424
Springfield, MA 01103
Phone: (413)737-6712
Fax: (413)737-2312
Dianne Fuller Doherty

## Michigan

Allegan County Economic Alliance
SBDC
Allegan Intermediate School Bldg.
2891 M-277
PO Box 277
Allegan, MI 49010-8042
Phone: (616)673-8442
Fax: (616)650-8042
Chuck Birr

Alpena Community College
SBDC
666 Johnson St.
Alpena, MI 49707
Phone: (517)356-9021
Fax: (517)354-7507
Carl Bourdelais

Arenac County Extension Service
SBDC
County Bldg.
PO Box 745
Standish, MI 48658
Phone: (517)846-4111

Association of Commerce and
Industry
SBDC
1 S. Harbor Ave.
PO Box 509
Grand Haven, MI 49417
Phone: (616)846-3153
Fax: (616)842-0379
Karen K. Benson

Battle Creek Area Chamber of
Commerce
SBDC
4 Riverwalk Centre
34 W. Jackson, Ste. A
Battle Creek, MI 49017
Phone: (616)962-4076
Fax: (616)962-4076
Kathy Perrett

Bay Area Chamber of Commerce
SBDC
901 Saginaw
Bay City, MI 48708
Phone: (517)893-4567
Fax: (517)893-7016
Cheryl Hiner

Branch County Economic Growth
Alliance
SBDC
20 Division St.
Coldwater, MI 49036
Phone: (517)278-4146
Fax: (517)278-8369
Joyce Elferdink

Buchanan Chamber of Commerce
SBDC
119 Main St.
Buchanan, MI 49107
Phone: (616)695-3291
Fax: (616)695-4250
Marlene Gauer

Center for Continuing Education-
Macomb Community College
SBDC
32101 Caroline
Fraser, MI 48026
Phone: (810)296-3516
Fax: (810)293-0427

Central Michigan University
Small Business Development Center
256 Applied Business Studies
Complex
Mt. Pleasant, MI 48859
Phone: (517)774-3270
Fax: (517)774-7992
Charles Fitzpatrick

Community Capital Development
Corp.
SBDC
Walter Ruether Center
711 N. Saginaw, Ste. 123
Flint, MI 48503
Phone: (810)239-5847
Fax: (810)239-5575
Kim Yarber

Downriver Small Business
Development Center
15100 Northline Rd.
Southgate, MI 48195
Phone: (313)281-0700
Fax: (313)281-3418
Paula Boase

Ferris State University
Small Business Development Center
330 Oak St.
West 115
Big Rapids, MI 49307
Phone: (616)592-3553
Fax: (616)592-3539
Lora Swenson

First Step, Inc.
Small Business Development Center
2415 14th Ave., S.
Escanaba, MI 49829
Phone: (906)786-9234
Fax: (906)786-4442
David Gillis

Genesis Center for Entrepreneurial
Development
SBDC
111 Conant Ave.
Monroe, MI 48161
Phone: (313)243-5947
Fax: (313)242-0009
Dani Topolski

Grand Valley State University
SBDC
Seidman School of Business, Ste.
718S
301 W. Fulton St.
Grand Rapids, MI 49504

Phone: (616)771-6693
Fax: (616)458-3872
Carol R. Lopucki

Gratiot Area Chamber of Commerce
SBDC
110 W. Superior St.
PO Box 516
Alma, MI 48801-0516
Phone: (517)463-5525

Greater Gratiot Development, Inc.
Small Business Center
136 S. Main
Ithaca, MI 48847
Phone: (517)875-2083
Fax: (517)875-2990
Don Schurr

Greater Niles Economic Development
Fund
SBDC
1105 N. Front St.
Niles, MI 49120
Phone: (616)683-1833
Fax: (616)683-7515
Chris Brynes

Harbor County Chamber of
Commerce
SBDC
3 W. Buffalo
New Buffalo, MI 49117
Phone: (616)469-5409
Fax: (616)469-2257

Hastings Industrial Incubator
SBDC
1035 E. State St.
Hastings, MI 49058
Phone: (616)948-2305
Fax: (616)948-2947
Joe Rahn

Huron County Economic
Development Corp.
Small Business Development Center
Huron County Bldg., Rm. 303
250 E. Huron
Bad Axe, MI 48413
Phone: (517)269-6431
Fax: (517)269-7221
Carl Osentoski

Huron Shores Campus
SBDC
5800 Skeel Ave.
Oscoda, MI 48750
Phone: (517)739-1445

Fax: (517)739-1161
Dave Wentworth

Jackson Business Development
Center
SBDC
414 N. Jackson St.
Jackson, MI 49201
Phone: (517)787-0442
Fax: (517)787-3960
Duane Miller

Kalamazoo College
Small Business Development Center
Stryker Center for Management
Studies
1327 Academy St.
Kalamazoo, MI 49006-3200
Phone: (616)337-7350
Fax: (616)337-7415
Carl R. Shook

Kirtland Community College
SBDC
10775 N. St. Helen Rd.
Roscommon, MI 48653
Phone: (517)275-5121
Fax: (517)275-8745
John Loiacano

Lake Michigan College
Corporation and Community
Development Department
Small Business Development Center
2755 E. Napier
Benton Harbor, MI 49022-1899
Phone: (616)927-8179
Fax: (616)927-8103
Milton E. Richter

Lansing Community College
Small Business Development Center
Continental Bldg.
333 N. Washington Sq.
PO Box 40010
Lansing, MI 48901-7210
Phone: (517)483-1921
Fax: (517)483-9803
Deleski Smith

Lapeer Development Corp.
Small Business Development Center
449 McCormick Dr.
Lapeer, MI 48446
Phone: (810)667-0080
Fax: (810)667-3541
Patricia Crawford Lucas

Lenawee County Chamber of
Commerce
SBDC
202 N. Main St., Ste. A
Adrian, MI 49221-2713
Phone: (517)266-1488
Fax: (517)263-6065
Sally Pinchock

Livingston County Small Business
Development Center
131 S. Hyne
Brighton, MI 48116
Phone: (810)227-3556
Fax: (810)227-3080
Dennis Whitney

Macomb Community College
SBDC
14500 12 Mile Rd.
Warren, MI 48093
Phone: (810)445-7348
Fax: (810)445-7316
Geary Maiurini

Macomb County Business Assistance
Network
Small Business Development Center
115 S. Groesbeck Hwy.
Mt. Clemens, MI 48043
Phone: (810)469-5118
Fax: (810)469-6787
Donald L. Morandi

Midland Chamber of Commerce
SBDC
300 Rodd St.
Midland, MI 48640
Phone: (517)839-9901
Fax: (517)835-3701
Sam Boeke

MMTC SBDC
2901 Hubbard Rd.
PO Box 1485
Ann Arbor, MI 48106-1485
Phone: (313)769-4110
Fax: (313)769-4064
Bill Loomis

Muskegon Economic Growth
Alliance
Small Business Development Center
230 Terrace Plz.
PO Box 1087
Muskegon, MI 49443-1087
Phone: (616)722-3751
Fax: (616)728-7251
Mert Johnson

North Central Michigan College
SBDC
800 Livingston Blvd.
Gaylord, MI 49735
Phone: (517)731-0071

Northern Lakes Economic Alliance
SBDC
1048 East Main St.
PO Box 8
Boyne City, MI 49712-0008
Phone: (616)582-6482
Fax: (616)582-3213
Thomas Johnson

Northwest Michigan Council of
Governments
Small Business Development Center
2200 Dendrinos Dr.
PO Box 506
Traverse City, MI 49685-0506
Phone: (616)929-5000
Fax: (616)929-5017
Richard J. Beldin

Northwestern Michigan College
Small Business Development Center
Center for Business and Industry
1701 E. Front St.
Traverse City, MI 49686
Phone: (616)922-1717
Fax: (616)922-1722
Cheryl Troop

Oakland Count Small Business
Development Center
SOC Bldg.
4555 Corporate Dr., Ste. 201
PO Box 7085
Troy, MI 48098
Phone: (810)641-0088
Fax: (810)267-3809
Daniel V. Belknap

Oceana County Economic
Development Corp.
SBDC
100 State St.
PO Box 168
Hart, MI 49420-0168
Phone: (616)873-7141
Fax: (616)873-5914
Charles Persenaire

Ottawa County Economic
Development Office, Inc.
Small Business Development Center
6676 Lake Michigan Dr.
PO Box 539

Allendale, MI 49401-0539
Phone: (616)892-4120
Fax: (616)895-6670
Ken Rizzio

The Right Place Program
SBDC
820 Monroe NW, Ste. 350
Grand Rapids, MI 49503-1423
Phone: (616)771-0571
Fax: (616)458-3768
Raymond P. DeWinkle

Saginaw County Chamber of
Commerce
SBDC
901 S. Washington Ave.
Saginaw, MI 48601
Phone: (517)752-7161
Fax: (517)752-9055
James Bockelman

Saginaw Future, Inc.
Small Business Development Center
301 E. Genesee, 3rd Fl.
Saginaw, MI 48607
Phone: (517)754-8222
Fax: (517)754-1715
Matthew Hufnagel

Saginaw Valley State University
Small Business Development Center
7400 Bay Rd.
University Center, MI 48710-0001
Phone: (517)791-7746
Fax: (517)249-1955
Christine Greve

St. Clair County Community College
Small Business Development Center
800 Military St., Ste. 320
Port Huron, MI 48060-5015
Phone: (810)982-9511
Fax: (810)982-9531
Todd Brian

South Haven Chamber of Commerce
SBDC
300 Broadway
South Haven, MI 49090
Phone: (616)637-5171
Fax: (616)639-1570
Larry King

Sterling Heights Area Chamber of
Commerce
Small Business Development Center
12900 Hall Rd., Ste. 110
Sterling Heights, MI 48313

Phone: (810)731-5400
Fax: (810)731-3521
Lillian Adams-Yanssens

Traverse Bay Economic Development
Corp.
Small Business Development Center
202 E. Grandview Pkwy.
PO Box 387
Traverse City, MI 49684
Phone: (616)946-1596
Fax: (616)946-2565
Charles Blankenship

Traverse City Area Chamber of
Commerce
Small Business Development Center
202 E. Grandview Pkwy.
PO Box 387
Traverse City, MI 49684
Phone: (616)947-5075
Fax: (616)946-2565
Matthew Meadors

Tuscola County Economic
Development Corp.
Small Business Development Center
194 N. State St., Ste. 200
Caro, MI 48723
Phone: (517)673-2849
Fax: (517)673-2517
James McLoskey

University of Detroit-Mercy
Small Business Development Center
Commerce and Finance Bldg., Rm.
105
4001 W. McNichols
PO Box 19900
Detroit, MI 48219-0900
Phone: (313)993-1115
Fax: (313)993-1052
Ram Kesavan

Warren-Center Line Sterling Heights
Chamber of Commerce
SBDC
30500 Van Dyke, No.118
Warren, MI 48093
Phone: (313)751-3939
Fax: (313)751-3995
Janet E. Masi

Warren - Centerline - Sterling Heights
Chamber of Commerce
Small Business Development Center
30500 Van Dyke, Ste. 118
Warren, MI 48093
Phone: (313)751-3939

Fax: (313)751-3995
Janet Masi

Washtenaw Community College
SBDC
740 Woodland
Saline, MI 48176
Phone: (313)944-1016
Fax: (313)944-0165
Kathleen Woodard

Wayne State University
Michigan Small Business
Development Center
2727 Second Ave., Ste. 107
Detroit, MI 48201
Phone: (313)964-1798
Fax: (313)964-3648
E-mail:
stateoffice@misbdc.wayne.edu.
Website: http://www.bizserve.com/
sbdc
Ronald R. Hall, Director

West Shore Community College
Small Business Development Center
Business and Industrial Development
Institute
3000 N. Stiles Rd.
PO Box 277
Scottville, MI 49454-0277
Phone: (616)845-6211
Fax: (616)845-0207
Mark Bergstrom

## Minnesota

Central Lakes College
Small Business Development Center
501 W. College Dr.
Brainerd, MN 56401
Phone: (218)825-2028
Fax: (218)828-2053
Pamela Thomsen

Century College
SBDC
3300 Century Ave., N., Ste. 200-D
White Bear Lake, MN 55110-1894
Phone: (612)773-1794
Fax: (612)779-5802
Ernie Brodtmann

Dakota County Technical College
SBDC
1300 145th St. E.
Rosemount, MN 55068
Phone: (612)423-8262
Fax: (612)423-8761
Tom Trutna

Department of Trade and Economic
Development
Minnesota SBDC
500 Metro Sq.
121 7th Pl. E.
St. Paul, MN 55101-2146
Phone: (612)297-5770
Fax: (612)296-1290
Mary Kruger

Hennepin Technical College
SBDC
1820 N. Xenium Ln.
Plymouth, MN 55441
Phone: (612)550-7218
Fax: (612)550-7272
Danelle Wolf

Hibbing Community College
Small Business Development Center
1515 E. 25th St.
Hibbing, MN 55746
Phone: (218)262-6703
Fax: (218)262-6717
Jim Antilla

Itasca Development Corp.
Grand Rapids Small Business
Development Center
19 NE 3rd St.
Grand Rapids, MN 55744
Phone: (218)327-2241
Fax: (218)327-2242
Kirk Bustrom

Minnesota Department of Trade and
Economic Development
Small Business Development Center
500 Metro Square
121 7th. Pl. E
St. Paul, MN 55101-2146
Phone: (612)297-5770
Free: 800-657-3858
Fax: (612)296-1290
Website: http://www.dted.state.mn.us
Mary Kruger, Director

Minnesota Project Innovation
Small Business Development Center
111 3rd Ave. S., Ste. 100
Minneapolis, MN 55401
Phone: (612)347-6751
Fax: (612)338-3483
Pat Dillon

Minnesota Technology, Inc.
Small Business Development Center
Olcott Plaza Bldg., Ste. 140
820 N. 9th St.

Virginia, MN 55792
Phone: (218)741-4241
Fax: (218)741-4249
John Freeland

Moorhead State University
Small Business Development Center
1104 7th Ave. S.
MSU Box 303
Moorhead, MN 56563
Phone: (218)236-2289
Fax: (218)236-2280
Len Sliwoski

Normandale Community College
(Bloomington)
Small Business Development Center
9700 France Ave. S
Bloomington, MN 55431
Phone: (612)832-6398
Fax: (612)832-6352
Scott Harding

Northwest Technical College
SBDC
905 Grant Ave., SE
Bemidji, MN 56601
Phone: (218)755-4286
Fax: (218)755-4289
Susan Kozojed

Owatonna Incubator, Inc.
SBDC
560 Dunnell Dr., Ste. 203
PO Box 505
Owatonna, MN 55060
Phone: (507)451-0517
Fax: (507)455-2788
Ken Henrickson

Pine Technical College
Small Business Development Center
1100 4th St.
Pine City, MN 55063
Phone: (320)629-7340
Fax: (320)629-7603
John Sparling

Pottery Business and Tech. Center
Small Business Development Center
2000 Pottery Pl. Dr., Ste. 339
Red Wing, MN 55066
Phone: (612)388-4079
Fax: (612)385-2251
Marv Bollum

Rainy River Community College
Small Business Development Center
1501 Hwy. 71

International Falls, MN 56649
Phone: (218)285-2255
Fax: (218)285-2239
Tom West

Region Nine Development
Commission
SBDC
410 Jackson St.
PO Box 3367
Mankato, MN 56002-3367
Phone: (507)389-8863
Fax: (507)387-7105
Jill Miller

Rochester Community and Tech.
College
Small Business Development Center
Riverland Hall
851 30th Ave. SE
Rochester, MN 55904
Phone: (507)285-7425
Fax: (507)285-7110
Michelle Pyfferoen

St. Cloud State University
Small Business Development Center
720 4th Ave. S.
St. Cloud, MN 56301-3761
Phone: (320)255-4842
Fax: (320)255-4957
Dawn Jensen-Ragnier

Southeast Minnesota Development
Corp.
SBDC
111 W. Jessie St.
PO Box 684
Rushford, MN 55971
Phone: (507)864-7557
Fax: (507)864-2091
Terry Erickson

Southwest State University
Small Business Development Center
Science and Technical Resource
Center, Ste. 105
1501 State St.
Marshall, MN 56258
Phone: (507)537-7386
Fax: (507)387-7105
Jack Hawk

University of Minnesota at Duluth
Small Business Development Center
School of Business and Economics,
Rm. 150
10 University Dr.
Duluth, MN 55812-2496

Phone: (218)726-8758
Fax: (218)726-6338
Lee Jensen

University of St. Thomas
SBDC
Mail Stop 25H 225
Ste. MPL 100
Minneapolis, MN 55403
Phone: (612)962-4500
Fax: (612)962-4810
Gregg Schneider

Wadena Chamber of Commerce
SBDC
222 2nd St., SE
Wadena, MN 56482
Phone: (218)631-1502
Fax: (218)631-2396
Paul Kinn

## Mississippi

Alcorn State University
SBDC
552 West St.
PO Box 90
Lorman, MS 39096-9402
Phone: (601)877-6684
Fax: (601)877-6256
Sharon Witty

Copiah-Lincoln Community College
Small Business Development Center
11 County Line Circle
Natchez, MS 39120
Phone: (601)445-5254
Fax: (601)446-1221
Bob D. Russ

Delta State University
Small Business Development Center
PO Box 3235 DSU
Cleveland, MS 38733
Phone: (601)846-4236
Fax: (601)846-4235
David Holman

East Central Community College
SBDC
Broad St.
PO Box 129
Decatur, MS 39327
Phone: (601)635-2111
Fax: (601)635-4031
Ronald Westbrook

Hinds Community College
Small Business Development Center/
International Trade Center

1500 Raymond Lake Rd., 2nd Fl.
Raymond, MS 39154
Phone: (601)857-3536
Fax: (601)857-3474
Marguerite Wall

Holmes Community College
SBDC
412 W. Ridgeland Ave.
Ridgeland, MS 39157
Phone: (601)853-0827
Fax: (601)853-0844
John Deddens

Itawamba Community College
Small Business Development Center
653 Eason Blvd.
Tupelo, MS 38801
Phone: (601)680-8515
Fax: (601)680-8547
Rex Hollingsworth

Jackson State University
Small Business Development Center
Jackson Enterprise Center, Ste. A-1
931 Hwy. 80 W
Box 43
Jackson, MS 39204
Phone: (601)968-2795
Fax: (601)968-2796
Henry Thomas

Jones County Junior College
SBDC
900 Court St.
Ellisville, MS 39437
Phone: (601)477-4165
Fax: (601)477-4166
Gary Suddith

Meridian Community College
Small Business Development Center
910 Hwy. 19 N
Meridian, MS 39307
Phone: (601)482-7445
Fax: (601)482-5803
Mac Hodges

Mississippi Contract Procurement
Center
SBDC
3015 12th St.
PO Box 610
Gulfport, MS 39502-0610
Phone: (601)864-2961
Fax: (601)864-2969
C. W. "Skip" Ryland

Mississippi Delta Community College
SBDC

PO Box 5607
Greenville, MS 38704-5607
Phone: (601)378-8183
Fax: (601)378-5349
Chuck Herring

Mississippi Delta Community College
Small Business Development Center
PO Box 5607
Greenville, MS 38704-5607
Phone: (601)378-8183
Fax: (601)378-5349
Chuck Herring

Mississippi Gulf Coast Community
College
SBDC
Jackson County Campus
PO Box 100
Gautier, MS 39553
Phone: (601)497-7723
Fax: (601)497-7788
Janice Mabry

Mississippi State University
Small Business Development Center
1 Research Bldg., Ste 201
PO Drawer 5288
Mississippi State, MS 39762
Phone: (601)325-8684
Fax: (601)325-4016
Sonny Fisher

Mississippi Valley State University
Affiliate SBDC
PO Box 992
Itta Bena, MS 38941
Phone: (601)254-3601
Fax: (601)254-6704
Dr. Jim Breyley

Northeast Mississippi Community
College
SBDC
Holiday Hall, 2nd Fl.
Cunningham Blvd.
Booneville, MS 38829
Phone: (601)720-7448
Fax: (601)720-7464
Kenny Holt

Northwest Mississippi Community
College
SBDC
DeSoto Ctr.
5197 W.E. Ross Pkwy.
Southaven, MS 38671
Phone: (601)280-7648
Fax: (601)280 7648
Jody Dunning

Pearl River Community College
Small Business Development Center
5448 U.S. Hwy. 49 S.
Hattiesburg, MS 39401
Phone: (601)544-0030
Fax: (601)544-9149
Heidi McDuffie

Southwest Mississippi Community
College
SBDC
College Dr.
Summit, MS 39666
Phone: (601)276-3890
Fax: (601)276-3883
Kathryn Durham

University of Mississippi
Mississippi SBDC
N.C.P.A., Rm. 1082
University, MS 38677
Phone: (601)234-2120
Fax: (601)232-4220
Michael Vanderlip

University of Mississippi
SBDC
Old Chemistry Bldg., Ste. 216
University, MS 38677
Phone: (601)232-5001
Fax: (601)232-5650
Walter D. Gurley, Jr.

University of Mississippi
Small Business Development Center
Old Chemistry Bldg., Ste. 216
University, MS 38677
Phone: (601)232-5001
Free: 800-725-7232
Fax: (601)232-5650
E-mail: msbdc@olemiss.edu
Website: http://www.olemiss.edu/
depts/mssbdc
Walter "Doug" Gurley, Jr., Director

University of Southern Mississippi
Small Business Development Center
136 Beach Park Pl.
Long Beach, MS 39560
Phone: (601)865-4578
Fax: (601)865-4581
Lucy Betcher

## Missouri

Audrain County Extension Center
SBDC
Courthouse, 4th Fl.
101 Jefferson

Mexico, MO 65265
Phone: (573)581-3231
Fax: (573)581-2766
Virgil Woolridge

Boone County Extension Center
SBDC
1012 N. Hwy. UU
Columbia, MO 65203
Phone: (573)445-9792
Fax: (573)445-9807
Mr. Casey Venters

Camden County
SBDC Extension Center
113 Kansas
PO Box 1405
Camdenton, MO 65020
Phone: (573)882-0344
Fax: (573)884-4297
Jackie Rasmussen

Cape Girardeau County
SBDC Extension Center
815 Hwy. 25S
PO Box 408
Jackson, MO 63755
Phone: (573)243-3581
Fax: (573)243-1606
Richard Sparks

Center for Technology Transfer and
Economic Development
Nagogami Ter., Bldg. 1, Rm. 104
Rolla, MO 65401-0249
Phone: (573)341-4559
Fax: (573)346-2694
Fred Goss

Central Missouri State University
Center for Technology
Grinstead, No. 75
Warrensburg, MO 64093-5037
Phone: (816)543-4402
Fax: (816)747-1653
Cindy Tanck

Central Missouri State University
SBDC
Grinstead, No. 9
Warrensburg, MO 64093-5037
Phone: (816)543-4402
Fax: (816)543-8159
Wes Savage

Chillicothe City Hall
SBDC
715 Washington St.
Chillicothe, MO 64601-2229

Phone: (660)646-6920
Fax: (660)646-6811
Nanette Anderjaska

Cole County Extension Center
SBDC
2436 Tanner Bridge Rd.
Jefferson City, MO 65101
Phone: (573)634-2824
Fax: (573)634-5463
Mr. Chris Bouchard

East Central Missouri/St. Louis
County
Extension Center
121 S. Meramac, Ste. 501
Clayton, MO 63105
Phone: (314)889-2911
Fax: (314)854-6147
Carole Leriche-Price

Franklin County
SBDC Extension Center
414 E. Main
PO Box 71
Union, MO 63084
Phone: (573)583-5141
Fax: (573)583-5145
Rebecca How

Hannibal Satellite Center
Hannibal, MO 63401
Phone: (816)385-6550
Fax: (816)385-6568

Howell County
SBDC Extension Center
217 S. Aid Ave.
West Plains, MO 65775
Phone: (417)256-2391
Fax: (417)256-8569
Mick Gilliam

Jefferson County
Courthouse, Annex No. 203
Extension Center
Courthouse, Annex 203
725 Maple St.
PO Box 497
Hillsboro, MO 63050
Phone: (573)789-5391
Fax: (573)789-5059

Mineral Area College
SBDC
PO Box 1000
Park Hills, MO 63601-1000
Phone: (573)431-4593
Fax: (573)431-2144

E-mail: sbdc-fr@ext.missouri.edu
Eugene Cherry

Missouri PAC - Eastern Region
SBDC
3830 Washington Ave.
St. Louis, MO 63108
Phone: (314)534-4413
Fax: (314)534-3237
E-mail: mopstl@ext.missouri.edu
Ken Konchel

Missouri PAC - Southeastern
Missouri State University
SBDC
222 N. Pacific
Cape Girardeau, MO 63701
Phone: (573)290-5965
Fax: (573)651-5005
George Williams

Missouri Southern State College
Small Business Development Center
Matthews Hall, Ste. 107
3950 Newman Rd.
Joplin, MO 64801-1595
Phone: (417)625-9313
Fax: (417)625-9782
E-mail: sbdc-j@ext.missouri.edu
Jim Krudwig

MO PAC-Central Region
University of Missouri-Columbia
SBDC
University Pl., Ste. 1800
1205 University Ave.
Columbia, MO 65211
Phone: (573)882-3597
Fax: (573)884-4297
E-mail: mopcol@ext.missouri.edu
Morris Hudson

Northwest Missouri State University
Small Business Development Center
423 N. Market St.
Maryville, MO 64468-1614
Phone: (660)562-1701
Fax: (660)582-3071
Brad Anderson

Pettis County
Extension Center
1012A Thompson Blvd.
Sedalia, MO 65301
Phone: (816)827-0591
Fax: (816)827-4888
Betty Lorton

Phelps County
SBDC Extension Center

Courthouse
200 N. Main
PO Box 725
Rolla, MO 65401
Phone: (573)364-3147
Fax: (573)364-0436
Paul Cretin

Randolph County
Extension Center
417 E. Urbandale
Moberly, MO 65270
Phone: (816)263-3534
Fax: (816)263-1874
Ray Marshall

Rockhurst College
Small Business Development Center
1100 Rockhurst Rd.
VanAckeren Hall, Rm. 205
Kansas City, MO 64110-2508
Phone: (816)501-4572
Fax: (816)501-4646
Rhonda Gerke

St. Louis County
Extension Center
207 Marillac, UMSL
8001 Natural Bridge Rd.
St. Louis, MO 63121
Phone: (314)553-5944
John Henschke

St. Louis / St. Charles County
Economic Council
SBDC Extension Center
260 Brown Rd.
St. Peters, MO 63376
Phone: (314)970-3000
Fax: (314)274-3310
Tim Wathen

St. Louis University
Small Business State University
SBDC
3750 Lindell Blvd.
St. Louis, MO 63108-3412
Phone: (314)977-7232
Fax: (314)977-7241
E-mail: sbdc-stl@ext.missouri.edu
Virginia Campbell

Southeast Missouri State University
Small Business Development Center
University Plaza
MS 5925
Cape Girardeau, MO 63701
Phone: (573)290-5965
Fax: (573)651-5005

E-mail: sbdc-cg@ext.missouri.edu
Frank "Buz" Sutherland

Southwest Missouri State University
Center for Business Research
Small Business Development Center
901 S. National
Box 88
Springfield, MO 65804-0089
Phone: (417)836-5685
Fax: (417)836-7666
Jane Peterson

Telecommunications Community
Resource Center
Longhead Learning Center
Small Business Development Center
1121 Victory Ln.
3019 Fair St.
Poplar Bluff, MO 63901
Phone: (573)840-9450
Fax: (573)840-9456
Judy Moss

Thomas Hill Enterprise Center
SBDC
1409 N. Prospect Dr.
PO Box 246
Macon, MO 63552
Phone: (816)385-6550
Fax: (816)562-3071
Jane Vanderham

Truman State University
Small Business Development Center
100 E. Norman
Kirksville, MO 63501-4419
Phone: (816)785-4307
Fax: (816)785-4357
E-mail: sbdc-k@ext.missouri.edu
Glen Giboney

University of Missouri
Missouri SBDC System
1205 University Ave., Ste. 300
Columbia, MO 65211
Phone: (573)882-0344
Fax: (573)884-4297
E-mail: sbdc-mso@ext.missouri.edu
Max E. Summers

University of Missouri—Columbia
Small Business Development Center
300 University Pl.
Columbia, MO 65211
Phone: (573)882-0344
Fax: (573)884-4297
Max E. Summers, Director

University of Missouri—Columbia
Small Business Development Center
University Pl., Ste. 1800
1205 University Ave.
Columbia, MO 65211
Phone: (573)882-7096
Fax: (573)882-6156
E-mail: sbdc-c@ext.missouri.edu
Frank Siebert

University of Missouri at Rolla
SBDC
Nagogami Terrace, Bldg. 1, Rm. 104
Rolla, MO 65401-0249
Phone: (573)341-4559
Fax: (573)341-6495
E-mail: sbdc-rt@ext.missouri.edu
Fred Goss

Washington County SBDC
102 N. Missouri
Potosi, MO 63664
Phone: (573)438-2671
Fax: (573)438-2079
LaDonna McCuan

## Montana

Bozeman Small Business
Development Center
222 E. Main St., Ste. 102
Bozeman, MT 59715
Phone: (406)587-3113
Fax: (406)587-9565
Michele DuBose

Butte Small Business Development
Center
305 W. Mercury, Ste. 211
Butte, MT 59701
Phone: (406)782-7333
Fax: (406)782-9675
John Donovan

Havre Small Business Development
Center
PO Box 170
Havre, MT 59501
Phone: (406)265-9226
Fax: (406)265-5602
Randy Hanson

High Plains Development Authority
Great Falls SBDC
710 1st. Ave. N.
PO Box 2568
Great Falls, MT 59403
Phone: (406)454-1934
Fax: (406)454-2995
Suzie David

Kalispell Small Business
Development Center
PO Box 8300
Kalispell, MT 59901
Phone: (406)758-5412
Fax: (406)758-6582
Dan Manning

Missoula Small Business
Development Center
127 N. Higgins, 3rd Fl.
Missoula, MT 59802
Phone: (406)728-9234
Fax: (406)721-4584
Brett George

Montana Department of Commerce
Montana SBDC
1424 9th Ave.
PO Box 200505
Helena, MT 59620
Phone: (406)444-2463
Fax: (406)444-1872
Ralph Kloser

Montana Department of Commerce
Small Business Development Center
1424 9th Ave.
Helena, MT 59620
Phone: (406)444-4780
Fax: (406)444-1872
E-mail: rkloser@mt.gov
Ralph Kloser, Director

Montana Tradepost Authority
Small Business Development Center
2722 3rd Ave., Ste. W300
115 N. Broadway, 2nd Fl.
Billings, MT 59101
Phone: (406)256-6871
Fax: (406)256-6877
Tom McKerlick

Sidney Small Business Development
Center
123 W. Main
Sidney, MT 59270
Phone: (406)482-5024
Fax: (406)482-5306
Dwayne Heintz

## Nebraska

Chadron State College
SBDC
Administration Bldg.
1000 Main St.
Chadron, NE 69337
Phone: (308)432-6282

Fax: (308)432-6430
Cliff Hanson

Mid-Plains Community College
SBDC
416 N. Jeffers, Rm. 26
North Platte, NE 69101
Phone: (308)534-5115
Fax: (308)534-5117
Dean Kurth

Nebraska Small Business
Development Center
Omaha Business and Technology
Center
2505 N. 24 St., Ste. 101
Omaha, NE 68110
Phone: (402)595-3511
Fax: (402)595-3524
Tom McCabe

Peru State College
SBDC
T.J. Majors Hall, Rm. 248
Peru, NE 68421
Phone: (402)872-2274
Fax: (402)872-2422
Jerry Brazil

University of Nebraska at Kearney
SBDC
Welch Hall
19th St. and College Dr.
Kearney, NE 68849-3035
Phone: (308)865-8344
Fax: (308)865-8153
Susan Jensen

University of Nebraska at Lincoln
SBDC
1135 M St., No. 200
11th and Cornhusker Hwy.
Lincoln, NE 68521
Phone: (402)472-3358
Fax: (402)472-3363
Cliff Mosteller

University of Nebraska at Omaha
Nebraska Business Development
Center
College of Business Administration,
Rm. 407
60th & Dodge Sts.
CBA Rm. 407
Omaha, NE 68182
Phone: (402)554-2521
Fax: (402)554-3747
Robert Bernier

University of Nebraska at Omaha
Nebraska Small Business
Development Center
CBA Rm. 407
60th & Dodge Streets
Omaha, NE 68182-0248
Phone: (402)554-2521
Fax: (402)554-3473
Website: http://
www.nbdc.unomaha.edu
Robert Bernier

University of Nebraska at Omaha
Peter Kiewit Conference Center
SBDC
1313 Farnam-on-the-Mall, Ste. 132
Omaha, NE 68182-0248
Phone: (402)595-2381
Fax: (402)595-2385
Nate Brei

Wayne State College
SBDC
Gardner Hall
1111 Main St.
Wayne, NE 68787
Phone: (402)375-7575
Fax: (402)375-7574
Loren Kucera

Western Nebraska Community
College
SBDC
Nebraska Public Power Bldg., Rm.
408
1721 Broadway
Scottsbluff, NE 69361
Phone: (308)635-7513
Fax: (308)635-6596
Ingrid Battershell

## Nevada

Carson City Chamber of Commerce
Small Business Development Center
1900 S. Carson St., Ste. 100
Carson City, NV 89701
Phone: (702)882-1565
Fax: (702)882-4179
Larry Osborne

Great Basin College
Small Business Development Center
1500 College Pkwy.
Elko, NV 89801
Phone: (702)753-2205
Fax: (702)753-2242
John Pryor

Incline Village Chamber of
Commerce
SBDC
969 Tahoe Blvd.
Incline Village, NV 89451
Phone: (702)831-4440
Fax: (702)832-1605
Sheri Woods

Las Vegas SBDC
SBDC
3720 Howard Hughes Pkwy., Ste. 130
Las Vegas, NV 89109
Phone: (702)734-7575
Fax: (702)734-7633
Robert Holland

Nevada Small Business Development
Center
University of Nevada at Reno
College of Business Administration/
032
Business Bldg., Rm. 411
Mail Stop 032
Reno, NV 89557-0100
Phone: (702)784-1717
Fax: (702)784-4337
Website: http://www.scs.unr.edu/
nfbdc
Sam Males, Director

North Las Vegas Small Business
Development Center
19 W. Brooks Ave., Ste. B
North Las Vegas, NV 89030
Phone: (702)399-6300
Fax: (702)895-4095
Janis Stevenson

Tri-County Development Authority
Small Business Development Center
50 W. 4th St.
PO Box 820
Winnemucca, NV 89446
Phone: (702)623-5777
Fax: (702)623-5999
Teri Williams

University of Nevada at Las Vegas
Small Business Development Center
4505 Maryland Pkwy.
Box 456011
Las Vegas, NV 89154-6011
Phone: (702)895-0852
Fax: (702)895-4095
Nancy Buist

University of Nevada at Reno
Small Business Development Center

College of Business Administration
Nazir Ansari Business Bldg., Rm. 411
Reno, NV 89557-0100
Phone: (702)784-1717
Fax: (702)784-4337
E-mail: nsbdc@scs.unr.edu
Sam Males

### New Hampshire

Keene State College
Small Business Development Center
Mail Stop 210
Keene, NH 03435-2101
Phone: (603)358-2602
Fax: (603)358-2612
Gary Cloutier

Littleton Small Business
Development Center
120 Main St.
Littleton, NH 03561
Phone: (603)444-1053
Fax: (603)444-5463
Liz Ward

Manchester Small Business
Development Center
1000 Elm St., 14th Fl.
Manchester, NH 03101
Phone: (603)624-2000
Fax: (603)634-2449
Bob Ebberson

New Hampshire Small Business
Development Center
1 Indian Head Plz., Ste. 510
Nashua, NH 03060
Phone: (603)886-1233
Fax: (603)598-1164
Bob Wilburn

Office of Economic Initiatives
SBDC
1000 Elm St., 14th Fl.
Manchester, NH 03101
Phone: (603)634-2796
E-mail: ahj@hopper.unh.edu
Amy Jennings

Plymouth State College
Small Business Development Center
Outreach Center, MSC24A
Plymouth, NH 03264-1595
Phone: (603)535-2523
Fax: (603)535-2850
Janice Kitchen

SBDC
18 S. Main St., Ste. 3A

Rochester, NH 03867
Phone: (603)330-1929
Fax: (603)330-1948

University of New Hampshire
Small Business Development Center
108 McConnell Hall
Durham, NH 03824-3593
Phone: (603)862-2200
Fax: (603)862-4876
E-mail: mec@christa.unh.edu
Website: http://www.mv.com/ipusers/
nhsbdc
Mary Collins, Director

### New Jersey

Bergen County Community College
SBDC
400 Paramus Rd., Rm. A333
Paramus, NJ 07652-1595
Phone: (201)447-7841
Fax: (201)447-7495
Melody Irvin

Brookdale Community College
Small Business Development Center
Newman Springs Rd.
Lincroft, NJ 07738
Phone: (732)842-1900
Fax: (732)842-0203
Larry Novick

Greater Atlantic City Chamber of
Commerce
Small Business Development Center
1301 Atlantic Ave.
Atlantic City, NJ 08401
Phone: (609)345-5600
Fax: (609)345-1666
William R. McGinley

Kean College
Small Business Development Center
East Campus, Rm. 242
Union, NJ 07083
Phone: (908)527-2946
Fax: (908)527-2960
Mira Kostak

Mercer County Community College
Small Business Development Center
West Windsor Campus
1200 Old Trenton Rd.
PO Box B
Trenton, NJ 08690
Phone: (609)586-4800
Fax: (609)890-6338
Herb Spiegel

New Jersey Small Business
Development Center
Rutgers Graduate School of
Management
49 Bleeker St.
University Heights
Newark, NJ 07102-1993
Phone: (973)353-1927
Fax: (973)353-1110
Website: http://www.nj.com/njsbdc
Brenda B. Hopper, Director

Rutgers University
New Jersey SBDC
Graduate School of Management
49 Bleeker St.
Newark, NJ 07102
Phone: (973)353-5950
Fax: (973)353-1110
Brenda B. Hopper

Rutgers University At Camden
Small Business Development Center
227 Penn St., 3rd Fl., Rm. 334
Camden, NJ 08102
Phone: (609)757-6221
Fax: (609)225-6231
Patricia Peacock

Warren County Community College
Small Business Development Center
Skylands 475
Rte. 57 W.
Washington, NJ 07882-9605
Phone: (908)689-9620
Fax: (908)689-2247
James Smith

### New Mexico

Albuquerque Technical-Vocational
Institute
Small Business Development Center
525 Buena Vista SE
Albuquerque, NM 87106
Phone: (505)224-4246
Fax: (505)224-4251
Ray Garcia

Clovis Community College
Small Business Development Center
417 Schepps Blvd.
Clovis, NM 88101
Phone: (505)769-4136
Fax: (505)769-4190
Sandra Taylor-Smith

Dona Ana Branch Community
College
Small Business Development Center

3400 S. Espina St.
Dept. 3DA, Box 30001
Las Cruces, NM 88003-0001
Phone: (505)527-7601
Fax: (505)527-7515
Terry Sullivan

Eastern New Mexico University at
Roswell
Small Business Development Center
57 University Ave.
PO Box 6000
Roswell, NM 88201-6000
Phone: (505)624-7133
Fax: (505)624-7132
Eugene D. Simmons

Luna Vocational-Technical Institute
Small Business Development Center
Camp Luna Site
Hot Springs Blvd.
PO Box 1510
Las Vegas, NM 87701
Phone: (505)454-2595
Fax: (505)454-2588
Don Bustos

Mesa Technical College
Small Business Development Center
911 S. 10th St.
Tucumcari, NM 88401
Phone: (505)461-4413
Fax: (505)461-1901
Carl Reiney

New Mexico Junior College
Small Business Development Center
5317 Lovington Hwy.
Hobbs, NM 88240
Phone: (505)392-5549
Fax: (505)392-2527
Don Leach

New Mexico State University at
Alamogordo
Small Business Development Center
2230 Lawrence Blvd.
Alamogordo, NM 88310
Phone: (505)434-5272
Fax: (505)439-3643
Dwight Harp

New Mexico State University at
Carlsbad
Small Business Development Center
301 S. Canal St.
PO Box 1090
Carlsbad, NM 88220
Phone: (505)887-6562

Fax: (505)885-0818
Larry Coalson

New Mexico State University at
Grants
Small Business Development Center
709 E. Roosevelt Ave.
Grants, NM 87020
Phone: (505)287-8221
Fax: (505)287-2125
Clemente Sanchez

Northern New Mexico Community
College
Small Business Development Center
1002 N. Onate St.
Espanola, NM 87532
Phone: (505)747-2236
Fax: (505)757-2234
Ralph Prather

San Juan College
Small Business Development Center
4601 College Blvd.
Farmington, NM 87402
Phone: (505)599-0528
Fax: (505)599-0385
Cal Tingey

Santa Fe Community College
New Mexico SBDC
6401 Richards Ave.
Santa Fe, NM 87505
Phone: (505)438-1362
Frce: 800-281-SBDC
Fax: (505)471-1469
Roy Miller

Santa Fe Community College
New Mexico Small Business
Development Center
6401 Richards Ave.
Santa Fe, NM 87505
Phone: (505)428-1343
Free: 800-281-7232
Fax: (505)428-1469
J. Roy Miller, Director

South Valley SBDC
SBDC
70 4th St. SW, Ste. A
Albuquerque, NM 87102
Phone: (505)248-0132
Fax: (505)248-0127
Steven Becerra

University of New Mexico at Gallup
Small Business Development Center
103 W. Hwy. 66

Gallup, NM 87305
Phone: (505)722-2220
Fax: (505)863-6006
Elsie Sanchez

University of New Mexico at Los
Alamos
Small Business Development Center
901 18th St., No. 18
PO Box 715
Los Alamos, NM 87544
Phone: (505)662-0001
Fax: (505)662-0099
Jay Wechsler

University of New Mexico at
Valencia
Small Business Development Center
280 La Entrada
Los Lunas, NM 87031
Phone: (505)925-8980
Fax: (505)925-8987
David Ashley

Western New Mexico University
Small Business Development Center
PO Box 2672
Silver City, NM 88062
Phone: (505)538-6320
Fax: (505)538-6341
Linda K. Jones

## New York

Baruch College
Mid-Town Outreach Center
SBDC
360 Park Ave. S., Rm. 1101
New York, NY 10010
Phone: (212)802-6620
Fax: (212)802-6613
Cheryl Fenton

Binghamton University
Small Business Development Center
PO Box 6000
Binghamton, NY 13902-6000
Phone: (607)777-4024
Fax: (607)777-4029
E-mail: sbdcbu@spectra.net
Joanne Bauman

Bronx Community College
Small Business Development Center
McCracken Hall, Rm. 14
W. 181st St. & University Ave.
Bronx, NY 10453
Phone: (718)563-3570

Fax: (718)563-3572
Adi Israeli

Bronx Outreach Center
Con Edison
SBDC
560 Cortlandt Ave.
Bronx, NY 10451
Phone: (718)563-9204
David Bradley

Canton Outreach Center (SUNY)
Jefferson Community College
SBDC
Canton, NY 13617
Phone: (315)386-7312
Fax: (315)386-7945

Clinton Community College
SBDC
Lake Shore Rd., Rte. 9 S.
136 Clinton Point Dr.
Plattsburgh, NY 12901
Phone: (518)562-4260
Fax: (518)563-9759
Merry Gwynn

Cobleskill Outreach Center
SBDC
SUNY Cobleskill
Warner Hall, Rm. 218
Cobleskill, NY 12043
Phone: (518)234-5528
Fax: (518)234-5272
Peter Desmond

College of Staten Island
SBDC
Bldg. 1A, Rm. 111
2800 Victory Blvd.
Staten Island, NY 10314-9806
Phone: (718)982-2560
Fax: (718)982-2323
Dr. Martin Schwartz

Corning Community College
Small Business Development Center
24 Denison Pkwy. W
Corning, NY 14830
Phone: (607)962-9461
Free: 800-358-7171
Fax: (607)936-6642
Bonnie Gestwicki

Downtown Brooklyn Outreach Center
Kingsborough Community College
SBDC
395 Flatbush Ave., Extension Rm.
413

Brooklyn, NY 11201
Phone: (718)260-9783
Fax: (718)260-9797
Stuart Harker

Dutchess Outreach Center
SBDC
Fishkill Extension Center
2600 Rte. 9, Unit 90
Fishkill, NY 12524-2001
Phone: (914)897-2607
Fax: (914)897-4653

East Harlem Outreach Center
SBDC
145 E. 116th St., 3rd Fl.
New York, NY 10029
Phone: (212)346-1900
Fax: (212)534-4576
Anthony Sanchez

Geneva Outreach Center
SBDC
122 N. Genesee St.
Geneva, NY 14456
Phone: (315)781-1253
Sandy Bordeau

Harlem Outreach Center
SBDC
163 W. 125th St., Rm. 1307
New York, NY 10027
Phone: (212)346-1900
Fax: (212)534-4576
Anthony Sanchez

Hempstead Outreach Center
SBDC
269 Fulton Ave.
Hempstead, NY 11550
Phone: (516)564-8672
Fax: (516)481-4938
Lloyd Clarke

Jamestown Community College
Small Business Development Center
525 Falconer St.
PO Box 20
Jamestown, NY 14702-0020
Phone: (716)665-5754
Free: 800-522-7232
Fax: (716)665-6733
Irene Dobies

Jefferson Community College
Small Business Development Center
Coffeen St.
Watertown, NY 13601
Phone: (315)782-9262

Fax: (315)782-0901
John F. Tanner

Kingsborough Community College
Small Business Development Center
2001 Oriental Blvd., Bldg. T4, Rm.
4204
Manhattan Beach
Brooklyn, NY 11235
Phone: (718)368-4619
Fax: (718)368-4629
Edward O'Brien

Kingston Small Business
Development Center
1 Development Ct.
Kingston, NY 12401
Phone: (914)339-0025
Fax: (914)339-1631
Patricia La Susa

Long Island University at
Southhampton/Southampton Outreach
Center
SBDC
Abney Peak, Montauk Hwy.
Southampton, NY 11968
Phone: (516)287-0059
Fax: (516)287-8287
George Tulmany

Manufacturing Field Office
SBDC
Rensselaer Technology Park
385 Jordan Rd.
Troy, NY 12180-7602
Phone: (518)286-1014
Fax: (518)286-1006
Bill Brigham

Mercy College/Westchester Outreach
Center
SBDC
555 Broadway
Dobbs Ferry, NY 10522-1189
Phone: (914)674-7485
Fax: (914)693-4996
Tom Milton

Mid-Town Outreach Ctr.
Baruch College
SBDC
360 Park Ave. S. Rm. 1101
New York, NY 10010
Phone: (212)802-6620
Fax: (212)802-6613
Barrie Phillip

Niagara County Community College
at Sanborn
Small Business Development Center
3111 Saunders Settlement Rd.
Sanborn, NY 14132
Phone: (716)693-1910
Fax: (716)731-3595
Richard Gorko

Niagara Falls Satellite Office
SBDC / International Trade Center
Carborundum Center
345 3rd St.
Niagara Falls, NY 14303-1117
Phone: (716)285-4793
Fax: (716)285-4797

Onondaga Community College
Small Business Development Center
Excell Bldg., Rm. 108
4969 Onondaga Rd.
Syracuse, NY 13215-1944
Phone: (315)498-6070
Fax: (315)492-3704
Robert Varney

Pace University
Small Business Development Center
1 Pace Plz., Rm. W483
New York, NY 10038
Phone: (212)346-1900
Fax: (212)346-1613
Ira Davidson

Rockland Community College
Small Business Development Center
145 College Rd.
Suffern, NY 10901-3620
Phone: (914)356-0370
Fax: (914)356-0381
Thomas J. Morley

SBDC Outreach Small Business
Resource Center
222 Bloomingdale Rd., 3rd Fl.
White Plains, NY 10605-1500
Phone: (914)644-4116
Fax: (914)644-2184
Kathleen Cassels

State University Institute of
Technology
Small Business Development Center
PO Box 3050
Utica, NY 13504-3050
Phone: (315)792-7546
Fax: (315)792-7554
David Mallen

State University of New York
New York Small Business
Development Center
State University Plz., Rm. S-523
Albany, NY 12246
Phone: (518)443-5398
Free: 800-732-SBDC
Fax: (518)465-4992
Website: http://
www.smallbiz.suny.edu/nysbdc.htm
James L. King, Director

State University of New York
Small Business Development Center
74 N. Main St.
Brockport, NY 14420
Phone: (716)637-6660
Fax: (716)637-2102
Wilfred Bordeau

State University of New York at
Albany
Small Business Development Center
Draper Hall, Rm. 107
135 Western Ave.
Albany, NY 12222
Phone: (518)442-5577
Fax: (518)442-5582
Peter George, III

State University of New York at
Buffalo
Small Business Development Center
Bacon Hall 117
1300 Elmwood Ave.
Buffalo, NY 14222
Phone: (716)878-4030
Fax: (716)878-4067
Susan McCartney

State University of New York at
Farmingdale
Small Business Development Center
Campus Commons Bldg.
2350 Route 110
Farmingdale, NY 11735
Phone: (516)420-2765
Fax: (516)293-5343
Joseph Schwartz

State University of New York (Suny)
New York SBDC
Suny Plaza, S-523
Albany, NY 12246
Phone: (518)443-5398
Free: 800-732-SBDC
Fax: (518)465-4992
E-mail: kingjl@cc.sunycentral.edu
James L. King

Suffolk County Community College
Riverhead Outreach Center
SBDC
Orient Bldg., Rm. 132
Riverhead, NY 11901
Phone: (516)369-1409
Fax: (516)369-3255
Al Falkowski

SUNY at Brockport
SBDC
Sibley Bldg.
228 E. Main St.
Rochester, NY 14604
Phone: (716)232-7310
Fax: (716)637-2182

Suny Geneseo Outreach Center
SBDC
South Hall, No. 111
1 College Circle
Geneseo, NY 14454
Phone: (716)245-5429
Fax: (716)245-5430
Charles VanArsdale

SUNY Institute of Technology at
Utica/Rome
SBDC
PO Box 3050
Utica, NY 13504-3050
Phone: (315)792-7546
Fax: (315)792-7554
David Mallen

SUNY at Oswego
Operation Oswego County
SBDC
44 W. Bridge St.
Oswego, NY 13126
Phone: (315)343-1545
Fax: (315)343-1546

SUNY at Stony Brook
SBDC
Harriman Hall, Rm. 103
Stony Brook, NY 11794-3775
Phone: (516)632-9070
Fax: (516)632-7176
Judith McEvoy

York College/City University of New
York
Small Business Development Center
Science Bldg., Rm. 107
94-50 159th St.
Jamaica, NY 11451
Phone: (718)262-2880
Fax: (718)262-2881
James A. Heyliger

## North Carolina

**Appalachian State University**
Small Business and Technology
Development Center (Northwestern
Region)
Walker College of Business
2123 Raley Hall
Boone, NC 28608
Phone: (704)262-2492
Fax: (704)262-2027
Bill Parrish

**Asheville SBTDC**
Haywood St.
PO Box 2570
Asheville, NC 28805
Phone: (704)251-6025
Fax: (704)251-6025

**Catawba Valley Region**
SBTDC
514 Hwy. 321 NW, Ste. A
Hickory, NC 28601
Phone: (704)345-1110
Fax: (704)326-9117
Rand Riedrich

**East Carolina University**
Small Business and Technology
Development Center (Eastern Region)
Willis Bldg.
300 East 1st St.
Greenville, NC 27858-4353
Phone: (919)328-6157
Fax: (919)328-6992
Walter Fitts

**Elizabeth City State University**
Small Business and Technology
Development Center (Northeastern
Region)
1704 Weeksville Rd.
PO Box 874
Elizabeth City, NC 27909
Phone: (919)335-3247
Fax: (919)335-3648
Wauna Dooms

**Fayetteville State University**
Cape Fear Small Business and
Technology Development Center
PO Box 1334
Fayetteville, NC 28302
Phone: (910)486-1727
Fax: (910)486-1949
Dr. Sid Gautam

**NC Small Business and Technology
Development Center**
University of North Carolina
333 Fayetteville Steet Mall, Ste. 1150
Raleigh, NC 27601-1742
Phone: (919)715-7272
Free: 800-2580-UNC
Fax: (919)715-7777
Website: http://www.sbtdc.org
Scott R. Daugherty, Director

**North Carolina A&T State University**
Northern Piedmont Small Business
and Technology Development Center
(Eastern Region)
C. H. Moore Agricultural Research
Center
1601 E. Market St.
PO Box D-22
Greensboro, NC 27411
Phone: (910)334-7005
Fax: (910)334-7073
Cynthia Clemons

**North Carolina SBTDC**
SBDC
333 Fayette St. Mall, Ste. 1150
Raleigh, NC 27601
Phone: (919)715-7272
Fax: (919)715-7777
Scott R. Daugherty

**North Carolina State University**
Capital Region
SBTDC
MCI Small Business Resource Center
800 S. Salisbury St.
Raleigh, NC 27601
Phone: (919)715-0520
Fax: (919)715-0518
Mike Seibert

**North Carolina Wesleyan College**
SBTDC
3400 N. Wesleyan Blvd.
Rocky Mount, NC 27804
Phone: (919)985-5130
Fax: (919)977-3701

**Pembroke State University**
Office of Economic Development and
SBTDC and SBDC
Pembroke, NC 28372
Phone: (910)521-6603
Fax: (910)521-6550

**University of North Carolina at
Chapel Hill**

**Central Carolina Regional Small
Business Development Center**
608 Airport Rd., Ste. B
Chapel Hill, NC 27514
Phone: (919)962-0389
Fax: (919)962-3291
Dan Parks

**University of North Carolina at
Charlotte**
Small Business and Technology
Development Center (Southern
Piedmont Region)
The Ben Craig Center
8701 Mallard Creek Rd.
Charlotte, NC 28262
Phone: (704)548-1090
Fax: (704)548-9050
George McAllister

**University of North Carolina at
Wilmington**
Small Business and Technology
Development Center (Southeast
Region)
601 S. College Rd.
Cameron Hall, Rm. 131
Wilmington, NC 28403
Phone: (910)395-3744
Fax: (910)350-3990
Mike Bradley

**University of North Carolina at
Wilmington**
Southeastern Region
SBTDC
601 S. College Rd.
Wilmington, NC 28403
Phone: (910)395-3744
Fax: (910)350-3014
Dr. Warren Guiko

**Western Carolina University**
Small Business and Technology
Development Center (Western
Region)
Center for Improving Mountain
Living
Bird Bldg.
Cullowhee, NC 28723
Phone: (704)227-7494
Fax: (704)227-7422
Allan Steinburg

**Winston-Salem State University**
Northwestern Piedmont Region Small
Business and Technology Center
PO Box 13025
Winston Salem, NC 27110

Phone: (910)750-2030
Fax: (910)750-2031
Bill Dowe

## North Dakota

Bismarck Regional Small Business
Development Center
700 E. Main Ave., 2nd Fl.
Bismarck, ND 58502
Phone: (701)328-5865
Fax: (701)250-4304
Jan M. Peterson

Devils Lake Outreach Center
SBDC
417 5th St.
Devils Lake, ND 58301
Free: 800-445-7232
Gordon Synder

Dickinson Regional Small Business
Development Center
Small Business Development Center
314 3rd Ave. W
Drawer L
Dickinson, ND 58602
Phone: (701)227-2096
Fax: (701)225-0049
Bryan Vendsel

Grafton Outreach Center
Red River Regional Planning Council
SBDC
PO Box 633
Grafton, ND 58237
Free: 800-445-7232
Gordon Snyder

Grand Forks Regional Small Business
Development Center
202 N. 3rd St., Ste. 200
The Hemmp Center
Grand Forks, ND 58203
Phone: (701)772-8502
Fax: (701)772-9238
Gordon Snyder

Jamestown Outreach Center
North Dakota Small Business
Development Center
210 10th St. SE
PO Box 1530
Jamestown, ND 58402
Phone: (701)252-9243
Fax: (701)251-2488
Jon Grinager

Minot Regional Small Business
Development Center
SBDC
900 N. Broadway, Ste. 300
Minot, ND 58703
Phone: (701)852-8861
Fax: (701)858-3831
Brian Argabright

Procurement Assistance Center
SBDC
PO Box 1309
Fargo, ND 58107-1309
Phone: (701)237-9678
Free: 800-698-5726
Fax: (701)237-9734
Eric Nelson

Tri-county Economic Development
Corp.
Fargo Regional Small Business
Development Center
657 2nd Ave. N, Rm. 279
PO Box 1309
Fargo, ND 58103
Phone: (701)237-0986
Fax: (701)237-9734
Jon Grinager

University of North Dakota
North Dakota SBDC
118 Gamble Hall
University Station, Box 7308
Grand Forks, ND 58202-7308
Phone: (701)777-3700
Free: 800-445-7232
Fax: (701)777-3225
Walter "Wally" Kearns, Director

Williston Outreach Center
SBDC
PO Box 2047
Williston, ND 58801
Free: 800-445-7232
Bryan Vendsel

## Ohio

Akron Regional Development Board
Small Business Development Center
1 Cascade Plz., 8th Fl.
Akron, OH 44308-1192
Phone: (330)379-3170
Fax: (330)379-3164
Charles Smith

Ashtabula County Economic
Development Council, Inc.
Small Business Development Center

36 W. Walnut St.
Jefferson, OH 44047
Phone: (216)576-9134
Fax: (216)576-5003
Sarah Bogardus

Central Ohio Manufacturing
SBDC
1250 Arthur E. Adams Dr.
Columbus, OH 43221
Phone: (614)688-5136
Fax: (614)688-5001

Clermont County Chamber of
Commerce
Clermont County Area SBDC
4440 Glen Este-Withamsville Rd.
Cincinnati, OH 45245
Phone: (513)753-7141
Fax: (513)753-7146
Matt VanSant

Dayton Area Chamber of Commerce
Small Business Development Center
Chamber Plz.
5th & Main Sts.
Dayton, OH 45402-2400
Phone: (937)226-8239
Fax: (937)226-8254
Harry Bumgarner

Department of Development
CIC of Belmont County
Small Business Development Center
100 E. Main St.
St. Clairsville, OH 43950
Phone: (614)695-9678
Fax: (614)695-1536
Mike Campbell

Department of Development
Ohio SBDC
77 S. High St., 28th Fl.
Columbus, OH 43216-1001
Phone: (614)466-2711
Fax: (614)466-0829
Holly I. Schick

EMTEC/Southern Area
Manufacturing
SBDC
3155 Research Park, Ste. 206
Kettering, OH 45420
Phone: (513)258-6180
Fax: (513)258-8189
Harry Bumgarner

Enterprise Center
Small Business Development Center

129 E. Main St.
PO Box 756
Hillsboro, OH 45133
Phone: (937)393-9599
Fax: (937)393-8159
Bill Grunkemeyer

Enterprise Development Corp.
SBDC
900 E. State St.
Athens, OH 45701
Phone: (614)592-1188
Fax: (614)593-8283
Karen Patton

Greater Cleveland Growth
Association
Small Business Development Center
200 Tower City Center
50 Public Sq.
Cleveland, OH 44113-2291
Phone: (216)621-1294
Fax: (216)621-4617
JoAnn Uhlik

Greater Columbus Area Chamber of
Commerce
Central Ohio SBDC
37 N. High St.
Columbus, OH 43215-3065
Phone: (614)225-6910
Fax: (614)469-8250
Linda Steward

Greater Steubenville Chamber of
Commerce
Jefferson County Small Business
Development Center
630 Market St.
PO Box 278
Steubenville, OH 43952
Phone: (614)282-6226
Fax: (614)282-6285
Tim McFadden

Kent State University Partnership
SBDC
College of Business Administration,
Rm. 300A
Summit and Terrace
Kent, OH 44242
Phone: (330)672-2772
Fax: (330)672-2448
Linda Yost

Kent State University/Salem Campus
SBDC
2491 State Rte. 45 S.
Salem, OH 44460

Phone: (330)332-0361
Fax: (330)332-9256
Deanne Taylor

Kent State University/Stark Campus
SBDC
6000 Frank Ave., NW
Canton, OH 44720
Phone: (330)499-9600
Fax: (330)494-6121
Annette Chunko

Lake County Economic Development
Center
SBDC
Lakeland Community College
7750 Clocktower Dr.
Kirtland, OH 44080
Phone: (216)951-1290
Fax: (216)951-7336
Cathy Haworth

Lawrence County Chamber of
Commerce
Small Business Development Center
U.S. Rte. 52 & Solida Rd.
PO Box 488
South Point, OH 45680
Phone: (740)894-3838
Fax: (740)894-3836
Lou-Ann Walden

Lima Technical College
Small Business Development Center
West Central Office
545 W. Market St., Ste. 305
Lima, OH 45801-4717
Phone: (419)229-5320
Fax: (419)229-5424
Gerald J. Biedenharn

Lorain County Chamber of
Commerce
SBDC
6100 S. Boadway
Lorain, OH 44053
Phone: (216)233-6500
Dennis Jones

Marietta College
SBDC
213 Fourth St., 2nd Fl.
Marietta, OH 45750
Phone: (614)376-4832
Fax: (614)376-4832
Emerson Shimp

Marion Area Chamber of Commerce
SBDC
206 S. Prospect St.

Marion, OH 43302
Phone: (614)387-0188
Fax: (614)387-7722
Lynn Lovell

Miami University
Small Business Development Center
Department of Decision Sciences
336 Upham Hall
Oxford, OH 45056
Phone: (513)529-4841
Fax: (513)529-1469
Dr. Michael Broida

Mid-Ohio Small Business
Development Center
246 E. 4th St.
PO Box 1208
Mansfield, OH 44901
Phone: (419)521-2655
Free: 800-366-7232
Fax: (419)522-6811
Barbara Harmony

Northern Ohio Manufacturing
SBDC
Prospect Park Bldg.
4600 Prospect Ave.
Cleveland, OH 44103-4314
Phone: (216)432-5300
Fax: (216)361-2900
Gretchen Faro

Northwest Private Industry Council
SBDC
197-2-B1 Park Island Ave.
Defiance, OH 43512
Phone: (419)784-6270
Fax: (419)782-6273
Don Wright

Northwest Technical College
Small Business Development Center
1935 E. 2nd St., Ste. D
Defiance, OH 43512
Phone: (419)784-3777
Fax: (419)782-4649
Don Wright

Ohio Department of Development
Small Business Development Center
77 S. High St., 28th Fl.
Columbus, OH 43215-6108
Phone: (614)466-2711
Free: 800-848-1300
Fax: (614)466-0829
Holly I. Schick, Director

Ohio University Innovation Center
Small Business Development Center

Enterprise & Technical Bldg., Rm.
155
20 East Circle Dr.
Athens, OH 45701
Phone: (614)593-1797
Fax: (614)593-1795
Debra McBride

Ohio Valley Minority Business
Association
SBDC
1208 Waller St.
PO Box 847
Portsmouth, OH 45662
Phone: (614)353-8395
Fax: (614)353-3695
Clemmy Womack

Springfield Small Business
Development Center
300 E. Auburn Ave.
Springfield, OH 45505
Phone: (937)322-7821
Fax: (937)322-7824
Ed Levanthal

Terra Community College
Small Business Development Center
North Central Fremont Office
1220 Cedar St.
Fremont, OH 43420
Phone: (419)334-8400
Fax: (419)334-9414
Joe Wilson

Toledo Small Business Development
Center
300 Madison Ave., Ste. 200
Toledo, OH 43604-1575
Phone: (419)243-8191
Fax: (419)241-8302
Wendy Gramza

Tuscarawas SBDC
300 University Dr., NE
Kent State University
300 University Dr., NE
New Philadelphia, OH 44663-9447
Phone: (330)339-3391
Fax: (330)339-2637
Tom Farbizo

University of Cincinnati
SBDC
1111 Edison Ave.
Cincinnati, OH 45216-2265
Phone: (513)948-2051
Fax: (513)948-2109
Mark Sauter

Upper Valley Joint Vocational School
Small Business Development Center
8811 Career Dr.
N. Country Rd., 25A
Piqua, OH 45356
Phone: (937)778-8419
Free: 800-589-6963
Fax: (937)778-9237
Jon Heffner

Women's Business Development
Center
SBDC
2400 Cleveland Ave., NW
Canton, OH 44709
Phone: (330)453-3867
Fax: (330)773-2992

Women's Entrepreneurial Growth
Organization
Small Business Development Center
Buckingham Bldg., Rm. 55
PO Box 544
Akron, OH 44309
Phone: (330)972-5179
Fax: (330)972-5513
Dr. Penny Marquette

Women's Network
SBDC
1540 West Market St., Ste. 100
Akron, OH 44313
Phone: (330)864-5636
Fax: (330)884-6526
Marlene Miller

Wright State University/Dayton
SBDC
Center for Small Business Assistance
College of Business
Rike Hall, Rm. 120C
Dayton, OH 45435
Phone: (937)873-3503
Dr. Mike Body

Wright State University—Lake
Campus
Small Business Development Center
West Central Office
7600 State Rte. 703
Celina, OH 45882
Phone: (419)586-0355
Free: 800-237-1477
Fax: (419)586-0358
Tom Knapke

WSOS Community Action
Commission, Inc.
Wood County SBDC

121 E. Wooster St.
PO Box 539
Bowling Green, OH 43402
Phone: (419)352-3817
Fax: (419)353-3291
Pat Fligor

Youngstown State University
SBDC
241 Federal Plaza W.
Youngstown, OH 44503
Phone: (330)746-3350
Fax: (330)746-3324
Patricia Veisz

Youngstown/Warren SBDC
Region Chamber of Commerce
180 E. Market St., Ste. 225
Warren, OH 44482
Phone: (330)393-2565
Jim Rowlands

Zanesville Area Chamber of
Commerce
Mid-East Small Business
Development Center
217 N. 5th St.
Zanesville, OH 43701
Phone: (614)452-4868
Fax: (614)454-2963
Bonnie J. Winnett

## Oklahoma

Carl Albert College
Small Business Development Center
1507 S. McKenna
Poteau, OK 74953
Phone: (918)647-4019
Fax: (918)647-1218
Dean Qualls

East Central University
Small Business Development Center
1036 E. 10th St.
Ada, OK 74820
Phone: (405)436-3190
Fax: (405)436-3190
Frank Vater

Langston University Center
Small Business Development Center
Minority Assistance Center
Hwy. 33 E.
Langston, OK 73050
Phone: (405)466-3256
Fax: (405)466-2909
Robert Allen

Lawton Satellite
Small Business Development Center
American National Bank Bldg.
601 SW D Ave., Ste. 209
Lawton, OK 73501
Phone: (405)248-4946
Fax: (405)355-3560
Jim Elliot

Northeastern Oklahoma A&M
Miami Satellite
SBDC
Dyer Hall, Rm. 307
215 I St.
Miami, OK 74354
Phone: (918)540-0575
Fax: (918)540-0575
Hugh Simon

Northeastern Oklahoma State
University
Oklahoma Small Business
Development Center
Tahlequah, OK 74464
Phone: (918)458-0802
Fax: (918)458-2105
Danielle Coursey

Northwestern Oklahoma State
University
Small Business Development Center
709 Oklahoma Blvd.
Alva, OK 73717
Phone: (405)327-8608
Fax: (405)327-0560
Clance Doelling

Phillips University
Small Business Development Center
100 S. University Ave.
Enid, OK 73701
Phone: (405)242-7989
Fax: (405)237-1607
Bill Gregory

Rose State College
SBDC
Procurement Speciality Center
6420 Southeast 15th St.
Midwest City, OK 73110
Phone: (405)733-7348
Fax: (405)733-7495
Judy Robbins

Southeastern Oklahoma State
University
Small Business Development Center
517 University
Station A, Box 2584

Durant, OK 74701
Phone: (580)924-0277
Free: 800-522-6154
Fax: (580)920-7471
E-mail: gpennington@sosu.edu
Dr. Grady Pennington

Southwestern Oklahoma State
University
Small Business Development Center
100 Campus Dr.
Weatherford, OK 73096
Phone: (405)774-1040
Fax: (405)774-7091
Chuck Felz

Tulsa Satellite
Small Business Development Center
State Office Bldg.
616 S. Boston, Ste. 100
Tulsa, OK 74119
Phone: (918)583-2600
Fax: (918)599-6173
Jeff Horvath

University of Central Oklahoma
Small Business Development Center
115 Park Ave.
Oklahoma City, OK 73102-9005
Phone: (405)232-1968
Fax: (405)232-1967
E-mail: sbdc@aix1.ucok.edu
Website: http://www.osbdc.org/
osbdc.htm
Susan Urbach, Director

## Oregon

Blue Mountain Community College
Small Business Development Center
37 SE Dorion
Pendleton, OR 97801
Phone: (541)276-6233
Fax: (541)276-6819
Gerald Wood

Central Oregon Community College
Small Business Development Center
2600 NW College Way
Bend, OR 97701
Phone: (541)383-7290
Fax: (541)317-3445
Bob Newhart

Chemeketa Community College
Small Business Development Center
365 Ferry St. SE
Salem, OR 97301
Phone: (503)399-5088

Fax: (503)581-6017
Tom Nelson

Clackamas Community College
Small Business Development Center
7616 SE Harmony Rd.
Milwaukie, OR 97222
Phone: (503)656-4447
Fax: (503)652-0389
Jan Stennick

Clatsop Community College
Small Business Development Center
1761 N. Holladay
Seaside, OR 97138
Phone: (503)738-3347
Fax: (503)738-7843
Lori Martin

Columbia Gorge Community College
SBDC
400 E. Scenic Dr., Ste. 257
The Dalles, OR 97058
Phone: (541)298-3118
Fax: (541)298-3119
Mr. Bob Cole

Eastern Oregon State College
Small Business Development Center
Regional Services Institute
1410 L Ave.
La Grande, OR 97850
Phone: (541)962-3391
Free: 800-452-8639
Fax: (541)962-3668
John Prosnik

Lane Community College
Oregon SBDC
44 W. Broadway, Ste. 501
Eugene, OR 97401-3021
Phone: (541)726-2250
Fax: (541)345-6006
Website: http://www.efn.org/~osbdcn
Dr. Edward Cutler, Director

Linn-Benton Community College
Small Business Development Center
6500 SW Pacific Blvd.
Albany, OR 97321
Phone: (541)917-4923
Fax: (541)917-4445
Dennis Sargent

Mount Hood Community College
Small Business Development Center
323 NE Roberts St.
Gresham, OR 97030
Phone: (503)667-7658

Fax: (503)666-1140
Don King

Oregon Coast Community College
Small Business Development Center
4157 NW Hwy. 101, Ste. 123
PO Box 419
Lincoln City, OR 97367
Phone: (541)994-4166
Fax: (541)996-4958
Guy Faust

Oregon Institute of Technology
Small Business Development Center
3201 Campus Dr. S. 314
Klamath Falls, OR 97601
Phone: (541)885-1760
Fax: (541)885-1855
Jamie Albert

Portland Community College
Small Business Development Center
2701 NW Vaughn St., No. 499
Portland, OR 97209
Phone: (503)978-5080
Fax: (503)228-6350
Robert Keyser

Portland Community College
Small Business International Trade
Program
121 SW Salmon St., Ste. 210
Portland, OR 97204
Phone: (503)274-7482
Fax: (503)228-6350
Tom Niland

Rogue Community College
Small Business Development Center
214 SW 4th St.
Grants Pass, OR 97526
Phone: (541)471-3515
Fax: (541)471-3589
Lee Merritt

Southern Oregon State College/
Ashland
Small Business Development Center
Regional Services Institute
Ashland, OR 97520
Phone: (541)482-5838
Fax: (541)482-1115
Liz Shelby

Southern Oregon State College/
Medford
Small Business Development Center
Regional Services Institute
332 W. 6th St.

Medford, OR 97501
Phone: (541)772-3478
Fax: (541)734-4813
Liz Shelby

Southwestern Oregon Community
College
Small Business Development Center
2110 Newmark Ave.
Coos Bay, OR 97420
Phone: (541)888-7100
Fax: (541)888-7113
Jon Richards

Tillamook Bay Community College
Small Business Development Center
401 B Main St.
Tillamook, OR 97141
Phone: (503)842-2551
Fax: (503)842-2555
Kathy Wilkes

Treasure Valley Community College
Small Business Development Center
650 College Blvd.
Ontario, OR 97914
Phone: (541)889-6493
Fax: (541)881-2743
Kathy Simko

Umpqua Community College
Small Business Development Center
744 SE Rose
Roseburg, OR 97470
Phone: (541)672-2535
Fax: (541)672-3679
Terry Swagerty

## Pennsylvania

Bucknell University
Small Business Development Center
126 Dana Engineering Bldg., 1st Fl.
Lewisburg, PA 17837
Phone: (717)524-1249
Fax: (717)524-1768
Charles Knisely

Bucks County SBDC Outreach Center
2 E. Court St.
Doylestown, PA 18901
Phone: (215)230-7150
Bruce Love

Clarion University of Pennsylvania
Small Business Development Center
Dana Still Bldg., Rm. 102
Clarion, PA 16214
Phone: (814)226-2060

Fax: (814)226-2636
Dr. Woodrow Yeaney

Duquesne University
Small Business Development Center
Rockwell Hall, Rm. 10, Concourse
600 Forbes Ave.
Pittsburgh, PA 15282
Phone: (412)396-6233
Fax: (412)396-5884
Dr. Mary T. McKinney

Gannon University
Small Business Development Center
120 W. 9th St.
Erie, PA 16501
Phone: (814)871-7714
Fax: (814)871-7383
Ernie Post

Indiana University of Pennsylvania
SBDC
208 Eberly College of Business
Indiana, PA 15705
Phone: (412)357-7915
Fax: (412)357-5985
Dr. Tony Palamone

Kutztown University
Small Business Development Center
2986 N. 2nd St.
Harrisburg, PA 17110
Phone: (717)720-4230
Fax: (717)720-4262
Katherine Wilson

LaSalle University
Small Business Development Center
1900 W. Olney Ave.
Box 365
Philadelphia, PA 19141
Phone: (215)951-1416
Fax: (215)951-1597
Andrew Lamas

Lehigh University
Small Business Development Center
Rauch Business Ctr., No. 37
621 Taylor St.
Bethlehem, PA 18015
Phone: (610)758-3980
Fax: (610)758-5205
Dr. Larry A. Strain

St. Francis College
Small Business Development Center
Business Resource Center
Loretto, PA 15940
Phone: (814)472-3200

*Business Plans Handbook, Volume 8*

Fax: (814)472-3202
Edward Huttenhower

St. Vincent College
Small Business Development Center
Alfred Hall, 4th Fl.
300 Fraser Purchase Rd.
Latrobe, PA 15650
Phone: (412)537-4572
Fax: (412)537-0919
Jack Fabean

Temple University
Small Business Development Center
1510 Cecil B. Moore Ave.
Philadelphia, PA 19121
Phone: (215)204-7282
Fax: (215)204-4554
Geraldine Perkins

University of Pennsylvania
Small Business Development Center
The Wharton School
423 Vance Hall
3733 Spruce St.
Philadelphia, PA 19104-6374
Phone: (215)898-1219
Fax: (215)573-2135
E-mail:
pasbdc@atcwharton.upenn.edu
Website: http://www.libertynet.org/
pasbdc
Gregory L. Higgins, Jr., Director

University of Pittsburgh
Small Business Development Center
The Joseph M. Katz Graduate School
of Business
208 Bellefield Hall
315 S. Bellefield Ave.
Pittsburgh, PA 15213
Phone: (412)648-1544
Fax: (412)648-1636
Ann Dugan

University of Scranton
Small Business Development Center
St. Thomas Hall, Rm. 588
Scranton, PA 18510
Phone: (717)941-7588
Fax: (717)941-4053
Elaine M. Tweedy

West Chester University
SBDC
319 Anderson Hall
211 Carter Dr.
West Chester, PA 19383
Phone: (610)436-2162
Fax: (610)436-2577

Wilkes University
Small Business Development Center
Hollenback Hall
192 S. Franklin St.
Wilkes Barre, PA 18766-0001
Phone: (717)831-4340
Free: 800-572-4444
Fax: (717)824-2245
Jeffrey Alves

**Puerto Rico**

Puerto Rico Small Business
Development Center
Edificio Union Plaza, Ste. 701
416 Ponce de Leon Ave.
Hato Rey, PR 00918
Phone: (787)763-6811
Fax: (787)763-4629

Small Business Development Center
Edificio Union Plaza, Ste. 701
416 Ponce de Leon Ave.
Hato Rey, PR 00918
Phone: (787)763-6811
Fax: (787)763-4629
Carmen Marti

University of Puerto Rico at
Mayaguez
Small Business Development Center
Mayaguez Campus
Box 5253, College Station
Mayaguez, PR 00681
Phone: (809)834-3790
Fax: (809)834-3790
Carmen Marti, Director

**Rhode Island**

Bell Atlantic Telecommunications
Center
1150 Douglas Pke.
Smithfield, RI 02917-1284
Phone: (401)232-0220
Fax: (401)232-0242
Kate Dolan

Bristol County Chamber of
Commerce
SBDC
PO Box 250
Warren, RI 02885-0250
Phone: (401)245-0750
Fax: (401)245-0110
Samuel Carr

Bryant College
Export Assistance Center

SBDC
1150 Douglas Pike
Smithfield, RI 02917
Phone: (401)232-6407
Fax: (401)232-6416
Raymond Fogarty

Bryant College
Rhode Island SBDC
1150 Douglas Pike
Smithfield, RI 02917-1284
Phone: (401)232-6111
Fax: (401)232-6933
Douglas H. Jobling

Bryant College
Rhode Island Small Business
Development Center
1150 Douglas Pke.
Smithfield, RI 02917-1284
Phone: (401)232-6111
Fax: (401)232-6933
Website: http://www.ri-sbdc.com
Richard Brussard, Director

Bryant College
Small Business Development Center
30 Exchange Terrace, 4th Fl.
Providence, RI 02903-1793
Phone: (401)831-1330
Fax: (401)274-5410
Ann Marie Marshall

Central Rhode Island Chamber of
Commerce
SBDC
3288 Post Rd.
Warwick, RI 02886-7151
Phone: (401)732-1100
Fax: (401)732-1107
Mr. Elizabeth Kroll

Enterprise Community SBDC/BIC
550 Broad St.
Providence, RI 02907
Phone: (401)272-1083
Fax: (401)272-1186
Simon Goudiaby

Entrepreneurship Training Program
Bryant College
SBDC
1150 Douglas Pike
Smithfield, RI 02917-1284
Phone: (401)232-6115
Fax: (401)232-6933
Sydney Okashige

Fishing Community Program Office
SBDC

PO Box 178
Narragansett, RI 02882
Phone: (401)783-2466
Angela Caporelli

Newport County Chamber of
Commerce
E. Bay Small Business Development
Center
45 Valley Rd.
Middletown, RI 02842-6377
Phone: (401)849-6900
Fax: (401)841-0570
Samuel Carr

Northern Rhode Island Chamber of
Commerce
SBDC
6 Blackstone Valley Pl., Ste. 105
Lincoln, RI 02865-1105
Phone: (401)334-1000
Fax: (401)334-1009
Shelia Hoogeboom

South County SBDC
QP/D Industrial Park
35 Belver Ave., Rm. 212
North Kingstown, RI 02852-7556
Phone: (401)294-1227
Fax: (401)294-6897
Elizabeth Kroll

### South Carolina

Charleston SBDC
5900 Core Dr., Ste. 104
North Charleston, SC 29406
Phone: (803)740-6160
Fax: (803)740-1607
Merry Boone

Clemson University
Small Business Development Center
College of Business and Public
Affairs
425 Sirrine Hall
Box 341392
Clemson, SC 29634-1392
Phone: (803)656-3227
Fax: (803)656-4869
Becky Hobart

Coastal Carolina College
Small Business Development Center
School of Business Administration
PO Box 261954
Conway, SC 29526-6054
Phone: (803)349-2170
Fax: (803)349-2455
Tim Lowery

Florence-Darlington Technical
College
Small Business Development Center
PO Box 100548
Florence, SC 29501-0548
Phone: (803)661-8256
Fax: (803)661-8041
David Raines

Greenville Manufacturing Field
Office
SBDC
53 E. Antrim Dr.
Greenville, SC 29607
Phone: (803)271-3005

Small Business Development Center
University of South Carolina
College of Business Administration
Hipp Bldg.
1710 College St.
Columbia, SC 29208
Phone: (803)777-4907
Fax: (803)777-4403
Website: http://sbdcweb.badm.sc.edu
John Lenti, Director

South Carolina State College
Small Business Development Center
School of Business Administration
Algernon Belcher Hall
300 College Ave.
Campus Box 7176
Orangeburg, SC 29117
Phone: (803)536-8445
Fax: (803)536-8066
John Gadson

Spartanburg Chamber of Commerce
Small Business Development Center
105 Pine St.
PO Box 1636
Spartanburg, SC 29304
Phone: (803)594-5080
Fax: (803)594-5055
John Keagle

University Center
Upstate Area Office Small Business
Development Center
216 S. Pleasantburg Dr., Rm. 140
Greenville, SC 29607
Phone: (864)250-8894
Fax: (864)250-8897

University of South Carolina
College of Business Administration
South Carolina SBDC
Hipp Bldg.

1710 College St.
Columbia, SC 29208
Phone: (803)777-4907
Fax: (803)777-4403
John Lenti

University of South Carolina
Small Business Development Center
College of Business Administration
Columbia, SC 29208
Phone: (803)777-5118
Fax: (803)777-4403
James Brazell

University of South Carolina at Aiken
Aiken Small Business Development
Center
171 University Pkwy.
Box 9
Aiken, SC 29801
Phone: (803)641-3646
Fax: (803)641-3647
Jackie Moore

University of South Carolina at
Beaufort
Small Business Development Center
800 Carteret St.
Beaufort, SC 29902
Phone: (803)521-4143
Fax: (803)521-4142
Martin Goodman

University of South Carolina at Hilton
Head
Small Business Development Center
1 College Center Dr.
10 Office Park Rd.
Hilton Head, SC 29928-7535
Phone: (803)785-3995
Fax: (803)785-3995
Pat Cameron

Upper Savannah Council of
Government
Small Business Development Center
Exchange Building
222 Phoenix St., Ste. 200
PO Box 1366
Greenwood, SC 29648
Phone: (803)941-8071
Fax: (803)941-8090
George Long

Winthrop University
Winthrop Regional Small Business
Development Center
College of Business Administration
118 Thurmond Bldg.

Rock Hill, SC 29733
Phone: (803)323-2283
Fax: (803)323-4281
Nate Barber

## South Dakota

Aberdeen Small Business
Development Center (Northeast
Region)
620 15th Ave., SE
Aberdeen, SD 57401
Phone: (605)626-2565
Fax: (605)626-2667
Belinda Engelhart

Pierre Small Business Development
Center
105 S. Euclid, Ste. C
Pierre, SD 57501
Phone: (605)773-5941
Fax: (605)773-5942
Greg Sund

Rapid City Small Business
Development Center (Western
Region)
444 N. Mount Rushmore Rd., Rm.
208
Rapid City, SD 57701
Phone: (605)394-5311
Fax: (605)394-6140
Carl Gustafson

Sioux Falls Region
SBDC
405 S. 3rd Ave., Ste. 101
Sioux Falls, SD 57104
Phone: (605)367-5757
Fax: (605)367-5755
Wade Bruin

University of South Dakota
Small Business Development Center
School of Business
414 E. Clark St.
Vermillion, SD 57069-2390
Phone: (605)677-5287
Fax: (605)677-5427
Steve Tracy, Jr., Director

University of South Dakota
South Dakota SBDC
School of Business
414 E. Clark
Vermillion, SD 57069
Phone: (605)677-5498
Fax: (605)677-5272
E-mail: sbdc@sundance.usd.edu
Robert E. Ashley, Jr.

Watertown Small Business
Development Center
124 1st. Ave., NW
PO Box 1207
Watertown, SD 57201
Phone: (605)886-7224
Fax: (605)882-5049
Belinda Engelhart

## Tennessee

Austin Peay State University
Small Business Development Center
College of Business
Clarksville, TN 37044
Phone: (615)648-7764
Fax: (615)648-5985
John Volker

Chattanooga State Technical
Community College
SBDC
100 Cherokee Blvd., No. 202
Chattanooga, TN 37405-3878
Phone: (423)752-1774
Fax: (423)752-1925
Donna Marsh

Cleveland State Community College
Small Business Development Center
PO Box 3570
Cleveland, TN 37320-3570
Phone: (423)478-6247
Fax: (423)478-6251
Don Green

Dyersburg State Community College
Small Business Development Center
1510 Lake Rd.
Dyersburg, TN 38024-2450
Phone: (901)286-3201
Fax: (901)286-3271
Bob Wylie

East Tennessee State University
College of Business
SBDC
PO Box 70625
Johnson City, TN 37614-0625
Phone: (423)929-5630
Fax: (423)461-7080
Bob Justice

Four Lakes Regional Industrial
Development Authority
SBDC
PO Box 63
Hartsville, TN 37074-0063
Phone: (615)374-9521

Fax: (615)374-4608
Dorothy Vaden

Jackson State Community College
Small Business Development Center
McWherter Center, Rm. 213
2046 N. Parkway St.
Jackson, TN 38301-3797
Phone: (901)424-5389
Fax: (901)425-2641
David L. Brown

Knoxville Area Chamber Partnership
International Trade Center
SBDC
Historic City Hall
601 W. Summit Hill Dr.
Knoxville, TN 37902-2011
Phone: (423)632-2990
Fax: (423)521-6367
Richard Vogler

Lambuth University
SBDC
705 Lambuth Blvd.
Jackson, TN 38301
Phone: (901)425-3326
Fax: (901)425-3327
Phillip Ramsey

Middle Tennessee State University
Small Business Development Center
Chamber of Commerce Bldg.
501 Memorial Blvd.
PO Box 487
Murfreesboro, TN 37129-0001
Phone: (615)898-2745
Fax: (615)890-7600
Patrick Geho

Pellissippi State Technical
Community College
Small Business Development Center
Historic City Hall
601 W. Summit Hill Dr.
Knoxville, TN 37902-2011
Phone: (423)632-2980
Fax: (423)971-4439
Teri Brahams

Small Business Development Center
(Columbia)
Maury County Chamber of
Commerce Bldg.
106 W. 6th St.
PO Box 8069
Columbia, TN 38402-8069
Phone: (615)898-2745
Fax: (615)893-7089
Eugene Osekowsky

Southeast Tennessee Development
District
Small Business Development Center
25 Cherokee Blvd.
PO Box 4757
Chattanooga, TN 37405-0757
Phone: (423)266-5781
Fax: (423)267-7705
Sherri Bishop

Tennessee State University
Small Business Development Center
College of Business
330 10th Ave. N.
Nashville, TN 37203-3401
Phone: (615)963-7179
Fax: (615)963-7160
Billy E. Lowe

Tennessee Technological University
SBDC
College of Business Administration
PO Box 5023
Cookeville, TN 38505
Phone: (931)372-3648
Fax: (931)372-6249
Dorothy Vaden

University of Memphis
International Trade Center
SBDC
320 S. Dudley St.
Memphis, TN 38152-0001
Phone: (901)678-4174
Fax: (901)678-4072
Philip Johnson

University of Memphis
Tennessee Small Business
Development Center
South Campus, Bldg. 1, Rm. 101
Campus Box 526324
Memphis, TN 38152-0001
Phone: (901)678-2500
Fax: (901)678-4072
E-mail: gmickle@cc.memphis.edu
Website: http://
www.tsbdc.memphis.edu
Dr. Kenneth J. Burns, Director

Walters State Community College
Tennessee Small Business
Development Center
500 S. Davy Crockett Pkwy.
Morristown, TN 37813
Phone: (423)585-2675
Fax: (423)585-2679
Jack Tucker

## Texas

Abilene Christian University
Small Business Development Center
College of Business Administration
648 E. Hwy. 80
Abilene, TX 79601
Phone: (915)670-0300
Fax: (915)670-0311
Judy Wilhelm

Alvin Community College
Small Business Development Center
3110 Mustang Rd.
Alvin, TX 77511-4898
Phone: (713)388-4686
Fax: (713)388-4903
Gina Mattei

Angelina Community College
Small Business Development Center
Hwy. 59 S.
PO Box 1768
Lufkin, TX 75902
Phone: (409)639-1887
Fax: (409)639-3863
Brian McClain

Angelo State University
Small Business Development Center
2610 West Ave. N.
Campus Box 10910
San Angelo, TX 76909
Phone: (915)942-2098
Fax: (915)942-2096
Harlan Bruha

Best Southwest
SBDC
214 S, Main, Ste. 102A
Duncanville, TX 75116
Phone: (214)709-5878
Free: 800-317-7232
Fax: (214)709-6089
Herb Kamm

Best Southwest Small Business
Development Center
214 S. Main, Ste. 102A
Duncanville, TX 75116
Phone: (972)709-5878
Free: 800-317-7232
Fax: (972)709-6089
Neil Small

Blinn College
Small Business Development Center
902 College Ave.
Brenham, TX 77833

Phone: (409)830-4137
Fax: (409)830-4135
Phillis Nelson

Bonham Satellite
Small Business Development Center
SBDC
Sam Rayburn Library, Bldg. 2
1201 E. 9th St.
Bonham, TX 75418
Phone: (903)583-7565
Fax: (903)583-6706
Darroll Martin

Brazos Valley Small Business
Development Center
Small Business Development Center
4001 E. 29th St., Ste. 175
PO Box 3695
Bryan, TX 77805-3695
Phone: (409)260-5222
Fax: (409)260-5229
Sam Harwell

Brazosport College
Small Business Development Center
500 College Dr.
Lake Jackson, TX 77566
Phone: (409)266-3380
Fax: (409)265-3482
Patricia Leyendecker

College of the Mainland
Small Business Development Center
1200 Amburn Rd.
Texas City, TX 77591
Phone: (409)938-1211
Free: 800-246-7232
Fax: (409)938-7578
Elizabeth Boudreau

Courtyard Center for Professional and
Economic Development
Collin Small Business Development
Center
4800 Preston Park Blvd., Ste. A126
Box 15
Plano, TX 75093
Phone: (972)985-3770
Fax: (972)985-3775
Chris Jones

Dallas County Community College
North Texas SBDC
1402 Corinth St.
Dallas, TX 75215
Phone: 800-350-7232
Fax: (214)860-5813
Elizabeth (Liz) Klimback

Denton Small Business Development
Center
PO Drawer P
Denton, TX 76201
Phone: (254)380-1849
Fax: (254)382-0040
Carolyn Birkhead

El Paso Community College
Small Business Development Center
103 Montana Ave., Ste. 202
El Paso, TX 79902-3929
Phone: (915)831-4410
Fax: (915)831-4625
Roque R. Segura

Galveston College
Small Business Development Center
4015 Avenue Q
Galveston, TX 77550
Phone: (409)740-7380
Fax: (409)740-7381
Georgette Peterson

Grand Prairie Satellite
SBDC
Chamber of Commerce
900 Conover Dr.
Grand Prairie, TX 75053
Phone: (214)860-5850
Fax: (214)860-5857
Al Salgado

Grayson County College
Small Business Development Center
6101 Grayson Dr.
Denison, TX 75020
Phone: (903)463-8787
Free: 800-316-7232
Fax: (903)463-5437
Cynthia Flowers-Whitfield

Greater Corpus Christi Business
Alliance
Small Business Development Center
1201 N. Shoreline
Corpus Christi, TX 78401
Phone: (512)881-1847
Fax: (512)882-4256
Rudy Ortiz

Houston Community College System
Small Business Development Center
10450 Stancliff, Ste. 100
Houston, TX 77099
Phone: (281)933-7932
Fax: (281)568-3690
Joe Harper

Houston Community College System
Small Business Development Center
13600 Murphy Rd.
Stafford, TX 77477
Phone: (713)499-4870
Fax: (713)499-8194
Ted Charlesworth

Houston International Trade Center
Small Business Development Center
1100 Louisiana, Ste. 500
Houston, TX 77002
Phone: (713)752-8404
Fax: (713)756-1500
Mr. Carlos Lopez

International Assistance Center
SBDC
2050 Stemmons Fwy.
PO Box 420451
Dallas, TX 75258
Phone: (214)747-1300
Free: 800-337-7232
Fax: (214)748-5774
Beth Huddleston

Kilgore College
SBDC
Triple Creek Shopping Plaza
110 Triple Creek Dr., Ste. 70
Longview, TX 75601
Phone: (903)757-5857
Free: 800-338-7232
Fax: (903)753-7920
Brad Bunt

Kingsville Chamber of Commerce
Small Business Development Center
635 E. King
Kingsville, TX 78363
Phone: (512)595-5088
Fax: (512)592-0866
Marco Garza

Lamar University
Small Business Development Center
855 Florida Ave.
Beaumont, TX 77705
Phone: (409)880-2367
Fax: (409)880-2201
Gene Arnold

Laredo Development Foundation
Small Business Development Center
Division of Business Administration
616 Leal St.
Laredo, TX 78041
Phone: (956)722-0563
Fax: (956)722-6247
Araceli Lozano

LCRA Coastal Plains
SBDC
PO Box 148
Wharton, TX 77488
Phone: (409)532-1007
Fax: (409)532-0056
Lynn Polson

Lee College
Small Business Development Center
Rundell Hall
PO Box 818
Baytown, TX 77522-0818
Phone: (281)425-6309
Fax: (713)425-6309
Tommy Hathaway

Lower Colorado River Authority
Small Business Development Center
3701 Lake Austin Blvd.
PO Box 220
Austin, TX 78703
Phone: (512)473-3510
Fax: (512)473-3285
Larry Lucero

McLennan Community College
Small Business Development Center
401 Franklin
Waco, TX 76708
Phone: (254)714-0077
Free: 800-349-7232
Fax: (254)714-1668
Lu Billings

Middle Rio Grande Development
Council
Small Business Development Center
209 N. Getty St.
Uvalde, TX 78801
Phone: (830)278-2527
Fax: (830)278-2929
Sheri Rutledge

Midlothian SBDC
330 N. 8th St., Ste. 203
Midlothian, TX 76065-0609
Phone: (214)775-4336
Fax: (214)775-4337

Midwestern State University
Small Business Development Center
3410 Taft Blvd.
Wichita Falls, TX 76308
Phone: (817)397-4373
Fax: (817)397-4374
Tim Thomas

Navarro Small Business Development
Center
120 N. 12th St.
Corsicana, TX 75110
Phone: (903)874-0658
Free: 800-320-7232
Fax: (903)874-4187
Leon Allard

North Central Texas College
Small Business Development Center
1525 W. California
Gainesville, TX 76240
Phone: (254)668-4220
Free: 800-351-7232
Fax: (254)668-6049
Cathy Keeler

North Harris Montgomery
Community College District
Small Business Development Center
250 N. Sam Houston Pkwy. E.
Houston, TX 77060
Phone: (281)260-3174
Fax: (713)591-3513
Kay Hamilton

Northeast Texarkana
Small Business Development Center
PO Box 1307
Mt. Pleasant, TX 75455
Phone: (903)572-1911
Free: 800-357-7232
Fax: (903)572-0598
Bob Wall

Paris Junior College
Small Business Development Center
2400 Clarksville St.
Paris, TX 75460
Phone: (903)784-1802
Fax: (903)784-1801
Pat Bell, Dir.

Bill J. Priest Institute for Economic
Development
North Texas-Dallas Small Business
Development Center
1402 Corinth St.
Dallas, TX 75215
Phone: (214)860-5842
Free: 800-348-7232
Fax: (214)860-5881
Pamela Speraw

Sam Houston State University
Small Business Development Center
843 S. Sam Houston Ave.
PO Box 2058

Huntsville, TX 77341-3738
Phone: (409)294-3737
Fax: (409)294-3612
Bob Barragan

Small Business Development Center
for Enterprise Excellence
SBDC
7300 Jack Newell Blvd., S.
Fort Worth, TX 76118
Phone: (817)272-5930
Fax: (817)272-5932
Jo An Weddle

Sul Ross State University
Big Bend SBDC Satellite
PO Box C-47, Rm. 319
Alpine, TX 79832
Phone: (915)837-8694
Fax: (915)837-8104
Michael Levine

Tarleton State University
Small Business Development Center
College of Business Administration
Box T-0650
Stephenville, TX 76402
Phone: (817)968-9330
Fax: (817)968-9329
Jim Choate, Dir.

Tarrant County Junior College
Small Business Development Center
Mary Owen Center, Rm. 163
1500 Houston St.
Ft. Worth, TX 76102
Phone: (817)871-2068
Fax: (817)871-0031
David Edmonds

Technology Assistance Center
SBDC
1402 Corinth St.
Dallas, TX 75215
Phone: 800-355-7232
Fax: (214)860-5881
Pamela Speraw

Texas Center for Government
Contracting and Technology
Assistance
Small Business Development Center
1402 Corinth St.
Dallas, TX 75215
Phone: (214)860-5841
Fax: (214)860-5881
Gerald Chandler

Texas Tech University
Northwestern Texas SBDC

Spectrum Plaza
2579 S. Loop 289, Ste. 114
Lubbock, TX 79423
Phone: (806)745-3973
Fax: (806)745-6207
E-mail: odbea@ttacs.ttu.edu
Craig Bean

Trinity Valley Community College
Small Business Development Center
500 S. Prairieville
Athens, TX 75751
Phone: (903)675-7403
Free: 800-335-7232
Fax: (903)675-5199
Judy Loden, Dir.

Tyler Junior College
Small Business Development Center
1530 South SW Loop 323, Ste. 100
Tyler, TX 75701
Phone: (903)510-2975
Fax: (903)510-2978
Frank Viso, Dir.

University of Houston
Southeastern Texas SBDC
1100 Louisiana, Ste. 500
Houston, TX 77002
Phone: (713)752-8444
Fax: (713)756-1500
J.E. "Ted" Cadou

University of Houston
Southeastern Texas Small Business
Development Center
1100 Louisiana, Ste. 500
Houston, TX 77002
Phone: (713)752-8444
Fax: (713)756-1500
Website: http://
smbizsolutions.2uh.edu
Dr. Elizabeth Gatewood, Director

University of Houston
Texas Information Procurement
Service
Small Business Development Center
1100 Louisiana, Ste. 500
Houston, TX 77002
Phone: (713)752-8477
Fax: (713)756-1515
Jacqueline Taylor

University of Houston
Texas Manufacturing Assistance
Center (Gulf Coast)
1100 Louisiana, Ste. 500
Houston, TX 77002

Phone: (713)752-8440
Fax: (713)756-1500
Roy Serpa

University of Houston—Victoria
Small Business Development Center
700 Main Center, Ste. 102
Victoria, TX 77901
Phone: (512)575-8944
Fax: (512)575-8852
Carole Parks

University of Texas (Downtown San Antonio)
South Texas Border SBDC
1222 N. Main, Ste. 450
San Antonio, TX 78212
Phone: (210)458-2450
Fax: (210)458-2464
E-mail: rmckinle@utsadt.utsa.edu
Robert McKinley

University of Texas—Pan American
Small Business Development Center
1201 W. University Dr., Rm. BA-124
Center for Entrepreneurship &
Economic Development
Edinburg, TX 78539-2999
Phone: (956)316-2610
Fax: (956)316-2612
Juan Garcia

University of Texas—Permian Basin
Small Business Development Center
College of Management
4901 E. University Blvd.
Odessa, TX 79762
Phone: (915)552-2455
Fax: (915)552-2433
Arthur L. Connor, III

University of Texas at San Antonio
International Trade Center
SBDC
1222 N. Main, Ste. 450
San Antonio, TX 78212
Phone: (210)458-2470
Fax: (210)458-2464
Sara Jackson

University of Texas at San Antonio
Small Business Development Center
1222 N. Main St., Ste. 450
San Antonio, TX 78212
Phone: (210)458-2458
Fax: (210)458-2464
Judith Ingalls

West Texas A&M University
Small Business Development Center

T. Boone Pickens School of Business
1800 S. Washington, Ste. 209
Amarillo, TX 79102
Phone: (806)372-5151
Fax: (806)372-5261
Don Taylor

Western Bank and Trust Satellite
SBDC
PO Box 461545
Garland, TX 75046
Phone: (214)860-5850
Fax: (214)860-5857
Al Salgado

## Utah

Dixie College
Small Business Development Center
225 South 700 East
St. George, UT 84770-3876
Phone: (435)652-7751
Fax: (435)652-7870
Jill Ellis

Salt Lake City Small Business
Development Center
Salt Lake Community College
1623 S State St.
Salt Lake City, UT 84115
Phone: (801)957-3480
Fax: (801)957-3489
Mike Finnerty

Salt Lake Community College
Sandy SBDC
8811 South 700 East
Sandy, UT 84070
Phone: (435)255-5878
Fax: (435)255-6393
Barry Bartlett

Salt Lake Community College
SBDC
1623 S. State St.
Salt Lake City, UT 84115
Phone: (801)957-3480
Fax: (801)957-3489
Mike Finnerty

Snow College
Small Business Development Center
345 West 100 North
Ephraim, UT 84627
Phone: (435)283-7472
Fax: (435)283-6913
Russell Johnson

South Eastern Utah AOG
Small Business Development Center

Price Center
PO Box 1106
Price, UT 84501
Phone: (435)637-5444
Fax: (435)637-7336
Dennis Rigby

Southern Utah University
Small Business Development Center
351 W. Center
Cedar City, UT 84720
Phone: (435)586-5400
Fax: (435)586-5493
Derek Snow

Utah State University
Small Business Development Center
East Campus Bldg., Rm. 124
Logan, UT 84322
Phone: (435)797-2277
Fax: (435)797-3317
Franklin C. Prante

Utah State University Extension
Office
SBDC
987 E. Lagoon St.
Roosevelt, UT 84066
Phone: (435)722-2294
Fax: (435)789-3689
Mark Holmes

Utah Valley State College
Utah Small Business Development
Center
800 West 200 South
Orem, UT 84058
Phone: (435)222-8230
Fax: (435)225-1229
Chuck Cozzens

Weber State University
Small Business Development Center
School of Business and Economics
Ogden, UT 84408-3815
Phone: (435)626-6070
Fax: (435)626-7423
Bruce Davis

## Vermont

Addison County Economic
Development Corp.
SBDC
RD4, Box 1309A
Middlebury, VT 05753
Phone: (802)388-7953
Fax: (802)388-8066
James Stewart

Bennington County Industrial Corp.
SBDC
PO Box 357
North Bennington, VT 05257-0357
Phone: (802)442-8975
Fax: (802)442-1101
Chris Hunsinger

Brattleboro Development Credit
Corp.
SBDC
72 Cotton Mill Hill
PO Box 1177
Brattleboro, VT 05301-1177
Phone: (802)257-7731
Fax: (802)258-3886
William McGrath

Central Vermont Economic
Development Center
SBDC
PO Box 1439
Montpelier, VT 05601-1439
Phone: (802)223-4654
Fax: (802)223-4655
Donald Rowan

Franklin County Industrial
Development Corp.
SBDC
PO Box 1099
St. Albans, VT 05478-1099
Phone: (802)524-2194
Fax: (802)527-5258
Timothy J. Soule

Greater Burlington Industrial Corp.
Northwestern Vermont Small
Business Development Center
PO Box 786
Burlington, VT 05402-0786
Phone: (802)658-9228
Fax: (802)860-1899
Thomas D. Schroeder

Green Mountain Economic
Development Corporation
SBDC
PO Box 246
White River Jct., VT 05001-0246
Phone: (802)295-3710
Fax: (802)295-3779
Lenae Quillen-Blume

Lake Champlain Islands Chamber of
Commerce
SBDC
PO Box 213
North Hero, VT 05474-0213

Phone: (802)372-5683
Fax: (802)372-6104
Barbara Mooney

Lamoille Economic Development
Corp.
SBDC
Sunset Dr.
PO Box 455
Morrisville, VT 05661-0455
Phone: (802)888-4542
Chris D'Elia

Northeastern Vermont Small Business
Development Center
44 Main St.
PO Box 630
St. Johnsbury, VT 05819-0630
Phone: (802)748-1014
Fax: (802)748-1223
Charles E. E. Carter

Rutland Economic Development
Corp.
Southwestern Vermont Small
Business Development Center
256 N. Main St.
Rutland, VT 05701-0039
Phone: (802)773-9147
Fax: (802)773-2772
Wendy Wilton

Springfield Development Corp.
Southeastern Vermont Small Business
Development Center
PO Box 58
Springfield, VT 05156-0058
Phone: (802)885-2071
Fax: (802)885-3027
Steve Casabona

Vermont Small Business
Development Center
Vermont Technical College
PO Box 422
Randolph Center, VT 05060-0422
Phone: (802)728-9101
Free: 800-464-SBDC
Fax: (802)728-3026
Website: http://www.vtsbdc.org
Donald L. Kelpinski, Director

## Virgin Islands

University of the Virgin Islands
Small Business Development Center
Sunshine Mall
No.1 Estate Cane, Ste. 104
Frederiksted, VI 00840

Phone: (809)692-5270
Fax: (809)692-5629
Chester Williams

## Virginia

Arlington Small Business
Development Center
George Mason University, Arlington
Campus
4001 N. Fairfax Dr., Ste. 450
Arlington, VA 22203-1640
Phone: (703)993-8129
Fax: (703)430-7293
Paul Hall

Central Virginia Small Business
Development Center
918 Emmet St., N., Ste. 200
Charlottesville, VA 22903-4878
Phone: (804)295-8198
Fax: (804)295-7066
Robert A. Hamilton, Jr.

Department of Business Assistance
Small Business Development Center
707 East Main St. Ste. 300
Richmond, VA 23219
Phone: (804)371-8253
Fax: (804)225-3384
Website: http://www.vdba.org
Dr. Robert D. Smith

Department of Business Assistance
Virginia SBDC
707 E. Main St., Ste. 300
Richmond, VA 23219
Phone: (804)371-8253
Fax: (804)225-3384
Bob Wilburn

Flory Small Business Development
Center
10311 Sudley Manor Dr.
Manassas, VA 20109-2962
Phone: (703)335-2500
Linda Decker

George Mason University
Northern Virginia Small Business
Development Center
4031 University Dr., Ste. 200
Fairfax, VA 22030
Phone: (703)277-7700
Fax: (703)993-2126
Michael Kehoe

Greater Richmond Small Business
Development Center

1 N. 5th St., Ste. 510
Richmond, VA 23219
Phone: (804)648-7838
Free: 800-646-SBDC
Fax: (804)648-7849
Charlie Meacham

Hampton Roads Chamber of
Commerce
SBDC
400 Volvo Pkwy.
PO Box 1776
Chesapeake, VA 23320
Phone: (757)664-2590
Fax: (757)548-1835
William J. Holoran, Jr.

Hampton Roads Inc.
Small Business Development Center
525 Butler Farm Rd., Ste. 102
Hampton, VA 23666
Phone: (757)825-2957
Fax: (757)825-2960
James Carroll

James Madison University
Small Business Development Center
College of Business
Zane Showker Hall, Rm. 527
PO Box MSC 0206
Harrisonburg, VA 22807
Phone: (540)568-3227
Fax: (540)568-3106
Karen Wigginton

Longwood College (Farmville)
Small Business Development Center
515 Main St.
Farmville, VA 23909
Phone: (804)395-2086
Fax: (804)395-2359
Gerald L. Hughes, Jr.

Lord Fairfax Community College
SBDC
173 Skirmisher Ln.
PO Box 47
Middletown, VA 22645
Phone: (540)869-6649
Fax: (540)868-7002
Robert Crosen

Loudoun County Small Business
Development Center
Satellite Office of Northern Virginia
207 E. Holly Ave., Ste. 214
Sterling, VA 20164
Phone: (703)430-7222
Fax: (703)430-7258
Ted London

Lynchburg Regional Small Business
Development Center
147 Mill Ridge Rd.
Lynchburg, VA 24502-4341
Phone: (804)582-6170
Free: 800-876-7232
Fax: (804)582-6106
Barry Lyons

Mount Empire Community College
Southwest Small Business
Development Center
Drawer 700, Rte. 23, S.
Big Stone Gap, VA 24219
Phone: (540)523-6529
Fax: (540)523-2400
Tim Blankenbecler

New River Valley
SBDC
600-H Norwood St.
PO Box 3726
Radford, VA 24141
Phone: (540)831-6056
Fax: (540)831-6057
David Shanks

Rappahannock Region Small
Business Development Center
1301 College Ave.
Seacobeck Hall, Rm. 102
Fredericksburg, VA 22401
Phone: (540)654-1060
Fax: (540)654-1070
Jeffrey R. Sneddon

Regional Chamber Small Business
Development Center
Western Virginia SBDC Consortium
212 S. Jefferson St.
Roanoke, VA 24011
Phone: (540)983-0717
Fax: (540)983-0723
Ian Webb

SBDC Satellite Office of Longwood
PO Box 709
115 Broad St.
Martinsville, VA 24114
Phone: (540)632-4462
Fax: (540)632-5059
Ken Copeland

Small Business Development Center
of Hampton Roads, Inc. (Norfolk)
420 Bank St.
PO Box 327
Norfolk, VA 23501
Phone: (757)664-2528

Fax: (757)622-5563
Warren Snyder

South Boston Satellite Office of
Longwood
Small Business Development Center
515 Broad St.
PO Box 1116
South Boston, VA 24592
Phone: (804)575-0044
Fax: (804)572-1762
Vincent Decker

Southwest Virginia Community
College
Southwest Small Business
Development Center
PO Box SVCC, Rte. 19
Richlands, VA 24641
Phone: (540)964-7345
Fax: (540)964-5788
Jim Boyd

Virginia Eastern Shore Corp.
SBDC
36076 Lankford Hwy.
PO Box 395
Belle Haven, VA 23306
Phone: (757)442-7179
Fax: (757)442-7181

Virginia Highlands SBDC
Rte. 382
PO Box 828
Abingdon, VA 24212
Phone: (540)676-5615
Fax: (540)628-7576
Jim Tilley

Virginia Small Business Development
Center
Commonwealth of Virginia
Department of Economic
Development
901 E Byrd St., Ste. 1400
Richmond, VA 23219
Phone: (804)371-8253
Fax: (804)225-3384
Robert D. Wilburn

Warsaw Small Business Development
Center
Satellite Office of Rappahannock
5559 W. Richmond Rd.
PO Box 490
Warsaw, VA 22572
Phone: (804)333-0286
Free: 800-524-8915
Fax: (804)333-0187
John Clickener

Wytheville Community College
Wytheville Small Business
Development Center
1000 E. Main St.
Wytheville, VA 24382
Phone: (540)223-4798
Free: 800-468-1195
Fax: (540)223-4716
Rob Edwards

## Washington

Bellevue Small Business
Development Center
Bellevue Community College
3000 Landerholm Circle SE
Bellevue, WA 98007-6484
Phone: (425)643-2888
Fax: (425)649-3113
Bill Huenefeld

Big Bend Community College
Small Business Development Center
7662 Chanute St.
Moses Lake, WA 98837-3299
Phone: (509)762-6306
Fax: (509)762-6329
Ed Baroch

Centralia Community College
Small Business Development Center
600 W. Locust St.
Centralia, WA 98531
Phone: (360)736-9391
Fax: (360)730-7504
Joanne Baria

Columbia Basin College—TRIDEC
Small Business Development Center
901 N. Colorado
Kennewick, WA 99336
Phone: (509)735-6222
Fax: (509)735-6609
Blake Escudier

Columbia River Economic
Development Council
Small Business Development Center
217 SE 136th Ave., Ste. 105
Vancouver, WA 98660
Phone: (360)260-6372
Fax: (360)260-6369
Janet Harte

Edmonds Community College
Small Business Development Center
20000 68th Ave. W.
Lynnwood, WA 98036
Phone: (425)640-1435

Fax: (425)640-1532
Jack Wicks

International Trade Institute
North Seattle Community College
Small Business Development Center
2001 6th Ave., Ste. 650
Seattle, WA 98121
Phone: (206)553-0052
Fax: (206)553-7253
Ann Tamura

Port of Walla Walla SBDC
500 Tausick Way
Rte. 4, Box 174
Walla Walla, WA 99362
Phone: (509)527-4681
Fax: (509)525-3101
Rich Monacelli

Quest Small Business Development
Center
37 S. Wenatchee Ave., Ste. C
Industrial Bldg. 2, Ste. D.
Wenatchee, WA 98801-2443
Phone: (509)662-8016
Fax: (509)663-0455
Rich Reim

Skagit Valley College
Small Business Development Center
2405 College Way
Mount Vernon, WA 98273
Phone: (360)428-1282
Fax: (360)336-6116
Peter Stroosma

South Puget Sound Community
College
Small Business Development Center
721 Columbia St. SW
Olympia, WA 98501
Phone: (360)753-5616
Fax: (360)586-5493
Douglas Hammel

South Seattle Community College
Duwamish Industrial Education
Center
Small Business Development Center
6770 E. Marginal Way S
Seattle, WA 98108-3405
Phone: (206)768-6855
Fax: (206)764-5838
Henry Burton

Washington Small Business
Development Center (Seattle)
180 Nickerson, Ste. 207

Seattle, WA 98109
Phone: (206)464-5450
Fax: (206)464-6357
Warner Wong

Washington Small Business
Development Center (Tacoma)
950 Pacific Ave., Ste. 300
PO Box 1933
Tacoma, WA 98401-1933
Phone: (253)272-7232
Fax: (253)597-7305
Neil Delisanti

Washington State University
Small Business Development Center
College of Business & Economics
501 Johnson Tower
Pullman, WA 99164-4851
Phone: (509)335-1576
Fax: (509)335-0949
Website: http://www.sbdc.wsu.edu
Carol Riesenberg, Director

Washington State University
(Pullman)
Small Business Development Center
501 Johnson Tower
PO Box 644851
Pullman, WA 99164-4727
Phone: (509)335-1576
Fax: (509)335-0949
Carol Riesenberg

Washington State University
(Spokane)
Small Business Development Center
665 North Riverpoint Blvd.
Spokane, WA 99202
Phone: (509)358-7894
Fax: (509)358-7896
Richard Thorpe

Wenatchee Valley College
SBDC
PO Box 741
Okanogan, WA 98840
Phone: (509)826-5107
Fax: (509)826-1812
John Rayburn

Western Washington University
Small Business Development Center
College of Business and Economics
308 Parks Hall
Bellingham, WA 98225-9073
Phone: (360)650-4831
Fax: (360)650-4844
Tom Dorr

Yakima Valley College
Small Business Development Center
PO Box 1647
Yakima, WA 98907
Phone: (509)454-3608
Fax: (509)454-4155
Audrey Rice

### West Virginia

College of West Virginia
SBDC
PO Box AG
Beckley, WV 25802
Phone: (304)252-7885
Fax: (304)252-9584
Tom Hardiman

Fairmont State College
Small Business Development Center
1000 Technology Dr., Ste. 1120
Fairmont, WV 26554
Phone: (304)367-2712
Fax: (304)367-2717
Jack Kirby

Fairmont State College (Elkins
Satellite)
SBDC
10 Eleventh St., Ste. 1
Elkins, WV 26241
Phone: (304)637-7205
Fax: (304)637-4902
James Martin

Marshall University
Small Business Development Center
1050 4th Ave.
Huntington, WV 25755-2126
Phone: (304)696-6246
Fax: (304)696-6277
Edna McClain

Shepherd College
Small Business Development Center
120 N. Princess St.
Shepherdstown, WV 25443
Phone: (304)876-5261
Fax: (304)876-5467
Fred Baer

West Virginia Department Office
West Virginia SBDC
950 Kanawha Blvd. E., Ste. 200
Charleston, WV 25301
Phone: (304)558-2960
Free: (888)WVA-SBDC
Fax: (304)348-0127
Dr. Hazel Kroesser-Palmer

West Virginia Development Office
Small Business Development Center
950 Kanawha Blvd. E., 2nd Floor
Charleston, WV 25301
Phone: (304)558-2960
Fax: (304)558-0127
Dr. Hazel Kroesser, Director

West Virginia Institute of Technology
Small Business Development Center
Engineering Bldg., Rm. 102
Montgomery, WV 25136
Phone: (304)442-5501
Fax: (304)442-3307
James Epling

West Virginia Northern Community
College
Small Business Development Center
1701 Market St.
College Sq.
Wheeling, WV 26003
Phone: (304)233-5900
Fax: (304)232-0965
Ron Trevellini

West Virginia University
Fairmont State College Satellite
Small Business Development Center
PO Box 6025
Morgantown, WV 26506-6025
Phone: (304)293-5839
Fax: (304)293-7061
Sharon Stratton

West Virginia University
(Parkersburg)
Small Business Development Center
Rte. 5, Box 167-A
Parkersburg, WV 26101
Phone: (304)424-8277
Fax: (304)424-8315
Greg Hill

### Wisconsin

University of Wisconsin
Wisconsin SBDC
432 N. Lake St., Rm. 423
Madison, WI 53706
Phone: (608)263-7794
Fax: (608)263-7830
Erica McIntire

University of Wisconsin—Eau Claire
Small Business Development Center
Schneider Hall, Rm. 113
PO Box 4004
Eau Claire, WI 54702-4004

Phone: (715)836-5811
Fax: (715)836-5263
Fred Waedt

University of Wisconsin—Extension
Small Business Development Center
432 N. Lake St., Rm. 423
Madison, WI 53706-1498
Phone: (608)263-7794
Fax: (608)262-3878
Website: http://www.vwex.edu/sbdc
Erica Kauten, Director

University of Wisconsin—Green Bay
Small Business Development Center
Wood Hall, Rm. 480
2420 Nicolet Dr.
Green Bay, WI 54311
Phone: (920)465-2089
Fax: (920)465-2552
Jan Thornton

University of Wisconsin—La Crosse
Small Business Development Center
North Hall, Rm. 120
1701 Farwell St.
La Crosse, WI 54601
Phone: (608)785-8782
Fax: (608)785-6919
Jan Gallagher

University of Wisconsin—Madison
Small Business Development Center
975 University Ave., Rm. 3260
Grainger Hall
Madison, WI 53706
Phone: (608)263-2221
Fax: (608)263-0818
Neil Lerner

University of Wisconsin—Milwaukee
Small Business Development Center
161 W. Wisconsin Ave., Ste. 600
Milwaukee, WI 53203
Phone: (414)227-3240
Fax: (414)227-3142
Sara Thompson

University of Wisconsin—Oshkosh
Small Business Development Center
800 Algoma Blvd.
Oshkosh, WI 54901
Phone: (920)424-1453
Fax: (920)424-7413
John Mozingo

University of Wisconsin—Parkside
Small Business Development Center
Tallent Hall, Rm. 284

900 Wood Rd.
Kenosha, WI 53141-2000
Phone: (414)595-2189
Fax: (414)595-2471
Patricia Deutsch

University of Wisconsin—Stevens
Point
Small Business Development Center
Old Main Bldg., Rm. 103
Stevens Point, WI 54481
Phone: (715)346-3838
Fax: (715)346-4045
Vicki Lobermeier

University of Wisconsin—Superior
Small Business Development Center
1800 Grand Ave.
Superior, WI 54880-2898
Phone: (715)394-8352
Fax: (715)394-8592
Laura Urban

University of Wisconsin—
Whitewater
Small Business Development Center
2000 Carlson Bldg.
Whitewater, WI 53190
Phone: (414)472-3217
Fax: (414)472-5692
Carla Lenk

University of Wisconsin at
Whitewater
Wisconsin Innovation Service Center
SBDC
416 McCutchen Hall
Whitewater, WI 53190
Phone: (414)472-1365
Fax: (414)472-1600
E-mail: malewicd@uwwvax.uww.edu
Debra Malewicki

## Wyoming

Casper Small Business Development
Center
Region III
111 W. 2nd St., Ste. 502
Casper, WY 82601
Phone: (307)234-6683
Free: 800-348-5207
Fax: (307)577-7014
Leonard Holler

Cheyenne SBDC
Region IV
1400 E. College Dr.
Cheyenne, WY 82007-3298

Phone: (307)632-6141
Free: 800-348-5208
Fax: (307)632-6061
Arlene Soto

Northwest Community College
Small Business Development Center
Region II
146 South Bent St.
John Dewitt Student Center
Powell, WY 82435
Phone: (307)754-2139
Free: 800-348-5203
Fax: (307)754-0368
Dwane Heintz

Rock Springs Small Business
Development Center
Region I
PO Box 1168
Rock Springs, WY 82902
Phone: (307)352-6894
Free: 800-348-5205
Fax: (307)352-6876

Wyoming Small Business
Development Center
State Office
University of Wyoming
PO Box 3622
Laramie, WY 82071-3622
Phone: (307)766-3505
Free: 800-348-5194
Fax: (307)766-3406
Diane Wolverton

Wyoming Small Business
Development Center
University of Wyoming
PO Box 3922
Laramie, WY 82071-3922
Phone: (307)766-3505
Free: 800-348-5194
Fax: (307)766-3406
Diane Wolverton

# SERVICE CORPS OF RETIRED EXECUTIVES (SCORE) OFFICES

*This section contains a listing of all
SCORE offices organized alphabetically
by state/U.S. territory name, then by
agency name.*

## Alabama

SCORE Office (Alabama Capitol
City)
600 S. Court St.
Montgomery, AL 36104
Phone: (334)240-6868
Fax: (334)240-6869

SCORE Office (Baldwin County)
29750 Larry Dee Cawyer Dr.
Daphne, AL 36527
Phone: (334)928-5838

SCORE Office (East Alabama)
PO Box 2366
Opelika, AL 36803
Phone: (334)745-4861
E-mail: score636@hotmail.com
Website: http://www.angelfire.com/
sc/score636/

SCORE Office (Mobile)
PO Box 2187
Mobile, AL 36652
Phone: (334)433-6951
Fax: (334)431-8646

SCORE Office (North Alabama)
901 South 15th St, Rm. 201
Birmingham, AL 35294-2060
Phone: (205)934-6868
Fax: (205)934-0538

SCORE Office (Northeast Alabama)
PO Box 1087
Anniston, AL 36202
Phone: (256)237-3536

SCORE Office (Shoals)
612 S. Court
Florence, AL 35630
Phone: (256)764-7661

SCORE Office (Tuscaloosa)
2200 University Blvd.
Tuscaloosa, AL 35402
Phone: (205)758-7588

## Alaska

SCORE Office (Anchorage)
222 W. 8th Ave.
Anchorage, AK 99513-7559
Phone: (907)271-4022
Fax: (907)271-4545

## Arizona

SCORE Office (East Valley)
Federal Bldg., Rm. 104
26 N. MacDonald St.
Mesa, AZ 85201
Phone: (602)379-3100
Fax: (602)379-3143
E-mail: 402@aol.com
Website: http://
www.scorearizona.org/mesa/

SCORE Office (Lake Havasu)
PO Box 2049
Lake Havasu City, AZ 86405
Phone: (520)453-5951
E-mail: SCORE@ctaz.com
Website: http://
www.scorearizona.org/lake_havasu/

SCORE Office (Phoenix)
2828 N. Central Ave., Ste. 800
Central & One Thomas
Phoenix, AZ 85004
Phone: (602)745-7250
Fax: (602)745-7210
E-mail: e-mail@SCORE-phoenix.org
Website: http://www.score-
phoenix.org/

SCORE Office (Prescott Arizona)
1228 Willow Creek Rd., Ste. 2
Prescott, AZ 86301
Phone: (520)778-7438
Fax: (520)778-0812
E-mail: score@northlink.com
Website: http://
www.scorearizona.org/prescott/

SCORE Office (Tucson)
PO Box 2143
Tucson, AZ 85702
Phone: (520)670-5008
Fax: (520)670-5011
E-mail: score@azstarnet.com
Website: http://
www.scorearizona.org/tucson/

SCORE Office (Yuma)
281 W. 24th St., Ste. 116
Yuma, AZ 85364

Phone: (520)314-0480
E-mail: score@C2i2.com
Website: http://
www.scorearizona.org/yuma

## Arkansas

SCORE Office (Garland County)
Grand & Ouachita
PO Box 6090
Hot Springs, AR 71902
Phone: (501)321-1700

SCORE Office (Little Rock)
2120 Riverfront Dr., Rm. 100
Little Rock, AR 72202-1747
Phone: (501)324-5893
Fax: (501)324-5199

SCORE Office (Northwest Arkansas)
Glenn Haven Dr., No. 4
Ft. Smith, AR 72901
Phone: (501)783-3556

SCORE Office (Ozark)
1141 Eastwood Dr.
Fayetteville, AR 72701
Phone: (501)442-7619

SCORE Office (South Central)
201 N. Jackson Ave.
El Dorado, AR 71730-5803
Phone: (870)863-6113
Fax: (870)863-6115

SCORE Office (Southeast Arkansas)
PO Box 5069
Pine Bluff, AR 71611-5069
Phone: (870)535-7189
Fax: (870)535-1643

## California

SCORE Office (Antelope Valley)
4511 West Ave., No. M-4
Quartz Hill, CA 93536
Phone: (805)272-0087
E-mail: avscore@ptw.com
Website: http://www.score.av.org/

SCORE Office (Central California)
2719 N. Air Fresno Dr., Ste. 200
Fresno, CA 93727-1547
Phone: (559)487-5605
Fax: (559)487-5636

SCORE Office (Central Coast)
509 W. Morrison Ave.
Santa Maria, CA 93454
Phone: (805)347-7755

SCORE Office (Concord)
2151-A Salvio St., Ste. B
Concord, CA 94520
Phone: (510)685-1181
Fax: (510)685-5623

SCORE Office (Conejo Valley)
625 W. Hillcrest Dr.
Thousand Oaks, CA 91360
Phone: (805)499-1993
Fax: (805)498-7264

SCORE Office (Covina)
935 W. Badillo St.
Covina, CA 91723
Phone: (818)967-4191
Fax: (818)966-9660

SCORE Office (Culver City)
PO Box 707
Culver City, CA 90232-0707
Phone: (310)287-3850
Fax: (310)287-1350

SCORE Office (Danville)
380 Diablo Rd., Ste. 103
Danville, CA 94526
Phone: (510)837-4400

SCORE Office (Downey)
11131 Brookshire Ave.
Downey, CA 90241
Phone: (310)923-2191
Fax: (310)864-0461

SCORE Office (East Bay)
519 17th St., Ste 240
Oakland, CA 94612
Phone: (510)273-6611
Fax: (510)273-6015
E-mail: eastbayscore@yahoo.com
Website: http://www.eastbayscore.org

SCORE Office (El Cajon)
109 Rea Ave.
El Cajon, CA 92020
Phone: (619)444-1327
Fax: (619)440-6164

SCORE Office (El Centro)
1100 Main St.
El Centro, CA 92243
Phone: (619)352-3681
Fax: (619)352-3246

SCORE Office (Encinitas)
550 W. C St., Ste. 550
San Diego, CA 92101-3540
Phone: (619)557-7272
Fax: (619)557-5894

SCORE Office (Escondido)
720 N. Broadway
Escondido, CA 92025
Phone: (619)745-2125
Fax: (619)745-1183

SCORE Office (Fairfield)
1111 Webster St.
Fairfield, CA 94533
Phone: (707)425-4625
Fax: (707)425-0826

SCORE Office (Fontana)
17009 Valley Blvd., Ste. B
Fontana, CA 92335
Phone: (909)822-4433
Fax: (909)822-6238

SCORE Office (Foster City)
1125 E. Hillsdale Blvd.
Foster City, CA 94404
Phone: (415)573-7600
Fax: (415)573-5201

SCORE Office (Fremont)
2201 Walnut Ave., Ste. 110
Fremont, CA 94538
Phone: (510)795-2244
Fax: (510)795-2240

SCORE Office (Gardena)
1204 W. Gardena Blvd.
Gardena, CA 90247
Phone: (310)532-9905
Fax: (310)515-4893

SCORE Office (Glendora)
131 E. Foothill Blvd.
Glendora, CA 91740
Phone: (818)963-4128
Fax: (818)914-4822

SCORE Office (Golden Empire)
1706 Chester Ave., Ste. 200
Bakersfield, CA 93301
Phone: (661)322-5881
Fax: (661)322-5663

SCORE Office (Greater Chico Area)
1324 Mangrove St., Ste. 114
Chico, CA 95926
Phone: (530)342-8932
Fax: (530)342-8932

SCORE Office (Grover Beach)
177 S. 8th St.
Grover Beach, CA 93433
Phone: (805)489-9091
Fax: (805)489-9091

SCORE Office (Hawthorne)
12477 Hawthorne Blvd.
Hawthorne, CA 90250
Phone: (310)676-1163
Fax: (310)676-7661

SCORE Office (Hayward)
22300 Foothill Blvd., Ste. 303
Hayward, CA 94541
Phone: (510)537-2424

SCORE Office (Hemet)
1700 E. Florida Ave.
Hemet, CA 92544-4679
Phone: (909)652-4390
Fax: (909)929-8543

SCORE Office (Hesperia)
16367 Main St.
PO Box 403656
Hesperia, CA 92340
Phone: (619)244-2135

SCORE Office (Hollister)
321 San Felipe Rd., No. 11
Hollister, CA 95023

SCORE Office (Hollywood)
7018 Hollywood Blvd.
Hollywood, CA 90028
Phone: (213)469-8311
Fax: (213)469-2805

SCORE Office (Indio)
82503 Hwy. 111
PO Drawer TTT
Indio, CA 92202
Phone: (619)347-0676

SCORE Office (Inglewood)
330 Queen St.
Inglewood, CA 90301
Phone: (818)552-3206

SCORE Office (Inland Empire)
777 E. Rialto Ave.
Purchasing
San Bernardino, CA 92415-0760
Phone: (909)386-8278

SCORE Office (La Puente)
218 N. Grendanda St. D.
La Puente, CA 91744
Phone: (818)330-3216
Fax: (818)330-9524

SCORE Office (La Verne)
2078 Bonita Ave.
La Verne, CA 91750
Phone: (909)593-5265
Fax: (714)929-8475

SCORE Office (Lake Elsinore)
132 W. Graham Ave.
Lake Elsinore, CA 92530
Phone: (909)674-2577

SCORE Office (Lakeport)
PO Box 295
Lakeport, CA 95453
Phone: (707)263-5092

SCORE Office (Lakeside)
2150 Low Tree
Palmdale, CA 93551
Phone: (805)948-4518
Fax: (805)949-1212

SCORE Office (Lakewood)
5445 E. Del Amo Blvd., Ste. 2
Lakewood, CA 90714
Phone: (213)920-7737

SCORE Office (Lompoc)
330 N. Brand Blvd., Ste. 190
Glendale, CA 91203-2304
Phone: (818)552-3206
Fax: (818)552-3323

SCORE Office (Long Beach)
1 World Trade Center
Long Beach, CA 90831

SCORE Office (Los Alamitos)
901 W. Civic Center Dr., Ste. 160
Los Alamitos, CA 90720

SCORE Office (Los Altos)
321 University Ave.
Los Altos, CA 94022
Phone: (415)948-1455

SCORE Office (Los Angeles)
330 N. Brand Blvd., Ste. 190
Glendale, CA 91203-2304
Phone: (818)552-3206
Fax: (818)552-3323

SCORE Office (Los Banos)
222 S. Shepard St.
Sonora, CA 95370
Phone: (209)532-4212

SCORE Office (Manhattan Beach)
PO Box 3007
Manhattan Beach, CA 90266
Phone: (310)545-5313
Fax: (310)545-7203

SCORE Office (Menlo Park)
1100 Merrill St.
San Francisco, CA 94105
Phone: (415)325-2818
Fax: (415)325-0920

SCORE Office (Merced)
1632 N. St.
Merced, CA 95340
Phone: (209)725-3800
Fax: (209)383-4959

SCORE Office (Milpitas)
75 S. Milpitas Blvd., Ste. 205
Milpitas, CA 95035
Phone: (408)262-2613
Fax: (408)262-2823

SCORE Office (Montclair)
5220 Benito Ave.
Montclair, CA 91763

SCORE Office (Monterey Bay)
380 Alvarado St.
PO Box 1770
Monterey, CA 93940-1770
Phone: (831)648-5360

SCORE Office (Monterey Park)
485 N. Garey
Pomona, CA 91769

SCORE Office (Moreno Valley)
25480 Alessandro
Moreno Valley, CA 92553

SCORE Office (Morgan Hill)
25 W. 1st St.
PO Box 786
Morgan Hill, CA 95038
Phone: (408)779-9444
Fax: (408)778-1786

SCORE Office (Morro Bay)
880 Main St.
Morro Bay, CA 93442
Phone: (805)772-4467

SCORE Office (Mountain View)
580 Castro St.
Mountain View, CA 94041
Phone: (415)968-8378
Fax: (415)968-5668

SCORE Office (Napa)
1556 1st St.
Napa, CA 94559
Phone: (707)226-7455
Fax: (707)226-1171

SCORE Office (North Hollywood)
5019 Lankershim Blvd.
North Hollywood, CA 91601
Phone: (818)552-3206

SCORE Office (Northridge)
8801 Reseda Blvd.

Northridge, CA 91324
Phone: (818)349-5676

SCORE Office (Novato)
807 De Long Ave.
Novato, CA 94945
Phone: (415)897-1164
Fax: (415)898-9097

SCORE Office (Oceanside)
928 N. Coast Hwy.
Oceanside, CA 92054
Phone: (619)722-1534

SCORE Office (Ontario)
121 West B. St.
Ontario, CA 91762
Fax: (714)984-6439

SCORE Office (Orange County)
200 W. Santa Anna Blvd., Ste. 700
Santa Ana, CA 92701
Phone: (714)550-7369
Fax: (714)550-0191
Website: http://www.score114.org

SCORE Office (Oxnard)
PO Box 867
Oxnard, CA 93032
Phone: (805)385-8860
Fax: (805)487-1763

SCORE Office (Pacifica)
450 Dundee Way, Ste. 2
Pacifica, CA 94044
Phone: (415)355-4122

SCORE Office (Palm Desert)
72990 Hwy. 111
Palm Desert, CA 92260
Phone: (619)346-6111
Fax: (619)346-3463

SCORE Office (Palm Springs)
650 E. Tahquitz Canyon Way, Ste. D
Palm Springs, CA 92262-6706
Phone: (760)320-6682
Fax: (760)323-9426

SCORE Office (Palo Alto)
325 Forest Ave.
Palo Alto, CA 94301
Phone: (415)324-3121
Fax: (415)324-1215

SCORE Office (Pasadena)
117 E. Colorado Blvd., Ste. 100
Pasadena, CA 91105
Phone: (818)795-3355
Fax: (818)795-5663

SCORE Office (Paso Robles)
1225 Park St.
Paso Robles, CA 93446-2234
Phone: (805)238-0506
Fax: (805)238-0527

SCORE Office (Petaluma)
799 Baywood Dr., Ste. 3
Petaluma, CA 94954
Phone: (707)762-2785
Fax: (707)762-4721

SCORE Office (Pico Rivera)
9122 E. Washington Blvd.
Pico Rivera, CA 90660

SCORE Office (Pittsburg)
2700 E. Leland Rd.
Pittsburg, CA 94565
Phone: (510)439-2181
Fax: (510)427-1599

SCORE Office (Pleasanton)
777 Peters Ave.
Pleasanton, CA 94566
Phone: (510)846-9697

SCORE Office (Pomona)
485 N. Garey Ave.
Pomona, CA 91766
Phone: (909)622-1256

SCORE Office (Rancho Cucamonga)
8280 Utica, Ste. 160
Cucamonga, CA 91730
Phone: (909)987-1012
Fax: (909)987-5917

SCORE Office (Redwood City)
1675 Broadway
Redwood City, CA 94063
Phone: (415)364-1722
Fax: (415)364-1729

SCORE Office (Richmond)
3925 MacDonald Ave.
Richmond, CA 94805

SCORE Office (Ridgecrest)
PO Box 771
Ridgecrest, CA 93555
Phone: (619)375-8331
Fax: (619)375-0365

SCORE Office (Riverside)
3685 Main St., Ste. 350
Riverside, CA 92501
Phone: (909)683-7100

SCORE Office (Sacramento)
9845 Horn Rd., 260-B

Sacramento, CA 95827
Phone: (916)361-2322
Fax: (916)361-2164
E-mail: sacchapter@directcon.net
Website: http://www.learnwell.org/
~edu/score.shtml

SCORE Office (Salinas)
PO Box 1170
Salinas, CA 93902
Phone: (408)424-7611
Fax: (408)424-8639

SCORE Office (San Carlos)
San Carlos Chamber of Commerce
PO Box 1086
San Carlos, CA 94070
Phone: (415)593-1068
Fax: (415)593-9108

SCORE Office (San Diego)
550 West C. St., Ste. 550
San Diego, CA 92101-3500
Phone: (619)557-7272
Fax: (619)557-5894
Website: http://www.score-
sandiego.org

SCORE Office (San Francisco)
455 Market St., 6th Fl.
San Francisco, CA 94105
Phone: (415)744-6827
Fax: (415)744-6750
E-mail: sfscore@sfscore.
Website: http://www.sfscore.com

SCORE Office (San Gabriel)
401 W. Las Tunas Dr.
San Gabriel, CA 91776
Phone: (818)576-2525
Fax: (818)289-2901

SCORE Office (San Jose)
Deanza College
208 S. 1st. St., Ste. 137
San Jose, CA 95113
Phone: (408)288-8479
Fax: (408)535-5541

SCORE Office (San Luis Obispo)
4111 Broad St., Ste. A
San Luis Obispo, CA 93401
Phone: (805)547-0779

SCORE Office (San Mateo)
1021 S. El Camino, 2nd Fl.
San Mateo, CA 94402
Phone: (415)341-5679

SCORE Office (San Pedro)
390 W. 7th St.

San Pedro, CA 90731
Phone: (310)832-7272

SCORE Office (Santa Barbara)
PO Box 30291
Santa Barbara, CA 93130
Phone: (805)563-0084

SCORE Office (Santa Clara County)
84 W. Santa Clara St.
Entrepreneur Center, Ste. 100
San Jose, CA 95113
Phone: (408)288-8479
Fax: (408)494-0214
E-mail: svscore@Prodigy.net
Website: http://www.svscore.org

SCORE Office (Santa Maria)
614 S. Broadway
Santa Maria, CA 93454-5111
Phone: (805)925-2403
Fax: (805)928-7559

SCORE Office (Santa Monica)
501 Colorado, Ste. 150
Santa Monica, CA 90401
Phone: (310)393-9825
Fax: (310)394-1868

SCORE Office (Santa Rosa)
777 Sonoma Ave., Rm. 115B
Santa Rosa, CA 95404
Phone: (707)571-8342
Fax: (707)541-0331
Website: http://www.pressdemo.com/
community/score/score.html

SCORE Office (Scotts Valley)
4 Camp Evers Ln.
Scotts Valley, CA 95066
Phone: (408)438-1010
Fax: (408)438-6544

SCORE Office (Shasta)
737 Auditorium Dr.
Redding, CA 96099
Phone: (916)225-2770

SCORE Office (Simi Valley)
40 W. Cochran St., Ste. 100
Simi Valley, CA 93065
Phone: (805)526-3900
Fax: (805)526-6234

SCORE Office (Sonoma)
453 1st St. E
Sonoma, CA 95476
Phone: (707)996-1033

SCORE Office (South San Francisco)
445 Market St., Ste. 6th Fl.

South San Francisco, CA 94105
Phone: (415)744-6827
Fax: (415)744-6812

SCORE Office (Stockton)
401 N. San Joaquin St., Rm. 114
Stockton, CA 95202
Phone: (209)946-6293
Fax: (209)946-6294

SCORE Office (Taft)
314 4th St.
Taft, CA 93268
Phone: (805)765-2165
Fax: (805)765-6639

SCORE Office (Torrance)
3400 Torrance Blvd., Ste. 100
Torrance, CA 90503
Phone: (310)540-5858
Fax: (310)540-7662

SCORE Office (Truckee)
PO Box 2757
Truckee, CA 96160
Phone: (916)587-2757
Fax: (916)587-2439

SCORE Office (Tuolumne County)
39 North Washington St.
Sonora, CA 95370
Phone: (209)588-0128
Fax: (209)588-0673
E-mail: score@mlode.com

SCORE Office (Upland)
433 N. 2nd Ave.
Upland, CA 91786
Phone: (909)931-4108

SCORE Office (Vallejo)
2 Florida St.
Vallejo, CA 94590
Phone: (707)644-5551
Fax: (707)644-5590

SCORE Office (Van Nuys)
14540 Victory Blvd.
Van Nuys, CA 91411
Phone: (818)989-0300
Fax: (818)989-3836

SCORE Office (Ventura)
5700 Ralston St., Ste. 310
Ventura, CA 93003
Phone: (805)658-0484
Fax: (805)658-2252
E-mail: scoreven@jps.net
Website: http://www.jps.net/scoreven

SCORE Office (Visalia)
113 S. M St,
Tulare, CA 93274
Phone: (209)627-0766
Fax: (209)627-8149

SCORE Office (Vista)
201 E. Washington St.
Vista, CA 92084
Phone: (619)726-1122
Fax: (619)226-8654

SCORE Office (Watsonville)
PO Box 1748
Watsonville, CA 95077
Phone: (408)724-3849
Fax: (408)728-5300

SCORE Office (West Covina)
811 S. Sunset Ave.
West Covina, CA 91790
Phone: (818)338-8496
Fax: (818)960-0511

SCORE Office (Westlake)
30893 Thousand Oaks Blvd.
Westlake Village, CA 91362
Phone: (805)496-5630
Fax: (818)991-1754

SCORE Office (Yosemite)
1012 I St.
Modesto, CA 95354
Phone: (209)521-6177
Fax: (209)521-9373

## Colorado

SCORE Office (Colorado Springs)
2 N. Cascade Ave., Ste. 110
Colorado Springs, CO 80903
Phone: (719)636-3074
Website: http://www.cscc.org/
score02/index.html

SCORE Office (Denver)
US Custom's House, 4th Fl.
721 19th St.
Denver, CO 80202-2517
Phone: (303)844-3985
Fax: (303)844-6490
E-mail: score62@coredenver.org
Website: http://www.scoredenver.org

SCORE Office (Grand Junction)
2591 B & 3/4 Rd.
Grand Junction, CO 81503
Phone: (970)243-5242

SCORE Office (Gunnison)
608 N. 11th

Gunnison, CO 81230
Phone: (303)641-4422

SCORE Office (Minturn)
PO Box 2066
Vail, CO 81658
Phone: (970)476-1224

SCORE Office (Montrose)
1214 Peppertree Dr.
Montrose, CO 81401
Phone: (970)249-6080

SCORE Office (Pagosa Springs)
PO Box 4381
Pagosa Springs, CO 81157
Phone: (970)731-4890

SCORE Office (Pueblo)
302 N. Santa Fe
Pueblo, CO 81003
Phone: (719)542-1704
Fax: (719)542-1624
E-mail: score@bbci.com
Website: http://www.pueblo.org/score

SCORE Office (Ridgway)
143 Poplar Pl.
Ridgway, CO 81432

SCORE Office (Rifle)
0854 W. Battlement Pky., Apt. C106
Parachute, CO 81635
Phone: (970)285-9390

SCORE Office (Silverton)
PO Box 480
Silverton, CO 81433
Phone: (303)387-5430

SCORE Office (Tri-River)
1102 Grand Ave.
Glenwood Springs, CO 81601
Phone: (970)945-6589

## Connecticut

SCORE office (Greater Danbury)
246 Federal Rd.
Unit LL2, Ste. 7
Brookfield, CT 06804
Phone: (203)775-1151

SCORE Office (Bristol)
10 Main St. 1st. Fl.
Bristol, CT 06010
Phone: (203)584-4718
Fax: (203)584-4722

SCORE Office (Eastern Connecticut)
Administration Bldg., Rm. 313

PO 625
61 Main St. (Chapter 579)
Groton, CT 06475
Phone: (203)388-9508

SCORE Office (Fairfield County)
24 Beldon Ave., 5th Fl.
Norwalk, CT 06850
Phone: (203)847-7348
Fax: (203)849-9308

SCORE Office (Greater Bridgeport)
230 Park Ave.
Bridgeport, CT 06601-0999
Phone: (203)576-4369
Fax: (203)576-4388

SCORE Office (Greater Danbury)
246 Federal Rd., Unit LL2, Ste. 7
Brookfield, CT 06804
Phone: (203)775-1151

SCORE Office (Greater Hartford
County)
330 Main St.
Hartford, CT 06106
Phone: (860)251-7000
Fax: (860)240-4659
Website: http://www.score56.org

SCORE Office (Manchester)
20 Hartford Rd.
Manchester, CT 06040
Phone: (203)646-2223
Fax: (203)646-5871

SCORE Office (New Britain)
185 Main St., Ste. 431
New Britain, CT 06051
Phone: (203)827-4492
Fax: (203)827-4480

SCORE Office (New Haven)
25 Science Pk., Rm. 502
New Haven, CT 06511
Phone: (203)865-7645

SCORE Office (Old Saybrook)
146 Main St.
PO Box 625
Old Saybrook, CT 06475
Phone: (860)388-9508

SCORE Office (Simsbury)
Box 244
Simsbury, CT 06070
Phone: (203)651-7307
Fax: (203)651-1933

SCORE Office (Torrington)
23 North Rd.

Torrington, CT 06791
Phone: (203)482-6586

## Delaware

SCORE Office (Dover)
Treadway Towers
PO Box 576
Dover, DE 19903
Phone: (302)678-0892
Fax: (302)678-0189

SCORE Office (Lewes)
PO Box 1
Lewes, DE 19958
Phone: (302)645-8073
Fax: (302)645-8412

SCORE Office (Milford)
204 NE Front St.
Milford, DE 19963
Phone: (302)422-3301

SCORE Office (Wilmington)
824 Market St., Ste. 610
Wilmington, DE 19801
Phone: (302)573-6652
Fax: (302)573-6092
Website: http://
www.scoredelaware.com

## District of Columbia

SCORE Office (George Mason
University)
409 3rd St. SW, 4th Fl.
Washington, DC 20024
Free: 800-634-0245

SCORE Office (Washington DC)
1110 Vermont Ave. NW, 9th Fl.
Washington, DC 20043
Phone: (202)606-4000
Fax: (202)606-4225
E-mail: dcscore@hotmail.com
Website: http://www.scoredc.org/

## Florida

Clay County SCORE Office
Clay County Chamber of Commerce
1734 Kingsdey Ave.
PO Box 1441
Orange Park, FL 32073
Phone: (904)264-2651
Fax: (904)269-0363

SCORE Office (Bay County)
2500 Minnesota Ave.
Lynn Haven, FL 32444

Phone: (850)271-1108
Fax: (850)271-1109

SCORE Office (Bradenton)
2801 Fruitville, Ste. 280
Sarasota, FL 34237
Phone: (813)955-1029

SCORE Office (Central Florida)
5410 S. Florida Ave., No. 3
Lakeland, FL 33813
Phone: (863)619-5783

SCORE Office (Charlotte County)
201 W. Marion Ave., Ste. 211
Punta Gorda, FL 33950
Phone: (941)575-1818
E-mail: score@gls3c.com
Website: http://www.charlotte-
florida.com/business/scorepg01.htm

SCORE Office (Citrus County)
3810 S. Lecanto Hwy.
Bldg. P1-101
Lecanto, FL 34661
Phone: (352)621-0775

SCORE Office (Cocoa)
1600 Farno Rd., Unit 205
Melbourne, FL 32935
Phone: (407)254-2288

SCORE Office (Dade)
49 NW 5th St.
Miami, FL 33128
Phone: (305)371-6889
Fax: (305)374-1882
E-mail: score@netrox.net
Website: http://www.netrox.net/
~score/

SCORE Office (Daytona Beach)
921 Nova Rd., Ste. A
Holly Hills, FL 32117
Phone: (904)255-6889
Fax: (904)255-0229
E-mail: score87@n-jcenter.com

SCORE Office (DeLand)
336 N. Woodland Blvd.
DeLand, FL 32720
Phone: (904)734-4331
Fax: (904)734-4333

SCORE Office (Desota County
Chamber of Commerce)
16 South Velucia Ave.
Arcadia, FL 34266
Phone: (941)494-4033

SCORE Office (Emerald Coast)
19 W. Garden St., No. 325
Pensacola, FL 32501
Phone: (904)444-2060
Fax: (904)444-2070

SCORE Office (Ft. Lauderdale)
Federal Bldg., Ste. 123
299 E. Broward Blvd.
Ft. Lauderdale, FL 33301
Phone: (954)356-7263
Fax: (954)356-7145

SCORE Office (Gainesville)
101 SE 2nd Pl., Ste. 104
Gainesville, FL 32601
Phone: (352)375-8278
Fax: (352)375-5340

SCORE Office (Hialeah Dade
Chamber)
59 W. 5th St.
Hialeah, FL 33010
Phone: (305)887-1515
Fax: (305)887-2453

SCORE Office (Hillsborough)
4732 Dale Mabry Hwy. N, Ste. 400
Tampa, FL 33614-6509
Phone: (813)870-0125

SCORE Office (Jacksonville)
7825 Baymeadows Way, Ste. 100-B
Jacksonville, FL 32256
Phone: (904)443-1911
Fax: (904)443-1980
E-mail: scorejax@juno.com
Website: http://www.scorejax.org/

SCORE Office (Jacksonville Satellite)
3 Independent Dr.
Jacksonville, FL 32256
Phone: (904)366-6600
Fax: (904)632-0617

SCORE Office (Lake Sumter)
122 E. Main St.
Tavares, FL 32778-3810
Phone: (352)365-3556

SCORE Office (Lakeland)
100 Lake Morton Dr.
Lakeland, FL 33801
Phone: (941)686-2168

SCORE Office (Leesburg)
9501 US Hwy. 441
Leesburg, FL 34788-8751
Phone: (352)365-3556
Fax: (352)365-3501

SCORE Office (Manasota)
2801 Fruitville Rd., Ste. 280
Sarasota, FL 34237
Phone: (941)955-1029
Fax: (941)955-5581
E-mail: score116@gte.net
Website: http://www.score-
suncoast.org/

SCORE Office (Melbourne)
Melbourne Professional Complex
1600 Sarno, Ste. 205
Melbourne, FL 32935
Phone: (407)254-2288
Fax: (407)245-2288

SCORE Office (Merritt Island)
1600 Sarno Rd., Ste. 205
Melbourne, FL 32935
Phone: (407)254-2288
Fax: (407)254-2288

SCORE Office (Naples of Collier)
International College
2655 Northbrooke Dr.
Naples, FL 34119
Phone: (941)254-9440
Fax: (941)254-9441
E-mail: score@naples.net
Website: http://www.naples.net/clubs/
score/index.htm

SCORE Office (Ocala)
110 E. Silver Springs Blvd.
Ocala, FL 34470
Phone: (352)629-5959

SCORE Office (Orlando)
80 N. Hughey Ave.
Federal Bldg. Rm. 445
Orlando, FL 32801
Phone: (407)648-6476
Fax: (407)648-6425

SCORE Office (Palm Beach)
500 Australian Ave. S, Ste. 100
West Palm Beach, FL 33401
Phone: (561)833-1672
Fax: (561)833-1712

SCORE Office (Pasco County)
6014 US Hwy. 19, Ste. 302
New Port Richey, FL 34652
Phone: (727)842-4638

SCORE Office (St. Augustine)
1 Riberia St.
St. Augustine, FL 32084
Phone: (904)829-5681
Fax: (904)829-6477

SCORE Office (St. Petersburg)
800 W. Bay Dr., Ste. 505
Largo, FL 33712
Phone: (813)585-4571

SCORE Office (South Broward)
3475 Sheridian St., Ste. 203
Hollywood, FL 33021
Phone: (305)966-8415

SCORE Office (South Palm Beach)
1050 S. Federal Hwy., Ste. 132
Delray Beach, FL 33483
Phone: (561)278-7752
Fax: (561)278-0288

SCORE Office (Southeast Volusia)
115 Canal St.
New Smyrna Beach, FL 32168
Phone: (904)428-2449
Fax: (904)423-3512

SCORE Office (Southwest Florida)
The Renaissance
8695 College Pky., Ste. 345 - 346
Ft. Myers, FL 33919
Phone: (941)489-2935
Fax: (941)489-1170

SCORE Office (Space Coast)
Melbourne Professional Complex
1600 Sarno, Ste. 205
Melbourne, FL 32935
Phone: (407)254-2288
Fax: (407)254-2288

SCORE Office (Suncoast/Pinellas)
Airport Business Ctr.
4707 - 140th Ave. N, No. 311
Clearwater, FL 33762
Phone: (727)532-6800
Fax: (727)532-6800

SCORE Office (Tallahassee)
200 W. Park Ave.
Tallahassee, FL 32302
Phone: (850)487-2665

SCORE Office (Titusville)
2000 S. Washington Ave.
Titusville, FL 32780
Phone: (407)267-3036
Fax: (407)264-0127

SCORE Office (Treasure Coast)
Professional Center, Ste. 2
3220 S. US 1
Ft. Pierce, FL 34982
Phone: (561)489-0548

SCORE Office (Venice)
257 N. Tamiami Trl.
Venice, FL 34285
Phone: (941)488-2236
Fax: (941)484-5903

SCORE Office (Wildwood)
103 N. Webster St.
Wildwood, FL 34785

## Georgia

SCORE Office (Atlanta)
Harris Tower, Ste. 1900
233 Peachtree Rd. NE
Atlanta, GA 30303
Phone: (404)331-0121
Fax: (404)331-0138

SCORE Office (Augusta)
3126 Oxford Rd.
Augusta, GA 30909
Phone: (706)869-9100

SCORE Office (Brunswick)
4 Glen Ave.
St. Simons Island, GA 31520
Phone: (912)265-0620
Fax: (912)265-0629

SCORE Office (Columbus)
School Bldg.
PO Box 40
Columbus, GA 31901
Phone: (706)327-3654

SCORE Office (Dalton-Whitfield)
PO Box 1941
Dalton, GA 30722
Phone: (706)279-3383

SCORE Office (Gainesville)
PO Box 374
Gainesville, GA 30503
Phone: (770)532-6206
Fax: (770)535-8419

SCORE Office (Macon)
711 Grand Bldg.
Macon, GA 31201
Phone: (912)751-6160

SCORE Office (Savannah)
111 E. Liberty St., Ste. 103
Savannah, GA 31401
Phone: (912)652-4335
Fax: (912)652-4184
E-mail: info@scoresav.org
Website: http://www.scoresav.org

## Hawaii

SCORE Office (Hawaii, Inc.)
1111 Bishop St., Ste. 204
Honolulu, HI 96813
Phone: (808)522-8132
Fax: (808)522-8135
E-mail: hnlscore@juno.com

SCORE Office (Kahului)
250 Alamaha, Unit N16A
Kahului, HI 96732
Phone: (808)871-7711

SCORE Office (Maui, Inc.)
590 E. Lipoa Pkwy., Ste. 227
Kihei, HI 96753
Phone: (808)875-2380

## Idaho

SCORE Office (Eastern Idaho)
2300 N. Yellowstone, Ste. 119
Idaho Falls, ID 83401
Phone: (208)523-1022
Fax: (208)528-7127

SCORE Office (Treasure Valley)
1020 Main St., No. 290
Boise, ID 83702
Phone: (208)334-1696
Fax: (208)334-9353

## Illinois

SCORE Office (Bensenville)
1050 Busse Hwy. Suite 100
Bensenville, IL 60106
Phone: (708)350-2944
Fax: (708)350-2979

SCORE Office (Central Illinois)
402 N. Hershey Rd.
Bloomington, IL 61704
Phone: (309)644-0549
Fax: (309)663-8270
E-mail: webmaster@central-illinois-score.org
Website: http://www.central-illinois-score.org/

SCORE Office (Chicago)
Northwest Atrium Ctr.
500 W. Madison St., No. 1250
Chicago, IL 60661
Phone: (312)353-7724
Fax: (312)886-4879
Website: http://www.mcs.net/~bic/

SCORE Office (Chicago—Oliver Harvey College)
Pullman Bldg.
1000 E. 11th St., 7th Fl.
Chicago, IL 60628
Fax: (312)468-8086

SCORE Office (Danville)
28 W. N. Street
Danville, IL 61832
Phone: (217)442-7232
Fax: (217)442-6228

SCORE Office (Decatur)
Milliken University
1184 W. Main St.
Decatur, IL 62522
Phone: (217)424-6297
Fax: (217)424-3523
E-mail: charding@mail.millikin.edu
Website: http://www.millikin.edu/academics/Tabor/score.html

SCORE Office (Downers Grove)
925 Curtis
Downers Grove, IL 60515
Phone: (708)968-4050
Fax: (708)968-8368

SCORE Office (Elgin)
24 E. Chicago, 3rd Fl.
PO Box 648
Elgin, IL 60120
Phone: (847)741-5660
Fax: (847)741-5677

SCORE Office (Fox Valley)
144 N. Farnsworth Ave.
Aurora, IL 60505
Phone: (630)692-1162
Fax: (630)852-3127

SCORE Office (Freeport Area)
26 S. Galena Ave.
Freeport, IL 61032
Phone: (815)233-1350
Fax: (815)235-4038

SCORE Office (Galesburg)
292 E. Simmons St.
PO Box 749
Galesburg, IL 61401
Phone: (309)343-1194
Fax: (309)343-1195

SCORE Office (Glen Ellyn)
500 Pennsylvania
Glen Ellyn, IL 60137
Phone: (708)469-0907
Fax: (708)469-0426

SCORE Office (Grayslake)
19351 W. Washington St.
Grayslake, IL 60030
Phone: (708)223-3633
Fax: (708)223-9371

SCORE Office (Greater Alton)
Alden Hall
5800 Godfrey Rd.
Godfrey, IL 62035-2466
Phone: (618)467-2280
Fax: (618)466-8289
Website: http://www.altonweb.com/score/

SCORE Office (Greater Belvidere)
419 S. State St.
Belvidere, IL 61008
Phone: (815)544-4357
Fax: (815)547-7654

SCORE Office (Harrisburg)
303 S. Commercial
Harrisburg, IL 62946-1528
Phone: (618)252-8528
Fax: (618)252-0210

SCORE Office (Joliet)
100 N. Chicago
Joliet, IL 60432
Phone: (815)727-5371
Fax: (815)727-5374

SCORE Office (Kankakee)
101 S. Schuyler Ave.
Kankakee, IL 60901
Phone: (815)933-0376
Fax: (815)933-0380

SCORE Office (Macomb)
216 Seal Hall, Rm. 214
Macomb, IL 61455
Phone: (309)298-1128
Fax: (309)298-2520

SCORE Office (Matteson)
210 Lincoln Mall
Matteson, IL 60443
Phone: (708)709-3750
Fax: (708)503-9322

SCORE Office (Mattoon)
1701 Wabash Ave.
Mattoon, IL 61938
Phone: (217)235-5661
Fax: (217)234-6544

SCORE Office (Naperville)
131 W. Jefferson Ave.
Naperville, IL 60540

Phone: (708)355-4141
Fax: (708)355-8355

SCORE Office (Northbrook)
2002 Walters Ave.
Northbrook, IL 60062
Phone: (847)498-5555
Fax: (847)498-5510

SCORE Office (Northern Illinois)
515 N. Court St.
Rockford, IL 61103-6807
Phone: (815)962-0122
Fax: (815)962-0806

SCORE Office (Palos Hills)
10900 S. 88th Ave.
Palos Hills, IL 60465
Phone: (847)974-5468
Fax: (847)974-0078

SCORE Office (Peoria)
124 SW Adams, Ste. 300
Peoria, IL 61602
Phone: (309)676-0755
Fax: (309)676-7534

SCORE Office (Prospect Heights)
1375 Wolf Rd.
Prospect Heights, IL 60070
Phone: (847)537-8660
Fax: (847)537-7138

SCORE Office (Quad Cities)
622 19th St.
Moline, IL 61265
Phone: (309)797-0082
Fax: (309)757-5435
E-mail: score@qconline.com
Website: http://www.qconline.com/
business/score/

SCORE Office (Quincy Tri-State)
300 Civic Center Plz., Ste. 245
Quincy, IL 62301
Phone: (217)222-8093
Fax: (217)222-3033

SCORE Office (River Grove)
2000 5th Ave.
River Grove, IL 60171
Phone: (708)456-0300
Fax: (708)583-3121

SCORE Office (St. Charles)
103 N. 1st Ave.
St. Charles, IL 60174-1982
Phone: (847)584-8384
Fax: (847)584-6065

SCORE Office (Southern Illinois)
150 E. Pleasant Hill Rd.
Box 1
Carbondale, IL 62901
Phone: (618)453-6654
Fax: (618)453-5040

SCORE Office (Springfield)
511 W. Capitol Ave., Ste. 302
Springfield, IL 62704
Phone: (217)492-4416
Fax: (217)492-4867

SCORE Office (Sycamore)
112 Somunak St.
Sycamore, IL 60178
Phone: (815)895-3456
Fax: (815)895-0125

SCORE Office (University)
Hwy. 50 & Stuenkel Rd. Ste. C3305
University Park, IL 60466
Phone: (708)534-5000
Fax: (708)534-8457

## Indiana

SCORE Office (Anderson)
205 W. 11th St.
PO Box 469
Anderson, IN 46015
Phone: (765)642-0264

SCORE Office (Bloomington)
Star Center
216 W. Allen
Bloomington, IN 47403
Phone: (812)335-7334
E-mail: wtfische@indiana.edu
Website: http://
www.brainfreezemedia.com/
score527/

SCORE Office (Corydon)
310 N. Elm St.
Corydon, IN 47112
Phone: (812)738-2137
Fax: (812)738-6438

SCORE Office (Crown Point)
Old Courthouse Sq. Ste. 206
PO Box 43
Crown Point, IN 46307
Phone: (219)663-1800

SCORE Office (Elkhart)
418 S. Main St.
PO Box 428
Elkhart, IN 46515

Phone: (219)293-1531
Fax: (219)294-1859

SCORE Office (Evansville)
1100 W. Lloyd Expy., Ste. 105
Evansville, IN 47708
Phone: (812)426-6144

SCORE Office (Fort Wayne)
1300 S. Harrison St.
Ft. Wayne, IN 46802
Phone: (219)422-2601
Fax: (219)422-2601

SCORE Office (Gary)
973 W. 6th Ave., Rm. 326
Gary, IN 46402
Phone: (219)882-3918

SCORE Office (Hammond)
7034 Indianapolis Blvd.
Hammond, IN 46324
Phone: (219)931-1000
Fax: (219)845-9548

SCORE Office (Indianapolis)
429 N. Pennsylvania St., Ste. 100
Indianapolis, IN 46204-1873
Phone: (317)226-7264
Fax: (317)226-7259
E-mail: inscore@indy.net
Website: http://www.score-
indianapolis.org/

SCORE Office (Jasper)
PO Box 307
Jasper, IN 47547-0307
Phone: (812)482-6866

SCORE Office (Kokomo/Howard
Counties)
106 N. Washington St.
Kokomo, IN 46901
Phone: (765)457-5301
Fax: (765)452-4564

SCORE Office (Logansport)
300 E. Broadway, Ste. 103
Logansport, IN 46947
Phone: (219)753-6388

SCORE Office (Madison)
301 E. Main St.
Madison, IN 47250
Phone: (812)265-3135
Fax: (812)265-2923

SCORE Office (Marengo)
Rt. 1 Box 224D
Marengo, IN 47140
Fax: (812)365-2793

SCORE Office (Marion/Grant
Counties)
215 S. Adams
Marion, IN 46952
Phone: (765)664-5107

SCORE Office (Merrillville)
255 W. 80th Pl.
Merrillville, IN 46410
Phone: (219)769-8180
Fax: (219)736-6223

SCORE Office (Michigan City)
200 E. Michigan Blvd.
Michigan City, IN 46360
Phone: (219)874-6221
Fax: (219)873-1204

SCORE Office (Rensselaer)
104 W. Washington
Rensselaer, IN 47978

SCORE Office (Salem)
210 N. Main St.
Salem, IN 47167
Phone: (812)883-4303
Fax: (812)883-1467

SCORE Office (South Bend)
401 E. Colfax Ste. 120
South Bend, IN 46617-2735
Phone: (219)282-4350
Fax: (219)236-1056
E-mail: chair@southbend-score.org
Website: http://www.southbend-
score.org/

SCORE Office (South Central
Indiana)
4100 Charleston Rd.
New Albany, IN 47150-9538
Phone: (812)945-0266

SCORE Office (South East Indiana)
500 Franklin St.
Box 29
Columbus, IN 47201
Phone: (812)379-4457

SCORE Office (Valparaiso)
150 Lincolnway
Valparaiso, IN 46383
Phone: (219)462-1105
Fax: (219)469-5710

SCORE Office (Vincennes)
27 N. 3rd
PO Box 553
Vincennes, IN 47591
Phone: (812)882-6440
Fax: (812)882-6441

SCORE Office (Wabash)
PO Box 371
Wabash, IN 46992
Phone: (219)563-1168
Fax: (219)563-6920

## Iowa

SCORE Office (Burlington)
Federal Bldg.
300 N. Main St.
Burlington, IA 52601
Phone: (319)752-2967

SCORE Office (Cedar Rapids)
Lattner Bldg., Ste. 200
215 - 4th Ave. SE, No. 200
Cedar Rapids, IA 52401-1806
Phone: (319)362-6405
Fax: (319)362-7861

SCORE Office (Central Iowa)
Fisher Community College
709 S. Center
Marshalltown, IA 50158
Phone: (515)753-6645

SCORE Office (Council Bluffs)
PO Box 1565
Council Bluffs, IA 51502-1565
Phone: (712)325-1000

SCORE Office (Des Moines)
Federal Bldg., Rm. 749
210 Walnut St.
Des Moines, IA 50309-2186
Phone: (515)284-4760

SCORE Office (Dubuque)
10250 Sundown Rd.
Peosta, IA 52068
Phone: (319)556-5110

SCORE Office (Ft. Dodge)
Federal Bldg., Rm. 436
205 S. 8th St.
Ft. Dodge, IA 50501
Phone: (515)955-2622

SCORE Office (Illowa)
333 4th Ave. S
Clinton, IA 52732
Phone: (319)242-5702

SCORE Office (Independence)
110 1st. St. east
Independence, IA 50644
Phone: (319)334-7178
Fax: (319)334-7179

SCORE Office (Iowa City)
210 Federal Bldg.
PO Box 1853
Iowa City, IA 52240-1853
Phone: (319)338-1662

SCORE Office (Iowa Lakes)
122 W. 5th St.
Spencer, IA 51301
Phone: (712)262-3059

SCORE Office (Keokuk)
401 Main St.
Pierce Bldg., No. 1
Keokuk, IA 52632
Phone: (319)524-5055

SCORE Office (Northeast Iowa)
703 2nd St. E
Cresco, IA 52136
Phone: (319)547-3970

SCORE Office (River City)
15 West State St.
PO Box 1128
Mason City, IA 50401
Phone: (515)423-5724

SCORE Office (Sioux City)
Federal Bldg.
320 6th St.
Sioux City, IA 51101
Phone: (712)277-2324
Fax: (712)277-2325

SCORE Office (South Central)
SBDC, Indian Hills Community
College
525 Grandview Ave.
Ottumwa, IA 52501
Phone: (515)683-5127
Fax: (515)683-5263

SCORE Office (Southwest Iowa)
614 W. Sheridan
Shenandoah, IA 51601
Phone: (712)246-3260

SCORE Office (Vista)
119 W. 6th St.
Storm Lake, IA 50588
Phone: (712)732-3780

SCORE Office (Waterloo)
215 E. 4th
Waterloo, IA 50703
Phone: (319)233-8431

## Kansas

SCORE Office (Ark Valley)
205 E. 9th St.
Winfield, KS 67156
Phone: (316)221-1617

SCORE Office (Emporia)
811 Homewood
Emporia, KS 66801
Phone: (316)342-1600

SCORE Office (Golden Belt)
1307 Williams
Great Bend, KS 67530
Phone: (316)792-2401

SCORE Office (Hays)
PO Box 400
Hays, KS 67601
Phone: (913)625-6595

SCORE Office (Hutchinson)
1 E. 9th St.
Hutchinson, KS 67501
Phone: (316)665-8468
Fax: (316)665-7619

SCORE Office (McPherson)
PO Box 616
McPherson, KS 67460
Phone: (316)241-3303

SCORE Office (Salina)
606 Washington St.
Concordia, KS 66901
Phone: (785)243-4290
Fax: (785)243-1833

SCORE Office (Southeast Kansas)
404 Westminster Pl.
PO Box 886
Independence, KS 67301
Phone: (316)331-4741

SCORE Office (Southwest Kansas)
Dodge City Senior Center
2408 Central
Dodge City, KS 67801
Phone: (316)227-6943

SCORE Office (Topeka)
1700 College
Topeka, KS 66621
Phone: (785)231-1010

SCORE Office (Wichita)
271 W. 3rd St. N, Ste. 2500
Wichita, KS 67202
Phone: (316)269-6273
Fax: (316)269-6499

## Kentucky

SCORE Office (Ashland)
PO Box 830
Ashland, KY 41105
Phone: (606)329-8011
Fax: (606)325-4607

SCORE Office (Bowling Green)
812 State St.
PO Box 51
Bowling Green, KY 42101
Phone: (502)781-3200
Fax: (502)843-0458

SCORE Office (Glasgow)
301 W. Main St.
Glasgow, KY 42141
Phone: (502)651-3161
Fax: (502)651-3122

SCORE Office (Hazard)
B & I Technical Center
100 Airport Gardens Rd.
Hazard, KY 41701
Phone: (606)439-5856
Fax: (606)439-1808

SCORE Office (Lexington)
373 Waller Ave.
Lexington, KY 40504
Phone: (859)231-9902
Fax: (859)253-3190
E-mail:
scorelex@uky.campus.mci.net

SCORE Office (Louisville)
188 Federal Office Bldg.
600 Dr. Martin L. King Jr. Pl.
Louisville, KY 40202
Phone: (502)582-5976

SCORE Office (Madisonville)
257 N. Main
Madisonville, KY 42431
Phone: (502)825-1399
Fax: (502)825-1396

SCORE Office (Paducah)
Federal Office Bldg.
501 Broadway, Rm. B-36
Paducah, KY 42001
Phone: (270)442-5685

SCORE Office (Tri-Lakes)
508 Barbee Way
Danville, KY 40422-1548
Phone: (606)231-9902

## Louisiana

SCORE Office (Baton Rouge)
564 Laurel St.
PO Box 3217
Baton Rouge, LA 70801
Phone: (225)381-7130
Fax: (225)336-4306

SCORE Office (Central Louisiana)
802 3rd St.
PO Box 992
Alexandria, LA 71309
Phone: (318)442-6671

SCORE Office (Lafayette)
804 St. Mary Blvd., Drawer 51307
Lafayette, LA 70505-1307
Phone: (318)233-2705
Fax: (318)234-8671
E-mail: score302@aol.com

SCORE Office (Lake Charles)
120 W. Pujo St.
Lake Charles, LA 70601
Phone: (337)480-1199

SCORE Office (New Orleans)
365 Canal St., Ste. 2250
New Orleans, LA 70130
Phone: (504)589-2356
Fax: (504)589-2339

SCORE Office (North Shore)
PO Box 1458
Hammond, LA 70404
Phone: (504)345-4457
Fax: (504)345-4749

SCORE Office (Northeast Louisiana)
1900 N. 18th St., Ste. 440
Monroe, LA 71201
Phone: (318)323-0878
Fax: (318)323-9492

SCORE Office (Shreveport)
400 Edwards St.
Shreveport, LA 71101
Phone: (318)677-2536
Fax: (318)677-2541

## Maine

SCORE Office (Augusta)
40 Western Ave.
Augusta, ME 04330
Phone: (207)622-8509

SCORE Office (Bangor)
EMTC

354 Hogan Rd.
Bangor, ME 04401
Phone: (207)941-9707

SCORE Office (Central & Northern Arroostock)
24 Sweden St., Ste. 101
Caribou, ME 04736
Phone: (207)492-8010
Fax: (207)492-8010

SCORE Office (Lewiston-Auburn)
BIC of Maine-Bates Mill Complex
35 Canal St.
Lewiston, ME 04240-7764
Phone: (207)782-3708
Fax: (207)783-7745

SCORE Office (Maine Coastal)
PO Box 5352
Ellsworth, ME 04605-5352
Phone: (207)667-5800
E-mail: score@arcadia.net

SCORE Office (Oxford Hills)
150 Main St.
South Paris, ME 04281
Phone: (207)743-0499

SCORE Office (Penquis)
South St.
Dover Foxcroft, ME 04426
Phone: (207)564-7021

SCORE Office (Portland)
66 Pearl St., Rm. 210
Portland, ME 04101
Phone: (207)772-1147
Fax: (207)772-5581
E-mail: Score53@score.maine.org
Website: http://www.score.maine.org/chapter53/

SCORE Office (Western Mountains)
255 River St.
PO Box 252
Rumford, ME 04257-0252
Phone: (207)369-9976

## Maryland

SCORE Office (Baltimorc)
The City Crescent Bldg., 6th Fl.
10 S. Howard St.
Baltimore, MD 21201
Phone: (410)962-2233
Fax: (410)962-1805

SCORE Office (Bel Air)
108 S. Bond St.

Bel Air, MD 21014
Phone: (410)838-2020
Fax: (410)893-4715

SCORE Office (Bethesda)
7910 Woodmont Ave., Ste. 1204
Bethesda, MD 20814
Phone: (301)652-4900
Fax: (301)657-1973

SCORE Office (Bowie)
6670 Race Track Rd.
Bowie, MD 20715
Phone: (301)262-0920
Fax: (301)262-0921

SCORE Office (Dorchester County)
203 Sunburst Hwy.
Cambridge, MD 21613
Phone: (410)228-3575

SCORE Office (Frederick County)
43A S. Market St.
Frederick, MD 21701
Phone: (301)662-8723
Fax: (301)846-4427

SCORE Office (Gaithersburg)
9 Park Ave.
Gaithersburg, MD 20877
Phone: (301)840-1400
Fax: (301)963-3918

SCORE Office (Glen Burnie)
103 Crain Hwy. SE
Glen Burnic, MD 21061
Phone: (410)766-8282
Fax: (410)766-9722

SCORE Office (Hagerstown)
111 W. Washington St.
Hagerstown, MD 21740
Phone: (301)739-2015
Fax: (301)739-1278

SCORE Office (Laurel)
7901 Sandy Spring Rd. Ste. 501
Laurel, MD 20707
Phone: (301)725-4000
Fax: (301)725-0776

SCORE Office (Salisbury)
300 E. Main St.
Salisbury, MD 21801
Phone: (410)749-0185
Fax: (410)860-9925

SCORE Office (Southern Maryland)
2525 Riva Rd., Ste. 110
Annapolis, MD 21401
Phone: (410)266-9553

Fax: (410)573-0981
E-mail: score390@aol.com
Website: http://members.aol.com/score390/index.htm

SCORE Office (Upper Shore)
PO Box 1366
Easton, MD 21601
Phone: (410)822-4606
Fax: (410)822-7922

## Massachusetts

SCORE office (Bristol/Plymouth County)
53 N. 6th St., Federal Bldg.
Bristol, MA 02740
Phone: (508)994-5093

SCORE Office (Boston)
10 Causeway St., Rm. 265
Boston, MA 02222-1093
Phone: (617)565-5591
Fax: (617)565-5597
E-mail: boston-score-20@worldnet.att.net
Website: http://www.scoreboston.org/

SCORE Office (Bristol/Plymouth Counties)
53 N. 6th St., Federal Bldg.
New Bedford, MA 02740
Phone: (508)994-5093

SCORE Office (Cape Cod)
Independence Pk., Ste. 5B
270 Communications Way
Hyannis, MA 02601
Phone: (508)775-4884
Fax: (508)790-2540

SCORE Office (Carver)
12 Taunton Green, Ste. 201
Taunton, MA 02780
Phone: (508)824-4068
Fax: (508)824-4069

SCORE Office (Clinton Satellite)
1 Green St.
Clinton, MA 01510
Fax: (508)368-7689

SCORE Office (Greenfield)
PO Box 898
Greenfield, MA 01302
Phone: (413)773-5463
Fax: (413)773-7008

SCORE Office (Haverhill)
87 Winter St.

Haverhill, MA 01830
Phone: (508)373-5663
Fax: (508)373-8060

SCORE Office (Haverhill-Salem)
32 Derby Sq.
Salem, MA 01970
Phone: (508)745-0330
Fax: (508)745-3855

SCORE Office (Hudson Satellite)
PO Box 578
Hudson, MA 01749
Phone: (508)568-0360
Fax: (508)568-0360

SCORE Office (Lawrence)
264 Essex St.
Lawrence, MA 01840
Phone: (508)686-0900
Fax: (508)794-9953

SCORE Office (Leominster Satellite)
110 Erdman Way
Leominster, MA 01453
Phone: (508)840-4300
Fax: (508)840-4896

SCORE Office (NE Massachusetts)
100 Cummings Ctr., Ste. 101 K
Beverly, MA 01915
Phone: (978)922-9441
Website: http://www1.shore.net/
~score/

SCORE Office (Newburyport)
29 State St.
Newburyport, MA 01950
Phone: (617)462-6680

SCORE Office (North Adams)
820 N. State Rd.
Cheshire, MA 01225
Phone: (413)743-5100

SCORE Office (Pittsfield)
66 West St.
Pittsfield, MA 01201
Phone: (413)499-2485

SCORE Office (SE Massachusetts)
60 School St.
Brockton, MA 02401-4087
Phone: (508)587-2673
Fax: (508)587-1340
Website: http://
www.metrosouthchamber.com/
score.html

SCORE Office (Springfield)
1 Federal St.

Springfield Ent. Ctr.
Springfield, MA 01105
Phone: (413)785-0314

SCORE Office (Worcester)
33 Waldo St.
Worcester, MA 01608
Phone: (508)753-2929
Fax: (508)754-8560

## Michigan

SCORE Office (Allegan)
PO Box 338
Allegan, MI 49010
Phone: (616)673-2479

SCORE Office (Ann Arbor)
425 S. Main St., Ste. 103
Ann Arbor, MI 48104
Phone: (734)665-4433
Fax: (734)665-4191

SCORE Office (Battle Creek)
34 W. Jackson Ste. 4A
Battle Creek, MI 49017-3505
Phone: (616)962-4076
Fax: (616)962-6309

SCORE Office (Cadillac)
222 Lake St.
Cadillac, MI 49601
Phone: (231)775-9776
Fax: (231)768-4255

SCORE Office (Detroit)
477 Michigan Ave., Rm. 515
Detroit, MI 48226
Phone: (313)226-7947
Fax: (313)226-3448

SCORE Office (Flint)
708 Root Rd., Rm. 308
Flint, MI 48503
Phone: (810)233-6846

SCORE Office (Grand Rapids)
111 Pearl St. NW
Grand Rapids, MI 49503-2831
Phone: (616)771-0305
Fax: (616)771-0328
E-mail: scoreone@iserv.net
Website: http://www.iserv.net/
~scoreone/

SCORE Office (Holland)
480 State St.
Holland, MI 49423
Phone: (616)396-9472

SCORE Office (Jackson)
209 East Washington
PO Box 80
Jackson, MI 49204
Phone: (517)782-8221
Fax: (517)782-0061

SCORE Office (Kalamazoo)
346 W. Michigan Ave.
Kalamazoo, MI 49007
Phone: (616)381-5382
Fax: (616)384-0096
E-mail: score@nucleus.net

SCORE Office (Lansing)
117 E. Allegan
PO Box 14030
Lansing, MI 48901
Phone: (517)487-6340
Fax: (517)484-6910

SCORE Office (Livonia)
15401 Farmington Rd.
Livonia, MI 48154
Phone: (313)427-2122
Fax: (313)427-6055

SCORE Office (Madison Heights)
26345 John R
Madison Heights, MI 48071
Phone: (810)542-5010
Fax: (810)542-6821

SCORE Office (Monroe)
111 E. 1st
Monroe, MI 48161
Phone: (313)242-3366
Fax: (313)242-7253

SCORE Office (Mt. Clemens)
58 S/B Gratiot
Mt. Clemens, MI 48043
Phone: (810)463-1528
Fax: (810)463-6541

SCORE Office (Muskegon)
PO Box 1087
230 Terrace Plz.
Muskegon, MI 49443-1087
Phone: (231)722-3751
Fax: (231)728-7251

SCORE Office (Petoskey)
401 E. Mitchell St.
Petoskey, MI 49770
Phone: (231)347-4150

SCORE Office (Pontiac)
Executive Office Bldg.
1200 N. Telegraph Rd.

Pontiac, MI 48341
Phone: (810)975-9555

SCORE Office (Pontiac)
PO Box 430025
Pontiac, MI 48343
Phone: (810)335-9600

SCORE Office (Port Huron)
920 Pinegrove Ave.
Port Huron, MI 48060
Phone: (810)985-7101

SCORE Office (Rochester)
71 Walnut Ste. 110
Rochester, MI 48307
Phone: (810)651-6700
Fax: (810)651-5270

SCORE Office (Saginaw)
901 S. Washington Ave.
Saginaw, MI 48601
Phone: (517)752-7161
Fax: (517)752-9055

SCORE Office (Southfield)
21000 W. 10 Mile Rd.
Southfield, MI 48075
Phone: (810)204-3050
Fax: (810)204-3099

SCORE Office (Traverse City)
202 E. Grandview Pkwy.
PO Box 387
Traverse City, MI 49685-0387
Phone: (616)947-5075
Fax: (616)946-2565

SCORE Office (Upper Peninsula)
2581 I-75 Business Spur
Sault Ste. Marie, MI 49783
Phone: (906)632-3301

SCORE Office (Warren)
30500 Van Dyke, Ste. 118
Warren, MI 48093
Phone: (810)751-3939

## Minnesota

SCORE Office (Aitkin)
Aitkin, MN 56431
Phone: (218)741-3906

SCORE Office (Albert Lea)
202 N. Broadway Ave.
Albert Lea, MN 56007
Phone: (507)373-7487

SCORE Office (Austin)
PO Box 864

Austin, MN 55912
Phone: (507)437-4561
Fax: (507)437-4869

SCORE Office (Brainerd)
St. Cloud, MN 56301

SCORE Office (Central Area)
1527 Northway Dr.
St. Cloud, MN 56303
Phone: (320)240-1332
Fax: (320)255-9050
Website: http://www.scoreminn.org/

SCORE Office (Duluth)
UMD-CED Duluth Tech Village
11 E. Superior St., Ste. 210
Duluth, MN 55802
Phone: (218)726-7298
Fax: (218)726-6338
E-mail: duluth@scoreminn.org
Website: http://www.scoreminn.org

SCORE Office (Fairmont)
PO Box 826
Fairmont, MN 56031
Phone: (507)235-5547
Fax: (507)235-8411

SCORE Office (Minneapolis)
Firstar Bank Bldg., Ste. 103
8000 Hwy. 7
Minneapolis, MN 55426
Phone: (952)938-4570
Fax: (952)938-3926
Website: http://www.scoreminn.org/

SCORE Office (New Ulm)
1 N. Minnesota St.
PO Box 384
New Ulm, MN 56073
Phone: (507)233-4300

SCORE Office (Owatonna)
PO Box 331
Owatonna, MN 55060
Phone: (507)451-7970
Fax: (507)451-7972

SCORE Office (Red Wing)
2000 W. Main St., Ste. 324
Red Wing, MN 55066
Phone: (612)388-4079

SCORE Office (St. Paul)
1080 University Ave. W
St. Paul, MN 55104-4707
Phone: (651)632-8937
Fax: (651)632-8938
Website: http://www.scoreminn.org/

SCORE Office (South Metro)
350 Burnsville Pkwy., Ste. 400
Burnsville, MN 55337
Phone: (952)808-5595
Fax: (952)808-5596
E-mail: southmetro@scoreminn.org
Website: http://www.scoreminn.org/
southmetro/

SCORE Office (Southeastern
Minnesota)
220 S. Broadway, Ste. 100
Rochester, MN 55901
Phone: (507)288-1122
Fax: (507)282-8960
Website: http://www.scoreminn.org/

SCORE Office (Southwest
Minnesota)
112 Riverfront St.
Box 999
Mankato, MN 56001
Phone: (507)345-4519
Fax: (507)345-4451
Website: http://www.scoreminn.org/

SCORE Office (Winona)
Box 870
Winona, MN 55987
Phone: (507)452-2272
Fax: (507)454-8814

SCORE Office (Worthington)
1121 3rd Ave.
Worthington, MN 56187
Phone: (507)372-2919
Fax: (507)372-2827

## Mississippi

SCORE Office (Delta)
915 Washington Ave.
PO Box 933
Greenville, MS 38702
Phone: (662)378-3141
Fax: (662)378-3143

SCORE Office (Gulfcoast)
1 Government Plaza
2909 13th St., Ste. 203
Gulfport, MS 39501
Phone: (228)863-0054

SCORE Office (Jackson)
1st Jackson Center, Ste. 400
101 W. Capitol St.
Jackson, MS 39201
Phone: (601)965-5533

SCORE Office (Meridian)
5220 16th Ave.
Meridian, MS 39305
Phone: (601)482-4412

## Missouri

Chamber of Commerce (Cape
Girardeau)
PO Box 98
Cape Girardeau, MO 63702-0098
Phone: (314)335-3312

SCORE Office (Jefferson City)
213 Adams St.
PO Box 776
Jefferson City, MO 65102-0776
Phone: (573)634-3616

SCORE Office (Kansas City)
323 W. 8th St., Ste. 501
Kansas City, MO 64105
Phone: (816)374-6675
Fax: (816)374-6692
E-mail: SCOREBIC@AOL.COM
Website: http://www.crn.org/score/

SCORE Office (Lake of the Ozark)
University Extension
113 Kansas St.
PO Box 1405
Camdenton, MO 65020
Phone: (573)346-2644
Fax: (573)346-2694
E-mail: score@cdoc.net
Website: http://sites.cdoc.net/score/

SCORE Office (Lewis & Clark)
425 Spencer Rd.
St. Peters, MO 63376
Phone: (314)928-2900
Fax: (314)928-2900
E-mail: score01@mail.win.org

SCORE Office (Mexico)
111 N. Washington St.
Mexico, MO 65265
Phone: (314)581-2765

SCORE Office (Mid-Missouri)
1705 Halstead Ct.
Columbia, MO 65203
Phone: (573)874-1132

SCORE Office (Ozark-Gateway)
1486 Glassy Rd.
Cuba, MO 65453-1640
Phone: (573)885-4954

SCORE Office (St. Joseph)
3003 Frederick Ave.

St. Joseph, MO 64506
Phone: (816)232-4461

SCORE Office (St. Louis)
815 Olive St., Rm. 204
St. Louis, MO 63101-1569
Phone: (314)539-6600
Fax: (314)539-6200
E-mail: info@stlscore.org
Website: http://www.stlscore.org/

SCORE Office (Sedalia)
Lucas Place
323 W. 8th St., Ste.104
Kansas City, MO 64105
Phone: (816)374-6675

SCORE Office (Southeast Missouri)
Rte. 1, Box 280
Neelyville, MO 63954
Phone: (573)989-3577

SCORE Office (Springfield)
620 S. Glenstone, Ste. 110
Springfield, MO 65802-3200
Phone: (417)864-7670
Fax: (417)864-4108

SCORE Office (Tri-Lakes)
HCRI Box 85
Lampe, MO 65681
Phone: (417)858-6798

SCORE Office (Poplar Bluff Area)
806 Emma St.
Poplar Bluff, MO 63901
Phone: (573)686-8892

SCORE Office (Southeast Kansas)
1206 W. First St.
Webb City, MO 64870
Phone: (417)673-3984

SCORE Office (Tri-Lakes)
HC 1, Box 90-F
Blue Eye, MO 65611
Phone: (417)779-4151

## Montana

SCORE Office (Billings)
815 S. 27th St.
Billings, MT 59101
Phone: (406)245-4111

SCORE Office (Bozeman)
200 Commerce Way
Bozeman, MT 59715
Phone: (406)586-5421
Fax: (406)586-8286

SCORE Office (Butte)
1000 George St.
Butte, MT 59701
Phone: (406)723-3177

SCORE Office (Great Falls)
PO Box 2127
Great Falls, MT 59403
Phone: (406)761-4434
E-mail: scoregtf@in.tch.com

SCORE Office (Havre, Montana)
518 First St.
PO Box 308
Havre, MT 59501
Phone: (406)265-4383

SCORE Office (Helena)
Federal Bldg.
301 S. Park
Helena, MT 59626-0054
Phone: (406)441-1081

SCORE Office (Kalispell)
2 Main St.
Kalispell, MT 59901
Phone: (406)756-5271
Fax: (406)752-6665

SCORE Office (Missoula)
PO Box 632
Missoula, MT 59806
Phone: (406)327-8806
E-mail: score@safeshop.com
Website: http://missoula.bigsky.net/
score/

## Nebraska

SCORE Office (Central Nebraska)
PO Box 2288
Kearney, NE 68848-2288
Phone: (308)865-5675

SCORE Office (Columbus)
41 Stires Lake
Columbus, NE 68601
Phone: (402)564-2769

SCORE Office (Fremont)
92 W. 5th St.
Fremont, NE 68025
Phone: (402)721-2641

SCORE Office (Hastings)
Hastings, NE 68901
Phone: (402)463-3447

SCORE Office (Lincoln)
8800 O St.

Lincoln, NE 68520
Phone: (402)437-2409

SCORE Office (Norfolk)
3209 S. 48th Ave.
Norfolk, NE 68106
Phone: (402)564-2769

SCORE Office (North Platte)
3301 W. 2nd St., No. 44
North Platte, NE 69101
Phone: (308)532-4466

SCORE Office (Omaha)
11145 Mill Valley Rd.
Omaha, NE 68154
Phone: (402)221-3606
Fax: (402)221-7239
E-mail: infoctr@ne.uswest.net
Website: http://www.tandt.com/score/

SCORE Office (Panhandle)
150549 CR 30
Minatare, NE 69356
Phone: (308)632-2133
Website: http://www.tandt.com/
SCORE

### Nevada

SCORE Office (Carson City)
301 E. Stewart
PO Box 7527
Las Vegas, NV 89125
Phone: (702)388-6104

SCORE Office (Incline Village)
969 Tahoe Blvd.
Incline Village, NV 89451
Phone: (702)831-7327
Fax: (702)832-1605

SCORE Office (Las Vegas)
300 Las Vegas Blvd. S, Ste. 1100
Las Vegas, NV 89101
Phone: (702)388-6104

SCORE Office (Northern Nevada)
SBDC, College of Business
Administration
Univ. of Nevada
Reno, NV 89557-0100
Phone: (775)784-4436
Fax: (775)784-4337

### New Hampshire

SCORE Office (Concord)
143 N. Main St., Rm. 202A
PO Box 1258

Concord, NH 03301
Phone: (603)225-1400
Fax: (603)225-1409

SCORE Office (Dover)
299 Central Ave.
Dover, NH 03820
Phone: (603)742-2218
Fax: (603)749-6317

SCORE Office (Lakes Region)
67 Water St., Ste. 105
Laconia, NH 03246
Phone: (603)524-9168

SCORE Office (Merrimack Valley)
275 Chestnut St., Rm. 618
Manchester, NH 03103
Phone: (603)666-7561
Fax: (603)666-7925

SCORE Office (Monadnock)
34 Mechanic St.
Keene, NH 03431-3421
Phone: (603)352-0320

SCORE Office (Mt. Washington
Valley)
PO Box 1066
Conway, NH 03818
Phone: (603)447-4388
Fax: (603)447-9947

SCORE Office (North Country)
PO Box 34
Berlin, NH 03570
Phone: (603)752-1090

SCORE Office (Seacoast)
195 Commerce Way, Unit-A
Portsmouth, NH 03801-3251
Phone: (603)433-0575

SCORE Office (Upper Valley)
Citizens Bank Bldg., Rm. 310
20 W. Park St.
Lebanon, NH 03766
Phone: (603)448-3491
Fax: (603)448-1908
E-mail: billt@valley.net
Website: http://www.valley.net/
~score/

### New Jersey

SCORE Office (Bergen County)
327 E. Ridgewood Ave.
Paramus, NJ 07652
Phone: (201)599-6090
E-mail: nj-score@grizbiz.com
Website: http://www.nj-score.org/

SCORE Office (Chester)
5 Old Mill Rd.
Chester, NJ 07930
Phone: (908)879-7080

SCORE Office (Freehold)
36 W. Main St.
Freehold, NJ 07728
Phone: (908)462-3030
Fax: (908)462-2123

SCORE Office (Greater Princeton)
4 A George Washington Dr.
Cranbury, NJ 08512
Phone: (609)520-1776

SCORE Office (Greater Princeton)
216 Rockingham Row
Princeton Forrestal Village
Princeton, NJ 08540
Phone: (609)520-1776
Fax: (609)520-9107
E-mail: nj-score@grizbiz.com
Website: http://www.nj-score.org/

SCORE Office (Jersey City)
2 Gateway Ctr., 4th Fl.
Newark, NJ 07102
Phone: (973)645-3982
Fax: (973)645-2375

SCORE Office (Manalapan)
125 Symmes Dr.
Manalapan, NJ 07726
Phone: (908)431-7220

SCORE Office (Monmouth)
765 Newman Springs Rd.
Lincroft, NJ 07738
Phone: (732)224-2573
E-mail: nj-score@grizbiz.com
Website: http://www.nj-score.org/

SCORE Office (Newark)
2 Gateway Center, 15th Fl.
Newark, NJ 07102-5003
Phone: (973)645-3982
Fax: (973)645-2375
E-mail: nj-score@grizbiz.com
Website: http://www.nj-score.org

SCORE Office (North West)
Picantinny Innovation Ctr.
3159 Schrader Rd.
Dover, NJ 07801
Phone: (973)442-6400
Fax: (973)209-7252
E-mail: nj-score@grizbiz.com
Website: http://www.nj-score.org/

SCORE Office (Ocean County)
33 Washington St.
Toms River, NJ 08754
Phone: (732)505-6033
E-mail: nj-score@grizbiz.com
Website: http://www.nj-score.org/

SCORE Office (Pennsauken)
4900 Rte. 70
Pennsauken, NJ 08109
Phone: (609)486-3421

SCORE Office (Shrewsbury)
Hwy. 35
Shrewsbury, NJ 07702
Phone: (908)842-5995
Fax: (908)219-6140

SCORE Office (Somerset)
Raritan Valley Community College,
Box 3300
Somerville, NJ 08876
Phone: (908)218-8874
E-mail: nj-score@grizbiz.com.
Website: http://www.nj-score.org/

SCORE Office (Southern New
Jersey)
4900 Rte. 70
Pennsauken, NJ 08109-4792
Phone: (856)486-3421
E-mail: nj-score@grizbiz.com
Website: http://www.nj-score.org/

SCORE Office (Wall)
2700 Allaire Rd.
Wall, NJ 07719
Phone: (908)449-8877

SCORE Office (Wayne)
2055 Hamburg Tpke.
Wayne, NJ 07470
Phone: (201)831-7788
Fax: (201)831-9112

### New Mexico

SCORE Office (Albuquerque)
525 Buena Vista SE
Albuquerque, NM 87106
Phone: (505)272-7999
Fax: (505)272-7963

SCORE Office (Las Cruces)
Loretto Towne Center
505 S. Main St., Ste. 125
Las Cruces, NM 88001
Phone: (505)523-5627
Fax: (505)524-2101
E-mail: score.397@zianct.com

SCORE Office (Roswell)
Federal Bldg., Rm. 237
Roswell, NM 88201
Phone: (505)625-2112
Fax: (505)623-2545

SCORE Office (Santa Fe)
Montoya Federal Bldg.
120 Federal Place, Rm. 307
Santa Fe, NM 87501
Phone: (505)988-6302
Fax: (505)988-6300

### New York

SCORE Office (Auburn)
30 South St.
PO Box 675
Auburn, NY 13021
Phone: (315)252-7291
Fax: (315)255-3077

SCORE Office (Brookhaven)
3233 Rte. 112
Medford, NY 11763
Phone: (631)451-6563
Fax: (631)451-6925

SCORE Office (Buffalo)
Federal Bldg., Rm. 1311
111 W. Huron St.
Buffalo, NY 14202
Phone: (716)551-4301
Website: http://www2.pcom.net/
score/buf45.html

SCORE Office (Canandaigua)
Chamber of Commerce Bldg.
113 S. Main St.
Canandaigua, NY 14424
Phone: (716)394-4400
Fax: (716)394-4546

SCORE Office (Chatauqua)
101 W. 5th St.
Jamestown, NY 14701
Phone: (716)484-1101

SCORE Office (Chemung)
333 E. Water St., 4th Fl.
Elmira, NY 14901
Phone: (607)734-3358

SCORE Office (Clinton, Franklin,
Essex)
PO Box 310
Plattsburgh, NY 12901
Phone: (518)563-1000
Fax: (518)563-1028

SCORE Office (Dutchess)
1 Civic Center Plz.
Poughkeepsie, NY 12601
Phone: (914)454-1700

SCORE Office (Geneva)
Chamber of Commerce Bldg.
PO Box 587
Geneva, NY 14456
Phone: (315)789-1776
Fax: (315)789-3993

SCORE Office (Glens Falls)
84 Broad St.
Glens Falls, NY 12801
Phone: (518)798-8463
Fax: (518)745-1433

SCORE Office (Huntington Area)
151 W. Carver St.
Huntington, NY 11743
Phone: (516)423-6100

SCORE Office (Long Island City)
120-55 Queens Blvd.
Jamaica, NY 11424
Phone: (718)263-8961
Fax: (718)263-9032

SCORE Office (Melville)
35 Pinelawn Rd., Rm. 207-W
Melville, NY 11747
Phone: (516)454-0771

SCORE Office (Mt. Vernon)
4 N. 7th Ave.
Mt. Vernon, NY 10550
Phone: (914)667-7500

SCORE Office (Nassau County)
400 County Seat Dr., No. 140
Mineola, NY 11501
Phone: (516)571-3303
E-mail: Counse1998@aol.com
Website: http://members.aol.com/
Counse1998/Default.htm

SCORE Office (New York)
26 Federal Plz., Rm. 3100
New York, NY 10278
Phone: (212)264-4507
Fax: (212)264-4963
E-mail: score1000@erols.com
Website: http://users.erols.com/score-
nyc/

SCORE Office (Newburgh)
47 Grand St.
Newburgh, NY 12550
Phone: (914)562-5100

SCORE Office (Northeast)
1 Computer Dr. S
Albany, NY 12205
Phone: (518)446-1118
Fax: (518)446-1228

SCORE Office (Orange County)
40 Matthews St., No. 103
Goshen, NY 10924
Phone: (845)294-8080
Fax: (845)294-6121

SCORE Office (Owego)
188 Front St.
Owego, NY 13827
Phone: (607)687-2020

SCORE Office (Peekskill)
1 S. Division St.
Peekskill, NY 10566
Phone: (914)737-3600
Fax: (914)737-0541

SCORE Office (Penn Yan)
2375 Rte. 14A
Penn Yan, NY 14527
Phone: (315)536-3111

SCORE Office (Queens County)
Queens Borough Hall
120-55 Queens Blvd., Rm. 333
Kew Gardens, NY 11424
Phone: (718)263-8961
Fax: (718)263-9032

SCORE Office (Queens County City)
12055 Queens Blvd., Rm. 333
Borough Hall, NY 11424
Phone: (718)263-8961

SCORE Office (Rochester)
601 Keating Federal Bldg., Rm. 410
100 State St.
Rochester, NY 14614
Phone: (716)263-6473
Fax: (716)263-3146
Website: http://www.ggw.org/score/

SCORE Office (Saranac Lake)
30 Main St.
Saranac Lake, NY 12983
Phone: (315)448-0415

SCORE Office (South Tier
Binghamton)
Metro Center, 2nd Fl.
49 Court St.
PO Box 995
Binghamton, NY 13902
Phone: (607)772-8860

SCORE Office (Staten Island)
130 Bay St.
Staten Island, NY 10301
Phone: (718)727-1221

SCORE Office (Suffolk)
537 West Ln.
Aquebogue, NY 11931
Phone: (631)727-3200
Fax: (631)727-6712

SCORE Office (Syracuse)
401 S. Salina, 5th Fl.
Syracuse, NY 13202
Phone: (315)471-9393

SCORE Office (Tompkins County)
904 E. Shore Dr.
Ithaca, NY 14850
Phone: (607)273-7080

SCORE Office (Ulster)
One Development Ct., Rm. 101
Kingston, NY 12401
Phone: (914)687-5035
Fax: (914)687-5015
Website: http://www.scoreulster.org/

SCORE Office (Utica)
SUNY Institute of Technology, Route
12
PO Box 3050
Utica, NY 13504-3050
Phone: (315)792-7553

SCORE Office (Watertown)
518 Davidson St.
Watertown, NY 13601
Phone: (315)788-1200
Fax: (315)788-8251

SCORE Office (Westchester)
120 Bloomingdale Rd.
White Plains, NY 10605
Phone: (914)948-3907
Fax: (914)948-4645
E-mail: score@w-w-w.com
Website: http://w-w-w.com/score/

## North Carolina

SCORE Office (Asheboro)
317 E. Dixie Dr.
Asheboro, NC 27203
Free: (336)626-2626
Fax: (336)626-7077

SCORE Office (Asheville)
Federal Bldg., Rm. 259
151 Patton

Asheville, NC 28801-5770
Phone: (828)271-4786
Fax: (828)271-4786

SCORE Office (Chapel Hill)
104 S. Estes Dr.
PO Box 2897
Chapel Hill, NC 27514
Phone: (919)967-7075

SCORE Office (Charlotte)
200 N. College St., Ste. A-2015
Charlotte, NC 28202
Phone: (704)344-6576
Fax: (704)344-6769
E-mail:
CharlotteSCORE47@AOL.com
Website: http://www.charweb.org/
business/score/

SCORE Office (Coastal Plains)
PO Box 2897
Chapel Hill, NC 27515
Phone: (919)967-7075
Fax: (919)968-6874

SCORE Office (Down East)
312 S. Front St., Ste. 6
New Bern, NC 28560
Phone: (252)633-6688
Fax: (252)633-9608

SCORE Office (Durham)
411 W. Chapel Hill St.
Durham, NC 27701
Phone: (919)541-2171

SCORE Office (Gastonia)
PO Box 2168
Gastonia, NC 28053
Phone: (704)864-2621
Fax: (704)854-8723

SCORE Office (Greensboro)
400 W. Market St., Ste. 103
Greensboro, NC 27401-2241
Phone: (336)333-5399

SCORE Office (Henderson)
PO Box 917
Henderson, NC 27536
Phone: (919)492-2061
Fax: (919)430-0460

SCORE Office (Hendersonville)
Federal Bldg., Rm. 108
W. 4th Ave. & Church St.
Hendersonville, NC 28792
Phone: (828)693-8702
E-mail: score@circle.net

Website: http://www.wncguide.com/
score/Welcome.html

SCORE Office (High Point)
1101 N. Main St.
High Point, NC 27262
Phone: (336)882-8625
Fax: (336)889-9499

SCORE Office (Kinston)
PO Box 95
New Bern, NC 28561
Phone: (919)633-6688

SCORE Office (Outer Banks)
PO Box 1757
Kill Devil Hills, NC 27948
Phone: (252)441-8144

SCORE Office (Raleigh)
Century Post Office Bldg., Ste. 306
300 Fayetteville St. Mall
Raleigh, NC 27602
Phone: (919)856-4739
E-mail: jendres@ibm.net
Website: http://www.intrex.net/
score96/score96.htm

SCORE Office (Sandhills Area)
1480 Hwy. 15-501
PO Box 458
Southern Pines, NC 28387
Phone: (910)692-3926

SCORE Office (Sanford)
1801 Nash St.
Sanford, NC 27330
Phone: (919)774-6442
Fax: (919)776-8739

SCORE Office (Unifour)
PO Box 1828
Hickory, NC 28603
Phone: (704)328-6111

SCORE Office (Wilmington)
Corps of Engineers Bldg.
96 Darlington Ave., Ste. 207
Wilmington, NC 28403
Phone: (910)815-4576
Fax: (910)815-4658

## North Dakota

SCORE Office (Bismarck-Mandan)
700 E. Main Ave., 2nd Fl.
PO Box 5509
Bismarck, ND 58506-5509
Phone: (701)250-4303

SCORE Office (Fargo)
657 2nd Ave., Rm. 225
PO Box 3086
Fargo, ND 58108-3086
Phone: (701)239-5677

SCORE Office (Minot)
2201 15th St. SW
Minot, ND 58701
Phone: (701)852-6883
Fax: (701)852-6905

SCORE Office (Upper Red River)
202 N. 3rd St., Ste. 300
Grand Forks, ND 58203
Phone: (701)746-5851
Fax: (701)746-5748

## Ohio

SCORE Office (Akron)
1 Cascade Plz., 7th Fl.
Akron, OH 44308
Phone: (330)379-3163
Fax: (330)379-3164

SCORE Office (Ashland)
Gill Center
47 W. Main St.
Ashland, OH 44805
Phone: (419)281-4584

SCORE Office (Canton)
116 Cleveland Ave. NW, Ste. 601
Canton, OH 44702-1720
Phone: (330)453-6047

SCORE Office (Chillicothe)
165 S. Paint St.
Chillicothe, OH 45601
Phone: (614)772-4530

SCORE Office (Cincinnati)
Ameritrust Bldg., Rm. 850
525 Vine St.
Cincinnati, OH 45202
Phone: (513)684-2812
Fax: (513)684-3251
Website: http://
www.score.chapter34.org/

SCORE Office (Cleveland)
Eaton Center, Ste. 620
1100 Superior Ave.
Cleveland, OH 44114-2507
Phone: (216)522-4194
Fax: (216)522-4844

SCORE Office (Columbus)
2 Nationwide Plz., Ste. 1400

Columbus, OH 43215-2542
Phone: (614)469-2357
Fax: (614)469-5548
E-mail: info@scorecolumbus.org
Website: http://
www.scorecolumbus.org/

SCORE Office (Dayton)
Dayton Federal Bldg., Rm. 505
200 W. Second St.
Dayton, OH 45402-1430
Phone: (937)225-2887
Fax: (937)225-7667

SCORE Office (Defiance)
615 W. 3rd St.
PO Box 130
Defiance, OH 43512
Phone: (419)782-7946

SCORE Office (Findlay)
123 E. Main Cross St.
PO Box 923
Findlay, OH 45840
Phone: (419)422-3314

SCORE Office (Heart of Ohio)
377 W. Liberty St.
Wooster, OH 44691
Phone: (330)262-5735
Fax: (330)262-5745

SCORE Office (Licking County)
222 Price Rd.
Newark, OH 43055
Phone: (740)345-7458
Fax: (740)366-4097

SCORE Office (Lima)
147 N. Main St.
Lima, OH 45801
Phone: (419)222-6045
Fax: (419)229-0266

SCORE Office (Mansfield)
55 N. Mulberry St.
Mansfield, OH 44902
Phone: (419)522-3211

SCORE Office (Marietta)
Thomas Hall
Marietta, OH 45750
Phone: (614)373-0268

SCORE Office (Medina)
County Administrative Bldg.
144 N. Broadway
Medina, OH 44256
Phone: (216)764-8650

SCORE Office (Salem)
2491 State Rte. 45 S
Salem, OH 44460
Phone: (216)332-0361

SCORE Office (Tiffin)
62 S. Washington St.
Tiffin, OH 44883
Phone: (419)447-4141
Fax: (419)447-5141

SCORE Office (Toledo)
608 Madison Ave, Ste. 910
Toledo, OH 43604-1128
Phone: (419)259-7598
Fax: (419)259-6460

SCORE Office (Youngstown)
306 Williamson Hall
Youngstown, OH 44555
Phone: (330)746-2687

## Oklahoma

SCORE Office (Anadarko)
PO Box 366
Anadarko, OK 73005
Phone: (405)247-6651

SCORE Office (Ardmore)
PO Box 1585
Ardmore, OK 73402-1585
Phone: (580)226-2620

SCORE Office (Lawton)
4500 W. Lee Blvd., Bldg. 100, Ste. 107
Lawton, OK 73505
Phone: (580)353-8727
Fax: (580)250-5677

SCORE Office (Northeast Oklahoma)
210 S. Main
Grove, OK 74344
Phone: (918)787-2796
Fax: (918)787-2796
E-mail: Score595@greencis.net

SCORE Office (Oklahoma City)
210 Park Ave., No. 1300
Oklahoma City, OK 73102
Phone: (405)231-5163
Fax: (405)231-4876
E-mail: score212@usa.net

SCORE Office (Stillwater)
439 S. Main
Stillwater, OK 74074
Phone: (405)372-5573
Fax: (405)372-4316

SCORE Office (Tulsa)
616 S. Boston, Ste. 406
Tulsa, OK 74119
Phone: (918)581-7462
Fax: (918)581-6908
Website: http://www.ionet.net/
~tulscore/

## Oregon

SCORE Office (Bend)
4401 SW Williams Dr.
Powell Butte, OR 97753
Phone: (541)923-2849

SCORE Office (Florence)
3149 Oak St.
Florence, OR 97439
Phone: (503)997-8444
Fax: (503)997-8448

SCORE Office (Portland)
1515 SW 5th Ave., Ste. 1050
Portland, OR 97201
Phone: (503)326-3441
Fax: (503)326-2808
E-mail: gr134@prodigy.com

SCORE Office (Salem)
PO Box 4024
Salem, OR 97302-1024
Phone: (503)370-2896

SCORE Office (Southern Oregon)
PO Box 969
Medford, OR 97501
Phone: (541)776-4220
E-mail: pgr134f@prodigy.com

SCORE Office (Willamette)
1401 Willamette St.
PO Box 1107
Eugene, OR 97401-4003
Phone: (541)465-6600
Fax: (541)484-4942

## Pennsylvania

SCORE Office (Airport Area)
986 Brodhead Rd.
Moon Township, PA 15108-2398
Phone: (412)264-6270
Fax: (412)264-1575

SCORE Office (Altoona-Blair)
1212 12th Ave.
Altoona, PA 16601-3493
Phone: (814)943-8151

SCORE Office (Bucks County)
409 Hood Blvd.
Fairless Hills, PA 19030
Phone: (215)943-8850
Fax: (215)943-7404

SCORE Office (Butler County)
100 N. Main St.
PO Box 1082
Butler, PA 16003
Phone: (412)283-2222
Fax: (412)283-0224

SCORE Office (Central Pennsylvania)
200 Innovation Blvd., Ste. 242-B
State College, PA 16803
Phone: (814)234-9415
Fax: (814)234-6864
Website: http://countrystore.org/
business/score.htm

SCORE Office (Chester County)
Government Service Center, Ste. 281
601 Westtown Rd.
West Chester, PA 19382-4538
Phone: (610)344-6910
Fax: (610)344-6919
E-mail: score@locke.ccil.org

SCORE Office (Cumberland Valley)
75 S. 2nd St.
Chambersburg, PA 17201
Phone: (717)264-2935

SCORE Office (Delaware County)
602 E. Baltimore Pike
Media, PA 19063
Phone: (610)565-3677
Fax: (610)565-1606

SCORE Office (East Montgomery County)
Baederwood Shopping Center
1653 The Fairways, Ste. 204
Jenkintown, PA 19046
Phone: (215)885-3027

SCORE Office (Erie)
120 W. 9th St.
Erie, PA 16501
Phone: (814)871-5650
Fax: (814)871-7530

SCORE Office (Hanover)
146 Broadway
Hanover, PA 17331
Phone: (717)637-6130
Fax: (717)637-9127

SCORE Office (Harrisburg)
4211 Trindle Rd.
Camp Hill, PA 17011
Phone: (717)761-4304
Fax: (717)761-4315

SCORE Office (Harrisburg)
100 Chestnut, Ste. 309
Harrisburg, PA 17101
Phone: (717)782-3874

SCORE Office (Kittanning)
2 Butler Rd.
Kittanning, PA 16201
Phone: (412)543-1305
Fax: (412)543-6206

SCORE Office (Lancaster)
118 W. Chestnut St.
Lancaster, PA 17603
Phone: (717)397-3092

SCORE Office (Lebanon)
252 N. 8th St.
PO Box 899
Lebanon, PA 17042-0899
Phone: (717)273-3727
Fax: (717)273-7940

SCORE Office (Lehigh Valley)
Rauch Bldg. 37
Lehigh University
621 Taylor St.
Bethlehem, PA 18015
Phone: (610)758-4496
Fax: (610)758-5205

SCORE Office (Lewistown)
3 W. Monument Sq., Ste. 204
Lewistown, PA 17044
Phone: (717)248-6713
Fax: (717)248-6714

SCORE Office (Milton Area)
112 S. Front St.
Milton, PA 17847
Phone: (717)742-7341
Fax: (717)792-2008

SCORE Office (Mon-Valley)
435 Donner Ave.
Monessen, PA 15062
Phone: (412)684-4277
Fax: (412)684-7688

SCORE Office (Monroe County-
Stroudsburg)
556 Main St.
Stroudsburg, PA 18301
Phone: (717)421-4433

SCORE Office (Monroeville)
William Penn Plaza
2790 Mosside Blvd., Ste. 295
Monroeville, PA 15146
Phone: (412)856-0622
Fax: (412)856-1030

SCORE Office (North Central
Pennsylvania)
Executive Plaza
330 Pine St., Ste. 305
Williamsport, PA 17701
Phone: (717)322-3720
Fax: (717)322-1607
E-mail: score234@mail.csrlink.net
Website: http://www.lycoming.org/
score/

SCORE Office (Northeast)
8601 E. Roosevelt Blvd.
Philadelphia, PA 19152
Phone: (215)332-3400
Fax: (215)332-6050

SCORE Office (Philadelphia)
1315 Walnut St., Ste. 500
Philadelphia, PA 19107
Phone: (215)790-5050
Fax: (215)790-5057
E-mail: score46@bellatlantic.net
Website: http://www.pgweb.net/
score46/

SCORE Office (Pittsburgh)
Federal Bldg.
1000 Liberty Ave., Rm. 1314
Pittsburgh, PA 15222
Phone: (412)395-6560
Fax: (412)395-6562

SCORE Office (Reading)
601 Penn St.
Reading, PA 19601
Phone: (610)376-3497

SCORE Office (Scranton)
Oppenheim Bldg.
116 N. Washington Ave., Ste. 650
Scranton, PA 18503
Phone: (717)347-4611
Fax: (717)347-4611

SCORE Office (Tri-County)
801 N. Charlotte St.
Pottstown, PA 19464
Phone: (610)327-2673

SCORE Office (Uniontown)
140 S. Beeson Ave., Rm. 404
Uniontown, PA 15401

Phone: (412)437-4222
E-mail: uniontownscore@lcsys.net

SCORE Office (Warren County)
315 2nd Ave.
Warren, PA 16365
Phone: (814)723-9017

SCORE Office (Waynesboro)
323 E. Main St.
Waynesboro, PA 17268
Phone: (717)762-7123
Fax: (717)962-7124

SCORE Office (Westmoreland
County)
300 Fraser Purchase Rd.
Latrobe, PA 15650-2690
Phone: (412)539-7505
Fax: (412)539-1850

SCORE Office (Wilkes-Barre)
7 N. Wilkes-Barre Blvd.
Wilkes Barre, PA 18702-5241
Phone: (717)826-6502
Fax: (717)826-6287

SCORE Office (York)
Cyber Center
2101 Pennsylvania Ave.
York, PA 17404
Phone: (717)845-8830
Fax: (717)854-9333

**Puerto Rico**

SCORE Office (Puerto Rico & Virgin
Islands)
PO Box 12383-96
San Juan, PR 00914-0383
Phone: (787)726-8040
Fax: (787)726-8135

**Rhode Island**

SCORE Office (Barrington)
281 County Rd.
Barrington, RI 02806
Phone: (401)247-1920
Fax: (401)247-3763

SCORE Office (J.G.E. Knight)
380 Westminster St.
Providence, RI 02903
Phone: (401)528-4571
Fax: (401)528-4539
E-mail: feedback@ch13.score.org.
Website: http://chapters.score.org/
ch13

SCORE Office (Warwick)
3288 Post Rd.
Warwick, RI 02886
Phone: (401)732-1100
Fax: (401)732-1101

SCORE Office (Westerly)
74 Post Rd.
Westerly, RI 02891
Phone: (401)596-7761
Free: 800-732-7636
Fax: (401)596-2190

SCORE Office (Wickford)
8045 Post Rd.
North Kingstown, RI 02852
Phone: (401)295-5566
Fax: (401)295-8987

SCORE Office (Woonsocket)
640 Washington Hwy.
Lincoln, RI 02865
Phone: (401)334-1000
Fax: (401)334-1009

## South Carolina

SCORE Office (Aiken)
PO Box 892
Aiken, SC 29802
Phone: (803)641-1111
Free: 800-542-4536
Fax: (803)641-4174

SCORE Office (Anderson)
Anderson Mall
3130 N. Main St.
Anderson, SC 29621
Phone: (864)224-0453

SCORE Office (Coastal)
284 King St.
Charleston, SC 29401
Phone: (803)727-4778
Fax: (803)853-2529

SCORE Office (Grand Strand)
PO Box 2468
Myrtle Beach, SC 29578
Phone: (803)918-1079
Fax: (803)918-1083
E-mail: score381@aol.com

SCORE Office (Greenwood)
PO Drawer 1467
Greenwood, SC 29648
Phone: (864)223-8357

SCORE Office (Hilton Head Island)
PO Box 5647

Hilton Head, SC 29938
Phone: (843)785-7107
Fax: (843)785-7110

SCORE Office (Midlands)
Strom Thurmond Bldg., Rm. 358
1835 Assembly St.
Columbia, SC 29201
Phone: (803)765-5131
Fax: (803)765-5962
Website: http://
www.scoremidlands.org/

SCORE Office (Piedmont)
Federal Bldg., Rm. B-02
300 E. Washington St.
Greenville, SC 29601
Phone: (864)271-3638

SCORE Office (Spartanburg)
PO Box 1636
Spartanburg, SC 29304
Phone: (864)594-5000
Fax: (864)594-5055

## South Dakota

SCORE Office (Sioux Falls)
First Financial Center
110 S. Phillips Ave., Ste. 200
Sioux Falls, SD 57102-1109
Phone: (605)330-4231

SCORE Office (West River)
Rushmore Plz. Civic Ctr.
444 N. Mount Rushmore Rd., No. 204
Rapid City, SD 57701
Phone: (605)394-1707
Fax: (605)394-6140
E-mail: score@gwtc.net

## Tennessee

SCORE Office (Chattanooga)
Federal Bldg., Rm. 26
900 Georgia Ave.
Chattanooga, TN 37402
Phone: (423)752-5190
Fax: (423)752-5335

SCORE Office (Cleveland)
PO Box 2275
Cleveland, TN 37320
Phone: (423)472-6587
Fax: (423)472-2019

SCORE Office (Greater Knoxville)
Farragot Bldg., Ste. 224
530 S. Gay St.
Knoxville, TN 37902

Phone: (865)545-4203
E-mail: scoreknox@ntown.com
Website: http://www.scoreknox.org/

SCORE Office (Greeneville)
115 Academy St.
Greeneville, TN 37743
Phone: (423)638-4111
Fax: (423)638-5345

SCORE Office (Jackson)
Aeeas Bldg.
210 E. Chester St.
Jackson, TN 38301
Phone: (901)427-7900
Fax: (901)427-3942

SCORE Office (Kingsport)
151 E. Main St.
Kingsport, TN 37662
Phone: (423)392-8805

SCORE Office (Maryville)
201 S. Washington St.
Maryville, TN 37804-5728
Phone: (423)983-2241
Free: 800-525-6834
Fax: (423)984-1386

SCORE Office (Memphis)
Federal Bldg., Ste. 390
167 N. Main St.
Memphis, TN 38103
Phone: (901)544-3588
Fax: (901)544-0557

SCORE Office (Nashville)
50 Vantage Way, Ste. 201
Nashville, TN 37228-1500
Phone: (615)736-7621

SCORE Office (Northeast Tennessee)
1st Tennessee Bank Bldg.
2710 S. Roan St., Ste. 584
Johnson City, TN 37601
Phone: (423)461-8051
Fax: (423)461-8053

SCORE Office (Unicoi County)
PO Box 713
Erwin, TN 37650
Phone: (423)743-3000
Fax: (423)743-0942

SCORE Office (Upper Cumberland Center)
1225 S. Willow Ave.
Cookeville, TN 38501
Phone: (615)432-4111
Fax: (615)432-6010

## Texas

SCORE Office (Abilene)
2106 Federal Post Office and Court
Bldg.
Abilene, TX 79601
Phone: (915)677-1857

SCORE Office (Austin)
2501 S. Congress
Austin, TX 78701
Phone: (512)442-7235
Fax: (512)442-7528

SCORE Office (Bedford)
100 E. 15th St., Ste. 400
Ft. Worth, TX 76102
Phone: (817)871-6002

SCORE Office (Brazos Valley)
3000 Briarcrest, Ste. 302
Bryan, TX 77802
Phone: (979)776-8876
Fax: (979)776-8794
E-mail:
102633.2612@compuserve.com

SCORE Office (Brownsville)
3505 Boca Chica Blvd., Ste. 305
Brownsville, TX 78521
Phone: (210)541-4508

SCORE Office (Cleburne)
Watergarden Pl., 9th Fl., Ste. 400
Cleburne, TX 76031
Phone: (817)871-6002

SCORE Office (Corpus Christi)
651 Upper North Broadway, Ste. 654
Corpus Christi, TX 78477
Phone: (361)888-4322
Fax: (361)888-3418

SCORE Office (Dallas)
6260 E. Mockingbird
Dallas, TX 75214-2619
Phone: (214)828-2471
Fax: (214)821-8033

SCORE Office (East Texas)
RTDC
1530 SSW Loop 323, Ste. 100
Tyler, TX 75701
Phone: (903)510-2975
Fax: (903)510-2978

SCORE Office (El Paso)
10737 Gateway West
El Paso, TX 79935
Phone: (915)534-0541
Fax: (915)534-0513

SCORE Office (Ft. Worth)
100 E. 15th St., No. 400
Ft. Worth, TX 76102
Phone: (817)871-6002
Fax: (817)871-6031
E-mail: fwbac@onramp.net

SCORE Office (Garland)
2734 W. Kingsley Rd.
Garland, TX 75041
Phone: (214)271-9224

SCORE Office (Golden Triangle)
PO Box 3150
Beaumont, TX 77704
Phone: (409)838-6581
Fax: (409)833-6718

SCORE Office (Granbury Chamber
of Commerce)
416 S. Morgan
Granbury, TX 76048
Phone: (817)573-1622
Fax: (817)573-0805

SCORE Office (Houston)
9301 Southwest Fwy., Ste. 365
Houston, TX 77074
Phone: (713)773-6565
Fax: (713)773-6550

SCORE Office (Irving)
3333 N. MacArthur Blvd., Ste. 100
Irving, TX 75062
Phone: (214)252-8484
Fax: (214)252-6710

SCORE Office (Lower Rio Grande
Valley)
222 E. Van Buren, Ste. 500
Harlingen, TX 78550
Phone: (956)427-8533
Fax: (956)427-8537

SCORE Office (Lubbock)
1205 Texas Ave., Rm. 411D
Lubbock, TX 79401
Phone: (806)472-7462
Fax: (806)472-7487

SCORE Office (Midland)
Post Office Annex
200 E. Wall St., Rm. P121
Midland, TX 79701
Phone: (915)687-2649

SCORE Office (Orange)
1012 Green Ave.
Orange, TX 77630-5620
Phone: (409)883-3536

Free: 800-528-4906
Fax: (409)886-3247

SCORE Office (Plano)
1200 E. 15th St.
PO Drawer 940287
Plano, TX 75094-0287
Phone: (214)424-7547
Fax: (214)422-5182

SCORE Office (Port Arthur)
4749 Twin City Hwy., Ste. 300
Port Arthur, TX 77642
Phone: (409)963-1107
Fax: (409)963-3322

SCORE Office (Richardson)
411 Belle Grove
Richardson, TX 75080
Phone: (214)234-4141
Free: 800-777-8001
Fax: (214)680-9103

SCORE Office (San Antonio)
Federal Bldg., Rm. A527
727 E. Durango
San Antonio, TX 78206
Phone: (210)472-5931
Fax: (210)472-5935

SCORE Office (Texarkana)
PO Box 1468
Texarkana, TX 75504
Phone: (903)792-7191
Fax: (903)793-4304

SCORE Office (Waco)
401 Franklin Ave.
Waco, TX 76701
Phone: (254)754-8898
Fax: (254)756-0776
Website: http://www.brc-waco.com/

SCORE Office (Wichita Falls)
Hamilton Bldg.
PO Box 1860
Wichita Falls, TX 76307
Phone: (940)723-2741
Fax: (940)723-8773

## Utah

SCORE Office (Central Utah)
1071 E. Windsor Dr.
Provo, UT 84604
Phone: (801)226-0881

SCORE Office (Northern Utah)
160 N. Main
Logan, UT 84321
Phone: (435)752-2161

SCORE Office (Ogden)
324 25th St., No. 6104
Ogden, UT 84401
Phone: (801)625-5712
E-mail: score158@netscape.net

SCORE Office (Salt Lake)
169 East 100 South
Salt Lake City, UT 84111
Phone: (801)364-1331
Fax: (801)364-1310

SCORE Office (Southern Utah)
225 South 700 East
St. George, UT 84770
Phone: (801)652-7741

### Vermont

SCORE Office (Champlain Valley)
Winston Prouty Federal Bldg.
11 Lincoln St., Rm. 106
Essex Junction, VT 05452
Phone: (802)951-6762

SCORE Office (Marble Valley)
256 N. Main St.
Rutland, VT 05701-2413
Phone: (802)773-9147

SCORE Office (Montpelier)
87 State St., Rm. 205
PO Box 605
Montpelier, VT 05601
Phone: (802)828-4422
Fax: (802)828-4485

SCORE Office (Northeast Kingdom)
20 Main St.
PO Box 904
St. Johnsbury, VT 05819
Phone: (802)748-5101

### Virgin Islands

SCORE Office (St. Croix)
United Plaza Shopping Center
PO Box 4010, Christiansted
St. Croix, VI 00822
Phone: (809)778-5380

SCORE Office (St. Thomas-St. John)
Federal Bldg., Rm. 21
Veterans Dr.
St. Thomas, VI 00801
Phone: (809)774-8530

### Virginia

SCORE Office (Alleghany Satellite)
241 W. Main St.

Covington, VA 24426
Phone: (540)962-2178
Fax: (540)962-2179

SCORE Office (Arlington)
2009 N. 14th St., Ste. 111
Arlington, VA 22201
Phone: (703)525-2400

SCORE Office (Blacksburg)
141 Jackson St.
Blacksburg, VA 24060
Phone: (540)552-4061

SCORE Office (Bristol)
20 Volunteer Pkwy.
PO Box 519
Bristol, VA 24203
Phone: (540)989-4850
Fax: (540)989-4867

SCORE Office (Central Fairfax)
3975 University Dr., Ste. 350
Fairfax, VA 22030
Phone: (703)591-2450

SCORE Office (Central Virginia)
1001 E. Market St., Ste. 101
Charlottesville, VA 22902
Phone: (804)295-6712
Fax: (804)295-7066

SCORE Office (Fairfax)
8391 Old Courthouse Rd., Ste. 300
Vienna, VA 22182
Phone: (703)749-0400

SCORE Office (Falls Church)
PO Box 491
Falls Church, VA 22040
Phone: (703)532-1050
Fax: (703)237-7904

SCORE Office (Glenns)
Glenns Campus
Box 287
Glenns, VA 23149
Phone: (804)693-9650

SCORE Office (Greater Prince
William)
8963 Center St
Manassas, VA 20110
Phone: (703)368-4813
Fax: (703)368-4733

SCORE Office (Greater Vienna)
513 Maple Ave. West
Vienna, VA 22180
Phone: (703)281-1333
Fax: (703)242-1482

SCORE Office (Hampton Roads)
Federal Bldg., Rm. 737
200 Grandby St.
Norfolk, VA 23510
Phone: (757)441-3733
Fax: (757)441-3733
E-mail: scorehr60@juno.com

SCORE Office (Lynchburg)
Federal Bldg.
1100 Main St.
Lynchburg, VA 24504-1714
Phone: (804)846-3235
Fax: (804)846-1798

SCORE Office (Martinsvile)
115 Broad St.
Martinsville, VA 24112-0709
Phone: (540)632-6401
Fax: (540)632-5059

SCORE Office (Norfolk)
Federal Bldg., Rm. 737
200 Granby St.
Norfolk, VA 23510
Phone: (757)441-3733
Fax: (757)441-3733

SCORE Office (Northern Virginia)
1360 S. Pleasant Valley Rd.
Winchester, VA 22601
Phone: (540)662-4118

SCORE Office (Peninsula)
1919 Commerce Dr., Ste. 320
Hampton, VA 23666
Phone: (757)262-2000
Fax: (757)262-2009
E-mail: score100@seva.net

SCORE Office (Radford)
1126 Norwood St.
Radford, VA 24141
Phone: (540)639-2202

SCORE Office (Richmond)
Federal Bldg.
400 N. 8th St., Ste. 1150
PO Box 10126
Richmond, VA 23240-0126
Phone: (804)771-2400
Fax: (804)771-2764
E-mail: scorechapter12@yahoo.com
Website: http://www.cvco.org/score/

SCORE Office (Roanoke)
Federal Bldg., Rm. 716
250 Franklin Rd.
Roanoke, VA 24011
Phone: (540)857-2834

Fax: (540)857-2043
E-mail: scorerva@juno.com
Website: http://hometown.aol.com/
scorerv/Index.html

SCORE Office (Shenandoah Valley)
301 W. Main St.
Waynesboro, VA 22980
Phone: (540)949-8203
Fax: (540)949-7740
E-mail: score427@intelos.net

SCORE Office (Tri-Cities)
PO Drawer 1297
Hopewell, VA 23860
Phone: (804)458-5536
Fax: (804)458-1342

SCORE Office (Virginia Beach)
Chamber of Commerce
200 Grandby St., Rm 737
Norfolk, VA 23510
Phone: (804)441-3733

SCORE Office (Williamsburg)
201 Penniman Rd.
Williamsburg, VA 23185
Phone: (757)229-6511
Fax: (757)229-2047
E-mail: wacc@williamsburgcc.com

## Washington

SCORE Office (Bellingham)
101 E. Holly St.
Bellingham, WA 98225
Phone: (360)676-3307

SCORE Office (Clover Park)
PO Box 1933
Tacoma, WA 98401-1933
Phone: (206)627-2175

SCORE Office (Everett)
2702 Hoyt Ave.
Everett, WA 98201-3556
Phone: (206)259-8000

SCORE Office (Fort Vancouver)
1701 Broadway, S-1
Vancouver, WA 98663
Phone: (360)699-1079

SCORE Office (Gig Harbor)
3125 Judson St.
Gig Harbor, WA 98335
Phone: (206)851-6865

SCORE Office (Gray's Harbor)
506 Duffy St.

Aberdeen, WA 98520
Phone: (360)532-1924
Fax: (360)533-7945

SCORE Office (Kennewick)
PO Box 6986
Kennewick, WA 99336
Phone: (509)736-0510

SCORE Office (Mid-Columbia)
2 S. Chelan Ave.
Wenatche, WA 98801
Phone: (509)574-4944
Fax: (509)574-2943
Website: http://www.ellensburg.com/
~score/

SCORE Office (Puyallup)
322 2nd St. SW
PO Box 1298
Puyallup, WA 98371
Phone: (206)845-6755
Fax: (206)848-6164

SCORE Office (Seattle)
1200 6th Ave., Ste. 1700
Seattle, WA 98101
Phone: (206)553-7320
Fax: (206)553-7044
E-mail: score55@aol.com
Website: http://www.scn.org/civic/
score-online/index55.html

SCORE Office (Spokane)
801 W. Riverside Ave., No. 240
Spokane, WA 99201
Phone: (509)353-2820
Fax: (509)353-2600
E-mail: score@dmi.net
Website: http://www.dmi.net/score/

SCORE Office (Tacoma)
1101 Pacific Ave.
Tacoma, WA 98402
Phone: (253)274-1288
Fax: (253)274-1289

SCORE Office (Walla Walla)
500 Tausick Way
Walla Walla, WA 99362
Phone: (509)527-4681

## West Virginia

SCORE Office (Charleston)
1116 Smith St.
Charleston, WV 25301
Phone: (304)347-5463
E-mail: score256@juno.com

SCORE Office (Huntington)
1101 6th Ave., Ste. 220
Huntington, WV 25701-2309
Phone: (304)523-4092

SCORE Office (Marion County)
PO Box 208
Fairmont, WV 26555-0208
Phone: (304)363-0486

SCORE Office (Upper Monongahela
Valley)
1000 Technology Dr., Ste. 1111
Fairmont, WV 26555
Phone: (304)363-0486
E-mail: score537@hotmail.com

SCORE Office (Virginia Street)
1116 Smith St., Ste. 302
Charleston, WV 25301
Phone: (304)347-5463

SCORE Office (Wheeling)
1310 Market St.
Wheeling, WV 26003
Phone: (304)233-2575
Fax: (304)233-1320

## Wisconsin

SCORE Office (Beloit)
136 W. Grand Ave., Ste. 100
PO Box 717
Beloit, WI 53511
Phone: (608)365-8835
Fax: (608)365-9170

SCORE Office (Central Wisconsin)
700 Cypress Ave.
Marshfield, WI 54449
Phone: (715)387-0406

SCORE Office (Eau Claire)
Federal Bldg., Rm. B11
510 S. Barstow St.
Eau Claire, WI 54701
Phone: (715)834-1573
E-mail: score@ecol.net
Website: http://www.ecol.net/~score/

SCORE Office (Fond du Lac)
207 N. Main St.
Fond du Lac, WI 54935
Phone: (414)921-9500
Fax: (414)921-9559

SCORE Office (Fox Cities)
227 S. Walnut St.
PO Box 1855
Appleton, WI 54913

Phone: (920)734-7101
Fax: (920)734-7161

SCORE Office (Green Bay)
835 Potts Ave.
Green Bay, WI 54304
Phone: (414)496-8930
Fax: (414)496-6009

SCORE Office (Janesville)
20 S. Main St., Ste. 11
PO Box 8008
Janesville, WI 53547
Phone: (608)757-3160
Fax: (608)757-3170

SCORE Office (La Crosse)
712 Main St.
PO Box 219
La Crosse, WI 54602-0219
Phone: (608)784-4880

SCORE Office (Madison)
505 S. Rosa Rd.
Madison, WI 53719
Phone: (608)441-2820

SCORE Office (Manitowoc)
1515 Memorial Dr.
PO Box 903
Manitowoc, WI 54221-0903
Phone: (414)684-5575
Fax: (414)684-1915

SCORE Office (Milwaukee)
310 W. Wisconsin Ave., Ste. 425
Milwaukee, WI 53203
Phone: (414)297-3942
Fax: (414)297-1377

SCORE Office (Superior)
Superior Business Center Inc.
1423 N. 8th St.
Superior, WI 54880
Phone: (715)394-7388
Fax: (715)393-7414

SCORE Office (Waukesha)
223 Wisconsin Ave.
Waukesha, WI 53186-4926
Phone: (414)542-4249

SCORE Office (Wausau)
300 3rd St., Ste. 200
PO Box 6190
Wausau, WI 54402-6190
Phone: (715)845-6231

SCORE Office (Wisconsin Rapids)
2240 Kingston Rd.

Wisconsin Rapids, WI 54494
Phone: (715)423-1830

## Wyoming

SCORE Office (Casper)
Federal Bldg., No. 2215
100 East B St.
Casper, WY 82602
Phone: (307)261-6529
Fax: (307)261-6530

SCORE Office (Gillette)
222 S. Gillette Ave.
PO Box 3948
Gillette, WY 82717-3948
Phone: (307)682-6594

# VENTURE CAPITAL & FINANCING COMPANIES

*This section contains a listing of financing and loan companies in the United States and Canada. These listings are arranged alphabetically by country, state/territory/province, then by organization name.*

## CANADA

### Alberta

Native Venture Capital Company, Inc.
21 Artist View Point, Box 7
Site 25, RR 12
Calgary, AB, Canada T3E 6W3
Phone: (903)208-5380
Milt Pahl, President
Investment Types: Seed, startup, first stage, second stage, and leveraged buyout. Industry Preferences: Diversified.

### British Columbia

MDS Ventures Pacific, Inc.
555 W. Eighth Ave., Ste. 305
Vancouver, BC, Canada V5Z 1C6
Phone: (604)872-8464
Fax: (604)872-2977
E-mail: info@mds-ventures.com
Investment Types: Seed, research and development, startup, first and second stages. Industry Preferences: Medical and health related. Geographic Preferences: Western Canada and Northwestern U.S.

Nova Bancorp Group
1000-1075 W. Georgia St.
Vancouver, BC, Canada V6E 3C9
Phone: (604)681-0332
Fax: (604)681-5699
Ken Melnyk, Vice President
Investment Types: Seed, startup, first and second stages. Industry Preferences: Energy and natural resources. Geographic Preferences: Western U.S., Canada.

Ventures West Management Inc.
1285 W. Pender St., Ste. 280
Vancouver, BC, Canada V6E 4B1
Phone: (604)688-9495
Fax: (604)687-2145
Website: http://
www.ventureswest.com
Investment Types: Seed, research and development, startup, first and second stages. Industry Preferences: Diversified technology. Geographic Preferences: Western U.S., Canada.

### Ontario

Bailey & Company, Inc.
594 Spadina Ave.
Toronto, ON, Canada M5S 2H4
Phone: (416)921-6930
Fax: (416)925-4670
E-mail: bailey@interlog.com
Investment Types: Research and development, first stage, and special situations. Industry Preferences: Diversified technology. Geographic Preferences: No preference.

Enterprise Fund
65 Queen St. W, Ste. 1820
PO Box 17
Toronto, ON, Canada M5H 2M5
Phone: (416)362-9009
Fax: (416)360-8286
Website: http://
www.enterprisefund.com
Investment Types: Startup, first stage, second stage, mezzanine, and leveraged buyout. Industry Preferences: Diversified. Geographic Preferences: No preference.

Grieve, Horner, Brown & Asculai
8 King St. E, Ste. 1704
Toronto, ON, Canada M5C 1B5
Phone: (416)362-7668
Fax: (416)362-7660

Investment Types: Startup, first and second stages. Industry Preferences: Diversified. Geographic Preferences: Entire U.S. and Canada.

## Quebec

Business Development Bank of Canada
Venture Capital Division
Five Place Ville Marie, Ste. 600
Montreal, QC, Canada H3B 5E7
Phone: (514)283-1896
Fax: (514)283-5455
Investment Types: Early and late stages. Industry Preferences: Diversified technology. Geographic Preferences: No preference.

## Saskatchewan

Saskatchewan Government Growth Fund
1801 Hamilton St., Ste. 1210
Regina, SK, Canada S4P 4B4
Phone: (306)787-2994
Fax: (306)787-2086
E-mail: sggf@sk.sympatico.ca
Rob M. Duguid, Vice President, Investing
Investment Types: Startup, first stage, second stage, and mezzanine. Industry Preferences: Diversified.

## UNITED STATES

### Alabama

Cordova Ventures
4121 Carmichael Rd., Ste. 301
Montgomery, AL 36106
Phone: (334)271-6011
Fax: (334)260-0120
Website: http://www.cordovaventures.com
Investment Types: Second stage and mezzanine. Industry Preferences: Diversified. Geographic Preferences: Southeast.

FHL Capital Corp.
600 20th Street North
Suite 350
Birmingham, AL 35203
Phone: (205)328-3098
Fax: (205)323-0001
E-mail: fhl@scott.net

Kevin Keck, Vice President
Preferred Investment Size: Between $500,000 and $1,000,000. Investment Types: Mezzanine, leveraged buyout, and special situations. Geographic Preferences: Southeast.

FJC Growth Capital Corp.
200 W. Side Sq., Ste. 340
Huntsville, AL 35801
Phone: (256)922-2918
Fax: (256)922-2909
William B. Noojin, Vice President & General Manager
Preferred Investment Size: Between $100,000 and $500,000. Investment Types: Second stage. Industry Preferences: Hotel and resort, restaurant, and electronic equipment distribution. Does not consider turnarounds, start-ups, real estate development and agriculture. Geographic Preferences: Southeast.

Harbert Management Corp.
One Riverchase Pkwy. South
Birmingham, AL 35244
Phone: (205)987-5500
Fax: (205)987-5707
Charles P. Shook, IV, Investment Director
Preferred Investment Size: $5,000,000 to $25,000,000. Investment Types: Leveraged buyout, special situations and industry roll ups. Industry Preferences: Oil and gas not considered. Geographic Preferences: Entire U.S.

Hickory Venture Capital Corp.
301 Washington St. NW
Suite 301
Huntsville, AL 35801
Phone: (256)539-1931
Fax: (256)539-5130
E-mail: hvcc@hvcc.com
Website: http://www.hvcc.com
Preferred Investment Size: $1,000,000. Investment Types: First stage, second stage, mezzanine, and leverage buyout. Industry Preferences: Communications, computer-related, electronic components and instrumentation, energy/natural resources, genetic engineering, industrial products and equipment, medical/health related and transportation. Geographic

Preferences: Southeast, Southwest, Midwest, Gulf states and Middle Atlantic.

Jefferson Capital Fund
PO Box 13129
Birmingham, AL 35213
Phone: (205)324-7709
Fax: (205)252-7783
Lana E. Sellers, Managing Director
Preferred Investment Size: $500,000 to $5,000,000. Investment Types: Leveraged buyout, special situations and control block purchases. Industry Preferences: Telephone communications; consumer leisure and recreational products; consumer and industrial, medical and catalog specialty distribution; industrial products and equipment; medical/health related; publishing and education related. Geographic Preferences: Northeast, Southeast, Gulf states, and Middle Atlantic.

Private Capital Corp.
101 Brookwood Pl., 4th Fl.
Birmingham, AL 35209
Phone: (205)879-2722
Fax: (205)879-5121
Preferred Investment Size: $1,000,000 to $5,000,000. Investment Types: Startup, first stage, second stage, mezzanine, leveraged buyout, and special situations. Industry Preferences: Communications; computer related; industrial, and medical product distribution; electronic components and instrumentation; energy/natural resources; medical/health related; education; and finance and insurance. Geographic Preferences: Southeast.

Small Business Clinic of Alabama/AG Bartholomew & Associates
PO Box 231074
Montgomery, AL 36123-1074
Phone: (334)284-3640
Preferred Investment Size: $100,000 to $5,000,000. Investment Types: Startup, first stage, second stage, leveraged buyout, and special situations. Industry Preferences: Communications, computer related, consumer, distribution, industrial products and equipment, medical/health related, education, finance and

insurance, real estate, specialty consulting, and transportation. Geographic Preferences: Southeast.

Southern Development Council
4101 C Wall St.
Montgomery, AL 36106
Phone: (334)244-1801
Free: 800-499-3034
Fax: (334)244-1421
E-mail: sdci@sdcinc.org
Website: http://www.sdcinc.org
Statewide nonprofit financial packaging corporation. Helps small businesses arrange financing.

Tullis Dickerson & Company
2550 Cahaba Rd., Ste. 240
Birmingham, AL 35223
Phone: (205)870-1516
E-mail: lahjc@aol.com
Lynn Hohnke
Investment Types: Seed, research and development, startup, first stage, second stage, mezzanine, leveraged buyout, control block purchases, industry roll ups, and special situations. Industry Preferences: Computer related, genetic engineering, medical/health related, and agriculture. Geographic Preferences: National.

21st Century Health Ventures
One Health South Pkwy.
Birmingham, AL 35243
Phone: (256)268-6250
Fax: (256)970-8928
W. Barry McRae
Preferred Investment Size: $5,000,000. Investment Types: First stage, second stage and leveraged buyout. Industry Preferences: Medical/Health related. Geographic Preferences: Entire U.S.

## Arizona

Carmichael & Company, LLC
2929 N. Central Ave., Ste. 1500
Phoenix, AZ 85012
Phone: (602)266-8660
Website: http://www.carmichaelandco.com
Investment Types: Research and development, startup, first stage, second stage, mezzanine, and leveraged buyout. Industry

Preferences: Communications, computer related, consumer, medical/health related, and aerospace. Geographic Preferences: National.

The Columbine Venture Funds
6155 N. Scottsdale Rd., Ste. 100
Scottsdale, AZ 85250
Phone: (602)661-9222
Fax: (602)661-6262
Investment Types: Seed, research and development, startup, and first stage. Industry Preferences: Diversified technology. Geographic Preferences: Southwest, Rocky Mountains, and West Coast.

Coronado Venture Fund
PO Box 65420
Tucson, AZ 85728-5420
Phone: (520)577-3764
Fax: (520)299-8491
Preferred Investment Size: $100,000. Investment Types: Seed, startup, first and second stage. Industry Preferences: Communications, computer related, electronic components and instrumentation, genetic engineering, industrial products and equipment, medical and health related. Geographic Preferences: No preference for later stage financing. Southwest for seed and startup financing.

Gwynn Financial Services
7350 E. Stetson Dr., Ste. 108-A
Scottsdale, AZ 85251
Phone: (480)947-8700
Fax: (480)947-8766
E-mail: gwynnd@primenet.com
Preferred Investment Size: $250,000 to $5 million. Investment Types: First stage, second stage, mezzanine, and special situations. Industry Preferences: Communications, computer related, consumer, distribution, electronic components and instrumentation, energy/natural resources, genetic engineering, industrial products and equipment, medical/health related, agriculture, education, and finance. Geographic Preferences: Northwest, Midwest, Southwest, Rocky Mountains, West Coast.

McKellar & Co.
311 E. Rose Ln.
Phoenix, AZ 85012-1243
Phone: (602)277-1800
Fax: (602)277-0429
Winston P. McKellar, President
Preferred Investment Size: $250,000 to $5,000,000. Investment Types: First stage, second stage, mezzanine, leveraged buyout and special situations. Industry Preferences: Diversified. Geographic Preferences: Entire U.S.

Miller Capital Corp.
4909 E. McDowell Rd.
Phoenix, AZ 85008
Phone: (602)225-0504
Fax: (602)225-9024
E-mail: tmg@themillergroup.com
Website: http://www.themillergroup.com
Rudy R. Miller, Chairman and President
Preferred Investment Size: $1,000,000 to $5,000,000. Investment Types: First stage, second stage, mezzanine, and special situations. Industry Preferences: Communications, computer related, and distribution. Geographic Preferences: Entire U.S.

Southwest Venture Capital Network
One E. Camelback Rd.
Box 60756
Suite 1100
Phoenix, AZ 85082-0756
Phone: (602)263-2390
Preferred Investment Size: $100,000 to $250,000. Investment Types: Seed, startup, first and second stage. Industry Preferences: Diversified. Geographic Preferences: Southwest, Rocky Mountains.

Valley Ventures
6617155 N. Scottsdale Rd.
Suite 104
Scottsdale, AZ 85250-5412
Phone: (602)661-6600
Fax: (602)661-6262
Preferred Investment Size: $500,000 to $1,000,000. Investment Types: Second stage, mezzanine, and leveraged buyout. Industry Preferences: Diversified. Retailing, real estate, and professional services not considered. Geographic

Preferences: Southwest, Rocky Mountains, and Southern California.

W.B. McKee Securities Inc.
7702 E. Doubletree Ranch Rd.
Suite 230
Scottsdale, AZ 85258
Phone: (602)368-0333
Fax: (602)607-7446
E-mail: corpfin@wbmckee.com
Mark Jazwin, Corporate Finance
Preferred Investment Size: $1,000,000 to $5,000,000. Investment Types: Second stage, mezzanine, and leveraged buyout. Industry Preferences: Communications, computer related, consumer, distribution, electronic components and instrumentation, energy/natural resources, genetic engineering, industrial products and equipment, medical and health related, finance, and transportation. Geographic Preferences: Entire U.S.

## Arkansas

Roher Capital Group, LLC
21405 Walnut Grove Trail
Little Rock, AR 72223
Phone: (501)821-2885
Fax: (501)218-2513
E-mail: mroher@worldnet.att.net
Preferred Investment Size: $1,000,000 to $20,000,000. Investment Types: Second stage, mezzanine, leveraged buyout, special situations, control block purchases, and industry roll ups. Industry Preferences: Communications, consumer products, distribution, energy/natural resources and industrial products and equipment. Geographic Preferences: United States and Canada.

## California

Acacia Venture Partners
101 California St., Ste. 3160
San Francisco, CA 94111
Phone: (415)433-4200
Fax: (415)433-4250
Website: http://www.acaciavp.com
Brian Roberts, Senior Associate
Preferred Investment Size: $2,000,000 to $10,000,000. Investment Types: Seed, startup, first and second stage, mezzanine and leveraged buyout.

Industry Preferences: Computer, and medical/health related. Geographic Preferences: Entire U.S.

Accel Partners (San Francisco)
428 University Ave.
Palo Alto, CA 94301
Phone: (650)614-4800
Fax: (650)614-4880
Website: http://www.accel.com
Preferred Investment Size: $100,000 minimum. Investment Types: Seed, research and development, startup, first and second stage, mezzanine, leveraged buyout, special situations, and control block purchases. Industry Preferences: Communications, computer related, and electronic components and instrumentation. Geographic Preferences: No preference.

Access Venture Partners
4133 Mohr Ave., Ste. H
Pleasanton, CA 94566
Phone: (925)426-9574
Fax: (925)462-4398
Robert W. Rees, II, Managing Director
Preferred Investment Size: $250,000 to $5 million. Investment Types: Seed, startup, first stage, and special situations. Industry Preferences: Diversified. Real estate, oil and gas, motion pictures, and consulting services not considered. Geographic Preferences: Northwest, Southwest, Midwest, Rocky Mountains, and West Coast.

Acer Technology Ventures
2641 Orchard Pkwy.
San Jose, CA 95134
Phone: (408)433-4945
Fax: (408)433-5230
James C. Lu, Managing Director
Preferred Investment Size: $500,000 to $5,000,000. Investment Types: Seed, startup, first and second stage. Industry Preferences: Diversified. Geographic Preferences: Entire U.S. and Canada.

Advanced Technology Ventures
485 Ramona St., Ste. 200
Palo Alto, CA 94301
Phone: (650)321-8601
Fax: (650)321-0934

Steven Baloff, General Partner
Investment Types: Startup, first stage, second stage, and mezzanine. Industry Preferences: Diversified. Geographic Preferences: Natonal.

Advent International Corporation
2180 Sand Hill Rd., Ste. 420
Menlo Park, CA 94025
Phone: (650)233-7500
Fax: (650)233-7515
Investment Types: Startup, first and second stage, mezzanine, leveraged buyout, special situations, recaps, and acquisitions. Industry Preferences: Diversified. Geographic Preferences: Entire U.S. and Canada.

Alpine Technology Ventures
20300 Stevens Creek Boulevard, Ste. 495
Cupertino, CA 95014
Phone: (408)725-1810
Fax: (408)725-1207
E-mail: carol@alpineventures.com
Website: http://www.alpineventures.com
Preferred Investment Size: $500,000 to $6,000,000. Investment Types: Seed, startup, research and development, first and second stage, and mezzanine. Industry Preferences: Communications, computer related, distribution, electronic components and instrumentation, industrial products and equipment. Biotechnology and healthcare not considered. Geographic Preferences: California.

Alta Partners
One Embarcadero Center, Ste. 4050
San Francisco, CA 94111
Phone: (415)362-4022
Fax: (415)362-6178
E-mail: alta@altapartners.com
Website: http://www.altapartners.com
Jean Deleage, Partner
Preferred Investment Size: $1,000,000 to $10,000,000. Investment Types: Seed, startup, first and second stage, and mezzanine. Industry Preferences: Communications, computer related, distribution, electronic components and instrumentation, genetic engineering, industrial products and equipment, medical/health related. Real estate, oil and natural gas

exploration, and environmental not considered. Geographic Preferences: West Coast.

Applied Technology
1010 El Camino Real, Ste. 300
Menlo Park, CA 94025
Phone: (415)326-8622
Fax: (415)326-8163
Eugene Flath, General Partner
Investment Types: Seed, startup, first and second stage. Industry Preferences: Diversified. Geographic Preferences: Entire U.S.

Aspen Ventures
1000 Fremont Ave., Ste. 200
Los Altos, CA 94024
Phone: (650)917-5670
Fax: (650)917-5677
Website: http://
www.aspenventures.com
Alexander Cilento, Partner
Preferred Investment Size: $500,000 to $3,000,000. Investment Policies: Equity. Investment Types: Seed, research and development, startup, first and second stage, special situations. Industry Preferences: Communications, computer related, electronic components and instrumentation. Geographic Preferences: Southwest, and West Coast.

Asset Management Associates Inc.
2275 E. Bayshore, Ste. 150
Palo Alto, CA 94303
Phone: (650)494-7400
Fax: (650)856-1826
E-mail: postmaster@assetman.com
Website: http://www.assetman.com
Preferred Investment Size: $750,000 to $2,000,000. Investment Types: Seed, startup, and first stage. Industry Preferences: High technology. Geographic Preferences: Northeast, West Coast.

August Capital
2480 Sand Hill Rd., Ste. 101
Menlo Park, CA 94025
Phone: (650)234-9900
Fax: (650)234-9910
Andrew S. Rappaport, General Partner
Preferred Investment Size: $1,000,000 to $5,000,000. Investment Types:

Startup, first stage and special situations. Industry Preferences: Communications, computer related, distribution, and electronic components and instrumentation. Real estate, finance, and insurance not considered. Geographic Preferences: Northwest, Southwest, Rocky Mountains, and West Coast.

AVI Management Partners
1 First St., Ste. 2
Los Altos, CA 94022
Phone: (650)949-9862
Fax: (650)949-8510
Brian J. Grossi, General Partner
Preferred Investment Size: $100,000 to $3 million. Investment Policies: Equity only. Investment Types: Seed, startup, first and second stage, and special situations. Industry Preferences: High technology and electronic deals only. Geographic Preferences: West Coast, Silicon Valley/San Francisco Bay area.

Baccharis Capital Inc.
2420 Sand Hill Rd., Ste. 100
Menlo Park, CA 94025
Phone: (650)324-6844
Fax: (650)854-3025
Michelle von Roedelbronn
Preferred Investment Size: $250,000 to $1,000,000. Investment Types: Startup, first stage and second stage, mezzanine and special situations. Industry Preferences: Diversified. Geographic Preferences: West Coast.

BancBoston Capital / BancBoston Ventures
435 Tasso St., Ste. 250
Palo Alto, CA 94301
Phone: (650)470-4100
Fax: (650)853-1425
E-mail: mheymann@bkb.com
Investment Types: First and second stage, mezzanine, leveraged buyouts, special situations, and minority buyouts. Industry Preferences: Diversified. Geographic Preferences: Entire U.S. and Atlantic provinces of Canada.

Bangert Dawes Reade Davis & Thom
220 Montgomery St., Ste. 424
San Francisco, CA 94104
Phone: (415)954-9900

Fax: (415)954-9901
E-mail: bdrdt@pacbell.net
Lambert Thom, Vice President
Preferred Investment Size: $500,000 to $5,000,000. Investment Types: Second stage, mezzanine, leveraged buyout and special situations. Industry Preferences: Diversified. Geographic Preferences: No preference.

BankAmerica Ventures
950 Tower Ln., Ste. 700
Foster City, CA 94404
Phone: (650)378-6000
Fax: (650)378-6040
Anchie Y. Kuo, Managing Director
Preferred Investment Size: $1,000,000 to $12,000,000. Investment Types: Startup, first and second stage, and mezzanine. Industry Preferences: Communications, computer related, medical product distribution, electronic components and instrumentation, genetic engineering, and medical/health related. Retail, real estate, and oil and gas exploration not considered. Geographic Preferences: No preference.

Bastion Capital Corp.
1999 Avenue of the Stars, Ste. 2960
Los Angeles, CA 90067
Phone: (310)788-5700
Fax: (310)277-7582
E-mail: ga@bastioncapital.com
Website: http://
www.bastioncapital.com
James Villanueva, Vice President
Preferred Investment Size: $5,000,000 to $10,000,000. Investment Types: Leveraged buyout, special situations and control block purchases. Industry Preferences: Diversified. Real estate not considered. Geographic Preferences: Entire U.S. and Canada.

Bay Partners
10600 N. De Anza Blvd.
Cupertino, CA 95014-2031
Phone: (408)725-2444
Fax: (408)446-4502
E-mail: partners@baypartners.com
Bob Williams, General Partner
Preferred Investment Size: $1,000,000 to $5,000,000. Investment Types: Seed, startup, first and second stage. Industry Preferences:

Communications and computer related. Geographic Preferences: National.

Benchmark Capital
2480 Sand Hill Rd., Ste. 200
Menlo Park, CA 94025
Phone: (650)854-8180
Fax: (650)854-8183
E-mail: info@benchmark.com
Website: http://www.benchmark.com
Preferred Investment Size: $1,000,000 to $5,000,000. Investment Types: Seed, research and development, startup, first and second stage, and special situations. Industry Preferences: Communications, computer related, and electronic components and instrumentation. Medical/health related, environmental, and biotechnology not considered. Geographic Preferences: Southwest and West Coast.

Berkeley International Capital Corp.
650 California St., Ste. 2800
San Francisco, CA 94108-2609
Phone: (415)249-0450
Fax: (415)392-3929
Website: http://www.berkeleyvc.com
Arthur I. Trueger, Chairman
Preferred Investment Size: $3,000,000 to $15,000,000. Investment Types: Second stage, mezzanine, leveraged buyout and special situations. Industry Preferences: Communications, computer related, distribution, electronic components and instrumentation, industrial products and equipment, and medical/ health related. Geographic Preferences: Entire U.S.

Bessemer Venture Partners (Menlo Park)
535 Middlefield Rd., Ste. 245
Menlo Park, CA 94025
Phone: (650)853-7000
Fax: (650)853-7001
Investment Types: Seed, research and development, start-up, first stages, leveraged buyout, special situations, and control block purchases. Industry Preferences: Communications, computer related, consumer products, distribution, and electronics. Geographic Preferences: National.

BioVentures West LLC
2131 Palomar Airport Rd.
Carlsbad, CA 92009
Phone: (760)431-5104
Fax: (760)431-5105
E-mail: bobrobb123@msn.com
Robert Robb, President
Preferred Investment Size: $100,000 to $1,000,000. Investment Types: Seed, research and development, and startup. Industry Preferences: Genetic engineering, industrial products and equipment, and medical/health related. Geographic Preferences: West Coast.

Bluewater Capital Management Inc.
50 California St., Ste. 3200
San Francisco, CA 94111
Phone: (415)362-5007
Fax: (415)788-6763
Adam L. Rothstein
Preferred Investment Size: $1,000,000 to $25,000,000. Investment Types: Second stage, mezzanine, leveraged buyout, special situations, and control block purchases. Industry Preferences: Diversified high technology. Geographic Preferences: No preference.

Brad Peery Capital Inc.
145 Chapel Pkwy.
Mill Valley, CA 94941
Phone: (415)389-0625
Fax: (415)389-1336
Brad Peery, Chairman
Prefers communications and computer related industry. No geographical preference.

Brentwood Associates (Los Angeles)
11150 Santa Monica Blvd., Ste. 1200
Los Angeles, CA 90025
Phone: (310)477-7678
Fax: (310)477-1868
Preferred Investment Size: $2,000,000 to $5,000,000. Investment Types: Seed, startup, first and second stage, and mezzanine. Industry Preferences: Electronics and medical/health related. Geographic Preferences: Entire U.S. for later-stage, and within two hours of office for start-ups.

Brentwood Associates (Menlo Park)
3000 Sandhill Rd., Ste. 260
Menlo Park, CA 94025

Phone: (650)854-7691
Fax: (650)854-9513

Brentwood Venture Capital
1920 Main St., Ste. 820
Irvine, CA 92614
Phone: (949)251-1010
Fax: (949)251-1011
Preferred Investment Size: $2,000,000 to $5,000,000. Investment Types: Seed, startup, first and second stage, and mezzanine. Industry Preferences: Electronics and medical/health related. Geographic Preferences: Entire U.S. for later-stage, and within two hours of office for start-ups.

Burr, Egan, Deleage, and Co. (San Francisco)
1 Embarcadero Center, Ste. 4050
San Francisco, CA 94111
Phone: (415)362-4022
Fax: (415)362-6178
Private venture capital supplier. Invests start-up, expansion, and acquisitions capital nationwide. Principal concerns are strength of the management team; large, rapidly expanding markets; and unique products for services. Past investments have been made in the fields of biotechnology and pharmaceuticals, cable TV, chemicals/plastics, communications, software, computer systems and peripherals, distributorships, radio common carriers, electronics and electrical components, environmental control, health services, medical devices and instrumentation, and radio and cellular telecommunications. Primarily interested in medical, electronics, and media industries.

Burrill & Company
120 Montgomery St., Ste. 1370
San Francisco, CA 94104
Phone: (415)743-3160
Fax: (415)743-3161
Website: http:// www.burrillandco.com
David Collier, Managing Director
Preferred Investment Size: $500,000 to $5,000,000. Investment Types: Startup, first and second stage, and mezzanine. Industry Preferences:

Diversified. Geographic Preferences: No preference.

Buttonwood Capital Inc.
15250 Ventura Blvd., Ste. 520
Sherman Oaks, CA 94103
Phone: (818)981-2210
Fax: (818)981-2223
Curtice A. Cornell, Managing Director
Preferred Investment Size: $1,000,000 to $5,000,000. Investment Types: Second stage and leveraged buyout. Industry Preferences: Diversified high technology. Biotechnology not considered. Geographic Preferences: Entire U.S. and Canada.

The Cambria Group
1600 El Camino Real Rd., Ste. 155
Menlo Park, CA 94025
Phone: (650)329-8600
Fax: (650)329-8601
Website: http://www.cambriagroup.com
Paul L. Davies, III, Managing Principal
Preferred Investment Size: $500,000 to $1,000,000. Investment Types: Second stage, mezzanine, leveraged buyout, special situations, and control block purchases. Industry Preferences: Diversified. Computer related, financial services, retail, real estate, healthcare, and biotechnology not considered. Geographic Preferences: Entire U.S.

Canaan Partners
2884 Sand Hill Rd., Ste. 115
Menlo Park, CA 94025
Phone: (650)854-8092
Fax: (650)854-8127
Website: http://www.canaan.com
Preferred Investment Size: $1,00,000 to $5,000,000. Investment Types: First and second stage, mezzanine, leverage buyout, acquisition financing. Industry Preferences: Diversified. Geographic Preferences: No preference.

Capstone Ventures
3000 Sand Hill Rd., Bldg. One, Ste. 290
Menlo Park, CA 94025
Phone: (650)854-2523
Fax: (650)854-9010

E-mail: gfischer@capstonevc.com
Website: http://www.capstonevc.com
Eugene J. Fischer
Preferred Investment Size: $500,000 to $5,000,000. Investment Types: Startup, and first and second stage. Industry Preferences: Diversified high technology. Geographic Preferences: Midwest, Rocky Mountains, and West Coast.

Cascade Communications Ventures
60 E. Sir Francis Drake Blvd., Ste. 300
Larkspur, CA 94939
Phone: (415)925-6500
Fax: (415)925-6501
Preferred Investment Size: $1,000,000 to $5,000,000. Investment Types: Leveraged buyout and special situations. Industry Preferences: Communications. Geographic Preferences: Entire U.S.

Centex Securities Inc.
1020 Prospect St., Ste. 200
La Jolla, CA 92037
Phone: (619)456-8200
E-mail: regraves1@aol.com
Douglas Gale
Preferred Investment Size: $5,000,000 to $50,000,000. Investment Types: First and second stage, mezzanine, leveraged buyout, special situations, and control block purchases. Industry Preferences: Diversified. Geographic Preferences: No preference.

Charter Ventures
525 University Ave., Ste. 1500
Palo Alto, CA 94301
Phone: (415)325-6953
Fax: (415)325-4762
Preferred Investment Size: $250,000 maximum. Investment Types: Seed, startup, first and second stage, mezzanine, leveraged buyout, and special situations. Industry Preferences: Diversified. Geographic Preferences: No preference.

CMEA Ventures
235 Montgomery St., Ste. 920
San Francisco, CA 94401
Phone: (415)352-1520
Fax: (415)352-1524
Website: http://www.cmeaventures.com

Thomas R. Baruch, General Partner
Preferred Investment Size: $100,000 to $1,000,000. Investment Types: Seed, startup, first and second stage. Industry Preferences: Diversified high technology. Geographic Preferences: No preference.

Comdisco Venture Group (Silicon Valley)
3000 Sand Hill Rd., Bldg. 1, Ste. 155
Menlo Park, CA 94025
Phone: (415)854-9484
Fax: (415)854-4026
Preferred Investment Size: $250,000 to $500,000. Investment Types: Seed, startup, first and second stage, receivables, loans, and equipment leases. Industry Preferences: Diversified. Geographic Preferences: No preference.

Commtech International
535 Middlefield Rd., Ste. 200
Menlo Park, CA 94025
Phone: (650)328-0190
Fax: (650)328-6442
Preferred Investment Size: $100,000 to $250,000. Investment Types: Seed, startup, research and development. Industry Preferences: Diversified. Geographic Preferences: West Coast.

Communications Ventures
505 Hamilton Avenue, Ste. 305
Palo Alto, CA 94301
Phone: (650)325-9600
Fax: (650)325-9608
Website: http://www.comven.com
Preferred Investment Size: $500,000 to $5,000,000. Investment Types: Seed. Industry Preferences: Communications. Geographic Preferences: No preference.

Compass Technology Partners
1550 El Camino Real, Ste. 275
Menlo Park, CA 94025-4111
Phone: (650)322-7595
Fax: (650)322-0588
David G. Arscott, General Partner
Preferred Investment Size: $250,000 to $1,000,000. Investment Types: Mezzanine, leveraged buyout, and special situations. Industry Preferences: Diversified high technology. Geographic Preferences: National.

Comventures
505 Hamilton Ave., No. 305
Palo Alto, CA 94301
Phone: (650)325-9600
Fax: (650)325-9608
Website: http://www.comven.com
Michael Rolnick
Investment Types: Seed. Industry
Preferences: Communications and
computer related. Geographic
Preferences: National.

Convergence Partners
3000 Sand Hill Rd., Ste. 235
Menlo Park, CA 94025
Phone: (650)854-3010
Fax: (650)854-3015
Website: http://
www.convergencepartners.com
Preferred Investment Size: $100,000
to $5,000,000. Investment Types:
Seed, startup, research and
development, early and late stage, and
mezzanine. Industry Preferences:
Communications, computer related,
electronic components and
instrumentation, and interactive
media. Geographic Preferences: West
Coast.

Cornerstone Ventures
750 Menlo Ave., Ste. 350
Menlo Park, CA 94025
Phone: (650)473-9780
Fax: (650)473-9784
Preferred Investment Size: $1,000,000
to $5,000,000. Investment Types:
Second stage, mezzanine, leveraged
buyout, special situations, and control
block purchases. Industry
Preferences: Diversified technology.
Geographic Preferences: Southwest,
West Coast, and Western Canada.

Crosspoint Venture Partners
2925 Woodside Rd.
Woodside, CA 94062
Phone: (650)851-7600
Fax: (650)851-7661
E-mail: partners@crosspointvc.com
Preferred Investment Size: $100,000
to $5,000,000. Investment Types:
Seed and startup. Industry
Preferences: Communications,
computer related, and
communications and medical product
distribution. Geographic Preferences:

Northwest, Southwest, Rocky
Mountains, and West Coast.

Crosspoint Venture Partners (Irvine)
18552 MacArthur Blvd.
Irvine, CA 92612
Phone: (949)852-1611
Fax: (949)852-9804
E-mail: partners@crosspointvc.com
Website: http://
www.crosspointvc.com
Preferred Investment Size: $100,000
to $5,000,000. Investment Types:
Seed and startup. Industry
Preferences: Communications,
computer related, and
communications and medical product
distribution. Geographic Preferences:
Northwest, Southwest, Rocky
Mountains, and West Coast.

Dakota Capital
PO Box 1025
Menlo Park, CA 94025
Phone: (650)853-0600
Fax: (650)851-4899
E-mail: info@dakota.com
Stephen A. Meyer, General Partner
Preferred Investment Size: $250,000
to $1,000,000. Investment Types:
Early and later stages, and special
situations. Industry Preferences:
Diversified computer and
communications technology,
education, and publishing.
Geographic Preferences: National.

Davis Group
PO Box 69953
Los Angeles, CA 90069-0953
Phone: (310)659-6327
Fax: (310)659-6337
Roger W. Davis, Chairman
Preferred Investment Size: $100,000
minimum. Investment Types: Early
stages, leveraged buyouts, and special
situations. Industry Preferences:
Diversified. Geographic Preferences:
National.

Delphi Ventures
3000 Sand Hill Rd.
Bldg. One, Ste. 135
Menlo Park, CA 94025
Phone: (650)854-9650
Fax: (650)854-2961
Investment Types: Seed, startup, first
and second stage. Industry

Preferences: Genetic engineering,
medical/health related. Geographic
Preferences: Western U.S.

Developers Equity Capital Corp.
447 S. Robertson Blvd., Ste. 101
Beverly Hills, CA 90211
Phone: (310)550-7552
Fax: (310)550-7529
Preferred Investment Size: $100,000
to $500,000. Investment Types: Seed,
startup, and leverage buyout. Industry
Preferences: Diversified. Geographic
Preferences: Within two hours of
office.

Domain Associates
28202 Cabot Rd., Ste. 200
Laguna Niguel, CA 92677
Phone: (949)347-2446
Fax: (949)347-9720
Website: http://www.domainvc.com
Preferred Investment Size: $1,000,000
to $20,000,000. Investment Types:
Seed, first stage and second stage.
Industry Preferences: Electronics,
genetic engineering, and medical/
health related. Geographic
Preferences: Entire U.S.

Dominion Ventures, Inc.
44 Montgomery St., Ste. 4200
San Francisco, CA 94104
Phone: (415)362-4890
Fax: (415)394-9245
Preferred Investment Size: $1,000,000
to $10,000,000. Investment Types:
First and second stage, and
mezzanine. Industry Preferences:
Diversified. Geographic Preferences:
No preference.

Draper, Fisher, Jurvetson
400 Seaport Ct., Ste.250
Redwood City, CA 94063
Phone: (415)599-9000
Fax: (415)599-9726
E-mail: mail@draprvc.com
Website: http://www.draprvc.com
Karen Mostes
Investment Types: Seed, startup, and
first stage. Industry Preferences:
Communications, computer related,
electronic components and
instrumentation. Geographic
Preferences: West Coast.

Drysdale Enterprises
177 Bovet Rd., Ste. 600

San Mateo, CA 94402
Phone: (650)341-6336
Fax: (650)341-1329
E-mail: drysdale@aol.com
George M. Drysdale, President
Preferred Investment Size: $500,000
to $5,000,000. Investment Types:
First and second stage, mezzanine,
leveraged buyout, and special
situations. Industry Preferences:
Diversified. Geographic Preferences:
West Coast.

DSV Partners
1920 Main St., Ste. 820
Irvine, CA 92614
Phone: (949)475-4242
Fax: (949)475-1950
James R. Bergman, Partner
Preferred Investment Size: $1,000,000
maximum. Investment Types: Startup
and first stage. Industry Preferences:
Diversified. Real estate not
considered. Geographic Preferences:
Entire U.S.

El Dorado Ventures (Cupertino)
2400 Sand Hill Rd., Ste. 100
Menlo Park, CA 94025
Phone: (650)854-1200
Fax: (650)854-1202
Website: http://
www.eldoradoventures.com
Preferred Investment Size: $500,000
to $5,000,000. Investment Types:
Seed, startup, first and second stage.
Industry Preferences:
Communications, computer related,
electronics, and industrial products
and equipment. Geographic
Preferences: West Coast.

Eucalyptus Venture Management,
L.L.C.
1 Bush St., 12th Fl.
San Francisco, CA 94104
Phone: (415)371-4240
Fax: (415)439-3621
Bruce E. Crocker, Managing Director
Preferred Investment Size: $1,000,000
to $5,000,000. Investment Types:
Early and later stages. Industry
Preferences: Diversified computer and
communications technology, and
healthcare industry. Geographic
Preferences: National.

Far East Capital Corp.
350 S. Grand Ave., Ste. 1100
Los Angeles, CA 90071
Phone: (213)687-1361
Fax: (213)617-7939
E-mail:
free@fareastnationalbank.com
Preferred Investment Size: $100,000
to $250,000. Investment Types: First
stage, second stage, mezzanine, and
special situations. Industry
Preferences: Communications,
computer related, electronic
components and instrumentation,
genetic engineering, medical/health
related. Geographic Preferences: West
Coast.

Forrest, Binkley & Brown
840 Newport Ctr. Dr., Ste. 480
Newport Beach, CA 92660
Phone: (949)729-3222
Fax: (949)729-3226
Jeff Brown, Partner
Investment Types: First stage, second
stage, leveraged buyout, and special
situations. Industry Preferences:
Diversified. Communications,
computer related, consumer,
electronic components and
instrumentation, genetic engineering,
industrial products and equipment,
medical/health related, agriculture,
education, and finance. Geographic
Preferences: National.

Forward Ventures
9255 Towne Centre Dr.
San Diego, CA 92121
Phone: (858)677-6077
Fax: (858)452-8799
E-mail: info@forwardventure.com
Standish M. Fleming, Partner
Preferred Investment Size: $250,000
to $5,000,000. Investment Types:
Seed, research and development,
startup, first and second stage.
Industry Preferences: Genetic
engineering and medical/health
related. Geographic Preferences: West
Coast.

Gatx Capital
Four Embarcadero Center, Ste. 2200
San Francisco, CA 94904
Phone: (415)955-3200
Fax: (415)955-3449

Preferred Investment Size: $500,000
to $5,000,000. Investment Types:
Early and later stages, and leveraged
buyouts. Industry Preferences:
Diversified technologies, forestry, and
agriculture. Geographic Preferences:
National and Canada.

Glynn Ventures
3000 Sand Hill Rd., Bldg. 4, Ste. 225
Menlo Park, CA 94025
Phone: (650)854-2215
John W. Glynn, Jr., General Partner
Preferred Investment Size: $250,000
to $500,000. Investment Types: Later
stages. Industry Preferences:
Diversified computer and
communications technology, and
consumer services. Geographic
Preferences: East and West Coast.

Greylock Management (Palo Alto)
755 Page Mill Rd., Ste. A-100
Palo Alto, CA 94304-1018
Phone: (650)493-5525
Fax: (650)493-5575
Venture capital firm providing all
stages of financing. Areas of interest
include computer software,
communications, health,
biotechnology, publishing, and
specialty retail.

Hallador Venture Partners, L.L.C.
740 University Ave., Ste. 110
Sacramento, CA 95825-6710
Phone: (916)920-0191
Fax: (916)920-5188
E-mail: chris@hallador.com
Chris L. Branscum, Managing
Director
Preferred Investment Size: $250,000
to $1,000,000. Investment Types:
Early and later stages. Industry
Preferences: Diversified computer and
communications technology, and
electronic semiconductors.
Geographic Preferences: Western
U.S.

Hambrecht and Quist (San Francisco)
1 Bush St.
San Francisco, CA 94104
Phone: (415)439-3300
Fax: (415)677-7747
Prefers to invest in computer
technology, environmental

technology, and biotechnology. Investments from $500,000.

HMS Capital Partners
1 First St., Ste. 6
Los Altos, CA 94022
Phone: (650)917-0390
Fax: (650)917-0394
Preferred Investment Size: $100,000 to $500,000. Investment Types: Seed, startup, first stage, and leveraged buyout. Industry Preferences: Communications, computer related, electronics, and industrial products. Geographic Preferences: No preference.

Idanta Partners Ltd.
4660 La Jolla Village Dr., Ste. 850
San Diego, CA 92122
Phone: (619)452-9690
Fax: (619)452-2013
Preferred Investment Size: $500,000. Investment Types: Seed, startup, first and second stage. Industry Preferences: Diversified. Geographic Preferences: Entire U.S.

Idealab Capital Partners
130 W. Union St.
Pasadena, CA 91103
Phone: (626)535-2870
Fax: (626)535-2881
E-mail: venture.info@icp.com
Website: http://www.icp.com
Jim Armstrong, Principal
Preferred Investment Size: $500,000 to $4,000,000. Investment Types: Early stages. Industry Preferences: Data communications, Internet, retailing, and computer distribution. Geographic Preferences: National.

Inman and Bowman
4 Orinda Way, Bldg. D, Ste. 150
Orinda, CA 94563
Phone: (510)253-1611
Fax: (510)253-9037
Preferred Investment Size: $500,000 to $1,000,000. Investment Types: Startup, first and second stage. Industry Preferences: Diversified technology. Geographic Preferences: West Coast.

Institutional Venture Partners
3000 Sand Hill Rd., Bldg. 2, Ste. 290
Menlo Park, CA 94025
Phone: (650)854-0132

Fax: (650)854-5762
E-mail: litesci@ivp.com
Website: http://www.ivp.com
Preferred Investment Size: $500,000 to $5,000,000. Investment Types: Seed, startup, first and second stage, mezzanine, and special situations. Industry Preferences: Diversified. Geographic Preferences: Entire U.S.

Interwest Partners (Menlo Park)
3000 Sand Hill Rd., Bldg. 3, Ste. 255
Menlo Park, CA 94025-7112
Phone: (650)854-8585
Fax: (650)854-4706
Website: http://www.interwest.com
Preferred Investment Size: $1,000,000 to $17,500,000. Investment Types: Seed, research and development, startup, first and second stage, mezzanine, and special situations. Industry Preferences: Diversified. Oil and gas exploration and real estate not considered. Geographic Preferences: Entire U.S.

Jafco America Ventures, Inc.
505 Hamilton Ste. 310
Palto Alto, CA 94301
Phone: (650)463-8800
Fax: (650)463-8801
Website: http://www.jafco.com
Barry Schiffman, Pres.
Preferred Investment Size: $1,000,000 to $5,000,000. Investment Types: First and second stage and mezzanine. Industry Preferences: Diversified technology. Geographic Preferences: Entire U.S.

Kleiner Perkins Caufield & Byers (Menlo Park)
2750 Sand Hill Rd.
Menlo Park, CA 94025
Phone: (650)233-2750
Fax: (650)233-0300
Website: http://www.kpcb.com
Provides seed, start-up, second and third-round, and bridge financing to companies on the West Coast. Preferred industries of investment include electronics, computers, software, telecommunications, biotechnology, medical devices, and pharmaceuticals.

Kline Hawkes California SBIC, LP
11726 San Vicente Blvd., Ste. 300

Los Angeles, CA 90049
Phone: (310)442-4700
Fax: (310)442-4707
Robert M. Freiland, Partner
Preferred Investment Size: $1,000,000 to $10,000,000. Investment Types: Second stage, leveraged buyout, special situations, and inter-generational buyouts. Industry Preferences: Diversified technology. Geographic Preferences: Northwest, Southwest, and California.

Lawrence Financial Group
701 Teakwood
PO Box 491773
Los Angeles, CA 90049
Phone: (310)471-4060
Fax: (310)472-3155
E-mail: lnhurwitz@aol.com
Preferred Investment Size: $100,000 to $1,000,000. Investment Types: Late stages. Industry Preferences: Diversified. Geographic Preferences: West Coast.

Makenna Delaney & Sullivan, L.L.C.
5973 Avenida Encinas, Ste. 216
Carlsbad, CA 92008
Phone: (760)931-2500
Fax: (760)931-2503
E-mail: rs@venturefinance.com
Website: http://www.venturefinance.com
Robert Sullivan, CEO
Preferred Investment Size: $500,000 to $5,000,000. Investment Types: Early and later stages, leveraged buyout, and private placements. Industry Preferences: Diversified. Geographic Preferences: National and Canada.

Marwit Capital LLC
180 Newport Center Dr., Ste. 200
Newport Beach, CA 92660
Phone: (949)640-6234
Fax: (949)720-8077
Website: http://www.marwit.com
Thomas W. Windsor, Vice President
A small business investment corporation. Provides financing for leveraged buyouts, mergers, acquisitions, and expansion stages. Investments are in the $500,000 to $5 million range. Does not provide financing for start-ups or real estate ventures.

Matrix Partners
2500 Sand Hill Rd., Ste. 113
Menlo Park, CA 94025
Phone: (650)854-3131
Fax: (650)854-3296
Website: http://
www.matrixpartners.com
Andrew W. Verlahen, General Partner
Preferred Investment Size: $500,000
to $5,000,000. Investment Types:
Startup, first and second stage, and
leveraged buyout. Industry
Preferences: Communications,
computer related, and electronic
components and instrumentation.
Geographic Preferences: Entire U.S.

Mayfield Fund
2800 Sand Hill Rd.
Menlo Park, CA 94025
Phone: (650)854-5560
Fax: (650)854-5712
Preferred Investment Size: $250,000
to $5,000,000. Investment Types:
Seed, startup, first and second stage.
Industry Preferences: Diversified.
Real estate, oil and gas, and motion
pictures not considered. Geographic
Preferences: Northwest, East Coast,
Rocky Mountains, and West Coast.

McCown De Leeuw and Co. (Menlo
Park)
3000 Sand Hill Rd., Bldg. 3, Ste. 290
Menlo Park, CA 94025-7111
Phone: (650)854-6000
Fax: (650)854-0853
Robert B. Hellman, Managing
Member
Preferred Investment Size:
$20,000,000 minimum. Investment
Types: Leveraged buyout, special
situations, and recapitalization.
Industry Preferences: Diversified.
Geographic Preferences: Entire U.S.

Medicus Venture Partners
2882 Sand Hill Rd., Ste. 116
Menlo Park, CA 94025
Phone: (650)854-7100
Fax: (650)854-5700
E-mail: fred@medicusvc.com
Website: http://www.medicusvc.com
Fred Dotzler, General Partner
Preferred Investment Size: $100,000
to $5,000,000. Investment Types:
Early stages. Industry Preferences:
Genetic engineering and healthcare

industry. Geographic Preferences:
Western U.S.

Menlo Ventures
3000 Sand Hill Rd., Bldg. 4, Ste. 100
Menlo Park, CA 94025
Phone: (650)854-8540
Fax: (650)854-7059
H. DuBose Montgomery, General
Partner and Managing Director
Venture capital supplier. Provides
start-up and expansion financing to
companies with experienced
management teams, distinctive
product lines, and large growing
markets. Primary interest is in
technology-oriented, service,
consumer products, and distribution
companies. Investments range from
$1,000,000 to $2 million; also
provides capital for leveraged
buyouts.

Merrill Pickard Anderson & Eyre
2480 Sand Hill Rd., Ste. 200
Menlo Park, CA 94025
Phone: (650)854-8600
Fax: (650)854-8183
Preferred Investment Size: $5,000,000
maximum. Investment Types: Seed,
startup, first and second stage.
Industry Preferences: Diversified
technology. Geographic Preferences:
No preference.

National Investment Management,
Inc.
2601 Airport Dr., Ste.210
Torrance, CA 90505
Phone: (310)784-7600
Fax: (310)784-7605
E-mail: robins621@aol.com
Preferred Investment Size: $1,000,000
to $5,000,000. Investment Types:
Leveraged buyout. Industry
Preferences: Consumer products and
retailing, distribution, industrial
products and equipment, medical/
health related, and publishing. Real
estate deals not considered.
Geographic Preferences: Entire U.S.

NC Berkowitz & Co.
1095 Market St.
San Francisco, CA 94103
Phone: (415)255-9781
Fax: (415)255-9392
E-mail: nathaniels@yahoo.com

Nathaniel Berkowitz
Preferred Investment Size: $100,000
to $250,000. Investment Types: Seed,
startup, first stage, leveraged buyout,
and special situations. Industry
Preferences: Diversified. Geographic
Preferences: Entire U.S.

New Enterprise Associates (Menlo
Park)
2490 Sand Hill Rd.
Menlo Park, CA 94025
Phone: (650)854-9499
Fax: (650)854-9397
Ronald H. Kase, General Partner
Preferred Investment Size: $100,000
to $5,000,000. Investment Types:
Seed, startup, first and second stage,
mezzanine, and incubator. Industry
Preferences: Diversified technology.
Geographic Preferences: No
preference.

New Enterprise Associates (San
Francisco)
2490 Sand Hill Road
Menlo Park, CA 94025
Phone: (650)854-9499
Fax: (650)854-9397
Website: http://www.nea.com
Venture capital supplier. Concentrates
in technology-based industries that
have the potential for product
innovation, rapid growth, and high
profit margins.

New Vista Capital
540 Cowper St., Ste. 200
Palo Alto, CA 94301
Phone: (650)329-9333
Fax: (650)328-9438
E-mail: fgreene@nvcap.com
Frank Greene
Investment Types: Seed, startup, first
stage, second stage. Industry
Preferences: Diversified.
Communications, computer related,
energy/natural, medical and health
related. Geographic Preferences:
Western U.S., Rocky Mountains.

Newbury Ventures
535 Pacific Ave., 2nd Fl.
San Francisco, CA 94133
Phone: (415)296-7408
Fax: (415)296-7416
Website: http://
www.newburyven.com

Preferred Investment Size: $500,000 to $1,000,000. Investment Types: Early and later stages, and leveraged buyout. Industry Preferences: Diversified high technology. Geographic Preferences: Eastern and Western U.S. and Canada.

Norwest Venture Capital (Palo Alto)
245 Lytton Ave., Ste. 250
Palo Alto, CA 94301-1426
Phone: (650)321-8000
Fax: (650)321-8010
Charles B. Lennin, Partner
Preferred Investment Size: $2,000,000 to $3,000,000. Investment Types: Seed, startup, first and second stage, mezzanine, leveraged buyout, and special situations. Industry Preferences: Diversified. Geographic Preferences: No preference.

Novus Ventures
20111 Stevens Creek Blvd., Ste. 130
Cupertino, CA 95014
Phone: (408)252-3900
Fax: (408)252-1713
Dan Tompkins, Managing General Partner
Preferred Investment Size: $250,000 to $1 Million. Investment Types: First and second stage. Industry Preferences: Information technology. Geographic Preferences: Western U.S.

Nu Capital Access Group, Ltd.
7677 Oakport St., Ste. 105
Oakland, CA 94621
Phone: (510)635-7345
Fax: (510)635-7068
Preferred Investment Size: $500,000 to $2,500,000. Investment Types: Early and later stages, and special situations. Industry Preferences: Diversified consumer products and services, food and industrial product distribution. Geographic Preferences: Western U.S.

Oak Investment Partners
525 University Ave., Ste. 1300
Palo Alto, CA 94301
Phone: (650)614-3700
Fax: (650)328-6345
Website: http://www.oakinv.com
Preferred Investment Size: $250,000 to $5,000,000. Investment Types:

Seed, startup, first stage, leveraged buyout, and special situations. Industry Preferences: Communications, computer related, consumer restaurants and retailing, electronics, genetic engineering, and medical/health related. Geographic Preferences: No preference.

Onset Ventures
2400 Sand Hill Rd.
Cupertino, CA 94025
Phone: (650)529-0700
Fax: (650)529-0777
E-mail: menlopark@onset.com
Investment Types: Seed, startup, first stage, second stage. Industry Preferences: Communications, computer related, medical and health related. Geographic Preferences: California.

Opportunity Capital Partners
2201 Walnut Ave., Ste. 210
Fremont, CA 94538
Phone: (510)795-7000
Fax: (510)494-5439
Peter Thompson, Managing Partner
Preferred Investment Size: $750,000 to $2,500,000. Investment Types: Second stage, mezzanine, leveraged buyouts, and industry roll ups. Industry Preferences: Communications, consumer franchise businesses, electronics, industrial products, medical/health related, and transportation. Geographic Preferences: No preference.

Opportunity Capital Partners
2201 Walnut Ave., Ste. 210
Fremont, CA 94538
Phone: (510)795-7000
Fax: (510)494-5439
Peter Thompson, Managing Partner
Preferred Investment Size: $750,000 to $2,500,000. Investment Types: Second stage, mezzanine, leveraged buyout, and industry roll ups. Industry Preferences: Communications, franchise businesses, electronic components, industrial equipment and machinery, and medical/health related. Geographic Preferences: Entire U.S.

Paragon Venture Partners
3000 Sand Hill Rd., Bldg. 1, Ste. 275

Menlo Park, CA 94025
Phone: (650)854-8000
Fax: (650)854-7260
Private venture capital firm. Maximum investment is $500,000.

Pathfinder Venture Capital Funds (Menlo Park)
3000 Sand Hill Rd., Bldg. 1, Ste. 290
Menlo Park, CA 94025
Phone: (650)854-2523
Fax: (650)854-9010
E-mail: jahrens620@aol.com
Jack K. Ahrens, II, Investment Officer
Preferred Investment Size: $250,000 to $500,000. Investment Types: Seed, startup, first and second stage, mezzanine, leveraged buyout, and special situations. Industry Preferences: Diversified technology. Geographic Preferences: Entire U.S. and Canada.

Patricof & Co. Ventures, Inc. (Palo Alto)
2100 Geng Rd., Ste. 150
Palo Alto, CA 94303
Phone: (650)494-9944
Fax: (650)494-6751
Website: http://www.patricof.com
Preferred Investment Size: $5,000,000 to $25,000,000. Investment Types: Seed, startup, first and second stage, mezzanine, and leveraged buyout. Industry Preferences: Diversified. Geographic Preferences: No preference.

Phoenix Growth Capital Corp.
2401 Kerner Blvd.
San Rafael, CA 94901
Phone: (415)485-4569
Fax: (415)485-4663
E-mail: nnelson@phxa.com
Preferred Investment Size: $250,000 to $1,000,000. Investment Types: First and second stage, and mezzanine. Industry Preferences: Communications, computer related, consumer retailing, distribution, electronics, genetic engineering, medical/health related, education, publishing, and transportation. Geographic Preferences: Entire U.S.

Quest Ventures (San Francisco)
333 Bush St., Ste. 1750
San Francisco, CA 94104

Phone: (415)782-1414
Fax: (415)782-1415
E-mail: ruby@crownadvisors.com
Lucien Ruby, General Partner
Preferred Investment Size: $100,000
maximum. Investment Types: Seed
and special situations. Industry
Preferences: Diversified. Geographic
Preferences: No preference.

Redleaf Venture Management
14395 Saratoga Ave., Ste. 130
Saratoga, CA 95070
Phone: (408)868-0800
Fax: (408)868-0810
E-mail: nancy@redleaf.com
Website: http://www.redleaf.com
Robert von Goeben, Director
Preferred Investment Size: $1,000,000
to $4,000,000. Investment Policies:
Equity. Investment Types: Early and
late stage. Industry Preferences:
Internet business related. Geographic
Preferences: Northwest and Silicon
Valley.

Riordan Lewis & Haden
300 S. Grand Ave., 29th Fl.
Los Angeles, CA 90071
Phone: (213)229-8500
Fax: (213)229-8597
Preferred Investment Size: $2,000,000
to $20,000,000. Investment Types:
Leveraged buyouts, and special
situations. Industry Preferences:
Diversified. Geographic Preferences:
West Coast, within two hours of
office.

Robertson-Stephens Co.
555 California St., Ste. 2600
San Francisco, CA 94104
Phone: (415)781-9700
Fax: (415)781-2556
Website: http://
www.omegaadventures.com
Private venture capital firm.
Considers investments in any
attractive merging-growth area,
including product and service
companies. Key preferences include
health care, communications and
technology, biotechnology, software,
and information services. Maximum
investment is $5 million.

Rosewood Capital, L.P.
One Maritime Plaza, Ste. 1330

San Francisco, CA 94111-3503
Phone: (415)362-5526
Fax: (415)362-1192
Website: http://www.rosewoodvc.com
Kevin Reilly, Vice President
Preferred Investment Size: $1,000,000
to $3,000,000. Investment Policies:
Equity. Investment Types: Later
stages, leveraged buyout, and special
situations. Industry Preferences:
Consumer and Internet related.
Geographic Preferences: National.

Sandton Financial Group
21550 Oxnard St., Ste. 300
Woodland Hills, CA 91367
Phone: (818)702-9283
Preferred Investment Size: $100,000
to $250,000. Investment Types: Early
and later stages, and special
situations. Industry Preferences: No
preference. Geographic Preferences:
National and Canada.

Sequoia Capital
3000 Sand Hill Rd., Bldg. 4, Ste. 280
Menlo Park, CA 94025
Phone: (650)854-3927
Fax: (650)854-2977
E-mail: sequoia@sequoiacap.com
Website: http://www.sequoiacap.com
Private venture capital partnership
with $700 million under management.
Provides financing for all stages of
development of well-managed
companies with exceptional growth
prospects in fast-growth industries.
Past investments have been made in
computers and peripherals,
communications, health care,
biotechnology, and medical
instruments and devices. Investments
range from $100,000 for early stage
companies to $1 million for late stage
accelerates.

Sierra Ventures
3000 Sand Hill Rd., Bldg. 4, Ste. 210
Menlo Park, CA 94025
Phone: (650)854-1000
Fax: (650)854-5593
Preferred Investment Size: $1,000,000
maximum. Investment Types: Seed,
startup, first and second stage, and
leveraged buyout. Industry
Preferences: Diversified. Geographic
Preferences: East and West Coast.

Sigma Partners
2884 Sand Hill Rd., Ste. 121
Menlo Park, CA 94025-7022
Phone: (650)854-1300
Fax: (650)854-1323
E-mail: info@sigmapartners.com
Website: http://
www.sigmapartners.com
Lawrence G. Finch, Partner
Independent venture capital
partnership. Prefers to invest in the
following areas: communications,
computer hardware, computer
software, manufacturing, medical
equipment, and semiconductor capital
equipment. Avoids investing in
construction, hotels, leasing, motion
pictures, and natural resources.
Minimum initial commitment is
$2,000,000.

Silicon Valley Bank
3003 Tasman
Santa Clara, CA 95054
Phone: (408)654-7400
Fax: (408)727-8728
Investment Types: Startup, first stage,
second stage, mezzanine. Industry
Preferences: Diversified. Geographic
Preferences: National.

Sorrento Associates, Inc.
4370 LaJolla Village Dr., Ste. 1040
San Diego, CA 92122
Phone: (619)452-3100
Fax: (619)452-7607
Website: http://
www.sorrentoventures.com
Vincent J. Burgess, Vice President
Preferred Investment Size: $500,000
to $7,000,000. Investment Policies:
Equity only. Investment Types: Start-
up, first and second stage, leveraged
buyout, special situations, and control
block purchases. Industry
Preferences: Medicine, health,
communications, electronics, special
retail. Geographic Preferences: West
Coast.

Sprout Group (Menlo Park)
3000 Sand Hill Rd.
Bldg. 3, Ste. 170
Menlo Park, CA 94025
Phone: (650)234-2700
Fax: (650)234-2779
Investment Types: Seed, startup, first
and second stage, mezzanine,

leveraged buyout, and special situations. Industry Preferences: Diversified technology. Geographic Preferences: National.

Summit Partners (Palo Alto)
499 Hamilton Ave., Ste. 200
Palo Alto, CA 94301
Phone: (650)321-1166
Fax: (650)321-1188
Website: http://
www.summitpartners.com
Ernest K. Jacquet
Preferred Investment Size: $5,000,000 maximum. Investment Types: First and second stage, mezzanine, leveraged buyout, special situations, and control block purchases. Industry Preferences: Diversified. Geographic Preferences: Entire U.S. and Canada.

Sundance Venture Partners, L.P.
10600 North de Anza Blvd., Ste. 215
Cupertino, CA 95014
Phone: (408)257-8100
Preferred Investment Size: $100,000 to $250,000. Investment Types: First and second stage, mezzanine, leveraged buyout, special situations, and subordinated debt with warrants. Industry Preferences: No preference. Geographic Preferences: Southwest and West Coast.

Sutter Hill Ventures
755 Page Mill Rd., Ste. A-200
Palo Alto, CA 94304
Phone: (650)493-5600
Fax: (650)858-1854
E-mail: shv@shv.com
Preferred Investment Size: $100,000 to $2,000,000. Investment Types: Seed, startup, first and second stage, and purchase of secondary positions. Industry Preferences: Diversified. Geographic Preferences: Entire U.S.

TA Associates (Menlo Park)
70 Willow Rd., Ste. 100
Menlo Park, CA 94025
Phone: (650)328-1210
Fax: (650)326-4933
Michael C. Child, Managing Director
Private venture capital firm. Prefers technology companies and leveraged buyouts. Provides $5 million in investments. No geographical preference.

Technology Funding
2000 Alameda de las Pulgas, Ste. 250
San Mateo, CA 94403
Phone: (415)345-2200
Fax: (415)345-1797
Peter F. Bernardoni, Partner
Small business investment corporation. Provides primarily late first-stage, early second-stage, and mezzanine equity financing. Also offers secured debt with equity participation to venture capital backed companies. Investments range from $250,000 to $500,000.

Thompson Clive Inc.
3000 Sand Hill Rd., Bldg. 1, Ste. 185
Menlo Park, CA 94025-7102
Phone: (650)854-0314
Fax: (650)854-0670
E-mail: mail@tcvc.com
Website: http://www.tcvc.com
Greg Ennis, Principal
Preferred Investment Size: $500,000 to $1,000,000. Investment Types: Early and later stages, leveraged buyouts, and special situations. Industry Preferences: Diversified computer and communications technology, electronic instrumentation, genetic engineering, and education. Geographic Preferences: National and Western Canada.

Ticonderoga Capital Inc.
555 California St., No. 4950
San Francisco, CA 94104
Phone: (415)296-7900
Fax: (415)296-8956
Graham K Crooke, Partner
Preferred Investment Size: $5,000,000 maximum. Investment Types: Second stage, mezzanine, leveraged buyout, and consolidation strategies. Industry Preferences: Diversified. Geographic Preferences: Entire U.S. and Canada.

Trinity Ventures Ltd.
3000 Sand Hill Rd., Bldg. 1, Ste. 240
Menlo Park, CA 94025
Phone: (650)854-9500
Fax: (650)854-9501
Website: http://
www.trinityventures.com
Lawrence K. Orr, General Partner
Preferred Investment Size: $1,000,000 maximum. Investment Types: Startup,

first and second stage, mezzanine, and leveraged buyout. Industry Preferences: Communications, computer related, and consumer products, services, food and beverage, restaurants, and retailing. Geographic Preferences: Northwest, Southwest, Midwest, Rocky Mountains, and West Coast.

Triune Capital
1888 Century Park East, Ste. 1900
Los Angeles, CA 90067
Phone: (310)284-6800
Fax: (310)284-3290
Preferred Investment Size: $1,000,000 to $5,000,000. Investment Types: Late stage and special situations. Industry Preferences: Diversified technology. Geographic Preferences: West Coast.

Turner Venture Associates
268 Bush St., Penthouse 10
San Francisco, CA 94104-3402
Phone: (415)398-6325
Fax: (415)398-3220
Preferred Investment Size: $100,000 to $500,000. Investment Types: Early stages and special situations. Industry Preferences: Diversified technology and education. Geographic Preferences: West Coast.

21st Century Internet Venture Partners
Two South Park
2nd Floor
San Francisco, CA 94107
Phone: (415)512-1221
Fax: (415)512-2650
Website: http://www.21vc.com
Shawn Myers
Preferred Investment Size: $5,000,000 maximum. Investment Types: Seed, research and development, startup, first and second stage, mezzanine, leveraged buyout, and special situations. Industry Preferences: Diversified. Geographic Preferences: Entire U.S. and Canada.

2M Invest Inc.
1875 S. Grant St.
Suite 750
San Mateo, CA 94402
Phone: (650)655-3765
Fax: (650)372-9107

E-mail: 2minfo@2minvest.com
Website: http://www.2minvest.com
Preferred Investment Size: $500,000
to $5 million. Investment Types:
Startup. Industry Preferences:
Communications, computer related,
electronic components and
instrumentation. Non-information
technology companies not considered.
Geographic Preferences: West Coast.

**UnionBanCal Venture Corporation**
445 S. Figueroa St., 9th Fl.
Los Angeles, CA 90071
Phone: (213)236-4092
Fax: (213)236-6329
Investment Types: Second stage,
mezzanine, leveraged buyout, and
special situations. Industry
Preferences: Communications,
computer related. Geographic
Preferences: National.

**U.S. Venture Partners**
2180 Sand Hill Rd., Ste. 300
Menlo Park, CA 94025
Phone: (650)854-9080
Fax: (650)854-3018
Website: http://www.usvp.com
William K. Bowes, Jr., General
Partner
Preferred Investment Size: $500,000
to $5,000,000. Investment Types:
Seed, research and development,
startup, first and second stage, and
mezzanine. Industry Preferences:
Communications, computer related,
consumer products and services,
distribution, electronics, and medical/
health related. Geographic
Preferences: Northwest and West
Coast.

**USVP-Schlein Marketing Fund**
2180 Sand Hill Rd., Ste. 300
Menlo Park, CA 94025
Phone: (415)854-9080
Fax: (415)854-3018
Website: http://www.usvp.com
Venture capital fund. Prefers specialty
retailing/consumer products
companies.

**Vanguard Venture Partners**
525 University Ave., Ste. 600
Palo Alto, CA 94301
Phone: (650)321-2900
Fax: (650)321-2902

Donald F. Wood, Partner
Preferred Investment Size: $250,000
to $5,000,000. Investment Types:
Early stages. Industry Preferences:
Diversified computer and
communications technology, genetic
engineering, and healthcare.
Geographic Preferences: National.

**Venrock Associates**
2497 Sand Hill Rd., Ste. 200
Menlo Park, CA 94025
Phone: (650)561-9580
Fax: (650)561-9180
Website: http://www.venrock.com
Ted H. McCourtney, Managing
General Partner
Preferred Investment Size: $2,000,000
to $10,000,000. Investment Types:
Seed, research and development,
startup, first and second stage.
Industry Preferences: Diversified.
Geographic Preferences: No
preference.

**Ventana Growth Funds (Irvine)**
18881 Von Karman Ave., Ste. 1150
Irvine, CA 92612
Phone: (949)476-2204
Fax: (949)752-0223
E-mail: ventana@ventanaglobal.com
Scott A. Burri, Managing Director
Preferred Investment Size: $250,000
to $5,000,000. Investment Types:
First and second stage, and
mezzanine. Industry Preferences:
Diversified technology. Geographic
Preferences: Southwest.

**Venture Growth Associates**
2479 East Bayshore St., Ste. 710
Palo Alto, CA 94303
Phone: (650)855-9100
Fax: (650)855-9104
James R. Berdell, Managing Partner
Preferred Investment Size: $1,000,000
to $5,000,000. Investment Types:
Early and later stages, and special
situations. Industry Preferences:
Diversified technology, finance and
insurance. Geographic Preferences:
West Coast.

**VK Ventures**
600 California St., Ste.1700
San Francisco, CA 94111
Phone: (415)391-5600
Fax: (415)397-2744

David D. Horwich, Senior Vice
President
Preferred Investment Size: $100,000
to $250,000. Investment Types:
Second stage, mezzanine, and
leveraged buyout. Industry
Preferences: Diversified. Geographic
Preferences: West Coast.

**Walden Group of Venture Capital
Funds**
750 Battery St., Seventh Floor
San Francisco, CA 94111
Phone: (415)391-7225
Fax: (415)391-7262
Arthur Berliner
Preferred Investment Size: $1,000,000
to $7,000,000. Investment Types:
Seed, startup, first and second stage.
Industry Preferences: Diversified
technology. Geographic Preferences:
Entire U.S.

**Wedbush Capital Partners**
1000 Wilshire Blvd., Ste. 900
Los Angeles, CA 90017
Phone: (213)688-4545
Fax: (213)688-6642
Preferred Investment Size: $250,000
to $500,000. Investment Types: Later
stages, recapitalization and leveraged
buyouts. Industry Preferences:
Diversified computer technology,
consumer related, distribution, and
healthcare. Geographic Preferences:
West Coast.

**Weiss, Peck and Greer Venture
Partners L.P. (San Francisco)**
555 California St., Ste. 3130
San Francisco, CA 94104
Phone: (415)622-6864
Fax: (415)989-5108
Website: http://www.wpgvp.com
Peter Nich, General Partner
Preferred Investment Size: $500,000
to $2,000,000. Investment Types:
Seed, startup, first and second stage,
and mezzanine. Industry Preferences:
Diversified technology. Geographic
Preferences: No preference.

**Wells Fargo Equity Capital, Inc.**
One Montgomery St.
West Tower, Ste. 2530
San Francisco, CA 94104
Phone: (415)396-5700
Fax: (415)765-1569

E-mail: greenr@wellsfargo.com
Investment Types: Leveraged buyout.
Industry Preferences: Consumer,
industrial products and equipment,
medical/health related, and
publishing. Geographic Preferences:
Western U.S.

Westar Capital (Costa Mesa)
949 South Coast Dr., Ste. 650
Costa Mesa, CA 92626
Phone: (714)481-5160
Fax: (714)481-5166
Alan Sellers, General Partner
Preferred Investment Size: $3,000,000
to $10,000,000. Investment Types:
Leveraged buyouts, special situations,
control block purchases, and industry
roll ups. Industry Preferences:
Diversified. Does not consider sports,
real estate, oil and gas, hospitality,
gaming, or airlines. Geographic
Preferences: Northwest, Southwest,
Rocky Mountains, and West Coast.

Western States Investment Group
9191 Towne Ctr. Dr., Ste. 310
San Diego, CA 92122
Phone: (619)678-0800
Fax: (619)678-0900
Investment Types: Seed, research and
development, startup, first stage,
leveraged buyout. Industry
Preferences: Computer related,
consumer, electronic components and
instrumentation, medical/health
related. Geographic Preferences:
Western U.S.

Western Technology Investment
2010 N. First St., Ste. 310
San Jose, CA 95131
Phone: (408)436-8577
Fax: (408)436-8625
E-mail: mktg@westerntech.com
Investment Types: Seed, research and
development, startup, first stage,
second stage, mezzanine, leveraged
buyout, and special situations.
Industry Preferences: Diversified.
Geographic Preferences: National.

Windward Ventures
PO Box 7688
Thousand Oaks, CA 91359-7688
Phone: (805)497-3332
Fax: (805)497-9331

Investment Types: Seed, startup, first
stage, second stage. Industry
Preferences: Communications,
computer related, electronic
components and instrumentation,
genetic engineering, industrial
products and equipment, medical and
health related. Geographic
Preferences: West Coast.

Woodside Fund
850 Woodside Dr.
Woodside, CA 94062
Phone: (650)368-5545
Fax: (650)368-2416
Website: http://
www.woodsidefund.com
Matthew Bolton, Analyst
Investment Types: Seed, startup, first
stage, second stage, and special
situations. Industry Preferences:
Diversified technology. Geographic
Preferences: Western U.S.

Worldview Technology Partners
435 Tasso St., Ste. 120
Palo Alto, CA 94301
Phone: (650)322-3800
Fax: (650)322-3880
John Boyle, General Partner
Investment Types: Seed, research and
development, startup, first stage,
second stage, mezzanine. Industry
Preferences: Diversified technology.
Geographic Preferences: National.

## Colorado

Access Venture Partners
8787 Turnpike Dr., Ste. 260
Westminster, CO 80030
Phone: (303)426-8899
Fax: (303)426-8828
E-mail: robert.rees@juno.com
Robert W. Rees, Managing Director
Investment Types: Seed, startup, first
stage, and special situations. Industry
Preferences: Diversified. Geographic
Preferences: Western and Midwestern
U.S.

Boranco Management, L.L.C.
1528 Hillside Dr.
Fort Collins, CO 80524-1969
Phone: (970)221-2297
Fax: (970)221-4787
Preferred Investment Size: $100,000.
Investment Types: Early and late

stage. Industry Preferences:
Agricultural and animal
biotechnology. Geographic
Preferences: Within two hours of
office.

The Centennial Funds
1428 15th St.
Denver, CO 80202-1318
Phone: (303)405-7500
Fax: (303)405-7575
Website: http://www.centennial.com
Preferred Investment Size: $250,000
to $5,000,000. Investment Types:
Seed, startup, first and second stage,
and national consolidations. Industry
Preferences: Diversified. Geographic
Preferences: No preference.

Century Capital Group
6530 S. Yosemite St.
Englewood, CO 80111-5128
Phone: (303)796-2600
Fax: (303)796-2612
Preferred Investment Size: $100,000
to $250,000. Investment Types:
Second stage, mezzanine, leveraged
buyout, and special situations.
Industry Preferences: Diversified.
Geographic Preferences: Rocky
Mountain area and Canada.

Chase Capital Partners
108 S. Frontage Rd. W, Ste. 307
Vail, CO 81657
Phone: (970)476-7700
Fax: (970)476-7900
Preferred Investment Size: $5,000,000
to $100,000,000. Investment Types:
Startup, first and second stage,
mezzanine, leveraged buyout, and
special situations. Industry
Preferences: Diversified. Geographic
Preferences: Entire U.S. and Canada.

The Columbine Venture Funds
5460 S. Quebec St., Ste. 270
Englewood, CO 80111
Phone: (303)694-3222
Fax: (303)694-9007
Preferred Investment Size: $100,000
to $250,000. Investment Types: Seed,
research and development, startup,
and first stage. Industry Preferences:
Diversified technology. Geographic
Preferences: Southwest, Rocky
Mountains, and West Coast.

CVM Equity Funds
4845 Pearl East Cir., Ste. 300
Boulder, CO 80301
Phone: (303)440-4055
Fax: (303)440-4636
E-mail: gbloomer@cvmequity.com
Gary Bloomer, Managing Partner
Investment Types: Seed, startup, first
stage. Industry Preferences:
Diversified. Geographic Preferences:
Southwest, Rocky Mountains.

Dean & Associates
4362 Apple Way
Boulder, CO 80301
Fax: (303)473-9900
Investment Types: First stage, second
stage, and mezzanine. Industry
Preferences: Internet related.
Geographic Preferences: Western
U.S.

Holden Capital, L.L.C.
6300 S. Syracruse Way, Ste. 484
Englewood, CO 80111
Phone: (303)694-0268
Fax: (303)694-1707
E-mail: block@vailsys.com
Preferred Investment Size: $250,000
to $5,000,000. Investment Types:
Early and late stage, and leveraged
buyout. Industry Preferences:
Diversified. Geographic Preferences:
National.

Investment Securities of Colorado,
Inc.
4605 Denice Dr.
Englewood, CO 80111
Phone: (303)796-9192
Preferred Investment Size: $100,000
to $300,000. Investment Types: Seed
and startup. Industry Preferences:
Electronic components, industrial
controls and sensors, healthcare
industry. Geographic Preferences:
Rocky Mountain area.

Kinship Partners
6300 S. Syracuse Way, Ste. 484
Englewood, CO 80111
Phone: (303)694-0268
Fax: (303)694-1707
E-mail: block@vailsys.com
Preferred Investment Size: $250,000
to $1,000,000. Investment Types:
Seed, startup, and early stage.
Industry Preferences: Diversified

computer and communication
technology, specialty retailing,
genetic engineering, and healthcare.
Geographic Preferences: Within two
hours of office.

New Venture Resources
445C E. Cheyenne Mtn. Blvd.
Colorado Springs, CO 80906-4570
Phone: (719)598-9272
Fax: (719)598-9272
Jeffrey M. Cooper, Managing
Director
Preferred Investment Size: $100,000
to $250,000. Investment Types: Seed
and startup. Industry Preferences:
Diversified technology. Geographic
Preferences: Southwest, Rocky
Mountains.

Rocky Mountain Capital Partners
1125 17th St., Ste. 2260
Denver, CO 80202
Phone: (303)291-5200
Fax: (303)291-5327
Investment Types: Mezzanine and
leveraged buyout. Industry
Preferences: Diversified.
Communications, computer related,
consumer, distribution, electronic
components and instrumentation, and
industrial products and equipment.
Geographic Preferences: Western
U.S.

Roser Ventures LLC
1105 Spruce St.
Boulder, CO 80302
Phone: (303)443-6436
Fax: (303)443-1885
Website: http://
www.roserventures.com
Steven T. Joanis, Associate
Investment Types: Startup, first stage,
second stage, and special situations.
Industry Preferences:
Communications, computer related,
distribution, electronic components
and instrumentation, energy/natural
resources, industrial products and
equipment, medical and health
related. Geographic Preferences:
National.

Sequel Venture Partners
4430 Arapahoe Ave., Ste. 220
Boulder, CO 80303
Phone: (303)546-0400

Fax: (303)546-9728
E-mail: tom@sequelvc.com
Website: http://www.sequelvc.com
Kinney Johnson, Partner
Preferred Investment Size: $100,000
to $5,000,000. Investment Types:
Seed, startup, and early stage.
Industry Preferences: Diversified
technology. Geographic Preferences:
Rocky Mountains.

Wolf Ventures
50 South Steele St., Ste. 777
Denver, CO 80209
Phone: (303)321-4800
Fax: (303)321-4848
E-mail:
businessplan@wolfventures.com
Website: http://
www.wolfventures.com
David O. Wolf
Preferred Investment Size: $500,000
to $3,000,000. Investment Types:
First stage, second stage, and special
situations. Industry Preferences:
Diversified. Geographic Preferences:
Rocky Mountains.

## Connecticut

ABP Acquisition Corporation
333 Ludlow St.
Stamford, CT 06902
Phone: (203)425-2931
Fax: (203)323-9453
E-mail: gskakel@aol.com
Investment Types: Seed, startup, first
stage, leveraged buyout, and special
situations. Industry Preferences:
Communications and computer
related. Geographic Preferences:
Eastern U.S., Midwest, Rocky
Mountains.

Advanced Materials Partners, Inc.
45 Pine St.
PO Box 1022
New Canaan, CT 06840
Phone: (203)966-6415
Fax: (203)966-8448
E-mail: wkb@amplink.com
Preferred Investment Size: $500,000
to $5,000,000. Investment Types:
Diversified early and late stage.
Industry Preferences: Diversified.
Geographic Preferences: National and
Canada.

Axiom Venture Partners
City Place II
185 Asylum St., 17th Fl.
Hartford, CT 06103
Phone: (860)548-7799
Fax: (860)548-7797
Investment Types: Startup, first stage, second stage, and later stages. Industry Preferences: Communications, computer related, distribution, genetic engineering, medical/health related. Geographic Preferences: National.

Baxter Associates, Inc.
PO Box 1333
Stamford, CT 06904
Phone: (203)323-3143
Fax: (203)348-0622
Preferred Investment Size: $100,000 to $500,000. Investment Types: Early and late stage. Industry Preferences: Radio and TV, franchise businesses, industrial and medical product distribution, chemicals and materials, genetic engineering, and specialty consulting. Geographic Preferences: National.

Beacon Partners Inc.
6 Landmark Sq., 4th Fl.
Stamford, CT 06901-2792
Phone: (203)359-5776
Fax: (203)359-5876
Investment Types: First stage, second stage, mezzanine, leveraged buyout, and turnarounds. Industry Preferences: Diversified. Geographic Preferences: Northeast.

Bio-Investigations, Ltd.
32 Country Way
PO Box 4041
Madison, CT 06443
Phone: (203)421-3697
Stewart B. Rosenberg, President
Preferred Investment Size: $100,000 to $500,000. Investment Types: Diversified early and late stage. Industry Preferences: Communications, computers, consumer, distribution, electronics, natural resources, genetic engineering, industrial products, and healthcare. Geographic Preferences: National.

Canaan Partners
105 Rowayton Ave.
Rowayton, CT 06853
Phone: (203)855-0400
Fax: (203)854-9117
Preferred Investment Size: $1,000,000 to $5,000,000. Investment Types: First and second stage, mezzanine, leveraged buyout, and acquisition financing. Industry Preferences: Diversified. Geographic Preferences: National.

Catterton Partners
9 Greenwich Office Park
Greenwich, CT 06830
Phone: (203)629-4901
Fax: (203)629-4903
E-mail: catterton@cattertonpartners.com
Andrew C. Taub
Investment Types: First stage, second stage, leveraged buyout, and special situations. Industry Preferences: Consumer products and services. Geographic Preferences: National.

Collinson, Howe, and Lennox, LLC
1055 Washington Blvd., 5th Fl.
Stamford, CT 06901
Phone: (203)324-7700
Fax: (203)324-3636
E-mail: info@chimedical.com
Investment Types: Seed, research and development, start-up, and first stage. Industry Preferences: Consumer health care products, medical products distribution, medical/health related. Geographic Preferences: National.

Connecticut Innovations, Inc.
999 West St.
Rocky Hill, CT 06067
Phone: (860)563-5851
Fax: (860)563-4877
E-mail: pamela.hartley@ctinnovations.com
Website: http://www.ctinnovations.com
Preferred Investment Size: $100,000 minimum. Investment Types: Early and late stage. Industry Preferences: Diversified technology. Geographic Preferences: Connecticut.

Conning & Company
City Place II

185 Asylum St.
Hartford, CT 06103-4105
Phone: (860)520-1238
Fax: (860)520-1299
E-mail: pe@conning.com
John B. Clinton, Executive Vice President
Investment Types: Startup, first stage, second stage, mezzanine, leveraged buyout, and special situations. Industry Preferences: Computer related. Geographic Preferences: National.

Consumer Venture Partners
3 Pickwick Plz.
Greenwich, CT 06830
Phone: (203)629-8800
Fax: (203)629-2019
E-mail: lcummin@consumer-venture.com
Linda Cummin, Business Manager
Preferred Investment Size: $500,000 to $5,000,000. Investment Types: Startup, first and second stage, and leveraged buyout. Industry Preferences: Internet related, consumer related, consumer and food distribution, education, and publishing. Geographic Preferences: Entire U.S.

Cove Associates, Ltd.
19 Pine Hill Ave.
Norwalk, CT 06855
Phone: (203)866-5251
Fax: (203)866-4099
Preferred Investment Size: $500,000 to $5,000,000. Investment Types: Later stage and leveraged buyout. Industry Preferences: Internet related, consumer products and services, and food and beverage products. Geographic Preferences: National.

The Crestview Investment and Financial Group
431 Post Rd. E, Ste. 1
Westport, CT 06880-4403
Phone: (203)222-0333
Fax: (203)222-0000
Norman Marland, Pres.
Investment Types: Seed, research and development, first stage, second stage, and mezzanine. Industry Preferences: Diversified. Geographic Preferences: National.

Enterprise Associates
200 Nyala Farms
Westport, CT 06880
Phone: (203)222-4594
Fax: (203)222-4592
E-mail:
vkontogouris@cognizantcorp.com
Investment Types: First stage.
Industry Preferences:
Communications, computer related.
Geographic Preferences: National.

First New England Capital
100 Pearl St.
Hartford, CT 06103
Phone: (860)293-3333
Fax: (860)293-3338
E-mail:
info@firstnewenglandcapital.com
Website: http://
www.firstnewenglandcapital.com
Investment Types: Mezzanine,
leveraged buyout, and special
situations. Industry Preferences:
Consumer, distribution, energy/
natural resources, industrial products
and equipment. Geographic
Preferences: Eastern and midwestern
U.S.

James B Kobak & Co.
Four Mansfield Place
Darien, CT 06820
Phone: (203)656-3471
Fax: (203)655-2905
Preferred Investment Size: $100,000
maximum. Investment Types: Early
stage. Industry Preferences:
Publishing. Geographic Preferences:
National.

J.H. Whitney & Company
177 Broad St.
Stamford, CT 06901
Phone: (203)973-1400
Fax: (203)973-1422
Website: http://www.jhwhitney.com
Investment Types: First stage, second
stage, mezzanine, and leveraged
buyout. Industry Preferences:
Diversified technology. Geographic
Preferences: National.

James B. Kobak and Co.
Four Mansfield Place
Darien, CT 06820
Phone: (203)656-3471

Fax: (203)655-2905
Venture capital supplier and
consultant. Provides assistance to new
ventures in the communications field
through conceptualization, planning,
organization, raising money, and
control of actual operations. Special
interest is in magazine publishing.

Landmark Partners, Inc.
760 Hopmeadow St.
PO Box 188
Simsbury, CT 06070-0188
Phone: (860)651-9760
Fax: (860)651-8890
James P. McConnell, Partner
Preferred Investment Size: $500,000
to $5,000,000. Investment Types:
Special situations. Industry
Preferences: Communications.
Geographic Preferences: National.

LTI Venture Leasing
221 Danbury Rd.
Wilton, CT 06897
Phone: (203)563-1100
Fax: (203)563-1111
Website: http://www.ltileasing.com
Richard Livingston, Regional
Manager
Investment Types: Seed, startup, first
stage, second stage, mezzanine,
leveraged buyout. Industry
Preferences: Communications,
computer related, consumer,
electronic components and
instrumentation, industrial products
and equipment, medical and health
related. Geographic Preferences:
National.

Marketcorp Venture Associates, L.P.
(MCV)
274 Riverside Ave.
Westport, CT 06880
Phone: (203)222-3030
Fax: (203)222-3033
E. Bulkeley Griswold, General
Partner
Preferred Investment Size: $250,000
to $1,000,000. Investment Types:
First and second stage, mezzanine,
and leveraged buyout. Industry
Preferences: Consumer products and
services. Geographic Preferences:
Entire U.S.

Northeast Ventures
One State St., Ste. 1720
Hartford, CT 06103
Phone: (860)547-1414
Fax: (860)246-8755
Preferred Investment Size: $5,000,000
maximum. Investment Types:
Secondary. Industry Preferences:
Diversified technology and education.
Geographic Preferences: National.

Oak Investment Partners (Westport)
1 Gorham Island
Westport, CT 06880
Phone: (203)226-8346
Fax: (203)227-0372
Website: http://www.oakinv.com
Preferred Investment Size: $250,000
to $5,000,000. Investment Types:
Seed, startup, first stage, leveraged
buyout, and special situations.
Industry Preferences: Diversified
technology. Geographic Preferences:
National.

Orien Ventures
1 Post Rd.
Fairfield, CT 06430
Phone: (203)259-9933
Fax: (203)259-5288
Investment Types: Seed, research and
development. Industry Preferences:
Diversified technology. Geographic
Preferences: National.

Oxford Bioscience Partners
315 Post Rd. W
Westport, CT 06880-5200
Phone: (203)341-3300
Fax: (203)341-3309
William Greenman
Preferred Investment Size: $500,000
to $5,000,000. Investment Types:
Seed, research and development,
startup, first and second stage, and
mezzanine. Industry Preferences:
Genetic engineering and medical/
health related. Geographic
Preferences: Entire U.S.

Prince Ventures (Westport)
25 Ford Rd.
Westport, CT 06880
Phone: (203)227-8332
Fax: (203)226-5302
Preferred Investment Size: $500,000
to $1,000,000. Investment Types:
Seed, startup, first and second stage,

and leveraged buyout. Industry Preferences: Genetic engineering and medical/health related. Geographic Preferences: No preference.

Regulus International Capital Co., Inc.
140 Greenwich Ave.
Greenwich, CT 06830
Phone: (203)625-9700
Fax: (203)625-9706
E-mail: lee@chaossystems.com
Preferred Investment Size: $100,000.
Investment Types: Early stage.
Industry Preferences: Software, packaging and printing, chemicals and materials, and publishing. Geographic Preferences: National.

RFE Investment Partners
36 Grove St.
New Canaan, CT 06840
Phone: (203)966-2800
Fax: (203)966-3109
James A. Parsons, General Partner
Preferred Investment Size: $5,000,000 to $25,000,000. Investment Policies: Prefer equity investments. Investment Types: Later stage, expansion, acquisitions. Industry Preferences: Diversified. Geographic Preferences: Entire U.S.

Saugatuck Capital Co.
1 Canterbury Green
Stamford, CT 06901
Phone: (203)348-6669
Fax: (203)324-6995
Preferred Investment Size: $5,000,000 maximum. Investment Types: Second stage, mezzanine, leveraged buyout, special situations, and buyout or acquisition. Industry Preferences: Diversified. Geographic Preferences: Entire U.S.

Soundview Technology Group
22 Gatehouse Rd.
Stamford, CT 06902
Phone: (203)462-7200
Fax: (203)462-7350
Website: http://www.sndv.com
Brian Bristol, Managing Director
Preferred Investment Size: $100,000 to $500,000. Investment Types: Late stage and mezzanine. Industry Preferences: Diversified information

technology. Geographic Preferences: United States and Canada.

Summit Capital Markets
38 Sylvan Rd.
Madison, CT 06443
Phone: (203)245-6870
Fax: (203)245-6865
Rockwell D. Marsh, Managing Partner
Preferred Investment Size: $250,000 to $5,000,000. Investment Types: Late stage and buyouts. Industry Preferences: Consumer products, industrial products, electronics, and pharmaceuticals. Geographic Preferences: East Coast.

Sweeney & Company
PO Box 567
Southport, CT 06490
Phone: (203)255-0220
Fax: (203)255-0220
E-mail: sweeney@connix.com
Investment Types: Seed, research and development, startup, first stage, second stage, mezzanine, leveraged buyout, and special situations.
Industry Preferences: Diversified.
Geographic Preferences: Northeast U.S. and Eastern Canada.

TSG Ventures, L.L.C.
177 Broad St., 12th Fl.
Stamford, CT 06901
Phone: (203)406-1500
Fax: (203)406-1590
Cleveland A. Christophe, Managing Partner
Preferred Investment Size: $5,000,000 to $10,000,000. Investment Types: Second stage and leveraged buyout. Industry Preferences: Diversified. Geographic Preferences: Entire U.S. and Canada.

Windward Holdings.
38 Sylvan Rd.
Madison, CT 06443
Phone: (203)245-6870
Fax: (203)245-6865
Preferred Investment Size: $250,000 to $1,000,000. Investment Types: Late stage and special situations. Industry Preferences: Diversified distribution, electronics, and industrial products. Geographic Preferences: East Coast.

## Delaware

Blue Rock Capital
5803 Kennett Pike, Ste. A
Wilmington, DE 19807
Phone: (302)426-0981
Fax: (302)426-0982
Website: http://www.bluerockcapital.com
Preferred Investment Size: $250,000 to $3,000,000. Investment Types: Early stage. Industry Preferences: Communication, computer, semiconductors, and education. Geographic Preferences: Northeast, Middle Atlantic.

Delaware Innovation Fund
100 West 10th St., Ste. 413
Wilmington, DE 19801
Phone: (302)777-1616
Fax: (302)777-1620
David J. Freschman, President
Preferred Investment Size: $100,000 to $500,000. Investment Types: Early stage. Industry Preferences: Diversified technology. Geographic Preferences: Delaware.

## District of Columbia

Allied Capital Corp.
1919 Pennsylvania Ave. NW
Washington, DC 20006-3434
Phone: (202)331-2444
Fax: (202)659-2053
Website: http://www.alliedcapital.com
Tricia Daniels, Sales & Marketing
Preferred Investment Size: $3,000,000 to $25,000,000. Investment Types: Second stage, mezzanine, leveraged buyout, special situations, industry roll ups. Industry Preferences: Diversified. Geographic Preferences: No preference.

Atlantic Coastal Ventures, L.P.
3101 South St. NW
Washington, DC 20007
Phone: (202)293-1166
Fax: (202)293-1181
Website: http://www.atlanticcv.com
Preferred Investment Size: $1,000,000 to $2,000,000. Investment Types: Early and late stage. Industry Preferences: Communication and

computer related. Geographic
Preferences: East Coast.

Capitol Health Partners
2620 P St. NW
Washington, DC 20007
Phone: (202)342-6300
Fax: (202)342-6399
Robert Coppedge, Associate
Investment Types: Startup, first and
second stage. Industry Preferences:
Medical/health related. Geographic
Preferences: National.

Columbia Capital Group, Inc.
1660 L St. NW, Ste. 308
Washington, DC 20036
Phone: (202)775-8815
Fax: (202)223-0544
Erica Batie, Director of Investments
Preferred Investment Size: $100,000
to $250,000. Investment Types: Early
and late stage, and mezzanine.
Industry Preferences: Communication
and computer related, consumer
products and services, and education.
Geographic Preferences: Washington,
DC.

MultiMedia Broadcast Investment
Corp.
3101 South St. NW
Washington, DC 20007
Phone: (202)293-1166
Fax: (202)293-1181
E-mail: mbic@mmbic.com
Website: http://www.mmbic.com
Preferred Investment Size: $100,000
to $1,000,000. Investment Types:
Mezzanine, leveraged buyout, and
special situations. Industry
Preferences: Communications,
computer scanning, and electronics
equipment distribution. Geographic
Preferences: No preference.

Next Point Partners
701 Pennsylvania Ave. NW, Ste. 900
Washington, DC 20004
Phone: (202)434-7319
Fax: (202)434-7400
E-mail: mf@nextpoint.vc
Michael Faber, Managing General
Partner
Investment Types: First and second
stage. Industry Preferences:
Communications, computer related,

and electronic components.
Geographic Preferences: National.

Plaza Street Capital, L.P.
701 Pennsylvania Ave. NW
Washington, DC 20004
Phone: (202)434-7319
E-mail: mfaber@mintz.com
Preferred Investment Size: $500,000
to $5,000,000. Investment Types:
Early and late stage. Industry
Preferences: Communication and
computer related, consumer,
distribution, electronics, genetic
engineering, medical, and agriculture.
Geographic Preferences: National.

Wachtel & Co., Inc.
1101 4th St. NW
Washington, DC 20005-5680
Phone: (202)898-1144
Preferred Investment Size: $100,000
to $250,000. Investment Types: Early
and late stage. Industry Preferences:
Diversified. Geographic Preferences:
East Coast.

Winslow Partners LLC
1300 Connecticut Ave. NW, Ste. 850
Washington, DC 20036-1703
Phone: (202)530-5000
Fax: (203)530-5010
E-mail:
winslow@winslowpartners.com
Robert Chartener, Partner
Investment Types: First stage, second
stage, and leverage buyout. Industry
Preferences: Diversified. Geographic
Preferences: Eastern and Midwestern
U.S.

## Florida

Adventure Capital Corp.
PO Box 370531
Miami, FL 33137
Phone: (305)530-0046
Fax: (305)350-6826
E-mail: corp@adventurecapital.com
Website: http://
www.adventurecapital.com
Jeffrey M. Stoller, President
Preferred Investment Size: $100,000.
Investment Types: Early stage.
Industry Preferences: Communication
and computer related, and consumer

products and services. Geographic
Preferences: National.

Avery Business Development
Services
2506 St. Michel Ct.
Ponte Vedra, FL 32082
Phone: (904)285-6033
Investment Types: Seed, research and
development, startup, first stage,
second stage, leveraged buyout, and
special situations. Industry
Preferences: Diversified. Geographic
Preferences: National.

Bailey Capital
205 Worth Ave., Ste. 201
Palm Beach, FL 33480
Phone: (561)366-9223
Fax: (561)833-5825
E-mail: ibailey919@aol.com
Preferred Investment Size: $250,000
to $1,000,000. Investment Types:
Early and late stage. Industry
Preferences: E-commerce.
Geographic Preferences: Southeast.

Chartwell Capital Investors
1 Independent Dr., Ste. 3120
Jacksonville, FL 32202
Phone: (904)355-3519
Fax: (904)353-5833
E-mail: info@chartwellcap.com
Investment Types: First stage, second
stage and leveraged buyout. Industry
Preferences: Diversified. Geographic
Preferences: Southeast.

Financial Capital Resources, Inc.
3001 North Rocky Point Drive East,
Ste. 200
Tampa, FL 33607
Phone: (813)281-5486
Preferred Investment Size: $1,000,000
to $5,000,000. Investment Types:
Leveraged buyout. Industry
Preferences: Financial services.
Geographic Preferences: National.

Florida Venture Partners, Inc.
325 Florida Bank Plaza
100 W. Kennedy Blvd.
Tampa, FL 33602
Phone: (813)229-2294
Fax: (813)229-2028
Preferred Investment Size: $1,000,000
to $5,000,000. Investment Types:
Startup, first and second stage.

Industry Preferences: Diversified.
Geographic Preferences: Southeast.

Henry & Co.
8201 Peters Rd., Ste. 1000
Plantation, FL 33324
Phone: (954)797-7400
Preferred Investment Size: $500,000
to $1,000,000. Investment Types:
Early stage. Industry Preferences:
Healthcare industry. Geographic
Preferences: West Coast.

LM Capital Corp.
120 S. Olive, Ste. 400
West Palm Beach, FL 33401
Phone: (561)655-7186
Fax: (561)655-6587
E-mail: lmcap@aol.com
Preferred Investment Size: $1,000,000
to $5,000,000. Investment Types:
Leveraged buyout. Industry
Preferences: Diversified consumer
products and services.

North American Business
Development Co., L.L.C.
312 SE 17th St., Ste.300
Ft. Lauderdale, FL 33316
Phone: (954)463-0681
Fax: (954)527-0904
Website: http://
www.northamericanfund.com
PIS $2,000,000 to $16,000,000.
Investment Types: Leveraged buyout,
special situations, control block
purchases, industry roll ups, and small
business with growth potential.
Industry Preferences: No preference.
Geographic Preferences: Southeast
and Midwest.

Sigma Capital Corp.
22668 Caravelle Circle
Boca Raton, FL 33433
Phone: (561)368-9783
Preferred Investment Size: $250,000
to $1,000,000. Investment Types:
Early and late stage. Industry
Preferences: Diversified
communication and computer,
consumer products and services,
distribution, electronics, genetic
engineering, finance, and real estate.
Geographic Preferences: Southeast.

South Atlantic Venture Fund
614 W. Bay St.
Tampa, FL 33606-2704

Phone: (813)253-2500
Fax: (813)253-2360
E-mail: venture@southatlantic.com
Website: http://
www.southatlantic.com
Donald W. Burton, Chairman and
Managing Director
Preferred Investment Size: $1,500,000
to $7,500,000. Investment Types:
Startup, first and second stage,
mezzanine, special situations, and
control block purchases. Industry
Preferences: Diversified. Geographic
Preferences: Southeast, Middle
Atlantic, and Texas.

Taurus International Investments Inc.
1401 Manatee Ave. W
Bradenton, FL 34209
Phone: (941)795-6611
Fax: (941)362-4330
Investment Types: Seed, startup,
second stage, mezzanine, leveraged
buyout, and special situations.
Industry Preferences: Diversified.
Geographic Preferences: National.

Venture Capital Management Corp.
PO Box 2626
Satellite Beach, FL 32937
Phone: (407)777-1969
Preferred Investment Size: $100,000
to $250,000. Investment Types: Early
and late stage. Industry Preferences:
Diversified. Geographic Preferences:
National.

## Georgia

Alliance Technology Ventures
3343 Peachtree Rd. NE
East Tower, Ste. 1140
Atlanta, GA 30326
Phone: (404)816-4791
Fax: (404)816-4891
E-mail: info@atv.com
Website: http://www.atv.com
Preferred Investment Size: $250,000
to $1,000,000. Investment Types:
Early and late stage. Industry
Preferences: Diversified technology.
Geographic Preferences: Southeast.

Arete Ventures, L.L.C.
115 Perimeter Center Pl., Ste. 640
Atlanta, GA 30346
Phone: (770)399-1660
Fax: (770)399-1664

Preferred Investment Size: $500,000
to $5,000,000. Investment Types:
Startup, first and second stage, and
leveraged buyout. Industry
Preferences: Electric and gas utility
industry. Geographic Preferences: No
preference.

Bradford Ventures Ltd.
35 Valley Rd.
Atlanta, GA 30305
Phone: (404)869-0499
Fax: (404)869-9964
Investment Types: Seed, first stage,
second stage, and leveraged buyout.
Industry Preferences:
Communications, computer related,
electronic components and
instrumentation, industrial products
and equipment. Geographic
Preferences: Eastern states.

CGW Southeast Partners
12 Piedmont Center, Ste. 210
Atlanta, GA 30305
Phone: (404)816-3255
Fax: (404)816-3258
Richard L. Cravey, Managing Partner
Preferred Investment Size: $3,000,000
to $7,000,000. Investment Types:
Leveraged buyout. Industry
Preferences: Diversified. Geographic
Preferences: Southeastern U.S. and
Canada.

Cordova Ventures
2500 North Winds Pkwy., Ste. 475
Alpharetta, GA 30004
Phone: (678)942-0300
Fax: (678)942-0301
Website: http://
www.cordovaventures.com
Frank Dalton, Partner
Preferred Investment Size: $1,000,000
to $5,000,000. Investment Policies:
Equity and/or debt. Investment Types:
Second stage and mezzanine. Industry
Preferences: Diversified. Geographic
Preferences: Southeast.

EGL Holdings, Inc.
3495 Piedmont Rd., Bldg. 10, Ste.
412
Atlanta, GA 30305
Phone: (404)949-8300
Fax: (404)949-8311
Salvatore A. Massaro, Partner

Preferred Investment Size: $1,000,000 to $2,000,000. Investment Types: Mezzanine, leveraged buyout, industry roll ups, and development capital. Industry Preferences: Diversified. Geographic Preferences: Southeast and East Coast, Midwest.

Equity Capital Partners, Inc.
4330 Georgetown Sq., Ste. 502
Atlanta, GA 30338
Phone: (770)458-9966
Fax: (770)451-4408
E-mail: kg_ecp@mindspring.com
Katie Goodman, Marketing Associate
Preferred Investment Size: $750,000 to $4,000,000. Investment Types: Late stage, recaps, and industry roll ups. Industry Preferences: Diversified communication and computer technology, consumer products and services, distribution, electronics, and publishing. Geographic Preferences: Southeast, Southwest, Midwest, and East Coast.

Equity South Advisors
1790 The Lenox Bldg.
3399 Peachtree Rd. NE
Atlanta, GA 30326
Phone: (404)237-6222
Fax: (404)261-1578
Douglas L. Diamond, Managing Director
Preferred Investment Size: $2,000,000 to $3,000,000. Investment Types: Mezzanine, leveraged buyout, and control block purchases. Industry Preferences: Diversified. Geographic Preferences: Northeast, Southeast, Southwest, and East Coast.

Frontline Capital, Inc.
3475 Lenox Rd., Ste. 400
Atlanta, GA 30326
Phone: (404)240-7280
Fax: (404)240-7281
Preferred Investment Size: $500,000 to $5,000,000. Investment Types: Early stage. Industry Preferences: Diversified communication and computer technology, consumer products and services, distribution, electronics, and publishing. Geographic Preferences: Southeast.

J.P. Carey Asset Management
3343 Peachtree Rd., Ste. 500

Atlanta, GA 30319
Phone: (404)816-5339
E-mail: jpcarey@bellsouth.net
Scott Martin
Investment Types: Seed, startup, second stage, mezzanine, and special situations. Industry Preferences: Communications, computer related, medical and health related. Geographic Preferences: National.

Noro-Moseley Partners
4200 Northside Pkwy., Bldg. 9
Atlanta, GA 30327
Phone: (404)233-1966
Fax: (404)239-9280
Preferred Investment Size: $1,000,000 to $5,000,000. Investment Types: Startup, first and second stage, mezzanine, leveraged buyout, special situations, and control block purchases. Industry Preferences: Diversified. Geographic Preferences: Southeast.

Renaissance Capital Corp.
34 Peachtree St. NW, Ste. 2230
Atlanta, GA 30303
Phone: (404)658-9061
Fax: (404)658-9064
Preferred Investment Size: $200,000 to $450,000. Investment Types: Second stage, mezzanine, and leveraged buyout. Industry Preferences: Diversified. Geographic Preferences: Southeast.

River Capital, Inc.
Two Midtown Plaza
1360 Peachtree St. NE, Ste. 1430
Atlanta, GA 30309
Phone: (404)873-2166
Fax: (404)873-2158
Jerry D. Wethington
Preferred Investment Size: $1,000,000 to $15,000,000. Investment Types: Mezzanine and leveraged buyout. Industry Preferences: Diversified. Geographic Preferences: Southeast, Southwest, East Coast, Midwest, Gulf States, and Middle Atlantic.

State Street Bank & Trust Co.
3414 Peachtree Rd. NE, Ste. 1010
Atlanta, GA 30326
Phone: (404)364-9500
Fax: (404)261-4469

Investment Types: Leveraged buyout and special situations. Industry Preferences: Diversified technology. Geographic Preferences: National.

UPS Strategic Enterprise Fund
55 Glenlake Pkwy. NE
Atlanta, GA 30328
Phone: (404)828-7082
Fax: (404)828-8088
E-mail: jcacyce@ups.com
Preferred Investment Size: $100,000 to $1,000,000. Investment Types: Early and late stage. Industry Preferences: Diversified communication and computer technology, distribution, electronics, and transportation. Geographic Preferences: United States and Canada.

Venture First Associates
4811 Thornwood Dr.
Acworth, GA 30102
Phone: (770)928-3733
Fax: (770)928-6455
Preferred Investment Size: $500,000 to $5,000,000. Investment Types: Seed, startup, first and second stage. Industry Preferences: Diversified technology and consumer products and services. Geographic Preferences: Southeast.

## Hawaii

Pacific Century SBIC
130 Merchant St.
Honolulu, HI 96813
Phone: (808)537-8286
Fax: (808)521-7602
Frank Tokioka, Vice President
Preferred Investment Size: $100,000 to $250,000. Investment Types: Second stage, mezzanine, leveraged buyout, and special situations. Industry Preferences: Computer related, communications, consumer related, distribution, electronics, genetic engineering, and medical/health related. Geographic Preferences: Hawaii.

## Idaho

Sun Valley Ventures
160 Second St.
Ketchum, ID 83340

Phone: (208)726-5005
Fax: (208)726-5094
Investment Types: Second stage, leveraged buyout, and special situations. Industry Preferences: Diversified. Geographic Preferences: Entire U.S. and Canada.

## Illinois

ABN AMRO Capital Private Equity
208 S. La Salle St., 10th Fl.
Chicago, IL 60604
Phone: (312)855-7079
Fax: (312)553-6648
David Bogetz, Managing Director
Preferred Investment Size: $1,000,000 maximum. Investment Types: First and second stage, mezzanine, leveraged buyout, and special situations. Industry Preferences: Diversified. Geographic Preferences: Entire U.S.

Allstate Private Equity
3075 Sanders Rd., Ste. G5D
Northbrook, IL 60062-7127
Phone: (847)402-8247
Fax: (847)402-0880
William E. Engbers, Director
Preferred Investment Size: $5,000,000 maximum. Investment Types: Startup, first and second stage, mezzanine, leveraged buyout, and special situations. Industry Preferences: Diversified. Geographic Preferences: Entire U.S.

Alpha Capital Partners, Ltd.
122 S. Michigan Ave., Ste. 1700
Chicago, IL 60603
Phone: (312)322-9800
Fax: (312)322-9808
E-mail: acp@alphacapital.com
William J. Oberholtzer, Vice President
Preferred Investment Size: $500,000 maximum. Investment Types: First and second stage, leveraged buyout, and special situations. Industry Preferences: Diversified. Geographic Preferences: Midwest.

Ameritech Development Corp.
30 S. Wacker Dr., 37th Fl.
Chicago, IL 60606
Phone: (312)750-5083
Fax: (312)609-0244

Craig Lee, Director
Preferred Investment Size: $500,000 to $1,000,000. Investment Types: Startup, first and second stage. Industry Preferences: Communications, computer related, and electronics. Geographic Preferences: Entire U.S.

Apex Investment Partners
225 W. Washington, Ste. 1450
Chicago, IL 60606
Phone: (312)857-2800
Fax: (312)857-1800
E-mail: apex@apexvc.com
Website: http://www.apexvc.com
Preferred Investment Size: $500,000 to $7,000,000. Investment Types: Early and late stage. Industry Preferences: Diversified communication and computer technology, consumer products and services, distribution, electronics, and education. Geographic Preferences: United States and Canada.

Arch Venture Partners
8725 W. Higgins Rd., Ste. 290
Chicago, IL 60631
Phone: (773)380-6600
Fax: (773)380-6606
Website: http://www.archventure.com
Steven Lazarus, Managing Director
Preferred Investment Size: $100,000 to $1,000,000. Investment Types: Early stage. Industry Preferences: Diversified communication and computer technology, electronics, and genetic engineering. Geographic Preferences: National.

Batterson, Johnson and Wang Venture Partners
303 W. Madison St., Ste. 1110
Chicago, IL 60606-3309
Phone: (312)269-0300
Fax: (312)269-0021
E-mail: bvp@vcapital.com
Website: http://www.vcapital.com
Preferred Investment Size: $100,000 to $1,000,000. Investment Types: Seed, startup, first and second stage, mezzanine, and leveraged buyout. Industry Preferences: Diversified. Geographic Preferences: Entire U.S.

Batterson Venture Partners
303 W. Madison St., Ste. 1110

Chicago, IL 60606
Phone: (312)269-0300
Fax: (312)269-0021
E-mail: bvp@battersonvp.com
Website: http://www.battersonvp.com
Investment Types: Seed, startup, first stage, second stage. Industry Preferences: Communications, computer related, genetic engineering, medical and health related. Geographic Preferences: National.

Beecken, Petty & Co.
901 Warrenville Rd., Ste. 205
Lisle, IL 60532
Phone: (630)435-0300
Fax: (630)435-0370
E-mail: hep@bpcompany.com
Investment Types: Seed, startup, first and second stage. Industry Preferences: Communications, computer related, genetic engineering, medical and health related. Geographic Preferences: National.

William Blair Capital Partners, L.L.C.
222 W. Adams St., Ste. 1300
Chicago, IL 60606
Phone: (312)364-8250
Fax: (312)236-1042
E-mail: privateequity@wmblair.com
Website: http://www.wmblair.com
Maureen Naddy, Office Manager
Preferred Investment Size: $2,000,000 to $30,000,000. Investment Types: First and second stage, and leveraged buyout. Industry Preferences: Communications, computer related, consumer, electronics, energy/natural resources, genetic engineering, and medical/health related. Geographic Preferences: Entire U.S.

Brinson Partners, Inc.
209 S. LaSalle, Ste. 114
Chicago, IL 60604-1295
Phone: (312)220-7100
Fax: (312)220-7110
Thomas C. Dolson, Director
Preferred Investment Size: $1,000,000 to $2,000,000. Investment Types: First and second stage, and leveraged buyout. Industry Preferences: Diversified. Geographic Preferences: No preference.

The Capital Strategy Management Co.
233 S. Wacker Dr.

Box 06334
Chicago, IL 60606
Phone: (312)444-1170
Preferred Investment Size: $200,000 to $10,000,000. Investment Types: Early and late stage, leveraged buyout, and special situations. Industry Preferences: Diversified communication and computer technology, consumer products and services, distribution, electronics, and education. Geographic Preferences: Midwest.

The Cerulean Fund/WGC Associates, Inc.
1701 E. Lake Ave., Ste. 170
Glenview, IL 60025
Phone: (847)657-8002
Fax: (847)657-8168
E-mail: walnet@aol.com
Walter G. Cornett, III, Managing Director
Preferred Investment Size: $3,000,000 to $50,000,000. Investment Types: Leveraged buyout, special situations, control block purchases, and consolidation. Industry Preferences: Diversified. Geographic Preferences: Midwest, entire U.S. for leverage buyouts or consolidations.

Chicago Venture Partners
303 E. Wacker Dr., Ste. 311
Chicago, IL 60601
Phone: (312)297-7000
Fax: (312)819-9701
Website: http://www.chicagoventure.com
Investment Types: First and second stage, mezzanine. Industry Preferences: Communications, computer related, distribution, electronic components and instrumentation. Geographic Preferences: National.

Comdisco Ventures Group (Rosemont)
6111 N. River Rd.
Rosemont, IL 60018
Phone: (847)698-3000
Free: 800-321-1111
Fax: (847)518-5440
Preferred Investment Size: $250,000 to $500,000. Investment Types: Seed, startup, first and second stage, receivables, loans, and equipment

leases. Industry Preferences: Diversified. Geographic Preferences: No preference.

Continental Illinois Venture Corp.
231 S. LaSalle St., Seventh Fl.
Chicago, IL 60697
Phone: (312)828-8021
Fax: (312)987-0763
Gregory W. Wilson, Managing Director
Preferred Investment Size: $5,000,000 maximum. Investment Types: Leveraged buyout, special situations, control block purchases, industry consolidation. Industry Preferences: Diversified. Geographic Preferences: Entire U.S.

Duchossois Investments Limited, LLC
845 Larch Ave.
Elmhurst, IL 60126
Phone: (630)279-3600
Fax: (630)530-6051
Daniel Phelps, Senior Investment Officer
Investment Types: Startup, first and second stage. Industry Preferences: Diversified. Communications and computer related. Geographic Preferences: National.

Environmental Private Equity Fund II, L.P.
233 S. Wacker Pkwy., Ste. 9500
First Analysis Corp.
Chicago, IL 60606-3103
Phone: (312)258-1400
Fax: (312)258-0334
Preferred Investment Size: $250,000 to $5,000,000. Investment Types: Early and late stage, leveraged buyout, and special situations. Industry Preferences: Diversified communication and computer technology, consumer products and services, electronics, and natural resources. Geographic Preferences: National.

Essex Woodlands Health Ventures, L.P.
190 S. LaSalle St., Ste. 2800
Chicago, IL 60603
Phone: (312)444-6040
Fax: (312)444-6034
Marc S. Sandroff, Managing Director

Preferred Investment Size: $1,000,000 to $12,000,000. Investment Types: Startup and first stage. Industry Preferences: Healthcare. Geographic Preferences: No preference.

Evanston Business Investment Corp.
1840 Oak Ave.
Evanston, IL 60201
Phone: (847)866-1840
Fax: (847)866-1808
E-mail: t-parkinson@nwu.com
Website: http://www.ebic.com
Preferred Investment Size: $250,000 to $500,000. Investment Types: Early stage. Industry Preferences: Diversified communication and computer technology, consumer products and services, distribution, electronics, and education. Geographic Preferences: Chicago metropolitan area.

First Analysis Corp.
233 S. Wacker Dr., Ste. 9500
Chicago, IL 60606
Phone: (312)258-1400
Fax: (312)258-0334
Bret Maxwell, Managing Director
Preferred Investment Size: $1,000,000 to $10,000,000. Investment Types: Startup, first and second stage, leveraged buyout, special situations, and industry roll ups. Industry Preferences: Diversified. Geographic Preferences: No preference.

Frontenac Co.
135 S. LaSalle St., Ste.3800
Chicago, IL 60603
Phone: (312)368-0044
Fax: (312)368-9520
Website: http://www.frontenac.com
Preferred Investment Size: $10,000,000 to $50,000,000. Investment Types: Leveraged buyout and industry roll ups. Industry Preferences: Diversified. Geographic Preferences: Entire U.S.

Graystone Venture Partners, L.L.C.
One Northfield Plaza, Ste. 530
Northfield, IL 60093
Phone: (847)446-9460
Fax: (847)446-9470
Mathew B. McCall, Vice President
Preferred Investment Size: $250,000 to $3,000,000. Investment Types:

Early and late stage. Industry Preferences: Diversified communication and computer technology, consumer products and services, distribution, electronics, genetic engineering, and education. Geographic Preferences: National.

GTCR Golder Rauner, LLC
6100 Sears Tower
Chicago, IL 60606
Phone: (312)382-2200
Fax: (312)382-2201
Website: http://www.gtcr.com
Bruce V. Rauner
Preferred Investment Size: $10,000,000 maximum. Investment Types: Leveraged buyout, special situations, and industry consolidations. Industry Preferences: Diversified. Geographic Preferences: No preference.

IEG Venture Management, Inc.
70 West Madison
Chicago, IL 60602
Phone: (312)644-0890
Fax: (312)454-0369
Website: http://www.iegventure.com
Preferred Investment Size: $100,000 to $500,000. Investment Types: Seed, startup, first and second stage. Industry Preferences: Diversified. Geographic Preferences: Midwest.

JK&B Capital
205 N. Michigan Ave., Ste. 808
Chicago, IL 60601
Phone: (312)946-1200
E-mail: gspencer@jkbcapital.com
Preferred Investment Size: $500,000 to $5,000,000. Investment Types: Early and late stage, and mezzanine. Industry Preferences: Diversified communication and computer technology, consumer products and services, distribution, electronics, and finance and insurance. Geographic Preferences: National.

KB Partners
500 Skokie Blvd., Ste. 446
Northbrook, IL 60062
Phone: (847)714-0444
Fax: (847)714-0445
E-mail: keith@kbpartners.com
Keith Bank, Managing Partner

Investment Types: Seed, research and development, startup, and first stage. Industry Preferences: Diversified. Geographic Preferences: National.

Lake Shore Capital Partners
20 N. Wacker Dr., Ste. 2807
Chicago, IL 60606
Phone: (312)803-3536
Fax: (312)803-3534
Investment Types: First and second stage, mezzanine, and leveraged buyout. Industry Preferences: Diversified. Geographic Preferences: National.

Linc Capital, Inc.
303 E. Wacker Pkwy., Ste. 1000
Chicago, IL 60601
Phone: (312)946-1000
Fax: (312)938-4290
E-mail: bdemars@linccap.com
Martin E. Zimmerman, Chairman
Preferred Investment Size: $250,000 to $5,000,000. Investment Types: Early and late stage, mezzanine, and special situations. Industry Preferences: Diversified communication and computer technology, distribution, electronics, and finance and insurance. Geographic Preferences: National.

Madison Dearborn Partners, Inc.
3 First National Plz., Ste. 3800
Chicago, IL 60602
Phone: (312)895-1000
Fax: (312)895-1001
E-mail: invest@mdcp.com
Website: http://www.mdcp.com
Preferred Investment Size: $20,000,000 to $200,000,000. Investment Types: Leveraged buyout, special situations, control block purchases, and industry roll ups. Industry Preferences: Diversified. Geographic Preferences: Entire U.S. and Canada.

Marquette Venture Partners
520 Lake Cook Rd., Ste. 450
Deerfield, IL 60015
Phone: (847)940-1700
Fax: (847)940-1724
Website: http://www.marquetteventures.com
Preferred Investment Size: $500,000 to $5,000,000. Investment Types:

Startup, first and second stage. Industry Preferences: Diversified. Geographic Preferences: Entire U.S.

Mesirow Capital Partners SBIC, Ltd.
350 N. Clark St.
Chicago, IL 60610
Phone: (312)595-6099
Fax: (312)595-6211
Website: http://www.meisrowfinancial.com
Thomas E. Galuhn, Senior Managing Director
Preferred Investment Size: $1,000,000 to $5,000,000. Investment Types: Second stage, mezzanine, leveraged buyout, and later-stage financing. Industry Preferences: Diversified. Geographic Preferences: Entire U.S.

Motorola New Enterprises
1303 E. Algonquin Rd.
6th Floor Tower
Schaumburg, IL 60196-1065
Phone: (847)538-6986
Fax: (847)576-7185
Website: http://www.mot.com/mne
James Burke, New Business Development Manager
Investment Types: Startup, first and second stage. Industry Preferences: Diversified technology. Geographic Preferences: National.

Open Prairie Ventures
115 N. Neil St., Ste. 209
Champaign, IL 61820
Phone: (217)351-7000
Fax: (217)351-7051
E-mail: inquire@openprairie.com
Website: http://www.openprairie.com
Dennis D. Spice, Managing Member
Preferred Investment Size: $250,000 to $3,000,000. Investment Types: Seed and startup. Industry Preferences: Diversified communication and computer technology, distribution, electronics, and genetic engineering. Geographic Preferences: Midwest.

Platinum Venture Partners
1815 S. Meyers Rd., 5th Fl.
Oakbrook Terrace, IL 60181
Phone: (630)620-5000
Fax: (630)691-9134
E-mail: pvpinfo@platinum.com

Website: http://
www.platinumventures.com
Brenda Lee Johnson, Business
Manager
Investment Types: Startup, first stage,
second stage. Industry Preferences:
Diversified. Geographic Preferences:
National.

Polestar Capital, Inc.
180 N. Michigan Ave., Ste. 1905
Chicago, IL 60601
Phone: (312)984-9090
Fax: (312)984-9877
Website: http://www.polestarvc.com
Preferred Investment Size: $250,000
to $1,000,000. Investment Policies:
Primarily equity. Investment Types:
Early to later stages. Industry
Preferences: Communications,
computer related. Geographic
Preferences: Entire U.S.

Portage Venture Partners
1 Northfield Plz., Ste. 530
Northfield, IL 60093
Phone: (847)446-9460
Fax: (847)446-9470
Website: http://
www.portageventures.com
Matthew B. McCall, Vice President
Investment Types: Startup, first and
second stage. Industry Preferences:
Diversified technology. Geographic
Preferences: National.

Prince Ventures (Chicago)
10 S. Wacker Dr., Ste. 2575
Chicago, IL 60606-7407
Phone: (312)454-1408
Fax: (312)454-9125
Preferred Investment Size: $500,000
to $1,000,000. Investment Types:
Seed, startup, first and second stage,
leveraged buyout. Industry
Preferences: Genetic engineering and
medical/health related. Geographic
Preferences: No preference.

Prism Opportunity Fund
10 S. Wacker Dr., Ste. 3500
Chicago, IL 60606
Phone: (312)715-4525
Fax: (312)715-4800
Investment Types: First and second
stage, mezzanine, leveraged buyout,
and special situations. Industry

Preferences: Diversified technology.
Geographic Preferences: National.

Resource Financial Corporation
1905 LaSalle St., Ste. 850
Chicago, IL 60603
Phone: (312)673-7000
Fax: (312)673-7125
E-mail: info@resource-financial.com
Website: http://www.resource-
financial.com
Mark Teufel, Managing Director
Investment Types: First stage, second
stage, mezzanine, leveraged buyout,
and special situations. Industry
Preferences: Diversified. Geographic
Preferences: National.

Third Coast Capital
900 N. Franklin St., Ste. 850
Chicago, IL 60610
Phone: (312)337-3303
Fax: (312)337-2567
E-mail: manic@earthlink.com
Website: http://
www.thirdcoastcapital.com
Preferred Investment Size: $500,000
to $5,000,000. Investment Policies:
Venture leasing. Investment Types:
Early and late stage, and special
situations. Industry Preferences:
Diversified communication and
computer technology, consumer
franchise businesses, distribution,
electronics, and finance and
insurance. Geographic Preferences:
National.

Thomas Cressey Equity Partners
4460 Sears Tower
233 S. Wacker Dr.
Chicago, IL 60606
Phone: (312)777-4444
Fax: (312)777-4445
Investment Types: Leveraged buyouts
and special situations. Industry
Preferences: Diversified. Geographic
Preferences: National.

The Vencom Group, Inc.
2201 Waukegan Rd., Ste. E-200
Bannockburn, IL 60015
Phone: (847)374-7000
Fax: (847)374-1070
Website: http://www.vencom.com
James Otterback, President

Investment Types: Startup, first stage,
second stage, and mezzanine. Industry
Preferences: Communications and
computer related. Geographic
Preferences: National.

Ventana Financial Resources, Inc.
249 Market Sq.
Lake Forest, IL 60045
Phone: (847)234-3434
Preferred Investment Size: $100,000
to $1,000,000. Investment Types:
Early and late stage, and mezzanine.
Industry Preferences: Diversified
communication and computer
technology, consumer products and
services, distribution, electronics,
natural resources, genetic engineering,
and healthcare. Geographic
Preferences: Midwest, Southeast, and
Southwest.

Wind Point Partners (Chicago)
676 N. Michigan Ave., Ste. 3300
Chicago, IL 60611
Phone: (312)649-4000
Preferred Investment Size: $1,000,000
to $5,000,000. Investment Types:
Startup, first stage, leveraged buyout,
and special situations. Industry
Preferences: Diversified. Geographic
Preferences: Midwest.

## Indiana

Cambridge Ventures, L.P.
8440 Woodfield Crossing Blvd., No.
315
Indianapolis, IN 46240
Phone: (317)469-3927
Fax: (317)469-3926
Jean Wojtowicz, President
Preferred Investment Size: $100,000
maximum. Investment Types: Second
stage, mezzanine, and leveraged
buyout. Industry Preferences: No
preference. Geographic Preferences:
Midwest, within 200 miles of office.

CID Equity Partners
One American Square, Ste. 2850
Box 82074
Indianapolis, IN 46282
Phone: (317)269-2350
Fax: (317)269-2355
Website: http://www.cidequity.com
Chris Gough, Associate

Preferred Investment Size: $1,000,000 to $5,000,000. Investment Types: Early and late stage, and special situations. Industry Preferences: Diversified communication and computer technology, distribution, electronics, genetic engineering, natural resources, and finance and insurance. Geographic Preferences: Midwest.

Concept Development Associates
1408 Lark Dr.
PO Box 15245
Evansville, IN 47716-0245
Phone: (812)471-3334
Fax: (812)477-6499
Chuck Fray, Chairman
Investment Types: Seed, research and development, startup, first stage, second stage, and special situations. Industry Preferences: Diversified technology. Geographic Preferences: Eastern U.S.

First Source Capital Corp.
100 North Michigan St.
PO Box 1602
South Bend, IN 46601
Phone: (219)235-2180
Fax: (219)235-2227
Eugene L. Cavanaugh, Vice President
Preferred Investment Size: $200,000 maximum. Investment Types: Second stage, mezzanine, leveraged buyout, and special situations. Industry Preferences: Diversified. Geographic Preferences: Midwest.

Tier 4 Partners, L.L.C.
2421 Production Pkwy., Ste. 111
Indianapolis, IN 46241
Phone: (317)244-7429
Fax: (317)244-6401
David A. Shaw, CEO
Preferred Investment Size: $250,000 to $1,000,000. Investment Types: Early and late stage, and leveraged buyout. Industry Preferences: No preference. Geographic Preferences: Midwest, East and West Coast.

## Iowa

Aavin LLC
118 Third Ave. SE, Ste. 800
Cedar Rapids, IA 52401
Phone: (319)247-1072

Fax: (319)363-9519
Michael Reynoldson, Managing Director
Investment Types: First stage, second stage, mezzanine, leveraged buyout, and special situations. Industry Preferences: Diversified. Geographic Preferences: National.

Equity Dinamics
2116 Financial Center
Des Moines, IA 50309
Phone: (515)244-5746
Fax: (515)244-2346
Joe Dunham, Vice President
Preferred Investment Size: $250,000 to $5,000,000. Investment Policies: Equity. Investment Types: Early and late stage, and special situations. Industry Preferences: Diversified communication and computer technology, electronics, genetic engineering, and healthcare. Geographic Preferences: National.

InvestAmerica Investment Advisors, Inc.
101 2nd St. SE, Ste. 800
Cedar Rapids, IA 52401
Phone: (319)363-8249
Fax: (319)363-9683
Kevin F. Mullane, Vice President
Preferred Investment Size: $750,000 to $2,000,000. Investment Types: First and second stage, leveraged buyout, and special situations. Industry Preferences: Diversified. Geographic Preferences: Entire U.S.

Marshall Venture Capital
118 Third Ave. SE, Ste. 837
Cedar Rapids, IA 52401
Phone: (319)368-6675
Fax: (319)363-9515
Preferred Investment Size: $250,000 to $750,000. Investment Policies: Equity. Investment Types: Early and late stage, and special situations. Industry Preferences: Diversified communication and computer technology, consumer products and services, distribution, electronics, animal biotechnology, healthcare, and education. Geographic Preferences: National.

Pappajohn Capital Resources
2116 Financial Center

Des Moines, IA 50309
Phone: (515)244-5746
Fax: (515)244-2346
Website: http://www.pappajohn.com
Joe Dunham, President
Preferred Investment Size: $100,000 to $250,000. Investment Policies: Equity. Investment Types: Early and late stage, and special situations. Industry Preferences: Diversified communication and computer technology, electronics, genetic engineering, and healthcare. Geographic Preferences: National.

## Kansas

Enterprise Capital Management, Inc.
7400 West 110th St., Ste. 560
Overland Park, KS 66210
Phone: (913)327-8500
Fax: (913)327-8505
Preferred Investment Size: $500,000 to $1,000,000. Investment Types: Late stage and special situations. Geographic Preferences: Midwest.

Kansas Technology Enterprise Corp.
214 SW 6th, 1st Fl.
Topeka, KS 66603-3719
Phone: (785)296-5272
Fax: (785)296-1160
E-mail: ktec@ktec.com
Website: http://www.ktec.com
Preferred Investment Size: $50,000 to $500,000. Investment Types: Early stage. Industry Preferences: Diversified communication and computer technology, electronics, genetic engineering, and healthcare. Geographic Preferences: Within two hours of office.

Kansas Venture Capital, Inc. (Overland Park)
6700 Antioch Plz., Ste. 460
Overland Park, KS 66204
Phone: (913)262-7117
Fax: (913)262-3509
E-mail: jdalton@kvci.com
John S. Dalton, President
Preferred Investment Size: $250,000 to $1,500,000. Investment Types: First and second stage, mezzanine, leveraged buyout, turnaround, and recapitalization. Industry Preferences: Diversified. Real estate, oil and gas, and finance and insurance not

considered. Geographic Preferences: Kansas.

## Kentucky

Chrysalis Ventures, L.L.C.
1850 National City Tower
Louisville, KY 40202
Phone: (502)583-7644
Fax: (502)583-7648
E-mail:
bobsany@chrysalisventures.com
Preferred Investment Size: $500,000 to $5,000,000. Investment Types: Early and late stage. Industry Preferences: Diversified communication and computer technology, distribution, healthcare, and education. Geographic Preferences: Southeast and Midwest.

Humana Venture Capital
500 West Main St.
Louisville, KY 40202
Phone: (502)580-3922
Fax: (502)580-2051
E-mail: gemont@humana.com
George Emont, Director
Preferred Investment Size: $500,000 to $5,000,000. Investment Types: Early and late stage. Industry Preferences: Healthcare. Geographic Preferences: National.

Management Alternatives, Inc.
Summit Capital Group, Inc.
418 Knightsbridge Rd., Ste. 2
Louisville, KY 40206
Phone: (502)897-7733
Fax: (502)897-5838
Preferred Investment Size: $100,000 to $250,000. Investment Types: Early and late stage, and special situations. Industry Preferences: Communications, computer services, consumer products and services, distribution, forestry and fishing, and healthcare. Geographic Preferences: Southeast, Midwest.

Summit Capital Group, Inc.
6510 Glenridge Park Pl., Ste. 8
Louisville, KY 40222
Phone: (502)429-4515
Fax: (502)429-4518
Investment Types: Startup, first stage, second stage. Industry Preferences:

Diversified. Geographic Preferences: National.

## Louisiana

Advantage Capital Partners
LLE Tower
909 Poydras St., Ste. 2230
New Orleans, LA 70112
Phone: (504)522-4850
Fax: (504)522-4950
Website: http://
www.advantagecap.com
Steven T. Stull, President and
Managing Director
Preferred Investment Size: $1,000,000 to $6,000,000. Investment Types: Early and late stage, and special situations. Industry Preferences: Diversified. Geographic Preferences: North and Southeast, Midwest, and Gulf States.

Bank One Equity Investors, Inc.
451 Florida St.
Baton Rouge, LA 70801
Phone: (504)332-4421
Fax: (504)332-7377
Preferred Investment Size: $1,000,000 to $15,000,000. Investment Types: First and second stage, mezzanine, leveraged buyout, and special situations. Industry Preferences: Diversified. Geographic Preferences: Southeast, Southwest, and Gulf states.

Stonehenge Capital Corp.
451 Florida St.
Baton Rouge, LA 70801
Phone: (225)332-4421
Fax: (225)332-7377
Investment Types: First stage, second stage, mezzanine, leveraged buyout, and special situations. Industry Preferences: Communications, computer related, consumer, distribution, electronic components and instrumentation, energy/natural resources, genetic engineering, industrial products and equipment, medical and health related. Geographic Preferences: Southern U.S.

## Maine

Commwealth Bioventures, Inc.
4 Milk St.

Portland, ME 04101
Phone: (207)780-0904
Fax: (207)780-0913
E-mail: cbi4milk@aol.com
Investment Types: Seed. Industry Preferences: Biotechnology based start-ups. Geographic Preferences: East Coast.

The Maine Merchant Bank, L.L.C.
Two Monument Square
Portland, ME 04101
Phone: (207)772-8141
Fax: (207)761-4464
Douglas H. Bagin, President
Preferred Investment Size: $500,000 minimum. Investment Policies: Equity. Investment Types: Late stage, and leveraged buyout. Industry Preferences: No preference. Geographic Preferences: Midwest and eastern U.S.

## Maryland

ABS Ventures (Baltimore)
1 South St., Ste. 2150
Baltimore, MD 21202
Phone: (410)895-3895
Fax: (410)895-3899
Preferred Investment Size: $500,000 maximum. Investment Types: Startup, first and second stage, and mezzanine. Industry Preferences: Communications, computer related, genetic engineering, and medical/ health related. Geographic Preferences: Entire U.S.

Anthem Capital, L.P.
16 S. Calvert St., Ste. 800
Baltimore, MD 21202-1305
Phone: (410)625-1510
Fax: (410)625-1735
Preferred Investment Size: $500,000 to $1,000,000. Investment Types: Early and later stage. Industry Preferences: Diversified. Geographic Preferences: Middle Atlantic.

Arete Corporation
3 Bethesda Metro Ctr., Ste. 770
Bethesda, MD 20814
Phone: (301)657-6268
Fax: (301)657-6254
Website: http://www.arete-microgen.com

Jill Wilmoth
Investment Types: Seed. Industry
Preferences: Alternative energy.
Geographic Preferences: Entire U.S.
and Canada.

Armata Partners
300 E. Lombard St.
Baltimore, MD 21202
Phone: (410)727-4495
E-mail: armata@digen.com
Preferred Investment Size: $100,000
to $500,000. Investment Types:
Mezzanine, leveraged buyout, and
special situations. Industry
Preferences: Internet related,
restaurants, and education.
Geographic Preferences: Middle
Atlantic, Southeast.

Catalyst Ventures
1119 St. Paul St.
Baltimore, MD 21202
Phone: (410)244-0123
Fax: (410)752-7721
Preferred Investment Size: $500,000
maximum. Investment Policies:
Equity. Investment Types: Research
and development, and early stage.
Industry Preferences: Data
communications, biotechnology, and
medical related. Geographic
Preferences: Middle Atlantic.

Grotech Capital Group
9690 Deereco Rd., Ste. 800
Timonium, MD 21093
Phone: (410)560-2000
Fax: (410)560-1910
Website: http://www.grotech.com
Frank A. Adams, President and CEO
Preferred Investment Size: $1,000,000
to $5,000,000. Investment Types:
First and second stage, mezzanine,
leveraged buyouts, and special
situations. Industry Preferences:
Diversified. Geographic Preferences:
Southeast and Middle Atlantic.

Kinetic Ventures LLC
2 Wisconsin Cir., Ste. 620
Chevy Chase, MD 20815
Phone: (301)652-8066
Fax: (301)652-8310
Investment Types: Startup, first stage,
second stage, and mezzanine. Industry
Preferences: Diversified technology.
Geographic Preferences: National.

Maryland Venture Capital Trust
217 E. Redwood St., Ste. 2204
Baltimore, MD 21202
Phone: (410)767-6361
Fax: (410)333-6931
E-mail:
rblank@mdbusiness.state.md.us
Preferred Investment Size: $1,000,000
to $5,000,000. Investment Types:
Seed, startup, first and second stage.
Geographic Preferences: Maryland.

New Enterprise Associates
(Baltimore)
1119 St. Paul St.
Baltimore, MD 21202
Phone: (410)244-0115
Fax: (410)752-7721
Website: http://www.nea.com
Frank A. Bonsal, Jr., Founding
Partner
Preferred Investment Size: $100,000
to $5,000,000. Investment Types:
Seed, startup, first and second stage,
mezzanine, and incubator. Industry
Preferences: Diversified. Geographic
Preferences: Entire U.S.

T. Rowe Price Threshold Partnerships
100 E. Pratt St.
Baltimore, MD 21202
Phone: (410)345-2000
Douglas O. Hickman, Managing
Director
Preferred Investment Size: $2,000,000
to $3,000,000. Investment Types:
Mezzanine, special situations,
expansion financing, and established
growing companies. Industry
Preferences: Diversified. Geographic
Preferences: Entire U.S.

Spring Capital Partners
16 W. Madison St.
Baltimore, MD 21201
Phone: (410)685-8000
Fax: (410)727-1436
E-mail: mailbox@springcap.com
Jay Wilson
Investment Types: Second stage,
mezzanine, and leveraged buyout.
Geographic Preferences: Mid-
Atlantic.

Technomart RGA
401 Washington Ave., Ste. 801
Baltimore, MD 21208
Phone: (410)828-6555

Fax: (410)828-6584
E-mail:
webmaster@technomartr.g.a.com
Investment Types: First stage,
leveraged buyout, and special
situations. Industry Preferences:
Diversified. Geographic Preferences:
National.

Triad Investor's Corp.
PO Box 16380
Baltimore, MD 21210
Phone: (410)467-1881
Fax: (410)467-1885
Barbara P. Melera, President
Preferred Investment Size: $100,000
to $1,000,000. Investment Types:
Seed, research and development,
startup, first and second stage.
Industry Preferences:
Communications, computer related,
electronics, energy/natural resources,
genetic engineering, medical and
health related. Geographic
Preferences: Middle Atlantic.

## Massachusetts

Adams, Harkness & Hill, Inc.
60 State St.
Boston, MA 02109
Phone: (617)371-3900
Tim McMahan, Managing Director
Preferred Investment Size: $500,000
to $1,000,000. Investment Types:
Late stage. Industry Preferences:
Computer, consumer, electronics,
genetic engineering, industrial
products and equipment, and medical.
Geographic Preferences: National.

Advanced Technology Ventures
(Boston)
281 Winter St., Ste. 350
Waltham, MA 02451
Phone: (781)290-0707
Fax: (781)684-0045
E-mail: info@atv-ventures.com
Website: http://www.atv-
ventures.com
Preferred Investment Size: $2,000,000
to $8,000,000. Investment Types:
Startup, first stage, second stage, and
mezzanine. Industry Preferences:
Diversified. Geographic Preferences:
No preference.

Advent International
75 State St., 29th Fl.
Boston, MA 02109
Phone: (617)951-9400
Fax: (617)951-0566
Website: http://
www.adventinernational.com
Dennis R. Costeilo, Chief Investment
Officer
Preferred Investment Size: $1,000,000
to $2,000,000. Investment Types:
Startup, first and second stage,
mezzanine, leveraged buyout, special
situations, recaps, and acquisitions.
Industry Preferences: Diversified.
Geographic Preferences: Entire U.S.
and Canada.

American Research and Development
30 Federal St.
Boston, MA 02110-2508
Phone: (617)423-7500
Fax: (617)423-9655
Maureen A. White, Administrative
Manager
Preferred Investment Size: $100,000
to $1,000,000. Investment Types:
Seed, startup, first and second stage,
and special situations. Industry
Preferences: Diversified technology.
Geographic Preferences: Northeast.

Ampersand Ventures
55 William St., Ste. 240
Wellesley, MA 02481
Phone: (617)239-0700
Fax: (617)239-0824
E-mail:
info@ampersandventures.com
Paul C. Zigman, Partner
Preferred Investment Size: $1,000,000
to $5,000,000. Investment Types:
Startup, first and second stage,
mezzanine, leveraged buyout, and
special situations. Industry
Preferences: Diversified. Geographic
Preferences: No preference.

Analog Devices, Inc.
1 Technology Way
PO Box 9106
Norwood, MA 02062-9106
Phone: (781)329-4700
Free: 800-262-5643
Website: http://www.analog.com
Venture capital supplier. Prefers to
invest in industries involved in analog
devices.

Applied Technology
1 Cranberry Hill
Lexington, MA 02421-7397
Phone: (617)862-8622
Fax: (617)862-8367
Ellie McCormack, Analyst
Preferred Investment Size: $100,000
to $2,000,000. Investment Types:
Seed, startup, first and second stage.
Industry Preferences: Diversified.
Geographic Preferences: Entire U.S.

Argo Global Capital
210 Broadway, Ste. 101
Lynnfield, MA 01940
Phone: (781)592-2550
Fax: (781)592-5230
Investment Types: Startup, first stage,
second stage, mezzanine, leveraged
buyout, and special situations.
Industry Preferences:
Communications. Geographic
Preferences: National.

Ascent Venture Management
255 State St., 5th Fl.
Boston, MA 02109
Phone: (617)227-9200
Fax: (617)227-9240
E-mail: info@ascentvp.com
Website: http://www.ascentvp.com
Leigh E. Michl, Managing Director
Investment Types: Seed, startup, first
stage, second stage, mezzanine, and
leveraged buyout. Industry
Preferences: Diversified. Geographic
Preferences: Eastern U.S.

Atlantic Capital
164 Cushing Highway
Cohasset, MA 02025
Phone: (617)383-9449
Fax: (617)383-6040
Preferred Investment Size: $100,000
to $500,000. Investment Policies:
Equity. Investment Types: Early
stage. Industry Preferences:
Diversified. Geographic Preferences:
National.

Atlantic Capital Corporation
44 School St., Ste. 410
Boston, MA 02108-4200
Phone: (617)227-9840
Fax: (617)227-8753
E-mail: info@atlanticcap.com
Website: http://www.atlanticcap.com

Investment Types: Seed, startup, first
stage, and leveraged buyout. Industry
Preferences: Diversified. Geographic
Preferences: National.

Atlas Venture
222 Berkeley St.
Boston, MA 02116
Phone: (617)859-9290
Fax: (617)859-9292
Website: http://www.atlasventure.com
Preferred Investment Size: $500,000
to $5,000,000. Investment Types:
Seed, research and development, first
and second stage, mezzanine, and
expansion. Industry Preferences:
Communications, computer, genetic
engineering, medical and health
related. Geographic Preferences:
Entire U.S. and Canada.

BancBoston Capital/BancBoston
Ventures
175 Federal St., 10th Fl.
Mail code 75-10-01
Boston, MA 02110
Phone: (617)434-2509
Fax: (617)434-1153
E-mail: cannovicki@bkb.com
Frederick M. Fritz, President and
Managing Director
Preferred Investment Size: $1,000,000
to $3,000,000. Investment Types:
First and second stage, mezzanine,
leveraged buyouts, special situations,
and minority buyouts. Industry
Preferences: Diversified. Geographic
Preferences: Entire U.S. and Atlantic
provinces of Canada.

Battery Ventures (Boston)
20 Williams St., Ste. 200
Wellesley, MA 02481
Phone: (781)577-1000
Fax: (781)577-1001
Website: http://www.battery.com
Morgan M. Jones
Preferred Investment Size: $1,000,000
to $10,000,000. Investment Types:
Seed, startup, first and second stage,
mezzanine, and leveraged buyout.
Industry Preferences:
Communications, computer, computer
and communications distribution.
Geographic Preferences: No
preference.

Bessemer Venture Partners
(Wellesley Hills)
83 Walnut St.
Wellesley Hills, MA 02481
Phone: (781)237-6050
Fax: (781)235-7576
E-mail: travis@bvpny.com
Website: http://www.bvp.com
Investment Types: Seed, research and development, start-up, first stages, leveraged buyout, special situations, and control block purchases. Industry Preferences: Communications, computer related, consumer products, distribution, and electronics. Geographic Preferences: National.

Boston Capital Ventures
Old City Hall
45 School St.
Boston, MA 02108
Phone: (617)227-6550
Fax: (617)227-3847
E-mail: info@bcv.com
Website: http://www.bcv.com
Alexander Wilmerding
Preferred Investment Size: $250,000 to $8,000,000. Investment Types: Startup, first and second stage. Industry Preferences: Diversified. Geographic Preferences: Entire U.S.

Boston Financial & Equity Corp.
20 Overland St.
PO Box 15071
Boston, MA 02215
Phone: (617)267-2900
Fax: (617)437-7601
E-mail: debbie@bfec.com
Deborah J. Monosson, Senior Vice President
Preferred Investment Size: $100,000 to $1,500,000. Investment Types: Early and late stage. Industry Preferences: Diversified. Geographic Preferences: National.

Boston Millennia Partners
30 Rowes Wharf
Boston, MA 02110
Phone: (617)428-5150
Fax: (617)428-5160
Website: http://
www.millenniapartners.com
Dana Callow, Managing General Partner
Preferred Investment Size: $1,000,000 to $15,000,000. Investment Policies:

Equity. Investment Types: Early and late stage. Industry Preferences: Communication, computer related, consumer services, natural resources, genetic engineering, medical, and education. Geographic Preferences: National.

Bristol Investment Trust
842A Beacon St.
Boston, MA 02215-3199
Phone: (617)566-5212
Fax: (617)267-0932
E-mail: bernardberkman@prodigy.net
Preferred Investment Size: $100,000 minimum. Investment Policies: Equity. Investment Types: Early and late stage. Industry Preferences: Restaurants, retailing, consumer distribution, medical/health, and real estate. Geographic Preferences: Northeast.

Burr, Egan, Deleage, and Co.
(Boston)
1 Post Office Sq., Ste. 3800
Boston, MA 02109
Phone: (617)482-8020
Fax: (617)482-1944
Preferred Investment Size: $1,000,000 to $5,000,000. Investment Types: No preference. Industry Preferences: Communications, computer, and medical/health related. Geographic Preferences: Entire U.S.

Cambridge/Samsung Partners
One Exeter Plaza
Ninth Fl.
Boston, MA 02116
Phone: (617)262-4440
Fax: (617)262-5562
Aashish Kalra, Associate
Preferred Investment Size: $100,000 minimum. Investment Policies: Equity. Investment Types: Early stage. Industry Preferences: Diversified. Geographic Preferences: National.

Charles River Ventures
1000 Winter St., Ste. 3300
Waltham, MA 02451
Phone: (781)487-7060
Fax: (781)487-7065
Website: http://www.crv.com
Richard M. Burnes, Jr., General Partner

Preferred Investment Size: $1,000,000 to $6,000,000. Investment Types: Seed, startup, first and second stage. Industry Preferences: Communications, computer, and electronics. Geographic Preferences: No preference.

Chestnut Partners, Inc.
One Financial Center, 28th Floor
Boston, MA 02111
Phone: (617)832-8600
Fax: (617)832-8610
E-mail: chestnut@chestnutp.com
Drew Zalkind, Senior Vice President
Preferred Investment Size: $100,000 to $1,000,000. Investment Types: Seed, research and development, startup, and first stage. Industry Preferences: Diversified. Geographic Preferences: No preference.

Claflin Capital Management, Inc.
10 Liberty Sq., Ste. 300
Boston, MA 02109
Phone: (617)426-6505
Fax: (617)482-0016
E-mail: venutre@clafcap.com
Rolf Stutz, General Partner
Preferred Investment Size: $100,000 to $170,000. Investment Types: Seed, startup, and first stage. Industry Preferences: Diversified. Geographic Preferences: Northeast.

Comdisco Venture Group (Waltham)
Totton Pond Office Center
400-1 Totten Pond Rd.
Waltham, MA 02451
Phone: (617)672-0250
Fax: (617)398-8099
Investment Types: Seed, startup, first and second stage, receivables, loans, and equipment leases. Industry Preferences: Diversified. Geographic Preferences: National.

Commonwealth Capital Ventures, L.P.
20 William St.
Wellesley, MA 02481
Phone: (781)237-7373
Fax: (781)235-8627
Website: http://www.ccvlp.com
Preferred Investment Size: $500,000 to $5,000,000. Investment Policies: Equity. Investment Types: Early and late stage. Industry Preferences:

Diversified communication and computer technology, consumer products and services, retailing, distribution, electronics, medical and health related. Geographic Preferences: New England.

Community Technology Fund
108 Bay State Rd.
Boston, MA 02215
Phone: (617)353-4550
Fax: (617)353-6141
E-mail: rcrawford@bu.edu
Website: http://www.bu.edu/ctf
Randall C. Crawford, Director
Investment Types: Seed, research and development, startup, first stage, and second stage. Industry Preferences: Diversified technology. Geographic Preferences: Northeast.

Comvest LLC
20 William St., Ste. 210
Wellesley, MA 02481
Phone: (781)239-7600
Fax: (781)239-0377
Investment Types: Startup, first and second stage. Industry Preferences: Communications and computer related. Geographic Preferences: National.

Corning Capital
121 High Street
Boston, MA 02110
Phone: (617)338-2656
Preferred Investment Size: $100,000 to $500,000. Investment Policies: Equity. Investment Types: Early and late stage. Industry Preferences: Diversified technology. Geographic Preferences: National.

Downer & Co.
211 Congress St.
Boston, MA 02110
Phone: (617)482-6200
Fax: (617)482-6201
E-mail: cdowner@downer.com
Website: http://www.downer.com
Charles W. Downer
Preferred Investment Size: $250,000 to $500,000. Investment Types: Early and late stage. Industry Preferences: Computer related, retailing, distribution, electronics, and healthcare. Geographic Preferences: Northeastern U.S. and Canada.

Eastech Management Co., Inc.
30 Federal St.
Boston, MA 02110
Phone: (617)423-1096
Fax: (617)695-2699
Michael H. Shanahan, Partner
Preferred Investment Size: $250,000 to $1,000,000. Investment Types: Seed, startup, first and second stage. Industry Preferences: Communications, computer, electronics, and industrial controls and sensors. Geographic Preferences: Northeast.

Fidelity Ventures
82 Devonshire St., Mail Zone R25C
Boston, MA 02109
Phone: (617)563-9160
Fax: (617)476-5015
Neal Yanofsky, Vice President
Preferred Investment Size: $500,000 to $5,000,000. Investment Types: Startup, first and second stage, leveraged buyout, and special situations. Industry Preferences: Diversified. Geographic Preferences: Northeast.

Fowler, Anthony & Company
20 Walnut St.
Wellesley, MA 02481
Phone: (781)237-4201
Fax: (781)237-7718
Investment Types: Seed, startup, first stage, second stage, and mezzanine. Industry Preferences: Diversified. Geographic Preferences: Entire U.S. and Canada.

GCC Investments
1300 Boylston St.
Chestnut Hill, MA 02467
Phone: (617)975-3200
Fax: (617)975-3201
Michael Greeley, Senior Vice President
Investment Types: First stage, second stage, mezzanine, leveraged buyout, and special situations. Industry Preferences: Diversified. Geographic Preferences: Entire U.S. and Canada.

Gemini Investors
20 William St.
Wellesley, MA 02481
Phone: (781)237-7001
Fax: (781)237-7233

C. Redington Barrett, III, Managing Director
Investment Types: Second stage, mezzanine, leveraged buyout, and special situations. Industry Preferences: Diversified. Geographic Preferences: National.

Greylock Management Corp. (Boston)
1 Federal St.
Boston, MA 02110-2065
Phone: (617)423-5525
Fax: (617)482-0059
David B. Aronoff
Preferred Investment Size: $500,000 to $5,000,000. Investment Types: Startup, first and second stage, mezzanine, leveraged buyout, and special situations. Industry Preferences: Diversified. Geographic Preferences: No preference.

Gryphon Ventures
222 Berkeley St., Ste.1600
Boston, MA 02116
Phone: (617)267-9191
Fax: (617)267-4293
E-mail: all@gryphoninc.com
Andrew J. Atkinson, Vice President
Investment Types: Startup, first stage, second stage. Industry Preferences: Energy/natural resources, genetic engineering, and industrial products and equipment. Geographic Preferences: National.

Halpern, Denny & Co.
500 Boylston St.
Boston, MA 02116
Phone: (617)536-6602
Fax: (617)536-8535
David P. Malm, Partner
Investment Types: First stage, second stage, mezzanine, and leveraged buyouts. Industry Preferences: Energy/natural resources, genetic engineering, industrial products and equipment. Geographic Preferences: National.

Harbourvest Partners, LLC
1 Financial Center, 44th Fl.
Boston, MA 02111
Phone: (617)348-3707
Fax: (617)350-0305
Kevin Delbridge, Managing Partner

Preferred Investment Size: $5,000,000 maximum. Investment Types: First and second stage, mezzanine, and leveraged buyout. Also invests in other funds and partnerships. Industry Preferences: Diversified. Geographic Preferences: No preference.

Highland Capital Partners
2 International Pl.
Boston, MA 02110
Phone: (617)531-1500
Fax: (617)531-1550
E-mail: info@hcp.com
Website: http://www.hcp.com
Keith Benjamin, General Partner
Preferred Investment Size: $500,000 to $5,000,000. Investment Types: Seed, research and development, startup, first and second stage, mezzanine, special situations, control block purchases, and consolidations. Industry Preferences: Communications, computer, genetic engineering, and medical/health related. Geographic Preferences: Entire U.S.

M/C Venture Partners
75 State St., Ste. 2500
Boston, MA 02109
Phone: (617)345-7200
Fax: (617)345-7201
Matthew J. Rubins
Preferred Investment Size: $5,000,000 to $25,000,000. Investment Types: Startup, first and second stage, and industry roll ups. Industry Preferences: Communications. Geographic Preferences: Entire U.S. and Canada.

M/C Venture Partners
75 State St., Ste. 2500
Boston, MA 02109
Phone: (617)345-7200
Fax: (617)345-7201
Matthew J. Rubins
Investment Types: Startup, first stage, second stage, and industry roll ups. Industry Preferences: Communications. Geographic Preferences: National.

Massachusetts Capital Resources Co.
420 Boylston St.
Boston, MA 02116
Phone: (617)536-3900

Fax: (617)536-7930
William J. Torpey, Jr., President
Preferred Investment Size: $250,000 to $1,000,000. Investment Policies: Equity. Investment Types: Late stage. Industry Preferences: No preference. Geographic Preferences: Northeast.

Massachusetts Technology Development Corp. (MTDC)
148 State St.
Boston, MA 02109
Phone: (617)723-4920
Fax: (617)723-5983
E-mail: jhodgman@mtdc.com
Website: http://www.mtdc.com
John F. Hodgman, President
Preferred Investment Size: $100,000 to $500,000. Investment Types: Seed, startup, first and second stage. Industry Preferences: Diversified. Geographic Preferences: Northeast.

Matrix Partners
Bay Colony Corporate Center
1000 Winter St., Ste.4500
Waltham, MA 02451
Phone: (781)890-2244
Fax: (781)890-2288
Website: http://www.matrixpartners.com
Andrew Marcuvitz, General Partner
Preferred Investment Size: $500,000 to $5,000,000. Investment Types: Startup, first and second stage, and leveraged buyout. Industry Preferences: Diversified. Geographic Preferences: Entire U.S.

MDT Advisers, Inc.
125 Cambridge Park Dr.
Cambridge, MA 02140-2314
Phone: (617)234-2200
Fax: (617)234-2210
Michael E. A. O'Malley
Preferred Investment Size: $500,000 to $5,000,000. Investment Types: Startup, first and second stage, mezzanine, leveraged buyout, special situations, and secondaries. Industry Preferences: Diversified. Geographic Preferences: No preference.

Milk Street Ventures
9 Harcourt, Ste. 206
Boston, MA 02116
Phone: (617)345-7228
Fax: (617)345-7201

E-mail: paschober@aol.com
Investment Types: Startup, first stage, second stage, and mezzanine. Industry Preferences: Communications and computer related, Geographic Preferences: National.

New Health Ventures
100 Summer St., 4th Fl.
Mail Stop 01-04
Boston, MA 02110
Phone: (617)832-4741
Fax: (617)832-4630
Investment Types: Startup, first stage, second stage, and special situations. Industry Preferences: Genetic engineering, medical and health related. Geographic Preferences: National.

North Bridge Venture Partners
950 Winter St. Ste. 4600
Waltham, MA 02451
Phone: (781)290-0004
Fax: (781)290-0999
E-mail: eta@nbvp.com
Preferred Investment Size: $100,000 to $6,000,000. Investment Types: Seed, research and development, startup, first and second stage. Industry Preferences: Communications, computer related, distribution, and electronics. Geographic Preferences: Entire U.S.

Norwest Venture Capital
40 William St., Ste. 305
Wellesley, MA 02481-3902
Phone: (781)237-5870
Fax: (781)237-6270
Investment Types: Seed, startup, first and second stage, mezzanine, leveraged buyout, and special situations. Industry Preferences: Diversified. Geographic Preferences: National.

OneLiberty Ventures
150 Cambridge Park Dr.
Boston, MA 02140
Phone: (617)492-7280
Fax: (617)492-7290
Website: http://www.oneliberty.com
Edwin M. Kania, Jr., General Partner
Preferred Investment Size: $500,000 to $5,000,000. Investment Policies: Equity. Investment Types: Early and late stage. Industry Preferences:

Diversified technology. Geographic Preferences: Entire U.S. and Canada.

**Palmer Service Corp.**
200 Unicorn Park Dr.
Woburn, MA 01801
Phone: (781)933-5445
Fax: (781)933-0698
Preferred Investment Size: $250,000 to $1,000,000. Investment Types: Startup, first and second stage, and special situations. Industry Preferences: Communications, computer, energy/natural resources, industrial, education, finance, and publishing. Geographic Preferences: Northeast, Southeast, Southwest, East Coast, Midwest, and Middle Atlantic.

**Pharm-Eco Laboratories, Inc.**
128 Spring St.
Lexington, MA 02421
Phone: (781)861-9303
Fax: (781)861-9386
Investment Types: Seed, research and development, startup, and first stage. Industry Preferences: Pharmaceuticals. Geographic Preferences: National.

**Pioneer Capital Corp.**
60 State St.
Boston, MA 02109
Phone: (617)422-4947
Fax: (617)742-7315
Website: http://www.pioneer-capital.com
C. W. Dick, Partner
Preferred Investment Size: $500,000 to $5,000,000. Investment Types: Seed, startup, first and second stage, mezzanine, and leveraged buyout. Industry Preferences: Diversified. Geographic Preferences: East Coast.

**Polaris Venture Partners**
Bay Colony Corporate Ctr.
1000 Winter St., Ste. 3500
Waltham, MA 02451
Phone: (781)290-0770
Fax: (781)290-0880
E-mail: partners@polarisventures.com
Website: http://www.polarisventures.com
Michael Hirschland
Investment Types: Seed, startup, first and second stages. Industry

Preferences: Information technology, medical and health related. Geographic Preferences: National.

**Prism Venture Partners**
100 Lowder Brook Dr., Ste. 2500
Westwood, MA 02090
Phone: (781)302-4000
Fax: (781)302-4040
E-mail: dwbaum@prismventure.com
Investment Types: Startup, first stage, second stage, and mezzanine. Industry Preferences: Communications, computer related, electronic components and instrumentation, medical and health. Geographic Preferences: National.

**Royalty Capital Management**
5 Downing Rd.
Lexington, MA 02421-6918
Phone: (781)861-8490
Investment Types: Startup, first stage, second stage, leveraged buyout, and special situations. Industry Preferences: Diversified. Geographic Preferences: Northeast.

**Sage Management Group**
44 South Street
PO Box 2026
East Dennis, MA 02641
Phone: (508)385-7172
Fax: (508)385-7272
E-mail: sagemgt@capecod.net
Charles Bauer
Preferred Investment Size: $500,000 to $1,000,000. Investment Policies: Equity. Investment Types: Early and late stage. Industry Preferences: Diversified technology. Geographic Preferences: National.

**Seacoast Capital Partners**
55 Ferncroft Rd.
Danvers, MA 01923
Phone: (978)750-1300
E-mail: gdeli@seacoastcapital.com
Website: http://www.seacoastcapital.com
Thomas Gorman, Managing Director
Preferred Investment Size: $2,000,000 to $15,000,000. Investment Policies: Loans and equity investments. Investment Types: Expansion, later stage. Industry Preferences: Diversified. Geographic Preferences: National.

**Seaflower Ventures**
Bay Colony Corporate Ctr.
1000 Winter St. Ste.1000
Waltham, MA 02451
Phone: (781)466-9552
Fax: (781)466-9553
E-mail: moot@seaflower.com
Alexander Moot, Partner
Investment Types: Seed, research and development, startup, first and second stage. Industry Preferences: Genetic engineering, industrial products and equipment, medical and health related. Geographic Preferences: Eastern U.S. and Midwest.

**Shawmut Capital Partners**
75 Federal St., 18th Fl.
Boston, MA 02110
Phone: (617)368-4900
Fax: (617)368-4910
Website: http://www.shawmutcapital.com
Glenn Dixon, Managing Director
Investment Types: Startup, first stage, second stage, mezzanine, leveraged buyout, and special situations. Industry Preferences: Financial services and applications. Geographic Preferences: Entire U.S. and Canada.

**Softbank Capital Partners**
10 Langley Rd., Ste. 202
Newton Center, MA 02459
Phone: (617)928-9300
Fax: (617)928-9305
E-mail: clax@bvc.com
Investment Types: Seed, startup, first stage, second stage, mezzanine, leveraged buyout, and special situations. Industry Preferences: Communications and Internet. Geographic Preferences: Entire U.S. and Canada.

**Solstice Capital**
33 Broad St., 3rd Fl.
Boston, MA 02109
Phone: (617)523-7733
Fax: (617)523-5827
E-mail: solticecapital@solcap.com
Henry Newman, Partner
Investment Types: Startup, first stage and second stage. Industry Preferences: Diversified. Geographic Preferences: National.

Spectrum Equity Investors
One International Pl., 29th Fl.
Boston, MA 02110
Phone: (617)464-4600
Fax: (617)464-4601
William Collatos, Managing General
Partner
Investment Types: Seed, startup, first
stage, second stage, mezzanine,
leveraged buyout, and special
situations. Industry Preferences:
Communications and computer
related. Geographic Preferences:
National.

Spray Venture Partners
One Walnut St.
Boston, MA 02108
Phone: (617)305-4140
Fax: (617)305-4144
Preferred Investment Size: $50,000 to
$4,000,000. Investment Policies:
Equity. Investment Types: Early and
late stage. Industry Preferences:
Medical and health related, and
genetic engineering. Geographic
Preferences: National.

Stonebridge Technology Associates
10 Post Office Sq.
Boston, MA 02109
Phone: (617)357-1770
Fax: (617)357-4933
Website: http://www.stonebr.com
James Chung, Vice President
Investment Types: Startup, first stage,
second stage, and mezzanine. Industry
Preferences: Computer related and
communications. Geographic
Preferences: Northeast.

Summit Partners
600 Atlantic Ave., Ste. 2800
Boston, MA 02210-2227
Phone: (617)824-1000
Fax: (617)824-1100
Website: http://
www.summitpartners.com
Gregory Avis, Managing Partner
Preferred Investment Size: $5,000,000
maximum. Investment Types: First
and second stage, mezzanine,
leveraged buyout, special situations,
and control block purchases. Industry
Preferences: Diversified. Geographic
Preferences: Entire U.S. and Canada.

TA Associates, Inc. (Boston)
High Street Tower
125 High St., Ste. 2500
Boston, MA 02110
Phone: (617)574-6700
Fax: (617)574-6728
Brian Conway, Managing Director
Preferred Investment Size: $5,000,000
maximum. Investment Types:
Leveraged buyout, special situations,
control block purchases, and all stages
of business. Industry Preferences:
Diversified. Geographic Preferences:
No preference.

Trans National Ventures
133 Federal St.
Boston, MA 02110
Phone: (617)369-1200
Fax: (617)369-1063
E-mail: tnventures@tninternet.com
Investment Types: Seed, research and
development, startup, first stage,
second stage, mezzanine, leveraged
buyout, and special situations.
Industry Preferences: Consumer
services. Geographic Preferences:
Entire U.S. and Canada.

TTC Ventures
One Main St., 6th Fl.
Cambridge, MA 02142
Phone: (617)528-3137
Fax: (617)577-1715
E-mail: info@ttcventures.com
Investment Types: Seed, startup, first
stage, second stage, and mezzanine.
Industry Preferences: Computer
related. Geographic Preferences:
National.

TVM Techno Venture Management
101 Arch St., Ste. 1950
Boston, MA 02110
Phone: (617)345-9320
Fax: (617)345-9377
E-mail: info@tvmvc.com
John J. DiBello, Partner
Venture capital firm providing early
stage financing as well as mezzanine
and foreign market entry. Areas of
interest include high technology such
as software, communications,
medical, and biotechnology
industries. Preferred investment size
is $1 million to $3.5 million.

Venture Capital Fund of New
England
20 Walnut St., Ste. 120
Wellesley Hills, MA 02481-2175
Phone: (781)239-8262
Fax: (781)239-8263
E-mail: kjdvcfne3@aol.com
Kevin J. Dougherty, General Partner
Preferred Investment Size: $250,000
to $1,000,000. Investment Types:
Startup, first and second stage.
Industry Preferences: Diversified.
Geographic Preferences: Northeast,
New England.

Venture Investment Company
(VIMAC)
177 Milk St.
Boston, MA 02190-3410
Phone: (617)292-3300
Fax: (617)292-7979
E-mail: bzeisig@vimac.com
Mark Robinson, Partner
Investment Types: Seed, startup, first
and second stage. Industry
Preferences: Diversified technology.
Geographic Preferences: Northeast
U.S. and Ontario, Canada.

Zero Stage Capital
101 Main St., 17th Fl.
Cambridge, MA 02142
Phone: (617)876-5355
Fax: (617)876-1248
E-mail: zerostage@aol.com
Paul Kelley, Managing General
Partner
Preferred Investment Size: $50,000 to
$1,000,000. Investment Types: Early
and later stage. Industry Preferences:
Diversified technology. Geographic
Preferences: Northeast.

## Michigan

Arbor Partners, L.L.C.
130 South First St.
Ann Arbor, MI 48104
Phone: (734)668-9000
E-mail: jburr@arborpartners.com
Jason Burr, Associate
Preferred Investment Size: $500,000
to $10,000,000. Investment Policies:
Equity. Investment Types: Early and
late stage. Industry Preferences:
Diversified technology. Geographic
Preferences: National.

EDF Ventures
425 N. Main St.
Ann Arbor, MI 48104
Phone: (734)663-3213
Fax: (734)663-7358
E-mail: edf@edfvc.com
Mary Campbell, Partner
Investment Types: Seed, startup, first stage, second stage, mezzanine, and leveraged buyout. Industry Preferences: Diversified technology. Geographic Preferences: Midwest.

Enterprise Development Fund
425 North Main St.
Ann Arbor, MI 48104
Phone: (734)663-3213
Fax: (734)663-7358
E-mail: edf@edfvc.com
Mary L. Campbell, General Partner
Preferred Investment Size: $1,000,000 to $2,000,000. Investment Policies: Equity. Investment Types: Early and late stage. Industry Preferences: Diversified technology. Geographic Preferences: Great Lakes region.

Investcare Partners
31500 Northwestern Hwy., Ste. 120
Farmington Hills, MI 48334
Phone: (248)851-9200
Fax: (248)851-9208
E-mail: gma@gmacapital.com
Website: http://www.gmacapital.com
Malcolm Moss, Managing Director
Investment Types: Second stage and leveraged buyout. Industry Preferences: Medical and health related. Geographic Preferences: National.

Liberty Bidco Investment Corp.
30833 Northwestern Highway, Ste. 211
Farmington Hills, MI 48334
Phone: (248)626-6070
Fax: (248)626-6072
James Zabriskie, Vice President
Preferred Investment Size: $250,000 to $2,000,000. Investment Types: Late stage and special situations. Industry Preferences: Diversified. Geographic Preferences: Midwestern U.S. and Ontario, Canada.

Seaflower Ventures
5170 Nicholson Rd.
PO Box 474

Fowlerville, MI 48836
Phone: (517)223-3335
Fax: (517)223-3337
E-mail: gibbons@seaflower.com
M. Christine Gibbons, Partner
Investment Types: Seed, research and development, startup, first and second stage. Industry Preferences: Genetic engineering, industrial products and equipment, medical and health related. Geographic Preferences: Eastern U.S. and Midwest.

Tullis Dickerson & Company
303 Detroit St., Ste.301
Ann Arbor, MI 48104
Phone: (734)623-6300
E-mail: tactdco@aol.com
Investment Types: Seed, research and development, startup, first stage, second stage, mezzanine, leveraged buyout, control block purchases, industry roll ups, and special situations. Industry Preferences: Computer related, genetic engineering, medical/health related, and agriculture. Geographic Preferences: National.

Venture Funding, Ltd.
Fisher Bldg.
3011 West Grand Blvd., Ste. 321
Detroit, MI 48202
Phone: (313)871-3606
Fax: (313)873-4935
Monis Schuster, Vice President
Preferred Investment Size: $250,000 to $500,000. Investment Policies: Equity. Investment Types: Startup and special situations. Industry Preferences: Diversified. Geographic Preferences: National.

Wellmax, Inc.
3541 Bendway Blvd., Ste. 100
Bloomfield Hills, MI 48301
Phone: (248)646-3554
Fax: (248)646-6220
Preferred Investment Size: $100,000.
Investment Policies: Equity.
Investment Types: Early and late stage and special situations. Industry Preferences: Diversified. Geographic Preferences: Midwest, Southeast.

White Pines Management, L.L.C.
2401 Plymouth Rd., Ste. B
Ann Arbor, MI 48105

Phone: (734)747-9401
Fax: (734)747-9704
E-mail: ibund@whitepines.com
Preferred Investment Size: $1,000,000 to $4,000,000. Investment Types: Second stage, mezzanine, leveraged buyout, and special situations. Industry Preferences: Diversified. Geographic Preferences: Southeast and Midwest.

### Minnesota

Affinity Capital Management
1900 Foshay Tower
821 Marquette Ave.
Minneapolis, MN 55402
Phone: (612)904-2305
Fax: (612)204-0913
Preferred Investment Size: $250,000 to $1,100,000. Investment Types: Seed, research and development, startup, first and second stage, and mezzanine. Industry Preferences: Medical/Health related. Geographic Preferences: Midwest.

Artesian Capital
1700 Foshay Tower
821 Marquette Ave.
Minneapolis, MN 55402
Phone: (612)334-5600
Fax: (612)334-5601
E-mail: artesian@artesian.com
Frank B. Bennett, President
Preferred Investment Size: $100,000 to $500,000. Investment Types: Seed, research and development, and startup. Industry Preferences: Diversified. Geographic Preferences: Midwest.

Cherry Tree Investments, Inc.
7601 France Ave. S, Ste. 150
Edina, MN 55435
Phone: (612)893-9012
Fax: (612)893-9036
Gordon F. Stofer, Managing Partner
Preferred Investment Size: $100,000 to $5,000,000. Investment Types: Seed, startup, first and second stage, mezzanine, and management buyout. Industry Preferences: Diversified. Geographic Preferences: Midwest.

Coral Ventures
60 S. 6th St., Ste. 3510
Minneapolis, MN 55402

Phone: (612)335-8666
Fax: (612)335-8668
Website: http://
www.coralventures.com
Mark C. Headrick, Senior Associate
Preferred Investment Size: $100,000
to $8,000,000. Investment Types:
Seed, research and development,
startup, first and second stage, and
mezzanine. Industry Preferences:
Diversified technology. Geographic
Preferences: No preference.

Crescendo Venture Management,
L.L.C.
800 LaSalle Ave., Ste. 2250
Minneapolis, MN 55402
Phone: (612)607-2800
Fax: (612)607-2801
Website: http://www.iaiventures.com
Jeffrey R. Tollefson, Vice President
Preferred Investment Size: $250,000
to $5,000,000. Investment Types:
Startup, early and late stage. Industry
Preferences: Diversified information
technology. Geographic Preferences:
National.

Development Corp. of Austin
1900 Eighth Ave., NW
Austin, MN 55912
Phone: (507)433-0346
Fax: (507)433-0361
E-mail: dca@smig.net
Website: http://
www.spamtownusa.com
Preferred Investment Size: $100,000.
Investment Types: Startup and early
stage. Industry Preferences:
Diversified industrial products and
equipment. Geographic Preferences:
Minnesota.

The Food Fund, L.P.
5720 Smatana Dr., Ste. 300
Minnetonka, MN 55343
Phone: (612)939-3950
Fax: (612)939-8106
John Trucano, Managing General
Partner
Preferred Investment Size: $100,000
to $250,000. Investment Types:
Startup, first and second stage,
leveraged buyout, and special
situations. Industry Preferences:
Consumer food and beverage
products. Geographic Preferences:
Entire U.S.

Gideon Hixon Venture
1900 Foshay Tower
821 Marquette Ave.
Minneapolis, MN 55402
Phone: (612)904-2314
Fax: (612)204-0913
E-mail: bkwhitney@gideonhixon.com
Preferred Investment Size: $100,000
to $1,000,000. Investment Policies:
Equity. Investment Types: Startup,
early and late stage. Industry
Preferences: Diversified
communication and computer
technology, education, finance and
insurance, and publishing. Geographic
Preferences: Minnesota.

Medallion Capital, Inc.
7831 Glenroy Rd., Ste. 480
Minneapolis, MN 55439-3132
Phone: (612)831-2025
Stephen Lewis, Vice President
Investment Types: Second stage,
mezzanine, and leveraged buyout.
Industry Preferences: Diversified.
Geographic Preferences: National.

Medical Innovation Partners, Inc.
6450 City West Pkwy.
Eden Prairie, MN 55344-3245
Phone: (612)828-9616
Fax: (612)828-9596
Mark B. Knudson, Ph.D., Managing
Partner
Preferred Investment Size: $100,000
to $5,000,000. Investment Types:
Seed, startup, and first stage. Industry
Preferences: Medical technology and
healthcare. Geographic Preferences:
Northwest and Midwest.

Milestone Growth Fund, Inc.
401 2nd Ave. S., Ste. 1032
Minneapolis, MN 55401-2310
Phone: (612)338-0090
Fax: (612)338-1172
E-mail: milestone7@aol.com
Esperanza Guerrero-Anderson,
President and CEO
Preferred Investment Size: $200,000
to $500,000. Investment Types:
Second stage. Industry Preferences:
Communication, computer,
distribution, electronics, genetic
engineering, and industrial products
and equipment. Geographic
Preferences: Minnesota.

Northeast Ventures Corp.
802 Alworth Bldg.
Duluth, MN 55802
Phone: (218)722-9915
Fax: (218)722-9871
Greg Sandbulte, President
Preferred Investment Size: $100,000
to $500,000. Investment Policies:
Equity. Investment Types: Startup,
early and late stage. Industry
Preferences: No preference.
Geographic Preferences: Midwest.

Norwest Equity Partners V, L.P.
2800 Piper Jaffray Tower
222 S. 9th St.
Minneapolis, MN 55402-3388
Phone: (612)667-1650
Fax: (612)667-1660
Charles B. Lennin, Partner
Preferred Investment Size: $2,000,000
to $3,000,000. Investment Policies:
Equity. Investment Types: Start-up,
expansion, later stage. Industry
Preferences: Diversified. Geographic
Preferences: National.

Norwest Venture Capital
2800 Piper Jaffray Tower
222 S. 9th St.
Minneapolis, MN 55402-3388
Phone: (612)667-1650
Fax: (612)667-1660
Charles B. Lennin, Partner
Preferred Investment Size: $2,000,000
to $3,000,000. Investment Types:
Seed, startup, first and second stage,
mezzanine, leveraged buyout, and
special situations. Industry
Preferences: Diversified. Geographic
Preferences: Entire U.S.

Oak Investment Partners
(Minneapolis)
4550 Norwest Center
90 S. 7th St.
Minneapolis, MN 55402
Phone: (612)339-9322
Fax: (612)337-8017
Website: http://www.oakinv.com
Preferred Investment Size: $250,000
to $5,000,000. Investment Types:
Seed, startup, first stage, leveraged
buyout, and special situations.
Industry Preferences:
Communications, computer related,

consumer restaurants and retailing, electronics, and medical/health related. Geographic Preferences: Entire U.S.

Pathfinder Venture Capital Funds (Minneapolis)
7300 Metro Blvd., Ste. 585
Minneapolis, MN 55439
Phone: (612)835-1121
Fax: (612)835-8389
E-mail: jahrens620@aol.com
Jack K. Ahrens, II, Investment Officer
Preferred Investment Size: $250,000 to $500,000. Investment Types: Seed, startup, first and second stage, mezzanine, leveraged buyouts, and special situations. Industry Preferences: Diversified. Geographic Preferences: Entire U.S. and Canada.

Piper Jaffray Ventures, Inc.
222 S. 9th St.
Minneapolis, MN 55402
Phone: (612)342-5686
Fax: (612)337-8514
Preferred Investment Size: $1,000,000 to $5,000,000. Investment Types: First and second stage, and mezzanine. Industry Preferences: Computer and medical/health related. Geographic Preferences: Entire U.S.

St. Paul Venture Capital, Inc.
10400 Vicking Dr., Ste. 550
Eden Prairie, MN 55344
Phone: (612)995-7474
Fax: (612)995-7475
Barb Shronts
Preferred Investment Size: $500,000 to $2,000,000. Investment Types: Startup, early and late stage. Industry Preferences: Diversified. Geographic Preferences: National.

Shared Ventures, Inc.
6559 York Ave. S
Edina, MN 55435
Phone: (612)291-3411
Investment Types: Second stage, leveraged buyout, and special situations. Industry Preferences: Consumer, distribution, energy/natural resources, industrial products and equipment, medical and health related. Geographic Preferences: Midwest.

## Missouri

Bankers Capital Corp.
3100 Gillham Rd.
Kansas City, MO 64109
Phone: (816)531-1600
Fax: (816)531-1334
Lee Glasnapp, Vice President
Preferred Investment Size: $100,000 to $250,000. Investment Types: Leveraged buyout. Industry Preferences: Consumer product and electronics distribution, and industrial equipment and machinery. Geographic Preferences: Midwest.

Bome Investors, Inc.
8000 Maryland Ave., Ste. 1190
St. Louis, MO 63105
Phone: (314)721-5707
Fax: (314)721-5135
Gregory R. Johnson
Preferred Investment Size: $500,000 to $1,000,000. Investment Types: Startup, early and late stage. Industry Preferences: Diversified. Geographic Preferences: Midwest.

Capital for Business, Inc. (Kansas City)
11 S. Meramac St., Ste. 1430
St. Louis, MO 63105
Phone: (314)746-7427
Fax: (314)746-8739
Stephen B. Brown, Senior Vice President
Preferred Investment Size: $500,000 to $5,000,000. Investment Types: Mezzanine, leveraged buyout, special situations, control block purchases, and management buyouts. Industry Preferences: Diversified. Geographic Preferences: Midwest.

Capital for Business, Inc. (St. Louis)
11 S. Meramec St., Ste. 1430
St. Louis, MO 63105
Phone: (314)746-7427
Fax: (314)746-8739
Stephen B. Brown, Senior Vice President
Preferred Investment Size: $500,000 to $5,000,000. Investment Types: Mezzanine, leveraged buyout, special situations, control block purchases, and management buyouts. Industry Preferences: Diversified. Geographic Preferences: Midwest.

Gateway Venture Associates L.P.
8000 Maryland Ave., Ste. 1190
St. Louis, MO 63105
Phone: (314)721-5707
Fax: (314)721-5135
John S. McCarthy, Managing General Partner
Preferred Investment Size: $250,000 to $1,000,000. Investment Types: Second stage, mezzanine, leveraged buyout, special situations, control block purchases. Industry Preferences: Communications, computer related, and hospital and other institutional management. Geographic Preferences: Entire U.S.

InvestAmerica Investment Advisors, Inc. (Kansas City)
Commerce Tower
911 Main St., Ste. 2424
Kansas City, MO 64105
Phone: (816)842-0114
Fax: (816)471-7339
Kevin F. Mullane, Vice President
Preferred Investment Size: $750,000 to $2,000,000. Investment Types: First and second stage, leveraged buyout, and special situations. Industry Preferences: Diversified. Geographic Preferences: Entire U.S.

Kansas City Equity Partners
233 W. 47th St.
Kansas City, MO 64112
Phone: (816)960-1771
Fax: (816)960-1777
Nicole Garren
Investment Types: First stage, second stage, mezzanine, and leveraged buyout. Industry Preferences: Diversified. Geographic Preferences: Midwest.

## Montana

Bozeman Technology Incubator, Inc.
1320 Manley Rd.
Bozeman, MT 59715
Phone: (406)585-0665
Fax: (406)585-0723
E-mail: grg@mcn.net
Preferred Investment Size: $100,000 to $250,000. Investment Policies: Equity. Investment Types: Startup, early and late stage. Industry

Preferences: Software. Geographic Preferences: Rocky Mountains.

## Nebraska

Heartland Capital Fund, Ltd.
12020 Shamrock Plz., Ste. 200
Omaha, NE 68154
Phone: (402)778-5124
Fax: (402)778-5190
E-mail: hrtlndcptl@aol.com
John G. Gustafson, Vice President
Preferred Investment Size: $500,000 to $2,000,000. Investment Policies: Equity. Investment Types: Early and late stage. Industry Preferences: Diversified technology. Geographic Preferences: Southwest and Midwest.

World Investments, Inc.
World-Herald Sq.
Omaha, NE 68102
Phone: (402)444-1000
Website: http://www.worldinvestments.com
Investment Types: First stage, second stage, and mezzanine. Industry Preferences: Diversified technology. Geographic Preferences: Midwest, Rocky Mountains.

## Nevada

Development Financial Institute of Nevada, L.P.
PO Box 11464
Las Vegas, NV 89111-1464
Phone: (702)732-4966
Fax: (702)735-2912
Paula Rushiddin, Managing Partner
Preferred Investment Size: $100,000 to $1,000,000. Investment Types: Startup, early and late stage. Industry Preferences: Diversified technology and retailing. Geographic Preferences: United States and Western Canada.

Edge Capital Investment Company
1350 E. Flamingo Rd., Ste. 3000
Las Vegas, NV 89119
Phone: (702)428-3343
E-mail: jy@edgecapitaldirect.com
Website: http://www.vcedge.com
Investment Types: Seed, startup, first stage, second stage, mezzanine, leveraged buyout, and special situations. Industry Preferences: Diversified technology. Geographic Preferences: National.

NE2W, LLC
3752 Howard Hughes Pkwy., Ste. 201
Las Vegas, NV 89109
Phone: (702)868-4121
Fax: (702)792-0682
Website: http://www.ne2w.com
Investment Types: Seed, startup, first stage, and special situations. Industry Preferences: Communications, computer related, and real estate. Geographic Preferences: National.

## New Hampshire

Baldwin & Clarke Corporate Finance
116B S. River Rd.
Bedford, NH 03110
Phone: (603)668-4353
Fax: (603)622-1107
John Clarke, Jr., Partner
Investment Types: First stage, second stage, mezzanine, leveraged buyout, and special situations. Industry Preferences: Diversified. Geographic Preferences: Northeast.

## New Jersey

Accel Partners
1 Palmer Sq.
Princeton, NJ 08542
Phone: (609)614-4800
Fax: (609)614-4880
Website: http://www.accel.com
James W. Breyer, Managing General Partner
Investment Types: Early and late stage, leveraged buyout, and special situations. Industry Preferences: Communications, computer-related. Geographic Preferences: National.

Accel Partners (Princeton)
1 Palmer Sq.
Princeton, NJ 08542
Phone: (609)683-4500
Fax: (609)683-0384
Website: http://www.accel.com
Venture capital firm. Telecommunications software industries preferred. Minimum investment of $100,000 required.

AT & T Ventures
295 N. Maple Ave., Rm. 3353C1
Basking Ridge, NJ 07920
Phone: (908)221-3892
Fax: (908)630-1455

Investment Types: Seed, startup, first stage, second stage, and mezzanine. Industry Preferences: Diversified. Geographic Preferences: National.

BCI Advisors, Inc.
Glenpointe Center W.
Teaneck, NJ 07666
Phone: (201)836-3900
Fax: (201)836-6368
E-mail: info@bciadvisors.com
Website: http://www.bcipartners.com
Mark Hastings, General Partner
Preferred Investment Size: $3,000,000 to $20,000,000. Investment Types: Second stage and mezzanine. Industry Preferences: Diversified. Geographic Preferences: Entire U.S.

Capital Express, L.L.C.
Genesis Direct
1100 Valleybrook Ave.
Lyndhurst, NJ 07071
Phone: (201)438-8228
Fax: (201)438-5131
Niles Cohen
Preferred Investment Size: $250,000 to $2,000,000. Investment Policies: Equity. Investment Types: Early and late stage. Industry Preferences: Internet and consumer related. Geographic Preferences: East Coast.

Cardinal Health Partners
221 Nassau St.
Princeton, NJ 08542
Phone: (609)924-6452
Fax: (609)683-0174
Website: http://www.cardinalhealthpartners.com
Lisa Skeete Tatum, Associate
Investment Types: Seed, startup, first and second stage. Industry Preferences: Genetic engineering, medical and health related. Geographic Preferences: National.

The CIT Group/Equity Investments, Inc.
650 CIT Dr.
Livingston, NJ 07039
Phone: (973)740-5435
Fax: (973)740-5555
E-mail: cweiler@citigroup.com
Preferred Investment Size: $1,000,000 to $5,000,000. Investment Types: First and second stage, mezzanine, and leveraged buyout. Industry

Preferences: Radio and TV, consumer products and retailing, biotechnology research, chemicals and materials, plastics, and manufacturing. Geographic Preferences: Entire U.S.

Demuth, Folger & Wetherill
Glenpointe Center E., 5th Fl.
Teaneck, NJ 07666
Phone: (201)836-6000
Fax: (201)836-5666
E-mail: dfwmgmt@aol.com
Donald F. DeMuth, General Partner
Preferred Investment Size: $1,000,000 to $5,000,000. Investment Policies: Equity. Investment Types: Later stage. Industry Preferences: Healthcare, computer, communication, diversified. Geographic Preferences: National.

Domain Associates
One Palmer Sq., Ste. 515
Princeton, NJ 08542
Phone: (609)683-5656
Fax: (609)683-9789
Website: http://www.domainvc.com
Jason Holden, Associate
Investment Types: Seed, first and second stage. Industry Preferences: Electronic components and instrumentation, genetic engineering, industrial products and equipment, medical and health related. Geographic Preferences: National.

DSV Partners (Princeton)
221 Nassau St.
Princeton, NJ 08542
Phone: (609)924-6420
Fax: (609)683-0174
Preferred Investment Size: $1,000,000 maximum. Investment Types: Startup and first stage. Industry Preferences: Diversified. Geographic Preferences: Entire U.S.

Early Stage Enterprises
995 Route 518
Skillman, NJ 08558
Phone: (609)921-8896
Fax: (609)921-8703
Website: http://www.esevc.com
Ronald R. Hahn, Managing Director
Preferred Investment Size: $100,000 to $1,000,000. Investment Types: Seed, early and late stage. Industry Preferences: Diversified. Geographic

Preferences: Within two hours of office.

Edelson Technology Partners
300 Tice Blvd.
Woodcliff Lake, NJ 07675
Phone: (201)930-9898
Fax: (201)930-8899
Harry Edelson, Managing Partner
Preferred Investment Size: Seed, startup, first and second stage, and mezzanine. Industry Preferences: Diversified. Geographic Preferences: No preference.

Edison Venture Fund
1009 Lenox Dr., Ste. 4
Lawrenceville, NJ 08648
Phone: (609)896-1900
Fax: (609)896-0066
E-mail: info@edisonventure.com
Website: http://www.edisonventure.com
John H. Martinson, Managing Partner
Preferred Investment Size: $1,000,000 to $6,000,000. Investment Types: First and second stage, mezzanine, leveraged buyout, and industry rollups. Industry Preferences: Diversified. Geographic Preferences: Northeast and Middle Atlantic.

First Princeton Capital Corp.
One Garret Mountain Plaza, 9th Fl.
West Paterson, NJ 07424
Phone: (973)278-8111
Fax: (973)278-4290
Website: http://www.lytellcatt.net
Preferred Investment Size: $250,000 to $2,000,000. Investment Types: Early stage, mezzanine, and leveraged buyout. Industry Preferences: Diversified. Geographic Preferences: Northeast and East Coast.

Johnson & Johnson Development Corp.
One Johnson & Johnson Plz.
New Brunswick, NJ 08933
Phone: (732)524-3218
Fax: (732)247-5309
Sandra Hamilton, Director
Investment Types: Seed, startup, first and second stage. Industry Preferences: Genetic engineering, medical and health related. Geographic Preferences: National.

Johnston Associates, Inc.
181 Cherry Valley Rd.
Princeton, NJ 08540
Phone: (609)924-3131
Fax: (609)683-7524
E-mail: jaincorp@aol.com
Preferred Investment Size: $500,000 to $3,000,000. Investment Types: Seed, startup, and leveraged buyout. Industry Preferences: Science and healthcare industry. Geographic Preferences: Northeast.

Kemper Ventures
Princeton Forrest Village
155 Village Blvd.
Princeton, NJ 08540
Phone: (609)936-3035
Fax: (609)936-3051
Richard Secchia, Partner
Investment Types: Seed, research and development, startup, first and second stage. Industry Preferences: Computer related, medical and health related. Geographic Preferences: National.

MidMark Capital, L.P.
466 Southern Blvd.
Chatham, NJ 07928
Phone: (973)822-2999
Fax: (973)822-8911
E-mail: mfinlay@midmarkassoc.com
Website: http://www.midmarkcapital.com
Matthew W. Finlay, Vice President
Preferred Investment Size: $1,000,000 to $5,000,000. Investment Policies: Equity. Investment Types: Expansion, later stage. Industry Preferences: Diversified, communication, manufacturing, retail/service. Geographic Preferences: National.

NJS Partners, Inc.
18 Willow Ave.
Randolph, NJ 07869
Preferred Investment Size: $100,000. Investment Types: Seed, early stage, and special situations. Industry Preferences: Diversified. Geographic Preferences: National.

Penny Lane Partners
One Palmer Sq., Ste. 309
Princeton, NJ 08542
Phone: (609)497-4646
Fax: (609)497-0611

Investment Types: Second stage and leveraged buyouts. Industry Preferences: Computer related, genetic engineering, medical/health related, franchise, retail and real estate. Geographic Preferences: Eastern U.S.

Tappan Zee Capital Corp. (New Jersey)
201 Lower Notch Rd.
PO Box 416
Little Falls, NJ 07424
Phone: (973)256-8280
Fax: (973)256-2841
Jeffrey Birnberg, President
Preferred Investment Size: $100,000 to $250,000. Investment Types: Leveraged buyout, debt, and debt with equity secured. Industry Preferences: Consumer products, food and beverage products, franchise businesses, restaurants, distribution of communications and electronics equipment. Geographic Preferences: Within two hours of office.

Technology Management & Funding
707 State Rd.
Princeton, NJ 08540-1438
Phone: (609)921-2001
Fax: (609)497-0998
Website: http://www.tmflp.com
William Marder, Managing Director
Investment Types: Seed, startup, first stage, leveraged buyout, and special situations. Industry Preferences: Diversified. Geographic Preferences: National.

Westford Technology Ventures, L.P.
17 Academy St.
Newark, NJ 07102
Phone: (973)624-2131
Fax: (973)624-2008
Preferred Investment Size: $250,000 to $500,000. Investment Types: Startup, early and late stage. Industry Preferences: Diversified communication and computer technology, electronics, industrial products and equipment. Geographic Preferences: Eastern U.S.

## New Mexico

Bruce F. Glaspell & Associates
10400 Academy Rd. NE, Ste. 313

Albuquerque, NM 87111
Phone: (505)293-9590
Fax: (505)292-4258
Investment Types: Seed, research and development, startup, first stage, second stage, leveraged buyout, and special situations. Industry Preferences: Diversified. Geographic Preferences: Entire U.S. and Canada.

High Desert Ventures, Inc.
6101 Imparata St. NE, Ste. 1721
Albuquerque, NM 87111
Phone: (505)797-3330
Preferred Investment Size: $500,000 to $2,500,000. Investment Types: Startup and early stage. Industry Preferences: Diversified. Geographic Preferences: Northeast and Southwest.

New Business Capital Fund, Ltd.
5805 Torreon NE
Albuquerque, NM 87109
Phone: (505)822-8445
Preferred Investment Size: $100,000. Investment Policies: Equity. Investment Types: Seed and startup. Industry Preferences: Diversified. Geographic Preferences: New Mexico.

SRI Ventures
10400 Academy Rd. NE, Ste. 313
Albuquerque, NM 87111
Phone: (505)292-4505
Fax: (505)292-4528
Viviana Cloninger, General Partner
Investment Types: Seed, research and development, startup, and first stage. Industry Preferences: Diversified. Geographic Preferences: Entire U.S. and Canada.

Technology Ventures
1155 University Blvd. SE
Albuquerque, NM 87106
Phone: (505)246-2882
Fax: (505)246-2891
Beverly Bendicksen
Investment Types: Seed, startup, first and second stage. Industry Preferences: Diversified. Geographic Preferences: Southwest.

## New York

Aberlyn Holding Co., Inc.
500 Fifth Ave.

New York, NY 10110
Phone: (212)391-7750
Fax: (212)391-7762
Lawrence Hoffman, Chairman and CEO
Preferred Investment Size: $500,000 to $5,000,000. Investment Types: Startup, early and late stage. Industry Preferences: Diversified computer technology, food and beverage products, genetic engineering, and healthcare. Geographic Preferences: National.

Adler & Company
Venda Administrative Services
342 Madison Ave., Ste. 807
New York, NY 10173
Phone: (212)599-2535
Fax: (212)599-2526
E-mail: jnickse@aol.com
Jay Nickse, Treasurer & Chief Financial Officer
Investment Types: Startup, first and second stage. Industry Preferences: Diversified. Geographic Preferences: National.

Alimansky Capital Group, Inc.
605 Madison Ave., Ste. 300
New York, NY 10022-1901
Phone: (212)832-7300
Fax: (212)832-7338
Howard Duby, Managing Director
Investment Types: First stage, second stage, mezzanine, leveraged buyout, and special situations. Industry Preferences: Diversified. Geographic Preferences: Entire U.S. and Canada.

Alpha Capital Corporation
950 Third Ave.
New York, NY 10022
Phone: (212)838-1858
Fax: (212)838-1843
Investment Types: Seed, startup, first stage, second stage, mezzanine, leveraged buyout, and special situations. Industry Preferences: Diversified. Geographic Preferences: Northeast.

The Argentum Group
The Chyrsler Bldg.
405 Lexington Ave.
New York, NY 10174
Phone: (212)949-6262
Fax: (212)949-8294

Walter H. Barandiaran, Managing Dir.
Preferred Investment Size: $1,000,000 to $5,000,000. Investment Types: Second stage, mezzanine, leveraged buyout, and special situations. Industry Preferences: Diversified. Geographic Preferences: Entire U.S.

Arthur P. Gould & Co.
One Wilshire Dr.
Lake Success, NY 11020
Phone: (516)773-3000
Fax: (516)773-3289
Andrew Gould, Vice President
Investment Types: Seed, research and development, startup, first stage, second stage, mezzanine, and leveraged buyout. Industry Preferences: Diversified. Geographic Preferences: National.

Bedford Capital Corp.
18 East 48th St., Ste. 1800
New York, NY 10017
Phone: (212)688-5700
Fax: (212)754-4699
E-mail: info@bedfordnyc.com
Website: http://www.bedfordnyc.com
Ross M. Patten, Managing Director
Preferred Investment Size: $250,000 to $5,000,000. Investment Types: Early and late stage, and leveraged buyout. Industry Preferences: Diversified. Geographic Preferences: East Coast and Midwest.

Bessemer Venture Partners (Westbury)
1400 Old Country Rd., Ste. 407
Westbury, NY 11590
Phone: (516)997-2300
Fax: (516)997-2371
E-mail: bob@bvpny.com
Website: http://www.bvp.com
Preferred Investment Size: $500,000 maximum. Investment Types: Seed, research and development, startup, first and second stage, leveraged buyout, special situations, and control block purchases. Industry Preferences: No preference. Geographic Preferences: Entire U.S.

Bloom & Co.
950 Third Ave.
New York, NY 10022
Phone: (212)838-1858

Fax: (212)838-1843
Jack S. Bloom, President
Preferred Investment Size: $500,000 to $3,000,000. Investment Types: Startup, early and late stage. Industry Preferences: No preference. Geographic Preferences: Within two hours of office.

BT Capital Partners, Inc.
130 Liberty St., 34th Fl.
New York, NY 10006
Phone: (212)250-5563
Fax: (212)669-1749
Preferred Investment Size: $5,000,000 maximum. Investment Types: Second stage, mezzanine, leveraged buyouts, and special situations. Industry Preferences: Diversified. Geographic Preferences: No preference.

Carl Marks & Co.
135 E. 57th St.
New York, NY 10022
Phone: (212)909-8428
Fax: (212)980-2630
Robert Davidoff, Managing Director
Investment Types: First stage, second stage, mezzanine, leveraged buyout, and special situations. Industry Preferences: Diversified. Geographic Preferences: Entire U.S. and Canada.

Carmichael & Company
489 5th Ave., 7th Fl.
New York, NY 10017
Phone: (212)973-0110
Fax: (212)973-0440
Website: http://www.carmichaelandco.com
Investment Types: Research and development, startup, first stage, second stage, mezzanine, and leveraged buyout. Industry Preferences: Communications, computer related, consumer, medical/health related, and aerospace. Geographic Preferences: National.

CB Commercial, Inc.
560 Lexington Ave., 20th Fl.
New York, NY 10022
Phone: (212)207-6119
Fax: (212)207-6095
Website: http://www.cbcommercial.com

A small business investment company. Diversified industry preference.

Chase Capital Partners
380 Madison Ave., 12th Fl.
New York, NY 10017-2070
Phone: (212)622-3060
Fax: (212)622-3101
Preferred Investment Size: $5,000,000 to $100,000,000. Investment Types: Startup, first and second stage, mezzanine, leveraged buyout, and special situations. Industry Preferences: Diversified. Geographic Preferences: Entire U.S. and Canada.

Citicorp Venture Capital Ltd. (New York City)
399 Park Ave., 14th Fl.
Zone 4
New York, NY 10043
Phone: (212)559-1127
Fax: (212)888-2940
Preferred Investment Size: $5,000,000 maximum. Investment Types: Leveraged buyout. Industry Preferences: Diversified. Geographic Preferences: No preference.

CMNY Capital II, LP
135 E. 57th St.
New York, NY 10022
Phone: (212)909-8428
Fax: (212)980-2630
Preferred Investment Size: $250,000 to $500,000. Investment Types: First and second stage, mezzanine, leveraged buyout, special situations, and turnarounds. Industry Preferences: Diversified. Geographic Preferences: No preference.

Cohen & Co., L.L.C.
800 Third Ave.
New York, NY 10022
Phone: (212)317-2250
Fax: (212)317-2255
E-mail: nlcohen@aol.com
Neil L. Cohen, President
Preferred Investment Size: $500,000 to $5,000,000. Investment Types: Startup, early and late stage. Industry Preferences: Communications, consumer, distribution, electronics, energy, and healthcare. Geographic Preferences: National.

Cornerstone Equity Investors, L.L.C.
717 5th Ave., Ste. 1100
New York, NY 10022
Phone: (212)753-0901
Fax: (212)826-6798
Mark Rossi, Senior Managing Director
Preferred Investment Size: $5,000,000 maximum. Investment Types: Leveraged buyout, later stage equity, and special situations. Industry Preferences: Diversified. Geographic Preferences: No preference.

Creditanstalt SBIC
245 Park Ave., 27th Fl.
New York, NY 10167
Fax: (212)856-1699
Dennis O'Dowd, President

CW Group, Inc.
1041 3rd Ave., 2nd Fl.
New York, NY 10021
Phone: (212)308-5266
Fax: (212)644-0354
Website: http://www.cwventures.com
Walter Channing, Jr., Managing General Partner
Preferred Investment Size: $100,000 to $5,000,000. Investment Types: Seed, research and development, startup, first and second stage, special situations, and control block purchases. Industry Preferences: Specialize in the medical/health business. Geographic Preferences: Entire U.S.

DB Capital Parnters, Inc.
130 Liberty St., 25th Fl.
New York, NY 10006
Phone: (212)250-4648
Fax: (212)669-1749
Investment Types: Second stage, mezzanine, leveraged buyout, and special situations. Industry Preferences: Diversified. Geographic Preferences: National.

DH Blair Investment Banking Corp.
44 Wall St., 2nd Fl.
New York, NY 10005
Phone: (212)495-5000
Fax: (212)269-1438
J. Morton Davis, Chairman
Investment Types: Research and development, startup, first stage, and

leveraged buyout. Industry Preferences: Diversified. Geographic Preferences: National. Northwest, Southwest, Midwest, Rocky Mountains, and West Coast.

Dresdner Kleinwort Benson Private Equity Partnership
75 Wall St.
New York, NY 10005
Phone: (212)429-3131
Richard Wolf, Partner
Investment Types: Second stage, mezzanine, and leveraged buyout. Industry Preferences: Diversified. Geographic Preferences: National.

East River Ventures, L.P.
645 Madison Ave., 22nd Fl.
New York, NY 10022
Phone: (212)644-2322
Fax: (212)644-5498
Montague H. Hackett
Preferred Investment Size: $500,000 to $5,000,000. Investment Types: Early and late stage, and mezzanine. Industry Preferences: Diversified communication and computer technology, consumer services, and medical. Geographic Preferences: National.

Easton Capital Corporation
415 Madison Ave., 20th Fl.
New York, NY 10017
Phone: (212)702-0950
Fax: (212)702-0952
Website: http://www.eastoncapital.com
Investment Types: Startup, first stage, second stage, mezzanine, leveraged buyout, and special situations. Industry Preferences: Diversified. Geographic Preferences: Entire U.S. and Canada.

Elk Associates Funding Corp.
747 3rd Ave., Ste. 4C
New York, NY 10017
Phone: (212)355-2449
Fax: (212)759-3338
Gary C. Granoff, Pres.
Preferred Investment Size: $100,000 to $1,000,000. Investment Types: Second stage and leveraged buyout. Industry Preferences: Radio and TV, consumer franchise businesses, hotel and resort areas, and transportation.

Geographic Preferences: Southeast and Midwest.

EOS Partners, L.P.
320 Park Ave., 22nd Fl.
New York, NY 10022
Phone: (212)832-5800
Fax: (212)832-5815
E-mail: mfirst@eospartners.com
Website: http://www.eospartners.com
Mark L. First, Managing Director
Preferred Investment Size: $3,000,000. Investment Policies: Equity and equity-oriented debt. Investment Types: Expansion, later stage. Industry Preferences: Diversified. Geographic Preferences: Entire United States and Canada.

Euclid Partners
45 Rockefeller Plaza, Ste. 907
New York, NY 10111
Phone: (212)218-6880
Fax: (212)218-6877
E-mail: graham@euclidpartners.com
Website: http://www.euclidpartners.com
Preferred Investment Size: $500,000 to $5,000,000. Investment Types: Startup, first and second stage. Industry Preferences: Data communications, computer services, genetic engineering, and medical/health related. Geographic Preferences: No preference.

Evergreen Capital Partners, Inc.
150 East 58th St.
New York, NY 10155
Phone: (212)813-0758
Fax: (212)759-0486
E-mail: rysmith@evergreencapital.com
Preferred Investment Size: $500,000 to $5,000,000. Investment Types: Early and late stage, and special situations. Industry Preferences: Diversified. Geographic Preferences: National.

The Exeter Group
10 E. 53rd St.
New York, NY 10022
Phone: (212)872-1172
Fax: (212)872-1198
E-mail: exeter@usa.net
Karen J. Watai, Partner

Preferred Investment Size: $1,000,000 to $12,000,000. Investment Policies: Loans and equity investments. Investment Types: Expansion, later stage. Industry Preferences: Diversified. Geographic Preferences: National.

Exponential Business Development Co.
216 Walton St.
Syracuse, NY 13202-1227
Phone: (315)474-4500
Fax: (315)474-4682
E-mail: dirksonn@aol.com
Dirk E. Sonneborn, Partner
Preferred Investment Size: $100,000 to $250,000. Investment Types: Startup, early and late stage. Industry Preferences: No preference. Geographic Preferences: Northeast.

Financial Technology Research Corp.
518 Broadway
Penthouse
New York, NY 10012
Phone: (212)625-9100
Fax: (212)431-0300
E-mail: fintek@financier.com
Neal Bruckman, President
Investment Types: Seed, research and development, startup, first stage, second stage, and special situations. Industry Preferences: Diversified. Geographic Preferences: Entire U.S. and Canada.

First Charter Partners, Inc.
405 Park Avenue
New York, NY 10022
Phone: (212)644-9700
Fax: (212)644-3900
Eric Gilchrest, President
Preferred Investment Size: $500,000 to $5,000,000. Investment Types: Late stage and special situations. Industry Preferences: Diversified. Geographic Preferences: United States and Canada.

4C Ventures
237 Park Ave., Ste. 801
New York, NY 10017
Phone: (212)692-3680
Fax: (212)692-3685
Website: http://www.4cventures.com
Ted Hobart, Partner

Investment Types: Seed, research and development, startup, first and second stage. Industry Preferences: Communications, computer related, and consumer. Geographic Preferences: Entire U.S. and Canada.

Gabelli Multimedia Partners
One Corporate Center
Rye, NY 10580
Phone: (914)921-5395
Fax: (914)921-5031
E-mail: fsommer@gabelli.com
Preferred Investment Size: $250,000 to $500,000. Investment Policies: Equity. Investment Types: Startup, early and late stage. Industry Preferences: Diversified communications. Geographic Preferences: Northeast.

Generation Partners
551 Fifth Ave., Ste. 3100
New York, NY 10176
Phone: (212)450-8507
Fax: (212)450-8550
Website: http://www.genpartners.com
Preferred Investment Size: $1,000,000. Investment Types: Startup, early and late stage. Industry Preferences: Diversified communications and computer technology, consumer products and services, and industrial products and equipment. Geographic Preferences: United States and Canada.

Genesee Funding
70 Linden Oaks, 3rd Fl.
Rochester, NY 14625
Phone: (716)383-5550
Fax: (716)383-5305
Investment Types: Second stage, mezzanine, and leveraged buyout. Industry Preferences: Diversified. Geographic Preferences: Northeast.

Gerard Klauer Mattison
529 Fifth Ave.
New York, NY 10017
Phone: (212)885-4000
Fax: (212)338-8991
Nathan Schipper
Investment Types: Startup, first stage, second stage, and mezzanine. Industry Preferences: Diversified. Geographic Preferences: Entire U.S. and Canada.

Golub Associates, Inc.
230 Park Ave, 19th Fl.
New York, NY 10169
Phone: (212)207-1575
Fax: (212)207-1579
Evelyn Mordechai, Vice President
Investment Types: Second stage, mezzanine, leveraged buyout, and special situations. Industry Preferences: Diversified. Geographic Preferences: Eastern U.S.

The Growth Group
400 Park Ave., 14th Fl.
New York, NY 10022
Phone: (212)486-7722
Fax: (212)888-8856
Preferred Investment Size: $1,000,000 to $5,000,000. Investment Types: Startup, early and late stage. Industry Preferences: No preference. Geographic Preferences: United States and Canada.

Hambro International Equity Partners (New York)
650 Madison Ave., 21st Floor
New York, NY 10022
Phone: (212)223-7400
Fax: (212)223-0305
Preferred Investment Size: $2,500,000 to $5,000,000. Investment Types: First and second stage, and special situations. Industry Preferences: Genetic engineering, chemicals and materials, and medical/health related. Geographic Preferences: Entire U.S.

Harvest Partners, Inc.
280 Park Ave, 33rd Fl.
New York, NY 10017
Phone: (212)549-6300
Fax: (212)812-0100
Preferred Investment Size: $8,000,000 to $12,000,000. Investment Types: Leveraged buyout. Industry Preferences: Consumer products and services, communications, distribution, fiberoptics, and medical/health related. Geographic Preferences: No preference.

Harvest Partners, Inc. (New York)
280 Park Ave, 33rd Fl.
New York, NY 10017
Phone: (212)549-6300
Fax: (212)812-0100

Harvey P. Mallement, Managing Partner
Preferred Investment Size: $8,000,000 to $12,000,000. Investment Types: Leveraged buyout. Industry Preferences: Diversified. Geographic Preferences: No preference.

Herbert Young Securities, Inc.
98 Cuttermill Rd.
Great Neck, NY 11021
Phone: (516)487-8300
Fax: (516)487-8319
Herbert D. Levine, President
Preferred Investment Size: $100,000 to $5,000,000. Investment Types: Early and late stage. Industry Preferences: Diversified communications and computer technology, consumer products and services, electronics, genetic engineering, healthcare, and real estate. Geographic Preferences: National.

Holding Capital Group, Inc.
10 E. 53rd St., 30th Fl.
New York, NY 10022
Phone: (212)486-6670
Fax: (212)486-0843
James W. Donaghy, President
Preferred Investment Size: $5,000,000. Investment Types: Leveraged buyout. Industry Preferences: No preference. Geographic Preferences: Entire U.S.

Hudson Venture Partners
660 Madison Ave.
New York, NY 10021-8405
Phone: (212)644-9797
Fax: (212)644-7430
Marilyn Adler
Investment Types: First and second stages. Industry Preferences: Diversified. Geographic Preferences: Eastern U.S.

IBJS Capital Corp.
1 State St.
New York, NY 10004
Phone: (212)858-2019
Fax: (212)858-2768
George Zombeck, Chief Operating Officer
Preferred Investment Size: $2,000,000 maximum. Investment Types: Mezzanine, leveraged buyout, and

special situations. Industry Preferences: Consumer products and services, and chemicals and materials. Geographic Preferences: Entire U.S.

Inclusive Ventures, L.L.C.
14 Wall St., 26th Fl.
New York, NY 10005
Phone: (212)619-4000
Fax: (212)619-7202
Preferred Investment Size: $100,000 to $250,000. Investment Types: Seed and startup. Industry Preferences: Diversified computer technology. Geographic Preferences: National.

InterEquity Capital Partners, L.P.
220 5th Ave.
New York, NY 10001
Phone: (212)779-2022
Fax: (212)779-2103
E-mail: iecp@aol.com
Website: http://www.interequity-capital.com
Preferred Investment Size: $250,000 to $500,000. Investment Types: first and second stage, mezzanine, leveraged buyout, and special situations. Industry Preferences: Diversified. Geographic Preferences: Entire U.S.

International Paper Capital Formation, Inc. (Purchase)
2 Manhattanville Rd.
Purchase, NY 10577-2196
Phone: (914)397-1500
Fax: (914)397-1909
E-mail: comm@ipaper.com
Website: http://www.ipaper.com
A minority enterprise small business investment company.

International Real Returns
120 Wooster St.
New York, NY 10012
Phone: (212)905-8150
Fax: (212)905-8155
Investment Types: Startup, first stage, second stage, mezzanine, and leveraged buyout. Industry Preferences: Diversified. Geographic Preferences: National.

Josephberg, Grosz and Co., Inc.
810 Seventh Ave., 27th Fl.
New York, NY 10019
Phone: (212)974-9926
Fax: (212)397-5832

Preferred Investment Size: $1,000,000 to $5,000,000. Investment Types: Seed, research and development, startup, first and second stage, mezzanine, and leveraged buyout. Industry Preferences: Diversified. Geographic Preferences: Entire U.S.

J.P. Morgan Capital Corp.
60 Wall St.
New York, NY 10260-0060
Phone: (212)648-9000
Fax: (212)648-5002
Lincoln E. Frank, Chief Operating Officer
Preferred Investment Size: $5,000,000 maximum. Investment Types: Second stage and special situations. Industry Preferences: Diversified. Geographic Preferences: Entire U.S. and Canada.

Loeb Partners Corp.
61 Broadway, Ste. 2450
New York, NY 10006
Phone: (212)483-7000
Fax: (212)425-7090
Preferred Investment Size: $100,000 to $1,000,000. Investment Types: Startup, early and late stage. Industry Preferences: Diversified. Geographic Preferences: National.

Madison Investment Partners
660 Madison Ave.
New York, NY 10021
Phone: (212)223-2600
Fax: (212)223-8208
Investment Types: Second stage, leveraged buyout, and industry roll ups. Industry Preferences: Diversified. Geographic Preferences: National.

McCown, De Leeuw and Co. (New York)
65 E. 55th St., 36th Fl.
New York, NY 10022
Phone: (212)355-5500
Fax: (212)355-6283
Charles Ayres, Managing Member
Investment Types: Leveraged buyout, special situations, and recapitalization. Industry Preferences: Diversified. Geographic Preferences: National.

Mesa Partners, Inc.
34 S. Earie Ave.
PO Box 2187
Montak, NY 11954

Phone: (516)668-3603
Fax: (516)668-3605
E-mail: info@mesapartners.com
Website: http://
www.mesapartners.com
Ian Sacks
Investment Types: Seed, startup, first
stage, second stage, and industry roll
ups. Industry Preferences: Diversified.
Geographic Preferences: National.

Morgan Stanley Venture Partners
1221 Avenue of the Americas, 33rd
Fl.
New York, NY 10020
Phone: (212)762-7900
Fax: (212)762-8424
E-mail: msventures@ms.com
Website: http://www.msvp.com
David Hammer, Associate
Investment Types: Second stage,
mezzanine, and industry roll ups.
Industry Preferences: Diversified
technology. Geographic Preferences:
Entire U.S. and Canada.

Morgan Stanley Venture Partners
(New York)
1221 Avenue of the Americas, 33rd
Fl.
New York, NY 10020
Phone: (212)762-7900
Fax: (212)762-8424
E-mail: msventures@ms.com
Website: http://www.msvp.com
Preferred Investment Size: $3,000,000
to $40,000,000. Investment Types:
Second stage, mezzanine, industry
roll ups, and growth buyouts. Industry
Preferences: Communications,
computer related, computer and
electronics distribution, electronics,
and medical/health related.
Geographic Preferences: Entire U.S.
and Canada.

Nazem and Co.
645 Madison Ave., 12th Fl.
New York, NY 10022
Phone: (212)371-7900
Fax: (212)371-2150
E-mail: nazem@msn.com
Fred F. Nazem, Managing General
Partner
Preferred Investment Size: $500,000
to $5,000,000. Investment Types:
Seed, startup, first and second stage,
mezzanine, and special situations.

Industry Preferences: Diversified.
Geographic Preferences: No
preference.

NE2W, LLC
67 Wall St., Ste. 2411
New York, NY 10005
Phone: (212)859-3463
Fax: (877)968-8426
E-mail: info@ne2w.com
Website: http://www.ne2w.com
Paula White-Rushiddin, Managing
Partner
Investment Types: Seed, startup, first
stage, and special situations. Industry
Preferences: Communications,
internet, food and beverage, and real
estate. Geographic Preferences: Entire
U.S. and western Canada.

Needham Capital Management,
L.L.C.
445 Park Ave.
New York, NY 10022
Phone: (212)371-8300
Fax: (212)371-1450
Glen Alabanese, Chief Financial
Officer
Preferred Investment Size: $1,000,000
to $5,000,000. Investment Policies:
Equity. Investment Types: Later
stage. Industry Preferences:
Diversified technology. Geographic
Preferences: National.

New York State Science &
Technology Foundation
Small Business Technology
Investment Fund
99 Washington Ave., Ste. 1731
Albany, NY 12210
Phone: (518)473-9741
Fax: (518)473-6876
E-mail: jvanwie@empire.state.ny.us
Preferred Investment Size: $100,000
to $250,000. Investment Types:
Startup, early and late stage. Industry
Preferences: Diversified technology.
Geographic Preferences: New York
state.

Northwood Ventures LLC
485 Underhill Blvd., Ste. 205
Syosset, NY 11791
Phone: (516)364-5544
Fax: (516)364-0879
E-mail: northwood@northwood.com

Website: http://
www.northwoodventures.com
Paul Homer, Associate
Preferred Investment Size: $1,000,000
to $6,000,000. Investment Types:
First and second stage, leveraged
buyout, special situations, and
industry roll ups. Industry
Preferences: Diversified. Geographic
Preferences: Entire U.S.

Norwood Venture Corp.
1430 Broadway, Ste. 1607
New York, NY 10018
Phone: (212)869-5075
Fax: (212)869-5331
E-mail: nvc@mail.idt.net
Website: http://www.norven.com
Preferred Investment Size: $250,000.
Investment Types: Mezzanine,
leveraged buyout, and special
situations. Industry Preferences:
Diversified. Geographic Preferences:
National.

Paribas Principal, Inc.
787 7th Ave.
New York, NY 10019
Phone: (212)841-2115
Fax: (212)841-3558
Gary Binning
Preferred Investment Size:
$5,000,000. Investment Types:
Leveraged buyout, special situations,
and control block purchases. Industry
Preferences: Diversified. Geographic
Preferences: Entire U.S.

Patricof & Co. Ventures, Inc. (New
York)
445 Park Ave.
New York, NY 10022
Phone: (212)753-6300
Fax: (212)319-6155
Website: http://www.patricof.com
Preferred Investment Size: $5,000,000
to $25,000,000. Investment Types:
Seed, startup, first and second stage,
mezzanine, and leveraged buyout.
Industry Preferences: Diversified.
Geographic Preferences: No
preference.

The Pittsford Group
8 Lodge Pole Rd.
Pittsford, NY 14534
Phone: (716)223-3523

Investment Types: Startup, first and
second stage. Industry Preferences:
Diversified technology. Geographic
Preferences: Eastern U.S. and Canada.

The Platinum Group, Inc.
350 Fifth Ave, Ste. 7113
New York, NY 10118
Phone: (212)736-4300
Fax: (212)736-6086
Website: http://
www.platinumgroup.com
Michael Grant, Analyst
Investment Types: Startup, first stage,
second stage, and leveraged buyout.
Industry Preferences: Diversified.
Geographic Preferences: National.

Prospect Street Ventures
10 East 40th St., 44th Fl.
New York, NY 10016
Phone: (212)448-0702
Fax: (212)448-9652
E-mail: wkohler@prospectstreet.com
Edward Ryeom, Vice President
Preferred Investment Size: $1,000,000
to $3,000,000. Investment Types:
Early and later stage. Industry
Preferences: No preference.
Geographic Preferences: East and
West Coast.

Rand Capital Corp.
2200 Rand Bldg.
Buffalo, NY 14203
Phone: (716)853-0802
Fax: (716)854-8480
Allen F. Grum, President and CEO
Preferred Investment Size: $100,000
to $500,000. Investment Types: First
and second stage, mezzanine, and
leveraged buyout. Industry
Preferences: Diversified. Geographic
Preferences: Northeast.

Regent Capital Partners
505 Park Ave., Ste. 1700
New York, NY 10022
Phone: (212)735-9900
Fax: (212)735-9908
E-mail: ninamcle@aol.com
Investment Types: Second stage,
mezzanine, and leveraged buyout.
Industry Preferences:
Communications, consumer products
and services. Geographic Preferences:
National.

Rothschild Ventures, Inc.
1251 Avenue of the Americas, 51st
Fl.
New York, NY 10020
Phone: (212)403-3500
Fax: (212)403-3652
Scott T. Jones, Senior Vice President
Preferred Investment Size: $500,000
to $5,000,000. Investment Types:
Seed, research and development,
startup, first and second stage,
mezzanine, and leveraged buyout.
Industry Preferences: Diversified.
Geographic Preferences: Entire U.S.
and Canada.

Sandler Capital Management
767 Fifth Ave., 45th Fl.
New York, NY 10153
Phone: (212)754-8100
Fax: (212)826-0280
Preferred Investment Size: $500,000
to $5,000,000. Investment Policies:
Equity. Investment Types: Early and
late stage. Industry Preferences:
Diversified communication and
computer technology, consumer
products and services, education, and
publishing. Geographic Preferences:
United States and Canada.

Siguler Guff & Company
630 Fifth Ave., 16th Fl.
New York, NY 10111
Phone: (212)332-5100
Fax: (212)332-5120
Maria Boyazny, Associate
Investment Types: Startup, first stage,
second stage, mezzanine, leveraged
buyout, and special situations.
Industry Preferences: Diversified.
Geographic Preferences: National.

Spencer Trask Securities
535 Madison Ave.
New York, NY 10022
Phone: (212)355-5565
Fax: (212)751-3362
A. Emerson Martin, II, Senior
Managing Director
Investment Types: Startup, first stage,
second stage, and special situations.
Industry Preferences: Diversified.
Geographic Preferences: National.

Sperry, Mitchell & Co.
595 Madison Ave.
New York, NY 10022

Phone: (212)832-6628
Fax: (212)753-0757
Paul Sperry, Managing Director
Investment Types: First stage, second
stage, leveraged buyout, and special
situations. Industry Preferences:
Diversified. Geographic Preferences:
National.

Sprout Group (New York City)
277 Park Ave.
New York, NY 10172
Phone: (212)892-3600
Fax: (212)892-3444
E-mail: info@sproutgroup.com
Patrick J. Boroian, General Partner
Preferred Investment Size: $500,000
to $5,000,000. Investment Types:
Seed, startup, first and second stage,
mezzanine, leveraged buyout, and
special situations. Industry
Preferences: Diversified technology.
Geographic Preferences: Entire U.S.
and Atlantic provinces of Canada.

Sterling/Carl Marks Capital, Inc.
175 Great Neck Rd.
Great Neck, NY 11021
Phone: (516)482-7374
Fax: (516)487-0781
E-mail: stercrlmar@aol.com
Website: http://
www.serlingcarlmarks.com
Preferred Investment Size: $250,000
to $1,000,000. Investment Types:
Second stage and mezzanine. Industry
Preferences: Consumer related;
distribution of electronics equipment,
food and industrial products; and
industrial equipment and machinery.
Geographic Preferences: Northeast.

Tessler and Cloherty, Inc.
155 Main St.
Cold Spring, NY 10516
Phone: (914)265-4244
Fax: (914)265-4158
Anne Saunders, Manager
Preferred Investment Size: $250,000
to $1,000,000. Investment Types:
First and second stage, leveraged
buyouts, and special situations.
Industry Preferences: Precious metals.
Does not consider real estate,
publishing, or consumer related.
Geographic Preferences: Entire U.S.

Toronto Dominion Capital (USA)
31 W. 52nd St., 20th Fl.
New York, NY 10019
Phone: (212)827-7760
Fax: (212)974-8429
David Grossman, Associate
Investment Types: Startup, first stage,
second stage, mezzanine, and
leveraged buyout. Industry
Preferences: Diversified. Geographic
Preferences: Entire U.S. and Canada.

US Trust Company of New York
114 W.47th St.
New York, NY 10036
Phone: (212)852-3125
Fax: (212)852-3759
Jim Ruler
Investment Types: First stage, second
stage, mezzanine, and leveraged
buyout. Industry Preferences:
Diversified. Geographic Preferences:
National.

Vega Capital Corp.
45 Knollwood Rd.
Elmsford, NY 10523
Phone: (914)345-9500
Fax: (914)345-9505
Preferred Investment Size: $100,000
to $250,000. Investment Types:
Second stage, mezzanine, leveraged
buyout, special situations, and
collateralized loans. Industry
Preferences: Diversified. Geographic
Preferences: Northeast, Southeast, and
Middle Atlantic.

Venrock Associates
30 Rockefeller Plaza, Ste. 5508
New York, NY 10112
Phone: (212)649-5600
Fax: (212)649-5788
Website: http://www.venrock.com
Investment Types: Seed, research and
development, startup, first and second
stages. Industry Preferences:
Diversified. Geographic Preferences:
National.

Venture Capital Fund of America,
Inc.
509 Madison Ave., Ste. 812
New York, NY 10022
Phone: (212)838-5577
Fax: (212)838-7614
E-mail: mail@vcfa.com
Website: http://www.vcfa.com

Dayton T. Carr, General Partner
Preferred Investment Size: $100,000
to $1,000,000. Investment Types:
Secondary partnership interests.
Industry Preferences: Does not
consider tax shelters, real estate, or
direct investments in companies.
Geographic Preferences: Entire U.S.

Venture Opportunities Corp.
43 Round House Rd.
Bedford, NY 10506
Phone: (212)832-3737
Fax: (212)980-6603
E-mail: jerryvoc@aol.com
Jerry March, President
Preferred Investment Size: $100,000
maximum. Investment Types: Startup,
first and second stage, mezzanine,
leveraged buyout, and special
situations. Industry Preferences:
Diversified. Geographic Preferences:
Entire U.S.

Warburg Pincus Ventures, Inc.
466 Lexington Ave.
New York, NY 10017
Phone: (212)878-0600
Fax: (212)878-9351
Preferred Investment Size: $1,000,000
to $5,000,000. Investment Types:
Seed, startup, first and second stage,
mezzanine, leveraged buyouts, and
special situations. Industry
Preferences: Diversified. Geographic
Preferences: No preference.

Wasserstein Adelson Ventures L.P.
31 W. 52nd St., 27th Fl.
New York, NY 10019
Phone: (212)969-2700
Fax: (212)969-7879
Perry W. Steiner
Investment Types: Startup, first and
second stages. Industry Preferences:
Diversified. Geographic Preferences:
National.

Welsh, Carson, Anderson, & Stowe
320 Park Ave., Ste. 2500
New York, NY 10022-6815
Phone: (212)893-9500
Fax: (212)893-9575
Patrick J. Welsh, General Partner
Preferred Investment Size:
$10,000,000 for leveraged buyout.
Investment Types: Leveraged buyout
and special situations. Industry

Preferences: Computer related and
medical/health related. Geographic
Preferences: Entire U.S.

J. H. Whitney and Co. (New York)
630 Fifth Ave. Ste. 3225
New York, NY 10111
Phone: (212)332-2400
Fax: (212)332-2422
Website: http://www.jhwitney.com
James R. Matthews, Vice President
Preferred Investment Size: $1,000,000
to $5,000,000. Investment Types:
First and second stage, mezzanine,
and leveraged buyout. Industry
Preferences: No industry preference.
Geographic Preferences: Entire U.S.

Winthrop Ventures
74 Trinity Place, Ste. 600
New York, NY 10006
Phone: (212)422-0100
Cyrus Brown
Preferred Investment Size: $500,000
to $5,000,000. Investment Types:
Startup, early and late stage. Industry
Preferences: Diversified. Geographic
Preferences: National.

Wolfensohn Partners, L.P. (New
York)
590 Madison Ave., 32nd Fl.
New York, NY 10022
Phone: (212)849-8120
Fax: (212)849-8171
Jonathan E. Gold, Associate
$500,000 to $5,000,000. Investment
Types: Seed, research and
development, startup, first and second
stage, and special situations. Industry
Preferences: Diversified. Geographic
Preferences: No preference.

## North Carolina

The Aurora Funds, Inc.
2525 Meridian Pkwy., Ste. 220
Durham, NC 27713
Phone: (919)484-0400
Fax: (919)484-0444
Preferred Investment Size: $250,000
to $1,000,000. Investment Types:
Startup, early and late stage. Industry
Preferences: Diversified. Geographic
Preferences: Eastern United States.

Blue Ridge Investors L.P.
PO Box 21692

Greensboro, NC 27420
Phone: (336)370-0576
Fax: (336)274-4984
Edward McCarthy, Executive Vice
President
Investment Types: Second stage,
mezzanine, leveraged buyout, and
special situations. Industry
Preferences: Diversified. Geographic
Preferences: Eastern U.S.

Carolinas Capital Investment Corp.
1408 Biltmore Dr.
Charlotte, NC 28207
Phone: (704)375-3888
Fax: (704)375-6226
E-mail: ed@carolinacapital.com
Investment Types: Seed, research and
development, startup, first and second
stages. Industry Preferences:
Communications, electronic
components and instrumentation.
Geographic Preferences: North
Carolina, South Carolina.

First Union Capital Partners
1 1st Union Center
Charlotte, NC 28288-0732
Phone: (704)374-4656
Fax: (704)374-6711
L. Watts Hamrick, III, Partner
Preferred Investment Size: $1,000,000
to $5,000,000. Investment Types:
First and second stage, mezzanine,
leveraged buyout, special situations,
and control block purchases. Industry
Preferences: Diversified. Geographic
Preferences: No preference.

Intersouth Partners
One Copley Pkwy., Ste. 102
Morrisville, NC 27560
Phone: (919)544-6473
Fax: (919)544-6645
E-mail: info@intersouth.com
Investment Types: Seed, startup, first
and second stages. Industry
Preferences: Diversified. Geographic
Preferences: Southeast and
Southwest.

Kitty Hawk Capital
2700 Coltsgate Rd., Ste. 202
Charlotte, NC 28211
Phone: (704)362-3909
Fax: (704)362-2774
Stephen W. Buchanan, General
Partner

Preferred Investment Size: $500,000
to $5,000,000. Investment Types:
Startup, first and second stage.
Industry Preferences: Diversified.
Geographic Preferences: Southeast.

NationsBanc Leveraged Capital
Group
100 N. Tryon St., 10th Fl.
Charlotte, NC 28255
Phone: (704)386-8063
Fax: (704)386-6432
Doug Williamson, Managing Director
Preferred Investment Size: $3,000,000
to $5,000,000. Investment Policies:
Equity, sub debt with warrants.
Investment Types: Later stage,
expansion. Industry Preferences:
Diversified. Geographic Preferences:
National.

The North Carolina Enterprise Fund,
L.P.
3600 Glenwood Ave., Ste. 107
Raleigh, NC 27612
Phone: (919)781-2691
Fax: (919)783-9195
Charles T. Closson, President and
CEO
Preferred Investment Size: $1,000,000
to $2,000,000. Investment Policies:
Equity. Investment Types: Startup,
early and late stage. Industry
Preferences: Diversified. Real estate,
natural resources, and energy not
considered. Geographic Preferences:
North Carolina.

Ruddick Investment Co.
1800 Two First Union Center
Charlotte, NC 28282
Phone: (704)372-5404
Fax: (704)372-6409
Richard N. Brigden, Vice President
Preferred Investment Size: $250,000
to $1,000,000. Investment Types:
Early and late stage. Industry
Preferences: Diversified. Geographic
Preferences: Southeast.

## North Dakota

Fargo Cass County Economic
Development Corp.
406 Main Ave., Ste. 404
Fargo, ND 58103
Phone: (701)237-6132
Fax: (701)293-7819

E-mail: info@fedc.com
Website: http://www.fedc.com
Certified development company that
lends to small and medium-sized
businesses at fixed rates.

## Ohio

Banc One Capital Partners
(Columbus)
580 N. Fourth St., Ste. 450
Columbus, OH 43215
Phone: (614)227-6942
Fax: (614)227-6947
Suzanne B. Kriscunas, Managing
Director
Preferred Investment Size: $5,000,000
to $15,000,000. Investment Types:
Later stage, leveraged buyout, and
special situations. Industry
Preferences: Diversified. Geographic
Preferences: Entire U.S.

Battelle Venture Partners
505 King Ave.
Columbus, OH 43201
Phone: (614)424-7005
Fax: (614)424-4874
Investment Types: Startup, first and
second stage. Industry Preferences:
Diversified. Energy/natural resources,
industrial products and equipment.
Geographic Preferences: National.

Brantley Venture Partners
20600 Chagrin Blvd., Ste. 1150
Cleveland, OH 44122
Phone: (216)283-4800
Fax: (216)283-5324
Kevin J. Cook, Associate
Preferred Investment Size: $1,000,000
to $5,000,000. Investment Types:
Industry roll ups and leveraged build
ups. Industry Preferences: Diversified.
Geographic Preferences: Entire U.S.

Capital Technology Group, L.L.C.
400 Metro Place North, Ste. 300
Dublin, OH 43017
Phone: (614)792-6066
Fax: (614)792-6070
E-mail: info@capitaltech.com
Preferred Investment Size: $250,000
to $1,000,000. Investment Types:
Seed, early and late stage. Industry
Preferences: Diversified electronics,
alternative energy, and Internet

related. Geographic Preferences:
National.

**Clarion Capital Corp.**
1801 E. 9th St., Ste. 1120
Cleveland, OH 44114
Phone: (216)687-1096
Fax: (216)694-3545
Preferred Investment Size: $250,000
to $500,000. Investment Types: First
and second stage, leveraged buyout,
and private placements. Industry
Preferences: Diversified. Geographic
Preferences: East Coast, Midwest, and
West Coast.

**Crystal Internet Venture Fund, L.P.**
1120 Chester Ave., Ste. 418
Cleveland, OH 44114
Phone: (216)263-5515
Fax: (216)263-5518
E-mail: jf@crystalventure.com
Website: http://
www.crystalventure.com
Joseph Tzeng, Managing Director
Preferred Investment Size: $750,000
to $4,000,000. Investment Policies:
Equity. Investment Types: Seed, early
and late stage. Industry Preferences:
Diversified communications and
computer technology. Geographic
Preferences: National.

**Key Equity Capital Corp.**
127 Public Sq., 28th Fl.
Cleveland, OH 44114
Phone: (216)689-5776
Fax: (216)689-3204
Sean P. Ward, Vice President
Preferred Investment Size: $5,000,000
to $50,000,000. Investment Policies:
Willing to make equity investments.
Investment Types: Later stage.
Industry Preferences: Diversified.
Geographic Preferences: National.

**Morgenthaler Ventures**
Terminal Tower
50 Public Square, Ste. 2700
Cleveland, OH 44113
Phone: (216)621-3070
Fax: (216)621-2817
John D. Lutsi, General Partner
Preferred Investment Size: $1,000,000
to $12,000,000. Investment Types:
Startup, first and second stage,
leveraged buyout, special situations,
and industry roll ups. Industry

Preferences: Diversified. Geographic
Preferences: Entire U.S. and Canada.

**National City Capital**
1965 E. 6th St.
Cleveland, OH 44114
Phone: (216)575-2491
Fax: (216)575-9965
E-mail: nccap@aol.com
Website: http://www.nccapital.com
Carl E. Baldassarre, Managing
Director
Preferred Investment Size: $1,000,000
to $15,000,000. Investment Types:
Second stage, mezzanine, leveraged
buyout, special situations, industry
roll ups, management buyouts,
consolidations plays. Industry
Preferences: Diversified. Geographic
Preferences: Northeast, Southeast,
East Coast, Midwest, Middle Atlantic.

**Northwest Ohio Venture Fund**
4159 Holland-Sylvania R., Ste. 202
Toledo, OH 43623
Phone: (419)824-8144
Fax: (419)882-2035
E-mail: bwalsh@novf.com
Barry P. Walsh, Managing Partner
Preferred Investment Size: $250,000
to $1,000,000. Investment Types:
Seed, early and late stage. Industry
Preferences: Diversified. Does not
consider oil and gas exploration or
real estate. Geographic Preferences:
Midwest.

**The Ohio Partners LLC**
62 E. Board St., 3rd Fl.
Columbus, OH 43215
Phone: (614)621-1210
Fax: (614)621-1240
E-mail: mcox@ohiopartners.com
Investment Types: Startup, first and
second stage. Industry Preferences:
Computer related. Geographic
Preferences: Western U.S. and
Midwest.

**Primus Venture Partners, Inc.**
5900 LanderBrook Dr., Ste. 200
Cleveland, OH 44124-4020
Phone: (440)684-7300
Fax: (440)684-7342
E-mail: info@primusventure.com
Website: http://
www.primusventure.com
Jeffrey J. Milius, Investment Manager

Preferred Investment Size: $5,000,000
maximum. Investment Types: First
and second stage, startup, and
leveraged buyout. Industry
Preferences: Diversified. Geographic
Preferences: Entire U.S.

**River Cities Capital Funds**
221 E. 4th St., Ste. 2250
Cincinnati, OH 45202
Phone: (513)621-9700
Fax: (513)579-8939
Website: http://www.rccf.com
Preferred Investment Size: $1,000,000
to $6,000,000. Investment Policies:
Equity investments. Investment
Types: Early stage, expansion, later
stage. Industry Preferences:
Diversified. Geographic Preferences:
Southeast and Midwest.

**Senmend Medical Ventures**
4445 Lake Forest Dr., Ste. 600
Cincinnati, OH 45242
Phone: (513)563-3264
Fax: (513)563-3261
Investment Types: Second stage and
mezzanine. Industry Preferences:
Genetic engineering, medical and
health related. Geographic
Preferences: National.

**Walnut Capital Partners**
312 Walnut St., Ste. 1151
Cincinnati, OH 45202
Phone: (513)651-3300
Fax: (513)241-1321
Lawrence H. Horwitz
Preferred Investment Size: $500,000
to $5,000,000. Investment Types:
Early and late stage, and special
situations. Industry Preferences:
Consumer products and services, and
business marketing and services. Does
not consider high technology.
Geographic Preferences: United
States and Canada.

## Oklahoma

**Chisholm Private Capital, Inc.**
10830 E. 45th St., Ste. 307
Tulsa, OK 74146
Phone: (918)663-2500
Fax: (918)663-1140
James Bode, General Partner
Preferred Investment Size: $250,000
to $1,000,000. Investment Types:

Startup, early and late stage. Industry Preferences: Diversified communications and computer, consumer products and retailing, electronics, alternative energy, and medical. Geographic Preferences: Southwest.

Davis, Tuttle Venture Partners, L.P. (Tulsa)
320 S. Boston Ste.,1000
Tulsa, OK 74103-3703
Phone: (918)584-7272
Fax: (918)582-3404
Preferred Investment Size: $1,000,000 to $5,000,000. Investment Types: First and second stage, mezzanine, and leveraged buyout. Industry Preferences: Diversified. Geographic Preferences: Southwest.

Moore & Associates
1000 W. Wilshire Blvd., Ste. 370
Oklahoma City, OK 73116
Phone: (405)842-3660
Fax: (405)842-3763
Investment Types: Second stage, mezzanine, and leveraged buyout. Industry Preferences: Diversified technology. Geographic Preferences: National.

RBC Ventures
2627 E. 21st St.
Tulsa, OK 74114
Phone: (918)744-5607
Fax: (918)743-8630
K.Y. Vargas, Vice President
Preferred Investment Size: $250,000 to $5,000,000. Investment Policies: Equity. Investment Types: Late stage and special situations. Industry Preferences: Diversified transportation. Geographic Preferences: Southwest.

## Oregon

Olympic Venture Partners (Lake Oswego)
340 Oswego Pointe Dr., Ste. 200
Lake Oswego, OR 97034
Phone: (503)697-8766
Fax: (503)697-8863
E-mail: info@ovp.com
Website: http://www.ovp.com
Preferred Investment Size: $500,000 to $5,000,000. Investment Types:

Seed, startup, first and second stage. Industry Preferences: Communications, computer related, electronics, genetic engineering, and medical health related. Geographic Preferences: Western U.S.

Orca Capital
1200 NW Naito Pkwy., Ste. 500
Portland, OR 97209
Phone: (503)227-3055
Fax: (503)248-1713
Norman B. Duffett, President
Preferred Investment Size: $1,000,000. Investment Types: Early and late stage, and special situations. Industry Preferences: Diversified communications and computer, consumer food and beverage products, distribution, electronics, education, and publishing. Geographic Preferences: Northwest.

Oregon Resource and Technology Development Fund
4370 NE Halsey St., Ste. 233
Portland, OR 97213-1566
Phone: (503)282-4462
Fax: (503)282-2976
State chartered venture capital fund. Provides investment capital for early stage business finance and applied research and development projects that leads to commercially viable products.

Orien Ventures
14523 Westlake Dr., Ste. 6
Lake Oswego, OR 97035
Phone: (503)699-1680
Fax: (503)699-1681
Preferred Investment Size: $500,000 to $1,000,000. Investment Types: Startup, first and second stage, and mezzanine. Industry Preferences: Diversified. Geographic Preferences: No preference.

Shaw Venture Partners
400 SW 6th Ave., Ste. 1100
Portland, OR 97204-1636
Phone: (503)228-4884
Fax: (503)227-2471
Preferred Investment Size: $250,000 to $750,000. Investment Types: Seed, startup, first and second stage, leveraged buyout, and special situations. Industry Preferences:

Diversified. Geographic Preferences: Northwest and West Coast.

Utah Ventures II LP
10700 SW Beaverton-Hillsdale Hwy., Ste. 548
Beaverton, OR 97005
Phone: (503)574-4125
E-mail: adishlip@uven.com
Investment Types: Seed, startup, first and second stages. Industry Preferences: Diversified technology. Geographic Preferences: Western U.S. and Rocky Mountains.

## Pennsylvania

Adams Capital Management
518 Broad St.
Sewickley, PA 15143
Phone: (412)749-9454
Fax: (412)749-9459
Joel Adams, General Partner
Investment Types: Startup, first and second stages. Industry Preferences: Diversified technology. Geographic Preferences: National.

Aloe Investment Corp.
200 Eagle Rd., Ste. 308
Wayne, PA 19087
Phone: (610)254-9403
Fax: (610)254-9404
Preferred Investment Size: $100,000 minimum. Investment Types: Startup, early and late stage. Industry Preferences: Diversified communications and computer, consumer products, education and publishing. Geographic Preferences: Within two hours of office.

CEO Venture Fund
2000 Technology Dr., Ste. 160
Pittsburgh, PA 15219-3109
Phone: (412)687-3451
Fax: (412)687-8139
E-mail: ceofund@aol.com
Website: http://www.ceoventurefund.com
Ned Renzi, General Partner
Investment Types: Startup, first stage, second stage, leveraged buyout, and special situations. Industry Preferences: Diversified technology. Geographic Preferences: Middle Atlantic states.

CIP Capital, L.P.
435 Devon Park Dr., Bldg. 300

Wayne, PA 19087
Phone: (610)964-7860
Fax: (610)964-8136
Joseph M. Corr, President
Preferred Investment Size: $250,000
to $1,000,000. Investment Types:
First and second stage, leveraged
buyout, and special situations.
Industry Preferences: Diversified.
Geographic Preferences: Entire U.S.

Ecommunities LLC
3741 Walnut St., Ste. 220
Philadelphia, PA 19104
Phone: (215)840-4204
Investment Types: Seed, research and
development, startup, first stage,
second stage, mezzanine, leveraged
buyout, and special situations.
Industry Preferences: Diversified.
Geographic Preferences: National.

Greater Philadelphia Venture Capital
Corp.
351 East Conestoga Rd.
Wayne, PA 19087
Phone: (610)688-6829
Fax: (610)254-8958
Fred Choate, Manager
Preferred Investment Size: $100,000
to $250,000. Investment Types: Early
and late stage, and special situations.
Industry Preferences: Diversified.
Geographic Preferences: Middle
Atlantic.

Keystone Minority Capital Fund L.P.
1801 Centre Ave., Ste. 201
Williams Sq.
Pittsburgh, PA 15219
Phone: (412)338-2230
Fax: (412)338-2224
Earl Hord, General Partner
Investment Types: Startup, first stage,
second stage, mezzanine, and
leveraged buyout. Industry
Preferences: Diversified. Geographic
Preferences: Middle Atlantic states.

Keystone Venture Capital
1601 Market St., Ste.2500
Philadelphia, PA 19103
Phone: (215)241-1200
Fax: (215)241-1211
Peter Ligeti
Preferred Investment Size: $500,000
to $1,000,000. Investment Types:
First and second stage, mezzanine,

and leveraged buyout. Industry
Preferences: Diversified. Geographic
Preferences: Middle Atlantic.

Liberty Venture Partners
2005 Market St., Ste. 200
Philadelphia, PA 19103
Phone: (215)282-4484
Fax: (215)282-4485
E-mail: info@libertyvp.com
Website: http://www.libertyvp.com
Thomas Morse
Investment Types: Startup, first stage,
second stage, and mezzanine. Industry
Preferences: Diversified technology.
Geographic Preferences: National.

Loyalhanna Venture Funds
527 Cedar Way, Ste. 104
Oakmont, PA 15139
Phone: (412)820-7035
Fax: (412)820-7036
James H. Knowles, Jr.
Preferred Investment Size: $100,000
to $1,000,000. Investment Types:
First and second stage. Industry
Preferences: No preference.
Geographic Preferences: Entire U.S.

Mellon Ventures, Inc.
One Mellon Bank Ctr., Rm. 3200
Pittsburgh, PA 15258
Phone: (412)236-3594
Fax: (412)236-3593
Investment Types: Mezzanine,
leveraged buyout, and special
situations. Industry Preferences:
Diversified. Geographic Preferences:
National.

Meridian Venture Partners (Radnor)
The Radnor Court Bldg., Ste. 140
259 Radnor-Chester Rd.
Radnor, PA 19087
Phone: (610)254-2999
Fax: (610)254-2996
E-mail: mvpart@ix.netcom.com
Kenneth E. Jones
Preferred Investment Size: $1,000,000
to $5,000,000. Investment Types:
Second stage, leveraged buyout, and
special situations. Industry
Preferences: Diversified. Geographic
Preferences: East Coast and Middle
Atlantic.

Mid-Atlantic Venture Funds
125 Goodman Dr.
Bethlehem, PA 18015

Phone: (610)865-6550
Fax: (610)865-6427
E-mail: thebeste@net.bfp.org
Glen R. Bressner
Preferred Investment Size: $250,000
to $1,000,000. Investment Types:
Seed, research and development,
startup, first and second stage,
leveraged buyout. Industry
Preferences: Diversified. Geographic
Preferences: Middle Atlantic.

Patricof & Co. Ventures, Inc.
Executive Terrace Bldg.
455 S. Gulph Rd., Ste. 410
King of Prussia, PA 19406
Phone: (610)265-0286
Fax: (610)265-4959
Venture capital firm providing mid-
to later stage financing.

Penn Janney Fund, Inc.
1801 Market St., 11th Fl.
Philadelphia, PA 19103
Phone: (215)665-4447
Fax: (215)665-0820
Richard M. Fox, President
Preferred Investment Size: $250,000
to $1,000,000. Investment Types:
Second stage, mezzanine, leveraged
buyout, and special situations.
Industry Preferences: Diversified.
Geographic Preferences: Northeast,
West Coast, and Middle Atlantic.

Pennsylvania Growth Fund
5850 Ellsworth Ave., Ste. 303
Pittsburgh, PA 15232
Phone: (412)661-1000
Fax: (412)361-0676
Barry Lhomer, Partner
Preferred Investment Size: $300,000
to $2,000,000. Investment Types:
Late stage and special situations.
Industry Preferences: Diversified.
High technology not considered.
Geographic Preferences: Middle
Atlantic.

Philadelphia Ventures, Inc.
The Bellevue
200 S. Broad St.
Philadelphia, PA 19102
Phone: (215)732-4445
Fax: (215)732-4644
Walter M. Aikman, Managing
Director

Preferred Investment Size: $500,000 maximum. Investment Types: Startup, first and second stage, mezzanine, and leveraged buyout. Industry Preferences: Diversified technology. Geographic Preferences: Entire U.S.

PNC Equity Management Corp.
3150 CNG Tower
625 Liberty Ave.
Pittsburgh, PA 15222
Phone: (412)762-7035
Fax: (412)762-6233
Robert Daley, Associate
Preferred Investment Size: $2,000,000 to $20,000,000. Investment Types: Second stage, mezzanine, leveraged buyout, and industry roll ups. Industry Preferences: Diversified. Geographic Preferences: Eastern U.S. and Midwest.

Point Venture Partners
2970 USX Tower
600 Grant St.
Pittsburgh, PA 15219
Phone: (412)261-1966
Fax: (412)261-1718
Kent Engelmeier, General Partner
Investment Types: Startup, first stage, second stage, mezzanine, and leveraged buyout. Industry Preferences: Diversified. Geographic Preferences: Eastern and midwestern U.S.

Rockhill Ventures, Inc.
100 Front St., Ste. 1350
West Conshohocken, PA 19428
Phone: (610)940-0300
Fax: (610)940-0301
E-mail: hsbroderso@aol.com
Preferred Investment Size: $100,000 to $5,000,000. Investment Types: Seed, research and development, startup, first and second stage, virtual company strategy. Industry Preferences: Genetic engineering and medical/health related. Geographic Preferences: Eastern U.S.

Safeguard Scientifics, Inc.
800 The Safeguard Bldg.
435 Devon Park Dr.
Wayne, PA 19087
Phone: (888)733-1200
Fax: (610)293-0601
Website: http://www.safeguard.com

Private venture capital fund. Areas of interest include biotechnology, health care, information services, and high technology industries.

The Sandhurst Venture Fund, L.P.
351 E. Constoga Rd.
Wayne, PA 19087
Phone: (610)254-8900
Fax: (610)254-8958
Preferred Investment Size: $500,000 to $1,000,000. Investment Types: Second stage and leveraged buyout. Industry Preferences: Computer stores, disposable medical/health related, and industrial products. Geographic Preferences: East Coast and Middle Atlantic.

S.R. One, Ltd.
Four Tower Bridge
200 Barr Harbor Dr., Ste. 250
W. Conshohocken, PA 19428-2977
Phone: (610)567-1000
Fax: (610)567-1039
Elaines Jones, Investment Manager
Preferred Investment Size: $100,000 to $3,000,000. Investment Types: Seed, startup, first and second stage, leveraged buyout, and mezzanine. Industry Preferences: Healthcare and genetic engineering. Geographic Preferences: No preference.

TDH
919 Conestoga Rd., Bldg. 1, Ste. 301
Rosemont, PA 19010
Phone: (610)526-9970
Fax: (610)526-9971
J.B. Doherty, Managing General Partner
Preferred Investment Size: $1,000,000 to $5,000,000. Investment Types: Startup, first and second stage, mezzanine, and leveraged buyout. Industry Preferences: Diversified. Geographic Preferences: Eastern U.S. and Midwest.

TL Ventures
700 The Safeguard Bldg.
435 Devon Park Dr.
Wayne, PA 19087-1990
Phone: (610)971-1515
Fax: (610)975-9330
Website: http://www.tlventures.com
Pam Strisofsky,
pstrisofsky@tlventures.com

Investment Types: Seed, startup, second stage, mezzanine, and special situations. Industry Preferences: Diversified technology. Geographic Preferences: National.

## Puerto Rico

Advent-Morro Equity Partners
Banco Popular Bldg.
206 Tetuan St., Ste. 903
San Juan, PR 00902
Phone: (787)725-5285
Fax: (787)721-1735
Cyril L. Meduna, General Partner
Preferred Investment Size: $500,000 to $1,000,000. Investment Types: Early and late stage, and special situations. Industry Preferences: Diversified. Retail not considered. Geographic Preferences: Southeast and East Coast.

North America Investment Corp.
Mercantil Plaza, Ste. 813
PO Box 191831
San Juan, PR 00919
Phone: (787)754-6177
Fax: (787)754-6181
Marcelino D. Pastrana-Torres, President
Preferred Investment Size: $100,000 to $250,000. Investment Types: Second stage. Industry Preferences: Consumer products and retailing, consumer distribution, industrial equipment, therapeutic equipment, real estate, and transportation. Geographic Preferences: Puerto Rico.

## Rhode Island

Fleet Equity Partners
50 Kennedy Plaza, 12th Fl.
RI MO F12C
Providence, RI 02903
Phone: (401)278-6770
Fax: (401)278-6387
E-mail: fep@fleetequity.com
Website: http://www.fleetequity.com
Rory B. Smith, General Partner
Preferred Investment Size: $5,000,000 to $25,000,000. Investment Policies: Equity. Investment Types: Leverage buyouts, expansion. Industry Preferences: Media/communications, healthcare, printing, manufacturing. Geographic Preferences: National.

Manchester Humphreys, Inc.
40 Westminster St.
Providence, RI 02903
Phone: (401)454-0400
Fax: (401)454-0403
Investment Types: Leveraged buyout
and expansion financing. Industry
Preferences: Diversified. Geographic
Preferences: National.

## South Carolina

Capital Insights, L.L.C.
PO Box 27162
Greenville, SC 29616-2162
Phone: (864)242-6832
Fax: (864)242-6755
E-mail: jwarner@capitalinsights.com
Website: http://
www.capitalinsights.com
Preferred Investment Size: $500,000
to $5,000,000. Investment Policies:
Equity. Investment Types: Early and
late stage. Industry Preferences:
Communications and consumer-
related services. Geographic
Preferences: Southeast.

Florida Venture Partners, Inc.
201 Brookfield Pkwy., Ste. 100
Greenville, SC 29607
Phone: (864)272-6000
Investment Types: Startup, first and
second stage. Industry Preferences:
Diversified. Geographic Preferences:
Southeast.

Transamerica Mezzanine Financing
7 N. Laurens St., Ste. 603
Greenville, SC 29601
Phone: (864)232-6198
Fax: (864)241-4444
J. Phillip Falls, Investment Officer
Investment Types: Seed, startup, first
stage, second stage, and mezzanine.
Industry Preferences: Diversified
technology. Geographic Preferences:
Southeast.

## Tennessee

Capital Services & Resources, Inc.
5159 Wheelis Dr., Ste. 106
Memphis, TN 38117
Phone: (901)761-2156
Fax: (907)767-0060

Charles Y. Bancroft, Treasurer
Preferred Investment Size: $100,000
to $250,000. Investment Policies:
Equity. Investment Types: Late stage
and special situations. Industry
Preferences: Diversified. Geographic
Preferences: United States and
Canada.

Coleman Swenson-Hoffman, Booth
Inc.
237 2nd Ave. S
Franklin, TN 37064-2649
Phone: (615)791-9462
Fax: (615)791-9636
Larry H. Coleman, Ph.D., Managing
Partner
Preferred Investment Size: $1,000,000
to $7,000,000. Investment Types:
Seed, startup, first and second stage.
Industry Preferences: Healthcare
related. Geographic Preferences: No
preference.

Equitas L.P.
2000 Glen Echo Rd., Ste. 101
PO Box 158838
Nashville, TN 37215-8838
Phone: (615)383-8673
Fax: (615)383-8693
Preferred Investment Size: $500.000.
Investment Types: Later stage.
Industry Preferences: Diversified.
Geographic Preferences: Southeast
and East Coast.

Massey Burch Capital Corp.
310 25th Ave. N, Ste. 103
Nashville, TN 37203
Phone: (615)329-9448
Fax: (615)329-9237
E-mail: tcalton@masseyburch.com
Website: http://
www.masseyburch.com
Lucious E. Burch, IV, Partner
Preferred Investment Size: $500,000
to $2,000,000. Investment Types:
Seed, startup, first and second stage.
Industry Preferences: Communication
and computer related. Geographic
Preferences: Southern U.S. and
Middle Atlantic.

Sirrom Capital Corp.
500 Church St., Ste. 200
Nashville, TN 37219
Phone: (615)256-0701
Fax: (615)726-1208

Website: http://
www.sirromcapital.com
Kathy Harris, Vice President
Preferred Investment Size: $500,000
to $5,000,000. Investment Types:
Mezzanine and leveraged buyout.
Industry Preferences: Diversified.
Geographic Preferences: No
preference.

SSM Ventures
845 Crossover Ln., Ste. 140
Memphis, TN 38117
Phone: (901)767-1131
Fax: (901)767-1135
Website: http://
www.ssmventures.com
R. Wilson Orr, III
Investment Types: Startup, first stage,
second stage, mezzanine, leveraged
buyout, and special situations.
Industry Preferences: Diversified.
Geographic Preferences: Southeast
and Southwest U.S.

Valley Capital Corp.
Krystal Bldg.
100 W. Martin Luther King Blvd.,
Ste. 212
Chattanooga, TN 37402
Phone: (423)265-1557
Fax: (423)265-1588
Preferred Investment Size: $100,000
to $350,000. Investment Types:
Second stage, mezzanine, and
leveraged buyout. Industry
Preferences: Diversified. Geographic
Preferences: Southeast.

## Texas

Alliance Financial of Houston
218 Heather Ln.
Conroe, TX 77385-9013
Phone: (936)447-3300
Fax: (936)447-4222
Investment Types: Second stage,
mezzanine, leveraged buyout, and
special situations. Industry
Preferences: Sales, distribution, and
manufacturing. Geographic
Preferences: Gulf states.

Amerimark Capital Corp.
1111 W. Mockingbird, Ste. 1111
Dallas, TX 75247
Phone: (214)638-7878
Fax: (214)638-7612

E-mail: amerimark@amcapital.com
Website: http://www.amcapital.com
Investment Types: Second stage, mezzanine, and leveraged buyout. Industry Preferences: Diversified. Geographic Preferences: National.

AMT Venture Partners
8204 Elmbrook, Ste. 101
Dallas, TX 75247
Phone: (214)905-9757
Fax: (214)905-9761
Investment Types: First and second stages. Industry Preferences: Industrial products and equipment, electronic components and instruments. Geographic Preferences: National.

Arkoma Venture Partners
5950 Berkshire Lane, Ste. 1400
Dallas, TX 75225
Phone: (214)739-3515
Fax: (214)739-3572
E-mail: joelf@arkomavp.com
Joel Fontenot, Executive Vice President
Preferred Investment Size: $500,000 to $5,000,000. Investment Policies: Equity. Investment Types: Seed, early and late stage, and leveraged buyout. Industry Preferences: Diversified communications and computer, distribution, electronics, and industrial products and equipment. Geographic Preferences: National.

Austin Ventures, L.P.
114 W. 7th St., Ste. 1300
Austin, TX 78701
Phone: (512)485-1900
Fax: (512)476-3952
E-mail: info@ausven.com
Website: http://www.austinventures.com
Joseph C. Aragona, General Partner
Preferred Investment Size: $1,000,000 to $2,000,000. Investment Types: Seed, startup, first and second stage, leveraged buyout, and special situations. Industry Preferences: Diversified. Geographic Preferences: Southwest and Texas.

Banc One Capital Partners (Dallas)
3811 Turtle Creek Blvd., Ste. 1600
Dallas, TX 75219
Phone: (214)979-0650

Fax: (214)979-0769
Suzanne B. Kriscunas, Managing Director
Preferred Investment Size: $5,000,000 to $15,000,000. Investment Types: Second stage, mezzanine, leveraged buyout, special situations, recaps, and expansion financing for mature companies. Industry Preferences: Food, industrial, and medical product distribution; medical/health related; education; and transportation. Geographic Preferences: Entire U.S.

The Capital Network
3925 West Braker Lane, Ste. 406
Austin, TX 78759-5321
Phone: (512)305-0826
Fax: (512)305-0836
E-mail: davidg@ati.utexas.edu
Preferred Investment Size: $100,000. Investment Types: Seed, early and late stage, and special situations. Industry Preferences: Diversified. Geographic Preferences: United States and Canada.

Capital Southwest Corp.
12900 Preston Rd., Ste. 700
Dallas, TX 75230
Phone: (972)233-8242
Fax: (972)233-7362
Website: http://www.capitalsouthwest.com
Howard Thomas, Investment Associate
Preferred Investment Size: $1,000,000 to $6,000,000. Investment Types: First and second stage, leveraged buyout, special situations, and control block purchases. Industry Preferences: Diversified. Geographic Preferences: Entire U.S.

The Catalyst Group
3 Riverway, Ste. 770
Houston, TX 77056
Phone: (713)623-8133
Fax: (713)623-0473
E-mail: herman@thecatalystgroup.com
Website: http://www.thecatalystgroup.com
Rick Herman, Partner
Preferred Investment Size: $500,000 to $5,000,000. Investment Types: Second stage, mezzanine, leveraged buyout, and control block purchases.

Industry Preferences: Diversified. Geographic Preferences: No preference.

Cureton & Co., Inc.
1100 Louisiana, Ste. 3250
Houston, TX 77002
Phone: (713)658-9806
Fax: (713)658-0476
E-mail: chipcur@aol.com
Stewart Cureton, Jr., President
Preferred Investment Size: $1,000,000 to $25,000,000. Investment Types: First and second stage, leveraged buyout, and special situations. Industry Preferences: Diversified. Geographic Preferences: Southwest.

Davis, Tuttle Venture Partners (Dallas)
8 Greenway Plaza, Ste. 1020
Houston, TX 77046
Phone: (713)993-0440
Fax: (713)621-2297
Phillip Tuttle, Partner
Preferred Investment Size: $1,000,000 to $5,000,000. Investment Types: First and second stage, mezzanine, and leveraged buyout. Industry Preferences: Diversified. Geographic Preferences: Southwest.

First Capital Group Management Co., L.C.
750 East Mulberry St., Ste. 305
PO Box 15616
San Antonio, TX 78212
Phone: (210)736-4233
Fax: (210)736-5449
Jeffrey P. Blanchard, Managing Partner
Preferred Investment Size: $500,000 to $5,000,000. Investment Types: Second stage, mezzanine, leveraged buyout, and special situations. Industry Preferences: Diversified. Geographic Preferences: Southwest.

Hook Partners
13760 Noel Rd., Ste. 805
Dallas, TX 75240
Phone: (972)991-5457
Fax: (972)991-5458
E-mail: dhook@hookpartners.com
Website: http://www.hookpartners.com
David J. Hook

Preferred Investment Size: $100,000 maximum. Investment Types: Seed, research and development, startup, and first stage. Industry Preferences: Diversified. Geographic Preferences: Southwest and West Coast.

Houston Partners, SBIC
PO Box 2023
Houston, TX 77252-2023
Phone: (713)222-8600
Fax: (713)222-8932
A small business investment company. Diversified industry preference.

Interwest Partners (Dallas)
2 Galleria Tower
13455 Noel Rd., Ste. 1670
Dallas, TX 75240
Phone: (972)392-7279
Fax: (972)490-6348
Investment Types: Seed, research and development, startup, first and second stage, mezzanine, and special situations. Industry Preferences: Diversified. Oil and gas exploration and real estate not considered. Geographic Preferences: Entire U.S.

Kahala Investments, Inc.
8214 Westchester Dr., Ste. 715
Dallas, TX 75225
Phone: (214)987-0077
Fax: (214)987-2332
Lee R. Slaughter, Jr., President
Preferred Investment Size: $100,000 maximum. Investment Types: Mezzanine, leveraged buyout, special situations, control block purchases, industry roll ups, and private equity. Industry Preferences: Diversified. Geographic Preferences: Southeast and Southwest.

MESBIC Ventures Holding Co.
12655 N. Central Expy., Ste. 710
Dallas, TX 75243
Phone: (972)991-1597
Fax: (972)991-1647
Linda Roach, Senior Vice President
Preferred Investment Size: Up to $1,000,000. Investment Policies: Loans and/or equity. Investment Types: Expansion, later stage. Industry Preferences: Diversified. Geographic Preferences: Southwest.

NationsBank Capital Investors
901 Main St., 22nd Fl.
Dallas, TX 75202-2911
Phone: (214)508-0900
Fax: (214)508-0604
Doug Williamson, Managing Director
Preferred Investment Size: $3,000,000 to $5,000,000. Investment Types: Second stage, mezzanine, leveraged buyout, recaps, management buyouts, and expansion. Industry Preferences: Diversified. Geographic Preferences: Entire U.S.

North Texas MESBIC, Inc.
9500 Forest Lane, Ste. 430
Dallas, TX 75243
Phone: (214)221-3565
Fax: (214)221-3566
Preferred Investment Size: $100,000 to $250,000. Investment Types: Second stage, mezzanine, and leveraged buyout. Industry Preferences: Consumer food and beverage products, restaurants, retailing, consumer and food distribution. Geographic Preferences: Southwest.

Pacesetter/MESBIC Ventures Holding Co.
N. Central Plaza One
12655 N. Central Expy., Ste. 710
Dallas, TX 75243
Phone: (972)991-1597
Fax: (972)991-4770
E-mail: mesbic@gan.net
Verncen Russell, Associate
Investment Types: Second stage, mezzanine, and leveraged buyout. Industry Preferences: Diversified technology. Geographic Preferences: Southwest.

Phillips-Smith Specialty Retail Group
5080 Spectrum Dr., Ste. 805 W
Addison, TX 75001
Phone: (972)387-0725
Fax: (972)458-2560
E-mail: pssrg@aol.com
Website: http://www.phillips-smith.com
G. Michael Machens, General Partner
Preferred Investment Size: $1,000,000 to $5,000,000. Investment Types: Seed, startup, first and second stage, mezzanine, and leveraged buyout.

Industry Preferences: Retail related. Geographic Preferences: Entire U.S.

Richard Jaffe & Company, Inc,
7318 Royal Cir.
Dallas, TX 75230
Phone: (214)265-9397
Fax: (214)739-1845
E-mail: rjaffe@pssi.net
Richard R. Jaffe, President
Investment Types: Startup, first stage, leveraged buyouts, and special situations. Industry Preferences: Diversified. Geographic Preferences: Southwest.

Sevin Rosen Funds
13455 Noel Rd., Ste. 1670
Dallas, TX 75240
Phone: (972)702-1100
Fax: (972)702-1103
E-mail: info@srfunds.com
Website: http://www.srfunds.com
John V. Jaggers, Partner
Preferred Investment Size: $1,000,000 to $10,000,000. Investment Types: Seed, research and development, startup, and first stage. Industry Preferences: Diversified technology. Geographic Preferences: Entire U.S.

Southwest Venture Group
10878 Westheimer, Ste. 178
Houston, TX 77042
Phone: (713)827-8947
Free: (713)461-1470
David M. Klausmeyer, Partner
Investment Types: Early and late stages. Industry Preferences: Diversified. Geographic Preferences: National.

Southwest Venture Partners/Hixven Partners
16414 San Pedro, Ste. 345
San Antonio, TX 78232
Phone: (210)402-1200
Fax: (210)402-1221
E-mail: swvp@aol.com
Preferred Investment Size: $500,000 to $5,000,000. Investment Types: Startup, first and second stage. Industry Preferences: Diversified. Geographic Preferences: Southwest and Gulf states.

Stratford Capital Partners, L.P.
300 Crescent Ct., Ste. 500
Dallas, TX 75201

Phone: (214)740-7377
Fax: (214)720-7393
E-mail: stratcap@hmtf.com
Michael D. Brown, Managing Partner
Preferred Investment Size: $3,000,000
to $9,000,000. Investment Policies:
Equity, sub debt with equity.
Investment Types: Expansion, later
stage, acquisition. Industry
Preferences: Manufacturing,
distribution, diversified. Geographic
Preferences: National.

Sunwestern Investment Group
12221 Merit Dr., Ste. 935
Dallas, TX 75251
Phone: (972)239-5650
Fax: (972)701-0024
Preferred Investment Size: $500,000
to $1,000,000. Investment Types:
Second stage, leveraged buyout, and
special situations. Industry
Preferences: Diversified. Geographic
Preferences: Southwest and West
Coast.

Techxas Ventures LLC
8920 Business Park Dr.
Austin, TX 78759
Phone: (512)343-0118
Fax: (512)343-1879
E-mail: bruce@techxas.com
Website: http://www.techxas.com
Bruce Ezell, General Partner
Investment Types: Seed, startup, first
stage, second stage, and special
situations. Industry Preferences:
Diversified technology. Geographic
Preferences: Texas.

Triad Ventures
AM Fund
4600 Post Oak Place, Ste. 100
Houston, TX 77027
Phone: (713)627-9111
Fax: (713)627-9119
Preferred Investment Size: $250,000
maximum. Investment Types: First
and second stage, and mezzanine.
Industry Preferences: Medical,
consumer, computer-related.
Geographic Preferences: Southwest
and Texas.

Ventex Management, Inc.
3417 Milam St.
Houston, TX 77002-9531
Phone: (713)659-7870

Fax: (713)659-7855
Preferred Investment Size: $1,000,000
to $5,000,000. Investment Types:
Second stage, mezzanine, leveraged
buyout, and special situations.
Industry Preferences: Diversified.
Geographic Preferences: Southwest.

Wingate Partners
750 N. St. Paul St., Ste. 1200
Dallas, TX 75201
Phone: (214)720-1313
Fax: (214)871-8799
Preferred Investment Size: $5,000,000
maximum. Investment Types:
Leveraged buyout and control block
purchases. Industry Preferences:
Diversified. Geographic Preferences:
Entire U.S. and Canada.

## Utah

First Security Business Investment
Corp.
15 East 100 South, Ste. 100
Salt Lake City, UT 84111
Phone: (801)246-5688
Fax: (801)246-5740
Preferred Investment Size: $250,000.
Investment Policies: Loans and/or
equity. Investment Types: Expansion,
later stage. Industry Preferences:
Diversified. Geographic Preferences:
West Coast, Rocky Mountains.

Travis Capital, Inc.
39 Market St., Ste. 200
Salt Lake City, UT 84101
Phone: (801)355-4321
Fax: (801)521-9142
E-mail: ntravis@traviscapital.com
Elliot R. Travis, President
Preferred Investment Size: $1,000,000
to $5,000,000. Investment Types:
Early and late stage, and leveraged
buyout. Industry Preferences:
Diversified communications and
computer, consumer products and
services, publishing, and
transportation. Geographic
Preferences: National.

Utah Ventures II, L.P.
423 Wakara Way, Ste. 206
Salt Lake City, UT 84108
Phone: (801)583-5922
Fax: (801)583-4105

James C. Dreyfous, Managing
General Partner
Preferred Investment Size: $100,000
to $3,000,000. Investment Types:
Seed, startup, first and second stage.
Industry Preferences: Diversified
technology. Geographic Preferences:
Northwest, Southwest, Rocky
Mountains, and West Coast.

Wasatch Venture Corp.
1 S. Main St., Ste. 1400
Salt Lake City, UT 84133
Phone: (801)524-8939
Fax: (801)524-8941
E-mail: mail@wasatchvc.com
Todd Stevens, Manager
Preferred Investment Size: $250,000
to $2,000,000. Investment Policies:
Equity and debt. Investment Types:
Early stage. Industry Preferences:
High technology. Geographic
Preferences: Western U.S.

## Vermont

Green Mountain Capital, L.P.
RD 1, Box 1503
Waterbury, VT 05676
Phone: (802)244-8981
Fax: (802)244-8990
Website: http://www.gmtcap.com
Michael Sweatman, President
Preferred Investment Size: $100,000
to $500,000. Investment Types:
Second stage and mezzanine. Industry
Preferences: Technology,
communications. Geographic
Preferences: Northeast.

North Atlantic Capital Corp.
76 Saint Paul St., Ste. 600
Burlington, VT 05401
Phone: (802)658-7820
Fax: (802)658-5757
E-mail: gpeters@together.net
Website: http://
www.northatlanticcapital.com
Investment Types: Second stage,
mezzanine, and leveraged buyout.
Industry Preferences: Diversified
technology. Geographic Preferences:
Northeast.

## Virginia

Calvert Social Venture Partners
402 Maple Ave. W

Vienna, VA 22180
Phone: (703)255-4930
Fax: (703)255-4931
E-mail: calven2000@aol.com
John May, Managing General Partner
Investment Types: Startup, first and
second stages. Industry Preferences:
Diversified. Geographic Preferences:
Middle Atlantic states.

Continental SBIC
PO Box 3723
Arlington, VA 22203
Phone: (703)527-5200
Fax: (703)527-3700
Michael W. Jones, Senior Vice
President
Preferred Investment Size: $100,000
to $1,000,000. Investment Types:
Second stage, mezzanine, leveraged
buyout, and special situations.
Industry Preferences: Diversified.
Geographic Preferences: Northeast,
Southeast, Middle Atlantic, and
Central Canada.

Fairfax Partners
8000 Towers Crescent Dr., Ste. 940
Vienna, VA 22182
Phone: (703)847-9486
Fax: (703)847-0911
E-mail:
bgouldey@fairfaxpartners.com
Bruce K. Gouldey, Managing
Director
Investment Types: Startup, first stage,
second stage, and leveraged buyout.
Industry Preferences: Computer
related, Medical and health related.
Geographic Preferences: Middle
Atlantic States.

Novak Biddle Venture Partners
1897 Preston White Dr.
Reston, VA 20191
Phone: (703)264-7904
Fax: (703)264-1438
E-mail: roger@novakbiddle.com
Roger Novak, General Partner
Investment Types: Seed, startup, first
stage, second stage, and special
situations. Industry Preferences:
Communications and computer
related. Geographic Preferences:
Eastern U.S.

Oxford Venture Finance LLC
Alexandria, VA 22314

Phone: (703)519-4900
Fax: (703)519-4910
E-mail: oxford133@aol.com
Investment Types: Seed, research and
development, startup, first stage,
second stage, and mezzanine. Industry
Preferences: Diversified technology.
Geographic Preferences: National.

Spacevest
11911 Freedom Dr., Ste. 500
Reston, VA 20190
Phone: (703)904-9800
Fax: (703)904-0571
E-mail: spacevest@spacevest.com
Website: http://www.spacevest.com
Roger P. Widing, Managing Director
Preferred Investment Size: $500,000
to $5,000,000. Investment Policies:
Equity. Investment Types: Early and
late stage. Industry Preferences:
Diversified. Geographic Preferences:
National.

Strategic Technology Investors, LLC
4001 N. Ninth St., Ste. 306
Arlington, VA 22203
Free: 800-331-8545
Roy Morris
Investment Types: Seed, research and
development, startup, and first stage.
Industry Preferences: Diversified
technology. Geographic Preferences:
Northeast and Middle Atlantic states.

Virginia Capital
9 S. 12th St., Ste. 400
Richmond, VA 23219
Phone: (804)648-4802
Fax: (804)648-4809
E-mail: webmaster@vacapital.com
Justin Marriott, Associate
Investment Types: Late stages.
Industry Preferences:
Communications, consumer, medical
and health related. Geographic
Preferences: Southeast.

Walnut Capital Corp. (Vienna)
8000 Towers Crescent Dr., Ste.1070
Vienna, VA 22182
Phone: (703)448-3771
Fax: (703)448-7751
Preferred Investment Size: $100,000
to $500,000. Investment Types:
Startup, first and second stage,
mezzanine, and leveraged buyout.

Industry Preferences: Diversified.
Geographic Preferences: No
preference.

**Washington**

Columbia Basin Ventures, L.L.C.
8911 Grandridge Blvd., Ste. A
Kennewick, WA 99336
Phone: (509)783-4227
Fax: (509)783-4612
Richard J. Reisinger, Vice President
Preferred Investment Size: $100,000
to $500,000. Investment Types: Early
and late stage. Industry Preferences:
Diversified. Geographic Preferences:
Eastern Washington.

Encompass Ventures
777 108th Ave. NE, Ste. 2300
Bellevue, WA 98004
Phone: (425)486-3900
Fax: (425)486-3901
E-mail: info@evpartners.com
Website: http://
www.encompassventures.com
Sam Gupta, General Partner
Investment Types: Research and
development, startup, first and second
stages. Industry Preferences:
Computer related, medical and health
related. Geographic Preferences:
Western U.S. and Canada.

Fluke Venture Partners
11400 SE Sixth St., Ste. 230
Bellevue, WA 98004
Phone: (425)453-4590
Fax: (425)453-4675
E-mail: gabelein@flukeventures.com
Website: http://
www.flukeventures.com
Dennis Weston, Managing Director
Investment Types: Startup, first stage,
second stage, and mezzanine. Industry
Preferences: Diversified. Geographic
Preferences: Northwest.

Frazier & Company
601 Union St., Ste. 3300
Seattle, WA 98101
Phone: (206)621-7200
Fax: (206)621-1848
E-mail: jon@frazierco.com
Jon Gilbert, General Partner
Investment Types: Early and late
stages. Industry Preferences: Medical

and health related. Geographic Preferences: National.

Kirlan Venture Capital, Inc.
221 First Ave. W, Ste. 108
Seattle, WA 98119-4223
Phone: (206)281-8610
Fax: (206)285-3451
E-mail: bill@kirlanventure.com
Website: http://
www.kirlanventure.com
Investment Types: First stage, second stage, and mezzanine. Industry Preferences: Diversified technology. Geographic Preferences: Western U.S. and Canada.

Materia Venture Associates, L.P.
3435 Carillon Pointe
Kirkland, WA 98033-7354
Phone: (425)822-4100
Fax: (425)827-4086
Preferred Investment Size: $250,000 to $1,000,000. Investment Types: Startup, first and second stage, and mezzanine. Industry Preferences: Advanced industrial products and equipment. Geographic Preferences: Entire U.S.

McGoodwin James & Co.
119 S. Main St., Ste. 300
Seattle, WA 98104-3430
Phone: (206)428-4000
E-mail: jay@mcgoodwin.com
Investment Types: Seed and startup. Industry Preferences: Computer related, medical and health related. Geographic Preferences: National.

Northwest Venture Associates
221 N. Wall St., Ste. 628
Spokane, WA 99201
Phone: (509)747-0728
Fax: (509)747-0758
Christopher Brookfield
Investment Types: Seed, research and development, startup, first stage, second stage, and mezzanine. Industry Preferences: Diversified. Geographic Preferences: Northwest and Rocky Mountains.

Olympic Venture Partners (Kirkland)
2420 Carillon Pt.
Kirkland, WA 98033
Phone: (425)889-9192
Fax: (425)889-0152
E-mail: info@ovp.com

Website: http://www.ovp.com
Preferred Investment Size: $500,000 to $5,000,000. Investment Types: Seed, startup, first and second stage. Industry Preferences: Diversified technology. Geographic Preferences: Western U.S. and Canada.

Pacific Northwest Partners SBIC, L.P.
305 108th Ave. NE, 2nd Fl.
Bellevue, WA 98004
Phone: (425)455-9967
Fax: (425)455-9404
Preferred Investment Size: $5,000,000 maximum. Investment Policies: Private equity investments. Investment Types: Seed through later stage. Industry Preferences: Diversified, retail, healthcare, technology. Geographic Preferences: Western U.S.

Phoenix Partners
1000 2nd Ave., Ste. 3600
Seattle, WA 98104
Phone: (206)624-8968
Fax: (206)624-1907
E-mail: djohnsto@interserv.com
William B. Horne, Chief Financial Officer
Preferred Investment Size: $500,000 to $2,000,000. Investment Types: Seed, research and development, startup, first and second stage, and mezzanine. Industry Preferences: Diversified. Geographic Preferences: No preference.

Tredegar Investments
701 Fifth Ave., Ste. 6501
Seattle, WA 98104
Phone: (206)652-9240
Fax: (206)652-9250
Website: http://
www.tredgarinvestments.com
Steven M. Johnson, President
Preferred Investment Size: $250,000 to $5,000,000. Investment Policies: Equity. Investment Types: Seed, early and late stage. Industry Preferences: Diversified technology. Geographic Preferences: National.

Voyager Capital
800 5th St., Ste. 4100
Seattle, WA 98103
Phone: (206)470-1180
Fax: (206)470-1185

E-mail: info@voyagercap.com
Website: http://www.voyagercap.com
Erik Benson, Senior Associate
Preferred Investment Size: $500,000 to $4,000,000. Investment Policies: Equity. Investment Types: Startup, early and late stage. Industry Preferences: Diversified communications and computer related. Geographic Preferences: West Coast and Western Canada.

## West Virginia

Catterton Partners
10 Hale St., Ste. 205
Charleston, WV 25301
Phone: (304)345-5500
Fax: (304)345-3528
Investment Types: First stage, second stage, and leveraged buyout. Industry Preferences: Diversified. Consumer, distribution. Geographic Preferences: Entire U.S. and Canada.

## Wisconsin

Capital Investment, Inc.
1009 W. Glen Oaks Ln., Ste. 103
Mequon, WI 53092
Phone: (262)241-0303
Fax: (262)241-8451
E-mail: dmayer@capitalinvestmentsinc.com
Website: http://
www.capitalinvestmentsinc.com
Preferred Investment Size: $500,000 to $1 million. Investment Policies: Subordinated debt with warrant. Investment Types: Expansion, later stage. Industry Preferences: Diversified. Geographic Preferences: Midwest and Southwest.

Capital Investments, Inc.
1009 West Glen Oaks Lane, Ste. 103
Mequon, WI 53092
Phone: (414)241-0303
Fax: (414)241-8451
E-mail: dmayer@capitalinvestmentsinc.com
Website: http://
www.capitalinvestmentsinc.com
Preferred Investment Size: $500,000 to $1,000,000. Investment Types: Second stage, mezzanine, and leveraged buyout. Industry Preferences: Diversified. Geographic Preferences: Southwest and Midwest.

Future Value Venture, Inc.
2821 North 4th St., Ste. 526
Milwaukee, WI 53212-2300
Phone: (414)264-2252
Fax: (414)264-2253
William Beckett, President
Preferred Investment Size: $100,000
to $250,000. Investment Types: First
and second stage, and mezzanine.
Industry Preferences: No preference.
Geographic Preferences: Entire U.S.

GCI
20875 Crossroads Cir., Ste. 100
Waukesha, WI 53186
Phone: (262)798-5080
Fax: (262)798-5087
Investment Types: First stage, second
stage, and leveraged buyout. Industry
Preferences: Diversified technology.
Geographic Preferences: National.

Horizon Partners, Ltd.
225 E. Mason St., 6th Fl.
Milwaukee, WI 53202
Phone: (414)271-2200
Fax: (414)271-4016
Preferred Investment Size: $1,000,000
to $5,000,000. Investment Types:
Mezzanine. Industry Preferences:
Consumer products and services,
consumer distribution, electronic
components, chemicals and materials,
and publishing. Geographic
Preferences: Midwest.

Lubar and Co., Inc.
700 N. Water St., Ste. 1200
Milwaukee, WI 53202
Phone: (414)291-9000
Fax: (414)291-9061
David J. Lubar, Partner
Preferred Investment Size: $500,000
to $5,000,000. Investment Types:
Second stage, leveraged buyout,
special situations, and control block
purchases. Industry Preferences:
Diversified. Geographic Preferences:
Midwest.

M & I Ventures Corp.
770 N. Water St.
Milwaukee, WI 53202
Phone: (414)765-7910
Free: 800-342-2265
Fax: (414)765-7850
Diane Lau, Marketing Administrator

Preferred Investment Size: $1,000,000
to $5,000,000. Investment Types:
Mezzanine and leveraged buyout.
Industry Preferences: Diversified.
Geographic Preferences: Midwest.

Resource Financial Corporation
111 E. Kilbourn Ave., Ste. 1725
Milwaukee, WI 53202
Phone: (414)224-7000
Fax: (414)224-7015
E-mail: info@resource-financial.com
Website: http://www.resource-
financial.com
Investment Types: First stage, second
stage, mezzanine, leveraged buyout,
and special situations. Industry
Preferences: Diversified. Geographic
Preferences: National.

Venture Investors Management,
L.L.C.
University Research Park
505 S. Rosa Rd.
Madison, WI 53719
Phone: (608)441-2700
Fax: (608)441-2727
E-mail: roger@ventureinvestors.com
Website: http://
www.ventureinvesters.com
Scott Button, Partner
Preferred Investment Size: $250,000
to $1,000,000. Investment Types:
Seed, startup, first and second stage,
mezzanine, and special situations.
Industry Preferences: Diversified.
Geographic Preferences: Southeast
and Midwest.

Venture Investors of Wisconsin, Inc.
(Madison)
565 Science Dr., Ste. A
Madison, WI 53711-1071
Phone: (608)233-3070
Fax: (608)238-5120
E-mail: vi@ventureinvestors.com
Website: http://
www.ventureinvestors.com
Venture capital firm providing early-
stage financing to Wisconsin-based
companies with strong management
teams. Areas of interest include
biotechnology, software, analytical
instruments, medical products,
consumer products, and publishing
industries.

# Appendix C - Glossary of Small Business Terms

# Glossary of Small Business Terms

**Absolute liability**
Liability that is incurred due to product defects or negligent actions. Manufacturers or retail establishments are held responsible, even though the defect or action may not have been intentional or negligent.

**ACE**
*See* Active Corps of Executives

**Accident and health benefits**
Benefits offered to employees and their families in order to offset the costs associated with accidental death, accidental injury, or sickness.

**Account statement**
A record of transactions, including payments, new debt, and deposits, incurred during a defined period of time.

**Accounting system**
System capturing the costs of all employees and/or machinery included in business expenses.

**Accounts payable**
*See* Trade credit

**Accounts receivable**
Unpaid accounts which arise from unsettled claims and transactions from the sale of a company's products or services to its customers.

**Active Corps of Executives (ACE)**
*(See also Service Corps of Retired Executives)*
A group of volunteers for a management assistance program of the U.S. Small Business Administration; volunteers provide one-on-one counseling and teach workshops and seminars for small firms.

**ADA**
*See* Americans with Disabilities Act

**Adaptation**
The process whereby an invention is modified to meet the needs of users.

**Adaptive engineering**
The process whereby an invention is modified to meet the manufacturing and commercial requirements of a targeted market.

**Adverse selection**
The tendency for higher-risk individuals to purchase health care and more comprehensive plans, resulting in increased costs.

**Advertising**
A marketing tool used to capture public attention and influence purchasing decisions for a product or service. Utilizes various forms of media to generate consumer response, such as flyers, magazines, newspapers, radio, and television.

**Age discrimination**
The denial of the rights and privileges of employment based solely on the age of an individual.

**Agency costs**
Costs incurred to insure that the lender or investor maintains control over assets while allowing the borrower or entrepreneur to use them. Monitoring and information costs are the two major types of agency costs.

**Agribusiness**
The production and sale of commodities and products from the commercial farming industry.

**America Online**
*(See also Prodigy)*
An online service which is accessible by computer modem. The service features Internet access, bulletin boards, online periodicals, electronic mail, and other services for subscribers.

**Americans with Disabilities Act (ADA)**
Law designed to ensure equal access and opportunity to handicapped persons.

**Annual report**

*(See also Securities and Exchange Commission)*
Yearly financial report prepared by a business that adheres to the requirements set forth by the Securities and Exchange Commission (SEC).

**Antitrust immunity**

*(See also Collective ratemaking)*
Exemption from prosecution under antitrust laws. In the transportation industry, firms with antitrust immunity are permitted—under certain conditions—to set schedules and sometimes prices for the public benefit.

**Applied research**

Scientific study targeted for use in a product or process.

**Asians**

A minority category used by the U.S. Bureau of the Census to represent a diverse group that includes Aleuts, Eskimos, American Indians, Asian Indians, Chinese, Japanese, Koreans, Vietnamese, Filipinos, Hawaiians, and other Pacific Islanders.

**Assets**

Anything of value owned by a company.

**Audit**

The verification of accounting records and business procedures conducted by an outside accounting service.

**Average cost**

Total production costs divided by the quantity produced.

**Balance Sheet**

A financial statement listing the total assets and liabilities of a company at a given time.

**Bankruptcy**

*(See also Chapter 7 of the 1978 Bankruptcy Act; Chapter 11 of the 1978 Bankruptcy Act)*
The condition in which a business cannot meet its debt obligations and petitions a federal district court either for reorganization of its debts (Chapter 11) or for liquidation of its assets (Chapter 7).

**Basic research**

Theoretical scientific exploration not targeted to application.

**Basket clause**

A provision specifying the amount of public pension funds that may be placed in investments not included on a state's legal list (see separate citation).

**BBS**

*See* Bulletin Board Service

**BDC**

*See* Business development corporation

**Benefit**

Various services, such as health care, flextime, day care, insurance, and vacation, offered to employees as part of a hiring package. Typically subsidized in whole or in part by the business.

**BIDCO**

*See* Business and industrial development company

**Billing cycle**

A system designed to evenly distribute customer billing throughout the month, preventing clerical backlogs.

**Birth**

*See* Business birth

**Blue chip security**

A low-risk, low-yield security representing an interest in a very stable company.

**Blue sky laws**

A general term that denotes various states' laws regulating securities.

**Bond**

*(See also General obligation bond; Taxable bonds; Treasury bonds)*
A written instrument executed by a bidder or contractor (the principal) and a second party (the surety or sureties) to assure fulfillment of the principal's obligations to a third party (the obligee or government) identified in the bond. If the principal's obligations are not met, the bond assures payment to the extent stipulated of any loss sustained by the obligee.

**Bonding requirements**

Terms contained in a bond (see separate citation).

**Bonus**

An amount of money paid to an employee as a reward for achieving certain business goals or objectives.

**Brainstorming**

A group session where employees contribute their ideas for solving a problem or meeting a company objective without fear of retribution or ridicule.

**Brand name**

The part of a brand, trademark, or service mark that can be spoken. It can be a word, letter, or group of words or letters.

**Bridge financing**

A short-term loan made in expectation of intermediate-term or long-term financing. Can be used when a company plans to go public in the near future.

**Broker**

One who matches resources available for innovation with those who need them.

**Budget**

An estimate of the spending necessary to complete a project or offer a service in comparison to cash-on-hand and expected earnings for the coming year, with an emphasis on cost control.

**Bulletin Board Service (BBS)**

An online service enabling users to communicate with each other about specific topics.

**Business and industrial development company (BIDCO)**

A private, for-profit financing corporation chartered by the state to provide both equity and long-term debt capital to small business owners (see separate citations for equity and debt capital).

**Business birth**

The formation of a new establishment or enterprise. The appearance of a new establishment or enterprise in the Small Business Data Base (see separate citation).

**Business conditions**

Outside factors that can affect the financial performance of a business.

**Business contractions**

The number of establishments that have decreased in employment during a specified time.

**Business cycle**

A period of economic recession and recovery. These cycles vary in duration.

**Business death**

The voluntary or involuntary closure of a firm or establishment. The disappearance of an establishment or enterprise from the Small Business Data Base (see separate citation).

**Business development corporation (BDC)**

A business financing agency, usually composed of the financial institutions in an area or state, organized to assist in financing businesses unable to obtain assistance through normal channels; the risk is spread among various members of the business development corporation, and interest rates may vary somewhat from those charged by member institutions. A venture capital firm in which shares of ownership are publicly held and to which the Investment Act of 1940 applies.

**Business dissolution**

For enumeration purposes, the absence of a business that was present in the prior time period from any current record.

**Business entry**

*See* Business birth

**Business ethics**

Moral values and principles espoused by members of the business community as a guide to fair and honest business practices.

**Business exit**

*See* Business death

**Business expansions**

The number of establishments that added employees during a specified time.

**Business failure**

Closure of a business causing a loss to at least one creditor.

**Business format franchising**

*(See also Franchising)*

The purchase of the name, trademark, and an ongoing business plan of the parent corporation or franchisor by the franchisee.

**Business license**

A legal authorization issued by municipal and state governments and required for business operations.

**Business name**

*(See also Business license; Trademark)*

Enterprises must register their business names with local governments usually on a "doing business as" (DBA) form. (This name is sometimes referred to as a "fictional name.") The procedure is part of the business licensing process and prevents any other business from using that same name for a similar business in the same locality.

**Business norms**

*See* Financial ratios

**Business permit**

*See* Business license

**Business plan**

A document that spells out a company's expected course of action for a specified period, usually including a detailed listing and analysis of risks and uncertainties. For the small business, it should examine the proposed products, the market, the industry, the management policies, the marketing policies, production needs, and financial needs. Frequently, it is used as a prospectus for potential investors and lenders.

**Business proposal**

*See* Business plan

**Business service firm**

An establishment primarily engaged in rendering services to other business organizations on a fee or contract basis.

**Business start**

For enumeration purposes, a business with a name or similar designation that did not exist in a prior time period.

**Cafeteria plan**

*See* Flexible benefit plan

**Capacity**

Level of a firm's, industry's, or nation's output corresponding to full practical utilization of available resources.

**Capital**

Assets less liabilities, representing the ownership interest in a business. A stock of accumulated goods, especially at a specified time and in contrast to income received during a specified time period. Accumulated goods devoted to production. Accumulated possessions calculated to bring income.

**Capital expenditure**

Expenses incurred by a business for improvements that will depreciate over time.

**Capital gain**

The monetary difference between the purchase price and the selling price of capital. Capital gains are taxed at a rate of 28% by the federal government.

**Capital intensity**

*(See also Debt capital; Equity midrisk venture capital; Informal capital; Internal capital; Owner's capital; Secondhand capital; Seed capital; Venture capital)*

The relative importance of capital in the production process, usually expressed as the ratio of capital to labor but also sometimes as the ratio of capital to output.

**Capital resource**

The equipment, facilities and labor used to create products and services.

**Caribbean Basin Initiative**

An interdisciplinary program to support commerce among the businesses in the nations of the Caribbean Basin and the United States. Agencies involved include: the Agency for International Development, the U.S. Small Business Administration, the International Trade Administration of the U.S. Department of Commerce, and various private sector groups.

**Catastrophic care**

Medical and other services for acute and long-term illnesses that cost more than insurance coverage limits or that cost the amount most families may be expected to pay with their own resources.

**CDC**

*See* Certified development corporation

**CD-ROM**

Compact disc with read-only memory used to store large amounts of digitized data.

**Certified development corporation (CDC)**

A local area or statewide corporation or authority (for profit or nonprofit) that packages U.S. Small Business Administration (SBA), bank, state, and/or private money into financial assistance for existing business capital improvements. The SBA holds the second lien on its maximum share of 40 percent involvement. Each state has

Business Plans Handbook, Volume 8

at least one certified development corporation. This program is called the SBA 504 Program.

**Certified lenders**

Banks that participate in the SBA guaranteed loan program (see separate citation). Such banks must have a good track record with the U.S. Small Business Administration (SBA) and must agree to certain conditions set forth by the agency. In return, the SBA agrees to process any guaranteed loan application within three business days.

**Champion**

An advocate for the development of an innovation.

**Channel of distribution**

The means used to transport merchandise from the manufacturer to the consumer.

**Chapter 7 of the 1978 Bankruptcy Act**

Provides for a court-appointed trustee who is responsible for liquidating a company's assets in order to settle outstanding debts.

**Chapter 11 of the 1978 Bankruptcy Act**

Allows the business owners to retain control of the company while working with their creditors to reorganize their finances and establish better business practices to prevent liquidation of assets.

**Closely held corporation**

A corporation in which the shares are held by a few persons, usually officers, employees, or others close to the management; these shares are rarely offered to the public.

**Code of Federal Regulations**

Codification of general and permanent rules of the federal government published in the Federal Register.

**Code sharing**

*See* Computer code sharing

**Coinsurance**

*(See also Cost sharing)*

Upon meeting the deductible payment, health insurance participants may be required to make additional health care cost-sharing payments. Coinsurance is a payment of a fixed percentage of the cost of each service; copayment is usually a fixed amount to be paid with each service.

**Collateral**

Securities, evidence of deposit, or other property pledged by a borrower to secure repayment of a loan.

**Collective ratemaking**

*(See also Antitrust immunity)*

The establishment of uniform charges for services by a group of businesses in the same industry.

**Commercial insurance plan**

*See* Underwriting

**Commercial loans**

Short-term renewable loans used to finance specific capital needs of a business.

**Commercialization**

The final stage of the innovation process, including production and distribution.

**Common stock**

The most frequently used instrument for purchasing ownership in private or public companies. Common stock generally carries the right to vote on certain corporate actions and may pay dividends, although it rarely does in venture investments. In liquidation, common stockholders are the last to share in the proceeds from the sale of a corporation's assets; bondholders and preferred shareholders have priority. Common stock is often used in first-round start-up financing.

**Community development corporation**

A corporation established to develop economic programs for a community and, in most cases, to provide financial support for such development.

**Competitor**

A business whose product or service is marketed for the same purpose/use and to the same consumer group as the product or service of another.

**Computer code sharing**

An arrangement whereby flights of a regional airline are identified by the two-letter code of a major carrier in the computer reservation system to help direct passengers to new regional carriers.

**Consignment**

A merchandising agreement, usually referring to second-hand shops, where the dealer pays the owner of an item a percentage of the profit when the item is sold.

**Consortium**

A coalition of organizations such as banks and corporations for ventures requiring large capital resources.

**Consultant**

An individual that is paid by a business to provide advice and expertise in a particular area.

**Consumer price index**

A measure of the fluctuation in prices between two points in time.

**Consumer research**

Research conducted by a business to obtain information about existing or potential consumer markets.

**Continuation coverage**

Health coverage offered for a specified period of time to employees who leave their jobs and to their widows, divorced spouses, or dependents.

**Contractions**

*See* Business contractions

**Convertible preferred stock**

A class of stock that pays a reasonable dividend and is convertible into common stock (see separate citation). Generally the convertible feature may only be exercised after being held for a stated period of time. This arrangement is usually considered second-round financing when a company needs equity to maintain its cash flow.

**Convertible securities**

A feature of certain bonds, debentures, or preferred stocks that allows them to be exchanged by the owner for another class of securities at a future date and in accordance with any other terms of the issue.

**Copayment**

*See* Coinsurance

**Copyright**

A legal form of protection available to creators and authors to safeguard their works from unlawful use or claim of ownership by others. Copyrights may be acquired for works of art, sculpture, music, and published or unpublished manuscripts. All copyrights should be registered at the Copyright Office of the Library of Congress.

**Corporate financial ratios**

*(See also Industry financial ratios)*

The relationship between key figures found in a company's financial statement expressed as a numeric value. Used to evaluate risk and company performance. Also known as Financial averages, Operating ratios, and Business ratios.

**Corporation**

A legal entity, chartered by a state or the federal government, recognized as a separate entity having its own rights, privileges, and liabilities distinct from those of its members.

**Cost containment**

Actions taken by employers and insurers to curtail rising health care costs; for example, increasing employee cost sharing (see separate citation), requiring second opinions, or preadmission screening.

**Cost sharing**

The requirement that health care consumers contribute to their own medical care costs through deductibles and coinsurance (see separate citations). Cost sharing does not include the amounts paid in premiums. It is used to control utilization of services; for example, requiring a fixed amount to be paid with each health care service.

**Cottage industry**

*(See also Home-based business)*

Businesses based in the home in which the family members are the labor force and family-owned equipment is used to process the goods.

**Credit Rating**

A letter or number calculated by an organization (such as Dun & Bradstreet) to represent the ability and disposition of a business to meet its financial obligations.

**Customer service**

Various techniques used to ensure the satisfaction of a customer.

**Cyclical peak**

The upper turning point in a business cycle.

**Cyclical trough**

The lower turning point in a business cycle.

**DBA**

*See* Business name

**Death**

*See* Business death

**Debenture**

A certificate given as acknowledgment of a debt (see separate citation) secured by the general credit of the issuing corporation. A bond, usually without security, issued by a corporation and sometimes convertible to common stock.

**Debt**

*(See also Long-term debt; Mid-term debt; Securitized debt; Short-term debt)*

Something owed by one person to another. Financing in which a company receives capital that must be repaid; no ownership is transferred.

**Debt capital**

Business financing that normally requires periodic interest payments and repayment of the principal within a specified time.

**Debt financing**

*See* Debt capital

**Debt securities**

Loans such as bonds and notes that provide a specified rate of return for a specified period of time.

**Deductible**

A set amount that an individual must pay before any benefits are received.

**Demand shock absorbers**

A term used to describe the role that some small firms play by expanding their output levels to accommodate a transient surge in demand.

**Demographics**

Statistics on various markets, including age, income, and education, used to target specific products or services to appropriate consumer groups.

**Demonstration**

Showing that a product or process has been modified sufficiently to meet the needs of users.

**Deregulation**

The lifting of government restrictions; for example, the lifting of government restrictions on the entry of new businesses, the expansion of services, and the setting of prices in particular industries.

**Desktop Publishing**

Using personal computers and specialized software to produce camera-ready copy for publications.

**Disaster loans**

Various types of physical and economic assistance available to individuals and businesses through the U.S. Small Business Administration (SBA). This is the only SBA loan program available for residential purposes.

**Discrimination**

The denial of the rights and privileges of employment based on factors such as age, race, religion, or gender.

**Diseconomies of scale**

The condition in which the costs of production increase faster than the volume of production.

**Dissolution**

*See* Business dissolution

**Distribution**

Delivering a product or process to the user.

**Distributor**

One who delivers merchandise to the user.

**Diversified company**

A company whose products and services are used by several different markets.

**Doing business as (DBA)**

*See* Business name

**Dow Jones**

An information services company that publishes the Wall Street Journal and other sources of financial information.

**Dow Jones Industrial Average**

An indicator of stock market performance.

**Earned income**

A tax term that refers to wages and salaries earned by the recipient, as opposed to monies earned through interest and dividends.

**Economic efficiency**

The use of productive resources to the fullest practical extent in the provision of the set of goods and services that is most preferred by purchasers in the economy.

**Economic indicators**

Statistics used to express the state of the economy. These include the length of the average work week, the rate of unemployment, and stock prices.

**Economically disadvantaged**
*See* Socially and economically disadvantaged

**Economies of scale**
*See* Scale economies

**EEOC**
*See* Equal Employment Opportunity Commission

**8(a) Program**
A program authorized by the Small Business Act that directs federal contracts to small businesses owned and operated by socially and economically disadvantaged individuals.

**Electronic mail (e-mail)**
The electronic transmission of mail via phone lines.

**E-mail**
*See* Electronic mail

**Employee leasing**
A contract by which employers arrange to have their workers hired by a leasing company and then leased back to them for a management fee. The leasing company typically assumes the administrative burden of payroll and provides a benefit package to the workers.

**Employee tenure**
The length of time an employee works for a particular employer.

**Employer identification number**
The business equivalent of a social security number. Assigned by the U.S. Internal Revenue Service.

**Enterprise**
An aggregation of all establishments owned by a parent company. An enterprise may consist of a single, independent establishment or include subsidiaries and other branches under the same ownership and control.

**Enterprise zone**
A designated area, usually found in inner cities and other areas with significant unemployment, where businesses receive tax credits and other incentives to entice them to establish operations there.

**Entrepreneur**
A person who takes the risk of organizing and operating a new business venture.

**Entry**
*See* Business entry

**Equal Employment Opportunity Commission (EEOC)**
A federal agency that ensures nondiscrimination in the hiring and firing practices of a business.

**Equal opportunity employer**
An employer who adheres to the standards set by the Equal Employment Opportunity Commission (see separate citation).

**Equity**
*(See also Common Stock; Equity midrisk venture capital)*
The ownership interest. Financing in which partial or total ownership of a company is surrendered in exchange for capital. An investor's financial return comes from dividend payments and from growth in the net worth of the business.

**Equity capital**
*See* Equity; Equity midrisk venture capital

**Equity financing**
*See* Equity; Equity midrisk venture capital

**Equity midrisk venture capital**
An unsecured investment in a company. Usually a purchase of ownership interest in a company that occurs in the later stages of a company's development.

**Equity partnership**
A limited partnership arrangement for providing start-up and seed capital to businesses.

**Equity securities**
*See* Equity

**Equity-type**
Debt financing subordinated to conventional debt.

**Establishment**
A single-location business unit that may be independent (a single-establishment enterprise) or owned by a parent enterprise.

**Establishment and Enterprise Microdata File**
*See* U.S. Establishment and Enterprise Microdata File

**Establishment birth**
*See* Business birth

**Establishment Longitudinal Microdata File**
*See* U.S. Establishment Longitudinal Microdata File

**Ethics**
*See* Business ethics

**Evaluation**
Determining the potential success of translating an invention into a product or process.

**Exit**
*See* Business exit

**Experience rating**
*See* Underwriting

**Export**
A product sold outside of the country.

**Export license**
A general or specific license granted by the U.S. Department of Commerce required of anyone wishing to export goods. Some restricted articles need approval from the U.S. Departments of State, Defense, or Energy.

**Failure**
*See* Business failure

**Fair share agreement**
*(See also Franchising)*
An agreement reached between a franchisor and a minority business organization to extend business ownership to minorities by either reducing the amount of capital required or by setting aside certain marketing areas for minority business owners.

**Feasibility study**
A study to determine the likelihood that a proposed product or development will fulfill the objectives of a particular investor.

**Federal Trade Commission (FTC)**
Federal agency that promotes free enterprise and competition within the U.S.

**Federal Trade Mark Act of 1946**
*See* Lanham Act

**Fictional name**
*See* Business name

**Fiduciary**
An individual or group that hold assets in trust for a beneficiary.

**Financial analysis**
The techniques used to determine money needs in a business. Techniques include ratio analysis, calculation of return on investment, guides for measuring profitability, and break-even analysis to determine ultimate success.

**Financial intermediary**
A financial institution that acts as the intermediary between borrowers and lenders. Banks, savings and loan associations, finance companies, and venture capital companies are major financial intermediaries in the United States.

**Financial ratios**
*See* Corporate financial ratios; Industry financial ratios

**Financial statement**
A written record of business finances, including balance sheets and profit and loss statements.

**Financing**
*See* First-stage financing; Second-stage financing; Third-stage financing

**First-stage financing**
*(See also Second-stage financing; Third-stage financing)*
Financing provided to companies that have expended their initial capital, and require funds to start full-scale manufacturing and sales. Also known as First-round financing.

**Fiscal year**
Any twelve-month period used by businesses for accounting purposes.

**504 Program**
*See* Certified development corporation

**Flexible benefit plan**
A plan that offers a choice among cash and/or qualified benefits such as group term life insurance, accident and health insurance, group legal services, dependent care assistance, and vacations.

**FOB**
*See* Free on board

**Format franchising**
*See* Business format franchising; Franchising

**401(k) plan**
A financial plan where employees contribute a percentage of their earnings to a fund that is invested in stocks, bonds, or money markets for the purpose of saving money for retirement.

**Four Ps**
Marketing terms referring to Product, Price, Place, and Promotion.

**Franchising**
A form of licensing by which the owner—the franchisor—distributes or markets a product, method, or service through affiliated dealers called franchisees. The product, method, or service being marketed is identified by a brand name, and the franchisor maintains control over the marketing methods employed. The franchisee is often given exclusive access to a defined geographic area.

**Free on board (FOB)**
A pricing term indicating that the quoted price includes the cost of loading goods into transport vessels at a specified place.

**Frictional unemployment**
*See* Unemployment

**FTC**
*See* Federal Trade Commission

**Fulfillment**
The systems necessary for accurate delivery of an ordered item, including subscriptions and direct marketing.

**Full-time workers**
Generally, those who work a regular schedule of more than 35 hours per week.

**Garment registration number**
A number that must appear on every garment sold in the U.S. to indicate the manufacturer of the garment, which may or may not be the same as the label under which the garment is sold. The U.S. Federal Trade Commission assigns and regulates garment registration numbers.

**Gatekeeper**
A key contact point for entry into a network.

**GDP**
*See* Gross domestic product

**General obligation bond**
A municipal bond secured by the taxing power of the municipality. The Tax Reform Act of 1986 limits the purposes for which such bonds may be issued and establishes volume limits on the extent of their issuance.

**GNP**
*See* Gross national product

**Good Housekeeping Seal**
Seal appearing on products that signifies the fulfillment of the standards set by the Good Housekeeping Institute to protect consumer interests.

**Goods sector**
All businesses producing tangible goods, including agriculture, mining, construction, and manufacturing businesses.

**GPO**
*See* Gross product originating

**Gross domestic product (GDP)**
The part of the nation's gross national product (see separate citation) generated by private business using resources from within the country.

**Gross national product (GNP)**
The most comprehensive single measure of aggregate economic output. Represents the market value of the total output of goods and services produced by a nation's economy.

**Gross product originating (GPO)**
A measure of business output estimated from the income or production side using employee compensation, profit income, net interest, capital consumption, and indirect business taxes.

**HAL**
*See* Handicapped assistance loan program

**Handicapped assistance loan program (HAL)**
Low-interest direct loan program through the U.S. Small Business Administration (SBA) for handicapped persons. The SBA requires that these persons demonstrate that their disability is such that it is impossible for them to secure employment, thus making it necessary to go into their own business to make a living.

**Health maintenance organization (HMO)**
Organization of physicians and other health care professionals that provides health services to subscribers and their dependents on a prepaid basis.

**Health provider**
An individual or institution that gives medical care. Under Medicare, an institutional provider is a hospital, skilled nursing facility, home health agency, or provider of certain physical therapy services.

**Hispanic**
A person of Cuban, Mexican, Puerto Rican, Latin American (Central or South American), European Spanish, or other Spanish-speaking origin or ancestry.

**HMO**
*See* Health maintenance organization

**Home-based business**
*(See also Cottage industry)*
A business with an operating address that is also a residential address (usually the residential address of the proprietor).

**Hub-and-spoke system**
A system in which flights of an airline from many different cities (the spokes) converge at a single airport (the hub). After allowing passengers sufficient time to make connections, planes then depart for different cities.

**Human Resources Management**
A business program designed to oversee recruiting, pay, benefits, and other issues related to the company's work force, including planning to determine the optimal use of labor to increase production, thereby increasing profit.

**Idea**
An original concept for a new product or process.

**Import**
Products produced outside the country in which they are consumed.

**Income**
Money or its equivalent, earned or accrued, resulting from the sale of goods and services.

**Income statement**
A financial statement that lists the profits and losses of a company at a given time.

**Incorporation**
The filing of a certificate of incorporation with a state's secretary of state, thereby limiting the business owner's liability.

**Incubator**
A facility designed to encourage entrepreneurship and minimize obstacles to new business formation and growth, particularly for high-technology firms, by housing a number of fledgling enterprises that share an array of services, such as meeting areas, secretarial services, accounting, research library, on-site financial and management counseling, and word processing facilities.

**Independent contractor**
An individual considered self-employed (see separate citation) and responsible for paying Social Security taxes and income taxes on earnings.

**Indirect health coverage**
Health insurance obtained through another individual's health care plan; for example, a spouse's employer-sponsored plan.

**Industrial development authority**
The financial arm of a state or other political subdivision established for the purpose of financing economic development in an area, usually through loans to nonprofit organizations, which in turn provide facilities for manufacturing and other industrial operations.

**Industry financial ratios**
*(See also Corporate financial ratios)*
Corporate financial ratios averaged for a specified industry. These are used for comparison purposes and reveal industry trends and identify differences between the performance of a specific company and the performance of its industry. Also known as Industrial averages, Industry ratios, Financial averages, and Business or Industrial norms.

**Inflation**
Increases in volume of currency and credit, generally resulting in a sharp and continuing rise in price levels.

**Informal capital**
Financing from informal, unorganized sources; includes informal debt capital such as trade credit or loans from friends and relatives and equity capital from informal investors.

**Initial public offering (IPO)**
A corporation's first offering of stock to the public.

**Innovation**
The introduction of a new idea into the marketplace in the form of a new product or service or an improvement in organization or process.

**Intellectual property**
Any idea or work that can be considered proprietary in nature and is thus protected from infringement by others.

**Internal capital**
Debt or equity financing obtained from the owner or through retained business earnings.

**Internet**
A government-designed computer network that contains large amounts of information and is accessible through various vendors for a fee.

**Intrapreneurship**
The state of employing entrepreneurial principles to nonentrepreneurial situations.

**Invention**
The tangible form of a technological idea, which could include a laboratory prototype, drawings, formulas, etc.

**IPO**
*See* Initial public offering

**Job description**
The duties and responsibilities required in a particular position.

**Job tenure**
A period of time during which an individual is continuously employed in the same job.

**Joint marketing agreements**
Agreements between regional and major airlines, often involving the coordination of flight schedules, fares, and baggage transfer. These agreements help regional carriers operate at lower cost.

**Joint venture**
Venture in which two or more people combine efforts in a particular business enterprise, usually a single transaction or a limited activity, and agree to share the profits and losses jointly or in proportion to their contributions.

**Keogh plan**
Designed for self-employed persons and unincorporated businesses as a tax-deferred pension account.

**Labor force**
Civilians considered eligible for employment who are also willing and able to work.

**Labor force participation rate**
The civilian labor force as a percentage of the civilian population.

**Labor intensity**
*(See also Capital intensity)*
The relative importance of labor in the production process, usually measured as the capital-labor ratio; i.e., the ratio of units of capital (typically, dollars of tangible assets) to the number of employees. The higher the capital-labor ratio exhibited by a firm or industry, the lower the capital intensity of that firm or industry is said to be.

**Labor surplus area**
An area in which there exists a high unemployment rate. In procurement (see separate citation), extra points are given to firms in counties that are designated a labor surplus area; this information is requested on procurement bid sheets.

**Labor union**
An organization of similarly-skilled workers who collectively bargain with management over the conditions of employment.

**Laboratory prototype**
*See* Prototype

**LAN**
*See* Local Area Network

**Lanham Act**
Refers to the Federal Trade Mark Act of 1946. Protects registered trademarks, trade names, and other service marks used in commerce.

**Large business-dominated industry**
Industry in which a minimum of 60 percent of employment or sales is in firms with more than 500 workers.

**LBO**
*See* Leveraged buy-out

**Leader pricing**

A reduction in the price of a good or service in order to generate more sales of that good or service.

**Legal list**

A list of securities selected by a state in which certain institutions and fiduciaries (such as pension funds, insurance companies, and banks) may invest. Securities not on the list are not eligible for investment. Legal lists typically restrict investments to high quality securities meeting certain specifications. Generally, investment is limited to U.S. securities and investment-grade blue chip securities (see separate citation).

**Leveraged buy-out (LBO)**

The purchase of a business or a division of a corporation through a highly leveraged financing package.

**Liability**

An obligation or duty to perform a service or an act. Also defined as money owed.

**License**

*(See also Business license)*

A legal agreement granting to another the right to use a technological innovation.

**Limited partnerships**

*See* Venture capital limited partnerships

**Liquidity**

The ability to convert a security into cash promptly.

**Loans**

*See* Commercial loans; Disaster loans; SBA direct loans; SBA guaranteed loans; SBA special lending institution categories

**Local Area Network (LAN)**

Computer networks contained within a single building or small area; used to facilitate the sharing of information.

**Local development corporation**

An organization, usually made up of local citizens of a community, designed to improve the economy of the area by inducing business and industry to locate and expand there. A local development corporation establishes a capability to finance local growth.

**Long-haul rates**

Rates charged by a transporter in which the distance traveled is more than 800 miles.

**Long-term debt**

An obligation that matures in a period that exceeds five years.

**Low-grade bond**

A corporate bond that is rated below investment grade by the major rating agencies (Standard and Poor's, Moody's).

**Macro-efficiency**

*(See also Economic efficiency)*

Efficiency as it pertains to the operation of markets and market systems.

**Managed care**

A cost-effective health care program initiated by employers whereby low-cost health care is made available to the employees in return for exclusive patronage to program doctors.

**Management Assistance Programs**

*See* SBA Management Assistance Programs

**Management and technical assistance**

A term used by many programs to mean business (as opposed to technological) assistance.

**Mandated benefits**

Specific treatments, providers, or individuals required by law to be included in commercial health plans.

**Market evaluation**

The use of market information to determine the sales potential of a specific product or process.

**Market failure**

The situation in which the workings of a competitive market do not produce the best results from the point of view of the entire society.

**Market information**

Data of any type that can be used for market evaluation, which could include demographic data, technology forecasting, regulatory changes, etc.

**Market research**

A systematic collection, analysis, and reporting of data about the market and its preferences, opinions, trends, and plans; used for corporate decision-making.

**Market share**

In a particular market, the percentage of sales of a specific product.

**Marketing**
Promotion of goods or services through various media.

**Master Establishment List (MEL)**
A list of firms in the United States developed by the U.S. Small Business Administration; firms can be selected by industry, region, state, standard metropolitan statistical area (see separate citation), county, and zip code.

**Maturity**
*(See also Term)*
The date upon which the principal or stated value of a bond or other indebtedness becomes due and payable.

**Medicaid (Title XIX)**
A federally aided, state-operated and administered program that provides medical benefits for certain low-income persons in need of health and medical care who are eligible for one of the government's welfare cash payment programs, including the aged, the blind, the disabled, and members of families with dependent children where one parent is absent, incapacitated, or unemployed.

**Medicare (Title XVIII)**
A nationwide health insurance program for disabled and aged persons. Health insurance is available to insured persons without regard to income. Monies from payroll taxes cover hospital insurance and monies from general revenues and beneficiary premiums pay for supplementary medical insurance.

**MEL**
*See* Master Establishment List

**MESBIC**
*See* Minority enterprise small business investment corporation

**MET**
*See* Multiple employer trust

**Metropolitan statistical area (MSA)**
A means used by the government to define large population centers that may transverse different governmental jurisdictions. For example, the Washington, D.C. MSA includes the District of Columbia and contiguous parts of Maryland and Virginia because all of these geopolitical areas comprise one population and economic operating unit.

**Mezzanine financing**
*See* Third-stage financing

**Micro-efficiency**
*(See also Economic efficiency)*
Efficiency as it pertains to the operation of individual firms.

**Microdata**
Information on the characteristics of an individual business firm.

**Mid-term debt**
An obligation that matures within one to five years.

**Midrisk venture capital**
*See* Equity midrisk venture capital

**Minimum premium plan**
A combination approach to funding an insurance plan aimed primarily at premium tax savings. The employer self-funds a fixed percentage of estimated monthly claims and the insurance company insures the excess.

**Minimum wage**
The lowest hourly wage allowed by the federal government.

**Minority Business Development Agency**
Contracts with private firms throughout the nation to sponsor Minority Business Development Centers which provide minority firms with advice and technical assistance on a fee basis.

**Minority Enterprise Small Business Investment Corporation (MESBIC)**
A federally funded private venture capital firm licensed by the U.S. Small Business Administration to provide capital to minority-owned businesses (see separate citation).

**Minority-owned business**
Businesses owned by those who are socially or economically disadvantaged (see separate citation).

**Mom and Pop business**
A small store or enterprise having limited capital, principally employing family members.

**Moonlighter**
A wage-and-salary worker with a side business.

**MSA**
*See* Metropolitan statistical area

**Multi-employer plan**
A health plan to which more than one employer is required to contribute and that may be maintained through a collective bargaining agreement and required to meet standards prescribed by the U.S. Department of Labor.

**Multi-level marketing**
A system of selling in which you sign up other people to assist you and they, in turn, recruit others to help them. Some entrepreneurs have built successful companies on this concept because the main focus of their activities is their product and product sales.

**Multimedia**
The use of several types of media to promote a product or service. Also, refers to the use of several different types of media (sight, sound, pictures, text) in a CD-ROM (see separate citation) product.

**Multiple employer trust (MET)**
A self-funded benefit plan generally geared toward small employers sharing a common interest.

**NAFTA**
*See* North American Free Trade Agreement

**NASDAQ**
*See* National Association of Securities Dealers Automated Quotations

**National Association of Securities Dealers Automated Quotations**
Provides price quotes on over-the-counter securities as well as securities listed on the New York Stock Exchange.

**National income**
Aggregate earnings of labor and property arising from the production of goods and services in a nation's economy.

**Net assets**
*See* Net worth

**Net income**
The amount remaining from earnings and profits after all expenses and costs have been met or deducted. Also known as Net earnings.

**Net profit**
Money earned after production and overhead expenses (see separate citations) have been deducted.

**Net worth**
*(See also Capital)*
The difference between a company's total assets and its total liabilities.

**Network**
A chain of interconnected individuals or organizations sharing information and/or services.

**New York Stock Exchange (NYSE)**
The oldest stock exchange in the U.S. Allows for trading in stocks, bonds, warrants, options, and rights that meet listing requirements.

**Niche**
A career or business for which a person is well-suited. Also, a product which fulfills one need of a particular market segment, often with little or no competition.

**Nodes**
One workstation in a network, either local area or wide area (see separate citations).

**Nonbank bank**
A bank that either accepts deposits or makes loans, but not both. Used to create many new branch banks.

**Noncompetitive awards**
A method of contracting whereby the federal government negotiates with only one contractor to supply a product or service.

**Nonmember bank**
A state-regulated bank that does not belong to the federal bank system.

**Nonprofit**
An organization that has no shareholders, does not distribute profits, and is without federal and state tax liabilities.

**Norms**
*See* Financial ratios

**North American Free Trade Agreement (NAFTA)**
Passed in 1993, NAFTA eliminates trade barriers among businesses in the U.S., Canada, and Mexico.

**NYSE**
*See* New York Stock Exchange

**Occupational Safety & Health Administration (OSHA)**
Federal agency that regulates health and safety standards within the workplace.

**Optimal firm size**
The business size at which the production cost per unit of output (average cost) is, in the long run, at its minimum.

**Organizational chart**
A hierarchical chart tracking the chain of command within an organization.

**OSHA**
*See* Occupational Safety & Health Administration

**Overhead**
Expenses, such as employee benefits and building utilities, incurred by a business that are unrelated to the actual product or service sold.

**Owner's capital**
Debt or equity funds provided by the owner(s) of a business; sources of owner's capital are personal savings, sales of assets, or loans from financial institutions.

**P & L**
*See* Profit and loss statement

**Part-time workers**
Normally, those who work less than 35 hours per week. The Tax Reform Act indicated that part-time workers who work less than 17.5 hours per week may be excluded from health plans for purposes of complying with federal nondiscrimination rules.

**Part-year workers**
Those who work less than 50 weeks per year.

**Partnership**
Two or more parties who enter into a legal relationship to conduct business for profit. Defined by the U.S. Internal Revenue Code as joint ventures, syndicates, groups, pools, and other associations of two or more persons organized for profit that are not specifically classified in the IRS code as corporations or proprietorships.

**Patent**
A grant made by the government assuring an inventor the sole right to make, use, and sell an invention for a period of 17 years.

**PC**
*See* Professional corporation

**Peak**
*See* Cyclical peak

**Pension**
A series of payments made monthly, semiannually, annually, or at other specified intervals during the lifetime of the pensioner for distribution upon retirement. The term is sometimes used to denote the portion of the retirement allowance financed by the employer's contributions.

**Pension fund**
A fund established to provide for the payment of pension benefits; the collective contributions made by all of the parties to the pension plan.

**Performance appraisal**
An established set of objective criteria, based on job description and requirements, that is used to evaluate the performance of an employee in a specific job.

**Permit**
*See* Business license

**Plan**
*See* Business plan

**Pooling**
An arrangement for employers to achieve efficiencies and lower health costs by joining together to purchase group health insurance or self-insurance.

**PPO**
*See* Preferred provider organization

**Preferred lenders program**
*See* SBA special lending institution categories

**Preferred provider organization (PPO)**
A contractual arrangement with a health care services organization that agrees to discount its health care rates in return for faster payment and/or a patient base.

**Premiums**
The amount of money paid to an insurer for health insurance under a policy. The premium is generally paid periodically (e.g., monthly), and often is split between the employer and the employee. Unlike deductibles and coinsurance or copayments, premiums are paid for coverage whether or not benefits are actually used.

**Prime-age workers**
Employees 25 to 54 years of age.

**Prime contract**
A contract awarded directly by the U.S. Federal Government.

**Private company**
*See* Closely held corporation

**Private placement**
A method of raising capital by offering for sale an investment or business to a small group of investors (generally avoiding registration with the Securities and Exchange Commission or state securities registration agencies). Also known as Private financing or Private offering.

**Pro forma**
The use of hypothetical figures in financial statements to represent future expenditures, debts, and other potential financial expenses.

**Proactive**
Taking the initiative to solve problems and anticipate future events before they happen, instead of reacting to an already existing problem or waiting for a difficult situation to occur.

**Procurement**
*(See also 8(a) Program; Small business set asides)*
A contract from an agency of the federal government for goods or services from a small business.

**Prodigy**
*(See also America Online)*
An online service which is accessible by computer modem. The service features Internet access, bulletin boards, online periodicals, electronic mail, and other services for subscribers.

**Product development**
The stage of the innovation process where research is translated into a product or process through evaluation, adaptation, and demonstration.

**Product franchising**
An arrangement for a franchisee to use the name and to produce the product line of the franchisor or parent corporation.

**Production**
The manufacture of a product.

**Production prototype**
*See* Prototype

**Productivity**
A measurement of the number of goods produced during a specific amount of time.

**Professional corporation (PC)**
Organized by members of a profession such as medicine, dentistry, or law for the purpose of conducting their professional activities as a corporation. Liability of a member or shareholder is limited in the same manner as in a business corporation.

**Profit and loss statement (P & L)**
The summary of the incomes (total revenues) and costs of a company's operation during a specific period of time. Also known as Income and expense statement.

**Proposal**
*See* Business plan

**Proprietorship**
The most common legal form of business ownership; about 85 percent of all small businesses are proprietorships. The liability of the owner is unlimited in this form of ownership.

**Prospective payment system**
A cost-containment measure included in the Social Security Amendments of 1983 whereby Medicare payments to hospitals are based on established prices, rather than on cost reimbursement.

**Prototype**
A model that demonstrates the validity of the concept of an invention (laboratory prototype); a model that meets the needs of the manufacturing process and the user (production prototype).

**Prudent investor rule or standard**
A legal doctrine that requires fiduciaries to make investments using the prudence, diligence, and intelligence that would be used by a prudent person in making similar investments. Because fiduciaries make investments on behalf of third-party beneficiaries, the standard results in very conservative investments. Until recently, most state regulations required the fiduciary to apply this standard to each investment. Newer, more progressive regulations permit fiduciaries to apply this standard to the portfolio taken as a whole, thereby allowing a fiduciary to balance a

portfolio with higher-yield, higher-risk investments. In states with more progressive regulations, practically every type of security is eligible for inclusion in the portfolio of investments made by a fiduciary, provided that the portfolio investments, in their totality, are those of a prudent person.

**Public equity markets**

Organized markets for trading in equity shares such as common stocks, preferred stocks, and warrants. Includes markets for both regularly traded and nonregularly traded securities.

**Public offering**

General solicitation for participation in an investment opportunity. Interstate public offerings are supervised by the U.S. Securities and Exchange Commission (see separate citation).

**Quality control**

The process by which a product is checked and tested to ensure consistent standards of high quality.

**Rate of return**

*(See also Yield)*

The yield obtained on a security or other investment based on its purchase price or its current market price. The total rate of return is current income plus or minus capital appreciation or depreciation.

**Real property**

Includes the land and all that is contained on it.

**Realignment**

*See* Resource realignment

**Recession**

Contraction of economic activity occurring between the peak and trough (see separate citations) of a business cycle.

**Regulated market**

A market in which the government controls the forces of supply and demand, such as who may enter and what price may be charged.

**Regulation D**

A vehicle by which small businesses make small offerings and private placements of securities with limited disclosure requirements. It was designed to ease the burdens imposed on small businesses utilizing this method of capital formation.

**Regulatory Flexibility Act**

An act requiring federal agencies to evaluate the impact of their regulations on small businesses before the regulations are issued and to consider less burdensome alternatives.

**Research**

The initial stage of the innovation process, which includes idea generation and invention.

**Research and development financing**

A tax-advantaged partnership set up to finance product development for start-ups as well as more mature companies.

**Resource mobility**

The ease with which labor and capital move from firm to firm or from industry to industry.

**Resource realignment**

The adjustment of productive resources to interindustry changes in demand.

**Resources**

The sources of support or help in the innovation process, including sources of financing, technical evaluation, market evaluation, management and business assistance, etc.

**Retained business earnings**

Business profits that are retained by the business rather than being distributed to the shareholders as dividends.

**Revolving credit**

An agreement with a lending institution for an amount of money, which cannot exceed a set maximum, over a specified period of time. Each time the borrower repays a portion of the loan, the amount of the repayment may be borrowed yet again.

**Risk capital**

*See* Venture capital

**Risk management**

The act of identifying potential sources of financial loss and taking action to minimize their negative impact.

**Routing**

The sequence of steps necessary to complete a product during production.

**S corporations**

*See* Sub chapter S corporations

**SBA**
*See* Small Business Administration

**SBA direct loans**
Loans made directly by the U.S. Small Business Administration (SBA); monies come from funds appropriated specifically for this purpose. In general, SBA direct loans carry interest rates slightly lower than those in the private financial markets and are available only to applicants unable to secure private financing or an SBA guaranteed loan.

**SBA 504 Program**
*See* Certified development corporation

**SBA guaranteed loans**
Loans made by lending institutions in which the U.S. Small Business Administration (SBA) will pay a prior agreed-upon percentage of the outstanding principal in the event the borrower of the loan defaults. The terms of the loan and the interest rate are negotiated between the borrower and the lending institution, within set parameters.

**SBA loans**
*See* Disaster loans; SBA direct loans; SBA guaranteed loans; SBA special lending institution categories

**SBA Management Assistance Programs**
*(See also Active Corps of Executives; Service Corps of Retired Executives; Small business institutes program)*
Classes, workshops, counseling, and publications offered by the U.S. Small Business Administration.

**SBA special lending institution categories.**
U.S. Small Business Administration (SBA) loan program in which the SBA promises certified banks a 72-hour turnaround period in giving its approval for a loan, and in which preferred lenders in a pilot program are allowed to write SBA loans without seeking prior SBA approval.

**SBDB**
*See* Small Business Data Base

**SBDC**
*See* Small business development centers

**SBI**
*See* Small business institutes program

**SBIC**
*See* Small business investment corporation

**SBIR Program**
*See* Small Business Innovation Development Act of 1982

**Scale economies**
The decline of the production cost per unit of output (average cost) as the volume of output increases.

**Scale efficiency**
The reduction in unit cost available to a firm when producing at a higher output volume.

**SCORE**
*See* Service Corps of Retired Executives

**SEC**
*See* Securities and Exchange Commission

**SECA**
*See* Self-Employment Contributions Act

**Second-stage financing**
*(See also First-stage financing; Third-stage financing)*
Working capital for the initial expansion of a company that is producing, shipping, and has growing accounts receivable and inventories. Also known as Second-round financing.

**Secondary market**
A market established for the purchase and sale of outstanding securities following their initial distribution.

**Secondary worker**
Any worker in a family other than the person who is the primary source of income for the family.

**Secondhand capital**
Previously used and subsequently resold capital equipment (e.g., buildings and machinery).

**Securities and Exchange Commission (SEC)**
Federal agency charged with regulating the trade of securities to prevent unethical practices in the investor market.

**Securitized debt**
A marketing technique that converts long-term loans to marketable securities.

**Seed capital**
Venture financing provided in the early stages of the innovation process, usually during product development.

**Self-employed person**
One who works for a profit or fees in his or her own business, profession, or trade, or who operates a farm.

**Self-Employment Contributions Act (SECA)**
Federal law that governs the self-employment tax (see separate citation).

**Self-employment income**
Income covered by Social Security if a business earns a net income of at least $400.00 during the year. Taxes are paid on earnings that exceed $400.00.

**Self-employment retirement plan**
*See* Keogh plan

**Self-employment tax**
Required tax imposed on self-employed individuals for the provision of Social Security and Medicare. The tax must be paid quarterly with estimated income tax statements.

**Self-funding**
A health benefit plan in which a firm uses its own funds to pay claims, rather than transferring the financial risks of paying claims to an outside insurer in exchange for premium payments.

**Service Corps of Retired Executives (SCORE)**
*(See also Active Corps of Executives)*
Volunteers for the SBA Management Assistance Program who provide one-on-one counseling and teach workshops and seminars for small firms.

**Service firm**
*See* Business service firm

**Service sector**
Broadly defined, all U.S. industries that produce intangibles, including the five major industry divisions of transportation, communications, and utilities; wholesale trade; retail trade; finance, insurance, and real estate; and services.

**Set asides**
*See* Small business set asides

**Short-haul service**
A type of transportation service in which the transporter supplies service between cities where the maximum distance is no more than 200 miles.

**Short-term debt**
An obligation that matures in one year.

**SIC codes**
*See* Standard Industrial Classification codes

**Single-establishment enterprise**
*See* Establishment

**Small business**
An enterprise that is independently owned and operated, is not dominant in its field, and employs fewer than 500 people. For SBA purposes, the U.S. Small Business Administration (SBA) considers various other factors (such as gross annual sales) in determining size of a business.

**Small Business Administration (SBA)**
An independent federal agency that provides assistance with loans, management, and advocating interests before other federal agencies.

**Small Business Data Base**
*(See also U.S. Establishment and Enterprise Microdata File; U.S. Establishment Longitudinal Microdata File)*
A collection of microdata (see separate citation) files on individual firms developed and maintained by the U.S. Small Business Administration.

**Small business development centers (SBDC)**
Centers that provide support services to small businesses, such as individual counseling, SBA advice, seminars and conferences, and other learning center activities. Most services are free of charge, or available at minimal cost.

**Small business development corporation**
*See* Certified development corporation

**Small business-dominated industry**
Industry in which a minimum of 60 percent of employment or sales is in firms with fewer than 500 employees.

**Small Business Innovation Development Act of 1982**
Federal statute requiring federal agencies with large extramural research and development budgets to allocate a certain percentage of these funds to small research and development firms. The program, called the Small Business Innovation Research (SBIR) Program, is designed to stimulate technological innovation and make greater use of small businesses in meeting national innovation needs.

**Small business institutes (SBI) program**

Cooperative arrangements made by U.S. Small Business Administration district offices and local colleges and universities to provide small business firms with graduate students to counsel them without charge.

**Small business investment corporation (SBIC)**

A privately owned company licensed and funded through the U.S. Small Business Administration and private sector sources to provide equity or debt capital to small businesses.

**Small business set asides**

Procurement (see separate citation) opportunities required by law to be on all contracts under $10,000 or a certain percentage of an agency's total procurement expenditure.

**Smaller firms**

For U.S. Department of Commerce purposes, those firms not included in the Fortune 1000.

**SMSA**

*See* Metropolitan statistical area

**Socially and economically disadvantaged**

Individuals who have been subjected to racial or ethnic prejudice or cultural bias without regard to their qualities as individuals, and whose abilities to compete are impaired because of diminished opportunities to obtain capital and credit.

**Sole proprietorship**

An unincorporated, one-owner business, farm, or professional practice.

**Special lending institution categories**

*See* SBA special lending institution categories

**Standard Industrial Classification (SIC) codes**

Four-digit codes established by the U.S. Federal Government to categorize businesses by type of economic activity; the first two digits correspond to major groups such as construction and manufacturing, while the last two digits correspond to subgroups such as home construction or highway construction.

**Standard metropolitan statistical area (SMSA)**

*See* Metropolitan statistical area

**Start-up**

A new business, at the earliest stages of development and financing.

**Start-up costs**

Costs incurred before a business can commence operations.

**Start-up financing**

Financing provided to companies that have either completed product development and initial marketing or have been in business for less than one year but have not yet sold their product commercially.

**Stock**

*(See also Common stock; Convertible preferred stock)*
A certificate of equity ownership in a business.

**Stop-loss coverage**

Insurance for a self-insured plan that reimburses the company for any losses it might incur in its health claims beyond a specified amount.

**Strategic planning**

Projected growth and development of a business to establish a guiding direction for the future. Also used to determine which market segments to explore for optimal sales of products or services.

**Structural unemployment**

*See* Unemployment

**Sub chapter S corporations**

Corporations that are considered noncorporate for tax purposes but legally remain corporations.

**Subcontract**

A contract between a prime contractor and a subcontractor, or between subcontractors, to furnish supplies or services for performance of a prime contract (see separate citation) or a subcontract.

**Surety bonds**

Bonds providing reimbursement to an individual, company, or the government if a firm fails to complete a contract. The U.S. Small Business Administration guarantees surety bonds in a program much like the SBA guaranteed loan program (see separate citation).

**Swing loan**

*See* Bridge financing

**Target market**

The clients or customers sought for a business' product or service.

**Targeted Jobs Tax Credit**

Federal legislation enacted in 1978 that provides a tax credit to an employer who hires structurally unemployed individuals.

**Tax number**

*(See also Employer identification number)*

A number assigned to a business by a state revenue department that enables the business to buy goods without paying sales tax.

**Taxable bonds**

An interest-bearing certificate of public or private indebtedness. Bonds are issued by public agencies to finance economic development.

**Technical assistance**

*See* Management and technical assistance

**Technical evaluation**

Assessment of technological feasibility.

**Technology**

The method in which a firm combines and utilizes labor and capital resources to produce goods or services; the application of science for commercial or industrial purposes.

**Technology transfer**

The movement of information about a technology or intellectual property from one party to another for use.

**Tenure**

*See* Employee tenure

**Term**

*(See also Maturity)*

The length of time for which a loan is made.

**Terms of a note**

The conditions or limits of a note; includes the interest rate per annum, the due date, and transferability and convertibility features, if any.

**Third-party administrator**

An outside company responsible for handling claims and performing administrative tasks associated with health insurance plan maintenance.

**Third-stage financing**

*(See also First-stage financing; Second-stage financing)*

Financing provided for the major expansion of a company whose sales volume is increasing and that is breaking even or profitable. These funds are used for further plant expansion, marketing, working capital, or development of an improved product. Also known as Third-round or Mezzanine financing.

**Time deposit**

A bank deposit that cannot be withdrawn before a specified future time.

**Time management**

Skills and scheduling techniques used to maximize productivity.

**Trade credit**

Credit extended by suppliers of raw materials or finished products. In an accounting statement, trade credit is referred to as "accounts payable."

**Trade name**

The name under which a company conducts business, or by which its business, goods, or services are identified. It may or may not be registered as a trademark.

**Trade periodical**

A publication with a specific focus on one or more aspects of business and industry.

**Trade secret**

Competitive advantage gained by a business through the use of a unique manufacturing process or formula.

**Trade show**

An exhibition of goods or services used in a particular industry. Typically held in exhibition centers where exhibitors rent space to display their merchandise.

**Trademark**

A graphic symbol, device, or slogan that identifies a business. A business has property rights to its trademark from the inception of its use, but it is still prudent to register all trademarks with the Trademark Office of the U.S. Department of Commerce.

**Translation**

*See* Product development

**Treasury bills**

Investment tender issued by the Federal Reserve Bank in amounts of $10,000 that mature in 91 to 182 days.

**Treasury bonds**
Long-term notes with maturity dates of not less than seven and not more than twenty-five years.

**Treasury notes**
Short-term notes maturing in less than seven years.

**Trend**
A statistical measurement used to track changes that occur over time.

**Trough**
*See* Cyclical trough

**UCC**
*See* Uniform Commercial Code

**UL**
*See* Underwriters Laboratories

**Underwriters Laboratories (UL)**
One of several private firms that tests products and processes to determine their safety. Although various firms can provide this kind of testing service, many local and insurance codes specify UL certification.

**Underwriting**
A process by which an insurer determines whether or not and on what basis it will accept an application for insurance. In an experience-rated plan, premiums are based on a firm's or group's past claims; factors other than prior claims are used for community-rated or manually rated plans.

**Unfair competition**
Refers to business practices, usually unethical, such as using unlicensed products, pirating merchandise, or misleading the public through false advertising, which give the offending business an unequitable advantage over others.

**Unfunded accrued liability**
The excess of total liabilities, both present and prospective, over present and prospective assets.

**Unemployment**
The joblessness of individuals who are willing to work, who are legally and physically able to work, and who are seeking work. Unemployment may represent the temporary joblessness of a worker between jobs (frictional unemployment) or the joblessness of a worker whose skills are not suitable for jobs available in the labor market (structural unemployment).

**Uniform Commercial Code (UCC)**
A code of laws governing commercial transactions across the U.S., except Louisiana. Their purpose is to bring uniformity to financial transactions.

**Uniform product code (UPC symbol)**
A computer-readable label comprised of ten digits and stripes that encodes what a product is and how much it costs. The first five digits are assigned by the Uniform Product Code Council, and the last five digits by the individual manufacturer.

**Unit cost**
*See* Average cost

**UPC symbol**
*See* Uniform product code

**U.S. Establishment and Enterprise Microdata (USEEM) File**
A cross-sectional database containing information on employment, sales, and location for individual enterprises and establishments with employees that have a Dun & Bradstreet credit rating.

**U.S. Establishment Longitudinal Microdata (USELM) File**
A database containing longitudinally linked sample microdata on establishments drawn from the U.S. Establishment and Enterprise Microdata file (see separate citation).

**U.S. Small Business Administration 504 Program**
*See* Certified development corporation

**USEEM**
*See* U.S. Establishment and Enterprise Microdata File

**USELM**
*See* U.S. Establishment Longitudinal Microdata File

**VCN**
*See* Venture capital network

**Venture capital**
*(See also Equity; Equity midrisk venture capital)*
Money used to support new or unusual business ventures that exhibit above-average growth rates, significant potential for market expansion, and are in need of addi-

tional financing to sustain growth or further research and development; equity or equity-type financing traditionally provided at the commercialization stage, increasingly available prior to commercialization.

### Venture capital company

A company organized to provide seed capital to a business in its formation stage, or in its first or second stage of expansion. Funding is obtained through public or private pension funds, commercial banks and bank holding companies, small business investment corporations licensed by the U.S. Small Business Administration, private venture capital firms, insurance companies, investment management companies, bank trust departments, industrial companies seeking to diversify their investment, and investment bankers acting as intermediaries for other investors or directly investing on their own behalf.

### Venture capital limited partnerships

Designed for business development, these partnerships are an institutional mechanism for providing capital for young, technology-oriented businesses. The investors' money is pooled and invested in money market assets until venture investments have been selected. The general partners are experienced investment managers who select and invest the equity and debt securities of firms with high growth potential and the ability to go public in the near future.

### Venture capital network (VCN)

A computer database that matches investors with entrepreneurs.

### WAN

*See* Wide Area Network

### Wide Area Network (WAN)

Computer networks linking systems throughout a state or around the world in order to facilitate the sharing of information.

### Withholding

Federal, state, social security, and unemployment taxes withheld by the employer from employees' wages; employers are liable for these taxes and the corporate umbrella and bankruptcy will not exonerate an employer from paying back payroll withholding. Employers should escrow these funds in a separate account and disperse them quarterly to withholding authorities.

### Workers' compensation

A state-mandated form of insurance covering workers injured in job-related accidents. In some states, the state is the insurer; in other states, insurance must be acquired from commercial insurance firms. Insurance rates are based on a number of factors, including salaries, firm history, and risk of occupation.

### Working capital

Refers to a firm's short-term investment of current assets, including cash, short-term securities, accounts receivable, and inventories.

### Yield

*(See also Rate of return)*
The rate of income returned on an investment, expressed as a percentage. Income yield is obtained by dividing the current dollar income by the current market price of the security. Net yield or yield to maturity is the current income yield minus any premium above par or plus any discount from par in purchase price, with the adjustment spread over the period from the date of purchase to the date of maturity.

# Appendix D -
# Cumulative Index

# Index

Listings in this index are arranged alphabetically by business plan type (in bold), then alphabetically by business plan name. Users are provided with the volume number on which the plan begins.